NATIONAL GALLERY OF IRELAND
ILLUSTRATED SUMMARY CATALOGUE OF PRINTS AND SCULPTURE

NATIONAL GALLERY OF IRELAND

Illustrated Summary Catalogue of Prints and Sculpture

Edited by
Adrian Le Harivel
Compiled by
Susan Dillon, Frances Gillespie, Adrian Le Harivel and Wanda Ryan-Smolin

The National Gallery of Ireland

First published in 1988 by
The National Gallery of Ireland
Merrion Square, Dublin 2

British Library Cataloguing in Publication Data
National Gallery of Ireland
National Gallery of Ireland: illustrated
summary catalogue of prints and sculpture.
1. Sculpture — Exhibitions 2. Prints —
Exhibitions
I. Title II. Le Harivel, Adrian III. Dillon,
Susan
753' .074 NB60
ISBN 0-903162-41-5

Origination and Print Production by Printset & Design Ltd., Dublin
Printed in Ireland by Criterion Press Ltd., Dublin

CONTENTS

ACKNOWLEDGEMENT

In publishing this catalogue, which is the third and final catalogue in a series, the National Gallery of Ireland acknowledges the generous patronage of Allied Irish Banks plc, in supporting the project which has led to the entire collection in the National Gallery of Ireland being published in illustrated general format.

FOREWORD

At the time the National Gallery of Ireland was founded in 1854 no clear brief was established for the scope of the collections except in the most general way that the Gallery would be 'of Paintings, Sculpture and the Fine Arts'. The only sculptures in the Gallery at the time of its opening in 1864 were two nineteenth century copies of antique statues: the *Crouching Venus* and the *Spinario*; a larger-than-life size statue of the Irish railway magnate, William Dargan (whose generosity had led in part to the foundation of the Gallery); and a marble bust of the recently-deceased Roman Catholic Archbishop of Dublin (the last two being by Irish sculptors). There were no prints on display.

Over the decades since that time the Gallery has consistently collected sculpture and has had a policy of collecting engravings. As a glance at this Catalogue will show, emphasis has been laid on portrait sculpture and prints. This aspect of collecting followed the decision in 1884 to incorporate a 'Historical and Portrait' section within the Gallery.

The collection of portrait prints of 'eminent Irish men and women, as well as of others who, though not of Irish birth, have been politically or socially connected with Ireland or with her historical, literary, or artistic records' was greatly augmented in 1887. In that year over two hundred portrait prints were purchased at the first sale of the collection of John Chaloner Smith whose notable work, *British Mezzotint Portraits* was published between 1878 and 1884. Among the two hundred or so prints purchased by the Gallery from Smith's important collection were several by the distinguished Irish mezzotinters of the eighteenth century, McArdell, Brooks, Miller, Houston and others. The collection also included several prints after pictures by Irish painters such as Nathaniel Hone, Hugh Douglas Hamilton and Thomas Frye. The purchase of this nucleus of the print collection was made possible by the gift of £1,000 from Sir Edward Guinness, the Treasury having refused a special grant for the purpose. In 1888 almost one hundred further prints were added to the Collection from the second Chaloner Smith sale at a cost of £289 4s. Further significant acquisitions came in 1898 with the purchase of two hundred engravings from a Mr. P. Traynor in Dublin for the small sum of £10; and during the first decade of the present century a number of other substantial purchases were made. Since that time prints have consistently been collected though in relatively small numbers. The Collection as it now stands includes also some topographical engravings mainly of Irish locations, although traditionally the National Library of Ireland has taken responsibility for Irish topographical prints. As the Gallery is predominantly an Old Master Gallery it is appropriate that there should also be some old master prints, although these are in a minority. Several, however, are after pictures which are in our Collection, notably by such artists as Panini, Castiglione, Chardin and Metsu.

Purchases of sculpture for the Gallery have always concentrated on portrait sculpture, again for the national portrait collection. This means that within the Collection there is a strong emphasis on Irish sculpture, mainly of the nineteenth century with all the main sculptors such as Kirk, MacDowell, Foley, Hogan, Moore and Farrell represented. There is also among the Collection a substantial number of death masks. In more recent times with the resources of the Shaw Fund some individual pieces of European sculpture have been purchased with the intention that they would complement paintings in the galleries; and these include a bust by Duquesnoy and one attributed to Prieur, an eighteenth century Spanish group (in limewood) attributed to Villabrille y Ron and the *Pendule* of Renoir. The finest sculptures in the Collection have, however, been presented. With the Milltown Gift in 1902 came the exceptionally fine bronzes by Ferdinando Tacca after models by Giambologna as well as some other decorative sculpture, mainly of the nineteenth century. Hugh Lane bequeathed bronzes by Rodin, Barye, Dalou, Maillol and others; and Sir Alfred Chester Beatty presented busts by Bourdelle and Epstein. On his death in 1977, John Hunt bequeathed a collection of religious sculpture and they too are included in this Catalogue.

The *Illustrated Summary Catalogue of Prints and Sculpture* is one of a series of three catalogues which between them publish the entire collection in the National Gallery of Ireland: its publication completes the series. The Catalogue describes and illustrates all the engravings and sculpture in the Gallery as well as the few items of stained glass. This means that nearly three thousand individual prints, sixty engraved books and over three hundred sculptures are recorded. Extensive appendices list engravers, publishers, portrait sitters, views, donors and other information. The last catalogue of the Gallery to include any of the print collection was published in 1914 while an incomplete checklist of the sculpture was published in 1975. In the case of the present catalogue it is the first time that many of the items have ever been illustrated.

The compilation of the Catalogue has been a complex and enormous task carried out under the direction of Adrian Le Harivel. In examining and describing all the works he has been assisted by Susan Dillon, Frances Gillespie and Wanda Ryan-Smolin. Frances Bailey, Nicole Arnould, Veronika Montag and Nuala Fenton also contributed. During the compilation of the Catalogue a computer was installed in the Gallery (under the supervision of Raymond Keaveney) and the information contained in the Catalogue was entered on to a database which in turn provided the basis for the text. Many of the prints were specially conserved (under the supervison of Maighread McParland) prior to photography by Michael Olohan and Declan Emerson. For their dedication and diligence the Gallery is particularly grateful.

With the series of catalogues now completed it is a pleasure once again to thank Allied Irish Banks who generously provided the entire production costs of the first catalogue thereby enabling the entire proceeds of sale to be devoted to the production of the other catalogues in the series. Hopefully the publication of the *Illustrated Summary Catalogue of Prints and Sculpture* will lead to greater use being made of this part of the collections in the National Gallery of Ireland and a wider appreciation of the Gallery as a whole.

HOMAN POTTERTON,
Director, The National Gallery of Ireland
June 1988

GUIDE TO USING THE CATALOGUE

PRINTS

1. Prints are sorted alphabetically by originating **Artist** and ENGRAVER, with their dates (fl. if only period when working known) and national School (country they are associated with). This follows the format of the *National Gallery of Ireland Illustrated Summary Catalogue of Paintings* (1981) and *National Gallery of Ireland Illustrated Summary Catalogue of Drawings, Watercolours and Miniatures* (1983) and should assist users of the catalogue because of the number of portraits, landscapes and genre reproduced from the work of well-known artists. The *Liber Studiorum* by Turner and *Views* by T.S. Roberts are given in their published sequence to retain their coherence. A running head at the top of each page identifies the first print on it.

   Where there is an intermediary *COPYIST* of an artist's work for the engraver to work from, his name is inserted (with dates and national School) between artist and engraver. This does not affect the alphabetical sequence.

   Although one might expect that prints could be easily sorted because of the amount of information often found on them, in fact this is frequently erroneous. Artists or engravers' names are often missing or inaccurate. For this catalogue, where they are uncertain a question mark is inserted. With anonymous engravers the place published and date determines the national School and date.

   Appendix 2 is an alphabetical listing by engraver, with catalogue number, originating artist, short title and page number, so that it can be used as a catalogue in its own right.

2. Each print has a permanent catalogue number. In the National Gallery of Ireland numbering system, 10,000-11,999 and 20,000-21,199 (used in this catalogue to 20,839) are reserved for prints. Examples in the catalogue from engraved books (described in Appendix 8) are identified by a book number followed by a plate number in brackets [eg: 20,668(108)].

3. Unless there is a decorative border, only the image from a print is reproduced. All prints are lettered unless stated otherwise (with those cut down to the image this cannot always be determined).

4. *The title* - portrait sitters and views are described as when the print was issued, with maiden names, later titles, building alterations referred to briefly. Details of contemporary magazines and books in which the print appeared are also given (pl. for ...). Some prints were clearly removed *from* magazines and books and this is indicated also.

5. (after...) - where a print is derived from a dated oil painting, drawing, watercolour, sculpture or photograph (by signature, exhibition or written reference) and/or is located in a public collection, the information is given here. Many preparatory studies, done just for the engraver, do not of course survive. Mezzotint portraits were generally taken from an oil painting, but the picture may be either lost or in private ownership. Engravers and publishers also frequently stole or reworked prints by their rivals, to add further complication.

The following abbreviations are frequently used: BI (British Institution); BL (British Library); BM (British Museum); NG (National Gallery); NGI (National Gallery of Ireland); NGS (National Gallery of Scotland); NLI (National Library of Ireland); NMM (National Maritime Museum); NPG (National Portrait Gallery); RA (Royal Academy); RHA (Royal Hibernian Academy); RIA (Royal Irish Academy); RSBA (Royal Society of British Artists); SA (Society of Artists); SAI (Society of the Artists of Ireland); SNPG (Scottish National Portrait Gallery); V&A (Victoria and Albert Museum).

6. *INSCRIBED:* Dedications and informative inscriptions are included, but not the printed title and signatures which are often inaccurate. If the print is a proof (early impression before lettering was added) or lettered proof (as many 19th century prints claim to be), that is stated here.

7. Published: the name(s) of individuals and firms, the city (or cities) the print was published in and the date (as on the print or found from other sources) are given here. Further information about the publishers, also the addresses on their prints, can be found in Appendix 3. Some artist/printmakers issued their own prints privately, as is also indicated.

8. As in other National Gallery of Ireland catalogues, measurements are in centimetres, height x width. For prints an overall sheet measurement precedes a plate measurement (for intaglio processes), or image measurement (for woodcuts and lithographs).

9. Technique; as stated. The support is non-coloured paper unless described otherwise.

10. Provenance. How the print was acquired by the National Gallery of Ireland.

SCULPTURES

1. Sculptors are similarly catalogued in alphabetical order, with dates and national School.

2. The permanent catalogue numbers are in the 8000-9999 section of the National Gallery of Ireland numbering system (used in this catalogue to 8334).

3. *The title* describes the subject as for the Prints. In addition, it is noted where the piece is a model for a bronze, marble or plaster sculpture.

4. (after/copy from...) - where a preparatory model for a bronze or marble sculpture exists in a public collection (or was recorded at exhibition), this is mentioned here, also copies (full-size or reduced) from Classical sculpture or other sources.

5. Signatures, inscriptions, foundry marks and, where known, details of numbered series of casts are given, to aid comparison with replicas and variants.

6. There are no publishers for sculpture entries.

7. As in other National Gallery of Ireland catalogues, measurements are in centimetres. For *busts, statues and statuettes*, the height only is given, whereas width (wh.) and depth (dh.) are included for other pieces. For *marble busts* the height includes any socle (whose own height is given separately in brackets to enable comparison with variants without a socle). *Bronzes* are measured separately from marble or metal bases on which they were mounted by the sculptor or foundry. *Wax figurines* are measured separately from their presentation box. The diameter (diam.) is given for *reliefs*.

8. The material the sculpture is made from.

9. Provenance. How the sculpture was acquired by the National Gallery of Ireland.

ADRIAN LE HARIVEL
Curator of the Print Room

Prints Catalogue

OVERLEAF: *The Letter Writer* by Gabriel Metsu after the original in the NGI Cat. no. 4536 (Beit Collection). Engraved by John Burnett, when in the collection of Henry Philip Hope [NGI no. 20,673(37)]

A

Abbott, Lemuel Francis (1760-1803)
English School
BARNARD, WILLIAM S. (1774-1849)
ENGLISH SCHOOL

10,808
Charles James Fox, M.P., (1749-1806), Statesman, holding 'Articles of Peace' 1806
Published: W.S. Barnard, London, 10th October 1806
49.5 x 36 (plate cut)
Mezzotint
Purchased, London, 1st Chaloner Smith sale, 1887

Abbott, Lemuel Francis (1760-1803)
English School
CARDON, ANTHONY (1772-1813)
ANGLO-BELGIAN SCHOOL

11,117
General Sir Samuel Auchmuty, Bt., (1756-1822), later Commander-in-Chief in Ireland, (pl. for 'Royal Military Chronicle', 1811)
Published: J. Davis, London, 1st July 1811
21 x 13.2 (plate cut)
Line and stipple
Purchased, Dublin, Mr J.V. McAlpine, 1896

Abbott, Lemuel Francis (1760-1803)
English School
RIDLEY, WILLIAM (1764-1838)
ENGLISH SCHOOL

10,643
Admiral Sir Robert Kingsmill Bt., (1730-1805), (pl. for 'Naval Chronicle', 1801)
23.4 x 14.8 (plate cut)
Stipple
Acquired c.1908

Abresch, Franz (fl.1830s)
German School
BARTLETT, WILLIAM HENRY (1809-1854)
ENGLISH SCHOOL
BRANDARD, EDWARD PAXMAN (1819-1898)
ENGLISH SCHOOL

20,475
Belgrade, Yugoslavia, (pl. for W. Beattie's 'The Danube', 1844)
22 x 28.4 (plate 16.2 x 25.5)
Steel Engraving
Purchased, Lusk, Mr de Courcy Donovan, 1971

Abresch, Franz (fl.1830s)
German School
BARTLETT, WILLIAM HENRY (1809-1854)
ENGLISH SCHOOL
WALLIS, ROBERT (1794-1878)
ENGLISH SCHOOL

20,425
Sulina, at mouth of the River Danube, Romania, (pl. for W. Beattie's 'The Danube', 1844)
21.9 x 28.3 (plate cut)
Steel Engraving
Purchased, Lusk, Mr de Courcy Donovan, 1971

Allen (19th Century)
Irish School
ALLEN (19TH CENTURY)
IRISH SCHOOL

10,915
Rev. Theobald Mathew, (1790-1856), founder of the Temperance League of Ireland, administering the temperance pledge
Published: Allen's, Dublin
36.2 x 24.5 (image 36.1 x 24.4)
Lithograph
Acquired by 1913

Allingham, Charles (fl.1802-1812)
English School
RIDLEY, WILLIAM (1764-1838)
ENGLISH SCHOOL

20,834
Thomas Dermody, (1775-1802), Poet, (pl. for 'Monthly Mirror', September 1802)
(after an oil of 1802, NGI no. 138)
Published: Vernon & Hood, London, 31st August, 1802
13.5 x 8 (plate cut)
Stipple
Purchased, London, Mrs Noseda, 1875, (on reverse of oil no. 138)

Allom, Thomas (1804-1872)
English School
BENTLEY, JOSEPH CLAYTON (1809-1857)
ENGLISH SCHOOL

20,477
Castle Crag, Borrowdale Fells, from the village of Grange, Cumbria, (pl. for T. Rose's 'Cumberland', 1832)
Published: Fisher, Son & Co., London, 1832
14.5 x 22 (plate cut)
Steel Engraving
Purchased, Lusk, Mr de Courcy Donovan, 1971

Allom, Thomas (1804-1872)
English School
BRADSHAW, SAMUEL (FL.1832-1880)
ENGLISH SCHOOL

20,448(1)
Kentmere Head and Slate Quarries, Westmoreland, Cumbria, (previously pl. for T. Rose's 'Westmoreland', 1832)
Published: Fisher, Son & Co., London, 1838
28.3 x 22.1 (plate cut)
Steel Engraving
Purchased, Lusk, Mr de Courcy Donovan, 1971

Allom, Thomas (1804-1872)
English School
BRADSHAW, SAMUEL (FL.1832-1880)
ENGLISH SCHOOL

20,448(2)
Kendal, Cumbria from Green Bank, (previously pl. for T. Rose's 'Westmoreland', 1832)
Published: Fisher Son & Co., London, 1838 (with 20,448-1)
28.3 x 22.1 (plate cut)
Steel Engraving
Purchased, Lusk, Mr de Courcy Donovan 1971

Allom, Thomas (1804-1872)
English School
BUCKLE, D. (FL.1835-1847)
ENGLISH SCHOOL

20,419
Aydon Castle, Manor House, Northumberland, (previously pl. for T. Rose's 'Durham and Northumberland', 1832)
Published: Fisher, Son & Co., London, 1835
28.3 x 22.5 (plate cut)
Steel Engraving
Purchased, Lusk, Mr de Courcy Donovan, 1971

Allom, Thomas, (1804-1872)
English School
BUCKLE, D. (FL.1835-1847)
ENGLISH SCHOOL

20,420

Bynell Hall, Northumberland, (previously pl. for T. Rose's 'Durham and Northumberland', 1832)
Published: Fisher, Son & Co., London, 1835
28.3 x 22.5 (plate cut)
Steel Engraving
Purchased, Lusk, Mr de Courcy Donovan, 1971

Allom, Thomas (1804-1827)
English School
CHALLIS, EBENEZER (FL. 1831-1863)
ENGLISH SCHOOL

20,480
Mardale Head, Westmoreland, Cumbria, (pl. for T. Rose's 'Cumberland', 1832)
Published: Fisher, Son & Co., London, 1832
13.5 x 22.3 (plate cut)
Steel Engraving
Purchased, Lusk, Mr de Courcy Donovan, 1971

Allom, Thomas (1804-1872)
English School
CLARK, THOMAS (FL.1832-1840)
ENGLISH SCHOOL

20,279

Peveril Castle, near Castletown, Derbyshire, (pl. for T. Noble and T. Rose's 'Counties of Chester', 1836)
Published: Fisher, Son & Co., London & Paris, 1836
22.4 x 14.2 (plate cut)
Steel Engraving
Purchased, Lusk, Mr de Courcy Donovan, 1971

Allom, Thomas (1804-1872)
English School
KELSALL, W.H. (FL.1834-1857)
ENGLISH SCHOOL

20,456
View from Langdale Pikes, looking South East, Westmoreland, Cumbria, (previously pl. for T. Rose's 'Westmoreland', 1832)
Published: Fisher, Son & Co., London 1835
28.3 x 22.3 (plate cut)
Steel Engraving
Purchased, Lusk, Mr de Courcy Donovan, 1971

Allom, Thomas (1804-1872)
English School
KELSALL, W.H. (FL.1834-1857)
ENGLISH SCHOOL

20,457
View from Langdale Pikes, looking towards Bon Fell, Westmoreland, Cumbria, (previously pl. for T. Rose's 'Westmoreland', 1832)
Published: Fisher, Son & Co., London, 1835
28.3 x 22.3 (plate cut)
Steel Engraving
Purchased, Lusk, Mr de Courcy Donovan, 1971

Allom, Thomas (1804-1872)
English School
LACEY, SAMUEL (FL.1818-1857)
ENGLISH SCHOOL

20,263
High Force Waterfall on the River Tees, Co. Durham
Published: Fisher, Son & Co., London, 1835
22.3 x 28.2 (plate cut)
Steel Engraving
Purchased, Lusk, Mr de Courcy Donovan, 1971

Allom, Thomas (1804-1872)
English School
LE PETIT, WILLIAM A. (FL.1829-1857)
ENGLISH SCHOOL

20,451
Tintagel Castle and Head, Cornwall, (pl. for J. Britton and E.W. Brayley's 'Devonshire and Cornwall Illustrated', 1832)
Published: Fisher, Son & Co., London, 1832
28.5 x 22.1 (plate cut)
Steel Engraving
Purchased, Lusk, Mr de Courcy Donovan, 1971

Allom, Thomas (1804-1872)
English School
LE PETIT, WILLIAM A. (FL.1829-1857)
ENGLISH SCHOOL

20,452
Pentargon Bay Waterfall and Stone Quarry, near Boscastle, Cornwall, (pl. for J. Britton and E.W. Brayley's 'Devonshire and Cornwall Illustrated' 1832)
Published: Fisher, Son & Co., London, 1832
285 x 22.1 (plate cut)
Steel Engraving
Purchased, Lusk, Mr de Courcy Donovan, 1971

Allom, Thomas (1804-1872)
English School
REDAWAY, JAMES C. (FL.1818-1857)
ENGLISH SCHOOL

20,265
The Galilee Chapel, West End of Durham Cathedral, (previously pl. for T. Rose's 'Durham and Northumberland', 1832)
Published: Fisher, Son & Co., London, 1835
28.6 x 22.1 (plate cut)
Steel Engraving
Purchased, Lusk, Mr de Courcy Donovan, 1971

Allom, Thomas (1804-1872)
English School
REDAWAY, JAMES C. (FL.1818-1857)
ENGLISH SCHOOL

20,266
The Grotto in Castle Eden Dean, County Durham, (previously pl. for T. Rose's 'Durham and Northumberland', 1832)
Published: Fisher, Son & Co., London, 1835
28.6 x 22.1 (plate cut)
Steel Engraving
Purchased, Lusk, Mr de Courcy Donovan, 1971

Allom, Thomas (1804-1872)
English School
SANDS, ROBERT (1792-1855)
ENGLISH SCHOOL

20,398
Buttermere, Cumbria, (pl. for T. Rose's 'Cumberland', 1832)
Published: Fisher, Son & Co., London, 1832
14.1 x 22.4 (plate cut)
Steel Engraving
Purchased, Lusk, Mr de Courcy Donovan, 1971

Allom, Thomas (1804-1872)
English School
TOMBLESON, WILLIAM (FL.1814-1840)
ENGLISH SCHOOL

20,485
Colwith Force, Cumbria, (pl. for T. Rose's 'Cumberland', 1832)
Published: Fisher, Son & Co., London, 1832
22.1 x 14.5 (plate cut)
Steel Engraving
Purchased, Lusk, Mr de Courcy Donovan, 1971

Allom, Thomas (1804-1872)
English School
WALLIS, HENRY (1804-1890)
ENGLISH SCHOOL

20,284
Burnshead Hall, Westmoreland, (previously pl. for T. Rose's 'Westmoreland', 1832)
Published: Fisher, Son & Co., London, 1835
28.5 x 22.6 (plate cut)
Steel Engraving
Purchased, Lusk, Mr de Courcy Donovan, 1971

Allom, Thomas (1804-1872)
English School
WALLIS, HENRY (1804-1890)
ENGLISH SCHOOL

20,285
Clare Moss, from Little Langdale Head, Cumbria (previously pl. for T. Rose's 'Westmoreland', 1832)
Published: Fisher, Son & Co., London, 1835
28.5 x 22.6 (plate cut)
Steel Engraving
Purchased, Lusk, Mr de Courcy Donovan, 1971

Allom, Thomas (1804-1872)
English School
YOUNG, E. (FL. C.1832)
ENGLISH SCHOOL

20,262
Interior of Durham Cathedral from the Nine Altars
Published: Fisher, Son & Co., London, 1835
22.3 x 28.2 (plate cut)
Steel Engraving
Purchased, Lusk, Mr de Courcy Donovan, 1971

Allori, Alessandro (1535-1607)
Florentine School
BOREL, ANTOINE (1743-AFTER 1810)
FRENCH SCHOOL
TRIERRE, PHILIPPE (1756-C.1815)
FRENCH SCHOOL

20,723(7)
Venus and Cupid, (from 'Galerie du Palais Royal', Vol. I, École Florentine, 1786, see App. 8, no. 20,723)
(after an oil, Musée Fabre, Montpellier)
Published: J. Couché, also J. Bouilliard, Paris, 1786 (Printed: H. Perronneau)
55.5 x 33 (plate 41.6 x 28.5)
Line
Bequeathed, Judge J. Murnaghan, 1976

American School (19th century)
AMERICAN SCHOOL (19TH CENTURY)

10,723
Father Thomas Nicholas Burke, (1830-1883), Dominican preacher
Published: Haskell & Allen, Boston
46.1 × 34.3 (image 46.1 × 34.3)
Lithograph
Purchased, Dublin, Mr A. Roth, 1896

Amici, Domenico (1808-after 1858)
Roman School
AMICI, DOMENICO (1808-AFTER 1858)
ROMAN SCHOOL

20,734
The Arch of Janus below the Palatine Hill, Rome
30.1 × 43.5 (plate 22 x 28.9)
Line
Provenance Unknown

Amici, Domenico (1808-after 1858)
Roman School
AMICI, DOMENICO (1808-AFTER 1858)
ROMAN SCHOOL

20,735
The Arch of Septimus Severus in the Roman Forum, Rome
30.1 x 43.5 (plate 22 x 28.9)
Line
Provenance Unknown

Amici, Domenico (1808-after 1858)
Roman School
AMICI, DOMENICO (1808-AFTER 1858)
ROMAN SCHOOL

20,736

The Arch of Titus in the Roman Forum, Rome
30.1 x 43.5 (plate 22 x 29.1)
Line
Provenance Unknown

Amici, Domenico (1808-after 1858)
Roman School
AMICI, DOMENICO (1808-AFTER 1858)
ROMAN SCHOOL

20,737
The Pyramid of Caius Cestius by the Gate to Ostia, Rome
30.1 x 43.5 (plate 22 x 28.9)
Line
Provenance Unknown

Amici, Domenico (1808-after 1858)
Roman School
AMICI, DOMENICO (1808-AFTER 1858)
ROMAN SCHOOL

20,738
The Tomb of Cecilia Metella on the Appian Way, near Rome
30.1 x 43.5 (plate 22 x 28.9)
Line
Provenance Unknown

Amici, Domenico (1808-after 1858)
Roman School
AMICI, DOMENICO (1808-AFTER 1858)
ROMAN SCHOOL

20,739
The Column of Phocas in the Roman Forum, Rome
43.5 x 30.1 (plate 28.9 x 22)
Line
Provenance Unknown

Amici, Domenico (1808-after 1858)
Roman School
AMICI, DOMENICO (1808-AFTER 1858)
ROMAN SCHOOL

20,740
Trajan's Column in the Forum of Trajan, Rome
43.5 x 30.1 (plate 28.9 x 22)
Line
Provenance Unknown

Amici, Domenico (1808-after 1858)
Roman School
AMICI, DOMENICO (1808-AFTER 1858)
ROMAN SCHOOL

20,741
The Arch of Drusus on the Appian Way, Rome
30.1 x 43.5 (plate 22 x 28.9)
Line
Provenance Unknown

Amici, Domenico (1808-after 1858)
Roman School
AMICI, DOMENICO (1808-AFTER 1858)
ROMAN SCHOOL

20,742
The Arch of Gallienus near Piazza Vittorio Emanuel, Rome
30.1 x 43.5 (plate 22 x 28.9)
Line
Provenance Unknown

Amici, Domenico (1808-after 1858)
Roman School
AMICI, DOMENICO (1808-AFTER 1858)
ROMAN SCHOOL

20,743
The Arch of the Money Changers, or Settimio Severo on the Via Velabro, Rome
30.1 x 43.5 (plate 22.2 x 28.9)
Line
Provenance Unknown

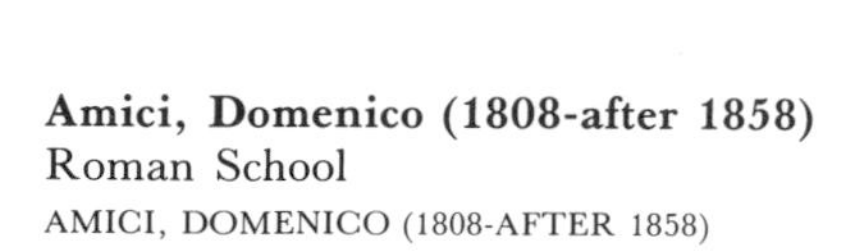

Amici, Domenico (1808-after 1858)
Roman School
AMICI, DOMENICO (1808-AFTER 1858)
ROMAN SCHOOL

20,744
Marcus Aurelius's Column on the Piazza Colonna, Rome
43.5 x 30.1 (plate 28.9 x 22)
Line
Provenance Unknown

Amici, Domenico (1808-after 1858)
Roman School
AMICI, DOMENICO (1808-AFTER 1858)
ROMAN SCHOOL

20,745
The Forum of Augustus with the Temple of Mars Ultor, Rome
43.5 x 30.1 (plate 28.9 x 22)
Line
Provenance Unknown

Amici, Domenico (1808-after 1858)
Roman School
AMICI, DOMENICO (1808-AFTER 1858)
ROMAN SCHOOL

20,746
The Temple of Venus and Rome above the Roman Forum, Rome
30.1 x 43.5 (plate 22 x 28.9)
Line
Provenance Unknown

Amici, Domenico (1808-after 1858)
Roman School
AMICI, DOMENICO (1808-AFTER 1858)
ROMAN SCHOOL

20,747
Ruins of the Temple of Minerva, the Forum of Nerva, Rome
30.1 x 43.5 (plate 22 x 29)
Line
Provenance Unknown

Amici, Domenico (1808-after 1858)
Roman School
AMICI, DOMENICO (1808-AFTER 1858)
ROMAN SCHOOL

20,748
The Arch of Constantine, Rome
30.1 x 43.5 (plate 22.5 x 29)
Line
Provenance Unknown

Amici, Domenico (1808-after 1858)
Roman School
AMICI, DOMENICO (1808-AFTER 1858)
ROMAN SCHOOL

20,749

The Tomb of P. Vibius Maranus, (so-called Tomb of Nero), Rome
30.1 x 43.5 (Plate 22 x 26.8)
Line
Provenance Unknown

Amici, Domenico (1808-after 1858)
Roman School
AMICI, DOMENICO (1808-AFTER 1858)
ROMAN SCHOOL

20,750
The Temple of Antoninus and Faustina, (now S. Lorenzo in Miranda), by the Sacred Way, Rome
30.1 x 43.5 (plate 22.2 x 28.9)
Line
Provenance Unknown

Amici, Domenico (1808-after 1858)
Roman School
AMICI, DOMENICO (1808-AFTER 1858)
ROMAN SCHOOL

20,751
The Basilica of Maxentius, in the Roman Forum, Rome
30.1 x 43.5 (plate 22.2 x 28.9)
Line
Provenance Unknown

Amici, Domenico (1808-after 1858)
Roman School
AMICI, DOMENICO (1808-AFTER 1858)
ROMAN SCHOOL

20,752
The Temple of Vesta by the River Tiber, Rome
30.1 x 43.5 (plate 22 x 28.9)
Line
Provenance Unknown

Amici, Domenico (1808-after 1858)
Roman School
AMICI, DOMENICO (1808-AFTER 1858)
ROMAN SCHOOL

20,753
The Porticus of Octavia below the Capitoline Hill, Rome
30.1 x 43.5 (plate 22 x 28.9)
Line
Provenance Unknown

Amici, Domenico (1808-after 1858)
Roman School
AMICI, DOMENICO (1808-AFTER 1858)
ROMAN SCHOOL

20,754
The Interior of the Colosseum, Rome
30.1 x 43.5 (plate 22 x 28.9)
Line
Provenance Unknown

Amici, Domenico (1808-after 1858)
Roman School
AMICI, DOMENICO (1808-AFTER 1858)
ROMAN SCHOOL

20,755
The Interior of S. Maria Maggiore, Rome
30.1 x 43.5 (plate 22 x 28.9)
Line
Provenance Unknown

Amici, Domenico (1808-after 1858)
Roman School
AMICI, DOMENICO (1808-AFTER 1858)
ROMAN SCHOOL

20,756
The Interior of the Pantheon, Rome
30.1 x 43.5 (plate 22 x 28.9)
Line
Provenance Unknown

Anelay, Henry (1817-1883)
English School
LINTON, WILLIAM JAMES (1812-1898)
ENGLISH SCHOOL

11,042
Defendants in the State Trial of 1844: Thomas Matthew Ray, (1800-1881), Secretary of the National, Repeal Association; Rev. Peter James Tyrell, (1792-1843) of Lusk, Co. Dublin; Rev. Thomas Tierney, (b.1790) of Clontibret, Co. Monaghan; Thomas Steele, (1788-1848), Repeal Warden-in-Chief for all Ireland; Daniel O'Connell M.P., (1775-1847), and John O'Connell M.P., (1810-1868); Richard Barret, Editor of 'The Pilot'; John, later Sir John Gray, (1815-1875), co-proprietor of 'Freeman's Journal' and Sir Charles Gavan Duffy M.P., (1816-1903)
INSCRIBED: Drawn upon the wood by H. Anelay and Engraved by W.J. Linton from original sketches taken expressly for the purpose.
Published: for the Proprietors, 1844
(Printed: Palmer & Clayton)
72 x 53 (image 67 x 45 approx)
Wood Engraving
Provenance Unknown

Aquila, Petrus (1650-1692)
Roman School
AQUILA, PETRUS (1650-1692)
ROMAN SCHOOL

20,684(4)
Allegory of the Flourishing of the Arts, (from 'Galerie Farnesianae', see App. 8, no. 20,684)
Published: J.J. de Rubeis, Rome
48 x 70.8 (plate 42 x 55.6)
Etching and line
Provenance Unknown

Archdeakon, Thomas (fl. c.1800)
Irish School
ARCHDEAKON, THOMAS (FL c.1800)
IRISH SCHOOL

11,919
King James II's Mint House, 27 Capel Street, (now demolished), birthplace of actor Thomas Sheridan
11.5 x 12 (plate cut)
Line
Presented, Mr W.G. Strickland, 1906

Arrowsmith, Thomas (fl.1792-1829)
English School
BARROW, T. (18TH CENTURY)
ENGLISH SCHOOL

11,315
Matthew Robinson-Morris, 2nd Baron Rokeby, (1713-1800)
(after a miniature)
Published: not before 1800
19.4 x 14.3 (plate cut)
Stipple and watercolour
Purchased, Dublin, Mr A. Roth, 1895

Ashton, Matthew (fl.1718-1728)
English School
BEARD, THOMAS (FL.C.1720 - C.1729)
IRISH SCHOOL

10,202
Hugh Boulter, P. Archbishop of Armagh, (1671-1742)
Published: 1728
25.2 x 24.8 (plate 35 x 24.4)
Mezzotint
Purchased, 1907

Astley, John (1730-1787)
English School
DIXON, JOHN (C.1740-1811)
IRISH SCHOOL

10,412
Francis Seymour-Conway, 16th Earl of Hertford, (1718-1794), Lord Lieutenant of Ireland, later 4th Marquess of Hertford
Published: c.1765
43 x 32.8 (plate 38 x 27.5)
Mezzotint
Acquired between 1890/98

Aubert, Jean Ernest (1824-1906)
French School
THIBAULT, CHARLES EUGENE (1835-AFTER 1880)
FRENCH SCHOOL

20,796
'La Rêverie'- Dreaming
(after an oil, Salon 1859)
Published: Virtue & Co. Ltd., London
33.5 x 24.7 (plate cut)
Line
Provenance Unknown

Aubry, Louis François (1767-1851)
French School
HUFFAM, T.W. (FL.1825-C.1855)
ENGLISH SCHOOL

11,171
Thomas Addis Emmet, (1764-1827), Lawyer, United Irishman and brother of Robert, (pl. for R. Madden's 'United Irishmen', 2nd series, 1843)
(after a miniature of 1803)
Published: Madden & Co., London, 1843
20.7 x 13.4 (plate 20 x 12.3)
Mezzotint
Purchased, Dublin, Mr P. Traynor, 1898

Aubry, Louis François (1767-1851)
French School
HUFFAM T.W. (FL.1825-C.1855)
ENGLISH SCHOOL

11,172
Thomas Addis Emmet, (1764-1827), Lawyer, United Irishman and brother of Robert, (pl. for R. Madden's 'United Irishmen', 2nd Series 1843), (another copy).
(after a miniature of 1803)
Published: Madden & Co., London, 1843
20.6 x 13.5 (plate 20 x 12.5)
Mezzotint
Purchased, Dublin, Mr P. Traynor, 1898

Aubry, Louis François (1767-1851)
French School
HUFFAM, T.W. (FL.1825-C.1855)
ENGLISH SCHOOL

11,173
Thomas Addis Emmet, (1764-1827), Lawyer, United Irishman, and brother of Robert, (pl. for R. Madden's 'United Irishmen', 2nd Series, 1843), (another copy)
(after a miniature of 1803)
Published: Madden & Co., London, 1843
21 x 13 (plate 20 x 12.5)
Mezzotint
Purchased, Dublin, Mr P. Traynor, 1898

B

B...., W.H.L. (19th Century)
English School
ENGLISH SCHOOL (19th CENTURY)

20,616
A Humanoid Oak in Richmond Park, London, (now felled)
10.4 x 7.6 (image 8.5 x 7)
Wood Engraving
Presented, Mrs D. Molloy, 1981

Bader, Augustin (fl.1835-1868)
French School
BADER, AUGUSTIN (FL.1835-1868)
FRENCH SCHOOL

20,400
The Zachringen Suspension Bridge at Fribourg, Switzerland, from the bank of the River Sarne
27.4 x 36.7 (image 19 x 28.6)
Lithograph
Purchased, Lusk, Mr de Courcy Donovan, 1971

Barbault, Jean (c.1705-1755)
French School
MONTAGU, DOMENICO (DIED C.1750)
ITALIAN SCHOOL

20,674(9)
Interior of the Portico of the Temple of Concorde, (from 'Les Plus Beaux Monuments de Rome Ancienne', 1761, see App. 8, no. 20,674)
Published: Bouchard & Gravier, Rome, 1761
52 x 37 (plate 35 x 24)
Etching
Bequeathed, Judge J. Murnaghan, 1976

Barber, Rupert (fl.1736-1772)
Irish School
WHEATLEY, SAMUEL (fl.1744-1771)
IRISH SCHOOL

11,376
Jonathan Swift, (1667-1745), Dean of St Patrick's Cathedral and Satirist
(after an etching of 1751, R. Barber/B. Wilson NGI no. 10,297)
19.7 x 12.2 (plate 15 x 9)
Line
Purchased, Dublin, Mr P. Traynor, 1898

Barber, Rupert (fl.1736-1772)
Irish School
WILSON, BENJAMIN (1721-1788)
ENGLISH SCHOOL

10,296

Jonathan Swift, (1667-1745), Dean of St Patrick's Cathedral, Dublin and Satirist
(after a chalk drawing)
1st State
Published: G. Faulkner, Dublin, 1751
17 x 9.5 (plate cut)
Etching
Provenance Unknown

Barber, Rupert (fl.1736-1772)
Irish School
WILSON, BENJAMIN (1721-1788)
ENGLISH SCHOOL

10,297
Jonathan Swift, (1667-1745), Dean of St Patrick's Cathedral, Dublin and Satirist, (frontispiece to Lord Orrery's 'Remarks on Life and Writings of Swift', 1752)
(after a chalk drawing)
2nd State
Published: G. Faulkner, Dublin, 1751
20.1 x 12.2 (plate 17.5 x 10.5)
Etching
Purchased, Dublin, Mr P. Traynor, 1898

Barocci, Federico (1526-1612)
Italian School
TOMKINS, PELTRO WILLIAM (1760-1840) and HODGSON, W.W. (19TH CENTURY)
ENGLISH SCHOOL
CARDON, ANTOINE (1772-1813)
ANGLO-BELGIAN SCHOOL

20,156
'La Madonna del Gatto' - The Holy Family with St John the Baptist, (pl. for the 'British Gallery of Pictures', 1818)
(after an oil, NG, London, first engraved 1577)
Published: Longman, Hurst Rees & Orme, also White & Co., also Cadell & Davies also P.W. Tomkins, London, January 1810
43.3 x 33 (plate cut)
Stipple
Purchased, Lusk, Mr de Courcy Donovan, 1971

Barocci, Federico (1526-1612)
Italian School
SADELER, AEGIDIUS (C.1570-1629)
FLEMISH SCHOOL

20,229
The Entombment of Christ
(after an oil of 1578-82, Santa Croce, Senigallia)
53.5 x 38.5 approx (plate cut)
Line
Purchased, Lusk, Mr de Courcy Donovan, 1971

Barralet, John James (1747-1815)
Irish School
BARRALET, JOHN JAMES (1747-1815)
IRISH SCHOOL

11,641
Harcourt Bridge, (at Charlemont Street), Grand Canal, Dublin
INSCRIBED: To the Right Honourable the Court of Directors of the Grand Canal Co. this view by Permission dedicated...
34 x 50.5 (plate cut)
Etching and aquatint
Acquired between 1904/1908

Barralet, John James (1747-1815)
Irish School
MILTON, THOMAS (1743-1827)
ENGLISH SCHOOL

11,604
The Vice-Regal Lodge, (Lord Lieutenant's Residence),(now Áras an Úachtaráin), Phoenix Park, Dublin, (pl. for T. Milton's 'The Seats and Demesnes of the Nobility and Gentry in Ireland', 1783-93)
INSCRIBED: Most Humbly dedicated to His Grace the Duke of Portland Lord Lieutenant of Ireland by Thos Milton

Published: J. Walter, London, for the author T. Milton in Dublin, 4th January 1783
16 x 20.5 (plate cut)
Line
Presented, Mr W.G. Strickland, 1906

Barralet, John James (1747-1815)
Irish School
MILTON, THOMAS (1743-1827)
ENGLISH SCHOOL

11,615
Leinster House Lawn, Dublin with a military parade, (pl. for T. Milton's 'The Seats and Demesnes of the Nobility and Gentry in Ireland', 1783-93)
INSCRIBED: Most humbly dedicated to his Grace the Duke of Leinster by Thos. Milton
Published: T. Milton, Dublin, 1783
19.7 x 26.8 (plate 13.2 x 20.3)
Line
Presented, Mr W.G. Strickland, 1906

Barralet, John James (1747-1815)
Irish School
MILTON, THOMAS (1743-1827)
ENGLISH SCHOOL

11,750
Leinster House Lawn, Dublin with a military parade, (pl. for T. Milton's 'The Seats and Demesnes of the Nobility and Gentry in Ireland', 1783-93)
INSCRIBED: Most Humbly Inscribed to His Grace the Duke of Leinster by Thos Milton

Published: J. Walter, London for the author T. Milton in Dublin, 1st January 1783
15.3 x 20.5 (plate cut)
Line
Provenance Unknown

Barralet, John James (1747-1815)
Irish School
STADLER, JOSEPH CONSTANTINE (FL.1780-1812)
GERMAN SCHOOL

11,643
Rutland Fountain, Merrion Square, Dublin
INSCRIBED: To her Grace Mary Isabella Duchess of Rutland this plate is most humbly inscribed by her devoted servant J. Blacquiere/This fountain for the use of the Poor of the City of Dublin, was Erected in honor of the Duke of Rutland, the late and much lamented Lord Lieutenant of Ireland...
Published: J. Blaquiere, Dublin, 1787
54 x 65.5 (plate 43.5 x 53)
Etching and aquatint with watercolour
Provenance Unknown

Barralet, John James (1747-1815)
Irish School
WARD THE ELDER, WILLIAM (1766-1826)
ENGLISH SCHOOL

11,654
The Preservation of Richard M'guire, 12th May 1781, after his balloon crashed in the sea off the Irish Coast, with, in the boat to the right, Lord Henry FitzGerald, (1761-1829), Mr Oliver and Mr Thornton
Published: T. Milton, London, also J.J. Barralet, Dublin, 4th June 1787
49.2 x 64.1 (plate 48.5 x 60.6)
Mezzotint
Purchased, London, 2nd Chaloner Smith sale, 1888

Barret the Younger, George (1767-1842)
Irish School
FREEBAIRN, ALFRED ROBERT (1794-1846)
ENGLISH SCHOOL

20,542
Classical Landscape at Sunset
Published: R. Ackermann, London
7.6 x 10.2 (plate cut)
Steel Engraving
Presented, Mrs D. Molloy, 1981

Barret the Younger, George (1767-1842)
Irish School
MELVILLE, HENRY (FL.1826-1877)
ENGLISH SCHOOL

20,248(89)
Retirement, (from 'The London Art and Union Prize Annual of 1846', see App. 8, no. 20,248)
Published: R.A. Sprigg, London, 1846
34.1 x 23.7 (plate cut)

Steel Engraving
Purchased, Lusk, Mr de Courcy Donovan, 1971

Barret the Younger, George (1767-1842)
Irish School
WALLIS, ROBERT (1794-1878)
ENGLISH SCHOOL

20,276
Evening near the Bavarian Alps
Published: Whittaker & Co., London; also G. Smith, Liverpool
9.9 x 16 (plate cut)
Steel Engraving
Purchased, Lusk, Mr de Courcy Donovan, 1971

Barrett, Jeremiah (fl.1753-1770)
Irish School
WATSON, JAMES (C.1740-1790)
ENGLISH SCHOOL

11,018
John Stacpoole of Cragbrien Castle, Co. Clare, (1674-1771), Landowner and Philanthropist
Published: not before 1771
46.5 x 36 (plate 43.3 x 28)
Mezzotint
Purchased, Dublin, Cranfield, 1876

Barron, Hugh (1747-1791)
English School
GREEN, VALENTINE (1739-1813)
ENGLISH SCHOOL

11,011
John Swan, (d. c.1782), Traveller
Published: H. Barron, London, lst May 1782
54.8 x 41.4 (plate 50.3 x 36.7)
Mezzotint
Purchased, London, lst Chaloner Smith sale, 1887

Barry, James (1741-1806)
Irish School
BARRY, JAMES (1741-1806)
IRISH SCHOOL

10,205
Self-Portrait (1802-c.04)
37.2 x 27 (plate 35.3 x 25.3)
Mezzotint
Purchased, Dublin, Bennett's, 1885

Barry, James (1741-1806)
Irish School
BARRY, JAMES (1741-1806)
IRISH SCHOOL

11,858
Jupiter and Juno on Mount Ida, (from Homer's 'Iliad')
(after an oil, RA 1773)
2nd State/INSCRIBED: Gazing he spoke and kindling at the view/His eager arms around the Goddess threw (Iliad 14)
Published: J. Barry, London, 1777
31.3 x 37.8 (plate 30.3 x 36)
Etching and aquatint
Presented, Mr W. Booth Pearsall, 1902

Barry, James (1741-1806)
Irish School
BARRY, JAMES (1741-1806)
IRISH SCHOOL

20,722(1)
Orpheus instructing a savage people in Theology and the Arts of social life, (from 'A series of etchings by James Barry', 1808, see App. 8, no. 20,722)
(after an oil mural of 1777-84, Royal Society of Arts, London)
3rd State
Published: firstly by J. Barry, London, 1791: this is re-issue by Colnaghi, London, 1808
(Printed: W. Bulmer & Co.)
49 x 67.3 (plate 41.6 x 50.5)
Etching and line
Provenance Unknown

Barry, James (1741-1806)
Irish School
BARRY, JAMES (1741-1806)
IRISH SCHOOL

20,722(2)
A Grecian Harvest-Home or Thanksgiving to the rural deities (from 'A series of etchings by James Barry', 1808, see App. 8, no. 20,722)
(after an oil mural of 1777-84, Royal Society of Arts, London)
4th State
Published: firstly by J. Barry, London, lst May 1791: this is re-issue by Colnaghi, London, 1808 (Printed: W. Bulmer & Co.)
49 x 67.3 (plate 41.4 x 50.5)
Etching and line
Provenance Unknown

Barry, James (1741-1806)
Irish School
BARRY, JAMES (1741-1806)
IRISH SCHOOL

20,722(3)
Crowning the Victors at Olympia, with Diagora of Athens held aloft by his sons, with portraits of William Pitt, lst Earl of Chatham, (1708-1778), as Pericles and Self-Portrait as Timanthes, (from 'A series of etchings by James Barry', 1808, see App. 8, no. 20,722)
(after an oil mural of 1777-84, Royal Society of Arts, London)
4th State
Published: firstly by J. Barry, London, lst May 1791: this is re-issue by Colnaghi, London, 1808 (Printed: W. Bulmer & Co.)
67.3 x 96 (plate 42 x 92.6)
Etching
Provenance Unknown

Barry, James (1741-1806)
Irish School
BARRY, JAMES (1741-1806)
IRISH SCHOOL

20,722(4)
The Thames or the Triumph of navigation, with Sir Walter Raleigh, (1552-1618), Sir Francis Drake, (1545-1596), Sebastian Cabot, (1477-1557), Captain James Cook, (1755-1812) and Dr Charles Burney, (1726-1814), (from 'A series of etchings by James Barry', 1808, see App. 8, no. 20,722)
(after an oil mural of 1777-84, Royal Society of Arts, London)
6th State
Published: firstly by J. Barry, London, lst May 1791: this is re-issue by Colnaghi, London, 1808 (Printed: W. Bulmer & Co.)
48 x 67.3 (plate 41.6 x 50.5)
Etching and line
Provenance Unknown

Barry, James (1741-1806)
Irish School
BARRY, JAMES (1741-1806)
IRISH SCHOOL

20,722(5)
The Distribution of Premiums in the Society of Arts, [with portraits of President, Robert Marsham, 2nd Baron Romney,(1712-1793), George Augustus Frederick, Prince of Wales, later King George IV, (1762-1830), Samuel Johnson, (1709-1784), Mrs Elizabeth Montague, (1720-1800), Dr William Hunter, (1741-1802), Georgina, Duchess of Devonshire, (1757-1806), Elizabeth, Duchess of Northumberland, (1716-1776) and Mary Isabella, Duchess of Rutland, (1756-1831)], (from 'A series of etchings by James Barry', 1808, see App. 8, no. 20,722)
(after an oil mural of 1777-84, Royal Society of Arts, London)
4th State
Published: firstly by J. Barry, London, Ist May 1791: this is re-issue by Colnaghi, London, 1808 (Printed: W. Bulmer & Co.)
49 x 67.3 (plate 41.6 x 50.5)
Etching and line
Provenance Unknown

Barry, James (1741-1806)
Irish School
BARRY, JAMES (1741-1806)
IRISH SCHOOL

20,722(6)
Elysium and Tartarus or the state of final retribution, (with 127 portraits of men of genius), (from 'A series of etchings by James Barry', 1808, see App. 8, no. 20,722)
(after an oil mural of 1777-84, Royal Society of Arts, London)
6th State
Published: firstly by J. Barry, London, 1st May 1791; this is re-issue by Colnaghi, London, 1808 (Printed: W. Bulmer & Co.)
67.3 x 96 (plate 41.5 x 91.4)
Etching and line
Provenance Unknown

Barry, James (1741-1806)
Irish School
BARRY, JAMES (1741-1806)
IRISH SCHOOL

20,722(7)
Reserved Knowledge, (enlarged detail from 'Elysium') with portraits of Sir Francis Bacon, (1561-1626), Nicolaus Copernicus, (1473-1543), Galileo Galilei, (1564-1642) and Sir Isaac Newton, (1642-1727), above Thales, (640-c.545BC), Rene Descartes, (1596-1650), Archimedes, (c.287-212BC), Bishop Robert Grouthead, (1175-1253), and Roger Bacon, (1214-1292), (from 'A series of etchings by James Barry', 1808, see App. 8, no. 20,722)
3rd State
Published: firstly by J. Barry, London, lst May 1795: this is re-issue by Colnaghi, London, 1808 (Printed: W. Bulmer & Co.)
94.4 x 67.5 (plate 71.5 x 46.8)
Etching and line
Provenance Unknown

Barry, James (1741-1806)
Irish School
BARRY, JAMES (1741-1806)
IRISH SCHOOL

20,722(8)
The Glorious Sextumvirate, (enlarged detail from, 'Elysium'), with portraits of Epaminondas, (411-362BC), Socrates, (469-399BC), Lucius Junius Brutus, (d.509BC), Marcus Cato the Younger, (85-46BC), Sir Thomas Moore, (1478-1538) and Marcus Junius Brutus, (c.85-42BC), below Christopher Columbus, (1445-1506), Anthony Cooper, 3rd Earl of Shaftesbury, (1671-1713), John Locke, (1632-1704), Zeno, (fl.5CBC), Aristotle, (384-323BC), Plato, (c.429-347BC), William Harvey, (1578-1657) and Hippocrates, (460-c.361BC), (from 'A series of etchings by James Barry', 1808, see App. 8, no. 20,722)
Published: firstly by J. Barry, London, lst May 1795: this is re-issue by Colnaghi, London, 1808 (Printed: W. Bulmer & Co.)
94.4 x 67.5 (plate 72.8 x 46.8)
Etching and line
Provenance Unknown

Barry, James (1741-1806)
Irish School
BARRY, JAMES (1741-1806)
IRISH SCHOOL

20,722(9)
Cecil Calvert, 1st Baron Baltimore, (?1582-1632) and a group of legislators, Lycurgus, (d. c.870BC), Numa Pompilius, (fl. 7CBC), William Penn, (1644-1718) and Marcus Aurelius, (121-180) and King Alfred the Great, (849-900), with Mary, Queen of Scots, (1542-1587) scattering flowers above, (from 'A series of etchings by James Barry', 1808, see App. 8, no. 20,722)
2nd State
Published: firstly by J. Barry, London, 2nd February, 1793: this is re-issue by Colnaghi, London, 1808 (Printed: W. Bulmer & Co.)
94.4 x 67.5 (plate 73.3 x 47.2)
Etching
Provenance Unknown

Barry, James (1741-1806)
Irish School
BARRY, JAMES (1741-1806)
IRISH SCHOOL

20,722(10)
Divine Justice, (enlarged detail from 'Elysium'), with the heads of Origen, (c.186-c.254), Blaise Pascal, (1623-1662), James Bossuet, (1627-1704), below Antoine Arnaud, (1612-1694), and Bishop Joseph Butler, (1692-1752), below St Charles Borromeo, (1538-1584), Emperors Trajan, (c.52-117) and Titus, (40-81), Czar Peter the Great, (1652-1725), King Henry IV, (1553-1610), Andrea Doria, (1468-1560), Scipio Africanus, (253-c.183BC), Cosmo de 'Medici, (1389-1464), Alexander the Great, (c.356-183), King Louis XIV, (1638-1715), and Pope Julius II, (d.1513), (from 'A series of etchings by James Barry, 1808, see App. 8, no. 20,722)
Issued privately by J. Barry, London, 1803: this is re-issue by Colnaghi, London, 1808
(Printed: W. Bulmer & Co.)
94.4 x 67.5 (plate 74.3 x 50.5)
Etching and line
Provenance Unknown

Barry, James (1741-1806)
Irish School
BARRY, JAMES (1741-1806)
IRISH SCHOOL

20,722(11)
The Angelic Guards, (revised detail from 'Elysium'), with portraits of King Charles I, (1600-1649), Jean-Baptiste Colbert, (1619-1683), Cassiodorus, (c.481-577), King Francis I, (1494-1547), and Marcus Agrippa, (c.63-12BC), below Joshua Reynolds, (1723-1792), Giles Hussey, (1710-1788), Annibale Carracci, (1560-1609), and Domenichino, (1581-1641), (from 'A series of etchings by James Barry', 1808, see App. 8, no. 20,722)
4th State
Published: firstly by J. Barry, London, c.1802: this is re-issue by Colnaghi & Co., London, 1808
(Printed: W. Bulmer & Co.)
94.3 x 67.5 (plate 74.3 x 50.2)
Etching and Line
Provenance Unknown

Barry, James (1741-1806)
Irish School
BARRY, JAMES (1741-1806)
IRISH SCHOOL

20,722(12)
Detail of the Diagorides Victors, (of 'Crowning the Victors at Olympia'), (from 'A series of etchings by James Barry', 1808, see App. 8, no. 20,722)
4th State
Published: firstly by J. Barry, London, 1st May 1795: this is re-issue by Colnaghi, London, 1808
(Printed: W. Bulmer & Co.)
94.3 x 67.5 (plate 74.3 x 47.4)
Etching
Provenance Unknown

Barry, James (1741-1804)
Irish School
BARRY, JAMES (1741-1804)
IRISH SCHOOL

20,722(13)

Sketches for two over-chimneys, intended to represent King George III, (1738-1820), recommending to both Houses of Parliament in 1761 a Bill for the independence of Judges: also Queen Charlotte, (1744-1818), at Windsor teaching children, (from 'A series of etchings by James Barry', 1808, see App. 8, no. 20,722)
5th State
Published: firstly by J. Barry, London, lst May 1791: this is re-issue by Colnaghi, London, 1808 (Printed: W. Bulmer & Co.)
49.8 x 67.5 (plate 42.2 x 51.6)
Etching
Provenance Unknown

Barry, James (1741-1806)
Irish School
BARRY, JAMES (1741-1806)
IRISH SCHOOL

20,722(14)
Queen Isabella of Spain, (1450-1504), Las Casas, (1474-1566), and Magellan, (c.1470-1521), (from 'A series of etchings by James Barry', 1808, see App. 8, no. 20,722)
2nd State
Published: firstly by J. Barry, London, 25th July 1800: this is a re-issue by Colnaghi, London, 1808 (Printed: W. Bulmer & Co.)
75.4 x 50.3 (plate 72 x 12.6)
Etching
Provenance Unknown

Barry, James (1741-1806)
Irish School
EDWARDS, WILLIAM CAMDEN (1777-1855)
ENGLISH SCHOOL

11,116
Self-Portrait as Timanthes, (pl. for A. Cunningham's 'The Lives of the most eminent British painters, sculptors and architects', 1830-33)
(after an oil of c.1780 and 1803, NGI no. 971)
Published: J. Murray, London, 1830
11.5 x 7.9 (plate cut)
Line
Provenance Unknown

Barry, James (1741-1806)
Irish School
HEATH, JAMES (1757-1834)
ENGLISH SCHOOL

10,712
Self-Portrait as Timanthes, (frontispiece for 'Transactions of the Royal Society of Arts', 1804)
(after an oil of c.1780 and 1803, NGI no. 971)
Published: The Society of Arts, London, 1804
31.8 x 29.8 (plate 25.3 x 21.7)
Line
Provenance Unknown

Barry, James (1741-1806)
Irish School
LEGAT FRANCIS (1755-1809)
SCOTTISH SCHOOL

20,712(40)
Lear weeping over the dead body of Cordelia, (Shakespeare's 'King Lear', Act V, scene 3), (from 'A Collection of Prints from Pictures painted for the purpose of illustrating the Dramatic Works of Shakespeare'. Vol. 2, 1803, see App. 8, no. 20,712)
(after an oil of 1786-87, Tate Gallery, London)
Published: J. & J. Boydell, London, 1st August 1792 (Printed: W. Bulmer & Co.)
51.5 x 67.5 (plate 50 x 64)
Line
Provenance Unknown

Barry, James (1741-1806)
Irish School
SCHIAVONETTI, LEWIS (1765-1810)
ANGLO-ITALIAN SCHOOL

20,722(15)

Pandora, (from 'A series of etchings by James Barry', 1808, see App. 8, no. 20, 722)
INSCRIBED: *Etched by Lewis Schiavonetti from a drawing by the late James Barry in the possession of Richard Horsman Solly Esq.*
Published: R.H. Solly, lst May 1810
67.5 x 96 (plate 49 x cut)
Etching
Provenance Unknown

Bartlett, William Henry (1809-1854)
English School
ADLARD, H. (Fl. 1828-1869)
ENGLISH SCHOOL

20,435
Pontoon Bridge linking Loughs Conn and Cullin, Co. Mayo, (pl. for N. Willis and S. Coyne's 'The Scenery and Antiquities of Ireland', 1842)
Published: G. Virtue, (for the Proprietor), London
22.2 x 28.4 (plate cut)
Steel Engraving
Purchased, Lusk, Mr de Courcy Donovan, 1971

Bartlett, William Henry (1809-1854)
English School
ADLARD, H. (FL.1828-1869)
ENGLISH SCHOOL

20,440
Luggala lodge, Lough Tay, Co. Wicklow, (pl. for N. Willis and S. Coyne's 'The Scenery and Antiquities of Ireland', 1842)
Published: G. Virtue, (for the Proprietors), London
22 x 28.4 (plate cut)
Steel Engraving
Purchased, Lusk, Mr de Courcy Donovan, 1971

Bartlett, William Henry (1809-1854)
English School
BENJAMIN, E. (1834-1846)
ENGLISH SCHOOL

20,437
Lismore Castle, Co. Waterford from the River Blackwater, (pl. for N. Willis and S. Coyne's 'The Scenery and Antiquities of Ireland', 1842)
Published: G. Virtue, (for the Proprietors), London
22.2 x 28.4 (plate cut)
Steel Engraving
Purchased, Lusk, Mr de Courcy Donovan, 1971

Bartlett, William Henry (1809-1854)
English School
BENTLEY, JOSEPH CLAYTON (1809-1851)
ENGLISH SCHOOL

20,601
The River Dargle, Co. Wicklow, (pl. for S.C. & A.M. Hall's 'Ireland, its Scenery, Character, etc.,' 1841-43, also for N.P. Wills and J.S. Coyne's 'The Scenery and Antiquities of Ireland', 1842)
Published: G. Virtue, (for the Proprietors), London
12.8 x 18.4 (plate cut)
Steel Engraving
Presented, Mrs D. Molloy, 1981

Bartlett, William Henry (1809-1854)
English School
CHALLIS, EBENEZER (fl.1831-1863)
ENGLISH SCHOOL

20,234
The Oak Room, Malahide Castle, Co. Dublin, (pl. for G. Virtue's 'Picturesque Beauties of Great Britain', 1832)
Published: G. Virtue, (for the Proprietors), London
22.3 x 28.4 (plate cut)
Line
Purchased, Lusk, Mr de Courcy Donovan, 1971

Bartlett, William Henry (1809-1854)
English School
COOKE, WILLIAM BERNARD (1778-1855)
ENGLISH SCHOOL

20,417

Baths of Saint-Gervais-Les Bains, Switzerland, (pl. for W. Beattie's 'Switzerland', 1836)
Published: G. Virtue, (for the Proprietor), London, 1835
27 x 21.5 (plate cut)
Steel Engraving
Purchased, Lusk, Mr de Courcy Donovan, 1971

Bartlett, William Henry (1809-1854)
English School
COUSEN, JOHN (1804-1880)
ENGLISH SCHOOL

20,438
Delphi Fishing Lodge, Lough Doo, Co. Mayo, (pl. for N. Willis and S. Coyne's 'The Scenery and Antiquities of Ireland', 1842)
Published: G. Virtue, (for the Proprietors), London
22 x 28.5 (plate cut)
Steel Engraving
Purchased, Lusk, Mr de Courcy Donovan, 1971

Bartlett, William Henry (1809-1854)
English School
COUSEN, JOHN (1804-1880)
ENGLISH SCHOOL

20,439
Delphi Fishing Lodge, Lough Doo, Co, Mayo, (pl. for N. Willis and S. Coyne's 'The Scenery and Antiquities of Ireland', 1842), (another copy)
Published: G. Virtue, (for the Proprietors), London
22.2 x 28.4 (plate cut)
Steel Engraving
Purchased, Lusk, Mr de Courcy Donovan, 1971

Bartlett, William Henry (1809-1854)
English School
COUSEN, JOHN (1804-1880)
ENGLISH SCHOOL

20,605
King John's Castle, Limerick, (pl. for S.C. and A.M. Hall's 'Ireland, its Scenery, Character, etc.', 1841-43)
Published: Hall, Virtue & Co., London
12 x 18.5 (plate cut)
Steel Engraving
Presented, Mrs D. Molloy, 1981

Bartlett, William Henry (1809-1854)
English School
HEATH, JAMES (1757-1834)
ENGLISH SCHOOL

11,749
The Equestrian Statue of King George II, (now removed), on South Mall, Cork, taken from the York Club House, (pl. for G.N. Wright's 'Ireland Illustrated', 1831)
Published: Fisher Son & Co., London, 1830
14 x 21.8 (plate cut)
Steel Engraving
Provenance Unknown

Bartlett, William Henry (1809-1854)
English School
HIGHAM, THOMAS (1796-1844)
ENGLISH SCHOOL

20,399
Scene on the River Orontes, near Suddeah, Syria, (pl. for J Carne's 'Syria', 1836-38)
Published: Fisher, Son & Co., London & Paris, 1836
22.3 x 28.3 (plate cut)
Steel Engraving
Purchased, Lusk, Mr de Courcy Donovan, 1971

Bartlett, William Henry (1809-1854)
English School
JORDAN, HENRY (Fl. 1829-1853)
ENGLISH SCHOOL

20,372
The Pays de Vaud from above Lausanne, Switzerland, (pl. for W. Beattie's 'Switzerland', 1836)
Published: G. Virtue, (for the Proprietor), London, 1836
21.6 x 27 (plate cut)
Steel Engraving
Purchased Lusk, Mr de Courcy Donovan, 1971

Bartlett, William Henry (1809-1854)
English School
RICHARDSON, GEORGE K. (Fl.1836-1891
ENGLISH SCHOOL

20,434
Powerscourt House, Co. Wicklow from above the River Dargle, (pl. for N. Willis and S. Coyne's 'The Scenery and Antiquities of Ireland' 1842)
Published: G. Virtue, (for the Proprietor), London
22.2 x 28.4 (plate cut)
Steel Engraving
Purchased, Lusk, Mr de Courcy Donovan, 1971

Bartlett, William Henry (1809-1854)
English School
RICHARDSON, GEORGE K. (FL. 1836-1891)
ENGLISH SCHOOL

20,436
Old Weir Bridge, Killarney, Co. Kerry, (pl. for N. Willis and S. Coyne's 'The Scenery and Antiquities of Ireland', 1842; also for S.C. and A.M. Hall's 'Ireland, its Scenery, Character etc.', 1841-43)
Published: G. Virtue, (for the Proprietors), London
22.1 x 28.2 (plate cut)
Steel Engraving
Purchased, Lusk, Mr de Courcy Donovan, 1971

Bartlett, William Henry (1809-1854)
English School
RICHARDSON, GEORGE K. (FL. 1836-1891
ENGLISH SCHOOL

20,600
The Salmon Leap at Leixlip, Co. Kildare, (pl. for N.P. Willis and J.S. Coyne's 'The Scenery and Antiquities of Ireland', 1842)
Published: G. Virtue, (for the Proprietors), London
14.2 x 19.5 (plate cut)
Steel Engraving
Presented, Mrs D. Molloy, 1981

Bartlett, William Henry (1809-1854)
English School
ROGERS, JOHN (C.1808-1888)
ENGLISH SCHOOL

20,514
Limerick Bridge and John's Castle, from the River Shannon, ('Specimens of Art', plate 15)
Published: J. McCormick, London
22.5 x 30.4 (plate 22 x 29)
Etching and mezzotint
Purchased, Lusk, Mr de Courcy Donovan, 1971

Bartlett, William Henry (1809-1854)
English School
STARLING, WILLIAM FRANCIS (FL. 1833-1845)
ENGLISH SCHOOL

20,453
Castle near Tripoli on the River Cadesha, (now Orontes), Syria, (previously pl. for J. Carne's 'Syria', 1836-38)
Published: Fisher Son & Co., London, 1842
22.2 x 28.5 (plate cut)
Steel Engraving
Purchased, Lusk, Mr de Courcy Donovan, 1971

Bartlett, William Henry (1809-1854)
English School
STEPHENSON, JAMES (1808-1886)
ENGLISH SCHOOL
20,455

Remains of the ancient port of Seleucia, at the mouth of the river Orontes, Turkey, (previously pl. for J. Carne's 'Syria', 1836-38)
Published: Fisher, Son & Co., London & Paris, 1841
22.5 x 28.5 (plate cut)
Steel Engraving
Purchased, Lusk, Mr de Courcy Donovan, 1971

Bartlett, William Henry (1809-1854)
English School
THOMPSON, D. (FL. 1832-1838)
ENGLISH SCHOOL

20,450
Besherrai village, Mount Lebanon, Syria, (previously pl. for J. Carne's 'Syria' 1836-38)
Published: Fisher Son & Co., London & Paris, 1841
22.3 x 28.5 (plate cut)
Steel Engraving
Purchased, Lusk, Mr de Courcy Donovan, 1971

Bartlett, William Henry (1809-54)
English School
TOPHAM, FRANCIS WILLIAM (1808-1877)
ENGLISH SCHOOL

11,763
St Patrick's Cathedral, Dublin from the North-East, (pl. for S.C. and A.M. Hall's 'Ireland, its Scenery, Character etc.', 1841-43)
15.7 x 20.7 (plate cut)
Steel Engraving
Provenance Unknown

Bartlett, William Henry (1809-1854)
English School
TOPHAM, FRANCIS WILLIAM (1808-1877)
ENGLISH SCHOOL

20,590
St Patrick's Cathedral, Dublin, from the North-East, (pl. for S.C. and A.M. Hall's 'Ireland, its Scenery, Character, etc.', 1841-43), (another copy)
13.1 x 17.5 (plate cut)
Steel Engraving
Presented, Mrs D. Molloy, 1981

Bartlett, William Henry (1809-1854)
English School
WALLIS, ROBERT (1794-1878)
ENGLISH SCHOOL

20,441
Istanbul, Turkey, from above The New Palace of Beshik-Tash, (pl. for J. Pardoe's 'The Beauties of the Bosphorus', 1839-40)
Published: G. Virtue, (for the Proprietors), London
21.8 x 28.2 (plate cut)
Steel Engraving
Purchased, Lusk, Mr de Courcy Donovan, 1971

Bartlett, William Henry (1809-1854)
English School
WINKLES, RICHARD (FL.1829-1836)
ENGLISH SCHOOL

11,771
St George's Church, Hardwicke Place, Dublin, (pl. for G.N. Wright's 'Ireland Illustrated', 1831)
Published: Fisher Son & Co., London, 1829
22.2 x 14.3 (pl. 21.9 x 14)
Steel Engraving
Provenance Unknown

Bartlett, William Henry (1809-1854)
English School
WINKLES, RICHARD (Fl.1829-1836)
ENGLISH SCHOOL

20,611
St George's Church, Hardwicke Place, Dublin, (pl. for G.N. Wright's 'Ireland Illustrated', 1831), (another copy)
Published: Fisher Son & Co.,

London, 1829
17.9 x 11.6 (plate cut)
Steel Engraving
Presented, Mrs D. Molloy, 1981

Bartlett, William Henry (1809-1854)
English School *and*
Creswick, Thomas (1811-1869)
English School
WILLMORE, JAMES TIBBETTS (1800-1863)
ENGLISH SCHOOL

20,418
Pissevache Cascade, in the Canton of Valais, Switzerland
Published: G. Virtue, (for the Proprietors), London, 1835
21.6 x 27 (plate cut)
Steel Engraving
Purchased, Lusk, Mr de Courcy Donovan, 1971

Bartolozzi, Francesco (1725-1815)
Anglo-Italian School
BARTOLOZZI, FRANCESCO (1725-1815)
ANGLO-ITALIAN SCHOOL

20,807
Two Amorini
48.4 x 30.2 (plate 25 x 18.4)
Stipple
Provenance Unknown

Baseley, C.I. (19th century)
English School
FINDEN, WILLIAM (1787-1852)
ENGLISH SCHOOL

10,769
Lady Alicia Conroy, (née Parsons 1815-1885), wife of Sir Edward Conroy, 2nd Bt. (pl. for W. Finden's 'Female Aristocracy of the Court of Queen Victoria', 1849)
Published: W. & E. Finden, (The Proprietors), London, lst October 1840
36 x 26.8 (plate 33.7 x 26)
Line and stipple
Purchased, 1908

Bassano Jacopo (1510-1592)
Venetian School
MONACO, PIETRO (FL. 1735-1775)
ITALIAN SCHOOL

11,488
The Departure of Abraham and his Family for Canaan
Published: P. Monaco, Venice
45 x 62 (plate 36.2 x 50.3)
Line and etching
Provenance Unknown

Bateman, James (1814-1849)
English School
ENGLEHEART, JONATHAN (Fl.1839-1853)
ENGLISH SCHOOL

11,873
'Don't you wish you may get it'
Published: Lloyd Brothers & Co., London, lst May 1851
35.1 x 44.5 (plate 32.4 x 41.3)
Line with watercolour and varnish
Provenance Unknown

Batoni, Pompeo (1708-1787)
Italian School
WATSON, JAMES (C.1740-1790)
IRISH SCHOOL

10,129
Augustus Henry Fitzroy, 3rd Duke of Grafton, (1735-1811), later British Prime Minister
(after an oil of 1762, Euston Hall, Suffolk)
35.6 x 25.7 (plate 35.2 x 25)
Mezzotint
Milltown Gift, 1902

Baudry, Paul Jacques Aimé (1828-1886)
French School
JACQUEMART, JULES FERDINAND (1837-1880)
FRENCH SCHOOL

11,380
Sir Richard Wallace Bt., (1818-1890), Connoisseur and Collector
Published: Gazette des Beaux-Arts, Paris (Printed: F. Lienard)
27.5 x 19.2 (plate cut)
Etching
Acquired by 1903

Baugniet, Charles (1814-1886)
Anglo-Belgian School
BAUGNIET, CHARLES (1814-1886)
ANGLO-BELGIAN SCHOOL

10,802
Admiral Sir William Henry Dillon, (1779-1857)
Published: London, 1854
52.8 x 37.5 (image 42.8 x 31)
Lithograph
Purchased, London,
Mr H.A.J. Breun, 1910

Baugniet, Charles (1814-1886)
Belgian School
BAUGNIET, CHARLES (1814-1886)
BELGIAN SCHOOL

10,901
Samuel Lover, (1797-1868), Artist, Composer and Author
(Printed: M. & N. Hanhart, London, 1844)
30.3 x 23.8 (image 27 x 21.2)
Lithograph
Purchased, 1907

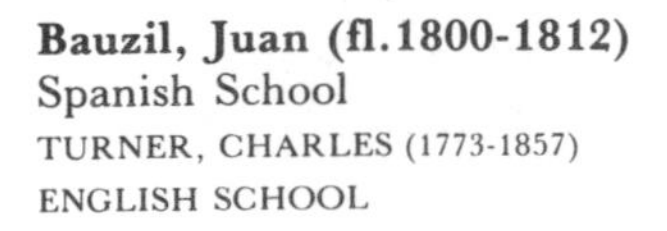

Bauzil, Juan (fl.1800-1812)
Spanish School
TURNER, CHARLES (1773-1857)
ENGLISH SCHOOL

10,507
Field-Marshal Arthur Wellesley, 1st Duke of Wellington, (1769-1852)
(derived from a watercolour, NPG, London)
Published: C. Turner, London, 16th April 1816
55.8 x 40.4 (plate cut)
Mezzotint
Acquired between 1904/8

Bazin, Charles-Louis (1802-1859)
French School
LAFOSSE, JEAN BAPTISTE ADELPHE (C.1810-1879)
FRENCH SCHOOL

11,875
Haydée, (no. 18 of a series)
Published: Bulla Freres et Jouy, Paris, Berlin and Barcelona, also E.

Gambart & Co., London.(Printed: Lemercier, Paris)
63 x 47 (plate 59 x 45 approx)
Deux Crayons lithograph
Provenance Unknown

Beechey, William (1753-1839)
English School
EARLOM, RICHARD (1743-1822)
ENGLISH SCHOOL

10,430
Captain Henry D'Esterre Darby, (d.1823), later an Admiral
INSCRIBED: *Engraved from the Original Picture in the possession of Sir John Darby Esqr. To whom This Plate is respectfully inscribed by his obliged & most obedient servant B.B. Evans*
Published: B.B. Evans, London, lst January 1801
50.5 x 36.5 (plate cut x 35.5)
Mezzotint
Presented, Mr A. Webb, 1903

Beechey, William (1753 -1839)
English School
WARD, JAMES (1769-1859)
ENGLISH SCHOOL

10,498
Charles Cornwallis, 1st Marquess of Cornwallis, (1738-1805), former Commander-in Chief in War with America, Governor General of Bengal, and Lord Lieutenant of Ireland, as a Knight of the Garter
(after an oil, RA 1799)
Published: A. De Pogg, London, 10th March 1799
67.4 x 48.4 (plate 66.3 x 46)
Mezzotint
Acquired between 1890/98

Behnes, William (1795-1864)
English School
MEYER, HENRY (C.1782-1847)
ENGLISH SCHOOL

11,553
Lady Sydney Morgan, (née Owenson, 1778-1859), Authoress, (pl. for E. Bell's 'La Belle Assemblée', August 1824)
(after a drawing)
Published: London, 1st August 1824
21.2 x 13.1 (plate cut)
Stipple
Acquired by 1909

Bell, John (1811-1895)
English School
ROFFE, F.R. (19TH CENTURY)
ENGLISH SCHOOL
ROFFE, WILLIAM (Fl.1848-1884)
ENGLISH SCHOOL

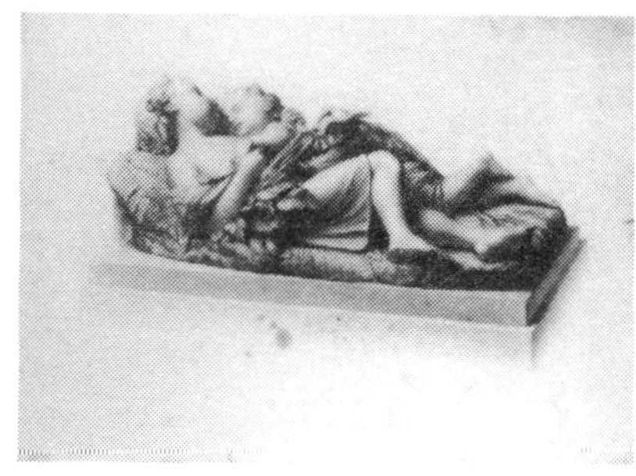

20,209
The Children in the Wood, (from the 'Art Journal', 1853)
(after a marble group, RA 1842)
Published: J.A. Virtue, London, 1853
23.4 x 32 (plate cut)
Steel Engraving
Purchased, Lusk, Mr de Courcy Donovan, 1971

Bella, Stefano della (1610-1664)
Italian School
BELLA, STEFANO DELLA (1610-1664)
ITALIAN SCHOOL

20,233

The Leopard (No. 9)
12 x 15 (plate 8.5 x 10.6)
Etching
Purchased, Lusk, Mr de Courcy
Donovan, 1971

Bella, Stefano della (1610-1664)
Italian School
BELLA, STEFANO DELLA (1610-1664)
ITALIAN SCHOOL

20,792
The Lion (No. 5)
12 x 15 (plate 8.6 x 10.8)
Etching
Purchased, Lusk, Mr de Courcy
Donovan, 1971

Bella, Stefano della (1610-1664)
Italian School
BELLA, STEFANO DELLA (1610-1664)
ITALIAN SCHOOL

20,793
The Ox (No. 13)
11.9 x 15.2 (plate 8.7 x 10.8)
Etching
Purchased, Lusk, Mr de Courcy
Donovan, 1971

Bella, Stefano Della (1610-1664)
Italian School
BELLA, STEFANO DELLA (1610-1664)
ITALIAN SCHOOL

20,794
The Doe (No. 15)
12 x 15.3 (plate 8.6 x 10.8)
Etching
Purchased, Lusk, Mr de Courcy
Donovan, 1971

Bella, Stefano della (1610-1664)
Italian School
BELLA, STEFANO DELLA (1610-1664)
ITALIAN SCHOOL

20,795
The Dromedary (No. 17)
12 x 15.4 (plate 8.7 x 10.8)
Etching
Purchased, Lusk, Mr de Courcy
Donovan, 1971

Belle, Alexis Simon (1674-1734)
French School
ENGLISH SCHOOL (18th CENTURY)

10,607
Rev. Charles Leslie, (1650-1722), Jacobite Religious Controversialist and Pamphleteer
(after an oil of c.1711)
13.5 x 7.6 (plate cut)
Line
Purchased, Dublin,
Mr J.V. McAlpine, 1909

Belle, Alexis Simon (1674-1734)
French School
?SIMON, JOHN (1675-1734)
ANGLO-FRENCH SCHOOL

11,413
Rev. Charles Leslie, (1650-1722), Jacobite Publisher, Religious Controversialist and Pamphleteer
(after an A.S. Belle/F. Chereau line engraving; example in NLI, Dublin, from an oil of c.1711)
34.5 x 25 (plate cut)
Mezzotint
Provenance Unknown

Bentley, Joseph Clayton (1809-1851)
English School
BENTLEY, JOSEPH CLAYTON (1809-1851)
ENGLISH SCHOOL

20,415
The Bridge at Pen-y-Gwryd, Wales, wtih Mount Snowdon beyond
Published: Simpkin & Marshall, also J.W. Stevens, London
21.4 x 27.5 (plate cut)
Steel Engraving
Purchased, Lusk, Mr de Courcy Donovan, 1971

Bentley, Joseph Clayton (1809-1851)
English School
BENTLEY, JOSEPH CLAYTON (1809-1851)
ENGLISH SCHOOL

20,610
The Bridge at Pen-y-Gwryd, Wales with Mount Snowdon beyond, (another copy)
Published: Simpkin & Marshall, also J.W. Stevens, London
12.3 x 16.1 (plate cut)
Steel Engraving
Presented, Mrs D. Molloy, 1981

Berchem, Nicolaes (1620-1683)
Dutch School
DUJARDIN, LOUIS (1808-1859)
FRENCH SCHOOL

20,618
Rustic Occupation
10.4 x 18.4 (image 9 x 13.5)
Wood Engraving
Presented, Mrs D. Molloy, 1981

Berchem, Nicolaes (1620-1683)
Dutch School
ENGLISH SCHOOL (18TH CENTURY)

20,135
Landscape with Shepherds
42 x 54 approx (plate cut)
Aquatint
Purchased, Lusk, Mr de Courcy Donovan, 1971

Berchem, Nicolaes (1620-1683)
Dutch School
?ENGLISH SCHOOL (18TH CENTURY)

20,547
Two Sheep
9.1 x 14.2 (plate cut)
Etching
Presented, Mrs D. Molloy, 1981

Berchem, Nicolaes (1620-1683)
Dutch School
?ENGLISH SCHOOL (18TH CENTURY)

20,548
Cattle, Milkmaid and goat
8.9 x 14.2 (plate cut)
Etching
Presented, Mrs D. Molloy, 1981

Berchem, Nicolaes (1620-1683)
Dutch School
ENGLISH SCHOOL (19TH CENTURY)

20,146
Peasants with Cattle and Sheep by a ruin
31.1 x 40.6 (plate cut)
Etching
Purchased, Lusk, Mr de Courcy Donovan, 1971

Berrettoni, Niccolo (1637-1682)
Italian School
CLAYTON THE ELDER, BENJAMIN (C.1754-1814)
IRISH SCHOOL

11,500

The Holy Family with St Anne and St John the Baptist
Published: Z. Jackson, Dublin
26.4 x 41.4 (plate 22.3 x 33)
Line
Provenance Unknown

Bewick, Thomas (1753-1828)
English School
THURSTON, JOHN (1774-1822)
ENGLISH SCHOOL
WORTHINGTON, WILLIAM HENRY(C.1795-C.1839)
ENGLISH SCHOOL

10,763
John Cunningham, (1729-1773), Actor and Poet, (pl. for 'Effigies Poetical', 1821)
INSCRIBED: *From a Drawing by Bewick, in the Possession of Miss Hornby*
Published: W. Walker, London, 1st September 1821
29.5 x 25.6 (plate 20 x 13.9)
Line
Purchased, Dublin, Mr J.V. McAlpine, 1909

Bewnes, William (1795-1864)
English School
LEWIS, FREDERICK CHRISTIAN (1779-1856)
ENGLISH SCHOOL

10,566
Richard Whateley, P. Archbishop of Dublin, (1787-1863)
Published: E. Graves & Co., late Colnaghi & Co., London, 18th April 1836
38.5 x 31.4 (plate 38 x 30.5)
Stipple
Purchased, Dublin, Mr J.V. McAlpine, 1913

Biasioli, Angelo (1790-1830)
Italian School
BIASIOLI, ANGELO (1790-1830)
ITALIAN SCHOOL

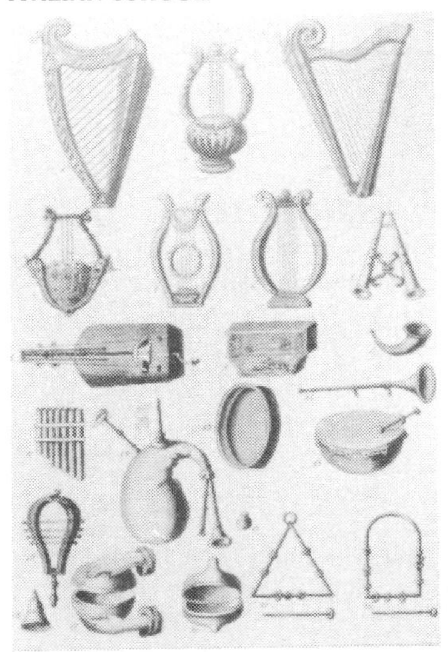

20,171
Twenty Two Musical Instruments
36.2 x 25.2 (plate 22.3 x 14)
Etching with watercolour
Purchased, Lusk, Mr de Courcy Donovan, 1971

Bigari, Angelo Mario (fl.1772-1792)
Italian School
MEDLAND, THOMAS (1755-1833)
ENGLISH SCHOOL

10,055
Christchurch Cathedral, Dublin and Chapter House, (now roofless), from the South-East, (pl. for F. Grose's 'The Antiquities of Ireland', 1791-95)
Published: S. Hooper, London, 1st October 1791
26 x 31 (plate 16.5 x 21.5)
Line
Presented, Mr W.G. Strickland, 1906

Bindon, Francis (c.1700-1765)
Irish School
BROOKS, JOHN (FL.1730-1756)
IRISH SCHOOL

10,044
Brigadier General Richard St George of Woodsgift, Co. Kilkenny, (d.1755)
Published: J. Brooks, Dublin, January 1744
36.6 x 26.8 (plate 34.7 x 25.3)
Mezzotint
Purchased, London, lst Chaloner Smith sale, 1887

Bindon, Francis (c.1700-1765)
Irish School
McARDELL, JAMES (1728/29-1765)
IRISH SCHOOL

10,026
Hugh Boulter, P. Archbishop of Armagh, (1672-1742)
(after an oil of 1742, Provost's House, Trinity College, Dublin)
INSCRIBED: *This Plate is most Humbly Dedicated to His Grace by his Grace's most Humble Servant Jno. Brooks*
Published: J. Brooks, Dublin, May 1742
50.5 x 37 (plate cut)
Mezzotint
Purchased, London, 1st Chaloner Smith sale, 1887

Bindon, Francis (c.1700-1765)
Irish School
MARTYN, JOHN (FL.1794-1765)
IRISH SCHOOL

10,279
'Carolan, the Celebrated Irish Bard', (Turlough O'Carolan, 1670-1738)
(after a replica of oil NGI no. 1344, c.1810)
INSCRIBED: *From a painting in the possession of Mr Hardiman, author of the History of Galway. Carolan, the celebrated Irish Bard. To his Excellency the Marquess Wellesley, K.G., Lord Lieutenant of Ireland etc., etc., This Print (by permission) is most respectfully inscribed by his most obedient Servant - John Martyn*
Published: J. Martyn, Dublin, 12th November 1822
34.6 x 26.4 (plate 28.6 x 21)
Line and stipple
Presumed Purchased, Dublin, Jones Salesroom, 1879

Bindon, Francis (c.1700-1765)
Irish School
MILLER, ANDREW (FL.1737-1763)
IRISH SCHOOL

10,024
Charles Cobbe, P. Archbishop of Dublin, (1687-1765)
INSCRIBED: *The most Revd. Charles Cobbe D.D. Lord Archbishop of Dublin, Primate & Metropolitan of IRELAND To whom this Plate is Humbly Dedicated by his Grace's much obliged and most obedient Sert. Mich:Forde*
Published: M. Ford, Dublin, 1746
35.1 x 25.1 (plate cut)
Mezzotint
Purchased, London, 1st Chaloner Smith sale, 1887

Bindon, Francis (c.1700-1765)
Irish School
MILLER, ANDREW (FL.1737-1763)
IRISH SCHOOL

10,052
Jonathan Swift, (1667-1745), Dean of St Patrick's Cathedral, Dublin, and Satirist
(after an oil of 1739, St Patrick's Cathedral Deanery)
Published: I. Orpin & P. Smith, Dublin, 1743
50 x 35.5 (plate cut)
Mezzotint
Purchased, London, 1st Chaloner Smith sale, 1887

Bindon, Francis (c.1700-1765)
Irish School
MILLER, ANDREW (FL.1737-1763)
IRISH SCHOOL

10,444

Charles Cobbe, P. Archbishop of Dublin, (1687-1765)
(?after an F. Bindon/A. Miller mezzotint, NGI no. 10,024)
Unlettered Proof
49.8 x 35.8 (plate 46.5 x 35.8)
Mezzotint
Purchased, Dublin, Mr A. Roth, 1900

Bindon, Francis (c.1700-1765)
Irish School
MILLER, ANDREW (FL.1737-1763)
IRISH SCHOOL

20,801
Jonathan Swift, (1667-1745), Dean of St Patrick's Cathedral Dublin and Satirist
(after an oil of 1739, St Patrick's Cathedral Deanery)
Unlettered proof
Published: ?1743
35.7 x 26.1 (plate 35.2 x 25.5)
Mezzotint
Purchased, London, 1st Chaloner Smith sale, 1887

Bindon, Francis (c.1700-1765)
Irish School
SCRIVEN, EDWARD (1775-1841)
ENGLISH SCHOOL

10,529
Jonathan Swift, (1667-1745), Dean of St Patrick's Cathedral, Dublin and Satirist, (pl. for W. M. Mason's 'The History and Antiquities of the Collegiate and Cathedral Church of St Patrick, near Dublin', 1819)
(after an oil of 1735, Howth Castle, Co. Dublin)
Lettered Proof
Published: W.M. Mason, Dublin, 1st August 1818
35.8 x 30.2 (plate 33.6 x 24.2)
Stipple and etching
Acquired between 1907/09

Bingham, Lady Margaret (later Countess of Lucan) (fl.1760-1814)
Irish School
McDOWALL (19TH CENTURY)
IRISH SCHOOL

11,291
Patrick Sarsfield, 1st Earl of Lucan, (d.1693)
(after an M. Bingham/J. & M. Tilliard line engraving, NGI no. 10,093)
25.4 x 17 (plate cut)
Line
Purchased, Dublin, Mr P. Traynor, 1898

Bingham, Lady Margaret (later Countess of Lucan) (fl.1760-1814)
Irish School
TILLIARD, JEAN BAPTISTE (1742-1813) *and* TILLIARD, Mme M. ANGELIQUE (?1743-1782, NÉE BREGEON)
FRENCH SCHOOL

10,093
Patrick Sarsfield, 1st Earl of Lucan, (d.1693)
(after a watercolour miniature)
INSCRIBED: After the Original picture in the possession of Sir Charles Bingham Bart. at Castlebar in the County of Mayo, in the Kingdom of Ireland
28 x 19.7 (plate cut)
Line
Presented, Sir John T. Gilbert, 1891

Black, G.B. (fl.1855-1861)
English School
BLACK, G.B. (FL.1855-1861)
ENGLISH SCHOOL

10,734
Richard Atkinson, Lord Mayor of Dublin, 1857 and 1861
(after an oil, RA 1855)
Published: London, 1861
52.3 x 43.8 (image 42 x 35 oval)
Lithograph
Purchased, Dublin,
Mr J.V. McAlpine, 1903

Blakey, Nicholas (fl.1747-1778)
Irish School
CATHELIN, LOUIS JACQUES (1739-1804)
FRENCH SCHOOL

20,770
Abbé Noel Antoine Pluche, (1688-1761), Theologian and Author
33.6 x 24.3 (plate 26.8 x 18.9)
Line
Presented, Mr D. Alexander, 1986

Blakiston, Douglas Y. (fl.1853-1865)
English School
ZOBEL, GEORGE. J. (1810-1881)
ENGLISH SCHOOL

11,007
Robert Bentley Todd, (1809-1860), Physician
Published: P. & D. Colnaghi, also Scott & Co., London, 1st November 1860
38 x 30.2 (plate 38 x 30.2)
Mezzotint
Purchased, Dublin, Mr A. Roth, 1897

Boel, Quirin (1620-1668)
Flemish School
BOEL, QUIRIN (1620-1668)
FLEMISH SCHOOL

10,276
Hugh Brady, Canon of St Peter's and President of St Anne's College, Louvain, Belgium
21 x 15.2 (plate cut)
Line
Purchased, Dublin,
Mr J.V. McAlpine, 1909

Bolognese School (17th century)
BOLOGNESE SCHOOL (17TH CENTURY)

20,228
The Assumption of the Virgin with six Apostles
55.5 x 37 (plate cut)
Line
Purchased, Lusk, Mr de Courcy Donovan, 1971

Bolognese School (18th century)
BOLOGNESE SCHOOL (18TH CENTURY)

10,515

Giovanni Ludovico Quadri, (d.1748), Bolognese Architectural Draughtsman and Engraver
17.5 x 11.8 (plate 12.3 x 10.5)
Etching
Provenance Unknown

?Bonaiuto, Andrea da (14th century)
Florentine School
ENGLISH SCHOOL (18TH CENTURY)

20,120
Giovanni Cimabue, (1240/50 - 1302), Artist
(after N. de l'Armissin's 1682 engraving of the Chapter House fresco, S. Maria Novella, Florence)
17.3 x 10.8 (plate cut)
Line
Purchased, Lusk, Mr de Courcy Donovan, 1971

Bonington, Richard Parkes (1802-1828)
English School
MILLER, WILLIAM (1796-1882)
ENGLISH SCHOOL

20,484
Sunset in the Pays de Caux, France, (titled 'Sea Shore Cornwall'), (previously pl. for 'The Keepsake', 1831)
(after a watercolour of 1828, Wallace Collection, London)
Published: Longman & Co., London, 1836
15.5 x 23.5 (plate cut)
Steel Engraving
Purchased, Lusk, Mr de Courcy Donovan, 1971

Bonington, Richard Parkes (1802-1828)
English School
MILLER, WILLIAM (1796-1828)
ENGLISH SCHOOL

20,589
Sunset in the Pays de Caux, France, (previously pl. for 'The Keepsake', 1831), (another copy)
(after a watercolour of 1828, Wallace Collection, London)
Published: Longman & Co., London, 1836
9.6 x 12.2 (plate cut)
Steel Engraving
Presented, Mrs D. Molloy, 1981

Bostok, John (fl.1826-1869)
English School
JENKINS, JOSEPH JOHN (1811-1885)
ENGLISH SCHOOL

10,913
Charles William Stewart, 3rd Marquess of Londonderry, (1778-1854), General, Statesman and Diplomat, (pl. for H.T. Ryall's 'Portraits of Eminent Conservatives and Statesman', 2nd series, 1846)
(after an oil of 1836)
Published: H.T. Ryall, also J. Fraser, also F.G. Moon, London, 1837
(Printed: Wilkinson & Dawe)
33.7 x 26.5 (plate 33.2 x 25.7)
Stipple
Acquired by 1903

Bowyer, Robert (1758-1834)
English School
BROMLEY, JOHN CHARLES (1795-1839)
ENGLISH SCHOOL

10,428

Frederick Augustus, Duke of York and Albany, (1763-1827), 2nd son of George II and Professional Soldier, against the Horse Guards Parade, London
Lettered Proof
Published: R. Bowyer & M. Parkes, London, 1828
52 x 36 (plate cut)
Mezzotint
Provenance Unknown

Bramer, Leonard (1596-1674)
Dutch School
CANOT, PIERRE CHARLES (1710-1777)
ANGLO-FRENCH SCHOOL

20,035
Pyramus and Thisbe - The Discovery of the Dead Lovers, (from Ovid's 'Metamorphoses')
INSCRIBED: To the Right Honourable Henry, Earl of Pembroke and Montgomery,/This Plate Engraved from an Original Picture of Leond. Bramer's is most humbly Inscribed by his Lordships most obedient, & most humble Servant,/John Boydell
Published: J. Boydell, London, 7th April 1768
54.5 x 76 (plate 45 x 55.7)
Line
Provenance Unknown

Brand, Johann Christian (1722-1795)
Austrian School
ALIAMET, JACQUES (1726-1788)
FRENCH SCHOOL

20,162
Near Sauverne, Alsace, France
INSCRIBED: Dédiée à Monsieur Rousseau du Réage/ Seigneur de la Goespierre, Secretair du Roi Honoraire & C/Par son tres humble Serviteur J. Aliamet
Published: J. Aliamet, Paris
22.5 x 28 (plate 20.5 x 26)
Line and etching
Purchased, Lusk, Mr de Courcy Donovan, 1971

Branwhite, Charles (1817-1880)
English School
LINTON, WILLIAM JAMES (1812-1898)
ENGLISH SCHOOL

20,626
Moel Siabod Mountain, N. Wales
18.6 x 24.5 (image 16.5 x 22)
Wood Engraving
Presented, Mrs D. Molloy, 1981

Bridgford, Thomas (1812-1878)
Irish School
GRIFFITHS, HENRY (FL.1835-1849)
ENGLISH SCHOOL

11,310
Sir Martin Archer Shee, (1769-1850), Portrait Painter and President of the Royal Academy, (pl, for 'Dublin university Magazine', Vol. XXVII, May 1846)
(after a chalk drawing, NGI no. 2027)
Published: J. McGlashan, Dublin, 1846
21.6 x 12.8 (plate cut)
Stipple
Purchased, Dublin, Mr J.V. McAlpine, 1913

Bridgford, Thomas (1812-1878)
Irish School
GRIFFITHS, HENRY (FL.1835-1849)
ENGLISH SCHOOL

11,312
Sir Martin Archer Shee, (1769-1880), Portrait Painter and President of the Royal Academy, (pl. for 'Dublin University Magazine', Vol. XXVII, May 1846), (another copy)
(after a chalk drawing, NGI no. 2027)
Published: J. McGlashan, Dublin, 1846
21.7 x 13.6 (plate cut)
Stipple
Purchased, Dublin, Mr J.V. McAlpine, 1913

Bridgford, Thomas (1812-1878)
Irish School
IRISH SCHOOL (1847)

11,237
Daniel Maclise, (1806-1870), Artist, (pl. for 'Dublin University Magazine', Vol. XXIX, May 1847)
(after a chalk drawing of 1844, NGI no. 2025)
Published: J. McGlashan, Dublin, 1847
22.3 x 14 (plate cut)
Stipple
Purchased, Mr P. Traynor, 1898

Bridgford, Thomas (1812-1878)
Irish School
P...., T. (19TH CENTURY)
IRISH SCHOOL

11,861
'The Masquerader', (Self-Portrait)
(after an oil, NGI no. 857)
Published: Allen's, Dublin
20 x 14.4 (image 14.5 x 12 approx)
Lithograph
Presented, Mr C. Tisdall, 1914

Bright, Henry, (1810-1873)
English School
DAY, WILLIAM (1797-1845)
ENGLISH SCHOOL *and*
HAGHE, LOUIS (1806-1885)
ANGLO-BELGIAN SCHOOL

20,222
Castle Entrance, (pl. for H. Bright's 'Drawing Book of Landscapes', 1843)
Published: Ackermann & Co., London, 1843 (Printed: W. Day & L. Haghe)
26.8 x 37.6 (image 18.5 x 27.5)
Lithograph
Purchased, Lusk, Mr de Courcy Donovan, 1971

Bright, Henry (1810-1873)
English School
DAY, WILLIAM (1747-1845)
ENGLISH SCHOOL *and*
HAGHE, LOUIS (1806-1885)
ANGLO-BELGIAN SCHOOL
20,347

A Cabin, (pl. for H. Bright's 'Drawing Book of Landscapes', 1843)
Published: Ackermann & Co., London, 1843 (Printed: W. Day & L. Haghe)
26.8 x 37.5 (image 18.5 x 27.5)
Lithograph
Purchased, Lusk, Mr de Courcy Donovan, 1971

?Brocas the Elder, Henry (1766-1838)
Irish School
BROCAS THE ELDER, HENRY (1766-1838)
IRISH SCHOOL

11,155
George IV, King of England, (1762-1830), Illustrating a Grand Royal Divertimento for the Pianoforte or Harp, to commemorate the Royal Visit to Dublin in 1821
Published: c.1821
16.2 x 16.2 (plate cut)
Stipple
Acquired between 1913/14

Brocas the Elder, Henry (1766-1838)
Irish School
BROCAS THE ELDER, HENRY (1766-1838)
IRISH SCHOOL

11,159
Thomas Grady, (d.c.1820), Poet, (pl. for his 'No. III or. the Nosegay....third letter of the Country Post-bag', 1816)

26 x 16.1 (plate 20.3 x 12.9)
Stipple
Purchased, London, 3rd Chaloner Smith sale, 1898

Brocas, Samuel Frederick (c.1792-1847)
Irish School
BROCAS THE YOUNGER, HENRY (C.1798-1873)
IRISH SCHOOL

11,703
The Custom House, Dublin, from the River Liffey
Published: J. Le Petit, Dublin, 1828
28.5 x 42.7 (plate cut)
Etching and line with watercolour
Provenance unknown

Brocas, Samuel Frederick (c.1792-1847)
Irish School
BROCAS THE YOUNGER, HENRY (C.1798-1873)
IRISH SCHOOL

11,944
Dublin Castle Gate between the Royal Exchange, (now City Hall), and Newcomen Bank, (now Civic Offices)
Published: J. Le Petit, Dublin
23.7 x 39 (plate cut)
Etching and line with watercolour
Purchased, Dublin, Mr J.V. McAlpine, 1901

Brocas, Samuel Frederick (c.1792-1847)
Irish School
BROCAS THE YOUNGER, HENRY (C.1798-1873)
IRISH SCHOOL

11,945
The Four Courts, Dublin looking down the River Liffey from Merchants Quay
(after a watercolour of 1818, NGI no. 2440)
Published: J. Le Petit, Dublin, 7th April 1818
31 x 47 (plate 26.3 x 42)
Etching and line with watercolour
Purchased, London, Mr L. Marks, 1898

Brocas, Samuel Frederick (c.1792-1847)
Irish School
BROCAS THE YOUNGER, HENRY (C.1798-1873)
IRISH SCHOOL

11,946
The Corn Exchange, (now offices), Burgh Quay, and Custom House, Dublin
Published: J. Le Petit, Dublin, also Wright & Bell, London, 1st July 1820
33 x 48.5 (plate 28 x 44.2)
Etching and line with watercolour
Purchased, London, Mr L. Marks, 1898

Brocas, Samuel Frederick (c.1792-1847)
Irish School
BROCAS THE YOUNGER, HENRY (C.1798-1873)
IRISH SCHOOL

11,947
D'Olier and Westmoreland Street, Dublin from Carlisle, (now O'Connell), Bridge
Published: J. Le Petit, Dublin, also Wright & Bell, London, 1st July 1820
Etching and line with watercolour
Purchased, Dublin, Mr A. Roth, 1900

Brocas, Samuel Frederick (c.1792-1847)
Irish School
BROCAS THE YOUNGER, HENRY (C.1798-1873)
IRISH SCHOOL

11,948
The General Post Office and Nelson Pillar, (now demolished), Sackville, (now O'Connell), Street, Dublin
(after a watercolour, V&A, London)
Published: J. Le Petit, Dublin
28.4 x 44.3 (pl. 26 x 41.7)
Etching and line with watercolour
Purchased, Dublin, Mr A. Roth, 1900

Brocas, Samuel Frederick (c.1792-1847)
Irish School
BROCAS THE YOUNGER, HENRY (C.1798-1873)
IRISH SCHOOL

11,949
The Lying-In, (now Rotunda), Hospital, The Rotunda and Rutland, (now Parnell), Square
Published: J. Le Petit, c.1820
31.7 x 48.5 (plate 28.2 x 44.2)
Etching and line with watercolour
Purchased, London, Mr L. Marks, 1898

Brocas, Samuel Frederick (c.1792-1847)
Irish School
BROCAS THE YOUNGER, HENRY (C.1798-1873)
IRISH SCHOOL

11,950
Dublin Castle Gate between the Royal Exchange, (now City Hall), and Newcomen Bank, (now Civic offices), (another copy)
Published: J. Le Petit, Dublin
36 x 52 (plate 27.5 x 44)
Etching and line with watercolour
Provenance Unknown

Brocas, Samuel Frederick (c.1792-1847)
Irish School
BROCAS THE YOUNGER, HENRY (C.1798-1873)
IRISH SCHOOL

11,951
The Royal Exchange, (now City Hall), and Dame Street, Dublin
Published: J. Le Petit, Dublin
36.4 x 51.3 (plate 26.8 x 42.2)
Etching and line with watercolour
Purchased, Dublin, Mr J.V. McAlpine, 1900

Brocas, Samuel Frederick (c.1792-1847)
Irish School
BROCAS THE YOUNGER, HENRY (C.1798-1873)
IRISH SCHOOL

11,952
Bank of Ireland, (formerly Parliament House), College Green, Dublin
Published: J. Le Petit, Dublin
27.6 x 43.8 (plate cut)
Etching and line with watercolour
Purchased, London, Mr L. Marks, 1898

Brocas, Samuel Frederick (c.1792-1847)
Irish School
BROCAS THE YOUNGER, HENRY (C.1798-1873)
IRISH SCHOOL

11,953
College Green, Dublin with Daly's Club House, (now rebuilt), Bank of Ireland, (formerly Parliament House), and Trinity College
Published: J. Le Petit, Dublin, 1828
31.5 x 47.5 (plate 27.5 x 41)
Etching and line with watercolour
Purchased, London, Mr L. Marks, 1898

Brocas, Samuel Frederick (c.1792-1847)
Irish School
BROCAS THE YOUNGER, HENRY (C.1798-1873)
IRISH SCHOOL

11,954
The Custom House, Dublin from the River Liffey, (another copy)
Published: J. Le Petit, Dublin, 1828
30 x 43 (plate cut)
Etching and line with watercolour
Purchased, London, Mr L. Marks, 1898

Brocas, Samuel Frederick (c.1792-1847)
Irish School
BROCAS THE YOUNGER, HENRY (C.1798-1873)
IRISH SCHOOL

11,955
The Chapel Royal, (now chapel of The Holy Trinity), Dublin Castle
(after a watercolour of 1818, V&A London)

Published: J. Le Petit, Dublin, 1828
32.5 x 47.5 (plate 29 x 42.9)
Etching and line with watercolour
Purchased, London, Mr L. Marks, 1898

Brocas, Samuel Frederick (c.1792-1847)
Irish School
BROCAS THE YOUNGER, HENRY (C.1798-1847)
IRISH SCHOOL

11,956
Trinity College, Dublin, from Westmoreland Street
(after a watercolour of 1818, NGI no. 2558)
Published: J. Le Petit, Dublin, 1829
31.7 x 48.3 (plate 27.6 43.5)
Etching with watercolour
Purchased, London, Mr L. Marks, 1898

Brocas, William (1794-1868)
Irish School
BROCAS, WILLIAM (1794-1868)
IRISH SCHOOL

10,264
Edward Bunting, (1773-1843), Musician and Collator of Irish Musical Airs
INSCRIBED: To the/Harp Societies of Dublin and Belfast/This plate is Most Respectfully Dedicated by their obedt. Servt./James Sidebotham
Published: J. Sidebotham, Dublin, 1st September 1811
42.5 x 28.5 (plate 35.3 x 25)
Stipple
Purchased, Dublin, Mr P. Traynor, 1898

Brocas, William (1794-1868)
Irish School
BROCAS, WILLIAM (1794-1868)
IRISH SCHOOL

10,965
Thomas McKenny, (1770-1849), Lord Mayor of Dublin, later a Baronet
(after a drawing)
Published: ?W. Brocas, Dublin, 1819
43.7 x 30 (plate 27.5 x 21.5)
Stipple
Purchased, London, 3rd Chaloner Smith sale, 1896

Brocas, William (1794-1868)
Irish School
BROCAS, WILLIAM (1794-1868)
IRISH SCHOOL

11,031
Sir John Andrew Stevenson, (1762-1833), Composer
INSCRIBED: To the/Harp Societies of Dublin and Belfast/This Plate is Most Respectfully Dedicated by their obedt. Sevt./James Sidebotham
Published: J. Sidebotham, Dublin, 6th September 1811
35 x 23.5 (plate cut)
Stipple and line
Acquired by 1913

Brocas, William (1794-1868)
Irish School
HAVELL THE ELDER, ROBERT (FL.1800-45)
ENGLISH SCHOOL *and*
HAVELL THE YOUNGER, ROBERT (FL.1820-50)
ENGLISH SCHOOL

11,638
'The National Bank, Dublin', (former Parliament House), and College Green
27.5 x 36.9 (plate cut)
Etching and aquatint
Purchased, Dublin, Mr J.V, McAlpine, 1904

Brocas, William (1794-1868)
Irish School
HAVELL THE ELDER, ROBERT (FL.1800-1840)
ENGLISH SCHOOL *and*
HAVELL THE YOUNGER, ROBERT
(FL.1820-1850)
ENGLISH SCHOOL

11,646
Trinity College, Dublin and the East Portico of the Bank of Ireland, (former entrance to House of Lords)
29 x 37 (plate 27.2 x 35.9)
Etching and aquatint
Provenance Unknown

Brocas, William (1794-1868)
Irish School
MARTYN, JOHN (FL.1794-1828)
IRISH SCHOOL

11,105
Rev. Thomas Betagh, (1739-1811), Jesuit Professor of Languages and Parish Priest of Sts. Michael and John's Church, Dublin
Published: c.1811
18 x 12.2 (plate cut)
Line and stipple
Purchased, Dublin, Mr P. Traynor, 1898

Brocas, William (1794-1868)
Irish School
MEYER, HENRY (1783-1847)
ENGLISH SCHOOL

10,658
Rev. Charles Robert Maturin, (1782-1824), Playwright and Novelist, (pl. for 'New Monthly Magazine and Universal Register', March 1819)
(after a drawing)
Published: H. Colburn, London, 1st March 1819
20.7 x 12.6 (plate cut)
Stipple
Purchased, London, 3rd Chaloner Smith sale, 1896

Brocas, William (1794-1868)
Irish School
MEYER, HENRY (C.1782-1847)
ENGLISH SCHOOL

10,937
Rev. Charles Robert Maturin, (1782-1824), Playwright and Novelist, (pl. for 'New Monthly Magazine and Universal Register', 1819), (another copy)
(after a drawing)
Published: H. Colburn, London, 1st March 1819
30.5 x 22.5 (plate 21 x 15.5)
Stipple
Purchased, London, 3rd Chaloner Smith sale, 1896

Brockedon, William (1787-1854)
English School
SANDS, JAMES (FL.1832-1844)
ENGLISH SCHOOL

20,442
Val Angrogna, near Turin, N. Italy, (pl. for D. Costello's 'Piedmont and Italy', c.1855)
Published: G. Vertue, London (for the Proprietors)
22.2 x 28.5 (plate cut)
Steel Engraving
Purchased, Lusk, Mr de Courcy Donovan, 1971

Brooke, Henry (1738-1806)
Irish School
CLAMP, R. (18TH CENTURY)
ENGLISH SCHOOL

11,107

Henry Brooke, (?1703-1783), Playwright, Novelist and the Artist's Uncle, (pl. for E. & S. Harding's 'The Biographical Mirror', 1793)
INSCRIBED: From the Original Picture in the Collection of Mr Harding Pall Mall.
Published: E. & S. Harding, London, 16th July 1793
18.7 x 12.3 (plate cut)
Stipple
Acquired by 1913

Brooke, William Henry (1772-1860)
English School
BROOKE, WILLIAM HENRY (1772-1860)
ENGLISH SCHOOL

11,507
'The Boy rose cautiously from the warrior's grasp', (pl. for 'Garanga')
Published: Collurin & Bentley, London, April 1830
12.1 x 19.3 (plate 11.9 x cut)
Etching
Provenance Unknown

Brooke, William Henry (1772-1860)
English School
BROOKE, WILLIAM HENRY (1772-1860)
ENGLISH SCHOOL

20,808
'Then mounting the noble horse, they bade farewell', (pl. for 'The Wahconda's Son')
9 x 13 (plate cut)
Etching
Presented, Miss I.C. Conan, 1918

Brooke, William Henry (1772-1860)
English School
BROOKE, WILLIAM HENRY (1772-1860)
ENGLISH SCHOOL

20,809
'In a moment multitudes of bright beings start up — "He is ours"!!!', (frontispiece for 'Garanga', Vol. 3)
14.7 x 9.1 (plate cut)
Etching
Presented, Miss I.C. Conan, 1918

Brooke, William Henry (1772-1860)
English School
BROOKE, WILLIAM HENRY (1772-1860)
ENGLISH SCHOOL

20,810
'She is gone! that beautiful form is but shadow', (frontispiece for 'Garanga', Vol. 2)
15 x 9.6 (plate cut)
Etching
Presented, Miss I.C. Conan, 1918

Brooke, William Henry (1772-1860)
English School
BROOKE, WILLIAM HENRY (1772-1860)
ENGLISH SCHOOL

20,811
'The Spirit breathed on her and she became stone', (pl. for 'Caverns of the Kickapoo')
9.1 x 13 (plate cut)
Etching
Presented, Miss I.C. Conan, 1918

Brooke, William Henry (1772-1860)
English School
BROOKE, WILLIAM HENRY (1772-1860)
ENGLISH SCHOOL

20,812
'I bore her away in my arms from the battle of warriors', (frontispiece for 'Garanga', Vol. 1)
13.7 x 7.7 (plate cut)
Etching
Presented, Miss I.C. Conan, 1918

Brooking, Charles (18th Century)
English School
BOWLES, JOHN (18TH CENTURY)
ENGLISH SCHOOL

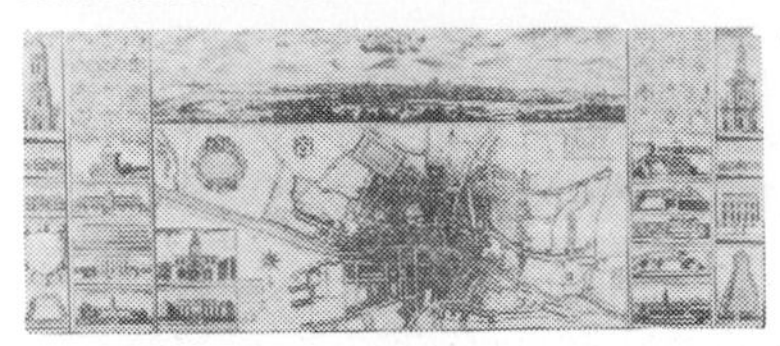

10,015
A Prospect of the City of Dublin from the North, Map and Elevations of Principal Buildings
1st State (without key to Prospect)
INSCRIBED: *To his Excellency/John Lord Carteret/Baron of Hawnes one of the Lords/of His Majesties Most Honourable/Privy Council & Lord Lieutenant/General/and General Governour/of His Majesties Kingdom of/Ireland/This Map is Humbly Dedicated/by Charles Brooking/1728*
Published: J. Bowles, London, 1728
59 x 143 (in three sections) (plate cut)
Line
Purchased, Dublin,
Mr J.V. McAlpine, 1900

Details from no. 10,015

Brooking, Charles (18th century)
English School
BOWLES, JOHN (18TH CENTURY)
ENGLISH SCHOOL

10,015(1)
The front of St Werburgh's church, Dublin, (now altered)

Brooking, Charles (18th century)
English School
BOWLES, JOHN (18TH CENTURY)
ENGLISH SCHOOL

10,015(2)
The Linen Hall, Dublin, (now demolished)

Brooking, Charles (18th century)
English School
BOWLES, JOHN (18TH CENTURY)
ENGLISH SCHOOL

10,015(3)
Dr Steevens's Hospital, Dublin, (now closed)

Brooking, Charles (18th century)
English School
BOWLES, JOHN (18TH CENTURY)
ENGLISH SCHOOL

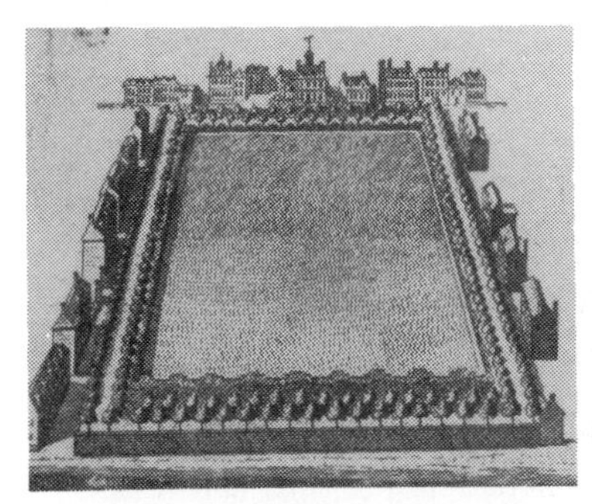

10,015(4)
Prospect of St Stephen's Green, Dublin

Brooking, Charles (18th century)
English School
BOWLES, JOHN (18TH CENTURY)
ENGLISH SCHOOL

10,015(5)
The Equestrian statue of King William III, (by Grinling Gibbons), on College Green, Dublin, (now destroyed)

Brooking, Charles (18th century)
English School
BOWLES, JOHN (18TH CENTURY)
ENGLISH SCHOOL

10,015(6)
The College Green front of Trinity College, Dublin, (now rebuilt)

Brooking, Charles (18th century)
English School
BOWLES, JOHN (18TH CENTURY)
ENGLISH SCHOOL

10,015(7)
The Library, Trinity College, Dublin

Brooking, Charles (18th century)
English School
BOWLES, JOHN (18TH CENTURY)
ENGLISH SCHOOL

10,015(8)
The Mansion House, Lord Mayor's residence, Dublin, (now refaced)

Brooking, Charles (18th century)
English School
BOWLES, JOHN (18TH CENTURY)
ENGLISH SCHOOL

10,015(9)
The Blew Coat Boys Hospital, Queen Street, Dublin, (now demolished)

Brooking, Charles (18th century)
English School
BOWLES, JOHN (18TH CENTURY)
ENGLISH SCHOOL

10,015(10)
The Tholsel, Skinners Row, Dublin, (now demolished)

Brooking, Charles (18th century)
English School
BOWLES, JOHN (18TH CENTURY)
ENGLISH SCHOOL

10,015(11)
The Poor House, James's Street, Dublin, (now demolished)

Brooking, Charles (18th century)
English School
BOWLES, JOHN (18TH CENTURY)
ENGLISH SCHOOL

10,015(12)
The Equestrian Statue of King George I, (by J. Van Nost the Elder; now at The Barber Institute, Birmingham), on Essex, (now rebuilt Grattan), Bridge, Dublin

Brooking, Charles (18th century)
English School
BOWLES, JOHN (18TH CENTURY)
ENGLISH SCHOOL

10,015(13)
Upper Yard, Dublin Castle, (now rebuilt)

Brooking, Charles (18th century)
English School
BOWLES, JOHN (18TH CENTURY)
ENGLISH SCHOOL

10,015(14)
The Custom House, Dublin, (now demolished)

Brooking, Charles (18th century)
English School
BOWLES, JOHN (18TH CENTURY)
ENGLISH SCHOOL

10,015(15)
The Royal, (now Collins), Barracks, Dublin, (centre demolished)

Brooking, Charles (18th century)
English School
BOWLES, JOHN (18TH CENTURY)
ENGLISH SCHOOL

10,015(16)
The Royal Hospital, Kilmainham, Dublin

Brooking, Charles (18th century)
English School
BOWLES, JOHN (18TH CENTURY)
ENGLISH SCHOOL

10,015(17)
The front of St Ann's church, Dawson Street, Dublin, (not as built)

Brooking, Charles (18th century)
English School
BOWLES, JOHN (18TH CENTURY)
ENGLISH SCHOOL

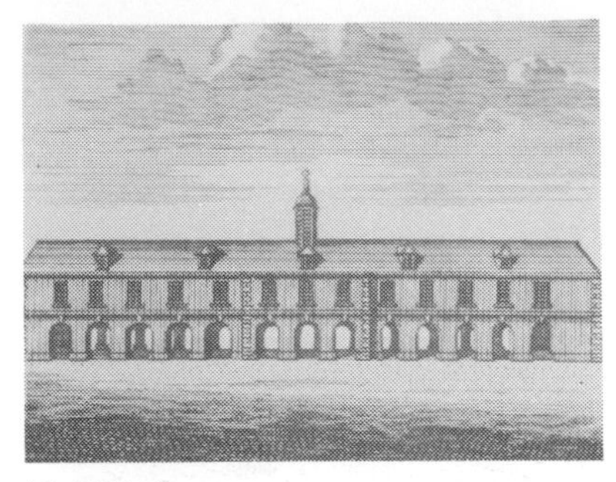

10,015(18)
The Corn Market House, Thomas Street, Dublin, (now demolished)

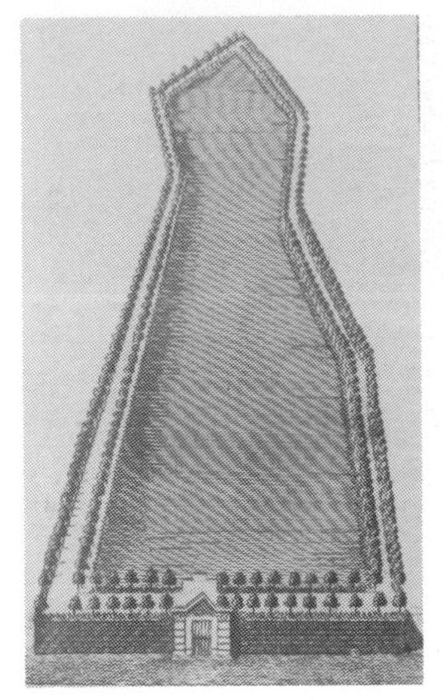

10,015(20)
Prospect of the City Basin, Dublin, (now rebuilt)

Brooking, Charles (18th century)
English School
BOWLES, JOHN (18TH CENTURY)
ENGLISH SCHOOL

10,015(19)
The Hospital in Stevens Street, Dublin, (now demolished)

Brooking, Charles (18th century)
English School
BOWLES, JOHN (18TH CENTURY)
ENGLISH SCHOOL

?Brooks, John (fl.1730-1756)
Irish School
BROOKS, JOHN (FL.1730-1756)
IRISH SCHOOL

10,117
So-called portrait of Rev. Samuel Madden, (1686-1765), Co-founder of the Dublin Society
Published: J. Brooks, Dublin, May 1747
39 x 27.5 (36.2 x 25.5)
Mezzotint
Purchased, London, 1st Chaloner Smith sale, 1887

?Brooks, John (fl.1730-1756)
Irish School
BROOKS, JOHN (FL.1730-1756)
IRISH SCHOOL

10,415
Henry Singleton, (fl.1726-1759), Lord Chief Justice of the Common Pleas in Ireland
Published: W. Herbert, London, not before 1740
50.2 x 35.5 (plate 49.8 x 34.8)
Mezzotint
Purchased, London, 1st Chaloner Smith sale, 1887

?Brooks, John (fl.1730-1756)
Irish School
BROOKS, JOHN (FL.1730-1756)
IRISH SCHOOL

10,434

Robert Jocelyn, Baron Newport, (1688-1756), Lord Chancellor of Ireland and later 1st Viscount Jocelyn
(after a J.B. Van Loo/J. Faber the Younger mezzotint of Sir Robert Walpole of c.1740, NGI no. 20,731 (62))
Published: T. Jefferys, also W. Herbert, London, 1744
51.3 x 36.1 (plate cut)
Mezzotint
Purchased, London, 1st Chaloner Smith sale, 1887

?Brooks, John (fl.1730-1756)
Irish School
BROOKS, JOHN (FL.1730-1756)
IRISH SCHOOL

20,802
Dr Cornelius Nary, (1660-1738), R.C. Priest and Author
35.7 x 25.7 (plate cut)
Mezzotint
Purchased, London, Rev. C. Lacy, 1914

Brown, C. (fl.1750s)
Irish School
BROOKS, JOHN (FL.1730-1756)
IRISH SCHOOL

10,481
Humphrey Butler, 4th Viscount and later 1st Earl of Lanesborough, (c.1700-1768)
Published: J. Brooks, Dublin
50 x 35 (plate 49.4 x 34.3)
Mezzotint
Purchased, London, Mr H.A.J. Breun, 1909

Brown, Mather (1761-1831)
Anglo-American School
HUDSON, HENRY (FL.1782-1800)
ENGLISH SCHOOL

10,246
George Macartney, 1st Earl Macartney, (1737-1806), Politician, former Chief Secretary for Ireland, Ambassador to Russia and China
Published: T. Simpson, London, 21st September 1796
38.6 x 28.2 (plate 37.8 x 27.5)
Mezzotint
Purchased, London, 1st Chaloner Smith sale, 1887

Brown, Mather (1761-1831)
Anglo-American School
ORME, DANIEL (?1766-?1832)
ENGLISH SCHOOL

20,104
George III, King of England, (1738-1802), and the Officers of State receiving the Turkish Ambassador, with (from left to right) James Cecil, Marquess of Salisbury, (1748-1823); Prime Minister William Pitt the Younger, (1759-1806); King George III; the Lord Chancellor; the Master of Ceremonies; William Wyndham Grenville, 1st Baron Grenville, (1759-1834); the Turkish Ambassador; Chevalier Mavrondi; Deriche Effendi; a Secretary and Interpreter
INSCRIBED: To his Grace the Duke of Leeds Governor of the United Turkey Company/This plate of His Majesty and the Officers of State receiving the Turkish Ambassador and suit/Is humbly dedicated by his Grace's most devoted servant, Dan. Orme.
Published: E. Orme, London, 1st January 1797
53.5 x 62 (plate 48.3 x 61.3)
Line and aquatint
Provenance Unknown

Brownrigg, John (18th century)
Irish School
FORD, JAMES (FL.1772-1812)
IRISH SCHOOL

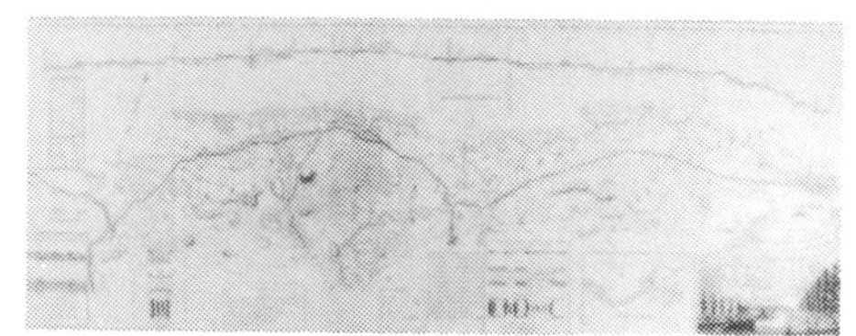

11,893

Map and Section of Grand Canal from Dublin to the river Barrow at Monasterevin, Co. Kildare
Published: J. Brownrigg, (Surveyor to the Grand Canal company), Dublin, 1788
58 x 133.3 (plate 52.5 x 132)
Etching
Purchased, 1914

Buck, Adam (1759-1833)
Irish School
ENGLISH SCHOOL (19TH CENTURY)

11,508
The Edgeworth Family including Maria Edgeworth, (1767-1849), Novelist, Richard Lovell Edgeworth, (1744-1817), and his third wife Elizabeth, (née Sneyd, d.1797)
(after a crayon drawing of 1787)
18.7 x 27.7 (image 18.7 x 27.7)
Lithograph
Acquired by 1901

Buck, Adam (1759-1833)
Irish School
HUFFAM, T.W. (FL.1825-C.1855)
ENGLISH SCHOOL

11,294
John Sheares, (1766-1798), United Irishman, Barrister, and brother of Henry Sheares, (pl. for R. Madden's 'United Irishmen', 2nd series, 1843)
(after a miniature)
Published: Madden & Co., London, 1843
20.1 x 12.3 (plate cut)
Mezzotint
Purchased, Dublin, Mr P. Traynor, 1898

?Buck, Adam (1759-1833)
Irish School
HUFFAM, T.W. (FL.1825-C.1855)
ENGLISH SCHOOL

11,295
Henry Sheares, (1753-1798), United Irishman, Barrister and Brother of John Sheares, (pl. for R. Madden's 'United Irishmen', 2nd series, 1843)
INSCRIBED: *From an original miniature in the possession of Mrs Sheares*
Published: Madden & Co., London, 1843
20.2 x 12.4 (plate cut)
Mezzotint
Purchased, Dublin, Mr P. Traynor, 1898

Buck, Adam (1759-1833)
Irish School
IRISH SCHOOL (1790)

11,134
Lord Henry FitzGerald, (1761-1829), son of the 1st Duke of Leinster and brother of Lord Edward FitzGerald, (pl. for 'Universal Magazine', May 1790)
(after an A. Buck/J. Mannin stipple of 1789)
Published: Universal Magazine, London, May 1790
17.5 x 12.1 (plate cut)
Stipple
Purchased, Mr R. Bateman, 1913

Buck, Adam (1759-1833)
Irish School
IRISH SCHOOL (1798)

10,585
Roger O'Connor, (1762-1834), United Irishman, Author and brother of Arthur O'Connor, (pl. for Walker's 'Hibernian Magazine', March, 1798 and Frontispiece for R. O'Connor's 'Chronicles of Eri', 1822)

Published: Hibernian Magazine, Dublin, March 1798
16 x 10.8 (plate cut)
Stipple
Purchased, Dublin, Mr P. Traynor, 1898

Buck, Adam (1759-1833)
Irish School
KIRKWOOD, JOHN (FL.1826-1853)
IRISH SCHOOL

10,673
Father Theobald Mathew, (1790-1856), founder of the Temperance Movement in Ireland
INSCRIBED: From the original by Buck in the possession of the Rev. D.B. Delany
Published: ?J. Kirkwood, Dublin, 1830/44
21.3 x 13.5 (plate 15 x cut)
Line
Purchased, Dublin, Mr P. Traynor, 1898

Buckner, Richard (fl.1820-1877)
English School
ZOBEL, GEORGE J. (1810-1881)
ENGLISH SCHOOL

10,772
General Sir George De Lacy Evans, M.P., (1787-1870)
Unlettered Proof
Published: Colnaghi, London, 1856
75 x 52.5 (plate 53 x 40.5)
Mezzotint
Purchased, Dublin, Mr J.V. McAlpine, 1913

Bull, Richard (fl.1777-1809)
Irish School
COLLYER, JOSEPH (1748-1827)
ENGLISH SCHOOL

10,753
Thomas Conolly, M.P., (1738-1803)
(after a miniature, RA 1796)
INSCRIBED: Dedicated by Permission to His Grace the/Duke of Leinster,/by his Grace's most devoted and very grateful Servt./R. Bull

Published: Diemar, London, 1st January 1796
30 x 22 (plate 20.2 x 13)
Stipple
Purchased, Browne & Phillips, 1907

Bull, Richard (fl.1777-1809)
Irish School
SEDGWICK, WILLIAM (1748-1800)
ENGLISH SCHOOL

11,194
Thomas Conolly, M.P., (1738-1803), Colonel of the Londonderry Militia, (pl. for Walker's 'Hibernian Magazine', May 1796)
(after a miniature, RA 1796)
Published: Hibernian Magazine, Dublin, May 1796
21 x 13.1 (plate 17.6 x 11.4)
Stipple
Purchased, Dublin, Mr P. Traynor, 1898

Burch the Younger, Henry Jacob (1763-after 1834)
English School
WARD, JAMES (1769-1859)
ENGLISH SCHOOL

10,718
William Henry West Betty, (1791-1874), Child Actor, aged 13
(after a miniature)
Published: W.H.W. Betty at Colnaghi & Co., London, 1st July 1805
39.1 x 29.2 (plate 38 x 28)
Mezzotint
Purchased, London, 2nd Chaloner Smith sale, 1888

Burghersh, Lady Priscilla (1793-1879)
English School
HODGETTS, THOMAS (FL.1801-1846)
ENGLISH SCHOOL

10,399
Anne, Countess of Mornington, (née Hill, 1742-1831), wife of the 1st Earl of Mornington, and mother of the 1st Duke of Wellington
INSCRIBED: *Engraved from the painting by Lady Burghersh in the possession of the Rt. Honble. Lord Maryborough/To whom by permission this print is most respectfully dedicated/by his Lordships Devoted and Humble Servants/Welch and Gwynn*
Published: Welch & Gwynn, London, 1st January 1839 (Printed: Lahee & Co.)
66.9 x 51 (plate 62.5 x 45)
Mezzotint
Purchased, Dublin, Mr J.V. McAlpine, 1901

Burlington, Dorothy, Countess of (1699-1758)
English School
FABER THE YOUNGER, JOHN (1684-1756)
ENGLISH SCHOOL

10,362
Lady Dorothy Boyle, Countess of Euston, (1724-1742), Daughter of the artist and the 3rd Earl of Burlington
(after a drawing of 1742)
INSCRIBED: *This was taken from a picture drawn seven weeks after her death (from memory)/by her most afflicted mother Dorothy Burlington*
Published: Dorothy, Countess of Burlington, as a private plate, 1744
36 x 26 (plate 33 x 23)
Mezzotint
Purchased, London, Mr H.J. Breun, 1910

Burns, Jean Douglas (b.1903)
Scottish School
BURNS, JEAN DOUGLAS (B.1903)
SCOTTISH SCHOOL

11,931
The Hunt Crossing a River
Issued by the artist (5/of 30), 1932
24 x 38 (image 16.6 x 30.5)
Woodcut
Provenance Unknown

Burton, Frederic William (1816-1900)
Irish School
LYNCH, JAMES HENRY (FL.1815-1868)
IRISH SCHOOL

11,076
Edward Pennefather, Baron Pennefather, (c.1774-1847), former Chief Justice of the Queen's Bench
(after a watercolour, RHA 1848)
(Printed: M. & N. Hanhart, London)
76.5 x 57 (image 55.5 x 35.5)
Lithograph
Purchased, Dublin, Mr J.V. McAlpine, 1899

Burton, Frederic William (1816-1900)
Irish School
SANDERS, GEORGE (1810-C.1876)
ENGLISH SCHOOL

10,815
Arthur Guinness of Beaumont, J.P., (1768-1855)
Published: T. Cranfield, Dublin
39.6 x 29.7 (plate cut)
Mezzotint
Purchased, Dublin,
Mr J.V. McAlpine, 1898

Burton, Frederic William (1816-1900)
Irish School
TEMPLETON, JOHN SAMUEL (FL.1830-1857)
IRISH SCHOOL

10,786
Thomas Osborne Davis, (1814-1845), Nationalist and Poet, co-founder of 'The Nation' newspaper
(after a pencil drawing, NGI no. 2032)
Published: J. Duffy, Dublin, not before 1845 (Printed: M. & N. Hanhart, London)
38.2 x 27.6 (image 18.2 x 14.6)
Lithograph
Bequeathed, Sir Charles Gavan Duffy, 1903

Bushe, Letitia (fl.1731-1757)
Irish School
BROWN, JOSEPH (FL.1854-1886)
ENGLISH SCHOOL

11,111
Self-Portrait, (pl. for Lady Llanover's 'Letters of Mrs Delany', 1861)
INSCRIBED: From an original miniature painted by herself/in the possession of the Rt. Honble Lady Llanover
Published: R. Bentley, London, 1861
21.8 x 15 (plate cut)
Line and stipple
Purchased, Dublin,
Mr J.V. McAlpine, 1904

Butin, Ulysse Louis Auguste (1837/38-1883)
French School
BUTIN, ULYSSE LOUIS AUGUSTE (1837/38-1883)
FRENCH SCHOOL

11,487
Waiting for the Fishing Boats: Saturday at Villerville
Published: L'Art, Paris 1875 (Printed: A. Salmon)
55 x 72 (plate 42.2 x59.5)
Etching
Provenance Unknown

Byrne, Charles (1757-c.1810)
Irish School
HUFFAM, T.W. (FL.1825-C.1855)
ENGLISH SCHOOL

10,646
Samuel Neilson, (1761-1803), United Irishman, (pl. for R. Madden's 'United Irishmen', 2nd series, 1843)
(after a miniature)
Published: Madden & Co., London, 1843
20.5 x 12.5 (plate cut)
Mezzotint
Purchased, Dublin, Mr P. Traynor, 1898

Byrne, Charles (1757-c.1810)
Irish School
HUFFAM, T.W. (FL.1825-1855)
ENGLISH SCHOOL

10,647
Samuel Neilson, (1761-1803), United Irishman, (pl. for R. Madden's 'United Irishmen', 2nd series, 1843), (another copy)
(after a miniature)
Published: Madden & Co., London, 1843
20.5 x 12.5 (plate cut)
Mezzotint
Presented, Dr T. Madden, 1901

Byrne, Patrick (1783-1864)
Irish School
RADCLYFFE, WILLIAM (1783-1855)
ENGLISH SCHOOL

11,609
The Choir of St Patrick's Cathedral, Dublin, before the 1863 Restoration, (pl. for W.M. Mason's 'History and Antiquities of the Collegiate and Cathedral Church of St Patrick near Dublin', 1819)
(after a drawing)
Lettered Proof
Published: W.M. Mason, Dublin, 1st July 1818
27.2 x 23 (plate cut x 22)
Steel Engraving
Presented, Dr E. MacDowel Cosgrave, 1907

Byrne, Patrick (1783-1864)
Irish School
RADCLYFFE, WILLIAM (1783-1855)
ENGLISH SCHOOL

11,759
The Choir of St Patrick's Cathedral, Dublin, before the 1863 Restoration, (pl. for W. M. Mason's 'History and Antiquities of the Collegiate and Cathedral Church of St Patrick near Dublin', 1819)
(after a drawing)
Published: W. M. Mason, Dublin, 1st July 1818
28.3 x 22.8 (plate cut)
Steel Engraving
Provenance Unknown

Byrne, Patrick (1783-1864)
Irish School
SMITH, W. (19TH CENTURY)
IRISH SCHOOL

11,608
South-East view of St Patrick's Cathedral, Dublin (frontispiece for W.M. Mason's 'History and Antiquities of the Collegiate and Cathedral Church of St Patrick near Dublin', 1819)
Lettered Proof
Published: W.M. Mason, Dublin, 1st July 1818
21 x 26.6 (plate cut)
Steel Engraving
Presented, Dr E. MacDowel Cosgrave, 1907

C

Cahill, T. (19th Century)
Irish School
IRISH SCHOOL (C.1827)

10,875
Sir Anthony Hart, (1754-1831), Lord Chancellor of Ireland, (frontispiece for 'Irish Law Recorder')
Published: Irish Law Recorder, Dublin
23.3 x 15.2 (plate cut)
Line
Purchased, Dublin,
Mr J.V. McAlpine, 1904

Calame, Alexandre (1810-1864)
Swiss School
CALAME, ALEXANDRE (1810-1864)
SWISS SCHOOL

20,145
A Lake, ('Oeuvres de A. Calame' no. 79)
Published: F. Delarue, Paris (Printed: Jacomme et Cie.)
38.9 x 55.8 (image 14.5 x 25)
Lithograph
Purchased, Lusk, Mr de Courcy Donovan, 1971

Calame, Alexandre (1810-1864)
Swiss School
CALAME, ALEXANDRE (1810-1864)
SWISS SCHOOL

20,337
Trees and Buildings by Water
(Printed: Jacomme et Cie., Paris)
40.3 x 32.1 (image 38 x 29)
Lithograph
Purchased, Lusk, Mr de Courcy Donovan, 1971

Calame, Alexandre (1810-1864)
Swiss School
CALAME, ALEXANDRE (1810-1864)
SWISS SCHOOL

20,340
Walnut Trees
Published: Goupil et Vibert, also H. Jeannin, Paris (Printed: Cattier, Paris)
49.5 x 37 approx. (image 39 x 29.4)
Lithograph
Purchased, Lusk, Mr de Courcy Donovan, 1971

Calame, Alexandre (1810-1864)
Swiss School
CALAME, ALEXANDRE (1810-1864)
SWISS SCHOOL

20,342
Ruined Castle on a Hill, (''Ecole du Paysagiste', no. 1)

Published: H. Jeannin, Paris, also Anaglyphic Co., London, 1st February, 1844. (Printed: Cattier, Paris)
29.6 x 36 (image 24.8 x 36)
Lithograph
Purchased, Lusk, Mr de Courcy Donovan, 1971

Calame, Alexandre (1810-1864)
Swiss School
CALAME, ALEXANDRE (1810-1864)
SWISS SCHOOL

20,343
River Landscape (no. 15)
Published: Goupil et Vibert, Paris; also E. Gambart Junin & Co., London, 1st October 1846. (Printed: Lemercier, Paris)
38.7 x 54.5 (image 26.6 x 38.8)
Lithograph
Purchased, Lusk, Mr de Courcy Donovan, 1971

Calame, Alexandre (1810-1864)
Swiss School
CALAME, ALEXANDRE (1810-1864)
SWISS SCHOOL

20,469
Figures on a country path
28.5 x 21.7 (image 24.5 x 20.5 approx)
Lithograph
Purchased, Lusk, Mr de Courcy Donovan, 1971

Calame, Alexandre (1810-1864)
Swiss School
CALAME, ALEXANDRE (1810-1864)
SWISS SCHOOL

20,470
River scene with trees, ('Oeuvres de A. Calame', no. 35)
(Printed: Jacomme et Cie, Paris)
27.8 x 22.4 (image 25.4 x 19.9)
Lithograph
Purchased, Lusk, Mr de Courcy Donovan, 1971

Calame, Alexandre (1810-1864)
Swiss School
CALAME, ALEXANDRE (1810-1864)
SWISS SCHOOL

20,487
Riverbank with trees, ('Oeuvres de A. Calame', no. 3)
(Printed: Jacomme et Cie., Paris)
24.2 x 35.5 (image 21.2 x 32.7)
Lithograph
Purchased, Lusk, Mr de Courcy Donovan, 1971

Calame, Alexandre (1810-1864)
Swiss School
CALAME, ALEXANDRE (1810-1864)
SWISS SCHOOL

20,489
Figures in Valley, ('L'Ecole du Paysagiste')
(Printed: Cattier, Paris)
27.3 x 39.3 (image 25 x 36.3)
Lithograph
Purchased, Lusk, Mr de Courcy Donovan, 1971

Calame, Alexandre (1810-1864)
Swiss School
CALAME, ALEXANDRE (1810-1864)
SWISS SCHOOL

20,490
Cattle in a Stream, ('L'Ecole du Paysagiste', no. 2)
Published: H. Jeannin, Paris, also Anaglyphic Co., London, 1st February, 1844 (Printed: Cattier, Paris)
29.8 x 39.9 (image 25 x 36.3)
Lithograph
Purchased, Lusk, Mr de Courcy Donovan, 1971

Calame, Alexandre (1810-1864)
Swiss School
CALAME, ALEXANDRE (1810-1864)
SWISS SCHOOL

20,491
Cattle in river valley ('L'Ecole du Paysagiste', no. 17)
Published: H. Jeannin, Paris
29.7 x 36.3 (image 25 x 36.3)
Lithograph
Purchased, Lusk, Mr de Courcy Donovan, 1971

Calame, Alexandre (1810-1864)
Swiss School
CALAME, ALEXANDRE (1810-1864)
SWISS SCHOOL

20,494
Figures by a tree ('L'Ecole du Paysagiste' no. 15)
(Printed: Cattier, Paris)
36.2 x 27.4 (image 33.4 x 25)
Lithograph
Purchased, Lusk, Mr de Courcy Donovan, 1971

Calame, Alexandre (1810-1864)
Swiss School
CALAME, ALEXANDRE (1810-1864)
SWISS SCHOOL

20,496
Woman on a tree-lined path, ('Oeuvres de A. Calame', no. 84).
(Printed: Jacomme et Cie., Paris)
24.8 x 29 (image 20.2 x 24.4)
Lithograph
Purchased, Lusk, Mr de Courcy Donovan, 1971

Calame, Alexandre (1810-1864)
Swiss School
CALAME, ALEXANDRE (1810-1864)
SWISS SCHOOL

20,497
Mountain pool ('Oeuvres de A. Calame', no. 16)
(Printed: Jacomme et Cie., Paris
23 x 29.5 (image 20.7 x 27.4)
Lithograph
Purchased, Lusk, Mr de Courcy Donovan, 1971

Calame, Alexandre (1810-1864)
Swiss School
CALAME, ALEXANDRE (1810-1864)
SWISS SCHOOL

20,498
River in torrent ('Oeuvres de A. Calame', no. 22).
(Printed: Jacomme et Cie., Paris)
20.4 x 31.1 (image 17.4 x 28)
Lithograph
Purchased, Lusk, Mr de Courcy Donovan, 1971

Calame, Alexandre (1810-1864)
Swiss School
CALAME, ALEXANDRE (1810-1864)
SWISS SCHOOL

20,499
River cascade ('Oeuvres de A. Calame', no. 42).
(Printed: Jacomme et Cie., Paris)
28.5 x 28.1 (image 18.8 x 25)
Lithograph
Purchased, Lusk, Mr de Courcy Donovan, 1971

Calame, Alexandre (1810-1864)
Swiss School
CALAME, ALEXANDRE (1810-1864)
SWISS SCHOOL

20,500

Lake at sunset
(Printed: Jacomme et Cie., Paris)
24 x 31.6 (image 21 x 28.3)
Lithograph
Purchased, Lusk, Mr de Courcy
Donovan, 1971

Calame, Alexandre (1810-1864)
Swiss School
CALAME, ALEXANDRE (1810-1864)
SWISS SCHOOL

20,505
Fishermen on a Riverbank, ('Etudes Progressives', no. 45).
Published: Goupil et Vibert; also
H. Jeannin, Paris (Printed: Cattier)
30.7 x 44.8 (image 20.3 x 29.6)
Lithograph
Purchased, Lusk, Mr de Courcy
Donovan, 1971

Calame, Alexandre (1810-1864)
Swiss School
CALAME, ALEXANDRE (1810-1864)
SWISS SCHOOL

20,506
Castle Ruins with Rustic Figures, ('Etudes Progressives', no. 42).
Published: Goupil et Vibert; also
H. Jeannin, Paris (Printed: Cattier)
30.7 x 44.8 (image 20.4 x 29.5)
Lithograph
Purchased, Lusk, Mr de Courcy
Donovan, 1971

Calame, Alexandre (1810-1864)
Swiss School
CALAME, ALEXANDRE (1810-1864)
SWISS SCHOOL

20,507
Women gathering firewood
Published: Goupil et Vibert; also
H. Jeannin, Paris (Printed: Cattier)
25.6 x 36.8 (image 25 x 36.2)
Lithograph
Purchased, Lusk, Mr de Courcy
Donovan, 1971

Calame, Alexandre (1810-1864)
Swiss School
CALAME, ALEXANDRE (1810-1864)
SWISS SCHOOL

20,508
Young Elms near a Tower
Published: Goupil et Vibert; also
H. Jeannin, Paris (Printed: Cattier)
35.8 x 43.7 (image 30 x 38.5)
Lithograph
Purchased, Lusk, Mr de Courcy
Donovan, 1971

Calame, Alexandre (1810-1864)
Swiss School
CALAME, ALEXANDRE (1810-1864)
SWISS SCHOOL

20,521
Windswept Forest
(Printed: Jacomme et Cie, Paris)
22.2 x 27.7 (image 18.5 x 23.8)
Lithograph
Purchased, Lusk, Mr de Courcy
Donovan, 1971

Calame, Alexandre (1810-1864)
Swiss School
CALAME, ALEXANDRE (1810-1864)
SWISS SCHOOL

20,652
The crest of a waterfall
(Printed: Cattier, Paris)
23.1 x 33.8 (image 21 x 33.8)
Lithograph
Presented, Mrs D. Molloy, 1981

Calame, Alexandre (1810-1864)
Swiss School *and*
Ferogio, François Fortune Antoine (1805-1888)
French School
CALAME, ALEXANDRE (1810-1864)
SWISS SCHOOL *and*
FEROGIO, FRANCOIS FORTUNE ANTOINE (1805-1888)
FRENCH SCHOOL

20,341
Weeping Willows (no. 13)
Published: Goupil et Vibert, also H. Jeannin, Paris; also Anaglyphic Co., London, 1st December, 1844. (Printed: Cattier, Paris)
34.2 x 42.3 (image 29.5 x 37.9)
Lithograph
Purchased, Lusk, Mr de Courcy Donovan, 1971

Calame, Alexandre (1810-1864)
Swiss School *and*
Ferogio, François Fortune Antoine (1805-1888)
French School
CALAME, ALEXANDRE (1810-1864)
SWISS SCHOOL *and*
FERGIO, FRANCOIS FORTUNE ANTOINE (1805-1888)
FRENCH SCHOOL

20,462
Chestnut Trees (no. 17)
Published: Goupil et Vibert, Paris, also H. Jeannin, Paris, also Anaglyphic Co., London, 1st December 1844 (Printed: Cattier, Paris)
45.8 x 32.7 (image 38 x 28.5)
Lithograph
Purchased, Lusk, Mr de Courcy Donovan, 1971

Calame, Alexandre (1810-1864)
Swiss School *and*
Ferogio, François Fortune Antoine (1805-1888)
French School
CALAME, ALEXANDRE (1810-1864)
SWISS SCHOOL *and*
FEROGIO, FRANCOIS FORTUNE ANTOINE (1805-1888)
FRENCH SCHOOL

20,488
Carob tree on a river bank
Published: Goupil et Vibert, Paris, also H. Jeannin, Paris, also Anaglyphic Co., London (Printed: Cattier, Paris)
32.5 x 41.6 (image 29.4 x 38.7)
Lithograph
Purchased, Lusk, Mr de Courcy Donovan, 1971

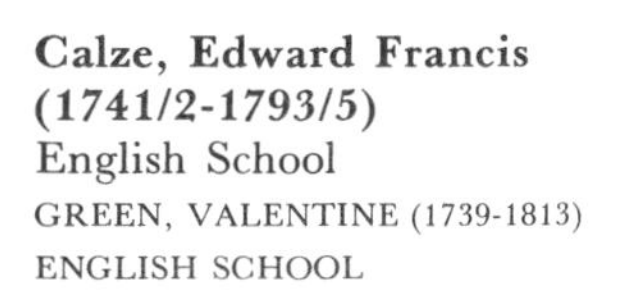

Calze, Edward Francis (1741/2-1793/5)
English School
GREEN, VALENTINE (1739-1813)
ENGLISH SCHOOL

10,382
Mrs Stephen Le Maistre, (née Mary Roche, 1741-1816), later Baroness Nolcken
Published: J. Boydell, London, 21st January 1771
43.2 x 31 (plate 41 x 29)
Mezzotint
Purchased, London, 1st Chaloner Smith sale, 1887

Cameron, David Young (1865-1945)
Scottish School
CAMERON, DAVID YOUNG (1865-1945)
SCOTTISH SCHOOL

11,682
The Isle of Arran, Scotland, (no. 14 of 20 subjects in 'Clyde Set')
Issued by the artist, 1889 (Printed: Messrs. Maclure, Macdonald & Co., Glasgow)
28 x 38 (plate 12.2 x 25)
Etching and drypoint
Provenance Unknown

Canaletto (1697-1768)
Venetian School
BROMLEY, JOHN CHARLES (1795-1839)
ENGLISH SCHOOL

20,333
The Rialto Bridge on the Grand Canal, Venice from the South (previously pl. for 'Gems of Art', 1824).
INSCRIBED: From the picture in the possession of James Stuart Wortley Esqr./Gems of Art plate 25.
Published: W.B. Cooke, London, 1st March 1825
30.3 x 44 (plate 19.6 x 25.2)
Aquatint
Purhased, Lusk, Mr de Courcy Donovan, 1971

Canaletto (1697-1768)
Venetian School
CHEVALIER, PIETRO (19TH CENTURY)
ITALIAN SCHOOL

20,390
Piazza S. Marco, Venice, from the North end of the Piazzetta
(after an oil, Royal Collection, Windsor Castle, or Canaletto/Vicentini etching)
Published: G.A. Habnit, Venice
20.8 x 29.7 (image 12.6 x 21.4)
Lithograph with watercolour and varnish
Purchased, Lusk, Mr de Courcy Donovan, 1971

Canova, Antonio (1757-1822)
Italian School
TOGNOLI, GIOVANNI (1786-1862)
ITALIAN SCHOOL
RICCIANI, ANTONIO (1775-1836)
ROMAN SCHOOL

20,714(16)
Napoleon I, (1769-1821), as Jupiter, (from 'Oeuvre de Canova', 1819, see App. 8, no. 20,714)
(after a marble statue of 1803-06, Apsley House, London)
Published: Rome, 1819
85 x 66 (plate 64.5 x 45.6)
Line
Provenance Unknown

Carlton, Thomas (fl.1670-1730)
Irish School
BEARD, THOMAS (FL.C.1720-C.1729)
IRISH SCHOOL

10,143
John Stearne, P. Bishop of Clogher, (1660-1745)
(derived from an oil of 1717)
Published: Dublin, 1729
36 x 26.6 (plate 34.2 x 25.3)
Mezzotint
Purchased, London, 1st Chaloner Smith sale, 1887

Carocci, G. (early 19th century)
Italian School
CAROCCI, G. (EARLY 19TH CENTURY)
ITALIAN SCHOOL

20,387
Florence cathedral and Baptistery, (pl. for undated bound volume with twenty three views of Florence)
23.1 x 30.6 (plate 17.8 x 22.8)
Etching and aquatint with watercolour
Purchased, Lusk, Mr de Courcy Donovan, 1971

Carocci, G. (early 19th century)
Italian School
CAROCCI, G. (EARLY 19TH CENTURY)
ITALIAN SCHOOL

20,392
Pisa Baptistery, N. Italy
29.8 x 21.7 (plate 24.5 x 15.3)
Etching and aquatint with watercolour
Purchased, Lusk, Mr de Courcy Donovan, 1971

Carpenter, Margaret Sarah (1793-1872)
English School
CARPENTER, WILLIAM (C.1818-1899)
ENGLISH SCHOOL

11,339
William Smith, (1808-1876), Printseller and Trustee of the National Portrait Gallery, London, (1858)
(after an oil, NPG, London)
21.8 x 14 (plate cut)
Etching
Acquired between 1913/14

Carpenter, Margaret Sarah (1793-1872)
English School
HODGETTS, THOMAS (FL.1801-1846)
ENGLISH SCHOOL

10,174
Major-General Sir Charles William Doyle, (1770-1842), Colonel of the 10th Royal Veteran Batallion
(after an oil, RA 1824; Museum of Fine Arts, Boston)
Lettered Proof
Published: Colnaghi Son & Co., London, 1827
45 x 35 (plate 31.8 x 24)
Mezzotint
Purchased, Dublin, Mr A. Roth, 1895

Carpenter, Richard Cromwell (1812-1855)
English School
BURY, THOMAS TALBOT (1811-1877)
ENGLISH SCHOOL

11,772
Carpenter's proposed restoration in 1847 of the Choir of St Patrick's Cathedral, Dublin, (from a set of six)
51.2 x 37.2 (image 43.2 x 30.4)
Lithograph
Presented, Mr C.J. McKean, 1918

Carr, John (1772-1832)
English School
MEDLAND, THOMAS (1755-1833)
ENGLISH SCHOOL

11,603
The Four Courts, Dublin, from Merchants Quay
Published: R. Phillips, London, 4th June 1806
28 x 43.5 (plate cut)
Aquatint
Provenance Unknown

Carr, John (1772-1832)
English School
TOMLINSON, JOHN (FL.1805-1824)
ENGLISH SCHOOL

11,692
The Four Courts, Dublin, from Merchants Quay
(after a J. Carr/T. Medland aquatint of 1806, NGI no. 11,603)
Published: Sherwood, Neely & Jones, London, 1820
20.8 x 26.8 (plate cut)
Line
Provenance Unknown

Carracci, Annibale (1560-1609)
Bolognese School
ENGLISH SCHOOL (19TH CENTURY)

20,268
Landscape with two figures at a shrine
(after a J.B. Massé etching of a drawing, The Louvre, Paris)
27.4 x 37.6 (plate 20.6 x 29)
Etching
Purchased, Lusk, Mr de Courcy Donovan, 1971

Carrick, Thomas Heathfield (1802-1875)
English School
HOLL THE YOUNGER, WILLIAM (1807-1871)
ENGLISH SCHOOL

10,289
Daniel O'Connell, M.P., (1775-1847), Statesman, (pl. for W. Cooke Taylor's 'National Portrait Gallery', 1844)
(after a watercolour miniature, RA 1844)
Published: Fisher, Son & Co., London, 26th June, 1844
21.8 x 10.4 (plate cut)
Line and stipple
Presented, Mr H. McDonnell, 1888

Carrick, Thomas Heathfield (1802-1875)
English School
HOLL THE YOUNGER, WILLIAM (1807-1871)
ENGLISH SCHOOL

10,597
Daniel O'Connell, M.P., (1775-1847), Statesman, (pl. for W. Cooke Taylor's 'National Portrait Gallery', 1844)
(after a watercolour minature, RA 1844)
Published: Fisher, Son & Co., London and Paris, 1844
21.1 x 13.4 (plate cut)
Line and stipple
Presented, Mr H. McDonnell, 1888

Carrick, Thomas Heathfield (1802-1875)
English School
HOLL THE YOUNGER, WILLIAM (1807-1871)
ENGLISH SCHOOL

10,972
Daniel O'Connell, M.P., (1775-1847), Statesman, (pl. for W. Cooke Taylor's 'National Portrait Gallery', 1844) (another copy of no. 10,289)
(after a watercolour minature, RA 1844)
Published: Fisher, Son & Co., London, 26th June, 1844
25.8 x 21.3 (plate cut)
Line and stipple
Provenance Unknown

Carrogis, Louis (1717-1806)
French School
?FRENCH SCHOOL (19TH CENTURY)

10,273
Laurence Sterne, (1713-1768), Author and Clergyman
(after a watercolour of 1762, NPG, London)
26.9 x 17.9 (image cut)
Lithograph and watercolour
Acquired between 1890/98

Carter the Elder, Thomas (fl.1729-1756)
English School
IRISH SCHOOL (18TH CENTURY)

11,642
Monument to William Conolly, (1662-1729), and his wife Katherine, (née Conyngham c.1662-1752), in the Conolly Mausoleum, Celbridge, Co. Kildare, 1736
51 x 35.5 (plate 51 x 35.5)
Mezzotint
Purchased, London, 2nd Chaloner Smith sale, 1888

Castellini, G. (fl.c.1800)
Italian School
CASTELLINI, G. (FL.C.1800)
ITALIAN SCHOOL

20,393
Interior of S. Lorenzo Maggiore, Milan, (pl. for G. Castellini's 'Principali Vedute di Milano e de Contorini')
25.5 x 36.3 (plate 16.5 x 22.3)
Aquatint and etching with watercolour
Purchased, Lusk, Mr de Courcy Donovan, 1971

Castiglione, Benedetto (1616-1690)
Genoese School
EARLOM, RICHARD (1743-1822)
ENGLISH SCHOOL
BOYDELL, JOHN (1719-1804)
ENGLISH SCHOOL

11,943
The Exposition of Cyrus - The Shepherdess Spako with the infant Cyrus
(after an oil of 1650s, NGI no. 994)
INSCRIBED: *This Print, engraved from the original picture, painted by Benedetto Castiglione, in the Collection of the Right Honourable/the Earl of Lincoln: is, with the deepest sense of Gratitude, most humbly dedicated to the subscribers and/Encouragers of this Undertaking - by their much obliged, and most obedient humble Servant,/John Boydell.*
Published: J. Boydell, London, 1st May 1765
55.7 x 40.8 (plate 51.6 x cut)
Line
Purchased, London, Portobello Market Antiques, 1983

Cattermole, George (1800-1868)
English School
BENTLEY, JOSEPH CLAYTON (1809-1851)
ENGLISH SCHOOL

20,444
Margaret meets Faustus in the Summer House, (from Goethe's 'Faust')
Published: Simpkin & Marshall; also J.W. Stevens (the Proprietor), London, 1830s
28.4 x 22.1 (plate cut)
Steel Engraving
Purchased, Lusk, Mr de Courcy Donovan, 1971

Cattermole, George (1800-1868)
English School
PAYNE, ALBERT HENRY (1812-1902)
ENGLISH SCHOOL

20,412
A Watermill in Westmoreland, Cumbria
Published: Simpkin & Marshall, also J.W. Stevens, London, 1834
27.4 x 21.6 (plate cut)
Steel Engraving
Purchased, Lusk, Mr de Courcy Donovan, 1971

Cattermole, George (1800-1868)
English School
SMITH, EDWARD (FL.1823-1851)
ENGLISH SCHOOL

20,152
Albert of Gierstein, Summoning Charles V, Duke of Burgundy, (1500-1558), to appear before the Vehme Court
(after a drawing)
Published: Simpkin & Marshall, also T.W. Stevens, London, 1830s
22.5 x 28.7 (plate cut)
Line and etching
Purchased, Lusk, Mr de Courcy Donovan, 1971

Catterson Smith the Elder, Stephen (1806-1872)
Irish School
COOPER, ROBERT (FL.1795-1836)
ENGLISH SCHOOL

10,981
Daniel O'Connell, M.P., (1775-1847), Statesman
Published: J. Robins, London & Dublin, 1st September, 1825
29.5 x 22.2 (plate 22.1 x 14.1)
Line and stipple
Acquired by 1898

Catterson Smith the Elder, Stephen (1806-1872)
Irish School
COOPER, ROBERT (FL.1795-1836)
ENGLISH SCHOOL

11,179
James Warren Doyle, R.C. Bishop of Kildare and Leighlin, (1786-1834)
(after a drawing)
24.7 x 15.6 (plate 19.7 x 13.5)
Stipple and etching
Purchased, Dublin, Mr P. Traynor, 1898

Catterson Smith the Elder, Stephen (1806-1882)
Irish School
COOPER, ROBERT (FL.1795-1836)
ENGLISH SCHOOL

11,289
Richard Lalor Sheil, M.P., (1791-1851), Lawyer, Politician and Playwright, (pl. for 'Dublin and London Magazine', April 1825)
(after a drawing)
Published: J. Robins, London, April 1825
22 × 14 (plate 13.2 × 12.3)
Stipple
Acquired by 1898

Catterson Smith the Elder, Stephen (1806-1872)
Irish School
IRISH SCHOOL (C.1830)

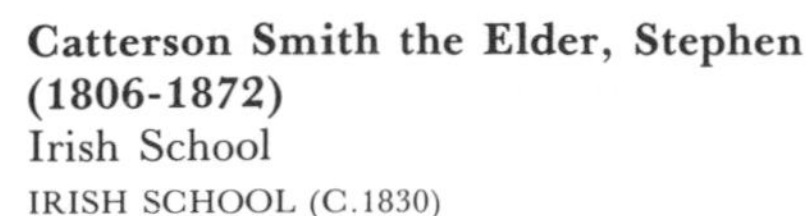

10,977
Daniel O'Connell, M.P., (1775-1847), Statesman
INSCRIBED: *Presented Gratuitously/to the Purchasers of/Carpenters Political Letter*
Published: Carpenter's Political Letter, c.1830
27.8 x 21.7 (plate cut)
Stipple
Purchased, Dublin, Dillon & Co., 1901

Catterson Smith the Elder, Stephen (1806-1872)
Irish School
JACKSON, JOHN RICHARDSON (1819-1877)
ENGLISH SCHOOL

10,441

Marcus Gervais Beresford, P. Archbishop of Armagh, (1801-1885), as Prelate of the Order of St Patrick
Published: T. Cranfield, Dublin, 15th November 1866
56.2 x 44.8 (plate 49.2 x 37)
Mezzotint, etching and stipple
Purchased, London, Mr G. Lausen, 1895

Catterson Smith the Elder, Stephen (1806-1872)
Irish School
JACKSON, JOHN RICHARDSON (1819-1877)
ENGLISH SCHOOL

11,556
Marcus Gervais Beresford, P. Archbishop of Armagh, (1801-1885), as Prelate of the Order of St Patrick (another copy)
Published: T. Cranfield, Dublin, 15th November 1866
66.2 x 52.5 (plate 49.2 x 37)
Mezzotint, etching and stipple
Provenance Unknown

Catterson Smith the Elder, Stephen (1806-1872)
Irish School
SANDERS, GEORGE (1810-C.1876)
ENGLISH SCHOOL

10,421
George William Frederick Villiers, (1800-1870), 4th Earl of Clarendon, Lord Lieutenant of Ireland, later Foreign Secretary
(after an oil of c.1849)
Published: T. Cranfield, Dublin, also Messrs. Lloyd Brothers & Co., London
57.5 x 46 (plate cut)
Mezzotint
Acquired between 1898/1904

Catterson Smith the Elder, Stephen (1806-1872)
Irish School
SANDERS, GEORGE (1810-C.1876)
ENGLISH SCHOOL

10,456
Francis Blackburne, (1782-1867), Lord Chancellor of Ireland
(after an oil, RHA 1848, when Chief Justice of the Queen's Bench)
Published: T. Cranfield, Dublin, March 1852
60.2 x 50 (plate 53.5 x 44)
Mezzotint
Purchased, London, Mr G. Lausen, 1895

Catterson Smith the Elder, Stephen (1806-1872)
Irish School
SANDERS, GEORGE (1810-C.1876)
ENGLISH SCHOOL

10,468
Augustus Frederick FitzGerald, 3rd Duke of Leinster, (1791-1874)
60 x 48 (plate cut)
Published: T. Cranfield, Dublin
Mezzotint
Purchased, Mr H. Naylor, 1905

Catterson Smith the Elder, Stephen (1806-1872)
Irish School
SANDERS, GEORGE (1810-C.1876)
ENGLISH SCHOOL

10,483
Sir Henry Marsh, (1790-1860), President, Royal College of Physicians of Ireland
Unlettered Proof
74 x 52.2 (plate 66 x 48.5)
Mezzotint
Acquired between 1898/1904

Catterson Smith the Elder, Stephen (1806-1872)
Irish School
SANDERS, GEORGE (1810-C.1876)
ENGLISH SCHOOL

10,505
Archibald William Montgomerie, 13th Earl of Eglinton and Winton, (1812-1861), Lord Lieutenant of Ireland
(after an oil, Dublin Castle)
Published; T. Cranfield, Dublin, not before 1852
64 x 51.3 (plate 55 x 43.5)
Mezzotint
Purchased, Dublin,
Mr J.V. McAlpine, 1900

Catterson Smith the Elder, Stephen (1806-1872)
Irish School
SANDERS, GEORGE (1810-C.1876)
ENGLISH SCHOOL

10,506
Richard Whateley, P. Archbishop of Dublin, (1787-1863)
(after an oil, RHA 1848)
Published: T. Cranfield, Dublin, April 1853
64.2 x 50.5 (plate 57.7 x 45)
Mezzotint
Purchased, London, Mr G. Lausen, 1895

Catterson Smith the Elder, Stephen (1806-1872)
Irish School
SANDERS, GEORGE (1810-C.1876)
ENGLISH SCHOOL

10,510
Lord John George de la Poer Beresford, P. Archbishop of Armagh, (1773-1862), against Trinity College, Dublin Campanile and Library
(after an oil, RHA 1854; Trinity College, Dublin)
Published: T. Cranfield, Dublin, 13th July 1857
91.5 x 58 (plate 84 x 53.5)
Mezzotint
Purchased, Dublin,
Mr J.V. McAlpine, 1899

Catterson Smith the Elder, Stephen (1806-1872)
Irish School
SANDERS, GEORGE (1810-C.1876)
ENGLISH SCHOOL

10,544
Sir Philip Crampton, Bt., (1777-1858), Surgeon
(after an oil, RHA 1850; Trinity College, Dublin)
Unlettered Proof
Published: T. Cranfield, Dublin 1857
61 x 46.8 (plate 58.3 x 45.7)
Mezzotint
Acquired by 1914

Catterson Smith the Elder, Stephen (1806-1872)
Irish School
SANDERS, GEORGE (1810-C.1876)
ENGLISH SCHOOL

10,690
Charles William Wall, (c.1783-1862), Vice-Provost and former Professor of Oriental Languages at Trinity College, Dublin
(after a tql oil, RHA, 1849; Trinity College, Dublin)
Published: Hodges & Smith, Dublin
38.6 x 31.2 (plate cut)
Mezzotint
Purchased, Mr R. Langton Douglas, 1906

Catterson Smith the Elder, Stephen (1806-1872)
Irish School
SANDERS, GEORGE (1810-C.1876)
ENGLISH SCHOOL

11,856
Field Marshal Sir Edward Blakeney, (1778-1868)
Unlettered Proof
58 x 44 (plate 57 x 43.4)
Mezzotint
Acquired between 1898/1904

Catterson Smith the Elder, Stephen (1806-1872)
Irish School
SANDERS, GEORGE (1810-C.1876)
ENGLISH SCHOOL

20,768
The Hon. Richard Ponsonby, P. Bishop of Derry and Raphoe, (1772-1853)
44 x 35.6 (plate cut)
Mezzotint
Provenance Unknown

Catterson Smith the Elder, Stephen (1806-1872)
Irish School
VINTER, JOHN ALFRED (C.1828-1905)
ENGLISH SCHOOL

10,190
Peter Purcell of Halverstown, (1788-1846), founder of the Royal Agricultural Improvement Society of Ireland
(after an oil, NGI no. 308)
Published: Day & Son, London
45.5 x 35.9 (image 35.2 x 27.6)
Lithograph
Provenance Unknown

Chalmers, George (c.1720-1791)
Scottish School
McARDELL, JAMES (1728-1765)
IRISH SCHOOL

10,087
Lieut.-General Baron William Blakeney, (1672-1761), former Lt. Governor of Minorca, later Baron Blakeney
(after an oil of 1755, SNPG, Edinburgh)
Published: G. Hawkins, London, 1756
34 x 23.8 (plate 33 x 22.8)
Mezzotint
Purchased, London, 3rd Chaloner Smith sale, 1896

Chalmers, George (c.1720-1791)
Scottish School
PURCELL, RICHARD (FL.1746-C.1766)
IRISH SCHOOL

10,163
Lieut.-General Baron William Blakeney, (1672-1761), former Lt. Governor of Minorca, later Baron Blakeney
(derived from an oil of 1755, SNPG, Edinburgh)
Published: J. Ryall & R. Withy, London, 1756
38.4 x 29.4 (plate 35 x 25)
Mezzotint
Purchased, Dublin, Mr J.V. McAlpine, 1901

Chalon, Alfred Edward (1780-1860)
English School
ARTLETT, RICHARD A. (1807-1873)
ENGLISH SCHOOL

10,814
Henrietta Frances, Countess de Grey, (née Cole, 1784-1848), wife of 1st Earl de Grey, (former 3rd Baron Grantham), daughter of 1st Earl of Enniskillen
Published: London, 1839
43.4 × 30 (plate 33.8 × 25.8)
Line and stipple
Provenance Unknown

Chalon, Alfred Edward (1780-1860)
English School
HINCHCLIFF, JOHN JAMES (1805-1875)
ENGLISH SCHOOL

10,326
Marguerite, Countess of Blessington, (née Power, 1789-1849), Writer and Socialite, and 2nd wife of 1st Earl of Blessington
39.8 x 29 (plate 23 x 16.6)
Line and stipple
Presented, Dr Moore Madden, 1900

Chalon, Alfred Edward (1780-1860)
English School
MOTE, WILLIAM HENRY (FL.1830-1858)
ENGLISH SCHOOL

11,309
Penelope, Princess of Capua, (née Smyth, from Ballintray, Co. Waterford), wife of Prince Charles of Capua, (pl. for Heath's 'Book of Beauty', 1842)
23.7 x 16 (plate cut)
Stipple
Purchased, 1908

Chalon, Alfred Edward (1780-1860)
English School
RYALL, HENRY THOMAS (1811-1867)
ENGLISH SCHOOL

10,361
Marguerite, Countess of Blessington, (née Power, 1789-1849), Writer and Socialite and 2nd wife of 1st Earl of Blessington
(after a watercolour of 1834; copy in NPG, London)

Published: C. Tilt and the Proprietor, London, 1836 (Printed: McQueen)
44.6 x 36.4 (plate 34.7 x 27.2)
Stipple
Purchased, Dublin, Mr A. Roth, 1896

Chalon, Alfred Edward (1780-1860)
English School
THOMSON, JAMES (1789-1850)
ENGLISH SCHOOL

10,336
Frances Anne, Marchioness of Londonderry, (née Vane-Tempest, 1800-1865), 2nd wife of the 3rd Marquess
Unlettered Proof
Published: not before 1819
43.5 x 30.2 (plate 33.7 x 26)
Line and stipple
Purchased, Dublin, Mr A. Roth, 1896

Chambers, George (1803-1840)
English School
BRANDARD, ROBERT (1805-1862)
ENGLISH SCHOOL

20,283
The North Foreland off Broadstairs, Kent
Published: S. Simpkin & Marshall; also R. Brandard, (The Proprietor), London
21.1 x 27 (plate cut)
Line
Purchased, Lusk, Mr de Courcy Donovan, 1971

Chappel, Alonzo (1828-1887)
American School
AMERICAN SCHOOL (1873)

10,773
Maria Edgeworth, (1767-1849), Novelist, (pl. for E. Duyckink's 'Portrait Gallery of Eminent Men & Women of Europe and America', 1873)
INSCRIBED: *From the original painting by Chappel in the possession of the publishers*
Published: Johnson, Wilson & Co., New York, 1873
27.5 x 21 (plate 27 x 20.8)
Stipple
Acquired by 1913

Chardin, Jean-Baptiste Siméon (1699-1779)
French School
LEPICIE THE ELDER, BERNARD FRANCOIS (1698-1755)
FRENCH SCHOOL

10,172
La Maîtresse d'Ecole (The Young Schoolmistress)
(after an oil of c.1735, NG, London; NGI oil no. 813 is a replica)
Published: P.L. de Surugue, Paris, 1740
21.7 x 20.8 (plate cut)
Line
Bequeathed, Sir Hugh Lane, 1918

Chardin, Jean-Baptiste Siméon (1699-1779)
French School
LEPICIE THE ELDER, BERNARD FRANCOIS (1698-1755)
FRENCH SCHOOL

11,490
La Ratisseuse (Woman cleaning vegetables)
(after an oil of c.1738, NG, Washington)
Published: Paris, 1742
38.9 x 28.6 (plate 38 x 27.2)
Line
Presumed presented, Mr T. Bodkin, 1925

Chardin, Jean-Baptiste Siméon (1699-1779)
French School
SURUGUE, PIERRE LOUIS (1710-1772)
FRENCH SCHOOL

11,522
Les Tours de Cartes (Card Tricks)
(after an oil, Salon 1739; NGI no. 478)
Published: P.L. Surugue, Paris, 1744
24.3 x 30.6 (plate cut)
Line
Presumed presented, Mr T. Bodkin, 1925

Chardin, Jean-Baptiste Siméon (1699-1779)
French School
SURUGUE, PIERRE LOUIS (1710-1772)
FRENCH SCHOOL

11,623
Les Tours de Cartes (Card Tricks)
(after an oil, Salon 1739; NGI no. 478)
INSCRIBED: *On vous séduit foible Jeunesse,/Par ces tours que vos yeux ne cessent d'admirer;/Dans le cours du bel âge ou vous aller entrer,/Craignes pour votre coeur mille autres tours d'adresse./ Danchet. Le tableau Original est dans le Cabinet de M. Chev. Despuechs.*
Published: P.L. Surugue, Paris, 1744
39.4 x 46.5 (plate 30.5 x 32.8)
Line
Presumed presented, Mr T. Bodkin, 1925

Chauveau, François (1613-1676)
French School
CHAUVEAU, FRANCOIS (1613-1676)
FRENCH SCHOOL

20,215
The Birth or Triumph of Cupid, (frontispiece for Ovid's 'Metamorphoses', 1676)
INSCRIBED: *D.D. A très noble et très Reverend. Seigneur Messire Nicolas Lumague. Seigneur de Villers. Soubs St. Leu de Serens, Abbé de Rille les Fougeres en Bretagne &c, Par son très humble Serviteur I van Merlen.*
Published: I. van Merlen, Antwerp, 1676
15.6 x 21.4 (plate cut)
Line
Purchased, Lusk, Mr de Courcy Donovan, 1971

Chesham, Francis (1749-1806)
English School
CHESHAM, FRANCIS (1749-1806)
ENGLISH SCHOOL

20,032
Moses striking the Rock
Published: E. Walker, also B. Evans, London, 12th August 1791
55.5 x 68.1 (plate 50.5 x 67)
Line
Provenance Unknown

Childs, George (fl.1826-1873)
English School
CHILDS, GEORGE (FL.1826-1873)
ENGLISH SCHOOL

20,167
Cottage near Lyndhurst, Hampshire
Published: Ackermann & Co., London, 1835
(Printed: G.E. Madeley)
27.8 x 37.6 (image 20 x 31)
Lithograph
Purchased, Lusk, Mr de Courcy Donovan, 1971

Childs, George (fl.1826-1873)
English School
CHILDS, GEORGE (FL.1826-1873)
ENGLISH SCHOOL

20,375
Near Mill Hill, N. London
Published: Ackermann & Co., London 1835 (Printed: G.E. Madeley)
27.5 x 38 (plate 23 x 32)
Lithograph
Purchased, Lusk, Mr de Courcy Donovan, 1971

Chinnery, George (1774-1852)
Irish School
BROCAS THE ELDER, HENRY (1766-1838)
IRISH SCHOOL

11,344
Anne, Viscountess Fitzgibbon, (née Whaley, fl.1786-1844), wife of future 1st Earl of Clare, at her spinning wheel, (pl. for Walker's 'Hibernian Magazine', March 1794)
Published: Hibernian Magazine, Dublin, March 1794
20.3 x 13 (plate cut)
Stipple
Purchased, Dublin, Mr P. Traynor, 1898

Chinnery, George (1774-1852)
Irish School
IRISH SCHOOL (1804)

11,246
Lieut. General Charles Vallancey, (1721-1812), Cartographer, Director of Engineers in Ireland and Architect of Queen's, (now Queen Maev), Bridge, Dublin, (pl. for his 'Collectanea De Rebus Hibernicis', 1804)
(after an oil, SAI 1800; RIA, Dublin)
21.3 x 14.6 (plate cut)
Stipple
Purchased, Dublin,
Mr J.V. McAlpine, 1913

Chinnery, George (1774-1852)
Irish School
IRISH SCHOOL (1804)

11,247
Lieut. General Charles Vallancey, (1721-1812), Cartographer, Director of Engineers in Ireland and Designer of Queen's, (now Queen Maev), Bridge, Dublin, (pl. for his 'Collectanea De Rebus Hibernicis', 1804), (another copy)
(after an oil, SAI 1800; RIA, Dublin)
24.4 x 15.8 (plate 23.3 x 14.6)
Stipple
Provenance Unknown

Ciceri, Eugène (1813-1890)
French School
CICERI, EUGENE (1813-1890)
FRENCH SCHOOL

20,240
A Boat on a Beach
Published: Goupil et Vibert, Paris; also the Anaglyphic Co., London, 1st April 1844 (Printed: Lemercier)
28.2 x 38.6 (image 17.3 x 27.9)
Lithograph
Purchased, Lusk, Mr de Courcy Donovan, 1971

Cipriani, Giovanni Battista (1727-1785/90)
Anglo-Italian School
BARTOLOZZI, FRANCESCO (1727-1815)
ANGLO-ITALIAN SCHOOL

11,957
Tancred Armenia and a Sheperdess, (from Tasso's 'Jerusalem Delivered')
Published: F. Bartolozzi, London, 1784
21.6 x 25.3 (plate cut)
Stipple in red
Milltown Gift, 1902

Cipriani, Giovanni Battista (1727-1785/90)
Anglo-Italain School
BARTOLOZZI, FRANCESCO (1727-1815)
ANGLO-ITALIAN SCHOOL

20,031

'E. D'Uccider se Stesso in Pensier Venne' - Orlando is prevented from stabbing himself, (pl. for Canto XL of L. Ariosto's 'Orlando Furioso', 1773)
Published: Birmingham, 1773
20.3 x 14.3 (plate cut)
Line
Provenance Unknown

Cipriani, Giovanni Battista (1727-1785)
Anglo-Italian School
BOVI, MARINO (1758-AFTER 1805)
ANGLO-ITALIAN SCHOOL

10,312
The Recording Angel
Published: M. Bovi, London, January 1797
27 x 21.6 (plate cut)
Coloured Stipple
Milltown Gift, 1902

?Clarget, N. (19th Century)
French School
TOURFAUT, LEON ALEXANDRE (FL.1876-1883)
FRENCH SCHOOL

11,723
The Four Courts, Dublin
25.2 x 32 (plate cut)
Line
Provenance Unknown

Claude Lorrain (1600-1682)
French School
ALLEN, THOMAS BAYLIE (1803-1870)
ENGLISH SCHOOL

20,245
Landscape with Cephalus and Procris reunited by Diana
(after an oil of 1645, NG, London)
Published: Jones & Co., London, 1832
22.5 x 28 (plate cut)
Line
Purchased, Lusk, Mr de Courcy Donovan, 1971

Claude Lorrain (1600-1682)
French School
BOYDELL, JOSIAH (1760-1817)
ENGLISH SCHOOL

20,718(1)
Self-Portrait, (from 'Liber Veritatis', Vol. 1, 1777, see App. 8, no. 20,718)
(after a chalk and wash drawing frontispiece for the 'Liber Veritatis', BM, London)
Published: J. Boydell, London, 25th March 1777 (Printed: W. Bulmer & Co.)
41.7 x 26 (plate 18 x 12.5)
Mezzotint
Bequeathed, Judge J. Murnaghan, 1976

Claude Lorrain (1600-1682)
French School
EARLOM, RICHARD (1743-1822)
ENGLISH SCHOOL

20,664(93)
Ascanius shooting the stag of Silvia, (pl. from 'Liber Veritatis', Vol. 3, 1817, see App. 8, no. 20,664)
(after an ink and wash drawing of 1678, Chatsworth House, Derbyshire of a 1682 oil, Ashmolean Museum, Oxford)
Published: Boydell & Co., London, 2nd May 1817 (Printed: J. Moyes)
27.5 x 41.5 (plate 24 x 29)
Etching and mezzotint
Bequeathed, Judge J. Murnaghan, 1976

Claude Lorrain (1600-1682)
French School
EARLOM, RICHARD (1743-1822)
ENGLISH SCHOOL

20,665(150)
Mercury charming Argus to sleep, (pl. from 'Liber Veritatis' vol. 2, 1777, see App. 8, no. 20,665)

(after an ink drawing in the 'Liber Veritatis', BM, London from a 1660 oil)
Published: J. Boydell, London, 2nd September 1776
26.8 x 41.4 (plate 20.7 x 25.7)
Etching and mezzotint
Bequeathed, Judge J. Murnaghan, 1976

Claude Lorrain (1600-1682)
French School
EARLOM, RICHARD (1743-1822)
ENGLISH SCHOOL

20,666(51)
The Delivery of St Peter out of Prison, (pl. from 'Liber Veritatis', Vol. I, 1777, see App. 8, no. 20,666)
(after an ink and wash drawing in the 'Liber Veritatis', BM, London)
Published: J. Boydell, London, 1st August 1774
26.8 x 41.2 (plate 20.7 x 25.7)
Etching and mezzotint
Bequeathed, Judge J. Murnaghan, 1976

Claude Lorrain (1600-1682)
French School
EARLOM, RICHARD (1743-1822)
ENGLISH SCHOOL

20,719(149)
Juno Committing Io to the care of Argus, (from 'Liber Veritatis', Vol. 2, 1777, see App. 8, no. 20,719)
(after an ink drawing in the 'Liber Veritatis', BM London, from an oil of 1660, NGI no. 763)
Published: J. Boydell, London, 2nd September 1776 (Printed: W. Bulmer & Co.)
27.1 x 24.1 (plate 20.5 x 25.7)
Etching and mezzotint
Bequeathed, Judge J. Murnaghan, 1976

Claude Lorrain (1600-1682)
French School
ENGLISH SCHOOL (1827)

20,242
Cephalus and Procris reunited by Diana, (pl. for 'Gems of Ancient Art', 1827)
(after an oil of 1664)
Published: Howlett & Brimmer, London, 1827
20.5 x 25 (plate 16.4 x 21.3)
Etching and aquatint
Purchased, Lusk, Mr de Courcy Donovan, 1971

Claude Lorrain (1600-1682)
French School
ENGLISH SCHOOL (1827)

20,427
Pastoral landscape with the Ponte Molle, (pl. for 'Gems of Ancient Art', 1827)
(after an oil of 1645, Birmingham City Museum and Art Gallery)
Published: Howlett & Brimmer, London, 1827
19.3 x 25.2 (plate 16.7 x 21.8)
Etching and aquatint
Purchased, Lusk, Mr de Courcy Donovan, 1971

Claude Lorrain (1600-1682)
French School
SMITH, WILLIAM RAYMOND (FL.1818-1848)
FRENCH SCHOOL

20,607
The Flight into Egypt
(after an oil of 1661, The Hermitage, Leningrad)
8.4 x 10.8 (plate cut)
Steel Engraving
Presented, Mrs D. Molloy, 1981

Style of **Claude Lorrain (1600-1682)**
French School
ENGLISH SCHOOL (19TH CENTURY)

20,553
Cattle crossing a river
16.1 x 23.2 (plate cut)
Steel Engraving
Presented, Mrs D. Molloy, 1981

Claudet, Antoine François Jean (1797-1867)
Anglo-French School
BOSLEY (19TH CENTURY)
ENGLISH SCHOOL

11,057
William Parsons, 3rd Earl of Rosse, (1800-1867), President of the Royal Society and Astronomer
(after a daguerreotype)
Lettered Proof
Published: A. Claudet, also Ackermann & Co., London, 1st September 1849
53.2 x 39.2 (image 26.8 x 22.5)
Lithograph
Purchased, Dublin, Mr A. Roth, 1895

Claudet, Antoine François Jean (?1797-1867)
Anglo-French School
ENGLISH SCHOOL (1846)

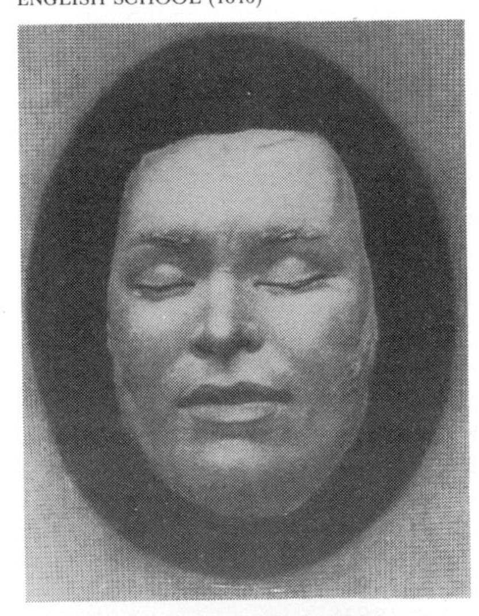

10,582
Death Mask of James O'Brien, United Irishman and Informer, hanged 1800, (pl. for R. Madden's 'United Irishmen', 3rd series, 1846)
(after a daguerreotype of J. Petrie's death mask of 1800)
Published: Madden & Co., London, 1846
20.1 x 11.9 (plate cut)
Mezzotint
Provenance Unknown

Claudet, Antoine François Jean (?1797-1867)
Anglo-French School
HUFFAM, T.W. (FL.1825-C.1855)
ENGLISH SCHOOL

10,660
Richard Robert Madden, (1798-1886), Writer and Anti-Slaver, (pl. for R. Madden's 'United Irishmen', 3rd series, 1846)
(after a daguerreotype)
Published: Madden & Co., London, 1846
21.6 x 12.6 (plate cut)
Mezzotint
Presented, Dr T. Moore Madden, 1901

Claudet, Antoine François Jean (?1797-1867)
Anglo-French
HUFFAM, T.W. (FL.1825-C.1855)
ENGLISH SCHOOL

10,661
Richard Robert Madden, (1798-1886), Writer and Anti-Slaver, (pl. for R. Madden's 'United Irishmen', 3rd series, 1846), (another copy)
(after a daguerreotype)
Published: Madden & Co., London, 1846
21.6 x 12.9 (plate cut)
Mezzotint
Purchased, Dublin, Mr P. Traynor, 1898

Clayton the Elder, Benjamin (c.1754-1814)
Irish School
CLAYTON THE ELDER, BENJAMIN (C.1754-1814)
IRISH SCHOOL

11,924
A Dutch Gabled House in Marrowbone Lane, Dublin, (demolished 1813)
9 x 10 (plate cut)
Line
Presented, Mr W.G. Strickland, 1906

Close the Elder, Samuel (fl.1770-1807)
Irish School
CLOSE THE ELDER, SAMUEL (FL.1770-1807)
IRISH SCHOOL

11,751
Montpelier Parade, Monkstown, Co. Dublin
(after a drawing)
(Printed: T. Bird, Dublin)
21.3 x 31.3 (plate 20.4 x 30.4)
Line
Provenance Unknown

Closterman, John Baptist (1660-1713)
Anglo-German School
SMITH, JOHN (1652-1742)
ENGLISH SCHOOL

10,229
Sir William Petty, (1623-1687), Physician to the Army in Ireland, Surveyor General and Political Economist
(after a tql oil c.1685, Earl of Shelburne Collection)
Published: J. Smith, London, 1696
38.7 x 28.8 (plate 34.8 x 25.8)
Mezzotint
Presumed purchased, Dublin, Jones Salesroom, 1879

Closterman, John Baptist (1660-1713)
Anglo-German School
SMITH, JOHN (1652-1742)
ENGLISH SCHOOL

10,930
General Thomas Maxwell, (d.1693), Commander of the Dragoons in Ireland
Published: J. Smith, London, 1692
34.6 x 25.4 (plate 34.2 x 24.8)
Mezzotint
Purchased, Dublin,
Mr J.V. McAlpine, 1899

Cocking, Thomas (fl.1783-1791)
English School
MEDLAND, THOMAS (1777-1822)
ENGLISH SCHOOL

11,927
Baggotrath Castle, Co. Dublin, (now demolished), (pl. for F. Grose's 'Antiquities of Ireland', 1791-95)
Published: S. Hooper, London, 14th June 1792
20 x 26.5 (plate 16.6 x 20)
Line
Presented, Dr E. MacDowel Cosgrave, 1907

Collier, William H. (c.1800-1847)
Irish School
O'NEILL, HENRY (1798-1880)
IRISH SCHOOL

10,789
William Hamilton Drummond, (1778-1865), Poet and Religious Controversialist
(after an oil, RHA 1846)
(Printed: M. & N. Hanhart, London)
41.6 x 31 (image 34.5 x 26.5)
Lithograph
Purchased, Dublin,
Mr J.V. McAlpine, 1911

Collins, Grenville (fl.1669-1696)
English School
ENGLISH SCHOOL (17TH CENTURY)

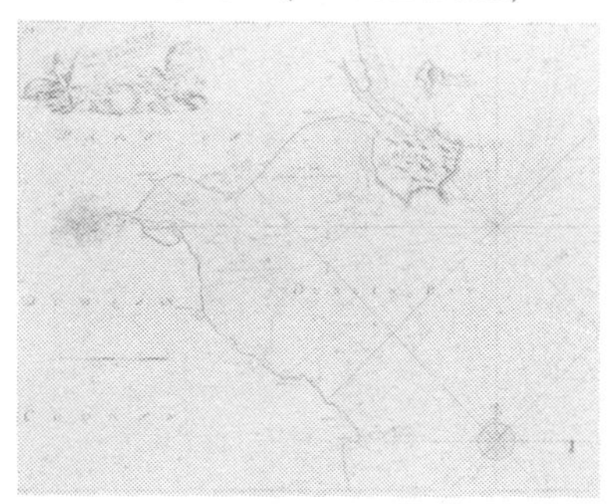

11,879
Dublin Bay and Part of Dublin County, (for a series of charts, 'Great Britain's Coasting Pilot', 1693)
INSCRIBED: To his Grace James/Duke of Ormond &c./This is humbly Dedicated and Presented,/by Capt. G. Collins

50.5 x 62 (plate 45.3 x 57.4)
Line and stipple
Acquired between 1898/1904

Collins, William (1788-1847)
English School
COLLINS, WILLIAM (1788-1847)
ENGLISH SCHOOL

20,330
The Prawn Fisher
Published: Rodwell & Martin, 1824, London (Printed: C. Hullmandel)
50 x 38 (image 36 x 30.3)
Lithograph
Purchased, Lusk, Mr de Courcy Donovan, 1971

Collins, William (1788-1847)
English School
FINDEN, EDWARD FRANCIS (1791-1857)
ENGLISH SCHOOL

20,383
'Happy as a King', (pl. for E. & W. Finden's 'Royal Gallery of British Art', 1838-49)
Published: E. & W. Finden, London, 1st May 1839
(Printed: McQueen)
28.2 x 38.5 (plate cut)
Steel Engraving
Purchased, Lusk, Mr de Courcy Donovan, 1971

Collins, William (1798-1847)
English School
OUTRIM, JOHN (FL.C.1840-1874)
ENGLISH SCHOOL

20,260
'Rustic Civility' - Children opening a country gate
(after an oil, RA 1832; V&A, London)
Published: Whitaker & Co., London, November 1835
14.2 x 20.5 (plate cut)
Steel Engraving
Purchased, Lusk, Mr de Courcy Donovan, 1971

Comerford, John (?1770-1832)
Irish School
CARDON, ANTHONY (1772-1813)
ANGLO-BELGIAN SCHOOL

11,220
Thomas Manners-Sutton, 1st Baron Manners, (1755-1842), Lord Chancellor of Ireland
(after a watercolour miniature, SAI 1810)
Unlettered Proof
Published: A. Cardon, London, 1811
16.2 x 13.7 (plate cut)
Stipple
Acquired by 1901

Comerford, John (?1770-1832)
Irish School
CARDON, ANTHONY (1772-1813)
ANGLO-BELGIAN SCHOOL

20,357
Thomas Manners-Sutton, 1st Baron Manners, (1756-1842), Lord Chancellor of Ireland, (another copy)
(after a watercolour miniature, SAI 1810)
Unlettered Proof
Published: A. Cardon, London, 1811
43.5 x 29.8 (plate 30.3 x 24.8)
Line and stipple
Purchased, Lusk, Mr de Courcy Donovan, 1971

Comerford, John (?1770-1832)
Irish School
CARVER, JOHN (FL. EARLY 19TH CENTURY)
ENGLISH SCHOOL

10,876
Gustavus Hume, (1730-1812), Irish State Surgeon and Speculative Builder
INSCRIBED: *In testimony of the great professional talents and unceasing attention to/Mercers Hospital during a period of more than half a Century the surviving/ Governors pay to his Memory this small but grateful tribute*
Published: not before 1812
34.1 x 25.1 (plate 23 x 17.2)
Stipple
Presented, Mr W.G. Strickland, 1906

Comerford, John (?1770-c.1832)
Irish School
COMERFORD, JOHN (1773-C.1835)
IRISH SCHOOL

11,327
Archibald Hamilton Rowan, (1751-1834), United Irishman
(after a drawing from life, Dublin, 1822)
(Printed: C.J. Hullmandel, London, 1822)
38.4 x 27.3 (image 19 x 15.6)
Lithograph
Purchased, Dublin, Mr P. Traynor, 1898

Comerford, John (?1770-1832)
Irish School
COOPER, ROBERT (FL.1795-1836)
ENGLISH SCHOOL

11,313
Thomas Spring Rice, M.P., (1790-1866), later Chancellor of the Exchequer and 1st Baron Monteagle
INSCRIBED: *Engraved by Cooper, from a drawing by Comerford/in the possession of Lady Theodoria Rice*
Published: J. Robins & Co., London and Dublin, 1st August 1825
18.6 x 12.1 (plate 18.4 x 12)
Stipple
Purchased, Dublin,
Mr J.V. McAlpine, 1896

Comerford, John (?1770-1832)
Irish School
COOPER, ROBERT (FL.1795-1836)
ENGLISH SCHOOL

11,314
Thomas Spring Rice, M.P., (1790-1866), later Chancellor of the Exchequer and 1st Baron Monteagle, (another copy)
INSCRIBED: *as no. 11,313*
Published: J. Robins & Co., London and Dublin, 1st August 1825
18.9 x 12.7 (plate 18.4 x 12)
Stipple
Purchased, Dublin,
Mr J.V. McAlpine, 1896

Comerford, John (?1770-1832)
Irish School
GRAVES, ROBERT (1798-1873)
ENGLISH SCHOOL

10,985
James Wandesford Butler, 19th Earl of Ormonde & Ossory, (1774-1838), later 1st Marquess of Ormonde
Published: London, 1823
31.1 x 24.7 (plate 21 x 31.8)
Etching
Acquired c.1903

Comerford, John (?1770-1832)
Irish School
HEAPHY, THOMAS (1775-1835)
ENGLISH SCHOOL

10,065
Daniel O'Connell, M.P., (1775-1847), Statesman, with the 'Catholic Rent' proposal to fund the Catholic Association
(after a drawing of 1824)
Published: J. Molteno, London, 14th June 1825 (Printed: Lahee)
42.2 x 32.5 (plate cut)
Stipple
Purchased, Dublin, Dillon & Co., 1901

Comerford, John (?1770-1832)
Irish School
HEATH, JAMES (1757-1834)
ENGLISH SCHOOL

10,687
Colonel Charles Vereker, M.P., (1768-1842), Constable of Limerick Castle, later 2nd Viscount Gort, (pl. for Sir J. Barrington's 'Historic Anecdotes and Secret Memoirs', 1809-15)

Published: G. Robinson, London, 1st August 1811
33.5 x 26.6 (plate 26 x 22)
Stipple
Acquired by 1901

Comerford, John (?1770-1832)
Irish School
HEATH, JAMES (1757-1834)
ENGLISH SCHOOL

10,708
John Blaquiere, 1st Baron de Blaquiere, (1732-1812), Irish Secretary of State, (pl. for Sir J. Barrington's 'Historic Anecdotes and Secret Memoirs', 1809-15)
INSCRIBED: From a drawing from life by Commerford, (sic) in the possession of Sir Jonah Barrington.
Published: G. Robinson, London, 1st August 1811
33.5 X 26.7 (plate 25.3 x 21.5)
Stipple
Acquired c.1896

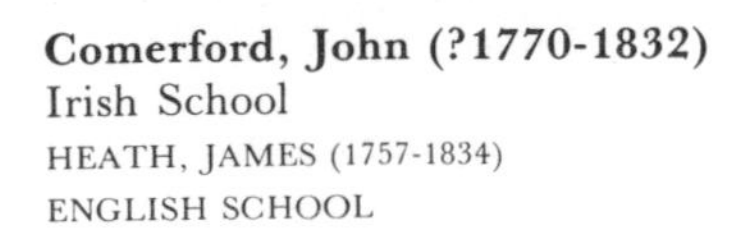

Comerford, John (?1770-1832)
Irish School
HEATH, JAMES (1757-1834)
ENGLISH SCHOOL

10,714
John Ball, Sergeant-at-Law, (pl. for Sir J. Barrington's 'Historic Anecdotes and Secret Memoirs', 1809-15)
INSCRIBED: From an original Drawing in possession of Sir Jonah Barrington
Published: G. Robinson, London, 1st March 1811
34.6 x 25.9 (plate 25.5 x 21.9)
Stipple
Acquired by 1895

Comerford, John (?1770-1832)
Irish School
HEATH, JAMES (1757-1834)
ENGLISH SCHOOL

10,748
Humphrey Butler, Politician, (pl. for Sir J. Barrington's 'Historic Anecdotes & Secret Memoirs' 1809-15)
INSCRIBED: From a drawing from life by

Commerford, (sic) in the possession of R. Power Esq.
Published: G. Robinson, London, 1st August 1811
33.5 x 26.5 (plate 25.2 x 21.5)
Stipple
Acquired by 1895

Comerford, John (?1770-1832)
Irish School
HEATH, JAMES (1757-1834)
ENGLISH SCHOOL

10,761
Charles Cornwallis, 1st Marquess Cornwallis, (1738-1805), Distinguished Officer, Governor General of India and Lord Lieutenant of Ireland, (pl. for Sir J. Barrington's 'Historic Anecdotes and Secret Memoirs, 1809-15)
INSCRIBED: From an original painting by Commerford (sic) in possession of Sir J. Barrington
Published: G. Robinson, London, 1st September 1809
34.5 x 28.5 (plate 25.3 x 21.3)
Stipple
Acquired by 1913

Comerford, John (?1770-1832)
Irish School
HEATH, JAMES (1757-1834)
ENGLISH SCHOOL

10,778
John Egan, (c.1750-1810), Lawyer and Chairman of Kilmainham, (pl. for Sir J. Barrington's 'Historic Anecdotes and Secret Memoirs', 1809-15)
INSCRIBED: From an original drawing by Comerford in possession of Sir Jonah Barrington
Published: G. Robinson, London, 1st August 1811
33.5 x 26.4 (plate 25 x 21.3)
Stipple
Acquired by 1901

Comerford, John (?1770-1832)
Irish School
HEATH, JAMES (1757-1834)
ENGLISH SCHOOL

10,793
Dr Patrick Duigenan, (1735-1816), Politician, (pl. for Sir J. Barrington's 'Historic Anecdotes and Secret Memoirs', 1809-15)
INSCRIBED: From an original drawing by Commerford (sic) in possession of Sir Jonah Barrington
Published: G. Robinson, London, 1st June 1810
34.8 x 27 (plate 25.3 x 21.5)
Stipple
Acquired by 1895

Comerford, John (?1770-1832)
Irish School
HEATH, JAMES (1757-1834)
ENGLISH SCHOOL

10,795
William Dickson, P. Bishop of Down and Connor, (1745-1804), (pl. for Sir J. Barrington's 'Historic Anecdotes and Secret Memoirs', 1809-15)
INSCRIBED: From an original painting in possession of Mrs Dickson
Published: G. Robinson, London, 1st June 1810
34.6 x 26.8 (plate 25.2 x 21.5)
Stipple
Acquired by 1895

Comerford, John (?1770-1832)
Irish School
HEATH, JAMES (1757-1834)
ENGLISH SCHOOL

10,803
James Fitzgerald, M.P., (1742-1835), formerly Prime Sergeant of Ireland, (pl. for Sir J. Barrington's 'Historic Anecdotes and Secret Memoirs', 1809-15)
INSCRIBED: From a drawing from life by Comerford (sic) in the possession of Sir Jonah Barrington
Published: G. Robinson, London, 1st August 1811
33.5 x 26.5 (plate 25 x 21.5)
Stipple
Acquired by 1898

Comerford, John (?1770-1832)
Irish School
HEATH, JAMES (1757-1834)
ENGLISH SCHOOL

10,811
John Fitzgibbon, 1st Earl of Clare, (1749-1802), Lord Chancellor of Ireland, (pl. for Sir J. Barrington's 'Historic Anecdotes and Secret Memoirs', 1809-15)
INSCRIBED: From an original painting by Commerford, (sic) in possession of Sir J. Barrington
Published: G. Robinson, London, 1st September 1809
33.2 x 25.5 (plate 26.5 x 21.5)
Stipple
Acquired by 1895

Comerford, John (?1770-1832)
Irish School
HEATH, JAMES (1757-1834)
ENGLISH SCHOOL

10,816
Thomas Gold, Barrister, (pl. for Sir J. Barrington's 'Historic Anecdotes and Secret Memoirs', 1809-15)
INSCRIBED: From an original drawing by Comerford in possession of Sir Jonah Barrington
Published: G. Robinson, London, 1st March 1811
34.8 x 26.4 (plate 25.4 x 21.3)
Stipple
Acquired by 1895

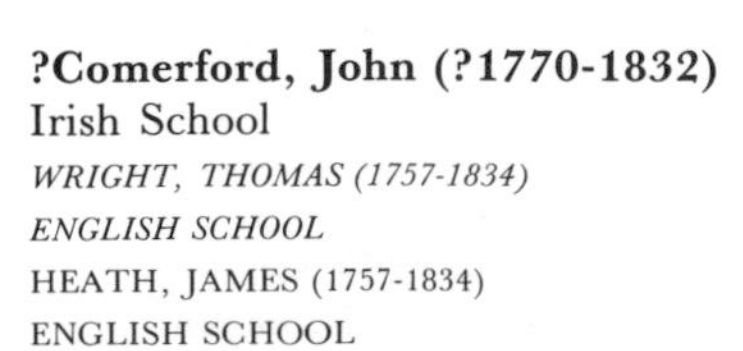

?Comerford, John (?1770-1832)
Irish School
WRIGHT, THOMAS (1757-1834)
ENGLISH SCHOOL
HEATH, JAMES (1757-1834)
ENGLISH SCHOOL

10,818
George Forbes, 6th Earl of Granard, (1760-1837), General, Opponent of the Act of Union, (pl. for Sir J. Barrington's 'Historic Anecdotes and Secret Memoirs', 1809-15)
Published: G. Robinson, London, 1st March 1815
34.2 x 27.3 (plate 25.4 x 21.3)
Stipple
Purchased, Mr W.V. Daniell, 1901

Comerford, John (?1770-1832)
Irish School
HEATH, JAMES (1757-1834)
ENGLISH SCHOOL

10,835
Henry Grattan, M.P., (1746-1820), Statesman, (pl. for 'The Kilkenny Private Theatre', 1825)
(after a drawing, 1808)

44.3 x 29.2 (plate 30.8 x 24.1)
Stipple
Acquired by 1898

Comerford, John (?1770-1832)
Irish School
HEATH, JAMES (1757-1834)
ENGLISH SCHOOL

10,836
Henry Grattan, M.P., (1746-1820), Statesman, (pl. for Sir J. Barrington's 'Historic Anecdotes and Secret Memoirs', 1809-15)
INSCRIBED: From an original drawing by Comerford in possession of Sir J. Barrington
Published: G. Robinson, London, 1st March 1811
34.5 x 26.2 (plate 25.4 x 21.5)
Stipple
Acquired by 1898

Comerford, John (?1770-1832)
Irish School
HEATH, JAMES (1757-1834)
ENGLISH SCHOOL

11,049
Lawrence Parsons, 2nd Earl of Rosse, (1758-1841), (pl. for Sir J. Barrington's 'Historic Anecdotes and Secret Memoirs', 1809-15)
INSCRIBED: From an original drawing by Comerford in possession of Sir Jonah Barrington
Published: G. Robinson, London, 1st June 1810
34.8 x 36.7 (plate 25.6 x 21.5)
Stipple
Acquired by 1903

Comerford, John (?1770-1832)
Irish School
HEATH, JAMES (1757-1854)
ENGLISH SCHOOL

20,790
Lawrence Parsons, 2nd Earl of Rosse, (1758-1841), Opponent of the Act of Union, (pl. for Sir J. Barrington's 'Historic Anecdotes and Secret Memoirs, 1809-1815), (another copy)
INSCRIBED: From an original drawing by Comerford in possession of Sir Jonah Barrington
Published: G. Robinson, London, 1st June 1810
19.8 x 13.6 (plate cut)
Stipple
Provenance Unknown

Comerford, John (?1770-1832)
Irish School
IRISH SCHOOL (1825)

10,557
Miss Smyth, (pl. for 'The Private Theatre of Kilkenny', 1825)
(after a drawing of 1808)
Unlettered Proof
36.8 x 26.8 (plate 30.5 x 24)
Stipple
Provenance Unknown

Comerford, John (?1770-1832)
Irish School
IRISH SCHOOL (1825)

10,716
William Beecher, amateur actor at the Kilkenny Theatre, (pl. for 'The Private Theatre of Kilkenny', 1825)
(after a drawing of 1808)
Unlettered Proof
36.2 x 26.3 (plate 30.2 x 24)
Stipple
Provenance Unknown

Comerford, John (?1770-1832)
Irish School
IRISH SCHOOL (1825)

10,747
Humphrey Butler, Politician, (pl. for 'The Private Theatre of Kilkenny', 1825)
(after a drawing of 1808)
Unlettered Proof
36.4 x 26.7 (plate 30.1 x 24)
Stipple
Acquired by 1895

Comerford, John (?1770-1832)
Irish School
IRISH SCHOOL (1825)

10,892
John Lyster, (pl. for 'The Private Theatre of Kilkenny', 1825)
(after a drawing of 1808)
Unlettered Proof
36.6 x 26.8 (plate 30.3 x 24)
Stipple
Provenance Unknown

Comerford, John (?1770-1832)
Irish School
IRISH SCHOOL (1825)

10,961
Thomas Moore, (1779-1852), Poet, (pl. for 'The Private Theatre of Kilkenny', 1825)
(after a drawing of 1808)
Unlettered Proof
34 x 26.3 (plate 30.5 x 23.8)
Stipple
Purchased, Dublin, Mr P. Traynor, 1898

Comerford, John (?1770-1832)
Irish School
IRISH SCHOOL (1825)

11,370
Richard Power, (Frontispiece for 'The Private Theatre of Kilkenny', 1825)
Unlettered Proof
(after a drawing of 1808)
30 x 24 (plate cut)
Stipple
Provenance Unknown

Comerford, John (?1770-1832)
Irish School
IRISH SCHOOL (1825)

11,371

George Routh, (pl. for 'The Private Theatre of Kilkenny', 1825)
(after a drawing of 1808)
Unlettered Proof
36.7 x 26.3 (plate 30. 4 x 24)
Stipple
Provenance Unknown

Comerford, John (?1770-1832)
Irish School
KIRKWOOD, JOHN (FL.1826-1853)
IRISH SCHOOL

11,270
Rev. Robert Walsh, (1772-1852), Author, (pl. for 'Dublin University Magazine', Vol. XV, February, 1840)
(after a drawing)
Published: W. Curry Junior & Co., Dublin
22.6 x 14.4 (plate cut)
Etching
Purchased, Dublin, Mr P. Traynor, 1898

Comerford, John (?1770-1832)
Irish School
LUPTON, THOMAS GOFF (1791-1873)
ENGLISH SCHOOL

10,798
William Downes, 1st Baron Downes, (1752-1826), Lord Chief Justice of Ireland
(after a miniature, exhibited RDS, 1825)
Published: not before 1826
37 x 28.5 (plate 36.7 x 27.7)
Mezzotint
Acquired between 1913/14

Comerford, John (?1770-1832)
Irish School
LYNCH, JAMES HENRY (FL.1815-1868)
IRISH SCHOOL

11,226
Henry Joy McCracken, (1767-1798), United Irishman, (pl. for R. Madden's 'United Irishmen', 2nd Series, 1843)
(after a miniature)
Unlettered Proof
Published: Madden & Co., London, 1843
22.3 x 14.3 (image 14.3 x 11.5)
Lithograph
Purchased, London, Mr H.A.J. Breun, 1911

Comerford, John (?1770-1832)
Irish School
LYNCH, JAMES HENRY (FL.1815-1868)
ENGLISH SCHOOL

11,329
Archibald Hamilton Rowan, (1751-1834), United Irishman, (pl. for R. Madden's 'United Irishmen', 2nd series, 1843)
(after J. Comerford/J. Comerford lithograph, NGI no. 11,327)
INSCRIBED: *From an original lithographic drawing presented by A.H.R. to Mr Willis*
Published: Madden & Co., London, 1843 (Printed: W. Day & L. Haghe)
19.6 x 12.5 (image 17 x 10)
Lithograph
Purchased, Dublin, Mr P. Traynor, 1898

Comerford, John (?1770-1832)
Irish School
MEYER, HENRY HOPPNER (1783-1847)
ENGLISH SCHOOL

11,152
James Gandon, (1743-1823), Architect
(after a drawing of 1805)
21.5 x 14.7 (plate cut)
Stipple
Acquired by 1911

Comerford, John (?1770-1832)
Irish School
MEYER, HENRY HOPPNER (1783-1847)
ENGLISH SCHOOL

10,200
George Ensor, (1769-1843), Political Writer
(after a drawing)
30.2 x 26.6 (plate 29.4 x 25)
Stipple
Purchased, Dublin, Mr A. Roth, 1896

Comerford, John (?1770-1832)
Irish School
PARKER, GEORGE (FL.1820-1834)
ENGLISH SCHOOL

10,986
James Wandesford Butler, 1st Marquess of Ormonde, (1774-1838), (pl. for W. Jerdan's 'National Portrait Gallery', 1830-34)
Published: Fisher Son & Co., London, 1830
26.9 x 18.2 (plate 23 x 14.8)
Stipple and line
Acquired c.1903

Comerford, John (?1770-1832)
Irish School
ROLLS, CHARLES (C.1800-C.1857)
ENGLISH SCHOOL

10,754
William Coppinger, P. Bishop of Cloyne and Ross, (1753-1831)
(after a drawing, NGI no. 2054)
60.7 x 44.3 (plate 43.3 x 33)
Line and stipple
Presented, Mr J.G. Robertson, 1883

Comerford, John (?1770-1832)
Irish School
SCRIVEN, EDWARD (1775-1841)
ENGLISH SCHOOL

10,679
Thomas Williams, Secretary to the Bank of Ireland
(after a miniature)
Lettered Proof
35.3 x 25.9 (plate 26.7 x 19.4)
Stipple
Purchased, Dublin, Mr A. Roth, 1897

Concanen, Alfred (19th Century)
English School
CHAVANE, E. (FL.1833-1850)
ENGLISH SCHOOL

11,620
The Wreck of the Queen Victoria on Howth Rocks, February 15th, 1853
Published: Read & Co., London
31 x 40 (plate 26.5 x 34.5)
Steel Engraving
Provenance Unknown

Constable, John (1776-1837)
English School
WARD THE YOUNGER, WILLIAM JAMES (1800-1840)
ENGLISH SCHOOL

10,231
Dr John Wingfield, (1760-1825), Prebendary of Worcester Cathedral and former Headmaster of Westminster School
(after an oil of 1818)
Published: P. Colnaghi, Son & Co., London, June 1827
48.9 x 37.8 (plate 35.4 x 25.2)
Mezzotint
Purchased, Mr D. Burke, 1949

Continental School (17th Century)
ENGLISH SCHOOL (1795)

11,206
Thomas Carve, (1590-?1672), Traveller, Army Chaplain and Notary Apostolic at St Stephen's Cathedral, Vienna
(after an M. Vliemayr line engraving of 1651; example in BM, London)
Published: W. Richardson, London, July 1795
14.2 x 10 (plate cut)
Line
Purchased, London, Mr A. Roth, 1898

Continental School (17th Century)
HARDING, SYLVESTER (1745-1809)
IRISH SCHOOL
GARDINER, WILLIAM NELSON (1766-1814)
IRISH SCHOOL

10,614
Count Anthony Hamilton, (?1646-1720), Writer and Soldier, (pl. for Count Hamilton's 'Memoirs of Count de Grammont', 1794 edition)
Published: E. & S. Harding, London, 1st October 1793
26.8 x 20.2 (plate cut)
Stipple
Purchased, Dublin, Mr J.V. McAlpine, 1899

Continental School (c.1620)
TURNER, CHARLES (1773-1857)
ENGLISH SCHOOL

10,869
James I, King of England, (1566-1625), his family, (Princes Henry and Charles, later King Charles I, Queen Anne of Denmark, Princesses Mary and Sophia), with the King and Queen of Bohemia and their children, (Frederick, Elizabeth, Rupert, Maurice, Charles, Louisa and Lewis)
Published: S. Woodburn, London, 1814
31 x 38.8 (plate cut)
Mezzotint
Purchased, Mr J.C. Nairn, 1900

Continental School (1730s)
IRISH SCHOOL (C.1847)

10,300
Dr Bartholomew Mosse, (1712-1759), Surgeon and founder of the Lying-in, (now Rotunda), Hospital, Dublin
(after an oil of 1730s, Rotunda Hospital, Dublin)
Published: Hodges & Smith, Dublin, c.1847
22.1 x 14.2 (plate cut)
Stipple
Purchased, Dublin, Mr P. Traynor, 1898

Continental School (19th Century)
CONTINENTAL SCHOOL (19TH CENTURY)

11,485
Domestic husbandry
23.5 x 28 (plate cut)
Line
Provenance Unknown

Continental School (19th Century)
HUFFAM, T.W. (FL.1825-C.1855)
ENGLISH SCHOOL

11,189
William Corbett, (1779-1842), United Irishman and French General, (pl. for R. Madden's 'United Irishmen', 3rd Series, 1846)
INSCRIBED: *From an original portrait in the possession of his Sister, Mrs Lyons*
Published: Madden & Co., London, 1846
21.1 x 13.6 (plate cut)
Aquatint and etching
Purchased, Dublin, Mr P. Traynor, 1898

Continental School (early 19th Century)
MAYER, CARL (1798-1868)
NUREMBERG SCHOOL

10,045
John Field, (1782-1837), Composer and Musician
Published: Schuberth & Niemeyer, Hamburg and Jtzehoe
16.5 x 11.8 (plate cut)
Stipple on steel
Purchased, Enniscorthy, Dr W.H. Grattan Flood, 1920

Cooke, John (fl.1818-1831)
?Irish School
COOKE, JOHN (FL.1818-1831)
?IRISH SCHOOL

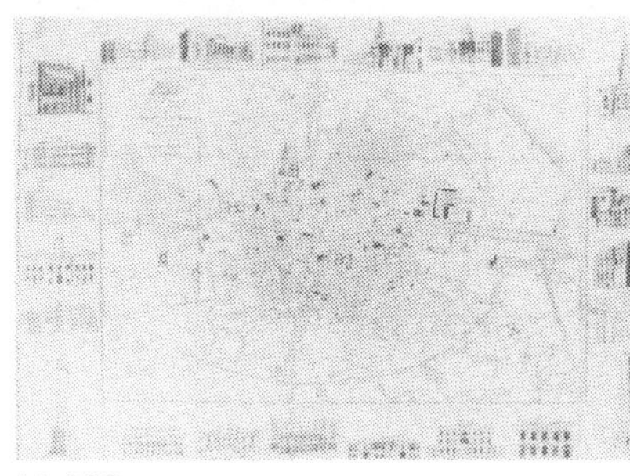

11,888
Cooke's Royal Map of Dublin (with vignettes of principal buildings)
INSCRIBED: *Dedicated by special permission to/His Most Gracious Majesty/King George the Fourth/on his visit to Ireland/corrected to 1831*
Published: G. Tyrrell, Dublin, 1831
50.2 x 71.3 (plate cut)
Line
Presented, Mr W.G. Strickland, 1906

Details from no. 11,888

Cooke, John (fl.1818-1831)
?Irish School
COOKE, JOHN (FL.1818-1831)
?IRISH SCHOOL

11,888(1)
The Bank of Ireland, (former Parliament House), College Green, Dublin

Cooke, John (fl.1818-1831)
?Irish School
COOKE, JOHN (FL.1818-1831)
?IRISH SCHOOL

11,888(2)
The Blue Coat Hospital, Blackhall Place, (now Incorporated Law Society), Dublin.

Cooke, John (fl.1818-1831)
?Irish School
COOKE, JOHN (FL.1818-1831)
?IRISH SCHOOL

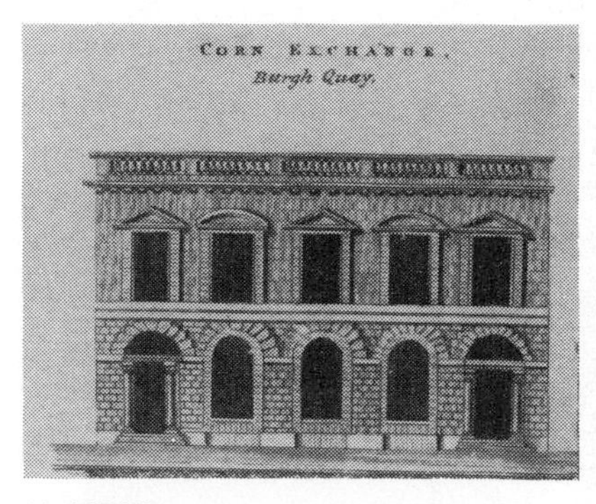

11,888(3)
The Corn Exchange, Burgh Quay, Dublin

Cooke, John (fl.1818-1831)
?Irish School
COOKE, JOHN (FL.1818-1831)
?IRISH SCHOOL

11,888(4)
The Custom House, Dublin

Cooke, John (fl.1818-1831)
?Irish School
COOKE, JOHN (FL.1818-1831)
?IRISH SCHOOL

11,888(7)
The Four Courts, Dublin

Cooke, John (fl.1818-1831)
?Irish School
COOKE, JOHN (FL.1818-1831)
?IRISH SCHOOL

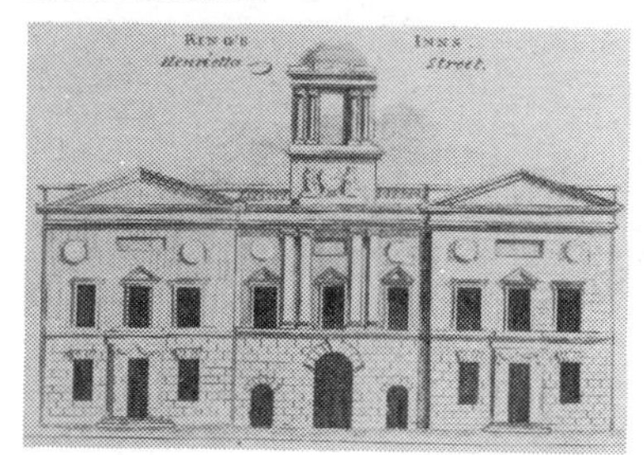

11,888(10)
The Kings Inns, Henrietta Street, Dublin

Cooke, John (fl.1818-1831)
?Irish School
COOKE, JOHN (FL.1818-1831)
?IRISH SCHOOL

11,888(5)
Dublin Castle Chapel and Record Tower

Cooke, John (fl.1818-1831)
?Irish School
COOKE, JOHN (FL.1818-1831)
?IRISH SCHOOL

11,888(8)
The General Post Office, Sackville Street, (now O'Connell Street), Dublin

Cooke, John (fl.1818-1831)
?Irish School
COOKE, JOHN (FL.1818-1831)
?IRISH SCHOOL

11,888(11)
The Linen Hall, (now demolished), Halston Street, Dublin

Cooke, John (fl.1818-1831)
?Irish School
COOKE, JOHN (FL.1818-1831)
?IRISH SCHOOL

11,888(6)
Upper Yard, Dublin Castle

Cooke, John (fl.1818-1831)
?Irish School
COOKE, JOHN (FL.1818-1831)
?IRISH SCHOOL

11,888(9)
Homes Hotel, (now demolished), Usshers Quay, Dublin

Cooke, John (fl.1818-1831)
?Irish School
COOKE, JOHN (FL.1818-1831)
?IRISH SCHOOL

11,888(12)
The Lying-In, (now Rotunda), Hospital and the Rotunda, Dublin

Cooke, John (fl.1818-1831)
?Irish School
COOKE, JOHN (FL.1818-1831)
?IRISH SCHOOL

11,888(13)
Interior of the Metropolitan Chapel, (now Pro-Cathedral), Dublin

Cooke, John (fl.1818-1831)
?Irish School
COOKE, JOHN (FL.1818-1831)
?IRISH SCHOOL

11,888(14)
Metropolitan Chapel, (now Pro-Cathedral), Dublin

Cooke, John (fl.1818-1831)
?Irish School
COOKE, JOHN (FL.1818-1831)
?IRISH SCHOOL

11,888(15)
Nelson Pillar, (now demolished), Sackville, (now O'Connell Street), Dublin

Cooke, John (fl.1818-1831)
?Irish School
COOKE, JOHN (FL.1818-1831)
?IRISH SCHOOL

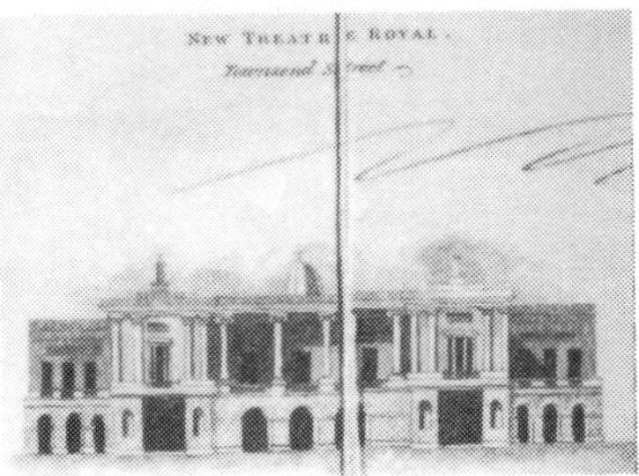

11,888(16)
New Theatre Royal, (now demolished), Hawkins Street, Dublin

Cooke, John (fl.1818-1831)
?Irish School
COOKE, JOHN (FL.1818-1831)
?IRISH SCHOOL

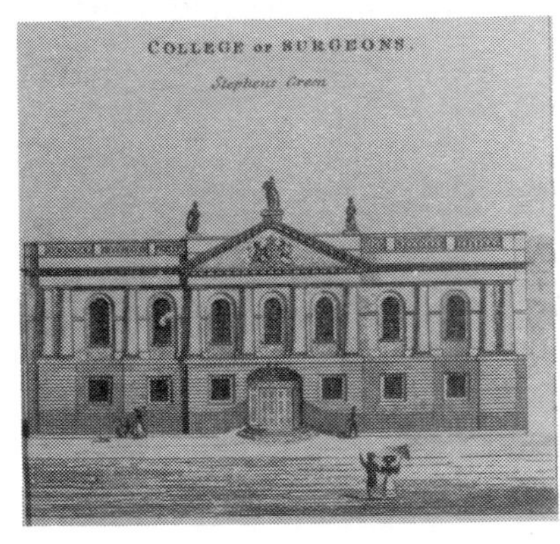

11,888(17)
Royal College of Surgeons, St Stephens Green, Dublin

Cooke, John (fl.1818-1831)
?Irish School
COOKE, JOHN (FL.1818-1831)
?IRISH SCHOOL

11,888(18)
Leinster House, Kildare Street, (now Dáil and Seanad), Dublin

Cooke, John (fl.1818-1831)
?Irish School
COOKE, JOHN (FL.1818-1831)
?IRISH SCHOOL

11,888(19)
Royal Exchange, Cork Hill, (now City Hall), Dublin

Cooke, John (fl.1818-1831)
?Irish School
COOKE, JOHN (FL.1818-1831)
?IRISH SCHOOL

11,888(20)
St George's Church, Hardwicke Place, Dublin

Cooke, John (fl.1818-1831)
?Irish School
COOKE, JOHN (FL.1818-1831)
?IRISH SCHOOL

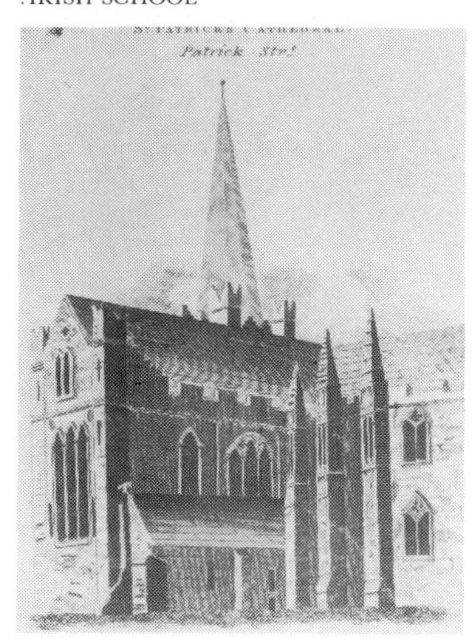

11,888(21)
St Patrick's Cathedral, Dublin, South Transept

Cooke, John (fl.1818-1831)
?Irish School
COOKE, JOHN (FL.1818-1831)
?IRISH SCHOOL

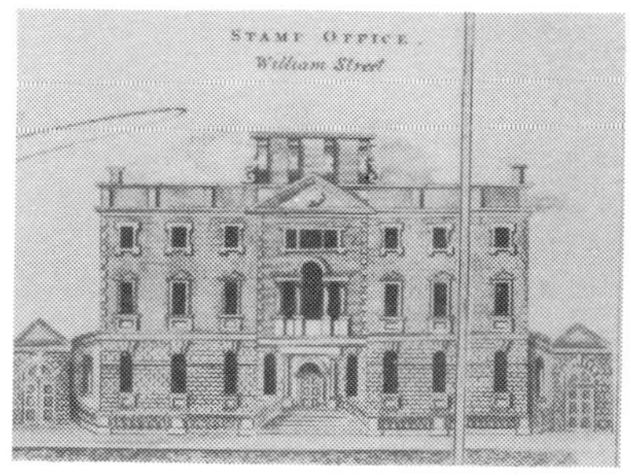

11,888(22)
The Stamp Office, (Powerscourt House), William Street South, Dublin

Cooke, John (fl.1818-1831)
?Irish School
COOKE, JOHN (FL.1818-1831)
?IRISH SCHOOL

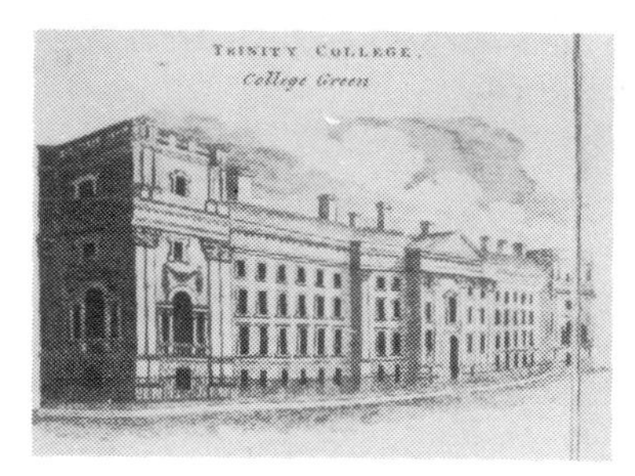

11,888(23)
Trinity College, Dublin, Entrance front

Cooke, John (fl.1818-1831)
?Irish School
COOKE, JOHN (FL.1818-1831)
?IRISH SCHOOL

11,888(24)
The Wellington Testimonial, Phoenix Park, Dublin

Cooper, Abraham (1787-1868)
English School
RADDON, WILLIAM (FL.1817-1862)
ENGLISH SCHOOL

20,615
A Mule Pheasant, (pl. for the 'New Sporting Magazine', June 1832)
Published: Baldwin & Cradock (for the proprietors of the 'New Sporting Magazine'), London, June 1832
13.7 x 22 (plate cut)
Line
Presented, Mrs D. Molloy, 1981

Cooper, Samuel (1609-1672)
English School
BROOKSHAW, RICHARD (1736-1804)
ENGLISH SCHOOL

11,393
Oliver Cromwell, (1599-1658), Lord Protector of England
(after a drawing of c.1655, Chatsworth, Derbyshire)
Published: J. Bowles, London
15.6 x 11.7 (plate 15.2 x 11.3)
Mezzotint
Purchased, London, 1st Chaloner Smith sale, 1887

Cooper, Samuel (1609-1672)
English School
BULFINCH, JOHN (FL.C.1680-C.1721)
ENGLISH SCHOOL
COOPER, RICHARD (1730-1820)
ENGLISH SCHOOL

11,392
Oliver Cromwell, (1599-1658), Lord Protector of England
(from an ink and wash drawing, NGI no. 2028 after a miniature of c.1653; Duke of Buccleuch collection)
Published: J. Caulfield, London, 1st October 1810
25.3 x 17.5 (plate cut)
Stipple
Acquired 1913

Cooper, Samuel (1609-1672)
English School
ENGLISH SCHOOL (1806)

11,050
John Robartes, Baron Robartes of Truro, (1606-1685), later 1st Earl of Radnor, Lord Lieutenant of Ireland, Speaker of the House of Lords
(after a watercolour miniature)
Published: J. Scott, London, 20th May 1806
26.7 x 21.8 (plate 19 x 14)
Stipple
Bequeathed, Miss E. Hone, 1912

Cooper, Samuel (1609-1672)
English School
VANDERGUCHT, MICHAEL (1660-1725)
ANGLO-FLEMISH SCHOOL

10,636
Henry Treton, (1611-1651), Cromwellian General and Lord Deputy of Ireland, (pl. for E. Ward's 'History of the Grand Rebellion', 1713)
(after a watercolour miniature of 1649, Fitzwilliam Museum, Cambridge)
18.8 x 11.1 (plate 17.6 x 10.1)
Line
Acquired by 1903

Cooper, Thomas Sydney (1803-1902)
English School
COOPER, THOMAS SYDNEY (1803-1902)
ENGLISH SCHOOL

20,165
Cattle Grazing
Published: T. McLean, London, 1st August 1837 (Printed: A. Ducôte)
33.8 x 43.5 (image 28.5 x 37.8)
Lithograph
Purchased, Lusk, Mr de Courcy Donovan, 1971

Cooper, Thomas Sydney (1803-1902)
English School
COOPER, THOMAS SYDNEY (1803-1902)
ENGLISH SCHOOL

20,169
Shire Horses, (pl. for T.S. Cooper's 'Drawing Book of Animals and Rustic Groups', 1853)
Published: S. & J. Fuller, London (Printed: A. Ducôte & Stephens)
27.8 x 38 (image 18 x 28)
Lithograph
Purchased, Lusk, Mr de Courcy Donovan, 1971

Cooper, Thomas Sydney (1803-1902)
English School
COOPER, THOMAS SYDNEY (1803-1902)
ENGLISH SCHOOL

20,170
'Halt at the Bell Inn', (pl. for T.S. Cooper's 'Drawing Book of Animals and Rustic Groups', 1853)
Published: S. & J. Fuller, London
(Printed: A. Ducôte & Stephens)
27.6 x 38 (image 18 x 29)
Lithograph
Purchased, Lusk, Mr de Courcy Donovan, 1971

Cooper, Thomas Sydney (1803-1902)
English School
COOPER, THOMAS SYDNEY (1803-1902)
ENGLISH SCHOOL

20,174
Donkeys, (pl. for T.S. Cooper's 'Drawing Book of Animals and Rustic Groups', 1853)
Published: S. & J. Fuller, London
(Printed: A. Ducôte & Stephens)
27.5 x 37.8 (image 14 x 23)
Lithograph
Purchased, Lusk, Mr de Courcy Donovan, 1971

Cooper, Thomas Sydney (1803-1902)
English School
COOPER, THOMAS SYDNEY (1803-1902)
ENGLISH SCHOOL

20,243
Deer, (pl. for T.S. Cooper's 'Drawing Book of Animals and Rustic Groups', 1853)
Published: S. & J. Fuller, London
(Printed: A. Ducôte & Stephens)
27 x 38.3 (image 14.5 x 24 approx)
Lithograph
Purchased, Lusk, Mr de Courcy Donovan, 1971

Cooper, Thomas Sydney (1803-1902)
English School
COOPER, THOMAS SYDNEY (1803-1902)
ENGLISH SCHOOL

20,345
Sheep and Carthorses, (pl. for T.S. Cooper's 'Drawing Book of Animals and Rustic Groups, 1853)
Published: S. & J. Fuller, London
(Printed: A. Ducôte & Stephens)
24.3 x 27.8 (image 20 x 24.5)
Lithograph
Purchased, Lusk, Mr de Courcy Donovan, 1971

Cooper, Thomas Sydney (1803-1902)
English School
COOPER, THOMAS SYDNEY (1803-1902)
ENGLISH SCHOOL

20,402
A Donkey and a Donkey with Rider, (pl. for T.S. Cooper's 'Drawing Book of Animals and Rustic Groups', 1853)
Published: S. & J. Fuller, London
(Printed: A. Ducôte & Stephens)
38 x 27.9 (image 31.5 x 24.5)
Lithograph
Purchased, Lusk, Mr de Courcy Donovan, 1971

Cope, Charles West (1811-1890)
English School
COPE, CHARLES WEST (1811-1890)
ENGLISH SCHOOL

10,957

11,388
Edmund Boyle, Lord Dungarvan, (1767-1856), later 8th Earl of Cork and Ossery, with his brothers, Charles Boyle, (1776-1800), and Courtney Boyle, (1770-1844), (left to right)
(after a drawing of c.1780)
Published: J. Jones, London, 4th April 1786
30.3 x 22.3 (plate cut)
Stipple
Purchased, London, 3rd Chaloner Smith sale, 1896

Corsi, G. (fl. early 19th Century)
Italian School
CORSI, G. (FL. EARLY 19TH CENTURY)
ITALIAN SCHOOL

20,388
The Cathedral and Leaning Tower of Pisa, N. Italy
Published: N. Volki, Florence
23 x 27.5 (plate 14.5 x 19)
Line
Purchased, Lusk, Mr de Courcy Donovan, 1971

Cosway, Richard (1742-1821)
English School
LANE, WILLIAM (1746-1819)
ENGLISH SCHOOL

11,340
Mrs Frances Abington, (née Barton, 1737-1815), Actress
Published: Dickenson & Co., London, 1790
16.4 x 9.9 (plate cut)
Lithograph
Milltown Gift, 1902

Cosway, Richard (1742-1821)
English School
SAILLIAR, LEWIS (1748-C.1795)
ENGLISH SCHOOL

10,140
George, Prince of Wales, (1762-1830), later King George IV of England, against Westminster Abbey, London
Published: R. Cosway, London
40.3 x 28.4 (plate 32.6 x 23.3)
Stipple
Milltown Gift, 1902

Cosway, Richard (1742-1821)
English School
SMITH, JOHN RAPHAEL (1752-1812)
ENGLISH SCHOOL

11,665
'Wisdom directing Beauty and Virtue to Sacrifice at the Altar of Diana' - Juliana, Countess of Carrick (née Boyle, c.1728-1814), wife of the 1st Earl and her daughters Lady Margaret Carrick, (1748-1775; wife of Armar Lowry-Corry) and Lady Harriet Carrick, (1750-1785; wife of future Viscount Mountgarret)
Published: S. Hooper also J.R. Smith, London, 15th April 1773
38 x 60 (plate 35.8 x 50.7)
Mezzotint
Purchased, 2nd Chaloner Smith sale, 1888

Cotes, Francis (1726-1770)
English School
BROOKSHAW, RICHARD (1736-1804)
ENGLISH SCHOOL

11,150

Elizabeth, Duchess of Hamilton and Brandon, (née Gunning 1734-1770), wife of the 6th Duke, later Duchess of Argyll then Baroness Hamilton; sister of Maria and Catherine and daughter of James Gunning, (1st State)
(after F. Cotes/J. McArdell mezzotint of 1752, NGI no. 10,343)
15.4 x 11.8 (plate cut x 11.5)
Mezzotint
Purchased, London, 1st Chaloner Smith sale, 1887

Cotes, Francis (1726-1770)
English School
BROOKSHAW, RICHARD (1736-1804)
ENGLISH SCHOOL

11,151
Elizabeth, Duchess of Hamilton and Brandon, (née Gunning, 1734-1770), wife of 6th Duke of Hamilton, later Duchess of Argyll then Baroness Hamilton; sister of Maria and Catherine and daughter of James Gunning, (2nd State)
(after an F. Cotes/J. McArdell mezzotint of 1752, NGI no. 10,343)
Published: R. Sayer, London, not before 1769
14.9 x 11.5 (plate cut)
Mezzotint
Purchased, London, 1st Chaloner Smith sale, 1887

Cotes, Francis (1726-1770)
English School
HOUSTON, RICHARD (1721-1775)
IRISH SCHOOL

10,342
Elizabeth, Duchess of Hamilton and Brandon, (née Gunning, 1734-1770), wife of 6th Duke; later Duchess of Argyll, then Baroness Hamilton; sister of Marie and Catherine and daughter of James Gunning
(partly from a pastel of 1751, when Miss Gunning, NPG London)
Published: ?R.Houston, London
32.7 x 22.6 (plate cut)
Mezzotint
Purchased, London, 1st Chaloner Smith sale, 1887

Cotes, Francis (1726-1770)
English School
HOUSTON, RICHARD (1721-1775)
IRISH SCHOOL

10,359
Catherine Gunning, (1735-1773), later Mrs Robert Travis; sister of Maria and Elizabeth and daughter of James Gunning
(after a pastel of 1751)
Published: J. Bowles & Son, London
32.2 x 23.2 (plate 32 x 22.1)
Mezzotint
Purchased, London, 1st Chaloner Smith sale, 1887

Cotes, Francis (1726-1770)
English School
McARDELL, JAMES (1728/29-1765)
IRISH SCHOOL

10,343
Elizabeth, Duchess of Hamilton and Brandon, (née Gunning 1734-1770), wife of the 6th Duke; later Duchess of Argyll, then Baroness Hamilton; sister of Maria and Catherine and daughter of James Gunning, (companion print to F. Cotes/J. McArdell no. 10,374)
(after a pastel of 1751, when Miss Gunning, NPG London)
Published: J. McArdell, London, 6th April 1752
32.5 x 22.2 (plate cut)
Mezzotint
Purchased, London, 1st Chaloner Smith sale, 1887

Cotes, Francis (1726-1770)
English School
McARDELL JAMES (1728/29-1765)
IRISH SCHOOL

Creswick, Thomas (1811-1869)
English School
HILL, R. (FL.1841-1843)
ENGLISH SCHOOL

20,503
Torc mountain, from Dinis island, Muckross Lake, Killarney County Kerry, (pl. for S.C. and A.M. Hall's 'Ireland, its Scenery, Character etc.', 1841-43)
Published: How & Parsons, London
(Printed: A. Adlard)
25.4 x 17.1 (plate cut)
Steel Engraving
Purchased, Lusk, Mr de Courcy Donovan, 1971

Creswick, Thomas (1811-1869)
English School
WALLIS, ROBERT (1794-1878)
ENGLISH SCHOOL

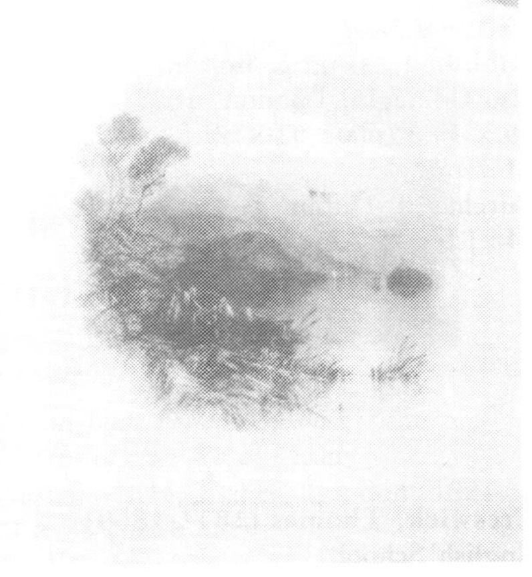

20,504
Lough Leane, (Lower Lake), Killarney, County Kerry, (pl. for S.C. and A.M. Hall's 'Ireland, its Scenery, Character, etc.', 1841-43)
Published: How & Parsons, London
(Printed: A. Adlard)
25.4 x 17.1 (plate cut)
Steel Engraving
Purchased, Lusk, Mr de Courcy Donovan, 1971

Creswick, Thomas (1811-1869)
English School
WILLMORE, JAMES TILBITTS (1800-1863)
ENGLISH SCHOOL

11,697
12, Aungier Street, Dublin, birthplace of the Poet Thomas Moore, (1779-1852), (now refaced)
Published: Longman & Co., London
22.6 x 14.9 (plate cut)
Line
Provenance Unknown

Creswick, Thomas (1811-1860)
English School
LACEY, SAMUEL (FL.1818-1857)
ENGLISH SCHOOL

20,518
'Evening', View of a River with Classical Buildings
Published: E. Lacey, London
11.1 x 17.8 (plate cut)
Steel Engraving
Purchased, Lusk, Mr de Courcy Donovan, 1971

Creswick, Thomas (1811-1869)
English School
WALLIS, ROBERT (1794-1878))
ENGLISH SCHOOL

20,513
Glengariff Castle and Bantry Bay, Co Cork
Published: How & Parsons, London, c.1841 (Printed: A. Adlard)
17.2 x 25.4 (plate cut)
Steel Engraving
Purchased, Lusk, Mr de Courcy Donovan, 1971

Crewe, Emma (18th Century)
English School
WHITE, CHARLES WILLIAM (FL.1750-1785)
ENGLISH SCHOOL

11,859
The Good Mother reading a story
Published: C. White, London, March 1783

29.2 x 29.2 (plate 28.5 x 29)
Line
Provenance Unknown

Croker, Thomas Crofton (1798-1857)
English School
PHILLIPS, I. (19TH CENTURY)
ENGLISH SCHOOL

20,805
The Spectacle Seller
Published: 1819
12.4 x 10.8 (image cut)
Lithograph
Provenance Unknown

Crowley, Nicholas Joseph (1819-1857)
Irish School
SHARPE, CHARLES WILLIAM (1818-1899)
ENGLISH SCHOOL

11,605
Fortune Telling by Cup Tossing
(after an oil, BI 1843)
INSCRIBED: This plate engraved from the original picture purchased by the Royal Irish Art union. Is given as an additional Engraving to the Members of that Society for the year 1842.
Published: For the Proprietors, Members of the Royal Irish Art Union, 1842
26.5 x 31.5 (plate cut)
Line
Provenance Unknown

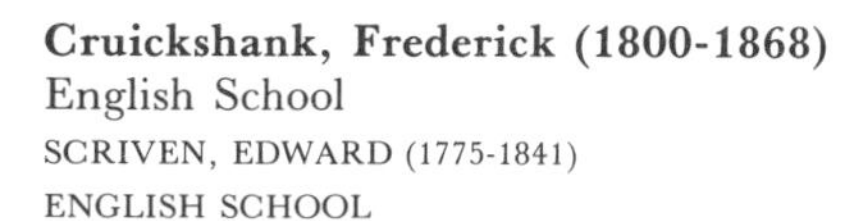

Cruickshank, Frederick (1800-1868)
English School
SCRIVEN, EDWARD (1775-1841)
ENGLISH SCHOOL

11,036
Frederick Shaw, M.P., (1799-1876), Recorder for Dublin, later Sir Frederick Shaw, 2nd Bt., (pl. for H.T. Ryall's 'Portraits of Eminent Conservatives and Statesmen', 1836)
(after a drawing)
Published: H.T. Ryall, also J. Fraser, also F.G. Moon, London, 1836
(Printed: Wilkinson & Dawe)
34.5 x 26.5 (plate 34 x 26)
Line and stipple
Acquired by 1903

Cullen, John (1761-1825/30)
Irish School
MAGUIRE, PATRICK (FL.1783-1820)
IRISH SCHOOL

10,602
Edward Lysaght, Barrister and Author, (1763-1811), (frontispiece for his 'Poems', 1811)
(after a drawing from recollection)
19.2 x 11.5 (plate 17.6 x 11.2)
Stipple
Purchased, Dublin, Mr P. Traynor, 1898

Cuming, William (1769-1852)
Irish School
ENGLEHEART, TIMOTHY STANFIELD (1803-1879)
ENGLISH SCHOOL

10,628
So-called Portrait of Edward Hudson, (1779/80-1833), United Irishman and Musician
(after an oil of 1797, NGI no. 305)

Published: Madden & Co., London, c.1843
23.5 x 16.1 (plate 21 x 14)
Line
Acquired c.1908

Cuming, William (1769-1852)
Irish School
?IRISH SCHOOL (19TH CENTURY)

11,325
General Sir John Doyle Bt., (1756-1834/35)
(after a W. Cuming/W. Ward mezzotint of 1797, NGI no. 10,780)
20.5 x 12.7 (plate 17.9 x 11.4)
Line and stipple
Provenance Unknown

Cuming, William (1769-1852)
Irish School
SMITH, JOHN RAPHAEL (1752-1812)
ENGLISH SCHOOL

10,192
James Cuffe, Baron Tyrawley, (1748-1821), Barrack-Master General and First Commissioner of the Board of Works in Ireland
Published: W. Cuming, Dublin also J.R. Smith, London, 20th March 1802
38.9 x 28.3 (plate 38 x 27.8)
Mezzotint
Purchased, London, Mr G. Lausen, 1895

Cuming, William (1769-1852)
Irish School
TURNER, CHARLES (1773-1857)
ENGLISH SCHOOL

10,547
Richard Annesley, 2nd Earl Annesley, (1745-1824), Commissioner of the Excise in Ireland
Published: W. Cuming, Dublin, 1st July 1806
51.5 x 35.7 (plate 51 x 35.2)
Mezzotint
Purchased, Dublin,
Mr J.V. McAlpine, 1906

Cuming, William (1769-1852)
Irish School
WARD THE ELDER, WILLIAM (1766-182[illegible]
ENGLISH SCHOOL

10,457
Edward Cooke, (1755-1820), Under-Secretary of State for Ireland
Hand Lettered Proof
Published: G. Holmes, London, 1799
53.1 x 38 (plate 50 x 31.5)
Mezzotint
Purchased, Dublin, Mr A. Roth, 1895

Cuming, William (1769-1852)
Irish School
WARD THE ELDER, WILLIAM (1766-1826)
ENGLISH SCHOOL

10,780
Lieut.-Colonel John Doyle, (1756-1834/35), Secretary at War, later Ger[illegible]l Sir John Doyle Bt.
P[illegible]lished: T. Nugent, London, also [illegible]. Allen, Dublin
59 x 44 (plate 38 x 28)
Mezzotint
Purchased, London,
Mr H.A.J. Breun, 1909

Cuming, William (1769-1852)
English School
WARD THE ELDER, WILLIAM (1766-1826)
ENGLISH SCHOOL

10,797
Lieut.-Colonel John Doyle, (c.1750-1834/35), Secretary at War, later General Sir John Doyle, Bt., (another copy)
Published: T. Nugent, London also W. Allen, Dublin, 4th September 1797
44 x 34 (plate 38 x 28)
Mezzotint
Provenance Unknown

Cunningham, Patrick (fl.1748-1774)
Irish School
IRISH SCHOOL (C.1770)

11,287
Jonathan Swift, (1667-1745), Dean of St Patrick's Cathedral and Satirist
(after a marble bust of 1766, St Patrick's Cathedral, Dublin)
13.6 x 8.4 (plate 12.8 x cut)
Line
Purchased, Dublin, Mr P. Traynor, 1898

Cuyp, Aelbert (1620-1691)
Dutch School
BENTLEY, JOSEPH CLAYTON (1809-1851)
ENGLISH SCHOOL

20,161
'A Sunny Day', (pl. for S.C. Hall's 'Gems of European Art', 1846, and for the 'Art Journal', 1868)
(after an oil of c.1660, Dulwich College Picture Gallery, London)
Published: G. Virtue, (for the Proprietors), London, 1846
26.2 x 31 (plate cut)
Steel Engraving
Purchased, Lusk, Mr de Courcy Donovan, 1971

Cuyp, Aelbert (1620-1691)
Dutch School
WESTALL, WILLIAM (1781-1850)
ENGLISH SCHOOL
MEDLAND, THOMAS (1755-1833)
ENGLISH SCHOOL *and*
BAILEY, JOHN (1750-1819)
ENGLISH SCHOOL

20,324
'An Aquatic Fête at Dort' - The Landing of Prince Frederick Henry at Nijmegen, Holland
(from a drawing after an oil of c.1655, Mertoun House, Scotland)
Published: Longman, Hurst, Rees, Orme & Brown, Also J. White; also Cadell & Davis; also P.W. Tomkins, London, 31st March, 1813
34 x 43 (plate cut)
Aquatint
Purchased, Lusk, Mr de Courcy Donovan, 1971

D

D'Agar, Charles (1669-1723)
French School
SIMON, JOHN (1675-1751)
ANGLO-FRENCH SCHOOL

10,730
Baroness Frances Carteret, (née Worsley, 1693/4-1743), 1st wife of Baron John Carteret
2nd State
Published: J. Bowles & Son, London, c.1760
37.3 x 26.8 (plate 35.3 x 25.6)
Mezzotint
Purchased, London, 2nd Chaloner Smith sale, 1888

D'Agar, Charles (1669-1723)
French School
SIMON, JOHN (1675-1751)
ANGLO-FRENCH SCHOOL

10,731
Baroness Frances Carteret, (née Worsley, 1693/4-1743), 1st wife of Baron John Carteret
1st State
Published: J. Bowles, London
32.3 x 25 (plate cut)
Mezzotint
Purchased, London, 2nd Chaloner Smith sale, 1888

Dahl, Michael (?1659-1743)
Anglo-Swedish School
BEARD, THOMAS (FL.1720-1729)
IRISH SCHOOL

10,063
William King, P. Archbishop of Dublin, (1650-1729)
Published: 1729
37.6 x 24.9 (plate 33.9 x 24.7)
Mezzotint
Purchased, London, 1st Chaloner Smith sale, 1887

?Dahl, Michael (?1659-1743)
Anglo-Swedish School
ENGLISH SCHOOL (EARLY 18TH CENTURY)

10,568
James Butler, 2nd Duke of Ormonde, (1665-1745)
21.8 x 16.7 (plate 20.3 x 15.2)
Mezzotint
Acquired between 1896/99

Dahl, Michael (?1659-1743)
Anglo-Swedish School
FABER THE YOUNGER, JOHN (1684-1756)
ENGLISH SCHOOL

10,125
Hugh Howard, (1675-1737), Artist and Antiquary
(after an oil of 1723)
Published: J. Faber the Younger, London, 1737
32.7 x 22.9 (plate 32.5 x 22.7)
Mezzotint
Purchased, Dublin, Mr J.V. McAlpine, 1899

Dahl, Michael (?1659-1743)
Anglo-Swedish School
PELHAM, PETER (C.1680-1751)
ENGLISH SCHOOL

10,569
James Butler, 2nd Duke of Ormonde, (1665-1745)
(after a tql oil of 1714, NPG, London)
Published: E. Cooper, London
19.9 x 14.5 (plate cut)
Mezzotint
Purchased, London, 1st Chaloner Smith sale, 1887

Dahl, Michael (?1659-1743)
Anglo-Swedish School
SIMON, JOHN (1675-1751)
ANGLO-FRENCH SCHOOL

10,822
Prince George of Denmark, (1653-1708), Consort of Queen Anne
(after a tql oil of c.1705, NPG, London)
Published: E. Cooper, London
33.7 x 24.7 (plate cut)
Mezzotint
Purchased, London, 2nd Chaloner Smith sale, 1888

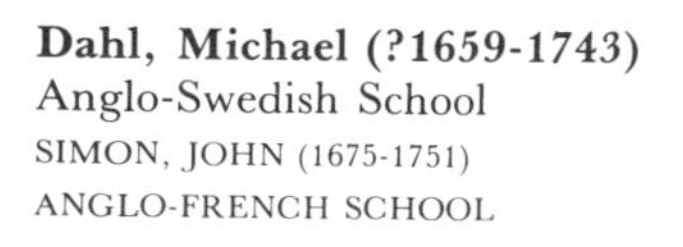

Dahl, Michael (?1659-1743)
Anglo-Swedish School
SIMON, JOHN (1675-1751)
ANGLO-FRENCH SCHOOL

10,995
James Butler, 2nd Duke of Ormonde, (1665-1745)
(after an oil of 1714, NPG, London)
Published: E. Cooper, London
36.8 x 25.7 (plate cut)
Purchased, London, 2nd Chaloner Smith sale, 1888

Danby, Thomas (1818-1886)
Irish School
SMITH, JOHN ORRIN (1799-1843)
ENGLISH SCHOOL

20,628
A Moonlight Feast
13.8 x 23.8 (image 12.5 x 23.2)
Wood Engraving
Presented, Mrs D. Molloy, 1981

Dance, George (1741-1825)
English School
DANIELL, WILLIAM (1769-1837)
ENGLISH SCHOOL

10,049
Thomas Barnard, (1728-1806), P. Bishop of Limerick, (pl. for 'A Collection of Portraits sketched from life since the Year 1793 by George Dance', 1809-14)
(after a pencil drawing of 15th June 1793, Ashmolean, Oxford)
Published: W. Daniell, London, 1st July 1812
40 x 29.5 (plate 27 x 20.3)
Soft-ground etching
Purchased, Dublin, Mr J.V. McAlpine, 1909

Dance, George (1741-1825)
English School
DANIELL, WILLIAM (1769-1837)
ENGLISH SCHOOL

10,196
James Barry, (1741-1806), Artist, (pl. for 'A Collection of Portraits sketched from life since the year 1793 by George Dance', 1809-14)
(after a black chalk drawing of 2nd April 1793, RA Collection, London)
Published: W. Daniell, London, 1st July 1809
31.6 x 24.9 (plate 27 x 20.1)
Soft-ground etching
Acquired between 1890/98

Dance, George (1741-1825)
English School
DANIELL, WILLIAM (1769-1837)
ENGLISH SCHOOL

10,746
James Caulfeild, 1st Earl of Charlemont, (1728-1799)
(after a drawing)
Published: W. Daniell, London, 2nd April 1814
48.7 x 33.2 (plate cut)
Soft-ground etching
Acquired by 1898

Dance, George (1741-1825)
English School
DANIELL, WILLIAM (1769-1837)
ENGLISH SCHOOL

10,902
Robert Stewart, 1st Marquess of Londonderry, (1739-1821)
(after a drawing, 28th May 1816)
38.3 x 28.2 (plate 27.3 x 20.4)
Soft-ground etching
Purchased, Dublin, Mr A. Roth, 1895

Dance, Nathaniel (1734-1811)
English School
BARTOLOZZI, FRANCESCO (1727-1815)
ANGLO-ITALIAN SCHOOL

10,819
Francis Grose, (1731-1791), Antiquarian and Watercolourist
(after a 1787 drawing, SNPG, Edinburgh: see p. 243)
Published: F. Bartolozzi, London, 1801
43.5 x 29.8 (plate 28 x 20.8)
Line
Purchased, Dillon & Co., 1901

Dance, Nathaniel (1734-1811)
English School
BURKE, THOMAS (1749-1815)
IRISH SCHOOL

10,999
Frederick North, Lord North, (1732-1792), British Prime Minister, later 2nd Earl of Guilford, (in Lord Chancellor's robes)
(after an oil, NPG, London)
Published: W.W. Ryland, London, 23rd May 1775
57.2 x 43.3 (plate 53.7 x 40.3)
Mezzotint
Purchased, London, 1st Chaloner Smith sale, 1887

Dance, Nathaniel (1734-1811)
English School
BURKE, THOMAS (1749-1815)
IRISH SCHOOL

11,000
Frederick North, Lord North, (1732-1792), Prime Minister, later 2nd Earl of Guilford
(after a tql oil, NPG, London, but with the Garter star)
Published: W.W. Ryland, London, 20th September 1775
57 x 43 (plate 50.2 x 35.3)
Mezzotint
Purchased, London, 1st Chaloner Smith sale, 1887

Dance, Nathaniel (1735-1811)
English School
DICKINSON, WILLIAM (1746-1823)
ENGLISH SCHOOL

10,462
Molyneux Shuldham, 1st Baron Shuldham, (1717-1798), Vice-Admiral of the White
Published: W. Dickinson & T. Watson, London, 2nd April 1780
49.8 x 36.5 (plate 45.5 x 33)
Mezzotint
Purchased, London, 1st Chaloner Smith sale, 1887

Dance, Nathaniel (1734-1811)
English School
RIDLEY, WILLIAM (1764-1838)
ENGLISH SCHOOL

10,669
Arthur Murphy, (1727-1805), Dramatist, (pl. for 'European Magazine', August 1805)
(after a tql oil of 1777, NPG, London)
Published: J. Asperne, London, 1st August 1805
21.8 x 14 (plate 16.2 x 11.2)
Stipple
Purchased, Dublin, Mr P. Traynor, 1898

Dance, Nathaniel (1734-1811)
English School
JACKSON, JOHN (1778-1831)
ENGLISH SCHOOL
SCRIVEN, EDWARD (1775-1841)
ENGLISH SCHOOL

10,925
Arthur Murphy, (1727-1805), Writer and Actor, (pl. for T. Cadell & W. Davies's 'Contemporary Portraits', 1822)
(after an oil, NGI no. 959)
Published: T. Cadell & W. Davies,

London, 1st June 1815
52.1 x 35 (plate 38.1 x 31.5)
Stipple
Provenance Unknown

Dance, Nathaniel (1734-1811)
English School
WARD THE ELDER, WILLIAM (1766-1826)
ENGLISH SCHOOL

10,474
Arthur Murphy, (1727-1805), Writer and Actor
(after an oil of 1777, NPG, London)
Published: J. Thompson, London, 5th October 1805
54.6 x 39 (plate 50.5 x 35.2)
Mezzotint
Acquired between 1879/90

Daniell, William (1769-1837)
English School
BRANDARD, ROBERT (1805-1862)
ENGLISH SCHOOL

20,609
Oriental Birds, (pl. for 'The Oriental Annual', 1836)
(after a drawing)
Published: E. Churton, (for the Proprietor), London, 1st October 1836
19.4 x 12.3 (plate cut)
Steel Engraving
Presented, Mrs D. Molloy, 1981

Daniell, William (1769-1837)
English School
DANIELL, WILLIAM (1769-1837)
ENGLISH SCHOOL

11,860
The Harbour Lighthouse, Holyhead, Wales, (now demolished)
(after a drawing)
Published: Longman & Co; also W. Daniell, London, 2nd January 1815
25.4 x 36.2 (plate 22.5 x 30.2)
Aquatint with watercolour
Presented, City of Dublin Steam Packet Co., 1924

Dawe, George (1781-1829)
English School
DEAN, T.A. (FL.1773-1840)
ENGLISH SCHOOL

10,894
Edmond Henry Pery, 1st Earl of Limerick, (1758-1844)
Lettered Proof
Published: For the Proprietors by J. Fraser, London, 1803 (Printed: McQueen)
43.4 x 29.8 (plate 33.3 x 25.3)
Line and stipple
Purchased, Mr W.V. Daniell, 1901

Dawe, George (1781-1829)
English School
DEAN, T.A. (FL.1773-1840)
ENGLISH SCHOOL

10,895
Edmond Henry Pery, 1st Earl of Limerick, (1758-1844), (another copy)
Lettered Proof
Published: For the Proprietors by J. Fraser, London, not before 1803 (Printed: McQueen)
44.2 x 30 (plate 33.3 x 25.3)
Line and stipple
Purchased, Dublin,
Mr J.V. McAlpine, 1904

Dawe, George (1781-1829)
English School
LEWIS THE ELDER, FREDERICK CHRISTIAN (1779-1856)
ENGLISH SCHOOL

10,991
Miss Eliza O'Neill, (1791-1872), Actress, as Juliet in Shakespeare's 'Romeo and Juliet', (Act 2, scene 2); later Lady Wrixon-Becher, wife of Sir William
(after an oil, RA 1816)
Published: G. Dawe, London, 30th May 1816
56.1 x 43 (plate 41.7 x 34)
Stipple
Acquired by 1910

Dawe, George (1781-1829)
English School
MAILE, GEORGE (1800-1842)
ENGLISH SCHOOL

10,423
William Beresford, 1st Baron Decies, P. Archbishop of Tuam, (1743-1819)
Published: G. Dawe, London, 20th May 1815 (Printed: Lahee)
59.5 x 42.8 (plate 50.5 x 35.5)
Mezzotint
Purchased, 1906

Day, E (19th century)
English School
CORBOULD, EDWARD HENRY (1815-1905)
ENGLISH SCHOOL
HOLL, FRANCIS (1815-1884)
ENGLISH SCHOOL

10,736
Prince Albert of Saxe-Coburg-Gotha, (1819-1861), Consort of Queen Victoria
(after a photograph)
Published: J. Mitchell London, 1862
(Printed: McQueen)
35 x 23 (plate cut)
Line and stipple
Acquired by 1913

Day, John George (1854-1931)
Irish School
DAY, JOHN GEORGE (1854-1931)
IRISH SCHOOL

11,419
John Redmond, M.P., (1856-1918), Leader of Home Rule Party
Dated in pencil 4th April 1914
27.7 x 21.7 (plate 22.5 x 17.4)
Etching
Presented, Mrs K. S. Roche, Mrs D.E.H. Westby and Mr E.P.J. Westby, 1976

Dayes, Edward (1763-1804)
English School
GAUGAIN, THOMAS (1748-C.1805)
ANGLO-FRENCH SCHOOL *and*
MITAN, JAMES (1776-1822)
ENGLISH SCHOOL

20,033
Reapers, with Canterbury Cathedral, Kent in the distance
Published: S. Morgan, London, July 1808
49.7 x 63.5 (plate 43 x 50.8)
Stipple and etching
Provenance Unknown

Dayes, Edward (1763-1804)
English School
NOBLE, SAMUEL (1779-1853)
ENGLISH SCHOOL

20,430
Middleham Castle, Yorkshire, (pl. for the 'Works of the Late Edward Hayes' containing 'An Excursion through the Principal Parts of Derbyshire and Yorkshire', 1805)

Published: Mrs Dayes, London, 25th May 1805
20.5 x 26.5 (plate 15.8 x 21)
Line
Purchased, Lusk, Mr de Courcy Donovan, 1971

Dayes, Edward (1763-1804)
English School
SMITH, JOSEPH CLARENDON (1778-1810)
ENGLISH SCHOOL

20,411
Dovedale, Derbyshire, (pl. for 'The Works of the Late Edward Dayes' containing 'An Excursion through the principal parts of Derbyshire and Yorkshire', 1805)
Published: Mrs Dayes, London, 25th May 1805
20.4 x 26.5 (plate 15.8 x 20.9)
Etching and Line
Purchased, Lusk, Mr de Courcy Donovan, 1971

Deane, Thomas Newenham (1828-1899)
Irish School *and*
Woodward, Benjamin (1815-1861)
Irish School
ROGERS, JAMES EDWARD (1838-1896)
IRISH SCHOOL

11,737
Dublin drinking fountains for Beresford Place and Parkgate Street, (both demolished), (from 'The Dublin Builder', 1st February, 1861)
Published: The Dublin Builder, Dublin, 1st February 1861
19.8 x 28 (image 15.6 x 23.2)
Wood Engraving
Provenance Unknown

Decamps, Alexandre Gabriel (1803-1860)
French School
DECAMPS, ALEXANDRE GABRIEL (1803-1860)
FRENCH SCHOOL

20,332
A Turkish village - asses at Boulac
(after an oil of 1833, Wallace Collection, London)
Published: A.G. Decamps, 1847
31 x 44.6 (plate 22.1 x 30)
Etching
Purchased, Lusk, Mr de Courcy Donovan, 1971

De Graves, Philip (17th century)
English School
SIMON, JOHN (1675-1751)
ANGLO-FRENCH SCHOOL

10,032
Henry Massue de Ruvigny, 2nd Marquess de Ruvigny and 1st Earl of Galway, (1648-1720), Williamite General
Published: E. Cooper, London, c.1704
37.3 x 26.6 (plate 34.8 x 25.2)
Mezzotint
Purchased, London, 2nd Chaloner Smith sale, 1888

De Grifft (18th century)
?Irish School
BROCAS THE ELDER, HENRY (1766-1838)
IRISH SCHOOL

10,667
Mr Moss, (fl.1777-1817), Actor, in the character of Midas from O'Hara's play
20.3 x 13 (plate 20 x 12.2)
Line
Purchased, Dublin, Mr. P. Traynor, 1898

De Hooghe, Romeyn (1645-1708)
Anglo-Dutch School
DE HOOGHE, ROMEYN (1645-1708)
ANGLO-DUTCH SCHOOL

11,655
The Battle of the Boyne, below the Flight of King James II from Ireland on the 12th July, 1690

Published: Callard, Amsterdam
50.5 x 59.7 (plate cut)
Etching
Purchased, Dublin
Mr J.V. McAlpine, 1900

De Hooghe, Romeyn (1645-1708)
Anglo-Dutch School
DE HOOGHE, ROMEYN (1645-1708)
ANGLO-DUTCH SCHOOL

11,846
The Departure from Holland of William, Prince of Orange, (1650-1702), on 2nd November 1688, to become King William III of England
Published: J. Tangena, Leiden, 13th November 1688
52 x 60.5 (plate 49 x 59.1)
Etching
Presented, C. R. Howard, 6th Earl of Wicklow, 1884

De Hooghe, Romeyn (1645-1708)
Anglo-Dutch School
DE HOOGHE, ROMEYN (1645-1708)
ANGLO-DUTCH SCHOOL

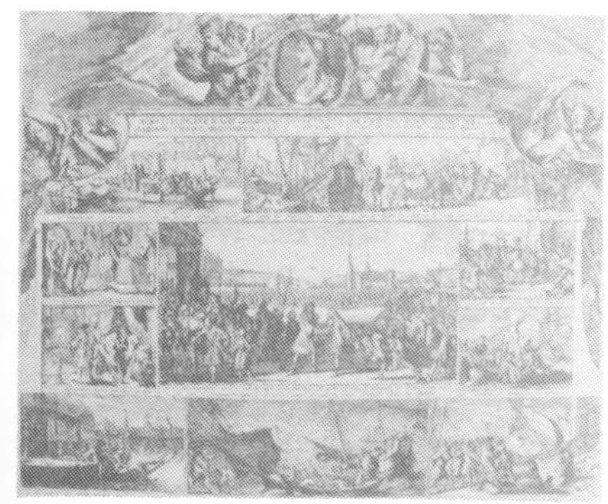

11,847
'Herstelling der Waere Godsdienst ...' - The Restoration of the true Religion and Constitution in Great Britain by H.R.H. King William III, (1650-1702); with the Flight from Court of King James II, (1633-1701), and his Queen Mary Beatrice, (1658-1718), with their Family
Published: J. Tangena, Leiden
51.7 x 61 (plate 48 x 57.7)
Etching
Presented, C. R. Howard, 6th Earl of Wicklow, 1884

Details from no. 11,847

De Hooghe, Romeyn (1645-1708)
Anglo-Dutch School
DE HOOGHE, ROMEYN (1645-1708)
ANGLO-DUTCH SCHOOL

11,847(1)
William III, King of England, (1650-1702)

De Hooghe, Romeyn (1645-1708)
Anglo-Dutch School
DE HOOGHE, ROMEYN (1645-1708)
ANGLO-DUTCH SCHOOL

11,847(2)
Mary Beatrice of Modena, (1658-1718), Queen of James II, and the Prince of Wales, (future so-called James III, 1688-1766), escape from Whitehall Palace, London

De Hooghe, Romeyn (1645-1708)
Anglo-Dutch School
DE HOOGHE, ROMEYN (1645-1708)
ANGLO-DUTCH SCHOOL

11,847(3)
They Board the French ship L'Assurance at Gravesend

De Hooghe, Romeyn (1645-1708)
Anglo-Dutch School
DE HOOGHE, ROMEYN (1645-1708)
ANGLO-DUTCH SCHOOL

11,847(4)
They Land at Calais, France, en route to meet Louis XIV, King of France, (1638-1715), at Saint-Germain-en Laye

De Hooghe, Romeyn (1645-1708)
Anglo-Dutch School
DE HOOGHE, ROMEYN (1645-1708)
ANGLO-DUTCH SCHOOL

11,847(5)
James II refuses at first, but later convenes a free Parliament

De Hooghe, Romeyn (1645-1708)
Anglo-Dutch School
DE HOOGHE, ROMEYN (1645-1708)
ANGLO-DUTCH SCHOOL

11,847(6)
James II throws the Rights of Parliament in the fire

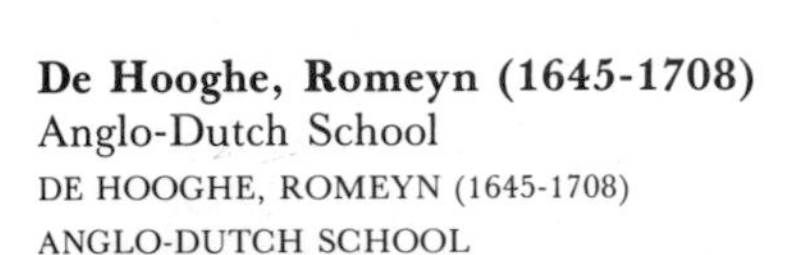

De Hooghe, Romeyn (1645-1708)
Anglo-Dutch School
DE HOOGHE, ROMEYN (1645-1708)
ANGLO-DUTCH SCHOOL

11,847(7)
James II Flees by night from the Court with the Royal Seal and crosses the River Thames

De Hooghe, Romeyn (1645-1708)
Anglo-Dutch School
DE HOOGHE, ROMEYN (1645-1708)
ANGLO-DUTCH SCHOOL

11,847(8)
James II Attempts to Board a Ship at Sheepey Island

De Hooghe, Romeyn (1645-1708)
Anglo-Dutch School
DE HOOGHE, ROMEYN (1645-1708)
ANGLO-DUTCH SCHOOL

11,847(9)
James II is Liberated at Feversham, Kent, by Louis de Duras, 1st Earl of Feversham, (?1640-1709)

De Hooghe, Romeyn (1645-1708)
Anglo-Dutch School
DE HOOGHE, ROMEYN (1645-1708)
ANGLO-DUTCH SCHOOL

11,847(10)
James II escapes from Rochester and arrives at Ambleteuse, France

De Hooghe, Romeyn (1645-1708)
Anglo-Dutch School
DE HOOGHE, ROMEYN (1645-1708)
ANGLO-DUTCH SCHOOL

11,847(11)
James II travels by way of Boulogne to Paris and Saint-Germain-en-Laye

De Hooghe, Romeyn (1645-1708)
Anglo-Dutch School
DE HOOGHE, ROMEYN (1645-1708)
ANGLO-DUTCH SCHOOL

11,847(12)
Louis XIV Receives James II at Saint-Germain-en-Laye a day after the Queen's Arrival, with the Prince of Wales, the Bastards of the King, some Catholic Lords and Priests in Attendance

De Hooghe, Romeyn (1645-1708)
Anglo-Dutch School
DE HOOGHE, ROMEYN (1648-1708)
ANGLO-DUTCH SCHOOL

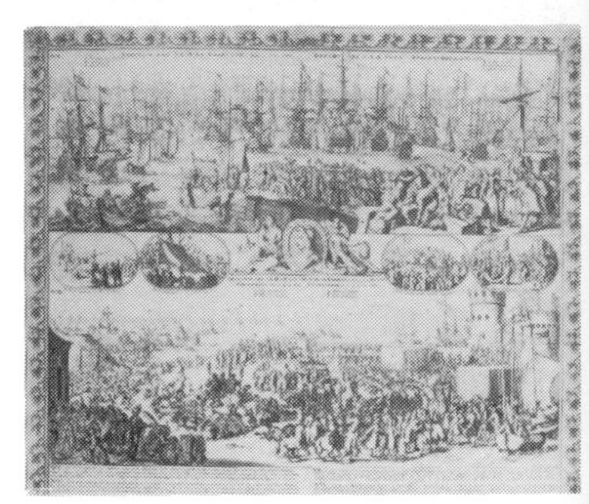

11,849
The Departure from Holland of William, Prince of Orange, (1650-1702), future King William III of England, on the 2nd November, 1688 and his arrival in England, 15th November 1688
Published: J. Danckerts, Amsterdam
52.8 x 63.4 (plate 50.3 x 60)
Line
Presented, C.R. Howard,
6th Earl of Wicklow, 1884

Details from no. 11,849

De Hooghe, Romeyn (1645-1708)
Anglo-Dutch School
DE HOOGHE, ROMEYN (1645-1708)
ANGLO-DUTCH SCHOOL

11,849(1)
The Arrival of William, Prince of Orange, (1650-1702), at Brixham, Devon, 15th November 1688

De Hooghe, Romeyn (1645-1708)
Anglo-Dutch School
DE HOOGHE, ROMEYN (1645-1708)
ANGLO-DUTCH SCHOOL

11,849(2)
William, Prince of Orange, (1650-1702), enters a tent

De Hooghe, Romeyn (1645-1708)
Anglo-Dutch School
DE HOOGHE, ROMEYN (1645-1708)
ANGLO-DUTCH SCHOOL

11,849(3)
Medallion of William III, King of England, (1650-1702), flanked by Justice and Minerva

De Hooghe, Romeyn (1645-1708)
Anglo-Dutch School
DE HOOGHE, ROMEYN (1645-1708)
ANGLO-DUTCH SCHOOL

11,849(4)
William, Prince of Orange, (1650-1702), arrives at London

De Hooghe, Romeyn (1645-1708)
Anglo-Dutch School
DE HOOGHE, ROMEYN (1644-1708)
ANGLO-DUTCH SCHOOL

11,849(5)
Mary, Princess of Orange, (1662-1694), arrives in England, 12th February 1689

De Hooghe, Romeyn (1645-1708)
Anglo-Dutch School
DE HOOGHE, ROMEYN (1645-1708)
ANGLO-DUTCH SCHOOL

11,882
Reception of Her Royal Highness Mary, Princess of Orange, (1662-1694), as Queen Mary II of England, on 12th February, 1689
Published: J. Tangena, Leyden
46.6 x 55.8 (plate cut)
Line
Provenance Unknown

De Koster, Simon (1767-1831)
Anglo-Dutch School
TOWNLY, CHARLES (1746-1800)
ENGLISH SCHOOL

10,953
George Macartney, 1st Viscount and later 1st Earl Macartney, (1737-1806), former Chief Secretary for Ireland and Ambassador to Russia and China
Published: J. Brydon, London, 2nd April 1793
68.4 x 45.3 (plate 68.4 x 43.5)
Mezzotint
Purchased, London, 2nd Chaloner Smith sale, 1888

Delacroix, Eugène (1798-1863)
French School
CARRED, LUCIEN DANIEL (FL.1873-1882)
FRENCH SCHOOL

11,495
The Barque of Dante, (Dante and Virgil)
(after an oil of 1822, The Louvre, Paris)
(Printed: A. Clément, Paris)
30.3 x 43.5 (plate 27 x 34.7)
Etching
Provenance Unknown

Delaroche, Paul (1797-1856)
French School
HENRIQUEL-DUPONT, LOUIS PIERRE (1797-1892)
FRENCH SCHOOL

11,484
The Deposition
(after an oil, c.1852)
Published: Goupil & Co. Ltd., Paris, Berlin & New York, 1st February 1856
39.8 x 62 (plate 33.5 x 55.5)
Line
Provenance Unknown

Delaroche, Paul (1797-1856)
French School
MARTINET, ACHILLE LOUIS (1806-1877)
FRENCH SCHOOL

11,486
'Marie Dans Le Désert' - The Virgin and Child
(after an oil of 1844, Wallace Collection, London)
Published: Bulla Frères et Jouy, Paris, Berlin, Barcelona, New York, also Gambart & Co., London, 1850
(Printed: Drouart, Paris)
54.3 x 36 (plate 48.6 x 30.1)
Line
Provenance Unknown

Denning, Stephen Poyntz (c.1787-1864)
English School
CHAPMAN, JOHN WATKINS (1832-1903)
ENGLISH SCHOOL

10,360
Princess, (later Queen), Victoria, (1819-1901), aged 4
(after an oil of 1823, Dulwich Picture Gallery, London)
Published: Shepherd Bros, London, 1901
40 x 30 (plate 32.1 x 26.2)
Mezzotint
Purchased, London, Shepherd Bros., 1902

Derby, William (1786-1847)
English School
MOLLISON, JAMES (FL.1833-1846)
ENGLISH SCHOOL

10,764
Adam Clarke, (?1762-1832), Wesleyan Minister and Theologian
(after a drawing)
Published: T.T. and J. Tegg, London
32.4 x 23.8 (plate 29 x 20.3)
Line and stipple
Purchased, Dublin,
Mr J.V. McAlpine, 1909

De Saint Aubyn, Augustin (1736-1807)
French School
CARDON, ANTHONY (1772-1813)
ANGLO-BELGIAN SCHOOL

11,167
Abbé Henry Essex Edgeworth de Fermont, (1745-1807), former Confessor of King Louis XVI
Published: R. Hunter, London, 14th May 1815
20 x 12.3 (plate cut)
Stipple
Purchased, Dublin,
Mr J.V. McAlpine, 1896

?Devilliers, Hyacinthe Rose (b.1808)
French School
DEVILLIERS, HYACINTHE ROSE (B.1808)
ENGLISH SCHOOL

20,102
Vulcan's Forge
61.6 x 46 (plate 45.3 x 36)
Etching
Provenance Unknown

Devis, Anthony William (1762-1822)
English School
COOPER, ROBERT (FL. 1795-1836)
ENGLISH SCHOOL

11,118
Lady Catherine Annesley, (b.1790), (pl. for Bell's 'La Belle Assemblée, December 1811)
Published: La Belle Assemblée, London, December 1811
28.6 x 19.3 (plate 21.7 x 15.3)
Line and stipple
Purchased, Dublin, Mr A. Roth, 1896

Devis, Arthur William (1762-1822)
English School
MEYER, HENRY HOPPNER (1783-1847)
ENGLISH SCHOOL

10,409
Eliza O'Neill, (1791-1872), Actress, as Belvidera in C. Otway's 'Venice Preserved'; later Lady Wrixon-Becher, wife of Sir William
(after an oil of 1816, Wolverhampton Art Gallery)
INSCRIBED: *To Her Royal Highness Princess Charlotte, This Plate is respectfully Dedicated, with permission, /By Her Royal Highnesses obedient and devoted servant, Arthur William Devis*
Published: Messrs, Boydell and Co., London, 1st January 1816
72 x 44 (plate 70 x 40)
Mezzotint
Acquired between 1904/08

De Wint, Peter (1784-1849)
English School
FINDEN, EDWARD FRANCIS (1791-1857)
ENGLISH SCHOOL

20,520
Distant view of Skiddaw, Cumbria, from Bassenthwaite Lake, (pl. for Lord Byron's 'Guy Mannering' 1832)
Published: C. Tilt, London, June 1830
17 x 23.4 (plate cut)
Steel Engraving
Purchased, Lusk, Mr de Courcy Donovan, 1971

De Wint, Peter (1784-1849)
English School
FLOYD, WILLIAM (1832-1859)
ENGLISH SCHOOL

20,493
Goodrich Castle, Herefordshire, from the river Wye, (pl. for 'Gallery of Modern British Artists', 1834)
Published: Simkin & Marshall, also R. Brandard, (the Proprietor), London
21 x 26.9 (plate cut)
Line and etching
Purchased, Lusk, Mr de Courcy Donovan, 1971

De Wint, Peter (1784-1849)
English School
KERNOT, JAMES HARFIELD (FL.1828-1849)
ENGLISH SCHOOL

20,382
The Forest Hall Mountains, (pl. for 'Gallery of the Society of Painters in Watercolours', 1833)
Published: C. Tilt, London, 1832
27.8 x 38.2 (plate 18.2 x 25.5)
Steel Engraving
Purchased, Lusk, Mr de Courcy Donovan, 1971

Dicksee, John Robert (1817-1905)
English School
DICKSEE, JOHN ROBERT (1817-1905)
ENGLISH SCHOOL

20,111

Padre Alessandro Gavazzi, (1804-1889)
Published: J.R. Dicksee & Ackerman & Co., also C. Gilpin, London, 22nd July 1851 (Printed: M. & N. Hanhart)
50 x 45.5 (image 47.8 x 35.4)
Lithograph
Purchased, Lusk, Mr de Courcy Donovan, 1971

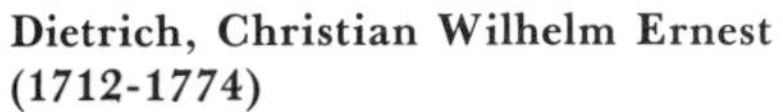

Dietrich, Christian Wilhelm Ernest (1712-1774)
German School
FOSSEYEUX, JEAN-BAPTISTE (1752-1824)
FRENCH SCHOOL

20,158
'The Dutch Violinist'
Published: Lenoir, Paris
37 x 26.3 (plate 25 x 19.2)
Line
Purchased, Lusk, Mr de Courcy Donovan, 1971

Dighton, Richard (1795-1889)
English School
DIGHTON, RICHARD (1795-1880)
ENGLISH SCHOOL

10,908
Francis Gerard Lake, 2nd Viscount Lake, (1772-1836), Major-General
(after a drawing of May 1818)
Published: T. McLean, London, 1818
30.4 x 22.2 (plate 27.7 x 19.7)
Etching with watercolour
Acquired c.1903

Dodd, Daniel (fl.1761-1780)
English School
COOK, THOMAS (C.1744-1818)
ENGLISH SCHOOL

11,095
Spranger Barry, (1719-1777), Actor, speaking the prologue to H. Jones's 'The Earl of Essex'
Published: Fielding & Walker, London, 28th November 1779
20 x 13 (plate 17 x 10.8)
Line
Acquired by 1910

Dodd, Daniel (fl.1761-1780)
English School
COOK, THOMAS (C.1744-1818)
ENGLISH SCHOOL

11,282
Richard Brinsley Sheridan, (1751-1816), Playwright, Actor and later Politician, speaking the prologue to J. Addison's 'Cato'
Published: Fielding and Walker, London, 3rd February 1780
20.1 x 13 (plate 17.2 x 10.9)
Line
Acquired between 1913/14

Dodd, Daniel (fl.1761-1790)
English School
SIBELIUS, GERARD (D.1785)
DUTCH SCHOOL

11,058
Margaret Caroline Rudd, (née Youngson d.1779), mistress of Daniel Perreau the forger
Published: W. Humphrey, London, 2nd December 1775, price 2s 6d
34.8 x 25 (plate cut)
Line
Purchased, London, Mr G. Lausen, 1895

?Dodd, Daniel (fl.1761-1780)
English School
?WALKER, JAMES (1748-1808)
ENGLISH SCHOOL

11,093
Ann Barry, (née Street, 1734-1801), Actress, wife of Spranger Barry, speaking the Occasional Prologue before J. Horne's play 'Douglas'
Published: Fielding & Walker, London, 12th February 1780
20 x 13.2 (plate 17.7 x 12)
Line and stipple
Acquired by 1913

Dodd, Daniel (fl.1761-1780)
English School
WALKER, JAMES (1748-1808)
ENGLISH SCHOOL

11,225
Charles Macklin, (c.1700-1797), Actor, as Sir Gilbert Wrangle, speaking his farewell Epilogue to C. Cibber's 'The Refusal' in 1753
Published: Fielding & Walker, London, 20th November 1779
20 x 13 (plate 17.5 x 11.9)
Line
Acquired by 1896

Doré, Louis Christophe Paul Gustave (1832-1883)
Anglo-French School
LAPLANTE, CHARLES (FL.1861-1903)
FRENCH SCHOOL

20,694(72)
The Death of Samson, (from 'The Doré Gallery', see App. 8, no. 20,694)
Published: Cassell, Petter & Galpin, London, Paris and New York
37.1 x 28.2 (image 24.7 x 19.6)
Lithograph
Provenance Unknown

D'Orsay, Alfred Guillaume Gabriel (?1798-1852)
French School
D'ORSAY, ALFRED GUILLAUME GABRIEL (?1798-1852)
FRENCH SCHOOL

10,757
Sir Philip Crampton, Bt., (1777-1858), Surgeon
(after a drawing, 12th August 1841)
Published: J. Mitchell, London, ?1841
(Printed: J. Graf)

37.9 x 27.5 (image 21.2 x 16.2)
Lithograph
Purchased 1909

D'Orsay, Alfred Guillaume Gabriel (?1798-1852)
Anglo-French School
D'ORSAY, ALFRED GUILLAUME GABRIEL (?1798-1852)
ANGLO-FRENCH SCHOOL

10,859
James Sheridan Knowles, (1784-1862), Actor, Author and Playwright
(after a drawing, 1st December 1839)
Published: J. Mitchell, London
38.2 x 27.8 (image 21 x 16.5)
Lithograph
Acquired by 1913

D'Orsay, Alfred Guillaume Gabriel (?1798-1852)
Anglo-French School
D'ORSAY, ALFRED GUILLAUME GABRIEL (?1798-1852)
ANGLO-FRENCH SCHOOL

11,066
William Grattan Tyrone Power, (1797-1841), Actor
(after a drawing of 19th October 1839)
Published: J. Mitchell, London, 1839
(Printed: J. Graf)
37.8 x 27.5 (image 24 x 19.2)
Lithograph
Purchased 1909

D'Orsay, Alfred Guillaume Gabriel (?1798-1852)
French School
D'ORSAY, ALFRED GUILLAUME GABRIEL (?1798-1852)
FRENCH SCHOOL

11,067
Richard Wingfield, 6th Viscount Powerscourt, (1815-1844)
(after a drawing of July 1841)
Published: J. Mitchell, London
36.5 x 27.3 (image 36.5 x 27.3)
Lithograph
Acquired c.1903

D'Orsay, Alfred Guillaume Gabriel (?1798-1852)
French School
D'ORSAY, ALFRED GUILLAUME GABRIEL (?1798-1852)
FRENCH SCHOOL

11,410
Walter Savage Landor, (1775-1864), Writer
(after a drawing, 1839)
Published: J. Mitchell, London 1839
Lithograph
Bequeathed, Mr E. Martyn, 1924

Dou, Gerard (1613-1675)
Dutch School
ENGLISH SCHOOL (19TH CENTURY)

20,159

Old Couple reading the Bible
(after an oil, c.1645, The Louvre, Paris)
Published: Allan Bell & Co., London
32.5 x 25.4 (plate cut)
Line
Purchased, Lusk, Mr de Courcy Donovan, 1971

Doussin-Dubreuil (fl.1841-1845)
Franco-Irish School
FRENCH SCHOOL (19TH CENTURY)

10,976
Daniel O'Connell, M.P., (1775-1847), Statesman
(after a daguerreotype taken in Dublin)
Published: D'Aubert et Cie, Paris
34 x 28.7 (image 25.7 x 20.5)
Lithograph
Acquired c.1908

Doussin-Dubreuil (fl.1841-1845)
Franco-Irish School
STADLER, JOHANN (1804-1859)
AUSTRIAN SCHOOL

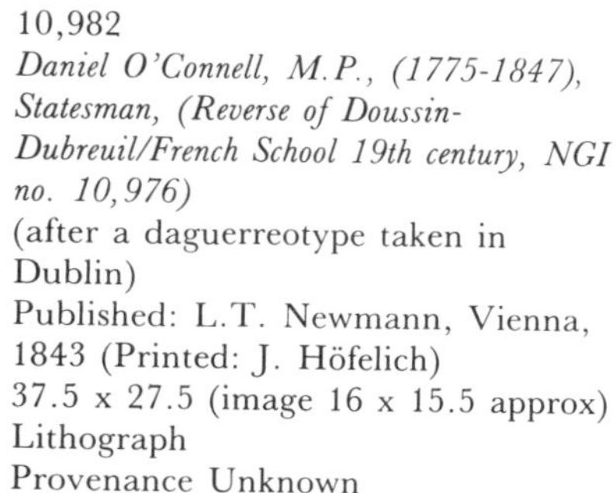

10,982
Daniel O'Connell, M.P., (1775-1847), Statesman, (Reverse of Doussin-Dubreuil/French School 19th century, NGI no. 10,976)
(after a daguerreotype taken in Dublin)
Published: L.T. Newmann, Vienna, 1843 (Printed: J. Höfelich)
37.5 x 27.5 (image 16 x 15.5 approx)
Lithograph
Provenance Unknown

Downman, John (1750-1824)
English School
BARTOLOZZI, FRANCESCO (1727-1815)
ANGLO-ITALIAN SCHOOL

10,320
Henrietta Frances, Viscountess Duncannon, (née Spencer 1761-1821), wife of Viscount Duncannon, later 3rd Earl of Bessborough
INSCRIBED: *Engraved by F. Bartolozzi after an original/drawing made by Mr. Downman for the scenery at Richmond House Theatre*
Published: R. Cribb, London, 1st January 1797
31.4 x 25.5 (plate 27.8 x 22.2)
Stipple
Purchased, London, 3rd Chaloner Smith sale, 1896

Doyle, John ('HB') (1797-1868)
Irish School
DOYLE, JOHN ('HB') (1797-1868)
IRISH SCHOOL

10,035
'The Catholic Triumvirate' - Honest Jack Lawless, (1773-1837), Daniel O'Connell, M.P., (1775-1847) and Richard Lalor Sheil, (1791-1851)
(after a drawing, NGI no. 2082)
Published: E. McLean, London, 1830
33 x 25 (image 31 x 23.5)
Lithograph
Presented, Dublin, Mr H.E. Doyle, 1873

Doyle, John (1797-1868)
Irish School
DOYLE, JOHN (1797-1868)
IRISH SCHOOL

11,158
Francis Grose, (?1731-1791), Antiquarian and Watercolourist
(after N. Hone; see p. 243)
28.4 x 20.4 (plate 19.2 x 11)
Etching
Bequeathed, Miss E. Hone, 1912

Doyle, John (1797-1868)
Irish School
DOYLE, JOHN (1797-1868)
IRISH SCHOOL

11,403
'The Darranane Conjurer or More Wigs on the Green' — Daniel O'Connell, M.P., (1775-1847), conjures up supporters for his Anti-Union Agitation; John Philpot Curran, (1750-1817), Henry Grattan, M.P., (1746-1820), William Saurin, (c.1757-1839), Attorney General, Thomas Bisle, M.P. and William Conyngham Plunket, 1st Baron Plunket, (1764-1854), Lord Chancellor of Ireland
Published: T. McLean, London, 7th October 1830
29.3 x 42.4 (image 24 x 35.4)
Lithograph
Purchased, Mr Miller, 1893

Doyle, John ('HB') (1797-1868)
Irish School
DOYLE, JOHN ('HB') (1797-1868)
IRISH SCHOOL

11,544(55)
'The Rejected of all' - Daniel O'Connell, M.P., (1775-1847), rejects the clean sweep proposed by Henry Brougham, 1st Baron Brougham, (1778-1868), as do Queen Victoria, (1819-1901), William Lamb, 2nd Viscount Melbourne, (1779-1848), Sir Robert Peel, (1788-1850), and Arthur Wellesley, 1st Duke of Wellington, (1769-1852), (from an album see App. 8, no. 11,544)
Published: Messrs Fores, London
29.2 x 43 (image 22 x 33)
Lithograph
Milltown Gift, 1902

Doyle, John ('HB') (1797-1868)
Irish School
DOYLE, JOHN ('HB') (1797-1868)
IRISH SCHOOL

11,544(56)
'John Gilpin' - Prime Minister Charles Grey, 2nd Earl Grey, (1764-1845), riding roughshod with his Reform Bill, followed by Daniel O'Connell, M.P., (1775-1847), (from an album, see App. 8, no. 11,544)
Published: T. McLean London, 13th May 1831 (Printed: C. Motte)
29 x 43 (image 25.2 x 38)
Lithograph
Milltown Gift, 1902

Doyle, John ('HB') (1797-1868)
Irish School
DOYLE JOHN ('HB') (1797-1868)
IRISH SCHOOL

11,544(57)
'The Horatii and the Curiatii' - Henry Brougham, 1st Baron Brougham, (1778-1868), and supporters William Conyngham Plunket, 1st Baron Plunket (1764-1854) and Henry Fox, 3rd Baron Holland, (1773-1840), against Arthur Wellesley, 1st Duke of Wellington, (1769-1852), Ernest Augustus, Duke of Cumberland, (1771-1851) and William Frederick, Duke of Gloucester, (1776-1834), (from an album, see App. 8, no. 11,544)
Published: T. McLean, London, 22nd April 1834 (Printed: A. Ducôte)
29 x 43 (image 25 x 36)
Lithograph
Milltown Gift, 1902

Doyle, John ('HB') (1797-1868)
Irish School
DOYLE, JOHN ('HB') (1797-1868)
IRISH SCHOOL

11,544(58)
'The upsetting of the Reform Coach' - William Lamb, 2nd Viscount Melbourne, (1779-1848), is reassured by fellow traveller Daniel O'Connell, M.P., (1775-1847), while Prime Minister Charles Grey, 2nd Earl Grey, (1764-1845), cries out, (from an album, see App. 8, no. 11,544)

Published: T. McLean, London, 4th June 1834 (Printed: A. Ducôte)
29 x 43 (image 25.3 x 36.5)
Lithograph
Milltown Gift, 1902

Doyle, John ('HB') (1797-1868)
Irish School
DOYLE, JOHN ('HB') (1797-1868)
IRISH SCHOOL

11,544(59)
'The Rival Newsmongers or Anticipated effects of the new alterations in the Stamp Duties' - John Bull, Sawney and Paddy on the Union coach petitioned by Torys and Daniel O'Connell, M.P., (1775-1847), with William Lamb, 2nd Viscount Melbourne, (1779-1848) as driver and John Russell, 1st Earl Russell, (1792-1878) as hostler, (from an album, see App. 8, no 11,544)
Published: T. McLean, London, 26th July 1836 (Printed: A Ducôte)
29 x 43 (image 24.7 x 33)
Lithograph
Milltown Gift, 1902

Doyle, John ('HB') (1797-1868)
Irish School
DOYLE, JOHN ('HB') (1797-1868)
IRISH SCHOOL

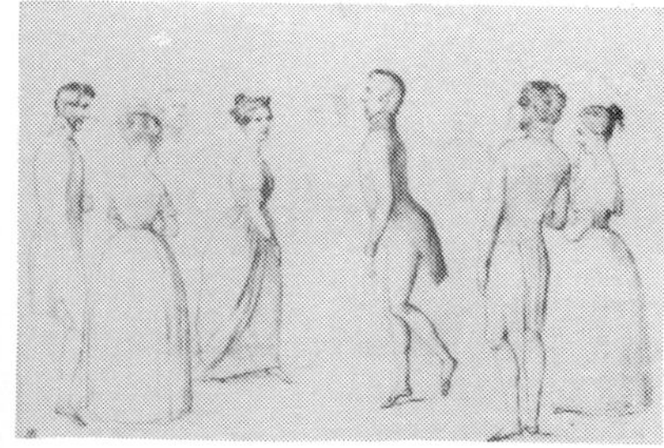

11,544(60)
'A Ballroom scene' - Queen Victoria, (1819-1901), dances with Constantine Phipps, 1st Marquess of Normandy, (1797-1868), Lord Lieutenant of Ireland, (from an album, see App. 8, no. 11,544)
Published: T. McLean, London, 3rd July 1838 (Printed: A. Ducôte)
29 x 43 (image 24 x 35)
Lithograph
Milltown Gift, 1902

Doyle, John ('HB') (1797-1868)
Irish School
DOYLE, JOHN ('HB') (1797-1868)
IRISH SCHOOL

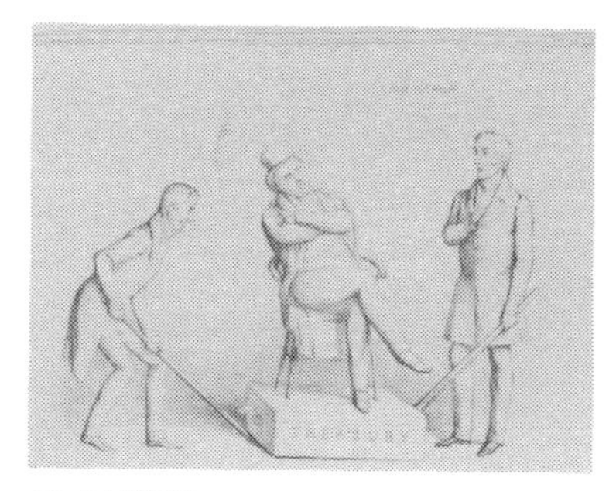

11,544(61)
'A Contrast' - William Lamb, 2nd Viscount Melbourne, (1779-1848), British Prime Minister, asleep in the Treasury Box, while Henry Brougham, 1st Baron Brougham, (1778-1868), tries to upset him, opposed by Arthur Wellesley, 1st Duke of Wellington, (1769-1852), (from an album, see App. 8, no. 11,544)
(after a black chalk and ink drawing, BM, London)
Published: T. McLean, London, 19th November 1838 (Printed: A. Ducôte)
29 x 43 (image 24.2 x 32)
Lithograph
Milltown Gift, 1902

Doyle, John ('HB') (1797-1868)
Irish School
DOYLE, JOHN ('HB') (1797-1868)
IRISH SCHOOL

11,544(62)
'A Council of War' - Daniel O'Connell, M.P. (1775-1847), explains his plan of attack to Irish Secretary George Howard, Viscount Morpeth, (1773-1848), Hugh Fortescue, 4th Baron Fortescue, (1783-1861), and Lord Lieutenant of Ireland Constantine Phipps, 1st Marquess of Normandy, (1797-1863), (from an album, see App. 8, no. 11,544)
Published: T. McLean, London, 12th March 1839 (Printed: A. Ducôte)
29 x 43 (image 24.6 x 33.2)
Lithograph
Milltown Gift, 1902

Doyle, John ('HB') (1797-1868)
Irish School
DOYLE, JOHN ('HB') (1797-1868)
IRISH SCHOOL

11,544(63)
'HB Discovered in his Studio' - John Singleton Copley, 1st Baron Lyndhurst, (1772-1863), watches Henry Brougham, 1st Baron Brougham (1778-1868), paint an unusually flattering portrait of Hugh Fortescue, 4th Baron Fortescue, (1783-1861), having completed one of Daniel O'Connell, M.P., (1775-1847), as a serpent, (from an album, see App. 8, no. 11,544)
Published: T. McLean, London, 26th March 1839 (Printed: A. Ducôte)
29 x 43 (image 24.2 x 34.5)
Lithograph
Milltown Gift, 1902

Doyle, John ('HB') (1797-1868)
Irish School
DOYLE, JOHN ('HB') (1797-1868)
IRISH SCHOOL

11,544(64)
'An Irish Subject' - Daniel O'Connell, M.P., (1775-1847), shies at the Bill for renewal of the Bank of Ireland charter and alarms Prime Minister William Lamb, 2nd Viscount Melbourne, (1779-1848), Queen Victoria, (1819-1901) and John Russell, 1st Earl Russell, (1792-1878), on an Irish car driven by Thomas Spring-Rice, later 1st Baron Monteagle, (1790-1866) (from an album, see App. 8, no. 11,544)
Published: T. McLean, London, 1st August 1839 (Printed: A. Ducôte)
29 x 43 (image 25.2 x 37.3)
Lithograph
Milltown Gift, 1902

Doyle, John ('HB') (1797-1868)
Irish School
DOYLE, JOHN ('HB') (1797-1868)
IRISH SCHOOL

11,544(65)
'The Road to Ruin' - Queen Victoria, (1819-1901) and William Lamb, 2nd Viscount Melbourne, (1779-1848), are alarmed as John Russell, 1st Earl Russell, (1792-1878), and Thomas Spring-Rice, later 1st Baron Monteagle, (1790-1866), try to restrain Daniel O'Connell, M.P. (1775-1847), (from an album, see App. 8, no. 11,544)
(after an ink and pencil drawing, BM, London)
Published: T. McLean, London, 26th August 1834 (Printed: A. Ducôte)
29 x 43 (image 25 x 38.8)
Lithograph
Milltown Gift, 1902

Doyle, John ('HB') (1797-1868)
Irish School
DOYLE, JOHN ('HB') (1797-1868)
IRISH SCHOOL

11,544(66)
'Another heavy blow....', - Prime Minister William Lamb, 2nd Viscount Melbourne, (1779-1848), prepares to resolve the constitutional crisis, watched by Queen Victoria, (1819-1901), Prince Albert, (1819-1861) and Daniel O'Connell, M.P., (1775-1847), (from an album, see App. 8, no 11,544)
Published: T. McLean, London, 8th November 1839 (Printed: A. Ducôte)
29 x 43 (image 24.5 x 34.5)
Lithograph
Milltown Gift, 1902

Doyle, John ('HB') (1797-1868)
Irish School
DOYLE, JOHN ('HB') (1797-1868)
IRISH SCHOOL

11,544(67)
'Omnibus Race' - The Tory Coach with John Bull inside passes that of the Whigs containing Queen Victoria and Prince Albert, (1819-1861) and driven by Daniel O'Connell, M.P., (1775-1847), with horses George Howard, Viscount Morpeth, (1773-1848), and John Russell, 1st Earl Russell, (1792-1878), (from an album, see App. 8, no 11,544)
(after a pencil and ink drawing, BM, London)
Published: T. McLean, London, 9th April 1840 (Printed; A. Ducôte)
29 x 43 approx. (image 25.8 x 34.2)
Lithograph
Milltown Gift, 1902

Doyle, John ('HB') (1797-1868)
Irish School
DOYLE, JOHN ('HB') (1797-1868)
IRISH SCHOOL

11,852
'Friar Tuck and Little John (again)' - Daniel O'Connell, M.P., (1775-1847), carried by John Russell, 1st Earl Russell, (1792-1878), (giving assistance in defeating breach of privilege motion in Parliament)
Published: T. McLean, London, 10th May 1836 (Printed: A. Ducôte)
28.5 x 38.1 (image 23.5 x 34)
Lithograph
Purchased, Mr Miller, 1893

Doyle, John ('HB') (1797-1868)
Irish School
DOYLE, JOHN ('HB') (1797-1868)
IRISH SCHOOL

11,853
'A Classical Subject' - Daniel O'Connell, M.P., (1775-1847), John Russell, 1st Earl Russell, (1792-1878) and George Howard, Viscount Morpeth, (1773-1848), observed by Sir Robert Peel, (1788-1850) and Edward George Stanley, (1799-1869), later 14th Earl of Derby
Published: T. McLean,
26 Haymarket, 10th May 1836
(Printed: A. Ducôte)
28.8 x 36.5 (image 24 x 33)
Lithograph
Purchased, Mr Miller, 1893

Doyle, John ('HB') (1797-1868)
Irish School
DOYLE, JOHN ('HB') (1797-1868)
IRISH SCHOOL

11,854
'A Pitiful Looking Group' - Daniel O'Connell, M.P., (1775-1847) attempting to pay off election expenses with Henry Warburton as the tame beast, Joseph Hume as the begging dog and John Russell, 6th Duke of Bedford, (1766-1839), with his son John Russell, 1st Earl Russell, (1792-1878)
Published: T. McLean, London,
22nd June 1836 (Printed: A. Ducôte)
28.7 x 36.7 (image 23.5 x 32)
Lithograph
Purchased, Mr Miller, 1893

Doyle, John ('HB') (1797-1868)
Irish School
DOYLE, JOHN ('HB') (1797-1868)
IRISH SCHOOL

11,891
'The Irish Tutor', Daniel O'Connell, M.P., (1775-1847), with his scholars William Lamb, 2nd Viscount Melbourne, (1779-1848), Henry Petty-Fitzmaurice, 3rd Marquess of Lansdowne, (1780-1863), John William Ponsonby, Viscount Duncannon, (1781-1847), later 4th Earl of Bessborough, John Russell, 1st Earl Russell, (1792-1878) and Thomas Spring Rice, (1790-1966), later 1st Baron Monteagle
Published: T. McLean, London,
29th April 1836
28.9 x 38.2 (image 24 x 34.5)
Lithograph
Purchased, Mr Miller, 1893

Drouais-Germain, Jean (1763-1788)
French School
DUVAL, LOUIS (FL. C.1800)
FRENCH SCHOOL

20,106
Christ and the Woman of Cana
(after an oil of 1784, The Louvre, Paris)
Unlettered Proof
46.8 x 61 (plate 32.3 x 42)
Etching
Provenance Unknown

Drulin, Antoine (1802-1869)
French School
DRULIN, ANTOINE (1802-1869)
FRENCH SCHOOL

20,401
The Zachringen Suspension Bridge over the River Sarine at Fribourg, Switzerland, from the Hotel Zachringen
26.7 x 36.8 (image 17.5 x 25.9)
Lithograph
Purchased, Lusk, Mr de Courcy Donovan, 1971

Drummond, Rose Emma (fl.1815-1837)
English School
HOPWOOD THE YOUNGER, JAMES (1795-AFTER 1825)
ENGLISH SCHOOL

11,006
Mary Tighe, (née Blachford 1772-1810), Poetess, (pl. for 'Ladies Monthly Museum', 1818)
(after a watercolour miniature)
Published: Dean & Munday, London,
1st February 1818
29 x 22.2 (plate 18.7 x 12)
Stipple
Purchased, Dublin, Mr P. Traynor, 1898

Drummond, Samuel (1765-1844)
English School
BARNARD, WILLIAM (1774-1849)
ENGLISH SHOOL

10,493
Sir Jerome Fitzpatrick, (d.1810), Inspector General of Health to the Army, with the plan of a county prison at his feet
Published: R. Finnell, London, not before 1799
64 x 41.8 (plate 64 x 40.9)
Mezzotint
Purchased, London, 1st Chaloner Smith sale, 1887

Drummond, Samuel (1765-1844)
English School
BLOOD, T. (FL.1814-1823)
ENGLISH SCHOOL

10,579
Eliza O'Neill, (1791-1872), Actress, later Lady Wrixon-Becher, wife of Sir William, (pl. for 'The European Magazine', December, 1814)
Published: J. Asperne, London, 1st December 1814
22.5 x 13.7 (plate 17.5 x 12.5)
Stipple
Purchased, Dublin, Mr P. Traynor, 1898

Drummond, Samuel (1765-1844)
English School
IRISH SCHOOL (1798)

10,668
Arthur Murphy, (1727-1805), Dramatist, (pl. for Walker's 'Hibernian Magazine', December 1798)
Published: Hibernian Magazine, Dublin, December 1798
20 x 12 (plate 16 x cut)
Stipple
Purchased, Dublin, Mr P. Traynor, 1898

Drummond, Samuel (1765-1844)
English School
MEYER, HENRY (1782-1847)
ENGLISH SCHOOL

11,261
Charles Phillips, (1787-1859), Barrister and Writer, (pl. for 'European Magazine', December 1816)
Published: J. Asperne, London, 1st December 1816
22.5 x 13.5 (plate 16.5 x 11)
Stipple
Purchased, Dublin, Mr P. Traynor, 1898

Drummond, Samuel (1765-1844)
English School
RIDLEY, WILLIAM (1764-1838)
ENGLISH SCHOOL

11,136
William Thomas Fitzgerald, (?1759-1829), Patriotic Versifier, (pl. for 'European Magazine', April 1804)
Published: J. Asperne, London,

1st April 1804
16.5 x 11.6 (plate cut)
Stipple
Purchased, Dublin, Mr A. Roth, 1901

Drummond, Samuel (?1770-1844)
English School
RIDLEY, WILLIAM (1764-1838)
ENGLISH SCHOOL *and*
HOLL THE ELDER, WILLIAM (1771-1838)
ENGLISH SCHOOL

11,204
Andrew Cherry, (1762-1812), Actor and Playwright, (pl. for the 'European Magazine', April 1806)
Published: J. Asperne, London, 31st March 1806
22 x 13.7 (plate 16 x 11)
Stipple
Purchased, Dublin, Mr P. Traynor, 1898

Drummond, Samuel (1765-1844)
English School
THOMSON, JAMES (1789-1850)
ENGLISH SCHOOL

11,278
Peter Turnerelli, (1774-1839), Sculptor, modelling a bust of George III, King of England, (1738-1820), (pl. for 'European Magazine', June 1821)
Published: Executors of the late J. Asperne, (for the 'European Magazine'), London, 1st June 1821
21.5 x 13.3 (plate cut)
Stipple
Acquired c.1903

Drummond, William (fl.1800-1850)
English School
EGLETON, WILLIAM HENRY (FL.1833-1862)
ENGLISH SCHOOL

11,336
Miss Marguerite A. Power, (?1815-1867), niece of Lady Blessington, (pl. for Heath's 'Book of Beauty', 1842)

Unlettered Proof
43.3 x 30.1 (plate 25.8 x 17.3)
Line
Purchased, 1908

Dubufe, Claude Marie (1790-1864)
French School
DUBUFE, CLAUDE MARIE (1790-1864)
FRENCH SCHOOL

20,088
'La Douleur' - Melancholy (the recipient of a letter and medal from a loved one after the Battle of Wagram)
Published: Lucarne Giraldon-Bovinez, Paris also R.G. Jones, London
(Printed: Lucarme)
54.7 x 36 (image 40.2 x 26.5)
Lithograph
Provenance Unknown

Du Pan, Barthélémy (1712-1763)
Anglo-Swiss School
FORD, MICHAEL (FL.1742-1765)
IRISH SCHOOL

10,157

William Stanhope, 1st Earl of Harrington, (c.1683-1756), Lord Lieutenant of Ireland
INSCRIBED: This plate of his Excellencys is Humbly dedicated to Lieut. Genl. St. George by his most obt Humble Servant/Mich Ford
Published: M. Ford, Dublin, 1749
37 x 26.5 (plate 34.3 x 24.2)
Mezzotint
Acquired between 1890/98

Dupéchez, Charles (fl.1908-after 1931)
English School
DUPECHEZ, CHARLES (FL.1908-AFTER 1931)
ENGLISH SCHOOL

10,889
Timothy Michael Healy, M.P., (1855-1931), first Governor-General of the Irish Free State
Issued by the Artist, ?1931
38 x 28.2 (plate 26 x 22.7)
Etching
Presented, London, Mr C. Dupéchez, the artist, 1931

Dusart, Cornelis (1660-1704)
Dutch School
BROWNE, JOHN (1741-1801)
ENGLISH SCHOOL *and*
WOOLLETT, WILLIAM (1735-1785)
ENGLISH SCHOOL

20,085
The Jocund Peasants
INSCRIBED: Engraved after a Capital Picture of the same size by Cornelis Du Sart in the collection of/Joshua Reynolds Esqr. F.R.S. & D.S.A.G.B. to whom this plate is Inscribed, by his obliged humble Servt/W. Woollett
Published: W. Woollett, also R. Sayer & J. Bennett, also J. Boydell, London, 1st May 1767
60 x 43 (plate 50.4 x 38.8)
Line and etching
Provenance Unknown

Dutch School (17th Century)
Dutch School
GEISSLER, JOHANN-MARTIN FRIEDRICH (1778-1853)
GERMAN SCHOOL

20,105
Accident at Milking Time
46.5 x 62 (plate 31.8 x 43.5)
Etching
Provenance Unknown

Dutch School (1689)
DUTCH SCHOOL (C.1689)

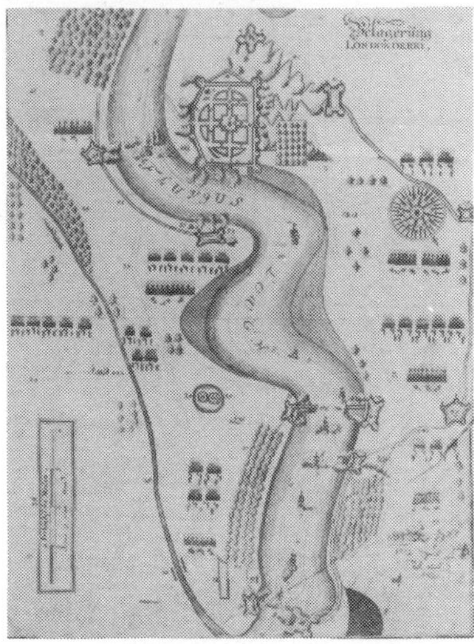

11,819
'Belägerung Londonderry', (Aerial view of the Siege of Derry in 1689; key missing), (pl. for 'Theatrum Europaeum', 1698)
38.7 x 33.3 (plate 35.6 x 26.4)
Line
Purchased, Mr W.V. Daniell, 1913

Dutch School (1689)
DUTCH SCHOOL (C.1689)

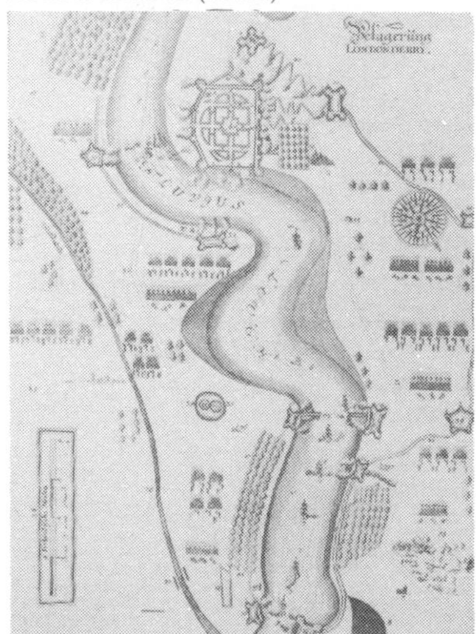

20,835
'Belägerung Londonderry', (Aerial view of the Siege of Derry in 1689; key missing), (pl. for 'Theatrum Europaeum', 1698), (another copy)
36.8 x 31.1 (plate 35.6 x 26.4)
Line
Presented, Munich, Mr N. O'Siochain, 1985

Dutch School (c.1690)
DUTCH SCHOOL (C.1690)

11,274
Richard Talbot, Earl and Titular Duke of Tyrconnel, (1630-1691), Lord Lieutenant of Ireland
18.3 x 14.3 (plate cut)
Line
Purchased, Dublin, Mr A. Roth, 1896

Dutch School (c.1690)
DUTCH SCHOOL (C.1690)

11,865
James II, former King of England, (1633-1701), lands at Kinsale Co. Cork, 12th March, 1689, and holds a parliament of French and Irish
15 x 18.8 (plate cut)
Etching
Provenance Unknown

Dutch School (c.1690)
DUTCH SCHOOL (C.1690)

11,866
James II, former King of England, (1633-1701), and the Earl D'Avaux are Defeated by the Protestants at Enniskillen, Co. Fermanagh
15.8 x 18.9 (plate cut)
Etching
Provenance Unknown

Dutch School (1691)
TANGENA, JOHANNES (17TH CENTURY)
DUTCH SCHOOL

10,004
The siege and taking of Athlone, Co. Westmeath, 2nd July 1691, by the Williamite General, Godert de Ginkel, (1643-1703), later 1st Earl of Athlone
Published: J. Tangena, Leiden, 1691
52.4 x 63.4 (plate cut)
Etching
Acquired by 1879

Dutch School (1691)
TANGENA, JOHANNES (17TH CENTURY)
DUTCH SCHOOL
DUTCH SCHOOL (C.1691)

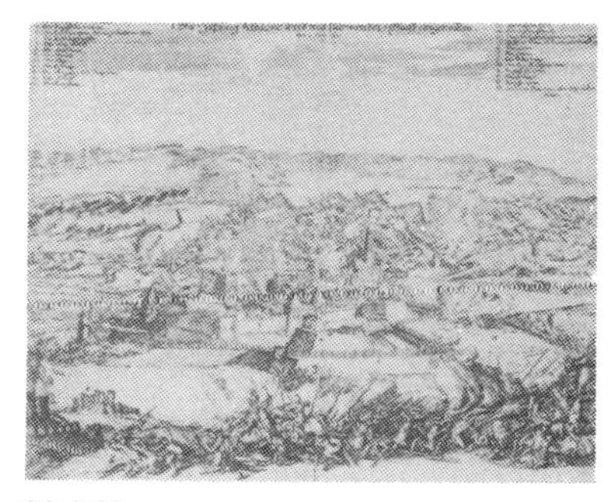

20,762
'Die Festung Athlone wird mit sturmende Hand eingenommen' - The Taking of Athlone, 2nd July 1691, (pl. for 'Theatrum Europeum', 1698)
(after a Dutch School 1691/J. Tangena line engraving of 1691, NGI no. 10,004)
33 x 38.7 (plate 31.2 x cut)
Line
Presented, Munich, Mr N. O'Siochain, 1985

?Dutch School (18th Century)
ENGLISH SCHOOL (19TH CENTURY)

20,643
Scene outside an Inn
16 × 19.5 (plate cut)
Line
Presented, Mrs D. Molloy, 1981

E

Eastlake, Charles Lock (1793-1865)
English School
MOTE, WILLIAM HENRY (FL.1830S-1850S)
ENGLISH SCHOOL

10,891
Miss Blanche Augusta Bury, later Mrs Lyons, Grand-daughter of Elizabeth Gunning, Duchess of Argyll, (pl. for W. Finden's 'Portraits of the Female Aristocracy of the Court of Queen Victoria', 1849)
Unlettered Proof
Published: W. Finden, London, 1839
60.2 x 44.4 (plate 36.2 x 26.7)
Line and stipple
Purchased, Dublin, Mr A. Roth, 1896

Eccard, John Giles (fl.c.1740-1779)
Anglo-German School
MILLER, ANDREW (FL.1737-1763)
IRISH SCHOOL

10,367
Margaret, (Peg), Woffington, (1718-1760), Actress
(after an oil, c.1745, ex-Malahide Castle, Co. Dublin)
Published: A. Miller, 1745
32.4 x 22.9 (plate cut)
Mezzotint
Purchased, London, 1st Chaloner Smith sale, 1887

Eccard, John Giles (fl.c.1740-1779)
Anglo-German School
PEARSON, JOHN (1777-1813)
ENGLISH SCHOOL

11,250
Margaret (Peg) Woffington, (1718-1760), Actress, (pl. for 'European Magazine', February 1795)
INSCRIBED: from an original painting by Eckhart in the possession of Charles Bedford Esquire
Published: J. Sewell, London, 1st February 1795
22.5 x 14.3 (plate 17.6 x 11.4)
Stipple
Acquired between 1913/14

Eddis, Eden Upton (1812-1901)
English School
ZOBEL, GEORGE J. (1810-1881)
ENGLISH SCHOOL

10,813
Hugh Fortescue, 2nd Earl Fortescue, (1783-1861), former Lord Lieutenant of Ireland
(after an oil of c.1839, when 4th Baron Fortescue)
Published: not before 1856
62.5 x 50.2 (plate 53.5 x 41.5)
Mezzotint
Acquired by 1913

Edridge, Henry (1769-1821)
English School
SCHIAVONETTI, LEWIS (1765-1810)
ANGLO-ITALIAN SCHOOL

10,951
George Macartney, 1st Earl Macartney, (1737-1806), former Chief Secretary for Ireland and Ambassador to Russia and China, (frontispiece for Barrow's 'Public Life of Earl Macartney', 1807)
(after a pastel, RA 1801)
Published: Cadell & Davies, London, 1st May 1807
29.1 x 22 (plate 27.9 x 22)
Stipple
Purchased, Dublin, Mr A. Roth, 1901

Edwards, Edward (1738-1806)
English School
NEWTON, JAMES (1748-1804)
ENGLISH SCHOOL

20,216
The Entrance to Strawberry Hill, (pl. for H. Walpole's 'The Works of Horatio Walpole, Earl of Orford', 1798)
25.7 x 20 (plate cut)
Line
Purchased, Lusk, Mr de Courcy Donovan, 1971

Elliot, Captain Robert James (fl.1784-1849)
English School
AUSTIN, SAMUEL (1796-1834)
ENGLISH SCHOOL
LE PETIT, WILLIAM (FL.1847-1880)
ENGLISH SCHOOL

20,356
Mah Chung Keow, Canton, China, (pl. for E. Roberts 'Views in the East', 1830-33)
Published: Fisher, Son & Co., London, 1831
25.1 x 32.4 (plate 17.3 x 24)
Steel Engraving
Purchased, Lusk, Mr de Courcy Donovan, 1971

Ellys, John (c.1701-1757)
English School
FABER THE YOUNGER, JOHN (C.1684-1756)
ENGLISH SCHOOL

10,219
Robert Wilks, (1665-1732), Actor Manager
(after an oil of 1732)
Published: T. Bowles, also J. Faber, London, 1732/33
40 x 28.3 (plate 35.2 x 25.2)
Mezzotint
Acquired by 1914

English School (15th century)
CARTER, JOHN (1748-1817)
ENGLISH SCHOOL
BASIRE THE ELDER, JAMES (1730-1802)
ENGLISH SCHOOL

10,766
Thomas Cranley, (c.1337-1417), Chancellor of Oxford University and later Archbishop of Dublin, (pl. for J. Carter's 'Specimens of English Ecclesiastical Costume', 1817)
(after a brass, New College Chapel, Oxford)
48.8 x 31.4 (plate 47 x 29.8)
Line
Purchased, Dublin, Mr J.V. McAlpine, 1899

?English School (16th century)
B..., A. (17TH CENTURY)
CONTINENTAL SCHOOL

10,046
John Bale, P. Bishop of Ossory, (1495-1563), Controversial Theologian
(after a print of 1620, example in BM, London)
21 x 13 (plate 16 x 11.6)
Line
Purchased, Dublin,
Mr J.V. McAlpine, 1909

English School (16th century)
POWLE, GEORGE (FL.1764-1771)
ENGLISH SCHOOL
GREEN, VALENTINE (1739-1813)
ENGLISH SCHOOL

10,290
Sir John Perrot, (1527-1592, said to be a son of King Henry VIII), Soldier and Lord Deputy of Ireland, (pl. for J. Nash's 'Worcestershire', 1776)
Published: 1st January 1776.
Issued on same sheet with Lady Dorothy Pakington, (now detached)
16.6 x 10.2 (plate cut)
Mezzotint
Acquired by 1903

English School (16th century)
HUMPHREY, OZIAS (1742-1810)
ENGLISH SCHOOL

11,135
'The Fair Geraldine', - Elizabeth Fitzgerald, Countess of Lincoln, (c.1528-1590), 2nd wife of the 1st Earl of Lincoln and daughter of the 9th Earl of Kildare
(after an oil, NGI no. 1195)
17.6 x 13.5 (plate cut)
Stipple
Acquired c.1908

?English School (16th century)
VAN DE PASSE, WILLEM (C.1598-1637)
ANGLO-GERMAN SCHOOL *and*
VAN DE PASSE, MAGDALENA (C.1600-C.1640)
ANGLO-GERMAN SCHOOL

11,037
Sir Henry Sidney, (1529-1586), Lord Deputy of Ireland, father of Sir Philip Sidney, (page from H. Holland's 'Herwologia', 1620)
29 x 18.3 (plate 16 x 11)
Line
Provenance Unknown

English School (c.1560)
HOUBRAKEN, JACOBUS (1698-1780)
AMSTERDAM SCHOOL

11,942
Thomas Howard, 4th Duke of Norfolk, (1536-1572), (artist given as Holbein)
INSCRIBED: In the Collection of Mr Richardson
Published: 1735
36.6 x 23.2 (plate cut)
Line
Provenance Unknown

English School (c.1580)
HARDING, GEORGE PERFECT (C.1780-1853)
ENGLISH SCHOOL
GREATBACH, WILLIAM (1802-C.1865)
ENGLISH SCHOOL

11,052
Sir William Russell, (1553-1613), later 1st Baron Russell of Thornhaugh, Lord Deputy of Ireland, (previously pl. for G.P. Harding's 'Ancient Historical Pictures', 1844)
(after a watercolour, NGI no. 19,217, from an oil at Woburn Abbey, Bedfordshire)
Published: G.P. Harding, London, 1st January 1845
48.5 x 33 (plate 33 x 23)
Line
Purchased, Dublin,
Mr J.V. McAlpine, 1904

?English School (17th century)
CROSS THE ELDER, THOMAS (FL.1632-1682)
ENGLISH SCHOOL

10,304
George Webb, P. Bishop of Limerick, (1581-1642), (Re-engraved as frontispiece for his 'The Practice of Quietness', 1705 Edition)
12 x 7 (plate cut)
Line
Acquired between 1898/1904

English School (17th century)
DE WILDE, SAMUEL (1748-1832)
ENGLISH SCHOOL

10,059
Sir William Parsons, (?1570-1650), Surveyor-General and Lord Justice of Ireland
Published: W. Humphrey, London, 29th May 1777
27.6 x 21.3 (plate 24.8 x 20)
Mezzotint
Purchased, London, 1st Chaloner Smith sale, 1887

English School (17th century)
ENGLISH SCHOOL (17TH CENTURY)

11,395
Oliver Cromwell, (1599-1658), Lord Protector of England
13 x 10 (plate cut)
Mezzotint
Purchased, London, 2nd Chaloner Smith sale, 1888

English School (17th century)
ENGLISH SCHOOL (17TH CENTURY)

11,820
London from Southwalk on the South bank of the River Thames before the Great Fire
22.1 x 32.8 (plate cut)
Line
Provenance Unknown

English School (17th century)
ENGLISH SCHOOL (1795)

10,872
Richard Head, (c.1637-c.1686), Author, Bookseller and Gambler, (pl. for J. Caulfield's 'Portraits, Memoirs and Characters of Remarkable Persons', 1820)
(re-issue of anonymous 17th century print; example in BM, London)
Published: J. Caulfield, London, 1795
26.6 x 20.2 (plate 16.6 x 9.7)
Line
Acquired c.1903

English School (17th century)
ENGLISH SCHOOL (1810)

10,610
Miles Corbet, (d.1662), Lawyer and Regicide, Chief Baron of the Exchequer in Ireland
(after R. Cooper's line engraving, example in BM, London)
Published: W. Richardson Junior, London, 9th February 1810
15.3 x 11 (plate cut)
Line
Provenance Unknown

English School (17th century)
ENGLISH SCHOOL (1815)

10,733
Elizabeth de Clare, (c.1291-1360), Grand-daughter of Edward I and Founder of Clare College Cambridge, (pl. for R. Ackermann's 'History of the Colleges of Cambridge', 1815)
(after an oil, Clare College, Cambridge)
Published: R. Ackermann, London, 1815
30.3 x 22.4 (plate cut)
Line and stipple
Purchased, Dublin, Mr A. Roth, 1898

English School (17th century)
ENGLISH SCHOOL (C.1816)

10,618
Colonel John Hewson, (d.1662), Parliamentary Commander and Regicide, (pl. for S. Woodburn's 'Gallery of Rare Portraits', 1816)
INSCRIBED: *From an original painting*
18 x 14.2 (plate cut)
Mezzotint
Provenance Unknown

English School (17th century)
FAITHORNE THE YOUNGER, WILLIAM (1656-C.1710)
ENGLISH SCHOOL *and*
VERTUE, GEORGE (1684-1756)
ENGLISH SCHOOL

10,771
Henry Hare, 2nd Baron Coleraine, (1636-1708), Antiquary & Author
36.2 x 23 (plate cut)
Line
Purchased, Dublin, Mr A. Roth, 1901

English School (17th century)
FAITHORNE, WILLIAM (1616-1691)
ENGLISH SCHOOL

11,275
Jeremy Taylor, (1613-1667), P. Bishop of Down, Connor and Dromore, with a vision of Heaven and Hell, (frontispiece for his 'Holy Living', 1653)
12.9 x 13.8 (plate cut)
Line
Purchased, Dublin,
Mr J.V. McAlpine, 1909

English School (17th century)
GOLE, JACOBUS (1660-1737)
DUTCH SCHOOL

10,340
Mary II, Queen of England, (1662-1694)
Published: N. Visscher, not before 1694
46.5 x 33.9 (plate 44.2 x 32.2)
Mezzotint
Purchased, London, 1st Chaloner Smith sale, 1887

English School (17th Century)
GOLE, JACOBUS (1660-1737)
DUTCH SCHOOL

10,564
Rev. George Walker, (1618-1690), Governor of Londonderry during the siege of 1689, killed at the Battle of the Boyne
Published: J. Gole, Amsterdam, c.1689
28.5 x 21 (plate cut)
Mezzotint
Purchased, London, 1st Chaloner Smith sale,1887

English School (17th century)
LENS, BERNARD (1659-1725)
ENGLISH SCHOOL

10,921
Mary II, Queen of England, (1662-1694), in her Coronation Robes
Published: E. Cooper, London, not before 1689
27 x 18.6 (plate cut)
Mezzotint
Purchased, London 1st Chaloner Smith sale 1887

English School (17th century)
MARSHALL, WILLIAM (FL.1591-1649)
ENGLISH SCHOOL

11,005
James Ussher, P. Archbishop of Armagh, (1581-1656), (frontispiece for his 'Body of Divinity', 1647)
Published: G. Bader, ?1647
27.8 x 16.5 (plate 27.4 x 15.8)
Line
Acquired by 1913

English School (17th century)
MILLER, ANDREW (1737-1763)
IRISH SCHOOL

10,133

James Ussher, P. Archbishop of Armagh, (1581-1656), (with ladies teaching a child in the border)
(after a G. Vertue line engraving of 1738: example in BM, London)
Published: A. Miller, also P. Smith, Dublin, 1744
35 x 24 (plate cut)
Mezzotint
Purchased, London, 1st Chaloner Smith sale, 1887

English School (17th century)
MILLER, ANDREW (FL.1737-1763)
IRISH SCHOOL

10,335
So-called portrait of Elizabeth I, Queen of England, (1533-1603), (artist given as Isaac Oliver)
Published: A. Miller also P. Smith, Dublin, 1744
35.7 x 26 (plate 35 x 25.5)
Mezzotint
Acquired between 1890/98

English School (17th century)
NUNZER, ENGELHARD (D.1733)
GERMAN SCHOOL

11,260
Rev. George Walker, (1618-1690), Governor of Londonderry during the Siege of 1689, killed at the Battle of the Boyne
17.5 x 12.8 (plate cut)
Line
Acquired by 1901

English School (17th century)
PELHAM, P. (C.1680-1751)
ENGLISH SCHOOL

11,022
So-called portrait of Jonathan Swift, (1667-1745), Dean of St Patrick's Cathedral, Dublin and Satirist
(face altered from J. Simon mezzotint of Benjamin Pratt)
Published: J. Bowles, London
36.5 x 25.8 (plate 35 x 24.8)
Mezzotint
Purchased, London. 2nd Chaloner Smith sale 1888

English School (17th century)
RAVENET THE ELDER, SIMON FRANCOIS (1706-1774)
ANGLO- FRENCH SCHOOL

11,205
Ulick de Burgh, 2nd Earl of St Albans and 1st Marquess of Clanricarde, (1604-1657), Lord Deputy of Ireland, (pl. for T.G. Smollett's 'A Complete History of England', 1757)
20.7 x 12.8 (plate 10.8 x 10.4)
Line
Acquired between 1913/14

English School (17th century)
SCHENCK, PIETER (1660-1718/19)
DUTCH SCHOOL

10,998
So-called portrait of James Butler, 2nd Duke of Ormonde, (1665-1745)
Published: P. Schenck, Amsterdam
28.4 x 22.6 (plate 24.6 x 18.2)
Mezzotint
Purchased, Dublin, Mr A. Roth, 1895

English School (17th century)
STURT, JOHN (1658-1730)
ENGLISH SCHOOL

10,051
Ezekiel Hopkins, P. Bishop of Derry, (1634-1690)
Published: c.1691
26.5 x 17.6 (plate 25.4 x 17.3)
Line
Purchased, Dublin, Mr A. Roth, 1897

English School (17th century)
STURT, JOHN (1658-1730)
ENGLISH SCHOOL

10,627
Ezekiel Hopkins, P. Bishop of Derry, (1634-1690), (frontispiece for his 'Sermons', 1691)
20 x 15.5 (plate 15.3 x 10.6)
Line
Purchased, Dublin, Mr P. Traynor, 1898

English School (17th century)
VANDERGUCHT, MICHAEL (1660-1725)
ANGLO-FLEMISH SCHOOL

10,625
Ezekiel Hopkins, P. Bishop of Derry, (1634-1690), (frontispiece for his 'Death Disarmed', 1712)
18 x 10.4 (plate cut)
Line
Purchased, Dublin, Mr P. Traynor, 1898

English School (17th century)
VANDERGUCHT, MICHAEL (1660-1725)
ANGLO-FLEMISH SCHOOL

10,626
Ezekiel Hopkins, P. Bishop of Derry, (1634-1690), (frontispiece for his 'Death Disarmed', 1712), (another copy)
18.7 x 10.7 (plate cut)
Line
Acquired by 1913

English School (17th century)
VERTUE, GEORGE (1684-1750)
ENGLISH SCHOOL

10,124
Sir James Ware, (1594-1666), Antiquary and Historian, (frontispiece to 'The Whole Works of Sir James Ware', 1739-64)
29.9 x 17 (plate 29.9 x 17)
Line
Purchased, Dublin
Mr J.V. McAlpine, 1906

10,537
Henry Boyle, M.P., (1682-1764), Speaker of the Irish House of Commons, later 1st Earl of Shannon
4th State
Published: T. Jefferys, also W. Herbert, London, c.1742
34.7 x 24.5 (plate cut)
Mezzotint
Purchased, London, 1st Chaloner Smith sale, 1887

English School (c.1740)
BROOKS, JOHN (FL.1730-1756)
IRISH SCHOOL

10,538
Henry Boyle, M.P., (1682-1764), Speaker of the Irish House of Commons, later 1st Earl of Shannon
2nd State (no publisher given)
35 x 24.7 (plate 34.8 x 24.6)
Mezzotint
Purchased, London, 1st Chaloner Smith sale, 1887

English or Irish School (c.1741)
BROOKS, JOHN (FL.1730-1756)
IRISH SCHOOL

10,197
John Bowes, (1690-1767), Lord Chief Baron of the Exchequer in Ireland, later 1st Baron Bowes of Clonlyon, Co. Meath and Lord High Chancellor of Ireland
Published: J. Brooks, Dublin, ?1743
36 x 25 (plate 35.2 x 24.3)
Mezzotint
Purchased, London, 1st Chaloner Smith sale, 1887

English or Irish School (c.1760)
HOUSTON, RICHARD (C.1721-1775)
IRISH SCHOOL

10,127
James Gunning of Castle Coote, Co. Roscommon, (d.1767), father of the celebrated beauties, Elizabeth, Maria and Catherine, (with medallion portrait of his daughter, Maria)
Published: not before 1760
30 x 22.8 (plate 13.5 x 22.7)
Mezzotint and print
Purchased, London, 1st Chaloner Smith sale, 1887

English School (c.1774)
HUMPHREY, WILLIAM (C.1740-1795)
ENGLISH SCHOOL

11,228
John Methuen, (?1650-1706), Ambassador to Portugal and Lord Chancellor of Ireland
Published: W. Humphrey, London, 1774
14.9 x 11.3 (plate cut)
Mezzotint
Provenance Unknown

English School (c.1780)
RIDLEY, WILLIAM (1764-1838)
ENGLISH SCHOOL

10,656
Francis Rawdon, 2nd Earl of Moira, (1754-1826), later 1st Marquess of Hastings, (pl. for 'European Magazine', August 1811)
Published: J. Asperne, London, 1st August 1811
20.6 x 12.8 (plate 13.8 x 10.2)
Stipple
Purchased, Dublin, Mr P. Traynor, 1898

English School (c.1780)
RIDLEY, WILLIAM (1764-1838)
ENGLISH SCHOOL

10,657
Francis Rawdon, 2nd Earl of Moira, (1754-1826), later 1st Marquess of Hastings, (pl. for 'European Magazine', August 1811), (another copy)
Published: J. Asperne, London, 1st August 1811
23 x 14.2 (plate 13.8 x 10.2)
Stipple
Purchased, Dublin, Mr P. Traynor, 1898

English School (c.1785)
ENGLISH SCHOOL (1785)

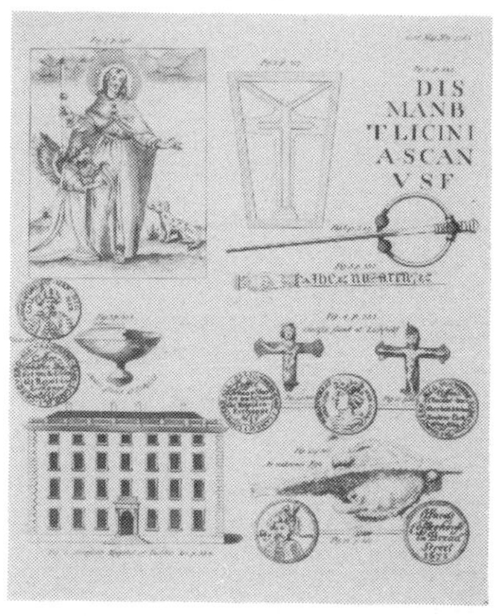

11,836
Sheet of Illustrations: French Woodcut of St Roch and an Angel, a Chalice found at Lichfield, a Thistle Brooch, Penal Crosses, a Coffin lid, Shop Signs, Simpson's Hospital, Great Britain Street, (now demolished), and an unknown fish, (pl. from 'Gentleman's Magazine', May 1785)
Published: Gentleman's Magazine, London, May 1785
25.3 x 21.5 (plate 22.2 x 20)
Line
Provenance Unknown

English School (c.1786)
ENGLISH SCHOOL (1786)

10,514
Captain, (later General), Sir Charles Asgill, Bt.,(1762/3-1823), (pl. for J. Andrews' 'History of the War with America, France, Spain and Holland' 1785-86)
Published: J. Fielding, London, 1st April 1786
18 x 11.7 (plate cut x 11.2)
Line
Provenance Unknown

English School (c.1786)
ENGLISH SCHOOL (1786)

10,517
Admiral Richard Kempelfelt, (1718-1782), (pl. for J. Andrews' 'History of the War with America, France, Spain and Holland', 1785-86)
Published: J. Fielding, London, 27th April 1786
17.8 x 11.5 (plate 17.5 x cut)
Line and stipple
Provenance Unknown

English School (c.1786)
ENGLISH SCHOOL (1786)

10,518

Admiral Sir Edward Hughes, (1720-1794), (pl. for J. Andrews's 'History of the War with America, France, Spain and Holland', 1785-86)
Published: J. Fielding, London, 12th May 1786
17.7 x 11 (plate cut)
Line
Provenance Unknown

English School (1790s)
ENGLISH SCHOOL (1790S)

10,652
John Toler, (1745-1831), Chief Justice of the Comman Pleas in Ireland, later 1st Earl of Norbury
19.2 x 11.5 (plate 15.5 x cut)
Stipple
Purchased, Dublin, Mr P. Traynor, 1898

English School (late 18th century)
ENGLISH SCHOOL (LATE 18TH CENTURY)

11,114

Bruce - There he is!
26.3 x 16.8 (plate 21 x 13.4)
Stipple
Purchased, London, 3rd Chaloner Smith sale, 1896

English School (late 18th century)
KINGSBURY, HENRY (FL. 1775-1798)
ENGLISH SCHOOL

10,275
Edmund Burke, M.P., (1729-1797), Writer and Statesman
Published: Lee & Hurst, London, 30th April 1798
25 x 17.6 (plate cut)
Mezzotint
Acquired between 1898/1904

English School (19th century)
ENGLISH SCHOOL (19TH CENTURY)

10,634

John Gale Jones, (1769-1838), Surgeon and Orator
Published: not before 1810
20.8 x 12.6 (plate 17.8 x 11)
Stipple
Provenance Unknown

English School (19th century)
ENGLISH SCHOOL (19TH CENTURY)

10,884
Mrs Samuel Carter Hall, (née Anna Maria Fielding, 1800-1881), Novelist and Travel writer
36.2 x 28.2 (plate 33.3 x 25.5)
Stipple and line
Acquired by 1901

English School (19th century)
ENGLISH SCHOOL (19TH CENTURY)

11,407

Robert Emmet, (1778-1803), 'The Irish Patriot'
Published: S. Lipschitz, London
69.6 x 53 (image 55 x 41)
Lithograph with watercolour
Provenance Unknown

?English School (19th century)
?ENGLISH SCHOOL (19TH CENTURY)

11,499
Elisha witnessing the Assumption of Elijah
26.5 x 30.6 (plate cut)
Line and stipple
Provenance Unknown

English School (19th century)
ENGLISH SCHOOL (19TH CENTURY)

20,039
Elizabeth, Queen of Edward IV, giving up her son, Edward V to Cardinal Bourchier, to keep company with his brother in the Tower of London
Published: Colnaghi & Co., London
33 x 44.8 (plate cut)
Stipple
Provenance Unknown

English School (19th century)
ENGLISH SCHOOL (19TH CENTURY)

20,144
Ladies in Turkish dress by a river
12.8 x 19 (plate cut)
Steel Engraving
Purchased, Lusk, Mr de Coursy Donovan, 1971

English School (19th century)
ENGLISH SCHOOL (19TH CENTURY)

20,163
Resting Cow
22.5 x 27.6 (plate 12.7 x 21.1)
Stipple and aquatint
Purchased, Lusk, Mr de Courcy Donovan, 1971

English School (19th century)
ENGLISH SCHOOL (19TH CENTURY)

20,197
Title page of the Illustrated Catalogue of the Exhibition of the Industry of all Nations, 1851
Published: Virtue and Co., London
32 x 23.6 (plate cut)
Stipple and line
Purchased, Lusk, Mr de Courcy Donovan, 1971

English School (19th century)
ENGLISH SCHOOL (19TH CENTURY)

20,220
A Cow
22.3 x 27.5 (plate 12.5 x 21)
Aquatint
Purchased, Lusk, Mr de Courcy Donovan, 1971

English School (19th century)
ENGLISH SCHOOL (19TH CENTURY)

20,320
'The Gipsies Retreat'
Published: Ackermann & Co., London,
1st September 1845
33.7 x 50.6 (image 28.3 x 39)
Lithograph
Purchased, Lusk, Mr de Courcy Donovan, 1971

English School (19th century)
ENGLISH SCHOOL (19TH CENTURY)

20,321
'Rustic Conversation'
Published: Ackermann & Co., London, 15th September 1845
Lithograph
Purchased, Lusk, Mr de Courcy Donovan, 1971

English School (19th century)
ENGLISH SCHOOL (19TH CENTURY)

20,346
Trees from life by Annibale Carracci and Titian
Published: Chapman & Hall, London
37.8 x 27.4 (image 34 x 25 approx)
Lithograph
Provenance Unknown

English School (19th century)
ENGLISH SCHOOL (19TH CENTURY)

20,349
A Harbour and fishing boats on a beach
13.5 x 19 (image 12 x 16.5)
Lithograph
Purchased, Lusk, Mr de Courcy Donovan, 1971

English School (19th century)
ENGLISH SCHOOL (19TH CENTURY)

20,363
Figures by a shrine
Unlettered Proof
30.1 x 43.5 (plate 15.1 x 22.7)
Steel Engraving
Purchased, Lusk, Mr de Courcy Donovan, 1971

English School (19th century)
ENGLISH SCHOOL (19TH CENTURY)

20,364
Valley below a hill town
Unlettered Proof
30.6 x 38.2 (plate 15.1 x 22.7)
Steel Engraving
Purchased, Lusk, Mr de Courcy Donovan, 1971

English School (19th century)
ENGLISH SCHOOL (19TH CENTURY)

20,416
Harbour at low tide
18.6 x 27 (plate 15.2 x 22.5)
Steel Engraving
Purchased, Lusk, Mr de Courcy Donovan, 1971

English School (19th century)
ENGLISH SCHOOL (19TH CENTURY)

20,515
Claverton Churchyard, near Bath, Somerset
7.5 x 12 (plate cut)
Steel Engraving
Purchased, Lusk, Mr de Courcy Donovan, 1971

English School (19th century)
ENGLISH SCHOOL (19TH CENTURY)

20,516
Southampton, Hampshire
8.2 x 12.1 (plate cut)
Steel Engraving
Purchased, Lusk, Mr de Courcy Donovan, 1971

English School (19th century)
ENGLISH SCHOOL (19TH CENTURY)

20,568
A wooden bridge over a stream
16.7 x 22.7 (cut to image)
Lithograph
Presented, Mrs D. Molloy, 1981

English School (19th century)
ENGLISH SCHOOL (19TH CENTURY)

20,574
Osteria - Playing at Bowls (pl. from 'The Illustrated London News')
Published: Illustrated London News
15.7 x 22.9 (image 14.5 x 23)
Wood Engraving
Presented, Mrs D. Molloy, 1981

English School (19th century)
ENGLISH SCHOOL (19TH CENTURY)

20,584
Cabinet work (1)
31.6 x 23.8 (cut to image)
Lithograph
Presented, Mrs D. Molloy, 1981

English School (19th century)
ENGLISH SCHOOL (19TH CENTURY)

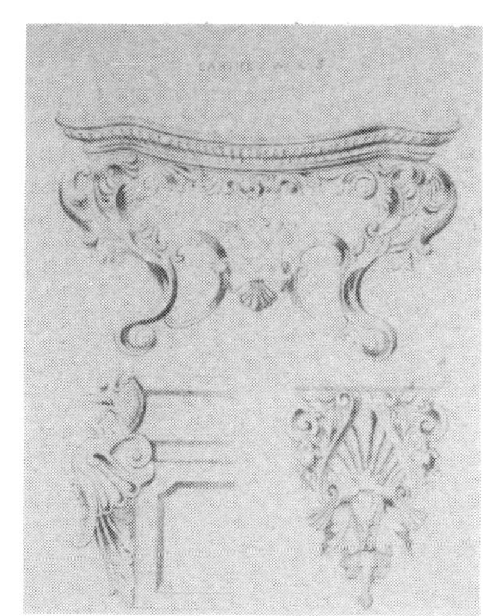

20,585
Cabinet work (2)
29.4 x 24.3 (cut to image)
Lithograph
Presented, Mrs D. Molloy, 1981

English School (19th century)
ENGLISH SCHOOL (19TH CENTURY)

20,586
Iron work (1)
31.8 x 25.5 (cut to image)
Lithograph
Presented, Mrs D. Molloy, 1981

English School (19th Century)
ENGLISH SCHOOL (19TH CENTURY)

20,587
Iron Work (2)
31.8 x 25.5 (image 31.8 x 25.5 approx)
Lithograph
Presented, Mrs D. Molloy, 1981

English School (19th century)
ENGLISH CENTURY (19TH CENTURY)

20,608
Windsor Castle, Berkshire from the River Thames
6.7 x 10.8 (plate cut)
Steel Engraving
Presented, Mrs D. Molloy, 1981

English School (19th century)
ENGLISH SCHOOL (19TH CENTURY)

20,614
Types of clouds
13.6 x 18.8 (plate cut)
Line
Presented, Mrs D. Molloy, 1981

English School (19th century)
ENGLISH SCHOOL (19TH CENTURY)

20,617
The Gipsy Child, (from E.C. Routledge's poem)
9.5 x 10.6 (image 8.5 x 10)
Wood Engraving
Presented, Mrs D. Molloy, 1981

English School (19th century)
ENGLISH SCHOOL (19TH CENTURY)

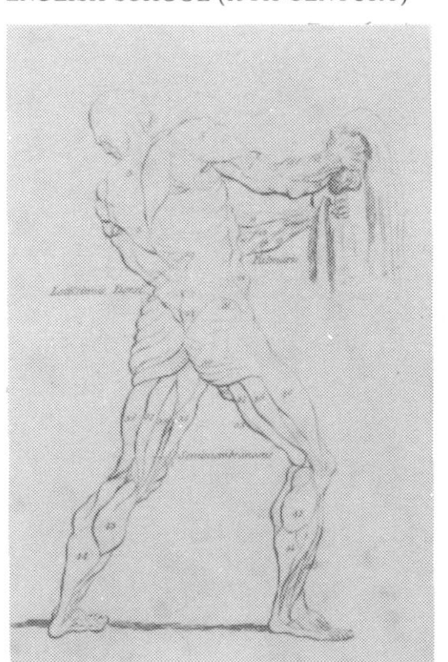

20,646
Ecorché Figure
10.5 x 6.8 (plate cut)
Line
Presented, Mrs D. Molloy, 1981

English School (19th century)
ENGLISH CENTURY (19TH CENTURY)

20,651
Two hounds running
12.5 x 19.4 (image 12 x 19.4 approx)
Lithograph
Presented, Mrs D. Molloy, 1981

English School (19th century)
GRIFFITHS , HENRY (FL.1835-1849)
ENGLISH SCHOOL

11,306
Sir Robert Henry Sale, (1782-1845), celebrated Colonel in the Afghanistan Wars, (pl. for 'Dublin University Magazine', Vol. XXVIII, August 1846)
Published: J. McGlashan, Dublin, 1846
21.7 x 13.4 (plate cut)
Stipple
Purchased, Dublin,
Mr J.V. McAlpine, 1913

English School (19th century)
GRIFFITHS, HENRY (FL.1835-1849)
ENGLISH SCHOOL

11,307
Sir Robert Henry Sale, (1782-1845), Celebrated Colonel in the Afghanistan Wars, (pl. for 'Dublin University Magazine', Vol. XXVIII, August 1846), (another copy)
Published: J. McGlashan, Dublin, 1846
21.3 x 13.4 (plate cut)
Stipple
Purchased, Dublin, Mr J.V. McAlpine, 1913

English School (19th century)
?LANGER, THEODOR (1819-1895)
GERMAN SCHOOL

10,918
Sir Richard Mayne, (1796-1868), Police Commissioner
(after a photograph)
38.7 x 29.3 (plate 24.7 x 18.5)
Line
Acquired by 1903

English School (19th century)
MORRIS & CO. (19TH CENTURY)
ENGLISH SCHOOL

10,482
Arthur MacMorrough Kavanagh, M.P., (1831-1839), Politican and Sportsman
Lettered Proof
Published: Morris & Co., London, not before 1889
59.5 x 44.5 (image 35 x 26.2)
Lithograph
Purchased, Miss Ashford, 1918

English School (19th century)
?PRIOR, THOMAS ABIEL (1809-1886)
ENGLISH SCHOOL

11,372
George Hamilton Gordon, 4th Earl of Aberdeen, (1784-1860), British Prime Minister; Edward George Stanley, 14th Earl of Derby, (1799-1869), British Prime Minister; Richard Cobden, (1804-1865), Statesman; Rowland Hill, (1795-1879), originator of the Penny Post
22.6 x 15 (plate cut)
Line
Provenance Unknown

English School (19th century)
READ, WILLIAM (FL.1824-1837)
ENGLISH SCHOOL

10,779
Robert Emmet, (1778-1803), Patriot, in court during his trial on the 19th September 1803
50.6 x 38.2 (plate 40.7 x 30)
Line and stipple
Purchased, Dublin, Mr J.V. McAlpine, 1898

English School (early 19th century)
DARTON THE YOUNGER, WILLIAM (EARLY 19TH CENTURY)
ENGLISH SCHOOL

20,662
Seven illustrations to extracts from O. Goldsmith's poem 'The Deserted Village'
Published: W. & T. Darton, London,

11th Febuary 1809
34.2 x 43 (plate cut)
Line and print
Provenance Unknown

?English School (early 19th century)
?ENGLISH SCHOOL (EARLY 19TH CENTURY)

11,425
Figures with Offerings
28.2 diam. (plate cut)
Etched border and stipple centre, plus watercolour
Provenance Unknown

?English School (early 19th century)
?ENGLISH SCHOOL (EARLY 19TH CENTURY)

11,426
Abundance and Cupid
29 diam. (plate cut)
Etched border and stipple centre, plus watercolour
Provenance Unknown

?English School (early 19th century)
?ENGLISH SCHOOL (EARLY 19TH CENTURY)

20,826
Diana preparing for the Chase
18.4 x 12 (plate cut)
Line
Provenance Unknown

English School (c.1800)
ENGLISH SCHOOL (C.1800)

10,874
Sir Anthony Hart, (?1754-1831), Lord Chancellor of Ireland
Published: G. Humphreys, for the Proprietor, London
34.8 x 23.5 (plate 30 x 20)
Stipple and etching with watercolour
Acquired by 1913

English School (c.1810)
TARDIEU, AMBROSE (1788-1841)
FRENCH SCHOOL

11,074
Charles Phillips, (?1787-1859), Barrister and Writer
Published: A. Tardieu, Paris
29.7 x 22 (plate 19.7 x 11.5)
Line and stipple
Acquired by 1913

English School (c.1813)
IRISH SCHOOL (1813)

10,655
Francis Rawdon, 2nd Earl of Moira, (1754-1826), later 1st Marquess of Hastings and Governor of Bengal, (pl. for 'Dublin Magazine', May 1813)
Published: Dublin Magazine, Dublin, May 1813

21.4 x 13.1 (plate 19 x 12.1)
Stipple
Purchased, Dublin, Mr P. Traynor, 1898

English School (c.1815)
ENGLISH SCHOOL (1815)

11,353
Napoleon I, Emperor of France, (1769-1821), (pl. for C. Kelly's 'History of the French Revolution', 1817)
Published: T. Kelly, London, 25th February 1815
26.3 x 19.4 (plate cut)
Line
Provenance Unknown

English School (c.1815)
ENGLISH SCHOOL (1815)

11,357
Francis I, Emperor of Austria, (1768-1835), (pl. for C. Kelly's 'History of the French Revolution', 1817)
Published: T. Kelly, London, 10th May 1815
26.4 x 20.8 (plate cut)
Line
Provenance Unknown

English School (c.1815)
ENGLISH SCHOOL (1815)

11,358
Matvei Ivanovitch, Count Platov, (1757-1818), in the Uniform of a Cossack General, (pl. for C. Kelly's 'History of the French Revolution', 1817)
Published: T. Kelly, London, 8th July 1815
26.3 x 20.4 (plate cut)
Line
Provenance Unknown

English School (c.1815)
ENGLISH SCHOOL (1815)

11,359
Henry William Paget, 2nd Earl of Uxbridge, (1768-1854), later 1st Marquess of Anglesey and Lord Lieutenant of Ireland
Published: T. Kelly, London, 16th September 1815
26.3 x 20.9 (plate cut)
Line
Provenance Unknown

English School (c.1815)
ENGLISH SCHOOL (1815)

11,362
Arthur Wellesley, 1st Duke of Wellington, (1769-1852), later British Prime Minister, (pl. for C. Kelly's 'History of the French Revolution', 1817)
Published: T. Kelly, London, 18th February 1815
26.3 x 20.9 (plate cut)
Line
Provenance Unknown

English School (c.1815)
ENGLISH SCHOOL (1815)

11,363
Frederick William III, (1770-1840), King of Prussia, (pl. for C. Kelly's 'History of the French Revolution', 1817)
Published: T. Kelly, London,
22nd July 1815
26.2 x 20.1 (plate cut)
Line
Provenance Unknown

English School (c.1815)
ENGLISH SCHOOL (1815)

11,365
Jean Victor Moreau, (1764-1813), French General, (pl. for C. Kelly's 'History of the French Revolution', 1817)
Published: T. Kelly, London,
17th February 1815
26.3 x 20.3 (plate cut)
Line
Provenance Unknown

English School (c.1815)
ENGLISH SCHOOL (1815)

11,367
Alexander I, Emperor of Russia, (1777-1825), (pl. for C. Kelly's 'History of the French Revolution', 1817)
Published: T. Kelly, London,
13th January 1815
26.2 x 20.1 (plate cut)
Line
Provenance Unknown

English School (c.1815)
ENGLISH SCHOOL (1815)

11,364
William Frederick, Duke of Brunswick, (d.1815), Prussian general, (cf. Byron's 'Childe Harold', canto 3, 1816), (pl. for C. Kelly's 'History of the French Revolution', 1817)
Published: T. Kelly, London,
28th October 1815
26.2 x 19.7 (plate cut)
Line
Provenance Unknown

English School (c.1815)
ENGLISH SCHOOL (1815)

11,366
Prince Gebhard Lebrecht von Blücher, (1742-1819), Prussian Field-Marshal, (pl. for C. Kelly's 'History of the French Revolution', 1817)
Published: T. Kelly, London,
11th March 1815
26.2 x 28.2 (plate cut)
Line
Provenance Unknown

English School (c.1815)
ENGLISH SCHOOL (1815)

11,368
Charles Philip, Prince Schwarzenberg, (1771-1820), Austrian Field Marshal, subsequently Commander in Chief of the Allied Grand Army of Bohemia, (pl. for C. Kelly's 'History of the French Revolution', 1817)
Published: T. Kelly, London,
23rd December 1815

26.2 x 20.2 (plate cut)
Line
Provenance Unknown

English School (c.1815)
ENGLISH SCHOOL (1815)

11,369
Sir Thomas Picton, (1758-1815), English General killed at Waterloo, (pl. for C. Kelly's 'History of the French Revolution', 1817)
Published: T. Kelly, London, 9th December 1815
26.2 x 20.2 (plate cut)
Line
Provenance Unknown

English School (c.1815)
ENGLISH SCHOOL (1816)

11,354
'The Duke of Brunswick', in fact Rowland Hill, 1st Viscount Hill, (1772-1842), (pl. for C. Kelly's 'History of the French Revolution', 1817)
Published: T. Kelly, London, 14th April 1816
26.2 x 20.8 (plate cut)
Line
Provenance Unknown

English School (c.1815)
ENGLISH SCHOOL (1816)

11,355
Frederick William Von Bülow, (1755-1816), Prussian General, (pl. for C. Kelly's 'History of the French Revolution', 1817)
Published: T. Kelly, London, 3rd February 1816
26.2 x 19.9 (plate cut)
Line
Provenance Unknown

English School (c.1815)
ENGLISH SCHOOL (1816)

11,356
Prince William of Orange, (1792-1849), A.D.C. to the Duke of Wellington at Waterloo, later King William II of the Netherlands, (pl. for C. Kelly's 'History of the French Revolution', 1817)
Published: T. Kelly, London, 21st July 1816
26.4 x 20.1 (plate cut)
Line
Provenance Unknown

English School (c.1815)
ENGLISH SCHOOL (1816)

11,360
The Battle of Waterloo, 1815: a dismounted Life Guardsman fighting a Cuirassier whom he slew and rode off with his horse, (pl. for C. Kelly's 'History of the French Revolution', 1817)
Published: T. Kelly, London, 3rd August 1816
26.3 x 19.5 (plate cut)
Line
Provenance Unknown

English School (c.1815)
ENGLISH SCHOOL (1816)

11,361
George III, King of England, (1738-1820), against Windsor Castle, Berkshire, (pl. for C. Kelly's 'History of the French Revolution', 1817)
Published: T. Kelly, London, 27th April 1816
26.2 x 19.8 (plate cut)
Line
Provenance Unknown

English School (c.1819)
ENGLISH SCHOOL (1819)

10,098
Michael Nolan, (fl.1787-1827), Barrister and Legal Author
Published: W. Cribb, London, 1819
20.4 x 13.5 (plate 17.7 x 11.2)
Stipple
Purchased, Dublin, Mr J.V. McAlpine, 1906

English School (1828)
ENGLISH SCHOOL (1828)

11,401
'The Humble Candidate' - Daniel O'Connell, (1775-1847), Jack Lawless, (1773-1837), and Charles James Patrick Mahon, 'The O'Gorman Mahon', (1800-1891), in Ennis during the 1828 election campaign, with O'Connell prostrate before R.C. Rev. Dr McMahon (posted as a letter, franked on verso 16 July 1828)
Published: T. McLean, London, 1828
30. 5 x 23.9 (image 24.2 x 22)
Lithograph
Purchased, Dublin, Mr A. Roth, 1896

English School (1829)
ENGLISH SCHOOL (1829)

20,596
The Gun-Tower and Gatehouse, Kenilworth Castle, Warwickshire
13.3 x 23 (image 13.3 x 23)
Lithograph
Presented, Mrs D. Molloy, 1981

English School (1829)
ENGLISH SCHOOL (1829)

20,597
The Keep of Kenilworth Castle, Warwickshire from the Tilt-Yard
17.6 x 24.5 (image 17.6 x 24.5)
Lithograph
Presented, Mrs D. Molloy, 1981

English School (1829)
ENGLISH SCHOOL (1829)

20,598
The Keep of Kenilworth Castle, Warwickshire, from the South-West
14.7 x 22.4 (cut to image)
Lithograph
Presented, Mrs D. Molloy, 1981

English School (c.1830)
ENGLISH SCHOOL (1830)

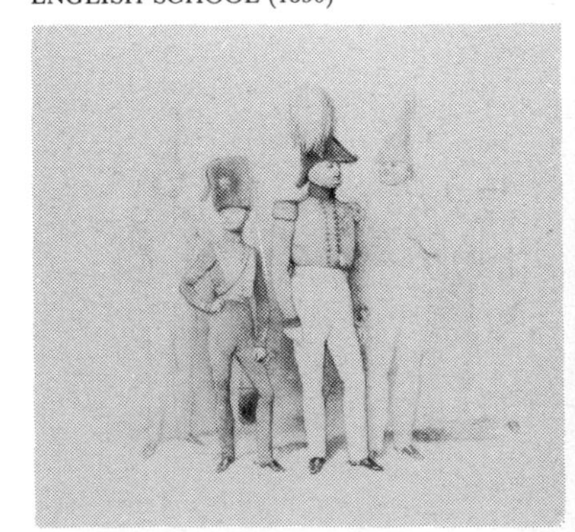

10,703
William IV, King of England, (1765-1837), as he appeared at the Reviews in St James' Park, London Lettered Proof

Published: J. Dickinson, London, November 1830 (Printed: C.J. Hullmandel)
26.2 x 30.2 (image 17.8 x 22.2)
Lithograph
Acquired by 1913

English School (c.1830)
ENGLISH SCHOOL (C.1830)

20,604
Triumphal Arch, dedicated to the Fine Arts
19.8 x 14.1 (image 16 x 12)
Lithograph
Presented, Mrs D. Molloy, 1981

English School (1830s)
JENKINSON (19TH CENTURY)
ENGLISH SCHOOL

11,060
Lieut.-Colonel Alexander Perceval, M.P., (1787-1858), later Serjeant-at-Arms of the House of Lords, (pl. for H. Ryall's 'Portraits of Eminent Conservative Statesmen, 2nd series', 1846)
36.4 x 27 (plate 33 x 26)
Stipple and line
Purchased, Dublin, Mr A. Roth, 1898

English School (1830s)
JENKINSON (19TH CENTURY)
ENGLISH SCHOOL

11,061
Lieut.-Colonel Alexander Perceval, M.P., (1787-1858), later Serjeant-at-Arms of the House of Lords, (pl. for H. Ryall's 'Portraits of Eminent Conservative Statesmen, 2nd series', 1846), (another copy)
Published: G. Virtue, London, 1846
35.3 x 27.3 (plate 33.5 x 25.8)
Stipple and line
Purchased, 1909

English School (c.1833)
HOLL, BENJAMIN (1808-1884)
ENGLISH SCHOOL

10,962
Thomas Moore, (1779-1852), Poet
INSCRIBED: *Presented gratis on Saturday May 4 1833/ to the/Purchasers of No. 10 of/ The Critic./ a New liberal, impartial and independent literary Journal*
Published: Penny National Library Office, London, 4th May 1833 (Printed: H. Martin)
25.2 x 22 (plate 19.7 x 12.5)
Stipple
Provenance Unknown

English School (c.1835)
ENGLISH SCHOOL (1835)

20,325
A Cottage at Ringwood, Hampshire
Published: Ackermann & Co., London, 1835 (Printed: G.E. Madeley)
27.5 x 37.9 (image 22.5 x 31 approx)
Lithograph
Purchased, Lusk, Mr de Courcy Donovan, 1971

English School (1836)
SMITH & GRAVES (19TH CENTURY)
IRISH SCHOOL

11,548
Bill-head for James Trevor, Military and Merchant tailor to His Grace The Duke of Northumberland, at Clifford Street, London, (illustrated), and 26, St Andrew Street, opposite the Round Church, Dublin, (illustrated; now rebuilt)
14 x 24 (plate cut)
Line
Provenance Unknown

English School (1840)
ENGLISH SCHOOL (1840)

11,040
Dr William Stokes, (1804-1878), Physician and Antiquary
Published: Day & Haghe, London, 1840
32.6 x 27.3 (image 18 x 19.5 approx)
Lithograph
Purchased, Dublin,
Mr J.V. McAlpine, 1903

English School (c.1840)
ENGLISH SCHOOL (C.1840)

20,543
Clumber, Nottinghamshire, (now demolished)
18.9 x 29.8 (image 18.9 x 29.8)
Lithograph
Presented, Mrs D. Molloy, 1981

English School (c.1840)
ENGLISH SCHOOL (C.1840)

20,650
The home of Peter Locke King, M.P.
17.5 x 25.5 (image 17.5 x 25.5)
Lithograph
Presented, Mrs D. Molloy, 1981

English School (c.1850)
BROWN, JOSEPH (FL.1854-1886)
ENGLISH SCHOOL

11,335
Sir Henry Pottinger Bt., (1789-1856), fought in India and China, Colonial Governor
Published: J.S. Virtue, London
25.5 x 16 (plate cut)
Line
Acquired c.1908

English School (c.1850)
ENGLISH SCHOOL (C.1850)

11,382
'Regina's Maids of Honour' - Queen Victoria, (1819-1901), and her Maids of Honour
21.3 x 27.7 (plate cut)
Etching
Provenance Unknown

English School (c.1850)
WEGER, AUGUST (1823-1892)
GERMAN SCHOOL

10,858
James Sheridan Knowles, (1784-1862), Actor, Author and Playwright
(after a photograph, c.1850)
Published: Baumgärtners Buchhandlung, Leipzig
29 x 22.6 (plate cut)
Line and stipple
Provenance Unknown

English School (c.1860)
ENGLISH SCHOOL (C.1860)

10,608
Samuel Lover, (1797-1868), Artist and Author
19.7 x 12.7 (plate cut)
Stipple
Purchased, 1909

English School (c.1860)
ENGLISH SCHOOL (C.1860)

10,988
Edward, Prince of Wales, (1841-1910), later King Edward VII of England
32.3 x 21.1 (image 32.3 x 21.1 approx)
Coloured lithograph
Acquired 1913/14

English School (1862)
ENGLISH SCHOOL (1862)

20,571
Edward, Prince of Wales' visit to Egypt: a portion of the Royal party leaving the encampment at Djizeh for the pyramids, (pl. from' The Illustrated London News', 1862)
Published: Illustrated London News, 1862
24.5 x 35.5 (image 23.7 x 34.8)
Wood Engraving
Presented, Mrs D. Molloy, 1981

English School (1864)
ENGLISH SCHOOL (1864)

11,595
The Lord Lieutenant of Ireland, George William Frederick Howard, 7th Earl of Carlisle, (1802-1864), opening the National Gallery of Ireland, (pl. from the 'Illustrated London News', 13th February 1864)
Published: The Illustrated London News, 13th February 1864
21.6 x 28.3 (image 19 x 26)
Wood Engraving
Provenance Unknown

English School (c.1867)
ENGLISH SCHOOL (1867)

20,627
December - 'The Sick Boy', (pl. from 'Bow Bells Almanack', December, 1867)
Published: Bow Bells Almanack, London, December 1867
16.2 x 25.3 (image 14.2 x 21.5)
Wood Engraving
Presented, Mrs D. Molloy, 1981

English School (c.1869)
ENGLISH SCHOOL (1869)

20,576
St Mungo's Well, Glasgow Cathedral, Scotland, (pl. from 'The Illustrated London News', 1869)
Published: Illustrated London News, 1869
16.8 x 10 (image 15.5 x 9.6)
Wood Engraving
Presented, Mrs D. Molloy, 1981

English School (c.1877)
M. & N. HANHART (FL. C.1820-1865)
ENGLISH SCHOOL

10,429
George Augustus Chichester May, (1815-1892), Lord Chief Justice of Ireland
Published: not before 1877
59.5 x 43.5 (plate cut)
Mezzotint
Presented, Mrs E.C. May, 1905

English School (c.1889)
ENGLISH SCHOOL (1889)

20,621
Mother and child, (pl. from 'Pen & Pencil', 11th May 1889)
Published: Pen & Pencil, London, 11th May 1889
30.8 x 23.5 (image 22.2 x 21)
Wood Engraving
Presented, Mrs D. Molloy, 1981

English School (late 19th century)
ENGLISH SCHOOL (LATE 19TH CENTURY)

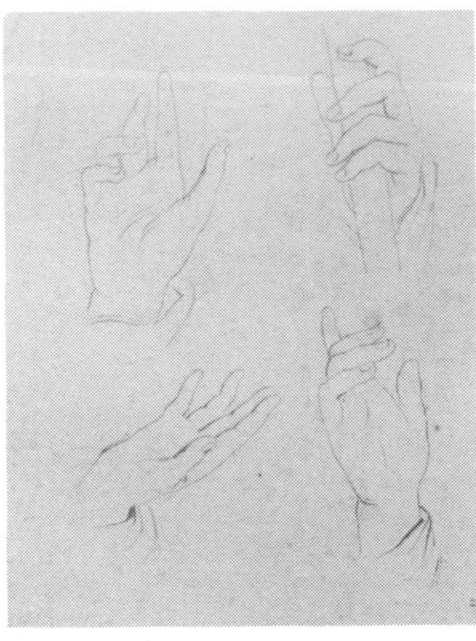

20,645
Hand Studies
14 x 18.4 (image 10.5 x 17 approx)
Lithograph
Presented, Mrs D. Molloy, 1981

English School (20th century)
ENGLISH SCHOOL (20TH CENTURY)

11,471
House and grounds
18.5 x 34.5 (plate 17.5 x 31.5)
Etching
Provenance Unknown

English School (20th century)
ENGLISH SCHOOL (20TH CENTURY)

11,472
House and garden
12.5 x 17.6 (plate 10 x 15)
Etching
Provenance Unknown

Evans, William (fl.1797-1856)
English School
FOX, CHARLES (1794-1849)
ENGLISH SCHOOL

20,153
The Fisherman's Hut
Published: C. Tilt, London, 1833
28 x 22.3 (plate 19.5 x 26)
Steel Engraving
Purchased, Lusk, Mr de Courcy Donovan, 1971

Evans, William (fl.1797-1856)
English School
PICART, CHARLES (1780-1837)
ENGLISH SCHOOL

10,707
James Barry, (1741-1806), Artist, (frontispiece for 'The Works of James Barry', 1809)
(after a black chalk drawing, NPG, London, from a life cast of c.1806)
Published: T. Cadell & W. Davies, London, 11th February 1811
35.8 x 28.8 (plate cut)
Stipple
Presented, Mr H.A. Johnston between 1879/90

Faber the Younger, John (c.1684-1756)
English School
FABER THE YOUNGER, JOHN (C.1684-1756)
ENGLISH SCHOOL

10,017
John Boyle, 5th Earl of Orrery, Baron Boyle of Marston, (1707-1762), later 6th Earl of Cork and Orrery, (with Marston Hall, Somerset in the background)
Published: ?J. Faber the Younger, London, 1741
36 x 25.8 (plate 35.5 x 25.2)
Mezzotint
Purchased, London, 1st Chaloner Smith sale, 1887

Faden, William (fl.1776-?1845)
English School
FADEN, WILLIAM (FL.1776-?1845)
ENGLISH SCHOOL

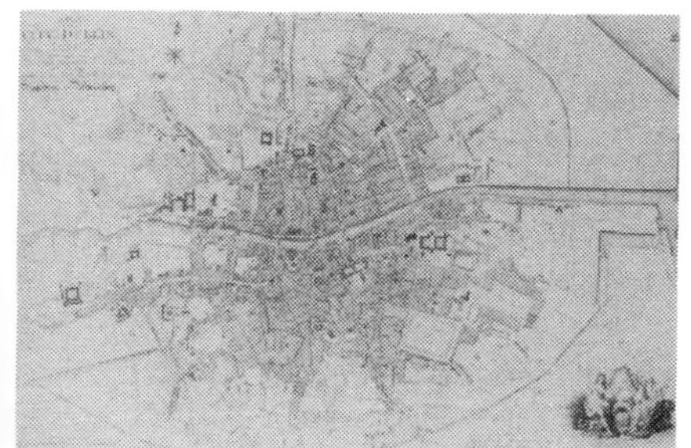

11,887
Map of Dublin in 1797
Published: W. Faden, London, 2nd January 1797, sold by W. Allen & J. Archer, Dublin
57.8 x 77.8 (plate 50.5 x 77.4)
Line
Provenance Unknown

Fairland, Thomas (1804-1852)
English School
FAIRLAND, THOMAS (1804-1852)
ENGLISH SCHOOL

20,352
The Meeting of the Waters, Co. Wicklow, (Rivers Avonmore and Avonbeg)
Published: J. McCormick, London (Printed: T. Fairland)
25.7 x 35.3 (image 23 x 27)
Lithograph
Purchased, Lusk, Mr de Courcy Donovan, 1971

?Faithorne the Elder, William (1616-1691)
English School
FAITHORNE THE ELDER, WILLIAM (1616-1691)
ENGLISH SCHOOL

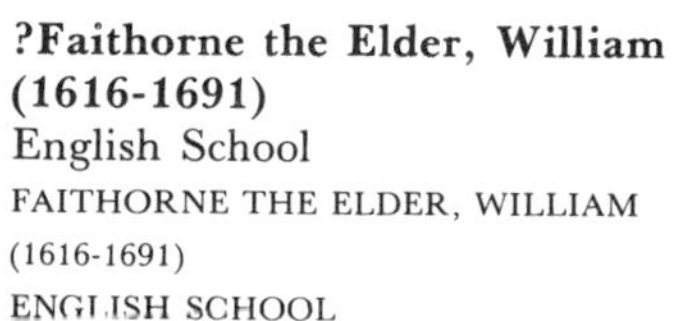

10,832
Valentine Greatrakes, (1629-1683), Cromwellian soldier in Ireland and Faith-healer
28.3 x 21.7 (plate 18.8 x 14.3)
Line
Acquired c.1903

Fayram, John (fl.1713-1743)
English School
FABER THE YOUNGER, JOHN (1684-1756)
ENGLISH SCHOOL

10,193

William Stanhope, Lord Harrington, (?1683-1756), Statesman, Diplomat, later 1st Earl of Harrington and Lord Lieutenant of Ireland
Published: J. Faber the Younger, London, c.1731
36 x 26 (plate 35 x 25)
Mezzotint
Purchased, 1907

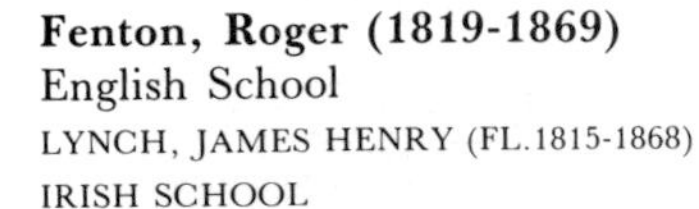

Fenton, Roger (1819-1869)
English School
LYNCH, JAMES HENRY (FL.1815-1868)
IRISH SCHOOL

10,263
Lieut.-General Sir George de Lacy Evans, M.P., (1787-1870), Celebrated Soldier and Radical Politician
(after a photograph)
Published: Goupil et Cie, Paris, also P. and D. Colnaghi & Co., London, 12th February 1855 (Printed: Day & Son)
44.6 x 35 (image 27.8 x 22.6)
Lithograph
Purchased, Dublin, Mr A. Roth, 1896

20,147
Studies of Figures in Landscapes
Published: F. Delarue, Paris also Gambart, Junin & Co., London, 15th March 1845 (Printed: Lemercier)
31.5 x 48.2 (plate cut)
Lithograph
Purchased, Lusk, Mr de Courcy Donovan, 1971

Ferogio, François Fortune Antoine (1805-1888)
French School
FEROGIO, FRANÇOIS FORTUNE ANTOINE (1805-1888)
FRENCH SCHOOL

20,148
The Spring
Published: Paris, 1845 (Printed: Lemercier)
36.3 x 53 (image 31.5 x 49.6)
Lithograph
Purchased, Lusk, Mr de Courcy Donovan, 1971

20,308
'Le Bois Mort' - Dead wood
Published: Paris, 1845 (Printed: Lemercier)
38.7 x 53.6 (image 32.7 x 49.3)
Lithograph
Purchased, Lusk, Mr de Courcy Donovan, 1971

Ferogio, François Fortune Antoine (1805-1888)
French School
FEROGIO, FRANÇOIS FORTUNE ANTOINE (1805-1888)
FRENCH SCHOOL

20,309
'La Clairiére' - The clearing
Published: Paris, 1845 (Printed: Lemercier)
38.7 x 52.6 (image 33.5 x 49.5)
Lithograph
Purchased, Lusk, Mr de Courcy Donovan, 1971

Ferogio, François Fortune Antoine (1805-1888)
French School
FERROGIO, FRANÇOIS FORTUNE ANTOINE, (1805-1888)
FRENCH SCHOOL

Ferogio, François Fortune Antoine (1805-1888)
French School
FEROGIO, FRANÇOIS FORTUNE ANTOINE (1805-1888)
FRENCH SCHOOL

Ferogio, François Fortune Antoine (1805-1888)
French School
FEROGIO, FRANÇOIS FORTUNE ANTOINE (1805-1888)
FRENCH SCHOOL

20,310
A landscape with figures on a pathway
Published: F. Delarue, Paris, also Gambart, Junin & Co., London, (Printed: Lemercier)
48.8 x 31.6 (image 37 x 28)
Lithograph
Purchased, Lusk, Mr de Courcy Donovan, 1971

Ferogio, François Fortune Antoine (1805-1888)
French School
FEROGIO, FRANÇOIS FORTUNE ANTOINE (1805-1888)
FRENCH SCHOOL

20,311
Figures resting by a Stream
Published: F. Delarue, Paris; also E. Gambart, London (Printed: Lemercier)
31.5 x 48.8 (image 24 x 40)
Lithograph
Purchased, Lusk, Mr de Courcy Donovan, 1971

Ferogio, François Fortune Antoine (1805-1888)
French School
FEROGIO, FRANÇOIS FORTUNE ANTOINE (1805-1888)
FRENCH SCHOOL

20,312
A Couple on a Mountain Path
Published: F. Delarue, Paris, also Gambart Junin & Co., London (Printed: Lemercier)
48.5 x 31.3 (image 36 x 27, approx)
Lithograph
Purchased, Lusk, Mr de Courcy Donovan, 1971

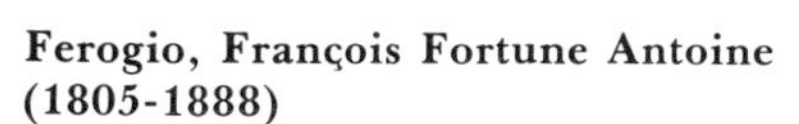

Ferogio, François Fortune Antoine (1805-1888)
French School
FEROGIO, FRANÇOIS FORTUNE ANTOINE (1805-1888)
FRENCH SCHOOL

20,313
A Boy and a Donkey on a Path, ('Etude aux deux crayons', no. 35)
Published: J. Bulla & F. Delarue, also Anaglyphic Co., London, 1st August 1844 (Printed: Lemercier)
48.4 x 31.7 (image 36 x 24 approx)
Lithograph
Purchased, Lusk, Mr de Courcy Donovan, 1971

Ferogio, François Fortune Antoine (1805-1888)
French School
FEROGIO, FRANÇOIS FORTUNE ANTOINE (1805-1888)
FRENCH SCHOOL

20,314
A Woodcutter resting with his horse and dog, ('La Campagne', no. 24)
Published: Bulla & Delarue, also Anaglyphic Co., London, 20th June 1844
31.2 x48.2 (image 25 x 37)
Lithograph
Purchased, Lusk, Mr de Courcy Donovan, 1971

Fildes, Luke (1847-1927)
English School
ENGLISH SCHOOL (1880)

20,578
Illustration to A.B. Edward's 'Lord Brackenbury', serialised in 'The Graphic'
Published: The Graphic, London, 15th May 1880
41.8 x 31.5 (image 22.6 x 17.5)
Wood Engraving
Presented, Mrs D. Molloy, 1981

11,549
The Secretary of State's House above the River Liffey at Palmerston, Co. Dublin, (now rebuilt), (pl. for J. Fisher's 'Scenery of Ireland', 1796)
Published: J. Fisher, Dublin, 1792
22 x 29 (plate 19.5 x 27.6)
Sepia Aquatint
Purchased, Dublin, Mr J. McGlade, 1964

11,639
Dublin and Islandbridge from the Magazine Hill in Phoenix Park (pl. for J. Fisher's 'Scenery of Ireland' 1796)
3rd State, Tonal Contrast strengthened
Published: J. Fisher, January 1792
Sepia Aquatint
Presented, Mr J. Culwick, 1901

Fischer Von Erlach, Johann Bernard (1656-1723)
German School
GERMAN SCHOOL (C.1725)

20,670(61)
The New Church of St Charles Borromeo, Vienna, (from 'Erstes Buch von einige Gebäude....', 1725, see App. 8, no. 20,670)
Published: Leipzig, 1725
37.5 x 51 (plate 34 x 43.3)
Line
Provenance Unknown

Fisher, Jonathan (fl.1763-1809)
Irish School
FISHER, JONATHAN (FL.1763-1809)
IRISH SCHOOL

11,628
Dublin Harbour from Poolbeg Lighthouse, looking towards the city, (pl. for J. Fisher's 'Scenery of Ireland', 1796)
Published: J. Fisher, Dublin, January, 1792
28.3 x 39.5 (plate 20.8 x 28.5)
Aquatint
Presented, Mr J. Culwick, 1901

Fisher, Jonathan (fl.1763-1809)
Irish School
FISHER, JONATHAN (FL.1763-1809)
IRISH SCHOOL

11,719
Dublin and Islandbridge from the Magazine Hill in Phoenix Park, (pl. for J. Fisher's 'Scenery of Ireland', 1796)
2nd State (Unlettered proof in NLI, Dublin)
Published: J. Fisher, Dublin, January 1792
28.2 x 45 (plate cut)
Sepia Aquatint
Provenance Unknown

Fisher, Jonathan (fl.1763-1809)
Irish School
FISHER, JONATHAN (FL.1763-1809)
IRISH SCHOOL

Fisher, Jonathan (fl.1763-1809)
Irish School
FISHER, JONATHAN (FL.1763-1809)
IRISH SCHOOL

Fitzgerald, Rev. William (19th century)
Irish School
FITZGERALD, REV. WILLIAM (19TH CENTURY)
IRISH SCHOOL

20,771
A Beggar Playing a Trumpet
23.2 x 13.2 (plate 8.2 x 4.5)
Etching
Presented, Mr W. Booth Persall, 1902

Fitzgerald, Rev. William (19th century)
Irish School
FITZGERALD, REV. WILLIAM (19TH CENTURY)
IRISH SCHOOL

20,772
A Cavalier
23.2 x 13.3 (plate 8 x 4.4)
Etching
Presented, Mr W. Booth Persall, 1902

Fitzgerald, Rev. William (19th century)
Irish School
FITZGERALD, REV. WILLIAM (19TH CENTURY)
IRISH SCHOOL

20,773
A Fisherman on a Pier
22.5 x 20.5 (plate 11.8 x 8)
Etching
Presented, Mr W. Booth Persall, 1902

Fitzgerald, Rev. William (19th century)
Irish School
FITZGERALD, REV. WILLIAM (19TH CENTURY)
IRISH SCHOOL

20,774
A Winged Figure Fishing
23.6 x 20.2 (plate 12 x 7.9)
Etching
Presented, Mr W. Booth Persall, 1902

Fitzgerald, Rev. William (19th century)
Irish School
FITZGERALD, REV. WILLIAM (19TH CENTURY)
IRISH SCHOOL

20,775
A Winged Figure Holding a Fishing Rod
22.5 x 20.4 (plate 11.8 x 8)
Etching
Presented, Mr W. Booth Persall, 1902

Fitzgerald, Rev. William (19th century)
Irish School
FITZGERALD, REV. WILLIAM (19TH CENTURY)
IRISH SCHOOL

20,776
A Man's Head in Profile
22.4 x 20 (plate 11.8 x 8)
Etching
Presented, Mr W. Booth Persall, 1902

Fitzgerald, Rev. William (19th century)
Irish School
FITZGERALD, REV. WILLLIAM (19TH CENTURY)
IRISH SCHOOL

20,777
Inundation; The Bemused Pot-Boy
22.9 x 19.6 (plate 9.6 x 6.5)
Etching
Presented, Mr W. Booth Persall, 1902

Fitzgerald, Rev. William (19th century)
Irish School
FITZGERALD, REV. WILLLIAM (19TH CENTURY)
IRISH SCHOOL

20,778
Success, the Happy Sportsman
22.8 x 22.4 (plate 9.7 x 6.7)
Etching
Presented, Mr W. Booth Persall, 1902

Fitzgerald, Rev. William (19th century)
Irish School
FITZGERALD, REV. WILLIAM (19TH CENTURY)
IRISH SCHOOL

20,779
Pantomime Figures?
23.1 x 20.4 (plate 9.7 x 6.6)
Etching
Presented, Mr W. Booth Persall, 1902

Fitzgerald, Rev. William (19th century)
Irish School
FITZGERALD, REV. WILLIAM (19TH CENTURY)
IRISH SCHOOL

20,780
A Drunken Fisherman
22.8 x 20.3 (plate 10.5 x 7.8)
Etching
Presented, Mr W. Booth Persall, 1902

Fitzgerald, Rev. William (19th century)
Irish Schoool
FITZGERALD, REV. WILLIAM (19TH CENTURY)
IRISH SCHOOL

20,781
The Angel of Death with a Soul
22.7 x 20.5 (plate 11.7 x 8)
Etching
Presented, Mr W. Booth Persall, 1902

Fitzgerald, Rev. William (19th century)
Irish School
FITZGERALD, REV. WILLIAM (19TH CENTURY)
IRISH SCHOOL

20,782
An Angel and a Figure with a Dove
23.2 x 20.5 (plate 11.8 x 8)
Etching
Presented, Mr W. Booth Persall, 1902

Fitzgerald, Rev. William (19th century)
Irish School
FITZGERALD, REV. WILLIAM (19TH CENTURY)
IRISH SCHOOL

20,783
Faces in the Dark
23 x 20.3 (plate 11.8 x 8)
Etching
Presented, Mr W. Booth Persall, 1902

Fitzgerald, Rev. William (19th century)
Irish School
FITZGERALD, REV. WILLIAM (19TH CENTURY)
IRISH SCHOOL

20,784
Fairies Riding on a Mouse's Back
23 x 20.3 (plate 9.7 x 6.5)
Etching
Presented, Mr W. Booth Persall, 1902

Fitzgerald, Rev. William (19th century)
Irish School
FITZGERALD, REV. WILLIAM (19TH CENTURY)
IRISH SCHOOL

20,785
A Tramp
22.5 x 20 (plate 11.8 x 8)
Etching
Presented, Mr W. Booth Persall, 1902

Fitzgerald, Rev. William (19th century)
Irish School
FITZGERALD, REV. WILLIAM (19TH CENTURY)
IRISH SCHOOL

20,786
A Wreck on a Beach
14 x 23 (plate 4.5 x 8.2)
Etching
Presented, Mr W. Booth Persall, 1902

Fitzgerald, Rev. William (19th century)
Irish School
FITZGERALD, REV. WILLIAM (19TH CENTURY)
IRISH SCHOOL

20,787
Dancing Nymphs in a Garden
20.4 x 23 (plate 8.1 x 11.9)
Etching
Presented, Mr W. Booth Persall, 1902

Fitzgerald, Rev. William (19th century)
Irish School
FITZGERALD, REV. WILLIAM (19TH CENTURY)
IRISH SCHOOL

20,788
An Artist Surrounded By Fairies, (?Self-Portrait)
23.8 x 19.9 (plate 12.1 x 8)
Etching
Presented, Mr W. Booth Persall, 1902

Fitzpatrick, Patrick (fl.1761-1788)
Irish School
ROBERTS, P. (FL.1795-1828)
ENGLISH SCHOOL

11,145
Profile of Henry Grattan, M.P., (1746-1820)
(after a drawing)
Published: H. Smith, London, 1st August 1797
17.9 x 11.5 (plate cut)
Stipple
Acquired between 1913/14

Fitzpatrick, Thomas (1860-1912)
Irish School
FITZPATRICK, THOMAS (1860-1912)
IRISH SCHOOL

11,059
David Robert Plunket, M.P., (1838-1919), later 1st Baron Rathmore, (supplement to 'The Union', 12th February 1887)
Published: The Union, Dublin, 12th February 1887
53 x 43.4 (image 21 x 24 approx)
Lithograph
Acquired c.1908

Fogarty, John (19th century)
Irish School
HAVELL THE ELDER, ROBERT (FL.1800-1840)
ENGLISH SCHOOL *and*
HAVELL THE YOUNGER, ROBERT (FL.1820-1850)
ENGLISH SCHOOL

11,842
Derrynane Abbey, Co. Kerry, home of Daniel O' Connnell, M.P., (1775-1847), with O'Connell and friends in foreground
(after a watercolour of c.1831)
Published: R. Havell, London, 28th July 1833
52 x 64.6 (plate cut)
Etching and aquatint
Provenance Unknown

Foley, John Henry (1818-1874)
Irish School
ROFFE, F.R. (19TH CENTURY)
ENGLISH SCHOOL
ROFFE, WILLIAM (FL.1848-1884)
ENGLISH SCHOOL

20,210
Ino and Bacchus, (from the 'Art Journal', 1849)
(after a marble group, RA 1840)
INSCRIBED: From the group in marble by J.H. Foley/ In the Collection of the Right Honourable the Earl of Ellesmere/ in the exhibition of the Industry of all Nations
Published: J.S. Virtue, London, 1849
23.5 x 32 (plate cut)
Steel Engraving
Purchased, Lusk, Mr de Courcy Donovan, 1971

Ford, James (fl.1772-1812)
Irish School
FORD, JAMES (FL.1772-1812)
IRISH SCHOOL

11,624
The Grand Canal Hotel, (now Portobello House), Portobello, Dublin
Published: ?1811
16.6 x 25.4 (plate 11.8 x 16.8)
Line and aquatint
Presented, Mr W.G. Strickland, 1906

Ford, James (fl.1772-1812)
Irish School
FORD,JAMES (FL.1772-1812)
IRISH SCHOOL

11,625
The New Stamp Office, Dublin, (Powerscourt House, William Street South)
Published: ?1811
15.5 x 18.5 (plate 11.8 x 16.8)
Line and aquatint
Presented, Mr W.G. Strickland, 1906

?Ford, James (fl.1772-1812)
Irish School
FORD, JAMES (FL.1772-1812)
IRISH SCHOOL

11,694
Dublin and the Royal Infirmary, (now Army G.H.Q.), from the Salute Battery, Phoenix Park
20.3 x 26.8 (plate 17.5 x 25.5)
Line
Provenance Unknown

Forrester, Joseph James (1809-1861)
English School
CHILDS, GEORGE (FL.1826-1875)
ENGLISH SCHOOL

20,592
Sierra Convent, above the River Duoro, Oporto, Portugal
Published: R.J. Lane, London
14.7 x 20 (image 14.7 x 20 approx)
Lithograph
Presented, Mrs D. Molloy, 1981

Forrester, Joseph James (1809-1861)
English School
CHILDS, GEORGE (FL.1826-1875)
ENGLISH SCHOOL

20,593
S. Antonio Convent, beside the river Duoro, Oporto, Portugal
Published: R.J. Lane, London
15.6 x 19.9 (image 15.6 x 19.9 approx)
Lithograph
Presented, Mrs D. Molloy, 1981

Forrester, Joseph James (1809-1861)
English School
CHILDS, GEORGE (FL.1826-1875)
ENGLISH SCHOOL

20,594
Interior of S. Niccolo, Oporto, Portugal
Published: R.J. Lane, London
20.2 x 15.3 (image 20.2 x 15.3 approx)
Lithograph
Presented, Mrs D. Molloy, 1981

Forrester, Joseph James (1809-1861)
English School
CHILDS, GEORGE (FL.1826-1875)
ENGLISH SCHOOL

20,595
Oporto and the River Douro, Portugal, from the Arabido
Published: R.J. Lane, London
14.7 x 20 (image 14.7 x 20)
Lithograph
Presented, Mrs D. Molloy, 1981

Fossati, Giorgio (1706-1778)
Italian School
VON DALL'ARMI, ANDREAS (1788-1846)
GERMAN SCHOOL

20,759(9)
The Temples of Concord and Vespasian in the Roman Forum, Rome, (from 'Ruins of Rome', Vol. 1, see App. 8, no. 20,759)
Published: S. Rosi, Rome
28.8 x 43 (image 18.2 x 21)
Lithograph
Provenance Unknown

Fossati, Giorgio (1706-1778)
Italian School
VON DALL'ARMI, ANDREAS (1788-1846)
GERMAN SCHOOL

20,760(6)
The Temple of Venus and Rome above the Roman Forum, Rome, (from 'Ruins of Rome', Vol. 2, see App. 8, no. 20,760)
Published: S. Rosi, Rome
29.1 x 44 (image 18.5 x 23)
Lithograph
Provenance Unknown

Foster, Miles Birket (1825-1899)
English School
VIZETELLY, HENRY (1820-1894)
ENGLISH SCHOOL

20,577
March primrose and palm gathering
15.4 x 13.7 (cut to image)
Wood Engraving
Presented, Mrs D. Molloy, 1981

Foster, Thomas (1798-1826)
Irish School
WARD THE YOUNGER, WILLIAM JAMES (1800-1840)
ENGLISH SCHOOL

10,249
Thomas Elrington, P. Bishop of Leighlin and Ferns, (1760-1835), Theologian and former Provost of Trinity College Dublin
(after an oil of 1820, Trinity College, Dublin)
Published: E. Graves & Co., late Colnaghi & Co., London, 2nd May 1836
51.8 x 39.7 (plate 37 x 28)
Mezzotint
Presented: Mr J. Elrington Ball, 1903

Foster, Thomas (1798-1826)
Irish School
WARD THE YOUNGER, WILLIAM JAMES (1800-1840)
ENGLISH SCHOOL

20,126
Dr Thomas Elrington, P. Bishop of Leighlin and Ferns (1760-1835), Theologian and former Provost of Trinity College, Dublin

(after an oil of 1820, Trinity College, Dublin)
Published: E. Graves, London, 2nd May 1836
39.5 x 29 (plate 37 x 28)
Mezzotint
Purchased, Lusk, Mr de Courcy Donovan, 1971

Foy, William (1791-after 1861)
English School
FOGGO, GEORGE (1793-1869)
ENGLISH SCHOOL

10,857
Rev. James Knox, (b.1756)
(after an oil of 1844)
Lettered Proof
Printed: M. & N. Hanhart
40.3 x 27 (image 34 x 26)
Lithograph
Purchased, London, Mr H.A.J. Breun, 1909

Fradelle, Henri Joseph (1778-1865)
Anglo-French School
DUNCAN, ANDREW (1795-AFTER 1845)
ENGLISH SCHOOL

0,057
Chastelard playing the lute to Mary Queen of Scots
(after an oil, BI 1821)
INSCRIBED: *To his Most Gracious Majesty George the Fourth This Engraving is with His Permission dedicated by his most obedient, humble and grateful servant H. Fradelle*
Published: Moon, Bay and Graves, London, 15th June 1830 (Printed: McQueen)
52 x 71 (plate 35 x 40)
Line
Provenance Unknown

Fragonard, Alexandre Evariste (1780-1850)
French School
BARATHIER (19TH CENTURY)
FRENCH SCHOOL

20,101
Le Récit - The Recitation
Printed: Villain, Paris
49.5 x 72 (image 41.8 x 64.6)
Coloured lithograph
Provenance Unknown

Fragonard, Honoré (1732-1806)
French School
ENGLISH SCHOOL (1827)

20,205
Annette at the age of fifteen, from Marmontel's 'Contes Moraux', (pl. for 'Gems of Ancient Art', 1827)
(after a lost oil pre-1774)
Published: Howlett & Brimmer, London, 1827
18.5 x 24 (plate 13.8 x 19.2)
Aquatint
Purchased, Lusk, Mr de Courcy Donovan, 1971

Franchini, Umberto (20th century)
Italian School
FRANCHINI, UMBERTO (20TH CENTURY)
ITALIAN SCHOOL

11,929
Figures (1), (from 'Arte Nel Evoluzione', 1973)
38.8 x 28.8 (image 29 x 20 approx)
Woodcut
Presented, Naples, Signor U. Franchini, the artist, 1973

Franchini, Umberto (20th century)
Italian School
FRANCHINI, UMBERTO (20TH CENTURY)
ITALIAN SCHOOL

20,823
Figures (2), (from 'Arte Nel Evoluzione', 1973)
Published: U. Franchini, Naples, 12th May 1973
38.8 x 28.8 (image 29 x 20 approx)
Woodcut
Presented, Naples, Signor U. Franchini, the artist, 1973

Franchini, Umberto (20th century)
Italian Schooll
FRANCHINI, UMBERTO (20TH CENTURY)
ITALIAN SCHOOL

20,824
Figures (3), (from 'Arte Nel Evoluzione', 1973)
Published: U. Franchini, Naples, 12th May 1973
38.8 x 28.8 (image 29.5 x 20 approx)
Woodcut
Presented, Naples, Signor U. Franchini, the artist, 1973

Franchini, Umberto (20th century)
Italian School
FRANCHINI, UMBERTO (20TH CENTURY)
ITALIAN SCHOOL

20,825
Figures (4), (from 'Arte Nel Evoluzione', 1973)
Published: U. Franchini, Naples, 12th May 1973
38.8 x 28.8 (image 29 x 20 approx)
Woodcut
Presented, Naples, Signor U. Franchini, the artist, 1973

Francia, François Thomas Louis (1772-1839)
French School
REEVE, R.G. (FL.1811-1837)
ENGLISH SCHOOL

11,496
Calais, N. France, seen from the Jetty
(after a watercolour of 1825, NGI no. 2109)
(Printed: Dumont)
28 x 37 (plate cut)
Aquatint and etching
Provenance Unknown

Fraser, Alexander (1786-1865)
Scottish School
BURNETT, JOHN (1784-1868)
SCOTTISH SCHOOL

20,550
Cattle
16.2 x 16.2 (plate 15.2 x 15.2)
Etching and drypoint
Presented, Mrs D. Molloy, 1981

French School (17th century)
FRENCH SCHOOL (17TH CENTURY)

20,117
Anthony, Count Hamilton, (c.1646-1720), Jacobite, Author of the Memoirs of his brother-in-law, Comte de Gramont
23.8 x 17.5 (plate cut)
Line
Purchased, Lusk, Mr de Courcy Donovan, 1971

French School (1634)
FRENCH SCHOOL (1634)

20,235
Louis XIII, King of France, (1601-1643), creating Chevaliers de St Michel, the day before the ceremony of the Order of St Esprit, (frontispiece for P.D. Hozier's 'Les Noms, Surnoms, Qualitez, Armes et Blazons des Chevaliers de l'Ordre du Saint Esprit créez par Louis le Juste, XIII du nom, Roy de France et de Navarre, á Fontainebleu, le 14 May 1633', 1634)
Published, M. Tavernier, Paris, 1634
27.5 x 17.6 (plate 24.2 x cut)
Line
Purchased, Lusk, Mr de Courcy Donovan, 1971

French School (18th century)
FRENCH SCHOOL (18TH CENTURY)

20,359
Archbishop François de Salignac, (1651-1715)
16.6 x 9.4 (plate cut)
Line and stipple
Purchased, Lusk, Mr de Courcy Donovan, 1971

French School (18th century)
GREEN, VALENTINE (1739-1813)
ENGLISH SCHOOL

11,034
Marie, Viscomtesse de Sarsfield, (née De Levis, fl.1766-1781)
Published: ?V. Green, London, not before 1781
40 x 31.5 (plate 35.5 x 28)
Mezzotint
Purchased, London, 1st Chaloner Smith sale, 1887

French School (18th century)
H...., P. (18TH CENTURY)
ENGLISH SCHOOL

11,320
Guillaume Thomas Raynal, (1713-96), French Historian, Author and Fellow of the Royal Society
19.8 × 11.8 (plate 16.2 x 10.8)
Line
Provenance Unknown

French School (18th century)
LEFEVRE, F. (18TH CENTURY)
FRENCH SCHOOL

10,878
General Lazare Hoche, (1768-1797), French Republican Army, Commander of the French forces in Ireland 1797
Published: Potrelle, Paris
36.8 x 22 (plate cut)
Stipple
Acquired by 1901

Giorgione (1477/78-1510)
Venetian School
TENIERS THE YOUNGER, DAVID (1610-1690)
FLEMISH SCHOOL
TROYEN, JAN VAN (C.1610-C.1666)
FLEMISH SCHOOL

20,716(10)
The Three Philosophers, (from 'Le Théatre des Peintres de David Teniers....', 1660, see App. 8, no. 20,716)
(after Teniers the Younger oil copy, NGI no. 390, from Giorgione oil of c.1508, Kunsthistorisches Museum, Vienna)
Published: D. Teniers the Younger, Brussels also H. Aertssens, Antwerp, 1660
40.8 x 26.9 (plate 21 x 30.5)
Etching
Provenance Unknown

Girardet, Karl (1813-1871)
French School
GIRARDET, KARL (1813-1871)
FRENCH SCHOOL

20,575
A landscape in Touraine, (pl. from 'The Illustrated London News')
Published: Illustrated London News
16.4 x 24 (image 15.3 x 23)
Wood Engraving
Presented, Mrs D. Molloy, 1981

Gleizes, Albert (1881-1953)
French School
GLEIZES, ALBERT (1881-1953)
FRENCH SCHOOL

11,566
Abstract Composition, (flames against skyscrapers)
Issued by the Artist, 1920
52.5 x 38.5 (image 37 x 28.8)
Lithograph
Bequeathed,
Miss R.S.R. Kirkpatrick, 1979

Gleizes, Albert (1881-1953)
French School
GLEIZES, ALBERT (1881-1953)
FRENCH SCHOOL

20,813
Abstract Composition, (flames against skyscrapers), (another copy)
INSCRIBED IN PENCIL: pour Mainie Jellett...
Issued by the Artist, 1920
58.9 x 49.5 (image 37 x 28.8)
Lithograph
Bequeathed,
Miss R.S.R. Kirkpatrick, 1979

Gluckman, Leon (fl.1843-1867)
Irish School
HANHART, M. AND N. (FL.C.1820-1865)
ENGLISH SCHOOL

10,119
John Mitchel, (1815-1875), Agitator and Author of 'Jail Journal'
(after a daguerreotype)
Published: L. Gluckman, Dublin, 10th May 1848
43.3 x 35.8 (image 26.4 x 20.9)
Lithograph
Presented, Mrs J. Martin, 1907

Gluckman, Leon (fl.1843-1867)
Irish School
HANHART, M. & N. (FL.C.1820-1865)
ENGLISH SCHOOL

10,524
John Mitchel, (1815-1875), Agitator and Author of 'Jail Journal', (another copy)
(after a daguerreotype)
Published: L. Gluckman, Dublin, 10th May 1848
57.2 x 38 (image 26.4 x 20.9)
Lithograph
Acquired 1913/14

Gluckman, Leon (fl.1843-1867)
Irish School
IRISH SCHOOL (1885)

20,217
Terence Bellew MacManus, (1823-1860), Patriot, as he stood in the Dock at Clonmel Courthouse, 11th October 1848, (pl. for 'Supplement to the Irish Fireside', 16th September 1885)
(after L. Gluckman/H. O'Neill lithograph, NGI no. 10,121)
Published: The Irish Fireside, 16th September 1885
25.8 x 18.9 (image 24.4 x 18.8)
Lithograph
Purchased, Lusk, Mr de Courcy Donovan, 1971

Gluckman, Leon (fl. 1843-1867)
Irish School
LYNCH, JAMES HENRY (FL.1815-1868)
IRISH SCHOOL

10,685
Sir William Robert Wills Wilde, (1815-1876), Surgeon and Antiquary, father of Oscar Wilde
(after a daguerreotype)
(Printed: M. & N. Hanhart, London)
48 x 35.8 (image 30 x 22.9)
Lithograph
Purchased, London, Mr H.A.J. Breun, 1910

Gluckman, Leon (fl.1843-1867)
Irish School
LYNCH, JAMES HENRY (FL.1815-1868)
IRISH SCHOOL

10,990
Patrick O'Donohue, (d.1854), Young Irelander, in the dock at Clonmel Court House, 23rd October 1848
(after a daguerreotype)
Published: L. Gluckman, Dublin, 1848
38.5 x 31.6 (image 27.5 x 22.5)
Lithograph
Purchased, Dublin, Mr J.V. McAlpine, 1899

Gluckman, Leon (fl.1843-1867)
Irish School
LYNCH, JAMES HENRY (FL.1815-1868)
IRISH SCHOOL

11,430

Published: L. Gluckman, Dublin, 1848
55.7 x 37.8 (image 27.9 x 22.9)
Lithograph
Provenance Unknown

Gluckman, Leon (fl.1843-1867)
Irish School
O'NEILL, HENRY (1798-1880)
IRISH SCHOOL

10,525
Charles Gavan Duffy, (1816-1903), Politician, Writer and Editor of 'The Nation' (another copy)
(after a daguerreotype)
Published: L. Gluckman, Dublin, 1848
56 x 37.8 (image 28 x 23.5)
Lithograph
Provenance Unknown

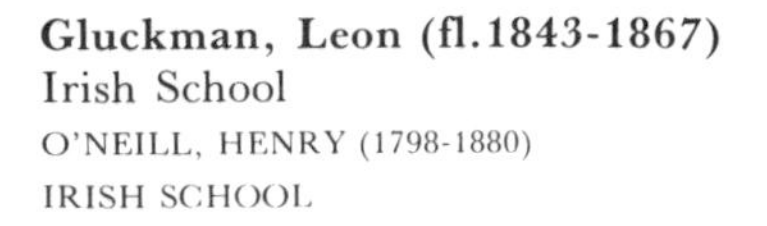

Gluckman, Leon (fl.1843-1867)
Irish School
O'NEILL, HENRY (1798-1880)
IRISH SCHOOL

10,526
John Martin, (1812-1875), Nationalist
(after a daguerreotype)
Published: L. Gluckman, Dublin, 1848
56 x 37.5 (image 26.5 x 21.7)
Lithograph
Presented, Mrs W. Mitchell Martin, 1906

Gluckman, Leon (fl.1843-1867)
Irish School
O'NEILL, HENRY (1798-1880)
IRISH SCHOOL

10,553
Terence Bellew McManus, (1823-1860), Young Irelander in the Dock at Clonmel Court House, 11th October 1848 (another copy)
(after a daguerreotype)
Dated by sitter, Richmond prison, 8th December 1848
Published: L. Gluckman, Dublin, 1848
44.8 x 33 (image 24.8 x 20.1)
Lithograph
Provenance Unknown

Gluckman, Leon (fl.1843-1867)
Irish School
O'NEILL, HENRY (1798-1880)
IRISH SCHOOL

10,710
George Baldwin, (d.c.1856), Registrar of the Court of Exchequer and Secretary of St Patrick's Masonic Lodge
(after a daguerreotype)
Published: T. Cranfield, Dublin
48.6 x 38 (image 26.2 x 20.8)
Lithograph
Provenance Unknown

Gluckman, Leon (fl.1843-1867)
Irish School
O'NEILL, HENRY (1798-1880)
IRISH SCHOOL

10,722
Lieut.-General Sir Edward Blakeney, (1778-1868)
(after a daguerreotype)
INSCRIBED: *To her Excellency the Countess of Clarendon this portrait of/Lieutenant General Sir Edward Blakeney,/Is by permission dedicated by her obedient humble servant/Leone Glukman*
Published: L. Gluckman, Dublin, 1848 (Printed: M. & N. Hanhart)
50.2 x 36.2 (image 42 x 31.5)
Lithograph
Purchased, Dublin, Mr J.V. McAlpine, 1903

Gluckman, Leon (fl.1843-1867)
Irish School
O'NEILL, HENRY (1798-1880)
IRISH SCHOOL

11,934
John Martin, (1812-1875), Nationalist, (another copy)
(after a daguerreotype)
Published: L. Gluckman, Dublin, 1848
53.4 x 38.2 (image 26.5 x 21.7)
Lithograph
Presented, Dr B. O'Brien, 1982

Gluckman, Leon (fl.1843-1867)
Irish School
O'NEILL, HENRY (1798-1880)
IRISH SCHOOL

11,935
Charles Gavan Duffy, (1816-1903), Nationalist and Editor of 'The Nation', (another copy)
(after a daguerreotype)
Published: L. Gluckman, Dublin, 1848
53.5 x 37.7 (image 28 x 23.5)
Lithograph
Presented, Dr B. O'Brien, 1982

Gluckman, Leon (fl.1843-1867)
Irish School
O'NEILL, HENRY (1798-1880)
IRISH SCHOOL

11,937
Richard O'Gorman, Junior, (1820-1895), Young Irelander, (another copy)
(after a daguerreotype)
Published: L. Gluckman, Dublin, 1848
54.8 x 37.8 (image 28 x 23.5)
Lithograph
Provenance Unknown

Gluckman, Leon (fl.1843-1867)
Irish School
O'NEILL, HENRY (1798-1880)
IRISH SCHOOL

11,938
Thomas Francis Meagher, (1823-1867), Nationalist, (another copy)
(after a daguerreotype)

Published: L. Gluckman, Dublin, 1848
53.4 x 37.8 (image 27.9 x 22.9)
Lithograph
Provenance Unknown

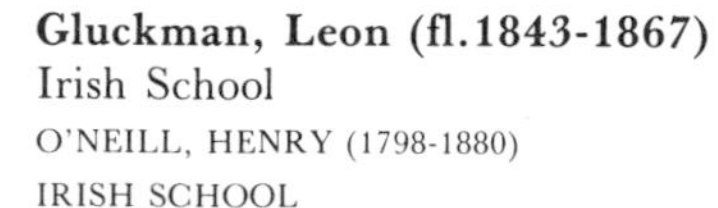

Gluckman, Leon (fl.1843-1867)
Irish School
O'NEILL, HENRY (1798-1880)
IRISH SCHOOL

11,940
Terence Bellew McManus, (1823-1860), Young Irelander in the Dock at Clonmel Court House, 11th October 1848,
(another copy)
(after a daguerreotype)
Dedicated by sitter in ink to William Smith O'Brien from Richmond prison, 23rd November 1848
Published: L. Gluckman, Dublin, 1848
54.7 x 37.9 (image 24.8 x 20.1)
Lithograph
Presented, Dr B. O'Brien, 1982

Gluckman, Leon (fl.1843-1867)
Irish School
READ & CO. (19TH CENTURY)
ENGLISH SCHOOL

10,306
Thomas Francis Meagher, (1823-1867), Nationalist
(after L. Gluckman/H. O'Neill lithograph NGI no. 11,938)
Published: Read & Co., London
37.7 x 28.6 (plate cut)
Line and stipple
Acquired between 1901/13

Goff, Robert Charles (1837-1922)
Irish School
GOFF, ROBERT CHARLES (1837-1922)
IRISH SCHOOL

11,871
The Riva Degli Schiavone, looking towards the Doges' Palace, Venice
Unlettered Proof
Issued after 1903
14 x 19.8 (plate 10 x 14.9)
Etching
Provenance Unknown

Goodall, Frederick (1822-1904)
English School
LINTON, HENRY DUFF (1815-1899)
ENGLISH SCHOOL

20,582
The Holy Well
18.5 x 24 (image 16.8 x 22.3)
Wood Engraving
Presented, Mrs D. Molloy, 1981

Goodridge, Sarah (1788-1852)
American School
DURAND, ASHER BROWN (1786-1886)
AMERICAN SCHOOL

11,297
Gilbert Charles Stuart, (1755-1828), Artist, (pl. for Longacre and Herring's 'National Portrait Gallery of Distinguished Americans', 1835-39)
(after a miniature)
Published: Longacre, Philadelphia, 1837
25.3 x 15.9 (plate cut)
Line
Acquired c.1903

Gordon, John Watson (1790-1864)
Scottish School
WALKER, WILLIAM (1791-1867)
ENGLISH SCHOOL *and*
COUSINS, SAMUEL (1801-1887)
ENGLISH SCHOOL

11,026
Daniel Sandford, (1766-1830), Bishop of Edinburgh
Published: W. Walker, (Private Plate), Edinburgh, 1st March 1829
56 x 38.5 (plate 39.5 x 30)
Etching & mezzotint
Acquired c.1908

Gosset, Isaac (1713-1799)
English School
HONE THE ELDER, NATHANIEL (1718-1784)
IRISH SCHOOL
BASIRE THE ELDER, JAMES (1730-1802)
ENGLISH SCHOOL

10,879
Benjamin Hoadly, Bishop of Winchester, (1676-1761), (frontispiece for his 'Works', 1773)
(after a wax model of 1756)
34.8 x 22.7 (plate 33.1 x 21.1)
Line
Bequeathed, Miss E. Hone, 1912

?Gower, George (1540-1596)
English School
BASIRE THE ELDER, JAMES (1730-1802)
ENGLISH SCHOOL

10,741
Sir William Brereton, 1st Baron Brereton of Laghlin, (1550-1631), Lord Justice of Ireland, (painted when Sir William)
(after an oil of 1579)
Lettered Proof
Published: Private Plate
30.3 x 22.4 (plate cut)
Line
Purchased, Dublin, Mr J.V. McAlpine, 1904

Grandsire, Pierre Eugène (1835-1905)
French School
BARBANT, CHARLES (FL.1863-1922)
FRENCH SCHOOL

20,619
Mount Etna, Sicily, from Il Bosco, (from 'The Sunday Magazine', 3rd November 1887)
Published: The Sunday Magazine, London, 3rd November 1887
16 x 24.9 (image 12.8 x 18.5)
Wood Engraving
Presented, Mrs D. Molloy, 1981

Grant, Francis (1803-1878)
English School
COUSINS, SAMUEL (1801-1887)
ENGLISH SCHOOL

10,485
Hugh Gough, 1st Viscount Gough, (1779-1869), Field-Marshal, as Commander-in-Chief in India
(after an oil, RA 1854)
Lettered Proof
Published: not before 1866
88.2 x 60 (plate 76.6 x 48.4)
Mezzotint
Purchased, London, H. Graves and Son, 1886

Grant, Francis (1810-1878)
English School
ZOBEL, GEORGE J. (1810-1881)
ENGLISH SCHOOL

11,043
Henry Montagu, 6th Baron Rokeby, (1798-1883), General
Unlettered Proof
68 x 50.6 (plate 53 x 40.8)
Mezzotint
Purchased, Dublin,
Mr J.V. McAlpine, 1904

Grattan, H. (19th century)
Irish School
GREIG, JOHN (FL.1801-1828)
ENGLISH SCHOOL

10,054
Christchurch Cathedral, Dublin, from beside St Michael's, (the latter now demolished except for tower)
14.5 x 22.9 (plate 10 x 15)
Line
Presented, Mr W. G. Strickland, 1906

Gravelot, Hubert François (1699-1773)
Anglo-French School
ENGLISH SCHOOL (1820)

11,133
Owen Farrel, (1716-?1742), the Irish Dwarf, (pl. for J. Caulfield's 'Portraits, Memoirs and Characters of Remarkable Persons', 1820)
(after an H.F. Gravelot/J. Hulett line of 1742, NGI no. 10,181)
Published: J. Caulfield, London
24 x 14.5 (plate cut)
Line
Acquired c.1903

Gravelot, Hubert François (1699-1773)
Anglo-French School
HULETT, JAMES (FL.1740-1771)
ENGLISH SCHOOL

10,181
Owen Farrel, the Irish Dwarf, (1716-?1742), against St Paul's Covent Garden, London
INSCRIBED: *Owen Farrel the Irish Dwarf. He was born in the county of Cavan: & in ye year 1716/was footman to a Colonel at Dublin: afterwards/was carried about for a show being but 3f-9in high,/yet so surprisingly strong, that he could carry/4 men, 2 sitting astride on each arm, and /perform several other feats of strength*
Published: J. Hulett, London, 27th May 1742
40 x 26.5 (plate 37 x 24)
Line
Purchased, Dublin,
Mr. J.V. McAlpine, 1909

Gravelot, Hubert François (1699-1773)
Anglo-French School
LE VASSEUR, JEAN CHARLES (1734-1816)
FRENCH SCHOOL

20,037
'Il s'éloigne, Il revient, il part désespéré, il part', (pl. for Ch. 9, of Voltaire's 'La Henriade', 1768)
27.1 x 20.5 (plate cut)
Etching
Provenance Unknown

Green, Benjamin Richard (1808-1876)
English School
LYNCH, JAMES HENRY (FL. 1815-1868)
IRISH SCHOOL

11,035
Frederick Shaw, M.P., (1799-1876), Recorder of Dublin, later Sir Frederick Shaw, 2nd Bt.
Published: A. Hall, London, not before 1832 (Printed: Day & Son)
44.2 x 30.8 (image 23 x 18)
Lithograph
Purchased, Dublin, Mr A. Roth, 1898

Gréther, Ulyssé (19th century)
French School
RAUNHEIM, HERMANN (1817-1895)
GERMAN SCHOOL

20,176
The Oath of the Grütli, 1307: Arnold de Melenthal, Walter Fürst and Werner Stauffacher
Published: Wild, Paris (Printed: Lemercier)
43 x 32.5 (image 19.2 x 14.2)
Coloured Lithograph
Purchased, Lusk, Mr de Courcy Donovan, 1971

Grey, Charles (1808-1892)
Irish School
GRIFFITHS, HENRY (FL.1835-1849)
ENGLISH SCHOOL

11,311
Dr Whitley Stokes, (1763-1845), Writer and former Professor of Medicine at Trinity College, (pl. for 'Dublin University Magazine', Vol. XXVI, August 1845)
(after a pencil drawing of ?1840, NGI no. 3788)
Published: W. Curry Junior & Co., Dublin
21.6 x 12.8 (plate cut)
Stipple
Acquired c.1903

?Grey, Charles (1808-1892)
Irish School
IRISH SCHOOL (1849)

11,202
Thomas Crofton Croker, (1798-1854), Author and Antiquarian, (pl. for 'Dublin University Magazine', Vol. XXXIV, August 1849)
Published: J. McGlashan, Dublin, 1849
21.5 x 13 (plate cut)
Etching
Acquired by 1903

Grey, Charles (1808-1892)
Irish School
IRISH SCHOOL (1849)

11,268
James Whiteside, (1804-1876), Lord

Chief Justice, (pl. for 'Dublin University Magazine', Vol. XXXIII, March 1849)
(after a pencil drawing, NGI no. 3789)
Published: J. McGlashan, Dublin, 1849
21.7 x 13.4 (plate cut)
Etching
Purchased, Dublin, Mr P. Traynor, 1898

Grey, Charles (1808-1892)
Irish School
IRISH SCHOOL (1849)

11,269
James Whiteside, (1804-1876), Lord Chief Justice, (pl. for 'Dublin University Magazine', Vol. XXXIII, March 1849), (another copy)
(after a pencil drawing, NGI no. 3789)
Published: J. McGlashan, Dublin, 1849
21.7 x 13.4 (plate cut)
Etching
Purchased, Dublin, Mr P. Traynor, 1898

Grey, Charles (1808-1892)
Irish School
IRISH SCHOOL (1850)

10,617
John Hogan, (1800-1858), Sculptor, (pl. for 'Dublin University Magazine', Vol. XXXV, January 1850)
Published: J. McGlashan, Dublin, 1850
21 x 13 (plate cut)
Etching
Purchased, Dublin, Mr P. Traynor, 1898

Grey, Charles (1808-1892)
Irish School
IRISH SCHOOL (1851)

10,666
Patrick MacDowell, (1799-1870), (pl. for 'Dublin University Magazine', Vol. XXXVIII, November 1851)
Published: J. McGlashan, Dublin 1851
21.8 x 13.5 (plate cut)
Etching
Purchased, Dublin, Mr J.V. McAlpine, 1913

Grey, Charles (1808-1892)
Irish School
IRISH SCHOOL (1851)

11,099
Michael William Balfe, (1808-1870), Composer, (pl. for 'Dublin University Magazine', Vol. XXXVIII, July 1851)
Published: J. McGlashan, Dublin, 1851
21.8 x 13.4 (plate cut)
Etching
Purchased, Dublin, Mr J.V. McAlpine, 1913

Grey, Charles (1808-1892)
Irish School
IRISH SCHOOL (1852)

10,641
James Sheridan Knowles, (1784-1862), Actor, Author and Playwright, (pl. for 'Dublin University Magazine', Vol. XL, October 1852)
?J. McGlashan, Dublin, 1852
22 x 13.7 (plate cut)
Etching
Purchased, Dublin,
Mr J.V. McAlpine, 1906

Grey, Charles (1808-1892)
Irish School
IRISH SCHOOL (1852)

11,271
Sir James Emerson Tennent, M.P., (1804-1869), Author, (pl. for 'Dublin University Magazine', Vol. XXXIX, January 1852)
Published: J. McGlashan, Dublin, 1852
21.6 x 13.5 (plate cut)
Etching
Purchased, Dublin,
Mr J.V. McAlpine, 1913

Grey, Charles (1808-1892)
Irish School
IRISH SCHOOL (1853)

11,421
Joseph Napier, M.P., (1804-1882), later Baronet, Lord Chancellor of Ireland and Vice-Chancellor of Dublin University, (pl. for 'Dublin University Magazine', Vol. XLI, March, 1853)
Published: J. McGlashan, Dublin, 1853
21.5 x 13.5 (plate cut)
Etching
Purchased, Dublin, Mr P. Traynor, 1898

Grey, Charles (1808-1892)
Irish School
IRISH SCHOOL (1853)

11,422
Joseph Napier, M.P., (1804-1882), later Baronet, Lord Chancellor of Ireland and Vice-Chancellor of Dublin University, (pl. for 'Dublin University Magazine', Vol. XLI, March 1853), (another copy)
Published: J. McGlashan, Dublin, 1853
22.6 x 14.2 (plate cut)
Etching
Purchased, Dublin, Mr P. Traynor, 1898

Grey, Charles (1808-1892)
Irish School
KIRKWOOD, JOHN (FL.1826-1853)
IRISH SCHOOL

10,613
William Rowan Hamilton, (1805-1865), Astronomer Royal and President of the

Royal Irish Academy, (pl. for 'Dublin University Magazine', Vol. XIX, January 1842)
Published: W. Curry Junior & Co., Dublin, 1842
21.5 x 13.2 (plate cut)
Etching
Purchased, Dublin, Mr. P. Traynor, 1898

Grey, Charles (1808-1892)
Irish School
KIRKWOOD, JOHN (FL.1826-1853)
IRISH SCHOOL

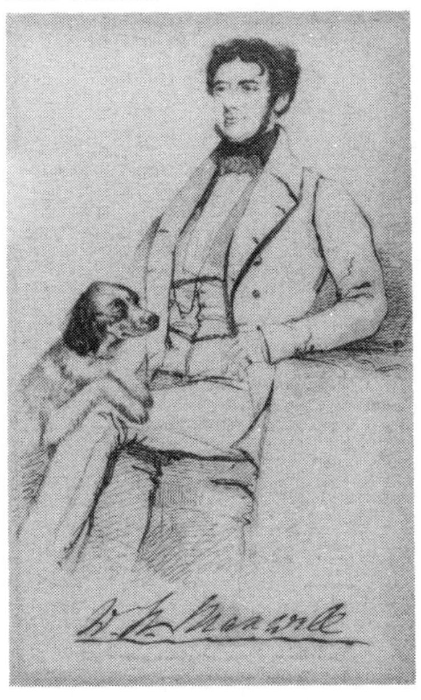

10,665
Rev. William Hamilton Maxwell, (1790-1850), Author, (pl. for 'Dublin University Magazine', Vol. XVIII, August 1841)
Published: W. Curry Junior & Co., Dublin, 1841
22.4 x 14.2 (plate 21 x 12.4)
Etching
Purchased, Dublin, Mr P. Traynor, 1898

Grey, Charles (1808-1892)
Irish School
KIRKWOOD, JOHN (FL.1826-1853)
IRISH SCHOOL

11,082
Charles Kendal Bushe, (1767-1843), Chief Justice of Ireland, (pl. for 'Dublin University Magazine', Vol. XVIII, July 1841)
Published: W. Curry Junior & Co., Dublin, 1841
22.3 x 14.3 (plate cut)
Etching
Purchased, Dublin,
Mr J.V. McAlpine, 1913

Grey, Charles (1808-1892)
Irish School
KIRKWOOD, JOHN (FL.1826-1853)
IRISH SCHOOL

11,090
Francis Blackburne, (1782-1867), Master of the Rolls, Lord Chancellor of Ireland, (pl. for 'Dublin University Magazine', Vol. XXIV, October 1844)
Published: W. Curry Junior & Co., Dublin, 1844
21.7 x 13.5 (plate cut)
Etching
Purchased, Dublin,
Mr J.V. McAlpine, 1913

?Grey, Charles (1808-1892)
Irish School
KIRKWOOD, JOHN (FL.1826-1853)
IRISH SCHOOL

11,100
Colonel William Blacker, (1775-1855), Vice-Treasurer of Ireland, (pl. for 'Dublin University Magazine', Vol. XVII, May 1841)
Published: W. Curry Junior & Co., Dublin, 1841
22.5 x 14 (plate cut)
Etching
Purchased, Dublin, Mr P. Traynor, 1898

Grey, Charles (1808-1892)
Irish School
KIRKWOOD, JOHN (FL.1826-1853)
IRISH SCHOOL

11,104
William Archer Butler, (1814-1845), Professor of Moral Philosophy at Trinity College, Dublin, (pl. for 'Dublin University Magazine', Vol. XVIII, April 1842)
Published: W. Curry Junior & Co., Dublin, 1842
21.7 x 13.5 (plate cut)
Etching
Purchased, Dublin, Mr J.V. McAlpine, 1913

Grey, Charles (1808-1892)
Irish School
KIRKWOOD, JOHN (FL.1826-1853)
IRISH SCHOOL

11,156
Charles Vereker, 2nd Viscount Gort, (1768-1842), (pl. for 'Dublin University Magazine' Vol. XIX, March 1842)
Published: W. Curry Junior & Co., Dublin, 1842
22 x 13.6 (plate cut)
Etching
Purchased, 1905

Grey, Charles (1808-1892)
Irish School
KIRKWOOD, JOHN (FL.1826-1853)
IRISH SCHOOL

11,161
Dr Robert James Graves, (1796-1853), Physician, (pl. for 'Dublin University Magazine', Vol. XIX, February 1842)
(after an ink drawing, NGI no. 3786)
Published: W. Curry Junior & Co., Dublin, 1842
21.3 x 13 (plate cut)
Etching
Purchased, Dublin, Mr P. Traynor, 1898

Grey, Charles (1808-1892)
Irish School
KIRKWOOD, JOHN (FL.1826-1853)
IRISH SCHOOL

11,192
John Wilson Croker, M.P., (1780-1857) Author, (pl. for 'Dublin University Magazine', Vol. XIX, June 1842)
Published: W. Curry Junior & Co., Dublin, 1842
22 x 13.7 (plate cut)
Etching
Acquired 1913

Grey, Charles (1808-1892)
Irish School
KIRKWOOD, JOHN (FL.1826-1853)
IRISH SCHOOL

11,216

William Carleton, (1798-69), Author with his Dog, (pl. for 'Dublin University Magazine, Vol. XVII, January 1841)
(after an ink drawing of 1840, NGI no. 3783)
Published: W. Curry Junior & Co., Dublin, 1841
21.3 x 12.8 (plate cut)
Etching
Purchased, Dublin, Mr P. Traynor, 1898

Grey, Charles (1808-1892)
Irish School
KIRKWOOD, JOHN (FL.1826-1853)
IRISH SCHOOL

11,217
William Carleton, (1798-1869), Author with his Dog, (pl. for 'Dublin University Magazine', Vol. XVII, January 1841), (another copy)
(after an ink drawing, NGI no. 3783)
Published: W. Curry Junior & Co. Dublin, 1841
21.5 x 13.4 (plate cut)
Etching
Purchased, Dublin, Mr P. Traynor, 1898

Grey, Charles (1808-1892)
Irish School
KIRKWOOD, JOHN (FL.1826-1853)
IRISH SCHOOL

11,227
Rev. George Miller, (1764-1848), Author, (pl. for 'Dublin University Magazine', Vol. XVII, June 1841)
Published: W. Curry Junior & Co., Dublin, 1841
21.3 x 13.4 (plate cut)
Etching
Purchased, Dublin, Mr P. Traynor, 1898

Grey, Charles (1808-1892)
Irish School
KIRKWOOD, JOHN (FL.1826-1853)
IRISH SCHOOL

11,273
Philip Meadows Taylor, (1808-1876), Administrator in India and Author, (pl. for 'Dublin University Magazine', Vol. XVII, April 1841)
(after an ink drawing of 1840, NGI no. 3784)
Published: W. Curry Junior & Co., Dublin, 1841
21.4 x 13.4 (plate cut)
Etching
Purchased, Dublin, Mr P. Traynor, 1898

Grey, Charles (1808-1892)
Irish School
KIRKWOOD, JOHN (FL.1826-1853)
IRISH SCHOOL

11,292
Percival Barton Lord, (1808-1840), Surgeon Writer and Diplomat, (pl. for 'Dublin University Magazine', Vol. XXI, September 1843)
Published: W. Curry Junior & Co., Dublin
21.7 x 13.5 (plate cut)
Etching
Purchased, Dublin, Mr J.V. McAlpine, 1913

Grey, Charles (1808-1892)
Irish School
KIRKWOOD, JOHN (FL.1826-1853)
IRISH SCHOOL

20,110
Dr Evory Kennedy (1806-1886)
(after an oil, RA 1841)
INSCRIBED: *Engraved from a picture painted expressly for his pupils on his retiring from the Mastership of the Dublin Lying-in Hospital*
Published: J. Kirkwood also T. Cranfield, Dublin
52 x 38 (plate 45.7 x 33)
Line
Purchased, Lusk, Mr de Courcy Donovan, 1971

Grey, Charles (1808-1892)
Irish School
PETERKIN, JAMES (19TH CENTURY)
IRISH SCHOOL

10,452
Daniel O'Connell, M.P., (1775-1847), Statesman, as Lord Mayor of Dublin in 1841-1842
(after an oil, RHA 1843)
INSCRIBED: *Dedicated to the Reform Corporations of Ireland by their obedient and humble servant/James Peterkin*
Published: J. Peterkin, Dublin, 12th March 1845
62.5 x 39 (plate 59.7 x 35.7)
Mezzotint and etching
Acquired between 1908/13

Grignon the Younger, Charles (1754-1804)
English School
MURPHY, JOHN (FL.1778-1820)
IRISH SCHOOL

10,166
Captain George Farmer, (1732-1779), who perished in an action with a French Frigate off Ushant
(after J. Murphy's drawing, BM, London, from an oil, RA 1778, now NPG, London)
Published: J. Boydell, London, 14th February 1780
40.5 x 30.5 (plate 37.7 x 28.1)
Mezzotint
Purchased, London, 1st Chaloner Smith sale, 1887

Gubbins, John (fl.1820s)
Irish School
O'REILLY, B. (19TH CENTURY)
IRISH SCHOOL

10,066
Daniel O'Connell, M.P., (1775-1847), Statesman
Published, B. O'Reilly, Dublin, 1st February 1823
31.4 x 22.9 (plate cut)
Line and stipple
Provenance Unknown

Gubbins, John (fl.1820s)
Irish School
QUILLEY, JOHN P. (FL.1823-1842)
ENGLISH SCHOOL

10,975
Daniel O'Connell, M.P., (1775-1847), Statesman
INSCRIBED: *This Portrait of Daniel O'Connell, Esqr./Is with respect Dedicated to J W. Fulton Esqr. the sincere friend/of Mr. O'Connell and Civil & Religious*

Liberty by his obliged Servant Thos. McLean
Published: T. McLean, London, 7th July 1829
35.7 x 25.5 (plate cut)
Mezzotint
Acquired by 1898

Guercino (1591-1666)
Italian School
TOFANELLI, AGOSTINO (1770-1834)
ITALIAN SCHOOL
LEONETTI, GIOVANNI BATTISTA (19TH CENTURY)
ITALIAN SCHOOL

11,659
David with the Head of Goliath
(after an oil of c.1636, Burghley House, Northants; NGI no. 1323 is a copy)
Published: A. Franzetti, Rome, 1804
43.7 x 55.9 (plate 40.5 x 49)
Line
Provenance Unknown

Guibal, Nicolas (1725-1784)
French School
MECHEL, CHRISTIAN DE (1737-1817)
SWISS SCHOOL

20,675(2)
The Genius of the Arts, (from 'La Gallerie Electorale de Düsseldorf', 1778, see App. 8, no. 20,675)
Published: C. de Mechel, Basle, also the Inspectors of the Electoral Galleries in Düsseldorf and Mannheim, 1777
29.5 x 37.2 (plate 9.1 x 13.5)
Line
Bequeathed, Judge J. Murnaghan, 1976

Gwim, James (fl.1720-1769)
Irish School
JACKSON, MICHAEL (FL.1736-C.1753)
IRISH SCHOOL

10,134
Spranger Barry, (1719-1777), Actor, as Macbeth in Act 2, Scene 3 of Shakespeare's Play
Published: ?M. Jackson, London, 1753
35 x 24.8 (plate 34.4 x 24.2)
Mezzotint
Purchased, London, 1st Chaloner Smith sale, 1887

H

Hackert, Johann Philipp (1737-1807)
German School
HACKERT, GEORG ABRAHAM (1755-1805)
GERMAN SCHOOL

20,769
The Temple of Sibyl or Vesta, Tivoli, near Rome
INSCRIBED: *Dediée à Son Excellence Madame La Comtesse Shawronsky/née d'Engelhard Dame de Portrait de S.M. Imple. de toutes les Russies/Par son très humble, et très Obeissant Serviteur George Hackert,/à Naples chez l'Auteur Graveur de Roi, avec Privelège.*
Published: G.A. Hackert, Naples, not before 1786
45.4 x 36.7 (plate cut)
Line and etching
Presented, Frederick Lawless, 5th Baron Cloncurry, 1929

Haines, William (1778-1848)
English School
SCRIVEN, EDWARD (1775-1841)
ENGLISH SCHOOL

11,218
John Croker, Surveyor-General of Customs and Excise in Ireland, father of John Wilson Croker
(probably after a miniature)
27.7 x 17.1 (plate 20.8 x 14.5)
Stipple and line
Acquired by 1913

Hamilton, Gavin (1723-1798)
Scottish School
FABER THE YOUNGER, JOHN (C.1684-1756)
ENGLISH SCHOOL

10,393
Elizabeth, Duchess of Hamilton and Brandon, wife of the 6th Duke, (née Gunning 1734-1790), later Duchess of Argyll and Baroness Hamilton; sister of Maria and Catherine and daughter of James Gunning (1st State)
(after an oil of 1752, Lennoxlove, Haddington, Scotland)
Published: J. Faber the Younger, London, 1753
50.5 x 35.2 (plate cut)
Mezzotint
Purchased, London, 1st Chaloner Smith sale, 1887

Hamilton, Gavin (1723-1798)
Scottish School
FABER THE YOUNGER, JOHN (C.1684-1756)
ENGLISH SCHOOL

10,834
Elizabeth, Duchess of Hamilton and Brandon, wife of the 6th Duke, (née Gunning, 1734-1790), later Duchess of Argyll and Baroness Hamilton; sister of Maria and Catherine and daughter of James Gunning (2nd State)
(after a wl oil of 1752, Lennoxlove,

Hamilton, Hugh Douglas (1739-1808)
Irish School
FITTLER, JAMES (1758-1835)
ENGLISH SCHOOL

10,897
David (Digges) La Touche, M.P., of Marlay, Co. Dublin, (1729-1817), Banker and Privy Counsellor
(after an oil, SAI 1804)
Unlettered Proof
Published: not before 1817
48.2 x 36.6 (plate cut)
Line
Purchased, Dublin, Cranfield, 1876

Hamilton, Hugh Douglas (1739-1808)
Irish School
GREEN, VALENTINE (1739-1813)
ENGLISH SCHOOL

10,182
William Burton Conyngham, (1733-1796), Teller of the Irish Exchequer and Treasurer of the Royal Irish Academy
(after a pastel, NGI no. 7242)
Published: London, 1780
39.2 x 28.5 (plate 35.2 x 25)
Mezzotint
Purchased, London, 1st Chaloner Smith sale, 1887

Hamilton, Hugh Douglas (1739-1808)
Irish School
HEATH, JAMES (1757-1834)
ENGLISH SCHOOL

10,286
Richard Marley, P. Bishop of Waterford, (d.1802), (pl. for Sir J. Barrington's 'Historic Anecdotes and Secret Memoirs', 1809-15)
(after an oil ?c.1800; H. Hone NGI no. 2158 is a reduced copy)
Published: G. Robinson, London, 1st June 1810
34.7 x 26.3 (plate 25.3 x 21.6)
Stipple
Acquired by 1914

Hamilton, Hugh Douglas (1739-1808)
Irish School
COMERFORD, JOHN (?1770-1832)
IRISH SCHOOL
HEATH, JAMES (1757-1834)
ENGLISH SCHOOL

10,715
Sir Jonah Barrington, (1760-1834), Judge and Author, (pl. for Sir J. Barrington's 'Historic Anecdotes and Secret Memoirs', 1809-15)
Published: G. Robinson, London, 1st August 1811
33.4 x 26.3 (plate 25.6 x 21.7)
Stipple
Acquired by 1903

Hamilton, Hugh Douglas (1739-1808)
Irish School
MAGUIRE, PATRICK (FL.1783-1820)
IRISH SCHOOL
HEATH, JAMES (1757-1834)
ENGLISH SCHOOL

10,783
Richard Dawson, M.P., (d.1807), Father of 2nd Baron Cremorne, (pl. for Sir J. Barrington's 'Historic Anecdotes and Secret Memoirs', 1809-15)
INSCRIBED: From an original Painting by

Hamilton, in the possession of the Countess of Aldborough
Published: G. Robinson, London, 1st March 1812
33.6 x 26.4 (plate 25 x 21)
Stipple
Acquired by 1898

Hamilton, Hugh Douglas (1739-1808)
Irish School
MAGUIRE, PATRICK (FL.1783-1820)
IRISH SCHOOL
HEATH, JAMES (1757-1834)
ENGLISH SCHOOL

10,863
Arthur Wolfe, 1st Viscount Kilwarden, (1739-1803), Chief Justice of the Kings Bench in Ireland, (pl. for Sir J. Barrington's 'Historic Anecdotes and Secret Memoir's, 1809-15)
Published: G. Robinson, London, 1st March 1811
34.6 x 26.3 (plate 25.1 x 21.6)
Stipple
Provenance Unknown

Hamilton, Hugh Douglas (1739-1808)
Irish School
HEATH, JAMES (1757-1834)
ENGLISH SCHOOL

10,947
Francis Rawdon, 2nd Earl of Moira, (1754-1826), later 1st Marquess of Hastings, (pl. for Sir J. Barrington's 'Historic Anecdotes & Secret Memoirs', 1809 15)
(after a wl oil, Exh. 1804; Castle Forbes, Co. Longford)
Published: G. Robinson, London, 1st September 1809
34.6 x 28.5 (plate 25.3 x 21.5)
Stipple
Acquired by 1898

Hamilton, Hugh Douglas (1739-1808)
Irish School
HEISSIG, FRANZ CARL (FL. FROM 1770)
GERMAN SCHOOL

10,752
Anne, Countess of Cork and Orrery, (née Courtney, 1742-1785), 1st wife of 7th Earl
(after H.D. Hamilton/J. Watson mezzotint of 1771, NGI no. 10,334)
Published: F.C. Hessig, Augsburg
29.8 x 19.8 (plate 29.3 x 18.9)
Mezzotint
Acquired by 1913

Hamilton, Hugh Douglas (1739-1808)
Irish School
HOUSTON, RICHARD (C.1721-1775)
IRISH SCHOOL

10,153
Isaac Barré, M.P., (1726-1802), Orator and former Officer in Canada
(after a pastel)
Published: Dublin, R. Sayer, London, 2nd July 1771
40.5 x 29.2 (plate 37.7 x 27)
Mezzotint
Purchased, London, 1st Chaloner Smith sale, 1887

?Hamilton, Hugh Douglas (1739-1808)
Irish School
IRISH SCHOOL (18TH CENTURY)

10,619
Wills Hill, 1st Earl of Hillsborough, (1718-1793), later 1st Marquess of Downshire
Published: not before 1781
21 x 12.8 (plate 17.5 x 10.5)
Line
Provenance Unknown

Hamilton, Hugh Douglas (1739-1808)
Irish School
KNIGHT, CHARLES (1743-C.1826)
ENGLISH SCHOOL

10,082
William Newcome, P. Archbishop of Armagh, (1729-1800)
(after an oil of 1798, Pembroke College, Oxford)
Published: C. Knight, London, 1st November 1803
45.4 x 35.2 (plate 40.5 x 30)
Line and stipple
Purchased, Dublin, Mr J.V. McAlpine, 1896

Hamilton, Hugh Douglas (1739-1808)
Irish School
LIGHTFOOT, PETER (1805-1885)
ENGLISH SCHOOL

10,640
Arthur Wolfe, 1st Viscount Kilwarden, (1739-1803), Chief Justice of Ireland
(after an oil of c.1795, NGI no. 578)
Published: not before 1803
22.7 x 14.4 (plate cut)
Line
Purchased, Dublin, Mr P. Traynor, 1898

Hamilton, Hugh Douglas (1739-1808)
Irish School
SHERWIN, JOHN KEYSE (1751-1790)
ENGLISH SCHOOL

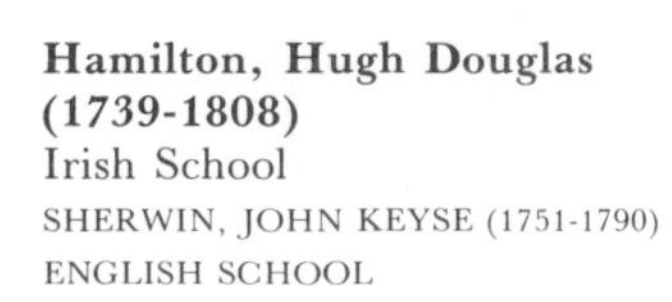

10,896
David (Digges) La Touche of Bellevue, Co. Wicklow, (1703-1785)
(after a pastel)
Published: not before 1785
43.4 x 33.4 (plate 30.7 x 24.1)
Line
Purchased, London, Maggs Bros., 1904

Hamilton, Hugh Douglas (1739-1808)
Irish School
TURNER, CHARLES (1773-1857)
ENGLISH SCHOOL

10,207
Charles Broderick, P. Archbishop of Cashel, (1761-1822)
Unlettered Proof
Published: C. Turner, London, 1823
49.2 x 35.5 (plate 38.8 x 30.5)
Mezzotint
Acquired between 1898/1904

Hamilton, Hugh Douglas (1739-1808)
Irish School
WARD THE ELDER, WILLIAM (1766-1826)
ENGLISH SCHOOL

10,050
Rev. Walter Blake Kirwan, (1754-1805), preaching on behalf of the Female Orphan House, Dublin
(after an oil of c.1800, destroyed)
Published: W. Allen, Dublin, also Colnaghi, London, 1st January 1806
69.5 x 75 (plate 61 x 68)
Mezzotint
Purchased, Dublin, Mr R. Langton Douglas, 1906

Hamilton, Hugh Douglas (1739-1808)
Irish School
WATSON, JAMES (C.1740-1790)
IRISH SCHOOL

10,334
Anne, Countess of Cork and Orrery, (née Courtenay, 1742-1785), 1st wife of 7th Earl
Published: R. Sayer, London, 4th December 1771
38.9 x 29.9 (plate 38.2 x 28)
Mezzotint
Purchased, London, 2nd Chaloner Smith sale, 1888

Hammond, Sir T. (19th century)
English School
ENGLISH SCHOOL (1822)

11,596
The Entrance of George IV, King of England, (1762-1830), into the Upper Yard, Dublin Castle, 17th August 1821
(after a drawing)
Published: Colnaghi & Co., London, 1st May 1822
25 x 36 (image 17 x 21.5)
Lithograph
Provenance Unknown

Hammond, Sir T. (19th century)
English School
ENGLISH SCHOOL (1822)

11,698
The Entrance of George IV, King of England, (1762-1830), into the Upper Yard, Dublin Castle, 17th August 1821
Proof with lettering and notes in pencil
24.2 x 34 (image 17 x 21.5)
Lithograph
Provenance Unknown

Harding, James Duffield (1798-1863)
English School
GOODALL, EDWARD (1795-1870)
ENGLISH SCHOOL

20,381
Italy, (Classical Ruins)
Published: C. Tilt, London, 1832
27.8 x 38 (plate 18.4 x 24.8)
Steel Engraving
Purchased, Lusk, Mr de Courcy Donovan, 1971

Harding, James Duffield (1798-1863)
English School
HARDING, JAMES DUFFIELD (1798-1863)
ENGLISH SCHOOL

20,182
Rainham Marshes, Kent
Published: C. Tilt, London
27.4 x 37.4 (image 18.8 x 27.5)
Lithograph
Purchased, Lusk, Mr de Courcy Donovan, 1971

Harding, James Duffield (1798-1863)
English School
HARDING, JAMES DUFFIELD (1798-1863)
ENGLISH SCHOOL

20,183
Capel Curig and Mount Snowdon, N. Wales
Published: C. Tilt, London
27.4 x 37.4 (image 19.5 x 27.5)
Lithograph
Purchased, Lusk, Mr de Courcy Donovan, 1971

Harding, James Duffield (1798-1863)
English School
HARDING, JAMES DUFFIELD (1798-1863)
ENGLISH SCHOOL

20,184
Cottage at Penhurst, Kent
Published: C. Tilt, London
27.4 x 37.4 (image 18.4 x 27.5)
Lithograph
Purchased, Lusk, Mr de Courcy Donovan, 1971

Harding, James Duffield (1798-1863)
English School
HARDING, JAMES DUFFIELD (1798-1863)
ENGLISH SCHOOL

20,185
Farmhouse at Alphington near Exeter, Devon
Published: C. Tilt, London
27.4 x 37.4 (image 18.6 x 27)
Lithograph
Purchased, Lusk, Mr de Courcy Donovan, 1971

Harding, James Duffield (1798-1863)
English School
HARDING, JAMES DUFFIELD (1798-1863)
ENGLISH SCHOOL

20,186
Dorney Common and the River Thames, Buckinghamshire
Published: C. Tilt, London
27.4 x 37.4 (image 18.8 x 27.5)
Lithograph
Purchased, Lusk, Mr de Courcy Donovan, 1971

Harding, James Duffield (1798-1863)
English School
HARDING, JAMES DUFFIELD (1798-1863)
ENGLISH SCHOOL

20,187
The Beach at Etretat, Normandy, N. France
Published: C. Tilt, London
27.4 x 37.4 (image 18.9 x 27)
Lithograph
Purchased, Lusk, Mr de Courcy Donovan, 1971

Harding, James Duffield (1798-1863)
English School
HARDING, JAMES DUFFIELD (1798-1863)
ENGLISH SCHOOL

20,188
Farm buildings, Littlehampton, Sussex
Published: C. Tilt, London
27.4 x 37.4 (image 18.5 x 27.2)
Lithograph
Purchased, Lusk, Mr de Courcy Donovan, 1971

Harding, James Duffield (1798-1863)
English School
HARDING, JAMES DUFFIELD (1798-1863)
ENGLISH SCHOOL

20,189
Bookham Line, Surrey
Published: C. Tilt, London
27.4 x 37.4 (image 18.5 x 25.6)
Lithograph
Purchased, Lusk, Mr de Courcy Donovan, 1971

Harding, James Duffield (1798-1863)
English School
HARDING, JAMES DUFFIELD (1798-1863)
ENGLISH SCHOOL

20,190
Beach scene with boats and figures
Published: C. Tilt, London
27.4 x 37.4 (image 18 x 26)
Lithograph
Purchased, Lusk, Mr de Courcy Donovan, 1971

Harding, James Duffield (1798-1863)
English School
HARDING, JAMES DUFFIELD (1798-1863)
ENGLISH SCHOOL

20,191
Boats on the River Thames near Woolwich
Published: C. Tilt, London
27.4 x 37.4 (image 18.7 x 27)
Lithograph
Purchased, Lusk, Mr de Courcy Donovan, 1971

Harding, James Duffield (1798-1863)
English School
HARDING, JAMES DUFFIELD (1798-1863)
ENGLISH SCHOOL

20,192
Boats on the River Thames
Published: C. Tilt, London
27.4 x 37.4 (image 18.6 x 28)
Lithograph
Purchased, Lusk, Mr de Courcy Donovan, 1971

Harding, James Duffield (1798-1863)
English School
HARDING, JAMES DUFFIELD (1798-1863)
ENGLISH SCHOL

20,193
Andernach Castle on the River Rhine, Germany
Published: C. Tilt, London
27.4 x 37.4 (image 19.7 x 27.9)
Lithograph
Purchased, Lusk, Mr de Courcy Donovan, 1971

Harding, James Duffield (1798-1863)
English School
HARDING, JAMES DUFFIELD (1798-1863)
ENGLISH SCHOOL

20,194
Boppard, Germany, with the towers of the Parish Churches
Published: C. Tilt, London
27.4 x 37.4 (image 27 x 18.9)
Lithograph
Purchased, Lusk, Mr de Courcy Donovan, 1971

Harding, James Duffield (1798-1863)
English School
HARDING, JAMES DUFFIELD (1798-1863)
ENGLISH SCHOOL

20,195
Bradgate Park, Leicestershire
Published: C. Tilt, London
27.4 x 37.4 (image 19.4 x 27.5)
Lithograph
Purchased, Lusk, Mr de Courcy Donovan, 1971

Harding, James Duffield (1798-1863)
English School
HARDING, JAMES DUFFIELD (1798-1863)
ENGLISH SCHOOL

20,196
River scene with Willows and boy fishing
Published: C. Tilt, London
27.4 x 37.4 (image 18 x 25.6)
Lithograph
Purchased, Lusk, Mr de Courcy Donovan, 1971

Harding, James Duffield (1798-1863)
English School
HARDING, JAMES DUFFIELD (1798-1863)
ENGLISH SCHOOL

20,224
Fishing Boats by the Shore, (from 'C.J. Hullmandel's Lithographic Drawing Book for the year 1835')
(after a drawing of 1834)
Published: Ackermann & Co., London, 1835 (Printed: C.J. Hullmandel)
19.1 x 28 (image 17.5 x 26)
Lithograph
Purchased, Lusk, Mr de Courcy Donovan, 1971

Harding, James Duffield (1798-1863)
English School
HARDING, JAMES DUFFIELD (1798-1863)
ENGLISH SCHOOL

20,225
A Shepherd driving Sheep towards a Village, (from 'C.J. Hullmandel's 'Lithographic Drawing Book for the year 1835')
(after a drawing of 1834)
Published: Ackermann & Co., London, 1835 (Printed: C.J. Hullmandel)
18.9 x 27.6 (image 14.5 x 26 approx)
Lithograph
Purchased, Lusk, Mr de Courcy Donovan, 1971

Harding, James Duffield (1798-1863)
English School
HARDING, JAMES DUFFIELD (1798-1863)
ENGLISH SCHOOL

20,226
Oberwesel by the River Rhine, Germany, with the Ruins of Schonburg Castle beyond
Published: C. Tilt, London
27.7 x 38.8 (image 16.7 x 25)
Lithograph
Purchased, Lusk, Mr de Courcy Donovan, 1971

Harding, James Duffield (1798-1863)
English School
HARDING, JAMES DUFFIELD (1798-1863)
ENGLISH SCHOOL

20,249
Rustic House
16 x 22.8 (image 16 x 22.8)
Lithograph
Purchased, Lusk, Mr de Courcy Donovan, 1971

Harding, James Duffield (1798-1863)
English School
HARDING, JAMES DUFFIELD (1798-1863)
ENGLISH SCHOOL

20,259
An Ash at Greta Bridge, Yorkshire, (from J.D. Harding's 'The Park and Forest', 1841)
Published: T. McLean, London, 1841 (Printed: C.J. Hullmandel)
28.3 x 34.4 (image 27.4 x 39.4)
Lithograph
Purchased, Lusk, Mr de Courcy Donovan, 1971

Harding, James Duffield (1798-1863)
English School
HARDING, JAMES DUFFIELD (1798-1863)
ENGLISH SCHOOL

20,264(26)
Old Oak Trees, (from J.D. Harding's 'Lessons on Trees', see App. 8, no. 20, 264)
Published: Day & Son, London, 1852 (Printed: G. Barclay)
37.2 x 27.2 (image 24.5 x 34)
Lithograph
Purchased, Lusk, Mr de Courcy Donovan, 1971

Harding, James Duffield (1798-1863)
English School
HARDING, JAMES DUFFIELD (1798-1863)
ENGLISH SCHOOL

20,273
Abel and Oak in Epping Forest, Essex, (from J.D. Harding's 'The Park and the Forest', 1841)
Published: T. McLean, London, 1841
(Printed: C.J. Hullmandel)
36.5 X 53.8 (image 29.5 x 44)
Lithograph
Purchased, Lusk, Mr de Courcy Donovan, 1971

Harding, James Duffield (1798-1863)
English School
HARDING, JAMES DUFFIELD (1798-1863)
ENGLISH SCHOOL

20,274
Wych Elm and Firs at the junction of the Rivers Tees and Greta, Yorkshire, (from J.D. Harding's 'The Park and the Forest', 1841)
Published: T. McLean, London, 1841
(Printed: C.J. Hullmandel)
54 x 36.8 (image 48 x 35.5)
Lithograph
Purchased, Lusk, Mr de Courcy Donovan, 1971

Harding, James Duffield (1798-1863)
English School
HARDING, JAMES DUFFIELD (1798-1863)
ENGLISH SCHOOL

20,275
Cedars of Lebanon
37.8 x 54.9 (image 28.3 x 40.5)
Lithograph
Purchased, Lusk, Mr de Courcy Donovan, 1971

Harding, James Duffield (1798-1863)
English School
HARDING, JAMES DUFFIELD (1798-1863)
ENGLISH SCHOOL

20,296
Beech and Ash, Rokeby on the Greta, Yorkshire, (from J.D. Harding's 'The Park and the Forest', 1841)
Published: T. McLean, London, 1841
(Printed: C.J. Hullmandel)
36.8 x 53.9 (image 28.5 x 41)
Lithograph
Purchased, Lusk, Mr de Courcy Donovan, 1971

Harding, James Duffield (1798-1863)
English School
HARDING, JAMES DUFFIELD (1798-1863)
ENGLISH SCHOOL

20,297
Stone Pines in the Campagna, near Rome, (from J. D. Harding's 'The Park and the Forest', 1841)
Published: T. McLean, London, 1841
(Printed: C.J. Hullmandel)
53.8 x 36.8 (image 41.5 x 28)
Lithograph
Purchased, Lusk, Mr de Courcy Donovan, 1971

Harding, James Duffield (1798-1863)
English School
HARDING, JAMES DUFFIELD (1798-1863)
ENGLISH SCHOOL

20,298
Ash, Sycamore and Oak on the River Tees, Rokeby Park, Yorkshire, (from J.D. Harding's 'The Park and the Forest', 1841)

Published: T. McLean, London, 1841
(Printed: C.J. Hullmandel)
36.9 x 53.9 (image 28.5 x 41)
Lithograph
Purchased, Lusk, Mr de Courcy Donovan, 1971

Harding, James Duffield (1798-1863)
English School
HARDING, JAMES DUFFIELD (1798-1863)
ENGLISH SCHOOL

20,299
Beech Tree, Windsor Forest, Berkshire, (from J.D. Harding's 'The Park and the Forest', 1841)
Published: T. McLean, London, 1841
(Printed: C.J. Hullmandel)
36.8 x 53.8 (image 30 x 41.7)
Lithograph
Purchased, Lusk, Mr de Courcy Donovan, 1971

Harding, James Duffield (1798-1863)
English School
HARDING, JAMES DUFFIELD (1798-1863)
ENGLISH SCHOOL

20,300
Willow Tree at Henley-on-Thames, Oxfordshire, (from J.D. Harding's 'The Park and the Forest', 1841)
Published: T. McLean, London, 1841
(Printed: C.J. Hullmandel)
36.9 x 53.9 (image 28.5 x 40.7)
Lithograph
Purchased, Lusk, Mr de Courcy Donovan, 1971

Harding, James Duffield (1798-1863)
English School
HARDING, JAMES DUFFIELD (1798-1863)
ENGLISH SCHOOL

20,301
Elms at Pinner, London, (from J.D. Harding's 'The Park and the Forest', 1841)
Published: T. McLean, London, 1841
(Printed: C.J. Hullmandel)
53.8 x 36.7 (image 39.2 x 29)
Lithograph
Purchased, Lusk, Mr de Courcy Donovan, 1971

Harding, James Duffield (1798-1863)
English School
HARDING, JAMES DUFFIELD (1798-1863)
ENGLISH SCHOOL

20,302
Black Poplars, Great Munden Park, Hertfordshire, (from J.D. Harding's 'The Park and the Forest', 1841)
Published: T. McLean, London, 1841
(Printed: C.J. Hullmandel)
36.7 x 53.9 (image 29.5 x 44)
Lithograph
Purchased, Lusk, Mr de Courcy Donovan, 1971

Harding, James Duffield (1798-1863)
English School
HARDING, JAMES DUFFIELD (1798-1863)
ENGLISH SCHOOL

20,303
Birch and Oak trees at Birkland, Ullswater, Cumbria, (from J.D. Harding's 'The Park and the Forest', 1841)
Published: T. McLean, London, 1841
(Printed: C.J. Hullmandel)
53.8 x 36.8 (image 39.2 x 32.5)
Lithograph
Purchased, Lusk, Mr de Courcy Donovan, 1971

Harding, James Duffield (1798-1863)
English School
HARDING, JAMES DUFFIELD (1798-1863)
ENGLISH SCHOOL

20,304
Yew Tree in the Churchyard Crenhurst, Sussex, (from J.D. Harding's 'The Park and the Forest', 1841)
Published: T. McLean, London, 1841
(Printed: C.J. Hullmandel)
36.5 x 53.5 (image 28.7 x 39.5)
Lithograph
Purchased, Lusk, Mr de Courcy Donovan, 1971

Harding, James Duffield (1798-1863)
English School
HARDING, JAMES DUFFIELD (1798-1863)
ENGLISH SCHOOL

20,305
Sycamore Trees, Rokeby, Yorkshire, (from J.D. Harding's 'The Park and Forest', 1841)
Published: T. McLean, London, 1841
(Printed: C.J. Hullmandel)
54 x 37.5 (image 40.5 x 30.5)
Lithograph
Purchased, Lusk, Mr de Courcy Donovan, 1971

Harding, James Duffield (1798-1863)
English School
HARDING, JAMES DUFFIELD (1798-1863)
ENGLISH SCHOOL

20,306
Scotch Fir at Bielstein on the River Moselle, Germany, (from J.D. Harding's 'The Park and the Forest', 1841)
Published: T. McLean, London, 1841
(Printed: C.J. Hullmandel)
53.8 x 36.7 (image 39.5 x 29.4)
Lithograph
Purchased, Lusk, Mr de Courcy Donovan, 1971

Harding, James Duffield (1798-1863)
English School
HARDING, JAMES DUFFIELD (1798-1863)
ENGLISH SCHOOL

20,307
Plane Trees, Twickenham, London, (from J.D. Harding's 'The Park and the Forest', 1841)
Published: T. McLean, London, 1841
(Printed: C.J. Hullmandel)
36.6 x 54 (image 28 x 42)
Lithograph
Purchased, Lusk, Mr de Courcy Donovan, 1971

Harding, James Duffield (1797-1863)
English School
HARDING, JAMES DUFFIELD (1797-1863)
ENGLISH SCHOOL

20,355
Hastings Beach, Sussex
27.1 x 37.3 (image 18.8 x 27)
Lithograph
Purchased, Lusk, Mr de Courcy Donovan, 1971

Harding, James Duffield (1798-1863)
English School
HARDING, JAMES DUFFIELD (1798-1863)
ENGLISH SCHOOL

20,358
'Trèves on the Moselle', (Trier, Germany)
Published: Chapman & Hall, London
27.4 x 37.8 (plate 18 x 26.4)
Aquatint and etching
Purchased, Lusk, Mr de Courcy Donovan, 1971

Harding, James Duffield (1798-1863)
English School
HARDING, JAMES DUFFIELD (1798-1863)
ENGLISH SCHOOL

20,361
Ruined Castle above a River, (from J.D. Harding's 'Principles and Practice of Art', 1845)
Published: Chapman & Hall, London, 1845
27.7 x 37.6 (plate 23 x 29.8)
Steel Engraving
Purchased, Lusk, Mr de Courcy Donovan, 1971

Harding, James Duffield (1798-1863)
English School
HARDING, JAMES DUFFIELD (1798-1863)
ENGLISH SCHOOL

20,370
Ruined Castle above a River, (from J.D. Harding's 'Principles and Practice of Art', 1845)
Published: Chapman & Hall, London, 1845
27.7 x 37.7 (plate 22.9 x 29.5)
Mezzotint, etching and line
Purchased, Lusk, Mr de Courcy Donovan, 1971

Harding, James Duffield (1798-1863)
English School
HARDING, JAMES DUFFIELD (1798-1863)
ENGLISH SCHOOL

20,391
Hastings Beach, Sussex, (another copy)
27.3 x 37.4 (image 18.8 x 27)
Lithograph
Purchased, Lusk, Mr de Courcy Donovan, 1971

Harding, James Duffield (1798-1863)
English School
HARDING, JAMES DUFFIELD (1798-1863)
ENGLISH SCHOOL

20,405
Fishermen in a boat on a river - example 1, (from J.D. Harding's 'Principles and Practice of Art', 1845)
Published: Chapman & Hall, London, 1845
37.7 x 27.2 (plate cut)
Etching
Purchased, Lusk, Mr de Courcy Donovan, 1971

Harding, James Duffield (1798-1863)
English School
HARDING, JAMES DUFFIELD (1798-1863)
ENGLISH SCHOOL

20,406
Riverbank with fisherman - example 2, (from J.D. Harding's 'Principles and Practice of Art', 1845)
Published: Chapman & Hall, London, 1845
37.7 x 27.2 (plate cut)
Etching and mezzotint
Purchased, Lusk, Mr de Courcy Donovan, 1971

Harding, James Duffield (1798-1863)
English School
HARDING, JAMES DUFFIELD (1798-1863)
ENGLISH SCHOOL

20,407
Riverside scene with man driving sheep - example 1, (from J.D. Harding's 'Principles and Practice of Art', 1845)
Published: Chapman & Hall, London, 1845
37.8 x 27.7 (plate cut)
Etching and mezzotint
Purchased, Lusk, Mr de Courcy Donovan, 1971

Harding, James Duffield (1798-1863)
English School
HARDING, JAMES DUFFIELD (1798-1863)
ENGLISH SCHOOL

20,408
Riverside scene with man driving sheep - example 2, (from J.D. Harding's 'Principles and Practice of Art', 1845)
Published: Chapman & Hall, London, 1845

37.8 x 27.7 (plate cut)
Line and mezzotint
Purchased, Lusk, Mr de Courcy Donovan, 1971

Harding, James Duffield (1798-1863)
English School
HARDING, JAMES DUFFIELD (1798-1863)
ENGLISH SCHOOL

20,409
River with Distant Ruined Castle - example 1, (from J.D. Harding's 'Principles and Practice of Art', 1845)
Published: Chapman & Hall, London, 1845
37.7 x 27.6 (plate cut)
Etching and aquatint
Purchased, Lusk, Mr de Courcy Donovan, 1971

Harding, James Duffield (1798-1863)
English School
HARDING, JAMES DUFFIELD (1798-1863)
ENGLISH SCHOOL

20,410
Steamship Offshore - example 2, (from J.D. Harding's 'Principles and Practice of Art', 1845)
Published: Chapman & Hall, London, 1845
37.7 x 27.6 (plate cut)
Etching and aquatint
Purchase, Lusk, Mr de Courcy Donovan, 1971

Harding, James Duffield (1798-1863)
English School
HARDING, JAMES DUFFIELD (1798-1863)
ENGLISH SCHOOL

20,428
Near Feldkirch, Tyrol, Austria, (from J.D. Harding's 'Principles and Practice of Art', 1845)
Published: Chapman & Hall, London, 1845
21.8 x 29.3 (plate cut)
Etching and aquatint
Purchased, Lusk, Mr de Courcy Donovan, 1971

Harding, James Duffield (1798-1863)
English School
HARDING, JAMES DUFFIELD (1798-1863)
ENGLISH SCHOOL

20,446
Beach at Low Tide, (from J.D. Harding's 'Principles and Practice of Art', 1845)
Published: Chapman & Hall, London, 1845
37.9 x 27.5 (plate cut)
Line, etching and mezzotint
Purchased, Lusk, Mr de Courcy Donovan, 1971

Harding, James Duffield (1798-1863)
English School
HARDING, JAMES DUFFIELD (1798-1863)
ENGLISH SCHOOL

20,447
Hay Cart on a Country Road - example 2, (from J.D. Harding's 'Principles and Practice of Art', 1845)
Published: Chapman & Hall, London, 1845
37.9 x 27.5 (plate cut)
Line, etching and mezzotint
Purchased, Lusk, Mr de Courcy Donovan, 1971

Harding, James Duffield (1798-1863)
English School
HARDING, JAMES DUFFIELD (1798-1863)
ENGLISH SCHOOL

20,463
Coastal Scene - example 1, (from J.D. Harding's 'Principles and Practice of Art', 1845)
Published: Chapman & Hall, London, 1845
37.7 x 27.5 (plate cut)
Etching and aquatint
Purchased, Lusk, Mr de Courcy Donovan, 1971

Harding, James Duffield (1798-1863)
English School
HARDING, JAMES DUFFIELD (1798-1863)
ENGLISH SCHOOL

20,464
Coastal Scene - example 2, (from J.D. Harding's 'Principles and Practice of Art', 1845)
Published: Chapman & Hall, London, 1845
37.8 x 27.6 (plate cut)
Etching and aquatint
Purchased, Lusk, Mr de Courcy Donovan, 1971

Harding, James Duffield (1798-1863)
English School
HARDING, JAMES DUFFIELD (1798-1863)
ENGLISH SCHOOL

20,465
Coastal Scene, - example 3, (from J.D. Harding's 'Principles and Practice of Art', 1845)
Published: Chapman & Hall, London, 1845
37.8 x 27.6 (plate cut)
Etching and drypoint
Purchased, Lusk, Mr de Courcy Donovan, 1971

Harding, James Duffield (1798-1863)
English School
HARDING, JAMES DUFFIELD (1798-1863)
ENGLISH SCHOOL

20,579
Sleeping man against a tree trunk
14.8 x 23.8 (image 14.4 x 23.8 approx)
Lithograph
Presented, Mrs D. Molloy, 1981

?Harding, James Duffield (1798-1863)
English School
?HARDING, JAMES DUFFIELD (1798-1863)
ENGLISH SCHOOL

20,580
Victoria Beech Tree
Published: Day & Haghe, London
18.9 x 10.5 (cut to image)
Lithograph
Presented, Mrs D. Molloy, 1981

Harding, James Duffield (1798-1863)
English School
HARDING, JAMES DUFFIELD (1798-1863)
ENGLISH SCHOOL

20,581
Gartmore, Scotland, with the River Kelty
Published: R. Ackermann, London, 1824
20.4 x 27.3 (image 20.4 x 27.3 approx)
Lithograph
Presented, Mrs D. Molloy, 1981

Harding, James Duffield (1798-1863)
English School
HARDING, JAMES DUFFIELD (1798-1863)
ENGLISH SCHOOL

20,649
Capel Curig and Mount Snowdon, N. Wales, (another copy)
Published: C. Tilt, London
19.5 x 27.5 (image 19.5 x 27.5)
Lithograph
Presented, Mrs D. Molloy, 1981

Harding, James Duffield (1798-1863)
English School
RADCLYFFE, WILLIAM (1783-1855)
ENGLISH SCHOOL

20,424
The campanile of the cathedral at Fiesole, Italy, (from J.D. Harding's 'Views of Italy, France and Switzerland', 1836)
Published: Fisher, Son & Co., London & Paris, 1836
28.3 x 22.2 (plate 23 x 15)
Steel Engraving
Purchased, Lusk, Mr de Courcy Donovan, 1971

Harding, James Duffield (1798-1863)
English School
SMITH, WILLIAM RAYMOND (FL.1818-1848)
ENGLISH SCHOOL

20,431
Dieppe, N. France
12.9 x 20.5 (plate cut)
Etching and line
Purchased, Lusk, Mr de Courcy Donovan, 1971

Harding, Sylvester (1745-1809)
English School
KNIGHT, CHARLES (1743-C.1826)
ENGLISH SCHOOL

10,920
John Monck Mason, M.P., (1726-1809), Commissioner of Revenue for Ireland and Shakespearean critic, (pl. for S. Harding's 'Shakespeare Illustrated', 1789-1793)
Published: E. Harding, London, 10th October 1791
27.7 x 22.1 (plate 19.2 x 14)
Stipple
Purchased, Dublin, Mr J.V. McAlpine, 1913

Hardy, James (fl.1832-1867)
English School
HUFFAM, T.W. (FL.1825-C.1855)
ENGLISH SCHOOL

10,934
Richard Robert Madden, (1798-1886), Author, Publilsher and Anti-Slaver
(after a drawing)
29.4 x 21.1 (plate 20.1 x 12.8)
Line and mezzotint
Purchased, Dublin, Mr P. Traynor, 1898

Hardy, James (fl.1832-1867)
English School
HUFFAM, T.W. (FL.1825-1855)
ENGLISH SCHOOL

10,935
Richard Robert Madden, (1798-1886), Author, Publisher and Anti-Slaver, (another copy)
(after a drawing)
29.4 x 20.7 (plate 20.1 x 12.8)
Line and mezzotint
Purchased, Dublin, Mr P. Traynor, 1898

Hardy, T. (fl.1792-1802)
English School
HARDY, T. (FL.1792-1802)
ENGLISH SCHOOL

10,103
John Moody, (1727?-1812), Comedy Actor
Published: T. Hardy, London, 12th June 1792
32.9 x 25.7 (plate 32.5 x 25.2)

Mezzotint
Presumed purchased, Dublin, Jones Salesroom, 1879

Hargreaves, Thomas (1774-1846)
English School
SMITH, EDWARD (FL.1823-1851)
ENGLISH SCHOOL

11,126
Lieut.-General John Devereaux, (1778-1860), of the Venezuelan Army
(after a miniature)
Published: E. Smith, Liverpool, September 1819
24.9 x 20.9 (plate cut)
Line
Acquired by 1903

Harlow, George Henry (1787-1819)
English School
MEYER, HENRY HOPPNER (C.1782-1847)
ENGLISH SCHOOL

20,122
Benjamin West, (1738-1820), Artist and President of the Royal Academy, (pl. for Golf & Northouse's 'London Magazine', April 1820)
(after a tql oil, RA, 1815)
Published: London Magazine, 1st April 1820
23 x 14.9 (plate cut)
Line and stipple
Purchased, Lusk, Mr de Courcy Donovan, 1971

Harlow, George Henry (1787-1819)
English School
SAY, WILLIAM (1768-1834)
ENGLISH SCHOOL

10,369
Cecil Frances, Countess of Wicklow, (née Hamilton, 1795-1860), wife of 4th Earl of Wicklow
Lettered Proof
Published: W. Say, London, 1st February 1819
40 x 30 (plate 35.5 x 25.5)
Mezzotint
Purchased, Dublin, Mr A. Roth, 1896

Harrington, Elizabeth, Countess of (c.1819-1912)
Irish School
M & N HANHART (FL.1820-1865)
ENGLISH SCHOOL

20,766
Isle O'Valla, Strangford Lough, Co. Down
(after a drawing)
Published: M & N Hanhart, London
28.5 x 37.9 (image 17.3 x 25.3)
Lithograph
Presented, Miss P. Quinlan, 1984

Harrington, Elizabeth, Countess of (c.1819-1912)
Irish School
HANHART, M & N (FL.1820-1865)
ENGLISH SCHOOL

20,767
Old Court, Strangford, Co. Down
(after a drawing)
Published: M & N Hanhart, London
28.5 x 37.9 (image 17.3 x 25.3)
Lithograph
Presented, Miss P. Quinlan, 1894

Harrison J.C. (fl.1882-1891)
English School
ATKINSON, GEORGE (1880-1941)
IRISH SCHOOL

10,502
Gerald Fitzgibbon, (1793-1882), Lord Justice of Appeal & Author
Published: The Benchers of the Honourable Society of Kings Inns, Dublin (Printed: G. Atkinson, Dublin)
73.6 x 46.6 (plate 60.8 x 35.1)
Mezzotint
Provenance Unknown

Haslock, J. (19th century)
English School
ROGERS, JOHN (FL.1820'S-1850'S)
ENGLISH SCHOOL

10,704
William Carr, 1st Viscount Beresford, (1768-1854), distinguished Officer, (pl. for W. Ryall's 'Eminent Conservative Statesmen', 2nd series, 1846)
Published: G. Virtue, London, 1846
36.1 x 25.9 (plate 34 x 25.3)
Line
Purchased, Dublin,
Mr J.V. McAlpine, 1896

Haverty, Joseph Patrick (1794-1864)
Irish School
HAVELL THE ELDER, ROBERT (FL.1800-1840)
ENGLISH SCHOOL *and*
HAVELL THE YOUNGER, ROBERT (FL.1820-1850)
ENGLISH SCHOOL

11,649
The Embarkation of George IV, King of England, (1762-1830), at Kingstown, (now Dun Laoghaire), 3rd September 1821
(from a J.L. Reilly sketch taken on the spot)
INSCRIBED: *To his Most Excellent Majesty George the Fourth King of Great Britain &c. &c. &c./This print, representing his Majesty's Embarkation at Kingstown on the 3rd September 1821,/ is with Gracious and Special permission humbly dedicated by his most faithful subject,/John Lushington Reilly*
Published: Hurst, Robinson & Co., also Colnaghi & Co., London, also R. Milliken, also Allen & Sons, Dublin, March 1823
47.3 x 67.2 (plate 46 x 67.2)
Aquatint and Etching
Provenance Unknown

Haverty, Joseph Patrick (1794-1864)
Irish School
HAVELL THE ELDER, ROBERT (FL.1800-1840)
ENGLISH SCHOOL *and*
HAVELL THE YOUNGER, ROBERT (FL.1820-1850)
ENGLISH SCHOOL

11,650
The Public Entry of George IV, King of England, (1762-1830), into Dublin 17th August 1821, by the Lying-in (now Rotunda) Hospital
(from a J. R. Reilly sketch taken on the spot)
INSCRIBED: To his most Excellent Majesty George the Fourth of Great Britain &c. &c. &c./This print, representing his Majesty's Public Entry into the City of Dublin on the 17th August 1821,/is with Gracious and Special Permission humbly dedicated by his Majesty's most faithful Subject, /John Lushington Reilly
Published: Hurst Robinson & Co., also Colnaghi & Co., London, also R. Milliken, also Allen & Sons, Dublin, March 1823
48.4 x 70.1 (plate x 67.2)
Aquatint and etching
Acquired between 1898/1904

Haverty, Joseph Patrick (1794-1864)
Irish School
HAVELL THE ELDER, ROBERT (FL.1800-1840)
ENGLISH SCHOOL *and*
HAVELL THE YOUNGER, ROBERT (FL.1820-1850)
ENGLISH SCHOOL

11,651
The Embarkation of George IV, King of England, (1762-1830), at Kingstown, (now Dun Laoghaire), 3rd September 1821, (another copy)
(from a J.R. Reilly sketch taken on the spot)
INSCRIBED: as on no. 11,649

Published: Hurst Robinson & Co., also Colnaghi & Co., London, also R. Milliken, also Allen & Sons, Dublin, March 1823
48.9 x 69.5 (plate 46 x 67.2)
Aquatint and Etching
Acquired between 1898/1904

Haverty, Joseph Patrick (1794-1864)
Irish School
HAVELL THE ELDER, ROBERT (FL.1800-1840) ENGLISH SCHOOL *and*
HAVELL THE YOUNGER, ROBERT (FL.1820-1850)
ENGLISH SCHOOL

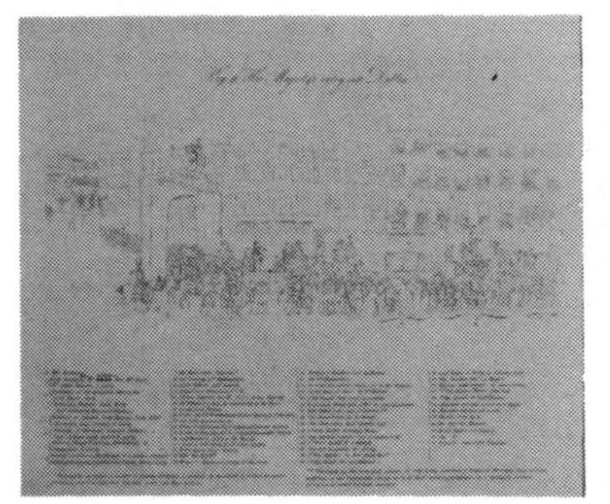

20,820
The Public Entry of George IV into Dublin, 17th August 1821, (key to aquatint, NGI no. 11,650)
28.2 x 33 (plate 26.4 x 31.2)
Etching
Provenance Unknown

Haverty, Joseph Patrick (1794-1864)
Irish School
HAVELL THE ELDER, ROBERT (FL.1800-1840) ENGLISH SCHOOL *and*
HAVELL THE YOUNGER, ROBERT (FL.1820-1850)
ENGLISH SCHOOL

20,821
The Embarkation of George IV at Kingstown, 3rd September 1821, (key to aquatint, NGI no. 11,651)
31.7 x 37.2 (plate 26.3 x 31)
Etching
Provenance Unknown

Haverty, Joseph Patrick (1794-1864)
Irish School
HAVERTY, JOSEPH PATRICK (1794-1864)
IRISH SCHOOL

10,794
James Warren Doyle, (1786-1834), R.C. Bishop of Kildare and Leighlin
(after an oil, RHA 1837; St Patrick's College, Carlow)
Lettered Proof
(Printed: C. J. Hullmandel, London)
29 x 23.8 (image 20 x 18.2)
Lithograph
Purchased, Dublin, Mr J.V. McAlpine 1901

Haverty, Joseph Patrick (1794-1864)
Irish School
HAVERTY, JOSEPH PATRICK (1794-1864)
IRISH SCHOOL

10,963
Father Thomas Maguire, (1792-1847), R.C. Priest of Innismagrath, Co. Leitrim and Controversialist
INSCRIBED: Drawn from Life on Stone
33 x 25.7 (image 27 x 22.5)
Lithograph
Presented, 1907

Haverty, Joseph Patrick (1794-1864)
Irish School
HAVERTY, JOSEPH PATRICK (1794-1864)
IRISH SCHOOL

10,969
Daniel O'Connell, M.P., (1775-1847), Statesman, O'Gorman Mahon, M.P., (1880-1891), and Thomas Steele, (1788-1848), Repealer
(after an oil from life)
Published: Molteno & Graves, London, 1829 (Printed: Engelmann Graf Coindet & Co.)
49.8 x 38 (image 40.5 x 30)
Lithograph
Purchased, Dublin, Mr A. Roth, 1898

Haverty, Joseph Patrick (1794-1864)
Irish School
HAVERTY, JOSEPH PATRICK (1794-1864)
IRISH SCHOOL

11,020
Catholic Agitation Group with Stephen Coppinger, Sir Thomas Wyse, M.P., (1791-1862), Diplomat and Author; Thomas Furlong, (1794-1827), Poet; Richard Lalor Sheil, M.P., (1791-1851), Playwright; Rev. F.J. L'Estrange; John Lawless, (1773-1837), Author; Michael Staunton, Proprietor of the 'Morning Register' and ?Self-Portrait
Published: Molteno & Graves, London, July 1829
39.2 x 39 (image 20 x 33.5)
Lithograph
Purchased, Dublin, Mr A. Roth, 1898

Haverty, Joseph Patrick (1794-1864)
Irish School
HAVERTY, JOSEPH PATRICK (1794-1864)
IRISH SCHOOL

11,857
'The Monster Meeting of the 20th September 1843, at Clifden in the Irish Highlands', showing Daniel O'Connell, M.P., (1775-1847), addressing his supporters
(after a drawing, RHA 1854)
INSCRIBED BY HAND: *This impression coloured by myself from the original picture and presented to J.A. N... by Jas Haverty*
Published: J.P. Haverty, London, 30th May 1845 (Printed: M & N Hanhart)
53.8 x 79.8 (image 39.5 x 66.5)
Lithograph with watercolour
Purchased, Miss Ray, 1905

Haverty, Joseph Patrick (1794-1864)
Irish School
WARD THE YOUNGER, WILLIAM JAMES (1800-1840)
ENGLISH SCHOOL

10,000
Daniel O'Connell, M.P., (1775-1847), Statesman
(after an oil of 1823-30, Reform Club, London)
Published: J. Haverty, London 1836 (Printed: Ross & Dixon)
73.5 x 45 (plate cut)
Mezzotint
Acquired by 1879

Haverty, Joseph Patrick (1794-1864)
Irish School
HAVERTY, JSOEPH PATRICK (1794-1864)
IRISH SCHOOL

11,695
Queenstown, (designed by Hosking & Son), proposed to be built on Killiney Hill, Co. Dublin, (never carried out)
?1st State
(Printed: J. Graf, London)
51.5 x 75.8 (image 35 x 64)
Lithograph
Presented, Mr F.E. Ball, 1905

Haverty, Joseph Patrick (1794-1864)
Irish School
HAVERTY, JOSEPH PATRICK (1794-1864)
IRISH SCHOOL

20,336
Queenstown, (designed by Hosking & Son), proposed to be built on Killiney Hill, Co. Dublin, (never carried out)
?2nd State
(Printed: J. Graf, London)
44.5 x 70.5 (image 35 x 64)
Lithograph
Provenance Unknown

Hawkins, E. (19th century)
English School
FINDEN, WILLIAM (1789-1852)
ENGLISH SCHOOL

10,943

Lady Flora Elizabeth Hastings, (1806-1839), daughter of the 1st Marquess of Hastings, (pl. for W. Finden's 'Female Aristocracy of the Court of Queen Victoria', 1849)
Published: W. & E. Finden, London, April 1840 (Printed: McQueen)
59.7 x 43.5 (plate 34.5 x 25.6)
Line and stipple
Purchased, Dublin, Mr A. Roth, 1896

Hayes, Edward (1797-1864)
Irish School
BELLIN, SAMUEL (1799-1864)
ENGLISH SCHOOL

10,870
Robert Holmes, (1765-1859), Lawyer and Brother-in-Law of Robert Emmet
INSCRIBED: *Engraved by desire of the Subscribers, Men of all parties and persuasions, the Admirers of his Learning, Talents, Integrity and Independence*
Issued as a Private Plate (Printed: W. Halton)
42.2 x 30.5 (plate cut)
Mezzotint
Purchased, Dublin,
Mr J.V. McAlpine, 1901

Hayes, Michael Angelo (1820-1877)
Irish School
HARRIS THE YOUNGER, JOHN (1791-1873)
ENGLISH SCHOOL

20,695
Getting Ready, Hearn's Hotel Clonmel: Car Travelling in the South of Ireland in the Year 1856
Published: Ackermann & Co., London, 1st December 1856
35 x 48.5 (plate ?27.5 x 38)
Aquatint and etching with watercolour
Purchased, London, The Parker Gallery, 1983

Hayes, Michael Angelo (1820-1877)
Irish School
HARRIS THE YOUNGER, JOHN (1791-1873)
ENGLISH SCHOOL

20,696
Arriving at the End of a Stage: Car Travelling in the South of Ireland in the Year 1856
Published: Ackermann & Co., London, 1st December 1856
35 x 48.5 (plate 27.5 x 38)
Aquatint and etching with watercolour
Purchased, London, The Parker Gallery, 1983

Hayes, Michael Angelo (1820-1877)
Irish School
HARRIS THE YOUNGER, JOHN (1791-1873)
ENGLISH SCHOOL

20,697
On the Road at Full Pace: Car Travelling in the South of Ireland in the Year 1856
Published: Ackermann & Co., London, 1st December 1856
35 x 48.5 (plate 27.3 x 38)
Aquatint and etching with watercolour
Purchased, London, The Parker Gallery, London 1983

Hayes, Michael Angelo (1820-1877)
Irish School
HARRIS THE YOUNGER, JOHN (1791-1873)
ENGLISH SCHOOL

20,698
Taking up a passenger: Car Travelling in the South of Ireland in the Year 1856
Published: Ackermann & Co., London, 1st December 1856
35 x 48.5 (plate 27.5 x 38)
Aquatint and etching with watercolour
Purchased, London, The Parker Gallery, 1983

Hayes, Michael Angelo (1820-1877)
Irish School
HARRIS THE YOUNGER, JOHN (1791-1873)
ENGLISH SCHOOL

20,699
Dropping a Passenger; Car Travelling in the South of Ireland in the Year 1856
Published: Ackermann & Co., London, 1st December 1856
35 x 48.5 (plate 27.5 x 38)
Aquatint and etching with watercolou
Purchased, London, The Parker Gallery, 1983

Hayes, Michael Angelo (1820-1877)
Irish School
HARRIS THE YOUNGER, JOHN (1791-1873)
ENGLISH SCHOOL

20,700
The Arrival at Waterford, Commins's Hotel: Car Travelling in the South of Ireland in the Year 1856
Published: Ackermann & Co., London, 1st December 1856
35 x 48.5 (plate 27.5 x 38)
Aquatint and etching with watercolour
Purchased, London, The Parker Gallery, 1983

Hayley, Thomas Alphonse (1780-1800)
English School
DENMAN, MARIA (1776-1861)
ENGLISH SCHOOL
WATSON, CAROLINE (1761-1814)
ENGLISH SCHOOL

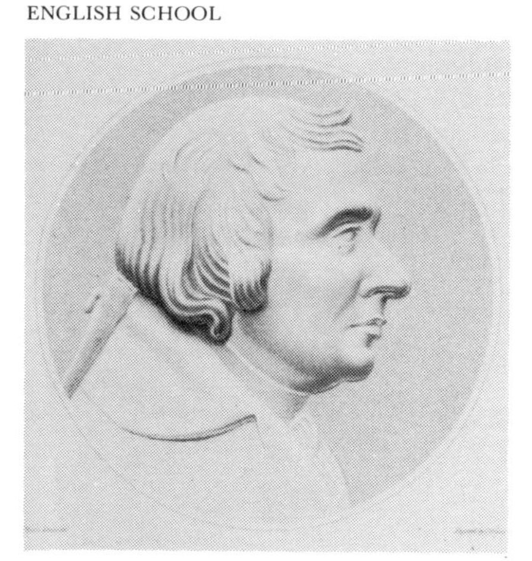

11,045
George Romney, (1734-1802), Artist, (pl. for W. Hayley's 'Life of Romney', 1809)
(after a medallion of 1795)
Published: T. Payne, London, 14th April 1809 (Printed: W. Mason)
27.1 x 20.5 (plate cut)
Stipple
Provenance Unknown

?Hayman, Francis (1708-1776)
English School
McARDELL, JAMES (1728/29-1765)
IRISH SCHOOL

10,104
James Quin, (1693-1766), Actor, as Shakespeare's Sir John Falstaff
Published: J. McArdell, London
35.6 x 25.3 (plate 35.3 x 24.9)
Mezzotint
Purchased, London, 1st Chaloner Smith sale, 1887

Hayman, Francis (1708-1776)
English School
McARDELL, JAMES (1728/29-1765)
IRISH SCHOOL

10,123
Henry Woodward, (1714-1777), Actor, as the Fine Gentleman in D. Garrick's 'Lethe'
(after a pencil drawing of c.1748, Fitzwilliam Museum, Cambridge)
Published: E. Griffin, London, not before 1748, price 6d
35.5 x 25.1 (plate 35.3 x 25.1)
Mezzotint
Purchased, London, 1st Chaloner Smith sale, 1887

Hayter, John (1800-1891)
English School
EGLETON, WILLIAM HENRY (FL.1833-1862)
ENGLISH SCHOOL

10,866
Frances Elizabeth, Viscountess Jocelyn, (née Cowper, 1820-1880), daughter of 5th Earl Cowper, widow of 1st Earl Roden
Published: not before 1841
36.6 x 26 (plate 33.5 x 25.3)
Line and stipple with watercolour
Purchased, Mr W.V. Daniell, 1901

Hayter, John (1800-1891)
English School
FINDEN, WILLIAM (1787-1852)
ENGLISH SCHOOL

10,727
Harriet Charlotte Beaujolais, Countess of Charleville, (née Campbell, fl. 1821-1848), wife of 3rd Earl of Charleville, (pl. for W. Finden's 'Female Aristocracy of the Court of Queen Victoria', 1849)
(after a drawing)
Published: The Proprietors, (W. & E. Finden), London, October 1841
36.6 x 26.8 (plate 34.5 x cut)
Stipple
Purchased, 1908

Hayter, John (1800-1891)
English School
LEWIS, FREDERICK CHRISTIAN (1779-1856)
ENGLISH SCHOOL

10,261
John Doherty, (1783-1850), Solicitor General for Ireland
(after a drawing)
Published: 1830
37.6 x 27.7 (plate 43.2 x 25.5)
Stipple
Purchased, Dublin, Mr P. Traynor, 1898

Hayter, John (1800-1891)
English School
MOTE, WILLIAM HENRY (FL.1830-1858)
ENGLISH SCHOOL

10,784
Miss Emily Mary Dawson, grand-daughter of the 1st Earl of Portarlington, later Mrs J.H. Wyndham King, (pl. for D. Bogue's 'Court Album', 1852)
(after a drawing)
Unlettered Proof
Published: D. Bogue, London
43.7 x 30 (plate 30.7 x 24)
Line and stipple
Purchased, 1908

Hayter, Stanley William (1901-1988)
English School
HAYTER, STANLEY WILLIAM (1901-1988)
ENGLISH SCHOOL

11,424(1)
'Still I', (from the first edition of Samuel Beckett's 'Still', 1974, see App. 8, no. 11,424)
Signed and dated in pencil 1973, 9/of 133
Published: M'Arte Edizioni, Milan, 1974
38 x 28.2 (plate 29.5 x 20.6)
Coloured Etching
Purchased, Dublin, The Neptune Gallery, 1975

Hayter, Stanley William (1901-1988)
English School
HAYTER, STANLEY WILLIAM (1901-1988)
ENGLISH SCHOOL

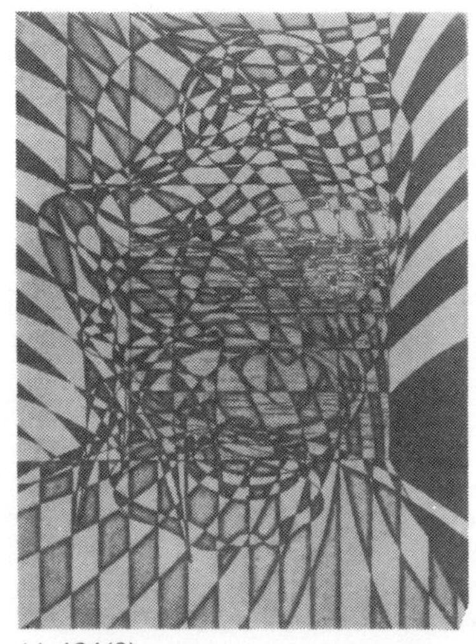

11,424(2)

'Still II', (from the the first edition of Samuel Beckett's 'Still', 1974, see App. 8, no. 11,424)
Signed and dated in pencil 1973, 9/of 133
Published: M'Arte Edizioni, Milan, 1974
37.7 x 28.2 (plate 29.4 x 21.4)
Coloured Etching
Purchased, Dublin, The Neptune Gallery, 1975

Hayter, Stanley William (1901-1988)
English School
HAYTER, STANLEY WILLIAM (1901-1988)
ENGLISH SCHOOL

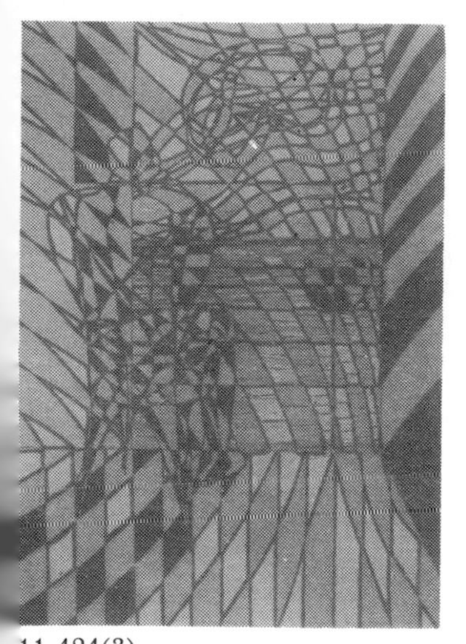

11,424(3)
'Still III', (from the first edition of Samuel Beckett's 'Still', 1974, see App. 8, no. 11,424)
Signed and dated in pencil 1973, 9/of 133
Published: M'Arte Edizioni, Milan, 1974
37.9 x 28.1 (plate 29.5 x 20.7)
Coloured Etching
Purchased, Dublin, The Neptune Gallery, 1975

Hayter, Stanley William (1901-1988)
English School
HAYTER, STANLEY WILLIAM (1901-1988)
ENGLISH SCHOOL

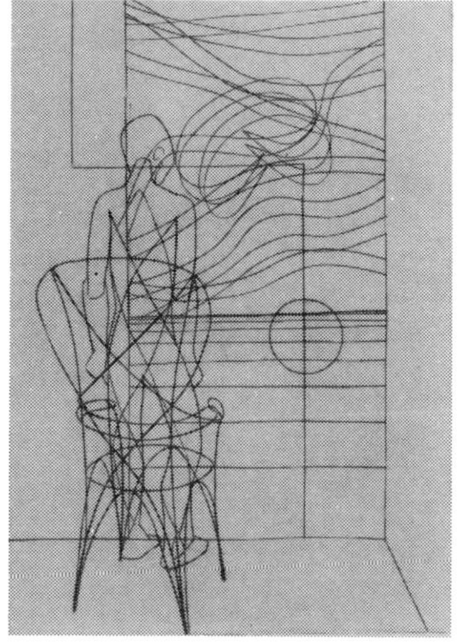

20,509
Study for 'Still I', (loose print included with NGI no. 11,424)
Signed and dated in pencil 1973 9/of 30
Published: M'Arte Edizioni, Milan, 1974
57 x 41 (plate 29.6 x 20.7)
Etching
Purchased, Dublin, The Neptune Gallery, 1975

Hayter, Stanley William (1901-1988)
English School
HAYTER, STANLEY WILLIAM (1901 1988)
ENGLISH SCHOOL

20,536
Study for 'Still II', (loose print included with NGI no. 11,424)
Signed and dated in pencil 1973, 9/of 30
Published: M'Arte Edizioni, Milan, 1974
57.4 x 40.6 (plate 29.8 x 21.5)
Etching
Purchased, Dublin, The Neptune Gallery, 1975

Hayter, Stanley William (1901-1988)
English School
HAYTER, STANLEY WILLIAM (1901-1988)
ENGLISH SCHOOL

20,829
Study for 'Still III', (loose print included with NGI no. 11,424)
Signed and dated in pencil 1973, 9/of 30
Published: M'Arte Edizioni, Milan, 1974
57.4 x 41.4 (plate 29.8 x 20.7)
Etching
Purchased, Dublin, The Neptune Gallery, 1975

Hearne, Thomas (1744-1817)
English School
POUNCY, BENJAMIN THOMAS (1772-1799)
ENGLISH SCHOOL

20,389

'In a Lane at Kenilworth', (with Kenilworth Castle), Warwickshire
Published: W. Lowry, (for W. Alexander), London, 2nd June 1798
28 x 35.4 (plate cut)
Etching
Purchased, Lusk, Mr de Courcy Donovan, 1971

Heemskerk, Marten (1498-1574)
Haarlem School
HEEMSKERK, MARTEN (1498-1574)
HAARLEM SCHOOL

20,710(1)
The Creation of Eve and the Temptation in the Garden, (from 'Heemskerck Engravings', see App. 8, no. 20,710)
Originally issued 1548
24.7 x 19.2 (plate cut)
Line
Provenance Unknown

Heffernan, Edward (19th century)
Irish School
IRISH SCHOOL (1868)

11,885
Dublin and its suburbs
Published: E. Heffernan, Dublin, 1st June 1868
56.6 x 72.6 (plate cut)
Line with varnish
Provenance Unknown

Details from no. 11,885

Heffernan, Edward (19th century)
Irish School
IRISH SCHOOL (1868)

11,885(1)
The Bank of Ireland, College Green, Dublin (former Parliament House)

Heffernan, Edward (19th century)
Irish School
IRISH SCHOOL (1868)

11,885(2)
The Chief Secretary's Lodge, Phoenix Park, Dublin, (now the residence of the American Ambassador)

Heffernan, Edward (19th century)
Irish School
IRISH SCHOOL (1868)

11,885(3)
The Custom House, Dublin

Heffernan, Edward (19th century)
Irish School
IRISH SCHOOL (1868)

11,885(4)
Dublin and Islandbridge from Phoenix Park

Heffernan, Edward (19th century)
Irish School
IRISH SCHOOL (1868)

11,885(5)
Dublin and Wicklow Railway Terminus, Harcourt Street, (now disused)

Heffernan, Edward (19th century)
Irish School
IRISH SCHOOL (1868)

11,885(6)
Dublin Castle Chapel and Record Tower

Heffernan, Edward (19th century)
Irish School
IRISH SCHOOL (1868)

11,885(7)
Upper Yard, Dublin Castle

Heffernan, Edward (19th century)
Irish School
IRISH SCHOOL (1868)

11,885(8)
Dublin from the Royal Hospital, Kilmainham

Heffernan, Edward (19th century)
Irish School
IRISH SCHOOL (1868)

11,885(9)
The Four Courts, Dublin

Heffernan, Edward (19th century)
Irish School
IRISH SCHOOL (1868)

11,885(10)
The General Post Office, Sackville Street, (now O'Connell Street), Dublin

Heffernan, Edward (19th century)
Irish School
IRISH SCHOOL(1868)

11,885(11)
The Great Southern and Western Railway Terminus, King's Bridge, (now Heuston Station), Dublin

Heffernan, Edward (19th century)
Irish School
IRISH SCHOOL (1868)

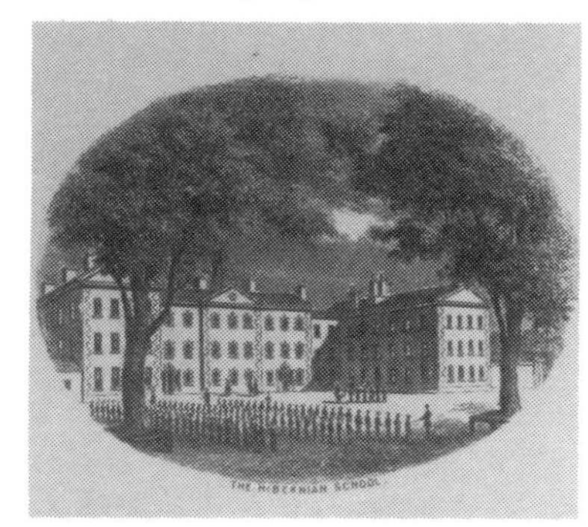

11,885(12)
The Hibernian School, (later St Mary's Hospital), Phoenix Park, Dublin

Heffernan, Edward (19th century)
Irish School
IRISH SCHOOL (1868)

11,885(13)
The River Liffey and Four Courts, Dublin from Ussher's Quay

Heffernan, Edward (19th century)
Irish School
IRISH SCHOOL (1868)

11,885(14)
The King's Inns, Dublin

Heffernan, Edward (19th century)
Irish School
IRISH SCHOOL (1868)

11,885(15)
The Rotunda Hospital and Assembly Rooms, (now the Gate Theatre), Dublin

Heffernan, Edward (19th century)
Irish School
IRISH SCHOOL (1868)

11,885(16)
The Royal Bank, (now Allied Irish Bank), Foster Place, Dublin

Heffernan, Edward (19th century)
Irish School
IRISH SCHOOL (1868)

11,885(17)
The Royal College of Surgeons, Dublin

Heffernan, Edward (19th century)
Irish School
IRISH SCHOOL (1868)

11,885(18)
The Royal Hospital, Kilmainham, Dublin

Heffernan, Edward (19th century)
Irish School
IRISH SCHOOL (1868)

11,885(19)
St Patrick's Cathedral, Dublin from the North West

Heffernan, Edward (19th century)
Irish School
IRISH SCHOOL (1868)

11,885(20)
Sackville, (now O'Connell), Street, Dublin with the General Post Office and Nelson Pillar, (now demolished)

Heffernan, Edward (19th century)
Irish School
IRISH SCHOOL (1868)

11,885(21)
Trinity College, Campanile, Dining Hall and Front Square

Heffernan, Edward (19th century)
Irish School
IRISH SCHOOL (1868)

11,885(22)
The Vice-Regal Lodge, (Lord Lieutenant's Residence, now Aras an Uachtaráin), Phoenix Park, Dublin

Heigeleg (19th century)
French School
FRENCH SCHOOL (1868)

20,087
Emilie
Published: Ostervale Ainé et Rittner, Paris, 1868 (Printed: Villain)
52.8 x 35.5 (image cut)
Lithograph
Provenance Unknown

Heil, Daniel van (1604-c.1662)
Flemish School
CAUKERCKEN, CORNELIS VAN (C.1625-1680)
FLEMISH SCHOOL

20,667(37)
Pieter Snayers, (1592-1667), (from 'The Portraits of the Most Eminent Painters and Other Famous Artists', 1739, see App. 8, no. 20,667)
Published: O. Payne also W.H. Toms, London, 1739
30.5 x 23.6 (plate 18 x 14.5)
Line
Provenance Unknown

Hellenistic School (1st century)
BOUILLON, PIERRE (1776-1831)
FRENCH SCHOOL
BERVIC (1756-1822)
FRENCH SCHOOL

20,683(59)
The Laocoon, (from 'Musée Francais - Statues', see App. 8, no. 20,683)
(after the classical marble, Vatican Museums, Rome)
Published: A. & W. Galignani, Paris also J.O. Robinson, London, 1807
(Printed: J. Didot L'Ainé, Paris)
61.5 x 44 (plate 42.3 x 31.5)
Line and etching
Provenance Unknown

Hellenistic School (1st century)
ENGLISH SCHOOL (1809)

20,653
The Laocoon
(after the classical marble, Vatican Museums, Rome)
Published: Boydell & Co., London, March 1809
38 x 26 (plate cut)
Stipple Engraving
Presented, Mrs D. Molloy, 1981

Henderson, John (1754-1845)
Irish School
FINDEN, WILLIAM (1787-1852)
ENGLISH SCHOOL

20,367
Lancaster and the River Lune, Lancashire, (pl. for E. Bain's 'History of Lancaster', 1836)
Lettered Proof
Published: Fisher, Son & Co., London, 1831
24.8 x 32.4 (plate 17.8 x 24.5)
Steel Engraving
Purchased, Lusk, Mr de Courcy Donovan, 1971

Herbert, James Dowling (1762/63-1837)
Irish School
BROCAS THE ELDER, HENRY (1766-1838)
IRISH SCHOOL

10,291

Luke Gardiner, 1st Viscount Mountjoy, (1745-1798), Colonel of the Dublin Militia
INSCRIBED: *To the County of Dublin Militia/This Print is Humbly Inscribed by their Obliged Servt./J. Dowling*
Published: J. Dowling, Dublin, 20th July 1798
26.5 x 19.2 (plate 25.2 x 17.6)
Stipple
Purchased, Dublin,
Mr J.V. McAlpine, 1911

Herbert, James Dowling (1762/63-1837)
Irish School
HUFFAM, T.W. (FL.1825-C.1855)
ENGLISH SCHOOL

10,633
Henry Jackson, United Irishman, (pl. for R. Madden's 'United Irishmen', 2nd series, 1843)
(after a watercolour miniature, Civic Museum, Dublin)
Published: Madden & Co., London, 1843
19.7 x 12.3 (plate cut)
Etching and mezzotint
Purchased, Dublin, Mr P. Traynor, 1898

Herbert, James Dowling (1762/63-1837)
Irish School
HUFFAM, T.W. (FL.1825-C.1855)
ENGLISH SCHOOL

10,671
Dr William James MacNeven, (1763-1841), (pl. for R. Madden's 'United Irishmen', 2nd series, 1843)
(after a drawing)
Published: Madden & Co., London, 1843
13.2 x 20.6 (plate cut)
Mezzotint
Purchased, Dublin, Mr P. Traynor, 1898

Herbert, James Dowling (1762/63-1837)
Irish School
HUFFAM, T.W. (FL.1825-C.1855)
ENGLISH SCHOOL

11,169
Thomas Addis Emmet, (1764-1827), Lawyer, United Irishman, brother of Robert, (pl. for R. Madden's 'United Irishmen', 2nd series, 1843)
(after a drawing of 1798)
Published: Madden & Co., London, 1843
21 x 12.4 (plate cut)
Mezzotint
Purchased, Dublin, Mr P. Traynor, 1898

Herbert, James Dowling (1762/63-1837)
Irish School
HUFFAM, T.W. (FL.1825-C.1855)
ENGLISH SCHOOL

11,170
Thomas Addis Emmet, (1764-1827), Lawyer, United Irishman and brother of Robert, (pl. for R. Madden's 'United Irishmen', 2nd series, 1843), (another copy)
(after a drawing of 1798)
Published: Madden & Co., London, 1843
21 x 24 (plate cut)
Mezzotint
Purchased, Dublin, Mr P. Traynor, 1898

Herbert, James Dowling (1762/63-1837)
Irish School
IRISH SCHOOL (1809)

10,589
Arthur O'Connor, M.P., (1763-1852), United Irishman and brother of Roger O'Connor, (pl. for 'Irish Magazine', April, 1809)
Published: Irish Magazine, Dublin, April 1809
20.8 x 12.6 (plate cut)
Stipple
Purchased, Dublin, Mr P. Traynor, 1898

Herbert, James Dowling (1762/63-1837)
Irish School
WARD THE ELDER, WILLIAM (1766-1826)
ENGLISH SCHOOL

:0,067
Arthur O'Connor, M.P., (1763-1852), United Irishman
Published: J.D. Herbert, London, 8th April 1798
38.6 x 28.9 (plate 38 x 28)
Mezzotint
Purchased, Dublin, Mrs Noseda, 1882

Herbert, John Rogers (1810-1890)
English School
SHENTON THE ELDER, HENRY CHAWNER (1803-1866)
ENGLISH SCHOOL

20,583
Olden Hospitality, (pl. for S.C. Hall's 'Gems of European Art', 1846)
Published: S.C. Hall, London
15.9 x 23.1 (plate cut)
Steel Engraving
Presented, Mrs D. Molloy, 1981

Hickey, John (1756-1795)
Irish School
WARD, JAMES (1769-1859)
ENGLISH SCHOOL

10,435
Edmund Burke, M.P., (1729-1797), Statesman and Writer
(after a marble bust, RA 1785 or 1791)
Published: J. Hickey, London
54.5 x 40 (plate 50.7 x 35.5)
Mezzotint
Purchased, Dublin, Mr J.V. McAlpine, 1899

Hickey, Thomas (1741-1824)
Irish School
HALL, JOHN (1739-1797)
ENGLISH SCHOOL

10,952
George Macartney, 1st Earl Macartney, (1737-1806), former Chief Secretary for Ireland and Ambassador to Russia and China, (frontispiece for Sir G. Staunton's 'An authentic account of the Embassy from the King of Great Britain to the Emperor of China', 1797)
(after an oil, RA 1792)
Published: G. Nichol, London, 12th April 1796
37 x 28 (plate 30.5 x 24.7)
Line
Acquired by 1901

Hickey, Thomas (1741-1824)
Irish School
HALPIN, PATRICK (FL.1755-1787)
IRISH SCHOOL

10,091
Charles Lucas, M.P., (1713-1771), Libertarian
(after an oil, Royal College of Physicians in Ireland, Dublin)
Published: P. Halpin, Dublin, 1711
33.7 x 24.8 (plate 32.8 x 23.9)
Line
Acquired between 1890/98

Hicks, George Elgar (fl.1848-1905)
English School
HICKS, GEORGE ELGAR (FL.1848-1905)
ENGLISH SCHOOL

20,181
Figure Studies, (from G.E. Hicks's 'Rustic Figures', ?1850)
Published: G. Rowney, London
(Printed: M. & N. Hanhart)
27.2 x 37.5 (image 22.2 x 29.2)
Lithograph
Purchased, Lusk, Mr de Courcy Donovan, 1971

Highmore, Joseph (1692-1780)
English School
FABER THE YOUNGER, JOHN (C.1684-1756)
ENGLISH SCHOOL

10,173
Abraham de Moivre, (1667-1754), Mathematician
(after an oil of 1736, Royal Society, London)
Published: J. Faber the Younger, London, also J. Brooks, Dublin c.1741
37.3 x 25.1 (plate 32.7 x 22.6)
Mezzotint
Acquired by 1903

Highmore, Joseph (1692-1780)
English School
HOPWOOD THE ELDER, JAMES (1752-1819)
ENGLISH SCHOOL

11,168
Thomas Emlyn, (1663-1744), first Unitarian Minister in England
14.2 x 19.3 (plate cut)
Stipple
Purchased, Dublin, Mr J.V. McAlpine, 1909

Highmore, Joseph (1692-1780)
English School
VANDERGUCHT, G. (1696-1776)
ANGLO-FLEMISH SCHOOL

10,282
Thomas Emlyn, (1663-1741), 1st Unitarian Minister in England, (frontispiece for his 'Sermons', 1742)
Published: not before 1741
24.9 x 13.7 (plate 19 x 11.1)
Line
Presented, Mr Shannon Millin, 1915

Hill, David Octavius (1802-1870)
Scottish School
FORREST, WILLIAM (1805-1889)
SCOTTISH SCHOOL

20,461
Auld Brig of Doon Bridge, Ayr, Scotland, (pl. for J. Wilson's & R. Chamber's 'The Land of Burns', 1840)
Published: Blackie & Son, Glasgow
(Printed: W. & D. Duncan)

22 x 28.4 (plate cut)
Steel Engraving
Purchased, Lusk, Mr de Courcy Donovan, 1971

Hill, David Octavius (1802-1870)
Scottish School
JEAVONS, THOMAS (C.1800-1867)
ENGLISH SCHOOL

20,460
Ellisland, near Dumfries, Scotland, (pl. for J. Wilson's & R. Chamber's 'The Land of Burns', 1840)
Published: Blackie & Son, Glasgow (Printed: W. & D. Duncan)
22.2 x 28.5 (plate cut)
Steel Engraving
Purchased, Lusk, Mr de Courcy Donovan, 1971

Hill, David Octavius (1802-1870)
Scottish School
RICHARDSON, WILLIAM (FL.1840-1877)
ENGLISH SCHOOL

:0,282
Barskimming on the River Ayr, Scotland', pl. for J. Wilson & R. Chamber's 'The Land of Burns', 1840)
Published: Blackie & Son, Glasgow, 1840 (Printed: W. & D. Duncan)
2.5 x 28.5 (plate cut)
Steel Engraving
Purchased, Lusk, Mr de Courcy Donovan, 1971

Hill, Thomas (1661-1734)
English School
WILLIAMS, ROBERT (FL.1680-1704)
ENGLISH SCHOOL

10,199
Godert de Ginkel, 1st Earl of Athlone, (1630-1703), Williamite General
Published: R. Williams, London, not before 1692
33.6 x 24.8 (plate cut)
Mezzotint
Purchased, London 2nd Chaloner Smith sale, 1888

Hills, Robert (1769-1844)
English School *and*
Robson, George Fennell (1788-1833)
English School
GIBBON, BENJAMIN PHELPS (1802-1851)
ENGLISH SCHOOL *and*
WEBB, EDWARD (1805-1854)
ENGLISH SCHOOL

20,362
Red Deer in the Pass of Glencoe, Scotland
Published: C. Tilt, London, 1833
38.1 x 27.8 (plate 25.3 x 18.9)
Steel Engraving
Purchased, Lusk, Mr de Courcy Donovan, 1971

Hills, T. (19th century)
English School
TYRRELL, EDWIN (19TH CENTURY)
ENGLISH SCHOOL

20,212
'The Cottage Door'
(after a drawing)
Published: N. Hailes, also Westley & Davis, London
16.4 x 10.2 (plate cut)
Steel Engraving
Purchased, Lusk, Mr de Courcy Donovan, 1971

Hincks, William (fl.1773-1797)
Irish School
HINCKS, WILLIAM (FL.1773-1797)
IRISH SCHOOL

11,637

Exterior of the Linen Hall, (now demolished), Dublin, (pl. XII from a set of prints describing the manufacture of Linen, first published 1782)
INSCRIBED: *To the very respectable the linen merchants and manufacturers of Ireland,/the conductors of that great and beneficial staple of our country;/this perspective view of the Linen Hall in Dublin,/with the boxes and bales of linen ready for exportation, the emblems of their industry/is dedicated by their obedient servant,/Wm. Hicks*
Published: R. Pollard, London, 20th June 1791
37.2 x 46 (plate 35 x 42.6)
Stipple
Provenance Unknown

Hoare, William (1706-1799)
English School
BROOKS, JOHN (FL.1730-1756)
IRISH SCHOOL

10,418
Philip Dormer Stanhope, 4th Earl of Chesterfield, (1694-1733), Lord Lieutenant of Ireland, in the robes of a Knight of the Garter
INSCRIBED: *This Plate is most humbly Dedicated to His Excellency,/By his Excellency, Most dutifull and Most Obedient servant John Brooks*
Published: J. Brooks, Dublin, November 1745
51.8 x 37.5 (plate 50.2 x 35.2)
Mezzotint
Acquired between 1890/98

Hoare, William (1706-1799)
English School
HOARE, WILLIAM (1706-1799)
ENGLISH SCHOOL

11,230
Hugh Percy, 2nd Earl of Northumberland, (1714-1786), Lord Lieutenant of Ireland, later 1st Duke of Northumberland
Published: R. Wilkinson, London, ?1764
10.2 x 7.6 (plate cut)
Etching
Purchased, Dublin, Mr P. Traynor, 1898

Hoare, William (1706-1799)
English School
HOUSTON, RICHARD (1721-1775)
IRISH SCHOOL

11,068
William Pitt the Elder, M.P., (1708-1778), Statesman, later 1st Earl of Chatham
(after an oil of c.1754)
Published: R. Houston, London, price 5s
40.2 x 29 (plate 39.2 x 28)
Mezzotint
Purchased, London, 1st Chaloner Smith Sale, 1887

Hoare, William (1706-1799)
English School
HOUSTON, RICHARD (1721-1775) - portrait
IRISH SCHOOL
WHEATLEY, SAMUEL (FL.1744-1771) - lettering
IRISH SCHOOL

Philip EARL OF Chesterfield,
SPEECH

10,445
Portrait of Lord Lieutenant of Ireland, Philip Dormer Stanhope, 4th Earl of Chesterfield, (1694-1773), at the head of his Speech of 8 October 1745 to the Irish Parliament
(portrait after a pastel of c.1740, NGI no. 6309 or replica in V&A London)
54 x 43.4 (plate 51.5 x 35.2)
Line and mezzotint with print
Purchased, London, 1st Chaloner Smith sale, 1887

Hoare, William (1706-1799)
English School
McARDELL, JAMES (1728/29-1765)
IRISH SCHOOL

10,180
Arthur Dobbs, (1689-1765), Governor of North Carolina
Published: H. Jouret, London, 1753/65
35.5 x 25 (plate cut)
Mezzotint
Purchased, London, 1st Chaloner Smith sale, 1887

Hoare, William (1706-1799)
English School
MILLER, ANDREW (FL.1737-1763)
IRISH SCHOOL

0,186
hilip Dormer Stanhope, 4th Earl of hesterfield, (1694-1773)
after a pastel, c.1740, NGI no. 6309 r replica in V&A London)
ublished: A. Miller, Dublin, 1746
1.5 x 22.3 (plate cut)
Iezzotint
urchased, Dublin,
Ir J.V. McAlpine, 1901

Hoare, William (1707-1792)
English School
SIMON, JOHN (1675-1751)
ANGLO-FRENCH SCHOOL

10,184
Philip Dormer Stanhope, 4th Earl of Chesterfield, (1694-1773)
(after a pastel of c.1740, NGI no. 6309 or replica in V&A, London)
Unlettered Proof
Published: London, c.1740
40 x 27.2 (plate 34.7 x 24.8)
Mezzotint
Purchased, London, 2nd Chaloner Smith sale, 1888

Hodgetts, Robert M. (fl.1826-1837)
English School
HODGETTS, ROBERT M. (FL.1826-1837)
ENGLISH SCHOOL

10,968

Daniel O'Connell, M.P., (1775-1847), Statesman
Published: S. Hollyer, for the Proprietor, London, 1st December 1843 (Printed: S. Hawkins)
55.2 x 40 (plate 43.6 x 34.4)
Mezzotint
Purchased, London, Mr G. Lausen, 1895

Hogan, John (1800-1858)
Irish School
WALSH, NICHOLAS (1839-1877)
IRISH SCHOOL

20,655
Thomas Osborne Davis, (1814-1845), Poet and Politician
(after a marble sculpture of 1852, City Hall, Dublin)
Published: London, 1863
56.8 x 44.4 (image 51 x 28.2 approx)
Lithograph
Provenance Unknown

Hogarth, William (1697-1764)
English School
ENGLISH SCHOOL (C.1750)

11,557

Marriage à la Mode, plate 1 - Lord Squanderfield's house and the marriage contract for his son
(after an oil of 1743, NG, London)
Published: C. Bowles, also R. Sayers, also R. Wilkinson, London, c.1750
26.5 x 36.5 (plate 25.7 x 36.5)
Line
Provenance Unknown

Hogarth, William (1697-1764)
English School
ENGLISH SCHOOL (C.1750)

11,558
Marriage à la Mode, plate 2 - Shortly after the marriage
(after an oil of 1743, NG, London)
Published: C. Bowles, also R. Sayers, also R. Wilkinson, London, c.1750
26.8 x 36.8 (plate 25.5 x 36.8)
Line
Provenance Unknown

Hogarth, William (1697-1764)
English School
ENGLISH SCHOOL (C.1750)

11,559
Marriage à la Mode, plate 3 - The visit to the quack doctor by the Viscount and his mistress
(after an oil of 1743, NG, London)
Published: C. Bowles, also R. Sayers, also R. Wilkinson, London, c.1750
26.6 x 36.8 (plate 26.4 x 36.8)
Line
Provenance Unknown

Hogarth, William (1697-1764)
English School
ENGLISH SCHOOL (C.1750)

11,560
Marriage à la Mode, plate 4 - The Countess's morning levée
(after an oil of 1743, NG, London)
Published: C. Bowles, also R. Sayers, also R. Wilkinson, London, c.1750
26.4 x 37 (plate 25.8 x 37)
Line
Provenance Unknown

Hogarth, William (1697-1764)
English School
ENGLISH SCHOOL (C.1750)

11,561
Marriage à la Mode, plate 5 - The killing of the Viscount by the Countess's lover
(after an oil of 1743, NG, London)
Published: C. Bowles, also R. Sayers, also R. Wilkinson, London, c.1750
26.5 x 37 (plate 25.5 x 37)
Line
Provenance Unknown

Hogarth, William (1697-1764)
English School
ENGLISH SCHOOL (C.1750)

11,562
Marriage à la Mode, plate 6 - The suicide of the Countess
(after an oil of 1743, NG, London)
Published: C. Bowles, also R. Sayers, also R. Wilkinson, London, c.1750
26.5 x 37.5 (plate 26.1 x 37.5)
Line
Provenance Unknown

Hogarth, William (1697-1764)
English School
ENGLISH SCHOOL (1784)

11,186
James Caulfeild, 1st Earl of Charlemont, (1728-99), Art Patron, Commander-in Chief of the Irish Volunteers, (pl. for 'European Magazine', February 1784)
(after an oil of 1759-64, Smith College, Northampton, Mass.)
Published: European Magazine, London, February 1784
17.8 x 11 (plate cut)
Line
Purchased, Dublin, Mr P. Traynor, 1898

Hogarth, William (1697-1764)
English School
ENGLISH SCHOOL (1784)

11,187
James Caulfeild, 1st Earl of Charlemont, (1728-99), Art Patron, Commander-in-Chief of the Irish Volunteers, (pl. for 'European Magazine', February 1784), (another copy)
(after an oil of 1759-64, Smith College, Northampton, Mass.)
Published: European Magazine, London, February 1784
21 x 14 (plate 17.7 x 11.5)
Line
Purchased, Dublin, Mr P. Traynor, 1898

Hogarth, William (1697-1764)
English School
HAYNES, JOSEPH (1760-1829)
ENGLISH SCHOOL

11,124
James Caulfeild, 1st Earl of Charlemont, (1728-1799), Art Patron
(after an oil of 1759-64, Smith College, Northampton, Mass.)
Unlettered Proof
Published: London, 1782
25.6 x 19.4 (plate 24.4 x 18)
Etching and stipple
Acquired by 1898

Hogarth, William (1697-1764)
English School
HOGARTH, WILLIAM (1697-1764)
ENGLISH SCHOOL

11,509
A Midnight Modern Conversation
(after an oil of c.1730, Paul Mellon Collection, U.S.A.)
3rd State
Published: W. Hogarth, London, not before 1732
41.5 x 54.3 (plate 34.3 x 47)
Line and etching
Presented, Mrs E. Bishop, 1942

Hogarth, William (1697-1764)
English School
HOGARTH, WILLIAM (1697-1764)
ENGLISH SCHOOL

11,510
Strolling actresses dressing in a Barn
(after an oil of 1737, destroyed)
4th State
Published: W. Hogarth, London, 25th March 1738
45.8 x 56.2 (plate cut)
Line and etching
Presented, Mrs E. Bishop, 1942

Hogarth, William (1697-1764)
English School
HOGARTH, WILLIAM (1697-1764)
ENGLISH SCHOOL

11,511
The First Stage of Cruelty, (Tom Nero torturing a dog in his youth)
(after a drawing, Paul Mellon Collection, U.S.A.)
Published: W. Hogarth, London, 1st February 1751, price 1s
40 x 35.7 (plate 38.2 x 32.4)
Line and etching
Presented, Mrs E. Bishop, 1942

Hogarth, William (1697-1764)
English School
HOGARTH, WILLIAM (1697-1764)
ENGLISH SCHOOL

11,512
The Second Stage of Cruelty, (Tom Nero beats his horse who has collapsed under the strain of the overcrowded coach)
(after a drawing, Pierpont Morgan Library, New York)
Published: W. Hogarth, London, 1st February 1751, price 1s

40 x 33.9 (plate 38.2 x 32.4)
Line and etching
Presented, Mrs E. Bishop, 1942

Hogarth, William (1697-1764)
English School
HOGARTH, WILLIAM (1697-1764)
ENGLISH SCHOOL

11,513
Cruelty in Perfection, (Tom Nero is caught for the murder of his mistress Ann Gill)
(after a drawing, Pierpont Morgan Library, New York)
Published: W. Hogarth, London, 1st February 1751, price 1s
40.1 x 34 (plate 38.2 x 32.4)
Line and etching
Presented, Mrs E. Bishop, 1942

Hogarth, William (1697-1764)
English School
HOGARTH, WILLIAM (1697-1764)
ENGLISH SCHOOL

11,514
The Reward of Cruelty, (Tom Nero's body is dissected after he has been hung)
(after a drawing, Pierpont Morgan Library, New York)
Published: W. Hogarth, London, 1st February 1751, price 1s
39.8 x 33.8 (plate 37.9 x 32)
Line and etching
Presented, Mrs E. Bishop, 1942

Hogarth, William (1697-1764)
English School
HOGARTH, WILLIAM (1697-1764)
ENGLISH SCHOOL

11,515
A Rake's Progress, Plate 3, (Rakewell at the Rose Tavern, Drury Lane)
(after an oil of 1733-34, Soane Museum, London)
3rd State
Published: W. Hogarth, London, 25th June 1735
43.7 x 54 (plate 35.4 x 40.7)
Line and etching
Presented, Mrs E. Bishop, 1942

Hogarth, William (1697-1764)
English School
HOGARTH, WILLIAM (1697-1764)
ENGLISH SCHOOL

11,516
A Rake's Progress, Plate 4, (Rakewell is rescued from the bailiffs outside St James' Palace by his former mistress)
(after an oil of 1733-34, Soane Museum, London)
2nd State
Published: W. Hogarth, London, 25th June 1735
43.4 x 55.5 (plate 35.7 x 40.5)
Line and etching
Presented, Mrs E. Bishop, 1942

Hogarth, William (1697-1764)
English School
HOGARTH, WILLIAM (1697-1764)
ENGLISH SCHOOL

11,517
A Rake's Progress, Plate 6, (Rakewell despairs having lost his wife's fortune gambling)
(after an oil of 1733-34, Soane Museum, London)
3rd State
Published: W. Hogarth, London, 25th June 1735
44.2 x 55 (plate 35.6 x 41)
Line and etching
Presented, Mrs E. Bishop, 1942

Hogarth, William (1697-1764)
English School
HOGARTH, WILLIAM (1697-1764)
ENGLISH SCHOOL

11,518

A Rake's Progress, Plate 7, (Rakewell is confined to the Fleet Debtors' Prison)
(after an oil of 1733-34, Soane Museum, London)
4th State
Published: W. Hogarth, London, 25th June 1735
43.3 x 51.2 (plate 35.6 x 41)
Line and etching
Presented, Mrs E. Bishop, 1942

Hogarth, William (1697-1764)
English School
HOGARTH, WILLIAM (1697-1764)
ENGLISH SCHOOL

11,519
A Rake's Progress, Plate 8, (Rakewell in a Mad House comforted by his mistress Sarah Young)
(after an oil of 1733-34, Soane Museum, London)
3rd State
Published: W. Hogarth, London, 1736
43.3 x 53.4 (plate 35.5 x 40.7)
Line and etching
Presented, Mrs E. Bishop, 1942

Hogarth, William (1697-1764)
English School
HOGARTH, WILLIAM (1697-1764)
ENGLISH SCHOOL

11,520
A Harlot's Progress, Plate 4, (Beating hemp in Bridewell Prison)
(after an oil of c.1731, destroyed)
1st State
Published: W. Hogarth, London, 1732
34 x 41 (plate 31.5 x 38.5)
Line and etching
Presented, Mrs E. Bishop, 1942

Hogarth, William (1697-1764)
English School
HOGARTH, WILLIAM (1697-1764)
ENGLISH SCHOOL

11,521
The Company of Undertakers, (Coat-of-Arms for Physicians)
2nd State
Published: W. Hogarth, London, 3rd March 1736, price 6d
26.9 x 18.6 (plate 26 x 17.8)
Line and etching
Presented, Mrs E. Bishop, 1942

Hogarth, William (1697-1764)
English School
MILLER, ANDREW (FL.1737-1763)
IRISH SCHOOL

10,436
Gustavus Hamilton, 2nd Viscount Boyle, (1710-1746)
(after an oil of 1735/40, Viscount Boyle Collection)
INSCRIBED: *To the Honble John Ponsonby Esq one of the Commissioners to his Majesty's Revenue in Ireland, this Plate is most humbly Dedicated by his honours/most obedient humble Servt./Andw. Miller*
Published: A. Miller, Dublin, not before 1743; price 2s 8.5d
51.2 x 36.6 (plate cut)
Mezzotint
Purchased, London, Mr H.A.J. Breun, 1910

Hogarth, William (1697-1764)
English School
MOORE, J. (FL.1831-1837)
ENGLISH SCHOOL

20,546

Satire on false perspective
(after a W. Hogarth/L. Sullivan line of 1754 from a lost drawing, c.1751)
INSCRIBED: *Whoever makes a design without the knowledge of perspective/Will be liable to such absurdities as are shown in this print*
18.8 x 13.5 (plate cut)
Line
Presented, Mrs D. Molloy, 1981

Holbrooke, William Henry (fl.1821-1848)
Irish School
HOLBROOKE, WILLIAM HENRY (FL.1821-1848)
IRISH SCHOOL

10,983
Daniel O'Connell, M.P., (1775-1847), Statesman, as Lord Mayor of Dublin
Published: W.H. Holbrooke, Dublin, 1842
46.5 x 32.7 (image 27.6 x 24.6)
Lithograph with watercolour
Purchased 1913

Holbrooke, William Henry (fl.1821-1848)
Irish School
HOLBROOKE, WILLIAM HENRY (FL.1821-1848)
IRISH SCHOOL

11,240
Daniel O'Connell, M.P., (1775-1847), Statesman, at the Bar of the House of Commons, refusing the Anti-Catholic declaration in 1829
(after a drawing)
Inscribed with handwritten Elegy for Daniel O'Connell by Richard Lalor Sheil
Published: W.H. Holbrooke, Dublin, not before 1832
24.8 x 19.8 (plate cut)
Line
Provenance Unknown

Holl the Younger, Frank (1845-1888)
English School
WEHRSCHMIDT, DANIEL ALBERT (1861-1932)
AMERICAN SCHOOL

11,855
Frederick Temple Blackwood, 1st Earl and later 1st Marquess of Dufferin and Ava, (1826-1902), Ambassador and Viceroy of India, (with etched remarque of a ship)
(after an oil, RA 1885)
Unlettered Proof
66.5 x 53.5 (plate 59.3 x 45.8)
Mezzotint (and etched remarque)
Presented, the sitter's widow, Harriet Georgina, Marchioness of Dufferin and Ava, 1902

Hollar, Wenceslaus (1607-1677)
Anglo-Czech School
HOLLAR, WENCESLAUS (1607-1677)
ANGLO-CZECH SCHOOL

20,763
The Execution of Thomas, Earl of Strafford, (1593-1641), on Tower Hill, London, 16th May 1641 (with key indicating Strafford and James Ussher, P. Archbishop of Armagh)
Published: W. Hollar, London, 1641
31.2 x 36.5 (plate 18.7 x 26.2)
Etching
Presented, Munich, Mr N. O'Siochain, 1985

Holmes, George (fl.1789-1804)
Irish School
WALKER, JAMES (1748-1808)
ENGLISH SCHOOL

11,689
Poolbeg Lighthouse, South Wall, Dublin Bay, (pl. for J. Walker's 'Union Magazine', May 1801)
Published: J. Walker, London, 1st May 1801
14.6 x 23 (plate 11 x 17.6)
Line
Provenance Unknown

Holmes, James (1777-1860)
English School
GAUCI, MAXIM (1775-1854)
ENGLISH SCHOOL

10,621
Arthur Marcus Cecil Hill, 3rd Baron Sandys, (1798-1863), son of the 2nd Marquess of Downshire
Unlettered Proof
18.7 x 16.9 (image 8.1 x 7.5)
Lithograph
Provenance Unknown

Home, Robert (1752-1834)
Irish School
BARTOLOZZI, FRANCESCO (1727-1815)
ANGLO-ITALIAN SCHOOL

0,692
'heobald Wolfe, (1710-1784), Barrister
after an oil of 1781)
NSCRIBED: From a picture in the Collection f Joseph Henry Esquire
'ublished: R. Livesay, London, 1785
7 x 21 (plate 26.8 x 21)
tipple
cquired by 1914

Home, Robert (1752-1834)
Irish School
BARTOLOZZI, FRANCESCO (1727-1815)
ANGLO-ITALIAN SCHOOL

10,693
Theobald Wolfe, (1710-1784), Barrister, (another copy)
(after an oil of 1781)
INSCRIBED: as no. 10,692
Published: R. Livesay, London, 1785
39.5 x 36.5 (plate 27 x 20.8)
Stipple
Acquired c.1903

Home, Robert (1752-1834)
Irish School
EVANS, WILLIAM (FL.1797-1856)
ENGLISH SCHOOL

11,085
Hugh Boyd, (1746-1794), Essayist
(after an oil)

Published: T. Cadell & W. Davies, London, 4th December 1799
23.6 x 13.7 (plate cut)
Stipple
Purchased, Dublin, Mr J.V. McAlpine, 1909

Home, Robert (1752-1834)
Irish School
?IRISH SCHOOL (18TH CENTURY)

10,931
William Molyneux, (1656-1698), Philosopher, Scientist and Politician
(after a wl oil of 1782-88, Examination Hall, Trinity College, Dublin)
Unlettered Proof
44.5 x 30.7 (plate 28.1 x 21.6)
Stipple and line
Purchased, Mr W.V. Daniell, 1901

Home, Robert (1752-1834)
Irish School
GREY, CHARLES (1808-1892)
IRISH SCHOOL
KIRKWOOD, JOHN (FL.1826-1853)
IRISH SCHOOL

11,254
James Ussher, P. Archbishop of Armagh, (1581-1656), (pl. for 'Dublin University Magazine', Vol. XVII, February 1841)
(after a drawing from an oil of 1782, Trinity College, Dublin)
Published: W. Curry Junior & Co., Dublin, 1841
21.6 x 14 (plate cut)
Etching
Purchased, Dublin, Mr P. Traynor, 1898

Home, Robert (1752-1834)
Irish School
RIDLEY, WILLIAM (1764-1888)
ENGLISH SCHOOL

11,084
Hugh Boyd, (1746-1794), Essayist, (pl. for 'European Magazine' May 1800)
(?after a drawing)
Published: J. Sewell, London, 1st May 1800
20.7 x 12.4 (plate 16 x 11.4)
Stipple
Purchased, Dublin, Mr J.V. McAlpine, 1909

Hone, Horace (1756-1825)
Irish School
BARTOLOZZI, FRANCESCO (1727-1815)
ANGLO-ITALIAN SCHOOL

10,309
Elizabeth, Countess of Lanesborough, (née La Touche, 1764-1788), wife of 3rd Earl
Published: E. Diemar, London, for H. Hone, Dublin, 12th August 1791
16.3 x 12.5 (plate cut)
Stipple
Bequeathed, Miss E. Hone, 1912

Hone, Horace (1756-1825)
Irish School
BARTOLOZZI, FRANCESCO (1727-1815)
ANGLO-ITALIAN SCHOOL

10,310
Mrs Sarah Siddons, (née Kemble, 1755-1831), Actress
(after a watercolour miniature of 1784, NGI no. 7318)
INSCRIBED: *Mrs Siddons from a picture/of the same size in the possession of/The Honble. Mrs O'Neill; to whom/this plate is most respectfully dedicated,/By her very obliged & most obedient humble servant/Horace Hone*
Published: F. Bartolozzi, London, (for H. Hone, Dublin), 1785
22.7 x 17.1 (plate cut)
Stipple
Bequeathed, Miss E. Hone, 1912

Hone, Horace (1756-1825)
Irish School
ENGLISH SCHOOL (1790)

11,322
Charles Manners, 4th Duke of Rutland, (1754-1787), former Lord Lieutenant of Ireland, (pl. for the 'Universal Magazine and Review', February 1790)
(after a watercolour miniature of 1787; NGI no. 2657 is a version in enamel)
Published: Universal Magazine and Review, London, February 1790
20.4 x 12.3 (plate 13.8 x 10.8)
Stipple
Acquired between 1913/14

Hone, Horace (1756-1825)
Irish School
HEATH, JAMES (1757-1834)
ENGLISH SCHOOL

10,742
James Caulfeild, 1st Earl of Charlemont, (1728-1799), Art Patron, (pl. for Sir J. Barrington's 'Historic Anecdotes and Secret Memoirs', 1809-15)
(after a miniature)
Published: G. Robinson, London, 1st June 1810
34.7 x 26.8 (plate 25.1 x 21.4)
Stipple
Acquired by 1898

Hone, Horace (1756-1825)
Irish School
HUFFAM T.W. (FL.1825-C.1855)
ENGLISH SCHOOL

11,137
Lord Edward FitzGerald, (1763-1798), Patriot, (pl. for R. Madden's 'United Irishmen', 2nd Series, 1843)
(after a watercolour miniature of c.1797, NPG, London; possibly from an H.D. Hamilton oil of 1796-98, NGI no. 195)
2nd State
Published: Madden & Co., London, 1843
21 x 12.5 (plate cut)
Mezzotint
Purchased, Dublin, Mr P. Traynor, 1898

Hone, Horace (1756-1825)
Irish School
HUFFAM, T.W. (FL.1825-C.1855)
ENGLISH SCHOOL

11,138
Lord Edward FitzGerald, (1763-1798), Patriot, (pl. for R. Madden's 'United Irishmen', 2nd Series, 1843)
(after a watercolour miniature of c.1797, NPG, London; possibly from an H.D. Hamilton oil of 1796-98, NGI no. 195)
1st State
Published: Madden & Co., London, 1843
21 x 12.5 (plate cut)
Mezzotint
Purchased, Dublin, Mr P. Traynor, 1898

Hone, Horace (1756-1825)
Irish School
MEYER, HENRY (C.1782-1847)
ENGLISH SCHOOL

10,833
James Gandon, (1743-1823), Architect, against the Custom House, Dublin, (frontispiece for T. Mulvany's 'The Life of James Gandon', 1846)
(after a watercolour miniature, NGI no. 2157)
36.3 x 25.4 (plate 23.3 x 18.4)
Stipple and etching
Bequeathed, Miss E. Hone, 1912

Hone, Horace (1756-1825)
Irish School
MEYER, HENRY HOPPNER (1783-1847)
ENGLISH SCHOOL

11,153
James Gandon, (1743-1823), Architect, (pl. for T. Mulvany's 'The Life of James Gandon', 1846)
(after a watercolour miniature, NGI no. 2157)
22.4 x 17.8 (plate 21.5 x 17)
Line and stipple
Bequeathed, Miss E. Hone, 1912

Hone, Horace (1756-1825)
Irish School
NUGENT, THOMAS (FL.1785-1798)
IRISH SCHOOL

10,743
James Caulfeild, 1st Earl of Charlemont, (1728-1799), Art Patron
(after a miniature)
Published: T. Nugent, (for H. Hone, Dublin), London, 1st February 1790
29.7 x 23.1 (plate 23.3 x 17.3)
Stipple
Provenance Unknown

Hone, Horace (1756-1825)
Irish School
NUGENT, THOMAS (FL.1785-1798)
IRISH SCHOOL

11,123
James Caulfeild, 1st Earl of Charlemont, (1728-1799), Art Patron, (another copy)
(after a miniature)
Published: T. Nugent, (for H. Hone, Dublin), London, 1st February 1790
23.6 x 17.7 (plate 23.3 x 17.3)
Stipple
Bequeathed, Miss E. Hone, 1912

Hone, Horace (1756-1825)
Irish School
SMITH, BENJAMIN (1775-1833)
ENGLISH SCHOOL

10,744
James Caulfeild, 1st Earl of Charlemont, (1728-1799), Art Patron, (pl. for T. Cadell & W. Davies's 'Contemporary Portraits', 1822)
(after a miniature)
Published: T. Cadell & W. Davies, London, 27th January 1814
44.8 x 53.3 (plate 37.8 x 32.7)
Stipple
Bequeathed, Miss E. Hone, 1912

Hone, Horace (1756-1825)
Irish School
SMITH, BENJAMIN (1775-1833)
ENGLISH SCHOOL

10,745
James Caulfeild, 1st Earl of Charlemont, (1728-1799), Art Patron, (pl. for T. Cadell & W. Davies' 'Contemporary Portraits', 1822), (another copy)
(after a miniature)
Published: T. Cadell & W. Davies, London, 27th January 1814
40.3 x 32.8 (plate 37.5 x 32.6)
Stipple
Acquired by 1898

Hone, Horace (1756-1825) - portrait
Irish School
B..., A. (19th century) - floral surround
English School
PHILLIPS, G.F. (FL.1815-1832) - portrait
ENGLISH SCHOOL
LEVENS T. (19TH CENTURY) - floral surround
ENGLISH SCHOOL

10,308
Mrs Sarah Siddons, (née Kemble, 1755-1831), Actress
(after a Hone enamel miniature, not located, copied from watercolour miniature, NGI no. 7318, of 1784)
INSCRIBED: *From a miniature in enamel in the Publishers Possession taken by the late H. Hone Esqr./Miniature Painter to His Majesty, shortly after Mrs. S.'s Debut*
Published: A. Bengo, London, 28th September 1825
20.5 x 14 (plate cut)
Stipple
Bequeathed, Miss E. Hone, 1912

?Hone the Elder, Nathaniel (1718-1784)
Irish School
BAILLIE, WILLIAM (1723-1810)
IRISH SCHOOL

10,225
Captain William Baillie, (1723-1810), Engraver and Connoisseur
38.8 x 41.4 (plate 31.5 x 33.7)
Stipple
Purchased, Dublin, Mr A. Roth, 1896

Hone the Elder, Nathaniel (1718-1784)
Irish School
BAILLIE, WILLIAM (1723-1810)
IRISH SCHOOL

10,532
'The Piping Boy' - John Camillus Hone, (1759-1836), son of the Artist
(after an oil, RA 1769; NGI no. 440)
Published: ?W. Baillie, London, 1st May 1771
29.3 x 22.5 (plate cut)
Mezzotint
Bequeathed, Miss E. Hone, 1912

Hone the Elder, Nathaniel (1718-1784)
Irish School
BAILLIE, WILLIAM (1723-1810)
IRISH SCHOOL

10,942
John Stuart, Baron Mountstuart, (1744-1814), later 1st Marquess of Bute
(after an oil) *2nd State*
Published: ?W. Baillie, London, 20th October 1779
29.6 x 21.1 (plate 28.2 x 19.5)
Stipple with watercolour
Bequeathed, Miss E. Hone, 1912

Hone the Elder, Nathaniel (1718-1784)
Irish School
BAILLIE, WILLIAM (1723-1810)
IRISH SCHOOL

10,944
John Stuart, Baron Mountstuart, (1744-1814), later 1st Marquess of Bute, 1st State
(after an oil)
Published: ?W. Baillie, London, 20th October 1779
28.4 x 20 (plate 28.2 x 19.5)
Stipple in red
Bequeathed, Miss E. Hone, 1912

Hone the Elder, Nathaniel (1718-1784)
Irish School
BAILLIE, WILLIAM (1723-1810)
IRISH SCHOOL

10,945
John Stuart, Baron Mountstuart, (1744-1814), later 1st Marquess of Bute 1st State
(after an oil)
Published: ?W. Baillie, London, 20th October 1779
27.9 x 19.8 (plate cut)
Stipple
Bequeathed, Miss E. Hone, 1912

Hone the Elder, Nathaniel (1718-1784)
Irish School
COOK, G. (FL.1840S)
ENGLISH SCHOOL

11,377

Madame Anna Zamparini, (b.?1754), Singer as Cecchina in N. Piccini's 'La Buona Figliuola', (pl. in stipple for J. Jesse's 'Memoirs of George Selwyn and his Contemporaries', 1843)
(after J. Finlayson's mezzotint of 1769, NGI no. 11,386)
Published: R. Bentley, London, 1843
29.2 x 20.4 (plate 23.2 x 14.6)
Line
Bequeathed, Miss E. Hone, 1912

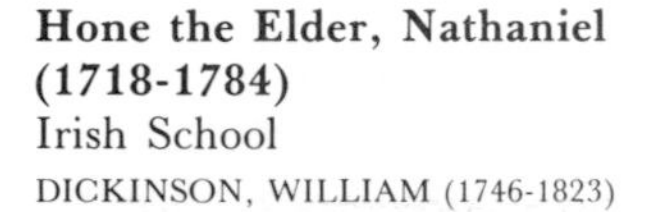

Hone the Elder, Nathaniel (1718-1784)
Irish School
DICKINSON, WILLIAM (1746-1823)
ENGLISH SCHOOL

11,002
Sir George Nares, (1716-1786), Justice of the Court of Common Pleas
Published: W. Dickinson, London, 10th April 1776
60 x 45.8 (plate 50.5 x 35.5)
Mezzotint
Bequeathed, Miss E. Hone, 1912

Hone the Elder, Nathaniel (1718-1784)
Irish School
ENGLISH SCHOOL (LATE 18TH CENTURY)

11,256
Rev. George Whitefield, (1714-1770), Methodist Preacher
(after a N. Hone/J. Greenwood mezzotint, NGI no. 10,680 of c.1769)
Published: Bowles and Carver, London
17.2 x 13.4 (plate 15.2 x 11.6)
Mezzotint
Bequeathed, Miss E. Hone, 1912

Hone the Elder, Nathaniel (1718-1784)
Irish School
FINLAYSON, JOHN (C.1730-C.1776)
ENGLISH SCHOOL

10,353
Eleanor or Mary Metcalfe, (b.1767/68), grand-daughter of the artist, with a Pomeranian dog, (commemorating their rescue from a burning house in Rome)
Published: J. Finlayson, London, 29th February 1772
55.5 x 41.2 (plate 50.3 x 35.5)
Mezzotint
Bequeathed, Miss E. Hone, 1912

Hone the Elder, Nathaniel (1718-1784)
Irish School
FINLAYSON, JOHN (C.1730-C.1776)
ENGLISH SCHOOL

10,933
Eleanor or Mary Metcalfe, (b.1767/68), grand-daughter of the artist, with a Pomeranian dog, (commemorating their rescue from a burning house in Rome), (another copy)
Published: J. Finlayson, London, 29th February 1772
51.5 x 37.7 (plate 50.3 x 35.3)
Mezzotint
Presented, Mrs C. Hone, 1925

Hone the Elder, Nathaniel (1718-1784)
Irish School
FINLAYSON, JOHN (C.1730-C.1776)
ENGLISH SCHOOL

11,386
Madame Anna Zamperini, (b.?1754), Singer, as Cecchina in N. Piccini's 'La Buona Figliuola'
(after an oil of 1767, Kedleston Hall, Derbyshire)
Published: H. Parker also J. Finlayson, London, 1st February 1769
34.3 x 27.8 (plate cut)
Mezzotint
Bequeathed, Miss E. Hone, 1912

Hone the Elder, Nathaniel (1718-1784)
Irish School
FISHER, EDWARD (1722-C.1785)
IRISH SCHOOL

0,070
elf-Portrait
after an oil of c.1747, NGI no. 1003)
ublished: London
6.2 x 27.2 (plate 32.8 x 23.4)
Mezzotint
Acquired between 1879/90

Hone the Elder, Nathaniel (1718-1784)
Irish School
FISHER, EDWARD (1722-C.1785)
IRISH SCHOOL

10,698
Self-Portrait (another copy)
(after an oil of c.1747, NGI no. 1003)
Published: London
37.5 x 27 (plate 32.8 x 23.4)
Mezzotint
Bequeathed, Miss E. Hone, 1912

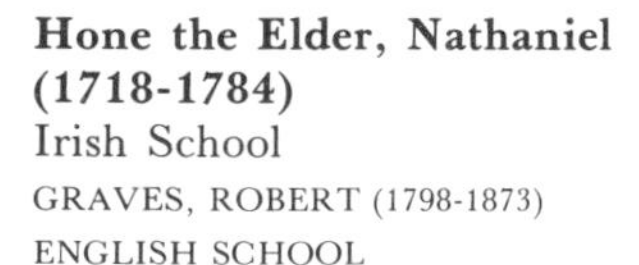

Hone the Elder, Nathaniel (1718-1784)
Irish School
GRAVES, ROBERT (1798-1873)
ENGLISH SCHOOL

11,277
James Turner, (born 1658), a beggar, aged 93, (pl. for J. Caulfield's 'Portraits, Memoirs and Characters of Remarkable Persons', 1820)
(after a miniature of 1751)
Published: J. Caulfield, London
17.6 x 12
Etching
Bequeathed, Miss E. Hone, 1912

Hone the Elder, Nathaniel (1718-1784)
Irish School
GREENWOOD, JOHN (1729-1792)
ANGLO-AMERICAN SCHOOL

10,329
Amelia Hone, the Artist's daughter, later Mrs Ambrose Rigg
Published: R. Sayer, London, 1st May 1771
39.2 x 27.1 (plate 35.2 x 25.3)
Mezzotint
Bequeathed, Miss E. Hone, 1912

Hone the Elder, Nathaniel (1718-1784)
Irish School
GREENWOOD, JOHN (1729-1792)
ANGLO-AMERICAN SCHOOL

10,680
Rev. George Whitefield, (1714-1770), Methodist preacher
(after an oil, SA 1768, destroyed 1943)
Published: Bowles & Carver, London, c.1769
35.8 x 25 (plate cut)
Mezzotint
Bequeathed, Miss E. Hone, 1912

Hone the Elder, Nathaniel (1718-1784)
Irish School
GREENWOOD, JOHN (1729-1792)
ANGLO-AMERICAN SCHOOL

10,695
Amelia Hone, the Artist's daughter, later Mrs Ambrose Rigg, (another copy)
Published: R. Sayer, London, 1st May 1771
36 x 25.6 (plate 35.5 x 25)
Mezzotint
Purchased, London, 1st Chaloner Smith sale, 1887

Hone the Elder, Nathaniel (1718-1784)
Irish School
GREENWOOD, JOHN (1729-1792)
ANGLO-AMERICAN SCHOOL

11,408
Lieut.-General the Hon. Philip Sherard, later 2nd Earl of Harborough, (1727-1790), accompanied by Captain William Tiffin, (d.1794) during the relief of a redoubt at the passage of the Brugher Muhl
(after an oil, RA 1782)
56 x 41 (plate 55.5 x 41)
Mezzotint
Bequeathed, Miss E. Hone, 1912

Hone the Elder, Nathaniel (1718-1784)
Irish School
HONE THE ELDER, NATHANIEL (1718-1784)
IRISH SCHOOL

10,072
Self-Portrait in a Fur Hat
(after an oil of 1747)
Published: N. Hone the Elder, London, 1747
35.6 x 25.1 (plate 35.3 x 25)
Mezzotint
Purchased, London, 1st Chaloner Smith sale, 1887

Hone the Elder, Nathaniel (1718-1784)
Irish School
HONE THE ELDER, NATHANIEL (1718-1784)
IRISH SCHOOL

11,276
James Turner, (born 1658), a beggar who valued his time at a shilling an hour, aged 93
(after a miniature of 1751)
Published: R. Wilkinson, London
15.6 x 15 (plate 5.8 x 5.4)
Etching
Bequeathed, Miss E. Hone, 1912

Hone the Elder, Nathaniel (1718-1784)
Irish School
HONE THE ELDER, NATHANIEL (1718-1784)
IRISH SCHOOL

11,848
'Monachum non facit cucullus' - Francis Grose, (1731-1791), Antiquary, Wit and Bon Viveur, with Theodosius Forrest, (1729-1784), Lawyer, Artist and Writer, as Capuchin Monks feasting at a table
(after an oil, RA 1770)
Published: N. Hone, London, 30th January 1772
36.7 x 46 (plate 36.4 x 45.6)
Mezzotint
Bequeathed, Miss E. Hone, 1912

Hone the Elder, Nathaniel (1718-1784)
Irish School
HUMPHREY, WILLIAM (C.1740-1795)
ENGLISH SCHOOL

0,696
The Spartan Boy' - John Camillus Hone, '1745-1836), son of the Artist
after an oil, RA 1775)
NSCRIBED: *Having stolen a Cub Fox, oncealed it under his garment, when being observ'd he suffer'd it to bite him mortally,/rather than undergo the disgrace of a discovery. 3rd State.* (Engraver given as W. Humphrey but probably J.R. Smith cf. no. 10,697).
Published: W. Humphrey, London, 18th July 1775
38.3 x 28 (plate 37.5 x 27.5)
Mezzotint
Purchased, London, 1st Chaloner Smith sale, 1887

Hone the Elder, Nathaniel (1718-1784)
Irish School
McARDELL, JAMES (1728/29-1765)
IRISH SCHOOL

10,755
Rev. Emmanuel Collins
33.8 x 23.5 (plate 32.7 x 22.8)
Mezzotint
Bequeathed, Miss E. Hone, 1912

Hone the Elder, Nathaniel (1718-1784)
Irish School
McARDELL JAMES (1728/29-1765)
ENGLISH SCHOOL

10,804
Sir John Fielding, (d.1780), Magistrate
(after an oil, ?SA 1762)
Published: Carey & Watson, London
29 x 28.5 (plate cut)
Mezzotint
Bequeathed, Miss E. Hone, 1919

Hone the Elder, Nathaniel (1718-1784)
Irish School
PHILLIPS, CHARLES (1737-AFTER 1783)
ENGLISH SCHOOL

10,378
Lydia Hone, (1760-1775), the Artist's eldest daughter
3rd State
Published: ?C. Phillips, London, 1771 (after 15th February)
43.3 x 31.6 (plate cut)
Mezzotint
Purchased, London, 1st Chaloner Smith sale, 1887

Hone the Elder, Nathaniel (1718-1784)
Irish School
PHILLIPS, CHARLES (1737-AFTER 1783)
ENGLISH SCHOOL

10,699
Lydia Hone, (1758-1773), the Artist's eldest daughter
4th State
Published: ?C. Phillips, London, 30th February 1771
43.6 x 32.1 (plate cut x 31.6)
Mezzotint
Purchased, London, 1st Chaloner Smith sale, 1887

Hone the Elder, Nathaniel (1718-1784)
Irish School
PICOT, VICTOR MARIE (1744-1805)
ANGLO-FRENCH SCHOOL

11,257
Rev. George Whitefield, (1714-1770), Methodist Preacher
(after an oil, SA 1768, destroyed 1943)
19.5 x 13.2 (plate 18 x 11.7)
Line
Bequeathed, Miss E. Hone, 1912

Hone the Elder, Nathaniel (1718-1784)
Irish School
POLLARD, ROBERT (1755-1838)
ENGLISH SCHOOL

10,777
General George Augustus Eliott, (1717-1790), later 1st Baron Heathfield, above a scene of the Siege of Gibraltar 1779-83
INSCRIBED: *From the original picture in the posession of William Fuller Esq.*
Published: T. Macklin, also R. Pollard, London, 29th October 1782
25.7 x 18.4 (plate cut)
Stipple
Bequeathed, Miss E. Hone, 1912

Hone the Elder, Nathaniel (1718-1784)
Irish School
PURCELL, RICHARD, (FL.1746-1766)
IRISH SCHOOL

10,322
Mrs Letitia Pilkington, (1712-1750, née Van Lewen), Adventuress and Author, (frontispiece for her book 'The Real Story of John Carteret Pilkington', 1760)
Published: London, c.1760
25.5 x 20 (plate cut x 19.5)
Mezzotint
Bequeathed, Miss E. Hone, 1912

Hone the Elder, Nathaniel (1718-1784)
Irish School
PURCELL, RICHARD (FL.1746-1766)
IRISH SCHOOL

11,069
Mrs Letitia Pilkington, (1712-1750, née Van Lewen), Adventuress and Author, (another copy)
Published: London, c.1760
26.3 x 19.5 (plate 26.3 x 19.5)

Mezzotint
Presented, Sir Walter Armstrong, 1892

Hone the Elder, Nathaniel (1718-1784)
English School
DANCE, NATHANIEL (1734-1811)
ENGLISH SCHOOL
RIDLEY, WILLIAM (1764-1838)
ENGLISH SCHOOL

11,157
Francis Grose, (1731-1791), Antiquarian and Watercolourist, (pl. for 'European Magazine', June 1797)
(after an N. Dance chalk drawing of 1787, SNPG, Edinburgh, from a lost oil)
Published: J. Sewell, London, 1st June 1797
21 x 12.9 (plate 20.5 x 12.1)
Stipple
Purchased, Dublin, Mr P. Traynor, 1898

Hone the Elder, Nathaniel (1718-1784)
Irish School
SMITH, JOHN RAPHAEL (1752-1812)
ENGLISH SCHOOL

10,330
Lydia Hone, (1760-1775), the Artist's eldest daughter
INSCRIBED: Her beauty hangs upon the cheek of Night, like a Rich Jewell in an Ethiops Ear
Published: R. Marshall, London, 1771
34.6 x 25.2 (plate cut x 25)
Mezzotint
Purchased, London, 2nd Chaloner Smith sale, 1888

Hone the Elder, Nathaniel (1718-1784)
Irish School
SMITH, JOHN RAPHAEL (1752-1812)
ENGLISH SCHOOL

10,697
'The Spartan Boy' - John Camillus Hone, (1745-1636), son of the Artist
(after an oil, RA 1775)
Published: T. Bradshaw also J.R. Smith, London, 18th July 1775
38 x 28 (plate 37.5 x 27.5)
Mezzotint
Bequeathed, Miss E. Hone, 1912

Hone the Elder, Nathaniel (1718-1784)
Irish School
SMITH, JOHN RAPHAEL (1752-1812)
ENGLISH SCHOOL

10,805
Sir John Fielding, (d.1780), Magistrate
(after an oil, ?SA 1762)
Published: J.R. Smith, London, 23rd November 1773
37.8 x 26.5 (plate cut)
Mezzotint
Bequeathed, Miss E. Hone, 1919

Hone the Elder, Nathaniel (1718-1784)
Irish School
SMITH, JOHN RAPHAEL (1752-1812)
ENGLISH SCHOOL

11,012
Rev. William Sclater, (d.1778), Rector of Bow Church, London
Published: W. Humphrey, London, 15th April 1777
39 x 28.7 (plate 38.3 x 27.7)
Mezzotint
Bequeathed, Miss E. Hone, 1912

Hone the Elder, Nathaniel (1718-1784)
Irish School
SMITH, JOHN RAPHAEL (1752-1812)
ENGLISH SCHOOL

11,414
'The Spartan Boy' - John Camillus Hone, (1745-1836), son of the Artist, (another copy)
(after an oil, RA 1775)
Published: T. Bradshaw also J.R. Smith, London, 18th July 1775
38 x 28 (plate 37.6 x 27.8)
Mezzotint
Presented, Mrs C. Hone, 1925

Hone the Elder, Nathaniel (1718-1784)
Irish School
WATSON, JAMES (C.1740-1790)
IRISH SCHOOL

10,068
'David the Shepherd Boy' - Horace Hone, (1756-1825), son of the Artist
(after an oil of 1771)
Unlettered Proof
Published: J. Bretherton, London, 1778
40.6 x 29.6 (plate 39 x 27.7)
Mezzotint
Purchased, London, 2nd Chaloner Smith sale, 1888

Hone the Elder, Nathaniel (1718-1784)
Irish School
WATSON, JAMES (C.1740-1790)
IRISH SCHOOL

10,139
The Brickdust Man
(after an oil, SA 1760)
Published: H. Parker & E. Bakewell, London
39.7 x 29.3 (plate 35 x 25.3)
Mezzotint
Bequeathed, Miss E. Hone, 1912

Hone the Elder, Nathaniel (1718-1784)
Irish School
WATSON, JAMES (C.1740-1790)
ENGLISH SCHOOL

10,700
'David the Shepherd Boy', - Horace Hone, (1756-1825), son of the Artist
(after an oil of 1771)
Published: J. Bretherton, London, 20th March 1778
38.6 x 27.8 (plate 38.4 x 27.6)
Mezzotint
Bequeathed, Miss E. Hone, 1912

Hone the Elder, Nathaniel (1718-1784)
Irish School
WATSON, JAMES (C.1740-1790)
ENGLISH SCHOOL

11,387
The Brickdust Man, (another copy)
(after an oil, SA 1760)
Published: H. Parker & E. Bakewell, London
33 x 25.4 (plate cut)
Mezzotint
Presented, Mrs C. Hone, 1925

Hook, James Clarke (1819-1907)
English School
WHYMPER, JOSIAH WOOD (1813-1903)
ENGLISH SCHOOL

20,630
A Dream of Ancient Venice
(after an oil, RA 1850)
20.2 x 18.2 (image 17.3 x 11.3)
Wood Engraving
Presented, Mrs D. Molloy, 1981

Hook, James Clarke (1819-1907)
English School
WHYMPER, JOSIAH WOOD (1813-1903)
ENGLISH SCHOOL

20,631
Market Morning
20.2 x 18.2 (image 11.1 x 16)
Wood Engraving
Presented, Mrs D. Molloy, 1981

Hooker, W.I. (19th century)
English School
HIGHAM, THOMAS (1796-1844)
ENGLISH SCHOOL

20,479
A cross at Paignton, Devon, (pl. for 'The Antiquarian Itinerary', 1817)
Published: W. Clarke, (for the Proprietors), London, 1st May 1817
14.2 x 22.5 (plate 10.3 x 15.5)
Line
Purchased, Lusk, Mr de Courcy Donovan, 1971

Hope, A. (19th century)
English School
GODBY, JAMES (FL.1790-1820)
ENGLISH SCHOOL

10,062
George Ponsonby, M.P., (1755-1817), Lord Chancellor of Ireland, (pl. for T. Cadell & W. Davies' 'Contemporary Portraits', 1822)
(after a drawing)
Published: T. Cadell and W. Davies, London, 11th February 1811
40.2 x 31.5 (plate 37.5 x 31.5)
Stipple
Purchased, Dublin, Mr J.V. McAlpine, 1899

Hoppner, John (1758-1810)
English School
CLINT, GEORGE (1770-1854)
ENGLISH SCHOOL

10,486
Sir Arthur Wellesley, (1769-1852), later 1st Duke of Wellington
(after an oil, RA 1806; Government House, Madras)

INSCRIBED: *From the original picture painted by order of the Civil and Military Servants of the Honble East India Company*
Published: T. Palser, London, 20th August 1814
77 x 49.5 (plate 69 x 45.5)
Mezzotint
Purchased, London, 1st Chaloner Smith sale, 1887

10,584
General Sir Ralph Abercromby, (1734-1801)
(after a wl oil, RA 1799; SNPG, Edinburgh)
20.6 x 11.5 (plate cut)
Stipple
Provenance Unknown

Hoppner, John (1758-1810)
English School
CLINT, GEORGE (1770-1854)
ENGLISH SCHOOL

11,070
William Pitt the Younger, M.P., (1759-1806), British Prime Minister
(after an oil of 1805)
Published: Colnaghi & Co., London, 20th January 1806
49 x 37.6 (plate 48 x 35.5)
Mezzotint
Provenance Unknown

Hoppner, John (1758-1810)
English School
EINSLIE, S. (FL.1785-1808)
ENGLISH SCHOOL

10,387
Ann Elizabeth, Countess of Aldborough, (née Henniker, fl.1788-1802), wife of the 2nd Earl
Published: S. Einslie, London, 1788
35.2 x 25.1 (plate 35 x 25)
Mezzotint
Purchased, London, 1st Chaloner Smith sale, 1887

10,386
Mrs Jordan, (née Dorothea Bland, 1762-1816), Actress, as Hypolita in Cibber's 'She Would and She Would Not'
(after an oil, RA 1791)
Published: J. Jones, London, 1st March 1791
41.3 x 30 (plate 38 x 27.8)
Mezzotint
Purchased, London, 1st Chaloner Smith sale, 1887

Hoppner, John (1758-1810)
English School
BARTOLOZZI, FRANCESCO (1727-1815)
ANGLO-ITALIAN SCHOOL
LANDSEER, HENRY (19TH CENTURY)
ENGLISH SCHOOL

10,949
Francis Rawdon, 2nd Earl of Moira, (1754-1826), later 1st Marquess of Hastings, as Acting Grand Master of the Freemasons

Hoppner, John (1758-1810)
English School
CLOSE THE ELDER, SAMUEL (FL.1770-1807)
IRISH SCHOOL

Hoppner, John (1758-1810)
English School
JONES, JOHN (1745-1797)
ENGLISH SCHOOL

INSCRIBED: *Dedicated by Permission to his Royal Highness George Prince of Wales &c., &c.,/By his Royal Highness obliged and obedient Servant Henry Landseer*
Published: G. Willanson, also H. Landseer, also Colnaghi, London, 20th February 1804
56.5 x 45.8 (plate cut)
Stipple
Purchased, 1907

Hoppner, John (1758-1810)
English School
PARK, THOMAS (C.1760-1834)
ENGLISH SCHOOL

10,408
Mrs Jordan, (née Dorothea Bland, 1762-1816), Actress, as Thalia the Comic Muse, supported by Euphrosyne, who represses the advances of a satyr
(after an oil, RA 1786; Royal Collection, Buckingham Palace
Published: T. Park, London, 1st August 1787
78.8 x 50 (plate 70 x 49)
Mezzotint
Purchased, London, 1st Chaloner Smith sale, 1887

Hoppner, John (1758-1810)
English School
PARK, THOMAS (C.1760-1834)
ENGLISH SCHOOL

11,415
Lord Henry FitzGerald, (1761-1829), Son of the 1st Duke of Leinster, as Don Felix in T. Park's 'The Wonder'
(after an oil, RA 1789)
Published: T. Park, London, ?1789
37 x 28 (plate 35.6 x 26.8)
Mezzotint
Purchased, London, 1st Chaloner Smith Sale, 1887

Hoppner, John (1758-1810)
English School
REYNOLDS THE ELDER, SAMUEL WILLIAM (1773-1835)
ENGLISH SCHOOL

10,469
Murrough O'Brien, 1st Marquess of Thomond, (1726-1808)
(after an oil, RA 1798)
Unlettered Proof
Published: Colnaghi and Co., London, 1808
53.8 x 38.5 (plate 50.5 x 35.3)
Mezzotint
Purchased, London, Mr H.A.J. Breun, 1909

Hoppner, John (1758-1810)
English School
TURNER, CHARLES (1773-1857)
ENGLISH SCHOOL

10,164
Vice-Admiral Sir Henry Blackwood, (1770-1832)
(after an oil of 1806, National Maritime Museum, Greenwich)
Published: C. Turner also Messrs. Colnaghi, Son & Co., London, 18th June 1833
45.2 x 35.1 (plate 35.7 x 25.5)
Mezzotint
Purchased, London, Mr G. Lausen, 1895

Hoppner, John (1758-1810)
English School
TURNER, CHARLES (1773-1857)
ENGLISH SCHOOL

10,453
Admiral Horatio Nelson, 1st Viscount Nelson, (1758-1805), against the Battle of Trafalgar
(after an oil of 1801-2, Royal Collection, St James's Palace)
Published: Colnaghi, London, 1806
70.5 x 47.7 (plate 64.1 x 41)
Mezzotint
Provenance Unknown

Hoppner, John (1758-1810)
English School
TURNER, CHARLES (1773-1857)
ENGLISH SCHOOL

10,812
John Fitzgibbon, 1st Earl of Clare, (1749-1802), Lord Chancellor of Ireland
Published: J. Jeffryes, London, 20th April 1802
40.4 x 28.7 (plate 35.4 x 25.1)
Mezzotint
Purchased, Dublin, Mr J.V. McAlpine, 1896

Hopson, Henry (fl.1780-1791)
Irish School
HOUSTON, H. H. (FL. C.1791)
IRISH SCHOOL

11,200
John Philpot Curran, (1750-1817), Orator and Master of the Rolls in Ireland, (pl. for 'Universal Magazine', February 1791)
Published: Universal Magazine, London, February 1791
21 x 12.7 (plate 15.6 x 10.5)
Stipple
Purchased, Dublin, Mr P. Traynor, 1898

Horsley, John Calcott (1817-1903)
English School
HARRAL, HORACE (FL.1862-1876)
ENGLISH SCHOOL

20,572
Checkmate - next move, (from 'The Illustrated London News', 1862)
(after an oil, RA 1862)
Published: Illustrated London News, 1862
25.3 x 36 (image 23.4 x 34)
Wood Engraving
Presented, Mrs D. Molloy, 1981

Howard, Hugh (1769-1847)
Irish School
EARLOM, RICHARD (1743-1822)
ENGLISH SCHOOL

10,431
Richard FitzWilliam, 7th Viscount FitzWilliam, (1745-1816), founder of the Fitzwilliam Museum Cambridge, Vice-Admiral of Leinster
(after a lost oil, copy in Fitzwilliam Museum, Cambridge)
Published: 1810
48.2 x 34 (plate 45.4 x 31.5)
Mezzotint
Purchased, London, 1st Chaloner Smith sale, 1887

Howard, Hugh (1675-1738)
Irish School
SMITH, JOHN (C.1652-1742)
ENGLISH SCHOOL

10,809

Arcangelo Corelli, (1653-1713), Composer and Violinist
(after an oil of c.1700, Royal Society of Musicians of Great Britain, London; NGI no. 773 is another version)
38 x 35.6 (plate 26.8 x 25)
Mezzotint
Provenance Unknown

Howard, Hugh (1675-1738)
Irish School
VANDERGUCHT, MICHAEL (1660-1725)
ANGLO-FLEMISH SCHOOL

10,729
Arcangelo Corelli, (1653-1713), Composer and Violinist
(after an oil of c.1700, Royal Society of Musicians of Great Britain, London; NGI no. 773 is another version)
30 x 22.5 (plate 25.7 x 18.6)
Line
Provenance Unknown

Howis the Elder, William (1804-1882)
Irish School
DICKINSON, LOWES (1819-1908)
ENGLISH SCHOOL

20,127
Sir James Dombrain, Inspector General of the Coast Guards in Ireland
(after an oil, RHA 1838)
Printed: C.J. Hullmandel
56 x 30 (image 29 x 23.4)
Lithograph
Purchased, Lusk, Mr de Coucry Donovan, 1971

Howis the Elder, William (1804-1882)
Irish School
DICKINSON, LOWES (1819-1908)
ENGLISH SCHOOL

20,128
Sir James Dombrain, Inspector General of the Coast Guards in Ireland, (another copy)
(after an oil, RHA 1838)
Printed: C.J. Hullmandel
56.3 x 38.2 (image 29 x 23.4)
Lithograph
Purchased, Lusk, Mr de Courcy Donovan, 1971

Howis the Elder, William (1804-1882)
Irish School
DICKINSON, LOWES (1819-1908)
ENGLISH SCHOOL

20,129
Sir James Dombrain, Inspector General of the Coast Guards in Ireland, (another copy)
(after an oil, RHA 1838)
Printed: C.J. Hullmandel
38.5 x 30.5 (image 29 x 23.4)
Lithograph
Purchased, Lusk, Mr de Courcy Donovan, 1971

Howis the Elder, William (1804-1892)
Irish School
DICKINSON, LOWES (1819-1908)
ENGLISH SCHOOL

20,130

11,537
Profile of a Young Man, (pl. for W. Huband's 'Critical and Familiar notices on the Art of Etching on Copper', 1810)
13.7 x 10.2 (plate 12.9 x 9.4)
Etching
Provenance Unknown

Huband, Willcocks (1776-1834)
Irish School
HUBAND, WILLCOCKS (1776-1834)
IRISH SCHOOL

11,539
'Attack, Hit, Duel, Sparring', Duelling by Sword, Pistols and Fisticuffs
12.8 x 13.8 (plate 10.8 x 12.6)
Etching
Provenance Unknown

Huband, Willcocks (1776-1834)
Irish School
HUBAND, WILLCOCKS (1776-1834)
IRISH SCHOOL

11,540
An Old Lady With a Pince-Nez
10.3 x 12.9 (plate 8.4 x 11.4)
Etching
Provenance Unknown

Hubert, Jean-Baptiste Louis (1801-after 1865)
French School
HUBERT, JEAN-BAPTISTE LOUIS (1801-AFTER 1865)
FRENCH SCHOOL

20,339
Green Oaks ('Etudes d'arbres par Hubert' no. 12)
Published: H. Jeannin, Paris
(Printed: Formentin et Cie., Paris)
44.6 x 35.4 (image 39.8 x 33.1)
Lithograph
Purchased, Lusk, Mr de Courcy Donovan, 1971

Huberti, Antonia (b.1914)
German School
HUBERTI, ANTONIA (B.1914)
GERMAN SCHOOL

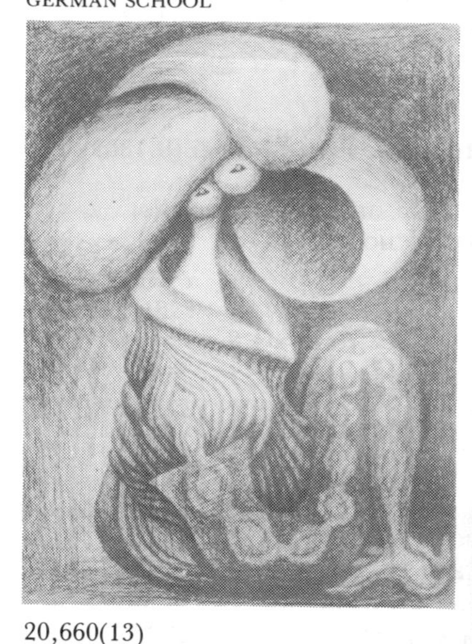

20,660(13)
The Head Gamekeeper's Courtesan, (from 'Zwanzig Farblithographien', see App. 8, no. 20,660)
Signed and numbered in pen 30/of 100
Published: F.J. Kohl-Weigand, St Ingbert, 29th March 1970
48.4 x 34.9 (image 48 x 34.5)
Lithograph with watercolour
Provenance Unknown

Hudson, Thomas (1701-1779)
English School
FABER THE YOUNGER, JOHN (C.1684-1756)
ENGLISH SCHOOL

10,111

James Quin, (1693-1766), Actor
Published: J. Faber the Younger, London, 1744, price ls 6d
36.2 x 25.1 (plate 33 x 23)
Mezzotint
Purchased, London, 1st Chaloner Smith sale, 1887

Hudson, Thomas (1701-1779)
English School
FABER THE YOUNGER, JOHN (C.1684-1756)
ENGLISH SCHOOL

10,709
Lieut.-General William Blakeney, (1672-1761), Lt. Governor of Minorca, later Baron Blakeney
Published: ?J. Faber The Younger, London, 1748
35.6 x 25.4 (plate cut)
Mezzotint
Purchased, Dublin, Mr J.V. McAlpine, 1901

Hudson, Thomas (1701-1779)
English School
FABER THE YOUNGER, JOHN (C.1684-1756)
ENGLISH SCHOOL

10,843
Major Foubert, (d.1743), Williamite Soldier and Director of a Royal Academy of Horsemanship
Published: J. Faber the Younger, London, 1740
44.6 x 35.7 (plate 33 x 22.6)
Mezzotint
Purchased, Mr J. Vickers, 1903

Hudson, Thomas (1701-1779)
English School
McARDELL, JAMES (1728/29-1765)
IRISH SCHOOL

10,114
Edward Maurice, (c.1690-1756), later P. Bishop of Ossory
35.6 x 25 (plate 35.4 x 25)
Mezzotint
Purchased, Mr J. Vickers, 1902

Hudson, Thomas (1701-1779)
English School
McARDELL, JAMES (1728/29-1765)
IRISH SCHOOL

10,168
John Perceval, 2nd Earl of Egmont, (1711-1770)
(after an oil, NPG, London)
Published: J. Short, London, 6th November 1764
42.4 x 32.8 (plate 38 x 28)
Mezzotint
Purchased, Dublin, Mr J.V. McAlpine, 1897

Hudson, Thomas (1701-1779)
English School
McARDELL, JAMES (1728/29-1765)
IRISH SCHOOL

10,189

George Townshend, (1724-1807), later 4th Viscount and 1st Marquess Townshend, also Lord Lieutenant of Ireland
(after an oil of c.1757, Castle Ashby, Northants)
40.2 x 28.2 (plate 39.8 x 27.8)
Mezzotint
Purchased, London, 1st Chaloner Smith sale, 1887

Hudson, Thomas (1701-1779)
English School
MCARDELL, JAMES (1728/29-1765)
IRISH SCHOOL

10,855
William King, (1685-1763), Oxford Scholar and Satirist
Published: c.1760
31.8 x 22.5 (plate cut)
Mezzotint
Purchased, London, 1st Chaloner Smith sale, 1887

Hudson, Thomas (1701-1779)
English School
RYLAND, WILLIAM WYNNE (1732-1783)
ENGLISH SCHOOL

11,258
Admiral Sir Peter Warren, (1703-1752), (pl. for T. G. Smollett's 'A Complete History of England', 1757)
(after a tql oil of c.1747, NPG, London)
Published: London, not before 1751
20.3 x 12.9 (plate 11.2 x 9.9)
Line
Acquired c.1908

Hunter, Robert (fl.1745-1803)
Irish School
DICKINSON, WILLIAM (1746-1823)
ENGLISH SCHOOL

10,454
John Bourke, 1st Baron Naas, (1705-1790), later 1st Earl of Mayo
Published: 1st November 1777
52.5 x 27 (plate 51 x 35.5)
Mezzotint
Acquired between 1890/98

Hunter, Robert (fl.1745-1803)
Irish School
DIXON, JOHN (C.1740-1804)
IRISH SCHOOL

10,158
Nicholas Taafe, 6th Viscount Taafe, (1677-1769), Lieut.-General in the Austrian Army
(after an oil, SA 1763)
INSCRIBED: *To his Excellency John Ponsonby Esq., Speaker of the Honourable House/of Commons and one of the Lords Justices and Genl. Governours of the Kingdom of Ireland./This plate is most humbly inscribed by his Excellency's most obedient humble servant/John Dixon*
Published: J. Dixon at T. Dixon's, Dublin, 1763
37.9 x 27.5 (plate 35 x 25)
Mezzotint
Purchased, London, 1st Chaloner Smith sale, 1887

Hunter, Robert (fl.1745-1803)
Irish School
FISHER, EDWARD (1722-C.1785)
IRISH SCHOOL

10,194
Simon Harcourt, 1st Earl Harcourt, (1714-1777), Lord Lieutenant of Ireland
(after an oil, NGI no. 1002)
Published: E. Fisher, London, 16th August 1775
36.4 x 26.2 (plate 35.6 x 25.3)
Mezzotint
Purchased, London, 1st Chaloner Smith sale, 1887

Hunter, Robert (fl.1745-1803)
Irish School
HARDING, SYLVESTER (1745-1808)
ENGLISH SCHOOL

10,670
Rev. Samuel Madden, (1686-1765), Co-founder of the Dublin Society, (pl. for 'European Magazine', April 1802)
(after a tql oil of 1755)
Published: L. Sewell, London, 1st April 1802
22.2 x 13.4 (plate 18.5 x cut)
Stipple
Acquired by 1913

Hunter, Robert (fl.1745-1803)
Irish School
HARDING, SYLVESTER (1745-1808)
ENGLISH SCHOOL

11,266
Nicholas Taafe, 6th Viscount Taafe, (1677-1769), General in Austrian Army
(after a wl oil of 1763)
Published: S. Harding, London, 4th April 1801
21.1 x 15.7 (plate 19.3 x 14)
Stipple
Purchased, Dublin, Mr P. Traynor, 1898

Hunter, Robert (fl.1745-1803)
Irish School
McARDELL, JAMES (1728/29-1765)
IRISH SCHOOL

10,220
Rev. John Mears, (c.1695-1767), Presbyterian Minister
39.5 x 27 (plate 36.2 x 24.7)
Mezzotint
Purchased, Dublin, Mr A. Roth, 1899

Hunter, Robert (fl.1745-1803)
Irish School
McARDELL, JAMES (1728/29-1765)
ENGLISH SCHOOL

10,440
Sir Charles Burton, M.P., (fl.1749-1775), as Lord Mayor of Dublin in 1753
Published: T. Sillcock, Dublin, 1753
51 x 36.7 (plate 51 (cut x 35.5)
Mezzotint
Purchased, London, 1st Chaloner Smith sale, 1887

Hunter, Robert (fl.1745-1803)
Irish School
PURCELL, RICHARD (FL.1746-1766)
ENGLISH SCHOOL

I

Inskipp, James (1790-1868)
English School
WAGSTAFF, CHARLES EDEN (1808-1850)
ENGLISH SCHOOL

20,150
Portrait of a Lady, (pl. for J. Inskipp's 'Studies of Heads from Nature', 1838)
Published: C. Tilt, (for the Proprietors), London, September 1834
36.5 x 29 (plate cut)
Line and stipple
Purchased, Lusk, Mr de Courcy Donovan, 1971

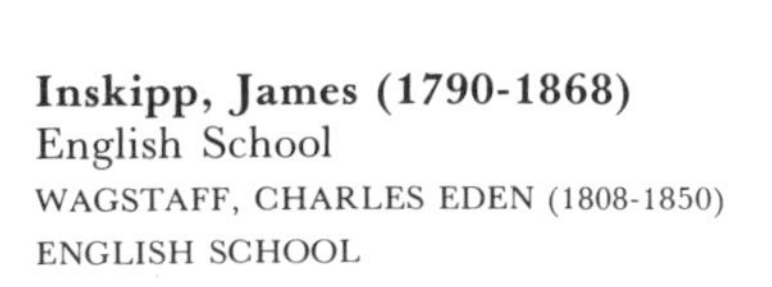

Inskipp, James (1790-1868)
English School
WAGSTAFF, CHARLES EDEN (1808-1850)
ENGLISH SCHOOL

20,164
Girl with a Sickle, (pl. for J. Inskipp's 'Studies of Heads from Nature', 1838)
Published: C. Tilt, (for the Proprietors) London, January 1835
(Printed: Reynolds & Allen)
43.8 x 33.4 (plate 36.7 x 29.2)
Line and stipple
Purchased, Lusk, Mr de Courcy Donovan, 1971

Inskipp, James (1790-1868)
English School
WAGSTAFF, CHARLES EDEN (1808-1850)
ENGLISH SCHOOL

20,166
A Girl holding a Dog, (pl. for J. Inskipp's 'Studies of Heads from Nature', 1838)
Published: C. Tilt, (for the Proprietors), London, 7th January 1835
38.9 x 29.5 (plate 36 x 28.5)
Line and stipple
Purchased, Lusk, Mr de Courcy Donovan, 1971

Irish School (17th century)
DICKSON, J. (FL.C.1660)
ENGLISH SCHOOL

10,305
Edward Parry, P. Bishop of Killaloe, (fl.1620-1650), (frontispiece for his 'David Restored, or an Antidote against the Prosperity of the Wicked', 1660)
15.5 x 9.4 (plate cut)
Line
Acquired by 1913

Irish School (17th century)
DUNKARTON, ROBERT (1744-AFTER 1811)
ENGLISH SCHOOL

11,112
Michael Boyle, P. Archbishop of Armagh, (?1609-1702), Lord Chancellor of Ireland
Published: S. Woodburn, London, 1813
28 x 18.5 (plate cut)
Mezzotint
Purchased, Dublin, Mr A. Roth, 1897

Irish School (17th century)
ENGLISH SCHOOL (17TH CENTURY)

10,574
'Chief Traytor of all Ireland' - Sir Phelim O'Neill, (?1604-1653), leader of the 1641 Irish Rebellion
24.9 x 19.3 (plate 16.8 x 13.1)
Line
Purchased, Dublin, Mr A. Roth, 1895

Irish School (17th century)
ENGLISH SCHOOL (1794)

11,003
John Yonge, (1589-1664), Irish Jesuit
Published: W. Richardson, London, 1794
32 x 24.5 (plate 15.4 x 12.2)
Line
Provenance Unknown

Irish School (c.1657)
BLOOTELING, ABRAHAM (1640-1690)
DUTCH SCHOOL

10,706
Cecil Calvert, 2nd Baron Baltimore, (1605/6-1675), aged 51
29.2 x 20.8 (plate 28 x 17.5)
Line
Purchased 1907

Irish School (c.1700)
SHERWIN, WILLIAM (1645-1711)
ENGLISH SCHOOL

10,301
William Sheridan, P. Bishop of Kilmore and Ardagh, (1636-1711), (frontispiece for his 'Sermons', 1704)
14.2 x 8.1 (plate cut)
Line
Purchased, Dublin,
Mr J.V. McAlpine, 1909

?Irish School (18th century)
BARCLAY (18TH CENTURY)
ENGLISH SCHOOL

11,680
Carlingford Castle, Carlingford Lough, Co. Louth
Published: A. Hogg, London
19.4 x 23 (plate cut)
Line
Presented, Mr E.J. McKean, 1918

?Irish School (18th century)
BARCLAY (18TH CENTURY)
ENGLISH SCHOOL

Irish School (c.1750)
SPOONER, CHARLES (C.1720-1767)
IRISH SCHOOL

10,221
Anthony Malone, (1700-1776), Lawyer, later Chancellor of the Exchequer in Ireland
Published: M. Williams; also M. Ford; also T. Wilkinson, Dublin, 1755, price 2s 6d
53.1 x 25.1 (plate 35 x 25)
Mezzotint
Purchased, London, 2nd Chaloner Smith sale, 1888

Irish School (c.1752)
IRISH SCHOOL (1752)

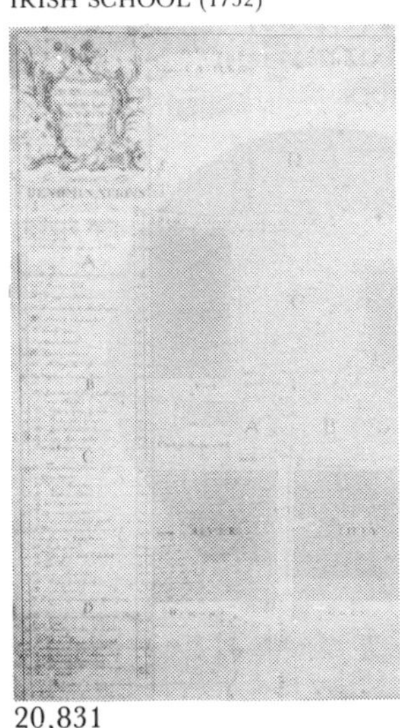

20,831
A survey of the present streets leading from the River Liffey to Dublin Castle
Published: 9th November 1752
63 x 37 (plate 61.5 x 35.5)
Line
Presented, Mr J.F. Fuller, 1914

Irish School (c.1753)
IRISH SCHOOL (1753)

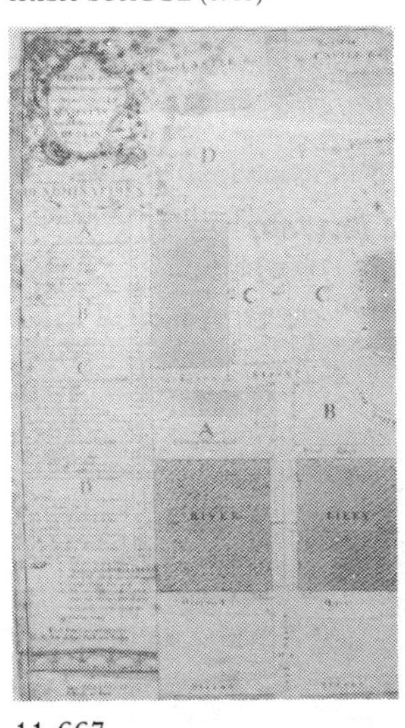

11,667
A Design for Opening Proper Streets or Avenues from the River Liffey to Dublin Castle
Published: 15th January 1753
62.8 x 37 (plate cut x 35)
Etching
Presented, Mr J. Fuller, 1914

Irish School (c.1754)
GRAVES, ROBERT (1798-1873)
ENGLISH SCHOOL

11,125
Crazy Crow, (George Hendrick, d.1762), of Dublin, (pl. for J. Caulfield's 'Portraits, Memoirs and Characters of Remarkable Persons', 1820)
(after an E. Lyons etching of 1754; example in NLI, Dublin)
30.7 x 23.6 (plate 25.3 x 15.7)
Line
Acquired c.1903

Irish School (c.1755)
COLE, B. (18TH CENTURY)
ENGLISH SCHOOL

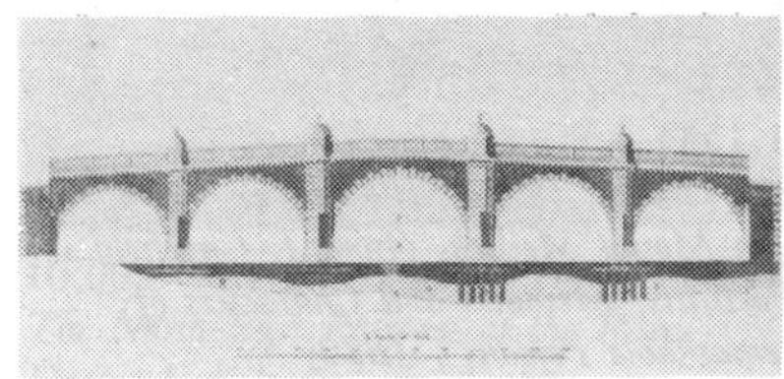

11,768
East Elevation and Section of Semple's Essex Bridge, Dublin, (now rebuilt Grattan Bridge)
Published: Gentleman's Magazine, London
21.8 x 33.6 (plate 17 x 32.2)
Line
Presented, Dr E. MacDowel Cosgrave, 1907

Irish School (c.1762)
IRISH SCHOOL (1762)

11,616
The Front of the original Blew-Coat Hospital, Queen Street, Dublin, (now demolished), (pl. for 'Dublin Magazine', August 1762)
Published: Dublin Magazine, August 1762
19 x 34.5 (plate 12.5 x 29)
Line
Provenance Unknown

Irish School (c.1768)
IRISH SCHOOL (1768)

20,729(1)
Heads, Faces & Animals, (from 'The Art of Drawing and Painting in Watercolours', 1768, see App. 8, no. 20, 729)
Published: J. Potts, Dublin, 1768
16.3 x 23 (plate cut)
Line and etching
Provenance Unknown

Irish School (1768/1781)
IRISH SCHOOL (1768/1781)

1,212
imon Luttrell, Baron Irnham, 1713-1787), later 1st Earl of arhampton
ublished: not before 1768
1.4 x 8.7 (plate cut)
ine
urchased, Mr H.A.J. Breun, 1909

rish School (c.1770)
RISH SCHOOL (18TH CENTURY)

10,138
Henry Flood, M.P., (1732-1791), Statesman and Orator
INSCRIBED: *From a miniature Portrait on the possession of the Rev'd Marcus Monck*
28.5 x 23 (plate 26.5 x 21.5)
Line
Acquired by 1913

Irish School (1770s)
DORRELL, EDMUND (1778-1857)
ENGLISH SCHOOL

10,593
Kane O'Hara, (1714-1782), Playwright and Musician
Published: W. Richardson, London, 1st November 1802
18.4 x 14.6 (plate 14.1 x 11.6)
Etching
Acquired by 1914

Irish School (c.1777)
IRISH SCHOOL (1777)

10,573
George Ogle, M.P., (1742-1814), Politician and Composer, (pl. for Walker's 'Hibernian Magazine', December 1777)
Published: Hibernian Magazine, Dublin, December 1777
21.3 x 13 (plate 17.8 x cut)
Line
Purchased, Dublin, Mr P. Traynor, 1898

Irish School (c.1777)
IRISH SCHOOL (1777)

11,331

Edmund Sexton Pery, (1719-1806), Speaker of the Irish House of Commons, later 1st Viscount Pery, (pl. for Walker's 'Hibernian Magazine', September 1777)
Published: Hibernian Magazine, Dublin, September 1777
21.1 x 12.8 (plate 18 x 11.5)
Line
Purchased, Dublin, Mr P. Traynor, 1898

Irish School (c.1778)
IRISH SCHOOL (1778)

11,342
Sir Edward Newenham, (1732-1814), M.P. for Co. Dublin, (pl. for Walker's 'Hibernian Magazine', March 1778)
Published: Hibernian Magazine, Dublin, March 1778
18.2 x 10.8 (plate cut)
Line
Purchased, Dublin, Mr P. Traynor, 1898

Irish School (c.1778)
IRISH SCHOOL (1778)

11,381
Luke Gardiner, (1745-1798), M.P. for Co. Dublin, later 1st Baron then 1st Viscount Mountjoy, (pl. for 'Hibernian Magazine', June 1778)
Published: Hibernian Magazine, Dublin, June 1778
21.5 x 13 (plate 18.3 x 11.7)
Line
Purchased, Dublin, Mr P. Traynor, 1898

Irish School (c.1779)
IRISH SCHOOL (1779)

10,651
Walter Hussey Burgh, (1742-1783), Chief Baron of the Exchequer in Ireland, (pl. for Walker's 'Hibernian Magazine', December 1779)
Published: Hibernian Magazine, Dublin, December 1779
19.6 x 12.6 (plate cut)
Line
Purchased, Dublin, Mr P. Traynor, 1898

Irish School (c.1779)
IRISH SCHOOL (1779)

11,110
Walter Hussey Burgh, (1742-1853), Chief Baron of the Exchequer in Ireland, (pl. for 'Hibernian Magazine', December 1779), (another copy)
Published: Hibernian Magazine, Dublin, December 1779
21.5 x 13 (plate 14.3 x 12.3)
Line
Purchased, Dublin, Mr P. Traynor, 1898

Irish School (c.1779)
IRISH SCHOOL (C.1779)

10,642

Sir Abraham King, Bt., late Lord Mayor of Dublin
Issued Privately c.1779
17 x 10.7 (plate 15.5 x 9.5)
Stipple
Purchased, Dublin, Mr P. Traynor, 1898

Irish School (c.1779)
IRISH SCHOOL (C.1800)

11,627
The Dublin Volunteers on College Green, 4th November, commemorating the birthday of King William III, (1650-1702)
Published: W. Allen, Dublin
24.5 x 38 (plate 17.5 x 27.5)
Line
Presented, Mr J.V. McAlpine, 1901

Irish School (c.1780)
IRISH SCHOOL (1780)

1,304
Villiam Petty, 2nd Earl of Shelburne, 1737-1805), Statesman, later British rime Minister and 1st Marquess of ansdowne
ublished: T. Walker, Dublin, 1780
20.9 x 13.2 (plate 17.5 x 12)
Line
Purchased, Dublin, Mr P. Traynor, 1898

Irish School (c.1780)
IRISH SCHOOL (C.1780)

11,146
Profile of Henry Grattan, M.P., (1746-1820), Statesman, in Volunteer Uniform
20.5 x 12.5 (plate 19 x cut)
Line
Purchased, Dublin, Mr P. Traynor, 1898

Irish School (c.1780)
IRISH SCHOOL (C.1780)

11,188
James Caulfeild, 1st Earl of Charlemont, (1728-1799), Art Patron, Commander-in-chief of the Irish Volunteers
Published: not before 1780
21 x 13.6 (plate 18 x 11.8)
Line
Purchased, Dublin, Mr P. Traynor, 1898

Irish School (c.1780)
IRISH SCHOOL (C.1780)

11,612
The Drawing of the Irish State Lottery at the Music Hall, 1780
11.5 x 18 (plate cut)
Line
Purchased, Dublin, Mr H. Naylor, 1909

Irish School (c.1782)
ENGLISH SCHOOL (1782)

11,147

Henry Grattan, M.P., (1746-1820), Statesman, (pl. for 'European Magazine', August 1782)
Published: J. Fielding, also J. Sewell, also J. Debrett, London, 1st August 1782
21.7 x 12.9 (plate 18 x cut)
Line
Purchased, Dublin, Mr P. Traynor, 1898

Irish School (1783)
IRISH SCHOOL (1783)

11,870
James Caulfeild, 1st Earl of Charlemont, (1728-1799) at the Provincial Reviews in the Phoenix Park, Dublin, 3rd June 1782
Published: Clarke, Dublin, November 1783 (Printed: Harpur, Leixlip)
105.5 x 84 (plate cut)
Line on linen
Presented, Dr E. MacDowel Cosgrave, 1907

Irish School (1784)
ENGLISH SCHOOL (1784)

11,626
The Dublin Volunteers on College Green, 4th November, commemorating the birthday of King William III, (1650-1702)
Published: London, for the Proprietor, 6th December 1784
33.4 x 43 (plate cut)
Line and aquatint
Presented, Mr J. Ribton Garstin, 1895

Irish School (1784)
ENGLISH SCHOOL (1784)

11,895
Dublin Castle Gateway, behind the Royal Exchange, (now City Hall) and Newcomen Bank, (now Civic Offices)
34.6 x 26.6 (plate cut)
Etching with watercolour
Purchased, Dublin, Mr H. Naylor, 1933

Irish School (1784)
ENGLISH SCHOOL (1784)

11,896
The Royal Exchange, (now City Hall), Cork Hill, Dublin
34.6 x 26.6 (plate cut)
Etching with watercolour
Purchased, Dublin, Mr H. Naylor, 1933

Irish School (1784)
ENGLISH SCHOOL (1784)

11,897
The Rotunda and the Lying-In, (now Rotunda), Hospital, Dublin
25.8 x 35 (plate cut)
Etching with watercolour
Purchased, Dublin, Mr H. Naylor, 1933

Irish School (1784)
ENGLISH SCHOOL (1784)

11,898
Trinity College and Parliament House, (now Bank of Ireland), College Green, Dublin
26.2 x 36 (plate cut)
Etching with watercolour
Purchased, Dublin, Mr II. Naylor, 1933

Irish School (1784)
ENGLISH SCHOOL (1784)

11,899
Essex Bridge, Dublin, (now rebuilt Grattan Bridge) and the Custom House, (now demolished)
24.5 x 34 (plate cut)
Etching with watercolour
Purchased, Dublin, Mr H. Naylor, 1933

Irish School (1784)
ENGLISH SCHOOL (1784)

11,900
The Dublin Volunteers on College Green, commemorating the birthday of King William III
25 x 35 (plate cut)
Etching with watercolour
Purchased, Dublin, Mr H. Naylor, 1933

Irish School (1784)
ENGLISH SCHOOL (1784)

11,901
Dublin and Islandbridge from the Magazine Hill in Phoenix Park
26 x 34.7 (plate cut)
Etching with watercolour
Purchased, Dublin, Mr H. Naylor, 1933

Irish School (c.1784)
IRISH SCHOOL (1784)

11,321
Charles Manners, 4th Duke of Rutland, (1754-1787), Lord Lieutenant of Ireland, (pl. for 'Hibernian Magazine', April 1784)
Dublin, April 1784
18.2 x 11.2 (plate cut)
Line
Acquired by 1895

Irish School (c.1785)
ENGLISH SCHOOL (1785)

11,706
Simpson's Hospital, (now demolished), Great Britain, (now Parnell), Street, Dublin, (from 'Gentleman's Magazine', May 1785)
Published: Gentleman's Magazine, London, May 1785
7 x 9 (plate cut)
Line
Provenance Unknown

Irish School (c.1785)
ENGLISH SCHOOL (1785)

11,915

West Front of of St. John's Church, Fishamble Street, Dublin, (now demolished), (from 'Gentleman's Magazine', August, 1785)
Published: Gentleman's Magazine, London, August 1785
8.1 x 7.8 (plate cut)
Line
Presented, Mr W.G. Strickland, 1906

Irish School (c.1785)
IRISH SCHOOL (1785)

11,129
Henry Flood, M.P., (1732-1791), (pl. for 'Hibernian Magazine', April 1785)
Published: Hibernian Magazine, Dublin, April 1785
21.6 x 13.2 (torn) (plate 18.5 x 10.8)
Line
Purchased, Dublin, Mr P. Traynor, 1898

Irish School (c.1786)
ENGLISH SCHOOL (1786)

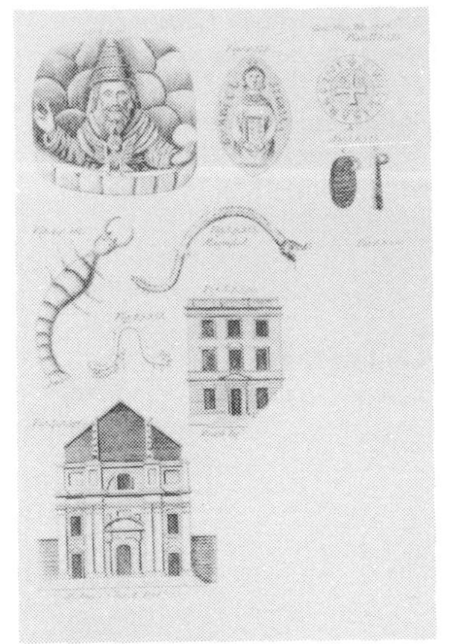

11,668
Ancient Church Customs, Seals, Aquatic Insects, The Meath Infirmary, (The Coombe, Dublin, now demolished), and the facade of St Ann's, Dawson Street, Dublin, (now rebuilt), (from 'Gentleman's Magazine', May 1786)
Published: Gentleman's Magazine, London, May 1786
21.2 x 12.9 (plate 18.7 x 12.5)
Line
Provenance Unknown

Irish School (c.1786)
ENGLISH SCHOOL (1786)

11,742
St Nicholas Within Church, Christchurch Place, Dublin, (now partially demolished), (from 'Gentleman's Magazine', May 1786; detached from NGI no. 11,668)
Published: Gentleman's Magazine, London, May 1786
11 x 6 (plate cut)
Line
Provenance Unknown

Irish School (c.1786)
ENGLISH SCHOOL (1786)

11,916
St Nicholas Within Church, Christchurch Place, (now partly demolished), (from 'Gentleman's Magazine', May 1786)
Published: Gentleman's Magazine, London, May 1786
Irregular shape 12.8 x 6.5 (plate cut)
Line
Presented, Mr W.G. Strickland, 1906

Irish School (c.1786)
ENGLISH SCHOOL (1786)

11,920

St Ann's Church, Dawson Street, Dublin, (later refaced), (from 'Gentleman's Magazine', May 1786)
Published: Gentleman's Magazine, London, May 1786
7.8 x 6.5 (plate cut)
Line
Presented, Mr W.G. Strickland, 1906

Irish School (c.1786)
IRISH SCHOOL (1786)

11,102
Timothy Brecknock, (1716-1786), associate of Adventurer and Politician George Robert Fitzgerald, in irons, (pl. for Walker's, 'Hibernian Magazine', June 1786)
Published: Hibernian Magazine, Dublin, June 1786
21 x 12.7 approx (plate 17.3 x 10.7)
Line
Provenance Unknown

Irish School (1787)
IRISH SCHOOL (1787)

1,613
Ticket for the Irish State Lottery 1787
21.5 x 13 (plate cut)
Line
Purchased, Dublin, Mr H. Naylor, 1909

Irish School (c.1787)
ENGLISH SCHOOL (1787)

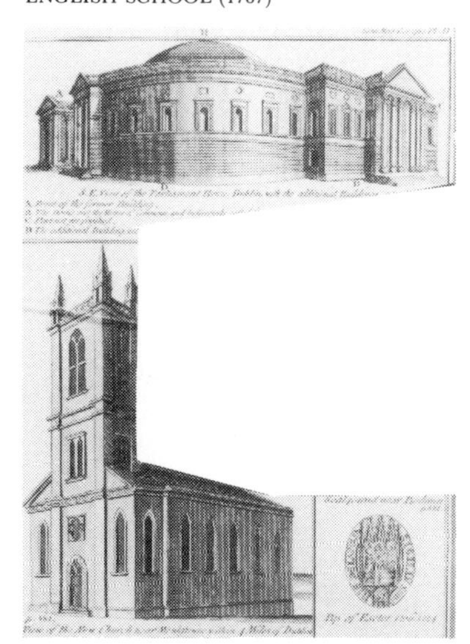

11,730
South-East view of the Parliament House, Dublin, (now Bank of Ireland), St John's Church, Monkstown, Co. Dublin, (now rebuilt), and the Bishop of Exeter's Seal, (from 'Gentleman's Magazine', October 1787)
Published: Gentleman's Magazine, London, October 1787
18.6 x 13 (plate cut)
Line
Provenance Unknown

Irish School (c.1787)
ENGLISH SCHOOL (1787)

11,731
South-East view of the Parliament House, Dublin, (now Bank of Ireland); the Secretary's House and the front of the Post Office, College Green, (now rebuilt); St John's Church, Monkstown, Co. Dublin, (now rebuilt), and the Bishop of Exeter's Seal, (from Gentleman's Magazine', October 1787)
Published: Gentleman's Magazine, London, October 1787
20.8 x 13.6 (plate 19 x 13.5)
Line
Provenance Unknown

Irish School (c.1787)
ENGLISH SCHOOL (1787)

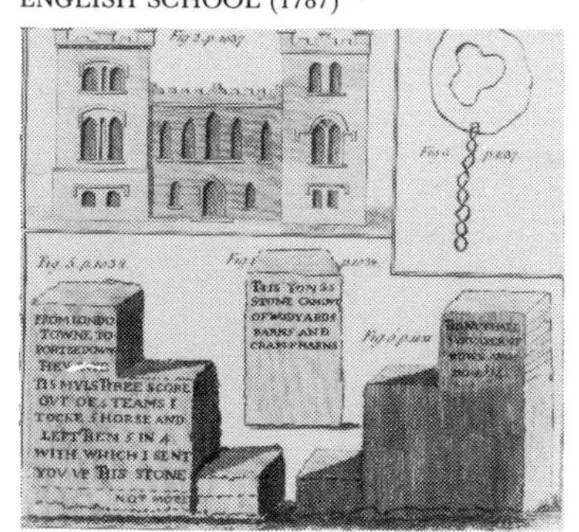

11,837
Sheet of Illustrations: Clontarf Castle, Co. Dublin, (now altered), a ball and chain, and three inscribed stones, (from 'Gentleman's Magazine', December, 1787)
Published: Gentleman's Magazine, London, December, 1787)

11.5 x 12.3 (plate cut)
Line
Provenance Unknown

Irish School (c.1787)
ENGLISH SCHOOL (1787)

11,913
The Post Office on College Green, (now rebuilt), (from 'Gentleman's Magazine', October 1787)
Published: Gentleman's Magazine, London, October 1787
8.2 x 9.2 irregular shape (plate cut)
Line
Presented, Mr W.G. Strickland, 1906

Irish School (c.1787)
ENGLISH SCHOOL (1787)

11,918
The Royal Charter School, Clontarf, (now demolished), (from 'Gentleman's Magazine', December 1787)
Published: Gentleman's Magazine, London, December 1787
7 x 12.2 (plate cut)
Line
Presented, Mr W.G. Strickland, 1906

Irish School (1788)
ENGLISH SCHOOL (1789)

11,756
Howth, Irelands Eye and Lambay Island from Kilmacud in 1788, (from 'Gentleman's Magazine', October 1789)
Published: Gentleman's Magazine, London, October 1789
12.5 x 20 (plate 12.4 x 18.7)
Line
Provenance Unknown

Irish School (c.1788)
ENGLISH SCHOOL (1788)

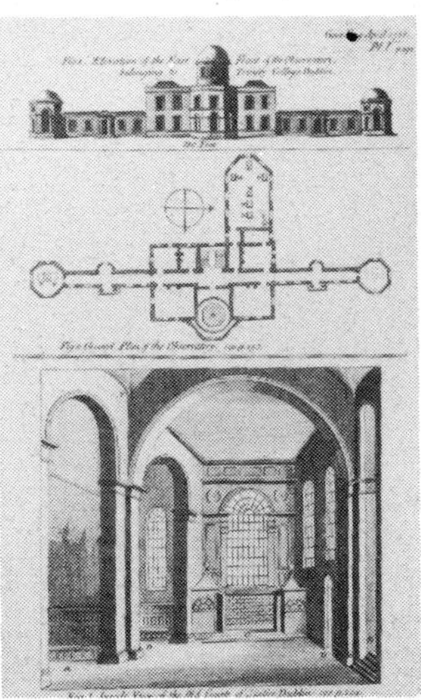

11,743
The east front and ground plan of Dunsink Observatory, Co. Dublin and inside the Old Courts of Justice, St Michael's Hill, (now demolished), (from 'Gentleman's Magazine', April 1788)
Published: Gentleman's Magazine, London, April 1788
20.7 x 12.7 (plate cut)
Line
Provenance Unknown

Irish School (c.1788)
ENGLISH SCHOOL (1788)

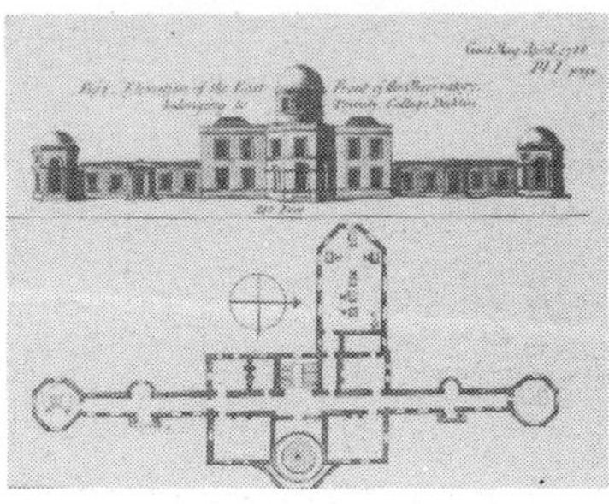

11,744
The east front and ground plan of Dunsink Observatory, Co. Dublin, (from 'Gentleman's Magazine', April 1788)
Published: Gentleman's Magazine, London, April 1788
10.1 x 12.6 (plate cut)
Line
Provenance Unknown

Irish School (c.1788)
ENGLISH SCHOOL (1788)

11,917
Castle Street, Dublin with the La Touche Bank, (now demolished) and Newcomen Bank, (now Civic offices), (from 'Gentleman's Magazine', December 1788)
Published: Gentleman's Magazine, London, December 1788
8.7 x 12.8 (plate cut)
Line
Presented, Mr W.G. Strickland, 1906

Irish School (c.1788)
ENGLISH SCHOOL (1788)

11,921

The Four Courts, St Michael's Hill, Dublin, (now demolished), showing the Court of Kings Bench, Court of Common Pleas, Screen of the Court of Chancery and Steps to the Court of Exchequer, (from 'Gentleman's Magazine', April 1788)
Published: Gentleman's Magazine, London, April 1788
10 x 12.5 (plate cut)
Line
Presented, Mr W.G. Strickland, 1906

Irish School (1789)
IRISH SCHOOL (1789)

11,546
Ticket to Public Assembly Rooms, (for Nicholas Wesby), with a tablet of the Frieze
8.5 x 15.5 (plate cut)
Line
Provenance Unknown

Irish School (c.1789)
ENGLISH SCHOOL (1789)

11,925
Smock Alley Theatre, Dublin, (now demolished), (from 'Gentleman's Magazine', London, June 1789)
Published: Gentleman's Magazine, London, June 1789
6.6 x 6.9 (plate cut)
Line
Presented, Mr W.G. Strickland, 1906

Irish School (c.1790)
ENGLISH SCHOOL (1790)

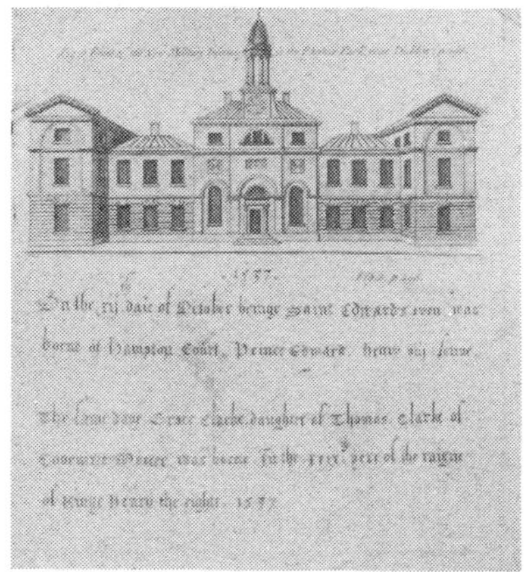

11,727
The Royal Military Infirmary, (now Army G.H.Q.), Phoenix Park, Dublin, (from 'Gentleman's Magazine', May 1790)
Published: Gentleman's Magazine, London, May 1790
13.8 x 13 (plate 13.4 x 12)
Line
Provenance Unknown

Irish School (c.1790)
ENGLISH SCHOOL (1790)

11,832
Dublin Architecture: the New Stamp Office, (now demolished); St Michan's Church Street; St Andrew's, Suffolk Street, (now rebuilt); Obelisk Fountain on St James's Street and smaller St James's Street Fountain, (now demolished), (from 'Gentleman's Magazine', November 1790)
Published: Gentleman's Magazine, London, November 1790
21.2 x 12.7 (plate 19.5 x 12.1)
Line
Provenance Unknown

Irish School (c.1790)
ENGLISH SCHOOL (1790)

11,923
Daly's Club House, Dame Street, (now rebuilt), (from 'Gentleman's Magazine', May 1790)
Published: Gentleman's Magazine, London, May 1790
7 x 12.7 (plate cut)
Line
Presented, Mr W.G. Strickland, 1906

Irish School (c.1790)
HUFFAM, T.W. (FL.1825-C.1855)
ENGLISH SCHOOL

11,272

Theobald Wolfe Tone, (1763-1798), United Irishman, as a Belfast Volunteer, (pl. for R. Madden's 'United Irishmen', 2nd series, 1843)
(after an oil, NGI no. 1784)
Published: Madden & Co., London, 1843
20.2 x 12.3 (plate cut)
Mezzotint and etching
Purchased, Dublin, Mr P. Traynor, 1898

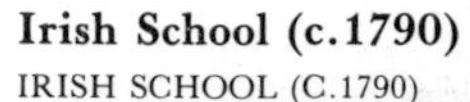

Irish School (c.1790)
IRISH SCHOOL (C.1790)

11,132
John Foster, (1740-1828), last Speaker of the Irish House of Commons, later 1st Baron Oriel
21.5 x 13 (plate 18 x 11.5)
Line
Purchased, Dublin, Mr P. Traynor, 1898

Irish School (1790s)
IRISH SCHOOL (EARLY 19TH CENTURY)

11,235
Thomas Moore, (1779-1852), Poet
18.2 x 11.8 (plate 13 x 11.6)
Stipple
Purchased, Dublin, Mr P. Traynor, 1898

Irish School (c.1791)
IRISH SCHOOL (1791)

11,083
William Brownlow, M.P., (1726-1794), (pl. for Walker's 'Hibernian Magazine', September 1791)
Published: Hibernian Magazine, Dublin, September 1791
19 x 11.5 (plate cut)
Line
Purchased, Dublin, Mr P. Traynor, 1898

Irish School (1792)
ENGLISH SCHOOL (1792)

11,720
The west side and north front of the Custom House, Dublin, (from 'Gentleman's Magazine', April 1792, with NGI no. 11,728)
Published: Gentleman's Magazine, London, April 1792
13 x 20.8, L-shaped (plate cut)
Line
Provenance Unknown

Irish School (1792)
ENGLISH SCHOOL (1792)

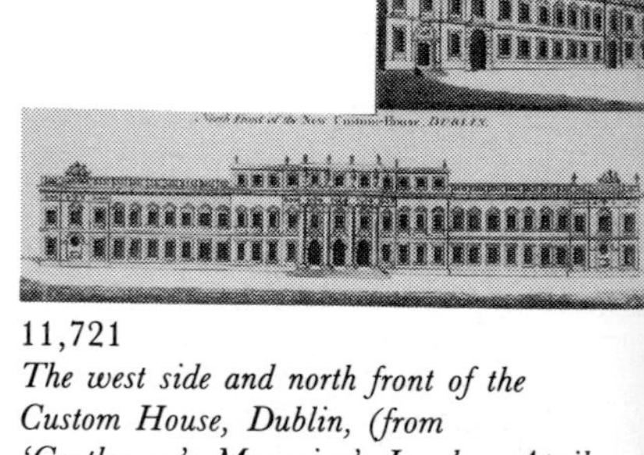

11,721
The west side and north front of the Custom House, Dublin, (from 'Gentleman's Magazine', London, April 1792), (another copy)
Published: Gentleman's Magazine, London, April 1792
13 x 21.6, L-shaped (plate cut)
Line
Provenance Unknown

Irish School (1792)
ENGLISH SCHOOL (1792)

11,728

Parliament House, Dublin, (now Bank of Ireland), with the House of Commons dome on fire, 27th February 1792, (from 'Gentleman's Magazine', April 1792, with NGI no. 11,720)
Published: Gentleman's Magazine, London, April 1792
7.3 x 11.2 (plate cut)
Line
Provenance Unknown

Irish School (1792)
ENGLISH SCHOOL (1792)

11,914
Parliament House, (now Bank of Ireland), College Green, Dublin, when in flames on the 27th February, 1792 and just before the dome fell in, (from 'Gentleman's Magazine', April 1792)
Published: Gentleman's Magazine, London, April 1792
7 x 11.8 (plate cut)
Line
Presented, Mr W.G. Strickland, 1906

Irish School (c.1792)
ENGLISH SCHOOL (1792)

11,177
Lieut.-Colonel John Hely-Hutchinson, M.P., (1757-1832) later 2nd Earl of Donoughmore, (pl. for 'Universal Magazine', April 1792)
Published: Universal Magazine, London, April 1792
21 x 12.6 (plate 16 x 12.2)
Line
Acquired 1913

Irish School (c.1792)
IRISH SCHOOL (1792)

11,091
Edward Byrne, President of the Catholic Committee, (pl. for Walker's 'Hibernian Magazine', November 1792)
Published: Hibernian Magazine, Dublin, November 1792
21.2 x 13.5 (plate 16.4 x 10.4)
Stipple
Purchased, Dublin, Mr P. Traynor, 1898

Irish School (c.1792)
IRISH SCHOOL (1792)

11,175
Count Theobald Dillon, (1745-1792), Brigadier-General of the Irish Brigade, killed mistakenly by his own troops, (pl. for Walker's 'Hibernian Magazine', July 1792)
Published: Hibernian Magazine, Dublin, July 1792
21.4 x 13.2 (plate 19.1 x 11.6)
Line
Acquired by 1903

Irish School (c.1793)
IRISH SCHOOL (1793)

11,245
George Frederick Nugent, 7th Earl of Westmeath, (1760-1814), as Father Luke in 'Poor Soldier', (pl. for Walker's 'Hibernian Magazine', April 1793)
Published: Hibernian Magazine, Dublin, April 1793
20.3 x 12.9 (plate 19.2 x 11.5)
Line with watercolour
Purchased, Dublin, Mr P. Traynor, 1898

Irish School (c.1792)
IRISH SCHOOL (C.1793)

10,580
So-called Portrait of Brigader-General Thomas O'Meara, (1750-1819), Commander of the French at Dunkirk against Frederick, Duke of York in 1793
(after line engraving NGI no. 11,175, of Count Dillon)
20.9 x 12.5 (plate 19 x 11.2)
Line
Acquired c.1908

Irish School (c.1794)
IRISH SCHOOL (1794)

11,328
Archibald Hamilton Rowan, (1751-1834), late President of the Society of United Irishmen of Dublin, (pl. for Walker's 'Hibernian Magazine', February 1794)
Published: Hibernian Magazine, Dublin, February 1794
20.3 x 13 (plate 19.2 x 12.5)
Line
Purchased, Dublin, Mr P. Traynor, 1898

Irish School (c.1795)
IRISH SCHOOL (1795)

10,578
M.E. O'Brien, (b.1772), Writer, (pl. for 'Sentimental and Masonic Magazine', May 1795)
Published: Sentimental and Masonic Magazine, Dublin, May 1795
20.8 x 12.8 (plate 15.6 x 9.5)
Stipple and line
Purchased, Dublin, Mr P. Traynor, 1898

Irish School (c.1795)
IRISH SCHOOL (1795)

11,139
William, Earl FitzWilliam, (1748-1833), former Lord Lieutenant of Ireland, (pl. for Walker's 'Hibernian Magazine', March 1795)
Published: Hibernian Magazine, Dublin, March 1795
16.2 x 11 (plate cut)
Line and stipple
Provenance Unknown

Irish School (c.1795)
IRISH SCHOOL (C.1795)

10,299
Rev. Thomas Campbell, (d.1795), Rector of Galoon and Chancellor of Clogher
Unlettered Proof
16.8 x 10 (plate cut)
Line and stipple
Presented, Mrs T.G. Moorehead, 1960

Irish School (c.1795)
IRISH SCHOOL (C.1795)

11,894

Rev. Thomas Campbell, Rector of Galoon, Co. Fermanagh and Chancellor of Clogher, (another copy)
Unlettered Proof
17 x 10 (plate cut)
Line
Acquired c.1908

Irish School (c.1796)
IRISH SCHOOL (C.1796)

11,602
The Opening of the new docks at Ringsend on St George's Day, 1796
19.9 x 25.8 (plate cut)
Line
Presented, Mr W.G. Strickland, 1906

Irish School (c.1797)
IRISH SCHOOL (1797)

10,588
Arthur O'Connor, M.P., (1763-1852), United Irishman, brother of Roger O'Connor
Published: 1797
.8 x 12.6 (plate cut)
Line and stipple
Purchased, Dublin, Mr P. Traynor, 1898

Irish School (c.1797)
IRISH SCHOOL (1797)

10,590
Arthur O'Connor, M.P., (1763-1852), United Irishman and brother of Roger O'Connor, (another copy)
Published: 1797
21 x 13 (plate 17.8 x 10.5)
Line and stipple
Purchased, Dublin, Mr P. Traynor, 1898

Irish School (1798)
HAMERTON, ROBERT JACOB (FL.1831-1858)
ENGLISH SCHOOL

10,615
Joseph Holt, (1756-1826), General of the Irish rebels in 1798, (frontispiece for C. Croker's 'Memoirs of Joseph Holt', 1838)
INSCRIBED: From an original picture in the possession of Sir William Betham - painted 1798
Published: H. Colburn, London
(Printed: W. Day & L. Haghe)
22.5 x 14.2 (image 12 x 11.5)
Lithograph
Purchased, Dublin, Mr P. Traynor, 1898

Irish School (1798)
IRISH SCHOOL (1798)

10,292
'The Unfortunate' Theobald Wolfe Tone, (1763-1798), Patriot, (pl. for 'Hibernian Magazine', November 1798)
(after a drawing taken at his trial, 10th November 1798)
Published: Hibernian Magazine, November 1798
20.8 x 11.8 (plate 17.6 x 10.8)
Line
Purchased, Dublin, Mr P. Traynor, 1898

Irish School (c.1798)
ENGLISH SCHOOL (1798)

11,679
Drogheda, Co. Louth on the River Boyne, from the East, (pl. for 'European Magazine', April 1798)

Published: J. Sewell, London, 1st April 1798
11.8 x 16.6 (plate cut)
Line
Provenance Unknown

Irish School (c.1798)
IRISH SCHOOL (C.1798)

10,648
James Napper Tandy, (1740-1803), United Irishman, when a French General
20.5 x 11.7 (plate 18.5 x 10.5)
Line
Purchased, Dublin, Mr P. Traynor, 1898

Irish School (c.1799)
IRISH SCHOOL (1799)

11,305
William Saurin, (1757-1839), Attorney General for Ireland, (pl. for 'Dublin Magazine', April 1799)
Published: Dublin Magazine, April 1799
11.3 x 8.2 (plate cut)
Stipple
Purchased, Dublin, Mr P. Traynor, 1898

Irish School (late 18th century)
ENGLISH SCHOOL (LATE 18TH CENTURY)

11,739
Sarah Bridge, (now Islandbridge), Kilmainham; Gavin Wilson, a Mason; a curious inscription, and a house elevation
Published: Gentleman's Magazine, London
13.7 x 12.5 (plate cut x 11.5)
Line
Provenance Unknown

Irish School (late 18th century)
IRISH SCHOOL (LATE 18TH CENTURY)

11,162
John Giffard, (1745-1819), Editor of the Dublin Journal and High Sheriff of Dublin
20.9 x 12.5 (plate 12.3 x 8.5)
Stipple
Purchased, Dublin, Mr P. Traynor, 1898

Irish School (late 18th century)
IRISH SCHOOL (LATE 18TH CENTURY)

11,316
William Wynne Ryland, (1732-1783), Engraver and Forger, popularised stipple engraving in England
21.5 x 12.3 (plate 17.9 x 10.8)
Line
Purchased, Dublin, Mr P. Traynor, 1898

Irish School (late 18th century)
IRISH SCHOOL (LATE 18TH CENTURY)

11,318

Captain Luke Ryan
20.8 x 13.2 (plate 17.8 x 11.8)
Line
Purchased, Dublin, Mr P. Traynor, 1898

Irish School (late 18th century)
IRISH SCHOOL (LATE 18TH CENTURY)

11,618
'Entrance to Phoenix Park, Dublin', (The Vice-Regal Lodge, Lord Lieutenant's Residence, now Áras an Uachtaráin)
21.8 x 27.6 (plate cut)
Etching and aquatint
Presented, Mr. W.G. Strickland, 1906

Irish School (late 18th century)
IRISH SCHOOL (LATE 18TH CENTURY)

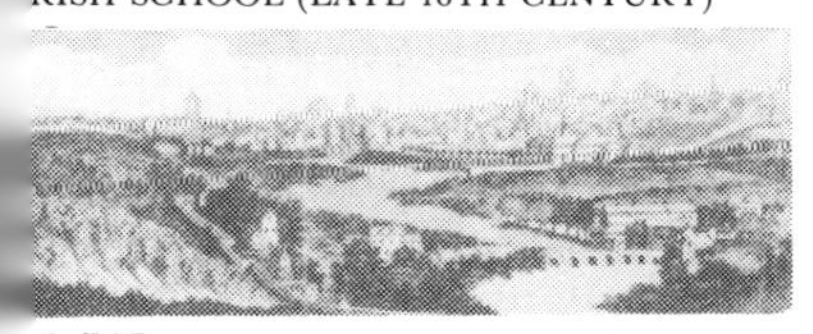

1,715
Dublin and Islandbridge from the Magazine Hill in Phoenix Park
1.6 x 27 (plate cut)
Line
Provenance Unknown

Irish School (late 18th century)
IRISH SCHOOL (LATE 18TH CENTURY)

1,738
The Floating Chapel, Ringsend Dock, Dublin
11 x 18.3 (plate cut)
Line
Provenance Unknown

Irish School (late 18th century)
ENGLISH SCHOOL (1799)

11,839
Dargle Glen and the River Dargle, near Kilbride, Co. Wicklow
Published: Laurie & Whittle, London, 12th September 1799
33 x 43 (plate 31 x 39.3)
Aquatint with watercolour
Purchased, London, Mr L. Marks, 1898

Irish School (late 18th century)
MAGUIRE, PATRICK, (FL.1783-1820)
IRISH SCHOOL

11,221
Leonard MacNally, (1752-1820), Barrister, Playwright and Political Informer, (pl. for 'Cyclopaedian Magazine', October, 1808)
Published: Cyclopaedian Magazine, Dublin, October 1808
15.8 x 11 (plate cut)
Stipple
Purchased, Dublin, Mr J.V. McAlpine, 1906

Irish School (late 18th century)
MAGUIRE, PATRICK (FL.1783-1820)
IRISH SCHOOL

11,555
John O'Neill, 1st Viscount O'Neill, (1740-1798), killed by the rebels at Antrim, 7th June 1798
Published: not before 1798
20 x 12.2 (plate 18.3 x 11)
Stipple
Purchased, Dublin, Mr P. Traynor, 1899

Irish School (late 18th century)
MYERS (18TH CENTURY)
ENGLISH SCHOOL

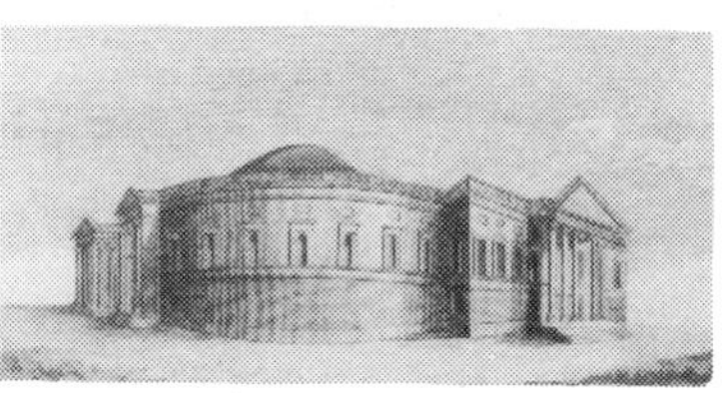

11,754
Parliament House, (now Bank of Ireland), Dublin, from the South-East, (from 'New London Magazine', March 1790)
Published: New London Magazine, March 1790
10.6 x 19 (plate cut)
Line
Presented, Dr E. MacDowel Cosgrave, 1907

Irish School (c.1800)
ENGLISH SCHOOL (1816)

11,231
Francis Moynan, R.C. Bishop of Cork, (1735-1815)
(after an oil, Lulworth Castle, Dorset)
Published: Keating, Braun & Keating, London, 1st November 1816
14.4 x 8.8 (plate cut)
Stipple
Purchased, Mr J.V. McAlpine, 1909

Irish School (c.1800)
TONE, CATHERINE SAMPSON (FL.1825-1858)
IRISH SCHOOL
GOGGINS, J.J. (19TH CENTURY)
IRISH SCHOOL

10,433
Wolfe Tone, (1763-1798), United Irishman, in French uniform
(after a C.J. Hullmandel lithograph of 1827; example in NLI, Dublin)
Published: J.J. Goggins, Dublin, 1898
67.7 x 49.8 (image 53 x 42 approx)
Lithograph
Provenance Unknown

Irish School (c.1800)
IRISH SCHOOL (C.1800)

10,581
James O'Brien, (d.1800), United Irishman and Informer 'with his working tools'
21.7 x 12.4 (plate cut)
Etching
Purchased, Dublin, Mr P. Traynor, 1898

Irish School (c.1800)
IRISH SCHOOL (C.1800)

11,181
Michael Dwyer, (1771-1826), United Irishman
8.2 x 7 (plate cut)
Stipple
Purchased, Dublin, Mr P. Traynor, 1898

Irish School (c.1800)
IRISH SCHOOL (C.1800)

11,718
Dublin from the South-West
Published: W. Allen, Dublin
18.2 x 28.2 (plate cut)
Etching
Provenance Unknown

Irish School (c.1800)
MAGUIRE, PATRICK (FL.1783-1820)
IRISH SCHOOL

10,293
Charles Thorp, (fl.1772-1820), Builder, Stuccodore and Lord Mayor of Dublin 1800-1801, (pl. for 'Hibernian Magazine', October 1800)
Published: Hibernian Magazine, October 1800
20.8 x 12.2 (plate 19.7 x cut)
Stipple
Acquired between 1903/13

Irish School (c.1800)
MEYER, HENRY HOPPNER (1782-1847)
ENGLISH SCHOOL

10,960
Thomas Moore, (1779-1852), Poet, (pl. for 'New Monthly Magazine and Universal Register', August 1818)
(after a miniature)
Unlettered Proof
36.4 x 29.7 (plate 19 x 13.9)
Stipple
Purchased, Dublin, Mr P. Traynor, 1898

Irish School (c.1800)
MEYER, HENRY HOPPNER (1782-1847)
ENGLISH SCHOOL

11,234
Thomas Moore, (1779-1852), Poet, (pl. for 'New Monthly Magazine and Universal Register', August 1818)
(after a miniature)
Published: H. Colburn, London, 1st August 1818
20.8 x 12.7 (plate 19 x cut)
Stipple
Purchased, Dublin, Mr P. Traynor, 1898

Irish School (19th century)
?BRANSTON, ALLEN ROBERT (1778-1827)
ENGLISH SCHOOL

20,639
Cahir Castle and Bridge over the River Suir, Co. Tipperary
10.3 x 14.2 (image 10.3 x 14.2)
Wood Engraving
Presented, Mrs D. Molloy, 1981

Irish School (19th century)
IRISH SCHOOL (19TH CENTURY)

11,241
The fatal shooting of D'Esterre, 1st February 1815, by Daniel O'Connell, (1775-1847), in a duel at Bishopscourt, Co. Kildare, 1815
12 x 20.5 (plate cut x 18.5)
Line
Provenance Unknown

Irish School (19th century)
IRISH SCHOOL (19TH CENTURY)

11,290
Richard Lalor Sheil, M.P., (1791-1851), Lawyer, Politician and Playwright
Published: J. Duffy, Dublin
20.4 x 12.6 (plate cut)
Line
Provenance Unknown

Irish School (19th century)
IRISH SCHOOL (19TH CENTURY)

11,411
Unidentified Man
48.8 x 42.2 (image 40 x 33)
Lithograph
Provenance Unknown

Irish School (19th century)
IRISH SCHOOL (19TH CENTURY)

11,635
Part of the old Walls of Londonderry, Co. Derry and two figures
16.4 x 12 (plate cut)
Etching with wash
Provenance Unknown

Irish School (19th century)
IRISH SCHOOL (19TH CENTURY)

11,636
Doorway of the medieval church at Maghera, Co. Derry
17.8 x 12.2 (plate cut)
Etching with wash
Provenance Unknown

Irish School (19th century)
IRISH SCHOOL (19TH CENTURY)

11,671
The Cromlech at Tubrid, Co. Kilkenny
INSCRIBED: *In Memoriam/ of John G.A. Prim this View of the Cromlech at Tubrid, in the County of Kilkenny/ is dedicated by the publisher James George Robertson/ Hon. Fell, R.S.A.I.*
Published: J.G. Robertson, Kilkenny
21.6 x 26.7 (plate 17.5 x 21.5)
Etching
Provenance Unknown

Irish School (19th century)
IRISH SCHOOL (19TH CENTURY)

11,672
The Cromlech at Harristown, Co. Kilkenny
INSCRIBED: *In Memoriam/ of the Rev. John J. Shearman P.P.M.R.I.A. this View of the Cromlech at Harristown/ in the County of Kilkenny is dedicated by the publisher James George Robertson*
Published: J.G. Robertson, Kilkenny
21.6 x 26.7 (plate 17 x 20.9)
Etching
Provenance Unknown

Irish School (19th century)
IRISH SCHOOL (19TH CENTURY)

11,673
Callan Church, Co. Kilkenny, (pl. for J.G. Robertson's 'Antiquities and Scenery of the County of Kilkenny', 1851)
INSCRIBED: *To the Revd. Dean Stephenson, this view of the Church-Callan/ is very respectfully inscribed by his Obt. Servant Wm. Robertson*
Published: W. Robertson, Kilkenny also J. Taylor, London (Printed: M. Allen)
37.8 x 44.6 (plate 26.4 x 34)
Aquatint
Provenance Unknown

Irish School (19th century)
IRISH SCHOOL (19TH CENTURY)

11,745
The Ruins of Rathmichael Monastery, Co. Dublin
21.5 x 23.8 (plate cut)
Etching on linen
Provenance Unknown

Irish School (19th century)
IRISH SCHOOL (19TH CENTURY)

11,746
Armoy Round Tower, Co. Antrim
21.5 x 23.4 (plate cut)
Etching on linen
Provenance Unknown

Irish School (19th century)
IRISH SCHOOL (19TH CENTURY)

11,760
The Choir of St Patrick's Cathedral, Dublin, before the 1863 Restoration
21.2 x 15 (plate cut)
Line
Provenance Unknown

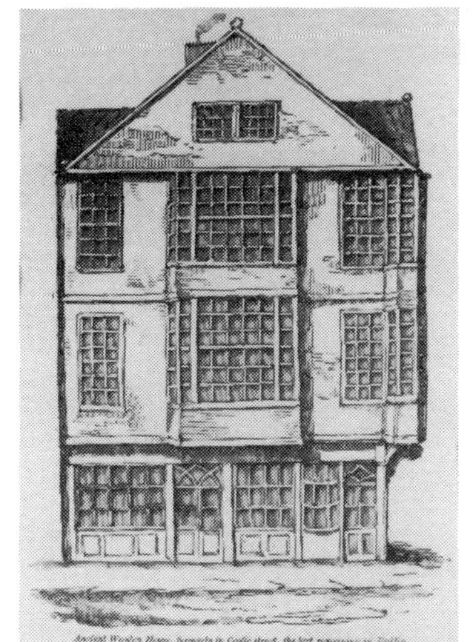

11,922
The last wooden house in Dublin on the corner of Castle and Werburgh Streets, (demolished 1812)
16.2 x 12.6 (plate cut)
Line
Presented, Mr W.G. Strickland, 1906

20,395
'Peace being Proclaimed, escaped from the Slaughter, landed at home'
37.5 x 27.4 (image 27 x 21.5)
Lithograph
Purchased, Lusk, Mr de Courcy Donovan, 1971

Irish School (19th century)
IRISH SCHOOL (19TH CENTURY)

1,867
'The Master of the Scrolls' - John Philpot Curran, (1750-1817), Judge and Orator
Published: W. McCleary, Dublin
8.5 x 22.1 (plate cut)
Purchased, Dublin,
Mr J.V. McAlpine, 1905

Irish School (19th century)
IRISH SCHOOL (19TH CENTURY)

20,394
'I fought for my country far, far from my true love'
37.5 x 27.5 (image 27 x 21)
Lithograph
Purchased, Lusk, Mr de Courcy Donovan, 1971

Irish School (19th century)
IRISH SCHOOL (19TH CENTURY)

20,396
'My sweet girl, I sought her'
37.4 x 27.5 (image 28 x 21.4)
Lithograph
Purchased, Lusk, Mr de Courcy Donovan, 1971

Irish School (19th century)
IRISH SCHOOL (19TH CENTURY)

Irish School (19th century)
IRISH SCHOOL (19TH CENTURY)

Irish School (19th century)
IRISH SCHOOL (19TH CENTURY)

20,555
Landscape
10 x 18.1 (plate cut)
Etching
Presented, Mrs D. Molloy, 1981

Irish School (19th century)
IRISH SCHOOL (19TH CENTURY)

20,622
Lombardy Poplars, (Pictorial effect)
11.1 x 18 (plate cut)
Etching
Presented, Mrs D. Molloy, 1981

Irish School (19th century)
IRISH SCHOOL (19TH CENTURY)

20,815
Ancient Tomb, Boreragh, Co. Londonderry
11.5 x 11.6 (plate cut)
Etching with wash
Provenance Unknown

Irish School (19th century)
IRISH SCHOOL (19TH CENTURY)

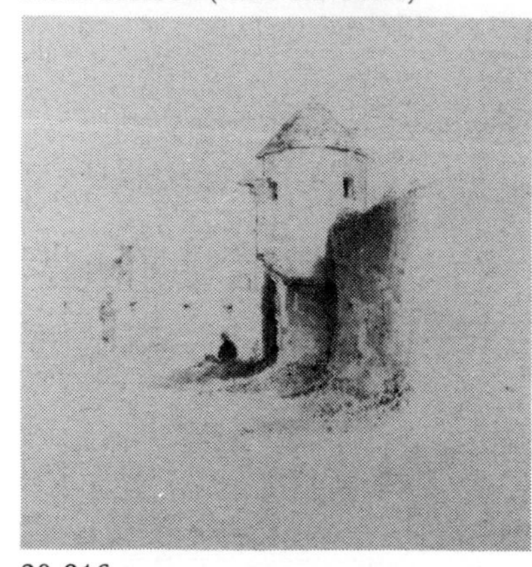

20,816
Part of the Old Walls of Londonderry and a seated figure
16.5 x 12.1 (plate cut)
Etching with wash
Provenance Unknown

Irish School (19th century)
IRISH SCHOOL (19TH CENTURY)

20,817
Doorways of the church at Maghera, Co. Londonderry
12 x 17.5 (plate cut)
Etching with wash
Provenance Unknown

Irish School (19th century)
IRISH SCHOOL (19TH CENTURY)

20,818
A damaged High Cross at Macosquin, Co. Londonderry
18 x 12.5 (plate cut)
Etching with wash
Provenance Unknown

Irish School (19th century)
IRISH SCHOOL (1847)

11,864
Edward Bunting, (1773-1843), Musician and Antiquary, (pl. for 'Dublin University Magazine', Vol. XXIX, January 1847)
Published: J. McGlashan, Dublin, 1847
27.7 x 23.4 (image 22 x 13.5)
Lithograph
Purchased, Dublin, Mr P. Traynor, 1898

Irish School (19th century)
JACKSON, M. (19TH CENTURY)
IRISH SCHOOL

11,729
Bank of Ireland, (formerly Parliament House), College Green and Trinity College, Dublin
27.2 x 18.3 (plate cut)
Line
Provenance Unknown

Irish School (19th century)
MARKS, J.I. (FL.1822-1839)
ENGLISH SCHOOL

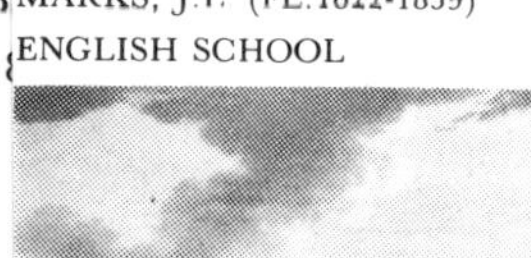

11,704
The Four Courts, Dublin from Merchant's Quay
11.8 x 19.4 (plate cut)
Etching and aquatint
Provenance Unknown

Irish School (19th century)
NEWMAN & CO., JOHN (FL.1860S-1870S)
ENGLISH SCHOOL

11,761
St Patrick's Cathedral, Dublin from the North-East
Published: J. Newman & Co., London
11.1 x 14.8 (plate cut)
Steel Engraving
Provenance Unknown

Irish School (19th century)
SLY, S. (FL.1833-1842)
ENGLISH SCHOOL

20,640
The Old Bridge, (now rebuilt), at Milltown, on the River Dodder, Dublin
8.5 x 13 (image 8.5 x 13)
Wood Engraving
Presented, Mrs D. Molloy, 1981

Irish School (19th century)
?SLY, S. (FL.1833-1842)
IRISH SCHOOL

20,641
Newbridge and the River Liffey, Co. Kildare
9.4 x 14.7 (image 9 x 13)
Wood Engraving
Presented, Mrs D. Molloy, 1981

Irish School (19th century)
SMITH, RICHARD (19TH CENTURY)
ENGLISH SCHOOL

11,280
William Power Le Poer-Trench, (1770-1839), P. Archbishop of Tuam, (pl. for 'Church Magazine', 1841)
Published: J. Hayward & Co., London, 1841
21.2 x 13.3 (plate cut)
Stipple
Acquired c.1908

?Irish School (19th century)
WEGER, T. (19TH CENTURY)
ENGLISH SCHOOL

10,900

T. Cadell & W. Davies' 'Contemporary Portraits', 1822)
INSCRIBED: From an original picture in his own possession
Published: T. Cadell & W. Davies, London, 1st March 1815
40.6 x 30.1 (plate 38 x cut)
Stipple
Presumed Purchased, Dublin, Jones Salesroom, 1879

Irish School (1806/1814)
LANE, JOHN BRYANT (1788-1868)
ENGLISH SCHOOL
FREEMAN, SAMUEL (1773-1857)
ENGLISH SCHOOL

10,770
John Philpot Curran, M.P., (1750-1817), as Master of the Rolls in Ireland, (pl. for T. Cadell & W. Davis' 'British Gallery of Contemporary Portraits', 1815-22), (another copy)
INSCRIBED: From an original picture in his own possession
Published: T. Cadell & W. Davies, London, 1st March 1815
42 x 31.8 (plate 38 x cut)
Stipple
Provenance Unknown

Irish School (1808)
IRISII SCHOOL (1808)

11,735
Charles Lennox, 9th Duke of Richmond, (1764-1819), Lord Lieutenant of Ireland, laying the first stone of Nelson Pillar, Dublin, February 15th, 1808
11.4 x 21.3 (plate 11.4 x 19.8)
Line
Provenance Unknown

Irish School (c.1808)
IRISH SCHOOL (1808)

10,587
Phelim O'Connor, (d.1315), King of Connaught, (pl. for 'Irish Catholic Magazine', January 1808)
Published: Irish Catholic Magazine, January 1808
19.5 x 11.9 (plate 14.3 x 9.6)
Stipple
Acquired c.1903

Irish School (c.1808)
IRISH SCHOOL (C.1808)

10,620
Edward Hay, (1761-1826), Writer and Agitator, member of the Royal Irish Academy
Published: not before 1808
20.1 x 14.5 (plate cut)
Stipple
Purchased, Dublin, Mr P. Traynor, 1898

Irish School (c.1809)
IRISH SCHOOL (1809)

11,343
Turlough O'Carolan, (1670-1738), Blind Harpist, (pl. for 'Irish Magazine', October 1809)
Published: W. Cox, Dublin, October 1809
18.1 x 11.6 (plate cut)
Stipple
Provenance Unknown

Irish School (c.1811)
BROCAS THE ELDER, HENRY (1766-1838)
IRISH SCHOOL

10,612
Hugh Douglas Hamilton, (1739-1808), Painter, (pl. for 'Hibernian Magazine', April 1811)
Published: Hibernian Magazine, Dublin, April 1811
21 x 12.8 (plate 19.2 x 12)
Stipple
Provenance Unknown

Irish School (c.1811)
IRISH SCHOOL (1811)

1,350
rthur James Plunkett, 8th Earl of ingall, (1759-1836), (pl. for 'Hibernian 1agazine', November 1811)
ublished: Hibernian Magazine,)ublin, November 1811
0.4 x 12.5 (plate 18.1 x 11.4)
tipple
rovenance Unknown

Irish School (c.1811)
IRISH SCHOOL (c.1811)

11,851
'A View of the Four Courts, Dublin'- William Downes, 1st Baron Downes, (1752-1826), Chief Justice of the King's Bench in Ireland; Thomas Manners-Sutton, 1st Baron Manners, (1755-1842), Lord Chancellor of Ireland: John Toler, 1st Earl of Norbury, (1745-1831), Chief Justice of the Common Pleas in Ireland and Standish O'Grady, 1st Viscount Guillamore, (1766-1840), Lord Chief Baron of the Exchequer in Ireland
Published: J. Sidebotham, Dublin, 1811
24 x 32 (plate cut)
Etching with watercolour
Provenance Unknown

Irish School (c.1813)
IRISH SCHOOL (1813)

10,598
Daniel O'Connell, (1775-1847), Statesman, when Counsellor defending John Magee, (pl. for 'Dublin Magazine', March 1813)
Published: Dublin Magazine, March 1813
20.9 x 12.6 (plate cut)
Stipple
Acquired by 1901

Irish School (c.1813)
IRISH SCHOOL (1813)

10,599
Daniel O'Connell, (1775-1847), Statesman, when Counsellor defending John Magee, (pl. for 'Dublin Magazine', March, 1813), (another copy)
Published: Dublin Magazine, March 1813
21.4 x 13.2 (plate cut)
Stipple
Acquired by 1901

Irish School (c.1814)
BLOOD, T. (FL.1814-1823)
ENGLISH SCHOOL

11,143
William Fletcher, (1750-1823), Judge of the Court of Common Pleas in Ireland, (pl. for 'European Magazine', January 1815)
(after an H. Brocas line and stipple, NGI no. 11,141)
Published: J. Asperne, London, 1st January 1815
22 x 12.9 (pl. 18 x cut)
Line and stipple
Provenance Unknown

Irish School (c.1814)
BROCAS THE ELDER, HENRY (1766-1838)
IRISH SCHOOL

11,141
William Fletcher, (1750-1823), Judge at the Court of Common Pleas in Ireland, (pl. for 'Dublin Monthly Museum', September 1814)
Published: Dublin Monthly Museum, September 1814
20.9 x 13 (plate 20 x cut)
Line and stipple
Purchased, Dublin, Mr P. Traynor, 1898

Irish School (c.1814)
BROCAS THE ELDER, HENRY (1766-1838)
IRISH SCHOOL

11,142
William Fletcher, (1750-1823), Judge at the Court of Common Pleas in Ireland, (pl. for 'Dublin Monthly Museum', September 1814), (another copy)
Published: Dublin Monthly Museum, September 1814
21.7 x 12.6 (plate 20 x cut)
Line and stipple
Purchased, Dublin, Mr P. Traynor, 1898

Irish School (c.1816)
ENGLISH SCHOOL (1816)

11,714
Dublin Bay and Howth from the North Strand, (pl. for A. Plumptre's 'Narrative of a Residence in Ireland during 1814 and 1815', 1817)
Published: H. Colburn, London, 1816
20.8 x 28.2 (plate cut)
Aquatint and etching
Provenance Unknown

Irish School (c.1817)
ENGLISH SCHOOL (1817)

11,741
St George's Church, Hardwicke Place, Dublin, (pl. for J. Warburton, J. Whitelaw and R. Walsh's 'History of the City of Dublin', 1818)
Published: T. Cadell & W. Davies, London, 21st August 1817
30.3 x 22.2 (plate 28.1 x 21.5)
Line
Presented, Mr W.G. Strickland, 1906

Irish School (c.1817)
ENGLISH SCHOOL (1817)

11,762
St Patrick's Cathedral, Dublin from the North-East, (pl. for J. Warburton, J. Whitelaw and R. Walsh's 'History of the City of Dublin', 1818)
Published: T. Cadell and W. Davies, London, 24th August 1817
22 x 30 (plate cut x 28)
Line
Presented, Mr W.G. Strickland, 1906

Irish School (c.1817)
ENGLISH SCHOOL (1817)

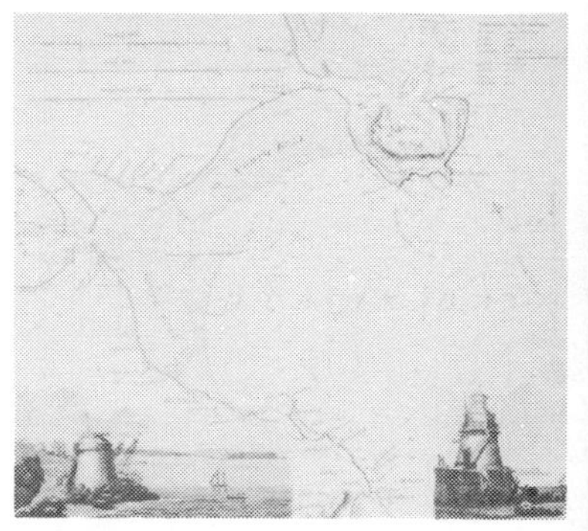

11,814
Nautical Map of Dublin Bay with vignettes of Seapoint Martello Tower and Poolbeg Light House, South Wall (pl. for J. Warburton, J. Whitelaw & R. Walsh's 'History of the City of Dublin', 1818)
(reduced version of Captain Bligh's 1800 survey)
Published: T. Cadell & W. Davies,

London, 28th August 1817
21.6 x 27.8 (plate cut x 25.5)
Line
Provenance Unknown

Irish School (c.1817)
ENGLISH SCHOOL (1817)

11,831
The Great Hall of the Foundling Hospital and Workhouse, Dublin, (later St Kevin's Hospital, now demolished), (pl. for J. Warburton, J. Whitelaw & R. Walsh's 'History of the City of Dublin', 1818)
Published: T. Cadell and W. Davies, London, 21st August 1817
13.6 x 19.6 (plate cut)
Line
Presented, Mr W.G. Strickland, 1906

Irish School (c.1818)
BRUNTON, B. (19TH CENTURY)
ENGLISH SCHOOL

11,767
South View of the Stove Tenter House, Weavers Square, Dublin, (now demolished), (from 'Gentleman's Magazine', February 1818)
Published: Gentleman's Magazine, London, February 1818
13.1 x 21.1 (plate 12.1 x 20.4)
Line
Provenance Unknown

Irish School (c.1820)
ENGLISH SCHOOL (19TH CENTURY)

11,088
John Banim, (1798-1842), Novelist, Poet and Dramatist
INSCRIBED: From the Picture in the possession of the family
Published: Blackie & Son, London, Glasgow & Edinburgh
24.5 x 16.7 (image 15.5 x 11)
Lithograph
Acquired between 1913/14

Irish School (c.1820)
IRISH SCHOOL (C.1820)

10,823
George IV, King of England, (1762-1830)
Published: J. Le Petit, Dublin, c.1820
42.6 x 36.5 (plate 37.5 x 27.3)
Line with watercolour
Acquired by 1913

Irish School (c.1820)
IRISH SCHOOL (C.1820)

11,736
The Royal College of Surgeons, St Stephens Green, Dublin, (later widened)
21.3 x 29.7 (plate 13.8 x 18.5)
Line
Presented, Dr E. MacDowel Cosgrave, 1907

Irish School (c.1820)
KELLY, THOMAS (FL.1799-1841)
IRISH SCHOOL

11,180
James Warren Doyle, (1786-1834), R.C. Bishop of Kildare and Leighlin
Published: Macgregor, Polson & Co., Dublin
22.1 x 14 (plate cut)
Line and stipple
Purchased, Dublin, Mr P. Traynor, 1898

Irish School (c.1823)
ENGLISH SCHOOL (1823)

10,600
Daniel O'Connell, (1775-1847), Statesman
Published: J. Robins & Co., London, 13th September 1823
21 x 12.5 (plate 16.7 x 10.8)
Line and stipple
Purchased, Dublin, Dillon & Co., 1901

10,989
Fergus O'Connor, M.P., (1794-1855), son of Roger O'Connor
51.2 x 38.1 (plate 47.3 x 34.5)
Line and stipple
Purchased, Mr J.V. McAlpine, 1898

Irish School (c.1840)
IRISH SCHOOL (C.1840)

11,862
Daniel O'Connell, M.P., (1775-1847), Statesman
12.8 x 10.2 (plate cut)
Mezzotint
Provenance Unknown

Irish School (c.1827)
IRISH SCHOOL (C.1827)

11,332
William Conyngham, 1st Baron Plunket, (1764-1854), Chief Justice of the Irish Common Pleas, later Lord Chancellor
24.6 x 20.5 (image 16 x 12 approx)
Lithograph
Provenance Unknown

Irish School (1830s)
READ, WILLIAM (FL.1824-1837)
ENGLISH SCHOOL

Irish School (c.1831)
IRISH SCHOOL (1831)

10,973
Daniel O'Connell, M.P., (1775-1847), Statesman
Published: T. McClean, London also C. Fleming, Dublin, 5th December 1831
31 x 23.3 (plate 25.6 x 21)
Line and stipple
Provenance Unknown

Irish School (1840s)
IRISH SCHOOL (1840S)

10,974
'The Liberator, Travelling' - Daniel O'Connell, M.P., (1775-1847), Statesman
Published: W.J. Kelly, Dublin
27.8 x 22.5 (image 13 x 10.7)
Lithograph
Presented, Mr H. Doyle, 1889

Irish School (c.1841)
KIRKWOOD, JOHN (FL.1823-1853)
IRISH SCHOOL

10,596
Daniel O'Connell, M.P., (1775-1847), Statesman, (pl. for 'Dublin University Magazine', Vol. XVII, March 1841)
Published: W. Curry Junior, Dublin, 1841
21.3 x 13.5 (plate cut)
Etching
Purchased, Dublin, Mr P. Traynor, 1898

Irish School (c.1841)
KIRKWOOD, JOHN (FL.1826-1853)
IRISH SCHOOL

1,109
ev. John Barrett, (1746-1821), Vice-rovost, Trinity College Dublin, against e Dining Hall and Rubrics, (pl. for 'Dublin University Magazine' Vol. XIX, September 1841)
Published: W. Curry Junior & Co., Dublin, 1841
22.8 x 14.3 (plate cut)
Etching
Purchased, Dublin, Mr P. Traynor, 1898

Irish School (c.1843)
HUFFAM, T.W. (FL.1825-C.1855)
ENGLISH SCHOOL

10,616
James Hope, (1764-1846), Nationalist, (pl. for R. Madden's 'United Irishmen', 2nd Series, 1843)
INSCRIBED: *From an original portrait in his possession*
Published: Madden & Co., London, 1843
20.2 x 12.2 (plate cut)
Mezzotint
Purchased, Dublin, Mr P. Traynor, 1898

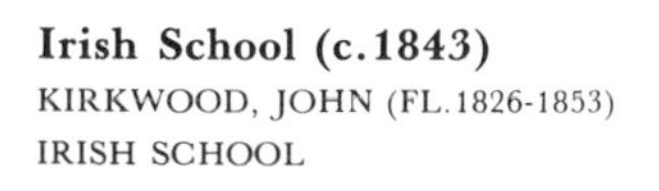

Irish School (c.1843)
KIRKWOOD, JOHN (FL.1826-1853)
IRISH SCHOOL

11,019
George Smith
38.8 x 32.4 (plate 29.2 x 23)
Etching
Provenance Unknown

Irish School (1846)
SMYTH (19TH CENTURY)
ENGLISH SCHOOL

11,878
Aerial View of the City of Dublin from the South East, (being no. 1 of a series of views of the principal capitals in Europe, presented gratis to the subscribers to the Illustrated London News, 1846)
Published: Illustrated London News, London, 1846
39.4 x 106.5 (image 35.6 x 103.7)
Wood Engraving
Acquired between 1908/14

Irish School (c.1847)
GRIFFITHS, HENRY (FL.1835-1849)
ENGLISH SCHOOL

11,178
John Doherty, (1783-1856), when Justice of the Common Pleas in Ireland, (pl. for 'Dublin University Magazine', Vol. XXIX, June 1847)
Published: McGlashan, Dublin 1847
22.6 x 14.2 (plate cut)
Stipple and etching
Purchased, Dublin, Mr P. Traynor, 1898

Irish School (c.1848)
GRIFFITHS, HENRY (FL.1835-1849)
ENGLISH SCHOOL

10,624
Robert Holmes, (1765-1859), Lawyer, brother-in-law of Robert Emmet, (pl. for 'Dublin University Magazine', Vol. XXXI, January 1848)
Published: J. McGlashan, Dublin, 1848
21.5 x 13.7 (plate cut)
Stipple
Purchased, Dublin, Mr P. Traynor 1898

Irish School (c.1850)
IRISH SCHOOL (1850)

11,378
Catherine Hayes, (c.1820-1851), Opera Singer, (pl. for 'Dublin University Magazine', Vol. XXXVI, November 1850)
Published: J. McGlashan, Dublin, 1850
22.7 x 14.4 (plate cut)
Etching
Purchased, Dublin,
Mr J.V. McAlpine, 1913

Irish School (c.1850)
IRISH SCHOOL (C.1850)

11,383
Rev. John Spratt, (1797-1871), Philanthropist, Provincial of Carmelite Order in Ireland, President of the Irish Total Abstinence Society
31.5 x 24.5 (image 25.8 x 24.5)
Lithograph
Acquired by 1903

Irish School (c.1850)
IRISH SCHOOL (C.1850)

11,766
The Interior of St Audeon's R.C. Church, High Street, Dublin
21.6 x 16.8 (image 13.9 x 12.6)
Wood Engraving
Provenance Unknown

Irish School (1853)
IRISH SCHOOL (1853)

11,630
The Great Industrial Exhibition, Leinster Lawn, Dublin, 1853, with vignette portrait of sponsor William Dargan, (1799-1867)
INSCRIBED: with illegible dedication to William Dargan
Published: Marlow Brothers, Dublin, 1853 (Printed: In the Exhibition by Marlow Brothers)

36.7 x 52.3 (image 28.5 approx x 49)
Coloured Lithograph
Purchased, Dublin,
Mr J.V. McAlpine, 1911

Irish School (1853)
IRISH SCHOOL (1853)

11,722
The Arrival of the Lord Lieutenant, Edward Granville Eliot, 3rd Earl of Saint Germans at the Dublin Great Exhibition, Leinster Lawn, Dublin, 1853
27.7 x 36.5 (plate 21.2 x 31.3)
Line
Presented, Dr E. MacDowel Cosgrave, 1907

Irish School (1861)
IRISH SCHOOL (1861)

20,554
A fatal omnibus accident in Dublin, 1861
20 x 26.1 (image 16.2 x 23.3)
Wood Engraving
Presented, Mrs D. Molloy, 1981

Irish School (c.1865)
MORISON & CO (FL.1865-1880)
IRISH SCHOOL

11,840
The New Presbyterian, (Findlater's), Church, Rutland, (now Parnell) Square, Dublin
55.9 x 37.9 (image 38 x 24.5)
Chromo-lithograph
Provenance Unknown

Irish School (c.1870)
McRAE, J.C. (19TH CENTURY)
?IRISH SCHOOL

10,284
Sir Charles Gavan Duffy, (1816-1903), Nationalist Politician in Ireland and Australia
(after a daguerreotype)
Published: Farrell & Son, Dublin
29.4 x 20.7 (plate cut)
Line
Provenance Unknown

Irish School (1880)
MORISON & CO. (FL.1865-1880)
IRISH SCHOOL

11,632
Theatre Royal, Hawkins Street, Dublin, on fire, 9th February 1880
(after a photograph)
Published: Dublin, 1880
34.2 x 47 (image 25.5 x 37)
Lithograph
Provenance Unknown

Irish School (c.1880)
IRISH SCHOOL (C.1880)

11,724
O'Connell, (formerly Carlisle), Bridge and Sackville, (now O'Connell), Street, Dublin
(after a print published by Messrs, Stark Brothers)
12.1 x 14.8 (cut to image)
Wood Engraving
Provenance Unknown

Irish School (1883)
IRISH SCHOOL (1883)

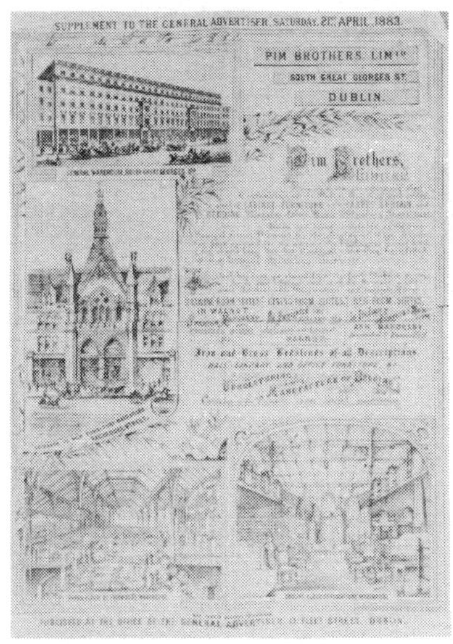

20,644
Advertisement for Pim Bros. Furniture Warehouses, South Great George's Street and Exchequer Street, (now rebuilt), (pl. from 'The General Advertiser', 21st April 1883)
Published: The General Advertiser, Dublin, 21st April 1883 (Printed: City Printing & Litho Co. Ltd.)
51 x 38 (image 50 x 37)
Lithograph
Presented, Mrs D. Molloy, 1981

Isabey, Eugène (1803-1886)
French School
SABATIER, LEON JEAN-BAPTISTE (FL.1827-1887)
FRENCH SCHOOL

20,316
Fishing Community, ('La Campagne', no.78)
Published: F. Delarue, Paris also E. Gambart Junin & Co., London
(Printed: Cattier, Paris)
30.3 x 47.4 (image 26.5 x 44.5)
Lithograph
Purchased, Lusk, Mr de Courcy Donovan, 1971

Isabey, Eugène (1803-1886)
French School
SABATIER, LEON JEAN-BAPTISTE (FL.1827-1887)
FRENCH SCHOOL

20,317
Boat under Repair with Figures, ('La Campagne', no. 74)
(Printed: Cattier, Paris)
47.3 x 30.9 (image 42 x 30 approx)
Lithograph
Purchased, Lusk, Mr de Courcy Donovan, 1971

Italian School (16th century)
CORR, MATHIEU ERIN (1805-1862)
FLEMISH SCHOOL

11,482
The Saviour of the World, (artist given as Leonardo da Vinci)
(after a painting on marble, formerly Antwerp Cathedral)
Published: M.E. Corr, Antwerp; also Goupil & Vibert, Paris; also E. Gambart & Co., London
72.5 x 55 (plate 52 x 42)
Line
Presented, Mr M. Corr van der Maeren, 1864

Italian School (16th century)
CORR, MATHIEU ERIN (1805-1862)
FLEMISH SCHOOL

20,806
The Saviour of the World, (artist given as Leonardo da Vinci), (another copy)
(after a painting on marble, formerly Antwerp Cathedral)
Published: M.E. Corr, Antwerp; also Goupil & Vibert, Paris; also E. Gambart & Co., London
86.5 x 61.3 (plate 52 x 42)
Line
Provenance Unknown

Italian School (c.1741)
ITALIAN SCHOOL (1741)

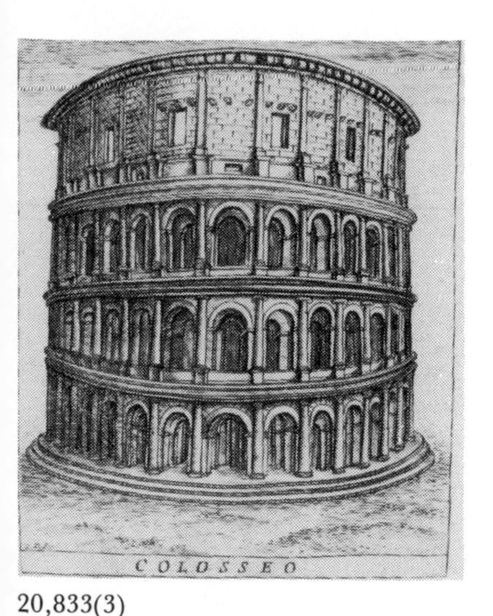

20,833(3)
The Colosseum, Rome, (a reconstruction), (from 'Roma Antica', 1741, see App. 8, no. 20,833)
Published: Rome, 1741 (Printed: Bornabo & Lazzarini)
17 x 15.4 (plate 13.5 x 10.8)
Etching
Provenance Unknown

Italian School (late 18th century)
RANCATI, ANTONIO (1748-1861)
ITALIAN SCHOOL

20,467
Chinese Porters
23.7 x 26.5 (plate 21.5 x 15.7)
Line with watercolour
Purchased, Lusk, Mr de Courcy Donovan, 1971

Italian School (late 18th century)
ZANCON, GAETANO (1771-1816)
ITALIAN SCHOOL

20,468
A Chinese building
26.5 x 37 (plate 16.5 x 22.8)
Line with watercolour
Purchased, Lusk, Mr de Courcy Donovan, 1971

Italian School (1856)
ITALIAN SCHOOL (1856)

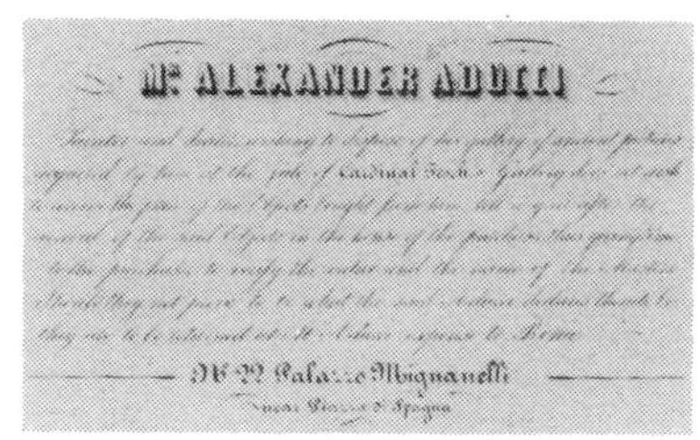
Mr ALEXANDER ADUCCI
No 22 Palazzo Mignanelli
near Piazza di Spagna

11,550
Trade Card of Alexander Aducci
INSCRIBED: Mr Alexander Aducci, Painter and dealer wishing to dispose of his Gallery of ancient pictures/acquired by him at the sale of Cardinal Fesch's Gallery does not wish/to receive the price of the objects bought from his till a year after the arrival of the/said Objects in the house of the purchaser, thus giving time/to the purchaser to verify the value and the name of the Masters./Should they not prove to be what the said Aducci declares them to be/they are to be returned at Mr Aducci's expense to Rome/No. 22 Palazzo Mignaelli/(near Piazza di Espagna)
7.3 x 11.5 (plate cut)
Etching
Presented, Mr A. Aducci, 1856

Ivory, Thomas (c.1730-1786)
Irish School
ROOKER, EDWARD (18TH CENTURY)
IRISH SCHOOL

11,669
Lord Charlemont's Casino at Marino, near Dublin (c.1772)
2nd State (dedication to 1st Earl of Charlemont cut)
43 x 64.8 (plate cut)
Line
Provenance Unknown

J

Jackson, John (1778-1831)
English School
FRY, WILLIAM THOMAS (1789-1831)
ENGLISH SCHOOL

10,260
Martin Archer Shee, (1760-1850), Artist, (pl. for T. Cadell & W. Davies's 'Contemporary Portraits' 1822)
(after a black chalk drawing with watercolour of c.1815, NPG, London)
Published: T. Cadell & W. Davies, London, 14th January 1817
42.3 x 33.5 (plate 37.8 x 33)
Stipple
Purchased, London, Mr J.V. McAlpine, 1899

Jackson, John (1778-1831)
English School
MEYER, HENRY HOPPNER (1783-1847)
ENGLISH SCHOOL

10,270
Charles Lennox, 4th Duke of Richmond, (1764-1819), Soldier and Lord Lieutenant of Ireland
INSCRIBED: *To the Duchess of Richmond this Plate is with permission Dedicated by Her Grace's/most obliged and humble Servant/H. Meyer.*
Lettered Proof
Published: H. Meyer, London, 25th May 1807
35.8 x 25.6 (plate 35.5 x 25)
Mezzotint
Acquired between 1890/98

Jackson, John (1778-1831)
English School
PAGE, ROBERT (19TH CENTURY)
ENGLISH SCHOOL

11,214
Rev. Adam Clarke, (?1762-1832), Wesleyan Minister and Biblical Commentator
Published: J. Robins & Co., London, 1st November 1823
21.1 x 12.3 (plate cut)
Stipple
Purchased, Dublin Mr P. Traynor, 1898

Jackson, John (1778-1831)
English School
THOMSON, JAMES (1789-1850)
ENGLISH SCHOOL

11,236
Thomas Moore, (1779-1852), Poet, (pl. for 'European Magazine', April 1824)
(after an oil of 1818, NGI no. 257)
Published: Sherwood & Co., London, April 1824
20.5 x 11.8 (plate cut)
Stipple
Purchased, Dublin, Mr P. Traynor, 1898

Jackson, John (1778-1831)
English School
WARD THE ELDER, WILLIAM (1766-1826)
ENGLISH SCHOOL

10,776
George James Welbore Agar Ellis, M.P., (1797-1833), later 1st Baron Dover and Trustee of the British Museum and the National Gallery, London
Published: Colnaghi & Co., London, 1st March 1823
36.8 x 26.4 (plate 35.3 x 25.2)
Mezzotint
Purchased, London, 2nd Chaloner Smith sale, 1888

Jackson, John (1778-1831)
English School
WOODMAN THE YOUNGER, RICHARD (1784-1859)
ENGLISH SCHOOL

10,118
John Flaxman, (1755-1826), Sculptor, pl. for C. Knight's 'Gallery of Portraits', 1833-37)
After an oil of c.1820, Althorp, (Northants)
INSCRIBED: From the original Picture by/John Jackson/in the possession of the Right Lord Dover/under the superintendence of the Society for the Diffusion of Useful knowledge
Published: C. Knight, London
27.5 x 19 (plate cut)
Stipple and mezzotint
Purchased, Lusk, Mr de Courcy Donovan, 1971

Jackson, Mason (1819-1903)
English School
ENGLISH SCHOOL (1865)

20,573
The Civil War in America: rendezvous of Mosby's men in the Pass of the Blue Ridge, Shenandoah Valley, (from 'The Illustrated London News', 1865)
Published: Illustrated London News, 1865
26.2 x 36 (image 23.6 x 34)
Wood Engraving
Presented, Mrs D. Molloy, 1981

Jacottet, Louis Julien (1806-after 1855)
French School *and*
Bayot, Adolphe Jean-Baptiste (1810-after 1866)
French School
JACOTTET, LOUIS JULIEN (1806-AFTER 1855)
FRENCH SCHOOL *and*
BAYOT, ADOLPHE JEAN-BAPTISTE (1810-AFTER 1866)
FRENCH SCHOOL

20,315
Figures resting by Trees, ('La Campagne', no.59)
Published: F. Delarue, Paris, also Gambart, Junin, & Co., London, 25th March 1845 (Printed: Lemercier, Paris)
49.1 x 31 (image 34 x 26.5 approx)
Lithograph
Purchased, Lusk, Mr de Courcy Donovan, 1971

Jagger, Charles (c.1770-1827)
English School
SANGSTER, SAMUEL (C.1804-1872)
ENGLISH SCHOOL

10,868
General Sir Henry Johnson, Bt., (1748-1835), defeated Irish rebels at New Ross, 1798
(after a miniature)

Published: not before 1835
43.7 x 29.8 (plate 31 x 23)
Line and stipple
Purchased, Dublin,
Mr J.V. McAlpine, 1909

Jenkins, Joseph John (1811-1885)
English School
WILLIAMSON, THOMAS (C.1800-1840)
ENGLISH SCHOOL

11,248
Princess Victoria, (1819-1901), later Queen Victoria of England, aged 12, (pl. for Bell's 'Weekly Messenger', 1st January 1832)
Lettered Proof
Published: Weekly Messenger, 1st January 1832
22.8 x 19.5 (plate cut x 15.8)
Stipple
Presented, Dublin,
Mr J.V. McAlpine, 1901

Jervas, Charles (c.1675-1739)
Irish School
BROOKS, JOHN (FL.1730-1756)
IRISH SCHOOL

10,148
Thomas Carter, M.P., (d.1763), Master of the Rolls in Ireland
34.9 x 25.5 (plate 34.7 x 25.4)
Mezzotint
Purchased, London, 1st Chaloner Smith sale, 1887

Jervas, Charles (c.1675-1739)
Irish School
BROOKS, JOHN (FL.1730-1756)
IRISH SCHOOL

10,242
Luke Gardiner, M.P., (d.1755), Vice-Treasurer of Ireland and building developer in Dublin
1st State
Published: J. Brooks, Dublin, c.1742
29.2 x 24.5 (plate cut)
Mezzotint
Purchased, London, 1st Chaloner Smith sale, 1887

Jervas, Charles (c.1675-1739)
Irish School
BROOKS, JOHN (FL.1730-1756)
IRISH SCHOOL

10,825
Luke Gardiner, M.P., (d.1755), Vice-Treasurer of Ireland and building developer in Dublin
2nd State
Published: T. Jefferys, also W. Herbert, London, c.1742
34.5 x 25.2 (plate 34.2 x 24.6)
Mezzotint
Purchased, London, 1st Chaloner Smith sale, 1887

Jervas, Charles (c.1675-1739)
Irish School
FOURDRINIER, PIERRE (FL.1728-1758)
ANGLO-FRENCH SCHOOL

10,019

William Conolly, (c.1662-1729), Speaker of the Irish House of Commons
(after an oil of c.1720, Castletown House, Co. Kildare)
Published: not before 1729
46 x 34 (plate cut)
Line
Purchased, Dublin, Mr J.V. McAlpine, 1898

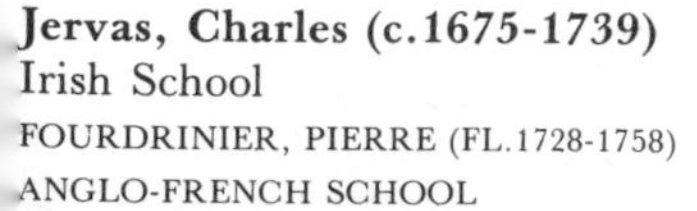

Jervas, Charles (c.1675-1739)
Irish School
FOURDRINIER, PIERRE (FL.1728-1758)
ANGLO-FRENCH SCHOOL

0,169
onathan Swift, (1667-1745), Dean of St 'atrick's Cathedral, Dublin and Satirist
after an oil of c.1718, NPG, London)
7 x 27.5 (plate 35.7 x 26.3)
ine
cquired between 1913/14

ervas, Charles (c.1675-1739)
ish School
URCELL, RICHARD (FL.1746-C.1766)
ISH SCHOOL

10,011
William King, P. Archbishop of Dublin, (1650-1729)
(probably after a J. Faber mezzotint of 1729; example in BM, London)
Published: T. Sillcock, Dublin, 1753
35.7 x 25.1 (plate cut)
Mezzotint
Purchased, London, 2nd Chaloner Smith sale, 1888

Jervas, Charles (c.1675-1739)
Irish School
SIMON, JOHN (1675-1751)
ANGLO-FRENCH SCHOOL

10,682
Philip Wharton, 1st Duke of Wharton, (1698-1731)
Published: J. Simon, London, not before 1718
36 x 26 (plate 35.5 x 25.7)
Mezzotint
Purchased, London, 2nd Chaloner Smith sale, 1888

Jervas, Charles (c.1675-1739)
Irish School
VERTUE, GEORGE (1684-1750)
ENGLISH SCHOOL

10,214
Jonathan Swift, (1667-1745), Dean of St Patrick's Cathedral, Dublin and Satirist
(after an oil of 1709-10, Bodleian Library, Oxford)
Published: 1715
35.4 x 25.4 (plate cut)
Line
Purchased, Dublin, Mr P. Traynor, 1898

Jervas, Charles (c.1675-1739)
Irish School
THURSTON, JOHN (1774-1822)
ENGLISH SCHOOL
WARREN, ALFRED WILLIAM (FL.1830S-1840S)
ENGLISH SCHOOL

11,285

Jonathan Swift, (1667-1745), Dean of St Patrick's Cathedral Dublin and Satirist
INSCRIBED: *From an original Picture in the Collection of/the Right Honorable the Earl of Bessborough*
17.8 x 13.5 (plate cut)
Line
Purchased, Dublin, Mr J.V. McAlpine, 1909

John, Augustus (1878-1961)
Welsh School
JOHN, AUGUSTUS (1878-1961)
WELSH SCHOOL

20,764
William Butler Yeats, (1865-1939), Poet and Dramatist
(after an oil of 1907, Manchester City Art Gallery)
Issued by the Artist, 1907; 23/of 50
28.5 x 21.5 (plate 17.5 x 12.3)
Etching and drypoint
Purchased, Dublin, James Adam & Sons, Ltd., 1984

Johnston, Francis (1760-1829)
Irish School
HAVELL THE ELDER, ROBERT (FL.1800-1840)
ENGLISH SCHOOL *and*
HAVELL THE YOUNGER, ROBERT (FL.1820-1850)
ENGLISH SCHOOL

11,705
The General Post Office, Sackville, (now O'Connell), Street, Dublin
Lettered Proof. INSCRIBED: *To the Right Honorable and Honorable the Post Masters General of Ireland./This view of the Post Office in Sackville Street Dublin, /is, with due respect, inscribed by their Lordships most obedient servant, Francis Johnston Architect.*
Published: R. Havell the Elder, London, 1st March 1824
51.8 x 74 (plate cut)
Aquatint and etching
Presented, Mr L. O'Callaghan, 1926

Jones, Edward (c.1775-1862)
Irish School
BROCAS THE ELDER, HENRY (1766-1838)
IRISH SCHOOL

11,301
Sir John Andrew Stevenson, (1762-1833), Composer, (pl. for 'Cyclopaedian Magazine', April 1807)
(after a miniature)
Published: Cyclopaedian Magazine, Dublin, April 1807
22.8 x 19.4 (plate 18.8 x 12.5)
Stipple
Purchased, London, 3rd Chaloner Smith sale, 1896

Jones, John Edward (1806-1862)
Irish School
RADCLYFFE, EDWARD (1809-1863)
ENGLISH SCHOOL

11,674
Monasterboice Monastery, near Drogheda, Co. Louth, (from J. D'Alton's 'History of Drogheda with its Environs; and an introductory memoir of the Dublin and Drogheda Railway', 1844)
Published: J. D'Alton, Dublin, 1844
22.8 x 14.3 (plate cut)
Steel Engraving
Provenance Unknown

Jones, John Edward (1806-1862)
Irish School
RADCLYFFE, EDWARD (1809-1863)
ENGLISH SCHOOL

11,675
Beaulieu House on the River Boyne, Drogheda, Co. Louth, (from J. D'Alton's 'History of Drogheda with its Environs; and an introductory memoir of the Dublin and Drogheda Railway', 1844)
Published: J. D'Alton, Dublin, 1844
14.2 x 22.5 (plate cut)
Steel Engraving
Provenance Unknown

Jones, John Edward (1806-1862)
Irish School
RADCLYFFE, EDWARD (1809-1863)
ENGLISH SCHOOL

11,676
Ruins of the Dominican Priory, Drogheda, Co. Louth, (from J. D'Alton's 'History of Drogheda with its Environs; and an introductory memoir of the Dublin and Drogheda Railway', 1844)
Published: J. D'Alton, Dublin, 1844
22.5 x 14.2 (plate cut)
Steel Engraving
Provenance Unknown

ones, John Edward (1806-1862)
rish School
ADCLYFFE, EDWARD (1809-1863)
NGLISH SCHOOL

1,677
rdgillan Castle, Balbriggan, Co. Dublin ith the Dublin and Drogheda Railway, rom J. D'Alton's 'History of Drogheda ith its Environs; and an introductory emoir of the Dublin and Drogheda ailway', 1844)
ublished: J. D'Alton, Dublin, 1844
.2 x 22.2 (plate cut)
eel Engraving
rovenance Unknown

Jones, John Edward (1806-1862)
Irish School
RADCLYFFE, EDWARD (1809-1863)
ENGLISH SCHOOL

11,678
Gormanstown Castle, Gormanstown, Co. Meath, (from J. D'Alton's 'History of Drogheda with its Environs; and an introductory memoir of the Dublin and Drogheda Railway', 1844)
Published: J. D'Alton, Dublin, 1844
14.2 x 22.6 (plate cut)
Steel Engraving
Provenance Unknown

Jones, John Edward (1806-1862)
Irish School
RADCLYFFE, EDWARD (1809-1863)
ENGLISH SCHOOL

11,685
Rush and the Skerries, Co. Dublin, with the Dublin and Drogheda railway, (from J. D'Alton's 'History of Drogheda with its Environs; and an introductory memoir of the Dublin and Drogheda Railway', 1844)
Published: J. D'Alton, Dublin, 1844
14.5 x 22.9 (plate cut)
Steel Engraving
Provenance Unknown

Jones, John Edward (1806-1862)
Irish School
RADCLYFFE, EDWARD (1809-1863)
ENGLISH SCHOOL

11,686
Portrane and Lambay Island, Co. Dublin, (from J. D'Alton's 'History of Drogheda with its Environs; and an introductory memoir of the Dublin and Drogheda Railway', 1844)
Published: J. D'Alton, Dublin, 1844
14.3 x 22.7 (plate cut)
Steel Engraving
Provenance Unknown

Jones, John Edward (1806-1862)
Irish School
RADCLYFFE, EDWARD (1809-1863)
ENGLISH SCHOOL

11,687
Malahide, Co. Dublin, with the Dublin and Drogheda railway, (from J. D'Alton's 'History of Drogheda with its Environs; and an introductory memoir of the Dublin and Drogheda Railway', 1844)
Published: J. D'Alton, Dublin, 1844
14.3 x 23 (plate cut)
Steel Engraving
Provenance Unknown

Jones, John Edward (1806-1863)
Irish School
RADCLYFFE, EDWARD (1809-1863)
ENGLISH SCHOOL

11,688

Malahide Castle, Co. Dublin, (from J. D'Alton's 'History of Drogheda with its Environs, and an introductory memoir of the Dublin and Drogheda Railway', 1844)
Published: J. D'Alton, Dublin, 1844
14.5 x 22.7 (plate cut)
Steel Engraving
Provenance Unknown

Jones, John Edward (1806-1862)
Irish School
RADCLYFFE, EDWARD (1809-1863)
ENGLISH SCHOOL

11,758
Lusk Church and Round Tower, Co. Dublin, (from J. D'Alton's 'History of Drogheda with its Environs; and an introductory memoir of the Dublin and Drogheda Railway', 1844)
Published: J. D'Alton, Dublin, 1844
(plate cut)
Steel Engraving
Provenance Unknown

Jones, Lieutenant Oliver John (?b.1813)
English School
DICKINSON & CO (19TH CENTURY)
ENGLISH SCHOOL

20,701
Her Majesty Queen Victoria's Tour through the Fleet in the Harbour of Cork on the 3rd of August 1849
INSCRIBED: *Publd. for the benefit of the Cork Masonic Female Orphan Asylum/ Dedicated to Coln. J.C. Chatterton K.H. /Provincial Grand Master of Munster SGIG 33rd.*
Published: Dickinson & Co., London
51 x 66 (image 37.5 x 55)
Lithograph with watercolour
Purchased, London, The Parker Gallery, 1983

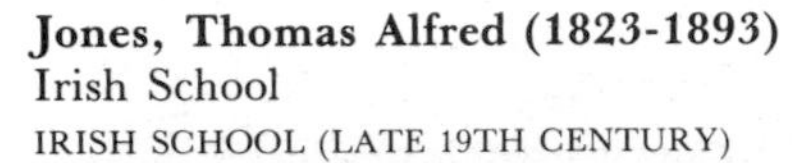

Jones, Thomas Alfred (1823-1893)
Irish School
IRISH SCHOOL (LATE 19TH CENTURY)

10,880
Robert J. Hunter
(after an oil, RHA 1883)
Unlettered Proof
Published: T. Cranfield, Dublin
43.3 x 35.5 (plate 44.2 x 35.4)
Etching
Acquired between 1913/14

Jones, William (fl.1744-1747)
Irish School
KING, GILES (FL.1732-1746)
ENGLISH SCHOOL

10,007
Howth, Co. Dublin from Beggars Bush; with key showing Ringsend, Irishtown, North and South Wall, Clontarf Island, Poolbeg, Sheds of Clontarf, Howth and Howth Castle
Published: J. Bowles, London, 1745
37 x 47.7 (plate cut)
Line
Purchased, Dublin, Mr P. Traynor, 1898

Jones, William (fl.1744-1747)
Irish School
MILLER, ANDREW (FL.1737-1763)
IRISH SCHOOL

10,074
Charles Lucas, (1713-1771), Libertarian
(after an oil of 1747)
Published: ?A. Miller, Dublin
35.9 x 25.5 (plate 35.5 x 25.5)
Mezzotint
Purchased, London, 1st Chaloner Smith sale, 1887

Jones, William (fl.1744-c.1749)
Irish School
MILLER, ANDREW (FL.1737-1763)
IRISH SCHOOL

10,480
Charles Lucas, (1713-1771), Libertarian
(after an oil of c.1749)
Published: ?A. Miller, Dublin
51 x 35 (plate 51 x 35)
Mezzotint
Purchased, London, 1st Chaloner Smith sale, 1887

Joseph, George Francis (1764-1846)
English School
FREEMAN, SAMUEL (1773-1857)
ENGLISH SCHOOL

10,639
rthur Wolfe, 1st Viscount Kilwarden (1739-1803), Chief Justice of Ireland, (pl. or J. Wills' 'Lives of Illustrious and Distinguished Irishmen', 1839-1847)
after a wl oil of 1820, Trinity College, Dublin)
Published: Macgregor, Polson, Sutherland & Co. Dublin, 1847
21.9 x 13.7 (plate cut)
Stipple
Purchased, Dublin, Mr P. Traynor 1898

Joseph, George Francis (1764-1846)
English School
SCRIVEN, EDWARD (1775-1841)
ENGLISH SCHOOL

11,029
Sir John Andrew Stevenson, (1762-1833), Composer
(after an oil, RA 1821, NGI no. 416)
Lettered Proof
Published: J. Willis, Dublin, 28th March 1822
46.7 x 33 (plate 37.8 x 26.4)
Line and stipple
Purchased, Dublin, Mr A. Roth, 1901

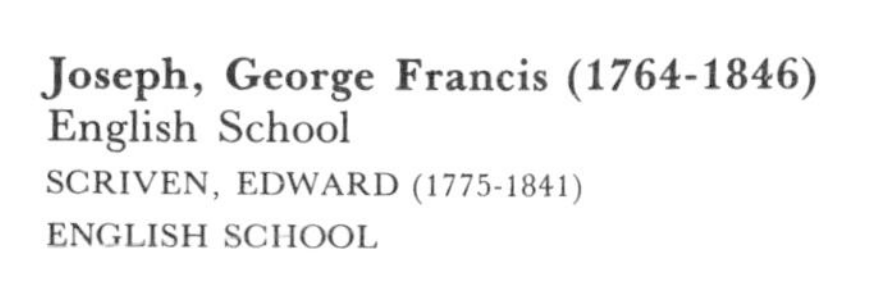

Joseph, George Francis (1764-1846)
English School
SCRIVEN, EDWARD (1775-1841)
ENGLISH SCHOOL

11,030
Sir John Andrew Stevenson, (1762-1833), Composer
(after an oil, RA 1821, NGI no. 416)
Unlettered Proof
45.2 x 31.2 (plate 37.8 x 26.4)
Line and stipple
Purchased, Dublin, Mr A. Roth, 1901

Jouvenet, Jean-Baptiste (1644-1717)
French School
EGLETON, WILLIAM HENRY (FL.1833-1860)
ENGLISH SCHOOL

20,529
The Miraculous Draught of Fishes
(after an oil of 1706, The Louvre, Paris)
12 x 17.9 (plate cut)
Line and stipple
Presented, Mrs D. Molloy, 1981

Joy, William (1803-1857/66)
English School
BRANDARD, JOHN (1812-1863)
ENGLISH SCHOOL

20,761
The Wreck of the Killarney Steamer off the Rennies, Co. Cork, Friday 26th January 1838
INSCRIBED: *This Print is dedicated by Permission to/Her Most Gracious Majesty the Queen/by the Author*
(Printed: J. Graf)
33 x 40.5 (image 25 x 35)
Lithograph with watercolour
Purchased, London, The Parker Gallery, 1984

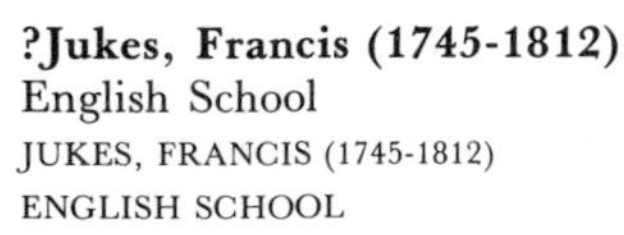

?Jukes, Francis (1745-1812)
English School
JUKES, FRANCIS (1745-1812)
ENGLISH SCHOOL

11,732
The Powder Magazine, Phoenix Park, Dublin
Published: F. Jukes, London
23 x 29 (plate 13.5 x 19.8)
Aquatint and etching
Provenance Unknown

?Jukes, Francis (1745-1812)
English School
JUKES, FRANCIS (1745-1812)
ENGLISH SCHOOL

11,733
The Powder Magazine, Phoenix Park, Dublin from across the River Liffey
Published: F. Jukes, London
24 x 29.7 (plate 13.7 x 19.8)
Aquatint and etching
Provenance Unknown

Julien, Bernard Romain (1802-1871)
French School
JULIEN, BERNARD ROMAIN (1802-1871)
FRENCH SCHOOL

11,874
A Young Middle-Eastern Woman
(Printed: Lemercier, Paris)
65.4 x 50.3 (image 53 x 42 approx)
Chromo-lithograph
Provenance Unknown

K

Kalf, Willem (1622-1693)
Dutch School
ENGLISH SCHOOL (19TH CENTURY)

20,636
Interior of a kitchen, (page from a magazine)
23.4 x 16.7 (image 13.9 x 13.1)
Wood Engraving
Presented, Mrs D. Molloy, 1981

Kauffmann, Angelica (1740-1807)
Anglo-Swiss School
BURKE, THOMAS (1749-1815)
IRISH SCHOOL

10,209
Frederick Augustus Hervey, P. Bishop of Derry and 4th Earl of Bristol, (1730-1803), seated against a view of Londonderry Cathedral, Co. Derry
(after an oil of 1790s, Ickworth House, Suffolk)
46.7 x 34.2 (plate 32.2 x 24.4)
Mezzotint
Purchased, Dublin, Mr J.V. McAlpine, 1910

Kauffmann, Angelica (1740-1807)
Anglo-Swiss School
BURKE, THOMAS (1749-1815)
IRISH SCHOOL

10,379
Charlotte Sophia, (née Mecklenburgh-Strelitz, 1744-1818), Queen of George III of England, raising the Genius of the Fine Arts
Published: W. W. Ryland, London, 23rd April 1772
47.5 x 38 (plate cut)
Mezzotint
Purchased, London, 1st Chaloner Smith sale, 1887

Kauffmann, Angelica (1740-1807)
Anglo-Swiss School
RIDLEY, WILLIAM (1764-1838)
ENGLISH SCHOOL

10,644
Self-Portrait aged about thirty, (pl. for 'European Magazine', May 1809)
Published: J. Asperne, London, 1st May 1809
21.5 x 12.8 (plate 14 x 10)
Stipple
Purchased, Dublin, Mr P. Traynor, 1898

Kauffmann, Angelica (1740-1807)
Anglo-Swiss School
WATSON, JAMES (C.1740-1790)
IRISH SCHOOL

10,392

Kauffmann/Watson

Lady Margaret Bingham, (née Smith, d.1814), wife of Lord Charles Bingham, later 1st Earl of Lucan
Published: J. Watson, London, 15th March 1775
51. x 38 (plate 49.3 x 38)
Mezzotint
Purchased, London, 2nd Chaloner Smith sale, 1888

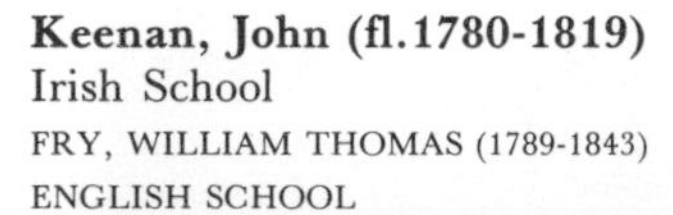

Keenan, John (fl.1780-1819)
Irish School
FRY, WILLIAM THOMAS (1789-1843)
ENGLISH SCHOOL

10,950
Dr James Macartney, (1770-1843), Professor of Anatomy and Surgery at Trinity College, Dublin
Published: Longman & Co., London also Hodges and McArthur, Dublin, September 1825
28.8 x 22 (plate cut)
Stipple
Provenance: Presented, Mrs Hepburn, 1918

Keere, Pieter van den (1571-after 1645)
Dutch School
KEERE, PIETER VAN DEN (1571-AFTER 1645)
DUTCH SCHOOL

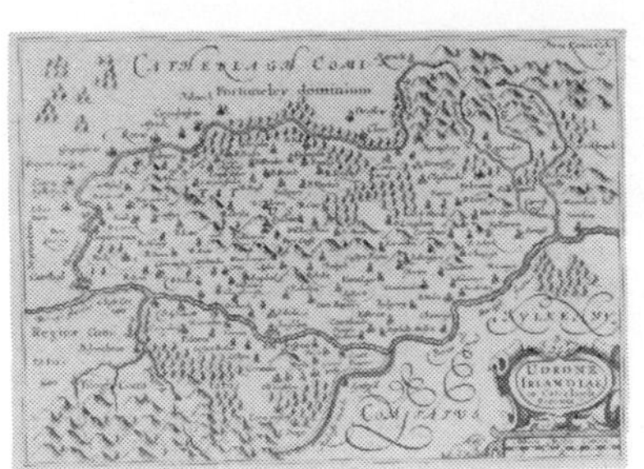

20,765
Map of the Barony of Idrone, Co. Carlow
Published: P. van den Keere, Amsterdam
24.7 x 36 (plate 18.6 x 25.7)
Line
Presented, Munich, Mr N. O'Siochain, 1985

Kelly, Thomas (fl.1799-1841)
Irish School
KELLY, THOMAS (FL.1799-1841)
IRISH SCHOOL

11,850
Union Street or Ease and Plenty; College Green imagined after the Act of Union, with Daly's Club, (now demolished), Ex-Parliament House, (now Bank of Ireland) and Trinity College, Dublin
Published: M. Williamson, Dublin, 9th May 1799
21.5 x 34.6 (plate cut)
Etching with watercolour
Purchased 1913

Kennedy, Mabel M. (20th century)
English School
KENNEDY, MABEL M. (20TH CENTURY)
ENGLISH SCHOOL

11,930
Landscape - Woods and River
30 x 42 (image 22.5 x 27.8)
Woodcut
Provenance Unknown

Kenny, Nicholas (c.1807-1856)
Irish School
LEWIS THE ELDER, FREDERICK CHRISTIAN (1779-1856)
ENGLISH SCHOOL

11,144
Henry Grattan, M.P., (1746-1820), Statesman, moving the Declaration of Irish Rights in 1782, (pl. for 'Memoir of the Life and Times of Henry Grattan', by his son Henry, 1839-46)
Published: H. Colburn, London, 1839
22 x 13.7 (plate cut)
Line and stipple
Purchased, Dublin, Mr P. Traynor, 1898

Ker, Sophia (19th century)
Irish School
TURNER, CHARLES (1773-1857)
ENGLISH SCHOOL

10,854
Richard Graves Ker of Red Hall, Ballycarry, Co. Antrim, (1756-1822)
(after a watercolour of 1805)
Published: C. Turner, London, 21st March 1822
35.2 x 27.1 (plate 33.1 x 25.5)
Mezzotint
Provenance Unknown

Kernoff, Harry (1900-1974)
Irish School
KERNOFF, HARRY (1900-1974)
IRISH SCHOOL

.1,932(7)
Bridge over the Mall, Westport, Co. Mayo, 1947, (from 'An Album of Kernoff Prints', see App. 8, no. 11,932)
ssued by the artist, 1947
24.2 x 29.4 (image 13.1 x 19.1)
Voodcut
Presented, Mr T. Ryan, P.R.H.A., 981

Kerseboom, Johann (fl.1680-1708)
English School
MILLER, ANDREW (FL.1737-1763)
IRISH SCHOOL

10,256
Hon. Robert Boyle, (1627-1691), Natural Philosopher, Scientist and Inventor of the Air-Pump, (seen in border)
(after Vertue's line engraving of 1740, in reverse; this in turn after either an unlocated oil or wl oil, c.1690, The Royal Society of Arts, London)
Published: P. Smith also A. Miller, Dublin, 1744
36.3 x 26.3 (plate 35.2 x 25.3)
Mezzotint
Purchased, London, 2nd Chaloner Smith sale, 1888

Kettle, Tilly (1735-1786)
English School
DE WILDE, SAMUEL (1748-1832)
ENGLISH SCHOOL

10,325
So-called Portrait of Mrs Ann Barry, (née Street, 1734-1801), Actress, wife of Spranger Barry
(after a T. Kettle/J. Watson mezzotint of Lady Molineux, taken from a c.1765 oil)
36.9 x 25.9 (plate 35.6 x 25.2)
Mezzotint
Purchased, London, 1st Chaloner Smith sale, 1887

Kettle, Tilly (1735-1786)
English School
DE WILDE, SAMUEL (FL.1748-1832)
ENGLISH SCHOOL

11,096
So-called portrait of Mrs Ann Barry, (nee Street, 1734-1801), Actress, wife of Spranger Barry
(after a T. Kettle/J. Watson mezzotint of Lady Molineux from a c.1765 oil: reduced size)
Published: J. Bowles, London
21.2 x 13.9 (plate 15.2 x 11.5)
Mezzotint
Purchased, London, 1st Chaloner Smith sale, 1887

Killigrew, Anne (1660-1685)
English School
BLOOTELING, ABRAHAM (1640-1690)
DUTCH SCHOOL

10,856
Self-Portrait
Published: A. Blooteling
26.1 x 18.6 (plate 25.9 x 18.4)
Mezzotint
Purchased, London, 1st Chaloner Smith sale, 1887

King, Giles (fl.1732-1746)
English School
BICKHAM THE YOUNGER, GEORGE (FL.1736-1758)
ENGLISH SCHOOL

10,531
James Annesley, (1715-1760), Claimant to the Anglesey Peerage
(after an oil, ?Dublin 1743)
Published: G. Bickham the Younger, London, March 1744
26 x 34 (plate cut)
Line
Purchased, 1909

Kirkwood, John (fl.1826-1853)
Irish School
KIRKWOOD, JOHN (FL.1826-1853)
IRISH SCHOOL

11,701
The Custom House, Dublin, with a paddle boat and the clipper 'Success'
(after a drawing)
Published: J. Kirkwood, Dublin, c.1830
31.3 x 41.7 (plate 26.5 x 30.5)
Line
Presented, Dr E. MacDowel Cosgrave, 1907

Kirkwood, John (fl.1826-1853)
Irish School
KIRKWOOD, JOHN (FL.1826-1853)
IRISH SCHOOL

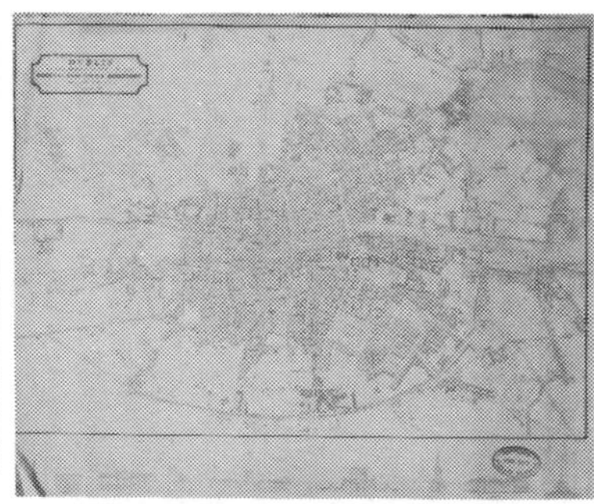

11,811
Plan of Dublin with elevations of Nelson Pillar, Homes Hotel, (both now demolished), the General Post Office, St Patrick's Cathedral, Custom House, Four Courts, St George's Church, (Hardwicke Place), Bank of Ireland, (College Green, former Parliament House), and The Wellington Testimonial, (Phoenix Park)
Published: General Post Office Directory, Dublin, c.1830
34 x 41 (plate cut)
Steel Engraving
Presented, Office of Public Works, 1909

Kneller, Godfrey (1646-1723)
Anglo-German School
BROOKS, JOHN (FL.1730-1756)
IRISH SCHOOL

10,223
William III, King of England, (1650-1702), above the King on horseback at the Battle of the Boyne
INSCRIBED: Done at the request of Joseph Sproule Esq., of Athlone
Published: W. Herbert also T. Jefferys, London, October 1744
35.8 x 23.4 (plate 35.3 x 23)
Mezzotint
Purchased, London, 1st Chaloner Smith sale, 1887

Kneller, Godfrey (1646-1723)
Anglo-German School
CHAMBARS, THOMAS (C.1724-1789)
IRISH SCHOOL

10,519

William III, King of England, (1650-1702)
(after a wl oil of c.1690, Royal Collection, St James's Palace)
15.2 x 9.2 (plate cut)
Line and etching
Provenance Unknown

Kneller, Godfrey (1646-1723)
Anglo-German School
ENGLISH SCHOOL (18TH CENTURY)

1,244
'homas Wharton, 1st Marquess of Vharton, (1648-1716), former Lord ieutenant of Ireland
after a G. Kneller/J. Houbraken line ngraving from an oil of 1715, NGP, ondon)
'ublished: J. Hinton, London
7.4 x 10.7 (plate cut)
ine
cquired by 1906

neller, Godfrey (1646-1723)
nglo-German School
BER THE YOUNGER, JOHN (1684?-1756)
GLISH SCHOOL

10,160
Sir Hans Sloane, Bt., (1660-1752), Physician and Naturalist
(after an oil of 1716, Royal Society, London)
Published: J. Faber the Younger, London 1729
36 x 26 (plate 34.7 x 24.8)
Mezzotint
Purchased, Dublin, Mr J. V. McAlpine, 1901

Kneller, Godfrey (1646-1723)
Anglo-German School
FABER THE YOUNGER, JOHN (1684-1756)
ENGLISH SCHOOL

10,676
Edward Hopkins, M.P., (d.1736), Commissioner of the Revenue in Ireland
(after an oil of c.1700)
Published: J. Faber the Younger, London, 1735
39.9 x 26.5 (plate 35.3 x 25.3)
Mezzotint
Acquired c.1908

Kneller, Godfrey (1646-1723)
Anglo-German School
FABER THE YOUNGER, JOHN (C.1684-1756)
ENGLISH SCHOOL

10,721
Richard Boyle, 2nd Viscount Shannon, (1675-1740), Field-Marshal
(after an oil of 1717, NPG, London)
Published: ?J. Faber The Younger, London 1733
34.8 x 24.8 (plate cut)
Mezzotint
Purchased, Dublin, Mr J.V. McAlpine, 1906

Kneller, Godfrey (1646-1723)
Anglo-German School
FABER THE YOUNGER, JOHN (C.1684-1756)
ENGLISH SCHOOL

10,826

George, Prince of Wales, (1683-1761), later King George II
(after a wl oil of 1716, Royal Collection, St James's Palace)
Published: T. Bowles, London
35.9 x 25.5 (plate 35.7 x 25.3)
Mezzotint
Purchased, London, 1st Chaloner Smith sale, 1887

Kneller, Godfrey (1646-1723)
German School
FABER THE YOUNGER, JOHN (C.1684-1756)
DUTCH SCHOOL

10,845
Charles Fitzroy, 2nd Duke of Grafton, (1683-1757), Statesman, former Lord Lieutenant of Ireland
(after an oil, c.1703, NPG, London)
Published: J. Faber the Younger, London 1731
47.2 x 29 (plate 35.4 x 25)
Mezzotint
Provenance Unknown

Kneller, Godfrey (1646-1723)
Anglo-German School
FABER THE YOUNGER, JOHN (C.1684-1756)
DUTCH SCHOOL

10,867
Admiral Sir John Jennings, M.P., (1664-1748), Governor of Greenwich Hospital
(after an oil of 1705, National Maritime Museum, Greenwich)
Published: J. Faber the Younger, London, 1722
36.4 x 25.9 (plate 35.5 x 25.2)
Mezzotint
Purchased, London, 1st Chaloner Smith sale, 1887

Kneller, Godfrey (1646-1723)
Anglo-German School
FABER THE YOUNGER, JOHN (C.1684-1756)
DUTCH SCHOOL

11,041
Sir Richard Steele, (1672-1729), Essayist and Politician
(after an oil of 1711, NPG, London)
Published: J. Faber the Younger, London, 1733
37 x 27 (plate 35.3 x 25.4)
Mezzotint
Purchased, 1906

Kneller, Godfrey (1646-1723)
Anglo-German School
FORD, MICHAEL (FL.1742-1765)
IRISH SCHOOL

10,504
William III, King of England, (1650-1702), and Frederick, 1st Duke of Schomberg, (1615-1690)
INSCRIBED: To His Excellency William Earl of Harrington, Lord Lieutenant General and General Governor of His Majesty's Kingdom of Ireland. This plate is humbly dedicated by his Excellency's/ most humble & Obedient servant/ Michael Ford
Published: M. Ford, Dublin, 4th November 1749, price 5s 5d
47 x 59.5 (plate 45.4 x 58.2)
Mezzotint
Purchased, London, 1st Chaloner Smith sale, 1887

Kneller, Godfrey (1646-1723)
Anglo-German School
GOLE, JACOBUS (1660-1737)
DUTCH SCHOOL

10,006

James II, King of England, (1633-1701)
(possibly after an oil of 1685)
33.3 x 25.7 (plate 34.4 x 25)
Mezzotint
Purchased, London, 1st Chaloner Smith sale, 1887

Kneller, George (1646-1723)
Anglo-German School
GOLE, JACOBUS (1660-1737)
DUTCH SCHOOL

11,024
Frederick Armand de Schomberg, 1st Duke of Schomberg, (1615-1690), Professional Soldier
?after a G. Kneller/ J. Smith mezzotint, of 1689, NGI no. 10,213)
Published: J. Gole, Amsterdam
25.3 x 19 (plate 24.8 x 18.6)
Mezzotint
Purchased, London, 1st Chaloner Smith sale, 1887

Kneller, Godfrey (1646-1723)
Anglo-German School
HAELWEGH, ADRIAEN (C.1637-C.1696)
DUTCH SCHOOL

10,224
'The Reverend and Valiant' George Walker, (1618-1690), Governor of Londonderry, who died at the Battle of the Boyne
(after an oil of c.1685)
Published: D. de la Feuille, Amsterdam
37.5 x 26.8 (plate cut)
Line
Purchased, Mr W.V. Daniell, 1901

Kneller, Godfrey (1646-1723)
Anglo-German School
HOUBRAKEN, JACOBUS (1698-1780)
AMSTERDAM SCHOOL

10,212
Laurence Hyde, 1st Earl of Rochester, (1642-1711), Politician, Ambassador and Lord Lieutenant of Ireland
(after an oil of c.1685)

INSCRIBED: *In the Collection of the Right Hon: The Earl of Burlington*
Published: J. and P. Knapton, London, 1741
46.1 x 30.5 (plate 37.3 x 25.3)
Line
Purchased, Dublin, Mr J.V. McAlpine, 1899

Kneller, Godfrey (1646-1723)
Anglo-German School
HOUBRAKEN, JACOBUS (1698-1780)
DUTCH SCHOOL

10,543
Queen Anne, (1665-1714), (pl. for T. G. Smollett's 'A Complete History of England', 1757)
(after a wl oil of 1702-3, Inner Temple, London)
8 x 14.5 (plate cut)
Line
Acquired between 1913/14

Kneller, Godfrey (1646-1723)
Anglo-German School
HOUBRAKEN, JACOBUS (1698-1780)
DUTCH SCHOOL

20,133
Lieut.-General Thomas Tollemache, (?1651-1694), (pl. for T. Birch's 'The Heads of Illustrious Persons of Great Britain', 1747-52)
(after a tql oil of c.1690, now lost; studio version at Ham House, London)
36.5 x 22.5 (plate cut)
Line
Purchased, Lusk, Mr de Courcy Donovan, 1971

Kneller, Godfrey (1646-1723)
Anglo-German School
McARDELL, JAMES (1728/29-1765)
IRISH SCHOOL

10,175
Lionel Cranfield Sackville, 1st Duke of Dorset, (1688-1765), Lord Lieutenant of Ireland
(after a wl oil of 1777, Knole, Kent)
Published: 1750
35.5 x 25.8 (plate 35.2 x 25)
Mezzotint
Purchased, London, 1st Chaloner Smith sale, 1887

Kneller, Godfrey (1646-1723)
Anglo-German School
MALONE, D. (FL. C.1748-1766)
IRISH SCHOOL

20,123
William III, King of England, (1650-1702), (frontispiece to N. Tindal's 'Continuation of Rapin's History of England, 1757-59 edition)
(after a wl oil of 1690, Royal Collection, St James's Palace)
19.2 x 12.3 (plate 17 x 10.6)
Line and etching
Purchased, Lusk, Mr de Courcy Donovan, 1971

Kneller, Godfrey (1646-1723)
Anglo-German School
MALONE, D. (FL.C.1748-1766)
IRISH SCHOOL

20,124
Queen Mary, (1662-1694), wife of William III, (frontispiece to Findal's 'History of England', 1728-47)
(after an oil of 1690, Royal Collection, St James's Palace)
19.3 x 12.3 (plate 17 x 10.6)
Line and stipple
Purchased, Lusk, Mr de Courcy Donovan, 1971

Kneller, Godfrey (1646-1723)
Anglo-German School
MILLER, ANDREW (FL.1737-1763)
IRISH SCHOOL

10,558

William III, (1650-1702), King of England, in Robes of State, (a Celebration of the Battle of the Boyne, 1st July, 1690)
(after a wl oil of 1690, Royal Collection, St James's Palace)
Published: ?A. Miller, Dublin, 1744
35.9 x 25.7 (plate cut)
Mezzotint
Acquired between 1890/98

Kneller, Godfrey (1646-1723)
Anglo-German School
PELHAM, PETER (1695-1751)
ENGLISH SCHOOL

0,997
William Cavendish, 1st Duke of Devonshire, (1640-1707), with a River God, (Print titled as James Butler, 2nd Duke of Ormonde)
after G. Kneller/I. Beckett mezzotint of an oil of c.1680, Burghley House, Northants)
Published: J. Bowles, London
4.3 x 25.5 (plate 34 x 25.2)
Mezzotint
Purchased, Dublin, Mr A. Roth, 396

neller, Godfrey (1646-1723)
nglo-German School
IOR, THOMAS ABIEL (1809-1886)
IGLISH SCHOOL

11,375
Queen Anne, (1665-1714), and her consort Prince George of Denmark, (1653-1708)
(Queen Anne after an oil of 1703, Inner Temple, London; Prince George after an oil of c.1700)
22.5 x 14.4 (plate cut)
Line
Provenance Unknown

Kneller, Godfrey (1646-1723)
Anglo-German School
ROBINSON, JOHN HENRY (1796-1871)
ENGLISH SCHOOL

10,570
James Butler, 2nd Duke of Ormonde, (1665-1745)
Published: Harding & Lepard, London, 1st October 1834
21.4 x 13.6 (plate cut)
Line and stipple
Purchased, Dublin, Mr P. Traynor, 1898

Kneller, Godfrey (1646-1723)
Anglo-German School
SCHENCK, PIETER (1660-1718/19)
DUTCH SCHOOL

10,821
George Prince of Denmark, (1635-1708), Consort of Queen Anne
(after a tql oil of c.1690)
Published: P. Schenck, Amsterdam, 1705
35.6 x 27 (plate 33.5 x 25.4)
Mezzotint
Purchased, London, 1st Chaloner Smith sale, 1887

Kneller, Godfrey (1646-1723)
Anglo-German School
SCRIVEN, EDWARD (1775-1841)
ENGLISH SCHOOL

10,533

James Butler, 1st Duke of Ormonde, (1610-1688), (pl. for E. Lodge's 'Portraits of Illustrious Personages of Great Britain', 1821-28)
Published: Harding, Mavor & Lepard, London, 1st April 1824
24.6 x 17.5 (plate cut)
Stipple
Provenance Unknown

?Kneller, Godfrey (1646-1723)
Anglo-German School
SIMON, JOHN (1675-1751)
ANGLO-FRENCH SCHOOL

10,021
Sir Constantine Phipps, (1656-1723), Lord Chancellor of Ireland
Published: J. Simon also H. Overton, London
40.6 x 28.6 (plate 34.6 x 25)
Mezzotint
Purchased, London, 2nd Chaloner Smith sale, 1888

Kneller, Godfrey (1646-1723)
Anglo-German School
SIMON, JOHN (1675-1751)
ANGLO-FRENCH SCHOOL

10,539
Joseph Addison, (1672-1719), Essayist and Poet
Published: J. Smith, London
36.2 x 26.2 (plate 35.5 x 25.6)
Mezzotint
Acquired by 1879

Kneller, Godfrey (1646-1723)
Anglo-German School
SIMON, JOHN (1675-1751)
ANGLO-FRENCH SCHOOL

10,732
John Cutts, 1st Baron Cutts of Gowran (1661-1707), General
(after an oil of c.1705)
36.9 x 27.4 (plate 36 x 26.4)
Mezzotint
Purchased, London, 2nd Chaloner Smith sale, 1888

Kneller, Godfrey (1646-1723)
Anglo-German School
SMITH, JOHN (1652-1742)
ENGLISH SCHOOL

10,002
James Butler, 2nd Duke of Ormonde, (1665-1745)
(after a wl oil of c.1695, Examination Schools, Oxford)
Published: J. Smith, London, 12th October 1702
39.4 x 28.5 (plate 34.5 x 25)
Mezzotint
Purchased, Dublin, Mr J.V. McAlpine, 1899

Kneller, Godfrey (1646-1723)
Anglo-German School
SMITH, JOHN (1652-1742)
ENGLISH SCHOOL

10,009

Edward Southwell, M.P., (1667/71-1730), Secretary of State for Ireland
Published: J. Smith, 1709
34.7 x 25.1 (plate 34.7 x 25)
Mezzotint
Purchased, London, 2nd Chaloner Smith sale, 1888

Kneller, Godfrey (1646-1723)
Anglo-German School
SMITH, JOHN (1652-1742)
ENGLISH SCHOOL

10,010
William Congreve, (1670-1729), Dramatist and Poet
(after an oil of 1709. NPG, London; NGI no. 4336 is a replica)
Published: J. Smith, London, 1710
35.6 x 26.1 (plate 34.7 x 25.1)
Mezzotint
Presumed purchased Dublin, Jones Saleroom, 1879

Kneller, Godfrey (1649-1723)
Anglo-German School
SMITH, JOHN (1652-1742)
ENGLISH SCHOOL

10,071
Sir John Perceval Bt., (1683-1748), later 1st Earl of Egmont and Governor of Georgia
(after an oil of 1704, Lambton Castle, Co. Durham)
Published: J. Smith, London, 1708
43.1 x 27.7 (plate 41.8 x 26.2)
Mezzotint
Purchased, Dublin, Mr G.J. Sweeny, 1897

Kneller, Godfrey (1646-1727)
Anglo-German School
SMITH, JOHN (1652-1742)
ENGLISH SCHOOL

10,095
James II, King of England, (1633-1701)
(after an oil of c.1685)
Published: J. Smith, London, 1697
35.2 x 25.3 (plate 34.5 x 24.7)
Mezzotint
Acquired by 1879

Kneller, Godfrey (1646-1723)
Anglo-German School
SMITH, JOHN (1652-1742)
ENGLISH SCHOOL

10,161
Sir Robert Southwell, (1635-1702), Secretary of State for Ireland and President of the Royal Society
(after a tql oil, Royal Society, London)
Published: J. Smith, London, 1704
34.7 x 25.2 (plate 34.2 x 24.7)
Mezzotint
Purchased, London, 2nd Chaloner Smith sale, 1888

Kneller, Godfrey (1646-1723)
Anglo-German School
SMITH, JOHN (1652-1742)
ENGLISH SCHOOL

10,213

Frederick Armand de Schomberg, 1st Duke of Schomberg, (1615-1690), Professional Soldier, killed at the Battle of the Boyne
(after an oil of ?1689, Brocklesby Hall, Lincolnshire)
Published: J. Smith, London, 1689
38.2 x 26.1 (plate 37.5 x 25.5)
Mezzotint
Presented, Mrs Noseda, 1882

10,226
Godert de Ginkel, 1st Earl of Athlone, (1630-1703), with the taking of Athlone, Co. Westmeath
(after an oil of ?1692, NGI no. 486)
Published: J. Smith, not before 1692
40 x 28 (plate 34.4 x 24.9)
Mezzotint
Presented, Mrs Noseda, 1882

Kneller, Godfrey (1646-1723)
Anglo-German School
SMITH, JOHN (1652-1742)
ENGLISH SCHOOL

10,238
Meinhardt Schomberg, Baron Tara, Earl of Bangor and Duke of Leinster, (1641-1719), Soldier, Inventor, later 3rd Duke of Schomberg
Published: J. Smith, London, 1693
Mezzotint
Purhcased, London, 2nd Chaloner Smith sale, 1888

Kneller, Godfrey (1646-1723)
Anglo-German School
SMITH, JOHN (1652-1742)
ENGLISH SCHOOL

10,218
Thomas Wharton, 1st Marquess of Wharton, (1648-1716), former Lord Lieutenant of Ireland
(after an oil of c.1715, NPG, London)
Published: J. Smith, London, ?1728
35.8 x 25.6 (plate 35.3 x 25.4)
Mezzotint
Purchased, Dublin, Mr J.V. McAlpine, 1906

Kneller, Godfrey (1646-1723)
Anglo-German School
SMITH, JOHN (1652-1742)
ENGLISH SCHOOL

10,227
'The Lord Euston' - Charles Fitzroy, Lord Euston, (1663-1757), later 2nd Duke of Grafton and Lord Lieutenant of Ireland
Published: J. Smith, London, 1689
33.4 x 25 (plate cut)
Mezzotint
Milltown Gift 1902

Kneller, Godfrey (1646-1723)
Anglo-German School
SMITH, JOHN (1652-1703)
ENGLISH SCHOOL

Kneller, Godfrey (1646-1723)
Anglo-German School
SMITH, JOHN (1652-1742))
ENGLISH SCHOOL

10,317

Elizabeth, Baroness Cutts, (née Pickering, 1678 or 79-1697), 2nd wife of Baron Cutts, who died in childbirth
(after an oil of c.1695, Chequers)
Published: 1698
22 x 17.6 (plate cut)
Mezzotint
Purchased, London, 2nd Chaloner Smith sale, 1888

Kneller, Godfrey (1646-1723)
Anglo-German School
SMITH, JOHN (1652-1742)
ENGLISH SCHOOL

0,333
lary, Duchess of Ormonde, (née Somerset, 665-1733), daughter of the 1st Duke of eaufort and 2nd wife of the 2nd Duke of rmonde, with her son, Thomas, Earl of ssory, (1686-1689)
after an oil of c.1688, Badminton louse, Avon)
ublished: J. Smith, London, 1693
4.5 x 25.2 (plate cut)
lezzotint
urchased, London, 1st Chaloner mith sale, 1887

neller, Godfrey (1646-1723)
nglo-German School
IITH, JOHN (1652-1742)
IGLISH SCHOOL

10,347
Mary, Duchess of Ormonde, (née Somerset, 1665-1733), daughter of the 1st Duke of Beaufort and 2nd wife of the 2nd Duke of Ormonde, with a negro page
(after an oil of c.1690)
Published: J. Smith, London, c.1690
42.2 x 27 (plate 42 x 26.7)
Mezzotint
Purchased, London, 2nd Chaloner Smith sale, 1888

Kneller, Godfrey (1646-1723)
Anglo-German School
SMITH, JOHN (1652-1742)
ENGLISH SCHOOL

10,534

Margaret, Countess of Ranelagh, (née Cecil, 1673-1727), 2nd wife of the 1st Earl of Ranelagh
(after an oil of c.1699)
Published: J. Smith, London
33.7 x 24.4 (plate cut)
Mezzotint
Purchased, London, 2nd Chaloner Smith sale, 1888

Kneller, Godfrey (1646-1723)
Anglo-German School
SMITH, JOHN (1652-1742)
ENGLISH SCHOOL

10,540
Caroline of Brandenburg-Ansbach, (1683-1737), Queen of King George II 2nd State
(after a wl oil of 1716, Royal Collection, Buckingham Palace, when Princess)
Published: J. Smith, London, not before 1727
34.7 x 25 (plate cut)
Mezzotint
Purchased, London, 2nd Chaloner Smith sale, 1888

Kneller, Godfrey (1646-1723)
Anglo-German School
SMITH, JOHN (1652-1742)
ENGLISH SCHOOL

10,728
Caroline of Brandenburg-Ansbach, (1683-1737), Princess of Wales, later Queen of King George II
1st State
(after a wl oil of 1716, Royal Collection, Buckingham Palace)
Published: J. Smith, London, 1717
34.9 x 25.1 (plate cut)
Mezzotint
Purchased, London, 2nd Chaloner Smith sale, 1888

Kneller, Godfrey (1646-1723)
Anglo-German School
SMITH, JOHN (1652-1742)
ENGLISH SCHOOL

10,785
Henry Nassau, Count D'Auverquerk, (1641-1708), husband of Madame D'Auverquerk
(after a tql oil of c.1700, Orange Nassau Museum Delft)
Published: J. Smith, London, 1706
35.5 x 26 (plate 34 x 25.5)
Mezzotint
Purchased, London, 2nd Chaloner Smith sale, 1888

Kneller, Godfrey (1646-1723)
Anglo-German School
SMITH, JOHN (1652-1742)
ENGLISH SCHOOL

10,904
Lucy, Viscountess Lisburne, (née Brydges d.1689), wife of 1st Viscount Lisburn, with putto symbolising abundance, in relief
(after an oil of 1686)
Published: J. Smith, London
53.4 x 39 (plate cut)
Mezzotint
Purchased, Dublin, Mr J.V. McAlpine, 1899

Kneller, Godfrey (1646-1723)
Anglo-German School
SMITH, JOHN (1652-1742)
ENGLISH SCHOOL

10,929
Mary of Modena, (1658-1718), Queen of King James II of England
(after a tql oil of c.1685, Chirk Castle, Wales)
Published: J. Smith, London
36.4 x 26.6 (plate 35 x 25.6)
Mezzotint
Acquired between 1890/98

Kneller, Godfrey (1646-1723)
Anglo-German School
SMITH, JOHN (1652-1742)
ENGLISH SCHOOL

10,996
James Butler, 2nd Duke of Ormonde, (1665-1745), General
Published: J. Smith, London, 1701
36.4 x 26.8 (plate 34.8 x 25.2)
Mezzotint
Acquired by 1879

?Kneller, Godfrey (1646-1720s)
Anglo-German School
TANJE, PIETER (1706-1761)
AMSTERDAM SCHOOL

10,994

John Churchill, 1st Duke of Marlborough, (1650-1722), General, with an allegory of Time Revealing Truth
Unlettered Proof
26.2 x 21.3 (plate 23.5 x 18.8)
Line
Purchased, Dublin, Mr A. Roth, 1896

Kneller, Godfrey (1646-1723)
Anglo-German School
VANDERBANCK, PETER (1649-1697)
ANGLO-DUTCH SCHOOL

10,414
Frederick Armand De Schomberg, (1615-1690), 1st Duke of Schomberg, Professional Soldier
INSCRIBED: *Offered by His most Humble Servant P. Vandrebanc (sic)*
Published: P. Vanderbanck, London, 1689
48.5 x 37 (plate 45.2 x 34.6)
Mezzotint
Presented, C.R. Howard, 6th Earl of Wicklow, 1884

Kneller, Godfrey (1646-1723)
Anglo-German School
VANDERBANCK, PETER (1649-1697)
ANGLO-DUTCH SCHOOL

10,565
Rev. George Walker, (1618-1690), Governor of Londonderry, during the Siege of 1689
(after an oil of c.1690)
Published: P. Vanderbanck, London, 1689
40.9 x 30.6 (plate cut)
Line
Presented, Mr H. Doyle, 1889

Kneller, Godfrey (1646-1723)
Anglo-German School
VANDERGUCHT, MICHAEL (1660-1725)
ANGLO-FLEMISH SCHOOL

11,213

William Congreve, (1670-1729), Dramatist and Poet, (frontispiece for his 'Letters on Love', 1718)
(after an oil of 1709, NPG, London; NGI no. 4336 is a replica)
19.7 x 12.3 (plate 12.8 x 8.2)
Line
Purchased, Dublin, Mr P. Traynor, 1898

Kneller, Godfrey (1646-1723)
German School
VERTUE, GEORGE (1684-1756)
ENGLISH SCHOOL

10,799
Lionel Cranfield Sackville, 1st Duke of Dorset, (1688-1765), formerly Lord Lieutenant of Ireland
(after a wl oil of 1717, Knole, Kent, Lord Sackville Collection)
Published: London 1744
43.5 x 29.3 (plate cut)
Line
Purchased, Dublin, Mr J.V. McAlpine, 1911

Kneller, Godfrey (1646-1723)
Anglo-German School *and*
Jervas, Charles (c.1675-1739)
Irish School

PRIOR, THOMAS ABIEL (1809-1886)
ENGLISH SCHOOL

11,346
Alexander Pope, (1688-1744), Poet; Joseph Addison, (1672-1719), Poet, Essayist and Statesman; Jonathan Swift, (1667-1745), Dean of St Patrick's Cathedral and Satirist
(Pope after a Kneller oil of 1722, Stanton Harcourt Manor, Oxfordshire; Addison after a Kneller oil of c.1712, NPG, London; Swift after a Jervas oil of c.1710, Bodleian, Oxford)
22.5 x 14.7 (plate cut)
Line
Provenance Unknown

Kneller, Godfrey (1646-1723)
Anglo-German School *and*
Worlidge, Thomas (1700-1766)
English School
PRIOR, THOMAS ABIEL (1809-1886)
ENGLISH SCHOOL

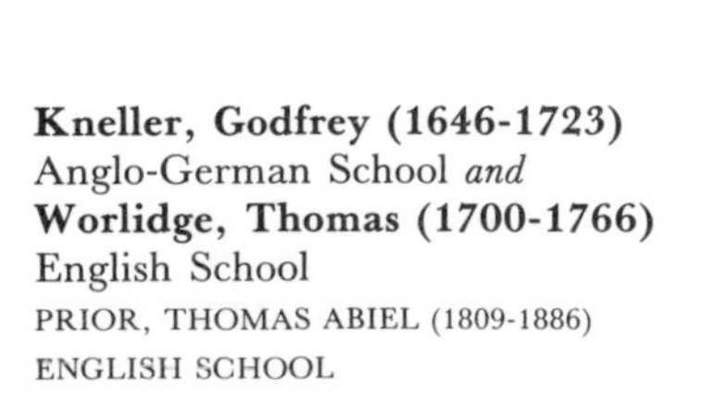

11,374
George I, King of England, (1660-1727), and George II, King of England, (1683-1760)
(George I after a wl oil of 1716, NPG, London; George II after a tql oil of c.1753, NPG, London)
22.5 x 14.5 (plate cut)
Line
Provenance Unknown

Knight, John Prescott (1803-1881)
English School
LUPTON, THOMAS GOFF (1791-1873)
ENGLISH SCHOOL

10,243
William Sharman Crawford, M.P., (1781-1861), Irish Radical and champion of R.C. Emancipation
(after an oil, RA 1843)
Published: T. Lupton, London, 1st August 1844
50 x 41.9 (plate 41 x 31)
Mezzotint
Presumed purchased, Dublin, Jones Saleroom, 1879

Kraus, Franz Anton (1705-1752)
German School
SORNIQUE, DOMINIQUE (1708-1756)
FRENCH SCHOOL

20,198
The Money Lender
INSCRIBED: *'L'Usuriere', Ramassez des Ducats, comptez-les, j'y consens,/Mais loin d'en être avare, il faut en faire usage,/Et vous souvenir qu'à votre âge/On doit bien payer les Galants.*
27.7 x 21.6 (plate 26 x 18.5)
Line
Purchased, Lusk, Mr de Courcy Donovan, 1971

?Kriehuber, Josef (1800-1876)
Austrian School
KRIEHUBER, JOSEF (1800-1876)
AUSTRIAN SCHOOL

10,938
Count Lavall G. Nugent, (1777-1862), Austrian Field Marshal and Prince of the Holy Roman Empire
Published: L.T. Neumann, Vienna, 1850
58.3 x 43 (image 39 x 30.4)
Lithograph
Presented, Mr H.E. Doyle, 1889

Kruger, Franz (1797-1857)
German School
KRUGER, FRANZ (1797-1857)
GERMAN SCHOOL

10,758
Frederick William Robert Stewart, Viscount Castlereagh, (1805-1872), later 4th Marquess of Londonderry
INSCRIBED: *From the original in the possession Arthur Magenis Esq.*
Published: Königl. Lith. Institut, Berlin, 1826
47.5 x 34 (image 24.8 x 22.8)
Lithograph
Acquired by 1901

Sir Samuel Cooke, Bt., Lord Mayor of Dublin in 1741
Unlettered Proof
Published: J. Brooks, Dublin, not before 1741
32.8 x 26 (plate cut x 25.1)
Mezzotint
Purchased, Dublin, Mr J.V. McAlpine, 1913

Latham, James (1696-1747)
Irish School
MILLER, ANDREW (FL.1744-1763)
IRISH SCHOOL

10,413
Eaton Stannard, M.P., (d.1755), Recorder in the Irish Parliament
(after an oil, NGI no. 4142)
INSCRIBED: *Eaton Stannard Esqr., Recorder of the Honble City of Dublin/ To Whom this Plate is most Humbly dedicated by his/most Obligd and most Obedient Humble Servt/Thos Sillcock*
Published: T. Sillcock, Dublin, not before 1733
49.5 x 35 (plate cut)
Mezzotint
Purchased, London, 1st Chaloner Smith sale, 1887

Latilla, Eugenio H. (c.1800-1859)
Italian School
HALL THE ELDER, HENRY BRYAN (1808-1884)
ANGLO-AMERICAN SCHOOL

10,967
Daniel O'Connell, M.P., (1775-1847), Statesman
INSCRIBED: *Presented to the Subscribers to The News August 20, 1837*
Published: J. Thompson, London, 20th August 1837
29.7 x 22.6 (plate 23.9 x 16.1)
Line and stipple
Purchased, Dillon & Co., 1901

Laurence, Samuel (1812-1884)
English School
GRIFFITHS, HENRY (FL.1835-1849)
ENGLISH SCHOOL

11,334
Sir Henry Pottinger Bt., (1789-1856), fought in India and China, Colonial Governor, (pl. for 'Dublin University Magazine', Vol. XXVIII, October 1846)
(after S. Laurence/H.Griffiths lithograph of 1842; example in NLI, Dublin)
Published: J. McGlashan, Dublin, 1846
21.8 x 13.5 (plate cut)
Stipple
Purchased, Dublin, Mr J.V. McAlpine, 1913

Lawrence, Thomas (1769-1830)
English School
AMSTRONG, COSMO (1781-1836)
ENGLISH SCHOOL

20,211
'The Mountain Daisy' - Lady Georgiana Fane, (d.1874), daughter of the 10th Earl of Westmoreland as a child, (pl. for 'The Amulet', 1829)
(after an oil of 1806, Tate Gallery, London)
Published: E. Lacey, London
16 x 9.6 (plate cut)
Line and etching
Purchased, Lusk, Mr de Courcy Donovan, 1971

Lawrence, Thomas (1769-1830)
English School
BOND, WILLIAM (FL.1799-1833)
ENGLISH SCHOOL

10,368
Mary, Countess of Inchiquin, (née Palmer, 1750-1820), 2nd wife of 4th Earl of Inchiquin, later 1st Marquess of Thomond
(after an oil, RA 1795)
Published: 4th Earl of Inchiquin, as a Private Plate
36 x 29 (plate 25.3 x 18.8)
Line and stipple
Purchased, Dublin, Mr J.V. McAlpine, 1901

Lawrence, Thomas (1769-1830)
English School
COCHRAN, JOHN (FL.1820S-1860S)
ENGLISH SCHOOL

10,955
Sir George Murray, M.P., (1772-1846), former Lieut.-General and Commander-in-Chief in Ireland, (pl. for H.T. Ryall's 'Portraits of Eminent Conservatives and Statesmen', 2nd series, 1846)
(after an oil of c.1815)
Published: R. Ryley & Co., also F.G. Moon, London, 1838 (Printed: Wilkinson & Dawe)
36.5 x 27.8 (plate 34 x 26.1)
Stipple
Purchased, Dublin, Mr A. Roth, 1898

Lawrence, Thomas (1769-1830)
English School
COUSINS, SAMUEL (1801-1887)
ENGLISH SCHOOL

10,057
Charles Grey, 2nd Earl Grey, (1764-1845), Statesman and later British Prime Minister
(after an oil of 1828, Lady Mary Howick Collection)
Published: Sir T. Lawrence, May 1829
52 x 39.7 (plate 40.9 x 28.2)
Mezzotint
Provenance Unknown

Lawrence, Thomas (1769-1830)
English School
COUSINS, SAMUEL (1801-1887)
ENGLISH SCHOOL

10,222
Richard Wellesley, 1st Marquess Wellesley, (1760-1842), Former Lord Lieutenant of Ireland
(after a wl oil, RA 1813, Royal Collection, Windsor Castle)
Unlettered Proof
Published: Welch & Gwynne, London, 1842
44 x 36 (plate 39 x 30.2)
Mezzotint
Presumed purchased, Dublin, Jones Salesroom, 1879

Lawrence, Thomas (1769-1830)
English School
COUSINS, SAMUEL (1801-1887)
ENGLISH SCHOOL

10,446

'Childhood's Companion', Julia Beatrice Peel, (c.1821-1893), daughter of Sir Robert Peel, later Countess of Jersey, wife of the 6th Earl
(after an oil, RA 1828; Hursley Park, Hampshire)
Published: Colnaghi & Puckle, London, 1st January 1841
50.8 x 41.4 (plate 46.8 x 36)
Mezzotint
Provenance Unknown

Lawrence, Thomas (1769-1830)
English School
COUSINS, SAMUEL (1801-1887)
ENGLISH SCHOOL

10,447
'Boyhood Reverie', Charles William Lambton, (1818-1831), later 1st Earl of Durham
(after an oil, RA 1825; Earl of Durham Collection)
Published: T. Boys, London, 1st March 1844
52 x 41.7 (plate 46.8 x 35.5)
Mezzotint
Provenance Unknown

Lawrence, Thomas (1769-1839)
English School
COUSINS, SAMUEL (1803-1887)
ENGLISH SCHOOL

10,509
Field-Marshal Arthur Wellesley, 1st Duke of Wellington, (1769-1852)
(after an oil, RA 1825; Wellington College, Berkshire)
Published: P. & D. Colnaghi & Co., London, 15th June 1845
80.6 x 51.6 (plate 78.5 x 49)
Mezzotint
Acquired between 1879/90

Lawrence, Thomas (1769-1830)
English School
DEAN, T.A. (FL.1783-1840)
ENGLISH SCHOOL

11,283
Major-General Sir Henry Torrens, (1779-1828), (pl. for W. Jerdan's 'National Portrait Gallery', 1830-34)
(after a C. Turner mezzotint of 1817, from a wl oil, RA 1816; Londonderry Town Hall)
Published: Fisher, Son & Co., London, 1829
30.3 x 23.3 (plate 22.5 x 14.2)
Line
Acquired c.1908

Lawrence, Thomas (1769-1830)
English School
DOO, GEORGE THOMAS (1800-1886)
ENGLISH SCHOOL

10,402
Lady Selina Meade, (d.1872), daughter of the 2nd Earl of Clanwilliam
(after an oil of 1819, Montalto, Co. Down)
Published: G.T. Doo, London, 1835
50.5 x 37.5 (plate 41.5 x 32.5)
Line
Purchased, Dublin, Mr A. Roth, 1896

Lawrence, Thomas (1769-1830)
English School
EVANS, T. (18TH CENTURY)
ENGLISH SCHOOL

?0,093
Horatio Walpole, 4th Earl of Orford, (1717-1797), (pl. for H. Walpole's 'The Works of Horatio Walpole, Earl of Orford', 1798)
(after a pencil drawing of 1795, NPG, London)
?6.1 x 20.6 (plate cut)
Stipple
Provenance Unknown

Lawrence, Thomas (1769-1830)
English School
FREEMAN, SAMUEL (1773-1857)
ENGLISH SCHOOL

?,199
John Philpot Curran, (1750-1817), Orator and Master of the Rolls in Ireland
(after an oil of 1799/1800)
Published; MacGregor, Polson & Co., Dublin; also D.G. Sutherland & Co., Belfast
22.2 x 14.2 (plate cut)
Stipple
Purchased, Dublin, Mr P. Traynor, 1898

Lawrence, Thomas (1769-1830)
English School
GILLER, WILLIAM (C.1805-1858)
ENGLISH SCHOOL

10,154
Philip Yorke, 3rd Earl of Hardwicke, (1757-1834), Former Lord Lieutenant of Ireland
(after an oil, RA 1830; Crichel House, Dorset)
Published: Hodgson & Graves, London, 1st November 1836
39.9 x 30.2 (plate 30.5 x 22.3)
Line and stipple
Purchased, Dublin,
Mr J.V. McAlpine, 1899

Lawrence, Thomas (1769-1830)
English School
GODBY, JAMES (FL.1790-1820)
ENGLISH SCHOOL

10,767
Lieut.-General Sir John Francis Cradock, (1762-1833), later 1st Baron Howden
(after a tql oil of c.1803)
Published: E. Orme, London, 2nd January 1809
35.5 x 25.9 (plate 26.5 x 20.2)
Stipple
Purchased, London,
Mr H.A.J. Breun, 1910

Lawrence, Thomas (1769-1830)
English School
GODBY, JAMES (FL.1790-1820)
ENGLISH SCHOOL

11,551
Miss Sydney Owenson, (1778-1859), later Lady Morgan, Authoress
(after a drawing, Apsley House, London)

Published: J.J. Stockdale, London, 13th February 1811
17.2 x 10 (plate cut)
Stipple
Acquired between 1913/14

Lawrence, Thomas (1769-1830)
English School
LANE, RICHARD JAMES (1800-1782)
ENGLISH SCHOOL

10,941
Lady Anne Lucy Nugent, (née Poulett, 1790-1848), wife of 3rd Baron Nugent, as the Lady in Milton's masque 'Comus'
(after an unfinished wl oil, begun 1813)
Published: J. Dickinson, London, October 1830 (Printed: C.J. Hullmandel)
35.2 x 31.5 (image 39 x 30.4)
Lithograph
Purchased, Dublin, Mr A. Roth, 1896

Lawrence, Thomas (1769-1830)
English School
LEWIS THE ELDER, FREDERICK CHRISTIAN (1779-1856)
ENGLISH SCHOOL

11,420
Self-Portrait, aged 35
(after a chalk drawing or watercolour miniature of c.1804)
Published: London, 1831
28.5 x 20.6 (plate 26.2 x cut)
Stipple
Provenance Unknown

Lawrence, Thomas (1769-1830)
English School
LUPTON, THOMAS (1791-1873)
ENGLISH SCHOOL

20,112
John Jebb, (1775-1873) P. Bishop of Limerick, Ardfert and Aghadoe
(after an oil of 1826)
Published: T. Lupton, London, 5th January 1830
39.5 x 28.2 (plate cut)
Mezzotint
Purchased, Lusk, Mr de Courcy Donovan, 1971

Lawrence, Thomas (1769-1830)
English School
MEYER, HENRY HOPPNER (1782/83-1847)
ENGLISH SCHOOL

11,198
John Philpot Curran, (1750-1817), Orator and Master of the Rolls in Ireland
(after an oil of 1799/1800)
Published: A. Constable & Co., Edinburgh, 20th April 1819
21.8 x 13.5 (plate 20.9 x 13.5)
Stipple
Purchased, Dublin, Mr P. Traynor, 1898

Lawrence, Thomas (1769-1830)
English School
PARRY, T.H. (19TH CENTURY)
ENGLISH SCHOOL

11,193

John Wilson Croker, M.P., (1780-1857), Author
(after an oil, RA 1825; NGI no. 300)
Published: Fisher, Son & Co., London, 1840
22.2 x 14.2 (plate cut)
Stipple
Purchased, Dublin, Mr P. Traynor, 1898

Lawrence, Thomas (1769-1830)
English School
WRIGHT, THOMAS (1792-1849)
ENGLISH SCHOOL
PICART, CHARLES (1780-C.1837)
ENGLISH SCHOOL

10,185
Lieutenant-General Sir Galbraith Lowry Cole, (1772-1842), later Governor of Mauritius and the Cape of Good Hope
Published: T. Cadell & W. Davies, London, 21st August 1816
42 x 33.5 (plate 38.5 x 32.5)
Stipple
Purchased, Dublin, Mr J.V. McAlpine, 1899

Lawrence, Thomas (1769-1830)
English School *and*
English School (c.1830)
PRIOR, THOMAS ABIEL (1809-1886)
ENGLISH SCHOOL

11,341
Three British Prime Ministers - William Lamb, 2nd Viscount Melbourne, (1779-1848), Henry Temple, 3rd Viscount Palmerston, (1784-1865), and John Russell, 1st Earl Russell, (1792-1878)
(Viscount Melbourne after a T. Lawrence hl oil of c.1805, NPG, London)
22.7 x 15.2 (plate cut)
Line
Provenance Unknown

Lawrence, Thomas (1769-1830)
English School
ROBINSON, JOHN HENRY (1796-1871)
ENGLISH SCHOOL

20,204
Psyche - Lady Henrietta Frances Grantham, (1784-1830), daughter of the 1st Earl of Enniskillen, wife of 3rd Baron Grantham, later 1st Earl de Gray
Published: J. Sharpe, London, 1838
17.3 x 12.2 (plate cut)
Line and etching
Purchased, Lusk, Mr de Courcy Donovan, 1971

Lawrence, Thomas (1769-1830)
English School
ROLLS, CHARLES (c.1800-c.1857)
ENGLISH SCHOOL

20,136
'The Morning Walk' - Mrs Elizabeth Allnutt, (née Douce, d.1810), and her daughter Anna, (1801-1828), (pl. for 'The Amulet', 1828)
(after an oil, RA 1798 and c.1803)
Lettered Proof
Published: The Proprietors of The Amulet, London, 1828
21.8 x 16.2 (plate 18.6 x 12.8)
Steel Engraving
Purchased, Lusk, Mr de Courcy Donovan, 1971

Lawrence, Thomas (1769-1830)
English School
SMITH, EDWARD (FL.1823-1851)
ENGLISH SCHOOL

11,265
Field-Marshal Arthur Wellesley, 1st Duke of Wellington, (169-1852), (pl. for McGregor's 'History of the French Revolution and the wars resulting from that event', 1816-27)
(after a wl oil of 1814-15, Royal Collection, Windsor Castle)
21.5 x 13 (plate cut)
Line
Acquired between 1913/14

Lawrence, Thomas (1769-1830)
English School
SMITH, JOHN RAPHAEL (1752-1812)
ENGLISH SCHOOL

10,058
John Philpot Curran, M.P., (1750-1817), Orator and Statesman
(after an oil of 1799/1800)
Published: 1801
41.5 x 33.3 (plate 37.6 x 30.2)
Mezzotint
Purchased, London, 2nd Chaloner Smith sale, 1888

Lawrence, Thomas (1769-1830)
English School
TURNER, CHARLES (1773-1857)
ENGLISH SCHOOL

10,107
John Porter, P. Bishop of Clogher, (d.1819)
(after an oil, Diocesan Collection, Clonboy)
Published: C. Turner, London, 10th October 1825
47 x 36.4 (plate 35.3 x 25.1)
Mezzotint
Purchased, London,
Mr J.V. McAlpine, 1904

Lawrence, Thomas (1769-1830)
English School
TURNER, CHARLES (1773-1857)
ENGLISH SCHOOL

10,458
Robert Stewart, Viscount Castlereagh, (1769-1822), later 2nd Marquess of Londonderry
(after an oil, RA 1814; Wynyard Park, Cleveland)
Published: C. Turner, London, 26th September 1814
65 x 48.8 (plate 56 x 40.5)
Mezzotint
Presumed purchased, Dublin, Jones Salesroom, 1879

Lawrence, Thomas (1769-1830)
English School
TURNER, CHARLES (1773-1857)
ENGLISH SCHOOL

10,689
Charles Whitworth, 1st Viscount, later 1st Earl Whitworth, (1752-1825), Lord Lieutenant of Ireland
(after an oil of 1807, The Louvre, Paris)
Published: Colnaghi & Co., London, 1814
54.2 x 39.1 (plate cut)
Mezzotint
Acquired by 1903

Lawrence, Thomas (1769-1830)
English School
TURNER, CHARLES (1773-1857)
ENGLISH SCHOOL

10,724
Lord John George De La Poer Beresford,
P. Archbishop of Armagh, (1773-1862),
Son of 1st Marquess of Waterford
(after an oil, RA 1830; Curraghmore,
County Waterford)
Published: C. Turner, London, 24th
March 1841
56.3 x 51 (plate 56.5 x 42)
Mezzotint
Purchased, Dublin,
Mr J.V. McAlpine, 1905

Lawrence, Thomas (1769-1830)
English School
TURNER, CHARLES (1773-1857)
ENGLISH SCHOOL

0,954
Sir John McMahon Bt., M.P.,
(1754-1817), Private Secretary and keeper
of the Privy Purse to the Prince Regent
(after an oil, RA 1814, one of three
known versions)
Published: C. Turner, for the
Proprietor, London, 16th February
1815
57.8 x 42.2 (plate 51.3 x 35.5)
Mezzotint
Acquired between 1898/1904

Lawrence, Thomas (1769-1830)
English School
TURNER, CHARLES (1773-1857)
ENGLISH SCHOOL

20,663
George Canning, M.P., (1770-1857),
British Prime Minister
Published: Colnaghi, Son & Co., also
C. Turner, London; also Giraldon
Bovinez, Paris; also Messrs. Allen,
Dublin, 1827
40 x 32 (plate 38 x 30.30)
Mezzotint
Provenance Unknown

Lawrence, Thomas (1769-1830)
English School
WAGSTAFF, CHARLES EDWARD (1808-1850)
ENGLISH SCHOOL

11,197
John Philpot Curran, M.P. (1750-1817),
Master of the Rolls in Ireland, (pl. for W.
Jerdan's 'National Portrait Gallery of
Illustrious and Eminent Personages of the
19th Century', 1830-34)
(after an oil of 1799/1800)
Published: Fisher, Son & Co.,
London, 1831
17.3 x 14.4 (plate cut)
Stipple
Purchased, Dublin, Mr P. Traynor,
1898

Lawrence, Thomas (1769-1830)
English School
WAGSTAFF, CHARLES EDWARD (1808-1850)
ENGLISH SCHOOL

20,804

11,479
Death Marching with the Revolutionaries
39.2 x 54 (plate 34 x 50)
Etching
Presented, Miss S.C. Harrison, 1904

Lehmann, Ludwig (1824-1901)
Danish School
TOMKINS, CHARLES ALGERNON (1821-1903)
ENGLISH SCHOOL

10,898
Charles William, 4th Duke of Leinster, (1819-1887)
(after an oil of 1876, NGI no. 1816)
Published: H. Graves & Co., London, 1st January 1884
40.5 x 32 (plate 37.5 x 29)
Mezzotint
Acquired by 1903

Lehmann, Ludwig (1824-1901)
Danish School
TOMKINS, CHARLES ALGERNON (1821-1903)
ENGLISH SCHOOL

10,905
Caroline, Duchess of Leinster, (née Lady Sutherland-Leveson-Gower, 1827-1887), wife of 4th Duke
(after an oil of 1876, NGI no. 1817)
Published: H. Graves & Co., London, 1st January 1884
40.5 x 32 (plate 37.5 x 29)
Mezzotint
Acquired by 1903

Leighton, Lady Mary (fl.1830-1864)
English School
LYNCH, JAMES HENRY (FL.1815-1868)
IRISH SCHOOL

10,893
'The Ladies of Llangollen' - Lady Eleanor Charlotte Butler, (1739-1829), daughter of 16th Earl of Ormonde, and Miss Sarah Ponsonby, (1757-1831)
Published: Day & Haghe, London, not before 1831
37.9 x 27.8 (image 22.4 x 18)
Coloured lithograph
Acquired by 1903

Leitch, William Leighton (1804-1883)
English School
FLOYD, WILLIAM (FL.1832-1859)
ENGLISH SCHOOL

20,281
Thurnberg Castle, called 'The Mouse' and Welmich on the River Rhine, Germany
Published: Fisher & Son, London & Paris
28.6 x 22.5 (plate cut)
Steel Engraving
Purchased, Lusk, Mr de Courcy Donovan, 1971

Leitch, William Leighton (1804-1883)
English School
SANDS, JAMES (FL.1832-1844)
ENGLISH SCHOOL

20,365
Argyro-Castro Castle, Albania
Published: Fisher, Son & Co., London & Paris
22.3 x 28.3 (plate cut)
Steel Engraving
Purchased, Lusk, Mr de Courcy Donovan, 1971

Leitch, William Leighton (1804-1883)
English School
SANDS, JAMES (FL.1832-1844)
ENGLISH SCHOOL

20,414
Isola di Garda, Lake Garda, N. Italy
Published: Fisher, Son & Co., London & Paris
22.4 x 28.4 (plate cut)
Steel Engraving
Purchased, Lusk, Mr de Courcy Donovan, 1971

ely, Peter (1618-1680)
nglo-Dutch School
ECKETT, ISAAC (1653-1719)
NGLISH SCHOOL

,080
illiam of Orange, Stadholder of Holland, 650-1702), later King William III of igland
fter an oil of 1677, Syon House, ondon)
ıblished: I. Beckett, London, 681/88
x 25 (plate cut)
ezzotint
ırchased, London, 1st Chaloner ıith sale, 1887

Lely, Peter (1618-1680)
Anglo-Dutch School
BECKETT, ISAAC (1653-1719)
ENGLISH SCHOOL

10,328
The Hon. Mary Fielding, (née Swift, d.1682), daughter of 1st Viscount Carlingford, wife of The Hon. Robert Fielding
Published: I. Beckett, London, ?1681/88
33.5 x 25.2 (plate cut)
Mezzotint
Purchased, London, 1st Chaloner Smith sale, 1887

Lely, Peter, (1618-1680)
Anglo-Dutch School
BECKETT, ISAAC (1653-1719)
ENGLISH SCHOOL

10,373
Elizabeth, Countess of Chesterfield, (née Butler, 1640-1665), daughter of the 1st Duke of Ormonde and 2nd wife of the 2nd Earl of Chesterfield
Published: I. Beckett, London, ?1681/88
36 x 26 (plate 34.5 x 25.2)
Mezzotint
Purchased, London, 1st Chaloner Smith sale, 1887

Lely, Peter (1618-1680)
Anglo-Dutch School
BECKETT, ISAAC (1653-1719)
ENGLISH SCHOOL

10,561
William of Orange, Stadholder of Holland, (1650-1702), later King William III of England, (variant of NGI no. 10,080)
(after an oil of 1677, Syon House, London)
Published: I. Beckett, London, ?1681/88
25.3 x 19.6 (plate 24.7 x 18.7)
Mezzotint
Purchased, London, 1st Chaloner Smith sale, 1887

Lely, Peter (1618-1680)
Anglo-Dutch School
BLOOTELING, ABRAHAM (1640-1690)
DUTCH SCHOOL

Stipple
Purchased, Dublin, Mr P. Traynor, 1898

Lely, Peter (1618-1680)
Anglo-Dutch School
GRIFFIER, JAN (C.1645-1718)
ANGLO-DUTCH SCHOOL

10,364
Mary of Modena, (1658-1718), Queen of King James II of England
36.2 x 27.1 (plate 34 x 25)
Mezzotint
Purchased, London, 1st Chaloner Smith sale, 1887

?Lely, Peter (1618-1680)
Anglo-Dutch School
LOMBART, PIERRE (1612-1682)
FRENCH SCHOOL

10,069
John Ogilby, (1600-1676), Author, Publisher, Master of the Revels in Ireland and Founder of the Werburgh Street Theatre, Dublin
(after an oil of c.1649, Bodleian Library, Oxford)
31.2 x 21.3 (plate cut)
Line
Presented, Mr T.H. Longfield, 1903

Lely, Peter, (1618-1680)
Anglo-Dutch School
LUTTERELL, EDWARD (FL.C.1673-1724)
IRISH SCHOOL

10,136
Arthur Capel, 1st Earl of Essex, (1631-1638)
(after an oil, Badminton House, Avon)
2nd State
Published: I. Lloyd, not before 1661
25 x 18 (plate 23.7 x 17.5)
Mezzotint
Purchased, London, 1st Chaloner Smith sale, 1887

Lely, Peter (1618-1680)
Anglo-Dutch School
LUTTERELL, EDWARD (FL.C.1673-1724)
IRISH SCHOOL

10,774
Arthur Capel, 1st Earl of Essex, (1631-1683)
(after an oil, Badminton House, Avon)
3rd State
Published: J. Smith, London
23.6 x 17.8 (plate cut)
Mezzotint
Purchased, London, 1st Chaloner Smith sale, 1887

Lely, Peter (1618-1680)
Anglo-Dutch School
McARDELL, JAMES (1728/29-1765)
ENGLISH SCHOOL

10,401
Elizabeth, Countess of Gramont, (née Hamilton, 1641-1708), Court Beauty
(after an oil of c.1663, Royal Collection, Hampton Court)
Published: E. Fisher with Ryland & Bryer, London
61.8 x 45.4 (plate 50 x 35)
Mezzotint
Acquired between 1879/90

?Lely, Peter (1618-1680)
Anglo-Dutch School
SCHENCK, PIETER (1660-1718/19)
DUTCH SCHOOL

10,560
William of Orange, Stadholder of Holland, (1650-1702), later King William III of England
Published: P. Schenck, Amsterdam
25.2 x 19.3 (plate 24.9 x 18.9)
Mezzotint
Purchased, London, 1st Chaloner Smith sale, 1887

Lely, Peter (1618-1680)
Anglo-Dutch School
VANDERBANCK, PETER (1649-1697)
ANGLO-FRENCH SCHOOL

1,418
Thomas Butler, Earl of Ossory, (1634-1680), son of the 1st Duke of Ormonde
(after an oil of c.1677, The Uffizi, Florence)
48.4 x 36.5 (plate 45 x 34)
Line
Purchased, London, Mr G. Lausen, 1895

Lely, Peter (1618-1680)
Anglo-Dutch School *and*
?Closterman, John (1660-1711)
English School
PRIOR, THOMAS ABIEL (1809-1886)
ENGLISH SCHOOL

11,373
Sir William Temple, (1628-1699), Statesman and Author; Sir Christopher Wren, (1632-1723), Architect; John Ray, (1627-1705), Naturalist
(Temple after an oil by Lely c.1660, NPG, London; Wren after an oil attrib. to Closterman c.1695, The Royal Society, London; Ray after an oil by unknown artist c.1680, NPG, London)
22.5 x 14.5 (plate cut)
Line and etching
Provenance Unknown

School of **Lely, Peter (1616-1686**
Anglo-Dutch School
WHITE, GEORGE (1676 OR 1689-1732)
ENGLISH SCHOOL

10,266
Erasmus Smith, (1611-1691), Merchant, London Alderman and Educational Benefactor in Ireland
(probably after an oil of 1666, Christ's Hospital, Horsham)
34.5 x 24.6 (plate 34.3 x 23.8)
Mezzotint
Purchased, London, 3rd Chaloner Smith sale, 1896

Le Pautre, Jean (1618-1682)
French School
LE PAUTRE, JEAN (1618-1682)
FRENCH SCHOOL

20,231
Diana and Adonis, (design for a Ceiling panel)
Published: P. Mariette, Paris
22 x 15 (plate cut)
Etching
Purchased, Lusk, Mr de Courcy Donovan, 1971

11,554
Denis Johnston, (1901-1984), Author and Playwright
Issued by the Artist, 1940
34 x 25 (image 26.5 x 24 approx)
Lithograph
Presented, Mrs S. Clarke, the Artist's sister, 1980

Linnell the Elder, John (1792-1882)
English School
LINNELL THE ELDER, JOHN (1792-1882)
ENGLISH SCHOOL

11,044
Thomas Spring Rice, M.P., (1790-1866), Chancellor of the Exchequer, later 1st Baron Monteagle
(after an oil, RA 1835)
Published: Frs. Graves & Co., late Colnaghi & Co., also J. Linnell, London, 15th March 1836
48.2 x 36.7 (plate 47.5 x 35.5)
Etching and mezzotint
Purchased, Dublin, Mr J.V. McAlpine, 1911

Linton, William (1791-1876)
English School
GOODALL, EDWARD (1795-1870)
ENGLISH SCHOOL

20,511
Naples, S. Italy, with Mount Vesuvius in the distance
10 x 16.2 (plate cut)
Steel Engraving
Purchased, Lusk, Mr de Courcy Donovan, 1971

Linton, William (1791-1876)
English School
WILLMORE, JAMES TILBITTS (1800-1863)
ENGLISH SCHOOL

20,139
The Ruins of Carthage with Caius Marcius in the foreground, (pl. for E & W Finden's 'Royal Gallery of British Art', 1838-49)
(after an oil, RSBA 1834)
INSCRIBED: *To the Right Honourable Charles Callis, Lord Western./This Engraving is with special permission/ respectfully dedicated by his Lordship's most obedient Servant/Edward Finden.*
Published: F.G. Moon, (for the proprietors), London, 1st January 1838
36.3 x 51.5 (plate 36 x 51.2)
Steel Engraving
Purchased, Lusk, Mr de Courcy Donovan, 1971

Liotard, Jean Etienne (1702-1789)
Swiss School
HOUSTON, RICHARD (1721-1775)
IRISH SCHOOL

10,384
So-called portrait of Maria, Countess of Coventry, (née Gunning, 1733-1760), wife of the 9th Earl
(after a wl pastel of 1752/54, Rijksmuseum, Amsterdam)
42 x 30.5 (plate cut)
Mezzotint
Purchased, London, 1st Chaloner Smith sale, 1887

Livesay, J. (19th century)
English School
WATKINS, W.G. (FL.1828-1848)
ENGLISH SCHOOL

20,429
Gainsborough, Lincolnshire
Published: J. Saunders, London & Lincoln, 1838
22.7 x 28.5 (plate 15.2 x 21)
Steel Engraving
Purchased, Lusk, Mr de Courcy Donovan, 1971

Livesay, Richard (1753-1823)
English School
DEAN, JOHN (C.1750-1798)
ENGLISH SCHOOL

10,464
James Caulfeild, 1st Earl of Charlemont, (1728-1799), Art Patron, as Commander-in-Chief of the Irish Volunteers
(after an oil of c.1783, NGI no. 4051 or replica in NPG, London)
Published: the Proprietor, London, also C. Callaghan, Dublin, 20th December 1785
63.5 x 43.5 (plate 58.5 x 39.9)
Mezzotint
Purchased, London, 1st Chaloner Smith sale, 1887

Locatelli, Andrea (1695-?1741)
Italian School
AUSTIN, WILLIAM (1721-1820)
ENGLISH SCHOOL

20,247(16)
Sts. Cosmas and Damian Church and the Colosseum, Rome, (from a bound copy of '28 Views of Rome and Environs', see App. 8, no. 20,247)
23.2 x 30.2 (plate 19.3 x 24.4)
Etching
Purchased, Lusk, Mr de Courcy Donovan, 1971

Lochée, John Charles (fl.1775-1790)
English School
CORNER, JOHN (FL.1778-1825)
ENGLISH SCHOOL

11,224
Charles Macklin, (c.1700-1797), Actor, (pl. for 'European Magazine', December 1787)
(after a medallion profile of ?1784; example in Wedgwood Museum, Barlaston, Stoke-on-Trent)
Published: J. Sewell, London, 1787
15 x 9.3 (plate cut)
Line
Purchased, Dublin,
Mr J.V. McAlpine, 1906

Lochée, John Charles (fl.1775-1790)
English School
HEATH, JAMES (1757-1834)
ENGLISH SCHOOL

11,281
Richard Brinsley Sheridan, M.P., (1751-1816), Playwright and Orator
(after a marble bust, RA 1790; V&A, London)
Published: W. Jones, Dublin, 1st February 1793
17.7 x 10.6 (plate cut)
Stipple
Purchased, Dublin, Mr P. Traynor, 1898

Lodder, William P.J. (fl.1783-1804)
English School
CARDON, ANTHONY (1772-1813)
ANGLO-BELGIAN SCHOOL

10,713
Major-General Sir Eyre Coote, (1762-?1824), Governor of Jamaica
Published: A. Cardon, London, 1805
30 x 21.5 (plate 24.8 x 17.5)
Stipple
Purchased, Dublin, Mr A. Roth, 1898

Loggan, David (c.1635-1692)
English School
SANDYS, EDWIN (FL.1685-1708)
IRISH SCHOOL

10,285
Sir William Petty, (1623-1687), Physician to the Army in Ireland, Surveyor-General and Political Economist, (frontispiece for his 'Hiberniae Delineatio', 1685)
(after a lost drawing of 1680)
23.5 x 17.3 (plate cut)
Line
Purchased, Dublin, Mr J.V. McAlpine, 1906

Lonsdale, James (1777-1839)
English School
TURNER, CHARLES (1773-1857)
ENGLISH SCHOOL

10,170
Michael Kelly, (1764-1826), Tenor and Musical Director
(after an oil, Garrick Club, London)
Published: Mr Sams, London, 14th June 1825
42.2 x 32.3 (plate 35.3 x 25.2)
Mezzotint
Purchased, London, Maggs Bros., 1905

Lotto, Lorenzo (c.1480-1556)
Venetian School
CRAIG, WILLIAM MARSHALL (FL.1788-1827)
ENGLISH SCHOOL
WRIGHT, JAMES HENRY (FL. 1808-1818)
ENGLISH SCHOOL

20,680(7)
The Virgin and Child and Sts. Peter, Jerome, Clare and Francis, (from 'Engravings of the most Noble The Marquis of Stafford's Collection of Pictures', see App. 8, no. 20,680)
(after an oil of c.1510, NGS, Edinburgh)
Published: Longman, Hurst, Rees, Orme & Brown, also White, also Cadell & Davies, also P.W. Tomkins, London, 1st June 1816 (Printed: Bensley & Son)
40 x 29.7 (plate cut)
Line
Provenance Unknown

Loutherbourg, Philippe de (1740-1812)
Anglo-French School
HUBAND, WILLCOCKS (1776-1834)
IRISH SCHOOL

11,542
A Drunken Peasant
11 x 12.6 (plate 10.8 x 12)
Etching
Provenance Unknown

Lover, Samuel (1797-1868)
Irish School
COOPER, ROBERT (FL.1795-1836)
ENGLISH SCHOOL

10,959
Lady Sydney Morgan, (née Owenson, 1778-1859), Authoress
(after a drawing)
Published: H. Colburn, 14th June 1825
51.2 x 34.3 (plate 32.3 x 24.1)
Stipple
Purchased, Dublin, Mr J.V. McAlpine, 1909

Lucas, John (1807-1874)
English School
LUCAS, JOHN (1807-1874)
ENGLISH SCHOOL

20,055
The Plague of Darkness - the Ninth Plague inflicted on the Egyptians
Published: Ritner & Goupil, Paris
(Printed: Aze)
42 x 57.4 (plate 31 x 38.7)
Mezzotint
Provenance Unknown

20,038
Christ among the Doctors, (artist given as Leonardo Da Vinci)
(after an oil, NG, London)
Published: M. Bovi, London, 1st March 1803
55.6 x 76.5 (plate 53 x 55.5)
Line and stipple
Provenance Unknown

Lüders, David (c.1710-1759)
Anglo-German School
McARDELL, JAMES (1728/29-1765)
IRISH SCHOOL

10,852
George William Frederick, Prince of Wales, (1738-1829), later King George III
(after an oil of 1751)
Published: J. McArdell, London
32.5 x 22.3 (plate cut)
Mezzotint
Purchased, London, 1st Chaloner Smith sale, 1887

Luini, Bernardino (1475-1532)
Italian School
BOVI, MARINO (1758-AFTER 1805)
ANGLO-ITALIAN SCHOOL

Lutterell, Edward (fl.c.1673-1724)
Irish School
LUTTERELL, EDWARD (FL.C.1673-1724)
IRISH SCHOOL

10,022
Rev. Francis Higgins, (1669-1728), Controversial Theologian and later P. Archdeacon of Cashel
Published: M. Lutterell, London, not before 1694
34.0 x 25.9 (plate 33.4 x 25.7)
Mezzotint
Purchased, London, 1st Chaloner Smith sale, 1887

M

M...., J. (18th century)
English School
?OKEY, SAMUEL (FL.1765-1780)
ANGLO-AMERICAN SCHOOL

10,327
'The Gunning Sisters' - Elizabeth, Duchess of Hamilton and Brandon, wife of the 6th Duke, (née Gunning, 1733-1790), with Maria, Countess of Coventry, wife of the 9th Earl, (née Gunning, 1733-1760), daughters of James Gunning
INSCRIBED: Hibernia long with Spleen beheld/Her favorite toasts by ours excell'd/Resolv'd t'outvie Britannias Fair/By her own Beauties, sent a Pair
Published: S. Okey, London, 1760s
25 x 35.3 (plate cut)
Mezzotint
Purchased, Mr H.A.J. Breun, 1911

Maas, Theodor (1659-1717)
Anglo-Dutch School
MAAS, THEODOR (1659-1717)
ANGLO-DUTCH SCHOOL

10,003
The Victory of King William III, (1650-1702), at the Battle of the Boyne, 1st July 1690
(after an oil of 1690, Welbeck Abbey, Nottinghamshire)
Published: E. Cooper, London
53 x 105.5 (plate cut)
Etching
Purchased, Paris, 1890

Maas, Theodor (1659-1717)
Anglo-Dutch School
MAAS, THEODOR (1659-1717)
ANGLO-DUTCH SCHOOL

20,800
The Victory of King William III, (1650-1702), at the Battle of the Boyne, 1st July 1690, (another copy)
(after an oil of 1690, Welbeck Abbey, Nottinghamshire)
Published: E. Cooper, London
53.5 x 103.5 (plate cut)
Etching
Provenance Unknown

McArdell, James (1728/29-1765)
Irish School
EARLOM, RICHARD (1743-1822)
ENGLISH SCHOOL

10,470
Self-Portrait (1765), while scraping his mezzotint of Van Dyck's 'Time and Cupid'
Published: R. Sayer, London, 20th April 1771
47.8 x 35.4 (plate 45 x 32.8)
Mezzotint
Purchased, London, 1st Chaloner Smith sale, 1887

MacDonald, Daniel (1821-1853)
Irish School
MACDONALD, DANIEL (1821-1853)
IRISH SCHOOL

10,916

Rev. Theobald Matthew, (1790-1856), founder of the Temperance League in Ireland
Published: Colnaghi, London, also, D. MacDonald, Cork
37.6 x 29.5 (plate cut)
Mezzotint
Presented, Mr W.G. Strickland, 1906

McEvoy, Ambrose (1878-1927)
English School
SICKERT, WALTER (1860-1942)
ENGLISH SCHOOL

11,448
'Pimlico' (1915)
2nd State
Issued by W. Sickert 1915; this is printed from the original plate by D. Strong for the Sickert Trust 1945/47
23.6 x 16 (plate 14.2 x 10)
Etching
Presented, The Sickert Trust, 1947

McInnes, Robert (1801-1886)
English School
BROWN, JOSEPH (FL.1854-1886)
ENGLISH SCHOOL

10,887
Thomas Hamilton, 9th Earl of Haddington, (1780-1858), Lord Lieutenant of Ireland, (pl. for H. Ryall's 'Portraits of Eminent Conservatives and Statesmen', 2nd series, 1846)
Published: G. Virtue, London, 1846
35 x 26 (plate cut)
Stipple
Purchased, Dublin, Mr J.V. McAlpine, 1913

Maclise, Daniel (1806-1870)
Irish School
DRUMMOND, WILLIAM (1800-1850)
ENGLISH SCHOOL

10,265
Sir William Betham, (1779-1853), Ulster King of Arms and Historian, (T. MacLean's 'Athenaeum portraits', no. 20')
(after a pencil drawing of 1827)
Published: T. McLean, London, February 1836 (Printed: Day & Haghe)
19.7 x 15.5 (image 15 x 14.5)
Lithograph
Purchased, Dublin, Mr A. Roth, 1895

Maclise, Daniel (1806-1870)
Irish School
KIRKWOOD, JOHN (FL.1826-1853)
IRISH SCHOOL

11,423
Thomas Moore, (1779-1852), Poet, (pl. for 'Dublin University Magazine', Vol. XIX, April 1842)
Published: W. Curry Junior & Co., Dublin
20.7 x 13 (plate cut)
Etching
Purchased, Dublin, Mr P. Traynor, 1898

Maclise, Daniel (1806-1870)
Irish School
MACLISE, DANIEL (1806-1870)
IRISH SCHOOL

10,288

'The Doctor' - William MaGinn, (1793-1842), Poet, Author, and Journalist, (pl. for Fraser's Magazine's 'A Gallery of Illustrious Literary Characters', 1830-38)
(after a pencil with watercolour study of 1830, NPG, London)
Published: J. Fraser, London, January 1831 (Printed: Engelmann, Graf & Coindet)
21 x 13 (image 19.5 x 12.5 approx)
Lithograph
Purchased, Dublin, Mr P. Traynor, 1898

Maclise, Daniel (1806-1870)
Irish School
MACLISE, DANIEL (1806-1870)
IRISH SCHOOL

10,601
Daniel O'Connell, (1775-1847), Statesman and Author of 'Agitation', with Richard Lalor Sheil, M.P., (1793-1851), Author of 'The Apostate', (pl. for Fraser's Magazine's 'A Gallery of Illustrious Literary Characters', 1830-38)
Published: J. Fraser, London, 1834
(Printed: Engelmann, Graf & Coindet)
21.2 x 13.1 (image 15 x 12.5 approx)
Lithograph
Provenance Unknown

Maclise, Daniel (1806-1870)
Irish School
MACLISE, DANIEL (1806-1870)
IRISH SCHOOL

10,675
Thomas Moore, (1779-1852), Poet, (pl. for Fraser's Magazine's 'A Gallery of Illustrious Literary Characters', 1830-38)
(after a drawing, V&A, London)
Published: J. Fraser, London, 1830
(Printed: Engelmann, Graf & Coindet)
21 x 13 (image 15.5 x 11.7 approx)
Lithograph
Acquired by 1906

MacManus, Henry (1810-1878)
Irish School
KIRKWOOD, JOHN (FL.1826-1853)
IRISH SCHOOL

11,302
Admiral Robert Stopford, (1768-1847), (pl. for 'Dublin University Magazine', Vol. XX, July 1842)
Published: W. Curry Junior & Co., Dublin
21.6 x 13.3 (plate cut)
Etching
Purchased, Dublin,
Mr J.V. McAlpine, 1913

Madden, Wyndham (fl.1766-1775)
Irish School
DICKINSON, WILLIAM (1746-1823)
ENGLISH SCHOOL

10,479
James Hewitt, 1st Baron Lifford, (1709-1789)
INSCRIBED: To the Right Honourable The Earl of Shelburne/One of His Majesty's Most honourable Privy Coucil/This plate is

humbly dedicated, as a noble encourager of the arts,/By His Lordships ever grateful devoted & faithful humble servant/Wyndham Madden
Published: W. Madden, Dublin also W. Dickinson, London, 1st December 1775
52.5 x 37.9 (plate 50.1 x 35.6)
Mezzotint
Purchased, London, 1st Chaloner Smith sale, 1887

Maes, Nicolaes (1634-1693)
Dutch School
LUPTON, THOMAS (1791-1873)
ENGLISH SCHOOL

0,326
The Surprise' - The Listening Housewife, from 'Gems of Art', 1824)
after an oil of 1655, Royal Collection, Buckingham Palace)
1.1 x 28.1 (plate 24.4 x 18.7)
Mezzotint
urchased, Lusk, Mr de Courcy Donovan, 1971

laguire, Charles E. (fl.c.1820)
ish School
AGUIRE, CHARLES E. (FL.C.1820)
ISH SCHOOL

11,838
Advertisement for Isaac Willis - music seller and pianoforte maker to H.M. George IV at the Royal Harmonic Saloon
Published: I. Willis, Dublin
16.6 x 20.5 (plate cut)
Line
Provenance Unknown

Maguire, James Robert (fl.1809-1850)
Irish School
HEATH, JAMES (1757-1834)
ENGLISH SCHOOL

10,881
Francis Hardy, M.P., (1751-1812), barrister, (pl. for Sir J. Barrington's 'Historic Anecdotes and Secret Memoirs' 1809-15)
INSCRIBED: *from an original drawing by J.R. Maguire in the possession of Sir J. Barrington*
Published: G. Robinson, London, 1st March 1811
34.5 x 26 (plate 25.2 x 21.5)
Stipple
Acquired by 1903

Maguire, Thomas Herbert (1821-1895)
Irish School
MAGUIRE, THOMAS HERBERT (1821-1895)
IRISH SCHOOL

10,684
Sir William Robert Wills Wilde, (1815-1876), Surgeon and Antiquary. father of Oscar Wilde
(after a drawing of 1847)
48.5 x 34 (image 29.5 x 22.8)
Lithograph
Purchased, London, Mr H.A.J. Breun, 1910

Maguire, Thomas Herbert (1821-1895)
English School
MAGUIRE, THOMAS HERBERT (1821-1895)
ENGLISH SCHOOL

10,871

Malton, James (c.1760-1803)
English School
MALTON, JAMES (C.1760-1803)
ENGLISH SCHOOL

11,577
Royal (now Collins) Barracks, Dublin, (pl. for J. Malton's 'A picturesque and descriptive view of the City of Dublin, described in a series of the most interesting scenes taken in the year 1791', 1799)
Published: J. Malton, London, July 1795
36.5 x 51 (plate 31.5 x 43)
Aquatint and etching
Acquired by 1904

Malton, James (c.1760-1803)
English School
MALTON, JAMES (C.1760-1803)
ENGLISH SCHOOL

11,580
The Provost's House, Trinity College, Dublin, (pl. for J. Malton's 'A picturesque and descriptive view of the City of Dublin, described in a series of the most interesting scenes taken in the year 1791', 1799)
Published: J. Malton, London, also G. Cowen, Dublin, February 1794
36 x 49.6 (plate 31 x 42.5)
Aquatint and etching
Acquired by 1904

Malton, James, (c.1760-1803)
English School
MALTON, JAMES (C.1760-1803)
ENGLISH SCHOOL

11,582
The Royal Military Infirmary, (now Army G.H.Q.), Phoenix Park, Dublin, (pl. for J. Malton's 'A picturesque and descriptive view of the City of Dublin, described in a series of the most interesting scenes taken in the year 1791', 1799)
Published: J. Malton, London, also G. Cowen, Dublin, July, 1794
36.2 x 50 (plate 30.2 x 42)
Aquatint and etching
Acquired by 1904

Malton, James (c.1760-1803)
English School
MALTON, JAMES (C.1760-1803)
ENGLISH SCHOOL

11,579
The West Front of St Patrick's Cathedral, Dublin, (pl. for J. Malton's 'A picturesque and descriptive view of the City of Dublin, described in a series of the most interesting scenes taken in the year 1791', 1799)
(after a watercolour of 1793, NGI no. 2620)
Published: J. Malton, London, also G. Cowen, Dublin, November 1793
36 x 51.6 (plate 30.5 x 42.3)
Aquatint and etching
Acquired by 1904

Malton, James (c.1760-1803)
English School
MALTON, JAMES (C.1760-1803)
ENGLISH SCHOOL

11,581
The Royal Hospital, Kilmainham, North Walk, (pl. for J. Malton's 'A picturesque and descriptive view of the City of Dublin, described in a series of the most interesting scenes taken in the year 1791', 1799)
Published: J. Malton, London, also G. Cowen, Dublin, February 1794
36 x 50.5 (plate 31 x 42.2)
Aquatint and etching
Acquired by 1904

Malton, James (c.1760-1803)
English School
MALTON, JAMES (C.1760-1803)
ENGLISH SCHOOL

11,583
Powerscourt House, William Street South, Dublin, (pl. J. Malton's 'A picturesque and descriptive view of the City of Dublin, described in a series of the most interesting scenes taken in the year 1791', 1799)
Published: J. Malton, London, July 1795
36 x 50 (plate 30.5 x 42))
Aquatint and etching
Acquired by 1904

Malton, James (c.1760-1803)
English School
MALTON, JAMES (C.1760-1803)
ENGLISH SCHOOL

11,585
The Rotunda and New Rooms, (now Gate Theatre), Dublin, (pl. for J. Malton's 'A picturesque and descriptive view of the City of Dublin, described in a series of the most interesting scenes taken in the year 1791', 1799)
Published: J. Malton, London, December 1795
36 x 50.5 (plate 31 x 43)
Aquatint and etching
Acquired by 1904

Malton, James (c.1760-1803)
English School
MALTON, JAMES (C.1760-1803)
ENGLISH SCHOOL

11,586
The Marine School, Dublin, (now demolished), looking up the River Liffey, (pl. J. Malton's 'A picturesque and descriptive view of the City of Dublin, described in a series of the most interesting scenes taken in the year 1791', 1799)
(after a watercolour, NGI no. 2704)
Published: J. Malton, London, June 1794
36 x 51 (plate 31 x 42.5)
Aquatint and etching
Acquired by 1904

Malton, James (c.1760-1803)
English School
MALTON, JAMES (C.1760-1803)
ENGLISH SCHOOL

11,587
St Stephen's Green gardens, Dublin, (now re-landscaped), (pl. for J. Malton's 'A picturesque and descriptive view of the City of Dublin, described in a series of the most interesting scenes taken in the year 1791', 1799)
Published: J. Malton, London, June 1796
36 x 52 (plate 31 x 43)
Aquatint and etching
Acquired by 1904

Malton, James (c.1760-1803)
English School
MALTON, JAMES (C.1760-1803)
ENGLISH SCHOOL

11,588
Dublin from the Magazine Fort, Phoenix Park, (pl. for J. Malton's 'A picturesque and descriptive view of the City of Dublin, described in a series of the most interesting scenes taken in the year 1791', 1799)
Published: J. Malton, London, July 1795
36.3 x 51.5 (plate 31.5 x 43.2)
Aquatint and etching
Acquired by 1904

Malton, James (c.1760-1803)
English School
MALTON, JAMES (C.1760-1803)
ENGLISH SCHOOL

11,591
The Blue-Coat Hospital, (now the Incorporated Law Society), Dublin, (pl. for J. Malton's 'A picturesque and descriptive view of the City of Dublin, described in a series of the most interesting scenes taken in the year 1791', 1799)
(after a watercolour, NGI no. 2706)
Published: J. Malton, London, March 1798
36.2 x 51.7 (plate 31.2 x 42.5)
Aquatint and etching
Acquired by 1904

Malton, James (c.1760-1803)
English School
MALTON, JAMES (C.1760-1803)
ENGLISH SCHOOL

11,592
The Four Courts, Dublin, looking up the River Liffey, (pl. for J. Malton's 'A picturesque and descriptive view of the City of Dublin, described in a series of the most interesting scenes taken in the year 1791', 1799)
(after a watercolour of 1793, NGI no. 7713)
Published: J. Malton, London, March 1799
38.2 x 52.4 (plate 31 x 43)
Aquatint and etching
Acquired by 1904

Malton, James (c.1760-1803)
English School
MALTON, JAMES (c.1760-1803)
ENGLISH SCHOOL

11,634
The Custom House, Dublin
1st state (1790)
26 x 37.3 (plate cut)
Etching with watercolour
Purchased, Sir James Linton, 1908

Malton, James (c.1760-1803)
English School
MALTON, JAMES (C.1760-1803)
ENGLISH SCHOOL

11,640
The Custom House, Dublin
2nd state
Published: J. Malton, London, also G. Cowen, Dublin, July 1792
31.2 x 43.3 (plate 31 x 41.8)
Aquatint and etching
Purchased, Dublin, Mr P. Traynor, 1899

Malton, James (c.1760-1803)
English School
MALTON, JAMES (C.1760-1803)
ENGLISH SCHOOL

11,690
Arms of the City of Dublin, (pl. for J. Malton's 'A picturesque and descriptive view of the City of Dublin, described in a series of the most interesting scenes taken in the year 1791', 1799)
Published: J. Malton, London, July 1792
52.8 x 35.8 (plate 42.2 x 31.1)
Aquatint and etching
Acquired by 1904

Malton, James (c.1760-1803)
English School
MALTON, JAMES (C.1760-1803)
ENGLISH SCHOOL

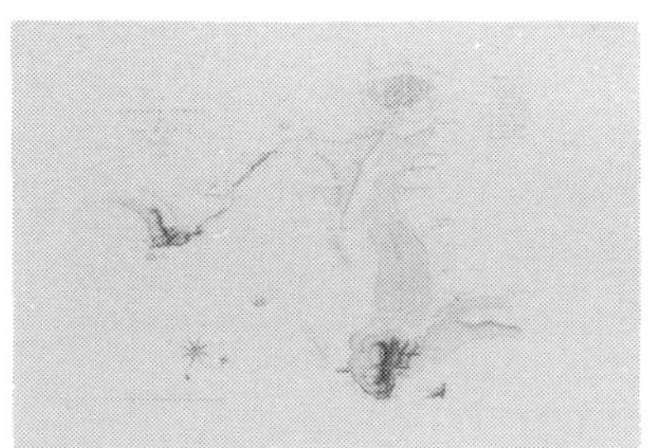

11,816
A Correct Survey of the Bay of Dublin, 1795
Published: J. Malton, London, December 1795
34.6 x 51 (plate 31.7 x 43.4)
Aquatint and line
Purchased 1908

Mansfield, Johann Georg (1764-1817)
Austrian School
MANSFIELD, JOHANN GEORG (1764-1817)
AUSTRIAN SCHOOL

11,103
George Count De Browne, (1698-1792), Professional Soldier, Governor of Livonia and Field Marshal in Russian Army
14.5 x 8.8 (plate cut)
Line
Presented, Mr H. Doyle, 1889

Maratta, Carlo (1625-1713)
Roman School
VALET, GUILLAUME (1632-1704)
FRENCH SCHOOL

10,144
Father Luke Wadding, (1632-1704), founder of the Irish College of St Isidore, Rome, (seen in background)

(after an oil of c.1650)
29.5 x 20.9 (plate cut)
Line
Presented, Rev. C.P. Meehan, 1884

Marieschi, Michele (1696-1743)
Venetian School
MARIESCHI, MICHELE (1696-1743)
VENETIAN SCHOOL

1,662
Piazza S. Marco, Venice, (pl. for Magnificentores selectioresque urbis Venetarium prospectus', 1741)
(possibly after an oil, NGI no. 473)
34.3 x 58 (plate 31 x 45)
Etching
Presented, Mr T.H. Longfield, 1898

Markham (18th century)
English School
BURFORD, THOMAS (FL.1741-1765)
ENGLISH SCHOOL

0,085
Jonathan Swift, (1667-1745), Dean of St Patrick's Cathedral, Dublin and Satirist
(2nd State of Markham/A. Van Haecken mezzotint of 1740, NGI no. 10,142)
Published: J. Bowles, London, 1744
36.5 x 26.1 (plate 35.2 x 24.8)
Mezzotint
Purchased, London, 2nd Chaloner Smith sale, 1888

Markham (18th century)
English School
BURFORD, THOMAS (FL.1741-1765)
ENGLISH SCHOOL

11,021
Jonathan Swift, (1667-1745), Dean of St Patrick's Cathedral, Dublin and Satirist
(3rd State of Markham/A. Van Haecken mezzotint of 1740, NGI no. 10,142)
Published: J. Bowles, London, 1744
39.5 x 27.7 (plate 35.2 x 25)
Mezzotint
Purchased, London, 2nd Chaloner Smith sale, 1888

Markham (18th Century)
English School
VAN HAECKEN, ALEXANDER (C.1701-1757)
ANGLO-DUTCH SCHOOL

10,142
Jonathan Swift, (1667-1745), Dean of St Patrick's Cathedral, Dublin and Satirist
(probably after an F. Bindon oil)
Published: ?A. Van Haecken, London, 25th February 1740
35 x 25 (plate cut)
Mezzotint
Purchased, London, 2nd Chaloner Smith sale, 1888

Marlow, William (1740-1813)
English School
GODFREY, (18TH CENTURY)
ENGLISH SCHOOL

20,095
North (Entrance) Front of Strawberry Hill, Middlesex, (pl. for H. Walpole's 'The Works of Horatio Walpole, Earl of Orford', 1798)
14.6 x 20.2 (plate cut)
Line and etching
Provenance Unknown

Marshall, I.F. (19th century)
English School
FAIRLAND, THOMAS (1804-1852)
ENGLISH SCHOOL

20,798
Cottage Charity
Published: Dean & Co., London
44.2 x 60.6 (image 29 x 35.5)
Lithograph with watercolour and varnish
Provenance Unknown

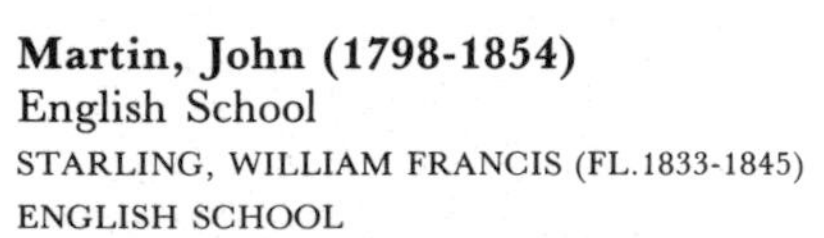

Martin, John (1798-1854)
English School
STARLING, WILLIAM FRANCIS (FL.1833-1845)
ENGLISH SCHOOL

20,397
Titus before Jerusalem, (from Shakespeare's 'Titus Andronicus', pl. for 'Illustrations of Shakespeare' 1833)
14 x 20.2 (plate cut)
Steel Engraving
Purchased, Lusk, Mr de Courcy Donovan, 1971

Masquerier, John James (1778-1855)
English School
SAY, WILLIAM (1768-1834)
ENGLISH SCHOOL

10,372
Eliza O'Neill, (1791-1872), Actress, later Lady Wrixon-Becher, wife of Sir William
(after an oil, NPG, London)
Lettered Proof
Published: for the Proprietors by D. Cox, London, 8th February 1815
40.5 x 30.6 (plate 35.5 x 25.3)
Mezzotint
Purchased, Dublin, Mrs Noseda, 1887

Masquerier, John James (1778-1855)
English School
TURNER, CHARLES (1773-1857)
ENGLISH SCHOOL

10,178
John de Blaquiere, 1st Baron de Blaquiere, (1732-1812), former Chief Secretary to the Lord Lieutenant of Ireland
(after an oil, RA 1803)
Published: C. Turner, London, 1st July 1803
43.8 x 33.8 (plate 38 x 28)
Mezzotint
Purchased, Dublin, Mr A. Roth, 1896

Matisse, Henri (1896-1954)
French School
MATISSE, HENRI (1896-1954)
FRENCH SCHOOL

20,839
'Danseuse reflétée dans la glace' - Ballet Dancer reflected in the mirror
Issued by the artist 1927, 31/of 50
32 x 40 (image 29 x 37 approx)
Lithograph
Presented, the Friends of the Nationa Collections of Ireland, 1938

Maull and Polyblank (19th century
English School
COCHRAN, JOHN (FL.1820S-1860S)
ENGLISH SCHOOL

11,243
Rev. William Urwick, (1791-1868), Non-conformist Divine and Chronicler
(after a photograph)
22 x 14 (plate cut)
Stipple
Acquired c.1908

Mayall, John (1810-1901)
Anglo-American School
MOORE, J. (FL.1851-1861)
ENGLISH SCHOOL

1,027
arry Sullivan, (1821-1891), Actor, as hakespeare's Hamlet, (Act 2, Sc. 2), (pl. or J. Tallis 'Drawing Room Table Book', 851)
after a daguerreotype)
ublished: J. Tallis & Co., London & ew York
3.7 x 30 (plate 28.5 x 23)
tipple
cquired c.1903

Mayall, John (1810-1901)
Anglo-American School
POUND, D.J. (FL.1842-1877)
ENGLISH SCHOOL

10,567
James Whiteside, M.P., (1804-1876), Lord Chief Justice of Ireland, (pl. for The Illustrated News of the World's 'The Drawing Room Portrait Gallery of Eminent Personages', 1859)
(after a photograph)
Published: Illustrated News of the World, London, 1859
36.4 x 26.5 (plate cut)
Line and stipple
Acquired between 1913/14

Mayall, John (1810-1901)
Anglo-American School
POUND, D.J. (FL.1842-1877)
ENGLISH SCHOOL

10,860
Sir Henry Singer Keating, M.P., (1804-1888), Solicitor-General and later Judge
(after a daguerreotype)
Published: 1850s
33.3 x 24.6 (plate cut)
Line and stipple
Acquired between 1913/14

Mayall, John (1810-1901)
Anglo-American School
POUND, D.J. (FL.1842-1877)
ENGLISH SCHOOL

10,927
Daniel Maclise, (1806-1870), Artist, (pl. for the Illustrated News of the World's 'The Drawing Room Portrait Gallery of Eminent Personages', 1859)
(after a daguerreotype)
Published: Illustrated News of the World, London, 1859
37.7 x 28.5 (plate cut)
Line and stipple
Purchased, Dublin, Mr P. Traynor, 1898

Mayall, John (1810-1901)
Anglo-American School
POUND, D.J. (FL.1842-1877)
ENGLISH SCHOOL

46.9 x 32.5 (plate cut)
Line
Bequeathed, Judge J. Murnaghan, 1976

Metsu, Gabriel (1629-1667)
Dutch School
CHATAIGNER, ALEXIS (1772-1817)
FRENCH SCHOOL

20,072
A Young Woman composing music
(after an oil of c.1662, Mauritshuis, The Hague)
62.5 x 46.2 (plate 43.5 x 32)
Etching
Provenance Unknown

Metz, Conrad Martin (1749-1827)
Anglo-German School
METZ, CONRAD MARITN (1749-1827)
ANGLO-GERMAN SCHOOL

20,236
Putti Playing with a Bird
Published: C.M. Metz, London, 1st March 1800
26.7 x 37.2 (plate 24.4 x 32.2)
Stipple
Purchased, Lusk, Mr de Courcy Donovan, 1971

Metz, Conrad Martin (1749-1827)
Anglo-German School
METZ, CONRAD MARTIN (1749-1827)
ANGLO-GERMAN SCHOOL

20,237
Putti Fishing
Published: C.M. Metz, London, 1st March 1800
27 x 37.1 (plate 21.5 x 29)
Stipple
Purchased, Lusk, Mr de Courcy Donovan, 1971

Metz, Conrad Martin (1749-1827)
Anglo-German School
METZ, CONRAD MARTIN (1749-1827)
ANGLO-GERMAN SCHOOL

20,238
Bacchic Putti
Published: C.M. Metz, London, 1st March 1800
27 x 37.1 (plate 24.7 x 31.5)
Stipple
Purchased, Lusk, Mr de Courcy Donovan, 1971

Metz, Conrad Martin (1749-1827)
Anglo-German School
METZ, CONRAD MARTIN (1749-1827)
ANGLO-GERMAN SCHOOL

20,239
Putti playing with Goats
Published: C.M. Metz, London, 1st March 1800
27.2 x 37 (plate 24.5 x 32)
Stipple
Purchased, Lusk, Mr de Courcy Donovan, 1971

Michelangelo (1475-1564)
Italian School
LEWIS THE ELDER, FREDERICK CHRISTIAN (1779-1856)
ENGLISH SCHOOL

20,720(28)
Study for the fresco of the Creation of Adam in the Sistine Chapel, Rome, (from the 'Italian School of Design', 1823, see App. 8, no. 20,720)
(after a red chalk drawing of c.1511, BM, London)
Published: W.Y. Ottley, London, 1st May 1818
48.8 x 33.5 (plate 27.1 x 33 approx)
Soft-ground etching
Provenance Unknown

?Miereveld, Michiel van (1567-1641)
Dutch School
DERBY, WILLIAM (1786-1847)
ENGLISH SCHOOL

SCRIVEN, EDWARD (1775-1841)
ENGLISH SCHOOL

10,782
Henry Danvers, 1st Earl of Danby, (1573-1644), Soldier and Statesman, (pl. for E. Lodge's 'Portraits of Illustrious Personages of Great Britain' 1821-28)
(after an oil, Woburn Abbey, Bedfordshire)
Published: Harding & Lepard, London, 1st June 1828
43 x 30 (plate 37.6 x 26.3)
Stipple
Purchased, Dublin, Mr J.V. McAlpine, 1906

Miers, John (?1758-1821)
English School
MIERS, JOHN (?1758-1821)
ENGLISH SCHOOL

10,668
A Gentleman in profile to left, (?John Wesley, 1709-1791, Methodist Preacher)
Published: J. Miers, Leeds, 1784
9.2 x 7.4 (plate cut)
Mezzotint (cut oval)
Miss Mary A. McNeill bequest, 1985

Mignard, Paul (1638/40-1691)
French School
VAN SOMER THE YOUNGER, PAUL (1649-C.1694)
ANGLO-DUTCH SCHOOL

10,321
Elizabeth, Countess of Meath, (née Lennard, 1644/45-1701), wife of the 3rd Earl
(after an oil of 1674/90)
Published: P. Van Somer the Younger, London
29.4 x 21.8 (plate 26 x 21.6)
Mezzotint
Purchased, London, 2nd Chaloner Smith sale, 1888

Mignard, Pierre (1612-1695)
French School
FAITHORNE THE YOUNGER, WILLIAM (1656-C.1710)
ENGLISH SCHOOL

11,025
Frederick Armand de Schomberg, (1615-1690), later 1st Duke of Schomberg, Professional Soldier
Published: G. Beckett, London, ?1681/88
27.5 x 21.1 (plate 23 x 15.5)
Mezzotint
Purchased, London, 1st Chaloner Smith sale, 1887

Miller, William (c.1740-c.1810)
English School
BIRRELL, O. (FL.1785-1800)
ENGLISH SCHOOL

11,345
François Joseph Paul, Comte De Grasse, (1723-1788), French Admiral defeated off Dominica, (pl. for J. Andrews' 'History of the War with America, France, Spain and Holland', 1785-86)
Published: J. Fielding, London,

6th October 1785
17.7 x 11.6 (plate cut)
Line
Provenance Unknown

Moll, Herman (1688-1745)
Anglo-Dutch School
MOLL, HERMAN (1688-1745)
ANGLO-DUTCH SCHOOL

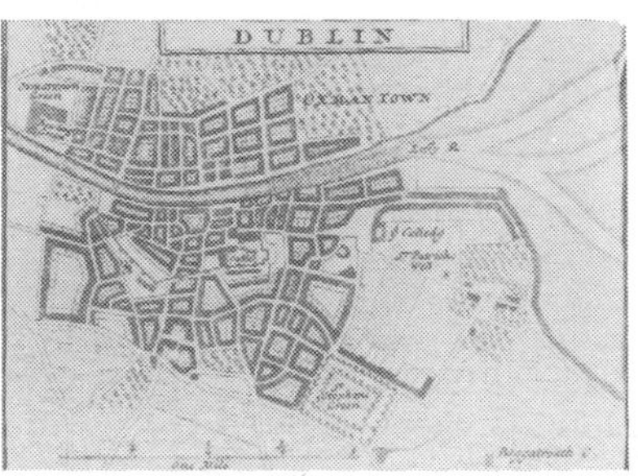

11,666
Map of Dublin in 1714
Published: H. Moll, London
10.2 x 13.7 (plate cut)
Etching
Presented, Dr E. MacDowel Cosgrave, 1907

Monvoisin, Raymond Auguste Qimsac (1794-1870)
French School
AUBRY-LECOMTE, HYACINTHE LOUIS VICTOR JEAN-BAPTISTE (1787-1858)
FRENCH SCHOOL
MOTTE, CHARLES ETIENNE PIERRE (1785-1836)
FRENCH SCHOOL

20,721(63)
A young Roman sleeping, (from 'Galerie Lithographiée.... ', see App. 8, no. 20, 721)
Published: J. Vatout et J.P. Quenot, Paris (Printed: C. Motte)
32.5 x 40.2 (image 29.6 x 37.5)
Lithograph
Bequeathed, Judge J. Murnaghan, 1976

Moore, John (fl.1831-1837)
English School
GAUCI, MAXIM (1775-1854)
ENGLISH SCHOOL

10,882
William Holmes, M.P., (1770-1851), Tory Whip
Published: M. Colnaghi, London, 1834 (Printed: Graf & Soret)
40.9 x 32.8 (image 26 x 24 approx)
Lithograph
Purchased, Dublin, Mr A. Roth, 1901

Moore, John (fl.1831-1837)
English School
SCRIVEN, EDWARD (1775-1841)
ENGLISH SCHOOL

11,039
Sir Edward Burtenshaw Sugden, (1781-1875), Lord Chancellor, later 1st Baron St Leonards, (pl. for H.T. Ryall's 'Portraits of Eminent Conservatives and Statesmen', 2nd series, 1846)
Published: R. Ryley, also J. Fraser, also F.G. Moon, London, 1837
38.2 x 28 (plate 33.8 x 26)
Line and stipple
Purchased, Dublin, Mr A. Roth, 1898

Moreau, Jean Michel (1741-1814)
French School
COURBE, WILBRODE NICOLAS MAGLOIRE (FL.1789-1814)
FRENCH SCHOOL

10,605
Trophime Gérard, Comte De Lally-Tolendal, (1751-1830), son of an Irish Jacobite General, former member of the French States General, (pl. for 'Collection des Portraits de Députés de l'Assemblée Nationale', 1789)
19.6 x 9.5 (plate cut)
Line
Acquired by 1903

Morland, George (1763-1804)
English School
ENGLISH SCHOOL (1827)

20,241
'A View in Leicestershire', (pl. for 'Gems of Ancient Art' 1827)
Published: Howlett & Brimmer, London, 1827
18.4 x 25.7 (plate 16.6 x 21.5)
Aquatint
Purchased, Lusk, Mr de Courcy Donovan, 1971

Moroni, Giambattista (1520/24-1578)
Bergamese School
CRAIG, WILLIAM MARSHALL (FL.1788-1828)
ENGLISH SCHOOL
TOMKINS, PELTRO WILLIAM (1760-1840)
ENGLISH SCHOOL

20,704(8)
'The School Master', (from 'Engravings of the Most Noble The Marquis of Stafford's Collection of Pictures in London', Vols. 1 and 2, 1818, see App. 8, no. 20,704)
(after an oil of c.1575, NG, Washington)
Published: Longman, Hurst, Rees, Orme & Brown, also J. White, also Cadell & Davies, also P.W. Tomkins, London, 1st August 1818 (Printed: Bensley & Son)
41.5 x 32 (plate cut)
Line
Bequeathed, Judge J. Murnaghan, 1976

?Morphey, Garret (fl.1680-1716)
Irish School
ENGLISH SCHOOL (1804)

11,337
(St) Oliver Plunkett, R.C. Archbishop of Armagh, (1629-1681)
INSCRIBED: From a Picture in Possession of the Publishers
Published: Keating, Brown and Co., London, 1st January 1804
30 x 35.3 (plate 21 x 28.2)
Stipple
Acquired by 1913

?Morphey, Garret (fl.1680-1716)
Irish School
IRISH SCHOOL (1808)

11,338
(St) Oliver Plunkett, R.C. Archbishop of Armagh, (1629-1681), (pl. for the 'Irish Magazine', March 1808)
Published: Irish Magazine, Dublin, March 1808
20.5 x 12.2 (plate 16.4 x 11.3)
Stipple
Acquired by 1913

?Morphey, Garret (fl.1680-1716)
Irish School
?LAURIE, ROBERT (C.1755-1836)
ENGLISH SCHOOL

10,201
(St) Oliver Plunkett, R.C. Archbishop of Armagh, (1629-1681)
(possibly after a drawing of 1681)
3rd State/INSCRIBED: From the original Portrait (in crayons) taken during his confinement in Newgate and now in the possession of the Revd. Doctor Campbell of Clogher
Published: not before 1790 (2nd State dated 1790)
36.3 x 28.6 (plate 28 x 20.7)
Mezzotint
Presented, Mrs T.G. Moorhead, 1960

?Morphey, Garret (fl.1680-1716)
Irish School
?LAURIE, ROBERT (C.1755-1836)
ENGLISH SCHOOL

11,073
(St) Oliver Plunkett, R.C. Archbishop of Armagh, (1629-1781)
(possibly after a drawing of 1681)
4th State/INSCRIBED: From the original Portrait (in crayons) taken during his confinement in Newgate and now in the possession of the Revd. Doctor Campbell of Clogher
Published: not before 1790 (2nd State dated 1790)
30 x 23 (plate 28.1 x 21)
Mezzotint
Purchased, 1887

Morphey, Garret (fl.1680-1716)
Irish School
VANDERVAART, JAN (1647-1721)
ANGLO-DUTCH SCHOOL

10,105
(St) Oliver Plunkett, R.C. Archbishop of Armagh, (1629-1681)
(after an oil of c.1681; NPG, London oil is probably a copy)
Published: T. Donbar, 1st July 1681
32.8 x 24.8 (plate cut)
Mezzotint
Purchased, London, 2nd Chaloner Smith sale, 1888

Mortimer, John Hamilton (1740-1779)
English School
BLYTH, ROBERT (1750-1784)
ENGLISH SCHOOL

20,034
The Captive, (of Sterne's 'A Sentimental Journey')
(after an ink drawing, SA 1774)
INSCRIBED: To Alexr. Wight Esqr. Advocate, This Plate is humbly Inscribed by His most obliged and most obedient Servant R. Blyth/From an Original Drawing of Mortimer, in the Collection of Richard Payne Knight Esq
Published: R. Blyth, London, 1st November 1781
43.3 x 58.4 (plate 32.5 x 41)
Etching
Provenance Unknown

Mortimer, John Hamilton (1740-1779)
English School
BLYTH, ROBERT (1750-1784)
ENGLISH SCHOOL

20,036
Two Figures wearing turbans - Banditti
INSCRIBED: To Sir William Forbes Bart. This plate is gratefully Inscribed by His much obliged and most obedient Servant, Robert Blyth/from an original Drawing of Mortimer in the Collection of Richard Payne Knight Esqr.-
Published: R. Blyth, London, November 1782
55.7 x 37.7 (plate 34.7 x 33.2)
Etching
Provenance Unknown

Mortimer, John Hamilton (1741-1779)
English School
BLYTH, ROBERT (1750-1784)
ENGLISH SCHOOL

20,066
Two Figures - a biblical scene
INSCRIBED: This plate is gratefully Inscribed by His most obedient Servant, Robert Blyth/From an original Drawing of Mortimer, in the Collection of Richard Payne Knight Esqr.
Published: R. Blyth, London, 1782
56 x 38 (plate 34.8 x 33)
Etching
Provenance Unknown

Mossop, William Stephen (1788-1827)
Irish School
?MOSSOP, WILLIAM STEPHEN (1788-1827)
IRISH SCHOOL

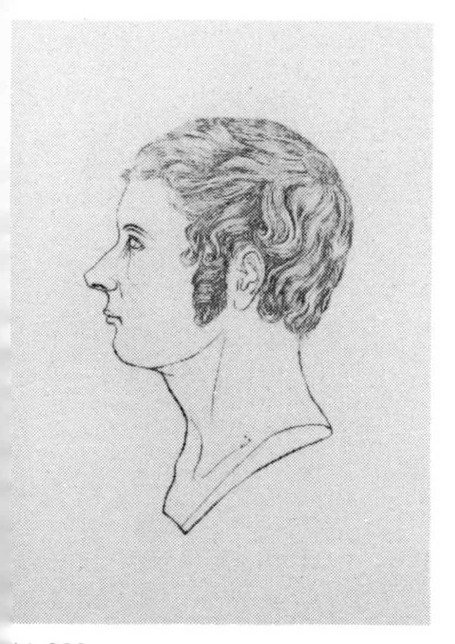

11,222
Self-Portrait of William Stephen Mossop, Medallist and first Secretary of the Royal Hibernian Academy
Unlettered Proof
Published: A. Smith, 1838
18.3 x 12.3 (plate 9.7 x 6.6)
Etching
Acquired between 1913/14

Mulcahy, Jeremiah Hodges (fl.1831-1889)
Irish School
ENGLISH SCHOOL (1859)

20,629
The Riot at the Limerick Elections
Published: Illustrated London News, 1859
5.3 x 18.2 (image 15 x 18)
Wood Engraving
Presented, Mrs D. Molloy, 1981

Mulcahy, Jeremiah Hodges (fl.1831-1889)
Irish School
MULCAHY, JEREMIAH HODGES (FL.1831-1889)
IRISH SCHOOL

20,168
A Grindstone and Waterwheel
Published: A. Hill, Edinburgh
(Printed: S. Leith)
33 x 43 (image 22.5 x 39.7)
Lithograph
Purchased, Lusk, Mr de Courcy Donovan, 1971

Mulcahy, Jeremiah Hodges (fl.1831-1889)
Irish School
MULCAHY, JEREMIAH HODGES (FL.1831-1889)
IRISH SCHOOL

20,323
Rothesay Pier, Isle of Bute, Scotland
Published: A. Hill, Edinburgh
(Printed: S. Leith)
32.8 x 43.3 (image 20.3 x 29.1)
Lithograph
Purchased, Lusk, Mr de Courcy Donovan, 1971

Mulcahy, Jeremiah Hodges (fl.1831-1889)
Irish School
WORRALL, JOHN (19TH CENTURY)
IRISH SCHOOL

20,524
Bakers Place Houses, Limerick (1856)
Working Proof
25.5 x 43 (image 19.5 x 34.2)
Lithograph
Presented, Mrs D. Molloy, 1981

Müller, Johann Sebastien (1715-1785)
Anglo-German School
MULLER, JOHANN SEBASTIEN (1715-1785)
ANGLO-GERMAN SCHOOL

11,347
Book Illustration
15.6 x 10.2 (plate cut)
Line
Provenance Unknown

?Mulrenin, Bernard (1803-1868)
?MULRENIN, BERNARD (1803-1868)
IRISH SCHOOL

10,971
Daniel O'Connell, M.P., (1776-1847), Statesman
Published: Allens, Dublin, not before 1828
37.6 x 26.4 (image 40.7 x 30)
Lithograph
Purchased, Dublin, Dillon & Co., 1901

Mulrenin, Bernard (1803-1868)
Irish School
MULRENIN, BERNARD (1803-1868)
IRISH SCHOOL

11,233
Henry William Paget, 1st Marquess of Anglesey, (1768-1854), Lord Lieutenant of Ireland, Distinguished Soldier
(probably after a miniature)
Published: London, not before 1828
(Printed: C.J. Hullmandel)
22 x 17 (plate cut)
Lithograph
Presented, Mr J.V. McAlpine, 1901

Mulvany, George Francis (1809-1869)
Irish School
EDWARDS, WILLIAM J. (FL.1843-1864)
ENGLISH SCHOOL

11,127
William Dargan, (1799-1867), Irish Industrialist, (frontispiece for Sproule's 'The Irish Industrial Exhibition of 1853', 1854)
Published: J. McGlashan, Dublin, 1854 (Printed: H. Wilkinson)
29.9 x 22.2 (plate cut x 21.2)
Line and stipple
Acquired by 1913

Mulvany, George Francis (1809-1869)
Irish School
FREEMAN, SAMUEL (1773-1857)
ENGLISH SCHOOL

10,645
Sir Robert Kane, (1809-1890), President of Queen's College, Cork
(after an oil, RHA 1849)
Published: W. Mackenzie, Glasgow, Edinburgh, London & New York
27.6 x 19 (plate cut)
Stipple
Purchased, Dublin, Mr P. Traynor, 1898

Murphy, A. (19th century)
Irish School
MURPHY, A. (19TH CENTURY)
IRISH SCHOOL

20,246
'Two Brooms for a halfpenny', (The Broomseller)
Published: M.H. & J.W. Allen, Dublin
34.3 x 24.1 (image 24 x 14)
Lithograph
Purchased, Lusk, Mr de Courcy Donovan, 1971

Murphy, John (fl.1778-1820)
Irish School
BOND, WILLIAM (FL.1799-1833)
ENGLISH SCHOOL

10,572
Rev. Arthur O'Leary, (1729-1802), Capuchin Friar, Preacher, Pamphleteer and Informer
(after a J. Murphy/G. Keating mezzotint of 1784, NGI no. 10,250)
Published: Longman & Co., also Keating & Brown, London, November 1822
18.2 x 12.4 (plate cut)
Stipple
Purchased, Dublin, Mr P. Traynor, 1898

Murphy, John (fl.1778-1820)
Irish School
KEATING, GEORGE (1762-1842)
IRISH SCHOOL

0,250
ev. Arthur O'Leary, (1729-1802), apuchin Friar, Preacher, Pamphleteer and former
ublished: G. Keating also W. ickinson, London, 23rd April 1784
37.9 x 27.4 (plate cut)
Mezzotint
Purchased, Mr J.H. North, 1894

Murphy, John (fl.1778-1820)
Irish School
MURPHY, JOHN (FL.1778-1820)
IRISH SCHOOL

10,541
Rev. James Archer, (fl.1789-1822), Catholic Preacher
(after a drawing)
Published: J. Murphy, London, 1st August 1791
35.6 x 25.6 (plate cut)
Mezzotint
Purchased, London, 1st Chaloner Smith sale, 1887

N

Napier, William Francis Patrick (1785-1860)
English School
ENGLISH SCHOOL (19TH CENTURY)

11,001
General Sir Charles James Napier, (1782-1853), Conqueror of Scinde and the Artist's brother
(after a drawing)
Published: T. & W. Boone, London, not before 1843
37.8 x 27.8 (image 14.2 x 10.4)
Lithograph
Acquired by 1903

Nash, Joseph (1808-1878)
English School
NASH, JOSEPH (1808-1878)
ENGLISH SCHOOL

11,497
The Interior of Kenilworth Castle Gate-House in the 16th century, (pl. for J. Nash's 'The Mansions of England in the Olden Time', c.1849)
(after a watercolour of 1840, NGI no. 2200)
38.1 x 56.6 (image 29 x 41.4)
Chromo-lithograph
Provenance Unknown

Nasmyth, Alexander (1758-1840)
Scottish School
FINDEN, EDWARD FRANCIS (1791-1857)
ENGLISH SCHOOL

20,360
The Tolbooth, Edinburgh, (now demolished), (cf. W. Scott's 'The Heart of Midlothian')
Published: C. Tilt, London, 1st August, 1830
17 x 23.3 (plate cut)
Line
Purchased, Lusk, Mr de Courcy Donovan, 1971

Nasmyth, Patrick (1787-1831)
Scottish School
LACEY, SAMUEL (FL.1818-1857)
ENGLISH SCHOOL

20,519
Arthur's Seat, Edinburgh, Scotland
Published: W. Marshall, London, 1828
10.5 x 14.7 (plate cut)
Steel Engraving
Purchased, Lusk, Mr de Courcy Donovan, 1971

Navez, François Joseph (1787-1869)
Belgian School
CORR, MATHIEU ERIN (1805-1862)
BELGIAN SCHOOL

11,483
Hagar and Her Son Ishmael in the Desert
Dated: 1832
71.5 x 52.2 (plate 53 x 41.5)
Line
Provenance Unknown

Neagle, John (1798-1865)
American School
THOMSON, JAMES (1789-1850)
ENGLISH SCHOOL

11,203
Matthew Carey, (1760-1839), Author, Philosopher and Antiquarian
(after a drawing)
INSCRIBED: *Private Plate, the Impressions for gratuitous presentation*
Issued by: W. Carey, London, 1822
19.8 x 11.3 (plate cut)
Stipple
Acquired c.1903

Nesfield, William Andrews (1793-1881)
English School
SANDS, JAMES (FL.1832-1844)
ENGLISH SCHOOL

10,421
Wressel Castle, Yorkshire
Published: Simkin & Marshall; also J.W. Stevens, London
28.5 x 22.2 (plate cut)
Steel Engraving
Purchased, Lusk, Mr de Courcy Donovan, 1971

Newenham, Frederick (1807-1859)
Irish School
LEWIS THE ELDER, FREDERICK CHRISTIAN (1779-1856)
ENGLISH SCHOOL

10,928
George Sandford, 3rd Baron Mountsandford, (1756-1846)
INSCRIBED: *To the Right Honorable Admiral Lord Gambier, G.C.B. &c., &c./This Portrait of George, Lord Mountsandford, sole founder of Sandford Church, &c. in the Diocese of Dublin;/Is respectfully dedicated by his Lordships/obliged humble servant/Frederick Newenham.*
Published: F. Newenham, London, 7th September 1831
30.2 x 22.8 (plate cut)
Stipple
Purchased, Dublin, Mr J.V. McAlpine, 1905

Newenham, Robert O'Callaghan (1770-1849)
Irish School
HARDING, JAMES DUFFIELD (1798-1863)
ENGLISH SCHOOL

11,610
St Patrick's Cathedral, Dublin, from St Sepulchre's Palace
(after a drawing)
Published: c.1830 (Printed: C. J. Hullmandel)
22 x 26.5 (image 15.5 x 20.5)
Lithograph
Presented, Dr E. MacDowel Cosgrave, 1907

Newenham, Robert O'Callaghan (1770-1849)
Irish School
HARDING, JAMES DUFFIELD (1798-1863)
ENGLISH SCHOOL

11,611
Interior of the South Transept of St Patrick's Cathedral, Dublin, (now restored)
Published: c.1830 (Printed: C.J. Hullmandel)
27.8 x 21.5 (image 21 x 17.5)
Lithograph
Presented, Dr E. MacDowel Cosgrave, 1907

Newenham, Robert O'Callaghan (1770-1849)
Irish School
HARDING, JAMES DUFFIELD (1797-1863)
ENGLISH SCHOOL

20,030
Reginald's Tower, Waterford, (pl. for R. O'C. Newenham's 'Picturesque views of the Antiquities of Ireland', 1830)
Published: T. & W. Boone, London, 1830 (Printed: C.J. Hullmandel)
22.5 x 28 (image 14.2 x 21)
Lithograph with watercolour
Purchased, London, The Parker Gallery, 1983

?Newman, J. (19th century)
English School
NEWMAN, J. (19TH CENTURY)
ENGLISH SCHOOL

20,642
Trinity College, Dublin
Published: J. Newman, London
11.3 x 15 (plate cut)
Line
Purchased, Mrs D. Molloy, 1981

Newton, Gilbert Stuart (1794-1835)
English School
GIBBS (19TH CENTURY)
ENGLISH SCHOOL

20,121
'La Pensierosa', (The Thinker)
Published: Whitaker & Co., for the Proprietor, London, November 1836
20.1 x 14.1 (plate cut)
Steel Engraving
Purchased, Lusk, Mr de Courcy Donovan, 1971

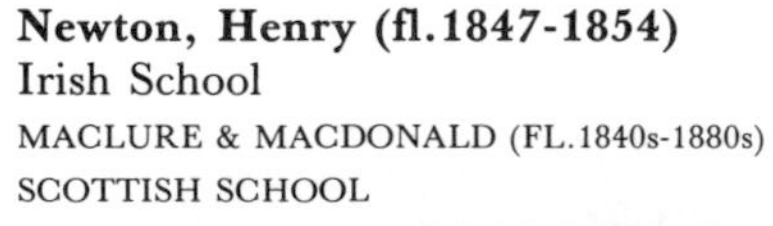

Newton, Henry (fl.1847-1854)
Irish School
MACLURE & MACDONALD (FL.1840s-1880s)
SCOTTISH SCHOOL

10,970
Daniel O'Connell, M.P., (1775-1847), Statesman
(after a watercolour, NLI, Dublin)
Published: A. Lesage, Dublin, also J. Finlay, Glasgow; also The Anaglyphic Co., London; also Goupil et Vibert, Paris; also L. Sackse, Berlin; also Baily & Ward, New York, 30th May 1844
50.6 x 38.4 (image 40.5 x 30)
Lithograph
Purchased, Dublin, Mr J.V. McAlpine, 1904

Newton, William John (1785-1869)
English School
POSSELWHITE, JAMES (1798-1884)
ENGLISH SCHOOL

10,885
George Alexander Hamilton, M.P., (1802-1871), founder of the Conservative Society of Ireland, (pl. for H. Ryall's 'Portraits of Eminent Conservatives and Statesmen', 2nd series, 1846)
Published: G. Virtue, London, 1846
36 x 26.8 (plate 32.7 x 25.3)
Stipple
Purchased, 1909

Newton, William John (1785-1869)
English School
POSSELWHITE, JAMES (1798-1884)
ENGLISH SCHOOL

10,886
George Alexander Hamilton, M.P., (1802-1871), founder of the Conservative Society of Ireland, (pl. for H. Ryall's 'Portraits of Eminent Conservatives and Statesmen', 2nd series, 1846), (another copy)
Published: G. Virtue, London, 1846
35 x 26.1 (plate 32.7 x 25.3)
Stipple
Purchased, Dublin, Mr J.V. McAlpine, 1913

Nicholson, Francis (1753-1844)
English School
HANSON, THOMAS FRAZER (1784-1828)
ENGLISH SCHOOL

10,076
Fanny with her puppies
INSCRIBED: A Favorite Bitch in the possession of C.J. Brandling Esqr. M.P/ to whom this Plate is (by Permission) respectfully dedicated
Published: G. Shirley, London, 1st May 1829
30.6 x 34.8 (plate 30.5 x 35)
Line
Provenance Unknown

Nixon, John (c.1760-1818)
English School
HARDING, EDWARD (1776-1796)
ENGLISH SCHOOL

10,576
O'Shauchnesey - a Dublin Beggar, (pl. for J. Nixon's 'Sketches from Nature', 1795)
(after a drawing of 1785)
Published: S. & E. Harding, London
15.8 x 10 (plate cut)
Line
Purchased, Dublin, Mr J.V. McAlpine, 1909

Nolel, T. (18th century)
Irish School
NOLEL, T. (18TH CENTURY)
IRISH SCHOOL

11,543
Counsellor Blackbourne at Dundalk Assizes in Ireland
Published: S. & E. Harding, London
16.2 x 24.6 (plate cut)
Etching
Provenance Unknown

Northcote, James (1746-1831)
English School
FITTLER, JAMES (1758-1835)
ENGLISH SCHOOL

10,473
Captain John MacBride, (d.1800), later an Admiral
Published: J. Fittler, March 1792
(Printed: J. Shovell)
61.2 x 46.2 (plate 49 x 37)
Line and stipple
Purchased, London, Mr H.A.J. Breun, 1909

Northcote, James (1746-1831)
English School
WARD, JAMES (1746-1859)
ENGLISH SCHOOL

10,210

William Henry West Betty, (1791-1874), Child Actor, aged 13
(after an oil, ?RA 1805; Petworth House, Sussex)
Published: W.H.W. Betty at Messrs. Colnaghi & Co., London, 16th March 1805
38.8 x 28.9 (plate 37.7 x 27.6)
Mezzotint
Purchased, London, 2nd Chaloner Smith sale, 1888

Nugent, Thomas (fl.1785-1798)
Irish School
ANNIS W.T. (FL.1798-1811)
ENGLISH SCHOOL

10,211
Edward Fitzgerald of New Park, Co. Wexford, (1770-1807), Revolutionary
(after a drawing of c.1798)
Lettered Proof
39.8 x 29.6 (plate 38 x 27.6)
Mezzotint
Purchased, London, 3rd Chaloner Smith sale, 1896

O

O'Donnell, Conn (18th century)
Irish School
BROCAS THE ELDER, HENRY (1766-1838)
IRISH SCHOOL

10,964
Father Thomas Maguire, (1792-1847), R.C. Priest of Innismagrath, Co. Leitrim and Controversialist
INSCRIBED: *To the R.C. Prelates, Clergy and Laity of Ireland, this Print is respectfully inscribed their obt. Servant C.O. Donel*
43.1 x 34 (plate 42 x 33.6)
Stipple and line
Purchased, London, 3rd Chaloner Smith sale, 1896

O'Kelly, F.J. (19th century)
Irish School
DEAN & CO (19TH CENTURY)
ENGLISH SCHOOL

10,594
Patrick O'Kelly, (fl.1842-1855), Historian and Author
Published: Dean & Co., London
22.2 x 14.3 (image 22.2 x 14.2)
Lithograph
Purchased, Dublin, Mr P. Traynor, 1898

O'Kelly, F.J. (19th century)
Irish School
DEAN & CO., (19TH CENTURY)
ENGLISH SCHOOL

10,595
Patrick O'Kelly, (fl.1842-1885), Historian and Author, (another copy)
Published: Dean & Co., London
22.3 x 14.2 (image 22.2 x 14.2)
Lithograph
Purchased, Dublin, Mr P. Traynor, 1898

Oldham, John (1779-1840)
Irish School
HEATH, JAMES (1757-1834)
ENGLISH SCHOOL

11,048
Robert Jocelyn, 2nd Earl of Roden, (1756-1820), Auditor-General of the Irish Exchequer, Knight of St Patrick
(after an ink drawing)
Published: Colnaghi & Co., also J.P. Thompson also Mr Heath, London, 1st September 1815
33.3 x 25.4 (plate 25.5 x 21.5)
Stipple
Acquired between 1913/14

Oliver, Isaac (?1556-1617)
English School
FRENCH SCHOOL (C.1600)

10,311
Elizabeth I, Queen of England, (1533-1603)
(after a C. Van der Passe the Elder line engraving of 1592, taken from I. Oliver's miniature of c.1588, V&A, London)
INSCRIBED: *C'est un miracle rare en l'Europe chrestienne/De voir Elizabeth la Roine des Anglois,/Mais, c'est bien plus de voir, que la grandeur maintienne /En la paix les petitz, et les grands, Soubz Ses Lois.*
Published: P. De la Houe, c.1600
20.9 x 12.9 (plate 17.2 x 12.6)
Line
Bequeathed, Miss E. Hone, 1912

?Oliver, Isaac (?1556-1617)
English School
TURNER, CHARLES (1773-1857)
ENGLISH SCHOOL

20,113
Elizabeth I, Queen of England, (1533-1603), 'in the superb Dress in which she went to St Paul's to return thanks for the Defeat of the Armada'
(after a drawing by I. Oliver or C. Van der Passe the Elder, Royal Collection, Windsor Castle)
Published: S. Woodburn, London
38 x 29.2 (plate cut)
Etching and aquatint
Purchased, Lusk, Mr de Courcy Donovan, 1971

Omer, Rowland (fl.1755-1767)
English School
HALPIN, PATRICK (FL.1755-1787)
IRISH SCHOOL

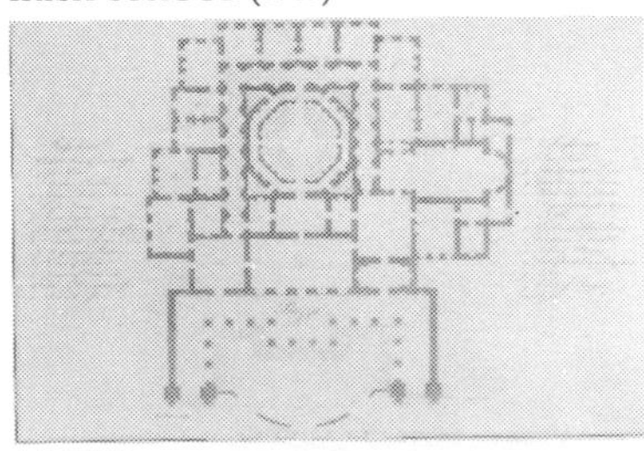

11,629
Elevation of the Front of Parliament House, (now Bank of Ireland), College Green, Dublin
Published: B. Scalé, Dublin 1767
41 x 51 (plate 36.8 x 47.8)
Line
Acquired by 1914

Omer, Rowland (fl.1755-1767)
Irish School
IRISH SCHOOL (1767)

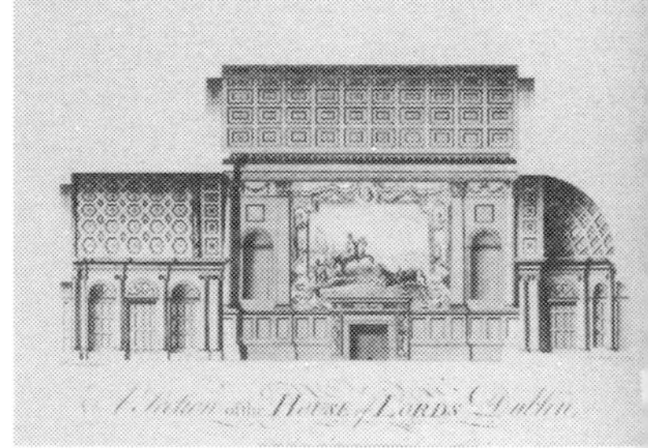

11,883
Plan of Parliament House, (now Bank of Ireland), Dublin
Published: B. Scalé, Dublin, 1767
41.4 x 51.9 (plate 36.5 x 47.3)
Presented, Dr E. MacDowel Cosgrave, 1907

Omer, Rowland (fl.1755-1767)
Irish School
MAZELL, PETER (FL.C.1761-1788)
ENGLISH SCHOOL

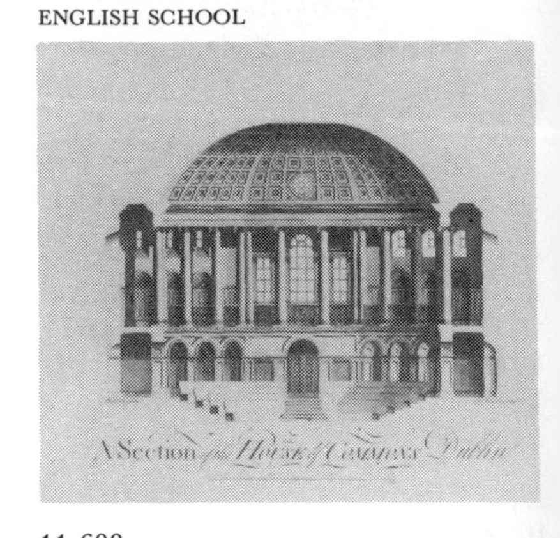

11,600
Section of the House of Commons, Dublin, (burnt down 1792)
Published: B. Scalé, Dublin, 1767
40.3 x 48 (plate 31.2 x 39)
Line
Presented, Mr J.V. McAlpine, 1901

Omer, Rowland (fl.1755-1767)
Irish School
MAZELL, PETER (FL.C.1761-1788)
ENGLISH SCHOOL

20,814
A Section of the House of Lords, (now Bank of Ireland), Dublin
Published: B. Scalé, Dublin, 1767
40.3 x 48.4 (plate 32.5 x 39.3)
Line
Provenance Unknown

O'Neill, Henry (1798-1880)
Irish School
O'NEILL, HENRY (1798-1880)
IRISH SCHOOL

10,980
Daniel O'Connell, M.P., (1775-1847), Statesman
(Printed: R. Martin, London)
26.7 x 21.6 (image 26.5 x 21.3 approx)
Lithograph
Acquired by 1901

O'Neill, Henry (1798-1880)
Irish School
TURNER, CHARLES (1773-1857)
ENGLISH SCHOOL

0,061
artholomew Lloyd, (1772-1837), Provost f Trinity College, Dublin and President of he Royal Irish Academy
after a drawing)
ublished: C. Turner, London, 20th ugust 1838
0.2 x 30.3 (plate 39 x 29.4)
lezzotint
urchased, Dublin, Mr J.V. IcApine, 1903

O'Neill, Mrs (18th century)
Irish School
ENGLISH SCHOOL (C.1790)

11,319
Mary Isabella, Duchess of Rutland, (née Lady Mary Somerset (1756-1831), wife of the 4th Duke of Rutland
Published: Universal Magazine and Review, London, c.1790
20.3 x 12.4 (plate 17.8 x 11.8)
Stipple
Purchased, Dublin, Mr P. Traynor, 1898

Opffer, Ivan (1897-1980)
Danish School
OPFFER, IVAN (1897-1980)
DANISH SCHOOL

20,837
William Butler Yeats, (1865-1939), Poet and Dramatist
(after a drawing taken in Copenhagen, 1923)
27.7 x 20 (image 25 x 18 approx)
Lithograph
Purchased, Mrs Opffer, the artist's widow, through Dr W. Gould, 1986

Opie, John (1761-1807)
English School
BARNEY, WILLIAM WHISTON (FL.1805-1810)
ENGLISH SCHOOL

10,177
John Denis Browne, 1st Marquess of Sligo, (1756-1809)
(after an oil, Westport House, Co. Sligo)
Published: W.W. Barney, London, 1st October 1806
38.3 x 27.3 (plate cut)
Mezzotint
Presented, Mrs Noseda, 1882

Opie, John (1761-1807)
English School
BROCAS THE ELDER, HENRY (1762-1837)
IRISH SCHOOL

11,223
Charles Macklin, (c.1700-1797), Actor
(after an oil of c.1792, Garrick Club, London, or J. Hopwood's stipple engraving of 1808, from it)
15.5 x 11.6 (plate cut)
Stipple
Purchased, London, 3rd Chaloner Smith sale, 1896

Os, Jan van (1744-1808)
Dutch School
CRAIG, WILLIAM MARSHALL (FL.1788-1827)
ENGLISH SCHOOL
BYRNE, ELIZABETH (FL.1809-1849)
ENGLISH SCHOOL

20,681(155)
Fruit and Flowers, (from 'Engravings of the most noble the Marquis of Stafford's Collection of Pictures in London', Vol. 4, see App. 8, no. 20,681)
(after an oil, Mertoun House, Scotland)
Published: Longman, Hurst, Rees, Orme & Brown, also J. White, also Cadell & Davies, also P.W. Tomkins, London, 1st May 1816
39.7 x 29.5 (plate cut)
Line
Bequeathed, Judge J. Murnaghan, 1976

Ostade, Adriaen van (1610-1685)
Dutch School
SWEBACH, JACQUES FRANÇOIS JOSE (1769-1823)
FRENCH SCHOOL
BOVINET (19TH CENTURY)
FRENCH SCHOOL

20,707(66)
The Schoolmaster, (from 'Musée Français - Ecole Allemande', see App. 8, no. 20,707)
Published: A. & W. Galignani, Paris, also J.O. Robinson, London (Printed: J. Didot L'Ainé, Paris)
60.5 x 45.8 (plate 41.5 x 30)
Line
Provenance Unknown

Ostade, Adriaen van (1610-1685)
Dutch School
HUBAND, WILLCOCKS (1776-1834)
IRISH SCHOOL

11,532
The Baker, (a different state is the frontispiece for W. Huband's 'Critical and Familiar Notices on the Art of Etching on Copper', 1810)
Issued privately by W. Huband, Dublin, c.1810
21.7 x 14 (plate 13 x 9)
Etching
Provenance Unknown

Ostade, Adriaen van (1610-1685)
Dutch School
HUBAND, WILLCOCKS (1776-1834)
IRISH SCHOOL

11,536
Peasant with a Pipe, (etched in reverse for W. Huband's 'Critical and Familiar Notices on the Art of Etching on Copper', 1810)
Issued privately by W. Huband, Dublin, c.1810
11 x 9.5 (plate cut)
Etching
Provenance Unknown

Ostade, Isaac van (1621-1649)
Dutch School
CANOT, PIERRE CHARLES (1710-1777)
FRENCH SCHOOL

20,090
A Country Wake
INSCRIBED: from the original picture painted by Isaac Ostade; in the collection of Paul Methuen Esq.
Published: J. Boydell, London, 1st January 1771
52.2 x 65 (plate 48 x 60.5)
Line
Provenance Unknown

Ottway, Thomas (18th century)
English School
FORD, MICHAEL (FL.1742-1765)
IRISH SCHOOL

:0,206
'ames Barry, 4th Earl of Barrymore, '1667-1747), Soldier and Politician
'ublished: M. Ford, Dublin, c.1753
:6.7 x 24.6 (plate 35.6 x 24.4)
Mezzotint
Acquired between 1879/90

Owen, William (1769-1825)
English School
WRIGHT, JOHN (C.1745-1820)
ENGLISH SCHOOL
MEYER, HENRY HOPPNER (1783-1847)
ENGLISH SCHOOL

10,751
John Wilson Croker, M.P., (1780-1857), Writer, (pl. for T. Cadell & W. Davies' 'Contemporary Portraits', 1822)
(after an oil, RA 1812; NPG, London)
Published: T. Cadell, London, 16th August 1822
42.7 x 32.8 (plate 39 x 32.3)
Stipple
Purchased, Dublin,
Mr J.V. McAlpine, 1906

Owen, William (1769-1825)
English School
REYNOLDS THE ELDER, SAMUEL WILLIAM (1773-1835)
ENGLISH SCHOOL

10,461
The Hon. William Stuart, P. Archbishop of Armagh, (1755-1822), son of the 3rd Earl of Bute
(after an oil, RA 1815, Archbishop's Palace, Armagh)
Published: T. Landley, Armagh, 1st January 1817
54.1 x 38.5 (plate 50.5 x 35.5)
Mezzotint
Purchased, Dublin,
Mr J.V. McAlpine, 1905

Owen, William (1769-1825)
English School
REYNOLDS THE ELDER, SAMUEL WILLIAM (1773-1835)
ENGLISH SCHOOL

10,701
The Hon. William Stuart, P. Archbishop of Armagh, (1755-1822), son of the 3rd Earl of Bute
(after an oil, RA 1815, Archbishop's Palace, Armagh)
Published: For S.W. Reynolds the Elder by Colnaghi & Co., London, 1st May 1816
50.2 x 35.2 (plate cut)
Mezzotint
Purchased, Dublin,
Mr J.V. McAlpine, 1905

P

Panini, Giovanni Paolo (1691/92-1765)
Italian School
DUMONT THE ELDER, JACQUES (1701-1781)
FRENCH SCHOOL
COCHIN, CHARLES NICOLAS (1715-1790)
FRENCH SCHOOL

11,656
Preparation for the fête and firework display in the Piazza Navona, Rome, 30th November 1729, on the birth of a Dauphin to King Louis XIV of France
(after an oil of 1729, NGI no. 95)
Published: C. Cochin, Paris
45.3 x 90 (plate cut)
Etching
Acquired c.1871

Panini, Giovanni Paolo (1691/92-1765)
Italian School
?FRENCH SCHOOL (18TH CENTURY)

20,544
Roman Capriccio with the Pyramid of Cestius
(after an oil of c.1720, Fontainebleau Museum)
14.5 x 10.8 (plate cut)
Line
Presented, Mrs D. Molloy, 1981

Parker, Henry Perle (1795-1873)
English School
GELLER, WILLIAM OVEREND (FL.1834-1857)
ENGLISH SCHOOL

20,056
Looking Out - a man with a pistol
Published: Ackermann & Co., London, 1st December 1836
71 x 58.6 (plate 59.3 x 46.5)
Mezzotint
Provenance Unknown

Parmentier, Joseph (1658-1730)
French School
FABER THE YOUNGER, JOHN (1684-1756)
ENGLISH SCHOOL

10,269
Sir James Reynolds, (1684-1747), Lord Chief Justice of the Common Pleas in Ireland, Chief Baron of the Exchequer in England
(after an oil of 1734)
Published: J. Faber the Younger, London, 1748
36.7 x 26.9 (plate 35.2 x 25)
Mezzotint
Purchased, Dublin, Mr J.V. McAlpine, 1901

?Parmigianino (1503-1540)
Italian School
ENGLISH SCHOOL (EARLY 19TH CENTURY

20,539
Figure Studies
14.8 x 19.4 (plate cut)
Etching and aquatint
Presented, Mrs D. Molloy, 1981

Pars, William (1742-1782)
English School
GODFREY (18TH CENTURY)
ENGLISH SCHOOL

20,096
The River Thames from the Terrace at Strawberry Hill, Middlesex, (pl. for H. Walpole's 'The Works of Horatio Walpole, Earl of Orford', 1798)
15.8 x 20 (plate cut)
Line and etching
Provenance Unknown

Pars, William (1742-1782)
English School
GODFREY (18TH CENTURY)
ENGLISH SCHOOL

20,097
East View of the Cottage Garden at Strawberry Hill, Middlesex, (pl. for H. Walpole's 'The Works of Horatio Walpole, Earl of Orford', 1798)
15.8 x 20 (plate cut)
Line and etching
Provenance Unknown

Pars, William (1742-1782)
English School
GODFREY, (18TH CENTURY)
ENGLISH SCHOOL

20,098
The Prior's Garden on the North Front, at Strawberry Hill, Middlesex, (pl. for H. Walpole's 'The Works of Horatio Walpole, Earl of Orford', 1798)
20 x 14 (plate cut)
Line and etching
Provenance Unknown

Pars, William (1742-1782)
English School
GODFREY, (18TH CENTURY)
ENGLISH SCHOOL

20,099
The River Thames and Teddington Road from the Great Bedchamber at Strawberry Hill, Middlesex, (pl. for H. Walpole's 'The Works of Horatio Walpole, Earl of Orford', 1798)
20 x 14 (plate cut)
Line and etching
Provenance Unknown

Patten, George (1801-1865)
English School
WAGSTAFF, CHARLES EDWARD (1808-1850)
ENGLISH SCHOOL

10,735
Prince Albert of Saxe-Coburg-Gotha, (1818-1861), Consort of Queen Victoria
(after an oil, RA 1840)
INSCRIBED: To his Serene Highness the Duke of Saxe Coburg Gotha, K.G./This Portrait of/His Royal Highness Prince Albert, K.G. &c./Is by special command/Most respectfully dedicated by His Serene Highness's/Most devoted and Obedient Humble Servants/Hodgson & Graves
Published: Hodgson & Graves, London, 24th May 1840
57.7 x 42.7 (plate 52.8 x 39.6)
Mezzotint
Acquired by 1903

Peale, Charles Wilson (1741-1827)
American School
MACKENZIE, E. (19TH CENTURY)
AMERICAN SCHOOL

10,674
General Richard Montgomery, (1736-1775), American Officer killed at Quebec
(after an oil, Pennsylvania Academy of the Fine Arts, Philadephia)
26.3 x 17 (plate cut)
Stipple
Purchased, Dublin,
Mr J.V. McAlpine, 1909

Pelletier, Joseph Laurent (1811-1892)
French School
PELLETIER, JOSEPH LAURENT (1811-1892)
FRENCH SCHOOL

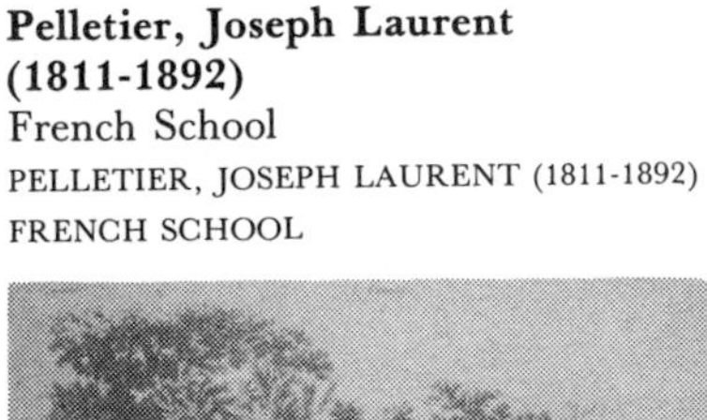

20,318
Rocks and Bushes, ('La campagne', no. 67)
Published: F. Delarue, Paris also Gambart Junin & Co., London, 15th March 1845
31.5 x 48.3 (image 26 x 38)
Purchased, Lusk, Mr de Courcy Donovan, 1971

Pelletier, Joseph Laurent (1811-1892)
French School
PELLETIER, JOSEPH LAURENT (1811-1892)
FRENCH SCHOOL

20,319
A Pathway leading to a Cottage
Published: F. Delarue, Paris also Gambard Junin & Co. London, 15th March 1845
31.4 x 84.5 (image 26 x 39)
Lithograph
Purchased, Lusk, Mr de Courcy Donovan, 1971

Pennell, Joseph (1860-1926)
American School
PENNELL, JOSEPH (1860-1926)
AMERICAN SCHOOL

11,454
Exeter and its Cathedral from the River Exe, Devon
Unlettered Proof
Issued by J. Pennell, 1905
28.5 x 38 (image 25 x 30.5)
Lithograph
Presented, New York, Mrs C. White, 1937

Pennell, Joseph (1860-1926)
American School
PENNELL, JOSEPH (1860-1926)
AMERICAN SCHOOL

11,455
Barnstaple, on the Taw Estuary, Devon
Unlettered Proof
28.6 x 38 (image 24.2 x 29.6)
Lithograph
Presented, New York, Mrs C. White, 1937

Pennell, Joseph (1860-1926)
American School
PENNELL, JOSEPH (1860-1926)
AMERICAN SCHOOL

11,456
Bideford on the River Torridge, Devon
Unlettered Proof
28 x 37.6 (image 17.8 x 28.66)
Lithograph
Presented, New York, Mrs C. White, 1937

Pennell, Joseph (1860-1926)
American School
PENNELL, JOSEPH (1860-1926)
AMERICAN SCHOOL

11,457
City Scene, Caissons, Vesey Street, New York
Unlettered Proof
Issued by J. Pennell, 1924
41 x 26.6 (plate 35 x 23.5)
Etching
Presented, New York, Mrs C. White, 1937

Pennell, Joseph (1860-1926)
American School
PENNELL, JOSEPH (1860-1926)
AMERICAN SCHOOL

11,458
The Valley of the River Dart, Devon
Unlettered Proof
8 x 29 (image 29.5 x 23.8)
Lithograph
Presented, New York, Dr W.J. Maloney, 1938

Pennell, Joseph (1860-1926)
American School
PENNELL, JOSEPH (1860-1926)
AMERICAN SCHOOL

11,459
Kensington Gardens, London
Unlettered Proof
Issued by J. Pennell, 1887
30.5 x 21.2 (plate 29.8 x 17.5)
Etching
Presented, New York, Mrs C. White, 1937

Pennell, Joseph (1860-1926)
American School
PENNELL, JOSEPH (1860-1926)
AMERICAN SCHOOL

11,460
The Times Building, Times Square, New York
Unlettered Proof
Issued by J. Pennell, 1904
36.5 x 25.9 (plate 30.2 x 21.4)
Etching
Presented, New York, Mrs C. White, 1937

Pennell, Joseph (1860-1926)
American School
PENNELL, JOSEPH (1860-1926)
AMERICAN SCHOOL

11,461
Pierpont Place and Montague Terrace, Brooklyn, New York
Unlettered Proof
Issued by J. Pennell, 1924
20.3 x 28.7 (plate 17.8 x 25)
Etching
Presented, New York, Mrs C. White, 1937

Pennell, Joseph (1860-1926)
American School
PENNELL, JOSEPH (1860-1926)
AMERICAN SCHOOL

11,462
'Hail America' - The Statue of Liberty, Hudson River, New York
Unlettered Proof
Issued by J. Pennell, 1908
29 x 42.5 (plate 21.4 x 37.7)
Mezzotint
Presented, New York, Mrs C. White, 1937

Pennell, Joseph (1860-1926)
American School
PENNELL, JOSEPH (1860-1926)
AMERICAN SCHOOL

11,463
'Out of My Brooklyn Window', New York
Unlettered Proof
Issued by J. Pennell, 1923
25.5 x 34.3 (plate 23.2 x 30.4)
Etching
Presented, New York, Mrs C. White, 1937

Pennell, Joseph (1860-1926)
American School
PENNELL, JOSEPH (1860-1926)
AMERICAN SCHOOL

11,464
Café
Unlettered Proof
Issued by J. Pennell, 1893
19.1 x 12.6 (plate 12 x 8)
Etching
Presented, New York, Mrs C. White, 1937

Pennell, Joseph (1860-1926)
American School
PENNELL, JOSEPH (1860-1926)
AMERICAN SCHOOL

11,465
Exeter Hall, The Strand, London, (now demolished)
Unlettered Proof
Issued by J. Pennell, 1905
36 x 25.5 (plate 28.2 x 20.5)
Etching
Presented, New York, Mrs C. White, 1937

Pennell, Joseph (1860-1926)
American School
PENNELL, JOSEPH (1860-1926)
AMERICAN SCHOOL

11,466
Sunset over Williamsburg Bridge, Brooklyn, New York
Unlettered Proof
Issued by J. Pennell, 1915
23.5 x 31 (plate 21.6 x 27.5)
Etching
Presented, New York, Mrs C. White, 1937

Pennell, Joseph (1860-1926)
American School
PENNELL, JOSEPH (1860-1926)
AMERICAN SCHOOL

11,467
Ilfracombe, Devon
Unlettered Proof
29 x 38 (image 22.2 x 27.8)
Lithograph
Presented, New York, Mrs C. White, 1937

Pennell, Joseph (1860-1926)
American School
PENNELL, JOSEPH (1860-1926)
AMERICAN SCHOOL

11,468
Fig Tree House, Lincoln's Inn, London
Unlettered Proof
Issued by J. Pennell, 1905
28.5 x 38.3 (plate 22.2 x 27.7)
Etching
Presented, New York, Mrs C. White, 1937

Pennell, Joseph (1860-1926)
American School
PENNELL, JOSEPH (1860-1926)
AMERICAN SCHOOL

1,469
lanhattan and Brooklyn Bridge, New ork
Jnlettered Proof
1.1 x 20 (plate 25.1 x 17.5)
tching
resented, New York, Mrs C. White, 937

ennell, Joseph (1860-1926)
merican School
ENNELL, JOSEPH (1860-1926)
MERICAN SCHOOL

,470
erminal Buildings, Cortland Street, New ork
nlettered Proof
3 x 47 (image 58.5 x 43)
ithograph
resented, New York, Mrs C. White, 37

Pennell, Joseph (1860-1926)
American School
PENNELL, JOSEPH (1860-1926)
AMERICAN SCHOOL

20,693(1)
Schiedam, Holland ,(from 'Lithography and Lithographers', see App. 8, no. 20, 693)
Unlettered Proof (53/of 58)
22.4 x 30.5 (image 18 x 27 approx)
Lithograph
Presented, Mrs B. Ganly, 1978

Perugino, Pietro (c.1450-1523)
Umbrian School
DUFLOS, CLAUDE (1662-1727)
FRENCH SCHOOL

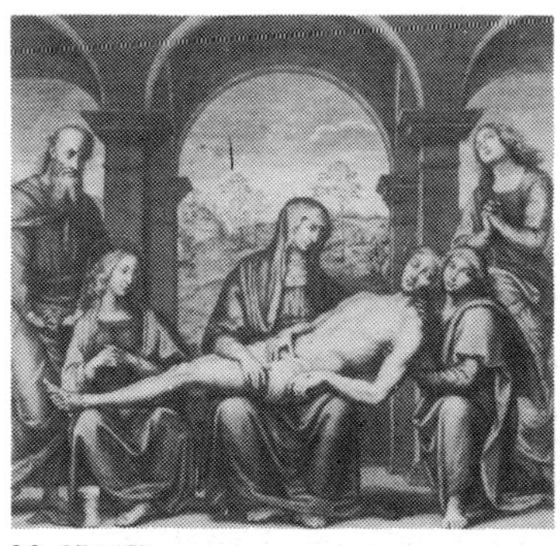

20,671(3)
The Pieta, (from 'Receuil d'Etampes d'après les plus beaux tableaux et d'après le plus beaux dessins qui sont en France dans la Cabinet du Roy', 1729, see App. 8, no. 20,671)
(after an oil of c.1495, NGI no. 942)
Published: L'Imprimerie Royale, Paris, 1729
61.6 x 46.4 (plate 32.5 x 33)
Etching and line
Provenance Unknown

Peters, Matthew William (1741-1814)
Irish School
HOUSTON, H.H. (FL.C.1791)
IRISH SCHOOL

11,601
An Angel carrying the spirit of a child to Heaven, (portraits of Mary Isabella, Duchess of Rutland, 1756-1831, wife of the 4th Duke, and Charlotte Dundas)
(after an oil, RA 1782; Burghley House, Northants)
Published: W. Allen, Dublin
34.5 x 25 (plate cut)
Stipple
Provenance Unknown

Peters, Matthew William (1741-1814)
Irish School
HOUSTON, H.H. (FL.C.1791)
IRISH SCHOOL

11,617

The Angel and Child arrived at the gates of Paradise
Published: W. Allen, Dublin
31.1 x 25 (plate cut)
Stipple
Provenance Unknown

Peters, Matthew William (1741-1814)
Irish School
MURPHY, JOHN (C.1748-1820)
IRISH SCHOOL

10,106
Matthew Peters, (1711-after 1776), Agricultural Author and the Artist's father
Published: J. Murphy, London, 1st November 1778
38.6 x 28.7 (plate 37.6 x 27.8)
Mezzotint
Purchased, London, 1st Chaloner Smith sale, 1887

Peters, Matthew William (1741-1814)
Irish School
HERBERT, JAMES DOWLING (1762-1837)
IRISH SCHOOL
REYNOLDS THE ELDER, SAMUEL WILLIAM (1773-1835)
ENGLISH SCHOOL

10,466
John O'Neill, 1st Viscount O'Neill, M.P., (1740-1798)
Published: not before 1798
55.8 x 40.5 (plate 50.8 x 35.2)
Mezzotint
Purchased, London, Mr G. Lausen, 1895

Peters, Matthew William (1741-1814)
Irish School
SIMON, PETER (C.1750-C.1810)
ENGLISH SCHOOL

20,686(16)
Hero, Ursula and Beatrice listening - Illustration to Shakespeare's 'Much Ado About Nothing' Act III, Scene I, (from 'A Collection of Prints from Pictures Painted for the purpose of illustrating the Dramatic Works of Shakespeare', Vol. 1, 1805, see App. 8, no. 20,686)
Published: J. & J. Boydell, London, 4th June 1790 (Printed: W. Bulmer & Co.)
67 x 52 (plate 64.1 x 46.5)
Line and stipple
Bequeathed, Judge J. Murnaghan, 1976

Peters, Matthew William (1741-1814)
Irish School
SMITH, JOHN RAPHAEL (1752-1812)
ENGLISH SCHOOL

10,348
The Hon. Mrs John O'Neill, (née Henrietta Boyle, 1756-1793), Poet and Patron of Mrs Siddons
Published: J.R. Smith, London, 6th August 1778
45.2 x 32.7 (plate cut)
Mezzotint
Purchased, London, 2nd Chaloner Smith sale, 1887

Peters, Matthew William (1741-1814)
Irish School
WATSON, JAMES (C.1740-1790)
IRISH SCHOOL

10,459
Sir William Robinson Bt., (1703-1785), brother of Baron Rokeby, P. Archbishop of Armagh
(after an oil of 1777, NGI no. 4053)
40 x 30 (plate 37.5 x 27.5)
Mezzotint
Presented, The Hon. F. Lawless, later 5th Baron Cloncurry, 1919

Peters, Wilhelm Otto (1851-after 1923)
Norwegian School
PETERS, WILHELM OTTO (1851-AFTER 1923)
NORWEGIAN SCHOOL

20,068
Norwegian Fishermen in a Tavern
Published: L'Art, Paris (Printed: A. Clément)
30.5 x 43.6 (plate 23.5 x 31)
Etching
Provenance Unknown

Petrie, George (1790-1866)
Irish School
BARBER, THOMAS (FL.1818-1846)
IRISH SCHOOL

10,056
The West View of Christchurch Cathedral, Dublin, (pl. for Cromwell's 'Excursions Through Ireland', 1820)
Published: Longman & Co., London, 1st September 1819
11.2 x 17.6 (plate 10.2 x 15.1)
Steel Engraving
Presented, Mr W.G. Strickland, 1906

Petrie, George (1790-1866)
Irish School
BARBER, THOMAS (FL.1818-1846)
ENGLISH SCHOOL

11,777
Trinity College, Dublin, and the East Portico of Bank of Ireland, (formerly House of Lords), (pl. for G.N. Wright's 'An Historical Guide to Ancient and Modern Dublin', 1821)
(after a wash study, RIA, Dublin)
Published: Baldwin, Cradock & Joy, London, August 1821 (Printed: R. Fenner)
9.5 x 16.8 (plate cut)
Steel Engraving
Presented, Dr E. MacDowel Cosgrave, 1907

Petrie, George (1790-1866)
Irish School
BARBER, THOMAS (FL.1818-1846)
IRISH SCHOOL

11,778
St George's Church, Hardwick Place, Dublin, (pl. for G.N. Wright's 'An Historical Guide to Ancient and Modern Dublin', 1821)
(after a wash study, RIA, Dublin)
Published: Baldwin, Cradock & Joy, London, August 1821 (Printed: R. Fenner)
9.7 x 15.6 (plate cut)
Steel Engraving
Presented, Dr E. MacDowel Cosgrave, 1907

Petrie, George (1790-1866)
Irish School
BARBER, THOMAS (FL.1818-1846)
ENGLISH SCHOOL

11,779
The New Theatre Royal, Hawkins Street, Dublin, (exterior as planned), (pl. for G.N. Wright's 'An Historical Guide to Ancient and Modern Dublin', 1821)
(after a wash study, RIA, Dublin)
Published: Baldwin, Cradock & Joy, London, August 1821 (Printed: R. Fenner)
9.8 x 16.3 (plate cut)
Steel Engraving
Presented, Dr E. MacDowel Cosgrave, 1907

Petrie, George (1790-1866)
Irish School
BARBER, THOMAS (FL.1818-1846)
ENGLISH SCHOOL

11,790
Sackville, (now O'Connell), Street with the General Post Office and Nelson Pillar, (now demolished), (pl. for G.N. Wright's 'An Historical Guide to Ancient and Modern Dublin', 1821)
(after a wash study, RIA, Dublin)
Published: Baldwin, Cradock & Joy, London, August 1821 (Printed: R. Fenner)
9.8 x 15.6 (plate cut)
Steel Engraving
Presented, Dr E. MacDowel Cosgrave, 1907

Petrie, George (1790-1866)
Irish School
BARBER, THOMAS (FL.1818-1846)
ENGLISH SCHOOL

11,792
Barrack Bridge, (now rebuilt); Queen's, (now Queen Maeve), Bridge and Richmond Tower, (now resited at Kilmainham), (pl. for T. Cromwell's 'Excursions through Ireland', 1820)
Published: Longman, London
7.5 x 9.2 (plate cut)
Steel Engraving
Presented, Dr E. MacDowel Cosgrave, 1907

Petrie, George (1790-1866)
Irish School
ENGLISH SCHOOL (1821)

11,780
The Lying-In, (now Rotunda), Hospital and the Rotunda, (pl. for G.N. Wright's 'An Historical Guide to Ancient and Modern Dublin', 1821)
(after a wash study, RIA, Dublin)
Published: Baldwin, Cradock & Joy, London, 1st August 1821 (Printed: R. Fenner)
10 x 16 (plate 9.5 x 15.3)
Steel Engraving
Presented, Dr E. MacDowel Cosgrave, 1907

Petrie, George (1790-1866)
Irish School
BARBER, T. (FL.1818-1846)
ENGLISH SCHOOL

11,791
Sackville, (now O'Connell), Street with the General Post Office and Nelson Pillar, (now demolished), (pl. for G.N. Wright's 'An Historical Guide to Ancient and Modern Dublin', 1821), (another copy)
(after a wash study, RIA, Dublin)
Published: Baldwin, Cradock & Joy, London, August 1821 (Printed: R. Fenner)
9 x 12.1 (plate cut)
Steel Engraving
Presented, Dr E. MacDowel Cosgrave, 1907

Petrie, George (1790-1866)
Irish School
ENGLISH SCHOOL (1821)

11,773
Dublin Castle Chapel and Record Tower, (pl. for G.N. Wright's 'An Historical Guide to Ancient and Modern Dublin', 1821)
(after a wash study, RIA, Dublin)
Published: Baldwin, Cradock & Joy, London, 1821 (Printed R. Fenner)
7.8 x 12 (plate cut)
Steel Engraving
Presented, Dr E. MacDowel Cosgrave, 1907

Petrie, George (1790-1866)
Irish School
ENGLISH SCHOOL (1821)

11,781
The Royal Exchange, (now City Hall), and Cork Hill, Dublin, (pl. for G.N. Wright's 'An Historical Guide to Ancient and Modern Dublin', 1821)
(after a wash study, RIA, Dublin)
Published: Baldwin, Cradock & Joy, London, August 1821 (Printed: R. Fenner)
10.2 x 16.2 (plate 9.7 x 15.3)
Steel Engraving
Presented, Dr E. MacDowel Cosgrave, 1907

Petrie, George (1790-1866)
Irish School
ENGLISH SCHOOL (1821)

11,783
The Four Courts and Richmond, (now O'Donovan Rossa), Bridge, Dublin, (pl. for G.N. Wright's 'An Historical Guide to Ancient and Modern Dublin', 1821)
(after a wash study, RIA, Dublin)
Published: Baldwin, Cradock & Joy, London, August 1821 (Printed: R. Fenner)
10 x 16.2 (plate 9.4 x 15.4)
Steel Engraving
Presented, Dr E. MacDowel Cosgrave, 1907

Petrie, George (1790-1866)
Irish School
ENGLISH SCHOOL (1821)

11,789
Dublin from the North near St Paul's, King Street, (pl. for G.N. Wright's 'An Historical Guide to Ancient and Modern Dublin', 1821)
Published: Baldwin, Cradock, & Joy, London, August 1821 (Printed: R. Fenner)
9.1 x 15.5 (plate cut)
Steel Engraving
Presented, Dr E. MacDowel Cosgrave, 1907

Petrie, George (1790-1866)
Irish School
GOODALL, EDWARD (1795-1870)
ENGLISH SCHOOL

11,774
Upper Castle Yard, Dublin Castle, (pl. for G.N. Wright's 'Ireland Illustrated', 1831)
INSCRIBED: To his Grace the Duke of Northumberland, Lord Lieutenant General, and General Governor of Ireland
Published: Fisher Son & Co., London, 1829
21.1 x 17.1 (plate cut)
Steel Engraving
Presented, Dr E. MacDowel Cosgrave, 1907

Petrie, George (1790-1866)
Irish School
ENGLISH SCHOOL (1821)

11,784
The King's Inns and Royal Canal Harbour, Dublin, (pl. for G.N. Wright's 'An Historical Guide to Ancient and Modern Dublin', 1821)
(after a wash study, RIA, Dublin)
Published: Baldwin, Cradock & Joy, London, August 1821
(Printed: R. Fenner)
10 x 15.8 (plate 9.4 x 15.3)
Steel Engraving
Presented, Dr E. MacDowel Cosgrave, 1907

Petrie, George (1790-1866)
Irish School
FIELDING, NEWTON (1799-1856)
ENGLISH SCHOOL

20,351
The Twelve Pins, Connemara, Co. Galway, (pl. for 'Picturesque sketches of some of the Finest Landscape and Coast Scenery of Ireland', 1835)
(after a watercolour of 1831, NGI no. 6027)
Published: W.F. Wakeman, Dublin, 1835
24.5 x 30.2 (plate 22.5 x 27.5)
Aquatint and watercolour
Purchased, Lusk, Mr de Courcy Donovan, 1971

Petrie, George (1790-1866)
Irish School
GOODALL, EDWARD (1795-1870)
ENGLISH SCHOOL

11,787
Dublin from Blaquiere Bridge on Royal Canal, (pl. for G.N. Wright's 'Ireland Illustrated', 1831)
INSCRIBED: To the Right Hon. The Earl of Blessington this Plate is most Respectfully Inscribed
Published: Fisher, Son & Co., London
14.4 x 23.2 (plate 14.2 x 21.8)
Steel Engraving
Presented, Dr E. MacDowel Cosgrave, 1907

Petrie, George (1790-1866)
Irish School
GOODALL, EDWARD (1795-1870)
ENGLISH SCHOOL

11,794
Sarah Bridge, (now Island Bridge), and the Wellington Testimonial, Phoenix Park, Dublin, (pl. for G.N. Wright's 'Ireland Illustrated', 1831)
INSCRIBED: *To the Right Hon. The Lord Viscount Palmerstown, This plate is most respectfully dedicated*
Published: Fisher Son & Co., London, 1828
13.7 x 20 (plate cut)
Steel Engraving
Presented, Dr E. MacDowel Cosgrave, 1907

Petrie, George (1790-1866)
Irish School
HIGHAM, THOMAS (1796-1844)
ENGLISH SCHOOL

11,775
St Patrick's Cathedral from the South-East, (pl. for G.N. Wright's 'An Historical Guide to Ancient and Modern Dublin', 1821)
Published: Baldwin, Cradock & Joy, London, August 1821 (Printed: R. Fenner)
9.4 x 14.4 (plate cut)
Steel Engraving
Presented, Dr E. MacDowel Cosgrave, 1907

Petrie, George (1790-1866)
Irish School
HIGHAM, THOMAS (1796-1844)
ENGLISH SCHOOL

20,791
Dunmow Castle, Co. Meath
Published: Longman & Co., London, 1st September 1820
11.1 x 16.8 (plate 10.1 x 15)
Steel Engraving
Purchased, Lusk, Mr de Courcy Donovan, 1971

Petrie, George (1790-1866)
Irish School
HIGHAM, THOMAS (1796-1844)
ENGLISH SCHOOL

11,700
Upper Castle Yard, Dublin Castle, (pl. for G.N. Wright's 'An Historical Guide to the Ancient and Modern City of Dublin', 1821)
Published: Baldwin, Cradock & Joy, London, August 1821 (Printed: R. Fenner)
9.5 x 16.3 (plate cut)
Steel Engraving
Presented, Dr E. MacDowel Cosgrave, 1907

Petrie, George (1790-1866)
Irish School
HIGHAM, THOMAS (1796-1844)
ENGLISH SCHOOL

11,793
King's, (now Sean Heuston), Bridge, Dublin
14.2 x 20.3 (plate cut)
Steel Engraving
Presented, Dr E. MacDowel Cosgrave, 1907

Petrie, George (1790-1866)
Irish School
RANSON, THOMAS FRAZER (1784-1828)
ENGLISH SCHOOL

10,048
Christchurch Cathedral, Dublin from the South-East, (for G.N. Wright's 'An Historical Guide to Ancient and Modern Dublin', 1821)
Published: Baldwin, Cradock & Joy, London, August 1821
8.5 x 11.9 (plate cut)
Steel Engraving
Provenance Unknown

Petrie, George (1790-1866)
Irish School
STORER, JAMES (1781-1853)
ENGLISH SCHOOL *and*
STORER, SARGENT HENRY (1795-1857)
ENGLISH SCHOOL

11,788
Dublin from the Magazine Hill in Phoenix Park
Published: Sherwood, Jones & Co., London, 1st September 1824
13.7 x 22.5 (plate cut)
Steel Engraving
Presented, Dr E. MacDowel Cosgrave, 1907

Petrie, George (1790-1866)
Irish School
WINKLES, BENJAMIN (FL.1829-1842)
ENGLISH SCHOOL

11,782
The Phoenix Pillar, Phoenix Park, Dublin
Published: Fisher, Son & Co., London, 1840 (re-issue of 1829 print)
20.4 x 14.2 (plate cut)
Steel Engraving
Presented, Dr E. MacDowel Cosgrave, 1907

Petrie, George (1790-1866)
Irish School
WINKLES, BENJAMIN (FL.1829-1842)
IRISH SCHOOL

11,786
College Street and the East Portico of Bank of Ireland, (formerly entrance to the House of Lords), (pl. for G.N. Wright's 'Ireland Illustrated', 1831)
INSCRIBED: *To Henry C. Sirr Esq. This Plate is Respectfully inscribed by His Obliged Friend G. Petrie*
Published: Fisher Son and Co., London, 1828
12.5 x 17.6 (plate cut)
Steel Engraving
Presented,, Dr E. MacDowel Cosgrave, 1907

Petrie, George (1790-1866)
Irish School
WINKLES, BENJAMIN (FL.1829-1842)
ENGLISH SCHOOL

11,776
The ruins of Lord Portlester's Chapel, St Audeon's Church, High Street, Dublin, (pl. for G.N. Wright's 'Ireland Illustrated', 1831)
After an ink and wash drawing, NGI No. 6002)
INSCRIBED: *To Sir Wm. Betham this Plate is Respectfully Inscribed*
Published: Fisher, Son & Co., London, 1829
15.1 x 22.5 (plate 14.7 x 21.9)
Line
Presented, Dr E. MacDowel Cosgrave, 1907

Petrie, George (1790-1866)
Irish School
WINKLES, BENJAMIN (FL.1829-1842)
ENGLISH SCHOOL

11,785
Bank of Ireland, (formerly the Parliament House), College Green, Dublin, (pl. for G.N. Wright's 'Ireland Illustrated', 1831)
Published: Fisher, Son & Co., London, 1829
13.3 x 22.5 (plate cut)
Steel Engraving
Presented, Dr E. MacDowel Cosgrave, 1907

Petrie, George (1790-1866)
Irish School
WINKLES, RICHARD (FL.1829-1836)
ENGLISH SCHOOL

20,612

Nelson Pillar, (now demolished), Sackville, (now O'Connell), Street, (pl. for G.N. Wright's 'Ireland Illustrated', 1831)
(? after an oil, NGI no. 4130)
Published: Fisher, Son & Co., London, 1831
17.8 x 11.7 (plate cut)
Steel Engraving
Presented, Mrs D. Molloy, 1981

Petrie, James (1750-1819)
Irish School
BROCAS THE ELDER, HENRY (1766-1838)
IRISH SCHOOL

10,262
Rev. John Austin, (1717-1784), Jesuit Preacher and Teacher
INSCRIBED: *To the Catholics of Dublin this plate is most Respectfully Inscribed by their very Obedient/Humble Servant/B. Corcoran*
Published: B. Corcoran, Dublin, 12th November 1792
39.2 x 28.3 (plate cut)
Line and stipple
Acquired between 1879/90

Petrie, James (1750-1819)
Irish School
ENGLISH SCHOOL (1843)

10,649
James Napper Tandy, (1740-1803) United Irishman, when a French General, (pl. for R. Madden's 'United Irishmen', 2nd series, 1843)
(after a J. Petrie stipple, NGI no. 10,456)
Published: Madden & Co., London, 1843
20.8 x 13.2 (plate cut)
Stipple
Purchased, Dublin, Mr P. Traynor, 1898

Petrie, James (1750-1819)
Irish School
ENGLISH SCHOOL (1846)

11,164
Robert Emmet, (1778-1803), United Irishman and Patriot, (pl. for R. Madden's 'United Irishmen', 3rd Series, 1846)
INSCRIBED: *From an original portrait drawn and engraved by Petrie*
Published: Madden & Co., London, 1846
21.3 x 12.8 (plate cut)
Stipple
Presented, Dr T. Moore Madden, 1901

Petrie, James (1750-1819)
Irish School
ENGLISH SCHOOL (1846)

11,165
Robert Emmet, (1778-1803), United Irishman and Patriot, (pl. for R. Madden's 'United Irishmen', 3rd Series 1846), (another copy)
INSCRIBED: *From an original portrait drawn and engraved by Petrie*
Published: Madden & Co., London, 1846
22 x 13 (plate cut)
Stipple
Purchased, Dublin, Mr P. Traynor, 1898

Petrie, James (1750-1819)
Irish School
CLAUDET, ANTOINE FRANCOIS JEAN (1797-1867)
ANGLO-FRENCH SCHOOL
ENGLISH SCHOOL (1846)

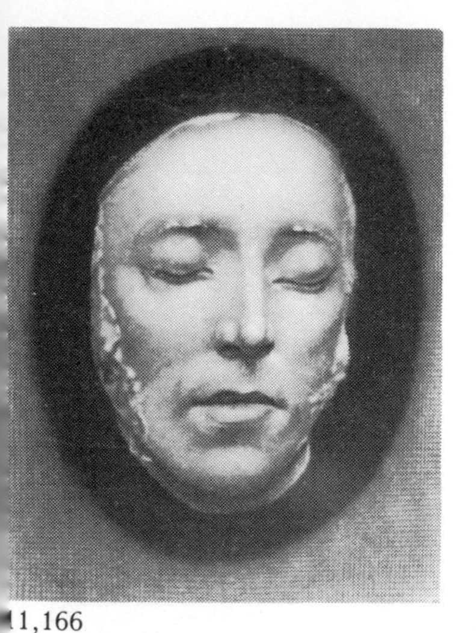

ı1,166
Death Mask of Robert Emmet, (1778-1803), United Irishman and Patriot, (pl. for R. Madden's 'United Irishmen', 3rd Series, 1846)
after a daguerreotype of a death nask, 1803, NGI no. 8130)
Published: Madden & Co., London, 846
1.5 x 13.7 (plate cut)
Mezzotint
Purchased, Dublin, P. Traynor, 1898

etrie, James (1750-1819)
rish School
NGLISH SCHOOL (1846)

,182
Michael Dwyer, (1771-1826), United Irishman, (pl. for R. Madden's 'United Irishmen', 3rd Series, 1846)
INSCRIBED: *from an original portrait drawn and engraved by Petrie*
Published: Madden & Co., London, 1846
21.5 x 12.6 (plate 21.5 x 12.6)
Mezzotint
Purchased, Dublin, Mr P. Traynor, 1898

Petrie, James (1750-1819)
Irish School
HEATH, JAMES (1757-1834)
ENGLISH SCHOOL

10,936
Major-General The Hon. Montague Mathew, (d.1819), son of the 1st Earl of Landaff, (pl. for Sir J. Barrington's 'Historic Anecdotes and Secret Memoirs', 1809-15)
INSCRIBED: *from an original drawing by Petrie in the possession of Sir J. Barrington*
Published: G. Robinson, London, 14th March 1811
34.6 x 26 (plate 25.4 x 21.6)
Stipple
Acquired by 1903

Petrie, James (1750-1819)
Irish School
HEATH, JAMES (1757-1834)
ENGLISH SCHOOL

10,940
James Napper Tandy, (1740-1803), United Irishman
INSCRIBED: *from a Drawing by J. Petrie in the possession of Sir J. Barrington*
Published: G. Robinson, London, 1st March 1815
35.4 x 27.5 (plate 25.3 x 21.3)
Stipple
Acquired by 1898

Petrie, James (1750-1819)
Irish School
IRISH SCHOOL (19TH CENTURY)

11,219
Robert Emmet, (1778-1803), Patriot
18.2 x 12.4 (plate 10 x 7.14)
Stipple and line
Provenance Unknown

Petrie, James (1750-1819)
Irish School
IRISH SCHOOL (1808)

10,650
James Napper Tandy, (1740-1803), United Irishman, when a French General, (pl. for 'Irish Magazine', September 1808)
(after a drawing)
Published: Irish Magazine, Dublin, September 1808
20.1 x 12.8 (plate cut)
Stipple
Purchased, Dublin, Mr P. Traynor, 1898

Petrie, James (1750-1819)
Irish School
IRISH SCHOOL (1808)

11,163
Robert Emmet, (1778-1803), United Irishman and Patriot, (pl. for 'Irish Magazine', November 1808)
Published: Irish Magazine, Dublin, November 1808
21 x 13.1 (plate 13.3 x 10.2)
Stipple
Purchased, Dublin, Mr P. Traynor, 1898

Petrie, James (1750-1819)
Irish School
MAGUIRE, PATRICK (FL.1783-1820)
IRISH SCHOOL

10,629
Henry Howley, (1775-1803), Patriot and accomplice of Robert Emmet
(after a pencil drawing of 1803, NLI, Dublin)
20.7 x 15.4 (plate 19.2 x 14.6)
Stipple
Purchased, Dublin, Mr P. Traynor, 1898

Petrie, James (1750-1819)
English School
MAGUIRE, PATRICK (FL.1783-1820)
IRISH SCHOOL

10,630
Henry Howley, (1775-1803), Patriot and accomplice of Robert Emmet, (another copy)
(after a pencil drawing of 1803, NLI, Dublin)
19.5 x 15 (plate 19.2 x 14.6)
Stipple
Purchased, Dublin, Mr P. Traynor, 1898

Petrie, James (1750-1819)
English School
MAGUIRE, PATRICK (FL.1783-1820)
IRISH SCHOOL

11,211
Henry Lawes Luttrell, 2nd Earl Carhampton, (1743-1821), Former Commander-in-Chief of the Army in Ireland, (pl. for 'Hibernian Magazine', December 1797)
(after a drawing)
Published: Hibernian Magazine, Dublin, December, 1797
19.9 x 11.7 (plate cut)
Stipple
Purchased, Mr P. Traynor, 1898

Petrie, James (1750-1819)
Irish School
PETRIE, JAMES (1750-1819)
IRISH SCHOOL

10,156
James Napper Tandy, (c.1740-1819), United Irishman, when a French General
(after a drawing)
Published: J. Petrie, Dublin, not before 1798
29 x 17.8 (plate 24 x 14.5)
Stipple
Purchased, Dublin, Mr J.V. McAlpine, 1904

Petrie, James (1750-1819)
Irish School *and*
Irish School (c.1803)
IRISH SCHOOL (C.1803)

1,352
The Speech from the dock by Robert Emmet, (1778-1803), Patriot, at his Trial on 19th September 1803
21.8 x 32.5 (plate cut)
Line
Purchased: Dublin, Mr J.V. McAlpine, 1913

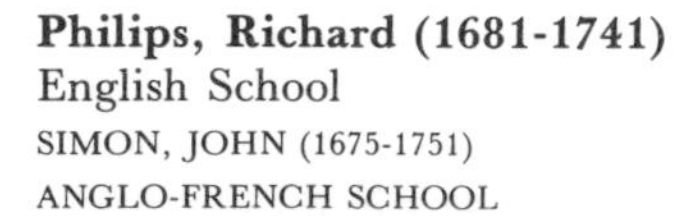

Philips, Richard (1681-1741)
English School
SIMON, JOHN (1675-1751)
ANGLO-FRENCH SCHOOL

10,694
Thomas Wilson, P. Bishop of Sodor and Man, (1663-1775), with a map of the Isle of Man
30.2 x 21.7 (plate cut)
Mezzotint
Purchased, 1906

Phillips, Henry Wyndham (1820-1868)
English School
COOK, HENRY R. (FL.1800-1845)
ENGLISH SCHOOL

11,079
Colonel William Blacker, (1775-1855), Vice-Treasurer of Ireland
Published: J. Rogerson, London, 1845
25.2 x 15 (plate cut)
Line and stipple
Purchased, London, Mr H.J. Breun, 1910

Phillips, Henry Wyndham (1820-1868)
English School
WALKER, WILLIAM (1791-1867)
ENGLISH SCHOOL

10,958

Sir Samuel Martin, (1801-1883), Baron of the Exchequer
Published: W. Walker, (as a private plate) London, 20th April 1853
42.8 x 30.5 (plate cut)
Mezzotint
Purchased, Dublin, Mr A. Roth, 1896

Phillips, Thomas (1770-1845)
English School
BROWN, JOSEPH (FL.1854-1886)
ENGLISH SCHOOL

10,844
Sir Robert FitzWygram Bt., M.P., (1773-1843), (pl. for H. Ryall's 'Portraits of Eminent Conservative Statesmen', 2nd series, 1846)
Published: G. Virtue, London, 1846
35 x 26 (plate cut)
Line and stipple
Acquired c.1908

Phillips, Thomas (1770-1845)
English School
BROWN, JOSEPH (FL.1854-1886)
ENGLISH SCHOOL

10,992
Charles Henry St John O'Neill, 1st Earl O'Neill, (1779-1841), Irish Postmaster General and Grandmaster of the Orange Order, (pl. for H. Ryall's 'Portraits of Eminent Conservative Statesmen', 2nd series, 1846)
Published: G. Virtue, London, 1846
22.5 x 29.2 (plate 33.2 x 25.3)
Stipple and line
Purchased, Mr W.V. Daniell, 1901

Phillips, Thomas (1770-1845)
English School
LANE, RICHARD JAMES (1800-1872)
ENGLISH SCHOOL

10,737

James Du Pré Alexander, Viscount Alexander, (1812-1855), later 3rd Earl of Caledon, in the dress he wore as page to His Majesty George IV at the installation of the Knights of St Patrick
Published: c.1821
37.9 x 26.7 (image 38 x 26.5)
Lithograph
Acquired by 1903

Phillips, Thomas (1770-1845)
English School
EVANS, WILLIAM (FL.1797-1856)
ENGLISH SCHOOL
MACKENZIE, K. (19TH CENTURY)
ENGLISH SCHOOL

10,801
Lieut.-General Lord John Hutchinson, (1757-1832), later 2nd Earl of Donoughmore, (pl. for T. Cadell & W. Davies' 'Contemporary Portraits', 1822)
INSCRIBED: *from an original picture by T. Phillips, Esq., R.A. in his own possession*
Published: T. Cadell & W. Davies, London, 9th June 1809
43 x 33.8 (plate 38 x 32.8)
Stipple
Purchased, Dublin, Mr A. Roth, 1895

Phillips, Thomas (1770-1845)
English School
TURNER, MRS MARY (1774-1850)
ENGLISH SCHOOL

10,926
William Marsden, (1754-1836), Numismatist and Writer
25.8 x 23 (plate 21 x 16.8)
Etching
Purchased, Dublin, Mr A. Roth, 1897

Piazzetta, Giovanni Battista (1682-1754)
Venetian School
KILLIAN, PHILIP ANDREAS (1714-1759)
GERMAN SCHOOL

20,218
The Three Marys at the Tomb
19.2 x 12.9 (plate cut)
Line
Purchased, Lusk, Mr de Courcy Donovan, 1971

Pickering, George (c.1794-1857)
English School
LE PETIT, WILLIAM A. (FL.1829-1857)
ENGLISH SCHOOL

20,458
Lakes Windermere, Esthwaithe and Coniston from the top of Loughrigg Fell, Cumbria, (previously pl. for T. Rose's 'Cumberland' 1832)
Published: Fisher, Son & Co., London, 1835
21.3 x 27.8 (plate cut)
Steel Engraving
Purchased, Lusk, Mr de Courcy Donovan, 1971

Pickering, George (c.1794-1857)
English School
MOTTRAM, CHARLES (1807-1876)
ENGLISH SCHOOL

20,486
Grasmere lake and village, Cumbria, (previously plate for T. Rose's 'Westmoreland', 1832)
Published: Fisher, Son & Co., London, 1833
15.1 x 22.5 (plate cut)
Steel Engraving
Purchased, Lusk, Mr de Courcy Donovan, 1971

Pickering, Henry (fl.c.1700-c.1750)
English School
FABER THE YOUNGER, JOHN (C.1684-1756)
ENGLISH SCHOOL

10,031
Margaret (Peg) Woffington, (1718-1760), Actress
Published: J. Faber the Younger, London, not before 1734
28 x 22.3 (plate cut)
Mezzotint
Purchased, London, 1st Chaloner Smith sale, 1887

Pickersgill, Henry William (1782-1875)
English School
COUSINS, HENRY (1809-1864)
ENGLISH SCHOOL

10,790
Thomas Drummond, (1797-1840), Under-Secretary for Ireland
Published: P. & D. Colnaghi, London, 20th June 1841
69.5 x 50.5 (plate 50.3 x 38)
Mezzotint
Purchased, Dublin, Mr J.V. McAlpine, 1911

Pillement, Jean (1727-1808)
French School
MAUGIN, MARGUERITE THERESE (1736-1787)
FRENCH SCHOOL

10,042
'Premiere vue D'Irelande' - a first view of Ireland
Published: Crepy, Paris
34.5 x 45 (plate 28.3 x 38)
Etching with watercolour
Purchased, Badische, Mr A.J. Onderdonk, 1969

Piloty, Karl (1826-1886)
German School
ENGLISH SCHOOL (1867)

20,632
The Nurse, (from 'Bow Bells Almanack', 17th July 1867)
Published: Bow Bells Almanack, London, 17th July 1867
31.4 x 22.6 (image 14 x 16.5)
Wood Engraving
Presented, Mrs D. Molloy, 1981

Pine, Robert Edge (c.1730-1788)
English School
BROOKSHAW, RICHARD (1736-1804)
ENGLISH SCHOOL

11,106
Mrs Elizabeth Bull, (fl.c.1770-c.1790), Printseller
Published: R. Sayer, London
16.5 x 12.7 (plate 15 x 11.2)
Mezzotint
Acquired between 1913/14

Pine, Robert Edge (1730-1788)
English School
DICKINSON, WILLIAM (1746-1823)
ENGLISH SCHOOL

10,686
James Worsdale, (?1692-1767), Portrait Painter, Actor and Author
Published: ?C. Bowles, London, 1769
38.8 x 28.7 (plate 38.6 x 28.1)
Mezzotint
Presented, Mr W.G. Strickland, 1906

Pine, Robert Edge (c.1730-1788)
English School
DICKINSON, WILLIAM (1746-1823)
ENGLISH SCHOOL

10,828
George II, King of England, (1683-1760)
(after an oil of 1759, Audley End, Essex)
Published: ?C. Bowles, London, 1766, price 5s
53.9 x 38.9 (plate 50.5 x 35.5)
Mezzotint
Purchased, London, 1st Chaloner Smith sale, 1887

Pinelli, Bartolomeo (1781-1835)
Italian School
PINELLI, BARTOLOMEO (1781-1835)
ITALIAN SCHOOL

20,709(3)
The grape gatherers, (from 'Nuova Raccolta....', 1816, see App. 8, no. 20,709)
Published: N. de Antoni & I. Pavon, Rome, 1816
26.8 x 39.8 (plate 21.5 x 29.2)
Etching
Purchased, Miss White, 1936

Piranesi, Giovanni Battista (1720-1778)
Italian School
PIRANESI, GIOVANNI BATTISTA (1720-1778)
ITALIAN SCHOOL

20,525
Temple of Pola, Istria, S. Italy, (pl. for G.B. Piranesi's 'Antichita Romane de Tempi della Repubblica e de Primi Imperatori', first published 1748)
12.5 x 25.5 (plate cut)
Etching
Presented, Mrs D. Molloy, 1981

Piranesi, Giovanni Battista (1720-1778)
Italian School
PIRANESI, GIOVANNI BATTISTA (1720-1778)
ITALIAN SCHOOL

20,526
The Arch of Augustus, Rimini, Italy, (pl. for G.B. Piranesi's 'Antichita Romane de Tempi della Repubblica e de Primi Imperatori', first published 1748)
13.5 x 26.5 (plate cut)
Etching
Presented, Mrs D. Molloy, 1981

Piranesi, Giovanni Battista (1720-1778)
Italian School
PIRANESI, GIOVANNI BATTISTA (1720-1778)
ITALIAN SCHOOLO

20,527
Ruins on the Campus Martius, Rome, 2nd frontispiece for G.B. Piranesi's 'Il Campo Marzio dell' Antica Roma', first published 1762)
19.5 x 29 (plate cut)
Etching
Presented, Mrs D. Molloy, 1981

Piranesi, Giovanni Battista (1720-1778)
Italian School
PIRANESI, GIOVANNI BATTISTA (1720-1778)
ITALIAN SCHOOL

20,528
Palace of the Venetian Ambassador, Piazza di San Marco, Rome, (pl. for G.B. Piranesi's 'Varie Vedute di Roma Antica e Modena', first published 1748)
13.5 x 19.5 (plate cut)
Etching
Presented, Mrs D. Molloy, 1981

Piranesi, Giovanni Battista (1720-1778)
Italian School
PIRANESI, GIOVANNI BATTISTA (1720-1778)
ITALIAN SCHOOL

20,530
Ruins of the Pontis Triumphalis on the River Tiber, (pl. for G.B. Piranesi's 'Il Campo Marzio dell' Antica Roma', first published 1762)
11.5 x 25.5 (plate cut)
Etching
Presented, Mrs D. Molloy, 1981

Piranesi, Giovanni Battista (1720-1778)
Italian School
PIRANESI, GIOVANNI BATTISTA (1720-1778)
ITALIAN SCHOOL

20,531
The Temple of Vespasian ruins, Roman Forum, Rome, (pl. for G.B. Piranesi's 'Il Antichita Romane'; first published 1756)
13 x 19.8 (plate cut)
Etching
Presented, Mrs D. Molloy, 1981

Piranesi, Giovanni Battista (1720-1778)
Italian School
PIRANESI, GIOVANNI BATTISTA (1720-1778)
ITALIAN SCHOOL

20,532
Tomb of the Scipios, Rome, (pl. for G.B. Piranesi's 'Antichita Romane de Tempi della Republica e de Primi Imperatori', first published 1748)
13.7 x 27 (plate cut)
Etching
Presented, Mrs D. Molloy, 1981

Piranesi, Giovanni Battista (1720-1778)
Italian School
PIRANESI, GIOVANNI BATTISTA (1720-1778)
ITALIAN SCHOOL

20,533
Back View of the Temple of Pola, in Istria, S. Italy, (pl. for G.B. Piranesi's 'Antichita Romane de Temp i della

Repubblica e de Primi Imperatori', first published 1748)
12.5 x 25.3 (plate cut)
Etching
Presented, Mrs D. Molloy, 1981

Piranesi, Giovanni Battista (1720-1778)
Italian School
PIRANESI, GIOVANNI BATTISTA (1720-1778)
ITALIAN SCHOOL

20,534
The Temple of Concord by the Capitol, Rome, (pl. for G.B. Piranesi's 'Il Antichita Romane', first published 1756)
14.1 x 21 (plate cut)
Etching
Presented, Mrs D. Molloy, 1981

Piranesi, Giovanni Battista (1720-1778)
Roman School
PIRANESI, GIOVANNI BATTISTA (1720-1778)
ROMAN SCHOOL

20,832
The Trevi Fountain, Rome (c.1773)
77.5 x 52.4 (plate 72 x 47.7)
Line and etching
Provenance Unknown

Pocock, Nicholas (1740-1821)
English School
HAVELL, DANIEL (FL.1812-1837)
ENGLISH SCHOOL *and*
HAVELL THE ELDER, ROBERT (FL.1800-1840)
ENGLISH SCHOOL

20,322
Fourth and fifth rate Men-of-War under courses, (composition from van de Velde the Younger)
(after a drawing)
Published: W. Soffe, London
34 x 49.1 (plate 22.7 x 49)
Aquatint and etching
Purchased, Lusk, Mr de Courcy Donovan, 1971

Pond, Arthur (c.1700-1758)
English School
McARDELL, JAMES (1728/29-1765)
IRISH SCHOOL

10,319
Margaret (Peg) Woffington, (1718-1760), Actress
23.5 x 33.5 (plate 22.8 x 32.9)
Mezzotint
Acquired by 1879

Pond, Arthur (c.1700-1758)
English School
McARDELL, JAMES (1728/29-1765)
IRISH SCHOOL

10,366
Margaret (Peg) Woffington, (1718-1760), Actress, (another copy)
34.6 x 25.4 (plate 33 x 23.7)
Mezzotint
Provenance Unknown

Pool, Robert (fl.1779-1809)
Irish School *and*
Cash, John (fl.c.1780)
Irish School
LODGE, JOHN (18TH CENTURY)
?IRISH SCHOOL

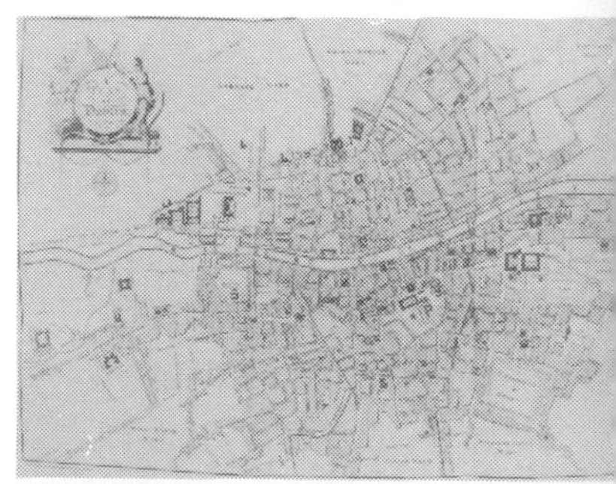

10,041(1)
Map of Dublin in 1780, (from 'Views of the most remarkable public buildings, monuments and other edifices in the city of Dublin', 1780, see App. 8, no. 10,041)
Published: 1780
34 x 37 (plate 32.2 x cut)
Line
Purchased, London, Sabin and Co., 1969

Pool, Robert (fl.1779-1809)
Irish School *and*
Cash, John (fl.c.1780)
Irish School
LODGE, JOHN (18TH CENTURY)
?IRISH SCHOOL

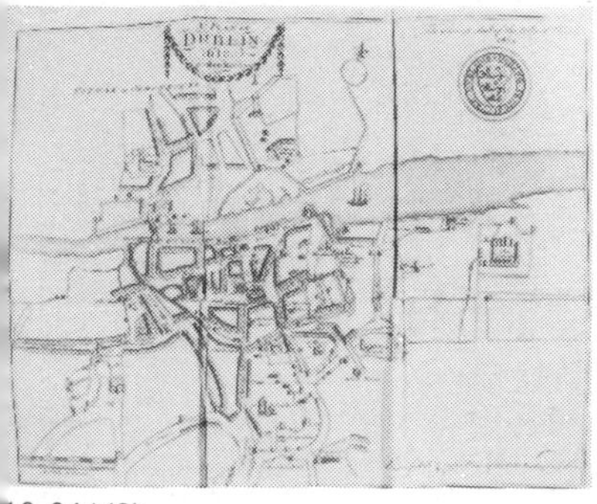

10,041(2)
Speed's Map of Dublin in 1610 with the ity seal from 1459, (from 'Views of the most remarkable public buildings, nonuments and other edifices in the city of Dublin', 1780, see App. 8, no. 10,041)
after a line engraving of 1611)
4 x 41 (plate 30.6 x cut)
Line
urchased, London, Sabin and Co., 1969

ool, Robert (fl.1779-1809)
rish School *and*
ash, John (fl.c.1780)
rish School
ODGE, JOHN (18TH CENTURY)
IRISH SCHOOL

0,041(3)
rontispiece: Grinling Gibbons's statue of Villiam III on College Green, Dublin, ow destroyed), (from 'Views of the most markable public buildings, monuments d other edifices in the city of Dublin', 780 see App. 8, no. 10,041)
ublished: 1st January 1780
7.5 x 18 (plate 19.2 x 12.2)
ine
urchased, London, Sabin and Co., 969

Pool, Robert (fl.1779-1809)
Irish School *and*
Cash, John (fl.c.1780)
Irish School
LODGE, JOHN (18TH CENTURY)
?IRISH SCHOOL

10,041(4)
Part of North Side of Dublin Castle, (The Bedford Tower, Upper Castle Yard and the Castle Gates), (from 'Views of the most remarkable public buildings, monuments and other edifices in the city of Dublin', 1780, see App. 8, no. 10,041)
18 x 23.5 (plate 14 x 20)
Line
Purchased, London, Sabin and Co., 1969

Pool, Robert (fl.1779-1809)
Irish School *and*
Cash, John (fl.c.1780)
Irish School
LODGE, JOHN (18TH CENTURY)
?IRISH SCHOOL

10,041(5)
The Garden Front of Dublin Castle's State Apartments, (from 'Views of the most remarkable public buildings, monuments and other edifices in the city of Dublin', 1780, see App. 8, no. 10,041)
Published: 1st March 1779
18 x 23.5 (plate 14 x 20)
Line
Purchased, London, Sabin and Co., 1969

Pool, Robert (fl.1779-1809)
Irish School *and*
Cash, John (fl.c.1780)
Irish School
LODGE, JOHN (18TH CENTURY)
?IRISH SCHOOL

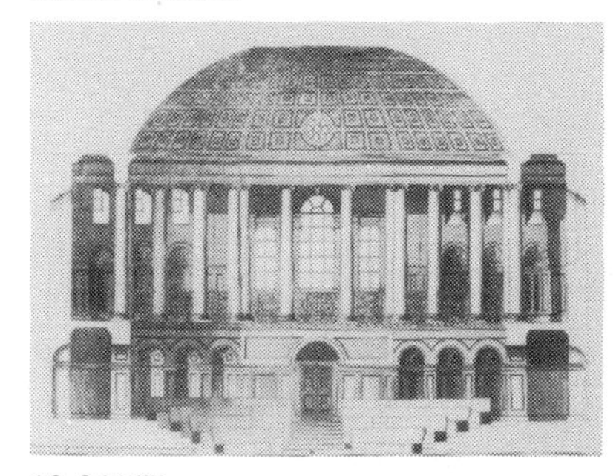

10,041(7)
Section of the House of Commons, Parliament House, Dublin, (now Bank of Ireland; rebuilt after 1792 fire), (from 'Views of the most remarkable public buildings, monuments and other edifices in the city of Dublin', 1780, see App. 8, no. 10,041)
Published: 1st March 1779
18 x 23.5 (plate 18 x 20)
Line
Purchased, London, Sabin and Co., 1969

Pool, Robert (fl.1779-1809)
Irish School *and*
Cash, John (fl.c.1780)
Irish School
LODGE, JOHN (18TH CENTURY)
?IRISH SCHOOL

10,041(8)
The East Front of Trinity College, Dublin, (from 'Views of the most remarkable public buildings, monuments and other edifices in the city of Dublin', 1780, see App. 8, no. 10,041)
Published: 1st March 1779
18 x 23.5 (plate 14 x 20)
Line
Purchased, London, Sabin and Co., 1969

Pool, Robert (fl.1779-1809)
Irish School *and*
Cash, John (fl.c.1780)
Irish School
LODGE, JOHN (18TH CENTURY)
?IRISH SCHOOL

10,041(9)
East Side of Principal or Front Square, Trinity College, Dublin, (the central spire was not built), (from 'Views of the most remarkable public buildings, monuments and other edifices in the city of Dublin', 1780, see App. 8, no. 10,041)
Published: 1st March 1779
18 x 23.5 (plate 14 x 20)
Line
Purchased, London, Sabin and Co., 1969

Pool, Robert (fl.1779-1809)
Irish School *and*
Cash, John (fl.c.1780)
Irish School
LODGE, JOHN (18TH CENTURY)
?IRISH SCHOOL

10,041(11)
The Provost's House, Trinity College, Dublin, (from 'Views of the most remarkable public buildings, monuments and other edifices in the city of Dublin', 1780, see App. 8, no. 10,041)
Published: 1st March 1779
18 x 23.5 (plate 14 x 20)
Line
Purchased, London, Sabin and Co., 1969

Pool, Robert (fl.1779-1809)
Irish School *and*
Cash, John (fl.c.1780)
Irish School
LODGE, JOHN (18TH CENTURY)
?IRISH SCHOOL

10,041(14)
Queen's, (now Queen Maev), Bridge above Essex, (now rebuilt Grattan), Bridge, Dublin, (from 'Views of the most remarkable public buildings, monuments and other edifices in the city of Dublin', 1780, see App. 8, no. 10,041)
Published: 1st March 1779
18 x 23.5 (plate 14 x 20)
Line
Purchased, London, Sabin and Co., 1969

Pool, Robert (fl.1779-1809)
Irish School *and*
Cash, John (fl.c.1780)
Irish School
LODGE, JOHN (18TH CENTURY)
?IRISH SCHOOL

10,041(10)
The Front of the Theatre, Trinity College, (the dome and statuary not carried out), (from 'Views of the most remarkable public buildings, monuments and other edifices in the city of Dublin', 1780, see App. 8, no. 10,041)
Published: 1st March 1779
18 x 23.5 (plate 14 x 20)
Line
Purchased, London, Sabin and Co., 1969

Pool, Robert (fl.1779-1809)
Irish School *and*
Cash, John (fl.c.1780)
Irish School
LODGE, JOHN (18TH CENTURY)
?IRISH SCHOOL

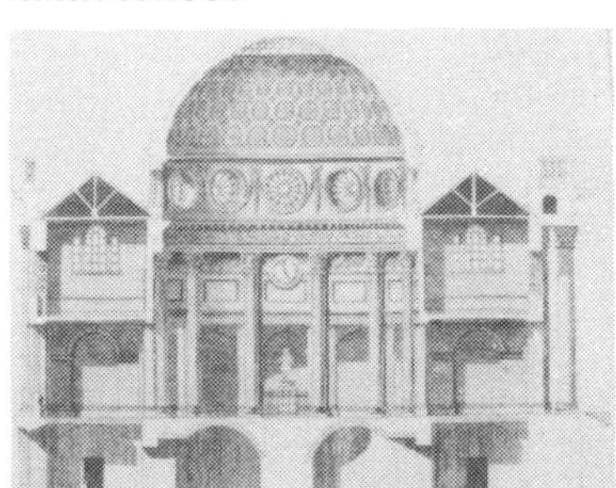

10,041(13)
Section of the Royal Exchange, (now City Hall), Cork Hill, Dublin, from East to West, (from 'Views of the most remarkable public buildings, monuments and other edifices in the city of Dublin', 1780, see App. 8, no. 10,041)
Published: January 1780
18 x 23.5 (plate 18 x 20)
Line
Purchased, London, Sabin and Co., 1969

Pool, Robert (fl.1779-1809)
Irish School *and*
Cash, John (fl.c.1780)
Irish School
LODGE, JOHN (18TH CENTURY)
?IRISH SCHOOL

10,041(15)
Newgate Gaol, (now demolished), Green Street, Dublin, (from 'Views of the most remarkable public buildings, monuments and other edifices in the city of Dublin', 1780, see App. 8, no. 10,041)
Published: 1st March 1779
18 x 23.5 (plate 14 x 20)
Line
Purchased, London, Sabin and Co., 1969

Pool, Robert (fl.1779-1809)
Irish School *and*
Cash, John (fl.c.1780)
Irish School
LODGE, JOHN (18TH CENTURY)
?IRISH SCHOOL

10,041(16)
The Marine School, (now demolished), Sir John Rogerson Quay, Dublin, (from 'Views of the most remarkable public buildings, monuments and other edifices in the city of Dublin', 1780, see App. 8, no. 10,041)
Published: 1st March 1779
18 x 23.5 (plate 14 x 20)
Line
Purchased, London, Sabin and Co., 1969

Pool, Robert (fl.1779-1809)
Irish School *and*
Cash, John (fl.c.1780)
Irish School
LODGE, JOHN (18TH CENTURY)
?IRISH SCHOOL

10,041(17)
The Lying-in, (now Rotunda), Hospital, Dublin, (from 'Views of the most remarkable public buildings, monuments and other edifices in the city of Dublin', 1780, see App. 8, no. 10,041)
Published: 1st March 1779
18 x 23.5 (plate 14 x 20)
Line
Purchased, London, Sabin and Co., 1969

Pool, Robert (fl.1779-1809)
Irish School *and*
Cash, John (fl.c.1780)
Irish School
LODGE, JOHN (18TH CENTURY)
?IRISH SCHOOL

10,041(19)
Dr Steevens's Hospital, Dublin, (now closed), (from 'Views of the most remarkable public buildings, monuments and other edifices in the city of Dublin', 1780, see App. 8, no. 10,041)
Published: 1st March 1779
18 x 23.5 (plate 14 x 20)
Line
Purchased, London, Sabin and Co., 1969

Pool, Robert (fl.1779-1809)
Irish School *and*
Cash, John (fl.c.1780)
Irish School
LODGE, JOHN (18TH CENTURY)
?IRISH SCHOOL

10,041(20)
Christchurch Cathedral, Dublin, from the North, (from 'Views of the most remarkable public buildings, monuments and other edifices in the city of Dublin', 1780, see App. 8, no. 10,041)
Published: 1st March 1779
18 x 23.5 (plate 14 x 20)
Line
Purchased, London, Sabin and Co., 1969

Pool, Robert (fl.1779-1809)
Irish School *and*
Cash, John (fl.c.1780)
Irish School
LODGE, JOHN (18TH CENTURY)
?IRISH SCHOOL

10,041(22)
The Facade of St Werburgh's Church, Werburgh Street, Dublin, (spire removed 1810), (from 'Views of the most remarkable public buildings, monuments and other edifices in the city of Dublin', 1780, see App. 8, no. 10,041)
Published: 1st March 1779
18 x 23.5 (plate 14 x 20)
Line
Purchased, London, Sabin and Co., 1969

Pool, Robert (fl. 1779-1809)
Irish School *and*
Cash, John (fl.c.1780)
Irish School
LODGE, JOHN (18TH CENTURY)
?IRISH SCHOOL

10,041(23)
The Facade of St Thomas's Church, Marlborough Street, Dublin, (now rebuilt), (from 'Views of the most remarkable public buildings, monuments and other edifices in

the city of Dublin', 1780, see App. 8, no. 10,041)
Published: 1st March 1779
18 x 23.5 (plate 14 x 20)
Line
Purchased, London, Sabin and Co., 1969

Pool, Robert (fl.1779-1809)
Irish School *and*
Cash, John (fl.c.1780)
Irish School
LODGE, JOHN (18TH CENTURY)
?IRISH SCHOOL

10,041(24)
The North Side of St Catherine's Church, Thomas Street, Dublin, (from 'Views of the most remarkable public buildings, monuments and other edifices in the city of Dublin', 1780, see App. 8, no. 10,041)
Published: 1st March 1779
18 x 23.5 (plate 14 x 20)
Line
Purchased, London, Sabin and Co., 1969

Pool, Robert (fl.1779-1809)
Irish School *and*
Cash, John (fl.c.1780)
Irish School
LODGE, JOHN (18TH CENTURY)
?IRISH SCHOOL

10,041(28)
The Monument, (by J. van Nost the Younger), to John, Baron Bowes of Clonlyon, (1690-1767), Lord Chancellor, in Christchurch Cathedral, Dublin, (now in the crypt), (from 'Views of the most remarkable public buildings, monuments and other edifices in the city of Dublin', 1780, see App. 8, no. 10,041)
Published: 1st March 1779
23.5 x 18 (plate 20 x 14)
Line
Purchased, London, Sabin and Co., 1969

Pool, Robert (fl.1779-1809)
Irish School *and*
Cash, John (fl.c.1780)
Irish School
LODGE, JOHN (18TH CENTURY)
?IRISH SCHOOL

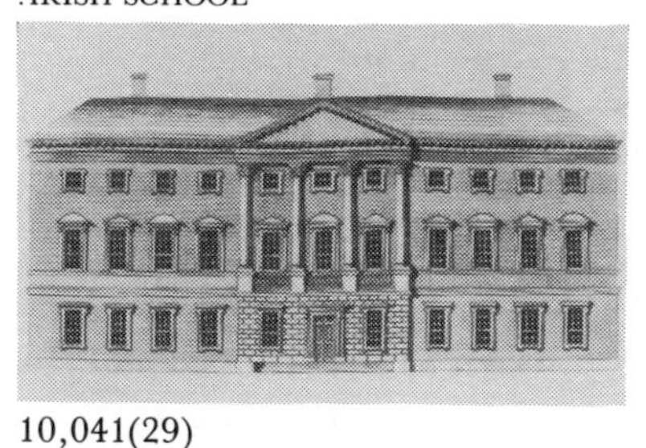

10,041(29)
The West Front of Leinster House, Kildare Street, (now the Dáil and Seanad), (from 'Views of the most remarkable public buildings, monuments and other edifices in the city of Dublin', 1780, see App. 8, no. 10,041)
Published: 1st January 1779
18 x 23.5 (plate 14 x 20)
Line
Purchased, London, Sabin and Co., 1969

Pool, Robert (fl.1779-1809)
Irish School *and*
Cash, John (fl.c.1780)
Irish School
LODGE, JOHN (18TH CENTURY)
?IRISH SCHOOL

10,041(30)
Lord Powerscourt's House, William Street South, Dublin, (from 'Views of the most remarkable public buildings, monuments and other edifices in the city of Dublin', 1780, see App. 8, no. 10,041)
Published: 1st March 1779
18 x 23.5 (plate 14 x 20)
Line
Purchased, London, Sabin and Co., 1969

Pool, Robert (fl.1779-1809)
Irish School *and*
Cash, John (fl.c.1780)
Irish School
LODGE, JOHN (18TH CENTURY)
?IRISH SCHOOL

10,041(31)
Lord Charlemont's House, Dublin, (now the Hugh Lane Municipal Gallery of Modern Art, Parnell Square), (from 'Views of the most remarkable public buildings, monuments and other edifices in the city of Dublin', 1780, see App. 8, no. 10,041)
Published: 1st March 1779
18 x 23.5 (plate 14 x 20)
Line
Purchased, London, Sabin and Co., 1969

Pool, Robert (fl.1779-1809)
Irish School *and*
Cash, John (fl.c.1780)
Irish School
LODGE, JOHN (18TH CENTURY)
?IRISH SCHOOL

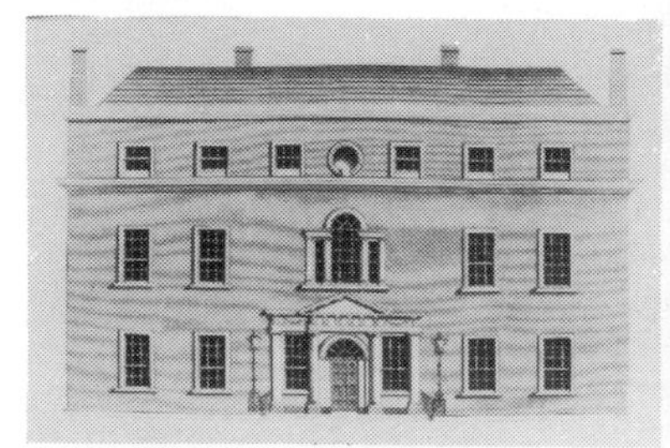

10,041(32)

Lord Tyrone's House, Marlborough Street, (now the Department of Education), (from 'Views of the most remarkable public buildings, monuments and other edifices in the city of Dublin', 1780, see App. 8, no. 10,041)
Published: 1st March 1799
23.5 x 18 (plate 14 x 20)
Line
Purchased: London, Sabin and Co., 1969

Pool, Robert (fl.1779-1809)
Irish School *and*
Cash, John (fl.c.1780)
Irish School
LODGE, JOHN (18TH CENTURY)
?IRISH SCHOOL

11,707
The Marine School, Sir John Rogerson's Quay, Dublin, (now demolished), (pl. for Z. Jackson's edition of J. Payne's 'New System of Universal Geography', 1793)
Published: Z. Jackson, Dublin
21.3 x 26.8 (plate 14 x 20)
Line
Provenance Unknown

Pool, Robert (fl.1779-1809)
Irish School *and*
Cash, John (fl.c.1780)
Irish School
LODGE, JOHN (18TH CENTURY)
?IRISH SCHOOL

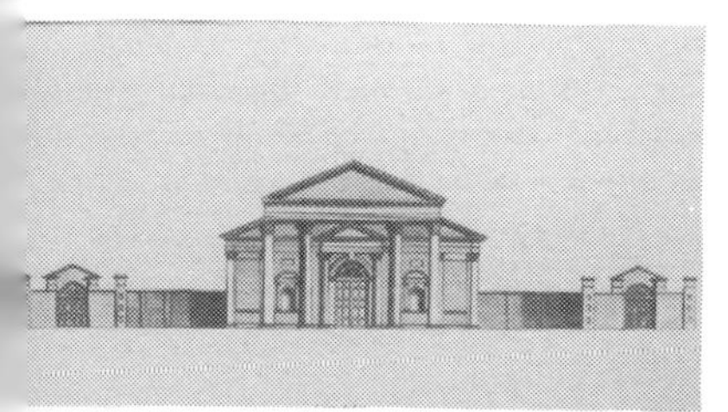

1,708
St Thomas's Church, Marlborough Street, Dublin, (now demolished), (pl. for Z. Jackson's edition of J. Payne's 'New System of Universal Geography', 1793)
Published: Z. Jackson, Dublin
21.4 x 26.8 (plate cut x 19.8)
Line
Provenance Unknown

Pool, Robert (fl.1779-1809)
Irish School *and*
Cash, John (fl.c.1780)
Irish School
LODGE, JOHN (18TH CENTURY)
?IRISH SCHOOL

11,709
East Side of Principal or Front Square, Trinity College, Dublin, (the central spire was not built), (pl. for Z. Jackson's edition of J. Payne's 'New System of Universal Geography', 1793)
Published: Z. Jackson, Dublin
15.2 x 21.8 (plate cut x 20)
Line
Provenance Unknown

Pool, Robert (fl.1779-1809)
Irish School *and*
Cash, John (fl.c.1780)
Irish School
LODGE, JOHN (18TH CENTURY)
?IRISH SCHOOL

11,710
The Provost's House, Trinity College, Dublin, (pl. for Z. Jackson's edition of J. Payne's 'New System of Universal Geography', 1793)
Published: Z. Jackson, Dublin
15.8 x 23.1 (plate cut x 20)
Line
Provenance Unknown

Pool, Robert (fl.1778-1809)
Irish School *and*
Cash, John (fl.c.1780)
Irish School
LODGE, JOHN (18TH CENTURY)
?IRISH SCHOOL

11,711
The East Front of Trinity College, Dublin, (pl. for Z. Jackson's edition of J. Payne's 'New System of Universal Geography', 1793)
Published: Z. Jackson, Dublin
19 x 24.3 (plate 14 x 20)
Line
Provenance Unknown

Pool, Robert (fl.1779-1809)
Irish School *and*
Cash, John (fl.c.1780)
Irish School
LODGE, JOHN (18TH CENTURY)
?IRISH SCHOOL

11,725
The west front of Leinster House, Kildare Street, Dublin, (now the Dáil and Seanad), (pl. for Z. Jackson's edition of J. Payne's 'New System of Universal Geography', 1793)
Published: Z. Jackson, Dublin
20.4 x 26.3 (plate cut x 20)
Line
Provenance Unknown

Pool, Robert (fl.1779-1809)
Irish School *and*
Cash, John (fl.c.1780)
Irish School
LODGE, JOHN (18TH CENTURY)
?IRISH SCHOOL

11,726
The Lying-In, (now Rotunda), Hospital, Dublin, (pl. for Z. Jackson's edition of J. Payne's 'New System of Universal Geography', 1793)
Published: Z. Jackson, Dublin
22 x 27 (plate 14 x 20)
Line
Provenance Unknown

Pool, Robert (fl.1779-1809)
Irish School *and*
Cash, John (fl.c.1780)
Irish School
LODGE, JOHN (18TH CENTURY)
?IRISH SCHOOL

11,734
Lord Powerscourt's House, William Street South, Dublin, (pl. for Z. Jackson's edition of J. Payne's 'New System of Universal Geography', 1793)
Published: Z. Jackson, Dublin
18.5 x 24.5 (plate 14.5 x 20)
Line
Provenance Unknown

Pool, Robert (fl.1779-1809)
Irish School *and*
Cash, John (fl. c.1780)
Irish School
LODGE, JOHN (18TH CENTURY)
?IRISH SCHOOL

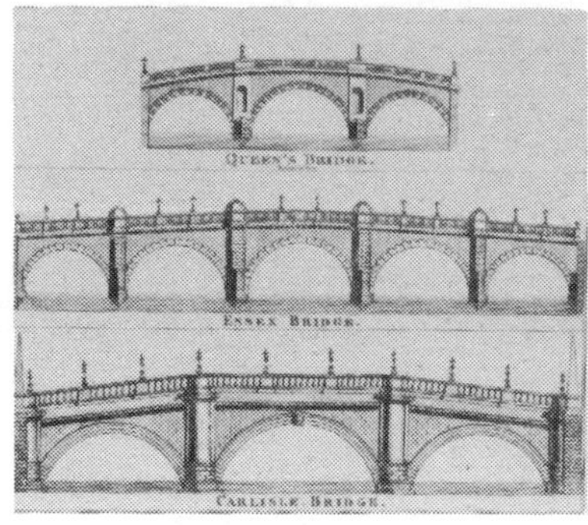

11,740
Queen's, (now Queen Maev), Bridge, Essex, (now rebuilt Grattan), Bridge and Carlisle, (now rebuilt O'Connell), Bridge, Dublin, (pl. for Z. Jackson's edition of J. Payne's 'New System of Universal Geography', 1793)
Published: Z. Jackson, Dublin
21.2 x 26.9 (plate 17.8 x 20.2)
Line
Provenance Unknown

Pool, Robert (fl.1779-1809)
Irish School *and*
Cash, John (fl.c.1780)
Irish School
TAYLOR THE ELDER, ISAAC (1730-1807)
ENGLISH SCHOOL

10,041(6)
Parliament House, (now Bank of Ireland), Dublin, (from 'Views of the most remarkable public buildings, monuments and other edifices in the city of Dublin', 1780, see App. 8, no. 10,041)
Published: 1st January 1780
18 x 23.5 (plate 16 x 20)
Line
Purchased, London, Sabin and Co., 1969

Pool, Robert (fl.1779-1809)
Irish School *and*
Cash, John (fl.c.1780)
?Irish School
TAYLOR THE ELDER, ISAAC (1730-1807)
ENGLISH SCHOOL

10,041(12)
North Front of the Royal Exchange, (now City Hall), Cork Hill, Dublin, (from 'Views of the most remarkable public buildings, monuments and other edifices in the city of Dublin', 1780, see App. 8, no. 10,041)
Published: 1st March 1779
18 x 23.5 (plate 16 x 20)
Line
Purchased, London, Sabin and Co., 1969

Pool, Robert (fl.1779-1809)
Irish School *and*
Cash, John (fl.c.1780)
Irish School
TAYLOR THE ELDER, ISAAC (1730-1807)
ENGLISH SCHOOL

10,041(18)
East Front of the Blue-Coat School, (now the Incorporated Law Society), Dublin, (from 'Views of the most remarkable public buildings, monuments and other edifices in the city of Dublin', 1780, see App. 8, no. 10,041)
Published: 1st February 1779
23.5 x 37 (plate 20 x 35)
Line
Purchased, London, Sabin and Co., 1969

Pool, Robert (fl.1779-1809)
Irish School *and*
Cash, John (fl.c.1780)
Irish School
TAYLOR THE ELDER, ISAAC (1730-1807)
ENGLISH SCHOOL

10,041(21)
St Patrick's Cathedral, Dublin, from the South-East, (from 'Views of the most remarkable public buildings, monuments and other edifices in the city of Dublin', 1780, see App. 8, no. 10, 041)
Published: 1778
18 x 23.5 (plate 16 x 20)
Line
Purchased, London, Sabin and Co., 1969

Pool, Robert (fl.1779-1809)
Irish School *and*
Cash, John (fl.c.1780)
Irish School
TAYLOR THE ELDER, ISAAC (1730-1807)
ENGLISH SCHOOL

10,041(25)
The Monument, (by J. Van Nost the Younger), to Thomas Smyth, P. Archbishop of Dublin, (1706-1777), in St Patrick's Cathedral, Dublin, (from 'Views of the most remarkable public buildings, monuments and other edifices in the city of Dublin', 1780, see App. 8, no. 10,041)
Published: 1778
23.5 x 18 (plate 20 x 16)
Line
Purchased, London, Sabin and Co., 1969

Pool, Robert (fl.1779-1809)
Irish School *and*
Cash, John (fl.c.1780)
Irish School
TAYLOR THE ELDER, ISAAC (1730-1807)
ENGLISH SCHOOL

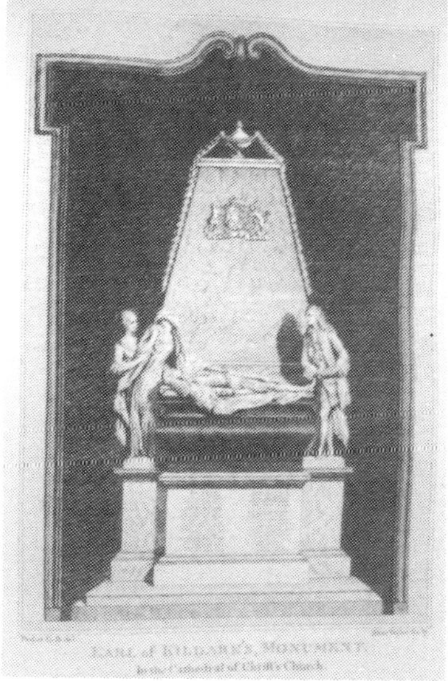

10,041(26)
The Monument, (by H. Cheere), in Christchurch Cathedral, Dublin to Robert FitzGerald, 19th Earl of Kildare, (1675-1744), mourned by his wife, Lady Mary Kildare, (née O'Brien 1692-1780), daughter Lady Margaretta, Countess of Hillsborugh, (1729-1766), and son James FitzGerald, (1722-1773), later 1st Duke of Leinster, (from 'Views of the most remarkable public buildings, monuments and other edifices in the city of Dublin', 1780, see App. 8, no. 10,041)
Published: 1st March 1779
23.5 x 18 (plate 20 x 15.5)
Line
Purchased, London, Sabin and Co., 1969

Pool, Robert (fl.1779-1809)
Irish School *and*
Cash, John (fl.c.1780)
Irish School
TAYLOR THE ELDER, ISAAC (1730-1807)
ENGLISH SCHOOL

10,041(27)
The Monument, (by J. Van Nost the Younger), to Thomas Prior, (c.1682-1751), in Christchurch Cathedral, Dublin, with a relief of Prior introducing the arts to Ireland, (from 'Views of the most remarkable public buildings, monuments and other edifices in the city of Dublin', 1780, see App. 8, no. 10,041)
Published: 1st March 1779
23.5 x 18 (plate 20 x 16.5)
Line
Purchased, London, Sabin and Co., 1969

Pool, Robert (fl.1779-1809)
Irish School *and*
Cash, John (fl.c.1780)
Irish School
TAYLOR THE ELDER, ISAAC (1730-1807)
ENGLISH SCHOOL

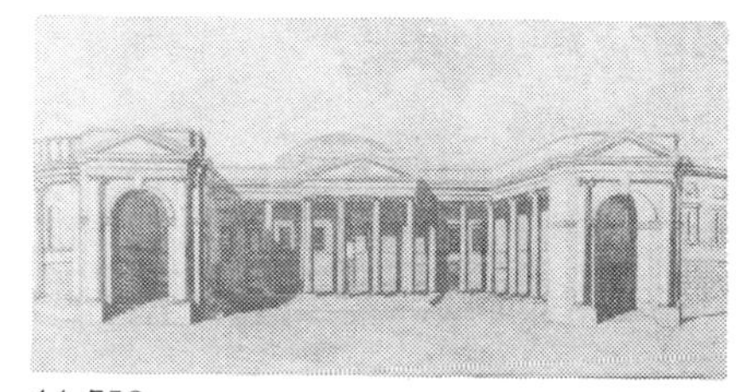

11,753
Parliament House, (now Bank of Ireland), College Green, Dublin, (pl. for Z. Jackson's edition of J. Payne's 'New

System of Universal Geography', 1793)
Published: Z. Jackson, Dublin
18.8 x 24 (plate cut x 20)
Line
Provenance Unknown

Pool, Robert (fl.1779-1809)
Irish School *and*
Cash, John (fl.c.1780)
Irish School
TAYLOR THE ELDER, ISAAC (1730-1807)
ENGLISH SCHOOL

11,755
The north front of the Royal Exchange, (now City Hall), Cork Hill, Dublin, (pl. for Z. Jackson's edition of J. Payne's 'New System of Universal Geography', 1793)
Published: Z. Jackson, Dublin
19.8 x 24.1 (plate cut x 20)
Line
Provenance Unknown

Pool, Robert (fl.1779-1809)
Irish School *and*
Cash, John (fl.c.1780)
Irish School
THOMAS, WILLIAM (FL.1780-1799)
ENGLISH SCHOOL

11,752
Parliament House, (now Bank of Ireland), College Green, Dublin (pl. for the 'European Magazine', April 1792)
(after a R. Pool & J. Cash/I.Taylor the Elder line engraving of 1st January 1780, NGI no. 10,041-16)
Published: J. Sewell, London, 1st April 1792
12.9 x 20.8 (plate 12.3 x 19.8)
Line
Provenance Unknown

Poole, Thomas R. (fl.1791-c.1821)
English School
ENGLISH SCHOOL (1791/1794)

10,609
Edmund Burke, M.P., (1729-1797), Writer and Statesman
(after a wax medallion of 1791, NPG, London)
20.3 x 12.2 (plate 16 x cut)
Line
Provenance Unknown

Poorter, Willem de (c.1603-1648)
Dutch School
BEYER, LEOPOLD (1784-1870)
AUSTRIAN SCHOOL

11,933
The Robing of Esther
(after an oil of late 1630s, NGI no. 380)
7.8 x 6.2 (plate cut)
Line
Presented, Sir Walter Armstrong, 1895, (on reverse of oil, NGI no. 380)

Pope, Alexander (1763-1835)
Irish School
CARDON, ANTHONY (1772-1813)
ANGLO-BELGIAN SCHOOL

10,135
Henry Tresham, (1751-1814), Artist (pl. for T. Cadell & W. Davies' 'Contemporary Portraits', 1822)
(after a drawing)
Published: T. Cadell & W. Davies, London, 27th January 1814
37.1 x 27 (plate cut)
Stipple
Purchased, London, Mr A. Roth, 1895

Pope, Alexander (1763-1835)
Irish School
ENGLISH SCHOOL (1807)

11,209
William Cook, (fl.1766-1824), Playwright, Author and Social Commentator, (pl. for 'Monthly Mirror', December 1807)
(after a miniature, RA 1791)
Published: Vernor, Hood & Sharpe, London, 1st December 1807
18.8 x 11.6 (plate 17.7 x 11)
Stipple
Purchased, Dublin,
Mr J.V. McAlpine, 1909

Pope, Alexander (1763-1835)
Irish School
GODBY, JAMES (FL.1790-1820)
ENGLISH SCHOOL

10,837
Henry Grattan, M.P., (1746-1820), Statesman, (pl. for T. Cadell & W. Davies' 'British Gallery of Contemporary Portraits', 1822)
(after a watercolour miniature, BM, London)
Published: T. Cadell & W. Davies, London, 1819
42.3 x 32.9 (plate 38.1 x 32.5)
Stipple
Provenance Unknown

Pope, Alexander (1763-1835)
Irish School
MARTYN, JOHN (FL.1794-1828)
IRISH SCHOOL

10,838
Henry Grattan, M.P., (1746-1820), Statesman
(after an A. Pope/E. Scriven line engraving of 1814, NGI no. 10,437)
29.8 x 22.1 (plate cut)
Line
Acquired by 1898

Pope, Alexander (1763-1835)
Irish School
MARTYN, JOHN (FL.1785-1828)
IRISH SCHOOL

11,148
Henry Grattan, M.P., (1746-1820), Statesman, (another copy)
(after an A. Pope/E. Scriven line engraving of 1814, NGI no. 10,437)
21.2 x 13.2 (plate cut)
Line
Acquired by 1898

Pope, Alexander (1763-1835)
Irish School
SCRIVEN, EDWARD (1775-1841)
ENGLISH SCHOOL

10,437
Henry Grattan, M.P., (1746-1820), holding a Petition from the Roman Catholics of Ireland, against Parliament House, Dublin
Lettered Proof. Dedicated to the Duke of Sussex
Published: A. Pope, London, 14th December 1814

50 x 36 (plate 47.5 x 34.8)
Line and stipple
Provenance Unknown

Pope-Stevens the Elder, Justin (fl.1743-1771)
Irish School
BROOKS, JOHN (FL.1730-1756)
IRISH SCHOOL

10,115
Daniel MacKercher, (d.1772), Solicitor of James Annesley
Published: J. Brooks, Dublin, 1744
35.2 x 25 (plate cut)
Mezzotint
Purchased, Dublin,
Mr J.V. McAlpine, 1906

Pope-Stevens the Elder, Justin (fl.1743-1771)
Irish School
BROOKS, JOHN (FL.1730-1756)
IRISH SCHOOL

10,208
James Annesley, (1715-1760), Claimant to the Annesley Peerage
Published: G. Smith, London, not before May 1744 (date on 1st State)
36 x 25.1 (plate 35.4 x 24.8)
Mezzotint
Purchased, London, 1st Chaloner Smith sale, 1887

Pope-Stevens the Elder, Justin (fl.1743-1771)
Irish School
MILLER, ANDREW (FL.1737-1763)
IRISH SCHOOL

10,099
Robert Jocelyn, Baron Newport, (c.1688-1756), Lord Chancellor of Ireland, later 1st Viscount Jocelyn
INSCRIBED: *Done from a painting in possession of the Honble Baron Mountney To whom this plate is most Humbly Dedicated by his Honours/most Obedient Humble Servant/Andrew Miller.*
Published: A. Miller, Dublin, 1747
35 x 25.5 (plate 34.8 x 25.4)
Mezzotint
Purchased, Dublin, 1907

Pope-Stevens the Elder, Justin (fl.1743-1771)
Irish School
MILLER, ANDREW (FL.1737-1763)
IRISH SCHOOL

10,511
Charles Tottenham, M.P., (1685-1758)
(after an oil of 1749)
Published: T. Sillcock, Dublin
51 x 34.5 (plate cut x 34)
Mezzotint
Purchased, London, 1st Chaloner Smith sale, 1887

Porter, H. (19th century)
English School
PORTER, H. (19TH CENTURY)
ENGLISH SCHOOL

20,797
Sheep by Moonlight
28.1 x 38.2 (plate 18.5 x 26.5)
Aquatint with watercolour
Acquired by 1913

Poussin, Nicolas (1594-1665)
French School
BERTAUX, H.G. (C.1750-C.1800)
FRENCH SCHOOL *and*
ROMANET, ANTOINE LOUIS (1742-AFTER 1810)
FRENCH SCHOOL

20,725(56)
Sacrament of Holy Eucharist, (from 'Galerie du Palais Royal', Vol. 3, 1808, see App. 8, no. 20,725)
(after an oil of 1647, Duke of Sutherland loan, NGS, Edinburgh)
Published: J. Couché, also Laporte, Paris, 1808 (Printed: H. Perronneau)
50.7 x 32.2 (plate 41.8 x 28.8)
Line
Bequeathed, Judge J. Murnaghan, 1976

Poussin, Nicolas (1594-1665)
French School
DUFRAINE (19TH CENTURY)
FRENCH SCHOOL
DUPLESSI-BERTAUX, JEAN (1747-1819)
FRENCH SCHOOL *and*
NIQUET, CLAUDE (C.1770-1831)
FRENCH SCHOOL

20,201
St John baptising in the Jordan (pl. from 'Galerie du Musée de France', 1814)
(after an oil of c.1636, The Louvre, Paris)
Published: A.M. Filhol (posthumously) Paris, 1814 (Printed: Gille Fils)
16.9 x 26.8 (plate cut)
Line and etching
Purchased, Lusk, Mr de Courcy Donovan, 1971

Poussin, Nicolas (1594-1665)
French School
ERTINGER, FRANZ (1640-1710)
FRENCH SCHOOL

20,545
The Andrians
(after an oil of c.1630, The Louvre, Paris)
10.7 x 15.4 (plate cut)
Line
Presented, Mrs D. Molloy, 1981

Poussin, Nicolas (1594-1665)
French School
FERRARO, GIOVANNI FRANCESCO (19TH CENTURY)
ROMAN SCHOOL

20,757(138)
The Entombment, (from 'Collection of the Best Works of Raphael, Poussin & Domenichino and other Celebrated Artists', see App. 8, no. 20,757)
(after an oil of c.1655, NGI no. 214)
Published: G.F. Ferrero, Rome
22.6 x 32 (plate 9 x 10.8)
Etching
Provenance Unknown

Poussin, Nicolas (1594-1665)
French School
FRAGONARD, ALEXANDRE EVARISTE (1780-1850)
FRENCH SCHOOL
GIRARDET, ABRAHAM (1764-1823)
SWISS SCHOOL

20,685(13)
The Rape of the Sabine Women, (pl. from 'Musée Français - Ecole Française', see App. 8, no. 20,685)
(after an oil of c.1635, The Louvre, Paris)
Published: A. & W. Galignani, Paris, also J.O. Robinson, London (Printed: Ramboz, Paris)
61.2 x 45.3 (plate 32.1 x 43.4)
Line
Provenance Unknown

Poussin, Nicolas (1594-1665)
French School
HEATH THE ELDER, CHARLES (1785-1848)
ENGLISH SCHOOL

20,726(14)
Penance, (from 'Engravings of the Most Noble the Marquis of Stafford's collection..', Vols. 1 & 2, 1818, see App. 8, no. 20,726)
(after an oil of 1647, Duke of Sutherland loan, NGS, Edinburgh)
Published: Longman, Hurst, Rees, Orme & Brown, also J. White, also Cadell & Davies also P.W. Tomkins London, 1st November 1816 (Printed: Bensley & Co.)
40.6 x 31.3 (plate cut)
Line
Presented, Mr G.F. Mulvany, 1868

Prout, Samuel (1783-1852)
English School
ALLEN, JAMES BAYLIS (1803-1876)
ENGLISH SCHOOL

20,459
Chillon Castle, Lake Geneva, Switzerland, (previously pl. for T. Rose's 'Tourist in Switzerland', 1830)
Published: Fisher, Son & Co., London, 1836
21.3 x 27.8 (plate 15 x 22.6)
Steel Engraving
Purchased, Lusk, Mr de Courcy Donovan, 1971

Prout, Samuel (1783-1852)
English School
GOODALL, EDWARD (1795-1870)
ENGLISH SCHOOL

20,366
The Doge's Palace and Piazzetta, Venice, from the Grand Canal
Published: C. Tilt, London, 1831
28 x 38.2 (plate 19.1 x 25.4)
Line
Purchased, Lusk, Mr de Courcy Donovan, 1971

Prout, Samuel (1783-1852)
English School
PROUT, SAMUEL (1783-1852)
ENGLISH SCHOOL

20,559
A Gothic archway, a timber-framed house, a shed, and a trough, (from S. Prout's 'Elementary drawing book of landscape and buildings', undated)
Published: R. Ackermann, London, April 1821
20.2 x 25.4 (image 19.5 x 24.5)
Lithograph
Presented, Mrs D. Molloy, 1981

Prout, Samuel (1783-1852)
English School
PROUT, SAMUEL (1783-1852)
ENGLISH SCHOOL

20,560
Farmyard at Lynmouth, Devon, (from S. Prout's 'Elementary drawing book of landscapes and buildings', undated)
Published: R. Ackermann, London, April 1821
20.7 x 30.2 (image 19.2 x 28.6)
Lithograph
Presented, Mrs D. Molloy, 1981

Prout, Samuel (1783-1852)
English School
PROUT, SAMUEL (1783-1852)
ENGLISH SCHOOL

20,561
Cottage near Chagford, Devon (from S. Prout's 'Elementary drawing book of landscape and buildings', undated)
Published: R. Ackermann, London
20.3 x 31.1 (image 18.9 x 28.8)
Lithograph
Presented, Mrs D. Molloy, 1981

Prout, Samuel (1783-1852)
English School
PROUT, SAMUEL (1783-1852)
ENGLISH SCHOOL

20,562
Cottage on Dartmoor, Devon, (from S. Prout's 'Elementary drawing book of landscape and buildings', undated)
Published: R. Ackermann, London
29.4 x 20.5 (image 27.5 x 19)
Lithograph
Presented, Mrs D. Molloy, 1981

Prout, Samuel (1783-1852)
English School
PROUT, SAMUEL (1783-1852)
ENGLISH SCHOOL

20,563

Cottage at Pennycross, (from S. Prout's 'Elementary drawing book of landscapes and buildings', undated)
Published: R. Ackermann, London
29.6 x 20.5 (image 7.7 x 19.4)
Lithograph
Presented, Mrs D. Molloy, 1981

Cottages at Glastonbury, Somerset, (from S. Prout's 'Elementary drawing book of landscapes and buildings', undated)
Published: R. Ackermann, London
20.9 x 29.8 (image 19.4 x 28.3)
Lithograph
Presented, Mrs D. Molloy, 1981

Mounts Olympus and Ossa from the Plains of Thessaly, Greece, (pl. for C. Wordsworth's, 'Greece', 1839)
17.2 x 25.1 (plate cut)
Steel Engraving
Purchased, Lusk, Mr de Courcy Donovan, 1971

Prout, Samuel (1783-1852)
English School
PROUT, SAMUEL (1783-1852)
ENGLISH SCHOOL

20,564
Cottage at Ideford, Devon, (from S. Prout's 'Elementary drawing book of landscapes and buildings', undated)
Published: R. Ackermann, London
29.6 x 19.9 (image 28.2 x 18.3)
Lithograph
Presented, Mrs D. Molloy, 1981

Prout, Samuel (1783-1852)
English School
PROUT, SAMUEL (1783-1852)
ENGLISH SCHOOL

20,565

Prout, Samuel (1783-1852)
English School
PROUT, SAMUEL (1783-1852)
ENGLISH SCHOOL

20,567
Cottages, (from S. Prout's 'Elementary drawing book of landscapes and buildings', undated)
Published: R. Ackermann, London
14.6 x 22.8 (cut to image)
Lithograph
Presented, Mrs D. Molloy, 1981

Purser, William (fl.1805-1839)
English School
BENTLEY, JOSEPH CLAYTON (1804-1851)
ENGLISH SCHOOL

20,200

Pyne, James Baker (1800-1870)
English School
BRANDARD, ROBERT (1805-1862)
ENGLISH SCHOOL

20,422
Water mill on the river Lynn, Devon
Published: Simpkin & Marshall, also J.W. Stevens, London
21.5 x 27.5 (plate cut)
Steel Engraving
Purchased, Lusk, Mr de Courcy Donovan, 1971

Pyne, James Baker (1800-1870)
English School
BRANDARD, ROBERT (1805-1862)
ENGLISH SCHOOL

20,492
Swansea Harbour, S. Wales
Published: Simpkin & Marshall, also R. Brandard, (The Proprietor), London
21.1 x 26.9 (plate cut)
Steel Engraving
Purchased, Lusk, Mr de Courcy Donovan, 1971

The Vatican Loggia painted by Raphael, (frontispiece from 'Logge del Vaticano', 1802, see App. 8, no. 20,676)
INSCRIBED: A sua Eccellza: il Sig. Barone Ermano de Schubart/Cav: dell Ordine di Dannebrogue Ciamberno: di S.M. il Re de Danimarca/suo inviato Straordinario Ministro Plenipotenziario/presso S.M. il Re della due Sicilie/Intendente Generale Relazioni Comerciali della Danimarca/nei porti d'Italia/Francesco Rainaldi D.D.D.
Published: N. de Antonio, Rome, 1802
65.4 x 46.4 (plate 54.4 x 37.1)
Line and stipple
Provenance Unknown

Raphael (1483-1520)
Italian School
DUTERTRE, ANDRE (1753-1842)
FRENCH SCHOOL
BEISSON, FRANCOIS JOSEPH ETIENNE (1759-1820)
FRENCH SCHOOL

20,679(18)
The Ecstasy of St Cecilia, (from 'Musée Français, Ecole Italienne', see App. 8, no. 20,679)
(after an oil of 1514, Pinacoteca Nazionale, Bologna)
Published: A. & W. Galignani, Paris, also J. O. Robinson, London
(Printed: J. Didot L'Ainé, Paris)
61 x 45.5 (plate 48 x 34.3)
Line
Provenance Unknown

Raphael (1483-1520)
Italian School
BIANCHI, SECONDO (18TH-19TH CENTURY)
ITALIAN SCHOOL

20,703(47)
The Meeting of Solomon and the Queen of Sheba, (from 'Les Cinquante deux tableaux....', 1788, see App. 8, no. 20, 703)
(after the Vatican Loggia fresco of 1518-19)
Published: J. Scudellari, Rome, 1788
26.5 x 39.6 (plate 19.2 x 24.2)
Line
Purchased, Miss White, 1936

Raphael (1483-1520)
Italian School
DORIGNY, NICOLAS (1652-1746)
ANGLO-FRENCH SCHOOL

20,678(15)
The Charge to St Peter - Feed my Lambs, (bound with 'La Galerie du Palais Luxembourg', see App. 8, no. 20,678)
(after a tapestry cartoon of 1515, Royal Collection loan to V&A, London)
Published: N. Dorigny, London, 1719
58.8 x 82.3 (plate 51.9 x 76.2)
Line
Provenance Unknown

Raphael (1483-1520)
Italian School
DUBOSC, CLAUDE (FL.C.1711-1740)
ANGLO-FRENCH SCHOOL

11,494
The Blinding of Elymas by St Paul
(after a tapestry cartoon of 1515, Royal Collection loan to V&A, London)
Published: c.1712
37.3 x 44.4 (plate 16.2 x 43.5)
Line
Provenance Unknown

Raphael (1483-1520)
Italian School
WICAR, JEAN-BAPTISTE (1762-1834)
FRENCH SCHOOL
DUPONCHEL, CHARLES EUGENE (B.1748)
FRENCH SCHOOL

20,687(46)
The Virgin and Child with St John, (from 'Galerie de Florence et du Palais Pitti', Vol. 1, 1789, see App. 8, no. 20,687)
(after an oil of 1514, Pitti Palace, Florence)
Published: E. Lacombe, Paris, 1789
52.6 x 33.5 (plate 27.7 x 3.5)
Line
Provenance Unknown

Raphael (1483-1520)
Italian School
HUBAND, WILLCOCKS (1776-1834)
IRISH SCHOOL

11,538
Elymas the Sorcerer Struck Blind, (pl. for W. Huband's 'Critical and Familiar notices on the Art of Etching on Copper', 1810)
(after a tapestry cartoon of 1515, Royal Collection loan to V&A, London)
Issued privately by W. Huband, Dublin, c.1810
13 x 12 (plate 11.9 x 11)
Etching
Provenance Unknown

Raphael (1583-1520)
Italian School
VENDENBERG (18TH CENTURY)
FRENCH SCHOOL
ROMANET, ANTOINE LOUIS (1742/3-AFTER 1810)
FRENCH SCHOOL

10,723(14)
The Virgin and Child, 'Bridgewater Madonna', (from 'Galerie du Palais Royal', Vol. 1, 1786, see App. 8, no. 10,723)
after an oil of 1506/09, Duke of Sutherland loan, NGS, Edinburgh)
Published: J. Couché, also J. Bouilliard, Paris, 1786 (Printed: H. Perronneau)
55.5 x 33 (plate 41.8 x 28.7)
Line
Bequeathed, Judge J. Murnaghan, 1976

Raphael, Joseph (1872-1950)
American School
RAPHAEL, JOSEPH (1872-1950)
AMERICAN SCHOOL

11,449
Tree Trunk and Bust on a Pedestal
13.2 x 18.3 (image 21 x 23 approx)
Linocut
Provenance Unknown

Raphael, Joseph (1872-1950)
American School
RAPHAEL, JOSEPH (1872-1950)
AMERICAN SCHOOL

11,450
Strolling Players against a view of Cannero, Lake Maggiore, Italy, 1938
23.3 x 26 (image 20 x 32 approx)
Linocut
Provenance Unknown

Raphael, Joseph (1872-1950)
American School
RAPHAEL, JOSEPH (1872-1950)
AMERICAN SCHOOL

11,451
S. Giorgio Maggiore, Venice, from across the Grand Canal, Easter 1938
25.2 x 37.5 (image 14 x 37 approx)
Linocut
Provenance Unknown

Raphael, Joseph (1872-1950)
American School
RAPHAEL, JOSEPH (1872-1950)
AMERICAN SCHOOL

11,452
Women of Lake Maggiore, N. Italy
23.2 x 41.3 (image 15 x 36 approx)
Linocut
Provenance Unknown

Raphael, Joseph (1872-1950)
American School
RAPHAEL, JOSEPH (1872-1950)
AMERICAN SCHOOL

11,453
Sailing Boats in a Harbour
19.3 x 27 (image 19 x 24.5 approx)
Linocut
Provenance Unknown

Razé, L.L. (19th century)
Anglo-French School
RAZE, L.L. (19TH CENTURY)
ANGLO-FRENCH SCHOOL

20,566
Rustic building
17.4 x 26.3 (image 17.4 x 26.3 approx)
Lithograph
Presented, Mrs D. Molloy, 1981

Razé, L.L. (19th century)
Anglo-French School
RAZE, L.L. (19TH CENTURY)
ANGL0-FRENCH SCHOOL

20,569
A ruined castle
Dated 1861
16.5 x 25.2 (image 16.5 x 25.2 approx)
Lithograph
Presented, Mrs D. Molloy, 1981

Razé, L.L. (19th century)
Anglo-French School
RAZE, L.L. (19TH CENTURY)
ANGLO-FRENCH SCHOOL

20,588
Buildings near the Porta Maggiore, Rome, (pl. for L.L. Razé's 'Easy studies', 1869)
32.7 x 22.7 (image 32.7 x 22.7 approx)
Lithograph on toned paper
Presented, Mrs D. Molloy, 1981

Read, Catherine (1723-1778)
English School
FINLAYSON, JOHN (C.1730-C.1776)
ENGLISH SCHOOL

10,391
Maria, Countess of Coventry, wife of the 9th Earl, (née Gunning, 1733-1760), sister of Catherine and Elizabeth, daughter of James Gunning
(after a pastel of 1771, Inverary Castle, Scotland)
Published: J. Finlayson, London, 15th May 1771
51.5 x 36.3 (plate 49.5 x 35)
Mezzotint
Purchased, London, 1st Chaloner Smith sale, 1887

Read, Catherine (1723-1778)
English School
FINLAYSON, JOHN (C.1730-C.1776)
ENGLISH SCHOOL

10,394
Elizabeth, Duchess of Argyll, wife of the 5th Duke, (née Gunning, 1734-1790; later Baroness Hamilton), sister of Catherine and Maria and daughter of James Gunning
(after a pastel, Inverary Castle, Scotland)
Published: J. Finlayson, London, 10th November 1770
51 x 35.5 (plate 50.3 x 35)
Mezzotint
Acquired between 1898/1904

Read, Catherine (1723-1778)
English School
HOUSTON, RICHARD (1721-1775)
IRISH SCHOOL

11,064
Harriet Powell, (d.1779), Actress, Singer and Courtesan, later Countess of Seaforth, wife of the 1st Earl
(after a pastel of 1760s)
Published: R. Sayer, London, 1st October 1769
51 x 35.7 (plate 50.2 x 35)
Mezzotint
Purchased, London, 1st Chaloner Smith sale, 1887

Rembrandt (1606-1669)
Dutch School
EARLOM, RICHARD (1743-1822)
ENGLISH SCHOOL

10,171
'Rembrandt's Mother' - a seated old woman with a veil
(after an oil of 1650s, Pushkin Museum, Moscow)
Published: J. Boydell, London
40.7 x 32.3 (plate 40 x 30.5)
Mezzotint
Bequeathed, V. Lawless, 4th Baron Cloncurry, 1929

Rembrandt (1606-1669)
Dutch School
ENGLISH SCHOOL (1827)

20,708(19)
Landscape with the Rest on the Flight into Egypt, (from 'Gems of Ancient Art', 1827, see App. 8, no. 20,708)
(after an oil of 1647, NGI no. 215)
Published: Howlett & Brimmer, London, 1827
31.8 x 24.7 (plate 16.4 x 21)
Aquatint
Bequeathed, Judge J. Murnaghan, 1976

Rembrandt (1606-1669)
Dutch School
WALKER, ANTHONY (1726-1765)
ENGLISH SCHOOL

11,506
The Angel departing from Tobit and his Family
(after an oil of 1637, The Louvre, Paris)
INSCRIBED: From a Picture painted by Rembrandt in the Collection of Nathaniel Hone, Esqr./To whom this Plate is Dedicated; by his much obliged & most humble servant,/J. Boydell
Published: J. Boydell, London, 1st May 1765
51.6 x 38.4 (plate 15.4 x 38.1)
Line
Bequeathed, Miss E. Hone, 1912

Rembrandt (1606-1669)
Dutch School
WOOD, JOHN (1720-1780)
ENGLISH SCHOOL

11,427
Landscape with Rest on the Flight into Egypt
(after an oil of 1647, NGI no. 215)
Published: October 1752
44.5 x 57.2 (plate 36.7 x 48.6)
Line
Presented, Mr J.C. Robinson, Surveyor of the Queen's pictures, 1883

After **Rembrandt (1606-1669)**
Dutch School
GROGAN, NATHANIEL (C.1740-1807)
IRISH SCHOOL

10,788

So-called Portrait of Catherine, Countess of Desmond, (née Fitzgerald c.1510-1604), 2nd wife of 12th Earl, (in fact an old woman, possibly Rembrandt's Mother, 1589-1640)
(after a copy of a lost oil, c.1629, Royal Collection, Windsor Castle)
INSCRIBED: *From an Original Family Picture of the same size/Painted on Board, in the possession of/The Right Honourable Maurice Fitz-Gerald, Knight of Kerry &c. &c./To whom this plate is most respectfully dedicated by his very obedient/and much obliged humble servant -/Henry Pelham.*
Published: H. Pelham, also E. Evans, London, 4th June 1806
44.5 x 31 (plate 36.8 x 23.7)
Aquatint
Purchased, London, Mr G. Lausen, 1895

Reni, Guido (1575-1642)
Bolognese School
ROSASPINA, FRANCESCO (1762-1841)
BOLOGNESE SCHOOL

20,682(62)
The Virgin and Child in Glory with the Protector Saints of Bologna, (from 'La Pinacoteca della Pontificia Accademia Delle belle Arti in Bologna', 1830, see App. 8, no. 20,682)
(after a painted silk banner of c.1630, Pinacoteca Nazionale, Bologna)
Published: F. Rosaspina, Bologna, 1830
46 x 29.8 (plate 36 x 23)
Line
Provenance Unknown

Retzsch, Friedrich Moritz August (1779-1857)
German School
RETZSCH, FRIEDRICH MORITZ AUGUST (1779-1857)
GERMAN SCHOOL

20,730(6)
Love Reposing, (from Retzsch's 'Fancies', 1834, see App. 8, no. 20,730)
Published: Saunders & Otley, London, May 1834
23 x 28.2 (plate 13 x 19.5)
Etching
Provenance Unknown

Reynolds, Joshua (1723-1792)
English School
BALDREY, JOSHUA KIRBY (1754-1828)
ENGLISH SCHOOL

11,047
Francis Rawdon Hastings, Baron Rawdon, (1754-1826), later 2nd Earl of Moira and 1st Marquess of Hastings
(after an undated oil)
Published: ?J.K. Baldrey, London, 1st June 1784
28.3 x 20.6 (plate 26 x 19)
Stipple
Presented, Mr R.B. Armstrong, 1911

Reynolds, Joshua (1723-1792)
English School
BARTOLOZZI, FRANCESO (1727-1815)
ANGLO-ITALIAN SCHOOL

10,313
Jane, Countess of Harrington, (née Fleming, 1755-1824), with her two eldest sons, Viscount Charles Petersham, (1780-1851), later 4th Earl of Harrington, and the Hon, Lincoln Edwin Robert Stanhope, (1781-1840)
(after an oil of 1786/87)
Unlettered Proof
Published: F. Bartolozzi, London, 1789
29.4 x 23.4 (plate cut)
Stipple
Milltown Gift, 1902

Reynolds, Joshua (1723-1792)
English School
BARTOLOZZI, FRANCESO (1727-1815)
ANGLO-ITALIAN SCHOOL

10,314

Jane, Countess of Harrington, (née Fleming, 1755-1824), with her two eldest sons, Viscount Charles Petersham, (1780-1851), later 4th Earl Harrington and the Hon, Lincoln Edwin Robert Stanhope, (1781-1840)
(after an oil of 1786/87)
Published: F. Bartolozzi, London, 1789
28.6 x 22.3 (plate cut)
Stipple
Milltown Gift, 1902

Reynolds, Joshua (1723-1792)
English School
BARTOLOZZI, FRANCESCO (1727-1815)
ANGLO-ITALIAN SCHOOL

10,315
Jane, Countess of Harrington, (née Fleming, 1755-1824), with her two eldest sons, Viscount Charles Petersham, (1780-1851), later 4th Earl of Harrington, and the Hon. Lincoln Edwin Robert Stanhope, (1781-1840)
(after an oil of 1786/87)
Published: F. Bartolozzi, London, 1789
35.6 x 28.5 (plate cut)
Coloured Stipple
Milltown Gift, 1902

Reynolds, Joshua (1723-1792)
English School
BROOKSHAW, RICHARD (1736-1804)
ENGLISH SCHOOL

11,097
Mrs William Bastard, (née Anne Worsley, d.1765)
(after an oil of 1755-57)
16.5 x 12.71.5) (plate 15.1 x 11.5)
Mezzotint
Acquired between 1913/14

Reynolds, Joshua (1723-1792)
English School
BROOKSHAW, RICHARD (1736-1804)
ENGLISH SCHOOL

11,098
Jacob Bouverie, Viscount Folkestone, (1750-1828), later 2nd Earl of Radnor
(after an oil of 1757)
Published: Ryland & Bryer, London
15.4 x 12 (plate 15.3 x 11.5)
Mezzotint
Provenance Unknown

Reynolds, Joshua (1723-1792)
English School
BROOKSHAW, RICHARD (1736-1804)
ENGLISH SCHOOL

11,201
Elizabeth and Sarah Crewe, (later Mrs John Hinchliff and Mrs Obediah Langton), sisters of future 1st Baron Crewe
(after an oil of 1766-67)
Published: J. Bowles, London
15.2 x 11.7 (plate 14.9 x 11.4)
Mezzotint
Acquired between 1913/14

Reynolds, Joshua (1723-1792)
English School
DEAN, JOHN (C.1750-1798)
ENGLISH SCHOOL

10,090
Thomas Leland, (1722-1785), Historian, Fellow of Trinity College, Dublin and Vicar of St Ann's Church, Dawson Street, Dublin
(after an oil of 1776)
Unlettered Proof
Published: J. Dean, London, 16th May 1777
37.3 x 35.4 (plate 27.3 x 25.1)
Mezzotint
Purchased, Dublin,
Mr J.V. McAlpine, 1906

Reynolds, Joshua (1723-1792)
English School
DEAN, JOHN (C.1750-1798)
ENGLISH SCHOOL

10,377
Lady Gertrude FitzPatrick, (c.1776-1841), daughter of the 2nd Earl of Upper Ossory, and sister of Lady Anne FitzPatrick
(after an oil of 1779, Columbus Gallery of Fine Arts, Ohio)
Published: W. Dickinson, London, 1st February 1782
50 x 37 (plate 45.5 x 32.7)
Mezzotint
Purchased, London, 1st Chaloner Smith sale, 1887

Reynolds, Joshua (1723-1792)
English School
DEAN, JOHN (C.1750-1798)
ENGLISH SCHOOL

10,911
Thomas Leland, (1722-1785), Historian
(after an oil of 1776)
Published: J. Dean, London, 16th May 1777
37.8 x 27.4 (plate 35.6 x 25.5)
Mezzotint
Purchased, Dublin, Mr A. Roth, 1896

Reynolds, Joshua (1723-1792)
English School
DICKINSON, WILLIAM (1746-1823)
ENGLISH SCHOOL

10,086
Thomas Percy, (1729-1811), Antiquarian, later Dean of Carlisle and Bishop of Dromore
(after an oil of 1773)
Published: London, 2nd February 1775
39.6 x 29.5 (plate 37.5 x 27.8)
Mezzotint
Purchased, London, 1st Chaloner Smith sale, 1887

Reynolds, Joshua (1723-1792)
English School
DICKINSON, WILLIAM (1746-1823)
ENGLISH SCHOOL

10,346
Emilia Olivia, Duchess of Leinster, (née Usher St George, 1759-1798), wife of the 2nd Duke of Leinster
(after an oil of 1779, NGI no. 4064)
Published: Dickinson & Watson, London, 12th November 1780
38.2 x 27.6 (plate 37.8 x 27.3)
Mezzotint
Purchased, London, 1st Chaloner Smith sale, 1887

Reynolds, Joshua (1723-1792)
English School
DICKINSON, WILLIAM (1746-1823)
ENGLISH SCHOOL

10,381
Mrs Richard Brinsley Sheridan, (née Elizabeth Ann Linley, 1754-1792), Singer, as St Cecilia

(after an oil of 1775, Waddesdon Manor, Buckinghamshire)
Published: W. Dickinson, also T. Watson, London, 21st May 1776
52.1 x 41.5 (plate 47 x 36)
Mezzotint with watercolour
Provenance Unknown

Reynolds, Joshua (1723-1792)
English School
DICKINSON, WILLIAM (1746-1823)
ENGLISH SCHOOL

10,407
Diana, Vicountess Crosbie, (1756-1814), (née Sackville-Germain), wife of Viscount Crosbie, later 2nd Earl of Glandore
(after an oil of 1781)
Published: London, 20th September 1779
54.2 x 38 (plate cut)
Mezzotint
Purchased, London, 1st Chaloner Smith sale, 1887

Reynolds, Joshua (1723-1792)
English School
DICKINSON, WILLIAM (1746-1823)
ENGLISH SCHOOL

10,490
Charles Manners, 4th Duke of Rutland, (1754-1787), Lord Lieutenant of Ireland
(after an oil of c.1784)
Published: W. Dickinson, London, 20th July 1791
65.3 x 39 (plate 64.9 x 38.2)
Mezzotint
Purchased, London, 1st Chaloner Smith sale, 1887

Reynolds, Joshua (1723-1792)
English School
DICKINSON, WILLIAM (1746-1823)
ENGLISH SCHOOL

11,028

Lady Mary Spencer, (née Beauclerk, 1743-1812), daughter of Lord Vere and wife of Lord Charles Spencer, (2nd son of 3rd Duke of Marlborough)
(after an oil of c.1775)
Published: W. Dickinson, at Mrs Sledges, London, 10th January 1776
50.8 x 35.5 (plate 50.7 x 35.4)
Mezzotint
Purchased, London, 1st Chaloner Smith sale, 1887

Reynolds, Joshua (1723-1792)
English School
DICKINSON, WILLIAM (1746-1823)
ENGLISH SCHOOL *and*
WATSON, THOMAS (1743-1781)
ENGLISH SCHOOL

10,853
George III, King of England, (1738-1820)
(after an oil of 1770-79, RA Collection, London)
Published: W. Dickinson & T. Watson, London, 25th April 1781
81.1 x 51 (plate cut)
Mezzotint
Purchased, London, 1st Chaloner Smith sale, 1887

Reynolds, Joshua (1723-1792)
English School
DIXON, JOHN (C.1740-1811)
IRISH SCHOOL

10,395
Lady Mary O'Brien, (1755-1831), daughter of future 1st Marquess of Thomond, later (suo jure) Countess of Orkney
(after an oil of 1773)
Published: W. W. Ryland, London, 29th September 1774
51.5 x 37 (plate 50.5 x 35)
Mezzotint
Purchased, London, 1st Chaloner Smith sale, 1887

Reynolds, Joshua (1723-1792)
English School
DIXON, JOHN (C.1740-1811)
IRISH SCHOOL

10,467
William Robert Fitzgerald, 2nd Duke of Leinster, (1749-1804)
(after an oil, RA 1775)
Published: J. Dixon, London, 25th April 1775
Mezzotint
Acquired by 1879

Reynolds, Joshua (1723-1792)
English School
DUNKARTON, ROBERT (1744-C.1811)
ENGLISH SCHOOL

10,484
James Hewitt, 1st Viscount Lifford, (1709-1789), Lord Chancellor of Ireland
(after an oil, RA 1789)
Published: T. Macklin, London, 1st January 1790
67 x 49.3 (plate 63.7 x 43.3)
Mezzotint
Purchased, London, 1st Chaloner Smith sale, 1887

Reynolds, Joshua (1723-1792)
English School
EDWARDS, WILLIAM CAMDEN (1777-1855)
ENGLISH SCHOOL

10,239
Self-Portrait
(after an oil of 1788, Royal Collection, Windsor Castle)
8.5 x 6.3 (plate cut)
Line
Provenance Unknown

Reynolds, Joshua (1723-1792)
English School
ENGLISH SCHOOL (1760S)

10,577
Nelly O'Brien, (d.1768), Courtesan
(after an oil, SA 1763; Wallace Collection, London)
Published: J. Bowles, London, 1760s
17.2 x 13.8 (plate 15.2 x 11.2)
Mezzotint
Provenance Unknown

Reynolds, Joshua (1723-1792)
English School
ENGLISH SCHOOL (C.1770)

11,140
Lady Charlotte FitzWilliam, (1746-1833), daughter of 1st Earl FitzWilliam
(after an oil of 1754, FitzWilliam family collection)
Published: R. Sayer, London, c.1770
35 x 11.5 (plate cut)
Mezzotint
Purchased, London, 1st Chaloner Smith sale, 1887

Reynolds, Joshua (1723-1792)
English School
ENGLISH SCHOOL (LATE 18TH CENTURY)

10,664

Edmond Malone, (1741-1812), Critic and Editor of Shakespeare, also of Reynolds' Literary Works
(after an oil of 1774-76)
20.1 x 13.3 (plate 15.5 x 11)
Stipple
Acquired by 1913

Reynolds, Joshua (1723-1792)
English School
ENGLISH SCHOOL (1811)

11,330
Dr Thomas Percy, (1729-1811), Dean of Carlisle and Bishop of Dromore, Antiquarian
(after an oil of 1773)
INSCRIBED: *Engraved from an Original Drawing in the possession of the late William Seward Esqr.*
Published: J. Asperne, London, 1st December 1811
20.5 x 13 (plate 16.5 x 11.1)
Stipple
Acquired by 1913

Reynolds, Joshua (1723-1792)
English School
FABER THE YOUNGER, JOHN (?1684-1756)
ENGLISH SCHOOL

10,176
William Cavendish, 3rd Duke of Devonshire, (1698-1755), former Lord Lieutenant of Ireland
(after an oil of 1753, Chatsworth House, Derbyshire)
Published: J. Faber the Younger, London, 1755
35 x 24.6 (plate cut)
Mezzotint
Purchased, London, 1st Chaloner Smith sale, 1887

Reynolds, Joshua (1723-1792)
English School
FISHER, EDWARD (1722-C.1785)
IRISH SCHOOL

10,357

Catherine Maria (Kitty) Fisher, (d.1767), Courtesan, Wit and Beauty
(after an oil of 1759, Petworth House, Sussex)
Published: J. Ewart, also R. Sayer, London, 17th July 1759
44.5 x 29.7 (plate 33.2 x 22.6)
Mezzotint
Provenance Unknown

Reynolds, Joshua (1723-1792)
English School
FISHER, EDWARD (1722-C.1785)
IRISH SCHOOL

10,363
Mrs Cyrus Trapaud, (née Catherine Plaistow, 1730-1803), Beauty
(after an oil of 1761)
Published: E. Fisher, London, 1762, price ls 6d
35 x 25 (plate 33 x 23.2)
Mezzotint
Purchased, London, 1st Chaloner Smith sale, 1887

Reynolds, Joshua (1723-1792)
English School
FISHER, EDWARD (1722-C.1785)
IRISH SCHOOL

10,545
Lawrence Sterne, (1713-1768), Author and Divine
Published: ?E. Fisher, London, 1761
(after an oil of 1760, NPG, London)
38.2 x 29.8 (plate 37.8 x 27.4)
Mezzotint
Acquired by 1879

Reynolds, Joshua (1723-1792)
English School
GREEN, VALENTINE (1739-1813)
ENGLISH SCHOOL

10,400
Jane, Countess of Harrington, (née Fleming, 1754/55-1824), wife of the 3rd Earl of Harrington
(after an oil of 1775, when Miss Fleming)
Published: V. Green, London, 1780
61.3 x 40.5 (plate 60 x 39)
Mezzotint
Milltown Gift, 1902

Reynolds, Joshua (1723-1792)
English School
GROZER, JOSEPH (C.1755-C.1799)
ENGLISH SCHOOL

10,252
William Wentworth, 2nd Earl FitzWilliam, (1748-1833), later Lord Lieutenant of Ireland
(after an oil of 1785)
Published: W. Austin, London, 31st March 1786
31 x 29.5 (plate 39.1 x 27.7)
Mezzotint
Purchased, Dublin, Mrs Noseda, 1886

Reynolds, Joshua (1723-1792)
English School
GROZER, JOSEPH (C.1755-C.1799)
ENGLISH SCHOOL

10,253

Frederick Ponsonby, Viscount Duncannon, (1758-1844), later 3rd Earl of Bessborough
(after an oil of 1785, Althorp, Northants)
Published: W. Austin, London, 31st March 1786
51.8 x 39.2 (plate 39 x 27.5)
Mezzotint
Purchased, Dublin, Mr R. Langton Douglas, 1906

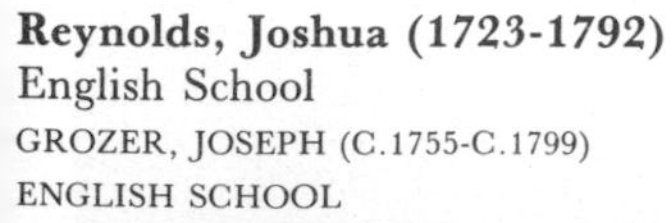

Reynolds, Joshua (1723-1792)
English School
GROZER, JOSEPH (C.1755-C.1799)
ENGLISH SCHOOL

10,390
Henrietta Frances, Viscountess Duncannon, (née Spencer, 1761-1821), wife of Viscount Duncannon, the future 3rd Earl of Bessborough
(after an oil of 1785, Althorp, Northants)
Published: W. Austin, London, 21st December 1785
41 x 29 (plate 39.2 x 27.7)
Mezzotint
Purchased, London, 1st Chaloner Smith sale, 1887

Reynolds, Joshua (1723-1792)
English School
GROZER, JOSEPH (C.1755-C.1799)
ENGLISH SCHOOL

10,762
John Crawford, M.P., (fl.1768-1814), ally of Charles James Fox
(after an oil of 1789)
39.5 x 29.3 (plate 37.5 x 27.7)
Mezzotint
Purchased, London, 1st Chaloner Smith sale, 1887

Reynolds, Joshua (1723-1792)
English School
GROZER, JOSEPH (C.1755-C.1799)
ENGLISH SCHOOL

10,768
Lord John Cavendish, (1732-1796), son of the 3rd Duke of Devonshire, Chancellor of the Exchequer
(after an oil of 1767-68)
Published: W. Austin, London, 31st March 1786
40.5 x 29 (plate 39 x 27.5)
Mezzotint
Purchased, London, 1st Chaloner Smtih sale, 1887

Reynolds, Joshua (1723-1792)
English School
HALL, JOHN (1739-1797)
ENGLISH SCHOOL

10,460
Richard Brinsley Sheridan, M.P., (1751-1816), Dramatist and Orator
(after an oil of 1788-89)
Published: J. Hall, London, 30th April 1791 (Printed: C. W. Richards)
57.2 x 42 (plate 51.9 x 38)
Line
Presumed purchased, Dublin, Jones Saleroom, 1879

Reynolds, Joshua (1723-1792)
English School
HARDY, THOMAS (FL.1792-1802)
ENGLISH SCHOOL

10,796
John Frederick Sackville, 3rd Duke of Dorset, (1745-1799), Diplomat
(after an oil of 1769, Knole House, Kent)

INSCRIBED: This Plate, after a Picture painted by Sir J. Reynolds during his Grace's Embassy/at the Court of France, is by Permission respectfully Inscribed to her Grace the/Duchess of Dorset, by her Grace's very obedient Servt./John Bridgman.
Published: J. Ginger, London, 9th April 1799
39.8 x 29 (plate 36 x 25.7)
Mezzotint
Purchased, London, 1st Chaloner Smith sale, 1887

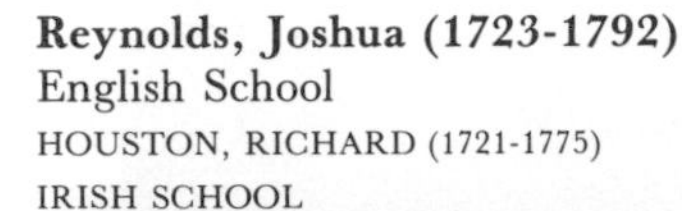

Reynolds, Joshua (1723-1792)
English School
HOUSTON, RICHARD (1721-1775)
IRISH SCHOOL

10,410
Richard Robinson, (1709-1794), P. Bishop of Kildare, later Archbishop of Armagh and 1st Baron Rokeby
(after an oil of 1761-63, Christchurch College Hall, Oxford)
Published: C. Bowles, also G. Woodfall, London, 1764
47.5 x 35.5 (plate 39.2 x 28)
Mezzotint
Acquired between 1898/1904

Reynolds, Joshua (1723-1792)
English School
HOUSTON, RICHARD (1721-1775)
IRISH SCHOOL

10,542
Princess Augusta, (1737-1813), sister of King George III, later Duchess of Brunswick
(after an oil of 1763)
Published: J. Bowles, also C. Bowles, London
17 x 12 (plate 15.3 x 11.5)
Mezzotint
Acquired by 1903

Reynolds, Joshua (1723-1792)
English School
HOUSTON, RICHARD (1721-1775)
IRISH SCHOOL

11,063
Harriet Powell, (d.1779), Actress and Singer, later Countess of Seaforth, as Leonara in I. Bickerstaffe's 'The Padlock'
(after an oil of 1769)
Published: R. Sayer, London, 1st May 1771
54 x 39 (plate 50.5 x 35.5)
Mezzotint
Purchased, London, 1st Chaloner Smith sale, 1887

Reynolds, Joshua (1723-1792)
English School
JONES, JOHN (C.1745-1797)
ENGLISH SCHOOL

10,089
Charles Bingham, 1st Baron of Lucan, (1735-1799), later 1st Earl of Lucan
(after an oil of 1780, Althorp, Northants)
Published: J. Jones, London, 1st December 1787
38.3 x 28 (plate 37.9 x 27.4)
Mezzotint
Acquired between 1898/1904

Reynolds, Joshua (1723-1792)
English School
JONES, JOHN (C.1745-1797)
ENGLISH SCHOOL

10,503

Francis Rawdon, Baron Rawdon, (1754-1825), later 2nd Earl of Moira and 1st Marquess of Hastings, as a Colonel and A.D.C. to King George III
(after an oil of 1789-90, Royal Collection, Buckingham Palace)
Published: J. Jones, London, 1792
63.5 x 39.7 (plate cut)
Mezzotint
Acquired between 1879/90

Reynolds, Joshua (1723-1792)
English School
JONES, JOHN (C.1745-1797)
ENGLISH SCHOOL

10,946
Francis Rawdon, 2nd Earl of Moira, (1754-1826), later 1st Marquess of Hastings
(after an oil of c.1789)
Published: J. Nichols, London, 1st January 1815
39.6 x 25.7 (plate 38 x cut)
Stipple
Purchased, Dublin,
Mr J.V. McAlpine, 1901

Reynolds, Joshua (1723-1792)
English School
JOSEY, RICHARD (1840/41-1906)
ENGLISH SCHOOL

10,903
Emelia Mary, Duchess of Leinster, (née Lennox, 1731-1814), wife of the 1st Duke of Leinster
(after an oil of 1775)
Published: H. Graves & Co., London, 1st August 1879
33.7 x 27 (plate 14 x 12)
Mezzotint
Presented, Lord Frederick FitzGerald, 1899

Reynolds, Joshua (1723-1792)
English School
KNIGHT, CHARLES (1743-C.1826)
ENGLISH SCHOOL

10,662
Edmond Malone, (1741-1812), Critic and Editor of Shakespeare, (pl. for S. Harding's 'Shakespeare Illustrated', 1789-93)
(after an oil of 1778, NPG, London)
Published: E. Harding, London, 30th July 1791
24.5 x 15.5 (plate 18.8 x 13.7)
Stipple
Purchased, Dublin,
Mr J.V. McAlpine, 1896

Reynolds, Joshua (1723-1792)
English School
KNIGHT, CHARLES (1743-C.1826)
ENGLISH SCHOOL

10,663
Edmond Malone, (1741-1812), Critic and Editor of Shakespeare, (pl. for S. Harding's 'Shakespeare Illustrated', 1789-93), (another copy)
(after an oil of 1778, NPG, London)
Published: E. Harding, London, 30th July 1791
28.6 x 16.4 (plate 18.8 x 13.7)
Stipple
Purchased, Dublin,
Mr J.V. McAlpine, 1896

Reynolds, Joshua (1723-1792)
English School
McARDELL, JAMES (1728/29-1765)
IRISH SCHOOL

Mr (later Sir) Richard Steele, M.P., (1672-1729), Playwright and Publisher
(after an oil of 1712, NPG, London)
Published: J. Smith, London, 1713
34.6 x 25.1 (plate 34.5 x 25)
Mezzotint
Presumed purchased, Dublin, Jones saleroom, 1879

Richmond, George (1809-1896)
English School
ADLARD, HENRY (FL.1825-1869)
ENGLISH SCHOOL

10,631
John Jebb, P. Bishop of Limerick, also of Ardfert and Aghadoe, (1775-1833), (frontispiece for C. Forster's 'Life of Bishop Jebb', 1836)
Published: J. Duncan, London, 1st April 1836
22 x 13.8 (plate cut)
Stipple
Acquired between 1913/14

Richmond, George (1809-1896)
English School
ARTLETT, RICHARD AUGUSTUS (1807-1873)
ENGLISH SCHOOL

10,155
Mr (later Sir) James Emerson Tennent, M.P., (1803-1869), (pl. for H.T. Ryall's 'Eminent Conservative Statesmen' 1836)
Published: H.J. Ryall, also J. Fraser, also F.C. Moon, London, 1836
(Printed: Wilkinson & Dawe)
40.6 x 31 (plate 32 x 25.3)
Stipple
Acquired, between 1898/1904

Richmond, George (1809-1896)
English School
HOLL, FRANCIS (1815-1884)
ENGLISH SCHOOL

10,425
George William Frederick Howard, 7th Earl of Carlisle, (1802-1864), Lord Lieutenant of Ireland
Published: not before 1855
49.5 x 40.6 (plate cut)
Stipple and line
Acquired by 1913

Richmond, William Blake (1842-1874)
English School
MILLER, JOHN DOUGLAS (1860-1903)
ENGLISH SCHOOL

10,188
Lord Frederick Charles Cavendish, (1836-1882), Chief Secretary for Ireland, murdered in Phoenix Park
(after an oil, RA 1874)
Published: H. Graves, London, 15th August 1883
45.7 x 35.5 (plate 49.7 x 31.5)
Mezzotint
Presented, Lady Cavendish, the sitter's widow, 1899

Rigaud, Hyacinthe (1659-1743)
French School
GUIBERT, FRANCOIS (FL.1786-1808)
FRENCH SCHOOL

20,725(76)
Charlotte Elizabeth de Baviere, Duchess of Orléans, (from 'Galerie du Palais Royal', Vol. 2, 1808, see App. 8, no. 20,725)
Published: J. Couché, also Laporte, Paris, 1808 (Printed: H. Perronneau)
50.7 x 32.2 (plate 41.8 x 28.8)
Line
Bequeathed, Judge J. Murnaghan, 1976

Rising, John (1753-1817)
English School
HINTON, W. (18TH CENTURY)
ENGLISH SCHOOL

11,262
Arthur Young, (1741-1820), Agriculturist and Traveller, (pl. for 'European Magazine', August 1795)
Published: J. Sewell, London, 23rd July 1795
21 x 13.1

Stipple
Purchased, Dublin, Mr P. Traynor, 1898

Roberts, David (1796-1864)
Scottish School
DAY, WILLIAM (1797-1845)
ENGLISH SCHOOL *and*
HAGHE, LOUIS (1806-1885)
ANGLO-BELGIAN SCHOOL

20,149
Encampment of Pilgrims at Jericho, 1st April 1839
INSCRIBED: Specimen of the vignette illustrations of The Holy Land , presented with the 'Art Union Monthly Journal'
Published: F.G. Moon, London
24.2 x 30 (image 23.5 x 30)
Lithograph
Purchased, Lusk, Mr de Courcy Donovan, 1971

Roberts, David (1796-1864)
Scottish School
FINDEN, EDWARD FRANCIS (1791-1857)
ENGLISH SCHOOL

20,272
Caerlaverock Castle, near Dumfries, Scotland, (cf. W. Scott's novel 'Guy Mannering')
Published: C. Tilt, London, August 1830
17 x 23.3 (plate cut)
Steel Engraving
Purchased, Lusk, Mr de Courcy Donovan, 1971

Roberts, David (1796-1864)
Scottish School
FREEBAIRN, ALFRED ROBERT (1794-1866)
SCOTTISH SCHOOL

20,371
St Vulfran's Church, Abbeville, across the River Somme, N. France
(after an oil, SA 1828)
Published: Whittaker & Co., London, also G. Smith, Liverpool
16.1 x 10 (plate cut)
Steel Engraving
Purchased, Lusk, Mr de Courcy Donovan, 1971

Roberts, David (1796-1864)
Scottish School
LE PETIT, WILLIAM A. (FL.1829-1857)
ENGLISH SCHOOL

20,443

Kelso Abbey, Scotland
Published: Simpkin & Marshall; also J.W. Stevens, London, 1st May 1834
27.8 x 22.6 (plate cut)
Steel Engraving
Purchased, Lusk Mr de Courcy Donovan, 1971

Roberts, Thomas (1748-1778)
Irish School
MILTON, THOMAS (1743-1827)
ENGLISH SCHOOL

20,277
Beau Parc and the River Boyne, Co. Meath, (pl. for T. Milton's 'The Seats and Demesnes of the Nobility and Gentry in Ireland', 1783-93)
(after an oil of c.1773, Beau-Parc, Co. Meath)
INSCRIBED: Most humbly Inscribed to Charles Lambart Esq. by Thos Milton
Published: J. Walter, London, for the author T. Milton in Dublin, 1st March 1785
19.1 x 25.2 (plate 15.5 x 20.2)
Line
Purchased, Lusk, Mr de Courcy Donovan, 1971

Roberts, Thomas (1748-1778)
Irish School
MILTON, THOMAS (1743-1827)
ENGLISH SCHOOL

20,295
The Weir in Lucan House Demesne, Co. Dublin, (previously pl. for T. Milton's 'The Seats and Demesnes of the Nobility and Gentry in Ireland', 1783-93)
(after an oil of c.1770, NGI no. 4465)
Published: W. Marshall, London, 1st July 1831
25 x 34.8 (plate 15.7 x 20)
Steel Engraving
Purchased, Lusk, Mr de Courcy Donovan, 1971

Roberts, Thomas Sautell (1760-1826)
Irish School
ALKEN, SAMUEL (FL.1780-1798)
ENGLISH SCHOOL

20,838(1)
East View of the City of Waterford, (from bound copy of T.S. Roberts's 'Views in the South of Ireland', issued in parts, 1795-99)
Published: T.S. Roberts, London, 10th December 1795
49.2 x 70.2 (plate 37.4 x 48.0)
Aquatint and etching
Purchased, London, Mr A. Thompson, 1986

Roberts, Thomas Sautell (1760-1826)
Irish School
ALKEN, SAMUEL (FL.1780-1798)
ENGLISH SCHOOL

20,838(2)
Lismore Castle, Co. Waterford, (from bound copy of T.S. Roberts's 'Views in the South of Ireland', issued in parts, 1795-99)
Published: T.S. Roberts, London, 10th December 1795
49.2 x 69.7 (plate 37.5 x 48.1)
Aquatint and etching
Purchased, London, Mr A. Thompson, 1896

Roberts, Thomas Sautell (1760-1826)
Irish School
EDY, JOHN WILLIAM (FL.1780-1798)
ENGLISH SCHOOL

20,838(3)
West view of the City of Waterford, (from bound copy of T.S. Roberts's 'Views in the south of Ireland', issued in parts, 1795-99)
Published: T.S. Roberts, London, 10th December 1795
49.0 x 70.2 (plate 35.1 x 46.5)
Aquatint and etching
Purchased, London, Mr A. Thompson, 1986

Roberts, Thomas Sautell (1760-1826)
Irish School
ALKEN, SAMUEL (FL.1780-1798)
ENGLISH SCHOOL

20,838(4)

Dunbrody Abbey, Co. Wexford, (from bound copy of T.S. Roberts's 'Views in the south of Ireland', issued in parts, 1795-99)
Published: T.S. Roberts, London, 1st August 1796
49.2 x 70.2 (plate 37.1 x 47.6)
Aquatint and etching
Purchased, London, Mr A. Thompson, 1986

Roberts, Thomas Sautell (1760-1826)
Irish School
EDY, JOHN WILLIAM (FL.1780-1820)
ENGLISH SCHOOL

0,838(5)
arrick Castle, Co. Tipperary, by the river uir, (from bound copy of T.S. Roberts's Views in the south of Ireland', issued in arts, 1795-99)
ublished: T.S. Roberts, London, 1st ugust 1796
9.3 x 69.8 (plate 35.4 x 46.8)
quatint and etching
urchased, London, Mr A. hompson, 1986

oberts, Thomas Sautell 1760-1826)
rish School
DY, JOHN WILLIAM (FL.1780-1798)
NGLISH SCHOOL

0,838(6)

The Entrance to Waterford Harbour, (from bound copy of T.S. Roberts's 'Views in the south of Ireland', issued in parts, 1795-99)
Published: T.S. Roberts, London, 1st August 1796
49.3 x 69.7 (plate 35.8 x 47.3)
Aquatint and etching
Purchased, London, Mr A. Thompson, 1986

Roberts, Thomas Sautell (1760-1826)
Irish School
EDY, JOHN WILLIAM (FL.1780-1798)
ENGLISH SCHOOL

20,838(7)
Blackrock Castle and the river Lee, Co. Cork, (from bound copy of T.S. Roberts's 'Views in the south of Ireland', issued in parts, 1795-99)
Published: T.S. Roberts, London, 1st August 1796
49.4 x 69.8 (plate 35.5 x 46.5)
Aquatint and etching
Purchased, London, Mr A. Thompson, 1986

Roberts, Thomas Sautell (1760-1826)
Irish School
ALKEN, SAMUEL (FL.1780-1798)
ENGLISH SCHOOL

20,838(8)

Blarney Castle, Co. Cork, (from bound copy of T.S. Roberts's 'Views in the south of Ireland', issued in parts, 1795-99)
Published: T.S. Roberts, London, 1st August 1796
49.1 x 69.8 (plate 37.2 x 47.6)
Aquatint and etching
Purchased, London, Mr A. Thompson, 1986

Roberts, Thomas Sautell (1760-1826)
Irish School
ALKEN, SAMUEL (FL.1780-1798)
ENGLISH SCHOOL

20,838(9)
Lower Glanmire on the river Glashaboy, Co. Cork, (from bound copy of T.S. Roberts's 'Views in the south of Ireland', issued in parts, 1795-99)
Published: T.S. Roberts, London, 1st August 1796
49.0 x 69.6 (plate 37.5 x 48.1)
Aquatint and etching
Purchased, London, Mr A. Thompson, 1986

Roberts, Thomas Sautell (1760-1826)
Irish School
ALKEN, SAMUEL (FL.1780-1798
ENGLISH SCHOOL

20,838(10)

City of Cork from the West, (from bound copy of T.S. Roberts's 'Views in the South of Ireland', issued in parts, 1795-99)
Published: T.S. Roberts, London, 1st July 1799
49.1 x 70.0 (plate 38.4 x 49.4)
Aquatint and etching
Purchased, London, Mr A. Thompson, 1986

Roberts, Thomas Sautell (1760-1826)
Irish School
ALKEN, SAMUEL (FL.1780-1798)
ENGLISH SCHOOL

20,838(11)
Eden Vale, Co. Wexford, (from bound copy of T.S. Roberts's 'Views in the south of Ireland', issued in parts, 1795-99)
Published: T.S. Roberts, London, 1st July 1799
49.8 x 70.1 (plate 37.9 x 48.0)
Aquatint and etching
Purchased, London, Mr A. Thompson, 1986

Roberts, Thomas Sautell (1760-1826)
Irish School
ALKEN, SAMUEL (FL.1780-1798)
ENGLISH SCHOOL

20,838(12)

Dromana, Co. Waterford, by the river Blackwater, (from bound copy of T.S. Roberts's 'Views in the South of Ireland', issued in parts, 1795-99)
Published: T.S. Roberts, London, 1st July 1799
49.4 x 70 (plate 38.1 x 48.1)
Aquatint and etching
Purchased, London, Mr A. Thompson, 1986

Roberts, Thomas Sautell (1760-1826)
Irish School
BLUCK, J. (FL.1791-1819)
ENGLISH SCHOOL

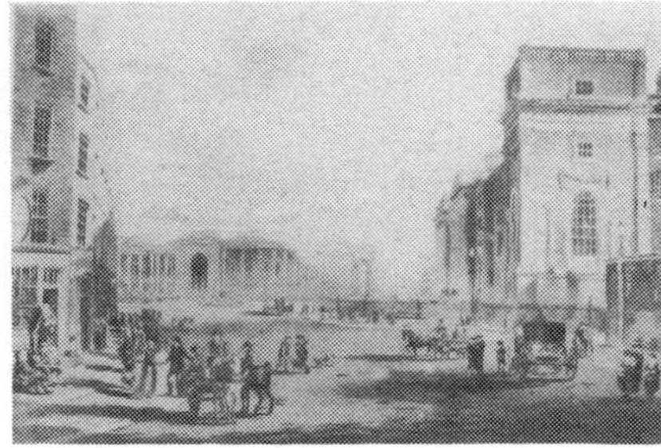

11,593
College Green, Dublin with Trinity College and the Bank of Ireland, (formerly Parliament House)
Published: R. Ackermann, London, 4th March 1807
63.2 x 93.5 (plate cut x 91.5)
Aquatint and etching with watercolour
Purchased, London, Mr L. Marks, 1907

Roberts, Thomas Sautell (1760-1826)
Irish School
BLUCK, J. (FL.1791-1819)
ENGLISH SCHOOL

11,653
Gold Mines in County Wicklow
Published: London, 19th May 1804
51 x 66 (plate 48.3 x 60.5)
Aquatint and etching with watercolour
Purchased, Dublin, Mr A. Roth, 1900

Roberts, Thomas Sautell (1760-1826)
Irish School
BLUCK, J. (FL.1791-1819)
ENGLISH SCHOOL

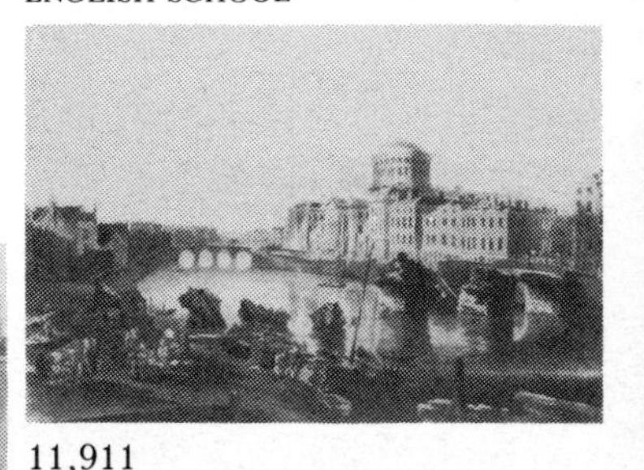

11,911
The Four Courts Dublin, from Wood Quay with the ruins of Coal Quay Bridge, (destroyed by floods, 1802)
(after a watercolour, SAI 1804 and/or RA 1805)
Published: 1807
48 x 65 (plate cut)
Aquatint and etching with watercolour
Acquired between 1908/14

Roberts, Thomas Sautell (1760-1826)
Irish School
HAVELL THE ELDER, ROBERT (FL.1800-1840)
ENGLISH SCHOOL *and*
HAVELL THE YOUNGER, ROBERT (FL.1820-1850)
ENGLISH SCHOOL

11,909
Dublin taken near the Custom House
INSCRIBED: *Dedicated to the Right Honble. the Commissioners of his Majesty's Revenue and Excise*
Published: Messrs. Boydell & Co.,

(for T. S. Roberts), London 1817
57.2 x 74.5 (plate 50 x 67)
Aquatint and etching with watercolour
Purchased, Dublin,
Mr J. V. McAlpine, 1904

Roberts, Thomas Sautell (1760-1826)
Irish School
HAVELL THE ELDER, ROBERT (FL.1800-1840)
ENGLISH SCHOOL *and*
HAVELL THE YOUNGER, ROBERT (FL.1820-1850)
ENGLISH SCHOOL

11,910
The General Post Office, Sackville, (now O'Connell), Street, Dublin
INSCRIBED: *Dedicated by Permission to his Majesty's Post Masters General of Ireland by their respectful and obedient servant/ James Del Vecchio*
Published: J. Del Vecchio, Dublin, 1818
48.1 x 65.8 (plate 46.4 x 59.5)
Aquatint and etching with watercolour
Purchased, London, Mr L. Marks, 1898

Roberts, Thomas Sautell (1760-1826)
Irish School
HAVELL THE ELDER, ROBERT (FL.1800-1840)
ENGLISH SCHOOL *and*
HAVELL THE YOUNGER, ROBERT (FL.1820-1850)
ENGLISH SCHOOL

11,912
The Four Courts, Dublin, from Merchants Quay
INSCRIBED: *Dedicated to the Right Honbl the Lord Chancellor the Right Honbly Honble the Judges of his Majestys Four Courts in Ireland Barristers at Law etc. etc.*
Published: A. Smith, (for T.S. Roberts), London, 1816
48 x 65 (plate cut)
Aquatint and etching
Purchased, Bath, Mr C. Gregory, 1905

Robertson, Andrew (1777-1845)
Scottish School
FINDEN, EDWARD FRANCIS (1791-1857)
ENGLISH SCHOOL

10,847
Lady Louisa Fortescue
(after a drawing)
Published: T.G. March, for the Proprietor, London, 1842 (Printed: McQueen)
36.5 x 26.4 (plate 34.6 x cut)
Line and stipple
Purchased, 1908

Robertson, Charles (1760-1821)
Irish School
AGAR, JOHN SAMUEL (?1770-AFTER 1835)
ENGLISH SCHOOL

10,324
Frances Thomasine, Countess Talbot, (née Lambart, 1782-1819), wife of the 3rd Earl Talbot
(after a watercolour miniature)
Published: The Proprietor, London, 10th May 1822
35.9 x 24.9 (34.6 x 25)
Stipple
Acquired between 1904/08

Robertson, Charles (1760-1821)
Irish School
PICART, CHARLES (1780-1837)
ENGLISH SCHOOL

10,800
George John Frederick Sackville, 4th Duke of Dorset, (1793-1815), against the Great Sugar Loaf Mountain, Co. Wicklow
Private Plate
50.8 x 37.5 (plate 48.3 x 35.5)
Line and stipple
Purchased, Dublin,
Mr J.V. McAlpine, 1911

Robertson, Mrs James (fl.1822-1849)
English School
POSSELWHITE, JAMES (1798-1884)
ENGLISH SCHOOL

11,308
Hester Catherine, Marchioness of Sligo, (née Lady de Burgh, 1800-1878), daughter of the 13th Earl of Clanricarde; wife of the 2nd Marquess of Sligo, (pl. for Bell's 'Court Magazine', 1832)
(after a watercolour miniature, RA 1831)
Published: E. Bull, London, 1832
21.1 x 13.2 (plate cut)
Stipple
Acquired by 1913

Robinson, John Charles (1824-1912)
English School
ROBINSON, JOHN CHARLES (1824-1912)
ENGLISH SCHOOL

20,082
Nine Barrow Down, Isle of Purbeck, Dorset, looking towards St Albans Head
(after a drawing of 1872)
31.5 x 44.2 (plate 11 x 25.8)
Etching
Provenance Unknown

Robinson, John Henry (1796-1871)
English School
CHILDS, GEORGE (FL.1826-1873)
ENGLISH SCHOOL

20,288
Evening Scene on the River Wye, near Chepstow, S. Wales
Published: Englemann & Co., London
28.1 x 38.1 (image 16.8 x 25.1)
Lithograph
Purchased, Lusk, Mr de Courcy Donovan, 1971

Robinson, John Henry (1796-1871)
English School
CHILDS, GEORGE (FL.1826-1873)
ENGLISH SCHOOL

20,289
The ruins of Caerphilly Castle, S. Wales, from the West
Published: Engelmann & Co., London
27.2 x 38 (image 16 x 24.8)
Lithograph
Purchased, Lusk, Mr de Courcy Donovan, 1971

Robinson, John Henry (1796-1871)
English School
CHILDS, GEORGE (FL.1826-1873)
ENGLISH SCHOOL

20,290
Chepstow Castle and bridge, S. Wales, on the River Wye, from Tutshill at sunset
Published: Engelmann, Graf, Coindet & Co., London, May 1831
27.8 x 38 (image 18 x 25)
Lithograph
Purchased, Lusk, Mr de Courcy Donovan, 1971

Robinson, John Henry (1796-1871)
English School
CHILDS, GEORGE (FL.1826-1873)
ENGLISH SCHOOL

20,291
North West View of St. Fagan's Castle, Wales, above the River Elai
Published: Englemann, Graf, Coindet & Co., London, January 1831
28 x 38.5 (image 20 x 29)
Lithograph
Purchased, Lusk, Mr de Courcy Donovan, 1971

Robinson, John Henry (1796-1871)
English School
CHILDS, GEORGE (FL.1826-1873)
ENGLISH SCHOOL

20,292
Manorbier Castle, S. Wales, from the North, in a Storm
Published: Englemann, Graf, Coindet & Co., London, May 1831
28.2 x 38.6 (image 17 x 24.5)
Lithograph
Purchased, Lusk, Mr de Courcy Donovan, 1971

Robinson, John Henry (1796-1871)
English School
CHILDS, GEORGE (FL.1826-1873)
ENGLISH SCHOOL

20,293
Ewenny Abbey, Wales, on the River Ewenny, from the South, during an Evening Shower
Published: Engelmann, Graf & Coindet, London, 1st January 1831
27.8 x 38 (image 16.6 x 25.6)
Lithograph
Purchased, Lusk, Mr de Courcy Donovan, 1971

Robinson, John Henry (1796-1871)
English School
CHILDS, GEORGE (FL.1826-1873)
ENGLISH SCHOOL

20,328
The Wreck of the Dunraven on the coast of Glamorganshire, Wales
Published: Englemann, Graf & Coindet, London, 1st January 1831
27.7 x 37.9 (image 17.5 x 25.5)
Lithograph
Purchased, Lusk, Mr de Courcy Donovan, 1971

Robinson, John Henry (1796-1871)
English School
CHILDS, GEORGE (FL.1826-1873)
ENGLISH SCHOOL

20,334
Kidwelly Town and Castle, S. Wales, on the River Gwendrath, from the West, near the Iron Works
Published: Engelmann, Graf, Coindet & Co., London, 1st February 1831
27.6 x 37.8 (image 16.4 x 24.4)
Lithograph
Purchased, Lusk, Mr de Courcy Donovan, 1971

Robinson, John Henry (1796-1871)
English School
CHILDS, GEORGE (FL.1826-1873)
ENGLISH SCHOOL

20,471
Webley Castle on the Gower peninsula, S. Wales, from the North, at noon
Published: Englemann, Graf, Coindet & Co., London, May 1837
27.1 x 38.1 (image 16.5 x 24.7)
Lithograph
Purchased, Lusk, Mr de Courcy Donovan, 1971

Robinson, John Henry (1796-1871)
English School
CHILDS, GEORGE (FL.1826-1873)
ENGLISH SCHOOL

20,473
Cilgerran Castle, above the River Teifi, S. Wales
Published: Englemann & Co., London
27.2 x 38 (image 18.2 x 25.4)
Lithograph
Purchased, Lusk, Mr de Courcy Donovan, 1971

Robinson, John Henry (1796-1871)
English School
CHILDS, GEORGE (FL.1826-1873)
ENGLISH SCHOOL

20,522
A Path above Oxwich bay, S. Wales, at Twilight
Published: Engelmann, Graf, Coindet & Co., London, May 1831
24.4 x 30.8 (image 16.4 x 24.7)
Lithograph
Purchased, Lusk, Mr de Courcy Donovan, 1971

Robinson, John Henry (1796-1871)
English School
ROBINSON, JOHN HENRY (1796-1871)
ENGLISH SCHOOL

20,474

Neath Abbey, S. Wales, from the North West
Published: Englemann, Graf, Coindet & Co., London, June 1830
27.8 x 38 (image 16.2 x 25.9)
Lithograph
Purchased, Lusk, Mr de Courcy Donovan, 1971

Robinson, John Henry (1796-1871)
English School
TEMPLETON, JOHN SAMUEL (FL.1830-1857)
IRISH SCHOOL

20,138
The River Towy near Grongor Hill, Wales, with a distant view of the ruins of Dynevor and Dryslwyn Castles
Published: Engelmann & Co., London
28.1 x 38 (image 16.4 x 25.4)
Lithograph
Purchased, Lusk, Mr de Courcy Donovan, 1971

Robinson, John Henry (1796-1871)
English School
TEMPLETON, JOHN SAMUEL (1819-1857)
IRISH SCHOOL

20,287
A Distant View of Swansea, S. Wales, and its harbour with Oystermouth Castle, from Poppet Hill, at Sunrise
Published: Engelmann, Graf, Coindet & Co., London, June 1830
27 x 38.2 (image 16.5 x 27.7)
Lithograph
Purchased, Lusk, Mr de Courcy Donovan, 1971

Robinson, John Henry (1796-1871)
English School
TEMPLETON, JOHN SAMUEL (FL.1819-1857)
IRISH SCHOOL

20,294
The Ruins of Caldecut Castle, S. Wales, from the East, during a storm
Published: Engelmann & Co., London
28 x 28 (image 16 x 24.8)
Lithograph
Purchased, Lusk, Mr de Courcy Donovan, 1971

Robinson, John Henry (1796-1871)
English School
TEMPLETON, JOHN SAMUEL (FL.1819-1857)
ENGLISH SCHOOL

20,368
The Ruins of Dynevor Castle, above the River Towy, Wales, at Morning
Published: Engelmann, Graf, Coindet & Co., London, May 1831
28 x 38.1 (image 16.5 x 26)
Lithograph
Purchased, Lusk, Mr de Courcy Donovan, 1971

Robinson, John Henry (1796-1871)
English School
TEMPLETON, JOHN SAMUEL (FL.1830-1857)
ENGLISH SCHOOL

20,472
Llanstephan Castle Village and ferry at the mouth of the River Towy, S. Wales
Published: Englemann, Graf, Coindet & Co., London, January 1831
27.8 x 37.8 (image 16.7 x 25)
Lithograph
Purchased, Lusk, Mr de Courcy Donovan, 1971

Robinson, Thomas (c.1770-1810)
Irish School
IRISH SCHOOL (1791)

11,242
Barry Yelverton, (1736-1805), later 1st Viscount Avonmore, as Lord Chief Baron of the Exchequer, (pl. for Walker's 'Hibernian Magazine', February 1791)
(after a wl oil of 1790)
Published: Hibernian Magazine, Dublin, February 1791
20.2 x 11.9 (plate 17 x 11)
Stipple
Provenance Unknown

Robinson, Thomas (c.1770-1810)
Irish School
RIDLEY, WILLIAM (1764-1838)
ENGLISH SCHOOL

11,174
Rev. William Cooper, Dissenting Minister in Dublin
Published: T. Williams, London, 1st February 1803
20.2 x 11.5 (plate 16.1 x 11.3)
Stipple
Acquired between 1913/14

Robinson, Thomas (c.1770-1810)
Irish School
ROBINSON, THOMAS (C.1770-1810)
IRISH SCHOOL

10,043
Barry Yelverton, (1736-1805), Chief Baron of the Exchequer, later 1st Viscount Avonmore, against his home Fortfield House, Terenure, Co. Dublin
(after an oil of 1792, St Louis City Art Museum)
Published: T. Robinson, Dublin, 1792
62.5 x 35.6 (plate cut)
Mezzotint and stipple
Purchased, Dublin, Mrs Daley, 1896

Robinson, William (1799-1839)
English school
BRETT, WILLIAM (FL.1820S)
ENGLISH SCHOOL *and*
COUSINS, SAMUEL (1801-1887)
ENGLISH SCHOOL

10,841
Thomas Philip Weddell Robinson, Baron Grantham, (1781-1859), later 2nd Earl De Grey and Lord Lieutenant of Ireland
(after an oil, RA 1827)
59.6 x 44.5 (plate 50.6 x 35.5)
Mezzotint
Purchased, Mr J.C. Nairn, 1900

Robinson, William (1799-1839)
English School
SCARLETT, DAVIS J. (1804-1845/46)
ENGLISH SCHOOL

10,775
John Willoughby Cole, 2nd Earl of Enniskillen, (1768-1840)
(after an oil, RA 1828)
Published: Colnaghi Sons & Co., London, 18th October 1829 (Printed: C.J. Hullmandel)
34.9 x 31.9 (image 33.8 x 30.18)
Lithograph
Purchased, Dublin, Mr A. Roth, 1896

Robson, George Fennell (1788-1833)
English School
FINDEN, EDWARD FRANCIS (1791-1857)
ENGLISH SCHOOL

20,478
Lochard, Scotland with Ben Lomond beyond, (pl. for C. Tilt's 'Landscape illustrations of the Waverly novels', 1832, cf. 'Rob Roy')
Published: C. Tilt, London, May 1830
17.1 x 23.1 (plate cut)
Steel Engraving
Purchased, Lusk, Mr de Courcy Donovan, 1971

Robson, George Fennell (1788-1833)
English School
FINDEN, EDWARD FRANCIS (1791-1857)
ENGLISH SCHOOL

20,481
Durham Castle and Cathedral, from the North-West, (pl. for C. Tilt's 'Landscape illustrations of the Waverly novels', 1832, cf. 'Heart of Midlothian')

Published: C. Tilt, London, August 1830
17.2 x 23.5 (plate cut)
Steel Engraving
Purchased, Lusk, Mr de Courcy Donovan, 1971

Robson, George Fennell (1788-1833)
English School
SMITH, WILLIAM RAYMOND (FL.1818-1848)
ENGLISH SCHOOL

20,386
Llyn Idwall, N. Wales
Published: C. Tilt, London, 1832
27.7 x 37.8 (plate 19 x 25.2)
Steel Engraving
Purchased, Lusk, Mr de Courcy Donovan, 1971

Rocque, John (c.1705-1762)
Anglo-French School
DURY, A. (18TH CENTURY)
IRISH SCHOOL *and*
HALPIN, PATRICK (FL.1755-1787)
IRISH SCHOOL

11,806
Survey of the City and Suburbs of Dublin with the Divisions of the Parishes, reduced from the large plan in four sheets by John Rocque
INSCRIBED: To John Rutland Esqr./This plan is most humbly inscribed/by his most obligd./humble servant/John Rocque
Published: J. Rocque, Dublin, 1757
61.5 x 89.5 (plate 51.5 x 72.5)
Line (drawn over in red ink)
Purchased, Dublin, Mr J.V. McAlpine, 1913

Rocque, John (c.1705-1762)
Anglo-French School
ENGLISH SCHOOL (1762)

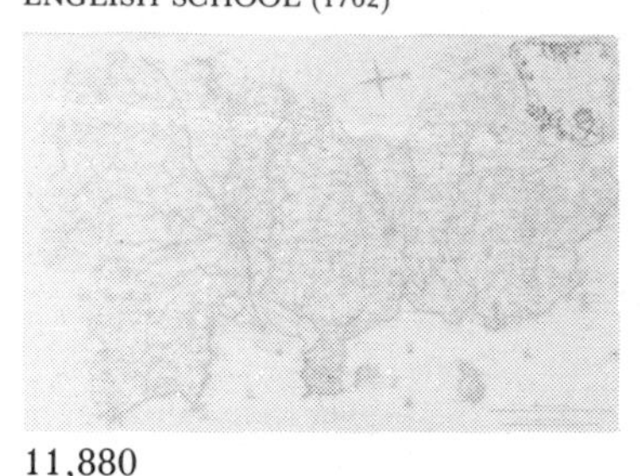

11,880
A Map of the County of Dublin divided in Barony's, reduced from an actual survey in four sheets
INSCRIBED: To the Right Honble/James Fitzgerald/Earl of Ophally etc. etc./This Map of the/ County of Dublin/is Dedicated by his/Lordships Most Obedt., &/Humble Servt. Mary Ann Rocque, 1762
Published: M. Rocque, London, 1762
47.4 x 66.8 (plate 44.3 x 64.5)
Line with watercolour
Presented, M. FitzGerald, 7th Duke of Leinster, 1913

Rocque, John (c.1705-1762)
Anglo-French School
ENGLISH SCHOOL (1799)

11,813
A Map of County Dublin divided in Barony's reduced from an actual survey in four sheets by John Rocque
Published: Laurie & Whittle, London, 25th March 1799
44 x 64.5 (plate cut)
Line with watercolour
Provenance Unknown

Rocque, John (c.1705-1762)
Anglo-French School
PERRET, J.J. (18TH CENTURY)
ENGLISH SCHOOL

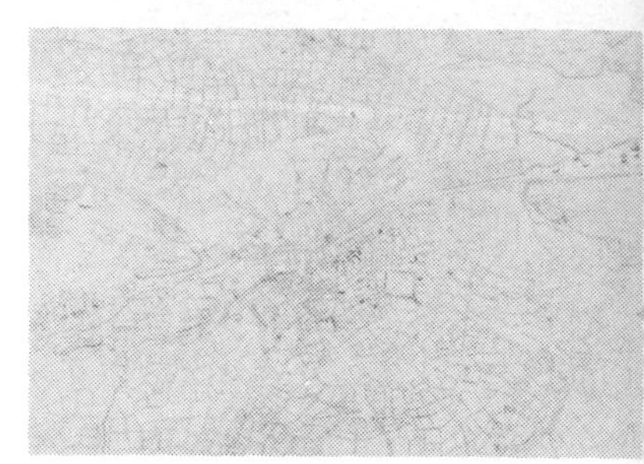

11,886
A Plan of the City of Dublin and Environs in 1753, on the same scale as London, Paris and Rome
Published: J. Rocque, Dublin, 1754/55
55.5 x 77 (plate 52 x 72.8)
Line
Presented, M. Fitzgerald, 7th Duke of Leinster, 1913

Roman (Antique)
BARTOLI, PIETRO SANTI (C.1635-1700)
ITALIAN SCHOOL

20,706(47)
Antique sepulche at Tivoli, near Rome, (from 'Gli Antichi Sepolcri....', 1768, see App. 8, no. 20,706)
Published: Rome, 1768
29 x 19 (plate 21 x 14.3)
Line
Provenance Unknown

Roman (Antique)
CONTINENTAL SCHOOL (19TH CENTURY)

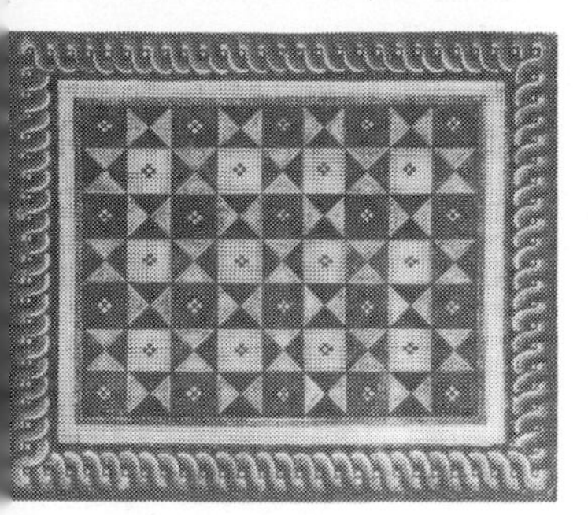

20,177
Abstract Mosaic
22.3 x 19.1 (plate cut)
Etching with watercolour
Purchased, Lusk, Mr de Courcy Donovan, 1971

Roman (Antique)
ENGLISH SCHOOL (19TH CENTURY)

20,557
Reclining faun
16.5 x 21.5 (plate cut)
Stipple Engraving
Presented, Mrs D. Molloy, 1981

Roman (Antique)
ITALIAN SCHOOL (17TH CENTURY)

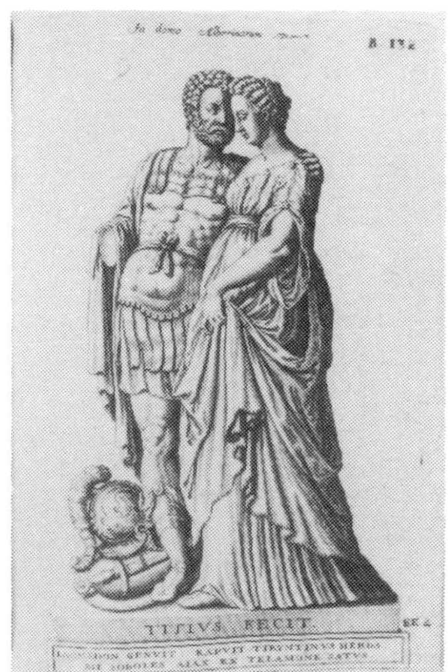

20,717(89)
Figures on a Roman sarcophagus, (from 'Petrus Lapidus...', see App. 8, no. 20,717)
29 x 19.5 (plate 27.5 x 17.5)
Line and etching
Provenance Unknown

Roman (Antique)
CONTINENTAL SCHOOL (19TH CENTURY)

0,178
Beware of the Dog' mosaic
after a mosaic, 'House of the Tragic oet', Pompeii, S. Italy)
3.9 x 21.8 (plate cut)
tching with watercolour
urchased, Lusk, Mr de Courcy onovan, 1971

?Roman (Antique)
ENGLISH SCHOOL (EARLY 19TH CENTURY)

20,654
Pegasus and Aurora
28.4 x 22.3 (plate cut)
Stipple
Presented, Mrs D. Molloy, 1981

Roman (Antique)
WICAR, JEAN BAPTISTE (1762-1834)
FRENCH SCHOOL
THOMAS, N. (c.1750-c.1812)
FRENCH SCHOOL

20,688(108)
The Young Faustina, (from the 'Galerie de Florence et du Palais Pitti', Vol. 2, 1789, see App. 8, no. 20,688)
(after the Roman Antique marble, The Uffizi, Florence)
Published: E. Lacombe, Paris, 1789
52.4 x 33.5 (plate 29.5 x 30.5)
Line
Provenance Unknown

Roman (Antique)
AUDENGERD, ROBERT VAN (1663-1743)
FLEMISH SCHOOL

20,221
Niobe mourning the death of her Children
(after a marble copy of lost Greek 4C BC marble, The Uffizi, Florence)
Published: D. de Rossi, Rome
36.1 x 23.3 (plate 34.2 x 21.3)
Line
Purchased, Lusk, Mr de Courcy Donovan, 1971

Romney, George (1734-1802)
English School
GREEN, VALENTINE (1739-1813)
ENGLISH SCHOOL

10,765
Richard Cumberland, (1732-1811), Playwright and Essayist
(after an oil of c.1768)
Published: J. Boydell, London, 28th October 1771
47.7 x 34.7 (plate 45.8 x 33.2)
Mezzotint
Purchased, London, 1st Chaloner Smith sale, 1887

Romney, George (1734-1802)
English School
JONES, JOHN (C.1745-1797)
ENGLISH SCHOOL

10,442
Edmund Burke, M.P., (1729-1797), Statesman and Writer
(after an oil of 1776)
Published: J. Jones, London, 10th December 1790
51.4 x 36 (plate 50.5 x 35)
Mezzotint
Purchased, London, 1st Chaloner Smith sale, 1887

Romney, George (1734-1802)
English School
JONES, JOHN (C.1745-1797)
ENGLISH SCHOOL

10,476
William Pitt the Younger, M.P., (1759-1806), Chancellor of the Exchequer, later British Prime Minister
(after an oil of 1783, Bayham Abbey, Kent)
Published: J. Jones, London, 20th May 1789
52.8 x 37.4 (plate 50.5 x 35.5)
Mezzotint
Purchased, London, 1st Chaloner Smith sale, 1887

Romney, George (1734-1802)
English School
JONES, JOHN (C.1745-1797)
ENGLISH SCHOOL

10,508

John Fane, 10th Earl of Westmoreland, (1759-1841), Lord Lieutenant of Ireland
(after an oil of 1789, Emmanuel College, Cambridge)
Published: J. Jones, London, 1st March 1792
57 x 42 (plate cut)
Mezzotint
Purchased, London, 1st Chaloner Smith sale, 1887

Romney, George (1734-1802)
English School
OGBORNE, JOHN (C.1755-1795)
ENGLISH SCHOOL

10,341
Mrs Jordan, (née Dorothy Bland, 1762-1816), Actress, as Peggy in 'The Country Dealer'
(after an oil of 1786-87)
Published: J. & J. Boydell, London, 21st June 1788
40 x 30 (plate 38 x 28.5)
Stipple
Purchased, Dublin, Mrs Noseda, 1882

Romney, George (1734-1802)
English School
COMERFORD, JOHN (?1770-1832)
IRISH SCHOOL
SCRIVEN, EDWARD (1775-1841)
ENGLISH SCHOOL

11,417
Mary Tighe, (née Blachford, 1772-1810), Poet, (frontispiece for her 'Psyche, or the Legend of Love', 1816 edition)
(after a Comerford miniature copy c.1810 of a Romney oil c.1795)
Published: Longman, London, June 1812
12.5 x 10.4 (plate cut)
Stipple
Purchased, Dublin, Mr P. Traynor, 1898

Romney, George (1734-1802)
English School
TOWNLEY, CHARLES (1746-1800)
ENGLISH SCHOOL

10,439
The Hon. John Forbes, (1714-1796), Admiral of the Fleet
(after an oil of 1778, NMM, Greenwich)
Published: C. Townley, London, 20th November 1796
50.8 x 38.4 (plate 45.6 x 33)
Mezzotint
Purchased, London, 2nd Chaloner Smith sale, 1888

Romney, George (1734-1802)
English School
WALKER, JAMES (1748-1808)
ENGLISH SCHOOL

10,864
Eyles Irwin, (c.1747-1817), Author
(after an oil of 1780)
Unlettered Proof
Published: J. Walker, London, 1780
26.3 x 20 (plate 25.1 x 19.1)
Mezzotint
Purchased, London, 2nd Chaloner Smith sale, 1888

Romney, George (1734-1802)
English School
COMERFORD, JOHN (?1770-1832)
IRISH SCHOOL
WATSON, CAROLINE (1761-1814)
IRISH SCHOOL

10,307
Mary Tighe, (née Blachford, 1772-1810), Poet, (frontispiece for her 'Psyche, or the Legend of Love', 1811)
(after a Comerford miniature copy, c.1810, of a Romney oil c.1795)
16.7 x 12.6 (plate cut)
Stipple
Purchased, Dublin, Mr P. Traynor, 1898

Romney, George (1734-1802)
English School
WATSON, CAROLINE (1761-1814)
ENGLISH SCHOOL

11,046
Three Self-Portraits, from 1782, 1795 and c.1775, (frontispiece for W. Hayley's 'Life of Romney', 1809)
(after an oil of 1782, NPG London; a 2nd oil and a watercolour miniature)
Published: T. Payne, London, 14th April 1809 (Printed: W. Mason)
27 x 19.3 (plate cut)
Stipple
Provenance Unknown

Room, Henry (1802-1850)
English School
COCHRAN, JOHN (FL.1821-1856)
ENGLISH SCHOOL

11,279
Charles Gostling Townley, (1781-1856), Author
21.4 x 13 (plate cut)
Line and stipple
Acquired c.1908

Rosa, Salvator (1615-1673)
Italian School
ENGLISH SCHOOL (18TH CENTURY)

20,551
Two warriors
(after a Rosa etching and drypoint of c.1656, example in Calcografia Nationale, Rome)
15.3 x 10 (plate cut)
Etching with wash
Presented, Mrs D. Molloy, 1981

?Rosa, Salvator (1615-1673)
Italian School
G..., A. (18TH CENTURY)
ENGLISH SCHOOL

20,335
Tree with carriage beyond
Published: 1759
44.4 x 31.2 (plate 43.5 x 30.5)
Etching
Purchased, Lusk, Mr de Courcy Donovan, 1971

Rosalba (1675-1757)
Venetian School
WEST, CHARLES (B.C.1750)
ENGLISH SCHOOL

20,731(136)
Diana, (from 'The Houghton Gallery', 1778, see App. 8, no. 20,731)
(after a pastel, The Hermitage, Leningrad)
Published: J. Boydell, London, 1st September 1785
58.2 x 52.3 (plate cut)
Stipple
Bequeathed, Judge J. Murnaghan, 1976

Ross, J. (19th century)
English School
MOTE, WILLIAM HENRY (FL.1830-1858)
ENGLISH SCHOOL

11,333
Elizabeth Frances Charlotte, Viscountess Powerscourt, (née Jocelyn 1813-1884), wife of 6th Viscount Powerscourt; later Marchioness of Londonderry, wife of 4th Marquess, (pl. for Heath's 'Book of Beauty', 1839)
Published: for the proprietor by Longman & Co., London, also Appleton & Co., New York
22 x 14.3 (plate cut)
Line and stipple
Acquired c.1903

Ross, William Charles (1794-1860)
English School
THOMSON, JAMES (1789-1850)
ENGLISH SCHOOL

10,806
Lady Elizabeth Ferguson
Published: E. Graves, late Colnaghi & Co., London, 2nd February 1836
43.6 x 29.8 (plate 25.9 x 19.3)
Line and stipple
Provenance Unknown

Rossi, Lucius (1846-1913)
French School
FRENCH SCHOOL (19TH CENTURY)

20,179
Cross Section and Plan of a Villa in the Roman Style
26.3 x 36.8 (plate 18.5 x 23.9)
Etching with watercolour
Purchased, Lusk, Mr de Courcy Donovan, 1971

Rossi, Lucius (1846-1913)
French School
FRENCH SCHOOL (19TH CENTURY)

20,180
Chinese Style Interior
26.3 x 37 (plate 15.8 x 22.1)
Etching with watercolour
Purchased, Lusk, Mr de Courcy Donovan, 1971

Rossi, Pasquale (1641-1718)
Italian School
CHATAIGNER, ALEXIS (1772-1817)
FRENCH SCHOOL

20,073
The School Mistress
(after an oil, The Louvre, Paris)
46.5 x 62 (plate 34.5 x 47)
Etching
Provenance Unknown

Rothschild, Baronne Charlotte de (1825-1899)
French School
CHAUVEL, THEOPHILE NARCISSE (1831-1910)
FRENCH SCHOOL

20,080
Buiten Singel, Amsterdam, Holland
Published: L'Art, Paris (Printed: F. Lienard)
30.5 x 44 (plate 24 x 32)
Etching
Provenance Unknown

Rothwell, Richard (1800-1868)
Irish School
HODGETTS, THOMAS (FL.1801-1846)
ENGLISH SCHOOL

10,792
Baroness Anna Dorothea Dufferin and Clandeboye, (née Foster, 1773-1865), wife of 2nd Baron
(after an oil, RHA 1828)
31.5 x 24.5 (plate cut)
Mezzotint
Purchased, 1907

Rothwell, Richard (1800-1868)
Irish School
LUCAS, DAVID (1802-1881)
ENGLISH SCHOOL

10,109
William Conyngham Plunket, 1st Baron Plunket, (1764-1854), Orator and former Lord Chancellor of Ireland
(after an oil, RA 1843)
Published: The Proprietor, London, 1844
39.2 x 28.7 (plate cut)
Mezzotint
Presented, Mr M. O'Shaughnessy, 1881

Rothwell, Richard (1800-1868)
Irish School
TEMPLETON, JOHN SAMUEL (FL.1830-1857)
IRISH SCHOOL

11,072
A Flower Seller (Artist's wife)
(after an oil of 1844, Fota House, Co. Cork)
Lettered Proof
(Printed: M.& N. Hanhart, London)
42.5 x 32.6 (image 35.4 x 27)
Lithograph
Purchased, Mrs L. Rogers, 1950

Rothwell, Richard (1800-1868)
Irish School
TURNER, CHARLES (1773-1857)
ENGLISH SCHOOL

10,554
Du Pré Alexander, 2nd Earl of Caledon, (1777-1839), 1st Governor of the Cape of Good Hope and Lord Lieutenant of Co. Tyrone
Published: C. Turner, for the Proprietor, London, 24th March 1840
69.3 x 51 (plate 36 x 25.5)
Mezzotint
Purchased, Dublin, Mr J.V. McAlpine, 1904

Rowbotham the Elder, Thomas Leeson (1783-1853)
English School
HAVELL, DANIEL (FL.1812-1837)
ENGLISH SCHOOL

11,647
Howth Head and Harbour, Co. Dublin, with the new pier and lighthouse, from Ireland's Eye
INSCRIBED: Dedicated with permission to Charles, Earl Whitworth, Lord Lieutenant of Ireland, &c. &c. &c.
Published: Colnaghi & Co., London, also J. Del Vecchio, Dublin, 15th September 1817
37.5 x 97.5 (plate 34.2 x 95)
Aquatint and etching
Purchased, Mr J.H. Kilgour, 1910

Rowbotham the Elder, Thomas Leeson (1783-1853)
English School
HAVELL, DANIEL (FL.1812-1837)
ENGLISH SCHOOL

11,648
Part of the Bay and City of Dublin, taken from Marino
INSCRIBED: Dedicated with permission to the Right Honourable the Countess of Charlemont
Published: Colnaghi & Co., London, also J. Del Vecchio, Dublin, 15th September 1817
37.5 x 97.8 (plate 34.5 x 94.8)
Aquatint and etching
Purchased, Mr J.H. Kilgour, 1910

Rowbotham the Elder, Thomas Leeson (1783-1853)
English School
HAVELL, DANIEL (FL.1812-1837)
ENGLISH SCHOOL

11,696
Howth Head and Harbour, Co. Dublin with the new pier and Lighthouse, from Ireland's Eye, (another copy)
INSCRIBED: Dedicated with permission, to Charles Earl Whitworth, Lord Lieutenant of Ireland, &c. &c. &c.
Published: Colnaghi & Co., London also J. Del Vecchio, Dublin, 15th September, 1817
36 x 97 (plate cut)
Aquatint and etching
Provenance Unknown

Rowe, George (1797-1864)
English School
ROWE, GEORGE (1797-1864)
ENGLISH SCHOOL

20,353
The Seven Churches, Glendalough, Co. Wicklow
Published: G. Rowe, Cheltenham
25.8 x 32 (image 17.5 x 25.7)
Lithograph
Purchased, Lusk, Mr de Courcy Donovan, 1971

Rowe, George (1797-1864)
English School
ROWE, GEORGE (1797-1864)
ENGLISH SCHOOL

20,354
Glenmalure, with the River Avonbeg, Co. Wicklow
Published: G. Rowe, Cheltenham
25.8 x 33 (image 18 x 25.6)
Lithograph
Purchased, Lusk, Mr de Courcy Donovan, 1971

Rowlandson, Thomas (1756-1827)
English School
HOPWOOD THE YOUNGER, JAMES (1795-AFTER 1825)
ENGLISH SCHOOL

10,586
Dr O'Meara, Clergyman friend of Frederick, Duke of York's mistress Mary Ann Clarke, (pl. for 'Trial of Duke of York', 1809)
Published: J. Stratford, London, 1809
12.8 x 9.8 (plate cut)
Stipple
Purchased, Dublin, Mr J.V. McAlpine, 1909

Rowlandson, Thomas (1756-1827)
English School
ROWLANDSON, THOMAS (1756-1827)
ENGLISH SCHOOL

11,409
Henry Munro, (c.1768-1798), Irish Rebel Commander defeated at Ballynahinch, Co. Down in 1798
Published: R. Ackermann, London, 1st July 1798
33.8 x 42 (plate 29 x 35)
Etching
Provenance Unknown

Etchings after the Tapestry series designed by Rubens depicting 'The History of Achilles', (from Homer's 'Iliad'). The original oil sketches of 1630 are now in the Boymans-van Beuningen Museum, Rotterdam. Copies for the engraver may have been done by Claude Dubosc (1682-1745)

Rubens, Peter Paul (1577-1640)
Flemish School
BARON, BERNARD (1696-1762 OR 66)
FRENCH SCHOOL

20,041
Achilles dipped into the River Styx by Thetis to make him invincible
Published: C. Bowles, London, 1724
68.5 x 50.4 (plate 44.4 x 33.6)
Line and etching
Presumed presented, Mr T. Bodkin, 1925

Rubens, Peter Paul (1577-1640)
Flemish School
BARON, BERNARD (1696-1762 OR 66)
FRENCH SCHOOL

20,042
Achilles Instructed by the Centaur Chiron
Published: C. Bowles, London, 1724
68.5 x 50.5 (plate 45.5 x 35.4)
Line and etching
Presumed presented, Mr T. Bodkin, 1925

Rubens, Peter Paul (1577-1640)
Flemish School
BARON, BERNARD (1696-1762 OR 66)
FRENCH SCHOOL

20,043
Achilles betrays himself while hiding among the daughters of Lycomedes
Published: C. Bowles, London, 1724
50 x 68.5 (plate 45 x 59.3)
Line and etching
Presumed presented, Mr T. Bodkin, 1925

Rubens, Peter Paul (1577-1640)
Flemish School
BARON, BERNARD (1696-1762 OR 66)
FRENCH SCHOOL

20,044
The Wrath of Achilles over returning Chryseis to Agamemnon watched by Pallas and Nestor
Published: C. Bowles, London, 1724
68.2 x 50 (plate 46 x 41.8)
Line and etching
Presumed presented, Mr T. Bodkin, 1925

Rubens, Peter Paul (1577-1640)
Flemish School
BARON, BERNARD (1696-1762 OR 66)
FRENCH SCHOOL

20,045
Thetis receives armour for Achilles from Vulcan, with Jupiter and Juno in background
Published: C. Bowles, London, 1724
50.3 x 68.5 (plate 45.5. x 48)
Line and etching
Presumed presented, Mr T. Bodkin, 1925

Rubens, Peter Paul (1577-1640)
Flemish School
BARON, BERNARD (1696-1762 OR 66)
FRENCH SCHOOL

20,046
Achilles aided by Apollo kills Hector and revenges Patroclus' death
Published: C. Bowles, London, 1724
50.5 x 68.5 (plate 45.5 x 48.3)
Line and etching
Presumed presented, Mr T. Bodkin, 1925

Rubens, Peter Paul (1577-1640)
Flemish School
BARON, BERNARD (1696-1762 OR 66)
FRENCH SCHOOL

20,047
The Death of Achilles, who is shot by Paris aided by Apollo and Cupid
Published: C. Bowles, London, 1724
58.7 x 50 (plate 46.5 x 41.5)
Line and etching
Presumed presented, Mr T. Bodkin, 1925

Rubens, Peter Paul (1577-1640)
Flemish School
ENGLISH SCHOOL (19TH CENTURY)

20,634
The Château at Steen
(after an oil of c.1630, Kunsthistorisches Museum, Vienna)
13.3 x 17.7 (image 11.4 x 16.3)
Wood Engraving
Presented, Mrs D. Molloy, 1981

Rubens, Peter Paul (1577-1640)
Flemish School
FRENCH SCHOOL (18TH CENTURY)

11,505
Peter Finding the Tribute Money
(after an oil of c.1617, Church of Our Lady, Mechlin)
Published: Esnauts, Paris also Rapilly, Coutances
28.2 x 36.8 (plate cut)
Line
Provenance Unknown

Rubens, Peter Paul (1577-1640)
Flemish School
CRAIG, WILLIAM MARSHALL (FL.1788-1828)
ENGLISH SCHOOL
HEATH, CHARLES (1785-1848)
ENGLISH SCHOOL

20,705(7)
Peace and War, (from 'Engravings of the Most Noble the Marquis of Stafford's Collection of Pictures in London', Vol.3, 1818, see App. 8, no. 20,705)
(after an oil of 1629-30, NG, London)
Published: Longman, Hurst, Rees, Orme & Brown; also Cadell and Davies; also P.W. Tomkins, London, 1st March 1815
41.6 x 32.3 (plate cut)
Line
Provenance Unknown

Rubens, Peter Paul (1577-1640)
Flemish School
NATTIER, JEAN MARC (1685-1766)
FRENCH SCHOOL
TROUVAIN, ANTOINE (1656-1708)
FRENCH SCHOOL

20,678(6)
The Marriage of Marie de Medici and Henry IV, (from 'La Galerie du Palais Luxembourg', see App. 8, no. 20,678)
(after an oil of 1622, The Louvre, Paris)
Published: J.M. Nattier, Paris
58.8 x 43.5 (plate 49.8 x 35.3)
Line
Provenance Unknown

After **Rubens, Peter Paul (1577-1640)**
Flemish School
LAMB, FRANCIS (19TH CENTURY)
SCOTTISH SCHOOL

11,661
Meleager and Atalanta or the Hunting of the Caledonian Boar
(after an oil, NGI no. 1705)
INSCRIBED: From an original Picture of Rubens in the Collection of the Hon. the Earl of Milltown Ireland to whom this Plate is Inscribed by his Lordships Most Obedt Humble Servant/Francis Lamb
Published: F. Lamb, Edinburgh, 1st August 1822
50 x 67.3 (plate cut)
Line
Milltown Gift, 1902

School of **Rubens, Peter Paul (1577-1640)**
Flemish School
BARON, BERNARD (1696-1762 OR 66)
FRENCH SCHOOL

20,040
Homage to Rubens - Frontispiece to Rubens' 'The History of Achilles'
(after a chalk drawing, NGI no. 2676)
INSCRIBED: Dedicated in Latin to Dr Richard Mead, then owner of the Rubens oil sketches
Published: C. Bowles, London, 1724
68 x 49.7 (plate 45.2 x 34)
Line and etching
Presumed presented, Mr T. Bodkin, 1925

Russell, Anthony (1663-1743)
English School
GRIBELIN, SIMON (1661/2-1733)
ANGLO-FRENCH SCHOOL

10,047
Charles Hickman, P. Bishop of Derry, (1648-1713), (frontispiece for his 'Sermons', 1724)
Published: J. Bonyer, London
17.9 x 10.4 (plate 17.4 x 9)
Line
Purchased, Dublin,
Mr J.V. McAlpine, 1909

Russell, John (1745-1806)
English School
SPILSBURY, JOHN (C.1730-1795)
ENGLISH SCHOOL

10,787
Rev. Richard De Courcy, (1744-1803), Chaplain to Lord Kinsale
Published: C. Bowles, London,
1st July 1770, price 2s
33.5 x 23.2 (plate 33 x 22.8)
Mezzotint
Purchased, London, 2nd Chaloner Smith sale, 1888

Rysbrack, John Michael (1694-1770)
Anglo-Flemish School
FABER THE YOUNGER, JOHN (C.1684-1756)
ENGLISH SCHOOL

10,027
The Hon. Robert Boyle, (1627-1691), Philosopher and Scientist
(after a marble bust of 1733, Royal Collection, Kensington Palace)
Published: T. & J. Bowles, London
35.6 x 25.3 (plate 35.2 x 25.1)
Mezzotint
Purchased, London, 1st Chaloner Smith sale, 1887

S

ıbatier, Etienne (fl.1831-1861)
ench School
ENCH SCHOOL (19TH CENTURY)

,466
ıe factory of Las Tous et Darbaste also Flour Mill of Antonin Brasovilié Fils a building of the Henry IV period at rac, S.W. France
ıblished: Goyer, Paris
.8 x 26.1 (image 15.8 x 22.8)
thograph
ırchased, Lusk, Mr de Courcy
ɔnovan, 1971

dler the Younger, William 782-1839)
sh School
ORER, JAMES (1781-1853)
GLISH SCHOOL *and*
RGENT, HENRY (1795-1857)
GLISH SCHOOL

,769
ɔlbeg Light House, South Wall, Dublin y
ter a drawing)
x 15.7 (plate cut)
ıe
ɔvenance Unknown

Sandby, Paul (1730-1809)
English School
COOK, THOMAS (C.1744-1818)
ENGLISH SCHOOL

20,029
King John's Castle and John's Bridge, (now rebuilt), Limerick, (pl. for 'The Virtuosi's Museum', 1778-81)
G. Kearsley, London, 2nd July 1780
22.5 x 28 (plate 15.9 x 20.5)
Line with watercolour
Purchased, London, The Parker Gallery, 1983

Sargent, John Singer (1856-1925)
American School
COLE, TIMOTHY (1852-1931)
AMERICAN SCHOOL

11,412
Woodrow Wilson, (1856-1924), President of the United States of America
(after an oil of 1917, NGI no. 817)
Unlettered Proof
Published: Arthur H. Hahlo & Co., New York, 1918
31 x 21.5 (plate cut)
Mezzotint
Purchased, New York, Arthur H. Hahlo & Co., 1919

Say, Frederick Richard (fl. 1825-1854)
English School
KIRKWOOD, JOHN (FL.1826-1853)
IRISH SCHOOL

11,293
Robert Jocelyn, 3rd Earl of Roden, (1788-1870), pointing to the Petition of the Protestants of Ireland, (pl. for 'Dublin University Magazine', Vol.XV, January 1840)
Published: W. Curry Junior & Co., Dublin, 1st January 1840
21.7 X 13.2 (plate cut)

Etching
Purchased, Dublin, Mr P. Traynor, 1898

Sayers, Reuben (1815-1888)
English School
PAYNE, GEORGE T. (FL.1838-1860)
ENGLISH SCHOOL

10,705
William Carr, 1st Viscount Beresford, (1768-1854), distinguished Officer
Published: R. Sayers, London, 1st March 1850
47.5 X 36.5 (plate 46.6 X 35.3)
Mezzotint
Purchased, Dublin,
Mr J.V. McAlpine, 1913

Scanlan, Robert Richard (fl.1826-1864)
Irish School
COOK, HENRY R. (FL.1800-1845)
ENGLISH SCHOOL

10,562
Field-Marshal Arthur Wellesley, 1st Duke of Wellington, (1769-1852)
(after a drawing of 1820s)
35.2 x 24.3 (plate cut)
Stipple
Purchased, 1913

Schenck, Peter (1660-1718/19)
Dutch School
SCHENCK, PETER (1660-1718/19)
DUTCH SCHOOL

10,865
James II, King of England, (1633-1701)
Published: P. Schenck, Amsterdam
27.9 X 21.5 (plate 24.5 x 18.5)
Mezzotint
Purchased, London, 1st Chaloner Smith sale, 1887

Schongauer, Martin (1445/50 -1491)
German School
ENGLISH SCHOOL (1826)

20,733(39)
The Virgin and Child, (from 'A Collection of Fac-Similes of Scarce and Curious Prints', Vol. 1, 1826, see App. 8, no. 20,733)
Published: Longman, Rees, Orme, Brown & Green, London, also Molteno, London, also Colnaghi & Co., London, 1826 (Printed: J. McCreery)
37.4 x 26.5 (plate 17.5 x 13)
Etching
Presented, Mr G.F. Mulvany, 1867

Schwartz, Christoph (c.1545-1592)
German and Venetian Schools
FRIEDEL, A. (19TH CENTURY)
ENGLISH SCHOOL

20,077
'Christ in the Hall of Judgement'-The Crowning with Thorns
INSCRIBED: From the original in possession of the publisher
Purchased: A. Friedel, London
49.5 x 34.6 (image 34.8 x 26.4)
Coloured lithograph
Provenance Unknown

Scott, Edmund (1758-c.1810)
English School
KNIGHT, CHARLES (1743-C.1876)
ENGLISH SCHOOL

11,051
Charles Lennox, 4th Duke of Richmond, (1764-1819), later Lord Lieutenant of Ireland and Governor General of Canada
Published: E. Scott, Brighton, 7th August 1807
33.5 x 25.1 (plate 26.3 x 19.5)
Stipple
Purchased, Dublin, Mr J.V. McAlpine, 1899

Seale, Richard William (fl.1732-1775)
English School
SEALE, RICHARD WILLIAM (FL.1732-1775)
ENGLISH SCHOOL

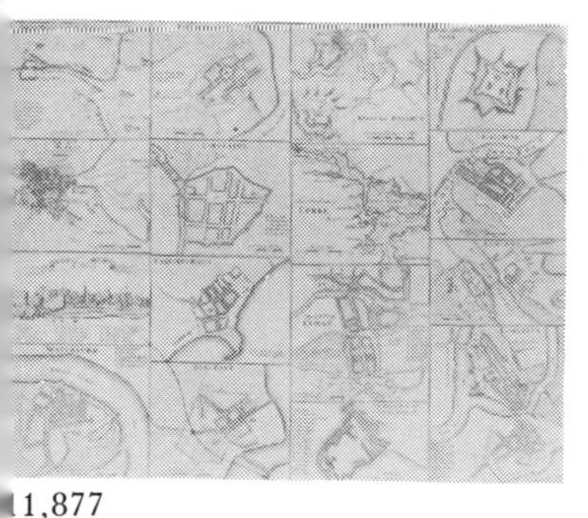

11,877
Plans of the Principal Towns, Forts and Harbours in Ireland - Drogheda, Co. Louth, with the Battle of the Boyne; Londonderry, Co. Derry; Kinsale Harbour, Co. Cork; Charlemont Fort, Co. Armagh; Dublin; Coleraine, Co. Derry; Cork Harbour, Co. Cork; Galway, Co. Galway; Kilkenny, Co. Kilkenny; Carrickfergus, Co. Antrim; Cork, Co. Cork; Athlone, Co Westmeath; Waterford, Co. Waterford; Belfast, Co. Antrim; Duncannon, Co. Wexford; Limerick, Co. Limerick, (pl. for 'Maps and plans of Tindal's Continuation of Rapin's History of England', 1785-c.90)
42.5 x 53.7 (plate 40.8 x 50)
Line
Provenance unknown

Sebastiano del Piombo (1485-1547)
Italian School
DELAUNAY, ROBERT (1749-1814)
FRENCH SCHOOL

20,723(22)
The Raising of Lazarus, (from 'Galerie Du Palais Royal', Vol. 1, 1786, see App. 8, no. 20,723)
(after an oil of 1517-19, NG, London)
Published: J. Couché also J. Bouilliard, Paris, 1786 (Printed: H. Perronneau)
55.5 x 33 (plate 41.9 x 29.8)
Line
Bequeathed, Judge J. Murnaghan, 1976

?Segar, William (fl.1585-1633)
English School
BELL, ROBERT CHARLES (1806-1872)
ENGLISH SCHOOL

11,053
So-called portrait of Sir Walter Raleigh, (1552-1618), (pendant to English School 1603/R.C. Bell, NGI no. 11,055)
(after an oil of 1598, NGI no. 281)
Published: not before 1830
36 x 28.5 (plate 28 x 23)
Line
Acquired by 1913

?Segar, William (fl.1585-1633)
English School
BELL, ROBERT CHARLES (1806-1872)
ENGLISH SCHOOL

11,054
So-called portrait of Sir Walter Raleigh, (1552-1618),(pendant to English School 1603/R.C. Bell NGI no. 11,055), (another copy)
(after an oil of 1598, NGI no. 281)
Published: not before 1830
44 x 30.5 (plate 28 x 23)
Line
Acquired by 1913

Sharpe, Louisa (1798-1843)
English School
EDWARDS, J.C. (FL.1821-1835)
ENGLISH SCHOOL

20,154
Juliet from Shakespeare's 'Romeo and Juliet', (pl. for 'The Keepsake', 1831)
Published: P. Fumagalli, Florence
28.3 x 22.8 (plate 22.5 x 15.2)
Steel Engraving
Purchased, Lusk, Mr de Courcy Donovan, 1971

Sharpe, Louisa (1798-1843)
English School
ROBINSON, HENRY (FL.1827-1872)
ENGLISH SCHOOL

20,157
The Maid of Athens, (of Byron's poem)
Published: P. Fumagalli, Florence
32 x 26 (plate 22.8 x 15.5)
Stipple
Purchased, Lusk, Mr de Courcy Donovan, 1971

Shee, Martin Archer (1769-1850)
Irish School
BLOOD, T. (FL.1814-1823)
ENGLISH SCHOOL

10,637
Walter Blake Kirwan, P. Dean of Killala, (1754-1805)
(after a wl oil, RA 1803; NGI no. 1129)
Published: Longman, London, 1814
14.7 x 8.9 (plate cut)
Stipple
Acquired between 1913/14

Shee, Martin Archer (1769-1850)
Irish School
CLINT, GEORGE (1770-1854)
ENGLISH SCHOOL

10,489
Walter Blake Kirwan, P. Dean of Killala, (1754-1805)
(after an oil, RA 1803; NGI no. 1129)
Published: G. Clint, London, 1st July 1806
75.8 x 50.6 (plate 71 x 45.5)
Mezzotint
Purchased, London, Mr G. Lausen, 1895

Shee, Martin Archer (1769-1850)
Irish School
CLINT, GEORGE (1770-1854)
ENGLISH SCHOOL

10,948

Francis Rawdon, 2nd Earl of Moira, (1754-1826), later 1st Marquess of Hastings
(after an oil, RA 1804; National Army Museum, Camberley)
Published: G. Clint, London, also P. Garof, Edinburgh, 1st May 1805
79 x 52.5 (plate 70.4 x 45.5)
Mezzotint
Provenance Unknown

Shee, Martin Archer (1769-1850)
Irish School
FORD, JAMES (FL.1772-1812)
RISH SCHOOL

0,274
homas Ryder, (1735-1790), Actor and Manager of Smock Alley Theatre, Dublin
after an oil of c.1790)
ublished: J. Ford, Dublin
8 x 22.5 (plate cut)
tipple
resented, Mr W.G. Strickland, 1906

hee, Martin Archer (1769-1850)
ish School
RIVEN, EDWARD (1775-1841)
GLISH SCHOOL

11,208
Lydia, Countess of Cavan, (née Arnold, d.1862), 2nd wife of the 2nd Earl of Cavan, (pl. J. Burke's 'The Portrait Gallery of Distinguished Females', 1833)
(after an oil, RA 1829)
Published: E. Bull, London (not before December 1829)
26.7 x 18.2 (plate 25.1 x cut)
Stipple
Acquired c.1903

Shee, Martin Archer (1769-1850)
Irish School
TURNER, CHARLES (1773-1857)
ENGLISH SCHOOL

10,487

William Robert Fitzgerald, 2nd Duke of Leinster, (1749-1804)
(after a reduced replica, NGI no. 569, of an oil, RA 1802; Masonic Hall, Dublin)
Published: 1804
70 x 50 (plate 66 x 46.3)
Mezzotint
Presumed purchased, Dublin, Jones Saleroom, 1879

Shee, Martin Archer (1769-1850)
Irish School
WARD THE ELDER, WILLIAM (1766-1826)
ENGLISH SCHOOL

10,100
John Henry Johnstone, (1749-1828), Actor and Singer as Sir Callaghan O'Brallaghan in Macklin's 'Love à La Mode'
(after an oil of 1803, Garrick Club, London)
Published: Messrs. Wards & Co., London, 26th September 1803
48.2 x 35.8 (plate 38.4 x 27.8)
Mezzotint
Purchased, Dublin,
Mr J.V. McAlpine, 1899

Shelley, Samuel (c.1750-1808)
English School
NUTTER, WILLIAM (1754-1802)
ENGLISH SCHOOL

11,094
Colonel Henry Barry, (1750-1822), Aide-de-Camp in N. America to Lord Rawdon
Published: London, 1789
15.8 x 12.5 (plate cut)
Stipple
Provenance Unknown

11,824(2)
Cambridge Terrace and the Coliseum, (now demolished), Regent's Park, London, (pl. for T.H. Shepherd's 'London and its Environs in the 19th century', 1829)
Published: Jones & Co., London, 5th January 1828 (with 11,824-2)
29 x 22.4 (plate 28.5 x 22, each view 8.8 x 15)
Line
Provenance Unknown

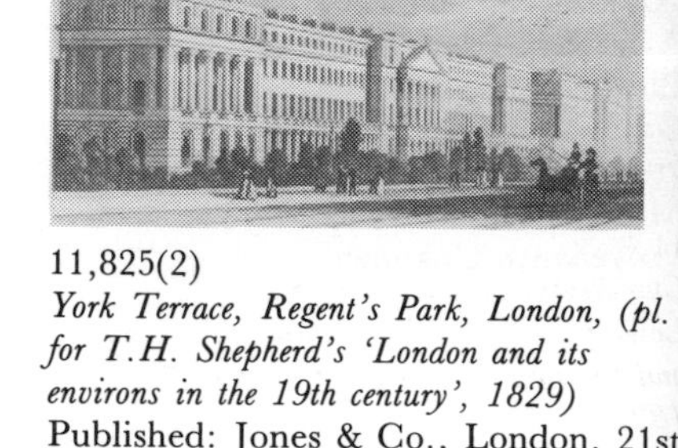

11,825(2)
York Terrace, Regent's Park, London, (pl. for T.H. Shepherd's 'London and its environs in the 19th century', 1829)
Published: Jones & Co., London, 21st July 1827 (with 11,825-2)
28.5 x 22.5 (plate 28.4 x 22, each view 9 x 15.4)
Line
Provenance Unknown

Shepherd, Thomas Hosmer (fl.1817-1840)
English School
ACON, ROBERT (FL.1818-1830)
ENGLISH SCHOOL

11,824(1)
Regent Street East, (now rebuilt), (pl. for T.H. Shepherd's 'London and its Environs in the 19th century', 1829)
Published: Jones & Co., London, 5th January 1828 (with 11,824-2)
29 x 22.4 (plate 28.5 x 22, each view 8.8 x 15)
Line
Provenance Unknown

Shepherd, Thomas Hosmer (fl.1817-1840)
English School
BARBER, THOMAS (FL.1818-1846)
ENGLISH SCHOOL

11,825(1)
A Villa for Regent's Park, London, (pl. for T.H. Shepherd's 'London and its environs in the 19th century', 1829)
INSCRIBED: *The residence of John Maberly Esq., M.P. to whom this plate is respectfully inscribed*
Published: Jones & Co., London, 21st July 1827 (with 11,825-2)
28.5 x 22.5 (plate 28.4 x 22, each view 9 x 15.4)
Line
Provenance Unknown

Shepherd, Thomas Hosmer (fl.1817-1840)
English School
TINGLE, JAMES (FL.1830-1860)
ENGLISH SCHOOL

11,823(1)
Hertford Villa, (now St Dunstans), Regent's Park, London, (pl. for T.H. Shepherd's 'London and its environs in the 19th century', 1829)
INSCRIBED: *The residence of the Marquess of Hertford to whom this plate is respectfully innscribed*
Published: Jones & Co., London, 15th December 1827 (with 11,823-2)
29 x 22.4 (plate 28 x 22, each view 8.5 x 14.5)
Line
Provenance Unknown

Shepherd, Thomas Hosmer (fl.1817-1840)
English School
ACON, ROBERT (FL. 1818-1830'S)
ENGLISH SCHOOL

Shepherd, Thomas Hosmer (fl.1817-1840)
English School
BARBER, THOMAS (FL.1818-1846)
ENGLISH SCHOOL

Shepherd, Thomas Hosmer (fl.1817-1840)
English School
TINGLE, JAMES (FL.1830-1860)
ENGLISH SCHOOL

11,823(2)
Cumberland Terrace, Regents Park, London, (pl. for T.H. Shepherd's 'London and its environs in the 19th century', 1829)
INSCRIBED: To John Nash Esq., Architect to the King. This plate is respectfully dedicated
Published: Jones & Co., London, 15th December 1827 (with 11,823-1)
29 x 22.4 (plate 28 x 22, each view 3.5 x 14.5)
Line
Provenance Unknown

Sherrard, Thomas (18th-19th century)
Irish School
IRISH SCHOOL (1803)

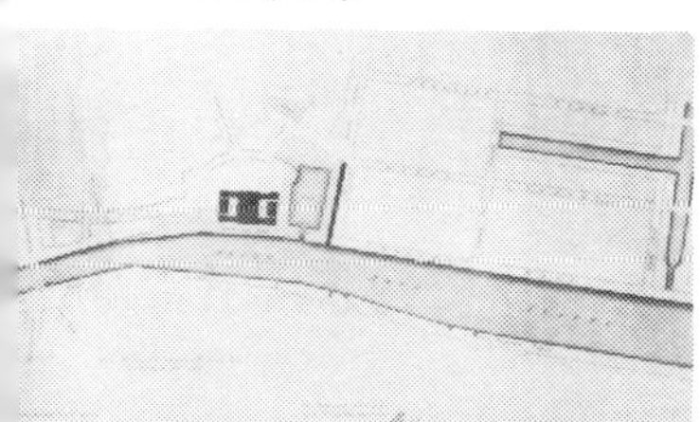

11,807
Survey of Dublin Quays near the Custom House
INSCRIBED: This map is a fac-simile of one/ in the Secretary Office Dublin Castle
72.3 x 59.5 (plate 40 x 56.7)
Line with watercolour
Purchased, Mr W.V. Daniell, 1913

Although numerous hands worked on the following Sherwin prints, only his name is given as engraver

Sherwin, John Keyse (1751-1790)
English School
SHERWIN, JOHN KEYSE (1751-1790)
ENGLISH SCHOOL

11,657
The Installation Banquet of the Knights of St Patrick in the Great Hall, Dublin Castle, 17th March 1783
(after an unfinished oil of c.1785)
5th State; Inscription same as for 4th State, no. 11,658
Published: R. Wilkinson, London, 17th March 1803
64 x 83.8 (plate 61 x 81.5)
Line
Presented, Sir Bernard Burke, 1873

Sherwin, John Keyse (1751-1790)
English School
SHERWIN, JOHN KEYSE (1751-1790)
ENGLISH SCHOOL

11,658
The Installation Banquet of the Knights of St Patrick in the Great Hall, Dublin Castle, 17th March 1783
(after an unfinished oil of c.1785)
4th State, INSCRIBED: Dedicated to the Most Nobel George Marquis of Buckingham, Knight of the Most Nobel Order of the Garter and 1783 Original Grand Master of the Most illustrious Order Of St. Patrick by his most obedient and humble servt. Robert Wilkinson/painted by the late J.K. Sherwin, Historical Engraver to his Majesty and to his Royal Highness The Prince of Wales and partly engraved by him and finished by others since his decease
Published: R. Wilkinson, London, 17th March 1803
68.5 x 87.8 (plate 61 x 80.1)
Line
Provenance Unknown

Sherwin, John Keyse (1751-1790)
English School
SHERWIN, JOHN KEYSE (1751-1790)
ENGLISH SCHOOL

11,827
The Installation Banquet of the Knights of St Patrick in the Great Hall, Dublin Castle, 17th March 1783
(after an unfinished oil of c.1785)
3rd state. Unlettered Proof (touches by F. Bartolozzi)
62.5 x 80 (plate 61 x cut)
Line
Presented, Mr J. Mulhall, 1907

Sherwin, John Keyse (1751-1790)
English School
SHERWIN, JOHN KEYSE (1751-1790)
ENGLISH SCHOOL

11,828
The Installation Banquet of the Knights of St Patrick in the Great Hall, Dublin Castle, 17th March 1785
(after an unfinished oil of c.1785)
1st state; Unlettered Proof, dated in pencil 12th March 1793
65 x 89.5 (plate 61 x 80.5)
Line
Presented, Mr J. Mulhall, 1907

Sherwin, John Keyse (1751-1790)
English School
SHERWIN, JOHN KEYSE (1751-1790)
ENGLISH SCHOOL

11,829
The Installation Banquet of the Knights of St Patrick in the Great Hall, Dublin Castle, 17th March 1783
(after an unfinished oil of c.1785)
2nd state; Unlettered Proof
64.5 x 84 (plate 61 x 80.5)
Line
Provenance unknown

?Shury the Elder, John (fl.1818-c.1849)
English School
SHURY THE ELDER, JOHN (1818-C.1849)
ENGLISH SCHOOL *and*
SHURY THE YOUNGER, JOHN
(FL.1834-C.1849)
ENGLISH SCHOOL

20,280
Brussels Gate and the River Dijle, Mechelen, Belgium, (pl. for 'Continental Tourist', 1849)
Published: Black & Armstrong, London
25 x 16.2 (plate 22.2 x 14.7)
Steel Engraving
Purchased, Lusk, Mr de Courcy Donovan, 1971

Sickert, Walter (1860-1942)
English School
SICKERT, WALTER (1860-1942)
ENGLISH SCHOOL

11,437
Old Heffel of Rowton House
(after an oil of c.1916, York City Art Gallery)
Printed from the original plate by David Strang for the Sickert Trust 1945/47
39.4 x 32.2 (plate 30.5 x 25)
Etching
Presented, The Sickert Trust, 1947

Sickert, Walter (1860-1942)
English School
SICKERT, WALTER (1860-1942)
ENGLISH SCHOOL

11,438
Noctes Ambroisanae, (The Gallery of the Middlesex Music Hall, London), (1906)
(after an oil of 1906, Nottingham Castle Museum)
2nd State
Printed from the original plate by David Strang for the Sickert Trust 1945/47
29.8 x 39.2 (plate 22.2 x 25.3)
Etching and aquatint
Presented, The Sickert Trust, 1947

Sickert, Walter (1860-1942)
English School
SICKERT, WALTER (1860-1942)
ENGLISH SCHOOL

11,439
'O Sole Mio', Maple Street, London, (c.1920)
Printed from the original plate by David Strang for the Sickert Trust 1945/47
39.4 x 32.2 (plate 30.5 x 25)
Etching
Presented, The Sickert Trust, 1947

Sickert, Walter (1860-1942)
English School
SICKERT, WALTER (1860-1942)
ENGLISH SCHOOL

11,440

Dressing for Church, (Wellington House, London)
Printed from the original plate by David Strang for the Sickert Trust 1945/47
23.5 x 17.7 (plate 17.7 x 12.4)
Etching
Presented, The Sickert Trust, 1947

Sickert, Walter (1860-1942)
English School
SICKERT, WALTER (1860-1942)
ENGLISH SCHOOL

11,441
Portrait of a Lady (1894)
Printed from the original plate by David Strang for the Sickert trust 1945/47
22.2 x 15.8 (plate 12.9 x 9.7)
Etching
Presented, The Sickert Trust, 1947

Sickert, Walter (1860-1942)
English School
SICKERT, WALTER (1860-1942)
ENGLISH SCHOOL

11,442
La Gaieté Montparnasse', (Gaieté Montparnasse Music Hall, Paris, 1919)
(after a chalk drawing of c.1907, Fitzwilliam Museum, Cambridge)
3rd State
Printed from the original plate by David Strang for the Sickert Trust 1945/47
23.3 x 15.1 (plate 13.5 x 10.9)
Etching
Presented, The Sickert Trust, 1947

Sickert, Walter (1860-1942)
English School
SICKERT, WALTER (1860-1942)
ENGLISH SCHOOL

11,443
The Old Hôtel Royal, Dieppe, (1894)
Printed from the original plate by David Strang for the Sickert Trust 1945/47
18 x 23.5 (plate 11.2 x 17.2)
Etching
Presented, The Sickert Trust, 1947

Sickert, Walter (1860-1942)
English School
SICKERT, WALTER (1860-1942)
ENGLISH SCHOOL

11,444
'Traghetti Di San Silvestro', (Gondolas of San Silvestro, Venice)
Printed from the original plate by David Strang for the Sickert Trust 1945/47
17.8 x 23.5 (plate 12.6 x 16.5)
Etching
Presented, The Sickert Trust, 1947

Sickert, Walter (1860-1942)
English School
SICKERT, WALTER (1860-1942)
ENGLISH SCHOOL

11,445
Maple Street, London (c.1920)
Printed from the original plate by David Strang for the Sickert Trust 1945/47
27.5 x 19.5 (plate 20 x 13)
Etching
Presented, The Sickert Trust, 1947

Sickert, Walter (1860-1942)
English School
SICKERT, WALTER (1860-1942)
ENGLISH SCHOOL

11,446
'Mon Bon Dodo'
Printed from the original plate by David Strang for the Sickert Trust 1945/47
16.6 x 18.7 (plate 19.9 x 11.6)
Etching
Presented, The Sickert Trust, 1947

Sickert, Walter (1860-1942)
English School
SICKERT, WALTER (1860-1942)
ENGLISH SCHOOL

11,447
'La Gaieté Rochechouard', (Gaieté Rochechouart Music Hall, Paris)
Printed from the original plate by David Strang for the Sickert Trust 1945/47
16.3 x 18.8 (plate 9.3 x 13.1)
Etching
Presented, The Sickert Trust, 1947

Simpson, John (1782-1847)
English School
TURNER, CHARLES (1773-1857)
ENGLISH SCHOOL

10,075
William Grattan Tyrone Power, (1797-1841), Actor and Playwright Unlettered Proof
Published: C. Simpson, London, 1833
42.8 x 33 (plate 35.7 x 25 .3)
Mezzotint
Purchased, Dublin, Mrs Noseda, Febuary 1887

Singleton, Henry (1766-1839)
English School
GODBY, JAMES (FL.1790-1820)
ENGLISH SCHOOL

20,059
The Departure of Cain and his Family, (S. Gessner's 'Death of Abel', Book V)
(after an oil, RA 1800)
Published: J. Murphy, London, 2nd January 1800
75.6 x 53.6 (plate 59.5 x51)
Line and stipple
Provenance Unknown

Singleton, Henry (1766-1839)
English School
GODBY, JAMES (FL.1800-1820)
ENGLISH SCHOOL

20,060
Adam bearing the murdered body of Abel, (S. Gessner's 'Death of Abel', Book IV)
(after an oil, RA 1797)
Published: J. Murphy, London, 1799
76 x 53.5 (plate 60 x 51)
Line and stipple
Provenance Unknown

Skillin, Samuel (c. 1819-1847)
Irish School
KIRKWOOD, JOHN (FL.1826-1853)
IRISH SCHOOL

10,287
William Maginn, (1793-1842), Poet, Author and Journalist, (pl for 'Dublin University Magazine', Vol.XX111, January 1844)

Published: W. Curry Junior, Dublin, 1844
22.7 x 15.3 (plate cut)
Etching
Purchased, Dublin, Mr P. Traynor, 1898

Slater, Joseph (fl.1772-1837)
English School
LEWIS THE ELDER, FREDERICK CHRISTIAN (1779-1856)
ENGLISH SCHOOL

1,389
George Robert Chinnery, (d.1825), Secretary of Embasssy to Portugal
8.9 x 34 (plate 28 x 22.7)
Stipple
Provenance Unknown

later, Joseph (fl.1772-1837)
nglish School
LATER, JOSEPH (FL.1772-1837)
NGLISH SCHOOL

0,271

John MacGregor Skinner, Captain of the Holyhead/Dún Laoghaire Mail Packet 'Escape', (1762-1832)
Published: C.J. Hullmandel, (for the Angelsea Hunting Club), London
30.8 x 25 (image 21 x 17)
Lithograph
Presented, Mr E. Watson, 1924

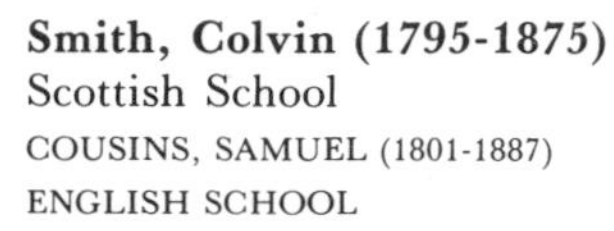

Smith, Colvin (1795-1875)
Scottish School
COUSINS, SAMUEL (1801-1887)
ENGLISH SCHOOL

10,097
Francis Jeffrey, (1773-1850), Lord Advocate and Founding Editor of 'The Edinburgh Review'
(after an oil, SNPG, Edinburgh)
Published: W. Walker, Edinburgh, May 1830
41.5 x 32.2 (plate 39.8 x 30.5)
Mezzotint
Provenance Unknown

Smith, John Raphael (1752-1812)
English School
SMITH, JOHN RAPHAEL (1752-1812)
ENGLISH SCHOOL

10,203
William Burgh, M.P., (1741-1808), Divine, brother-in-law of Walter Hussey Burgh
Published: J.R. Smith, London, also J. Wolstenholme, York, 21st June 1809
36 x 26.5 (plate cut)
Mezzotint
Purchased, Dublin, Mr J.V. McAlpine, 1900

Soest, Gerard (c.1600-1681)
Anglo-Dutch School
PURCELL, RICHARD (FL.1746-1766)
IRISH SCHOOL

10,053
Michael Boyle, P.Archbishop of Armagh, (c.1609-1702), Lord Chancellor of Ireland

INSCRIBED: *From an original in the possession of Mr William Wilks*
Published: W. Wilkinson, Dublin, not before 1702
37.1 x 25.7 (plate cut)
Mezzotint
Purchased, London, 2nd Chaloner Smith sale, 1888

10,846
The Hon. Susanna Fitzpatrick, (née Usher, fl.1748-1759)
(after a lost oil)
Published: London, ?1750
33.2 x 22.6 (plate 32.9 x 22.4)
Mezzotint
Purchased, London, 1st Chaloner Smith sale, 1887

Soest, Gerard (c.1600-1681)
Anglo-Dutch School
WALKER, EMMERY (17TH CENTURY)
ENGLISH SCHOOL

10,717
Colonel Thomas Blood, (1618-1680), Adventurer
(after an oil of c.1670, NPG, London)
33.4 x 26 (plate 24.2 x 17.5)
Mezzotint
Provenance Unknown

Soldi, Andrea (c.1703-1771)
Anglo-Italian School
McARDELL, JAMES (1728/29-1765)
IRISH SCHOOL

Specchi, Alessandro (1668-1729)
Italian School
SPECCHI, ALESSANDRO (1668-1729)
ITALIAN SCHOOL

20,677(2)
The Baldacchino by Bernini, St Peters, Rome, (from 'Views of Rome', see App. 8, no. 20,677)
Published: G. Rossi, Rome
74.3 x 50.6 (plate 66 x 36.3)
Line
Provenance Unknown

Speed, John (1552-1629)
English School
MALTON, JAMES (C.1760-1803)
ENGLISH SCHOOL

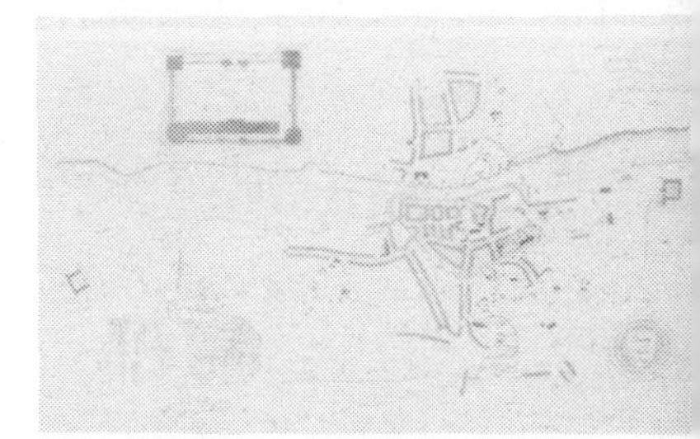

11,567
A Survey of Dublin as it stood in 1610, (pl. for J. Malton's 'A picturesque and descriptive view of the City of Dublin, described in a series of the most interesting scenes taken in the year 1791', 1799)
(after a line engraving of 1611; example in NLI, Dublin)
Published: J. Malton, London, July 1792
34.6 x 51 (plate 27.7 x 48)
Etching and aquatint
Acquired by 1904

Spencer, Countess Lavinia (1762-1831)
English School
BARTOLOZZI, FRANCESCO (1727-1815)
ANGLO-ITALIAN SCHOOL

10,352
Viscountess Henrietta Frances Duncannon, (née Spencer, 1761-1821), sister-in-law of the Artist and wife of Viscount Duncannon, future 3rd Earl of Bessborough
Published: W. Dickinson, London, 13th May 1787

52 x 37.6 (plate 33.5 x 23.4)
Etching
Purchased, Dublin,
Mr J.V. McAlpine, 1906

Spilsbury, John (c.1730-1795)
English School
SPILSBURY, JOHN (c.1730-1795)
ENGLISH SCHOOL

10,851
George William Frederick, Prince of Wales, (1738-1820), later King George III
INSCRIBED: To her Royal Highness, the Princess Dowager of Wales. This Plate is most humbly by Her Royal Highness's most devoted & Obedient humber Servt./Thos. Jeffreys./Done from an original painting in the possession of Thos. Jeffreys.
Published: T. Jeffreys, London, 4th June 1759
39.7 x 29 (plate 39.2 x 28.4)
Mezzotint
Purchased, London, 2nd Chaloner Smith sale, 1888

Sproule, Samuel (18th century)
Irish School
IRISH SCHOOL (1783)

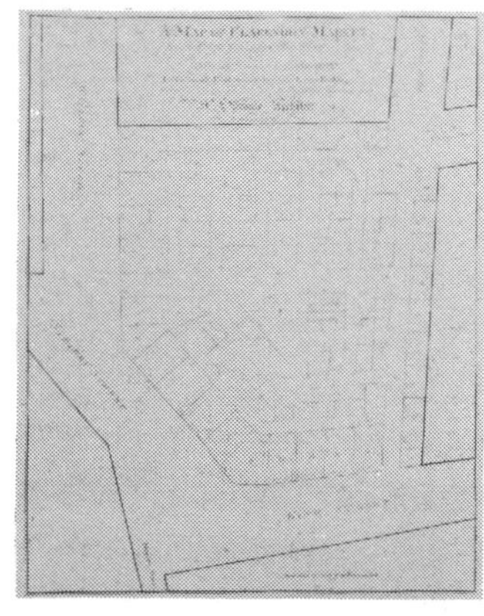

11,818
A map of proposed alterations to Clarendon Market, near St Stephen's Green, Dublin in 1783, (now demolished)
INSCRIBED: The Lots marked and Numbered are to be let for Building/ pursuant to a regular elevation the whole under the Inspection of/ Mr. Sproule Architect laid down by a Scale of 20 feet to an Inch
48 x 37.3 (plate 44.5 x 35)
Line
Purchased, Mr W. V. Daniell, 1913

Stanfield, William Clarkson (1793-1867)
English School
COUSEN, JOHN (1804-1880)
ENGLISH SCHOOL

20,208
Fecamp, Normandy, France, (pl. for Ritchie's 'Travelling Sketches on the Sea coast of France', in C. Heath's 'Picturesque Annuals', 1834)
(after a watercolour of c.1832)
Published: Longman & Co., London, 1834
17.1 x 24.2 (plate 15.5 x 23)
Steel Engraving
Purchased, Lusk, Mr de Courcy Donovan, 1971

Stanfield, William Clarkson (1793-1867)
English School
COUSEN, JOHN (1804-1880)
ENGLISH SCHOOL

20,213
The Storm
Published: Longman & Co., London
17.4 x 24.5 (plate 15.5 x 21.7)
Steel Engraving
Purchased, Lusk, Mr de Courcy Donovan, 1971

Stanfield, William Clarkson (1793-1869)
English School
GOODALL, EDWARD (1795-1870)
ENGLISH SCHOOL

20,495
Castello D'Ischia, Island of Ischia
Published: Art Union of London, 1845 (Printed: McQueen)
41.2 x 58.3 (plate cut)
Steel Engraving
Purchased, Lusk, Mr de Courcy Donovan, 1971

Stanfield, William Clarkson (1793-1867)
English School
LE PETIT, WILLIAM A. (FL.1829-1857)
ENGLISH SCHOOL

20,423
St Michael's Mount, Cornwall
Published: Simpkin & Marshall, (for the Proprietor), London
21.3 x 27.5 (plate cut)
Steel Engraving
Purchased, Lusk, Mr de Courcy Donovan, 1971

Stanfield, William Clarkson (1793-1867)
English School
MILLER, WILLIAM (1796-1882)
ENGLISH SCHOOL

20,207
'Homeward Bound', (leaving the River Mass, Holland), (pl. for C. Heath's 'Picturesque Annuals', 1833)
Published: Longman & Co., London
(Printed: McQueen)
12.4 x 19.5 (plate cut)
Steel Engraving
Purchased, Lusk, Mr de Courcy Donovan, 1971

Stanfield, William Clarkson (1793-1867)
English School
WALLIS, ROBERT (1794-1878)
ENGLISH SCHOOL

20,214
Boats near the island of Murano, Venice, (pl. for Ritchie's 'Travelling Sketches in the North of Italy', in C. Heath's 'Picturesque Annuals', 1832)
(after a watercolour of 1830, City of Manchester Art Galleries)
Published: Longman & Co., London, 1834
17.2 x 24.3 (plate 15.3 x 22.7)
Steel Engraving
Purchased, Lusk, Mr de Courcy Donovan, 1971

Stanfield, William Clarkson (1793-1867)
English School
WALLIS, ROBERT (1794-1878)
ENGLISH SCHOOL

20,413
Godesberg Castle above the River Rhine, Germany
Published: Longman & Co., London
17 x 24.5 (plate 15.3 x 22.5)
Steel Engraving
Purchased, Lusk, Mr de Courcy Donovan, 1971

Steel, Jeremiah (c.1780-after 1846)
English School
RIDLEY, WILLIAM (1764-1838)
ENGLISH SCHOOL *and*
HOLL THE ELDER, WILLIAM (1771-1838)
ENGLISH SCHOOL *and*
BLOOD, T. (FL.1814-1823)
ENGLISH SCHOOL

11,286
Dr Samuel Solomon
20 x 11.5 (plate 14 x 10)
Stipple
Provenance Unknown

Steen, Jan (1626-1679)
Dutch School
LE VILAIN, GERARD RENE (C.1740-1836)
FRENCH SCHOOL

20,074
'As the old sing, so twitter the young'
(after an oil of c.1655, Mauritshuis, The Hague)
46.5 x 62 (plate 34.5 x 40.3)
Line
Provenance Unknown

Stephanoff, Francis Philip (1788-1860)
English School
SCRIVEN, EDWARD (1775-1841)
ENGLISH SCHOOL

11,404
Admiral Sir Edmund Nagle, (1757-1830), as a Knight of the Order of the Bath, (pl. for Sir George Nayler's 'History of the Coronation of George IV', 1839)
Published: Sir George Nayler, London, January 1826
44.8 x 30.5 (image 31 x 18)
Aquatint and stipple
Purchased, Mr W. V. Daniell, 1901

Stevens, D. (18th century)
English School
FABER THE YOUNGER, JOHN (C.1684-1756)
ENGLISH SCHOOL

10,131
George I, King of England, (1660-1727), in Coronation Robes
Published: J. Bowles, London, 1722
36.7 x 26.0 (plate 35.7 x 25.4)
Mezzotint
Purchased, London, 1st Chaloner Smith sale, 1887

Stevenson, William (fl.1839-1844)
Irish School
KIRKWOOD, JOHN (FL.1826-1853)
IRISH SCHOOL

10,592
Rev. Caesar Otway, (1780-1842), Author, Antiquary and a founder of Christian Examiner, (pl. for 'Dublin University Magazine', Vol. XIV, October 1839)
Published: W. Curry Junior & Co., Dublin, 1st October 1839
21.5 x 13 (plate cut)
Etching
Purchased, Dublin, Mr P. Traynor, 1898

Stevenson, William (fl.1839-1844)
Irish School
KIRKWOOD, JOHN (FL.1828-1835)
IRISH SCHOOL

11,120
John Anster, (1793-1867), Author and Translator, (pl. for 'Dublin University Magazine', Vol.XIV, November 1839)
Published: W. Curry Junior & Co., Dublin, 1st November 1839
21.8 x 13.2 (plate cut)
Etching
Purchased, Dublin, Mr P. Traynor, 1898

Stevenson, William (fl.1839-1844)
Irish School
LUCAS, DAVID (1802-1881)
ENGLISH SCHOOL

10,033

Sir Philip Crampton Bt., (1777-1858), Surgeon
Published: A. Milliken, Dublin, 20th December 1842
55 x 41.7 (plate 51 x 38.4)
Mezzotint
Presented, Dublin, Mr S. Catterson Smith the Younger, 1884

Stevenson, William (fl.1839-1844)
Irish School
LUCAS, DAVID (1802-1881)
ENGLISH SCHOOL

10,116
Sir Philip Crampton Bt., (1777-1858), Surgeon, (with facsimile signature)
Published: A. Milliken, Dublin, 20th December 1842
53.4 × 41 (plate 51 × 38.4)
Mezzotint
Provenance Unknown

Stevenson, William (fl.1839-1844)
Irish School
LUCAS, DAVID (1802-1881)
ENGLISH SCHOOL

10,411
Charles Kendal Bushe, (1767-1843), Lord Chief Justice
INSCRIBED: *This Portrait is most/ respectfully inscribed to the Irish Bar, by the Publishers/Andrew Milliken*
Published: A. Milliken, Dublin, also F.G. Moon, London, 30th December 1841
Mounted
Stipple
Presumed purchased, Dublin, Jones Saleroom, 1879

Stevenson, William (fl.1839-1844)
Irish School
STEVENSON, WILLIAM (FL.1839-1844)
IRISH SCHOOL

11,115
Charles Kendal Bushe, (1767-1843), Lord Chief Justice
Published: W. Stevenson, Dublin, 1840
23 x 19.4 (image 19 x 15.5)
Lithograph
Presented, Mr M. O'Shaughnessey, 1881

Stewardson, Thomas (1781-1859)
English School
WARD THE ELDER, WILLIAM (1766-1826)
ENGLISH SCHOOL

10,450
George Canning, M.P., (1770-1827), Statesman and later Prime Minister
(after an oil, RA 1813)
INSCRIBED: *From an original in the possession of Jno Drinkwater Junr Esq. of Liverpool*
Published: W. Ward the Elder, London, 1st November 1813
54 X 38 (plate 50.5 x 35)
Mezzotint
Purchased, London, 2nd Chaloner Smith sale, 1888

Stewart, Anthony (1733-1846)
English School
WOOLNOTH, THOMAS (1785-C.1839)
ENGLISH SCHOOL

10,688
Princess Victoria, (1819-1903), later Queen Victoria of England
INSCRIBED: Dedicated by special permission to/Her Royal Highness the Duchess of Kent
Lettered Proof
Published: R. Ackermann, London, 1st February 1829
35.5 x 26.5 (plate 28 x 23)
Stipple
Acquired by 1901

Stewart, John (fl.1828-1865)
English School
ROBINSON, HENRY (FL.1827-1872)
ENGLISH SCHOOL

10,979
Daniel O'Connell, M.P., (1775-1847), Statesman
(after a drawing of c.1830)
35.4 x 24.9 (plate cut)
Line and stipple
Purchased, Dublin, Dillon & Co., 1901

Stewart, Robert (fl.1776-1801)
English School
SCOTT, EDMUND (C.1746-C.1801)
ENGLISH SCHOOL

11,038
Thomas Sheridan, (1719-1788), Actor, Theatre Manager and Lexicographer, father of Richard Brinsley Sheridan
Published: C. Dilly, London, 4th June 1789
27.2 x 21 (plate 25.6 x 16.8)
Stipple
Purchased, Dublin, Mr J. V. McAlpine, 1899

Stoker, Bartholomew (1763-1788)
Irish School
BROCAS THE ELDER, HENRY (1766-1838)
IRISH SCHOOL

11,176
Richard Hely-Hutchinson, 2nd Baron, later 1st Earl of Donoughmore, (1756-1825), (pl. for 'Sentimental and Masonic Magazine', August, 1792)
Published: Sentimental and Masonic Magazine, Dublin, August 1792
20.3 x 13 (plate 17.7 x 12.5)
Stipple
Purchased, Dublin, Mr P. Traynor, 1898

Stoker, Batholomew (1763-1788)
Irish School
SINGLETON, JOHN (fl.1788-1799)
ENGLISH SCHOOL

10,283
Robert Jephson, (1736-1803), Poet and Dramatist, (frontispiece for his poem 'Roman Portraits', 1794)
Published: G.G. and J. Robinson, London, 1st July 1794
30 x 21 (plate 26 x 20.3)
Stipple
Purchased, Dublin, Mr A. Roth, 1901

Stoker, Bartholomew (1763-1788)
Irish School
COMERFORD, JOHN (?1770-1832)
IRISH SCHOOL
WATTS, S. (18TH-19TH CENTURY)
ENGLISH SCHOOL

11,128
Henry Flood, M.P., (1732-1791), Statesman and Orator
(after a drawing)
22 x 14 (plate 16.5 x 10.2)
Line and etching
Purchased, Dublin, Mr P. Traynor, 1898

Stone, Ellen (fl.1874-1877)
English School
ROBINSON, HENRY (FL.1827-1872)
ENGLISH SCHOOL

20,155
Alice or the Black Riband
Published: Longman & Co., London
24.8 x 15.5 (plate 23.1 x 15.5)
Stipple
Purchased, Lusk, Mr de Courcy Donovan, 1971

Stone, Frank (1800-1859)
English School
ROBINSON, JOHN HENRY (1796-1871)
ENGLISH SCHOOL

10,370
Helena Selina, Baroness Dufferin and Clandeboye, (née Sheridan, 1807-1867), Writer, wife of 4th Baron Dufferin and Clandeboye, later Countess of Gifford, (pl for W. Finden's 'Female Aristocracy of the Court of Queen Victoria', 1849)
Published: W. & E. Finden, London, 1849
42.8 x 32.5 (plate 33.5 x 26)
Stipple
Purchased, Dublin, Mr A. Roth, 1896

Stoop, Dirck (1610-1686)
Dutch School
COOKE, GEORGE (1781-1834)
ENGLISH SCHOOL

20,540
Man leading an unwilling horse to water
Published: G. Cooke, London, 1815
11.7 x 19.2 (plate cut)
Etching
Presented, Mrs D. Molloy, 1981

Stoppelaer, Charles (fl.1703-1745)
Irish School
MILLER, ANDREW (FL.1737-1763)
IRISH SCHOOL

10,917
Joe Miller, (1684-1738), Comedian, as Teague in Sir R. Howard's 'The Committee'
(after an oil of 1738)
Published: ?A. Miller, London, 1739
38.8 x 27.8 (plate 35.2 x 25)
Mezzotint
Purchased, London 1st Chaloner Smith sale, 1887

Storer, James (1781-1852)
English School
STORER, JAMES (1781-1852)
ENGLISH SCHOOL

20,134
A Vaulted Passage and Part of the Ruins of St Bartholomew the Great, Smithfield, London
11 x 14.3 (plate cut)
Etching
Purchased, Lusk, Mr de Courcy Donovan, 1971

Stothard, Thomas (1755-1834)
English School
CARDON, ANTHONY (1772-1813)
FLEMISH SCHOOL

20,067
Catherine of France meets her future husband King Henry V of England, at the treaty of Troyes, 1420
Published: Colnaghi, Sala & Co., (late Torre), London, 1st July 1799
55 x 66 (plate 45.8 x 62.8)
Stipple
Provance Unknown

Strangways, Leonard R. (20th century)
Irish School
STRANGWAYS, LEONARD R. (20TH CENTURY)
IRISH SCHOOL

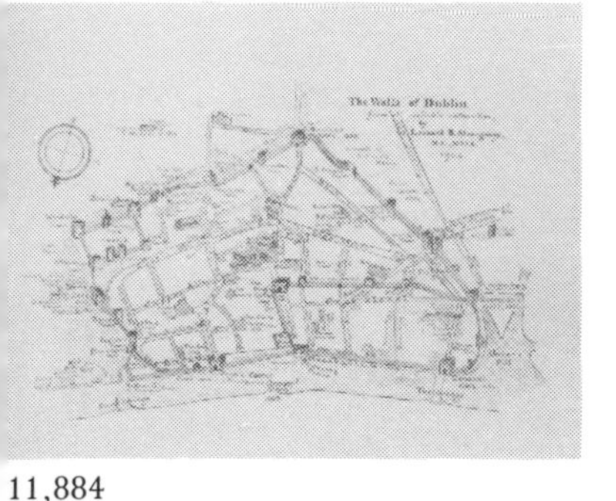

11,884
Map of Dublin within the Medieval City Walls
Published: 1904
29.8 x 36 (plate cut)
Etching
Provenance Unknown

Stuart, Gilbert Charles (1755-1828)
Anglo-American School
COLLYER, JOSEPH (1748-1827)
ENGLISH SCHOOL

10,118
Francis Rawdon Hastings, 2nd Earl of Moira, (1754-1826), later 1st Marquess of Hastings
INSCRIBED: *Engraved from the Original Picture,/in the possession of Dr Hayes*
Published: Darling & Thompson, also T. Simpson, also H. Ryland, also J. Collyer, London 11th June 1794
36.4 x 27.9 (plate 32.7 x 25.3)
Stipple
Purchased, London Mr J.V. McAlpine, 1905

Stuart, Gilbert Charles (1755-1828)
Anglo-American School
DICKINSON, WILLIAM (1746-1823)
ENGLISH SCHOOL

10,110
William Preston, P. Bishop of Ferns, (d. 1789)
Unlettered Proof
Published: not before 1789
37 x 27 (plate 36.7 x 26.4)
Mezzotint
Purchased, London, 1st Chaloner Smith sale, 1887

Stuart, Gilbert Charles (1755-1828)
Anglo-American School
EVANS, WILLIAM (FL.1797-1856)
ENGLISH SCHOOL

10,622
Hugh Hamilton, P. Bishop of Ossory, (1729-1805), (frontispiece for his 'Works', 1807)
Published: G. & W. Nicol, London, 1st May 1807
21.2 x 17 (plate cut)
Stipple
Purchased, London, 3rd Chaloner Smith sale, 1896

Stuart, Gilbert Charles (1755-1828)
Anglo-American School
FACIUS (C.1750-AFTER 1802)
ANGLO-GERMAN SCHOOL

20,665(1)
John Boydell, (1719-1804), Alderman of the City of London, engraver and publisher, (from 'Liber Veritatis', Vol 2, 1776, see App. 8, no. 20,665)
Published: J. & J. Boydell, London, 4th June 1802 (Printed: W. Bulmer & Co.)
41.5 27 (plate 22 x 16.3)
Line and stipple
Bequeathed, Judge J. Murnaghan, 1976

Stuart, Gilbert Charles (1755-1828)
American School
FARN, J. (18TH CENTURY)
ENGLISH SCHOOL

11,190
William Burton Conyngham, M.P. (1733-1796), Teller of the Exchange in Ireland, (pl. for 'European Magazine', March 1794)
(after G.C. Stuart/Schiavonetti line engraving of 1793; example in BM London)
Published; J. Sewell, London, 1st November 1793
21 x 12.5 (plate 17.7 x 11.5)
Line and Stipple
Purchased, Dublin, Mr P. Traynor, 1898

Stuart, Gilbert Charles (1755-1828)
American School
FARN, J (18TH CENTURY)
ENGLISH SCHOOL

11,191
William Burton Conyngham, (1733-1796), Teller of the Exchange in Ireland, (pl. for 'European Magazine', March 1794), (another copy)
(after a G.C. Stuart/L. Schiavonetti line engraving of 1793; example in BM, London)
Published: J. Sewell, London, 1st November 1793
21.4 x 13.5
Line and stipple
Purchased, Dublin, Mr P. Traynor, 1898

Stuart, Charles Gilbert (1755-1828)
Anglo-American School
EVANS, WILLIAM (FL.1797-1856)
ENGLISH SCHOOL
FRY, WILLIAM THOMAS (1789-1831)
ENGLISH SCHOOL

10,739
Isaac Barré, M.P., (1726-1802), Soldier and Vice-Treasurer of Ireland, (pl. for T. Cadell & W. Davies 'British Gallery of Contemporary Portraits', 1822)
(after an oil of 1785, Brooklyn Museum, New York)
Published: T. Cadell & W. Davies, London, 1st February 1817
38.4 x 31 (plate cut)
Stipple
Purchased, Dublin, Mr A. Roth, 1897

Stuart, Gilbert Charles (1755-1828)
Anglo-American School
HALL, JOHN (1739-1797)
ENGLISH SCHOOL

10,152

Isaac Barré, M.P., (1726-1802), Soldier and Vice-Treasurer of Ireland
(after an oil of 1785, Brooklyn Museum, New York)
Published: J. Hall, London, 5th April 1787 (Printed: C.E. Richards)
44.5 x 35.7 (plate 39.3 x 29)
Line
Purchased, Dublin, Mr A. Roth, 1896

Stuart, Gilbert Charles (1755-1828)
Anglo-American School
HODGES, CHARLES HOWARD (?1764-1837)
ENGLISH SCHOOL

0,092
Villiam Robert FitzGerald, 2nd Duke of einster, (1749-1804)
after an oil of c.1790, Montclair Art Auseum, New Jersey)
ublished: G. Cowen, Dublin and at . Macklin's, London, 2nd January 792
8.2 x 27.4 (plate cut)
Aezzotint
urchased, London, 1st Chaloner mith sale, 1887

tuart, Gilbert Charles (1755-1828)
nglo-American School
ODGES, CHARLES HOWARD (?1764-1837)
NGLISH SCHOOL

10,150
John Beresford, (1738-1805), First Commissioner of Revenue in Ireland
(after an oil of c.1790, Curraghmore House, Co. Waterford)
G. Cowen, Dublin and at T. Macklin's, London, 1st November 1790
38.2 x 28.1 (plate 37.6 x 27.5)
Mezzotint
Purchased, London, 1st Chaloner Smith sale, 1887

Stuart, Gilbert Charles (1775-1828)
Anglo-American School
HODGES, CHARLES HOWARD (?1764 -1837)
ENGLISH SCHOOL

10,217
Henry Grattan, M.P., (1746-1820), Statesman
(after an oil of c.1790, NGI no. 1163)
Published: G. Cowen, Dublin and at T. Macklin's, London, 15th November 1792
38 x 28.7 (plate cut x 27.5)
Mezzotint
Presented, Mr H. McManus, 1877

Stuart, Gilbert Charles (1775-1828)
Anglo-American School
HODGES, CHARLES HOWARD (?1764-1837)
ENGLISH SCHOOL

10,247
William Burton Conyngham, (1733-96), Teller of the Irish Exchequer and Treasurer of the Royal Irish Academy
(after an oil of c.1790, NGI no. 562)
Published: G. Cowen, Dublin and at T. Macklin's, London, 15th November 1792
50.7 x 41.5 (plate 38 x 28)
Mezzotint
Purchased, London, Mr G. Lausen, 1895

Stuart, Gilbert Charles (1775-1828)
American School
HODGES, CHARLES HOWARD (?1764-1837)
ENGLISH SCHOOL

10,251
William Brownlow, M.P. for Lurgan, (1726-1794), Musician
(after an oil of c.1790)
Published: G. Cowen, Dublin and at T. Macklin's, London, 2nd January 1792
37.4 x 27.3 (plate cut)
Mezzotint
Acquired between 1890/98

Stuart, Gilbert Charles (1775-1828)
Anglo-American School
HODGES, CHARLES HOWARD (?1764-1837)
ENGLISH SCHOOL

10,494
John FitzGibbon, (1749-1800), Lord Chancellor of Ireland, later 1st Earl of Clare
(after an oil of 1789, Cleveland Museum of Art, Ohio)
Published: G. Cowen, Dublin and at T. Macklin's, London, 20th September 1790
67.4 x 41.2 (plate 65.5 x 38)
Mezzotint
Purchased, London, 1st Chaloner Smith sale, 1887

Stuart, Gilbert Charles (1755-1828)
Anglo-American School
HODGES, CHARLES HOWARD (?1764-1837)
ENGLISH SCHOOL

10,501
John Foster, (1740-1828), last speaker of the Irish House of Commons, later 1st Baron Oriel
(after an oil of 1791, The Nelson-Atkins Museum of Art, Kansas City)
Published: G. Cowen, Dublin and at T. Macklin's, 2nd January 1792
58.1 x 39.7 (plate 38.5 x 57.2)
Mezzotint
Purchased, London, Mr R. Thomas, 1925

Stuart, Gilbert Charles (1755-1828)
Anglo-American School
HODGES, CHARLES HOWARD (?1764-1837)
ENGLISH SCHOOL

10,726
William Brownlow, M.P. for Lurgan, (1726-1794), Musician, (another copy)
(after an oil of c.1790)
Published: G. Cowen, Dublin and at T. Macklin's, London, 2nd January 1792
38.6 x 28.5 (plate 38 x 28)
Mezzotint
Purchased, London, 1st Chaloner Smith sale, 1887

Stuart, Gilbert Charles (1755-1828)
Anglo-American School
IRISH SCHOOL (C.1790)

10,635
'Leinster, the humane and great'- William Robert FitzGerald, 2nd Duke of Leinster, (1749-1804)

(after an oil of c.1790, Montclair Art Museum, New Jersey)
21 x 13.1 (plate 18.8 x 11.5)
Stipple
Provenance Unknown

Stuart, Gilbert Charles (1755-1828)
Anglo-American School
IRISH SCHOOL (C.1795)

10,079
'The Rt. Hon. Henry Grattan's answer to the Roman Catholic Address, Dublin, 1795, with portraits of (l-r), Henry Flood, M.P., Sir John Parnell, M.P., (1744-1801), Henry Grattan, M.P., (1746-1820), William Robert FitzGerald, 2nd Duke of Leinster, (1749-1804) and William Wentworth-FitzWilliam, 2nd Earl FitzWilliam, (1748-1833)
(Grattan after an oil of c.1790, NGI no. 1163; Leinster after an oil of c.1790, Montclair Art Museum, New Jersey)
Published: Dublin, c.1795
47 x 33.23 (plate 45.5 x 32.5)
Stipple and print
Provenance Unknown

Stuart, Gilbert Charles (1755-1828)
Anglo-American School
IRISH SCHOOL (1799)

11,131
John Foster, (1740-1828), last speaker of the House of Commons, later 1st Baron Oriel
(after a wl oil of 1791, Nelson Atkins Museum of Art, Kansas City)
INSCRIBED: Dedicated to the Glorious 111 Irish Commoners/who on the 26th of Jany. 1799 saved the Legislative/ Independance of their Country
20.7 x 12.8 (plate cut x 10)
Line and stipple
Purchased, Dublin, Mr P. Traynor, 1898

Stuart, Gilbert Charles (1755-1828)
Anglo-American School
LUPTON, THOMAS GOFF (1791-1873)
ENGLISH SCHOOL

20,664(1)
Richard Earlom, (1743-1822), Engraver, (frontispiece from 'Liber Veritatis', Vol 3, 1819, see App. 8, no. 20,664)
Published: Hurst Robinson & Co., successors to J. & J. Boydell, London, 1st February 1819
41.5 x 27.5 (plate cut)
Mezzotint
Bequeathed, Judge J. Murnaghan, 1976

?Stuart, Gilbert Charles (1755-1828)
Anglo-American School
MACKENZIE, FREDERICK (1787-1851)
SCOTTISH SCHOOL

11,130
John Fitzgibbon, 1st Earl of Clare, (1749-1802), Lord Chancellor of Ireland
(?after G. C. Stuart/C. Hodges mezzotint of 1790, NGI no. 10,494)
13.5 x 8.8 (plate cut)
Stipple
Acquired between 1913/14

Stuart, Gilbert Charles (1755-1828)
Anglo-American School
MAGUIRE, PATRICK (FL.1783-1820)
IRISH SCHOOL

10,277
John Foster, (1740-1828), Last Speaker of the Irish House of Commons, later 1st Baron Oriel
(after a wl oil of 1791, Nelson-Atkins Museum of Art, Kansas City)
Published: Henecy & Fitzpatrick, Dublin, 1799
43.7 x 25.8 (plate cut x 24.8)
Stipple
Presented, Mr W.G. Strickland, 1906

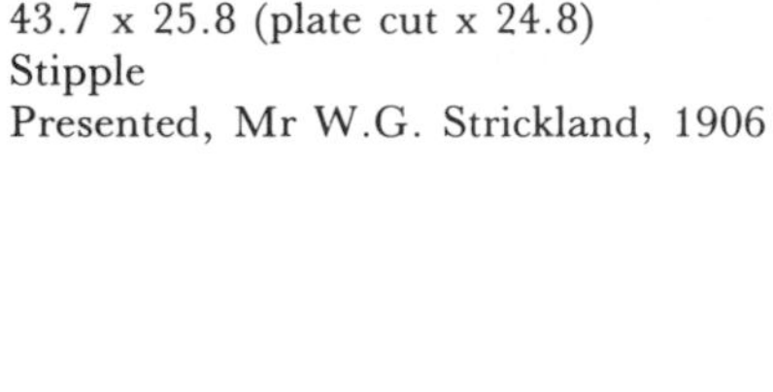

Stuart, Gilbert Charles (1755-1828)
Anglo-American School
SAY, WILLIAM (1768-1834)
ENGLISH SCHOOL

10,083
Charles Agar, P. Archbishop of Cashel, (1736-1809), later Archbishop of Dublin, 1st Viscount Somerton and 1st Earl of Normanton
(after an oil of 1783/93, Somerley, Hampshire)
Published: 1803
45.2 x 39 (plate 38.5 x 28.1)
Mezzotint
Purchased, London, 3rd Chaloner Smith sale, 1896

Stuart, Gilbert Charles (1755-1828)
Anglo-American School
SAY, WILLIAM (1768-1834)
ENGLISH SCHOOL

10,478
Edmond Sexton Pery, 1st Viscount Pery, (1719-1806), former Speaker of the Irish House of Commons
(after an oil of c.1790, ?NGI no 822)
Published: Colnaghi & Co., London, 20th July 1809
60.6 x 44.7 (plate 50.7 x 35)
Mezzotint
Purchased, London, 3rd Chaloner Smith sale, 1896

Stuart, Gilbert Charles (1755-1828)
Anglo-American School
WARD THE ELDER, WILLIAM (1766-1826)
ENGLISH SCHOOL

11,033
Robert Shaw, M.P., (1749-1796), Comptroller of the General Post Office
(after an oil of c.1790)
Published: W. Allen, Dublin, April 1797
38.5 x 28 (plate 37.7 x 27.8)
Mezzotint
Purchased, London, 3rd Chaloner Smith sale, 1896

Stuart, Gilbert Charles (1755-1828)
Anglo-American School
WARD THE ELDER, WILLIAM (1766-1826)
ENGLISH SCHOOL

10,268
Robert Shaw, M.P., (1749-1796), Banker, Comptroller of the Post Office
(after an oil of c.1790)
Unlettered Proof
38.1 x 28.2 (plate cut)
Mezzotint
Purchased, London, 3rd Chaloner Smith sale, 1896

Sullivan, Dennis (19th century)
Irish School
SULLIVAN, DENNIS (19TH CENTURY)
IRISH SCHOOL

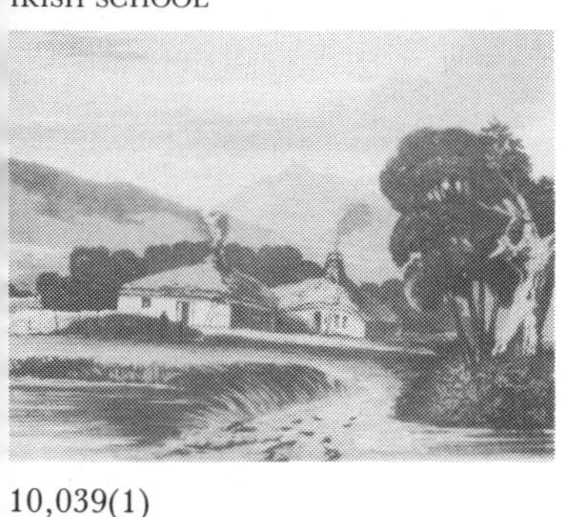

10,039(1)
Irish Cottages, ('Wretched Miserable Hovels'), Co. Wicklow (from 'A picturesque tour through Ireland', 1824, see App. 8, no. 10,039)
Published: T. McLean, London, 1824
(Printed: N. Lewis)
20.4 x 27 (plate 17.3 x 21)
Colour Aquatint
Purchased, Lewes, Bow Windows Bookshop, 1968

Sullivan, Dennis (19th century)
Irish School
SULLIVAN, DENNIS (19TH CENTURY)
IRISH SCHOOL

10,039(3)
Gold Mines, Avoca, Co. Wicklow. (from 'A picturesque tour through Ireland' 1824, see App. 8, no. 10,039)
Published: T. McLean, London, 1824
(Printed: N. Lewis)
20.4 x 27 (plate 17.3 x 21)
Colour Aquatint
Purchased, Lewes, Bow Windows Bookshop, 1968

Sullivan, Dennis (19th century)
Irish School
SULLIVAN, DENNIS (19TH CENTURY)
IRISH SCHOOL

10,039(5)
The House of St Molaise, Teampull More, the Abbey Church and Round Tower, Devinish, Lough Erne, Co. Fermanagh, (from 'A picturesque tour through Ireland', 1824, see App. 8, no. 10,039)
Published: T. McLean, London, 1824
(Printed: N. Lewis)
20.4 x 27 (plate 17.4 x 21)
Colour Aquatint
Purchased, Lewes, Bow Windows Bookshop, 1968

Sullivan, Dennis (19th century)
Irish School
SULLIVAN, DENNIS (19TH CENTURY)
IRISH SCHOOL

10,039(2)
Two ninth century Stone Crosses at Old Kilcullen, Co. Kildare. (from 'A picturesque tour through Ireland', 1824, see App. 8, no. 10,039)
Published: T. McLean, London, 1824
(Printed: N. Lewis)
20.4 x 27 (plate 17.5 x 20.5)
Colour Aquatint
Purchased, Lewes, Bow Windows Bookshop, 1968

Sullivan, Dennis (19th century)
Irish School
SULLIVAN, DENNIS (19TH CENTURY)
IRISH SCHOOL

10,039(4)
Lugnaquilla Mountain, Co. Wicklow. (from 'A picturesque tour through Ireland', 1824, see App. 8, no. 10,039)
Published: T. McLean, London, 1824
(Printed: N. Lewis)
20.4 x 27 (plate 17.8 x 21.8)
Colour Aquatint
Purchased, Lewes, Bow Windows Bookshop, 1968

Sullivan, Dennis (19th century)
Irish School
SULLIVAN, DENNIS (19TH CENTURY)
IRISH SCHOOL

10,039(6)
Monaincha Abbey, Co. Tipperary, (from 'A pictureqe tour through Ireland', 1824, see App. 8, no. 10,039)
Published: T. McLean, London, 1824
(Printed: N. Lewis)
20.4 x 27 (plate 17.8 x 22)
Colour Aquatint
Purchased Lewes, Bow Windows Bookshop, 1968

Sullivan, Dennis (19th century)
Irish School
SULLIVAN, DENNIS (19TH CENTURY)
IRISH SCHOOL

10,039(7)
Lough Leane, (Lower Lake) Killarney, Co. Kerry, (from 'A picturesque tour through Ireland', 1824, see App. 8, no. 10,039)
Published: T. McLean, London, 1824
(Printed: N. Lewis)
20.4 27 (plate 17.2 x 22.3)
Colour Aquatint
Purchased, Lewes, Bow Windows Bookshop, 1968

Sullivan, Dennis (19th century)
Irish School
SULLIVAN, DENNIS (19TH CENTURY)
IRISH SCHOOL

10,039(9)
Trim Castle, Co. Meath from across the river Boyne, (from 'A picturesque tour of Ireland' 1824, see App. 8, no. 10,039)
Published: T. McLean, London, 1824
(Printed: N. Lewis)
20.4 x 27 (plate 17.5 x 23)
Colour Aquatint
Purchased, Lewes, Bow Windows Bookshop, 1968

Sullivan, Dennis (19th century)
Irish School
SULLIVAN, DENNIS (19TH CENTURY)
IRISH SCHOOL

10,039(11)
Balregar Castle, Co. Louth, (from 'A picturesque tour through Ireland', 1824, see App. 8, no. 10,039)
Published: T. McLean, London, 1824
(Printed: N. Lewis)
20.4 x 27 (plate 17.6 x 22.8)
Colour Aquatint
Purchased, Lewes, Bow Windows Bookshop, 1968

Sullivan, Dennis (19th century)
Irish School
SULLIVAN, DENNIS (19TH CENTURY)
IRISH SCHOOL

10,039(8)
Aghaboe Abbey, Co. Laois (from 'A picturesque tour through Ireland,' 1824, see App. 8, no. 10,039)
Published: T. McLean, London, 1824
(Printed: N. Lewis)
20.4 x 27 (plate 17.3 x 21.5)
Colour Aquatint
Purchased, Lewes, Bow Windows Bookshop, 1968

Sullivan, Dennis (19th century)
Irish School
SULLIVAN, DENNIS (19TH CENTURY)
IRISH SCHOOL

10,039(10)
The Giant's Causeway, Co. Antrim, (from 'A picturesque tour through Ireland', 1824, see App. 8, no. 10,039)
Published: T. McLean, London, 1824
(Printed: N. Lewis)
20.4 x 27 (plate 17 x 22.4)
Colour Aquatint
Purchased, Lewes, Bow Windows Bookshop, 1968

Sullivan, Dennis (19th century)
Irish School
SULLIVAN, DENNIS (19TH CENTURY)
IRISH SCHOOL

10,039(12)
Roche Castle, Co. Louth, (from 'A picturesque tour through Ireland', 1824, see App. 8, no. 10,039)
Published: T. McLean, London, 1824
(Printed: N. Lewis)
20.4 x 27 (plate 17.5 x 21.5)
Colour Aquatint
Purchased, Lewes, Bow Windows Bookshop, 1968

Sullivan, Dennis (19th century)
Irish School
SULLIVAN, DENNIS (19TH CENTURY)
IRISH SCHOOL

10,039(13)
The entrance to Belfast Lough, (from 'A picturesque tour through Ireland', 1824, see App. 8, no. 10,039)
Published: T. McLean, London, 1824
(Printed: N. Lewis)
20.4 x 27 (plate 17 x 21.8)
Colour Aquatint
Purchased, Lewes, Bow Windows Bookshop, 1968

Sullivan, Dennis (19th century)
Irish School
SULLIVAN, DENNIS (19TH CENTURY)
IRISH SCHOOL

10,039(15)
The River Shannon, near Lough Derg, Co. Clare (from 'A picturesque tour through Ireland', 1824, see App. 8, no. 10,039)
Published: T. McLean, London, 1824
(Printed: N. Lewis)
20.4 x 27 (plate 17.6 x 23)
Colour Aquatint
Purchased, Lewes, Bow Windows Bookshop, 1968

Sullivan, Dennis (19th century)
Irish School
SULLIVAN, DENNIS (19TH CENTURY)
IRISH SCHOOL

10,039(17)
Downpatrick with St Patrick's Cathederal and the Quoile Valley, Co. Down (from 'A pictureque tour of Ireland,' 1824, see App. 8, no. 10,039)
Published: T.McLean, London, 1824
(Printed: N. Lewis)
20.4 x 27 (plate 17.7 x 22.2)
Colour Aquatint
Purchased, Lewes, Bow Windows Bookshop, 1968

Sullivan, Dennis (19th century)
Irish School
SULLIVAN, DENNIS (19TH CENTURY)
IRISH SCHOOL

10,039(14)
Belfast, Co. Antrim, from the Carrickfergus Road, (from 'A picturesque tour through Ireland', 1824, see App. no. 8, 10,039)
Published: T. McLean, London, 1824
(Printed: N. Lewis)
20.4 x 27 (plate 18.2 x 22)
Colour Aquatint
Purchased, Lewes, Bow Windows Bookshop, 1968

Sullivan, Dennis (19th century)
Irish School
SULLIVAN, DENNIS (19TH CENTURY)
IRISH SCHOOL

10,039(16)
The Mountains of Mourne, Co. Down, (from 'A picturesque tour through Ireland', 1824, see App. 8, no. 10,039)
Published: T. McLean, London, 1824
(Printed: N. Lewis)
20.4 x 27 (plate 17.5 x 21.2)
Colour Aquatint
Purchased, Lewes, Bow Windows Bookshop, 1968

Sullivan, Dennis (19th century)
Irish School
SULLIVAN, DENNIS (19TH CENTURY)
IRISH SCHOOL

10,039(18)
Lough Neagh, (from 'A picturesque tour through Ireland', 1824, see App. 8, no. 10,039)
Published: T. McLean, London, 1824
(Printed: N. Lewis)
20.4 x 27 (plate 18.2 x 22)
Colour Aquatint
Purchased, Lewes, Bow Windows Bookshop, 1968

Sullivan, Dennis (19th century)
Irish School
SULLIVAN, DENNIS (19TH CENTURY)
IRISH SCHOOL

10,039(19)
Carlingford Castle and Lough, Co. Louth, (from 'A picturesque tour through Ireland', 1824, see App. 8, no. 10,039)
Published: T. McLean, London, 1824
(Printed: N. Lewis)
20.4 x 27 (plate 17.5 x 21)
Colour Aquatint
Purchased, Lewes, Bow Window Bookshop, 1968

Sullivan, Dennis (19th century)
Irish School
SULLIVAN, DENNIS (19TH CENTURY)
IRISH SCHOOL

10,039(21)
The Salmon Leap, Leixlip, Co. Kildare, (from 'A picturesque tour through Ireland', 1824, see App. 8, no. 10,039)
Published: T. McLean, London, 1824
(Printed: N. Lewis)
20.4 x 27 (plate 17.2 x 21.4)
Colour Aquatint
Purchased, Lewes, Bow Windows Bookshop, 1968

Sullivan, Dennis (19th century)
Irish School
SULLIVAN, DENNIS (19TH CENTURY)
IRISH SCHOOL

10,039(23)
Bray Head, Co. Wicklow, (from 'A picturesque tour through Ireland', 1824, see App. 8, no. 10,039)
Published: T. McLean, London, 1824
(Printed: N. Lewis)
20.4 x 27 (plate 17.2 x 22.3)
Colour Aquatint
Purchased, Lewes, Bow Windows Bookshop, 1968

Sullivan, Dennis (19th century)
Irish School
SULLIVAN, DENNIS (19TH CENTURY)
IRISH SCHOOL

10,039(20)
Waterfall on the Mealagh River, near Bantry, Co. Cork, (from 'A picturesque tour through Ireland', 1824, see App. 8, no. 10,039)
Published: T. McLean, London, 1824
(Printed: N. Lewis)
20.4 x 27 (plate 17.5 x 23.2)
Colour Aquatint
Purchased, Lewis, Bow Windows Bookshop, 1968

Sullivan, Dennis (19th century)
Irish School
SULLIVAN, DENNIS (19TH CENTURY)
IRISH SCHOOL

10,039(22)
Dunamase Castle and Rock, Co. Laois, (from 'A picturesque tour through Ireland', 1824, see App. 8, no. 10,039)
Published: T. McLean, London, 1824
(Printed: N. Lewis)
20.4 x 27 (plate 17 x 22)
Colour Aquatint
Purchased, Lewes, Bow Windows Bookshop, 1968

Sullivan, Dennis (19th century)
Irish School
SULLIVAN, DENNIS (19TH CENTURY)
IRISH SCHOOL

10,039(24)
St Kelly's Castle on the River Blackwater, Co. Waterford, (from 'A picturesque tour through Ireland', 1824, see App. 8, no. 10,039)
Published: T. McLean, London, 1824
(Printed: N. Lewis)
20.4 x 27 (plate 17.2 x 21.1)
Colour Aquatint
Purchased, Lewes, Bow Windows Bookshop, 1968

Sullivan, Dennis (19th century)
Irish School
SULLIVAN, DENNIS (19TH CENTURY)
IRISH SCHOOL

10,039(25)
King John's Castle and John's Bridge, Limerick, (from 'A picturesque tour through Ireland', 1824, see App. 8, no. 10,039)
Published: T. McLean, London, 1824 (Printed: N. Lewis)
20.4 x 27 (plate 17.8 x 22)
Colour Aquatint
Purchased, Lewes, Bow Windows Bookshop, 1968

?Swiss School (19th century)
?SWISS SCHOOL (19TH SCHOOL)

20,648
The Grimsel Hospice by the Grimsel-See, Switzerland
.5 x 18.3 (plate cut)
Aquatint
Presented, Mrs D. Molloy, 1981

Syer, John (1815-1885)
English School
SYER, JOHN (1815-1885)
ENGLISH SCHOOL

20,223
Stormy Sea with Boats, (from 'Studies from the portfolios of Various Artists from Nature on Stone', 1851)
Published: G. Rowney & Co., London, 1851
23.7 x 33.5 (image 17.2 x 27.7)
Lithograph
Purchased, Lusk, Mr de Courcy Donovan, 1971

Syer, John (1815-1885)
English School
SYER, JOHN (1815-1885)
ENGLISH SCHOOL

20,348
Fishing Boats in a Cove, (from 'Studies from the Portfolios of Various Artists, drawn from Nature on Stone', 1851)
Published: C. Rowney & Co., London, 1851 (Printed: M. & N. Hanhart)
24 x 33.5 (image 18.2 x 26)
Lithograph
Purchased, Lusk, Mr de Courcy Donovan, 1971

Syer, John (1815-1885)
English School
SYER, JOHN (1815-1885)
ENGLISH SCHOOL

20,350
Bristol Docks, Avon, (from 'Studies from the Portfolios of Various Artists drawn from Nature on Stone', 1851)
Published: C. Rowney & Co., London, 1851 (Printed: M. & N. Hanhart)
23.9 x 33.4 (image 17.2 x 25.8)
Lithograph
Purchased, Lusk, Mr de Courcy Donovan, 1971

Syer, John (1815-1885)
English School
SYER, JOHN (1815-1885)
ENGLISH SCHOOL

20,369
A Beach near Weston-Super-Mare, Avon (from 'Studies from the Portfolios of Various Artists, drawn from Nature upon Stone', 1851)
Published: G. Rowney, London, 1851 (Printed: Day & Son)
Lithograph
Purchased, Lusk, Mr de Courcy Donovan, 1971

T

Taylor, Weld (fl.1836-1852)
English School
TAYLOR, WELD (FL.1836-1852)
ENGLISH SCHOOL

10,162
Philip Meadows Taylor, (1808-1876), Administrator in India, Author, amateur painter and the artist's brother
Published: ?W. Taylor, London
36.3 x 28.6 (image 23.5 x 19.3 approx)
Lithograph
Purchased, London, Mr W.V. Daniell, 1901

Taylor, William Benjamin (1781-1850)
Irish School
TAYLOR, WILLIAM BENJAMIN (1781-1850)
IRISH SCHOOL *and*
BLUCK, J. (FL.1791-1819)
ENGLISH SCHOOL

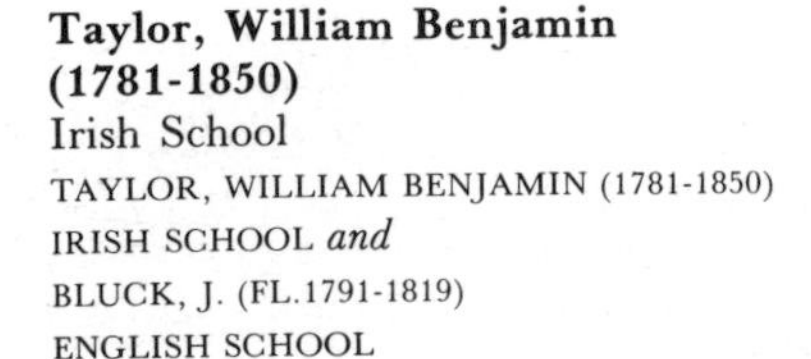

11,621
Front Square, Trinity College, Dublin at the Quarterly Examinations, (intended as pl. for a 'History of the University of Dublin')
Published: W.B. Taylor, Dublin, 1819
33 x 37 (plate 30 x 34.8)
Etching and aquatint with watercolour
Acquired between 1908/14

Taylor, William Benjamin (1781-1850)
Irish School
TAYLOR, WILLIAM BENJAMIN (1781-1850)
IRISH SCHOOL *and*
HAVELL THE ELDER, ROBERT (FL.1800-1840)
ENGLISH SCHOOL
and
HAVEL THE YOUNGER, ROBERT (FL.1820-1840)
ENGLISH SCHOOL

11,622
The Old Museum, Regent House, Trinity College, Dublin
Published: W.B. Taylor, Dublin, 1st October 1819
33 x 37 (plate 30 x 34.8)
Etching and aquatint with watercolour
Acquired between 1908/14

Tell, William (19th century)
Irish School
TELL, WILLIAM (19TH CENTURY)
IRISH SCHOOL

10,512
Hints and Hits No. 1: Moral Against Physical Force, the Scales of Repeal- Daniel O'Connell, M.P., (1775-1847), against Sir Robert Peel, (1788-1880), Arthur Wellesley, 1st Duke of Wellington, (1769-1852), and others
Published: J. McCormick, Dublin; plain 1d, coloured 2d
22.3 x 28.3 (image 15 x 19.5)
Wood Engraving
Provenance Unknown

Tell, William (19th century)
Irish School
TELL, WILLIAM (19TH CENTURY)
IRISH SCHOOL

10,513

Hints and Hits No. 2: 'Staggering Bob on his last legs' - Daniel O'Connell, M.P., (1775-1847), holding Prime Minister Sir Robert Peel, (1788-1850), on a lead while Arthur Wellesley, 1st Duke of Wellington, (1769-1852), lies knifed by Emancipation
Published: J. McCormick, Dublin, 1844: plain 1d, coloured 2d
22.3 x 28.2 (image 15 x 19)
Wood Engraving
Provenance Unknown

Teniers the Younger, David (1610-1690)
Flemish School
COOPER, ROBERT (FL.1795-1836)
ENGLISH SCHOOL

20,078
The Green Cap
(after an oil of 1637, Thyssen-Bornemisze collection, Lugano)
Published: London, 1813
28.8 x 27.2 (image 28.8 x 27.2)
Line and stipple
Provenance Unknown

Teniers the Younger, David (1610-1690)
Flemish School
DELAUNAY, ROBERT (1749-1814)
FRENCH SCHOOL

20,075
Bagpipes Player
(after an oil, The Louvre, Paris)
Published: 1803
623 x 46.5 (plate 48.5 x 35)
Etching
Provenance Unknown

Teniers the Younger, David (1610-1690)
Flemish School
DELAUNAY, ROBERT (1749-1814)
FRENCH SCHOOL

20,108
Smoker seated at table in Tavern
(after an oil of 1643, The Louvre, Paris)
Published: 1806
61 x 46 (plate 42.4 x 30.8)
Etching
Provenance Unknown

Teniers the Younger, David (1610-1690)
Flemish School
ENGLISH SCHOOL (19TH CENTURY)

20,160
The Flemish Ale House
25.2 x 35,7 (plate cut)
Steel Engraving
Purchased, Lusk, Mr de Courcy Donovan, 1971

Teniers the Younger, David (1610-1690)
Flemish School
HULBESTE, G. (EARLY 19TH CENTURY)
FRENCH SCHOOL

20,109
Tavern near a River
(after an oil, The Louvre, Paris)
46.8 x 61.5 (plate 29.5 x 47)
Etching
Provenance Unknown

Teniers the Younger, David (1610-1690)
Flemish School
LE BAS, JACQUES PHILIPPE (1707-1783)
FRENCH SCHOOL

20,084
The Entombment
(after an oil of c.1525, The Louvre, Paris)
Published: V. Jeanron et E. Charnez, Paris, 1846
41 x 52.8 (plate cut)
Line and etching
Provenance Unknown

Titian (c.1480-1575)
Venetian School
TARDIEU, NICOLAS HENRI (1674-1749)
FRENCH SCHOOL

20,672(7)
Noli me Tangere, (Jesus and Mary Magdalen), (from 'Recueil d'Estampes d'après les beaux tableaux et d'après les plus dessins qui sont en France', Vol. 2, see App. 8, no. 20,672)
(after an oil of c.1510, NG London)
Published: L'Imprimerie Royale, Paris, 1742
62.8 x 47 (plate 44 x 34.2)
Line and etching
Provenance Unknown

Titian (c.1480-1576)
Venetian School
VORSTERMANS THE YOUNGER, LUCAS (1624-1667)
FLEMISH SCHOOL

20,715
Ecce Homo
(after NGI oil no. 75 of c.1560 or a replica)
22.9 x 15.2 (plate cut)
Line
Provenance Unknown

School of **Titian (c.1480-1576)**
Venetian School
MURPHY, JOHN (FL.1778-1820)
IRISH SCHOOL

20,731(89)
So-called portraits of Titian's son and Nurse, (from 'The Houghton Gallery', 1788, see App. 8, no. 20,731)
(after an oil, The Hermitage, Leningrad)
Published: J. Boydell, London, 1st December 1778
67.2 x 52 (plate 50.3 x 35.5)
Mezzotint
Bequeathed, Judge J. Murnaghan, 1976

Tombleson, William (fl.1818-1840)
English School
LACEY, SAMUEL (FL.1818-1857)
ENGLISH SCHOOL

20,378
Chelsea Hospital, by the River Thames, London, (pl. for W.G. Fearnside's 'Tombleson's Thames', 1834)
Published: Tombleson & Co., London
22 x 28.9 (plate 17.8 x 22.8)
Steel Engraving
Purchased, Lusk, Mr de Courcy Donovan, 1971

Tombleson, William (fl.1818-1840)
English School
McCLATCHIE, A. (FL.1828-1834)
?SCOTTISH SCHOOL

20,377
Maidstone, on the River Medway, Kent, (pl. for W.G. Fearnside's 'Tombleson's Thames', 1834)
Published: Tombleson & Co., London; also Creuzbauer & Co., Germany
22.3 x 28.8 (plate 17.6 x 22.6)
Steel Engraving
Purchased, Lusk, Mr de Courcy Donovan, 1971

Tombleson, William (fl.1818-1840)
English School
PAYNE, ALBERT HENRY (1812-1902)
ENGLISH SCHOOL

20,278
The First Stone Bridge over the upper River Rhine, (pl. for W.G. Fearnside's 'Picturesque Beauties of the Rhine', 1832)
Published: Tombleson & Co., London
27.7 x 16.2 (plate 21.1 x 15.2)
Steel Engraving
Purchased, Lusk, Mr de Courcy Donovan, 1971

Tombleson, William (fl.1818-1840)
English School
SANDS, ROBERT (1792-1855)
ENGLISH SCHOOL

20,432
An Island near Henley-on-Thames, Berkshire, (pl. for W.G. Fearnside's 'Tombleson's Thames' 1834)
Published: Tombleson & Co., London; also Creuzbauer & Co., Germany
22.6 x 27.7 (plate 17.3 x 22.6)
Steel Engraving
Purchased, Lusk, Mr de Courcy Donovan, 1971

Tombleson, William (fl.1818-1840)
English School
TAYLOR, WILLIAM (FL.1832-1852)
ENGLISH SCHOOL

20,380
View near Greenwich, London, on the River Thames, (pl. for W.G. Fearnside's 'Tombleson's Thames', 1834)
Published: Tombleson & Co., London; also Creuzbauer & Co., Germany
21.9 x 28.5 (plate 17.7 x 22.6)
Steel Engraving
Purchased, Lusk, Mr de Courcy Donovan, 1971

Tombleson, William (fl.1818-1840)
English School
TOMBLESON, WILLIAM (FL.1818-1840)
ENGLISH SCHOOL

20,433
Clifton Hampden above the River Thames, Oxfordshire, (pl. for W.G. Fearnside's 'Tombleson's Thames', 1834)
Published: Tombleson & Co., London; also Creuzbauer & Co., Germany
22.8 x 27.9 (plate 17.5 x 22.9)
Steel Engraving
Purchased, Lusk, Mr de Courcy Donovan, 1971

Tombleson, William (fl.1818-1840)
English School
WINKLES, HENRY (FL.1818-1842)
ENGLISH SCHOOL

20,286
Waterfalls in the Gorge of the Roffla, Switzerland, (pl. for 'Tombleson's Upper Rhine', 1832)
Published: Tombleson & Co., London
25.7 x 15.8 (plate 20.7 x 15.2)
Steel Engraving
Purchased, Lusk, Mr de Courcy Donovan, 1971

Tombleson, William (fl.1818-1840)
English School
WINKLES, HENRY (FL.1818-1842)
ENGLISH SCHOOL

20,376
Rochester Castle by the River Medway, Kent, (pl. for W.G. Fearnside's 'Tombleson's Thames', 1834)
Published: Tombleson & Co., London; also Creuzbauer & Co., Germany
22.6 x 27.5 (plate 17.5 x 22.5)
Steel Engraving
Purchased, Lusk, Mr de Courcy Donovan, 1971

Tombleson, William (fl.1818-1840)
English School
WINKLES, HENRY (FL.1818-1842)
ENGLISH SCHOOL

20,379
Teddington Lock on the River Thames, London, (pl. for W.G. Fearnside's 'Tombleson's Thames', 1834)
Published: Tombleson & Co., London; also Creuzbauer & Co., Germany
22.7 x 28.1 (plate 17.1 x 22.5)
Steel Engraving
Purchased, Lusk, Mr de Courcy Donovan, 1971

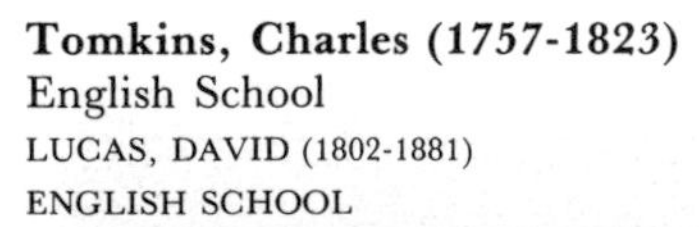

Tomkins, Charles (1757-1823)
English School
LUCAS, DAVID (1802-1881)
ENGLISH SCHOOL

20,327
The Beach at Dieppe, Normandy, France (after a drawing)
Published: S. Hollyer, London, 1830
26.3 x 37.9 (plate 14.2 x 17.1)
Mezzotint
Purchased, Lusk, Mr de Courcy Donovan, 1971

Tone, Catherine Samson (fl.1825-1858)
Irish School
ENGLISH SCHOOL (1846)

11,298
William Samson, (1764-1836), United Irishman and Barrister, father of the Artist, (pl. for R. Madden's 'United Irishmen', 3rd series, 1846)
Published: Madden & Co., London, 1846
21.6 x 12.9 (plate cut)
Mezzotint
Presented, Dr T. Moore Madden, 1901

Tone, Catherine Samson (fl.1825-1858)
Irish School
ENGLISH SCHOOL (1846)

11,299
William Samson, (1764-1836), United Irishman and Barrister, father of the Artist, (pl. for R. Madden's 'United Irishmen', 3rd series, 1846), (another copy)
Published: Madden & Co., London, 1846
21.5 x 12.9 (plate cut)
Mezzotint
Purchased, Dublin, Mr P. Traynor, 1898

Tone, Catherine Samson (fl.1825-1858)
Irish School
ENGLISH SCHOOL (1846)

11,300
William Samson, (1764-1836), United Irishman and Barrister, father of the Artist, (pl. for R. Madden's 'United Irishmen', 3rd series, 1846), (another copy)
Published: Madden & Co., London, 1846
20.7 x 12.9 (plate cut)
Mezzotint
Purchased, Dublin, Mr P. Traynor, 1898

Toussaint, Charles Henri (1849-1911)
French School
TOUSSAINT, CHARLES HENRI (1849-1911)
FRENCH SCHOOL

20,079
The Interior of Kings College Cambridge Chapel in 1879
36.2 x 26 (plate 28 x 20)
Etching
Provenance Unknown

Townsend, T.S. (fl.c.1880)
English School
TOWNSEND, T.S. (FL.C.1880)
ENGLISH SCHOOL

20,081
Dog on a Wooded Lane
36.3 x 25.9 (plate 20.2 x 15)
Etching
Provenance Unknown

Trotter, Eliza H. (fl.1800-1814)
Irish School
BROCAS THE ELDER, HENRY (1766-1838)
IRISH SCHOOL

11,071
Patrick Quin, (born c.1640), Harpist, (pl. for the 'Monthly Pantheon', October 1809)
Published: Monthly Pantheon, Dublin, October 1809
33 x 25.5. (image 9.5 x 8.5)
Zincograph copy of stipple and line
Acquired between 1913/14

Tudor, Joseph (?1695-1759)
Irish school
CARY, F. (18TH CENTURY)
IRISH SCHOOL

11,716
Dublin and Islandbridge from the Magazine Fort in Phoenix Park, (pl. for Millar's 'New Complete and Universal System of Geography')
(after a J. Tudor/T. Mason line engraving of 1753, (example in NLI, Dublin), with alterations)
Published: Millar
23.6 x 37.5 (plate 20.8 x 30.5)
Line
Presented, Dr E. MacDowel Cosgrave, 1907

Tudor, Joseph (?1695-1759)
Irish School
ENGLISH SCHOOL (1749)

11,614
The Illuminations and Fireworks to be exhibited at St Stephen's Green, Dublin on Thanksgiving Day for the general peace concluded at Aix-la-Chapelle, 1748, (pl. for the Universal Magazine, April, 1749)
(reduced from J. Tudor/T. Chambers print)
Published: J. Hinton, London, 1749
17 x 28 (plate 14.7 x 25.8)
Line
Presented, Mr J.V. McAlpine, 1901

Tudor, Joseph (?1695-1759)
English School
ENGLISH SCHOOL (1749)

11,712
The Illuminations and Fireworks to be exhibited at St Stephens Green, Dublin on Thanksgiving Day for the general peace concluded at Aix-la-Chapelle, 1748, (pl. for the 'Universal Magazine', April, 1749), (another copy)
Published: J. Hinton, London, 1749
19.7 x 27.6 (plate cut x 26.1)
Line
Presented, Mr J. Ribton Garstin, 1904

Tudor, Joseph (?1695-1759)
Irish School
ENGLISH SCHOOL (1774)

11,717
Dublin and Islandbridge from the Magazine Fort in Phoenix Park, (pl. for the 'Lady's Magazine', October 1774)
(after a J. Tudor/T. Mason line engraving of 1753, [example in NLI, Dublin], with alterations)
Published: Lady's Magazine, London, October 1774
13 x 21 (plate cut)
Line
Provenance Unknown

Tudor, Joseph (?1695-1759)
Irish School
?McARDELL, JAMES (1728/9-1765)
IRISH SCHOOL

10,008
The Old Library and Anatomy Theatre, (now demolished), Trinity College, Dublin, (No. 6 of 6 Views of Dublin)
Published: J. McArdell, London, 1753
31.4 x 45 (plate 24.6 x 39.3)
Line and etching
Presented, Dublin, Dr E. MacDowel Cosgrave, 1905

Tudor, Joseph (?1695-1759)
Irish School
?McARDELL, JAMES (1728/29-1765)
IRISH SCHOOL

11,906
Parliament House, (now Bank of Ireland), and College Green, Dublin, (no. 5 of 6 views of Dublin)
Published: R. Sayer, London, 1753
Stipple
Presented, Mr J.V. McAlpine, 1901

Tudor, Joseph (?1695-1759)
Irish School
PARR (18TH CENTURY)
ENGLISH SCHOOL

11,904
The Custom House, (now demolished), and Essex Bridge, (now rebuilt Grattan Bridge), Dublin, (no. 4 of 6 views of Dublin)
Published: R. Sayer, London, 1753
Stipple
Provenance Unknown

Tudor, Joseph (?1695-1759)
Irish School
PARR (18TH CENTURY)
ENGLISH SCHOOL

11,905
Upper Castle Yard, Dublin Castle, (no. 3 of 6 views of Dublin)
Published: R. Sayer, London, 1753
Stipple
Provenance Unknown

Tudor, Joseph (?1695-1759)
Irish School
SLACK (18TH CENTURY)
?IRISH SCHOOL

11,691
Dublin from the Magazine Fort in Phoenix Park, with a vignette of the Vice-Regal Lodge, (Lord Lieutenant's Residence), now Áras an Uachtaráin
(after a J. Tudor/T. Mason line engraving of 1753, [example in NLI, Dublin], with alterations)
23 x 38.3 (plate 20 x 27.7)
Line
Provenance Unknown

Tudor, Joseph (?1695-1759)
Irish School
WALKER, ANTHONY (1726-1765)
ENGLISH SCHOOL

11,903
Prospect of the Royal Barracks, Dublin, from St James's Church Yard, (no. 2 of 6 views of Dublin)
Published: R. Sayer, London, 1753
Stipple
Purchased, Dublin,
Mr J.V. McAlpine, 1914

Turner, Joseph Mallord William (1775-1851)
English School
ALLEN, JAMES BAYLIE (1803-1876)
ENGLISH SCHOOL

11,800

Le Havre, Normandy, France, (pl. for 'Turner's Annual Tour - The Seine', 1834)
(after a gouache of c.1832, Turner Bequest, London)
13.1 x 17 (plate cut)
Line
Provenance Unknown

Turner, Joseph Mallord William (1775-1851)
English School
ALLEN, JAMES BAYLIE (1803-1876)
ENGLISH SCHOOL

11,801
The River Seine from the terrace of the Château at Saint-Germain-en-Laye, near Paris, (pl. for 'Turner's Annual Tour- The Seine', 1835)
(after a gouache of c.1829, Turner Bequest, London)
Published: J. McCormick, London
14.4 x 16.8 (plate cut)
Line
Provenance Unknown

Turner, Joseph Mallord William (1775-1851)
English School
ALLEN, JAMES BAYLIS (1803-1876)
ENGLISH SCHOOL

20,482
The Château of Amboise, River Loire, France, (pl. for 'Turner's annual tour - The Loire', 1833)
Published: J. McCormack, London
17.4 x 24.8 (plate 15.4 x 22.8)
Steel Engraving
Purchased, Lusk, Mr de Courcy Donovan, 1971

Turner, Joseph Mallord William (1775-1851)
English School
BRANDARD, ROBERT (1805-1862)
ENGLISH SCHOOL

11,802
Rouen, Normandy, France, looking up the River Seine, (pl. for 'Turner's Annual Tour - The Seine', 1834)
(after a gouache of c.1832, Turner Bequest, London)
12 x 15.3 (plate cut)
Line
Provenance Unknown

Turner, Joseph Mallord William (1775-1851)
English School
BRANDARD, ROBERT (1805-1862)
ENGLISH SCHOOL

11,803
Rietz, near Saumur and the River Loire, France, (pl. for 'Turner's Annual Tour - The Loire', 1833)
(after a watercolour of c.1836, Ashmolean, Oxford)
(Printed: McQueen)
12.3 x 16 (plate cut)
Line
Provenance Unknown

Turner, Joseph Mallord William (1775-1851)
English School
BRANDARD, ROBERT (1805-1862)
ENGLISH SCHOOL

11,804
The Château of Tancarville with Quilleboeuf and the River Seine, Normandy, France, (pl. for 'Turner's Annual Tour - The Seine', 1834)
(after a gouache of c.1822, Turner Bequest, London)
12 x 15.8 (plate cut)
Line
Provenace Unknown

Turner, Joseph Mallord William (1775-1851)
English School
COUSEN, JOHN (1804-1880)
ENGLISH SCHOOL

11,799
Harfleur, France, (pl. for 'Turner's Annual Tour - The Seine', 1834)
(after a gouache of c.1832, Turner Bequest, London)
12.9 x 15.3 (plate cut)
Line
Provenance Unknown

Turner, Joseph Mallord William (1775-1851)
English School
CROSTICK, T. (FL.1820S)
ENGLISH SCHOOL

20,512

Fonthill Abbey, Wiltshire, (now demolished), from the south-Evening, (pl. for 'The Anniversary', 1829)
(after a watercolour, RA 1800; Montreal Museum of Fine Arts)
Published: J. Sharpe, London, 1st October 1828
12.3 x 19.5 (plate cut)
Steel Engraving
Purchased, Lusk, Mr de Courcy Donovan, 1971

Turner, Joseph Mallard William (1775-1851)
English School
PYE, JOHN (1782-1874)
ENGLISH SCHOOL

20,799
Ehrenbreitstein: The Bright Stone of Honour and Tomb of Marceau, (cf. Byron's 'Childe Harold')
(after an oil, RA 1835)
7.7 x 10.2 (plate cut)
Line
Provenance Unknown

Turner, Joseph Mallord William (1775-1851)
English School
RADCLYFFE, WILLIAM (1780-1855)
ENGLISH SCHOOL

11,798
Mantes-La-Jolie, France looking towards Notre-Dame Church from across the River Seine, (pl. for 'Turner's Annual Tour - The Seine', 1835)
(after a gouache of c.1832, Turner Bequest, London)
13.3 x 17 (plate cut)
Line
Provenance Unknown

Turner, Joseph Mallord William (1775-1851)
English School
TURNER, CHARLES (1773-1857)
ENGLISH SCHOOL

20,384
Totnes on the River Dart, Devon (pl. for W.B. Cooke's 'Rivers of England', 1827)
Published: W.B. Cooke, London, 1st March 1825
27.3 x 38.5 (plate 18.3 x 24.5)
Mezzotint
Purchased, Lusk, Mr de Courcy Donovan, 1971

Turner, Joseph Mallord Willilam (1775-1851)
English School
WALLIS, ROBERT (1794-1878)
ENGLISH SCHOOL

11,795
Tours, France, Looking towards the Old Bridge and Cathedral across the River Loire
12.4 x 16.1 (plate cut)
Line
Provenance Unknown

Turner, Joseph Mallord William (1775-1851)
English School
WILLMORE, JAMES TILBITTS (1800-1863)
ENGLISH SCHOOL

11,796
The Bridge at Pont de L'Arche on the River Seine, Normandy, France, (pl. for 'Turner's Annual Tour - The Seine', 1835)
(after a gouache of c.1832, Turner Bequest, London)
13.2 x 16.9 (plate cut)
Line
Provenance Unknown

Turner, Joseph Mallord William (1775-1851)
English School
WILLMORE, JAMES TILBITTS (1800-1863)
ENGLISH SCHOOL

11,797
The Château of Tancarville, Normandy, France, (pl. for 'Turner's Annual Tour - The Seine', 1834)
(after a gouache of c.1832, Turner Bequest, London)
13.1 x 17 (plate cut)
Line
Provenance Unknown

Turner, Joseph William Mallord (1775-1851)
English School
WILLMORE, JAMES TILBITTS (1800-1863)
ENGLISH SCHOOL

20,483

Le Havre, N. France
Published: Longman & Co., London
23.6 x 37.5 (plate 20.8 x 30.5)
Line
Presented, Dr E. MacDowel
Cosgrave, 1907

Turner, Joseph Mallord William
(1775-1851)
English School
WILLMORE, JAMES TILBITTS (1800-1863)
ENGLISH SCHOOL

20,599
Barnard Castle, Durham, in the moonlight (pl. for 'The Talisman', 1831)
(after a watercolour of c.1825, Yale
Center for British Art, New Haven)
9 x 12.2 (plate cut)
Steel Engraving
Presented, Mrs D. Molloy, 1981

Liber Studiorum
71 prints illustrating Historical,
Mountainous, Pastoral, Marine,
Architectural and Epic/Elegant
Pastoral landscapes. The preparatory
ink and sepia sketches are in the
Turner Bequest. Turner etched their
design onto the plate before the
mezzotinting and also finished some.

Turner, Joseph Mallord William
(1775-1851)
English School
TURNER, JOSEPH MALLORD WILLIAM
ENGLISH SCHOOL *and*
LASLING, J.C. (FL.1825-1833)
ENGLISH SCHOOL

11,958
Frontispiece to the Liber Studiorum, (Europa and Bull inset)
Published: J.M.W. Turner, London,
12th May 1812
30 x 44 (plate 21 x 29)
Etching and mezzotint
Presented Rev. S.A. Brooke, 1903

Turner, Joseph Mallord William
(1775-1851)
English School
TURNER, JOSEPH MALLORD WILLIAM
ENGLISH SCHOOL *and*
TURNER, CHARLES (1773-1857)
ENGLISH SCHOOL

11,959
Bridge and Cows (P)
Published: J.M.W. Turner, London,
11th June 1807
30 x 44 (plate 21 x 29)
Etching and mezzotint
Presented, Rev. S.A. Brooke, 1903

Turner, Joseph Mallord William
(1775-1851)
English School
TURNER, JOSEPH MALLORD WILLIAM
ENGLISH SCHOOL *and*
TURNER, CHARLES (1773-1857)
ENGLISH SCHOOL

11,960
Woman and Tambourine (EP)
Published: J.M.W Turner, London,
11th June 1807
21 x29 (plate 26.5 x 34.5)
Etching and mezzotint
Presented, Rev. S.A. Brooke, 1903

Turner, Joseph Mallord William
(1775-1851)
English School
TURNER, JOSEPH MALLORD WILLIAM
ENGLISH SCHOOL *and*
TURNER, CHARLES (1773-1857)
ENGLISH SCHOOL

11,961
Flint Castle, Wales (M)
Published: J.M.W. Turner, London,
11th June 1807
37.5 x 27 (plate 21 x 29)
Etching and mezzotint
Presented, Rev. S.A. Brooke, 1903

Turner, Joseph Mallord William
(1775-1851)
English School
TURNER, JOSEPH MALLORD WILLIAM
ENGLISH SCHOOL *and*
TURNER, CHARLES (1773-1857)
ENGLISH SCHOOL

11,962
Basle, Switzerland, from the River Rhine (A)
(after a drawing, Fonthill Sketchbook
of 1802; Turner Bequest, London)
Published: J.M.W. Turner, London,
11th June 1807
27.3 x 26.5 (plate 21 x 28.5)
Etching and mezzotint
Presented, Rev. S.A. Brooke, 1903

Turner, Joseph Mallord William (1775-1851)
English School
TURNER, JOSEPH MALLORD WILLIAM
ENGLISH SCHOOL *and*
TURNER, CHARLES (1773-1857)
ENGLISH SCHOOL

11,963
Jason and the Serpent (H)
(after an oil, RA 1802; Turner Bequest, London)
Published: J.M.W. Turner, London, 11th June 1807
39 x 25.8 (plate 20.7 x 28.8)
Etching and mezzotint
Presented, Rev. S.A. Brooke, 1903

Turner, Joseph Mallord William (1775-1851)
English School
TURNER, JOSEPH MALLORD WILLIAM
ENGLISH SCHOOL *and*
TURNER, CHARLES (1773-1857)
ENGLISH SCHOOL

11,965
Castle above the Meadows (EP)
Published: C. Turner, London, 20th February 1808
25.5 x 38.8 (plate 20.5 x 28.8)
Etching and mezzotint
Presented, Rev. S.A. Brooke, 1903

Turner, Joseph Mallord William (1775-1851)
English School
TURNER, JOSEPH MALLORD WILLIAM
ENGLISH SCHOOL *and*
TURNER, CHARLES (1773-1857)
ENGLISH SCHOOL

11,967
Ships in a Breeze (M)
(after the Egremont seapiece oil, RA 1802; Petworth House, Sussex)
Published: C. Turner, London, 20th February 1808
29.5 x 43.2 (plate 20.8 x 29)
Etching and mezzotint
Presented, Rev. S.A. Brooke, 1903

Turner, Joseph Mallord William (1775-1851)
English School
TURNER, JOSEPH MALLORD WILLIAM
ENGLISH SCHOOL *and*
TURNER, CHARLES (1773-1857)
ENGLISH SCHOOL

11,964
The Straw Yard (P)
Published: C. Turner, London, 20th February 1808
27 x 36.5 (plate 20.5 x 28.7)
Etching and mezzotint
Presented, Rev. S.A. Brooke, 1903

Turner, Joseph Mallord William (1775-1851)
English School
TURNER, JOSEPH MALLORD WILLIAM
ENGLISH SCHOOL *and*
TURNER, CHARLES (1773-1857)
ENGLISH SCHOOL

11,966
Mont St Gothard, Switzerland (MS)
(after a pencil drawing, Lake Thun sketchbook of 1802; Turner Bequest, London)
Published: C. Turner, London, 20th February 1808
29 x 43 (plate 20.8 x 29)
Etching and mezzotint
Presentd, Rev. S.A. Brooke, 1903

Turner, Joseph Mallord William (1775-1851)
English School
TURNER, JOSEPH MALLORD WILLIAM
ENGLISH SCHOOL *and*
TURNER, CHARLES (1773-1857)
ENGLISH SCHOOL

11,968
Holy Island Cathedral, (Lindisfarne Priory), Northumberland (A)
(after a drawing, North of England sketchbook of 1797; Turner Bequest, London)
Published: C. Turner, London, 20th February 1808
27 x 36.5 (plate 20.8 x 28.8)
Etching and mezzotint
Presented, Rev. S.A. Brooke, 1903

Turner, Joseph Mallord William (1775-1851)
English School
TURNER, JOSEPH MALLORD WILLIAM
ENGLISH SCHOOL *and*
TURNER, CHARLES (1773-1857)
ENGLISH SCHOOL

11,969
Pembury Mill, Kent (P)
Published: C. Turner, London, 10th June 1808
27 x 36.2 (plate 20.8 x 29)
Etching
Presented, Rev. S.A. Brooke, 1903

Turner, Joseph Mallord William (1775-1851)
English School
TURNER, JOSEPH MALLORD WILLIAM
ENGLISH SCHOOL *and*
TURNER, CHARLES (1773-1857)
ENGLISH SCHOOL

11,971
Dunstanborough Castle, Northumberland (A)
(after an oil, RA 1798; National Gallery of Victoria, Australia)
Published: C. Turner, London, 10th June 1808
29.2 x 36.8 (plate 20.8 x 29)
Etching and mezzotint
Presented, Rev. S.A. Brooke, 1903

Turner, Joseph Mallord William (1775-1851)
English School
TURNER, JOSEPH MALLORD WILLIAM
ENGLISH SCHOOL *and*
TURNER, CHARLES (1773-1857)
ENGLISH SCHOOL

11,973
The Fifth Plague of Egypt, (actually the Seventh, diseased cattle) (H)
(after an oil, RA 1800; Indianapolis Museum of Art)
Published: C. Turner, London, 10th June 1808
29.7 x 42.7 (plate 21 x 29)
Etching and mezzotint
Presented, Rev. S.A. Brooke, 1903

Turner, Joseph Mallord William (1775-1851)
English School
TURNER, JOSEPH MALLORD WILLIAM
ENGLISH SCHOOL *and*
TURNER, CHARLES (1773-1857)
ENGLISH SCHOOL

1,970
Walton Bridges, River Thames (EP)
Published: C. Turner, London, 10th June 1808
.8 x 41.2 (plate 20.8 x 29)
Etching and mezzotint
Presented, Rev. S.A. Brooke, 1903

Turner, Joseph Mallord William (1775-1851)
English School
TURNER, JOSEPH MALLORD WILLIAM
ENGLISH SCHOOL *and*
TURNER, CHARLES (1773-1857)
ENGLISH SCHOOL

11,972
Lake Thun, Switzerland (M)
Published: C. Turner, London, 20th May 1808
25 x 32.8 (plate 21 x 29)
Etching and mezzotint
Presented, Rev. S.A. Brooke, 1903

Turner, Joseph Mallord William (1775-1851)
English School
TURNER, JOSEPH MALLORD WILLIAM
ENGLISH SCHOOL *and*
TURNER, CHARLES (1773-1857)
ENGLISH SCHOOL

11,974
Farmyard with the Cock (P)
Published: C. Turner, London, 29th March 1809
27.4 x 36.4 (plate 20.9 x 29)
Etching and mezzotint
Presented, Rev. S.A. Brooke, 1903

Turner, Joseph Mallord William (1775-1851)
English School
TURNER, JOSEPH MALLORD WILLIAM
ENGLISH SCHOOL *and*
TURNER, CHARLES (1773-1857)
ENGLISH SCHOOL

11,975
Cora Linn falls on the River Clyde, Scotland (EP)
(after a watercolour, RA 1802; Walker Art Gallery, Liverpool)
Published: C. Turner, London, 29th March 1809
30.2 x 41.6 (plate 21 x 29.1)
Etching and mezzotint
Presented, Rev. S.A. Brooke, 1903

Turner, Joseph Mallord William (1775-1851)
English School
TURNER, JOSEPH MALLORD WILLIAM
ENGLISH SCHOOL *and*
TURNER, CHARLES (1773-1857)
ENGLISH SCHOOL

11,977
The Guardship at the Nore, off Sheerness, Kent, (The Leader Seapiece) (M)
(after an oil of c.1809)
Published: C. Turner, London, 29th March 1809
26 x 39.3 (plate 21 x 29)
Etching and mezzotint
Presented, Rev. S.A. Brooke, 1903

Turner, Joseph Mallord William (1775-1851)
English School
TURNER, JOSEPH MALLORD WILLIAM
ENGLISH SCHOOL *and*
SAY, WILLIAM (1768-1834)
ENGLISH SCHOOL

11,979
Juvenile Tricks (P)
Published: J.M.W. Turner, London, 1st January 1811
29.3 x 41.9 (plate 20.9 x 29)
Etching and mezzotint
Presented, Rev. S.A. Brooke, 1903

Turner, Joseph Mallord William (1775-1851)
English School
TURNER, JOSEPH MALLORD WILLIAM
ENGLISH SCHOOL

11,976
Little Devil's Bridge, Pass of St Gothard, Switzerland (M)
(after a watercolour, St Gothard and Mont Blanc Sketchbook of 1802; Turner Bequest, London)
Published: C. Turner, London, 29th March 1809
30 x 43.7 (plate 21 xd 29)
Etching and mezzotint
Presented, Rev. S.A. Brooke, 1903

Turner, Joseph Mallord William (1775-1851)
English School
TURNER, CHARLES (1773-1857)
ENGLISH SCHOOL

11,978
Morpeth, Northumberland (A)
Published: C. Turner, London, 29th March 1809
27.3 x 36.5 (plate 21 x 29)
Etching and mezzotint
Presented, Rev. S.A. Brooke, 1903

Turner, Joseph Mallord William (1775-1851)
English School
TURNER, JOSEPH MALLORD WILLIAM
ENGLISH SCHOOL *and*
DUNKARTON, ROBERT (1744-AFTER 1811)
ENGLISH SCHOOL

11,980
The Hindoo Worshipper (EP)
Published: J.M.W. Turner, London, 1st January 1811
29.6 x 44.5 (plate 21 x 29)
Etching and mezzotint
Presented, Rev. S.A. Brooke, 1903

Turner, Joseph Mallord William (1775-1851)
English School
TURNER, JOSEPH MALLORD WILLIAM
ENGLISH SCHOOL *and*
SAY, WILLIAM (1768-1834)
ENGLISH SCHOOL

11,981
The Coast of Yorkshire, near Whitby (M)
Published: J.M.W. Turner, London, 1st January 1811
27.4 x 36.7 (plate 20.9 x 29)
Etching and mezzotint
Presented, Rev. S.A. Brooke, 1903

Turner, Joseph Mallord William (1775-1851)
English School
TURNER, JOSEPH MALLORD WILLIAM
ENGLISH SCHOOL *and*
TURNER, CHARLES (1773-1857)
ENGLISH SCHOOL

11,983
London, from above the Royal Hospital, Greenwich (A)
(after an oil, RA 1809; Turner Bequest, London)
Published: J.M.W. Turner, London, 1st January 1811
27.4 x 36.8 (plate 20.9 x 29)
Etching and mezzotint
Presented, Rev. S.A. Brooke, 1903

Turner, Joseph Mallord William (1775-1851)
English School
TURNER, JOSEPH MALLORD WILLIAM
ENGLISH SCHOOL

11,985
Junction of the Rivers Severn and Wye, with Chepstow Castle (EP)
Published: J.M.W. Turner, London, 1st June 1811
29.2 x 44.7 (plate 21 x 29.1)
Etching, aquatint, roulette and mezzotint
Presented, Rev. S.A. Brooke, 1903

Turner, Joseph Mallord William (1775-1851)
English School
TURNER, JOSEPH MALLORD WILLIAM
ENGLISH SCHOOL *and*
DUNKARTON, ROBERT (1744-AFTER 1811)
ENGLISH SCHOOL

11,982
Hind Head, (Gibbet), Hill, Surrey, on the Portsmouth Road (M)
(after an ink drawing, Spithead sketchbook of 1807; Turner Bequest, London)
Published: J.M.W. Turner, London, 1st January 1811
29.3 x 42.9 (plate 21 x 29)
Etching and mezzotint
Presented, Rev. S.A. Brooke, 1903

Turner, Joseph Mallord William (1775-1851)
English School
TURNER, JOSEPH MALLORD WILLIAM
ENGLISH SCHOOL *and*
SAY, WILLIAM (1768-1834)
ENGLISH SCHOOL

11,984
Windmill and Lock, Grand Junction Canal at Southall Mill (P)
(after an oil, RA 1810)
Published: J.M.W. Turner, London, 1st June 1811
29.8 x 40.5 (plate 21.2 x 29.5)
Etching and mezzotint
Presented, Rev. S.A. Brooke, 1903

Turner, Joseph Mallord William (1775-1851)
English School
TURNER, JOSEPH MALLORD WILLIAM
ENGLISH SCHOOL *and*
SAY, WILLIAM (1768-1834)
ENGLISH SCHOOL

11,986
Marine Dabblers (M)
Published: J.M.W. Turner, London, 1st June 1811
29.7 x 44.2 (plate 21 x 29)
Etching and mezzotint
Presented, Rev. S.A. Brooke, 1903

Turner, Joseph Mallord William (1775-1851)
English School
TURNER, JOSEPH MALLORD WILLIAM
ENGLISH SCHOOL *and*
SAY, WILLIAM (1768-1834)
ENGLISH SCHOOL

11,987
Near Blair Athol, Scotland, on the River Garry (M)
Published: J.M.W. Turner, London, 1st June 1811
25.8 x 39.5 (plate 21.2 x 29.3)
Etching and mezzotint
Presented, Rev. S.A. Brooke, 1903

Turner, Joseph Mallord William (1775-1851)
English School
TURNER, JOSEPH MALLORD WILLIAM
ENGLISH SCHOOL *and*
DUNKARTON, ROBERT (1714-AFTER 1811)
ENGLISH SCHOOL

11,989
Young Anglers (P)
Published: J.M.W. Turner, London, 1st June 1811
29.4 x 41.8 (plate 21 x 29)
Etching and mezzotint
Presented, Rev. S.A. Brooke, 1903

Turner, Joseph Mallord William (1775-1851)
English School
TURNER, JOSEPH MALLORD WILLIAM
ENGLISH SCHOOL *and*
SAY, WILLIAM (1768-1834)
ENGLISH SCHOOL

11,991
Martello Towers, near Bexhill, Sussex (M)
Published: J.M.W. Turner, London, 1st June 1811
29.5 x 44.2 (plate 21 x 29)
Etching and mezzotint
Presented, Rev. S.A. Brooke, 1903

Turner, Joseph Mallord William (1775-1851)
English School
TURNER, JOSEPH MALLORD WILLIAM
ENGLISH SCHOOL *and*
HODGETTS, THOMAS (FL.1801-1846)
ENGLISH SCHOOL

11,988
Laufenburg, Switzerland, from the River Rhine (A)
(after a pencil drawing, Fonthill sketchbook, 1802; Turner Bequest, London)
Published: J.M.W. Turner, London, 1st June 1811
27.3 x 36.1 (plate 20.4 x 29)
Etching and mezzotint
Presented, Rev. S.A. Brooke, 1903

Turner, Joseph Mallord William (1775-1851)
English School
TURNER, JOSEPH MALLORD WILLIAM
ENGLISH SCHOOL *and*
EASLING, J.C. (FL.1825-1833)
ENGLISH SCHOOL

11,990
St Catherine's Hill and Chapel, near Guildford, Surrey (EP)
Published: J.M.W. Turner, London, 1st June 1811
28.5 x 42.5 (plate 21.4 x 29)
Etching and mezzotint
Presented, Rev. S.A. Brooke, 1903

Turner, Joseph Mallord William (1775-1851)
English School
TURNER, JOSEPH MALLORD WILLIAM
ENGLISH SCHOOL

11,992
Inverary Pier, Lock Fyne, Scotland (M)
Published: J.M.W. Turner, London 1st June 1811
30.5 x 44.7 (plate 21.5 x 29)
Etching, aquatint, roulette and mezzotint
Presented, Rev. S.A. Brooke, 1903

Turner, Joseph Mallord William (1775-1851)
English School
TURNER, JOSEPH MALLORD WILLIAM
ENGLISH SCHOOL *and*
HODGETTS, THOMAS (FL.1801-1846)
ENGLISH SCHOOL

11,993
From Spenser's 'Faerie Queen' (H)
Published: J.M.W. Turner, London, 1st June 1811
26.7 x 34.2 (plate 21 x 29)
Etching and mezzotint
Presented, Rev. S.A. Brooke, 1903

Turner, Joseph Mallord William (1775-1851)
English School
TURNER, JOSEPH MALLORD WILLIAM
ENGLISH SCHOOL *and*
SAY, WILLIAM (1768-1834)
ENGLISH SCHOOL

11,995
Hindu Ablutions, or Woman at Tank (EP)
Published: J.M.W. Turner, London, 1st February 1812
28.6 44.3 (plate 21.2 x 29.2)
Etching and mezzotint
Presented, Rev. S.A. Brooke, 1903

Turner, Joseph Mallord William (1775-1851)
English School
TURNER, JOSEPH MALLORD WILLIAM
ENGLISH SCHOOL *and*
ANNIS, W.T. (FL.1798-1811)
ENGLISH SCHOOL *and*
EASLING, J.C. (FL.1815-1833)
ENGLISH SCHOOL

11,997
Fishermen coming ashore at sunset (M)
(after an oil, RA 1797)
Published: J.M.W. Turner, London, 11th February 1812
29 x 39.8 (plate 21 x 29)
Etching and mezzotint
Presented, Rev. S.A. Brooke, 1903

Turner, Joseph Mallord William (1775-1851)
English School
TURNER, JOSEPH MALLORD WILLIAM
ENGLISH SCHOOL *and*
DUNKARTON, ROBERT, (1774-AFTER 1811)
ENGLISH SCHOOL

11,994
The Watermill (P)
Published: J.M.W. Turner, London 1st February 1812
29.5 x 44.8 (plate 21 x 29)
Etching and mezzotint
Presented, Rev. S.A. Brooke, 1903

Turner, Joseph Mallord William (1775-1851)
English School
TURNER, JOSEPH MALLORD WILLIAM
ENGLISH SCHOOL

11,996
The Rectory of Kirkstall Abbey, near Leeds, Yorkshire (A)
(after a watercolour, RA, 1798; Soane Museum, London)
Published: J.M.W. Turner, London, 11th February 1812
27.9 x 38.9 (plate 21 x 29)
Etching, aquatint, roulette and mezzotint
Presented, Rev. S.A. Brooke, 1903

Turner, Joseph Mallord William (1775-1851)
English School
TURNER, JOSEPH MALLORD WILLIAM
ENGLISH SCHOOL *and*
CLINT, GEORGE (1758-1810)
ENGLISH SCHOOL

11,998
Cephalus discovers he has killed his wife Procris (H)
Published: J.M.W. Turner, London, 14th February 1812
29.4 x 43.5 (plate 21.5 x29.2)
Etching and mezzotint
Presented, Rev. S.A. Brooke, 1903

Turner, Joseph Mallord William (1775-1851)
English School
TURNER, JOSEPH MALLORD WILLIAM
ENGLISH SCHOOL *and*
EASLING, J.C. (FL.1825-1833)
ENGLISH SCHOOL

11,999
Near Winchelsea, Sussex (P)
Published: J.M.W. Turner, London, 23rd April 1812
29.3 x 44 (plate 21 x 29)
Etching and mezzotint
Presented, Rev. S.A. Brooke, 1903

Turner, Joseph Mallord William (1775-1851)
English School
TURNER, JOSEPH MALLORD WILLIAM
ENGLISH SCHOOL

20,001
Calm (M)
Published: J.M.W. Turner, London, 23rd April 1812
27.5 x 33 (plate 21.5 x 30.2)
Etching, aquatint and mezzotint
Presented, Rev. S.A. Brooke, 1903

Turner, Joseph Mallord William (1775-1851)
English School
TURNER, JOSEPH MALLORD WILLIAM
ENGLISH SCHOOL *and*
DUNKARTON, ROBERT (1774-AFTER 1811)
ENGLISH SCHOOL

20,003
Rispah Protecting the bodies of her Sons, (H)
(after a now repainted oil, c.1808, Turner Bequest, London)
Published: J.M.W. Turner, London, 23rd April 1812
27.4 x 36.6 (plate 21 x 29)
Etching and mezzotint
Presented, Rev. S.A. Brooke, 1903

Turner, Joseph Mallord William (1775-1851)
English School
TURNER, JOSEPH MALLORD WILLIAM
ENGLISH SCHOOL *and*
LEWIS THE ELDER, FREDERICK CHRISTIAN (1779-1856)
ENGLISH SCHOOL

20,000
Bridge with Goats (EP)
Published: J.M.W. Turner, London, 23rd April 1812
27.3 x 36.5 (plate 21.2 x 29.2)
Etching and mezzotint
Presented, Rev. S.A. Brooke, 1903

Turner, Joseph Mallord William (1775-1851)
English School
TURNER, JOSEPH MALLORD WILLIAM
ENGLISH SCHOOL *and*
CLINT, GEORGE (1758-1810)
ENGLISH SCHOOL

20,002
Peat Bog, Scotland (M)
Published: J.M.W. Turner, London, 23rd April 1812
27.3 x 36.8 (plate 21 x 29)
Etching and mezzotint
Presented, Rev. S.A. Brooke, 1903

Turner, Joseph Mallord William (1775-1851)
English School
TURNER, JOSEPH MALLORD WILLIAM
ENGLISH SCHOOL *and*
EASLING, J.C. (FL.1825-1833)
ENGLISH SCHOOL

20,004
Hedging and Ditching (P)
Published: J.M.W. Turner, London, 23rd May 1812
30 x 45 (plate 21.1 x 29.1)
Etching and mezzotint
Presented, Rev. S.A. Brooke, 1903

Turner, Joseph Mallord William (1775-1851)
English School
TURNER, JOSEPH MALLORD WILLIAM
ENGLISH SCHOOL *and*
ANNIS, W.T. (FL.1798-1811)
ENGLISH SCHOOL

20,005
Chepstow Castle, Wales, from the River Wye (EP)
Published: J.M.W. Turner, London, 23rd May 1812
29 x 44.5 (plate 21.2 x 29.1)
Etching and mezzotint
Presented, Rev. S.A. Brooke, 1903

Turner, Joseph Mallord William (1775-1851)
English School
TURNER, JOSEPH MALLORD WILLIAM
ENGLISH SCHOOL

20,007
Mer de Glace, near Chamonix, Savoy, France (M)
(after a watercolour, St Gothard and Mont Blanc Sketchbook of 1802; Turner Bequest, London)
Published: J.M.W. Turner, London, 23rd May 1812
29.4 x 44.4 (plate 21.6 x 29.3)
Etching and mezzotint
Presented, Rev. S.A. Brooke, 1903

Turner, Joseph Mallord William (1775-1851)
English School
TURNER, JOSEPH MALLORD WILLIAM
ENGLISH SCHOOL *and*
LUPTON, THOMAS GOFF (1791-1873)
ENGLISH SCHOOL

20,009
Solway Moss near Carlisle, Cumberland, (scene of Scottish defeat, 1542) (P)
Published: J.M.W. Turner, London, 1st January 1816
29.7 x 42.8 (plate 21.7 x 29.1)
Etching and mezzotint
Presented, Rev. S.A. Brooke, 1903

Turner, Joseph Mallord William (1775-1851)
English School
TURNER, JOSEPH MALLORD WILLIAM
ENGLISH SCHOOL *and*
SAY, WILLIAM (1768-1834)
ENGLISH SCHOOL

20,006
Chain of the Alps from Grenoble to Chambery (M)
(after a pencil drawing, St Gothard and Mont Blanc Sketchbook, 1802; Turner Bequest, London)
Published: J.M.W. Turner, London, 23rd May 1812
27.3 x 36.7
Etching and mezzotint
Presented Rev. S.A. Brooke, 1903

Turner, Joseph Mallord William (1775-1851)
English School
TURNER, JOSEPH MALLORD WILLIAM
ENGLISH SCHOOL *and*
DAWE, HENRY (1790-1848)
ENGLISH SCHOOL

20,008
Rievaulx Abbey, Yorkshire (A)
Published: J.M.W. Turner, London, 23rd May 1812
29.5 x 44.5 (plate 21.8 x 30)
Etching and mezzotint
Presented, Rev. S.A. Brooke, 1903

Turner, Joseph Mallord William (1775-1851)
English School
TURNER, JOSEPH MALLORD WILLIAM
ENGLISH SCHOOL *and*
SAY, WILLIAM (1768-1834)
ENGLISH SCHOOL

20,010
Solitude, (with St Mary Magdalen) (EP)
Published: J.M.W. Turner, London, 12th May 1814
29 x 43.4 (plate 21 x 29)
Etching and mezzotint
Presented, Rev. S.A. Brooke, 1903

Turner, Joseph Mallord William (1775-1851)
English School
TURNER, JOSEPH MALLORD WILLIAM
ENGLISH SCHOOL *and*
DAWE, HENRY (1790-1848)
ENGLISH SCHOOL

20,011
Mill near the Grand Chartreuse, France (M)
(after a watercolour, St Gothard and Mont Blanc Sketchbook of 1802; Turner Bequest, London)
Published: J.M.W. Turner, 1st January 1816
29.7 x 42.5 (plate 21 x 29)
Etching and mezzotint
Presented, Rev. S.A. Brooke, 1903

Turner, Joseph Mallord William (1775-1851)
English School
TURNER, JOSEPH MALLORD WILLIAM
ENGLISH SCHOOL *and*
LUPTON, THOMAS GOFF (1791-1873)
ENGLISH SCHOOL

20,013
Dunblane Cathedral, Scotland, (now re-roofed), from the River Allan (A)
Published: J.M.W. Turner, London, 1st January 1816
29.2 x 43.5 (plate 21 x 29)
Etching and mezzotint
Presented, Rev. S.A. Brooke, 1903

Turner, Joseph Mallord William (1775-1851)
English School
TURNER, JOSEPH MALLORD WILLIAM
ENGLISH SCHOOL

20,015
Raglan Castle, Wales (EP)
Published: J.M.W. Turner, London, 1st January 1816
29 x 43 (plate 21.5 x 29.2)
Etching and mezzotint
Presented, Rev. S.A. Brooke, 1903

Turner, Joseph Mallord William (1775-1851)
English School
TURNER, JOSEPH MALLORD WILLIAM
ENGLISH SCHOOL

20,012
Fishing Boats entering Calais Harbour (M)
(after an oil of c.1803, Frick Collection, New York)
Published: J.M.W. Turner, London, 1st January 1816
29.5 x 42.7 (plate 21.5 x 20.1)
Etching and mezzotint
Presented, Rev. S.A. Brooke, 1903

Turner, Joseph Mallord William (1775-1851)
English School
TURNER, JOSEPH MALLORD WILLIAM
ENGLISH SCHOOL *and*
TURNER, CHARLES (1773-1857)
ENGLISH SCHOOL

20,014
Norham Castle, Scotland, from the River Tweed (P)
(after a watercolour of c.1798)
Published: J.M.W. Turner, London, 1st January 1816
21.6 x 30.4 (plate 21 x 29)
Etching and mezzotint
Presented, Rev. S.A. Brooke, 1903

Turner, Joseph Mallord William (1775-1851)
English School
TURNER, JOSEPH MALLORD WILLIAM
ENGLISH SCHOOL *and*
HODGETTS, THOMAS (FL.1801-1846)
ENGLISH SCHOOL

20,016
Ville de Thun, Switzerland, (A)
(after a pencil drawing, Lake Thun sketchbook of 1802; Turner Bequest, London)
Published: J.M.W. Turner, London, 1st January 1816
29.3 x 42.5 (plate 21 x 29.2)
Etching and mezzotint
Presented, Rev. S.A. Brooke, 1903

Turner, Joseph Mallord William (1775-1851)
English School
TURNER, JOSEPH MALLORD WILLIAM
ENGLISH SCHOOL

20,017
The Source of the River Arveiron near La Mer de Glace in the Valley of Chamounix, France (M)
Published: J.M.W. Turner, London, 1st January 1816
21.7 x 423 (plate 21.7 x 29.1)
Etching and mezzotint
Presented, Rev. S.A. Brooke, 1903

Turner, Joseph Mallord William (1775-1851)
English School
TURNER, JOSEPH MALLORD WILLIAM
ENGLISH SCHOOL *and*
SAY, WILLIAM (1768-1834)
ENGLISH SCHOOL

20,018
The Tenth Plague of Egypt, (Death of the First Born), (H)
(after an oil, RA 1802; Turner Bequest, London)
Published: J.M.W. Turner, London, 1st January 1816
29.9 x 38.4 (plate 21 x 29.1)
Etching and mezzotint
Presented, Rev. S.A. Brooke, 1903

Turner, Joseph Mallord William (1775-1851)
English School
TURNER, JOSEPH MALLORD WILLIAM
ENGLISH SCHOOL *and*
LUPTON, THOMAS GOFF (1791-1873)
ENGLISH SCHOOL

20,019
Watercress Gatherers (P)
Published: J.M.W. Turner, London, January 1819
29 x 44.1 (plate 21.7 x 29)
Etching and mezzotint
Presented, Rev. S.A. Brooke, 1903

Turner, Joseph Mallord William (1775-1851)
English School
TURNER, JOSEPH MALLORD WILLIAM
ENGLISH SCHOOL *and*
DAWE, HENRY (1790-1848)
ENGLISH SCHOOL

20,020
Alcove, (shooting lodge), Isleworth (EP)
Published: J.M.W. Turner, London, 1st January 1819
29.5 x 44 9plate 20.9 x 29)
Etching and mezzotint
Presented, Rev. S.A. Brooke, 1903

Turner, Joseph Mallord William (1775-1851)
English School
DAWE, HENRY (1790-1848)
ENGLISH SCHOOL

20,021
Chateau de St Michel, Bonneville, Savoy, France
(after a watercolour of c.1808, Turner Bequest, London)
Published: J.M.W. Turner, London, 1st January 1816
29.5 x 42.7 (plate 21.7 x 29.2)
Etching and mezzotint
Presented, Rev. S.A. Brooke, 1903

Turner, Joseph Mallord William (1775-1851)
English School
TURNER, JOSEPH MALLORD WILLIAM
ENGLISH SCHOOL *and*
TURNER, CHARLES (1773-1857)
ENGLISH SCHOOL

20,022
Inverary Castle and Town, Loch Fyne, Scotland (M)
(after a watercolour of c.1802, formerly Duke of Argyll's collection)
Published: J.M.W. Turner, London, 1st January 1816
30 x 44.2 (plate 21 x 29)
Etching and mezzotint
Presented, Rev. S.A. Brooke, 1903

Turner, Joseph Mallord William (1775-1851)
English School
TURNER, JOSEPH MALLORD WILLIAM
ENGLISH SCHOOL

20,023

Aesacus discarding Hesperia, (Ovid's 'Metamorphoses') (H)
Published: J.M.W. Turner, London, 1st January 1819
29.8 x 42.5 (plate 21 x 29)
Etching and mezzotint
Presented, Rev. S.A. Brooke, 1903

Turner, Joseph Mallord William (1775-1851)
English School
TURNER, JOSEPH MALLORD WILLIAM
ENGLISH SCHOOL *and*
REYNOLDS THE ELDER, SAMUEL WILLIAM (1773-1835)
ENGLISH SCHOOL

20,024
East Gate, Winchelsea, Sussex (P)
Published: J.M.W. Turner, London, January 1819
17.6 x 25.1 (plate cut)
Etching and mezzotint
Presented, Rev. S.A. Brooke, 1903

Turner, Joseph Mallord William (1775-1851)
English School
TURNER, JOSEPH MALLORD WILLIAM
ENGLISH SCHOOL *and*
SAY, WILLIAM (1768-1834)
ENGLISH SCHOOL

20,025
Isis, (rivers Isis and Thames near Windsor) (EP)
Published: J.M.W. Turner, London, 1st January 1819
29.8 x 43 (plate 21 x 29.2)
Etching and mezzotint
Presented, Rev. S.A. Brooke, 1903

Turner, Joseph Mallord Willian (1775-1851)
English School
TURNER, JOSEPH MALLORD WILLIAM
ENGLISH SCHOOL *and*
LUPTON, THOMAS GOFF (1791-1873)
ENGLISH SCHOOL

20,026
Ben Arthur, near Loch Lomond, Scotland (M)
Published: J.M.W. Turner, London, 1st January 1819
29.5 x 44 (plate 21 x 29)
Etching and mezzotint
Presented, Rev. S.A. Brooke, 1903

Turner, Joseph Mallord William (1778-1851)
English School
TURNER, JOSEPH MALLORD WILLIAM (1778-1851)
ENGLISH SCHOOL

20,027
Interior of a Church (A)
(after an oil of c.1797, Turner Bequest, London)
Published: J.M.W. Turner, London, 1st January 1819
19.5 x 27.2 (plate cut)
Soft-ground etching, roulette and mezzotint
Presented, Rev. S.A. Brooke, 1903

Turner, Joseph Mallord William (1775-1851)
English School
TURNER, JOSEPH MALLORD WILLIAM
ENGLISH SCHOOL *and*
REYNOLDS THE ELDER, SAMUEL WILLIAM (1773-1835)
ENGLISH SCHOOL

20,028
Christ and the Woman of Samaria (H)
Published: J.M.W. Turner, London, 1st January 1819
29.5 x 43.2 (plate 21 x 29)
Etching and mezzotint
Presented, Rev. S.A. Brooke, 1903

Tusch, Johann (1720 or 1738-1817)
Austrian School
ZUCCHI, LORENZO (1704-1779)
ITALIAN SCHOOL

10,084
John Sigismond Count Maguire, Irish General in Imperial Service and Governor of Dresden in 1760
Published: not before 1760
40.7 x 28.5 (plate 40 x 28.5)
Line
Purchased, Dublin, Bennetts, 1885

V

?Vaillant, Wallerant (1623-1677))
Dutch School
VAILLANT, WALLERANT (1623-1677)
DUTCH SCHOOL

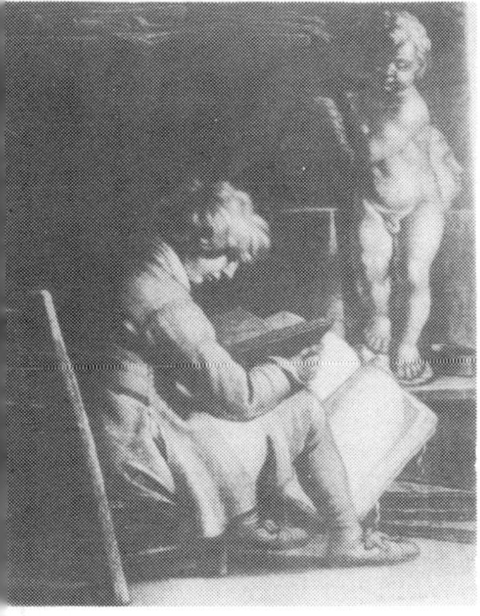

20,732(57)
A boy seated drawing a cast of Michelangelo's Christ child, (from 'A Collection of Engravings from Paintings and Drawings of the most Celebrated Masters', see App. 8, no. 20,732)
(after an oil of 1658, The Louvre, Paris; or replica in NG, London; both formerly in Irish collections)
Published: W. Vaillant, after 1658; this is re-issue by W.T. Gilling, London, 1807
41.4 x 28.5 (plate 27.5 x 21.5)
Mezzotint
Provenance Unknown

Van Bleeck, Pieter (fl.1723-1764)
Anglo-Dutch School
FABER THE YOUNGER, JOHN (1684-1756)
ENGLISH SCHOOL
ALAIS, WILLIAM JOHN (FL.1877-1894)
ENGLISH SCHOOL

11,121
Kitty Clive, (1711-1785), Actress, as Phillida in Cibber's 'Damon and Phillida'
(after a P. Van Bleeck/J. Faber the Younger mezzotint of 1734; example in BM, London)
22.5 x 14.5 (plate 13.3 x 10)
Line and stipple
Acquired c.1903

Van Bleeck, Pieter (fl.1723-1764)
Anglo-Dutch School
VAN BLEECK, PIETER (fl.1723-1764)
ANGLO-DUTCH SCHOOL

10,112
Owen Macswinny, (fl.1705-1754), Theatrical Manager, Playwright and Publisher
(after an oil of 1737)
Published: 1749
41.6 x 31.4 (plate 35.3 x 25.3)
Mezzotint
Purchased, Dublin, Mr J. Simington, 1898

Vanderbank, John (1694-1739)
English School
FABER THE YOUNGER, JOHN (C.1684-1756)
ENGLISH SCHOOL

10,548
Caroline of Brandenburg-Ansbach, (1683-1737), Queen of King George II
(after an oil of 1736, Goodwood House, Sussex)
INSCRIBED: From the Original, Painted for His Grace the Duke of Richmond & To whom this Plate is humbly Dedicated by His Grace's/Most Devoted Servt./John Faber
Published: J. Faber the Younger, London, 1739
53 x 35.4 (plate cut)

Mezzotint
Purchased, London, 1st Chaloner Smith sale, 1887

Vandercabel Adriaen (1630 or 31-1705)
Dutch School
REYNOLDS THE YOUNGER, SAMUEL WILLIAM (1794-1872)
ENGLISH SCHOOL

20,132
Sailing Boat
INSCRIBED: *From an Original Picture in the Possession of Lord Charles Townshend to whom the Plate is respectfully inscribed*
Published: S.W. Reynolds, London
30 x 44.3 (plate 18.9 x 22)
Aquatint
Purchased, Lusk, Mr de Courcy Donovan, 1971

Van Der Mijn, Francis (c.1719-1783)
Anglo-Dutch School
PURCELL, RICHARD (FL.1746-c.1766)
IRISH SCHOOL

10,683
So-called portrait of Margaret (Peg) Woffington
(after F. Van der Mijn/J. McArdell mezzotint; example in BM, London)
Published: R. Sayer, London
40 x 28.5 (plate 35.3 x 25.3)
Mezzotint
Purchased, 1906

Van Der Mijn, Francis (c.1719-1783)
Anglo-Dutch School
PURCELL, RICHARD (FL.1746-c.1766)
IRISH SCHOOL

11,249
So-called portrait of Margaret (Peg) Woffington
(after F. Van der Mijn/R. Purcell mezzotint; NGI no. 10,683)
Published: ?R. Sayer, London
14.9 x 11.8 (plate cut x 11.4)
Purchased, 1907

Vandervaart, Jan (1647-1721)
Anglo-Dutch School
FAITHORNE THE YOUNGER, WILLIAM (1656-C.1710)
ENGLISH SCHOOL

10,385
Mary II, Queen of England, (1662-1694)
Published: E. Cooper, London, 1698
35 x 26 (plate cut)
Mezzotint
Purchased, London, 1st Chaloner Smith sale, 1887

Vandervaart, Jan (1647-1721)
Anglo-Dutch School
VANDERVAART, JAN (1647-1721)
ANGLO-DUTCH SCHOOL

10,132
Edward Wetenhall, P. Bishop of Cork and Ross, (1637-1713), later Bishop of Kilmore and Ardagh
Unlettered Proof
Published: between 1678/99
37.5 x 28.7 (plate 34.3 x 24.8)
Mezzotint
Purchased, London, 2nd Chaloner Smith sale, 1888

Van Dongen, Kees (1877-1968)
Dutch School
FRENCH SCHOOL (20TH CENTURY)

11,565
'Oedipe Roi de Thebes de Saint Georges de Bouhelier' - Oedipus, King of Thebes poster for the Cirque D'Hiver, Paris
Published: Publicité Wall, Paris
229 x 156 (image 219.5 x 149)
Lithograph
Bequeathed, Miss R.S.R. Kirkpatrick, 1979

?Van Dyck, Anthony (1599-1641)
Flemish School
NATTIER, JEAN MARC (1685-1766)
FRENCH SCHOOL
AUDRAN, JEAN (1667-1756)
FRENCH SCHOOL

20,678(1)
Peter Paul Rubens, (1577-1640), Artist, (from 'La Galerie du Palais Luxembourg', see App. 8, no. 20,678)
Published: G. Duchange, Paris, 1710
58.8 x 43.5 (plate 50.1 x 35.2)
Line
Provenance Unknown

Van Dyck, Anthony (1599-1641)
Flemish School
BLOOTELING, ABRAHAM (1640-1690)
DUTCH SCHOOL

11,215
Prince Charles, (1630-1685), later King Charles II of England
(after an oil of the Royal family of c.1632, Royal Collection, Buckingham Palace)
Published: A. Blooteling, Amsterdam
19.8 x 13.6 (plate 19.5 x 13.3)
Mezzotint
Provenance Unknown

Van Dyck, Anthony (1599-1641)
Flemish School
BOYDELL, JOSHUA (1760-1817)
ENGLISH SCHOOL

10,556
Jane Wenman, (born c.1603), daughter of Sir Richard Wenman, later Mrs Arthur Goodwin, (incorrectly titled daughter of Lord Wenman), (pl. for 'The Houghton Gallery', 1778)
(after an oil of c.1639, The Hermitage, Leningrad)
Published: J. Boydell, London, 1st May 1779
39 x 27.7 (plate cut)
Mezzotint
Purchased, London, 1st Chaloner Smith sale, 1887

Van Dyck, Anthony (1599-1641)
Flemish School
BROWNE, ALEXANDER (FL.1660-1680)
ENGLISH SCHOOL

10,259

Thomas Wentworth, 1st Earl of Strafford, (1593-1641), Lord Lieutenant of Ireland
(after an oil of 1636, Petworth House, Sussex)
Publisher: A. Browne, London
37.7 x 27.4 (plate 34 x 25)
Mezzotint
Purchased, London, 1st Chaloner Smith sale, 1887

Van Dyck, Anthony (1599-1641)
Flemish School
BROWNE, ALEXANDER (FL.1660-1680)
ENGLISH SCHOOL

10,756
The five eldest children of King Charles I - Princess Ann, (1636-1640), Princess Elizabeth, (1635-1650), Prince Charles, later Charles II, (1630-1685), Prince James, Duke of York, later James II, (1633-1701), and Princess Mary, later mother of William III, (1631-1660)
(after an oil of 1637, Royal Collection, Windsor Castle)
Published: A. Browne, London
32.5 x 41 (plate cut)
Mezzotint
Purchased, London, 1st Chaloner Smith sale, 1887

Van Dyck, Anthony (1599-1641)
Flemish School
COOPER, RICHARD (1730-1820)
ENGLISH SCHOOL

10,546
The five eldest children of King Charles I - Princess Ann, (1636-1640), Princess Elizabeth, (1635-1650), Prince Charles, later Charles II, (1630-1685), Prince James, Duke of York, later James II, (1633-1701), and Princess Mary, later mother of William III, (1631-1660)
(after an oil of 1637, Royal Collection, Windsor Castle)
Published: R. Cooper the Younger, London, 1762
45 x 50 (plate cut)
Line
Milltown Gift, 1902

Van Dyck, Anthony (1599-1641)
Flemish School
CORR, MATHIEU ERIN (1805-1862)
FLEMISH SCHOOL

11,489
The Crucifixion
(after an oil of 1627, Koninklijk Museum Voor Schone Kunsten, Antwerp)
Published: M. E. Corr, Antwerp; also Goupil & Vibert, Paris, also P. & D. Colnaghi & Co., London, 1845
(Printed: Bougeard, Antwerp)
63.2 x 48 (plate 58.7 x 42.3)
Line and etching
Presented, Mr M. Corr van der Maeren, 1864

Van Dyck, Anthony (1599-1641)
Flemish School
BAMFYLDE, COPLESTON WARRE (1720-1791)
ENGLISH SCHOOL
ENGLISH SCHOOL (1814)

20,115
Sir Thomas Morgan, M.P., (d.1679), at the taking of Dunkirk, 1658
INSCRIBED: From a drawing in the Possession of Mr. Thos Coram
Published: G. Sheeton, London, 1st October, 1814
33 x 26.5 (plate 25 x 17.7)
Stipple
Purchased, Lusk, Mr de Courcy Donovan, 1971

Van Dyck, Anthony (1599-1641)
Flemish School
FABER THE YOUNGER, JOHN (C.1684-1756)
ENGLISH SCHOOL

10,096

James I, King of England, (1566-1625)
(after a wl oil of c.1632, Royal Collection, Windsor Castle, based on a P. Van Somer wl oil of 1618, Holyrood Palace)
Published: T. Bowles, London
35 x 25.5 (plate 34.7 x 25)
Mezzotint
Purchased, London, 1st Chaloner Smith sale, 1887

?Van Dyck, Anthony (1599-1641)
Flemish School
FABER THE YOUNGER, JOHN (1684-1756)
ENGLISH SCHOOL

20,244
An Apostle
INSCRIBED: *From the Original...Painting in the Collection of the Right Honourable/...Tyrconnell, Knight of the most honourable Order of the Ba.../*
Published: J. Faber the Younger, London
32.5 x 22.5 (plate cut)
Mezzotint
Purchased, Lusk, Mr de Courcy Donovan, 1971

Van Dyck, Anthony (1599-1641)
Flemish School
GALLE THE ELDER, CORNELIS (1576-1650)
FLEMISH SCHOOL

11,491
Frederick de Marselaer, Diplomat
(after an oil of c.1630, NGI no. 235)
30.6 x 20.4 (plate cut)
Line
Purchased, Brussels, 1876

Van Dyck, Anthony (1599-1641)
Flemish School
HOUBRAKEN, ARNOLD (1660-1719)
DUTCH SCHOOL
GUNST, PIETER VAN (1659-1724)
DUTCH SCHOOL

10,349
Katherine, (suo jure), Countess of Chesterfield, (née Wotton, fl.1628-1667)
(after an oil of 1636, painted when formerly the wife of self-styled Lord Henry Stanhope)
Published: P. van Gunst,
Amsterdam, not before 1713
51 x 31.7 (plate cut)
Line
Milltown Gift, 1902

Van Dyck, Anthony (1599-1641)
Flemish School
PONTIUS, PAUL (1603-1638)
FLEMISH SCHOOL

20,114
Hendrik van Balen the Elder, (?1573-1632), Artist and teacher of Van Dyck
(after a black chalk drawing of 1627/32, Chatsworth House, Derbyshire)
36.3 x 26.9 (plate 24.5 x 16)
Line
Purchased, Lusk, Mr de Courcy Donovan, 1971

Van Dyck, Anthony (1599-1641)
Flemish School
PONTIUS, PAUL (1603-1638)
FLEMISH SCHOOL

20,116
Jan Caspar Gevartius, (1593-1666), Philosopher and Historian
(after a black chalk drawing of 1627/35, Albertina, Vienna)
35.7 x 27.2 (plate 24.5 x 17)
Line
Purchased, Lusk, Mr de Courcy Donovan, 1971

Van Dyck, Anthony (1599-1641)
Flemish School
SIMON, JOHN (1675-1751)
ANGLO-FRENCH SCHOOL

10,248
Charles I, King of England, (1600-1649)
(after a wl oil of 1636, Royal Collection, Windsor Castle)
35.5 x 25.3 (plate cut)
Mezzotint
Purchased, London, 2nd Chaloner Smith sale, 1888

Van Dyck, Anthony (1599-1641)
Flemish School
FARRINGTON, GEORGE (1752-1790)
ENGLISH SCHOOL
WATSON, JAMES (C.1740-1790)
IRISH SCHHOOL

10,235
'Lord Chief Baron Wandesford' - Sir Rowland Wandesford, Attorney of the Ward of Courts, (pl. for 'The Houghton Gallery', 1788)
(after an oil of 1638, The Hermitage, Leningrad)
Published: J. Boydell, London, 1st December 1778
41.6 x 30.7 (plate cut)
Mezzotint
Presented, Mr M. O'Shaughnessy, 1881

Van Dyck, Anthony (1599-1641)
Flemish School
FARRINGTON, GEORGE (1752-1788)
ENGLISH SCHOOL
WATSON, JAMES (C.1740-1790)
IRISH SCHOOL

10,563
'Lord Chief Baron Wandesford' — Sir Rowland Wandesford, Attorney of the Ward of Courts, (pl. for 'The Houghton Gallery', 1788), (another copy)
(after an oil of 1638, The Hermitage, Leningrad)
Published: J. Boydell, London, 1st December 1778
40.7 x 30.5 (plate cut)
Mezzotint
Provenance Unknown

Van Loo, Jean-Baptiste (1684-1745)
Anglo-French School
FABER THE YOUNGER, JOHN (?1684-1756)
ENGLISH SCHOOL

10,120
Owen Macswinny, (fl.1705-1754), Theatrical Manager, Playwright and Publisher
(after an oil of 1737)
Published: ?J. Faber the Younger, London, 1752
37.5 x 26.8 (plate 35.3 x 25)
Mezzotint
Purchased, Mr J. G. Robertson, 1895

Van Loo, Jean-Baptiste (1684-1745)
French School
WATSON, JAMES (C.1740-1790)
IRISH SCHOOL

20,731(92)
Sir Robert Walpole, later 1st Earl of Orford, (from 'The Houghton Gallery', 1788, see App. 8, no. 20,731)
(after an oil, 1739, The Hermitage, Leningrad)
Published: J. & J. Boydell, London, 1st January 1788
67.2 x 52 (49.8 x 35)
Mezzotint
Bequeathed, Judge J. Murnaghan, 1976

Van Nost the Younger, John (c.1712-1780)
Irish School
SPOONER, CHARLES (C.1720-1767)
IRISH SCHOOL

10,013
Thomas Prior, (1682-1751), Founding Member and Secretary to the Dublin Society
(after a marble bust of 1751, Royal Dublin Society Collection, Dublin)
INSCRIBED: Thomas Prior Esqr./ Late Secretary to the Dublin Society./ To which Honble. Society this Plate is most Humbly inscribed by their Honours most/ Obedient Humble Servant Thos. Sillcock.
Published: T. Sillcock, Dublin, 1752
35.9 x 26.1 (plate 35 x 25.5)
Mezzotint
Purchased, London, 2nd Chaloner Smith sale, 1888

Van Nost the Younger, John (c.1712-1780)
Irish School
SPOONER, CHARLES (C.1720-1767)
IRISH SCHOOL

10,101
Rev. Samuel Madden, (1686-1765), Co-Founder of the Dublin Society
(after a marble bust of 1751, Royal Dublin Society Collection, Dublin)
INSCRIBED: Behold! in fact a Patriot - truly Great '/The Watchful Pilot of Hibernia's State,/Her present opulence, her growing Fame./Own Him the Fountain, Whence her Treasures Stream,/ This Little Draught the Portrait of his Face,/But Volumes only can his Vertue trace./Weeks.
Published: T. Sillcock, Dublin, 1752
36.2 x 26.5 (plate 35.1 x 25.5)
Mezzotint
Purchased, London, 2nd Chaloner Smith sale, 1888

Van Somer, Paul (c.1576-1621)
Anglo-Flemish School
HARDING, GEORGE PERFECT (c.1780-1853)
ENGLISH SCHOOL
BROWN, JOSEPH (FL.1854-1886)
ENGLISH SCHOOL

10,807
Henry Carey, 1st Viscount Falkland, (1576-1633), (previously pl. for G.P. Harding's 'Ancient Historical Pictures', 1844)
(after an oil of c.1620, Helmingham Hall, Suffolk)
Published: G.P. Harding, London, 1st January 1847
46.2 x 33 (pl. 35.5 x 24)
Stipple
Purchased, Dublin, Mr J.V. McAlpine 1904

Van Somer, Paul (c.1576-1621)
Anglo-Flemish School
GREEN, VALENTINE (1739-1813)
ENGLISH SCHOOL

10,443

Charles Blount, 8th Baron Mountjoy and 1st Earl of Devonshire, (1563-1606), Lord Deputy of Ireland, defeated Spanish at Kinsale
Published: J. Boydell, London, 2nd October 1775
55.5 x 36.8 (plate 54.5 x 35.6)
Mezzotint
Purchased, London, 1st Chaloner Smith sale, 1887

Velde the Younger, Willem van der (1633-1707)
Anglo-Dutch School
LUPTON, THOMAS GOFF (1791-1873)
ENGLISH SCHOOL

20,789
A Gale
INSCRIBED: from the picture in the Possession of George Morant Esq
28.3 x 41.2 (plate 19.7 x 25.4)
Aquatint and etching
Purchased, Lusk, Mr de Courcy Donovan, 1971

Venetian School (16th century)
HODGSON, W. (EARLY 19TH CENTURY)
ENGLISH SCHOOL
CARDON, ANTHONY (1772-1813)
ANGLO-BELGIAN SCHOOL

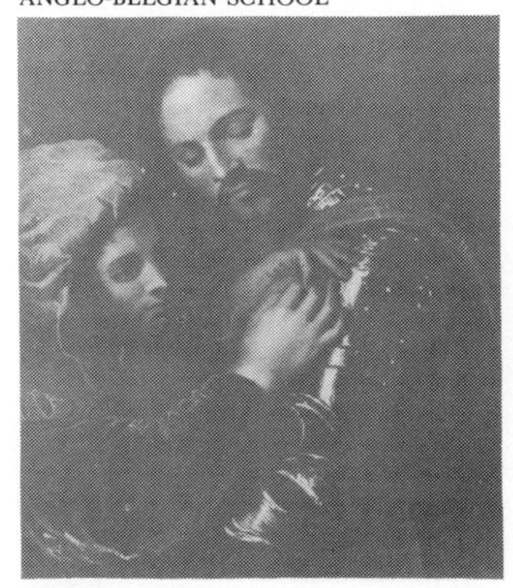

20,048
Knight and Page, (artist given as Giorgione)
(after an oil, Castle Howard, Yorkshire)
Published: Longman, Hurst, Rees, Orme & Brown, also White & Co., also Cadell & Davies, also P.W. Tomkins, London, 28th February 1811
44.6 x 34.3 (plate 44.2 x 54)
Line and stipple
Provenance Unknown

Verhulst, Charles Pierre (1774-1820)
Belgian School
ANSELIN, JEAN-LOUIS (1754-1823)
FRENCH SCHOOL

10,906
Trophime Gérard, Comte and Marquis de Lally-Tolendal, (1751-1830), son of an Irish Jacobite General, former member of the French States General
Published: J.L. Anselin, Paris, 1819
41.2 x 29.8 (plate cut)
Line
Acquired by 1903

Vermeyen, Jan Cornelisz (c.1500-1559)
German School
BOCOURT, ETIENNE GABRIEL (1821-AFTER 1883)
FRENCH SCHOOL

11,504
Portrait of a Man, (artist given as Holbein)
(after an oil, Alte Pinakothek, Munich)
Published: L'Art, Paris (Printed: F. Liénard)
44 x 30 (plate 28.7 x 21.2)
Etching
Provenance Unknown

Vigée-Le Brun, Elizabeth Louise (1755-1842)
French School
HART, G.J. (19TH CENTURY)
ENGLISH SCHOOL

11,876
Self-Portrait with her daughter Jeanne Lucie Louise, (1780-1819)
Unlettered Proof

73 x 53.1 (plate 53.2 x 38.5)
Chromo etching and mezzotint
Provenance Unknown

Vispré, Francis Xavier (1730-c.1790)
Anglo-French School
ENGLISH SCHOOL (18TH CENTURY)

11,183
Samuel Derrick, (1724-1769), Actor, Writer and Master of Ceremonies at Bath
21.4 x 13.4 (plate 6.8 x 6)
Line
Acquired by 1913

Von Breda, Carl Frederick (1759-1818)
Swedish School
REYNOLDS THE ELDER, SAMUEL WILLIAM (1773-1835)
ENGLISH SCHOOL

10,422
Thomas Hussey, (1741-1803), R.C. Bishop of Waterford and Lismore, 1st President of Maynooth College
Unlettered Proof
Published: Colnaghi & Co., London, 1796
50 x 36 (plate cut x 35)
Chromo-mezzotint
Presented, C. R. Howard, 4th Earl of Wicklow, 1884

Vouet, Simon (1540-1649)
French School
MASQUELIER LE JEUNE, NICOLAS FRANÇOIS JOSEPH (1760-1809)
FRENCH SCHOOL

20,058
The Flagellation, (artist given as Le Sueur)
(after an oil, The Louvre, Paris)
48 x 46.5 (plate 43.4 x 27.8
Line and stipple
Provenance Unknown

Published: R. van den Hoeye, Amsterdam
41.6 x 31.2 (plate 41.2 x 31.2)
Line and stipple (aquatint border)
Purchased, London, 1st Chaloner Smith sale, 1887

Walmsley, Thomas (1763-1806)
Irish School
CARTWRIGHT, WILLIAM (18TH CENTURY)
ENGLISH SCHOOL

20,702
Roughty Bridge, County Kerry
(after a gouache)
INSCRIBED: Miscellaneous Irish Scenery/Plate 4th
Published: J. Daniell & Co, London, 15th August 1806
46 x 57 (plate cut)
Aquatint
Purchased, London, The Parker Gallery, 1983

Walton & Co., C.W. (19th century)
English School
WALTON & CO., C.W. (19TH CENTURY)
ENGLISH SCHOOL

11,075
Mervyn Wingfield, 7th Viscount Powerscourt, (1836-1904)
(after a drawing)
Lettered Proof
Published: C.W. Walton & Co., London
59.5 x 44 (image 34 x 25.5)
Lithograph
Acquired, beween 1913/14

Ward, James (1769-1859)
English School
ENGLISH SCHOOL (1795)

20,089
Dog Attacking a rat
Published: T. Simpson, also Darling & Thompson, London, 1st January 1795
36.9 x 44 (plate cut)
Stipple
Provenance Unknown

Ward, Leslie Matthew (Spy) (1851-1922)
English School
BROOKS, VINCENT ROBERT ALFRED (1814-1885)
ENGLISH SCHOOL

11,078
Dion Boucicault, (1822-1890), Actor and Playwright, (pl. for 'Vanity Fair', 16th December 1882)
Published: V. Brooks, Day & Son, London, 1882
39 x 26.3 (image 31.3 x 18.5)
Coloured Lithograph
Acquired, c.1903

Watteau, Antoine (1684-1721)
French School
DUPUIS, CHARLES (1685-1742)
FRENCH SCHOOL

11,845
'L'Occupation selon L'âge' (To each age its occupation)
(after an oil of c.1718, now lost; NGI no. 1321 is a copy)
Published: Monsieur Hallée, Paris
40.2 x 25.1 (plate 38.1 x 44.3)
Line
Purchased, Naas, Mr T. Mansfield, 1956

Weidemann, Fredrich Wilhelm (1668-1750)
German School
SMITH, JOHN (1652-1742)
ENGLISH SCHOOL

10,719

Sophia Dorothea of Zell, (1666-1726), Queen of King George I of England
(after an oil of 1714)
Published: J. Smith, London, 1706
37.7 x 27.3 (plate 34.8 x 25)
Mezzotint
Acquired beween 1890/98

Weidemann, Frederick Wilhelm (1668-1750)
German School
SMITH, JOHN (C.1652-1742)
ENGLISH SCHOOL

11,184
Madame d'Auverquerck, (1639-1720), wife of Henry, Count d'Auverquerck
(after an oil of 1701)
Published: ?J. Smith, London
19.2 x 14.3 (plate 18.9 x 14)
Mezzotint
Purchased, London, 2nd Chaloner Smith sale, 1888

Weidemann, Frederich Wilhelm (1668-1750)
German School
SMITH, JOHN (C.1652-1742)
ENGLISH SCHOOL

11,185
Madame d'Auverquerck, (1639-1720), wife of Henry, Count d'Auverquerck
(after an oil of 1701)
Unlettered Proof
Published: ?J. Smith, London
19 x 14.2 (plate 18.9 x 14)
Mezzotint
Purchased, London, 2nd Chaloner Smith sale, 1888

West, Benjamin (1738-1820)
Anglo-American School
FISHER, EDWARD (1722-C.1785)
IRISH SCHOOL

10,850
George III, King of England, (1738-1820)
Published: E. Fisher, London, 1778
41.3 x 31.4 (plate 40 x 30.2)
Mezzotint
Purchased, London, 1st Chaloner Smith sale, 1887

West, Benjamin (1738-1820)
Anglo-American School
WOOLLETT, WILLIAM (1735-1785)
ENGLISH SCHOOL

11,664
The Destruction of the French Fleet at La Hogue, 1692
(after an oil, RA 1780)
44.5 x 61.2 (plate cut)
Line
Provenance Unknown

West, Francis Robert (c.1749-1809)
Irish School
WATSON, JAMES (C.1740-1790)
IRISH SCHOOL

10,236
Arthur Smyth, P. Archbishop of Dublin, (1706-1771)
(after an oil of 1771)
Published: London, ?1771
41.4 x 31.5 (plate 37.6 x 27.6)
Mezzotint
Purchased, London,
Mr H.A.J. Breun, 1909

West, Francis Robert (c.1749-1809)
Irish School
WATSON, JAMES (C.1740-1790)
IRISH SCHOOL

10,237
Arthur Smyth, P. Archbishop of Dublin, (1706-1771), (another copy)
(after an oil of 1771)
Published: London, ?1771
36.9 x 26.6 (plate cut)
Mezzotint
Provenance Unknown

West, Samuel (c.1810-after 1867)
Irish School
GELLER, WILLIAM OVEREND (FL.1834-1857)
ENGLISH SCHOOL

10,451
Rev. Theobald Mathew, (1790-1856), Founder of the Temperance Movement in Ireland
(after an oil, RA 1847)
INSCRIBED: respectfully dedicated to the members of the Temperance Societies throughout the World/by their Obed & Humble Servant/William Overend Geller
Published: W.O. Geller, London
62.2 x 50 (plate 55 x 40.8)
Mezzotint
Presented, London,
Sir Charles James Mathew, 1903

West, William Edward (early 19th century)
American School
SCRIVEN, EDWARD (1775-1840)
ENGLISH SCHOOL

20,658
Felicia Dorothea Hemans, (1793-1835), Poet, (frontispiece for her 'Works', 1839)
Published: W. Blackwood, London, 1839
20.7 x 17 (plate cut)
Stipple in black and brown with watercolour
Provenance Unknown

Westall, Richard (1765-1836)
English School
TURNER, CHARLES (1773-1857)
ENGLISH SCHOOL

20,445
The Cottage Door, (pl. for 'Gems of European Art', 1846)
Published: S.C. Hall, London
41.1 x 28.1 (plate 22.8 x 19)
Mezzotint
Purchased, Lusk, Mr de Courcy Donovan, 1971

Weyden, Rogier van der (c.1399-1464)
Flemish School
STRIXNER, NEPOMUK JOHANN (1782-1855)
GERMAN SCHOOL

20,758(34)
The Annunciation, (from 'Die Sammlung Alt-Nieder und Ober-Deutscher Gemälde', 1821, see App. 8, no. 20,758)
(after an oil, Alte Pinakothek, Munich)
Published: Stuttgart, 1821
56.7 x 29.9 (plate cut)
Lithograph
Provenance Unknown

Wheatley, Francis (1747-1801)
English School
COLLYER, JOSEPH (1748-1827)
ENGLISH SCHOOL

11,644
The Dublin Volunteers on College Green, 4th November 1779
(after a reduced w/c, V&A, London, from an oil of 1779, NGI no. 125)
Published: R. Lane, London, 10th May 1784
50 x 72.5 (plate 48.9 x 67.8)
Line
Acquired by 1879

Wheatley, Francis (1747-1801)
English School
COLLYER, JOSEPH (1748-1827)
ENGLISH SCHOOL

11,826
The Dublin Volunteers on College Green, 4th November 1779
(after a reduced w/c, V&A London, from an oil of 1779, NGI no. 125)
INSCRIBED: *To his Grace William Robert Fitzgerald, Duke of Leinster, &c, of the Kingdom of Ireland/and Visct. Leinster & Taplow of the Kingdom of Great Britain. This Plate is Inscribed by his Grace's most Obed. & much obligd humble Servt./R. Lane*
Published: R. Lane, London, 10th May 1784 and sold by J. Boydell
48.7 x 67.3 (plate cut)
Line
Acquired by 1914

Wheatley, Francis (1747-1801)
English School
ENGLISH SCHOOL (1801)

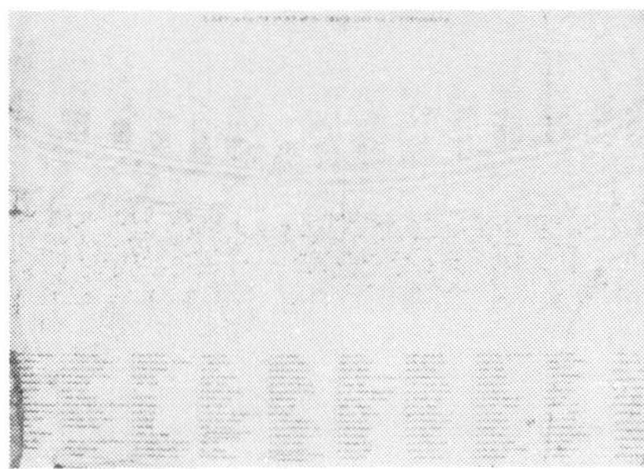

11,830
Key to the picture of the Irish House of Commons
(after an oil of 1780, Leeds City Art Galleries)
Published: W. Skelton, London, 26th February 1801
43.8 x approx 60 (plate cut)
Line and etching
Provenance Unknown

Wheatley, Francis (1747-1801)
English School
GREEN, VALENTINE (1739-1813)
ENGLISH SCHOOL

10,130
Henry Grattan, M.P., (1746-1820), Statesman, as Colonel of the Dublin Volunteers
(after an oil of 1780, NPG, London)
Published: V. Green, London, 10th September 1782
39.5 x 29.2 (plate 37.4 x 27.0)
Mezzotint
Presumed purchased, Dublin, Jones Salesroom, 1879

Wheatley, Francis (1747-1801)
English School
MALTON, THOMAS (1726-1801)
ENGLISH SCHOOL

11,645
Dublin Bay, (Coffee House, Dun Laoghaire)
Published: T. Malton, also W. Hinton, London, 30th December 1785
29.6 x 39.4 (plate cut)
Aquatint and etching
Provenance Unknown

Wheatley, Francis (1747-1801)
English School
MALTON, THOMAS (1726-1801)
ENGLISH SCHOOL

11,902
The Sheds of Clontarf, Dublin Bay
Published: T. Malton also W. Hinton, London, 30th December 1785
30 x 41 (plate 27.2 x 37.9)
Etching and aquatint
Provenance Unknown

Wheatley, Francis (1747-1801)
English School
MILTON, THOMAS (1743-1827)
ENGLISH SCHOOL

11,594
Lord Charlemont's Casino at Marino, near Dublin, (pl. for T. Milton's 'The Seats and Demesnes of the Nobility and Gentry in Ireland', 1783-93)
INSCRIBED: *Most humbly inscribed to the Earl of Charlemont, reviewing General and Commander/-in Chief of the Volunteer Forces of the whole Kingdom of Ireland/ by Thos. Milton*
Published: J. Walter, London, for the author T. Milton in Dublin, 1st July 1783
18 x 20 (plate 16 x 20.3)
Line
Presented, Dr E. MacDowel Cosgrave, 1907

Wheatley, Francis (1747-1801)
English School
MILTON, THOMAS (1743-1827)
ENGLISH SCHOOL

11,683
Howth Castle, Co. Dublin, (formerly pl. for T. Milton's 'The Seats and Demesnes of the Nobility and Gentry in Ireland', 1783-93)
Published: W. Marshall, London, 1st July 1831
22 x 28.5 (plate 15.5 x 20.2)
Line
Presented, Dr E. MacDowell Cosgrave, 1907

Wheatley, Francis (1747-1801)
English School
MILTON, THOMAS (1743-1827)
ENGLISH SCHOOL

11,684
Malahide Castle, County Dublin, (formerly pl. for T. Milton's 'The Seats and Demesnes of the Nobility and Gentry in Ireland, 1783-93)
(after a drawing of 1782, ex-Malahide Castle coll.)
Published: W. Marshall, London, 1st July 1831
22.7 x 28.8 (plate 16 x 20.4)
Line
Presented, Dr E. MacDowel Cosgrave, 1907

Wheatley, Francis (1747-1801)
English School
ROWLANDSON, THOMAS (1756-1827)
ENGLISH SCHOOL

11,503
Irish Peasants and Whiskey Tents at a Fair or A Group of Gypsies, (pl. for T. Rowlandson's, 'Imitations of Modern Drawings', undated)
(?after a watercolour of 1786 similar to NGI no. 2700)
48.4 x 30.2 (plate 21 x 25)
Etching
Provenance Unknown

White, George Francis (1804-1898)
English School
ALLOM, THOMAS (1804-1872)
ENGLISH SCHOOL *and*
KERNOT, JAMES HARFIELD (FL.1828-1849)
ENGLISH SCHOOL

20,454
Gungotri, the Sacred Source of the river Ganges, India, (pl. for R. Martin's 'Indian Empire', 1857)
Published: Fisher, Son & Co., London, 1840
21.7 x 27.5 (plate cut)
Steel Engraving
Purchased, Lusk, Mr de Courcy Donovan, 1971

White, Robert (1645-1703)
English School
WHITE, ROBERT (1645-1703)
ENGLISH SCHOOL

10,611
General Sir George Rawdon, Bt., (1604-1684), Campaigner in Ireland
Published: c.1667
22 x 17 (plate 16.6 x 11. 1)
Line
Presented, Mr G.F. Chittenden, 1898

Whymper, Edward (1840-1911)
English school
WHYMPER, EDWARD (1840-1911)
ENGLISH SCHOOL

20,269
The Scala Reggia of the Vatican, Rome, (from 'Sunday at Home', 1st March 1870)
Published: Sunday at Home, London, 1st March 1870
19.2 x 28 (image 14.9 x 21)
Wood Engraving
Purchased, Lusk, Mr de Courcy Donovan, 1971

Whymper, Edward (1840-1911)
English School
WHYMPER, EDWARD (1840-1911)
ENGLISH SCHOOL

20,270
The Nave of St Peter's Cathedral, Rome, (from 'Sunday at Home', 1st June 1870)
Published: Sunday at Home, London, 1st June 1870
27.9 x 19.5 (image 21.5 x 15.2)
Wood Engraving
Purchased, Lusk, Mr de Courcy Donovan, 1971

Wijnants, Jan (1631/32-1684)
Dutch School
ENGLISH SCHOOL (19TH CENTURY)

20,227
Edge of the Forest
(after an oil of 1668, The Louvre, Paris)
25.4 x 32 (plate cut)
Line and etching
Purchased, Lusk, Mr de Courcy Donovan, 1971

Wilkie, David (1785-1841)
Scottish School
MOSSE, G. (19TH CENTURY)
ENGLISH SCHOOL

11,663
The Village Holiday
(after an oil of 1809-11, Tate Gallery, London)
Published: H. Graves & Co., London, 20th January 1846
41 x 48.9 (plate cut)
Line
Provenance Unknown

Wilkie, David (1785-1841)
English School
SMITH, EDWARD (FL.1823-1851)
ENGLISH SCHOOL

20,219
The Jew's Harp, (pl. for S.C. Hall's 'Gems of European Art', 1846)
(after an oil of 1804)
Published: G. Virtue, for the Proprietors, London
37 x 27 (plate cut)
Steel Engraving
Purchased, Lusk, Mr de Courcy Donovan, 1971

Williams, George Augustus (fl.1841-1885)
English School
ENGLISH SCHOOL (19TH CENTURY)

20,501
Figures conversing on a country road
8.5 x 10.5 (plate cut)
Line and mezzotint
Purchased, Lusk, Mr de Courcy Donovan, 1971

Wills, James (fl.1740-1777)
English School
MILLER, ANDREW (FL. 1737-1763)
IRISH SCHOOL

10,018
Josiah Hort, P. Archbishop of Tuam, (1674-1751)
Published: ?A. Miller, Dublin, 1752
35.6 x 25.7 (plate 35.4 x 25)
Mezzotint
Purchased, London, 1st Chaloner Smith sale, 1887

Wilson, Benjamin (1721-1788)
English School
BASIRE, JAMES (1730-1802)
ENGLISH SCHOOL

10,404
Lady Anne Hussey Stanhope, (née Delaval, fl.1759-1811)
Published: London, 1st May 1772
51.5 x 35.8 (plate cut)
Line
Milltown Gift, 1902

Wilson, Benjamin (1721-1788)
English School
MCARDELL, JAMES (1728/29-1765)
IRISH SCHOOL

10,149
Simon Harcourt, 1st Earl Harcourt, (1714-1777), holding a plan of Nuneham, Oxfordshire, (later Lord Lieutenant of Ireland)
(after an oil of 1750, British Embassy, Bonn)
Unlettered Proof
35 x 24.5 (plate cut)
Mezzotint
Purchased, London, 1st Chaloner Smith sale, 1887

Wilson, Benjamin (1721-1788)
English School
MCARDELL, JAMES (1728/29-1765)
IRISH SCHOOL

10,677
Simon Harcourt, 1st Earl Harcourt, (1714-1777), holding a plan of Nuneham, Oxfordshire, (later Lord Lieutenant of Ireland)
(after an oil of 1750, British Embassy, Bonn)
35.8 x 25.4 (plate 35 x 25)
Mezzotint
Purchased London, 1st Chaloner Smith sale, 1887

Wilson, Benjamin (1721-1788)
English School
WILSON, BENJAMIN (1721-1788)
ENGLISH SCHOOl

10,128
Dr Bryan Robinson, (1680-1754), former President of the Royal College of Physicians
(after an oil of 1748/50, Trinity College, Dublin)
Published: B. Wilson, Dublin, 1750
37 x 27.5 (plate cut)
Etching
Purchased, Dublin, Mr J.V. McAlpine, 1904

Wilson, Benjamin (1721-1788)
English School
WILSON, BENJAMIN (1721-1788)
ENGLISH SCHOOL

0,388
Maria Gunning, (1733-1760), later Countess of Coventry, sister of Catherine and Elizabeth, daughter of James Gunning
Unlettered proof
Published: B. Wilson, Dublin, 1750
4.5 x 25.4 (plate 33 x 25)
Mezzotint
Purchased, London, 2nd Chaloner Smith sale, 1888

Wilson, Richard (1714-1782)
English School
MORRIS, THOMAS (FL.C.1750-1802)
ENGLISH SCHOOL

0,083
The Banks of the River Dee near Eaton Hall, Cheshire
(after an oil of c.1760, Barber Institute of Fine Arts, Birmingham)
Published: London, 1774
9.8 x 36.5 (plate cut)
Line
Provenance Unknown

Wilson, Richard (1714-1782)
English School
VARRALL, JOHN CHARLES (FL.1818-1848)
ENGLISH SCHOOL

20,552
The Destruction of the Children of Niobe
(after an oil of c.1765, destroyed)
13.1 x 18.2 (plate cut)
Steel Engraving
Presented, Mrs D. Molloy, 1981

Wilson, William (18th Century)
Irish School
BAKER, BENJAMIN (FL.1780-1824)
ENGLISH SCHOOL

11,812
Modern Plan of the City and Environs of Dublin 1798 with Vignette of the Custom House
INSCRIBED: This modern plan of the/City and Environs of/Dublin/including the Grand & Royal Canals, New Docks, &c. is by Permission, most respectfully/Inscribed, by her Ladyship's/humble & Obedient servent Wm. Wilson. Published as the act directs for/W. Wilson & sold by the Booksellers and Printersellers in London & Dublin
Published: W. Wilson, Dublin, 1st June 1798
44.7 x 52.8 (plate cut)
Line with watercolour
Provenance Unknown

Wissing, William (c.1656-1687)
Anglo-Dutch School
BECKETT, ISAAC (1653-1719)
ENGLISH SCHOOL

10,244
Henry Fitzroy, 1st Duke of Grafton, (1663-1690), (natural son of Charles II and Barbara Villiers, Duchess of Cleveland), in classical armour
(after an oil, Raby Castle, Co. Durham)
Unlettered Proof
Published: I. Beckett, London, ?1681/88
33 x 26 (plate 31.7 x 25)
Mezzotint
Purchased, London, 1st Chaloner Smith sale, 1887

Wissing, William (c.1656-1687)
Anglo-Dutch School
BECKETT, ISAAC (1653-1719)
ENGLISH SCHOOL

10,331

Amelia, Countess of Ossory, (née De Nassau, fl.1659-1688), wife of Thomas, Count of Ossory and mother of the 2nd Duke of Ormonde
Published: E. Cooper, London, ?1681/88
34 x 24.9 (plate cut)
Mezzotint
Purchased, London, 1st Chaloner Smith sale, 1887

Wissing, William (c.1656-1687)
Anglo Dutch School
BECKETT, ISAAC (1653-1719)
ENGLISH SCHOOL

10,993
Amelia, Countess of Ossory, (née De Nassau, fl.1659-1688), wife of Thomas, Count of Ossory and mother of the 2nd Duke of Ormonde, (another copy)
Published: E. Cooper, London, ?1681/88
31 x 24.5 (plate cut)
Mezzotint
Purchased, London, 1st Chaloner Smith sale, 1887

Wissing, William (c.1656-1687)
Anglo-Dutch School
BECKETT, ISAAC (1653-1719)
ENGLISH SCHOOL

11,863
Elizabeth, Countess of Kildare, (née Jones, 1665-1758), 2nd wife of the 18th Earl of Kildare
Unlettered Proof
Published: I. Beckett, London, ?1681/88
17.7 x 13.3 (plate 16.8 x 12.7)
Mezzotint
Purchased, London, 1st Chaloner Smith sale, 1887

Wissing, William (c.1656-1687)
Anglo-Dutch School
LENS, BERNARD (1659-1725)
ENGLISH SCHOOL

10,922
Mary II, Queen of England, (1662-1694)
Published: E. Cooper, London, not before 1689
43.8 x 26 (plate cut)
Mezzotint
Purchased, London, 1st Chaloner Smith sale, 1887

Wissing, William (c.1656-1687)
Anglo-Dutch School
SMITH, JOHN (1652-1742)
ENGLISH SCHOOL

10,559
William III, King of England, (1650-1702)
Published: E. Cooper, London, 1688
33.7 x 25.1 (plate cut)
Mezzotint
Acquired beween 1890/98

Wissing, William (c.1656-1687)
Anglo-Dutch School
SMITH, JOHN (1652-1742)
ENGLISH SCHOOL

10,691

Self-Portrait
Published: ?J. Smith, London, 1687
34.7 x 25.3 (plate 34.3 x 25.1)
Mezzotint
Purchased, London, 2nd Chaloner
Smith sale, 1888

Wissing, William (c.1656-1687)
Anglo-Dutch School
WILLIAMS, ROBERT (FL. 1680-1704)
ENGLISH SCHOOL

10,001
James Butler, 1st Duke of Ormonde, (1610-1688)
(after an oil, NPG, London)
Published: E. Cooper, London
3 x 24.4 (plate cut)
Mezzotint
Purchased, London, 2nd Chaloner
Smith sale, 1888

Wissing, William (c.1656-1687)
Anglo-Dutch School
WILLIAMS, ROBERT (FL.1680-1704)
ENGLISH SCHOOL

10,016
John Cutts, (1661-1707), Professional Soldier, later Baron Cutts of Gowran
(after an oil of c.1685, NPG, London)
Published: R. Williams, c.1685/90
33.3 x 24.5 (plate cut)
Mezzotint
Purchased, London 2nd Chaloner
Smith sale, 1888

Wivell the Elder, Abraham (1786-1849)
English School
LUPTON, THOMAS (1791-1873)
ENGLISH SCHOOL

10,824
George IV, King of England, (1762-1830)
INSCRIBED: Dedicated by Permission to/His Royal Highness the Duke of York,/by his obliged humble & devoted Servant,/William Sams
Published: W. Sams, London, 1st January 1824 (Printed: J. Lahee)
45.3 x 35.2 (plate 34 x 24.5)
Mezzotint
Acquired beween 1890/98

Wivell the Elder, Abraham (1786-1849)
English School
MEYER, HENRY HOPPNER (1783-1847)
ENGLISH SCHOOL

10,638
Michael Kelly, (?1764-1826), Singer and Composer, (frontispiece for his 'Reminiscences', 1825)
Unlettered Proof
Published: H. Colburn, London, 1825
24.5 x 16.9 (plate 22.7 x 15.3)
Stipple
Purchased, Dublin, Mr A. Roth, 1896

Wivell the Elder, Abraham (1786-1849)
English School
READ, WILLIAM (FL.1824-1837)
ENGLISH SCHOOL

10,583
Roger O'Connor, (1762-1834), United Irishman and Author, brother of Arthur O'Connor, 'Chief of the Prostrated People of his Nation'
Published: Sir Richard Phillips & Co., London
24.5 x 15.3 (plate 23.3 x 14.2)
Stipple
Purchased, Dublin, Mr J. V. McAlpine, 1898

Wivell the Elder, Abraham (1786-1849)
English School *and*
Lawrence, Thomas (1769-1830)
English School
?PRIOR, THOMAS ABIEL (1809-1886)
ENGLISH SCHOOL

11,384
Henry Brougham, M.P., (1778-1868), later Lord Chancellor and 1st Baron Brougham and Vaux; John Singleton Copley, (1772-1863), later Lord Chancellor and 1st Baron Lyndhurst; Robert Banks Jenkinson, 2nd Earl of Liverpool, (1770-1828), British Prime Minister
(Broughan after a Wivell drawing of 1820, engr. 1821; Copley after a Wivell drawing c.1820, engr. 1820; Liverpool after a Lawrence tql oil c.1820, Royal Collection, Windsor Castle)
22.8 x 15 (plate cut)
Line
Provenance Unknown

Wood, John (1801-1870)
English School
BROWN, JOSEPH (FL.1854-1886)
ENGLISH SCHOOL

10,840
Thomas Philip Weddell Robinson, 2nd Earl De Grey, (1781-1859), Statesman, later Lord Lieutenant of Ireland
(after an oil, RA 1837)
Published: R. Ryley, also J. Fraser, also F.G. Moon, London, 1837
(Printed: Wilkinson & Dawe)
40.4 x 28.6 (plate 34 x 25.7)
Stipple
Purchased, Dillon & Co., 1901

Wood, John (1801-1870)
English School
HOLL THE YOUNGER, WILLIAM (1807-1871)
ENGLISH SCHOOL

10,632
Dr James Johnson, (1777-1845), Physician to King William IV, (pl. for Pettigrew's 'Medical Portrait Gallery', 1838)
27.3 x 21 (plate cut)
Stipple
Acquired c.1903

Woodburn, Robert (d. 1803)
Irish School
DUNKARTON, ROBERT (1744- AFTER 1811)
ENGLISH SCHOOL

10,416
Major-General Henry Johnson, (1748-1835), Victor at New Ross, 1798
Published: R. Woodburn, Dublin also Colnaghi & Co., London, 4th June 1801
51.8 x 36.5 (plate 50.7 x 35.1)
Mezzotint
Purchased, 1914

oods, Isaac (1688/89-1752)
ıglish School
BER THE YOUNGER, JOHN (C.1684-1756)
GLISH SCHOOL

,029
ın Hoadly, P. Archbishop of Dublin, 578-1746), later Archbishop of Armagh
blished: J. Faber the Younger,
ndon, not before 1734
.7 x 25.2 (plate cut)
ezzotint
esumed purchased, Dublin, Jones
eroom, 1879

odward, George Montard 1760-1809)
glish School
GLISH SCHOOL (1808)

544(8)
iteness, (pl. for Earl of Chesterfield's averstie, or School of Modern Manners', 08, from Album of Caricatures, see App. no. 11,544)
CRIBED: I am sorry to intrude in this upt/manner-but do you know Sir you/are ed with my wife?/Sir I beg you ten usand pardons! Let me request you will eated and/she shall be at your service in course/of half an hour
6 x 35 (plate cut)
hing with watercolour
ltown Gift, 1902

Woodward, Thomas (1801-1852)
English School
SMITH, WILLIAM RAYMOND (FL.1818-1848)
ENGLISH SCHOOL *and*
ROBINSON, JOHN HENRY (1796-1871)
ENGLISH SCHOOL

20,331
'The Tempting Present'
(after an oil, RA 1822)
Published: Robinson & Co., London, 1st July 1824
41 x 58.6 (plate 32.1 x 35.3)
Line
Purchased, Lusk, Mr de Courcy Donovan, 1971

Worlidge, Thomas (1700-1766)
English School
HOUSTON, RICHARD (1721-1775)
IRISH SCHOOL

10,234
George II, King of England, (1683-1760)
(after an oil of c.1753, then belonged to publisher T. Jefferys; possibly the tql oil, NPG, London)
1st State
Published: R. Sayer, also T. Jefferys, London
44 x 32 (plate 39.5 x 27.5)
Mezzotint
Purchased, London, 1st Chaloner Smith sale, 1887

Worlidge, Thomas (1700-1766)
English School
HOUSTON, RICHARD (1721-1775)
IRISH SCHOOL

10,827
George II, King of England, (1683-1760)
(after an oil of c.1753, then belonged to publisher, T. Jefferys; possibly the tql oil NPG, London)
2nd State
Published: R. Sayer, also T. Jefferys, London
40 x 27.8 (plate cut)
Mezzotint
Purchased, London, 1st Chaloner Smith sale, 1887

Worlidge, Thomas (1700-1766)
English School
WHITE, CHARLES WILLIAM (C.1730-?1807)
ENGLISH SCHOOL

20,119
George II, King of England, (1683-1760), (pl. for J. Parson's 'Genuine Edition of Hume's England', 1794)
Published: J. Parsons, London, August 1971
14.6 x 8.9 (plate cut)
Stipple
Purchased, Lusk, Mr de Courcy Donovan, 1971

Worsdale, James (c.1692-1767)
English School
BROOKS, JOHN (FL.1730-1756)
IRISH SCHOOL

10,167
Samuel Grey, (d.1747), Commissioner of the Revenue in Ireland, (1st State)
Published: ?J. Brooks, Dublin, c.1742
34.8 x 25.4 (plate 34 x 24.3)
Mezzotint
Purchased, London, 1st Chaloner Smith sale, 1887

Worsdale, James (c.1692-1767)
English School
BROOKS, JOHN (FL.1730-1756)
IRISH SCHOOL

10,820
Samuel Grey, (d.1747), Commissioner of the Revenue in Ireland, (2nd State)
Published: T. Jefferys, also W. Herbert, London, c.1742
35.8 x 26 (plate 34 x 24.3)
Mezzotint
Purchased, London, 1st Chaloner Smith sale, 1887

Worsdale, James (c.1692-1767)
English School
BROOKS, JOHN (FL.1730-1756)
IRISH SCHOOL

11,062
The Hon. Mrs Jane Folliott Ponsonby, (née Taylor, d.1787)
Published: W. Herbert, London, not before 1744
34 x 24 (plate cut)
Mezzotint
Purchased, London, 1914

Worsdale, James (c.1692-1767)
English School
SIMON, JOHN (1675-1751)
ANGLO-FRENCH SCHOOL

10,215
Thomas Southerne, (1660-1746), Dramatist and Poet
(after an oil, ex-Earl of Cork's Collection)
Published: J. Simon, London, not before 1720
35.8 x 26 (plate 34.6 x 25)
Mezzotint
Purchased, Dublin, Mr J.V. McAlpine, 1901

Wouwerman, Philips (1619-1668)
Haarlem School
FILLOEUL, PIERRE (1690-1762)
FRENCH SCHOOL

20,689(25)
Travellers at an Inn, (from 'Oeuvres de P. Wouverman Hollandois', Vol. 1, 1737, see App. 8, no. 20,689)
Published: J. Moyreau, Paris, 1737
64.7 x 43.6 (plate 37.5 x 44.8)
Line
Bequeathed, Judge J. Murnaghan, 1976

Wouwerman, Philips (1619-1668)
Haarlem School
MOYREAU, JEAN (18TH CENTURY)
FRENCH SCHOOL

20,690(80)
The Departure for the Hunt, (from 'Oeuvres de P. Wouverman Hollandois' Vol. 2, 1756, see App. 8, no. 20,690)
Published: J. Moyreau, Paris, 1756
64.7 x 84.2 (plate 44.1 x 65.6)
Line
Bequeathed, Judge J. Murnaghan, 1976

Wright of Derby, Joseph (1734-1797)
English School
SMITH, JOHN RAPHAEL (1752-1812)
ENGLISH SCHOOL

10,406
The Children of Sir Walter Synnot of Co. Armagh; Marcus, (b.1771), Walter and Maria Eliza, (d.1800)
(after an oil of 1781)
Published: J.R. Smith, London, 25th April 1782
50.3 x 35.3 (plate cut x 35)
Mezzotint
Purchased, London, 2nd Chaloner Smith sale, 1888

Wyck, Jan (c.1640-1702)
Anglo-Dutch School
BROOKS, JOHN (FL.1730-1756)
IRISH SCHOOL

11,652
The Battle of the Boyne, 1st July 1690
Published: T. Kitchin, London, (reprint of Autumn 1747 mezzotint)
46.2 x 71.4 (plate 45.5 x 70)
Mezzotint
Acquired by 1914

Wyck, Jan (c.1640-1702)
Anglo-Dutch School
FABER THE YOUNGER, JOHN (C.1684-1756)
ENGLISH SCHOOL

10,420
King William III at the siege of Namur, Belgium, 1695
(after an oil possibly NGI no. 145)
INSCRIBED: *In Memory of our late Glorious Deliverer King William the III/ This plate (of the City and Castle of Namur taken 1695) is most Humbly Dedicated to the Superiour, Wardens, and the Rest of the Members of the Loyal and Friendly Society of the Blue and Orange./Done from the Original Painting once King William's now in the hands of the Bishop of Kildare/by a Member and their most Obliged Humble Servant/John Faber*
Published: J. Faber the Younger, London, 1743
35 x 50.2 (plate cut)
Mezzotint
Purchased, London, 1st Chaloner Smith sale, 1887

Yellowless, William (1796-1859)
Scottish School
WATTS, S. (18TH-19TH CENTURY)
ENGLISH SCHOOL

11,288
Charles Phillips, (1787-1859), Barrister and Writer
Published: W. Reynolds, London, 28th March 1819
33 x 23.3 (plate 19.8 x 15.5)
Line
Acquired by 1913

Zocchi, Giuseppe (1711-1767)
Italian School
ZOCCHI, GIUSEPPE (1711-1767)- figures
ITALIAN SCHOOL *and*
SGRILLI, BERNARDO SANSONE (FL.1733-1755)
ITALIAN SCHOOL

20,669(4)
Florence from across the River Arno, near the Porta S. Niccolo, (from 'Scelta di XXIV Vedute delle Principali Contrade

Piazze Chiese e Palazzi della alta di Firenze', see App. 8, no. 20, 669)
(after an ink and wash drawing, Pierpont Morgan Library, New York)
Published: G. Allegrini, Florence
57 x 72 (plate 51 x 68.5)
Line and etching
Provenance Unknown

Zoffany, Johann (1733-1810)
Anglo-German School
HOUSTON, RICHARD (C.1721-1775)
IRISH SCHOOL

10,350
Mrs Catherine Wodhull, (née Ingram, 1744-1808)
(after a wl oil)
Published: R. Sayers, London, 10th June 1772
43.6 x 32.7 (plate 38.5 x 27.7)
Mezzotint
Provenance Unknown

10,471
John Moody, (?1727-1812), Comedy Actor, as the Irish Priest, Father Foigard, in Farquhar's 'The Beaux Stratagem'
(after an oil, SA 1764)
Unlettered Proof
Published: I. Wesson, London
50.7 x 36.2 (plate 46 x 35)
Mezzotint
Purchased, London, 1st Chaloner Smith sale, 1887

Zoffany, Johann (1733-1810)
Anglo-German School
MARCHI, GIUSEPPE FILIPO LIBERATI (FL.1752-1808)
ANGLO-ITALIAN SCHOOL

Sculpture Catalogue

OVERLEAF: *Irish sculptor Peter Turnerelli modelling a bust of King George III.* Engraved after Samuel Drummond by James Thomson [NGI no. 11,278]

ams-Acton, John (1834-c.1892)
glish School
)9 *Charles James Patrick Mahon, M.P., (1800-1891), 'The O'Gorman Mahon', Adventurer and Soldier*
Signed: *John Adams Acton Fecit 1877*
75 ht., terracotta
Purchased, London, Mrs J. Adams-Acton, the sculptor's widow, 1912

dras, Catherine (1775-1860)
glish School
30 *Rose Rainey, (1728-1816), widow of Rev. Samuel Bruce*
Inscribed by former owner on label on back of case: *Modelled in wax/by Catherine Andreas* (sic) *of/Bristol/1799*
17 ht., painted wax figurine (in 33 ht. case)
Presented, Mrs M. B. Hutton, date unknown

gelis, Sabatino (b.1838)
apolitan School
39 *Dancing faun*
(copy of the Roman bronze from Pompeii, Museo Nazionale, Naples)
Foundry mark: *SAB. DEANGELIS & FILS. NAPLES*
78 ht., bronze
Presented, Mr J. F. D'Arcy, 1903

ily, Edward Hodges (1788-1867)
glish School
24 *Edmund Burke, M.P., (1729-1797), Statesman and Author*
(after J. Hickey's bust, c.1785)
Exhibited RA 1840
66 ht., marble (incl. 11ht. socle)
Purchased, Mr R. V. Bourke, 1924

rter, Richard (c.1824-1896)
sh School
36 *Charles Stewart Parnell, M.P., (1846-1891), Statesman*
(sculpted from photographs)
Signed: *RICHARD BARTER./SCULPTOR/1893*
33 ht., bronze (on 15.2 ht. yellow marble base)
Bequeathed, Miss S. Gorry, 1917

rye, Antoine Louis (1796-1875)
nch School
52 *Lion devouring a doe*
Signed: *BARYE*
33.4 ht. x 39 wh. x 12 dh., bronze
Bequeathed, Sir Hugh Lane, 1918

8109

8080

8224

8162

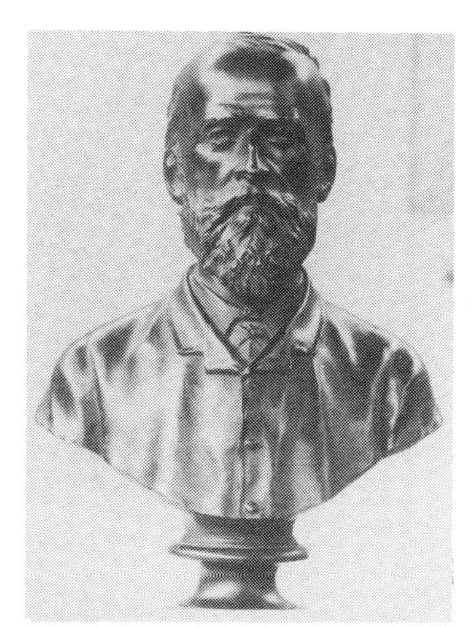
8086

8289

Barye

8163 *Tiger devouring a gazelle (1834)*
Signed: *BARYE*
32.5 ht. x 31.5 wh. x 12 dh., bronze
Bequeathed, Sir Hugh Lane, 1918

8163

8025

Bayser-Gratry, Marguerite (fl.1925-1939)
French School
8025 *William Gibson, 2nd Baron Ashbourne, (1868-1942)*
Signed: *Mlle Bayser G*
Foundry mark: *Cire/VALSUNA/perdue*
65 ht., bronze
Transferred from National Museum of Ireland, 1967

Behan, John (b.1932)
Irish School
8054 *Dan Breen, (1894-1969), Republican*
33 ht., bronze (on 8 ht. green marble base)
Presented, Mr J. Behan, the sculptor, 1968

8054

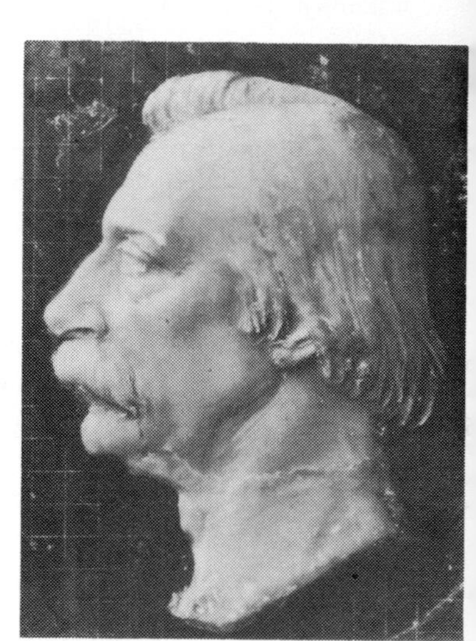

8157

Birch, Charles Bell (1832-1893)
English School
8157 *John Henry Foley, (1818-1874), Sculptor, (study for a plaster medallion, RA 1876, now NPG, London)*
14.5 ht. x 10.5 wh. approx., wax relief
Purchased, Mr G. Von Pirch, the artist's nephew, 1909

Boehm, Edgar (1834-c.1890)
English School
8148 *William Edward Hartpole Lecky, (1838-1903), Historian*
Signed: *By Sir Edgar Boehm 1890*
Inscribed: *W.E H. LECKY*
68 ht., bronze
Presented, Mrs Lecky, the sitter's widow, 1905

Bonnetain, Armand (1883-1973)
Belgian School
8169 *Brussels International Exhibition of 1935 plaquette*
Signed on both obverse and reverse: *BONNETAIN*
Inscribed on obverse: *EXPOSITION. UNIVERSELLE/ET. INTERNATIONALE/1935/ ALGEMEENE. WERELD. TENTOONSTELLUNG.*
6.5 x 8, gilt bronze
Provenance Unknown

8148

8169

:ributed to **Bourdelle, Emile Antoine**
361-1929)
:nch School
93 *Male Head*
37.5 ht., bronze (on 18.5 ht. green/black marble base)
Presented, Sir Alfred Chester Beatty, 1953

8093

:ributed to **Brustolon, Andrea (1662-1732)**
netian School
28 *Jardinière (1)*
198 ht., limewood (mother-of-pearl inlay in dragon's eyes)
Purchased, London, Heim, 1967

8028

29 *Jardinière (2)*
198 ht., limewood (mother-of-pearl inlay in dragon's eyes))
Purchased, London, Heim, 1967

8029

hool of **Caffieri, Jean Jacques (1725-1792)**
:nch School
51 *Portrait of a Woman (so-called portrait of Madame du Barry, 1746-1793)*
74 ht., marble (incl. 11.5 ht. socle)
Purchased, London, Mr P. Wallraf, 1968

8051

:er **Canova, Antonio (1757-1822)**
lian School
03 *A Sleeping Nymph*
(reduced copy of a marble c.1820, V&A, London)
23 ht. x 79 lh. x 33 dh., marble
Milltown Gift, 1902

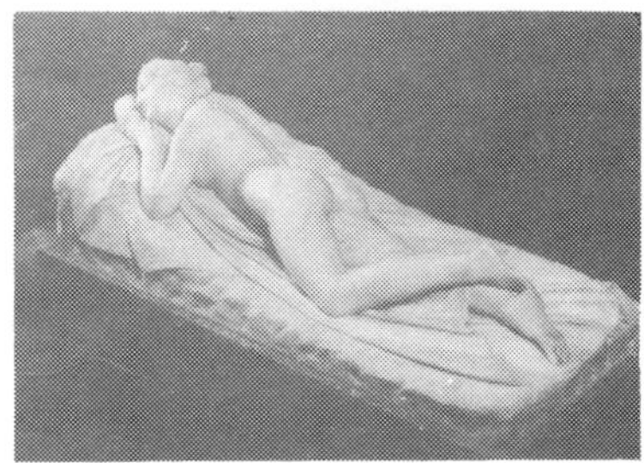
8103

rpeaux, Jean-Baptiste (1827-1875)
:nch School
40 *Empress Eugénie, (née Dona Eugenia Maria de Montigo de Guzman), wife of Emperor Napoleon III (c.1866)*
Signed: *J. B. Carpeaux*
37 ht., plaster
Bequeathed, Sir Hugh Lane, 1918

8040

Carre, Joseph S.M. (fl.1909-1914)
?French School
8106 *Nude Male Athelete*
Signed: *J... Carre*
46 ht., bronze
Presented, Captain Kelly, 1910

Cavaceppi, Bartolomeo (c.1716-1799)
Italian School
8242 *A Faun with grapes*
(reduced copy of the Classical rosso antico sculpture, Capitoline Museums, Rome)
Signed: *BARTOLOMEUS CAVACEPPI SCULP ROM 1751*
75 ht., marble
Milltown Gift, 1902

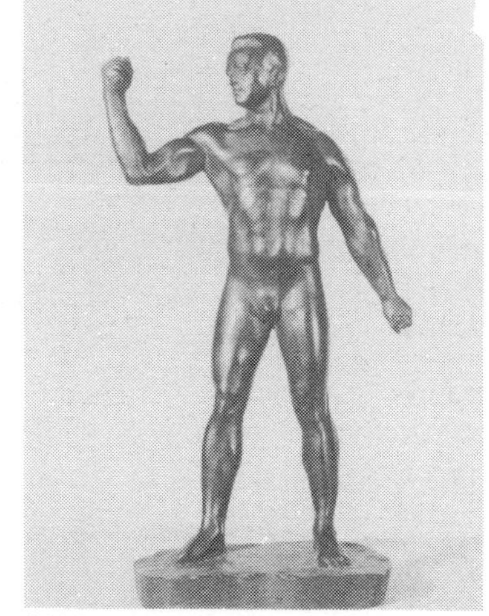

8106

8242

8243 *A Faun with a kid*
(reduced copy of the Classical marble sculpture, The Prado, Madrid)
Signed: *BARTOLOMEUS CAVACEPPI SCULP ROM 1751*
69 ht., marble
Milltown Gift, 1902

Chantrey, Francis (1781-1842)
English School
8151 *Richard Wellesley, 1st Marquess Wellesley, (1760-1842), Governor-General of India, Lord Lieutenant of Ireland, brother of 1st Duke of Wellington*
40 ht., bronze (on 11 ht. marble base)
Presented, Mr A. Montgomery, 1889

8243

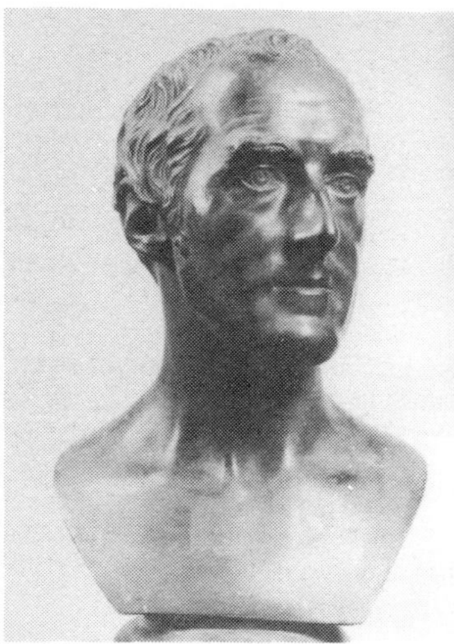

8151

School of **Chantrey, Francis (1781-1842)**
8241 *William Carr Beresford, 1st Viscount Beresford, (1768-1854), Peninsular War Officer*
72 ht. marble (incl. 13 ht. socle)
Presented, Sir Henry Pierce Bt., 1903

Chavalliaud, Leon Joseph (1858-1921)
French School
8189 *Rev. James Healy, (1825-1894)*
Signed: *L. Chavalliaud Sc./London 1895*
53.5 ht., bronze
Commissioned by and presented, Mr H. Y. Thompson, 1895

8241

8189

nnor, Jerome (1876-1943)
h School

2 *Plaque of Walt Whitman, (1819-1892), Poet, (model for a bronze, 1926)*
(probably from T. Eakins's 1891 photograph)
Signed: *JEROME CONNOR/SC.*
Inscribed on obverse: *WALT WHIT/MAN/COME/LOVELY AND/SOOTHING/DEATH/UNDULAT-E/ROUND THE/WORLD SERENE/LY ARRIVING. ARR/IVING IN THE DAY/IN THE NIGHT/TO ALL TO EACH/SOONER/OR LATER/DELICATE/DEATH*
Inscribed in pencil on reverse: *To AE - as a token /of our mutual regard/ for The Leaves of Grass/ from Jerome Connor/ April 1926*
25 diam., plaster
Purchased, Mr A. Denson, 1966

3 *Eamon de Valera, (1882-1975), Statesman and 3rd President of Ireland*
Signed indistinctly: *Jerome Connor*
37 ht., bronze (on 4 ht. green marble base)
Cast commissioned from Werner Schurmann, Dublin, by the Board of Governors and Guardians, after the original plaster loaned by the Late Mr F. Aiken, 1968

2 *Miss Brenda Charles*
Signed: *Jerome/Connor/DUBLIN*
50 ht., plaster and wax
Presented, Mr R. Charles, the sitter's brother, 1973

3 *Miss Brenda Charles*
Signed: *Jerome/Connor/DUBLIN*
Foundry mark:
DUBLIN/ART/FOUNDRY LTD/CAST 1973/(N.1)
49 ht., bronze
Cast commissioned from Dublin Art Foundry by the Board of Governors and Guardians after the original plaster, NGI no. 8232, 1973

ntinental School (18th century)

5 *Medallion of Maurice, Count de Lacy, (1740-1820), General of the Austrian Army*
Inscribed: *MAURITIUS COMES A LACY AUSTRIE SUPREMUS DUX*
9 diam., silvered plaster
Presented, Mr F. Stewart, 1912

plans, Joseph (20th century)
th African School

6 *George Bernard Shaw, (1856-1950), Author, Dramatist and Critic (1932)*
48 ht., bronze
Presented, Mr J. Coplans, the sculptor, 1952

8012

8053

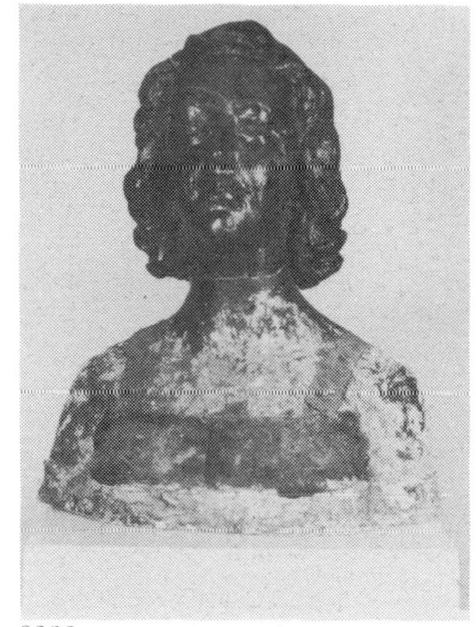

8232

8233

8165

8146

Cossos & Brontos

Cossos (19th century)
Greek School
and
Brontos (19th century)
Greek School

8185 *Sir Thomas Wyse, (1791-1862), Diplomat and British Minister in Athens*
Signed: *COSSOS/ET/BRONTOS/ATHENES*
55 ht., marble
Presented, Miss Wyse, the sitter's niece, 1907

8185

8050

Courbet, Gustave (1819-1877)
French School

8050 *Madame Buchon, (b.1841, née Helena Felicité Diziain), wife of the poet Max Buchon*
Foundry mark: *E. Godard Paris 4/6*
© *Alfred Daber Paris*
37 ht., bronze (on 8 ht. black marble base)
Purchased, Paris, Galerie Daber, 1968

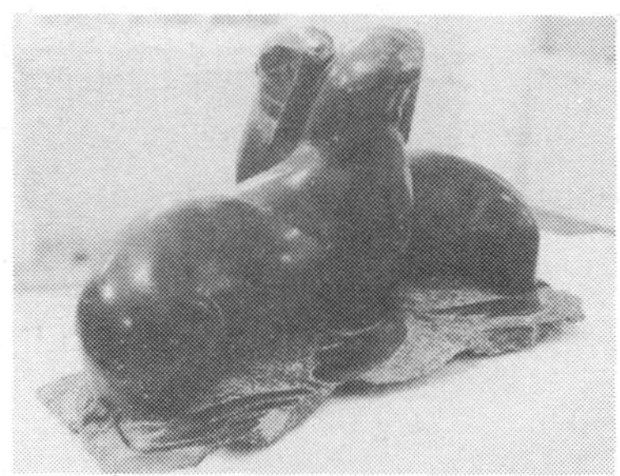
8079

8026

Cuairan, Francesco Lorencis (20th century)
South African School

8079 *Two Seals*
Signed: *CUAIRAN 1934*
35 ht. x 68 lh. x 25 dh., black basalt
Presented, The Friends of the National Collections of Ireland, 1938

Cunningham, Patrick (fl.1750-1774)
Irish School

8026 *Jonathan Swift, (1667-1745), Satirist and Dean of St Patrick's Cathedral, Dublin*
37 ht., marble (on 23 ht. grey marble base)
Purchased, London, Miss A. L. Cousins, 1901

Dalou, Aimé Jules (1838-1902)
French School

8056 *The Bather (c.1890)*
Signed: *DALOU*
Foundry mark: *CIRE/PERDUE/A.A. HEBRAND 4*
55 ht., bronze
Bequeathed, Sir Hugh Lane, 1918

8069 *Head of a Girl*
Signed: *Dalou*
Foundry mark: *CIRE/PERDUE/A. A. HEBRAND 7*
37.5 ht., bronze (on 13 ht. marble base)
Bequeathed, Sir Hugh Lane, 1918

8056

8069

vid D'Angers, Pierre Jean (1788-1856)
nch School
6 *Medallion of Dominique Jean Larrey, (1766-1841), Surgeon in Napoleon I's army*
Signed: *P. J. DAVID 18*[?37]
Inscribed: *D. J. LARREY*
17 diam., plaster
Provenance Unknown

Carnowsky, M. (19th century)
nch School
5 *Sir Charles Gaven Duffy, (1816-1903), Nationalist Politician in Ireland and Australia*
Signed: *M. de Carnowsky 5/91*
Inscribed: *C Gaven Duffy 1891* (facsimile signature)
52 ht. x 35 wh., terracotta relief
Presented, Miss Duffy, the sitter's daughter, 1904

tz, Ferdinand (1708-1777)
man School
1 *Chronos eating one of his children, (c.1764 garden sculpture from Schloss Sehof, near Bamberg)*
182.5 ht., sandstone
Purchased, London, Heim, 1970

noghue, John (1853-1903)
erican School
7 *The Young Sophocles leading the Chorus of Victory after the Battle of Salamis*
(after a plaster model sculpted 1885)
Signed: *J. DONOGHUE fc*
Foundry mark: *J. BARBEDIENNE Fondeur Paris 21*
114 ht., bronze
Presented, The Hon. Frederick Lawless, (later 5th Baron Cloncurry), 1926

Orsay, Count Alfred Guillaume Gabriel 01-1852)
nch School
2 *Statuette of Daniel O'Connell, M.P., (1775-1847), Statesmen*
Signed: *Comte D'Orsay Sculpt*
Dated: *1844*
63 ht., bronze
Purchased, London, J.W. Benson Ltd., 1908

yle-Jones, Francis William (1873-1938)
lish School
1 *Michael Collins, (1890-1922), Patriot*
Signed: *F. Doyle Jones 1923*
46 ht., bronze
Purchased, Mr F. W. Doyle-Jones, the sculptor, 1924

8166

8285

8081

8037

8142

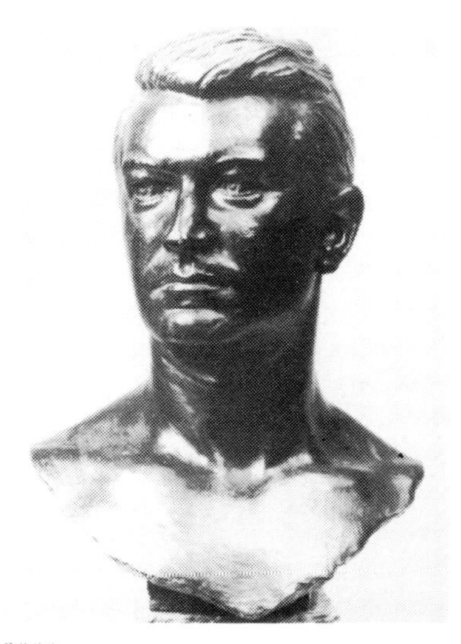

8001

Doyle-Jones

8003 *John Edward Redmond, M.P., (1856-1918)*
(replica of the Palace of Westminster, London, bronze)
Signed: *Francis Doyle Jones Sc/1910*
50 ht., bronze (on 16.5 ht. metal base)
Presented, Mr P. M. Stewart, in memory of his father Sir Halley Stewart's devotion to the cause of Home Rule for Ireland, 1931

8003

8030

Duquesnoy, François (1594-1643)
Flemish School
8030 *Cardinal Guido Bentivoglio, (1577-1644), Patron of Flemish Artists (c.1638)*
79 ht., marble (incl. 6 ht. socle)
Purchased, London, Heim, 1967

English School (early 19th century)
8231 *Mrs Sarah Siddons, (1755-1831), Actress, as Shakespeare's Lady Macbeth*
19.8 ht., painted wax (incl. wax column)
Presented, Edinburgh, Mr R. B. Armstrong, 1909

8231

8225

English School (19th century)
8225 *Elizabeth Stanhope*
Inscribed: *ELIZABETH WILLIAM STANHOPE*
70 ht., marble (incl. 11 ht. socle)
Milltown Gift, 1902

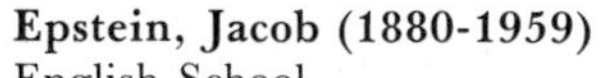

Epstein, Jacob (1880-1959)
English School
8074 *Fourth Portrait of Dolores (1923)*
25.5 ht, bronze
Presented, Sir Alfred Chester Beatty, 1953

8074

8044

Farrell, Thomas (1827-1900)
Irish School
8044 *Michael William Balfe, (1808-1870), Composer*
Signed: *T. Farrell R.H.A. Dublin 1878*
77 ht., marble
Commissioned and then presented by the Michael Balfe Memorial Committee, 1879

33 *Cast of death mask of John Mitchel, (1815-1875), Agitator and author of 'Jail Journey'*
33 ht., plaster
Purchased, Mr T. Farrell, the sculptor, 1907

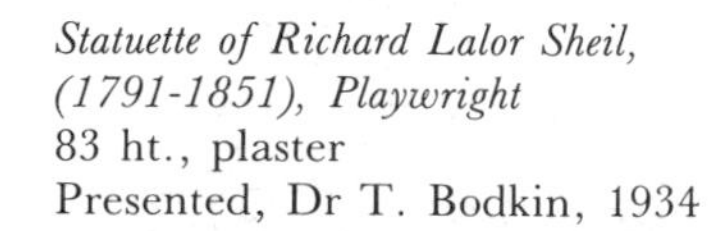

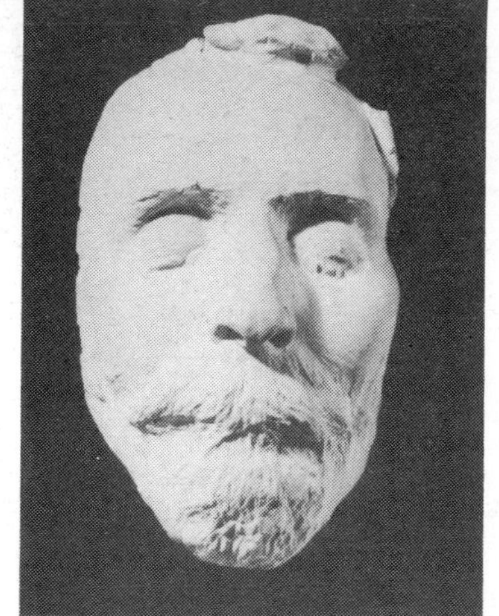

8133

83 *Statuette of Richard Lalor Sheil, (1791-1851), Playwright*
83 ht., plaster
Presented, Dr T. Bodkin, 1934

8183

95 *Cast of death mask of Alexander Martin, (1830-1884), Journalist and Proprietor of 'The Nation'*
26.5 ht., plaster
Presented, Serjeant A.M. Sullivan, 1921

8195

77 *William Dargan, (1799-1867), Railway magnate and sponsor of the 1853 Dublin Exhibition*
Signed: *THOMAS FARRELL R.H.A. Sculpt 1863*
258.5 ht., bronze
Presented, Dargan Committee for the National Gallery of Ireland, 1863

8277

mish School (17th century)

31 *Judith with the head of Holofernes*
34.4 ht. x 27.5 wh., pearwood
Bequeathed, Mr J. Hunt, 1977

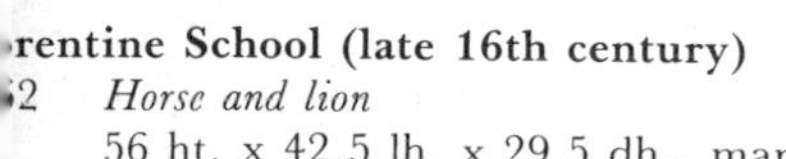

8331

rentine School (late 16th century)

52 *Horse and lion*
56 ht. x 42.5 lh. x 29.5 dh., marble
Purchased, London, Mr C. Humphris, 1969

8062

Foley, Edward (1814-1874)
Irish School

8249 *Portrait of a girl*
Signed: *E.A. FOLEY SCULP. 1873*
62.2 ht., marble (incl. 10.5 ht. socle)
Purchased, London, Fine Art Society Ltd., 1980

Foley, John Henry (1818-1874)
Irish School

8042 *Helen Faucit, (1817-1898), later Lady Martin, (wife of Sir Theodore Martin)*
(cast of 1843 marble bust, NPG, London)
Signed: *J.H. FOLEY Sculp. LONDON 1843*
Inscribed: *HELEN FAUCIT*
72 ht., plaster (incl. 11 ht. socle)
Purchased, Dublin, Mr K. Monaghan, 1967

8045 *Mrs Catherine Jane Prendergast, (née Annesley, 1811-1839)*
Signed: *J.H. FOLEY. Sc./LONDON 1845*
Inscribed: *CATHERINE. JANE. PRENDERGAST.*
62 ht., marble (incl. 12 ht. socle)
Presented, Major B.R. Cooper, the sitter's great-grandson, 1927

8191 *Statuette of Sir Dominic Corrigan, (1802-1880), Physician, (study for the 1869 marble, Royal College of Physicians, Dublin)*
Signed: *J.H. FOLEY RA 1863*
57 ht., plaster
Bequeathed, Lady Martin, the sitter's daughter, 1907

8200 *Statuette of Daniel O'Connell, M.P., (1775-1847), Statesman, (1860s study for the O'Connell Street, Dublin, monument, 1867-83)*
99 ht., plaster
Signed: *J.H. FOLEY R.A..../LONDON...*
Provenance Unknown

8251 *Equestrian statuette of Queen Victoria, (1819-1901)*
Signed: *J.H. FOLEY. RA. SC.*
Foundry mark: *ELKINGTON & Co FOUNDERS 1866*
44 ht., bronze
Purchased, London, Sotheby's, 1980

8249

8042

8045

8191

8200

8251

52 *Charles Graves, P. Bishop of Limerick, (1812-1899), (pendant to NGI no. 8269)*
Signed: *J.H. FOLEY. R.A. Sc.*
71 ht. x 63.5 wh., marble relief
Purchased, London, Sotheby's, 1980

8252

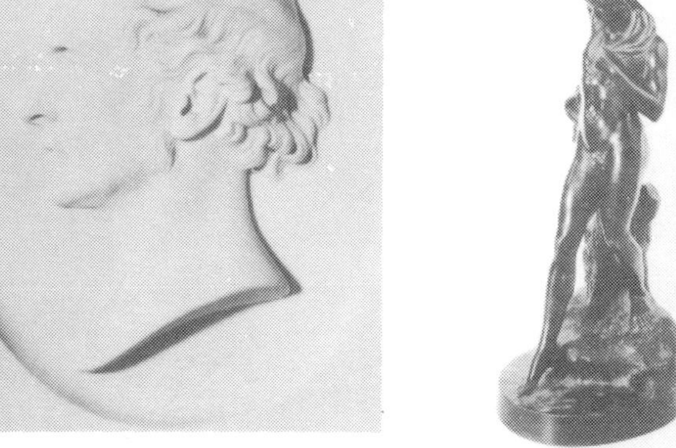

8257

57 *Youth at the stream*
(reduced version of the 1844 marble, Albert Hall, London)
Inscribed: *J.H. FOLEY. SCULP./EXCUTED*(sic) *FOR. THE. ART. UNION. OF. LONDON. 1846*
54.4 ht., bronze
Purchased, London, Christie's, 1981

58 *Caractacus or The Norseman*
(after the plaster maquette for the 1856 marble, both City of London Corporation)
Inscribed: *EXECUTED IN BRONZE BY J.H. HATFIELD/FOR THE ART-UNION OF LONDON 1894/FROM THE ORIGINAL BY J.H. FOLEY RA*
79 ht., bronze
Purchased, London, Christie's, 1982

8258

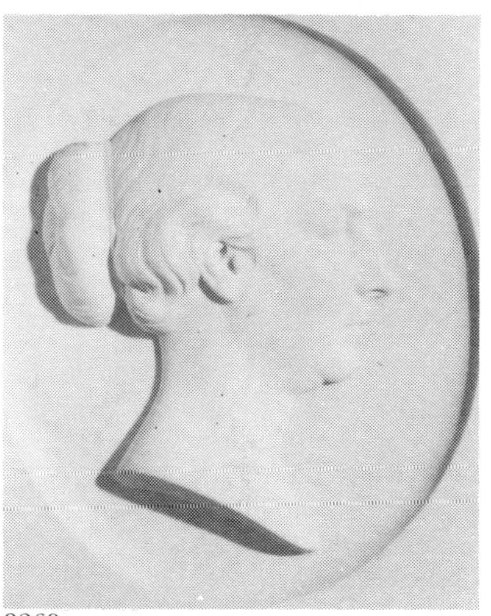

8269

59 *Mrs Charles Graves, (née Selina Cheyne, d.1873), wife of Bishop Graves, (pendant to NGI no. 8252)*
Signed: *J.H. FOLEY R.A. Sc.*
71 ht. x 63.5 wh., marble relief
Purchased, London, Sotheby's, 1980

rd, Edward Onslow (1852-1901)
glish School
43 *Sir Walter Armstrong, (1850-1915), Art Historian and Director of the National Gallery of Ireland·*
Exhibited RHA 1895
Signed: *E. Onslow Ford*
41 ht., bronze (on 21 ht. marble base)
Presented, Mr C.F. Armstrong, the sitter's son, 1924

8143

8330

nch School (16th century)
30 *Drinking vessel figurine representing Summer*
39.1 ht., silver gilt
Bequeathed, Mr J. Hunt, 1977

French School 17C

French School (17th century)

8332 *Mother and child (?Charity)*
43.2 ht., terracotta
Bequeathed, Mr J. Hunt, 1977

French School (late 17th century)

8333 *Cross*
63.5 ht. x 33.9 wh., rock crystal (with silver gilt mounts)
Bequeathed, Mr J. Hunt, 1977

8332

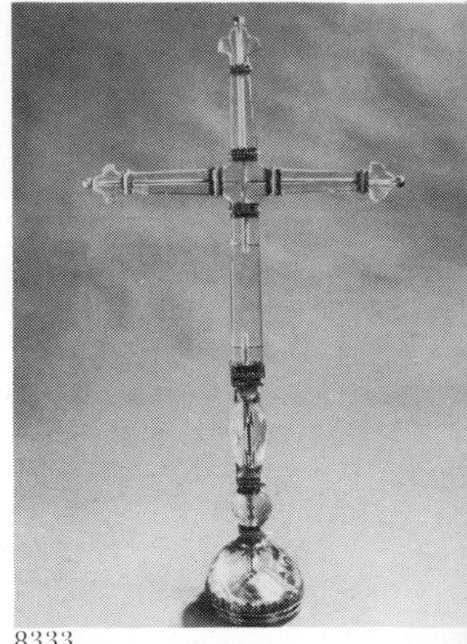

8333

8334 *Case for Cross, (NGI no. 8333), stamped with the dolphin emblem of the French Dauphin*
67.4 ht. x 36.2 wh., leather
Bequeathed, Mr J. Hunt, 1977

French School (19th century)

8102 *The Suicide of Cleopatra*
70 ht., marble
Milltown Gift, 1902

8334

8102

8310 *Female Head*
51 ht., bronze (on 20 ht. marble socle)
Transferred from the National Museum of Ireland, 1967

French or German School (c.1600)

8329 *Jester's bauble*
26.3 ht., ivory and wood (excluding bells)
Bequeathed, Mr J. Hunt, 1977

8310

8329

hagan, Lawrence (fl.1756-1817)
sh School
58 *Portrait of a Man wearing a medallion (1807)*
Signed: *L. GAHAGAN/FECIT. JUNE 1st/MDCCCVII*
Inscribed on medallion: *THE/TRIUMPH/OF/TRUTH*
60 ht., marble (incl. 9 ht. socle)
Purchased, London, Heim, 1968

58 *Sir Thomas Lawrence, (1769-1830), Artist*
Signed: *L. Gahagan Fecit 1812*
23 ht., bronze (on 6.5 ht. metal base)
Presented, Mr C. Humphris, 1970

8058

8068

efs, Guillaume (1805-1883)
lgian School
59 *The Repentant Magdalen*
Signed: *Gme Geefs Statuaire de S.M. le Roi des Belges. Bles 1841*
136 ht., marble
Purchased, London, Christie's, 1982

rman School (16th century)
27 *Crucifix*
120.5 ht. x 47.5 wh., wood with ivory *corpus* (inlaid with almandines)
Bequeathed, Mr J. Hunt, 1977

8259

8327

orkshop of **Ghiberti, Lorenzo (1378-1455)**
orentine School
49 *The Virgin and Child*
79 ht., terracotta
Purchased, London, Heim, 1968

lbert, Alfred (1854-1934)
glish School
77 *Mrs Eliza McLoghlin, (1863-1928)*
One of 6 casts made by Albert Toft of the Wurttemberg Electro Plate Co., 1909
Signed: *Alfred Gilbert Bruges/1906*
Inscribed: *Eliza McLoghlin/Eheu Fugaces!*
44.5 ht., bronze
Presented, Mrs E. McLoghlin, the sitter, 1921

8049

8077

Grant, Peter (b.1915)
Irish School
8009 *Joseph Mary Plunkett, (1887-1916), Patriot*
Signed: *Grant 1958*
54 ht., bronze
Presented, the Government, 1963

8009

Guillaume, Eugène (1833-1905)
French School
8192 *Paul Bert*
Signed: *EUGENE GUILLAUME 1887*
69 ht., bronze
Presented, Mrs W. O'Brien, 1932

8192

8193 *Madame Raffalovitch, (as a Greek goddess)*
Signed: *Eug. GUILLAUME/1884*
78 ht., bronze
Presented, Mrs W. O'Brien, the sitter's daughter, 1932

8193

Heffernan, James (1785-1847)
Irish School
8264 *Sir Francis Chantrey, (1781-1841), Sculptor*
(after F.W. Smith's 1826 marble bust, RA Collection, London)
Signed: *JS. HEFFERNAN SC. AFTER F.W. SMITH. 1843*
59 ht., marble (incl. 11.5 ht. socle)
Purchased, London, Christie's, 1982

8264

Herbert, Gwendolin (1878-1966)
Irish School
8306 *An Old Irish Woman (c.1907)*
27 ht., plaster
Purchased, Dublin, Mr P. Lamb, 1985

8306

Hewetson, Christopher (1739-1798)
Irish School
8063 *Sir Watkin Williams-Wynn Bt., (1749-1789), Traveller and Patron*
Signed: *CR. Hewetson Fect. 1769*
Inscribed: *SR. W.W. Winn.* (sic)
53 ht., terracotta
Purchased, London, Heim, 1969

8063

iggins, Joseph (1885-1925)
sh School

40 *Boy with a boat (1910)*
Cast in bronze for Fitzgerald Park, Cork, 1911
81 ht. x 41 lh. x 41 dh., plaster
Presented, Mrs M. Murphy, 1976

8240

ogan, John (1800-1858)
sh School

24 *Portrait of a Man*
Signed: *JH.* (in monogram)
61 ht., marble (incl. 9 ht. socle)
Purchased, Dublin, Wolfe Cherrick Antiques, 1967

8024

34 *Dr Daniel Murray, R.C. Archbishop of Dublin, (1768-1852), (1844)*
(after the plaster bust, Loreto Abbey, Rathfarnham)
Signed: *JH.* (in monogram)
68 ht., marble (incl. 13 ht. socle)
Presented, Rev. C. Burke, 1864

8034

47 *Anatomical study*
Signed: *J. HOGAN Sculpt.*
25 ht., alabaster
Purchased, Dublin, Messrs. Barry, 1957

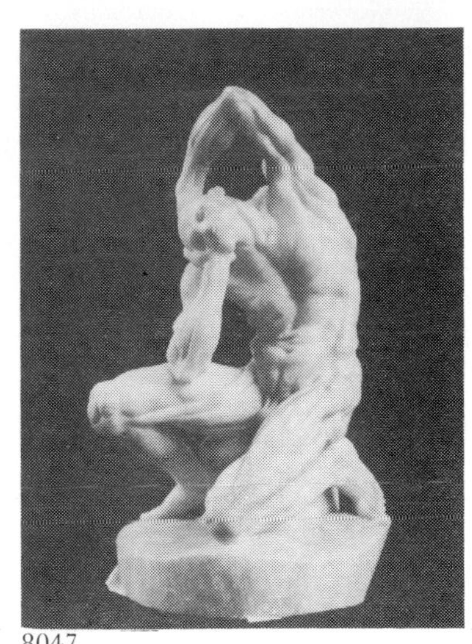

8047

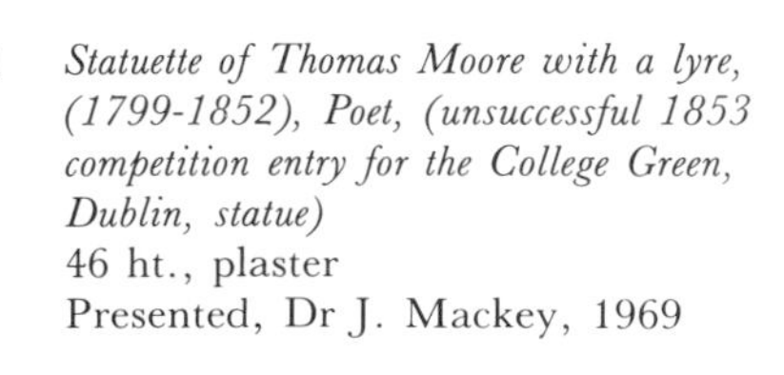

61 *Statuette of Thomas Moore with a lyre, (1799-1852), Poet, (unsuccessful 1853 competition entry for the College Green, Dublin, statue)*
46 ht., plaster
Presented, Dr J. Mackey, 1969

8061

31 *Cast of death mask of James Warren Doyle, R.C. Bishop of Kildare and Leighlin, (1786-1834)*
23.5 ht., plaster
Presented, Mrs H. Piatt, 1925

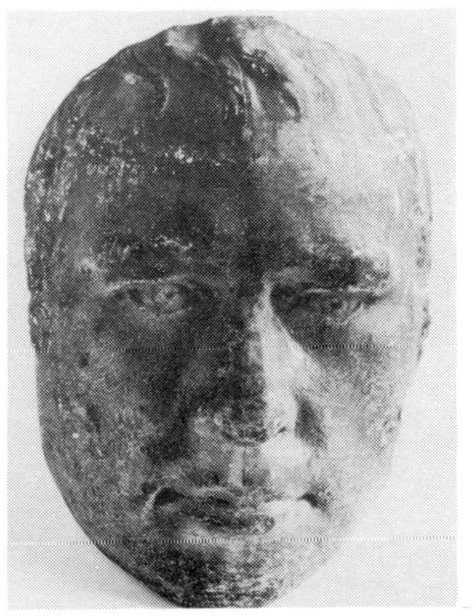

8131

Hogan

8196 *William Carleton, (1794-1869), Novelist (1855)*
Signed: *JH*(in monogram)*OGAN. LV.*
60 ht., plaster (incl. 9 ht. socle)
Purchased, Mr S. Shannon Millin, 1919

8196

8244

8244 *Statuette of Thomas Moore, (1799-1852), Poet, with a lyre, (unsuccessful 1853 competition entry for College Green statue, Dublin)*
(cast of plaster, NGI no. 8061)
Foundry mark:
DUBLIN/ART/FOUNDRY 1977
45.5 ht., bronze (on 5.3 ht. green marble base)
Cast commissioned by the Board of Governors and Guardians from Dublin Art Foundry after the original plaster, NGI no. 8061, 1977

8253 *Anatomical study of a head in profile*
Signed: *HOGAN Sculp.*
37 ht., wood
Purchased, Co. Kerry, Mrs J.D.H. Eddess, 1981

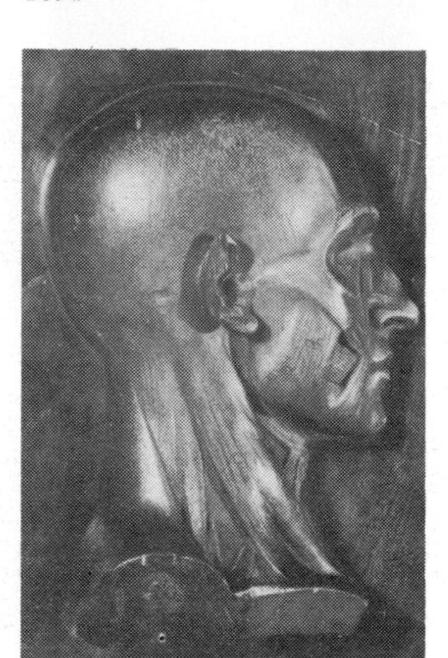
8253

8284

8284 *Statuette of Thomas Moore, (1799-1852), Poet, with a book, (alternative 1853 competition entry for the College Green statue, Dublin)*
47 ht., plaster (damaged)
Provenance Unknown

8291 *Anatomical study of a leg*
77.5 ht., wood
Provenance Unknown

Hughes, John (1865-1941)
Irish School

8097 *Sir Thomas Newenham Deane, (1828-1899), Architect (c.1900)*
44 ht., bronze (on 10.5 ht. green marble base)
Presented, Lady Deane, the sitter's widow, 1903

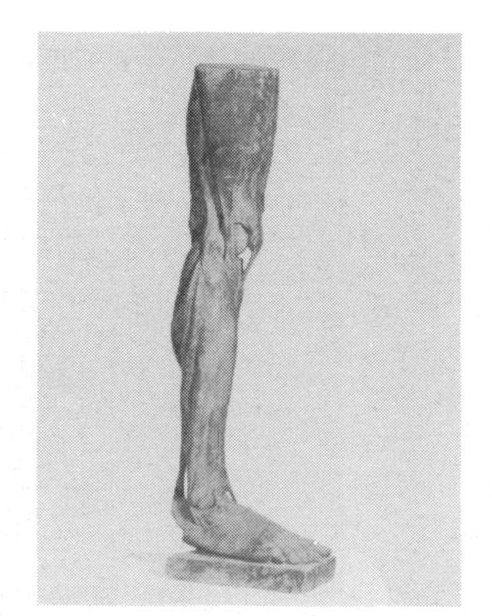
8291

8097

4 *Sir Frederic William Burton, (1816-1900), Artist and Director of the National Gallery, London*
(after a plaster life mask c.1850)
18.7 ht., marble
Purchased, the Executors of Miss M. Stokes, 1902

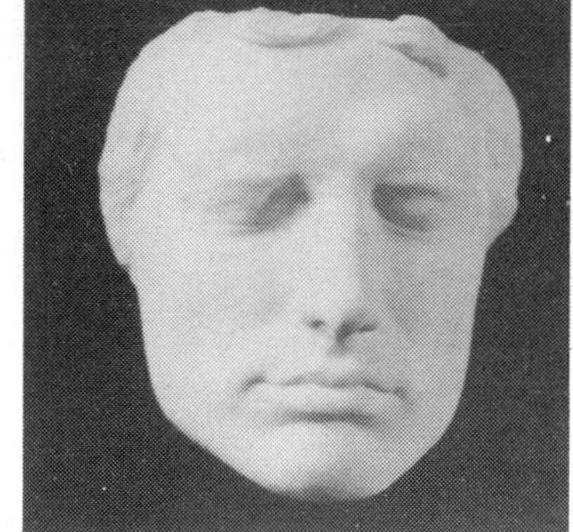
8134

8256

h School (c.1785)

6 *William Robert FitzGerald, 2nd Duke of Leinster, (1749-1804), as Colonel of the Dublin Volunteers*
58 ht., marble (incl. 10 ht. socle)
Presented, Mr H.P. McIlhenny, 1981

h School (1798)

8 *Cast of death mask of Theobald Wolfe Tone, (1763-1798), United Irishman*
21 ht., plaster
Purchased, Dublin, Mr P. Traynor, 1899

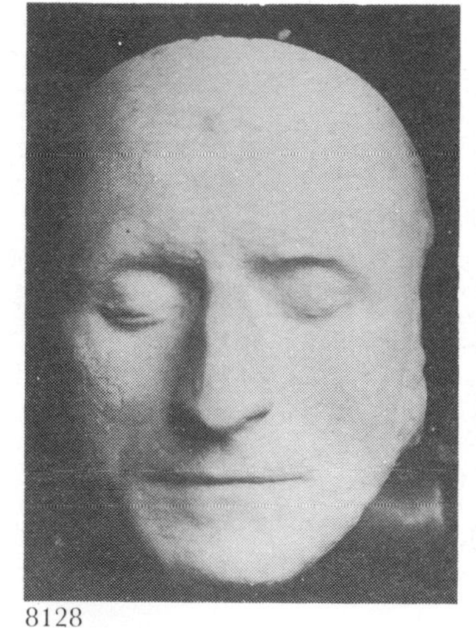
8128

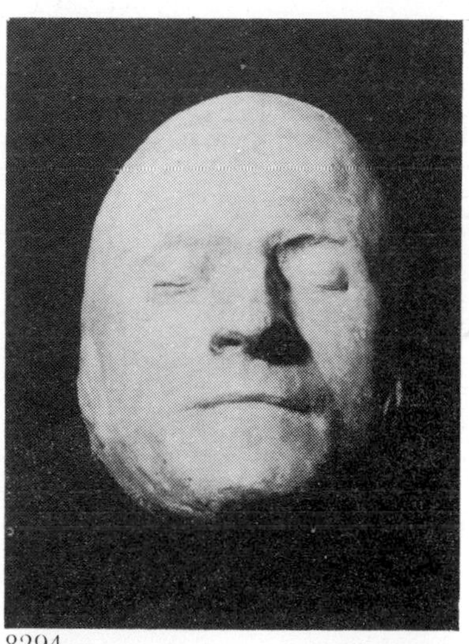
8294

4 *Cast of death mask of Theobald Wolfe Tone, (1763-1798), United Irishman, (another copy)*
21 ht., plaster
Provenance Unknown

h School (19th century)

1 *James Warren Doyle, R.C. Bishop of Kildare and Leighlin, (1786-1834)*
48.6 ht., plaster (incl. 8.5 ht. socle)
Purchased, Dublin, Mr R. Miller, 1896

8101

8234

4 *Samuel Lover, (1797-1868), Artist, Musician and Author*
17.5 ht., ceramic
Bequeathed, Mrs E. Herbert Bartlett, the sitter's great granddaughter, 1974

Irish School 19C

8283 *Portrait of a Young Lady*
72 ht., marble (incl. 17.5 ht. socle)
Provenance Unknown

8301 *Portrait of a Man with sideburns*
81 ht., plaster (incl. 11 ht. socle)
Provenance Unknown

8283

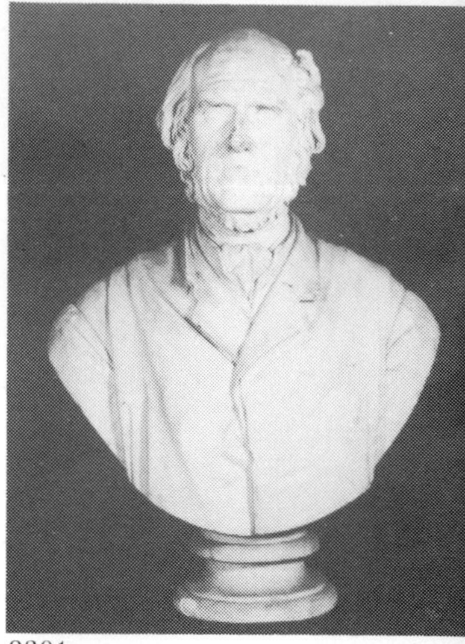

8301

Irish School (1817)

8132 *Cast of death mask of John Philpot Curran, (1750-1817), Lawyer*
Inscribed: *IPCurran*
32 ht., plaster
Presented, The Royal Hibernian Academy, 1912

Irish School (1866)

8154 *Cast of death mask of George Petrie, (1789-1866), Artist and Antiquary*
23.5 ht., plaster
Purchased, Dublin, Bennett's, Dr Kenny's Sale, 1900

8132

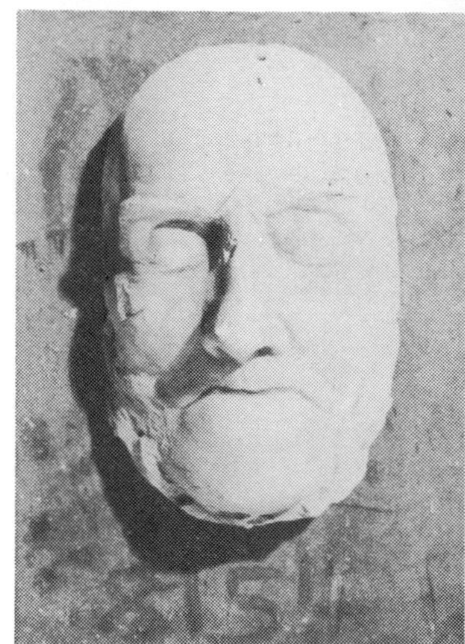

8154

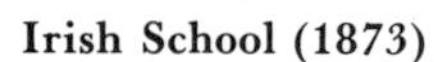

Irish School (1873)

8275 *Cast of death mask of Joseph Sheridan La Fanu, (1814-1873), Novelist and Journalist*
25 ht., plaster
Presented, Mr B. Le Faru, 1914

Irish School (1882)

8155 *Cast of death mask of Charles Joseph Kickham, (1826-1882), Fenian, Journalist and Author*
Inscribed: *Chs J. Kick/Au*
31 ht., plaster
Presented, Mrs H. Piatt, 1925

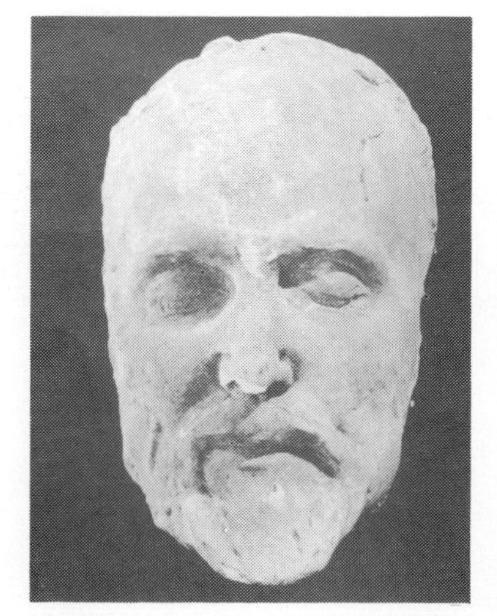

8275

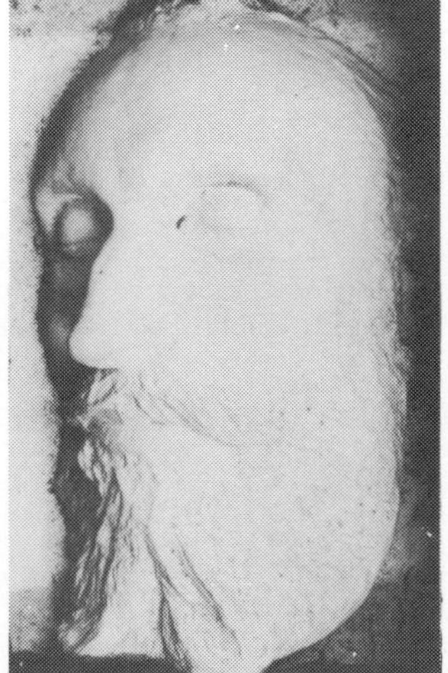

8155

06 *Cast of death mask of Charles Joseph Kickham, (1826-1882), Fenian, Journalist and Author, (another copy)*
Inscribed: *Chs J. Kickham/Died Augst. 22 '82*
40 ht., plaster
Provenance Unknown

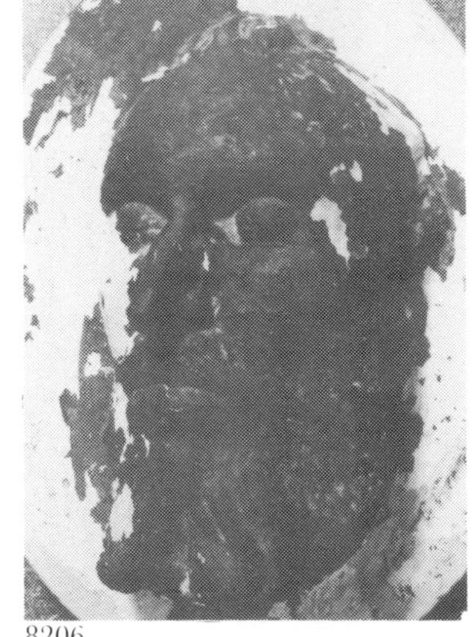

8206

8248

sh School (c.1919)

48 *Design for a seal for the National Gallery of Ireland*
5.6 diam., plaster
Provenance Unknown

sh School (1933)

29 *Cast of death mask of George Moore, (1852-1933), Novelist and Playwright*
25 ht., plaster
Transferred from the National Library of Ireland, 1968

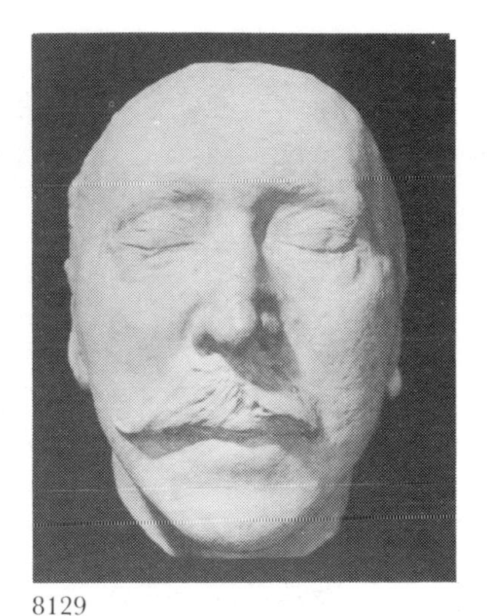

8129

8212

lian School (18th century)

12 *The Judgement of Paris*
14 ht. x 23.5 wh., boxwood
Milltown Gift, 1902

13 *Venus and Adonis surprised by Neptune*
13.6 ht. x 24 wh., boxwood
Milltown Gift, 1902

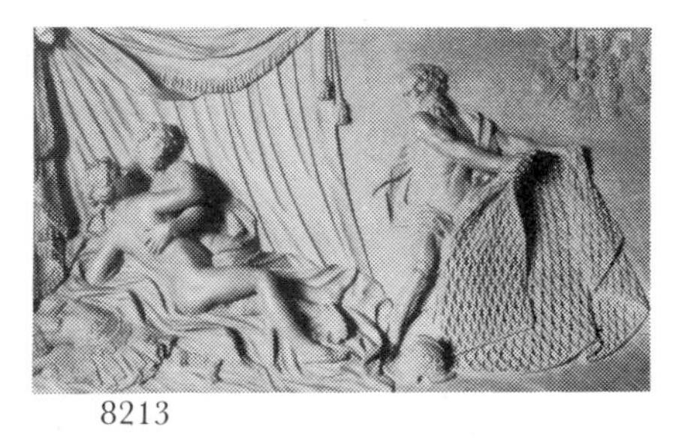

8213

lian School (late 18th century)

15 *Mars*
(after the 1570s statuette by Giambologna)
41 ht., bronze
Milltown Gift, 1902

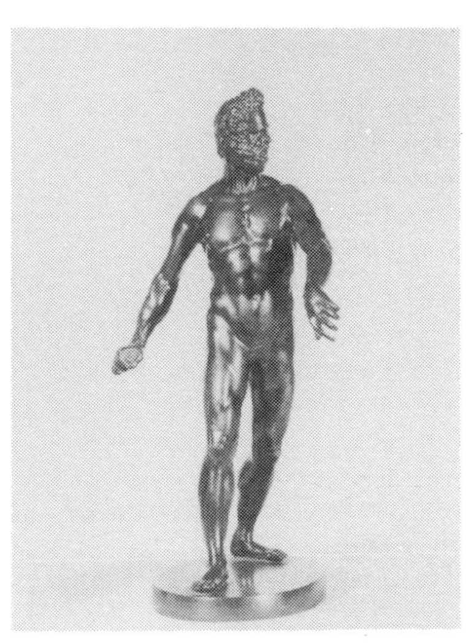

8115

Jones, John Edward (1806-1862)
Irish School
8204 *William Dargan, (1799-1867), Railway Magnate and sponsor of the 1853 Dublin Exhibition*
Signed: *J.E. Jones Sc./London 1854*
82.5 ht., marble (incl. 13.5 ht. socle)
Presented, Mr G.A. Phillips, 1905

8204

8208

8208 *Statuette*
Signed: *J.E. Jones Sculp... 186...*
51 ht., plaster
Provenance Unknown

After **Jones, John Edward (1806-1862)**
8071 *Daniel O'Connell, M.P., (1775-1847), Statesman*
(reduced copy of a marble bust RHA 1844)
Inscribed: *J.E. JONES Sculp. 1846/Reduced by B. Cheverton/Danl OConnell* (facsimile signature)
29 ht., marble (incl. 9.2 ht. marble socle)
Presented, Mr V. Scully, 1885

8071

8111

8111 *William Dargan, (1799-1867), Railway Magnate and sponsor of the 1853 Dublin Exhibition*
(reduced copy of a marble bust, NGI no. 8204)
Inscribed: *Dargan/JEJones Sc./Reduced by B. Cheverton*
22.5 ht., plaster
Provenance Unknown

Jorden, J.S. (fl.1827-1842)
Irish School
8237 *Daniel O'Connell, M.P., (1775-1847), Statesman (c.1829)*
Signed: *Jorden*
8.5 ht. x 5.5 wh. approx., painted wax relief (on glass)
Presented, Mrs A. Bodkin, 1974

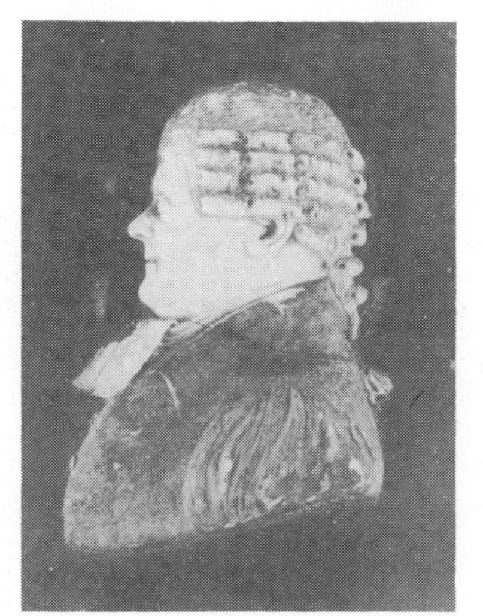
8237

Kelly, Oisín (1913-1981)
Irish School
8008 *Thomas Mac Donagh, (1878-1916), Poet, Dramatist and Patriot*
72 ht., bronze
Presented, The Government, 1963

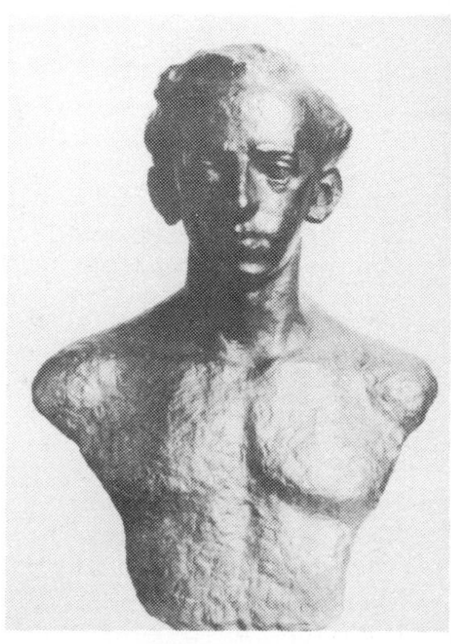
8008

62 *The Fate of the Children of Lir, (c.1961 maquette for the 1970 Garden of Remembrance, Parnell Square, Dublin bronze)*
(cast from wire and plaster maquette)
76.5 ht., bronze
Cast commissioned from Dublin Art Foundry by the Board of Governors and Guardians after the wire and plaster maquette, loaned by the artist's sons and daughters, 1983

8262

63 *Christopher Stephen ('Todd') Andrews, (1901-1985), Politician*
25 ht., terracotta
Presented, the sculptor's sons and daughters, in his memory, 1982

8263

irk, Thomas (1781-1845)
sh School

00 *Richard Brinsley Sheridan, (1751-1816), Dramatist and Politician*
Signed: *Thos. Kirk. R.H.A. Fecit. 1824.*
72 ht., marble
Purchased, Dublin, Messrs. Battersby & Co., 1943

8000

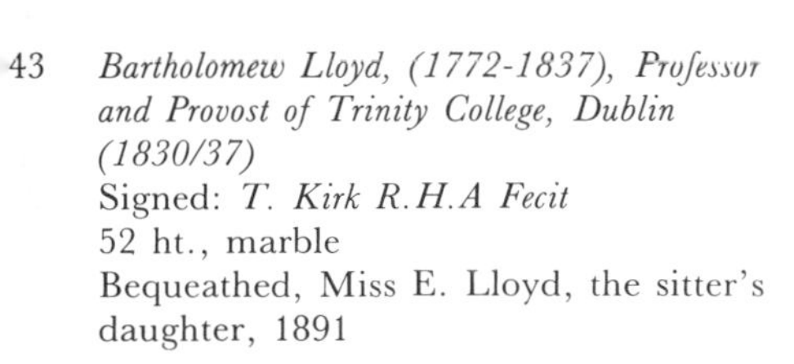

43 *Bartholomew Lloyd, (1772-1837), Professor and Provost of Trinity College, Dublin (1830/37)*
Signed: *T. Kirk R.H.A Fecit*
52 ht., marble
Bequeathed, Miss E. Lloyd, the sitter's daughter, 1891

8043

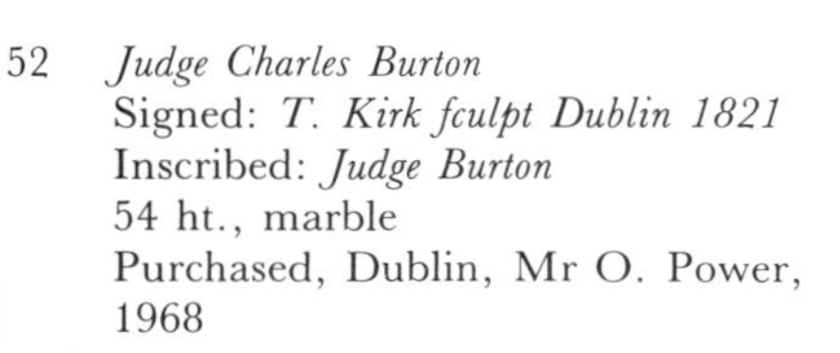

52 *Judge Charles Burton*
Signed: *T. Kirk fculpt Dublin 1821*
Inscribed: *Judge Burton*
54 ht., marble
Purchased, Dublin, Mr O. Power, 1968

96 *Classical Head*
Signed: *T. Kirk Sculpt 1821*
51 ht., alabaster
Purchased, Dublin, Hibernian Antiques, 1971

8052

8096

Kirk

8260 *Sir William Rowan Hamilton, (1805-1865), Mathematician and Astronomer Royal in Ireland*
Signed: *T. Kirk. R.H.A. Fecit/1830*
Inscribed: *Professor Hamilton 1830*
66 ht., marble (incl. 10.5 ht. socle)
Purchased, London, Hartley Fine Arts, 1982

8267 *Colonel Henry John Clements, M.P., (1781-1843)*
Signed: *T. KIRK. R.H.A. FECIT*
Inscribed: *COLONEL/CLEMENTS/1843*
59.5 ht., marble
Purchased, Co. Leitrim, Mr M. Clements, 1983

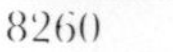

8260

8267

Lambert, Maurice (1901-1964)
English School

8064 *The Dove*
Signed: *ML* (in monogram)
21.5 ht., marble (on 9.7 ht. grey marble base)
Presented, Sir Alfred Chester Beatty, 1953

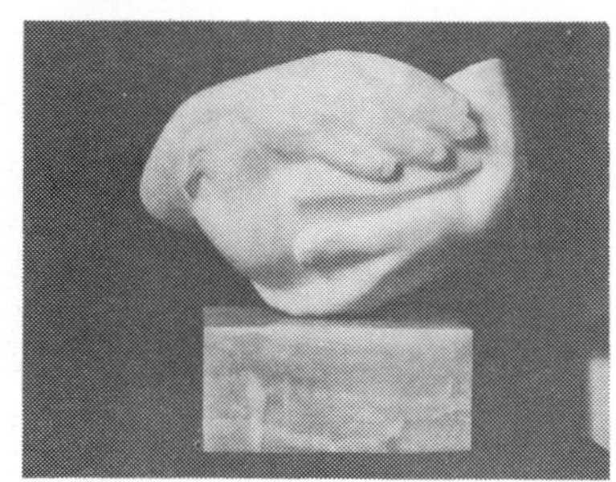

8064

After **Larson, William (17th century)**
English School

8095 *Equestrian Statuette of King James II, (1633-1701), (reduced copy of the destroyed 1685 bronze, formerly at Newcastle-upon-Tyne)*
Inscribed: *Baxter taught Wyck Drew Larson Embost & Cast it* (Larson reputedly studied Jan Wyck's pictures and consulted the equine specialist Nicholas Baxter)
64 ht. x 33.3 wh. x 19.7 dh., bronze
Purchased, London, Durlacher Bros., 1902

8095

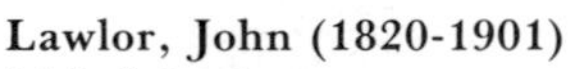

Lawlor, John (1820-1901)
Irish School

8083 *'The blind girl at Castle Cuille' (Longfellow)*
Signed: *J. LAWLOR 1876*
64 ht., marble
Purchased, London, Heim, 1971

8150 *Denny Lane, (1818-1895)*
Signed: *J LAWLOR SC 1889*
57 ht., plaster (incl. 8 ht. plinth)
Purchased, Mr W. Morrissey, 1955

8083

8150

1 *Bust of a Young Girl, (?'The Rose')*
Signed: *J. LAWLOR 1869*
54 ht., marble (incl. 10 ht. socle)
Purchased, London, Sotheby's, 1982

nn, Samuel Ferris (1834-1876)
h School
5 *William Ewart Gladstone, (1809-1898), British Prime Minister, (1865/67, to flank, with NGI no. 8236, the entrance to Messrs. Gilbey & Sons, 46-49 O'Connell Street Dublin; now demolished)*
41 diam., sandstone relief
Presented, English Property Company Ltd., 1974

6 *Henry John Temple, 3rd Viscount Palmerston, British Prime Minister, (1865/67, to flank, with NGI no. 8235, the entrance to Messrs. Gilbey & Sons, 46-49 O'Connell Street, Dublin; now demolished)*
41 diam., sandstone relief
Presented, English Property Company Ltd., 1974

cDonald, Lawrence (1799-1878)
ttish School
3 *Thomas Spring Rice, 1st Baron Monteagle, (1790-1866)*
Signed: *L. MACDONALD. FECIT. ROMA. 1843*
69 ht., marble (incl. 13.3 ht. socle)
Presented, Francis Spring Rice, 4th Baron Monteagle, the sitter's grandson, 1934

3 *Eurydice, (for the Saloon of Powerscourt House, Co. Wicklow)*
Signed: *L. MACDONALD FECIT. ROMA. 1837*
140 ht., marble
Purchased, Powerscourt, Christie's, Mr and Mrs R. Slazenger Sale, 1984

cDowell, Patrick (1799-1870)
h School
0 *A Girl Reading*
141 ht, marble
Signed: *MAC DOWELL SCULPT./1838.*
Purchased, Adare, Mr G. Stacpoole, 1980

8261

8235

8236

8203

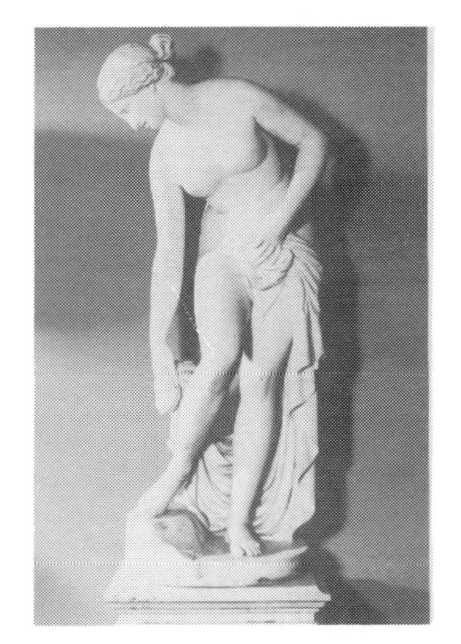
8303

8250

Mac Namara, Desmond (b.1918)
Irish School
8268 *Brendan Francis Behan, (1923-1964), Author and Playwright (1956)*
32 ht., bronze (on 6.5 ht. black marble base)
Cast commissioned from Dublin Art Foundry by the Board of Governors and Guardians after the original bronze cast, lent by a private collector, 1983

8268

Maillol, Aristide (1861-1944)
French School
8094 *Standing female nude*
Signed: *AM* (in monogram)
27 ht., bronze
Bequeathed, Sir Hugh Lane, 1918

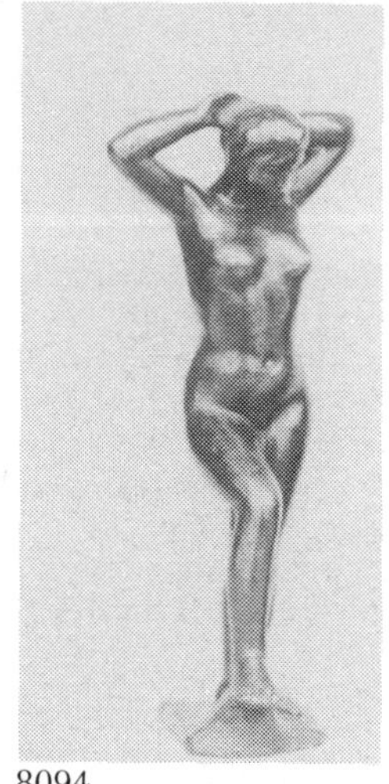
8094

8270 *Seated female nude with right arm on her forehead*
Signed: *ARISTIDE/MAILLOL*
21.5 ht., bronze
Bequeathed, Sir Hugh Lane, 1918

8270

8271 *Seated female nude holding her foot*
Signed: *AM* (in monogram)
21.8 ht., bronze
Bequeathed, Sir Hugh Lane, 1918

8271

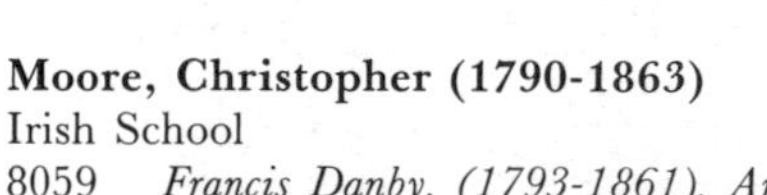

Moore, Christopher (1790-1863)
Irish School
8059 *Francis Danby, (1793-1861), Artist*
Signed: *Sept 1. 1827/Cr. Moore London*
65 ht., plaster (incl. 12.5 ht. plinth)
Presented, Mrs Gibbons, 1913

8059

8060 *Annie Hutton*
Signed: *C. MOORE Sc. LONDON 1854*
73 ht., marble (incl. 12 ht. socle)
Purchased, Miss M.B. Hutton, 1954

8060

55 *Richard Lalor Sheil, M.P., (1791-1851), Playwright and Politician, (engraved as frontispiece for W.T. McCullagh's 'Memoirs of Sheil', 1856)*
Signed: *C. MOORE. SC./LONDON. 1847*
59 ht., marble (incl. 9.5 ht. socle)
Presented, Henry Labouchere, 1st Baron Taunton, (who commissioned the bust), 1856

56 *William Conyngham Plunket, 1st Baron Plunket, (1764-1854), Lord Chancellor of Ireland*
Signed: *CHRR MOORE SCULP.*
Inscribed: *THE RT HON. LORD PLUNKET/AETATIS 77. 1841.*
63.5 ht., marble
Presented, Mr J. Healy, 1931

57 *Thomas Moore, (1779-1852), Poet*
Signed: *C. MOORE. SC. LONDON*
Inscribed: *BUST OF THOS MOORE ESQ 1842*
63 ht., marble (incl. 10 ht. socle)
Presented, James Molyneux Caulfeild, 3rd Earl of Charlemont, 1873

8 *George William Frederick Howard, 7th Earl of Carlisle, (1802-1864)*
Signed: *C. MOORE. SC./LONDON/1839*
68 ht., marble (incl. 10 ht. socle)
Purchased, Mrs N. Ball, 1890

8 *Louis Perrin, (1782-1864), Judge*
Signed: *C. MOORE. SC./LONDON 1843*
70 ht., marble
Purchased, Messrs. McMullan & Co., 1930

7 *William Conyngham Plunket, 1st Baron Plunket, (1764-1854), Lord Chancellor of Ireland*
Signed: *C. MOORE. SC./LONDON 1841* (raised letters)
Inscribed: *THE RT. HONBLE. LORD PLUNKET/AETATIS 77* (raised letters)
69.5 ht., plaster
Purchased, Mr J. Vicars, 1903

8065

8066

8067

8088

8108

8187

Moore

8265 *Anne, Countess of Charlemont, (née Bermingham, fl. 1802-1876), wife of the 2nd Earl of Charlemont*
Signed: *CHR. MOORE. Sc.*
Inscribed: *ANNE, COUNTESS OF CHARLEMONT.*
67.5 ht., marble (incl. 12.5 ht. socle)
Purchased, Co. Leitrim, Mr M. Clements, 1983

8266 *A Lady of the Caulfeild or Clements family*
Signed: *CR. MOORE. SCULP. 1859.*
70.5 ht., marble (incl. 12 ht. socle)
Purchased, Co. Leitrim, Mr M. Clements, 1983

8265

8266

8280 *Portrait of a Man, (possibly Thomas Moore, 1779-1852, Poet)*
71 ht., plaster (incl. 10 ht. plinth)
Provenance Unknown

8298 *John Doyle, ('HB'), (1797-1868), Artist and Political Cartoonist*
Signed: *CHRR. MOORE Sc.*
66 ht., plaster (incl. 10 ht. socle)
Purchased, Dublin, Mr R. Miller, 1896

8280

8298

Morbiducci, Publio (1889-1963)
Italian School

8170 *Medallion to mark the fifth centenary of the birth of artist Melozzo da Forli, (1438-1494), (angel on obverse, City Arms on reverse)*
Signed on obverse: *P. MORBI/DUCC*
Inscribed on obverse: *V. CENTENARIO DELLA NASCITA DI MELOZZO DA FORLI*
Inscribed on reverse: *ANNO XVI E.F./III IMP.*
41 diam., bronze
Presented, Forli Municipality, 1939

Mossop, William (1751-1805)
Irish School

8164 *James Caulfeild, 1st Earl of Charlemont, (1728-1799)*
9.5 ht., wax relief
Purchased, Tregaskis, 1903

8170

8164

14 *Patrick Sarsfield, (c.1650-1693), Earl of Lucan*
8.5 ht., wax relief
Purchased, Tregaskis, 1903

8214

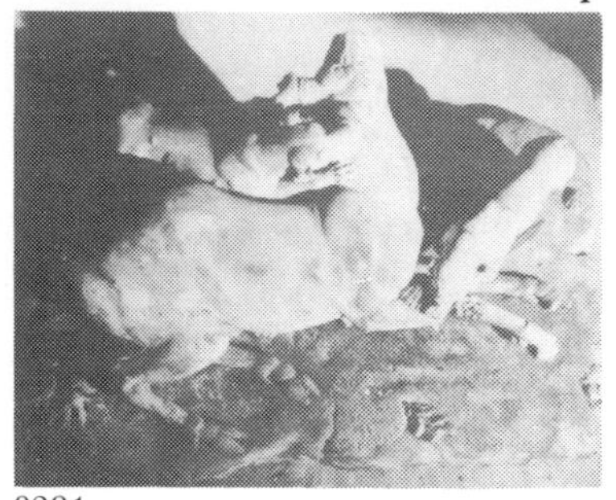

8281

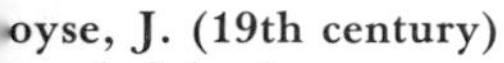

oyse, J. (19th century)
rench School
81 *The Hunted Stag*
34 ht. x 80 wh. x 51 dh., marble (very damaged)
Milltown Gift, 1902

unro, Alexander (1825-1871)
ottish School
16 *William Allingham, (1824-1889), Poet*
56 ht., plaster
Presented, Mr Fausset, 1908

8116

8006

urphy, Seamus (1907-1975)
sh School
)6 *James Conolly, (1870-1916), Patriot*
Signed: *SEAMUS MURPHY R.H.A. 1960*
Inscribed: *JAMES CONOLLY*
73 ht., bronze
Presented, the Government, 1963

32 *Frank O'Connor, (1903-1966), Author*
Signed: *SEAMUS MURPHY '57*
Inscribed: *FRANK O'CONNOR*
42.5 ht., bronze (on 8.5 ht. metal base)
Purchased, Mr S. Murphy, the sculptor, 1970

8082

8245

45 *Frederick May, (b.1911), Composer*
Signed: *S. Murphy R.H.A.*
Inscribed: *Frederick May Composer 1954*
31 ht., bronze (on 12.5 ht. black marble base)
Presented, Hon. G. de Brun, 1978

Murphy

8304 *Sean MacEntee, (1889-1984), Politician*
Signed: *S. MURPHY R.H.A. 1960*
Inscribed: *SEAN MACENTEE*
42 ht., bronze (on 11 ht. green marble base)
Presented, the MacEntee family, through Mrs Maire Cruise O'Brien, the sitter's daughter, 1984

8304

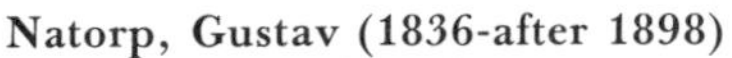

Natorp, Gustav (1836-after 1898)
Anglo-German School

8084 *Knuckle-bone player*
Signed: *G. Natorp./1893*
54 ht., bronze
Presented, Mr G. Natorp, the sculptor, 1896

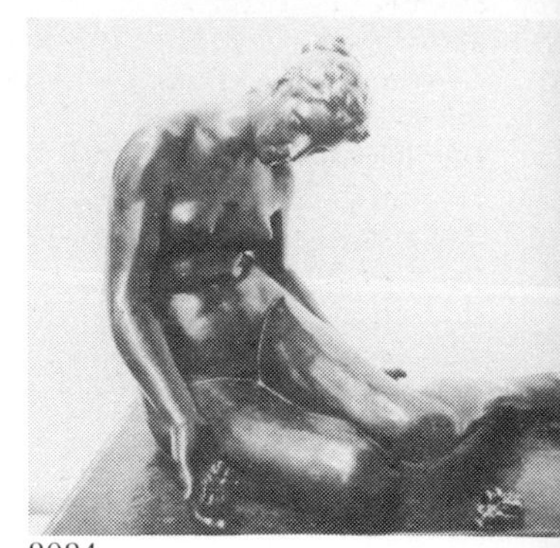

8084

O'Connor, Andrew (1874-1941)
American-Irish School

8238 *Desolation, (maquette for the bronze 'Triple Cross', 1926, now at Dun Laoghaire, Co. Dublin)*
79 ht., plaster
Presented, The Central Catholic Library, 1974

8238

O Murchadha, Domhnall (b.1914)
Irish School

8004 *Eamon Ceannt, (1882-1916), Patriot*
Signed: *DOMHNALL O MURCHADHA*
65 ht., bronze (on 4.5 ht. wooden base)
Presented, the Government, 1963

8004

Panormo, Constantine (c.1805-1852)
Irish School

8300 *Sir Edward Stanley, (1769-1851), Supporter of Irish Exhibitions and the Royal Dublin Society*
(cast of the 1844 marble, Royal Dublin Society Collection)
72 ht., plaster (incl. 10 ht. socle)
Presented, Mr E. Stanley Robertson, the sitter's grandson, 1906

8300

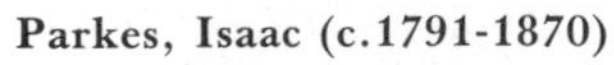

Parkes, Isaac (c.1791-1870)
Irish School

8158 *Medallion of Sir Edward Stanley, (1769-1851), Supporter of Irish Exhibitions and the Royal Dublin Society*
Signed on obverse: *I PARKES F*
Dated on reverse: *1844*
4.2 diam., bronze
Provenance Unknown

8158

rcy, Samuel (1750-1820)
sh School

57 *Charlotte Augusta, Princess of Wales, (1796-1817), daughter of the Prince Regent, later King George IV*
Inscribed on reverse of case: *Portrait of Princess/Charlotte of Wales 1815/Hold the frame paralell* (sic) */to Window that all the/Features May Catch Eaquel* (sic) */Light and Shade*
11 ht., painted wax figurine (in 25 diam. case)
Transferred from the National Museum of Ireland, 1968

8057

60 *Francis Rawdon Hastings, 2nd Earl of Moira and 1st Marquess of Hastings, (1754-1826), Statesman and Soldier*
15 ht., painted wax figurine (in 29.5 ht. case)
Presented, Mr R. B. Armstrong, 1907

8160

tributed to **Percy, Samuel (1750-1820)**
sh School

22 *Portrait of a Man in profile*
7.5 ht., painted wax relief (in 11.7 ht. x 9.5 wh. frame)
Miss Mary A. McNeill Bequest, 1985

8322

trie, James (c.1750-1819)
sh School

30 *Cast of death mask of Robert Emmet, (1778-1803), Patriot*
22 ht., plaster
Purchased, Dublin, Mr P. Traynor, 1899

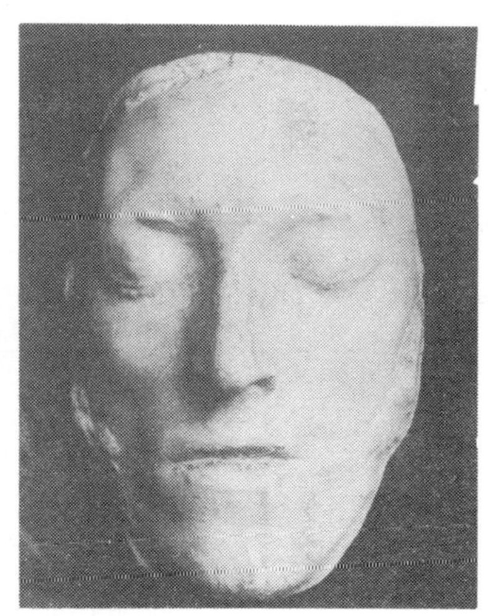
8130

93 *Cast of death mask of Robert Emmet, (1778-1803), Patriot, (another copy)*
22 ht., plaster
Provenance Unknown

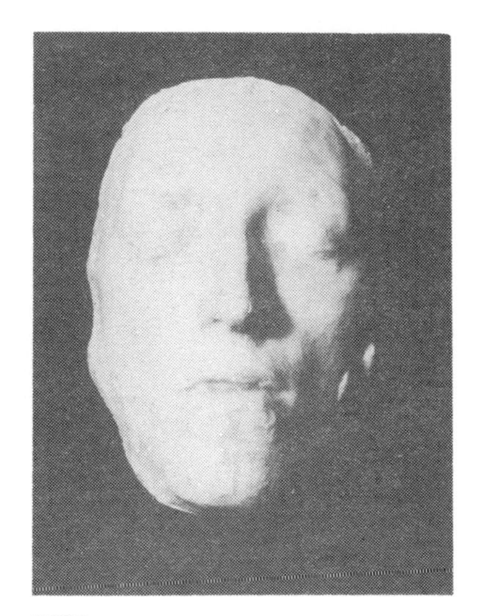
8293

amontini, Giovanni Battista .1725-?1762)
orentine School

10 *The Knife Sharpener (or so-called 'Listening Slave')*
(copy of the Classical marble from a lost 'Flaying of Marsyas' group, The Uffizi, Florence)
Signed: *JOHANNES PIAMONTINIUS/SCULP: FLORENT: MDMCCLIV*
70 ht. x 83.7 wh. x 37.7 dh., marble
Milltown Gift, 1902

8210

Piamontini

8211 *The Wrestlers*
(copy of the Classical marble, The Uffizi, Florence)
Signed: *JOHANNES PIAMONTINIUS/SCULP: FLORENT: MDCCLIV*
71 ht. x 74 wh. x 46.5 dh. approx., marble
Milltown Gift, 1902

8211

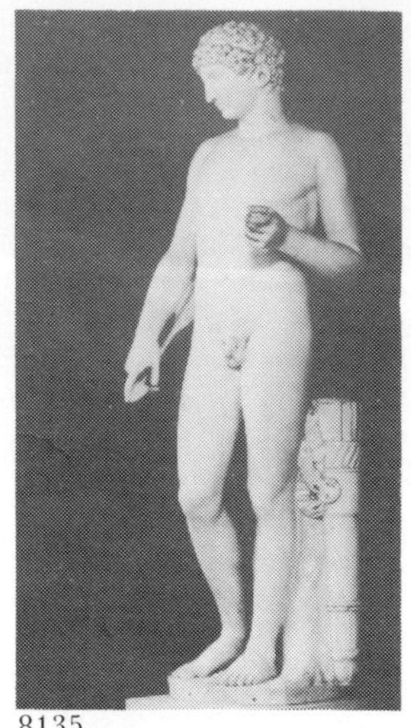
8135

Poncet, François Marie (1736-1797)
French School

8135 *Adonis (1784)*
(derived from the Classical marble of Apollo, The Louvre, Paris)
Signed: *F.M. PONCET. INV. F.*
165 ht., marble
Presented, F.W. FitzGerald, 4th Duke of Leinster, 1878

Power, Albert (c.1883-1945)
Irish School

8005 *Thomas James Clarke, (1858-1916), Patriot*
(cast from the plaster, NGI no. 8290)
Signed: *ALBERT G. POWER R.H.A.*
51 ht., bronze
Presented, the Government, 1963

8005

8007

8007 *Sean MacDiarmada, (1884-1916), Patriot*
Signed: *ALBERT G. POWER R.H.A.*
103 ht., bronze
Presented, the Government, 1963

8010 *Maquette for monument to Thomas Kettle, (1880-1916), Patriot, on St Stephen's Green, Dublin, completed 1926*
40 ht., painted plaster (ht. of bust 13)
Provenance Unknown

8010

8048 *William Butler Yeats, (1865-1939), Poet and Playwright*
(cast from the plaster, NGI no. 8292)
Signed: *A. POWER RHA 1939*
53 ht., bronze
Cast commissioned from Werner Schurmann, Dublin, by the Board of Governors and Guardians, after the original plaster, NGI no. 8292, 1968

8048

70 *Michael Collins, (1890-1922), Politican and Patriot*
Signed: *A. POWER/1936*
67 ht., bronze
Provenance Unknown

8070

8089

89 *The Fall of Icarus*
Exhibited RHA 1941
38 ht., marble
Purchased, Co. Wicklow, Mrs J. O'Reilly, 1950

90 *Connemara Trout*
Signed: *ALBERT POWER 1944*
48 ht., marble
Purchased, Mrs Fox Pym, 1949

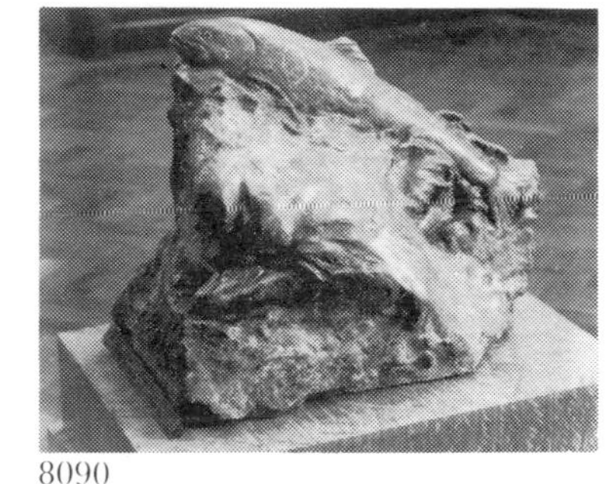

8090

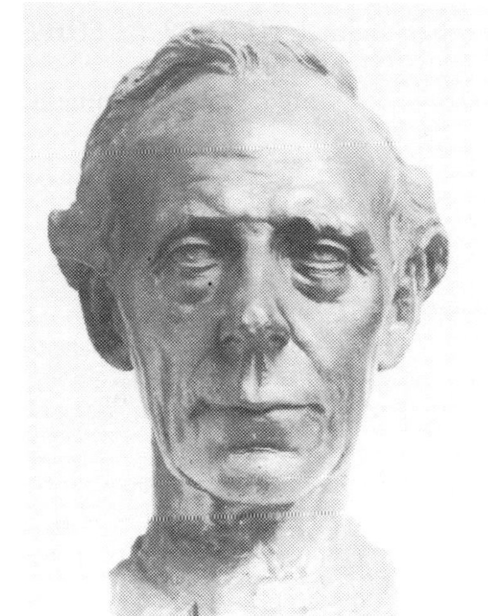

8099

99 *Dr Mannix, R.C. Archbishop of Melbourne, (1864-1963)*
Signed: *ALBERT G. POER/1921 DUBLIN*
35 ht., plaster
Provenance Unknown

00 *Arthur Griffith, (1872-1922), Founder of Sinn Fein*
Signed: *POWER 1922*
67 ht., bronze
Provenance Unknown

14 *Padraic O Conaire, (1882-1928), Author and Playwright in Irish*
Inscribed and Signed: *A. de Paor/ALBERT G. POWER RHA*
58 ht., plaster
Provenance Unknown

8100

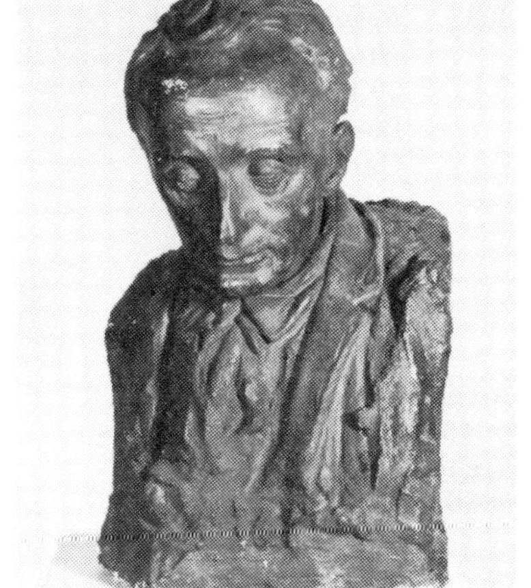

8114

Roman School 19C

8296 *Male Head*
41.5 ht., bronze
Transferred from the National Museum of Ireland, date unknown

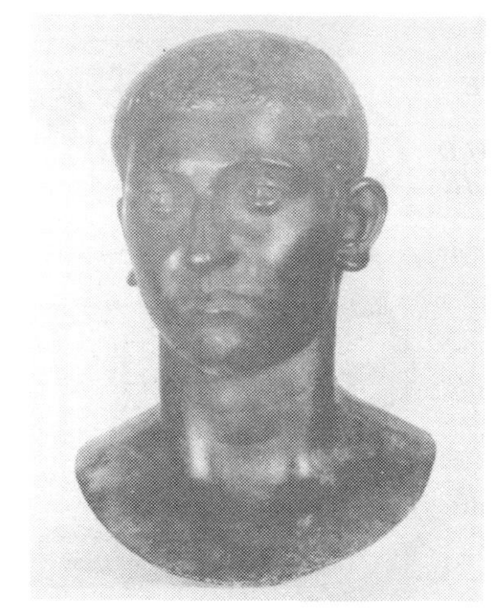

8296

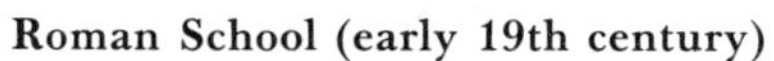

Roman School (early 19th century)

8112 *The dying Gladiator or Gaul*
(reduced copy of the Classical marble, Capitoline Museums, Rome)
18.5 ht., bronze
Milltown Gift, 1902

8112

8117 *The Borghese Gladiator*
(reduced copy of the Classical marble, The Louvre, Paris)
41 ht., bronze
Milltown Gift, 1902

8117

8126 *The Apoxyomenos or Athlete with a strigil*
(reduced copy of the Classical marble, Vatican Museums, Rome)
53 ht., bronze
Milltown Gift, 1902

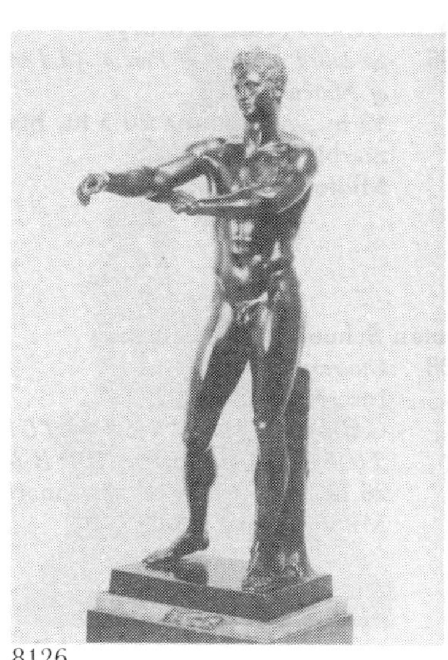

8126

8127 *The Laocoon*
(reduced copy of the Classical marble, Vatican Museums, Rome)
60.5 ht., bronze
Milltown Gift, 1902

8127

8144 *Apollo Belvedere*
(reduced copy of the Classical marble, Vatican Museums, Rome)
54.5 ht., bronze
Milltown Gift, 1902

8144

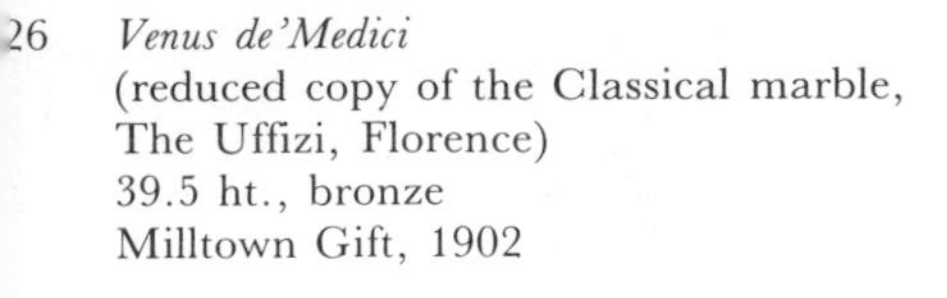

26 *Venus de'Medici*
(reduced copy of the Classical marble, The Uffizi, Florence)
39.5 ht., bronze
Milltown Gift, 1902

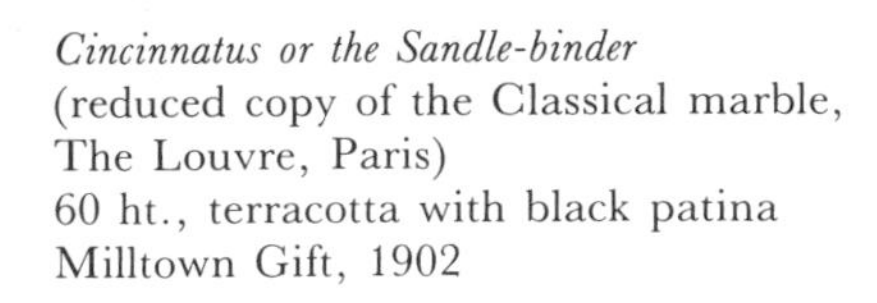

86 *Cincinnatus or the Sandle-binder*
(reduced copy of the Classical marble, The Louvre, Paris)
60 ht., terracotta with black patina
Milltown Gift, 1902

8226

8286

sandić, Toma (1878-1958)
goslavian School
68 *The Sculptor*
Signed: *T. ROSANDIC*
54 ht., bronze
Presented, Sir Alfred Chester Beatty, 1953

skell, Nicholas R. (fl.1861-1872)
glish School
07 *Seated Woman with a lyre, (possibly Erato, muse of lyric poetry)*
Signed: *N.R. ROSKELL. FECIT. 1864*
91 ht. x 75 wh. x 42 dh., marble
Milltown Gift, 1902

8168

8207

sbrack, John Michael (1694-1770)
nglo-Flemish School
15 *Portrait of a Man, (possibly Peter the Great, Czar of Russia, 1672-1725)*
Signed: *Mich. Rysbrack 1740*
62.2 ht., terracotta
Purchased, London, Heim, 1966

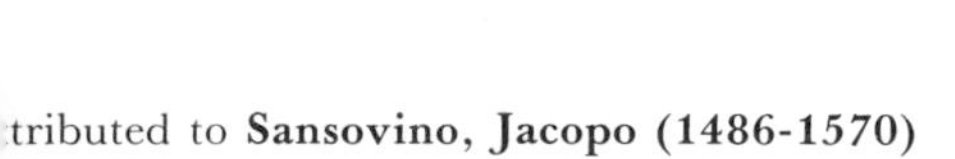

tributed to **Sansovino, Jacopo (1486-1570)**
enetian School
26 *Sanctus Bell with figure of St Jerome*
21 ht., gilt bronze
Bequeathed, Mr J. Hunt, 1977

8015

8326

Saunders, F. (19th century)
English School
8152 *Head of the Apollo Belvedere*
(copy of the Classical marble, Vatican Museums, Rome)
Signed: *F. Saunders. 1872.*
84 ht., marble (incl. 19.5 ht. socle)
Milltown Gift, 1902

8152

Sèvres (c.1820)
French School
8323 *An Officer*
Stamped: *Sevres*
7 ht., biscuit porcelain
Miss Mary A. McNeill bequest, 1985

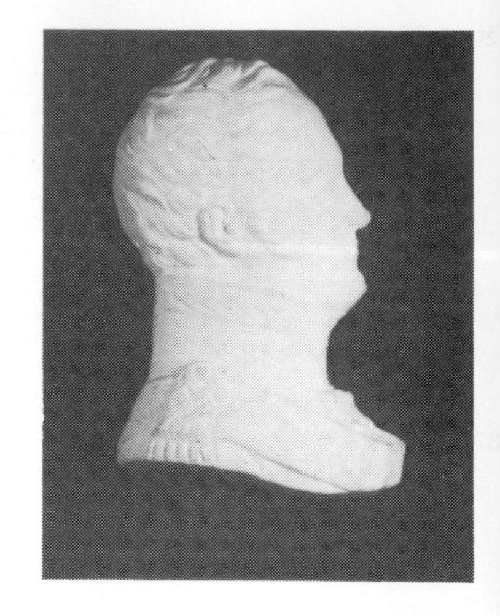
8323

Sheppard, Oliver (1864-1941)
Irish School
8046 *Kevin Christopher O'Higgins, (1892-1927), Politician*
Inscribed and signed: *Kevin O'Higgins/by/Oliver Sheppard/1932*
44.5 ht., bronze
Provenance Unknown

8046

8091 *'In mystery the Soul abides' (Matthew Arnold)*
Exhibited RHA 1913
Signed: *Oliver Sheppard*
Purchased, Dublin, Miss C. Sheppard, the sculptor's daughter, 1942

8091

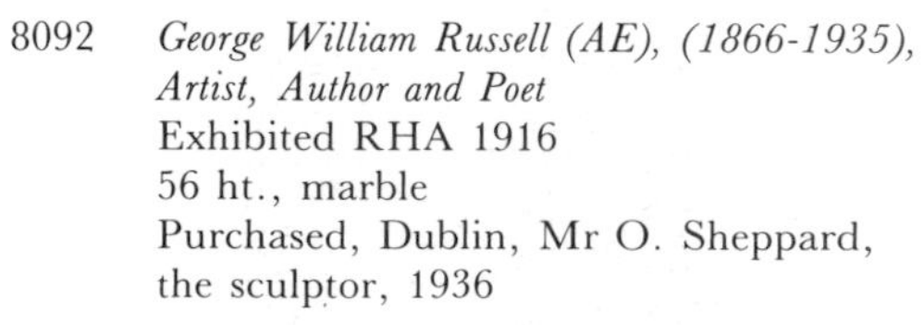
8092 *George William Russell (AE), (1866-1935), Artist, Author and Poet*
Exhibited RHA 1916
56 ht., marble
Purchased, Dublin, Mr O. Sheppard, the sculptor, 1936
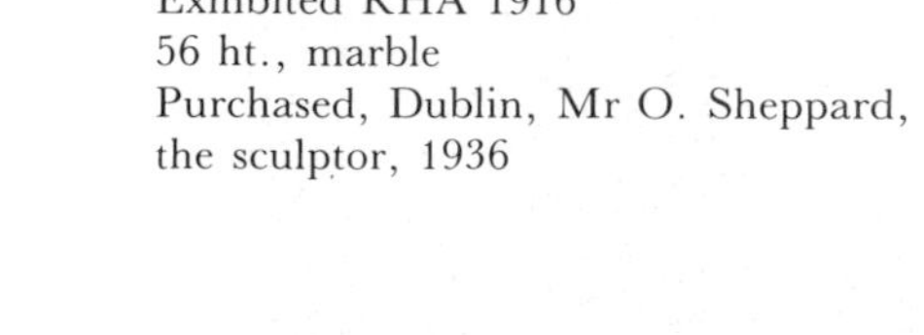

8092

8104 *Cathal Brugha, (1874-1922), Politician*
Signed: *OLIVER SHEPPARD RHA 1939*
Inscribed: *CATHAL BRUGHA*
72 ht., bronze
Presented, the Government, 1963

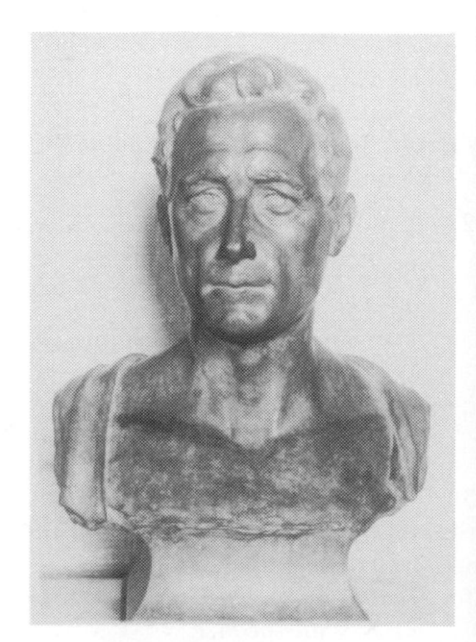
8104

36 *The Fate of the Children of Lir*
Bronze cast exhibited RHA 1917
Inscribed: *the.fate.of.the.children.of.lir*
78 ht. x 72 wh., bronze relief
Cast commissioned from Susses Frères, Paris, by the Board of Governors and Guardians, after the original plaster on loan, 1958

8136

8137

37 *Famine*
50.5 ht. x 50.5 wh., bronze relief
Cast commissioned from Susses Frères, Paris, by the Board of Governors and Guardians, after the original plaster on loan, 1958

59 *Plaque in honour of Sir John Thomas Banks, (c.1815-1908), Physician*
Bronze cast exhibited RHA 1907
Inscribed:
IN.HONOREM.JOHANNIS.BANKS.M. D.ORD.BALN.EQUITIS. COMMENDATORIS
25.9 diam., bronze relief
Presented, Miss Latterman, 1909

8159

11 *Mrs Oliver Sheppard, (née Rosaline Good, 1868-1931)*
42.5 ht., plaster
Presented, Miss C. Sheppard, the sculptor's and the sitter's daughter, 1985

8311

12 *Seated Old and Young Man, (maquette)*
25.8 ht., plaster
Presented, Miss C. Sheppard, the sculptor's daughter, 1985

8312

13 *Spring (?1890s)*
Bronze cast exhibited RHA 1921
Signed: *Oliver Sheppard*
72.5 ht., plaster
Presented, Miss C. Sheppard, the sculptor's daughter, 1985

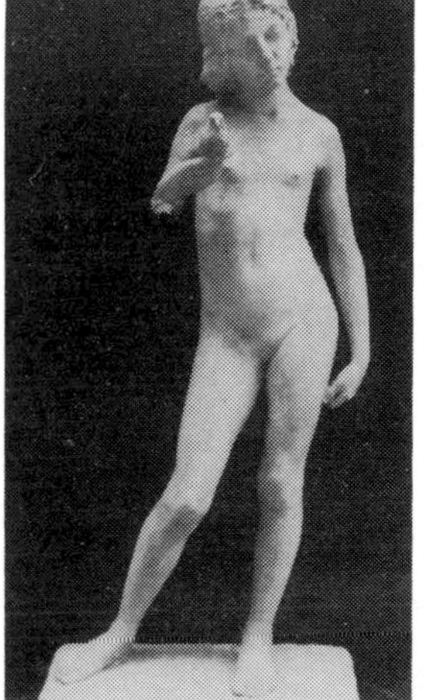

8313

Sheppard

8314 *Statuette*
Signed: *Oliver Sheppard 1924.*
51.5 ht., plaster
Presented, Miss C. Sheppard, the sculptor's daughter, 1985

8315 *Brothers*
Bronze cast exhibited RHA 1909
Signed: *Oliver Sheppard/1908.*
54 ht., plaster
Presented, Miss C. Sheppard, the sculptor's daughter, 1985

8314

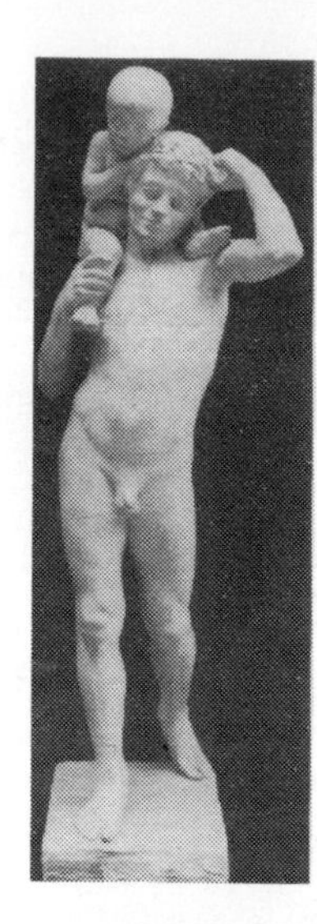
8315

8316 *Pastoral*
Bronze cast exhibited RHA 1927
Signed: *.LIVER SHEPPARD*
29.5 ht., plaster
Presented, Miss C. Sheppard, the sculptor's daughter, 1985

8317 *A seated Woman*
35 ht., plaster
Presented, Miss C. Sheppard, the sculptor's daughter, 1925

8316

8317

8318 *Peasant girl with gourds*
42 ht., plaster
Presented, Miss C. Sheppard, the sculptor's daughter, 1985

8319 *The Agony in the Garden, (probably model for a marble, c.1940)*
Signed: *OLIVER SHEPPARD*
26 ht. x 46 wh. x 16 dh., plaster
Presented, Miss C. Sheppard, the sculptor's daughter, 1985

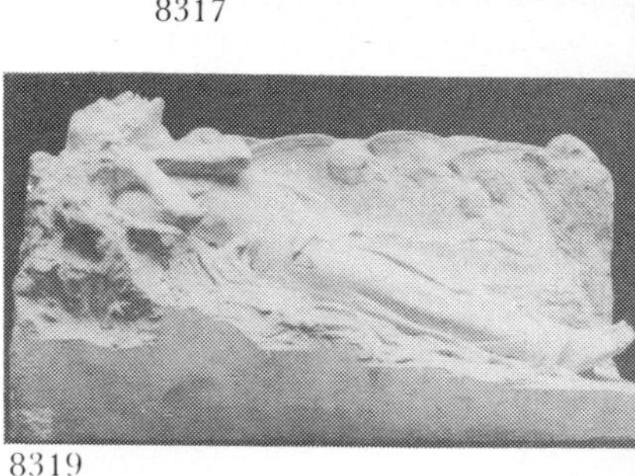
8319

8318

nith, Charles (20th century)
ıglish School
54 *Cast of the death mask of George Bernard Shaw, (1856-1950), Author, Playwright and Critic*
31 ht., plaster
Presented, The Trustees of the British Museum, 1981

8254

8038

nyth, Edward (1749-1812)
sh School
d

nyth, John (c.1773-1840)
sh School
38 *George III, King of England, (1738-1820)*
Exhibited jointly 1809
Signed: *Smyth Dublin*
59 ht., marble
Acquired between 1890/98

ldani, Massimiliano (1656-1740)
orentine School
22 *Executioner with the head of St John the Baptist*
(variant of 1570s *Mars* statuette by Giambologna)
41 ht., bronze
Milltown Gift, 1902

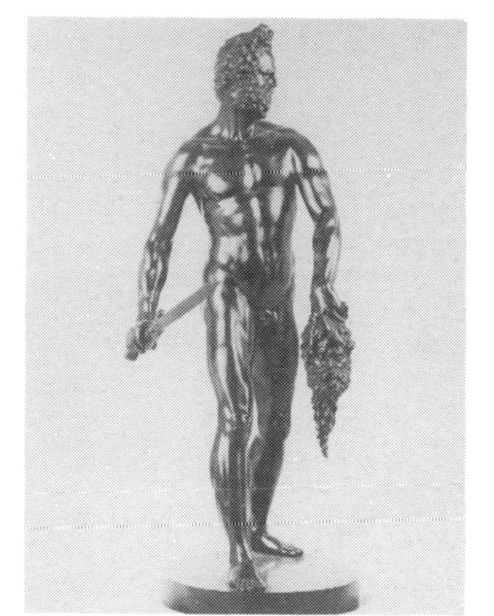

8122

8325

anish School (15th century)
25 *An Angel with the Arms of Castille and Leon*
73 ht., walnut
Bequeathed, Mr J. Hunt, 1977

anish School (1600/1650)
28 *Crucifix*
64.5 ht., gilt bronze with silver *corpus*
Bequeathed, Mr J. Hunt, 1977

anish or Italian School (c.1300)
24 *Altar or Processional Cross*
79.9 ht., bronze (with traces of gilding)
Bequeathed,, Mr J. Hunt, 1977

8328

8324

Spicer-Simson, Theodore (1871-1959)
English School

8138 *Medallion of George William Russell (AE), (1867-1935), Artist, Author and Poet, (model for bronze medallion, NGI no. 8219)*
Inscribed and signed: *AE by T. Spicer-Simson*
Also signed: *S-S* (in monogram)
Inscribed: *1922/AE* (in monogram)
10 diam., plasticine
Presented, Mr T. Spicer-Simson, the medallist, 1924

8139 *Medallion of Michael Collins, (1890-1922), Patriot, (model for bronze medallion, NGI no. 8216)*
Signed: *T. Spicer-Simson*
Also signed:*STS* (in monogram)
Inscribed: *Ad/1922/M/OC*
10 diam., plasticine
Presented, Mr T. Spicer-Simson, the medallist, 1924

8138

8139

8140 *Medallion of Lady Augusta Gregory, (1852-1932), Author and Playwright, (model for bronze medallion, NGI no. 8218)*
Inscribed and signed: *LADY GREGORY by T. SPICER-SIMSON*
7.6 diam., plasticine
Presented, Mr T. Spicer-Simson, the medallist, 1924

8141 *Medallion of Dr Douglas Hyde, (1860-1940), Scholar and 1st President of Ireland, (model for bronze medallion, NGI no. 8217)*
9.5 diam., plasticine
Presented, Mr T. Spicer-Simson, the medallist, 1924

8140

8141

8215 *Medallion of William Butler Yeats, (1865-1939), Poet and Playwright (1922)*
Signed: *T. S-S. A.D. MDCCCCXXII*
Inscribed: *W.B. YEATS*
10.7 diam., bronze
Purchased, Mr T. Spicer-Simson, the medallist, 1940

8216 *Medallion of Michael Collins, (1890-1922), Patriot*
(after the plasticine model, NGI no. 8139)
Signed: *STS* (in monogram)
Inscribed: *Ad/1922/M/O'C*
9.7 diam., bronze
Purchased, Mr T. Spicer-Simson, the medallist, 1940

8215

8216

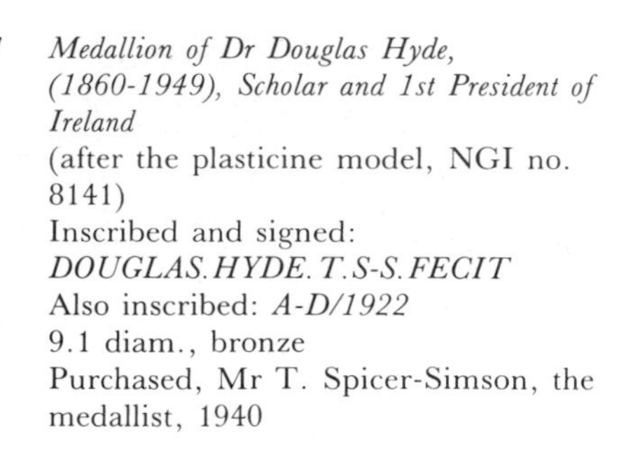
17 *Medallion of Dr Douglas Hyde, (1860-1949), Scholar and 1st President of Ireland*
(after the plasticine model, NGI no. 8141)
Inscribed and signed: *DOUGLAS.HYDE.T.S-S.FECIT*
Also inscribed: *A-D/1922*
9.1 diam., bronze
Purchased, Mr T. Spicer-Simson, the medallist, 1940

18 *Medallion of Lady Augusta Gregory, (1852-1932), Author and Playwright (1922)*
(after the plasticine model, NGI no. 8140)
Inscribed and signed: *LADY.GREGORY.T. S-S.FEC.MDCCCCXXII*
7.4 diam., bronze
Purchased, Mr T. Spicer-Simson, the medallist, 1940

19 *Medallion of George William Russell, ('AE') (1867-1935), Artist, Author and Poet*
(after the plasticine model, NGI no. 8138)
Signed: *S-S*
Inscribed: *1922/AE* (in monogram)
9.6 diam., bronze
Purchased, Mr T. Spicer-Simson, the medallist, 1940

20 *Medallion of James Stephens, (1883 1951), Poet and Novelist*
Signed: *T S-S/FEC*
Inscribed: *JAMES STEPHENS/1913*
10.2 diam., bronze
Purchased, Mr T. Spicer-Simson, the medallist, 1940

21 *Medallion of Padraic Colum, (1881-1971), Poet and Playwright*
Signed: *S-S A.D.1923*
Inscribed: *PADRAIC COLUM*
9.6 diam., bronze
Purchased, Mr T. Spicer-Simson, the medallist, 1940

22 *Medallion of Oliver St. John Gogarty, (1878-1957), Author*
Signed: *T.S-S/FEC*
Inscribed: *OSTJG* (in vertical monogram)
8.8 diam., bronze
Purchased, Mr T. Spicer-Simson, the medallist, 1940

8217

8218

8219

8220

8221

8222

Spicer-Simson

8223 *Medallion of Edward John Moreton Drax Plunkett, 18th Baron Dunsany, (1878-1957), (1922)*
Signed: *STS* (in monogram)
Inscribed: *LORD.DUNSANY/A.D. MDCCCCXXII*
10.4 diam., bronze
Purchased, Mr T. Spicer-Simson, the medallist, 1940

Stapleton, Michael (c.1740-1801)
Irish School
Unpainted casts of plaques used by the stuccodore Michael Stapleton from c.1770

8016 *Cupid bound*
(after A. Kauffmann/F. Bartolozzi Undated stipple or W.W. Ryland 1777 stipple)
96 diam., plaster
Purchased, Dublin, Mr G. Kenyon, 1966

8017 *The mounting of Cupid on a pedestal*
101 diam., plaster
Purchased, Dublin, Mr G. Kenyon, 1966

8018 *Cupid drawing Venus with swans*
58.5 ht. x 83 wh., plaster
Purchased, Dublin, Mr G. Kenyon, 1966

8019 *Flora*
(after the Classical marble, *The Farnese Flora*, Museo Nazionale, Naples)
75 ht. x 47.5 wh., plaster
Purchased, Dublin, Mr G. Kenyon, 1966

8020 *Venus in her bower*
69.2 ht. x 106 wh., plaster
Purchased, Dublin, Mr G. Kenyon, 1966

8223

8016

8017

8018

8019

8020

21 *Apollo with his Lyre*
96 ht. x 70 wh., plaster
Purchased, Dublin, Mr G. Kenyon, 1966

22 *Winter*
81.5 ht. x 57.5 wh., plaster
Purchased, Dublin, Mr G. Kenyon, 1966

23 *Diana in her chariot pulled by stags*
86 ht. x 115 wh., plaster
Purchased, Dublin, Mr G. Kenyon, 1966

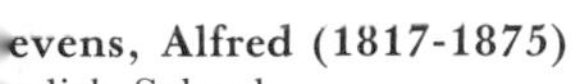

evens, Alfred (1817-1875)
nglish School

75 *Valour and Cowardice*
(cast of c.1857 small scale model for Wellington Monument, St Paul's Cathedral, London)
65 ht., bronze
Bequeathed, Sir Hugh Lane, 1918

76 *Truth and Falsehood*
(cast of c.1857 small scale model for Wellington Monument, St Paul's Cathedral, London)
59 ht., bronze
Bequeathed, Sir Hugh Lane, 1918

ones, Anthony (b.1934)
nglish School

05 *Liam O'Flaherty, (1896-1984), Author*
(cast of 1983 clay model)
Signed: *STONES 84*
Foundry mark: *D A F*
30 ht., bronze (on 15.5 ht. black marble base)
Cast commissioned from Dublin Art Foundry by the Board of Governors and Guardians after the original clay model loaned by Mr S. Cashman, 1984

8021

8022

8023

8075

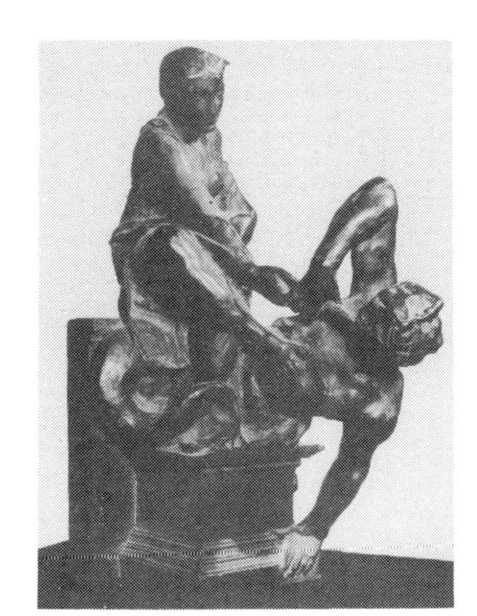

8076

8305

Stoyanovitch, Sreton (20th century)
Yugoslavian School

8167 *Head of an Old Woman*
Signed: *S. Stoyanovitch 1920*
Foundry mark: *LIVN... VOZDOYA BEOGRAD*
43 ht., bronze
Presented, Sir Alfred Chester Beatty, 1953

Tacca, Ferdinando (1619-1686)
Florentine School

8121 *Hercules slaying the Lernaean Hydra (c.1650)*
(derived from a c.1580 statuette by Giambologna)
40.2 ht., bronze with red-brown lacquer (on 14.5 ht. veined marble base)
Milltown Gift, 1902

8123 *Hercules and the Erymanthian Boar (c.1650)*
(derived from a c.1580 statuette by Giambologna)
44.8 ht., bronze with red-brown lacquer (on 14.5 ht. veined marble base)
Milltown Gift, 1902

8124 *Hercules slaying the Nemean Lion (c.1650)*
(derived from a c.1580 statuette by Giambologna)
32.3 ht., bronze with red-brown lacquer (on 14.5 ht. veined marble base)
Milltown Gift, 1902

8125 *Hercules with the Pillars (c.1650)*
(derived from a c.1580 statuette by Giambologna)
33.2 ht., bronze with red-brown lacquer (on 14.5 ht. veined marble base)
Milltown Gift, 1902

Tassie, James (1735-1799)
Scottish School

8320 *David Hume, (1711-1776), Philosopher and Historian*
Signed: *T*
Inscribed: *DAVID HUME*
Inscribed on original backing paper: *Edinburgh 21 June 1823/To Miss Edgeworth/from the Historians/ Nephew./David Hume* (and in a later hand) *Given to W W Fox*
7.5 ht., glass-paste relief
Miss Mary A. McNeill Bequest, 1985

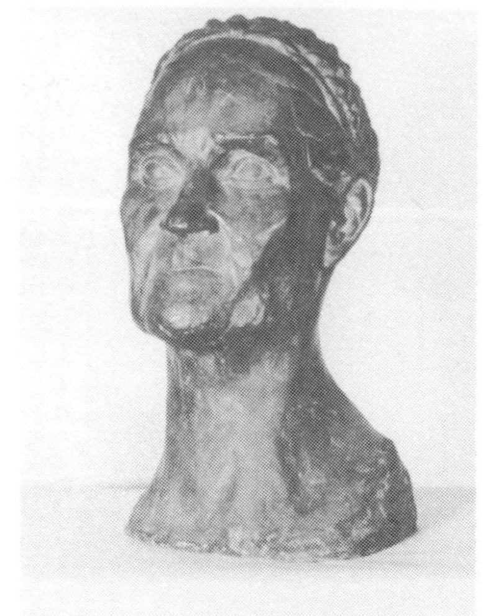
8167

8121

8123

8124

8125

8320

321 *David Stewart Erskine, 11th Earl of Buchan, (1742-1829)*
Signed: *Tassie F*
Inscribed: *D. S. BUCHANIAE COMES/1783*
8 ht., glass-paste relief (repaired)
Miss Mary A. McNeill Bequest, 1985

homas, John (1813-1862)
nglish School

.13 *Daniel Maclise, (1806-1870), Artist, (above a relief of Hibernia)*
Signed: *JOHN THOMAS LONDON SC.*
Inscribed: *DANIEL MACLISE R.A. 1859*
78 ht., marble
Purchased, Mrs Cox, 1874

.84 *Daniel Maclise, (1806-1870), Artist, (above a relief of Hibernia)*
Signed: *JOHN THOMAS/sc 1859*
Inscribed: *D. MACLISE R.A.*
78 ht., marble
Presented, Mrs M. R. Middleton, a friend of the sitter, 1892

hornycroft, Hamo (1850-1925)
nglish School

)98 *Edward Nugent Leeson, 6th Earl of Milltown, (1835-1890), as Lord Lieutenant of Co. Wicklow*
Signed: *HAMO THORNYCROFT APRIL 1879*
Inscribed: *EDWARD, 6TH EARL OF MILLTOWN.*
84 ht., plaster (incl. 13 ht. socle)
Milltown Gift, 1902

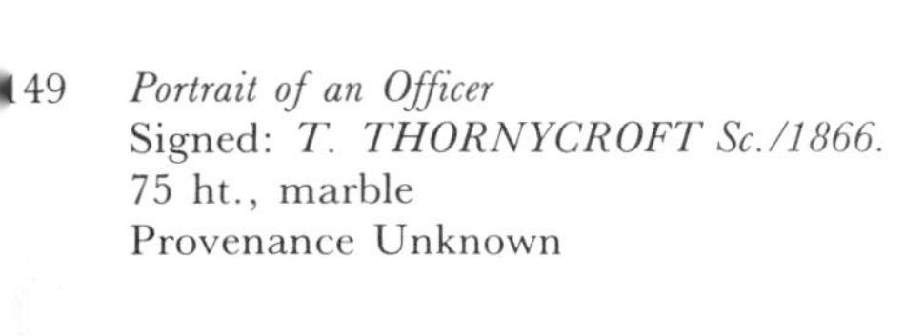

149 *Portrait of an Officer*
Signed: *T. THORNYCROFT Sc./1866.*
75 ht., marble
Provenance Unknown

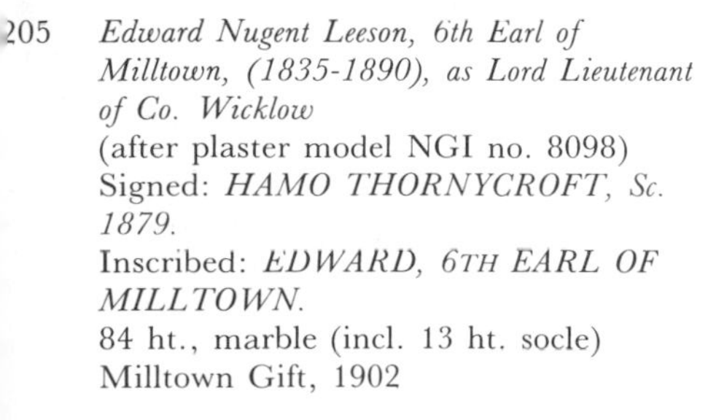

205 *Edward Nugent Leeson, 6th Earl of Milltown, (1835-1890), as Lord Lieutenant of Co. Wicklow*
(after plaster model NGI no. 8098)
Signed: *HAMO THORNYCROFT, Sc. 1879.*
Inscribed: *EDWARD, 6TH EARL OF MILLTOWN.*
84 ht., marble (incl. 13 ht. socle)
Milltown Gift, 1902

8321

8113

8184

8098

8149

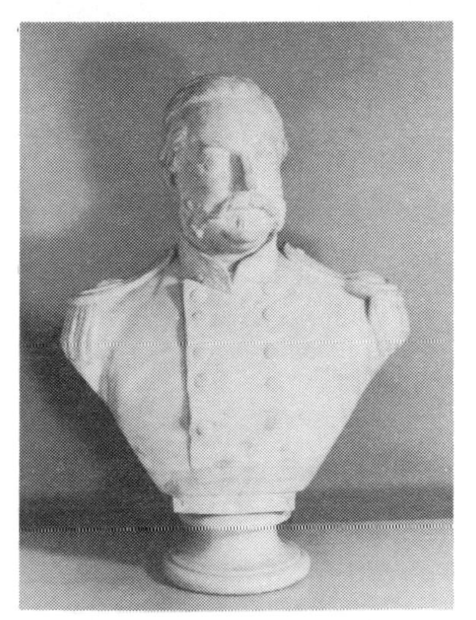

8205

After Thorvaldsen

After **Thorvaldsen, Bertel (1770-1844)**
Danish School

8110 *Venus with the apple*
(reduced copy of the 1813-16 marble, Thorvaldsens Museum, Copenhagen)
45.5 ht., bronze
Milltown Gift, 1902

8227 *A Shepherd Boy*
(reduced copy, probably French c.1830, of an 1817 marble, of which five versions are known)
43.5 ht., bronze
Milltown Gift, 1902

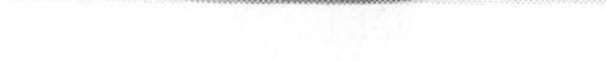

8110

8227

Troubetzkoy, Prince Paul (1866-1938)
Russian School

8105 *George Bernard Shaw, (1856-1950), Author, Playwright and Critic*
Signed: *1927 Paul Troubetzkoy*
Foundry mark: *Fonderia Faruffini & Co./Milano*
188 ht., bronze
Purchased, London, Colnaghi's, 1938

Turnerelli, Peter (1774-1839)
Irish School

8078 *Portrait of a Man*
(sculpted in marble 1821, Yale Center for British Art, New Haven)
Signed: *P. Turnerelli fecit/16 Jan. 1816*
57 ht., plaster (incl. 9.7 ht. socle)
Purchased, London, Cyril Humphris, 1970

8107 *Henry Grattan, (1746-1820), Statesman and Orator (1812)*
Signed: *P. Turnerelli Sculpr*
69 ht., marble (incl. 9.5 ht. socle)
Purchased, Dublin Library, 1882

8188 *Charles Kendal Bushe, (1767-1843), Politician and Lawyer*
Signed: *Turnerelli Fecit 1816*
72 ht., plaster (incl. 10 ht. socle)
Purchased, Mr J. Vicars, 1903

8105

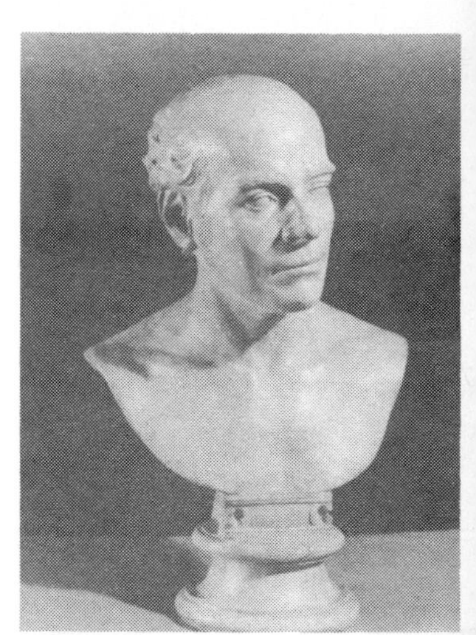

8078

8107

8188

)9 *John Thomas Troy, R.C. Archbishop of Dublin, (1739-1823)*
Signed: *Turnerelli fecit 1816*
75 ht., plaster (incl. 10 ht. socle)
Provenance Unknown

73 *Arthur Wellesley, 1st Duke of Wellington, (1769-1852), Field-Marshal and later British Prime Minister*
Signed: *P. TURNERELLI FECIT. 1816*
73 ht., marble (incl. 10.5 ht. socle)
Purchased, London, Sotheby's, 1984

8199

8273

74 *Field-Marshal Gebhard Lebrecht von Blücher, (1742-1819)*
Signed: *P. Turnerelli/Fecit 1815.*
71 ht., marble (incl. 11 ht. socle)
Purchased, London, Sotheby's, 1984

97 *Portrait of a Man*
51 ht., plaster
Provenance Unknown

8274

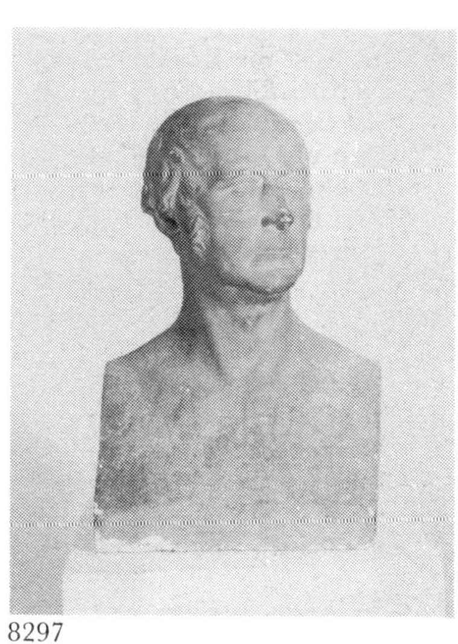
8297

Turnerelli, Peter (1774-1839)

28 *Henry Grattan, (1746-1820), Statesman and Orator*
(after a marble bust c.1812, example Bank of Ireland Collection, Dublin)
Inscribed: *Henry Grattan Esq./Irish Marble*
53.5 ht., marble (incl. 9 ht. socle)
Presented, Francis Spring Rice, 4th Baron Monteagle, 1935

nelli, Giacomo (19th century)
lian School

35 *Spinario or Boy extracting a thorn*
(copy of a Roman bronze, Capitoline Museums, Rome)
Signed: *Giacomo di Lepoldo Vanelli Scultore/in Carrara*
81 ht., marble
Presented, Mrs Carmichael, 1863

8228

8085

PPENDIX 1

TAINED GLASS

larke, Harry (1889-1931)
rish School

12,074 *The Song of the Mad Prince*
Signed: *HARRY CLARKE.1917*
34.3 × 17.7, stained glass
(set in a walnut cabinet by James Hicks of Dublin)
Purchased, Dublin, Mrs E. Jameson, 1987

12,074

12,071

Iand, Richard (fl.1780-1817)
rish School

12,071 *Halt at an Inn*
Signed: *Richd Hand 1785*
26.5 × 31, stained glass
Presented, the Friends of the National Collections of Ireland, 1974

Ione, Evie (1894-1955)
rish School

12,065 *Three Children in the Inferno*
23 diam., stained glass
Bequeathed, Miss R.S.R. Kirkpatrick, 1979

12,065

12,066 *The Cock and Pot (The Betrayal)*
55.5 × 33, stained glass
Bequeathed, Miss R.S.R. Kirkpatrick, 1979

12,066

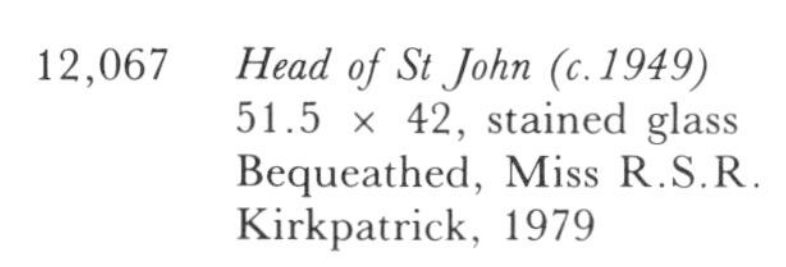
12,067 *Head of St John (c.1949)*
51.5 × 42, stained glass
Bequeathed, Miss R.S.R. Kirkpatrick, 1979

12,067

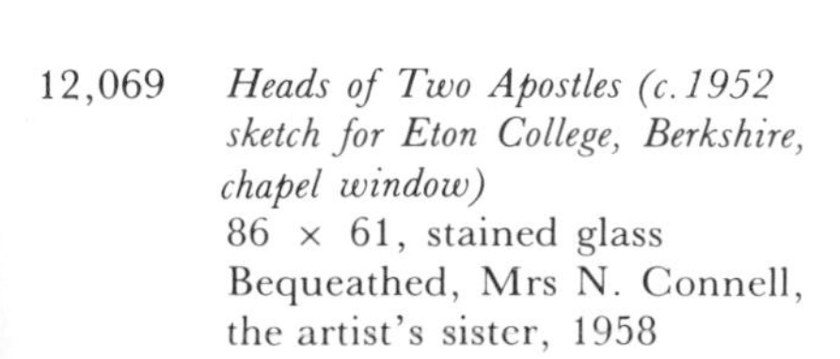
12,069 *Heads of Two Apostles (c.1952 sketch for Eton College, Berkshire, chapel window)*
86 × 61, stained glass
Bequeathed, Mrs N. Connell, the artist's sister, 1958

12,069

12,070 *Resurrection (c.1954)*
61.5 × 51, stained glass
Bequeathed, Mrs N. Connell, the artist's sister, 1958

12,070

Jervais, Thomas (fl.1760-1799)
Irish School

12,072 *View of an Estuary by moonlight (c.1780)*
(probably after A. van de Neer)
Signed: *Jervais*
20.3 × 28, stained glass
Presented, the Friends of the National Collections of Ireland, 1974

12,072

12,073 *Pastoral landscape*
28 × 20, stained glass
Presented, the Friends of the National Collections of Ireland, 1974

12,073

APPENDIX 2

ENGRAVERS' APPENDIX

An alphabetical list of engravers and copyists in the catalogue with the catalogue number(s) of their prints, the originating artist under whose name they are found, short title and page number.

The Chaloner Smith number and state (with any revision by Russell) are given for the 18th century mezzotint portraits which are such an important part of the collection.

Engraver	Artist	Short title	Page
ACON, ROBERT (FL.1818-1830s)			
ENGLISH SCHOOL			
11,824(1-2)	T.H. Shepherd	Regent's Park, London	474
ADLARD, HENRY (FL.1825-1869)			
ENGLISH SCHOOL			
10,631	G. Richmond	John Jebb	448
20,435	W.H. Bartlett	Pontoon Bridge, Co. Mayo	19
20,440	W.H. Bartlett	Luggala Lodge, Co. Wicklow	19
AGAR, JOHN SAMUEL (?1770-after 1835)			
ENGLISH SCHOOL			
10,324	C. Robertson	Countess Talbot	453
ALAIS, WILLIAM JOHN (FL.1877-1894)			
ENGLISH SCHOOL			
11,121	P. Van Bleeck	Kitty Clive	525
ALIAMET, JACQUES (1803-1876)			
FRENCH SCHOOL			
20,162	J.C. Brand	Near Saverne, Alsace, France	33
ALKEN, SAMUEL (FL.1780-1798)			
ENGLISH SCHOOL			
20,838 (1)	T. S. Roberts	Waterford	450
20,838 (2)	T. S. Roberts	Lismore Castle	450
20,838 (4)	T. S. Roberts	Dunbrody Abbey	450
20,838 (8)	T. S. Roberts	Blarney Castle	451
20,838 (9)	T. S. Roberts	Lower Glanmire	451
20,838 (10)	T. S. Roberts	Cork	451
20,838 (11)	T. S. Roberts	Eden Vale	452
20,838 (12)	T. S. Roberts	Dromona	452
ALLEN, JAMES BAYLIE (1803-1876)			
ENGLISH SCHOOL			
11,800	J.M.W. Turner	Le Havre, France	511
11,801	J.M.W. Turner	River Seine, near Paris	511
20,245	Claude Lorrain	Cephalus and Procris	66
20,459	S. Prout	Chillon Castle, Switzerland	422
20,482	J.M.W. Turner	Château of Amboise, France	511
ALLEN (19TH CENTURY)			
IRISH SCHOOL			
10,915	Allen	Rev. Theobald Mathew	2
ALLOM, THOMAS (1804-1872)			
ENGLISH SCHOOL			
20,454 *(COPYIST)*	G.F. White	Gungotri, India	540
AMERICAN SCHOOL (19TH CENTURY)			
10,723	American School 19C	Father Thomas Nicholas Burke	5

Engraver	Artist	Short title	Page
AMERICAN SCHOOL (1873)			
10,773	A. Chappel	Maria Edgeworth	63
AMICI, DOMENICO (1808-AFTER 1858)			
ROMAN SCHOOL			
20,734-20,756	D. Amici	Views of Ancient Rome	5-8
ANNIS, W.T. (FL.1798-1811)			
ENGLISH SCHOOL			
10,211	T. Nugent	Edward FitzGerald	384
(C.S.4)			
11,997	J.M.W. Turner	Fishermen	519
20,005	J.M.W. Turner	Chepstow Castle	521
ANSELIN, JEAN-LOUIS (1754-1823)			
FRENCH SCHOOL			
10,906	C.P. Verhulst	Comte de Lally-Tolendal	532
AQUILA, P. (18th CENTURY)			
ITALIAN SCHOOL			
20,684(4)	P. Aquila	Allegory of the Arts	9
ARCHDEAKON, THOMAS (FL. C.1800)			
IRISH SCHOOL			
11,919	T. Archdeakon	King James II's Mint House, Dublin	9
ARMSTRONG, COSMO (1781-1836)			
ENGLISH SCHOOL			
20,211	T. Lawrence	Lady Georgina Fane	332
ARMY LITHO SCHOOL (20th CENTURY)			
ENGLISH SCHOOL			
11,809	J. Thomas	The Taking of Enniskillen Castle	500
11,841	J. Thomas	Battle of Ballyshannon	500
ARTLETT, RICHARD AUGUSTUS (1807-1873)			
ENGLISH SCHOOL			
10,155	G. Richmond	James Emerson Tennent	448
10,814	A.E. Chalon	Countess de Grey	62
ATKINSON, GEORGE (1800-1941)			
IRISH SCHOOL			
10,502	J.C. Harrison	Gerard Fitzgibbon	211
AUBRY-LECOMTE, HYACINTHE LOUIS VICTOR JEAN-BAPTISTE (1787-1858)			
FRENCH SCHOOL			
20,721(63) *(COPYIST)*	R.A.Q. Monvoisin	Roman sleeping	374
AUDENGERD, ROBERT VAN (1663-1743)			
FLEMISH SCHOOL			
	Roman (Antique)	Niobe	460
AUDOUIN, PIERRE (1768-1822)			
FRENCH SCHOOL			
20,691(1)	Raphael	Virgin and Child with St John	425

Engraver	Artist	Short title	Page
ꓥUDRAN, JEAN (1667-1756)			
'RENCH SCHOOL			
?0,678(1)	?A. Van Dyck	Peter Paul Rubens	527
USTIN, SAMUEL (1796-1834)			
:NGLISH SCHOOL			
?0,351 *(COPYIST)*	R.J. Elliot	Mah Chung Keow, Canton, China	123
ꓥUSTIN, WILLIAM (1721-1820)			
:NGLISH SCHOOL			
?0,247(16)	A. Locatelli	Rome	355
....., A. (17TH CENTURY)			
:ONTINENTAL SCHOOL			
0,046	?English School 16C	Bishop John Bale	124
ADER, AUGUSTIN (FL. 1835-1868)			
'RENCH SCHOOL			
'0,411	A. Bader	Zachringen Suspension Bridge	11
AILEY, JOHN (1750-1819)			
:NGLISH SCHOOL			
?0,324	A. Cuyp	Landing of Prince Frederick at Nijmegen	97
AILLIE, (CAPTAIN) WILLIAM (1723-1810)			
RISH SCHOOL			
0,225	?N. Hone the Elder	William Baillie	237
0,532	N. Hone the Elder	John Camillus Hone	237
C.S.3; R.3 II/of III)			
0,942	N. Hone the Elder	Baron Mountstuart	237
0,944	N. Hone the Elder	Baron Mountstuart	237
0,945	N. Hone the Elder	Baron Mountstuart	237
AKER, BENJAMIN (FL.1780-1824)			
NGLISH SCHOOL			
1,812	W. Wilson	Plan of Dublin in 1798	543
ALDREY, JOSHUA KIRBY (1754-1828)			
NGLISH SCHOOL			
1,047	J. Reynolds	1st Marquess of Hastings	430
ALZAR, GIOVANNO (19TH CENTURY)			
TALIAN SCHOOL			
0,676(1)	Raphael	The Loggia of the Vatican	425
AMPFYLDE, COPPLESTONE WARRE			
720-1791)			
NGLISH SCHOOL			
0,115 *(COPYIST)*	A. Van Dyck	Sir Thomas Morgan	528
ARATHIER (19th CENTURY)			
RENCH SCHOOL			
0,101	A.E. Fragonard	The Recitation	163
ARBANT, CHARLES (FL.1863-1922)			
RENCH SCHOOL			
0,619	P.E. Grandsire	Mount Etna, Sicily	183

Engraver	Artist	Short title	Page
BARBER, THOMAS (FL.1818-1846) IRISH SCHOOL			
10,056	G. Petrie	Christchurch Cathedral, Dublin	397
11,777	G. Petrie	Trinity College, Dublin	397
11,778	G. Petrie	St George's Church, Dublin	397
11,779	G. Petrie	New Theatre Royal, Dublin	397
11,790	G. Petrie	Sackville Street, Dublin	398
11,791	G. Petrie	Sackville Street, Dublin	398
11,792	G. Petrie	Sackville Street, Dublin	398
11,825(1-2)	T.H. Shepherd	Regent's Park, London	474
BARCLAY (18TH CENTURY) ENGLISH SCHOOL			
11,680	?Irish School 18C	Carlingford Castle, Co. Louth	261
11,681	?Irish School 18C	Carlingford Castle, Co. Louth	262
BARNARD, WILLIAM S. (1774-1849) ENGLISH SCHOOL			
10,233 (C.S.2)	H.D. Hamilton	Walter Hussey Burgh	194
10,493 (C.S.4)	S. Drummond	Sir Jerome Fitzpatrick	118
10,808 (C.S.5)	L.F. Abbott	Charles James Fox	1
BARNEY, WILLIAM WHISTON (FL.1805-1810) ENGLISH SCHOOL			
10,177 (C.S.13 I/ofII)	J.Opie	1st Marquess of Sligo	387
BARON, BERNARD (1696-1762 or 66) FRENCH SCHOOL			
20,040-47	P.P. Rubens	'The History of Achilles'	466-467
BARRALET, JOHN JAMES (1747-1815) IRISH SCHOOL			
11,641	J.J. Barralet	Harcourt Bridge, Dublin	11, 641
BARROW, T. (18TH CENTURY) ENGLISH SCHOOL			
11,315	T. Arrowsmith	2nd Baron Rokeby	9
BARRY, JAMES (1741-1806) IRISH SCHOOL			
10,205	J. Barry	Self-Portrait	14
11,858	J. Barry	Jupiter and Juno on Mount Ida	14
20,722(1-14)	J. Barry	'A series of etchings'	14-18
BARTLETT, WILLIAM HENRY (1809-1854) ENGLISH SCHOOL			
20,425 *(COPYIST)*	F. Abresch	Sulina, Romania	1
20,475 *(COPYIST)*	F. Abresch	Belgrade, Yugoslavia	1
BARTOLI, PIETRO SANTI (C.1635-1700) ITALIAN SCHOOL			
20,706(47)	Roman Antique	Antique sepulchre	458

Engraver	Artist	Short title	Page
BARTOLOZZI, FRANCESCO (1727-1815) ANGLO-ITALIAN SCHOOL			
10,309	H. Hone	Countess of Lanesborough	234
10,310	H. Hone	Mrs Sarah Siddons	234
10,313	J. Reynolds	Countess of Harrington	430
10,314	J. Reynolds	Countess of Harrington	430
10,315	J. Reynolds	Countess of Harrington	431
10,320	J. Downman	Viscountess Duncannon	113
10,352	Countess L. Spencer	Viscountess Duncannon	480
10,692	R. Home	Theobald Wolfe Tone	233
10,693	R. Home	Theobald Wolfe Tone	233
10,702	H.D. Hamilton	1st Viscount Kilwarden	194
10,810	R. Cosway	Lord John Fitzgibbon	87
10,819	N. Dance	Captain Francis Grose	100
10,861	H.D. Hamilton	1st Viscount Kilwarden	195
10,862	H.D. Hamilton	1st Viscount Kilwarden	195
10,949	J. Hoppner	2nd Earl of Moira	246
11,606	J.H. Ramberg	'The Sorrows of Young Werther'	424
11,957	G.B. Cipriani	Tancred and Armenia	65
20,031	G.B. Cipriani	'Orlando Furioso'	65
20,103 *(COPYIST)*	?Titian	Cornelia	504
20,807	F. Bartolozzi	Two Armorini	23
BASIRE THE ELDER, JAMES (1730-1803) ENGLISH SCHOOL			
10,404	B. Wilson	Lady Anne Hussey Stanhope	542
10,741	?G. Gower	1st Baron Brereton	183
10,766	English School 15C	Thomas Cranley	183
10,879	I. Gossett	Bishop Benjamin Hoadly	183
20,535	English School 18C	Mausoleum of Augustus, Rome	132
BAUGNIET, CHARLES (1814-1866) ANGLO-BELGIAN SCHOOL			
10,802	C. Baugniet	Admiral Sir William Henry Dillon	24
10,901	C. Baugniet	Samuel Lover	24
BAYOT, ADOLPHE JEAN-BAPTISTE (1810-after 1866) FRENCH SCHOOL			
20,315	L.J. Jacottet & A.J.-B. Bayot	Figures resting by Trees	303
BEARD, THOMAS (FL.1720-1729) IRISH SCHOOL			
10,063 (C.S.5)	M. Dahl	Archbishop William King	98
10,143 (C.S.6)	T. Carlton	Bishop John Stearne	54
10,202 (C.S.1 I/of II)	M. Ashton	Archbishop Hugh Boulter	9
BEAUPARLANT, LEONIE-CHARLOTTE (FL.1885-1893) FRENCH SCHOOL			
11,502	C. Lapostolet	Le Port St Nicholas, Paris	330

Engraver	Artist	Short title	Page
11,207 (C.S.e II/of II)	P. Lely	Catherine of Braganza	346
11,215 (C.S.i II/of II)	A. Van Dyck	Charles II, King of England	527
11,263 (C.S.m.d. II/of II)	P. Lely	William of Orange	346
11,264 (C.S.m.b. R.m.b. II/ of II)	P. Lely	Mary, Princess of Orange	347
BLUCK, J. (FL.1791-1819) ENGLISH SCHOOL			
11,593	T.S. Roberts	College Green, Dublin	452
11,621	W.B. Taylor	Trinity College Dublin	498
11,653	T.S. Roberts	Goldmines in Co. Wicklow	452
11,911	T.S. Roberts	The Four Courts, Dublin	452
BLYTH, ROBERT (1750-1784) ENGLISH SCHOOL			
20,034	J.H. Mortimer	The Captive	376
20,036	J.H. Mortimer	Banditti	376
20,066	J.H. Mortimer	Two figures - a biblical scene	376
BOCOURT, ETIENNE GABRIEL (1821-AFTER 1883) FRENCH SCHOOL			
11,504	J.C. Vermeyen	Portrait of a Man	532
BOEL, QUIRIN (1620-1668) FLEMISH SCHOOL			
10,276	Q. Boel	Hugh Brady	31
BOIT, CHARLES (1663-1727) SWEDISH SCHOOL			
10,371 *(COPYIST)*	E. Lilly	Queen Anne	353
BOLOGNESE SCHOOL (17TH CENTURY)			
20,228	Bolognese School 17C	Assumption of the Virgin	31
BOLOGNESE SCHOOL (18TH CENTURY)			
10,515	Bolognese School	Giovanni Ludovico Quadri	31
BOND, WILLIAM (FL.1799-1833) ENGLISH SCHOOL			
10,368	T. Lawrence	Mary, Countess of Inchiquin	333
10,572	J. Murphy	Rev. Arthur O'Leary	379
BOREL, ANTOINE (1743-AFTER 1810) FRENCH SCHOOL			
20,723(7) *(COPYIST)*	A. Allori	Venus and Cupid	5
BOSLEY (19TH CENTURY) ENGLISH SCHOOL			
11,057	A.F.J. Claudet	3rd Earl of Rosse	68
BOUILLON, PIERRE (1776-18731) FRENCH SCHOOL			
20,683(59)*(COPYIST)*	Hellenistic School	The Laocoon	221

Engraver	Artist	Short title	Page
BOVI, MARINO (1758-AFTER 1805)			
ANGLO-ITALIAN SCHOOL			
10,312	G.B. Cipriani	The Recording Angel	66
20,038	B. Luini	Christ among the Doctors	357
20,103	?Titian	Cornelia	504
BOVINET (19TH CENTURY)			
FRENCH SCHOOL			
20,707(66)	A. Van Ostade	The Schoolmaster	388
BOWEN, EMANUEL (FL.1720-67)			
ENGLISH SCHOOL			
11,889	Irish School c.1728	Map of Dublin Harbour and Bay	266
BOYDELL, JOHN (1719-1804)			
ENGLISH SCHOOL			
10,294	H.D. Hamilton	Hugh Kelly	195
(C.S.4 I/of II)			
11,943	G.B. Castiglione	The Exposition of Cyprus	57
BOYDELL, JOSIAH (1760-1817)			
ENGLISH SCHOOL			
20,718 (1)	Claude Lorrain	Claude Lorrain	66
10,294	H.D. Hamilton	Hugh Kelly	195
10,556	A. Van Dyck	Jane Wenman	527
(C.S.5; R.5 II/ of II)			
BOWLES, JOHN (18TH CENTURY)			
ENGLISH SCHOOL			
10,015(1-20)	C. Brooking	Map of Dublin and details	40-42
BRADSHAW, SAMUEL (FL.1832-80)			
ENGLISH SCHOOL			
20,448(1)	T. Allom	Kentmere Head, Westmoreland	2
20,448(2)	T. Allom	Kendal, Cumbria	2
20,502	T. Creswick	The Gap of Dunloe, Co. Kerry	93
20,606	T. Creswick	The Gap of Dunloe, Co. Kerry	93
BRANDARD, EDWARD PAXMAN (1819-1898)			
ENGLISH SCHOOL			
20,475	F. Abresch	Belgrade, Yugoslavia	1
BRANDARD, JOHN (1812-1863)			
ENGLISH SCHOOL			
20,761	W. Joy	The Wreck of the Killarney Steamer	310
BRANDARD, ROBERT (1805-1862)			
ENGLISH SCHOOL			
11,802	J.M.W. Turner	Rouen, France	511
11,803	J.M.W. Turner	Rietz, France	511
11,804	J.M.W. Turner	Château of Tancarville,France	511
20,283	G. Chambers	North Foreland, Kent	63
20,422	J.B. Pyne	Water Mill on River Lynn, Devon	423
20,426	D. Cox	Sea-Coast	91
20,492	J. B. Pyne	Swansea Harbour	423
20,510	T. Creswick	Blackrock Castle	93
20,609	W. Daniell	Oriental Birds	102

Engraver	Artist	Short title	Page
10,760 (C.S.8; R.8 II/of III)	English or Irish 18C	Cornelius Callaghan	135
10,820 (C.S.12 II/of II; R.13 II/of III)	J. Worsdale	Samuel Grey	548
10,825 (C.S.12 II/of II)	C. Jervas	Luke Gardiner	304
10,899 (C.S.20; R.20 I/of II)	A. Lee	William Lingen	341
10,914 (C.S.28 post-II; R.28 III/of III)	J. Latham	Lady Helena Rawdon	331
11,062 (C.S.27 pre-II; R.27 II/of III)	J. Worsdale	The Hon. Mrs Folliott Ponsonby	548
11,652 (C.S.Class II:120)	J. Wyck	The Battle of the Boyne	549
20,802 (C.S.24 I/of II)	?J. Brooks	Dr Cornelius Nary	43
BROOKS, VINCENT ROBERT ALFRED (1814-1885) ENGLISH SCHOOL			
11,078	L.M. Ward	Dion Boucicault	536
BROOKSHAW, RICHARD (1736-1804) ENGLISH SCHOOL			
11,097 (C.S.1; R.1 II/of II)	J. Reynolds	Mrs William Bastard	431
11,098 (C.S.2)	J. Reynolds	J. Bouverie	431
11,106 (C.S.3)	R.E. Pine	Mrs Elizabeth Bull	408
11,150 (C.S.13 I/of II)	F. Cotes	Duchess of Hamilton & Brandon	88
11,151 (C.S.13 II/of II)	F. Cotes	Duchess of Hamilton & Brandon	89
11,201 (C.S.7)	J. Reynolds	Elizabeth and Sarah Crewe	431
11,393 (C.S.8 III/of III)	S. Cooper	Oliver Cromwell	83
BROWN, JOSEPH (FL.1854-1886) ENGLISH SCHOOL			
10,807	P. Van Somer	1st Viscount Falkland	531
10,840	J. Wood	2nd Earl De Grey	546
10,844	T. Phillips	Sir Robert Fitzwygram	406
10,887	R. McInnes	9th Earl of Haddington	359
10,992	T. Phillips	1st Earl O'Neill	406
11,111	L. Bushe	Self-Portrait	47
11,335	English School c.1850	Sir Henry Pottinger	135
BROWNE, ALEXANDER (FL.1660-1680) ENGLISH SCHOOL			
10,259 (C.S.39 I/of V)	A. Van Dyck	1st Earl of Strafford	527
10,756 (C.S.4 I/of II;R.4 II/of III)	A. Van Dyck	Children of King Charles I	528
10,759 (C.S.5 I/of III)	P. Lely	Charles II, King of England	347

Engraver	Artist	Short title	Page
BROWNE, JOHN (1741-1801) ENGLISH SCHOOL			
20,085	C. Dusart	The Jocund Peasants	120
BRUNTON, B. (19TH CENTURY) ENGLISH SCHOOL			
11,767	Irish School c.1818	Stove Tenter House, Dublin	295
BUCKLE, D. (FL.1835-1847) ENGLISH SCHOOL			
20,419	T. Allom	Aydon Castle, Northumberland	2
20,420	T. Allom	Bynell Hall, Northumberland	2
BULFINCH, JOHN (FL.C.1680-C.1741) *ENGLISH SCHOOL*			
11,392 *(COPYIST)*	S. Cooper	Oliver Cromwell	83
BURFORD, THOMAS (FL.1741-1765) ENGLISH SCHOOL			
10,085 (C.S.[Van Haecken]16 II/of III;R.[Van Haecken]16 II/of IV)	Markham	Dean Jonathan Swift	367
10,817 (C.S.9)	H. Hysing	Bishop Bonaventure Gifford	259
11,021 (C.S. [Van Haecken] 16 III/of III; R. [Van Haecken] III/of IV)	Markham	Dean Jonathan Swift	367
BURGESS, JAMES HOWARD (1817-1890) IRISH SCHOOL			
11,892	Irish School 18C	Kilkenny High Street	262
BURKE, THOMAS (1749-1815) IRISH SCHOOL			
?10,209	A. Kauffmann	Earl-Bishop of Derry	311
10,379 (C.S.1 I/of II; R.1 II/of III)	A. Kauffmann	Queen Charlotte Sophia	311
10,999 (C.S.6 I/of II; R.6 II/of IV)	N. Dance	Lord Frederick North	101
11,000 (C.S.7 I/of II)	N. Dance	Lord Frederick North	101
BURNETT, JOHN (1784-1868) SCOTTISH SCHOOL			
20,550	A. Fraser	Cattle	164
20,673(37)	G. Metsu	The Letter Writer	371
BURNS, JEAN DOUGLAS (B.1903) SCOTTISH SCHOOL			
11,931	J.D. Burns	The Hunt crossing a River	46
BURY, THOMAS TALBOT (1811-1877) ENGLISH SCHOOL			
11,772	R. Carpenter	St Patrick's Cathedral, Dublin	55
BUTIN, ULYSSE LOUIS AUGUSTE (1837 OR 38-1883) FRENCH SCHOOL			
11,487	U.L.A. Butin	Saturday at Villerville	47

Engraver	Artist	Short title	Page
BYRNE, ELIZABETH (FL.1809-1849)			
ENGLISH SCHOOL			
20,681(155)	J. Os	Fruit and Flowers	388
BYRNE, GEORGE (FL.1762-1791)			
IRISH SCHOOL			
10,603	A. Lee	John Leland	341
CALAME, ALEXANDRE (1810-1864)			
SWISS SCHOOL			
20,145	A. Calame	A Lake	49
20,337	A. Calame	Trees and building	49
20,340	A. Calame	Walnut trees	49
20,341	A. Calame & F.F.A. Ferogio	Weeping Willows	53
20,342	A. Calame	Ruined castle	49
20,343	A. Calame	River landscape	50
20,462	A. Calame & F.F.A. Ferogio	Chestnut trees	53
20,469	A. Calame	Figures on a path	50
20,470	A. Calame	River scene	50
20,487	A. Calame	River bank	50
20,488	A. Calame & F.F.A. Ferogio	Carob tree	53
20,489	A. Calame	Figures in a valley	50
20,490	A. Calame	Cattle	50
20,491	A. Calame	Cattle	51
20,494	A. Calame	Figures	51
20,496	A. Calame	Woman on a path	51
20,497	A. Calame	Mountain pool	51
20,498	A. Calame	River	51
20,499	A. Calame	River cascade	51
20,500	A. Calame	Lake at sunset	51
20,505	A. Calame	Fishermen	52
20,506	A. Calame	Castle ruins	52
20,507	A. Calame	Women gathering firewood	52
20,508	A. Calame	Young elms	52
20,521	A. Calame	Windswept forest	52
20,652	A. Calame	Waterfall	52
CAMERON, DAVID YOUNG (1865-1945)			
SCOTTISH SCHOOL			
11,682	D.Y. Cameron	The Isle of Arran, Scotland	53
CANOT, PIERRE CHARLES (1710-1777)			
ANGLO-FRENCH SCHOOL			
20,035	L. Bramer	Pyramus and Thisbe	33
20,090	I. Ostade	A Country Wake	389
CARDON, ANTHONY (1772-1813)			
ANGLO-BELGIAN SCHOOL			
10,135	A. Pope	Henry Tresham	418
10,318	R. Cosway	Madame Récamier	87
10,713	W.P.J. Lodder	Sir Eyre Coote	355
11,117	L.F. Abbot	General Sir Samuel Auchmuty	1
11,167	A. De Saint Aubyn	Abbé Henry Essex Edgeworth	108
11,220	J. Comerford	1st Baron Manners	70
20,048	Venetian School 16C	Knight and Page	532
20,067	T. Stothard	The Treaty of Troyes	487
20,156	F. Barocci	The Holy Family	12
20,357	J. Comerford	1st Baron Manners	70

ngraver	Artist	Short title	Page
AROCCI, G. (19TH CENTURY)			
TALIAN SCHOOL			
0,387	G. Carocci	Florence Cathedral	54
0,392	G. Carocci	Pisa Baptistery	54
ARPENTER, WILLIAM (C.1818-1899)			
NGLISH SCHOOL			
1,339	M. Carpenter	William Smith	55
ARRED, LUCIEN DANIEL (FL.1873-1882)			
RENCH SCHOOL			
1,495	E. Delacroix	The Barque of Dante	107
ARTER, JOHN (1748-1817)			
NGLISH SCHOOL			
0,766 *(COPYIST)*	English School 15C	Thomas Cranley	123
ARTWRIGHT, WILLIAM (18TH CENTURY)			
NGLISH SCHOOL			
0,702	T. Walmsley	Roughty Bridge, Co. Kerry	536
ARVER, JOHN (FL. EARLY 19TH ENTURY)			
NGLISH SCHOOL			
0,876	J. Comerford	Gustavus Hume	71
ARY, F. (18TH CENTURY)			
RISH SCHOOL			
1,716	J. Tudor	Dublin from Phoenix Park	509
ASTELLINI, G. (FL.C.1800)			
TALIAN SCHOOL			
0,393	G. Castellini	S. Lorenzo Maggiore, Milan	57
ATHELIN, LOUIS JACQUES (1739-1804)			
RENCH SCHOOL			
0,770	N. Blakey	Abbé Noel Antoine Pluche	31
AUKERCKEN, CORNELIS VAN .1625-1680)			
LEMISH SCHOOL			
0,667(37)	D. van Heil	Peter Snayers	221
HALLIS, EBENEZER (FL.1831-1863)			
NGLISH SCHOOL			
0,234	W. H. Bartlett	Malahide Castle	19
0,480	T. Allom	Mardale Head, Cumbria	3
HAMBARS, THOMAS (C.1724-1789)			
RISH SCHOOL			
0,519	G. Kneller	William III, King of England	314
HAPMAN, JOHN (FL.1792-1823)			
NGLISH SCHOOL			
0,910	A. Lee	Dr John Leland	342
HAPMAN, JOHN WATKINS (1832-1903)			
NGLISH SCHOOL			
0,360	S.P. Denning	Princess Victoria	108

Engraver	Artist	Short title	Page
CHATAIGNER, ALEXIS (1772-1817) FRENCH SCHOOL			
20,072	G. Metsu	Young Woman	372
20,073	P. Rossi	The School Mistress	463
CHAUVEAU, FRANCOIS (1613-1676) FRENCH SCHOOL			
11,493	Titian	The Supper at Emmaus	505
20,107	Titian	The Entombment	505
20,215	F. Chauveau	The Birth of Cupid	64
CHAUVEL, THEOPHILE NARCISSE (1831-1910) FRENCH SCHOOL			
20,080	Baronne C. Rothschild	Buiten Singel, Amsterdam	464
CHAVANE, E. (FL.C.1850) ENGLISH SCHOOL			
11,620	A. Concanen	Wreck of the Queen Victoria	78
CHESHAM, FRANCIS (1749-1806) ENGLISH SCHOOL			
20,032	F. Chesham	Moses striking the Rock	64
CHEVALIER, PIETRO (19TH CENTURY) ITALIAN SCHOOL			
20,390	Canaletto	Piazza S. Marco, Venice	54
CHILDS, GEORGE (FL.1826-1873) ENGLISH SCHOOL			
20,167	G. Childs	Cottage, Hampshire	64
20,288	J.H. Robinson	River Wye, Wales	454
20,289	J.H. Robinson	Caerphilly Castle, Wales	454
20,290	J.H. Robinson	Chepstow Castle, Wales	454
20,291	J.H. Robinson	St Fagan's Castle, Wales	454
20,292	J.H. Robinson	Manorbier Castle, Wales	454
20,293	J.H. Robinson	Ewenny Abbey, Wales	455
20,328	J.H. Robinson	Wreck of the Dun-Raven	455
20,334	J.H. Robinson	Kidwelly Town, Wales	455
20,375	G. Childs	Near Mill Hill, N. London	64
20,471	J.H. Robinson	Webley Castle, Wales	455
20,473	J.H. Robinson	Cilgerran Castle, Wales	455
20,522	J.H. Robinson	Oxwich Bay, Wales	455
20,592	J.J. Forrester	Sierra Convent, Oporto	161
20,593	J.J. Forrester	S. Antonio Convent, Oporto	161
20,594	J.J. Forrester	S. Niccolo, Oporto	161
20,595	J.J. Forrester	Oporto and River Duoro	162
CICERI, EUGENE (1813-1890) FRENCH SCHOOL			
20,240	E. Ciceri	Boat on a beach	65
CLAMP, R. (18TH CENTURY) ENGLISH SCHOOL			
11,107	H. Brooke	Henry Brooke	38
CLARK, THOMAS (FL.1832-1840) ENGLISH SCHOOL			
20,279	T. Allom	Peveril Castle, Derbyshire	3

ngraver	Artist	Short title	Page
LAUDET, ANTOINE FRANCOIS JEAN			
1797-1867)			
NGLO-FRENCH SCHOOL			
1,166 *(COPYIST)*	J. Petrie	Robert Emmet	402
LAYTON THE ELDER, BENJAMIN			
.1754-1814)			
RISH SCHOOL			
1,500	N. Berrettoni	Holy Family with Saints	27
1,924	B. Clayton the Elder	Marrowbone Lane House	68
LINT, GEORGE (1770-1854)			
NGLISH SCHOOL			
0,486	J. Hoppner	1st Duke of Wellington	245
0,489	M.A. Shee	Walter Blake Kirwan	472
0,948	M.A. Shee	2nd Earl of Moira	472
1,070	J. Hoppner	William Pitt the Younger	246
1,998	J.M.W. Turner	Cephalus and Procris	519
0,002	J.M.W. Turner	Peat bog, Scotland	520
LOSE THE ELDER, SAMUEL (FL.1770-1807)			
RISH SCHOOL			
0,584	J. Hoppner	General Sir Ralph Abercromby	246
1,751	S. Close the Elder	Monkstown, Co. Dublin	69
OCHIN, CHARLES NICOLAS (1715-1790)			
RENCH SCHOOL			
1,656	G.P. Panini	Preparation for a Fête in Rome	390
OCHRAN, JOHN (FL.1820s-1860s)			
NGLISH SCHOOL			
0,955	T. Lawrence	Sir George Murray	333
1,243	Maull & Polyblank	Rev. William Urwick	369
1,279	H. Room	Charles Gostling Townley	462
OLE, B. (18TH CENTURY)			
NGLISH SCHOOL			
1,768	Irish School c.1755	Essex Bridge, Dublin	268
OLE, TIMOTHY (1852-1931)			
MERICAN SCHOOL			
1,412	J.S. Sargent	Woodrow Wilson	469
OLLINS, WILLIAM (1788-1847)			
NGLISH SCHOOL			
0,330	W. Collins	The Prawn Fisher	70
OLLYER, JOSEPH (1748-1827)			
NGLISH SCHOOL			
0,118	G.C. Stuart	2nd Earl of Moira	487
0,753	R. Bull	Thomas Conolly	45
1,644	F. Wheatley	Dublin Volunteers in College Green	539
1,826	F. Wheatley	Dublin Volunteers in College Green	539

Engraver	Artist	Short title	Page
COMERFORD, JOHN (?1770-1832)			
IRISH SCHOOL			
10,307 *(COPYIST)*	G. Romney	Mary Tighe	462
10,715 *(COPYIST)*	H.D. Hamilton	Sir Jonah Barrington	196
11,327	J. Comerford	Archibald Hamilton Rowan	71
11,128 *(COPYIST)*	B. Stoker	Henry Flood	485
11,417 *(COPYIST)*	G. Romney	Mary Tighe	461
COMPARINI, L. (19TH CENTURY)			
ITALIAN SCHOOL			
20,676(1) *(COPYIST)*	Raphael	Vatican Loggia	425
CONDE, PIERRE (FL.1793-AFTER 1840)			
FRENCH SCHOOL			
10,137	R. Cosway	1st Earl of Clonmel	87
CONTINENTAL SCHOOL (19TH CENTURY)			
20,177	Roman Antique	Abstract mosaic	459
20,178	Roman Antique	'Beware of the dog' mosaic	459
11,485	Continental School 19C	Domestic Husbandry	80
COOK, G. (FL.1840s)			
ENGLISH SCHOOL			
11,377	N. Hone the Elder	Anna Zamparini	237
COOK, HENRY R. (FL.1800-1845)			
ENGLISH SCHOOL			
10,562	R.R. Scanlan	1st Duke of Wellington	470
11,079	H.W. Phillips	Colonel William Blacker	405
11,119	Mrs J. Mee	Countess of Antrim	370
COOK, THOMAS (C.1774-1818)			
ENGLISH SCHOOL			
11,095	D. Dodd	Spranger Barry	110
11,282	D. Dodd	Richard Brinsley Sheridan	110
20,029	P. Sandby	King John's Castle, Limerick	469
COOKE, GEORGE (1781-1834)			
ENGLISH SCHOOL			
20,373	A.V.D. Copley-Fielding	Southampton, Hampshire	86
20,540	D. Stoop	Horse being led to water	486
COOKE, JOHN (FL.1818-1831)			
?IRISH SCHOOL			
11,888(1-24)	J. Cooke	Cooke's Royal Map of Dublin	80-83
COOKE, WILLIAM BERNARD (1778-1855)			
ENGLISH SCHOOL			
20,417	W.H. Bartlett	Saint-Gervais-les-Bains	19
COOKE, WILLIAM JOHN (1797-1865)			
ENGLISH SCHOOL			
20,385	D. Cox	Calais Pier	91
20,517	A.V.D. Copley-Fielding	Brougham Castle, Cumbria	86

Engraver	Artist	Short title	Page
COOPER, RICHARD (1730-1820)			
ENGLISH SCHOOL			
10,316	English School 18C	Countess of Harrington	132
10,546	A. Van Dyck	The Children of Charles I	546
10,781	H.D. Hamilton	William Degane	195
11,392	S. Cooper	Oliver Cromwell	84
COOPER, ROBERT (FL.1795-1836)			
ENGLISH SCHOOL			
10,959	S. Lover	Lady Sydney Morgan	356
10,981	S. Catterson Smith the Elder	Daniel O'Connell	58
11,118	A.W. Davis	Lady Catherine Annesley	109
11,179	S. Catterson Smith the Elder	James Warren Doyle	58
11,289	S. Catterson Smith the Elder	Richard Lalor Sheil	58
11,313	J. Comerford	Thomas Spring Rice	71
11,314	J. Comerford	Thomas Spring Rice	71
20,078	D. Teniers the Younger	'The Green Cap'	499
COOPER, THOMAS SYDNEY (1803-1902)			
ENGLISH SCHOOL			
20,165	T.S. Cooper	Cattle Grazing	84
20,169	T.S. Cooper	Shire Horses	84
20,170	T.S. Cooper	Halt at 'The Bell' Inn	85
20,174	T.S. Cooper	Donkeys	85
20,243	T.S. Cooper	Deer	85
20,345	T.S. Cooper	Sheep and Carthorses	85
20,402	T.S. Cooper	Donkeys	85
COPE, CHARLES WEST (1811-1890)			
ENGLISH SCHOOL			
10,957	C.W. Cope	William Mulready	85
CORBOULD, EDWARD HENRY (1815-1905)			
ENGLISH SCHOOL			
10,736 *(COPYIST)*	E. Day	Prince Albert	103
CORLEY, CHARLES (19TH CENTURY)			
IRISH SCHOOL			
11,835	?C. Corley	General Post Office, Dublin	86
CORNER, JOHN (FL.1778-1825)			
ENGLISH SCHOOL			
11,224	J.C. Lochée	Charles Macklin	355
CORR, MATHIEU ERIN (1805-1862)			
FLEMISH SCHOOL			
11,482	Italian School 16C	The Saviour of the World	300
11,483	F.J. Navez	Hagar and her son Ishmael	380
11,489	A. Van Dyck	The Crucifixon	528
20,806	Italian School 16C	The Saviour of the World	300
CORSI, G. (FL. EARLY 19TH CENTURY)			
ITALIAN SCHOOL			
20,388	G. Corsi	Pisa Tower and Cathedral	88
COUCHÉ, JACQUES (1759-AFTER 1808)			
FRENCH SCHOOL			
20,724(11)	Titian	Death of Actaeon	505

Engraver	Artist	Short title	Page
COURBE, WILBRODE NICOLAS MAGLOIRE (FL.1789-1814)			
FRENCH SCHOOL			
10,605	J.M. Moreau	Comte de Lally-Tolendal	374
COUSEN, JOHN (1804-1880)			
ENGLISH SCHOOL			
11,799	J.M.W. Turner	Harfleur, France	511
20,208	W.C. Stanfield	Fécamp, Normandy	481
20,213	W.C. Stanfield	The Storm	481
20,438	W.H. Bartlett	Delphi Lodge, Co. Mayo	20
20,439	W.H. Bartlett	Delphi Lodge, Co. Mayo	20
20,605	W.H. Bartlett	King John's Castle, Limerick	20
COUSINS, HENRY (1809-1864)			
ENGLISH SCHOOL			
10,790	H.W. Pickersgill	Thomas Drummond	407
COUSINS, SAMUEL (1801-1887)			
ENGLISH SCHOOL			
10,057	T. Lawrence	2nd Earl Grey	333
10,097	C. Smith	Francis Jeffrey	479
10,222	T. Lawrence	1st Marquess Wellesley	333
10,446	T. Lawrence	Julia Beatrice Peel	333
10,447	T. Lawrence	1st Earl of Durham	334
10,485	F. Grant	1st Viscount Gough	183
10,509	T. Lawrence	1st Duke of Wellington	334
10,841	W. Robinson	Thomas Philip Weddell Robinson	457
10,888	G.W. Reynolds the Elder	General Sir George Hewitt	457
11,026	J.W. Gordon	Bishop Daniel Sandford	183
11,799	J.M.W. Turner	Harfleur, France	511
CRAIG, WILLIAM MARSHALL (FL1788-1828)			
ENGLISH SCHOOL			
20,680(7) *(COPYIST)*	L. Lotto	Virgin and Child	356
20,681(155) *(COPYIST)*	J. Os	Fruit and Flowers	388
20,704(8) *(COPYIST)*	G. Moroni	The School Master	375
20,705(7) *(COPYIST)*	P.P. Rubens	Peace and War	467
20,727(12) *(COPYIST)*	A.R. Mengs	Robert Woods	371
CROSS THE ELDER, THOMAS (FL.1632-1682)			
ENGLISH SCHOOL			
10,304	?English School 17C	George Webb	125
CROSTICK, T. (FL.1820s)			
ENGLISH SCHOOL			
20,512	J.M.W. Turner	Fonthill Abbey, Wiltshire	511
DALZIEL, EDWARD (1817-1905)			
ENGLISH SCHOOL			
11,390	L. S....	Archbishop Richard Whateley	328
DANCE, NATHANIEL (1734-1811)			
ENGLISH SCHOOL			
11,157 *(COPYIST)*	N. Hone the Elder	Francis Grose	243

Engraver	Artist	Short title	Page
DANIELL, WILLIAM (1769-1837)			
ENGLISH SCHOOL			
10,049	G. Dance	Bishop Thomas Barnard	100
10,196	G. Dance	James Barry	100
10,746	G. Dance	1st Earl of Charlemont	100
10,902	G. Dance	1st Marquess of Londonderry	100
11,860	W. Daniell	Holyhead Harbour Lighthouse	102
DARLING, WILLIAM (FL.1760-1790)			
ENGLISH SCHOOL			
20,661	English School 18C	The Poster's Guide from London to Dublin	133
DARTON THE YOUNGER, WILLIAM			
ENGLISH SCHOOL			
20,662	English School early 19C	Illustrations to 'The Deserted Village'	143
DAWE, HENRY (1790-1848)			
ENGLISH SCHOOL			
20,008	J.M.W.Turner	Rievaulx Abbey, Yorkshire	521
20,011	J.M.W.Turner	Mill near Grand Chartreuse	522
20,020	J.M.W.Turner	Alcove Shooting Lodge, London	523
20,021	J.M.W.Turner	Château de St Michel, Savoy	523
DAY, JOHN GEORGE (1854-1931)			
IRISH SCHOOL			
11,419	J.G. Day	John Redmond	103
DAY, WILLIAM (1797-1845)			
ENGLISH SCHOOL			
20,149	D. Roberts	Pilgrims at Jericho	449
20,222	H. Bright	Castle Entrance	34
20,347	H. Bright	A Cabin	34
DEAN & CO. (19TH CENTURY)			
ENGLISH SCHOOL			
10,594	F.J. O'Kelly	Patrick O'Kelly	385
10,595	F.J. O'Kelly	Patrick O'Kelly	385
DEAN, JOHN (C.1750-1798)			
ENGLISH SCHOOL			
10,090 (C.S.16 I/of II)	J. Reynolds	Dr Thomas Leland	431
10,377 (C.S.10 II/of II)	J. Reynolds	Lady Gertrude Fitzpatrick	432
10,464 (C.S.5 I/of II; R.5 III/of IV)	R. Livesay	1st Earl of Charlemont	355
10,549 (C.S.1 I/of II)	T. Gainsborough	8th Earl of Abercorn	169
10,911 (C.S.16 II/of II)	J. Reynolds	Dr Thomas Leland	432
DEAN, T.A. (FL.1773-1840)			
ENGLISH SCHOOL			
10,894	G. Dawe	1st Earl of Limerick	102
10,895	G. Dawe	1st Earl of Limerick	102
11,283	T. Lawrence	Sir Henry Torrens	334

Engraver	Artist	Short title	Page
DECAMPS, ALEXANDRE GABRIEL (1803-1860) FRENCH SCHOOL			
20,332	A.G. Decamps	A Turkish Village	104
DE HOOGHE, ROMEYN (1645-1708) ANGLO-DUTCH SCHOOL			
11,655	R. De Hooghe	Battle of the Boyne	104
11,846	R. De Hooghe	Departure of William III from Holland	105
11,847(1-12)	R. De Hooghe	Flight of James II and accession of William III	105-106
11,849(1-5)	R. De Hooghe	Departure of William III from Holland	106
11,882	R. De Hooghe	Reception of Mary, Princess of Orange	107
DELAUNAY, ROBERT (1749-1814) FRENCH SCHOOL			
20,075	D. Teniers the Younger	Bagpipes Player	499
20,108	D. Teniers the Younger	Smoker in a Tavern	499
20,723(22)	Sebastiano del Piombo	Raising of Lazarus	471
DENMAN, MARIA (1776-1861) ENGLISH SCHOOL			
11,045 (COPYIST)	T.A. Hayley	George Romney	215
DERBY, WILLIAM (1786-1847) ENGLISH SCHOOL			
10,782 *(COPYIST)*	?M.J. Miereveld	1st Earl of Danby	373
DEVILLIERS, HYACINTHE ROSE (B.1808) FRENCH SCHOOL			
20,102	?H.R. Devilliers	Forge of Vulcan	108
DE WILDE, SAMUEL (1748-1832) ENGLISH SCHOOL *(signed with pseud. J.S. Paul)*			
10,059 (C.S.4;R.4 II/of II)	English School 17C	Sir William Parsons	125
10,325 (C.S.1)	T. Kettle	Ann Barry	313
11,096 (C.S.2)	T. Kettle	So-called Ann Barry	313
DICKINSON, LOWES (1819-1908) ENGLISH SCHOOL			
20,127-131	W. Howis the Elder	Sir James Dombrain	249
DICKINSON, WILLIAM (1746-1823) ENGLISH SCHOOL			
10,086 (C.S.60 I/of V; R.60 II/of VI)	J. Reynolds	Dr Thomas Percy	432
10,110 (C.S.64 I/of II)	G.C. Stuart	William Preston	487
10,346 (C.S.43 I/of III; R.43 I/of IV)	J. Reynolds	Duchess of Leinster	432
10,381 (C.S.74 II/of III)	J. Reynolds	Mrs Richard Brinsley Sheridan	432
10,407 (C.S.14 II/of III; R.14 III/of IV)	J. Reynolds	Viscountess Crosbie	433

Engraver	Artist	Short title	Page
10,454 (C.S.52)	R. Hunter	1st Baron Naas	256
10,462 (C.S.75)	N. Dance	1st Baron Shuldham	101
10,479 (C.S.45)	W. Madden	1st Baron Lifford	360
10,490 (C.S.72 II/of III)	J. Reynolds	4th Duke of Rutland	433
10,686 (C.S.91 II/of II)	R.E. Pine	James Worsdale	408
10,828 C.C.26 II/of III)	R.E. Pine	George II, King of England	408
10,853 C.S.27 II/of II;R.27 II/of III)	J. Reynolds	George III, King of England	433
11,2382 (C.S.54 II/of II)	N. Hone the Elder	Sir George Nares	238
11,028 (C.S.77 II/of III)	J. Reynolds	Lady Charles Spencer	433
DICKINSON AND CO. (19TH CENTURY) ENGLISH SCHOOL			
20,701	O.J. Jones	Queen Victoria in Cork	308
DICKSEE, JOHN ROBERT (1817-1905) ENGLISH SCHOOL			
20,111	J.R. Dicksee	Padre Alessandro Gavazzi	109
DICKSON, J. (FL.C.1660) ENGLISH SCHOOL			
10,305	Irish School 17C	Edward Parry	260
DIGHTON, RICHARD (1795-1880) ENGLISH SCHOOL			
10,908	R. Dighton	2nd Viscount Lake	110
DILLON, P. (FL.1802-1815) IRISH SCHOOL			
10,623	Irish School early 19C	Christopher Hely-Hutchinson	290
DIXON, JOHN (C.1740-1811) IRISH SCHOOL			
10,014 (C.S.Class III.122)	Irish School 18C	Thomas Parnell	265
10,158 (C.S.32)	R. Hunter	6th Viscount Taaffe	256
10,395 (C.S.26 II/of II; R.26 III/of IV)	J. Reynolds	Mary O'Brien	434
10,412 (C.S.19 I/of II)	J. Astley	16th Earl of Hertford	10
10,467 (C.S.22 II/of III)	J. Reynolds	2nd Duke of Leinster	434
DIXON, T. (FL.1824-1842) ENGLISH SCHOOL			
11,693	W.M. Craig	Dublin from Foster Aquaduct	92
DOO, GEORGE THOMAS (1800-1886) ENGLISH SCHOOL			
10,402	T. Lawrence	Lady Selina Meade	334

Engraver	Artist	Short title	Page
DORIGNY, NICOLAS (1652-1746) FRENCH SCHOOL			
20,678(15)	Raphael	Charge to St Peter	426
DORRELL, EDMUND (1778-1857) ENGLISH SCHOOL			
10,593	Irish School 1770s	Kane O'Hara	269
D'ORSAY, COUNT ALFRED GUILLAUME GABRIEL (?1798-1852) FRENCH SCHOOL			
10,757	A.G.G. D'Orsay	Sir Philip Crampton	111
10,859	A.G.G. D'Orsay	James Sheridan Knowles	112
11,066	A.G.G. D'Orsay	Tyrone Power	112
11,067	A.G.G. D'Orsay	6th Viscount Powerscourt	112
11,410	A.G.G. D'Orsay	Walter Savage Landor	112
DOYLE, C. (19TH CENTURY) IRISH SCHOOL			
11,087	Irish School c.1806	S. Barrett	291
DOYLE, JOHN ('HB') (1797-1868) IRISH SCHOOL			
10,035	J. Doyle	'The Catholic Triumvirate'	113
11,158	J. Doyle	Francis Grose	114
11,403	J. Doyle	'The Darranane Conjurer'	114
11,544(59-67)	J. Doyle	Political Sketches	115-116
11,852-11,854	J. Doyle	Daniel O'Connell	116-117
11,891	J. Doyle	Daniel O'Connell	117
DREVET, PIERRE (1663-1738) FRENCH SCHOOL			
11,379	?R. Walker	Oliver Cromwell	534
DRULIN, ANTOINE (1802-1869) FRENCH SCHOOL			
20,401	A. Drulin	Zachringen Suspension Bridge	117
DRUMMOND, WILLIAM (1800-1850) ENGLISH SCHOOL			
10,265	D. Maclise	Sir William Betham	359
DUBOSC, CLAUDE (FL.C.1711-1740) ANGLO-FRENCH SCHOOL			
11,494	Raphael	The Blinding of Elymas	426
DUBUFE, CLAUDE MARIE (1790-1864) FRENCH SCHOOL			
20,088	C.M. Dubufe	Melancholy	119
DUFLOS, CLAUDE (1662-1727) FRENCH SCHOOL			
20,671(3)	P. Perugino	Pieta	395
DUFRAINE, (19TH CENTURY) *FRENCH SCHOOL*			
20,201 *(COPYIST)*	N. Poussin	St John baptising	421

Engraver	Artist	Short title	Page
DUJARDIN, LOUIS (1808-1859)			
FRENCH SCHOOL			
20,618	N. Berchem	Rustic Occupation	27
DUMONT THE ELDER, JACQUES (1701-1781)			
11,656 *(COPYIST)*	G.P. Panini	Preparation for a Fête in Rome	390
DUNCAN, ANDREW (1795-AFTER 1845)			
ENGLISH SCHOOL			
20,057	H.J. Fradelle	Mary, Queen of Scots	163
DUNKARTON, ROBERT (1744-AFTER 1811)			
ENGLISH SCHOOL			
10,416 (C.S.27; R.27 II/of II)	R. Woodburn	Major-General Henry Johnson	546
10,432 (C.S.7 II/of II)	J.S. Copley	2nd Earl of Bessborough	86
10,484 (C.S.29 I/of II; R.29 II/of III)	J. Reynolds	1st Viscount Lifford	434
11,112	Irish School 17C	Michael Boyle	261
11,980	J.M.W. Turner	The Hindoo Worshipper	516
11,982	J.M.W. Turner	Hindhead Hill, Surrey	517
11,989	J.M.W. Turner	Young Anglers	518
11,994	J.M.W. Turner	The Watermill	519
20,003	J.M.W. Turner	Rispah	520
DUPECHEZ, CHARLES (FL.1908-AFTER 1931)			
10,889	C. Dupéchez	Timothy Healy	120
DUPLESSI-BERTAUX, JEAN (1747-1819)			
FRENCH SCHOOL			
11,008	French School late 18C & J. Duplessi-Bertaux	Comte de Lally-Tolendal	166
20,201	N. Poussin	St John baptising	421
DUPONCHEL, CHARLES EUGENE (B.1748)			
FRENCH SCHOOL			
20,687(46)	Raphael	Virgin and Child	426
DUPONT, GAINSBOROUGH (1754-1797)			
ENGLISH SCHOOL			
10,496 (C.S.3 II/of II)	T. Gainsborough	Henry Seymour Conway	169
DUPUIS, CHARLES (1685-1742)			
FRENCH SCHOOL			
11,845	A. Watteau	L'Occupation selon L'Age	536
DURAND, ASHER BROWN (1796-1886)			
AMERICAN SCHOOL			
11,297	S. Goodridge	Gilbert Charles Stuart	182
DURY, A. (18TH CENTURY)			
IRISH SCHOOL			
11,806	J. Rocque	Map of Dublin, 1757	458
DUTCH SCHOOL (C.1689)			
11,819	Dutch School 1689	'Siege of Londonderry'	120
20,835	Dutch School 1689	'Siege of Londonderry'	120

Engraver	Artist	Short title	Page
DUTCH SCHOOL (C.1690)			
11,274	Dutch School c.1690	Richard Talbot	121
11,865	Dutch School c.1690	James II, King of England	121
11,866	Dutch School c.1690	James II, King of England	121
DUTCH SCHOOL (C.1691)			
20,762	Dutch School 1691	Taking of Athlone	121
DUTCH SCOOL (18TH CENTURY)			
10,245	R. Walker	Oliver Cromwell	535
DUTERTRE, ANDRE (1753-1842)			
FRENCH SCHOOL			
20,679(18) *(COPYIST)*	Raphael	The Ecstasy of St Cecilia	426
DUVAL, LOUIS (FL. C.1800)			
FRENCH SCHOOL			
20,106	J. Drouais-Germain	Christ and the woman of Cana	117
EARLOM, RICHARD (1743-1822)			
ENGLISH SCHOOL			
10,171	Rembrandt	'Rembrandt's Mother'	429
10,430	W. Beechey	Henry D'Esterre Darby	25
(C.S.11 I/of II)			
10,431	H. Howard	7th Viscount Fitzwilliam	248
(C.S.13 I/of II)			
10,470	J. McArdell	Self-Portrait	358
(C.S.28 1/of 11; R.28 II/III)			
10,912	Irish School 18C	Rev. Thomas Lendrum	262
(C.S.27 I/of II)			
11,943 (COPYIST)	G.B. Castiglione	The Exposition of Cyrus	57
20,664(93)	Claude Lorrain	Ascanius shooting the stag	66
20,665(150)	Claude Lorrain	Mercury charming Argus	66
20,666(51)	Claude Lorrain	The Delivery of St Peter	67
20,719(149)	Claude Lorrain	Juno Committing Io to Argus	67
EASLING, J.C. (FL.1825-1833)			
ENGLISH SCHOOL			
11,958	J.M.W. Turner	Liber Studiorum frontispiece	513
11,990	J.M.W. Turner	St Catherine's Hill, Surrey	518
11,997	J.M.W. Turner	Fishermen	519
11,999	J.M.W. Turner	Near Winchelsea, Sussex	520
20,004	J.M.W. Turner	Hedging and Ditching	520
EDWARDS, J.C.(FL.1821-1835)			
ENGLISH SCHOOL			
20,154	L. Sharpe	Juliet	472
EDWARDS, WILLIAM CAMDEN (1777-1855)			
ENGLISH SCHOOL			
10,239	J. Reynolds	Self-Portrait	434
11,116	J. Barry	Self-Portrait	18
EDWARDS, WILLIAM J. (FL.1843-1864)			
ENGLISH SCHOOL			
11,127	G.F. Mulvany	William Dargan	378

Engraver	Artist	Short title	Page
EDY, JOHN WILLIAM (FL.1810-1820)			
ENGLISH SCHOOL			
20,838 (3)	T.S. Roberts	Waterford	450
20,838 (5)	T. S. Roberts	Carrick Castle	451
20,838 (6)	T. S. Roberts	Waterford harbour	451
20,838 (7)	T. S. Roberts	Blackrock Castle	451
EGLETON, WILLIAM HENRY (FL.1833-1862)			
ENGLISH SCHOOL			
10,866	J. Hayter	Viscountess Jocelyn	215
11,336	W. Drummond	Miss Marguerite A. Power	119
20,529	J.B. Jouvenet	The Miraculous Draught of Fishes	309
EINSLIE, S. (FL.1785-1808)			
ENGLISH SCHOOL			
10,387 (C.S.1 II/of II)	J. Hoppner	Countess of Aldborough	246
ENGLEHEART, TIMOTHY STANFIELD (1803-1879)			
ENGLISH SCHOOL			
10,628	W. Cuming	so-called Edward Hudson	95
11,873	J. Bateman	'Don't you wish you may get it'	23
ENGLISH SCHOOL (17TH CENTURY)			
10,574	Irish School 17C	Sir Phelim O'Neil	261
11,251	?P. Lely	Archbishop James Ussher	347
11,252	English School c.1650	Archbishop James Ussher	130
11,394 (C.S.Class I:38)	?R. Walker	Oliver Cromwell	534
11,395 (C.S.Class I:40)	English School 17C	Oliver Cromwell	125
11,820	English School 17C	London	125
11,879	G. Collins	Dublin Bay	69
ENGLISH SCHOOL (1689)			
20,728	English School c.1689	Richard Baxter	131
ENGLISH SCHOOL (18TH CENTURY)			
10,272	English School 18C	James Quin	132
10,606	English School 18C	Lord Louth	132
10,607	A.S. Belle	Charles Leslie	26
10,659	English School 18C	Hon. Montagu Mathew	132
10,873	English School 18C	So-called Florence Hensey	132
11,183	F.X. Vispré	Samuel Derrick	533
11,244	G. Kneller	1st Marquess of Wharton	315
20,120	A. da Bonaiuto	Giovanni Cimabue	32
20,135	N. Berchem	Landscape with Shepherds	27
20,523	B. Langley	Architectural Frontispiece	330
20,537	English School 18C	River Tiber	133
20,538	English School 18C	Piazza S. Marco, Venice	133
20,547	N. Berchem	Two Sheep	27
20,548	N. Berchem	Milkmaid	27
20,551	S. Rosa	Figurines - Two Warriors	462
20,803	English School 18C	Naval Battle	133

Engraver	Artist	Short title	Page
ENGLISH SCHOOL (EARLY 18TH CENTURY)			
10,568 (R.Class II:76A)	?M. Dahl	2nd Duke of Ormonde	98
ENGLISH SCHOOL (1749)			
11,614	J. Tudor	Fireworks Display	509
11,712	J. Tudor	Fireworks Display	509
ENGLISH SCHOOL (1750)			
10,005	Irish School c.1750	Royal Hospital, Kilmainham	266
ENGLISH SCHOOL (c.1750)			
11,557-11,562	W. Hogarth	Marriage à la Mode	227
ENGLISH SCHOOL (1751)			
11,747	Irish School c.1750	Leixlip Castle, Co. Kildare	266
ENGLISH SCHOOL (1760s)			
10,577 (C.S.Class III)	J. Reynolds	Nelly O'Brien	434
ENGLISH SCHOOL (1762)			
11,880	J. Rocque	Map of County Dublin, 1762	458
ENGLISH SCHOOL (C.1770)			
11,140 (C.S.Class III)	J. Reynolds	Lady Charlotte FitzWilliam	435
ENGLISH SCHOOL (1774)			
11,717	J. Tudor	Dublin and Islandbridge	509
ENGLISH SCHOOL (1776)			
11,080	J. Latham	Bishop George Berkeley	331
ENGLISH SCHOOL (1782)			
11,147	Irish School 1782	Henry Grattan	271
ENGLISH SCHOOL (1784)			
11,186	W. Hogarth	1st Earl of Charlemont	228
11,187	W. Hogarth	1st Earl of Charlemont	229
11,626	Irish School 1784	Dublin Volunteers on College Green	272
11,895	Irish School 1784	Dublin Castle gateway	272
11,896	Irish School 1784	The Royal Exchange, Dublin	272
11,897	Irish School 1784	The Lying-in Hospital, Dublin	272
11,898	Irish School 1784	Trinity College, Dublin	273
11,899	Irish School 1784	Essex Bridge, Dublin	273
11,900	Irish School 1784	College Green, Dublin	273
11,901	Irish School 1784	Dublin and Islandbridge	273
ENGLISH SCHOOL (1785)			
11,706	Irish School c.1785	Simpson's Hospital, Dublin	273
11,836	English School c.1785	Magazine Illustrations	137
11,915	Irish School c.1785	St John's Church, Dublin	273

Engraver	Artist	Short title	Page
ENGLISH SCHOOL (1786)			
10,514	English School c.1786	Sir Charles Asgill	137
10,517	English School c,1786	Richard Kempenfelt	137
10,518	English School c.1786	Sir Edward Hughes	137
11,668	Irish School c.1786	Dublin Buildings	274
11,742	Irish School c.1786	St Nicholas Within Church	274
11,916	Irish School c.1786	St Nicholas Within Church	274
11,920	Irish School c.1786	St Anne's Church, Dublin	274
ENGLISH SCHOOL (1787)			
11,730	Irish School c.1787	Parliament House, Dublin	275
11,731	Irish School 1787	Parliament House, Dublin	275
11,837	Irish School c.1787	Clontarf Castle, Co. Dublin	275
11,913	Irish School c.1787	Post Office, College Green	276
11,918	Irish School c.1787	Royal Charter School, Clontarf	276
ENGLISH SCHOOL (1788)			
11,743	Irish School c.1788	Dunsink Observatory	276
11,744	Irish School c.1788	Dunsink Observatory	276
11,917	Irish School c.1788	Castle Street, Dublin	276
11,921	Irish School c.1788	The Four Courts, Dublin	276
ENGLISH SCHOOL (1789)			
11,756	Irish School 1788	Howth and Ireland's Eye	276
11,925	Irish School c.1789	Smock Alley Theatre, Dublin	277
ENGLISH SCHOOL (C.1790)			
11,319	Mrs O'Neill	Duchess of Rutland	387
ENGLISH SCHOOL (1790)			
11,322	H. Hone	4th Duke of Rutland	234
11,727	Irish School c.1790	Royal Military Infirmary, Dublin	277
11,832	Irish School c.1790	Dublin Architecture	277
11,923	Irish School c.1790	Daly's Club House, Dublin	277
ENGLISH SCHOOL (1790s)			
10,652	English School 1790s	John Toler	138
ENGLISH SCHOOL (1792)			
11,177	Irish School c.1792	John Hely-Hutchinson	279
11,720	Irish School 1792	Custom House, Dublin	278
11,721	Irish School 1792	Custom House, Dublin	278
11,728	Irish School 1792	Parliament House, Dublin	278
11,914	Irish School 1792	Parliament House, Dublin	279
ENGLISH SCHOOL (1791/94)			
10,609	T.R. Poole	Edmund Burke	418
ENGLISH SCHOOL (1794)			
11,003	Irish School 17C	John Yonge	261
ENGLISH SCHOOL (1795)			
10,872	English School 1795	Richard Head	125
11,206	Continental School	Thomas Carve	79
20,089	J. Ward	Dog attacking a rat	536
ENGLISH SCHOOL (1798)			
11,679	Irish School c.1798	Drogheda, Co. Louth	281

Engraver	Artist	Short title	Page
ENGLISH SCHOOL (1799)			
11,813	J. Rocque	Map of Co. Dublin, 1799	458
11,839	Irish School late 18C	Dargle Glen, Co. Wicklow	283
ENGLISH SCHOOL (LATE 18TH CENTURY)			
10,664	J. Reynolds	Edmund Malone	435
11,114	English School late 18C	Bruce	138
11,239	English School 1602	Sir Walter Raleigh	130
11,256	N. Hone the Elder	Rev. Whitefield	238
11,739	Irish School late 18C	Sarah Bridge	282
ENGLISH SCHOOL (C.1800)			
10,874	English School c.1800	Sir Anthony Hart	144
11,210	M. Gheeraerts the Younger	1st Earl of Totnes	174
ENGLISH SCHOOL (19TH CENTURY)			
10,634	English School 19C	John Gale Jones	138
10,880	T.A. Jones	Robert Hunter	308
10,884	English School 19C	Mrs Samuel Carter Hall	138
11,001	W.F.P. Napier	General Sir James Napier	380
11,080	Irish School c.1820	John Banim	295
11,407	English School 19C	Robert Emmet	138
11,499	?English School 19C	Elisha and Elijah	139
11,508	A. Buck	The Edgeworth Family	44
20,039	English School 19C	Elizabeth, Queen of Edward IV	139
20,144	English School 19C	Ladies in Turkish Dress	139
20,146	N. Berchem	Peasants with Cattle and Sheep	27
20,159	G. Dou	Old Couple reading the Bible	112
20,160	D. Teniers the Younger	Flemish Ale House	499
20,163	English School 19C	Resting Cow	139
20,197	English School 19C	Catalogue title page	139
20,220	English School 19C	Cow	139
20,227	J. Wijnants	Edge of the Forest	541
20,268	A. Carracci	Two figures at a shrine	55
20,320	English School 19C	'The Gypsies' Retreat'	139
20,321	English School 19C	'Rustic Conversation'	140
20,346	English School 19C	Trees from Carracci and Titian	140
20,349	English School 19C	Harbour and Fishing Boats	140
20,363	English School 19C	Figures	140
20,364	English School 19C	Valley	140
20,416	English School 19C	Harbour	140
20,501	G.A.Williams	Figures	541
20,515	English School 19C	Claverton Churchyard, Somerset	141
20,516	English School 19C	Southampton, Hampshire	141
20,553	Style of Claude Lorrain	Cattle	67
20,557	Roman Antique	Reclining Faun	459
20,568	English School 19C	Wooden Bridge	141
20,574	English School 19C	Osteria	141
20,584	English School 19C	Cabinet work	141
20,585	English School 19C	Cabinet work	141
20,586	English School 19C	Iron work	141
20,587	English School 19C	Iron work	142
20,608	English School 19C	Windsor Castle, Berkshire	142
20,614	English School 19C	Types of Clouds	142
20,616	W.H. B....	Richmond Park, London	11
20,617	English School 19C	'The Gipsy Child'	142
20,620	R. L....	Peter John Locke King	328

Engraver	Artist	Short title	Page
20,634	P.P. Rubens	The Château de Steen	467
20,636	W. Kalf	Interior of a Kitchen	311
20,643	?Dutch School 18C	Scene outside an Inn	121
20,646	English School 19C	Figure Ecorché	142
20,651	English School 19C	Two Hounds Running	142
ENGLISH SCHOOL (EARLY 19TH CENTURY)			
11,425	English Early 19C	Figures with Offerings	144
11,426	English Early 19C	Abundance and Cupid	144
20,539	?Parmigianino	Figure studies	390
20,654	?Antique Roman	Pegasus and Aurora	459
20,826	?English Early 19C	Diana Preparing for the Chase	144
ENGLISH SCHOOL (1801)			
11,830	F. Wheatley	Irish House of Commons	539
ENGLISH SCHOOL (1803)			
10,750	Circle of M. Gheeraerts the Younger	1st Earl of Cork	175
ENGLISH SCHOOL (1804)			
10,278	English School 1653	Bishop John Richardson	131
11,337	?G. Morphey	Archbishop Oliver Plunkett	375
ENGLISH SCHOOL (1806)			
11,050	S. Cooper	Baron Robartes	84
ENGLISH SCHOOL (1807)			
11,209	A. Pope	William Cook	419
ENGLISH SCHOOL (1808)			
11,544(8)	G.M. Woodward	Politeness	547
ENGLISH SCHOOL (1809)			
20,653	Hellenistic School 1C	The Laocoon	221
ENGLISH SCHOOL (1810)			
10,610	English School 17C	Miles Corbet	126
ENGLISH SCHOOL (1811)			
11,330	J. Reynolds	Thomas Percy	435
ENGLISH SCHOOL (1814)			
20,115	A. Van Dyck	Sir Thomas Morgan	528
ENGLISH SCHOOL (1815)			
10,733	English School 17C	Elizabeth de Clare	126
11,353	English School c.1815	Napoleon I, Emperor of France	145
11,357	English School c.1815	Francis I, Emperor of Austria	145
11,358	English School c.1815	Count Platov	145
11,359	English School c.1815	2nd Earl of Uxbridge	145
11,362	English School c.1815	1st Duke of Wellington	145
11,363	English School c.1815	King of Prussia	146
11,364	English School c.1815	Duke of Brunswick	146
11,365	English School c.1815	Jean Victor Moreau	146
11,366	English School c.1815	Field-Marshal Blücher	146
11,367	English School c.1815	Alexander I, Emperor of Russia	146
11,368	English School c.1815	Prince Schwarzenberg	146
11,369	English School c.1815	Sir Thomas Picton	147

Engraver	Artist	Short title	Page
ENGLISH SCHOOL (1816)			
11,231	Irish School c.1800	Francis Moynan	284
11,354	English School c.1815	1st Viscount Hill	147
11,355	English School c.1815	Frederick William Von Bülow	147
11,356	English School c.1815	Prince William of Orange	147
11,360	English School c.1815	Battle of Waterloo	147
11,361	English School c.1815	George III, King of England	148
11,714	Irish School c.1816	Dublin Bay	294
ENGLISH SCHOOL (C.1816)			
10,618	English School 17C	Colonel John Hewson	126
ENGLISH SCHOOL (1817)			
11,741	Irish School c.1817	St George's Church, Dublin	294
11,762	Irish School c.1817	St Patrick's Cathedral, Dublin	294
11,764	J. Malton	St Patrick's Cathedral, Dublin	362
11,814	Irish School c.1817	Map of Dublin Bay	294
11,831	Irish School c.1817	Foundling Hospital, Dublin	295
ENGLISH SCHOOL (1819)			
10,098	English School c.1819	Michael Nolan	148
ENGLISH SCHOOL (1820)			
11,133	H.F. Gravelot	Owen Farrell	184
ENGLISH SCHOOL (1821)			
11,773	G. Petrie	Dublin Castle Chapel	398
11,780	G. Petrie	Lying-in Hospital, Dublin	398
11,781	G. Petrie	The Royal Exchange, Dublin	398
11,783	G. Petrie	The Four Courts, Dublin	399
11,784	G. Petrie	The King's Inns, Dublin	399
11,789	G. Petrie	Dublin from the North	399
ENGLISH SCHOOL (1822)			
11,596	Sir T. Hammond	George IV, King of England	199
11,698	Sir T. Hammond	George IV, King of England	199
ENGLISH SCHOOL (1823)			
10,600	Irish School c.1823	Daniel O'Connell	295
ENGLISH SCHOOL (1824)			
11,303	English School 18C	Mrs Frances Sheridan	133
ENGLISH SCHOOL (1826)			
20,733(39)	M. Schongauer	Virgin and Child	470
ENGLISH SCHOOL (1827)			
20,205	H. Fragonard	Annette aged fifteen	163
20,241	G. Morland	View in Leicestershire	375
20,242	Claude Lorrain	Cephalus and Procris	67
20,427	Claude Lorrain	Pastoral landscape	67
20,708(19)	Rembrandt	Rest on the flight into Egypt	429
ENGLISH SCHOOL (1828)			
11,401	English School 1828	'The Humble Candidate'	148
ENGLISH SCHOOL (1829)			
20,596	English School 1829	Kenilworth Castle, Warwickshire	148
20,597	English School 1829	Kenilworth Castle, Warwickshire	148
20,598	English School 1829	Kenilworth Castle, Warwickshire	148

Engraver	Artist	Short title	Page
ENGLISH SCHOOL (1830)			
10,703	English School c.1830	William IV, King of England	148
20,604	English School c.1830	Triumphal Arch	149
ENGLISH SCHOOL (1835)			
20,325	English School c.1835	Cottage at Ringwood, Hampshire	149
ENGLISH SCHOOL (C.1839)			
11,065	E. Landseer	Margaret Powell	329
ENGLISH SCHOOL (1840)			
11,040	English School 1840	Dr William Stokes	150
20,543	English School c.1840	Clumber, Nottinghamshire	150
20,650	English School c.1840	The Home of Peter Locke King	150
ENGLISH SCHOOL (1843)			
10,649	J. Petrie	James Napper Tandy	402
ENGLISH SCHOOL (1846)			
10,582	A.F.J. Claudet	James O'Brien	68
11,164	J. Petrie	Robert Emmet	402
11,165	J. Petrie	Robert Emmet	402
11,166	J. Petrie	Robert Emmet	402
11,182	J. Petrie	Michael Dwyer	403
11,298	C.S. Tone	William Samson	508
11,299	C.S. Tone	William Samson	508
11,300	C.S. Tone	William Samson	508
ENGLISH SCHOOL (C.1850)			
11,382	English School c. 1850	Victoria, Queen of England	150
ENGLISH SCHOOL (1859)			
20,629	J.H. Mulcahy	Riot at Limerick elections	377
ENGLISH SCHOOL (C.1860)			
10,608	English School c.1860	Samuel Lover	151
10,988	English School c.1860	Edward, Prince of Wales	151
ENGLISH SCHOOL (1861)			
20,570	P. Levin	Interior of a Kursaal	352
ENGLISH SCHOOL (1862)			
20,571	English School 1862	Prince of Wales in Egypt	151
ENGLISH SCHOOL (1864)			
11,595	English School 1864	Opening of NGI	151
ENGLISH SCHOOL (1865)			
20,573	M. Jackson	The American Civil War	303
ENGLISH SCHOOL (1867)			
20,627	English School (c.1867)	The Sick Boy	151
20,632	K. Piloty	The Nurse	408
20,633	F. Geefs	The Young Mother	171
ENGLISH SCHOOL (1869)			
20,576	English School c.1869	St Mungo's Well, Scotland	151

Engraver	Artist	Short title	Page
ENGLISH SCHOOL (1880)			
20,578	L. Fildes	Illustration	156
ENGLISH SCHOOL (C.1889)			
20,621	English School c.1889	Mother and child	152
ENGLISH SCHOOL (LATE 19TH CENTURY)			
20,645	English School late 19C	Hand studies	152
ENGLISH SCHOOL (20TH CENTURY)			
11,471	English School 20C	House and grounds	152
11,472	English School 20C	House and grounds	152
ERTINGER, FRANZ (1640-1710)			
FRENCH SCHOOL			
20,545	N. Poussin	The Andrians	421
ESDALL, WILLIAM (FL.1766-1795)			
IRISH SCHOOL			
11,149	Irish School 18C	David Garrick	262
EVANS, T. (18TH CENTURY)			
ENGLISH SCHOOL			
20,093	T. Lawrence	4th Earl of Orford	335
EVANS, WILLIAM (FL.1797-1856)			
ENGLISH SCHOOL			
10,622	G.C. Stuart	Bishop Hugh Hamilton	487
10,801 *(COPYIST)*	T. Phillips	2nd Earl of Donoughmore	406
10,739 *(COPYIST)*	C.G. Stuart	Isaac Barré	488
11,085	R. Home	Hugh Boyd	233
FABER THE YOUNGER, JOHN (C.1684-1756)			
ENGLISH SCHOOL			
10,017 (C.S.272)	J. Faber the Younger	5th Earl of Orrery	153
10,027 (C.S.125)	J.M. Rysbrack	Hon. Robert Boyle	468
10,029 (C.S. 189 II/of II)	I. Woods	Archbishop John Hoadly	547
10,031 (C.S.392 II/of II)	H. Pickering	Margaret Woffington	407
10,096 (C.S.201; R.201 I/of II)	A. Van Dyck	James I, King of England	528
10,111 (C.S.301)	T. Hudson	James Quin	254
10,120 (C.S.231 Pre-I/of III)	J.B. Van Loo	Owen Macswinny	530
10,125 (C.S.193 II/of II)	M. Dahl	Hugh Howard	99
10,131 (C.S.154 I/of II)	D. Stevens	George I, King of England	483
10,160 (C.S.328 II/of II)	G. Kneller	Sir Hans Sloane	315
10,173 (C.S.113 post-III)	J. Highmore	Abraham de Moivre	224
10,176 (C.S.114 I/of III; R.114 II/of IV)	J. Reynolds	3rd Duke of Devonshire	435

Engraver	Artist	Short title	Page
10,193 (C.S.181)	J. Fayram	1st Earl of Harrington	153
10,219 (C.S.383 II/of II)	J. Ellys	Robert Wilks	123
10,240 (C.S.90 I/of III)	J. Latham	Sir Samuel Cooke	331
10,269 (C.S.302)	J. Parmentier	Sir James Reynolds	390
10,362 (C.S.38; R.38 II/of II)	Countess of Burlington	Lady Dorothy Boyle	46
10,393 (C.S.174 I/ofII)	G. Hamilton	Duchess of Hamilton & Brandon	193
10,403 (C.S.123 II/of II)	M. Gheeraerts the Younger	so-called Elizabeth I, Queen of England	174
10,420 (C.S.387 II/of II)	J. Wyck	William III, King of England	549
10,548 (C.S.63 I/of II)	J. Vanderbank	Caroline of Brandenburg-Ansbach	525
10,676 (C.S.208[between 41/42])	G. Kneller	Edward Hopkins	315
10,709 (C.S.35 I/of II; R.35 II/of III)	T. Hudson	General William Blakeney	255
10,721 (C.S.208[27])	G. Kneller	2nd Viscount Shannon	315
10,826 (C.S.155 I/ofII; R.155 I/of III)	G. Kneller	George, Prince of Wales	315
10,834 (C.S.174 II/of II; R.174 III/of III)	G. Hamilton	Duchess of Hamilton & Brandon	193
10,843 (C.S.137)	T. Hudson	Major Foubert	255
10,845 (C.S.208[4])	G. Kneller	2nd Duke of Grafton	316
10,867 (C.S.203 I/of II)	G. Kneller	Admiral Sir John Jennings	316
11,041 (C.S.208[31])	G. Kneller	Sir Richard Steele	316
11,121 (COPYIST)	P. Van Bleeck	Kitty Clive	521
20,244	?A. Van Dyck	An Apostle	529
FACIUS (C.1750-AFTER 1802) ANGLO-GERMAN SCHOOL			
20,665(1)	G.C. Stuart	John Boydell	488
FADEN, WILLIAM (FL.1776-?1845) ENGLISH SCHOOL			
11,887	W. Faden	Map of Dublin, 1797	153
FAIRLAND, THOMAS (1804-1852) ENGLISH SCHOOL			
20,352	T. Fairland	Meeting of the Waters	153
20,798	?L.F.Marshall	Cottage Charity	368
FAITHORNE THE ELDER, WILLIAM (1616-1691) ENGLISH SCHOOL			
10,771	English School 17C	2nd Baron Coleraine	126
10,832	?W. Faithorne	Valentine Greatrakes	153
11,253	?P.Lely	Archbishop James Ussher	347
11,275	English School 17C	Bishop Jeremy Taylor	126

Engraver	Artist	Short title	Page
FAITHORNE THE YOUNGER, WILLIAM (1656-c.1710) ENGLISH SCHOOL			
10,385 (C.S.24)	J. Vandervaart	Mary II, Queen of England	526
11,025 (C.S.34)	P. Mignard	1st Duke of Schomberg	373
FARN, J. (18TH CENTURY) ENGLISH SCHOOL			
11,190	G.C. Stuart	William Burton Conyngham	488
11,191	G.C. Stuart	William Burton Conyngham	488
FARRINGTON, GEORGE (1752-1788) ENGLISH SCHOOL			
10,235 *(COPYIST)*	A. Van Dyck	Sir Rowland Wandesford	530
10,563 *(COPYIST)*	A. Van Dyck	Sir Rowland Wandesford	530
FEROGIO, FRANCOIS FORTUNE ANTOINE (?1805-1888) FRENCH SCHOOL			
20,147	F.F.A. Ferogio	Figures in landscapes	154
20,148	F.F.A. Ferogio	The Siring	154
20,308	F.F.A. Ferogio	Dead wood	154
20,309	F.F.A. Ferogio	The Clearing	154
20,310	F.F.A. Ferogio	Landscapes with figures	155
20,311	F.F.A. Ferogio	Figures resting by a stream	155
20,312	F.F.A. Ferogio	Couple on a mountain path	156
20,313	F.F.A. Ferogio	Boy and donkey on a path	156
20,314	F.F.A. Ferogio	Woodcutter resting	156
20,341	A. Calame & F.F.A. Ferogio	Weeping Willows	53
20,462	A. Calame & F.F.A. Ferogio	Chesnut trees	53
20,488	A. Calame & F.F.A. Ferogio	Carob tree	53
FERRERO, GIOVANNI FRANCESCO (19TH CENTURY) ROMAN SCHOOL			
20,757(138)	N. Poussin	The Entombment	421
FIELDING, NEWTON (1799-1856) ENGLISH SCHOOL			
20,351	G. Petrie	The Twelve Pins, Connemara	399
FILLOEUL, PIERRE (1690-1762) FRENCH SCHOOL			
20,689(25)	P. Wouverman	Travellers at an Inn	548
FINDEN, EDWARD FRANCIS (1791-1837) ENGLISH SCHOOL			
10,847	A. Robertson	Lady Louisa Grace Fortescue	453
20,272	D. Roberts	Caerlaverock Castle, Scotland	449
20,360	A. Nasmyth	The Tolbooth, Edinburgh	380
20,383	W. Collins	'Happy as a King'	70
20,478	G.F. Robson	Loch Ard, Scotland	457
20,481	G.F. Robson	Durham Castle	457
20,520	P. De Wint	Skiddaw, Cumbria	109
20,591	A.V.D. Copley-Fielding	Goodrich Castle, Herefordshire	86

Engraver	Artist	Short title	Page
FINDEN, WILLIAM (C.1787-1852) ENGLISH SCHOOL			
10,727	J. Hayter	Harriet Charlotte Beaujolais	216
10,769	C.I. Baseley	Lady Alicia Conroy	23
10,943	E. Hawkins	Lady Flora Elizabeth Hastings	213
20,329	E. Landseer	Highlander's Cottage	329
20,367	J. Henderson	Lancaster	221
FINLAYSON, JOHN (C.1730-C.1776) ENGLISH SCHOOL			
10,353 (C.S.11 II/of II))	N. Hone the Elder	Eleanor or Mary Metcalfe	238
10,391 (C.S.4)	C. Read	Countess of Coventry	428
10,394 (C.S.1 I/of III)	C. Read	Duchess of Hamilton & Brandon	428
10,933 (C.S.11 II/of II)	N. Hone the Elder	Eleanor or Mary Metcalfe	238
11,386 (C.S.20 II/of II)	N. Hone the Elder	Anna Zamparini	239
FISHER, EDWARD (1722-C.1785) IRISH SCHOOL			
10,070 (C.S.30 I/of II)	N. Hone the Elder	Self-Portrait	239
10,194 (C.S.25)	R. Hunter	1st Earl Harcourt	257
10,357 (C.S.18a)	J. Reynolds	Catherine Maria Fisher	435
10,363 (C.S.58 II/of V)	J. Reynolds	Mrs Cyrus Trapaud	436
10,545 (C.S.56 I/of IV; R.56 II/of V)	J. Reynolds	Lawrence Sterne	436
10,698 (C.S.30 I/of II)	N. Hone the Elder	Self-Portrait	239
10,850 (C.S.21 I/of III)	B. West	George III, King of England	537
FISHER, JONATHAN (FL.1763-1809) IRISH SCHOOL			
11,549	J. Fisher	Secretary of State's House	156
11,628	J. Fisher	Dublin Harbour	156
11,639	J. Fisher	Dublin and Islandbridge	156
11,719	J. Fisher	Dublin and Islandbridge	156
FITTLER, JAMES (1758-1835) ENGLISH SCHOOL			
10,473	J. Northcote	Captain John MacBride	383
10,897	H.D. Hamilton	David La Touche	196
FITZGERALD, REV. WILLIAM (19TH CENTURY) IRISH SCHOOL			
20,771	Rev. W. Fitzgerald	Beggar playing a trumpet	157
20,772	Rev. W. Fitzgerald	A Cavalier	157
20,773	Rev. W. Fitzgerald	A Fisherman	157
20,774	Rev. W. Fitzgerald	Winged figure fishing	157
20,775	Rev. W. Fitzgerald	Winged figure with rod	157
20,776	Rev. W. Fitzgerald	Man's head	158

Engraver	Artist	Short title	Page
20,777	Rev. W. Fitzgerald	Inundation	158
20,778	Rev. W. Fitzgerald	Success	158
20,779	Rev. W. Fitzgerald	Pantomime figures	158
20,780	Rev. W. Fitzgerald	A drunken fisherman	158
20,781	Rev. W. Fitzgerald	Angel of death	159
20,782	Rev. W. Fitzgerald	Angel and a figure	159
20,783	Rev. W. Fitzgerald	Faces	159
20,784	Rev. W. Fitzgerald	Fairies on a mare's back	159
20,785	Rev. W. Fitzgerald	A tramp	159
20,786	Rev. W. Fitzgerald	A wreck on the beach	159
20,787	Rev. W. Fitzgerald	Dancing nymphs	160
20,788	Rev. W. Fitzgerald	Artist and fairies	160
FITZPATRICK, THOMAS (1860-1912)			
IRISH SCHOOL			
11,059	T. Fitzpatrick	David Robert Plunket	160
FLOYD, WILLIAM (FL.1832-1859)			
ENGLISH SCHOOL			
20,281	W.L. Leitch	Thurnberg Castle, Germany	344
20,493	P. De Wint	Goodrich Castle, Herefordshire	109
FOGGO, GEORGE (1793-1869)			
ENGLISH SCHOOL			
10,857	W. Foy	Rev. James Knox	163
FORD, JAMES (FL.1772-1812)			
IRISH SCHOOL			
10,274	M.A. Shee	Thomas Ryder	473
11,624	J. Ford	Grand Canal Hotel, Portobello	161
11,625	J. Ford	The New Stamp Office, Dublin	161
11,694	?J. Ford	Dublin from Phoenix Park	161
11,893	J. Brownrigg	Map of Grand Canal, 1788	43
FORD, MICHAEL (FL.1742-1765)			
IRISH SCHOOL			
10,157 (C.S.8 II/of II)	B. Du Pan	1st Earl of Harrington	119
10,206 (C.S.1 II/of II)	T. Ottway	4th Earl of Barrymore	389
10,500 (COPYIST)	R. Walker	Oliver Cromwell	535
10,504 (C.S.12)	G. Kneller	William III, King of England	316
FORREST, WILLIAM (1805-1889)			
SCOTTISH SCHOOL			
20,461	D.O. Hill	Auld Brig of Doon bridge	224
FOSSEYEUX, JEAN-BAPTISTE (1752-1824)			
FRENCH SCHOOL			
20,158	C.W.E. Dietrich	The Dutch Violinist	110
FOURDRINIER, PIERRE (D.1758)			
ANGLO-FRENCH SCHOOL			
10,019	C. Jervas	William Conolly	304
10,169	C. Jervas	Dean Jonathan Swift	305

Engraver	Artist	Short title	Page
FOX, CHARLES (1794-1849)			
ENGLISH SCHOOL			
20,153	W. Evans	The Fisherman's Hut	152
FRAGONARD, ALEXANDRE EVARISTE (1780-1850)			
FRENCH SCHOOL			
20,685(14)*(COPYIST)*	N. Poussin	Rape of the Sabine women	421
FRANCHINI, UMBERTO (20TH CENTURY)			
ITALIAN SCHOOL			
11,929	U. Franchini	Figures (1)	163
20,823	U. Franchini	Figures (2)	164
20,824	U. Franchini	Figures (3)	164
20,825	U. Franchini	Figures (4)	164
FREEBAIRN, ALFRED ROBERT (1794-1846)			
SCOTTISH SCHOOL			
20,371	D. Roberts	St Vulfran's Church, Abbeville	449
20,542	G. Barret the Younger	Classical Landscape	13
FREEMAN, SAMUEL (1773-1857)			
ENGLISH SCHOOL			
10,151	Irish School 1806/14	John Philpot Curran	291
10,639	G.F. Joseph	1st Viscount Kilwarden	309
10,645	G.F. Mulvany	Sir Robert Kane	378
10,770	Irish School 1806/14	John Philpot Curran	292
11,009	Titani	2nd Marquess of Thomond	504
11,010	Titani	2nd Marquess of Thomond	504
11,199	T. Lawrence	John Philpot Curran	335
11,255	?P. Lely	Archbishop James Ussher	347
FRENCH SCHOOL (17TH CENTURY)			
20,117	French School 17C	Count Anthony Hamilton	164
20,230	J. Thierry	The Triumph of Amphitrite	500
FRENCH SCHOOL (C.1600)			
10,311	I. Oliver	Elizabeth I, Queen of England	386
FRENCH SCHOOL (1634)			
20,235	French School 1634	Louis XIII, King of France	165
FRENCH SCHOOL (18TH CENTURY)			
11,505	P.P. Rubens	Peter finding the Tribute Money	467
20,359	French School 18C	Archbishop François de Salignac	165
20,544	G.P. Panini	Roman Capriccio	390
FRENCH SCHOOL (1799)			
10,877	French School c.1799	General Lazare Hoche	166
FRENCH SCHOOL (19TH CENTURY)			
?10,273	L. Carrogis	Laurence Sterne	56
10,976	Doussin-Dubreuil	Daniel O'Connell	113
20,179	L. Rossi	Plan of Roman style villa	463
20,180	L. Rossi	Chinese style interior	463
20,466	E. Sabatier	Factory, Nérac, France	469
20,556	French School 19C	Studies of Ears	166
20,558	French School 19C	Head of a Woman	167

Engraver	Artist	Short title	Page
FRENCH SCHOOL (1868)			
20,087	Heigeleg	Emilie	220
FRENCH SCHOOL (20TH CENTURY)			
11,565	K. Van Dongen	Poster	527
FRIEDEL, A. (19TH CENTURY)			
ENGLISH SCHOOL			
20,077	C. Schwartz	The Crowning with thorns	470
FRY, WILLIAM THOMAS (1789-1831)			
ENGLISH SCHOOL			
10,260	J. Jackson	Martin Archer Shee	302
10,739	G.C. Stuart	Isaac Barré	488
10,950	J. Keenan	James Macartney	312
FRYE, THOMAS (1710-1762)			
IRISH SCHOOL			
10,298	T. Frye	Self-Portrait	167
(C.S.7 II/of II; R.7 III/of III)			
10,465	T. Frye	Self-Portrait	167
(C.S.6; R.6 II/of II)			
10,550	T. Frye	Frederick, Prince of Wales	167
(C.S.5)			
10,551	T. Frye	Queen Charlotte Sophia	168
(C.S.2)			
10,552	T. Frye	Self-Portrait	168
(C.S.6; R.6 II/of II)			
FUSSELL, JOSEPH (1818-1912)	F.R. Lee	River Scene, N. Wales	342
ENGLISH SCHOOL			
G...., A. (18TH CENTURY)			
?ENGLISH SCHOOL			
20,335	?S. Rosa	Tree and Carriage	462
GAINER, J. (FL.1772-1779)			
IRISH SCHOOL			
10,108	G. Gaven	John Ponsonby	171
(C.S.1 II/of II)			
GALLE THE ELDER, CORNELIS (1576-1650)			
FLEMISH SCHOOL			
11,491	A. Van Dyck	Frederick de Marsalaer	529
GARDINER, WILLIAM NELSON (1766-1814)			
IRISH SCHOOL			
10,614	Continental School 17C	Count Anthony Hamilton	79
GAUCI, MAXIM (1775-1854)			
ENGLISH SCHOOL			
10,621	J. Holmes	3rd Baron Sandys	233
10,882	J. Moore	William Holmes	374
GAUGAIN, THOMAS (1748-C.1805)			
ANGLO-FRENCH SCHOOL			
20,033	E. Dayes	Reapers	103

Engraver	Artist	Short title	Page
GEISSLER, JOHANN MARTIN FRIEDRICH (1778-1853)			
GERMAN SCHOOL			
20,105	Dutch School 17C	Accident at milking time	120
GELLER, WILLIAM OVEREND (FL.1834-1857)			
ENGLISH SCHOOL			
10,451	S. West	Rev. Theobald Mathew	538
20,056	H.P. Parker	Man with a pistol	390
GERMAN SCHOOL (C.1725)			
20,670(61)	J.B. Fischer Von Erlach	St Charles Borromeo Church, Vienna	156
GERMAN SCHOOL (19TH CENTURY)			
11,834	German School 19C	Royal College of Surgeons	173
GETHIN, PERCY FRANCIS (1875-1916)			
ENGLISH SCHOOL			
11,428	P.F. Gethin	Musicians	173
11,429	P.F. Gethin	James E. Hawkins	173
11,480	P.F. Gethin	Peat bog	174
11,619	P.F. Gethin	Travelling Circus, Co. Clare	174
11,869	P.F. Gethin	A South German Farm	174
GIBBON, BENJAMIN PHILLIPS (1802-1851)			
ENGLISH SCHOOL			
20,362	R. Hills & G.F. Robson	Deer in Scotland	225
GIBBS (19TH CENTURY)			
ENGLISH SCHOOL			
20,121	G.S. Newton	The Thinker	382
GILLER, WILLIAM (C.1805-1858)			
ENGLISH SCHOOL			
10,154	T. Lawrence	3rd Earl of Hardwicke	335
GILLRAY, JAMES (1757-1815)			
ENGLISH SCHOOL			
10,939	J. Gillray	James Napper Tandy	175
11,545	J. Gillray	The Union Club	175
GIRARDET, ABRAHAM (1764-1823)			
SWISS SCHOOL			
20,685(14)	N. Poussin	Rape of the Sabine women	421
GIRARDET, KARL (1813-1871)			
GERMAN SCHOOL			
20,575	K. Girardet	Landscape	176
GLEIZES, ALBERT (1881-1953)			
FRENCH SCHOOL			
11,566	A. Gleizes	Abstract Composition	176
20,813	A. Gleizes	Abstract Composition	176
GLOVER, GEORGE (1618-AFTER 1652)			
ENGLISH SCHOOL			
10,281	English School c.1645	Archbishop James Ussher	130

Engraver	Artist	Short title	Page
GRIFFIER, JAN (c.1645-1718)			
ANGLO-DUTCH SCHOOL			
10,364 (C.S.6; R.6 II/of II)	P. Lely	Mary of Modena	348
GRIFFITHS, HENRY (FL.1835-1849)			
ENGLISH SCHOOL			
10,624	Irish School c.1848	Robert Holmes	298
11,178	Irish School c.1847	John Doherty	298
11,306	English School 19C	Sir Robert Henry Sale	142
11,307	English School 19C	Sir Robert Henry Sale	143
11,310	T. Bridgford	Sir Martin Archer Shee	33
11,311	C. Grey	Dr Whitley Stokes	185
11,312	T. Bridgford	Sir Martin Archer Shee	33
11,334	S. Lawrence	Sir Henry Pottinger	332
GROGAN, NATHANIEL (C.1740-1807)			
IRISH SCHOOL			
10,788	After Rembrandt	So-called Countess of Desmond	429
GROZER, JOSEPH (?1755-?1799)			
ENGLISH SCHOOL			
10,252 (C.S.11 II/of IV; R.11 either III/of IV or IV/of V)	J. Reynolds	2nd Earl FitzWilliam	436
10,253 (C.S.9 II/of III; R.9 III/of IV)	J. Reynolds	3rd Earl of Bessborough	436
10,390 (C.S.8 II/of II)	J. Reynolds	Viscountess Duncannon	437
10,762 (C.S.7; R.7 II/of II)	J. Reynolds	John Crawford	437
10,768 (C.S.5 I/of II; R.5 II/of III)	J. Reynolds	Lord John Cavendish	437
GUIBERT, FRANCOIS (FL.1786-1808)			
FRENCH SCHOOL			
20,725(76)	H. Rigaud	Duchess of Orleans	449
GUNST, PIETER VAN (1659-1724)			
DUTCH SCHOOL			
10,349	A. Van Dyck	Countess of Chesterfield	529
H...., P. (18TH CENTURY)			
ENGLISH SCHOOL			
11,320	French School 18C	Guillaume Raynal	165
HACKERT, GEORG ABRAHAM (1755-1805)			
GERMAN SCHOOL			
20,769	J.P. Hackert	Temple of the Sibyl, Tivoli	193
HAELWEGH, ADRIAEN (C.1637-C.1696)			
DUTCH SCHOOL			
10,224	G. Kneller	George Walker	317
HAGHE, WILLIAM LOUIS (1806-1885)			
ENGLISH SCHOOL			
20,149	D. Roberts	Pilgrims at Jericho	449
20,222	H. Bright	Castle Entrance	34
20,347	H. Bright	A Cabin	34

Engraver	Artist	Short title	Page
HALL, JOHN (1739-1797)			
ENGLISH SCHOOL			
10,152	G.C. Stuart	Isaac Barré	488
10,460	J. Reynolds	Richard Brinsley Sheridan	437
10,952	T. Hickey	1st Earl Macartney	223
11,195	Irish School 18C	Bishop Richard Chenevix	263
HALL THE ELDER, HENRY BRYAN (1808-1884)			
ANGLO-AMERICAN SCHOOL			
10,967	E.H. Latilla	Daniel O'Connell	332
HALPIN, PATRICK (FL.1755-1787)			
IRISH SCHOOL			
10,091	T. Hickey	Charles Lucas	224
11,629	R. Omer	The Parliament House, Dublin	386
11,806	J. Rocque	Survey of Dublin, 1757	458
HAMERTON, ROBERT JACOB (FL.1831-1858)			
ENGLISH SCHOOL			
10,615	Irish School 1798	Joseph Holt	281
?HANBURY, MICHAEL (FL.1748-1756)			
IRISH SCHOOL			
10,141	Irish School c.1750	Jack Haugh	267
HANHART, M. AND N. (FL.C.1820-1865)			
ENGLISH SCHOOL			
10,119	L. Gluckman	John Mitchel	176
10,429	English School c.1877	George Augustus Chichester May	152
10,524	L. Gluckman	John Mitchel	177
20,766	Countess of Harrington	Isle O'Valla	210
20,767	Countess of Harrington	Old Court	210
HARDING, EDWARD (1776-1796)			
ENGLISH SCHOOL			
10,576	J. Nixon	O'Shauchnesey	383
HARDING, GEORGE PERFECT (C.1780-1853)			
ENGLISH SCHOOL			
10,807	P. Van Somer	1st Viscount Falkland	531
11,052 *(COPYIST)*	English School c.1580	1st Baron Russell	125
HARDING, JAMES DUFFIELD (1798-1863)			
ENGLISH SCHOOL			
11,610	R.O'C. Newenham	St Patrick's Cathedral, Dublin	381
11,611	R.O'C. Newenham	St Patrick's Cathedral, Dublin	381
20,030	R.O'C. Newenham	Reginald's Tower, Waterford	382
20,182	J.D. Harding	Rainham Marshes, Kent	199
20,183	J.D. Harding	Capel Curig, N. Wales	200
20,184	J.D. Harding	Cottage at Penshurst, Kent	200
20,185	J.D. Harding	Farmhouse at Alphington, Devon	200
20,186	J.D. Harding	Dorney Common, Buckinghamshire	200
20,187	J.D. Harding	Beach at Etretat, France	200
20,188	J.D. Harding	Farm Buildings, Littlehampton	200
20,189	J.D. Harding	Bookham Lane, Surrey	200
20,190	J.D. Harding	Beach Scene	201
20,191	J.D. Harding	Boats on the River Thames	201
20,192	J.D. Harding	Boats on the River Thames	201
20,193	J.D. Harding	Andernach Castle, Germany	201

Engraver	Artist	Short title	Page
20,194	J.D. Harding	Boppard, Germany	201
20,195	J.D. Harding	Bradgate Park, Leicestershire	201
20,196	J.D. Harding	River Scene with Willows	201
20,224	J.D. Harding	Fishing boats by the shore	202
20,225	J.D. Harding	Shepherd driving sheep	202
20,226	J.D. Harding	Oberwesel on the River Rhine	202
20,249	J.D. Harding	Rustic scene	202
20,259	J.D. Harding	Ash tree, Greta Bridge	202
20,264	J.D. Harding	Old oak trees	202
20,273	J.D. Harding	Abel and oak, Epping Forest	203
20,274	J.D. Harding	Wych Elms and Firs, Yorkshire	203
20,275	J.D. Harding	Cedars of Lebanon	203
20,296-307	J.D. Harding	Harding's Trees	203-205
20,355	J.D. Harding	Hastings Beach, Sussex	205
20,358	J.D. Harding	Trier, Germany	205
20,361	J.D. Harding	Ruined Castle	206
20,370	J.D. Harding	Ruined Castle	206
20,391	J.D. Harding	Hastings Beach, Sussex	206
20,405	J.D. Harding	Fisherman	206
20,406	J.D. Harding	Fisherman	206
20,407	J.D. Harding	Riverside scene	206
20,408	J.D. Harding	River Scene	206
20,409	J.D. Harding	River with ruined castle	207
20,410	J.D. Harding	Steamship	207
20,428	J.D. Harding	Near Feldkirch, Tyrol	207
20,446	J.D. Harding	Beach at low tide and Haycart	207
20,447	J.D. Harding	Hay Cart on a Country Road	207
20,463	J.D. Harding	Coastal scene	207
20,464	J.D. Harding	Coastal scene	208
20,465	J.D. Harding	Coastal scene	208
20,579	J.D. Harding	Sleeping man	208
?20,580	?J.D. Harding	Victoria Beech Tree	208
20,581	J.D. Harding	Gartmore, Scotland	208
20,649	J.D. Harding	Capel Curig, N. Wales	208
HARDING, SYLVESTER (1745-1808)			
ENGLISH SCHOOL			
10,614 (COPYIST)	Continental School 17C	Count Anthony Hamilton	79
10,670	R. Hunter	Rev. Samuel Madden	257
11,266	R. Hunter	6th Viscount Taaffe	257
HARDY, T. (FL.1792-1802)			
ENGLISH SCHOOL			
10,103 (C.S.6 II/of II)	T. Hardy	John Moody	209
10,796 (C.S.2 II/of II)	J. Reynolds	3rd Duke of Dorset	437
HARRAL, HORACE (FL.1862-1876)			
ENGLISH SCHOOL			
20,572	J.C. Horsley	'Checkmate - next move'	248
HARRIS THE YOUNGER, JOHN (1791-1873)			
ENGLISH SCHOOL			
20,695	M.A. Hayes	Hearn's Hotel, Clonmel	214
20,696	M.A. Hayes	End of a Stage	214
20,697	M.A. Hayes	On the Road	214
20,698	M.A. Hayes	Taking up a Passenger	214
20,699	M.A. Hayes	Dropping a Passenger	214
20,700	M.A. Hayes	Arrival at Waterford	215

ngraver	Artist	Short title	Page
IART, G.J. (19TH CENTURY) NGLISH SCHOOL			
1,876	E.L. Vigée-Le Brun	Self-Portrait	532
IAVELL, DANIEL (FL.1812-1837) NGLISH SCHOOL			
1,647	T.L. Rowbotham the Elder	Howth Head and Harbour	464
1,648	T.L. Rowbotham the Elder	Dublin and Bay from Marino	465
1,696	T.L. Rowbotham the Elder	Howth Head and Harbour	465
0,322	N. Pocock	Men-of-War	410
IAVELL THE ELDER, ROBERT FL.1800-1840) NGLISH SCHOOL			
0,322	N. Pocock	Men-of-War	410
IAVELL THE ELDER, ROBERT FL.1800-1840) NGLISH SCHOOL nd IAVELL THE YOUNGER, ROBERT FL.1820-1850) NGLISH SCHOOL			
1,622	W.B. Taylor	Old Museum, Trinity College	498
1,638	W. Brocas	The National Bank, Dublin	37
1,646	W. Brocas	Trinity College, Dublin	38
1,649	J.P. Haverty	The Embarkation of King George IV at Kingstown	211
1,650	J.P.Haverty	The Entry of King George IV into Dublin	211
1,651	J.P. Haverty	The Embarkation of King George IV at Kingstown	211
1,705	F. Johnston	The General Post Office, Dublin	306
1,842	J. Fogarty	Derrynane Abbey, Co. Kerry	160
1,909	T.S. Roberts	Dublin from near Custom House	452
1,910	T.S. Roberts	General Post Office, Dublin	453
1,912	T.S. Roberts	The Four Courts, Dublin	453
0,820	J.P. Haverty	Key to no. 11,650	212
0,821	J.P. Haverty	Key to no. 11,651	212
IAVERTY, JOSEPH PATRICK (1794-1864) RISH SCHOOL			
0,794	J.P. Haverty	Bishop James Warren Doyle	212
0,963	J.P. Haverty	Father Thomas Maguire	212
0,969	J.P. Haverty	Daniel O'Connell	212
1,020	J.P. Haverty	Catholic Agitation Group	213
1,695	J.P. Haverty	Design for Queenstown	213
1,857	J.P. Haverty	The Monster Meeting	213
0,336	J.P. Haverty	Design for Queenstown	213
IAYNES, JOSEPH (1760-1829) NGLISH SCHOOL			
1,124	W. Hogarth	1st Earl of Charlemont	229
IAYTER, STANLEY WILLIAM (1901-1988) NGLISH SCHOOL			
1,424(1-3)	S.W. Hayter	Plates from 'Still'	216-217
0,509	S.W. Hayter	Study for 'Still I'	217
0,536	S.W. Hayter	Study for 'Still II'	217
0,829	S.W. Hayter	Study for 'Still III'	217

Engraver	Artist	Short title	Page
HEAPHY, THOMAS (1775-1835)			
ENGLISH SCHOOL			
10,065	J. Comerford	Daniel O'Connell	72
HEATH, CHARLES (1785-1848)			
ENGLISH SCHOOL			
20,705(7)	P.P. Rubens	Peace and War	467
20,726(14)	N. Poussin	Penance	421
HEATH, JAMES (1757-1834)			
ENGLISH SCHOOL			
10,286	H.D. Hamilton	Bishop Richard Marlay	196
10,687	J. Comerford	2nd Viscount Gort	72
10,708	J. Comerford	1st Baron de Blaquiere	72
10,712	J. Barry	Self-Portrait	18
10,714	J. Comerford	John Ball	72
10,715	H.D. Hamilton	Sir Jonah Barrington	196
10,742	H. Hone	1st Earl of Charlemont	235
10,748	J. Comerford	Humphrey Butler	72
10,761	J. Comerford	1st Marquess Cornwallis	73
10,778	J. Comerford	John Egan	73
10,783	H.D. Hamilton	Richard Dawson	196
10,793	J. Comerford	Dr Patrick Duigenan	73
10,795	J. Comerford	Bishop William Dickson	73
10,803	J. Comerford	James Fitzgerald	74
10,811	J. Comerford	1st Earl of Clare	74
10,816	J. Comerford	Thomas Gold	74
10,818	?J. Comerford	6th Earl of Granard	74
10,835	J. Comerford	Henry Grattan	74
10,836	J. Comerford	Henry Grattan	75
10,863	H.D. Hamilton	1st Viscount Kilwarden	197
10,881	J.R. Maguire	Francis Hardy	361
10,936	J. Petrie	Major General Montague Matthew	403
10,940	J. Petrie	James Napper Tandy	403
10,947	H.D. Hamilton	2nd Earl of Moira	197
11,048	J. Oldham	2nd Earl of Roden	385
11,049	J. Comerford	2nd Earl of Rosse	75
11,281	J.C. Lochee	Richard Brinsley Sheridan	355
11,749	W.H. Bartlett	George II Equestrian statue	20
20,790	J. Comerford	2nd Earl of Rosse	75
HEEMSKERCK, MARTEN (1498-1574)			
HAARLEM SCHOOL			
20,710(1)	M. Heemskerk	The Creation of Eve and Temptation in the Garden	218
HEISSIG, FRANZ CARL (FL.FROM 1770)			
GERMAN SCHOOL			
10,752	H.D. Hamiltonn	Anne, Countess of Cork and Orrery	197
HENRIQUEL-DUPONT, LOUIS PIERRE (1797-1892)			
FRENCH SCHOOL			
11,484	P. Delaroche	The Deposition	108
HERBERT, JAMES DOWLING (1762-1837)			
IRISH SCHOOL			
10,466 *(COPYIST)*	M.W. Peters	1st Viscount O'Neill	396

Engraver	Artist	Short title	Page
HICKS, GEORGE ELGAR (FL.1848-1905)			
ENGLISH SCHOOL			
20,181	G.E. Hicks	Figure studies	224
HIGHAM, THOMAS (1796-1844)			
ENGLISH SCHOOL			
11,700	G. Petrie	Dublin Castle	400
11,775	G. Petrie	St Patrick's Cathedral, Dublin	400
11,793	G. Petrie	King's Bridge, Dublin	400
20,399	W.H. Bartlett	Orontes River, Syria	20
20,479	W.I. Hocker	Cross at Paignton, Devon	245
20,791	G. Petrie	Dunmow Castle, Co. Meath	400
HILL, R. (FL.1841-1843)			
ENGLISH SCHOOL			
20,503	T. Creswick	Torc Mountain, Co. Kerry	94
HINCHCLIFF, JOHN JAMES (1805-1875)			
ENGLISH SCHOOL			
10,326	A.E. Chalon	Countess of Blessington	62
HINCKS, WILLIAM (FL.1773-1797)			
IRISH SCHOOL			
11,637	W. Hincks	The Linen Hall, Dublin	225
HINTON, W. (18TH CENTURY)			
ENGLISH SCHOOL			
11,262	J. Rising	Arthur Young	449
HOARE, WILLIAM (1706-1799)			
ENGLISH SCHOOL			
11,230	W. Hoare	2nd Earl of Northumberland	226
HODGES, CHARLES HOWARD (?1764-1837)			
ENGLISH SCHOOL			
10,092 (C.S.23 II/of II)	G.C. Stuart	2nd Duke of Leinster	489
10,150 (C.S.3 I/of II; R.3 II/of III)	G.C. Stuart	John Beresford	489
10,217 (C.S.16a II/of III)	G.C. Stuart	Henry Grattan	489
10,247 (C.S.9)	G.C. Stuart	William Burton Conyngham	489
10,251 (C.S.5)	G.C. Stuart	William Brownlow	490
10,494 (C.S.14 I/of II)	G.C. Stuart	John Fitzgibbon	490
10,501 (C.S.15 pre-I/of III)	G.C. Stuart	John Foster	490
10,726 (C.S.5; R.5 II/of II)	G.C. Stuart	William Brownlow	490
HODGETTS, ROBERT M. (FL.1826-1837)			
ENGLISH SCHOOL			
10,968	R.M. Hodgetts	Daniel O'Connell	227

Engraver	Artist	Short title	Page
HODGETTS, THOMAS (FL.1801-1846) ENGLISH SCHOOL			
10,174	M.S. Carpenter	Sir Charles Doyle	55
10,230	T.C. Thompson	Dr William Bruce	501
10,399	Lady P. Burghersh	Anne, Countess of Mornington	46
10,792	R. Rothwell	Baroness Anna Dufferin and Clandeboye	464
11,988	J.M.W. Turner	Laufenburg, Switzerland	518
11,993	J.M.W. Turner	From Spenser's 'Fairy Queen'	519
20,016	J.M.W. Turner	Ville de Thun, Switzerland	522
HODGSON, W.W. (FL. EARLY 19TH CENTURY) ENGLISH SCHOOL			
20,048 *(COPYIST)*	Venetian School 16C	Knight and Page	532
20,156 *(COPYIST)*	F. Barocci	The Holy Family	12
HOGARTH, WILLIAM (1697-1764) ENGLISH SCHOOL			
11,509	W. Hogarth	A Midnight Modern Conversation	229
11,510	W. Hogarth	Strolling Actresses in a barn	229
11,511-514	W. Hogarth	Four stages of Cruelty	229-230
11,515-519	W. Hogarth	5 plates of a Rake's Progress	230-231
11,520	W. Hogarth	Plate 4 of a Harlot's Progress	231
11,521	W. Hogarth	The Company of Undertakers	231
HOLBROOKE, WILLIAM HENRY (FL.1821-1848) IRISH SCHOOL			
10,983	W.H. Holbrooke	Daniel O'Connell	232
11,240	W.H. Holbrooke	Daniel O'Connell	232
HOLL, BENJAMIN (1808-1884) ENGLISH SCHOOL			
10,962	English School c.1833	Thomas Moore	149
HOLL, FRANCIS (1815-1884) ENGLISH SCHOOL			
10,425	G. Richmond	7th Earl of Carlisle	448
10,736	E. Day	Prince Albert	103
HOLL THE ELDER, WILLIAM (1771-1838) ENGLISH SCHOOL			
11,204	S. Drummond	Andrew Cherry	119
11,286	J. Steele	Dr Samuel Solomon	482
HOLL THE YOUNGER, WILLIAM (1807-1871) ENGLISH SCHOOL			
10,289	T.H. Carrick	Daniel O'Connell	56
10,597	T.H. Carrick	Daniel O'Connell	56
10,632	J. Wood	Dr James Johnson	546
10,972	T.H. Carrick	Daniel O'Connell	56
HOLLAR, WENCESLAS (1607-1677) ANGLO-CZECH SCHOOL			
20,763	W. Hollar	The Execution of Thomas, Earl of Strafford	232

Engraver	Artist	Short title	Page
HONE THE ELDER, NATHANIEL (1718-1784)			
IRISH SCHOOL			
10,072 (C.S.3;R.3 II/of II)	N. Hone the Elder	Self-Portrait	240
10,879 (COPYIST)	I. Gosset	Benjamin Hoadly	183
11,276	N. Hone the Elder	James Turner	240
11,848 (C.S.2 II/of II; R.2 III/of III)	N. Hone the Elder	Francis Grose	241
HOPWOOD THE ELDER, JAMES (1752-1819)			
ENGLISH SCHOOL			
11,168	J. Highmore	Thomas Emlyn	224
HOPWOOD THE YOUNGER, JAMES (1795-AFTER 1825)			
ENGLISH SCHOOL			
10,586	T. Rowlandson	Dr O'Meara	465
11,006	R.F. Drummond	Mrs Mary Tighe	117
HOUBRAKEN, ARNOLD (1660-1719)			
DUTCH SCHOOL			
10,349 *(COPYIST)*	A. Van Dyck	Countess of Chesterfield	529
HOUBRAKEN, JACOBUS (1698-1780)			
DUTCH SCHOOL			
10,212	G. Kneller	1st Earl of Rochester	317
10,543	G. Kneller	Queen Anne	317
10,839	R. Walker	Lt.-General Fleetwood	535
10,987	M. Maingaud	1st Earl of Orkney	362
11,942	English School c.1560	4th Duke of Norfolk	124
20,133	G. Kneller	Lt.-General Tollemache	318
HOUSTON, H.H. (FL.C.1791)			
IRISH SCHOOL			
11,200	H. Hopson	John Philpot Curran	248
11,601	M.W. Peters	Angel and child	395
11,617	M.W. Peters	Angel and child	395
HOUSTON, RICHARD (C.1721-1775)			
IRISH SCHOOL			
10,127 (C.S.56 II/of II)	English or Irish c.1760	James Gunning	136
10,153 (C.S.5 I/of II)	H.D. Hamilton	Isaac Barré	197
10,234 (C.S.39 I/of III; R.39 I/of II - C.S.39 II is another print)	T. Worlidge	George II, King of England	547
10,342 (C.S.59 I/of III)	F. Cotes	Duchess of Hamilton and Brandon	89
10,350 (C.S.125 I/of II)	J. Zoffany	Mrs Catherine Wodhull	550
10,359 (C.S.55 II/of II)	F. Cotes	Catherine Gunning	89
10,384 (C.S.31 I/of II; R.31 I/of III)	J.E. Liotard	So-called Countess of Coventry	354
10,410 (C.S.102 pre-II; R.102 III/of VI)	J. Reynolds	1st Baron Rokeby	438

Engraver	Artist	Short title	Page
10,445 (C.S.28)	W. Hoare	4th Earl of Chesterfield	226
10,542 (C.S.4)	J. Reynolds	Princess Augusta	438
10,827 (C.S.39 II/of III; R.39 II/of II - C.S.39 III is another print)	T. Worlidge	George II, King of England	547
11,063 (C.S.100 II/of II;R.100 III/of III)	J. Reynolds	Harriet Powell	438
11,064 (C.S.99 II/of II)	C. Read	Harriet Powell	429
11,068 (C.S.92 I/of III R.92b/of f)	W. Hoare	1st Earl of Chatham	226
HOWIS THE ELDER, WILLIAM (1804-1882) IRISH SCHOOL			
20,172	W. Howis the Elder	Cart, horses and dogs	250
20,173	W. Howis the Elder	Sheep, a cow and a sheep-dog	250
20,175	W. Howis the Elder	A calf and a boy with pitcher	250
20,253	W. Howis the Elder	Bridge over a mountain stream	250
20,256	W. Howis the Elder	A castle by a river	251
20,257	W. Howis the Elder	Bridge over a mountain stream	251
20,258	W. Howis the Elder	Bridge over a mountain stream	251
HOWIS THE YOUNGER, WILLIAM (1827-1857) IRISH SCHOOL			
20,250	W. Howis the Younger	Millhouse on the Liffey	251
20,251	W. Howis the Younger	Millhouse on the Liffey	251
20,252	W. Howis the Younger	Ruined Castle	251
20,254	W. Howis the Younger	Ruined Castle and river	251
20,255	W. Howis the Younger	Ruined Castle and river	252
HUBAND, GEORGE JOSEPH (B.1809) IRISH SCHOOL			
11,523	G.J. Huband	Halloween scarecrow	252
11,524	G.J. Huband	Banditti	252
11,525	G.J. Huband	Banditti among ruins	252
11,526	G.J. Huband	At the Barber's	252
11,527	G.J. Huband	Lady and Gentleman dancing	252
11,528	G.J. Huband	Two connoisseurs	252
11,529	G.J. Huband	Pantomime clowns	253
11,530	G.J. Huband	Head of an ass	253
11,541	G.J. Huband	Two connoisseurs	253
HUBAND, WILLCOCKS (1776-1834) IRISH SCHOOL			
11,532	A. Ostade	The Baker	388
11,533	W. Huband	A Man	253
11,534	W. Huband	A Blacksmith	253
11,535	W. Huband	A Cart Horse	253
11,536	A. Ostade	Peasant with a pipe	388
11,537	W. Huband	Head of a man	254
11,538	Raphael	Elymas struck blind	427
11,539	W. Huband	Duelling	254
11,540	W. Huband	Old Lady with pince-nez	254
11,542	P. Loutherbourg	A drunken peasant	356

Engraver	Artist	Short title	Page
HUBERT, JEAN-BAPTISTE LOUIS (1801-AFTER 1865) FRENCH SCHOOL			
20,339	J.B.L. Hubert	Green Oaks	254
HUBERTI, ANTONIA (B.1914) GERMAN SCHOOL			
20,660(13)	A. Huberti	The Head Gamekeeper's Courtesan	254
HUDSON, HENRY (FL.1782-1800) ENGLISH SCHOOL			
10,246 (C.S.6 II/of III R.6 II/of IV)	M. Brown	Lord George Macartney	43
HUFFAM, T.W. (FL.1825-C.1855) ENGLISH SCHOOL			
10,616	Irish School c.1843	James Hope	297
10,633	J.D. Herbert	Henry Jackson	222
10,646	C. Byrne	Samuel Neilson	47
10,647	C. Byrne	Samuel Neilson	48
10,660	A.F.C. Claudet	Richard Robert Madden	68
10,661	A.F.C. Claudet	Richard Robert Madden	68
10,671	J.D. Herbert	William James MacNeven	222
10,934	J. Hardy	Richard Robert Madden	209
10,935	J. Hardy	Richard Robert Madden	209
11,137	H. Hone	Lord Edward FitzGerald	235
11,138	H. Hone	Lord Edward FitzGerald	235
11,169	J.D. Herbert	Thomas Addis Emmet	222
11,170	J.D. Herbert	Thomas Addis Emmet	222
11,171	L.F. Aubry	Thomas Addis Emmet	10
11,172	L.F. Aubry	Thomas Addis Emmet	10
11,173	L.F. Aubry	Thomas Addis Emmet	10
11,189	Continental School 19C	William Corbett	80
11,272	Irish School c.1790	Theobald Wolfe Tone	277
11,294	A. Buck	John Sheares	44
11,295	?A. Buck	Henry Sheares	44
11,326	Irish School c.1803	Thomas Russell	290
HULBESTE, G. (FL. EARLY 19TH CENTURY) ?FRENCH SCHOOL			
20,109	D. Teniers the Younger	Tavern near a River	499
HULETT, JAMES (FL.1740-1771) ENGLISH SCHOOL			
10,181	H.F. Gravelot	Owen Farrell	184
HUMPHREY, OZIAS (1742-1810) ENGLISH SCHOOL			
11,135	English School 16C	'The Fair Geraldine'	124
HUMPHREY, WILLIAM (C.1740-1795) ENGLISH SCHOOL			
10,696 (C.S.9;R.85a III/of III)	N. Hone the Elder	John Camillus Hone	241
11,228 (C.S.12)	English School c.1774	John Methuen	136

Engraver	Artist	Short title	Page
IRISH SCHOOL (1793)			
11,245	Irish School c.1793	7th Earl of Westmeath	279
IRISH SCHOOL (C.1793)			
10,580	Irish School c.1792	Thomas O'Meara	280
IRISH SCHOOL (1794)			
11,328	Irish School c.1794	Archibald Hamilton Rowan	280
IRISH SCHOOL (1795)			
10,578	Irish School c.1795	M.E. O'Brie	280
11,139	Irish School c.1795	2nd Earl Fitzwilliam	280
IRISH SCHOOL (C.1795)			
10,079	G.C. Stuart	Grattan's answer to RC Address	491
10,299	Irish School c.1795	Rev. Thomas Campbell	280
11,894	Irish School c.1795	Rev. Thomas Campbell	280
IRISH SCHOOL (C.1796)			
11,602	Irish School c.1796	Ringsend New Docks	281
IRISH SCHOOL (1797)			
10,588	Irish School c.1797	Arthur O'Connor	281
10,590	Irish School c.1797	Arthur O'Connor	281
IRISH SCHOOL (1798)			
10,292	Irish School 1798	Theobald Wolfe Tone	281
10,585	A. Buck	Roger O'Connor	44
10,668	S. Drummond	Arthur Murphy	118
IRISH SCHOOL (c.1798)			
10,648	Irish School late 18C	James Napper Tandy	282
IRISH SCHOOL (1799)			
11,131	G.C. Stuart	John Foster	491
11,305	Irish School c.1799	William Saurin	282
IRISH SCHOOL (LATE 18TH CENTURY)			
11,162	Irish School late 18C	John Giffard	282
11,296	Irish School 18C	Rev. Walter Shirley	265
11,316	Irish School late 18C	William Wynne Ryland	282
11,318	Irish School late 18C	Captain Luke Ryan	282
11,618	Irish School late 18C	Entrance to Phoenix Park	283
11,715	Irish School late 18C	Dublin and Islandbridge	283
11,738	Irish School late 18C	Floating Chapel, Ringsend, Dublin	283
11,839	Irish School late 18C	Dargle Glen and River	283
IRISH SCHOOL (C.1800)			
10,581	Irish School c.1800	James O'Brien	284
11,181	Irish School c.1800	Michael Dwyer	284
11,627	Irish School c.1779	The Dublin Volunteers	271
11,718	Irish School c.1800	Dublin from South-west	284
IRISH SCHOOL (19TH CENTURY)			
11,219	J. Petrie	Robert Emmet	403
11,241	Irish School 19C	Shooting of D'Esterre	285
11,290	Irish School 19C	Richard Lalor Sheil	285
11,325	W. Cuming	General Sir John Doyle	96
11,411	Irish School 19C	Unidentified man	285
11,635	Irish School 19C	Old Walls of Londonderry	286

Engraver	Artist	Short title	Page
11,636	Irish School 19C	Doorway of Church at Maghera	286
11,671	Irish School 19C	Cromlech at Tubrid	286
11,672	Irish School 19C	Cromlech at Harristown	286
11,673	Irish School 19C	Callan Church	286
11,745	Irish School 19C	Rathmichael Monastery ruins	286
11,746	Irish School 19C	Armoy Round Tower	286
11,760	Irish School 19C	St Patrick's Cathedral, Dublin	287
11,867	Irish School 19C	John Philpot Curran	287
11,922	Irish School 19C	Wooden House, Dublin	287
20,394	Irish School 19C	'I fought for my country'	287
20,395	Irish School 19C	'Peace being proclaimed'	287
20,396	Irish School 19C	'My Sweet Girl'	287
20,555	Irish School 19C	Landscape	287
20,622	Irish School 19C	Lombardy Poplars	288
20,815	Irish School 19C	Ancient tomb, Boreragh	288
20,816	Irish School 19C	Old Walls, Londonderry	288
20,817	Irish School 19C	Banagher Church	288
20,818	Irish School 19C	High Cross, Macosquin	288
IRISH SCHOOL (EARLY 19TH CENTURY)			
11,235	Irish School 1790s	Thomas Moore	278
IRISH SCHOOL (C.1801)			
11,238	Irish School c.1801	George Ponsonby	290
IRISH SCHOOL (1803)			
11,323	Irish School c.1803	Thomas Russell	290
11,324	Irish School c.1803	Thomas Russell	291
11,352	J. Petrie & Irish School c.1803	Robert Emmet	405
11,807	T. Sherrard	Survey of Dublin Quays	475
IRISH SCHOOL (1804)			
11,246	G. Chinnery	Lt.-General Charles Vallancey	65
11,247	G. Chinnery	Lt.-General Charles Vallencey	65
IRISH SCHOOL (1804/06)			
11,348	Irish School 1804/06	The Devil and the Jack-Ass	291
11,349	Irish School 1804/06	A Ta-Whang Feast	291
IRISH SCHOOL (1805)			
11,351	Irish School c.1805	Rev. Archibald Douglas	291
IRISH SCHOOL (1808)			
10,587	Irish School c.1808	Phelim O'Connor	292
10,650	J. Petrie	James Napper Tandy	404
11,163	J. Petrie	Robert Emmet	404
11,338	?G. Morphey	Archbishop Oliver Plunkett	375
11,735	Irish School 1808	9th Duke of Richmond	292
IRISH SCHOOL (c.1808)			
10,620	Irish School c.1808	Edward Day	292
IRISH SCHOOL (1809)			
10,589	J.D. Herbert	Arthur O'Connor	223
11,343	Irish School 1809	Turlough O'Carolan	292
IRISH SCHOOL (c.1811)			
11,851	Irish School c.1811	The Four Courts	293

Engraver	Artist	Short title	Page
JACKSON, JOHN RICHARDSON (1819-1877) ENGLISH SCHOOL			
10,441	S. Catterson Smith the Elder	Marcus Gervais Beresford	58
11,556	S. Catterson Smith the Elder	Marcus Gervais Beresford	59
JACKSON, M. (19TH CENTURY) ?IRISH SCHOOL			
11,729	Irish School 19C	Bank of Ireland, Dublin	289
JACKSON, MASON (1819-1903) ENGLISH SCHOOL			
20,647	F.R. Lee	River Scene, North Wales	342
JACKSON, MICHAEL (FL.1736-C.1753) IRISH SCHOOL			
10,134 (C.S.1 I/of II)	J. Gwim	Spranger Barry	192
JACOTTET, LOUIS JULIEN (1806-AFTER 1855) FRENCH SCHOOL			
20,315	L.J. Jacottet & A.J.B. Bayot	Figures resting by Trees	303
JACQUEMART, JULES FERDINAND (1837-1880) FRENCH SCHOOL			
11,380	P.J.A. Baudry	Sir Richard Wallace	24
JAZET, JEAN PIERRE MARIE (1788-1871) FRENCH SCHOOL			
20,100	French School 19C	'La Bonne Nouvelle'	167
JEAVONS, THOMAS (C.1800-1867) ENGLISH SCHOOL			
20,460	D.O. Hill	Ellisland, Scotland	225
JENKINS, JOSEPH JOHN (1811-1885) ENGLISH SCHOOL			
10,913	J. Bostok	3rd Marquess of Londonderry	32
JENKINSON (19TH CENTURY) ENGLISH SCHOOL			
11,060	English School 1830s	Lt.-Colonel Alexander Perceval	149
11,061	English School 1830s	Lt.-Colonel Alexander Perceval	149
JOHN, AUGUSTUS (1879-1961) WELSH SCHOOL			
20,764	A. John	W.B. Yeats	306
JONES, JOHN (FL. 1740-1770) ENGLISH SCHOOL			
11,633	Irish School c.1750	Sackville Street, Dublin	267

Engraver	Artist	Short title	Page
JONES, JOHN (C.1745-1797) ENGLISH SCHOOL			
10,089 (C.S.48 II/of II)	J. Reynolds	1st Baron Lucan	438
10,386 (C.S.4 I/of II)	J. Hoppner	Mrs Jordan	246
10,442 (C.S.11 I/of II; R.11 II/of III)	G. Romney	Edmund Burke	460
10,476 (C.S.63 I/of II)	G. Romney	William Pitt the Younger	460
10,499 (C.S.14; R.14 III/of IV)	D. Gardner	1st Marquess Cornwallis	170
10,503 (C.S.67 I/of III)	J. Reynolds	2nd Earl of Moira	438
10,508 (C.S.82 I/of II)	G. Romney	10th Earl of Westmoreland	460
10,946	J. Reynolds	2nd Earl of Moira	439
?11,388	R. Cosway	Edmund Boyle	88
JORDAN, HENRY (FL.1829-1853) ENGLISH SCHOOL			
20,372	W.H. Bartlett	Pays de Vaud, Switzerland	20
JOSEY, RICHARD (1840/41-1906) ENGLISH SCHOOL			
10,903	J. Reynolds	Duchess of Leinster	439
11,077	E. Crawford	J. Scott Porter	92
JUKES, FRANCIS (1745-1812) ENGLISH SCHOOL			
11,732	?F. Jukes	Powder Magazine, Phoenix Park	310
11,733	?F. Jukes	Powder Magazine, Phoenix Park	310
JULIEN, BERNARD ROMAIN (1802-1871) FRENCH SCHOOL			
11,874	B.R. Julien	A Young Woman	310
KEATING, GEORGE (1762-1842) IRISH SCHOOL			
10,250 (C.S.8)	J. Murphy	Rev. Arthur O'Leary	379
KEERE, PIETER VAN DEN (1571-AFTER 1645) DUTCH SCHOOL			
20,765	P. van den Keere	Map of Barony of Idrone	312
KELLY, THOMAS (FL.1799-1841) IRISH SCHOOL			
11,180	Irish School c.1820	James Warren Doyle	295
11,850	T. Kelly	College Green, Dublin	312
KELSALL, W.H. (FL.1834-1857) ENGLISH SCHOOL			
20,456	T. Allom	View from Langdale Pikes	3
20,457	T. Allom	View from Langdale Pikes	3

Engraver	Artist	Short title	Page
KENNEDY, MABEL M. (20TH CENTURY) ENGLISH SCHOOL			
11,930	M.M. Kennedy	Woods and river	312
KERNOFF, HARRY (1900-1974) IRISH SCHOOL			
11,932(7)	H. Kernoff	Westport, Co Mayo	313
KERNOT, JAMES HARFIELD (FL.1828-1849) ENGLISH SCHOOL			
20,382	P. De Wint	The Forest Hall Mountains	109
20,454	G.F. White	Gungotri, India	540
KING, GILES (FL.1732-1746) ENGLISH SCHOOL			
10,007	W. Jones	Howth from Beggars Bush	308
KILIAN, PHILIP ANDREAS (1714-1759) GERMAN SCHOOL			
20,218	G.B. Piazzetta	Three Marys at the Tomb	407
KINGSBURY, HENRY (FL.1775-1798) ENGLISH SCHOOL			
10,275 (C.S.3)	English School late 18C	Edmund Burke	138
KIRKWOOD, JOHN (FL.1826-1853) IRISH SCHOOL			
10,287	S. Skillin	William Maginn	478
10,592	W. Stevenson	Rev. Caesar Otway	483
10,596	Irish School c.1841	Daniel O'Connell	297
10,613	C. Grey	William Rowan Hamilton	187
10,665	C. Grey	William Hamilton Maxwell	188
10,673	A. Buck	Rev. Theobald Mathew	45
11,019	Irish School c.1843	George Smith	297
11,082	C. Grey	Charles Kendal Bushe	188
11,090	C. Grey	Francis Blackburne	188
11,100	?C. Grey	Colonel William Blacker	188
11,104	C. Grey	William Archer Butler	189
11,109	Irish School c.1841	John Barrett	297
11,120	W. Stevenson	John Anster	483
11,156	C. Grey	2nd Viscount Gort	189
11,161	C. Grey	Dr Robert Graves	189
11,192	C. Grey	John Wilson Croker	189
11,216	C. Grey	William Carleton	189
11,217	C. Grey	William Carleton	190
11,227	C. Grey	Rev. George Miller	190
11,254	R. Home	Archbishop James Ussher	234
11,270	J. Comerford	Rev. Robert Walsh	77
11,273	C. Grey	Philip Meadows Taylor	190
11,292	C. Grey	Percival Barton Lord	190
11,293	F. R.Say	3rd Earl of Roden	469
11,302	H. MacManus	Robert Stopford	360
11,423	D. Maclise	Thomas Moore	359
11,701	J. Kirkwood	The Custom House, Dublin	314
11,811	J. Kirkwood	Plan of Dublin c.1830	314
20,110	C. Grey	Dr Evory Kennedy	191

Engraver	Artist	Short title	Page
KLIPPHAHN, JOHANN (1815-1892)			
GERMAN SCHOOL			
20,062	German School 1490/1530	Court cupboard	172
20,063	German School 1519	Drinking cup and cover	173
KNIGHT, CHARLES (1743-C.1826)			
ENGLISH SCHOOL			
10,082	H.D. Hamilton	Archbishop William Newcome	198
10,662	J. Reynolds	Edmund Malone	439
10,663	J. Reynolds	Edmund Malone	439
10,920	S. Harding	Hon. John Monck Mason	209
11,051	E. Scott	4th Duke of Richmond	471
KRIEHUBER, JOSEF (1800-1876)			
AUSTRIAN SCHOOL			
10,938	?J. Kriehuber	Count Lavall G. Nugent	327
KRUGER, FRANZ (1797-1857)			
GERMAN SCHOOL			
10,758	F. Kruger	Viscount Castlereagh	327
LACEY, SAMUEL (FL.1818-1857)			
ENGLISH SCHOOL			
20,263	T. Allom	Waterfall on the River Tees	3
20,378	W. Tombleson	Chelsea Hospital, London	506
20,476	H. Gastineau	Porth Yr Ogof, Wales	171
20,518	T. Creswick	River and Classical Buildings	94
20,519	P. Nasmyth	Arthur's Seat, Edinburgh	380
LAFITTE, LOUIS LAFITTE (1770-1828)			
FRENCH SCHOOL			
20,725(74)	C. Le Brun	Hercules with Diomedes' horses	340
LAFOSSE, JEAN BAPTISTE ADOLPHE (C.1810-1879)			
FRENCH SCHOOL			
11,875	C.L. Bazin	Haydée	24
LAMB, FRANCIS (19TH CENTURY)			
SCOTTISH SCHOOL			
11,661	Studio of P.P. Rubens	Meleager and Atalanta	467
LANDSEER, HENRY (19TH CENTURY)			
ENGLISH SCHOOL			
10,949	J. Hoppner	2nd Earl of Moira	246
LANE, JOHN BRYANT (1788-1868)			
ENGLISH SCHOOL			
10,151 *(COPYIST)*	Irish School 1806/14	John Philpot Curran	291
10,770 *(COPYIST)*	Irish School 1806/14	John Philpot Curran	292
LANE, RICHARD JAMES (1800-1872)			
ENGLISH SCHOOL			
10,737	T. Phillips	Viscount Alexander	406
10,941	T. Lawrence	Lady Anne Nugent	336
LANE, WILLIAM (1746-1819)			
ENGLISH SCHOOL			
11,340	R. Cosway	Mrs Frances Abington	88

Engraver	Artist	Short title	Page
LANG, KARL (1818-1878) GERMAN SCHOOL			
20,830	K. Lang	Summer	330
?LANGER, THEODOR (1819-1895) GERMAN SCHOOL			
10,918	English School 19C	Sir Richard Mayne	143
LANGLEY, BATTY (1696-1751) ENGLISH SCHOOL			
20,523	B. Langley	Architectural Frontispiece	330
LAPLANTE, CHARLES (FL.1861-1903) FRENCH SCHOOL			
20,694(72)	L.C.P.G. Doré	Death of Samson	111
LASSOUQUERE, JEAN PAULIN (1810-AFTER 1847) ANGLO-FRENCH SCHOOL			
10,555	J.P. Lassouquère	1st Duke of Wellington	330
LAURENT, PIERRE LOUIS HENRI (1779-1844) FRENCH SCHOOL			
20,070	E. Le Sueur	Raymond Diocres answers	352
20,071	E. Le Sueur	St Bruno teaching Theology	352
?LAURIE, ROBERT (C.1755-1836) IRISH SCHOOL			
10,201 (C.S.7 III/of IV; possibly a 17C print)	?G. Morphey	Archbishop Oliver Plunkett	375
11,073 (C.S.7 IV/of IV)	?G. Morphey	Archbishop Oliver Plunkett	376
LE BAS, JACQUES PHILIPPE (1707-1783) FRENCH SCHOOL			
11,868	D. Teniers the Younger	The Artist and his family	500
20,678(14)	N.N. Coypel	Diana	92
LEFEBVRE, VALENTIN (C.1642-C.1680) ITALO-FLEMISH SCHOOL			
11,481	Titian	Martyrdom of St Peter Martyr	505
11,492	Titian	Virgin of the Cherries	505
11,498	Titian	St John the Baptist	505
LEFEVBRE, F. (18TH CENTURY) FRENCH SCHOOL			
10,878	French School 18C	General Lazare Hoche	165
LEGAT, FRANCIS (1741-1806) SCOTTISH SCHOOL			
20,712(40)	J. Barry	Lear weeping over Cordelia	18

Engraver	Artist	Short title	Page
LEGROS, ALPHONSE (1837-1911) FRENCH SCHOOL			
11,473	A. Legros	The Burning Cottage	343
11,474	A. Legros	Peasants Taken away by Death	343
11,475	A. Legros	Triumph of Death	343
11,476	A. Legros	Death pursuing peasants	343
11,477	A. Legros	Death strikes the eldest son	343
11,478	A. Legros	Death with Revolutionaries	343
11,479	A. Legros	Death marching	344
LEMAITRE, AUGUSTIN FRANCOIS (1797-1870) FRENCH SCHOOL			
11,699	J. Malton	Upper Yard, Dublin Castle	362
11,702	J. Malton	The Custom House, Dublin	362
11,765	J. Malton	St Patrick's Cathedral, Dublin	363
LEMERCIER, ALFRED LEON (FL.C.1863) FRENCH SCHOOL			
20,054	H.L. Garnier	A Country scene	171
LENS, BERNARD (1659-1725) ENGLISH SCHOOL			
10,921 (C.S.14)	English School 17C	Mary II, Queen of England	127
10,922 (C.S.13 III/of III)	W. Wissing	Mary II, Queen of England	544
LEONETTI, GIOVANNI BATTISTA (19TH CENTURY) ITALIAN SCHOOL			
11,659	Guercino	David with head of Goliath	192
LE PAUTRE, JEAN (1618-1682) FRENCH SCHOOL			
20,231	J. Le Pautre	Diana and Adonis	349
20,232	J. Le Pautre	Assumption of the Virgin	350
LE PETIT, WILLIAM A. (FL.1829-1857) ENGLISH SCHOOL			
20,356	R.J. Elliot	Mah Chung Keow, Canton, China	123
20,423	W.C. Stanfield	St Michael's Mount, Cornwall	482
20,443	D. Roberts	Kelso Abbey, Scotland	449
20,451	T. Allom	Tintagel Castle, Cornwall	3
20,452	T. Allom	Pentargon Waterfall, Cornwall	4
20,458	G. Pickering	The Lakes, Cumbria	407
LEPICIE THE ELDER, BERNARD FRANCOIS (1698-1755) FRENCH SCHOOL			
10,172	J.-B.S. Chardin	'La Maîtresse D'École'	63
11,490	J.-B.S. Chardin	'La Ratisseuse'	63
LE PRINCE, JEAN-BAPTISTE (1734-1781) FRENCH SCHOOL			
20,711(36)	J.B. Le Prince	Woman and Children	350

Engraver	Artist	Short title	Page
LEROUGE, JEAN NICOLAS (B.C.1776) FRENCH SCHOOL			
20,086	D. Teniers the Younger	Peasants in an Inn	500
LEROUX, EUGENE (1807-1863) FRENCH SCHOOL			
20,143	E. Leroux	A Knight and a Monk	350
LESSORE, THERESE (1844-1945) ENGLISH SCHOOL			
11,431	T. Lessore	Music Hall Audience	351
11,432	T. Lessore	Cafe Exterior	351
11,433	T. Lessore	The Laundry	351
11,434	T. Lessore	On the Railway Station	351
11,435	T. Lessore	Women Working	351
11,436	T. Lessore	Waiting at the Station	351
LEVACHEZ, CHARLES FRANCOIS GABRIEL (1760-1830) FRENCH SCHOOL			
11,008	French School late 18C & J. Duplessi-Bertaux	Trophime Gérard	166
LE VASSEUR, JEAN CHARLES (1734-1816) FRENCH SCHOOL			
20,037	H. Gravelot	'La Henriade'	184
LEVENS, T. (19TH CENTURY) ENGLISH SCHOOL			
10,308	H. Hone	Mrs Sarah Siddons	236
LE VILAIN, GERARD RENE (C.1740-1836) FRENCH SCHOOL			
20,074	J. Steen	'As the Old Sing'	482
LEWIS (THE ELDER), FREDERICK CHRISTIAN (1779-1856) ENGLISH SCHOOL			
10,261	J. Hayter	John Doherty	216
10,566	W. Bewnes	Archbishop Richard Whateley	28
10,928	F. Newenham	3rd Baron Mountsandford	381
10,991	G. Dawe	Miss Eliza O'Neill	103
11,144	N. Kenny	Henry Grattan	312
11,389	J. Slater	George Robert Chinnery	479
11,420	T. Lawrence	Self-Portrait	336
20,000	J.M.W. Turner	Bridge with goats	520
20,199	E. Landseer	'Cottage Industry'	329
20,720(28)	Michelangelo	Study for the Creation of Adam	372
LEWIS, JAMES (FL.1813-1837) ENGLISH SCHOOL			
10,978	J. Lewis	Daniel O'Connell	352
LIGHTFOOT, PETER (1805-1885) ENGLISH SCHOOL			
10,640	H.D. Hamilton	1st Viscount Kilwarden	198

Engraver	Artist	Short title	Page
LINES, SAMUEL RESTALL (1804-1883)			
ENGLISH SCHOOL			
20,261	S.R. Lines	An Oak and druid's temple	353
20,344	S.R. Lines	Fir trees	353
20,374	S.R. Lines	Oak trees	353
LINES, VINCENT HENRY (1909-1968)			
ENGLISH SCHOOL			
11,554	V.H. Lines	Denis Johnston	354
LINNELL THE ELDER, JOHN (1792-1882)			
ENGLISH SCHOOL			
11,044	J. Linnell the Elder	Thomas Spring Rice	354
LINTON, HENRY DUFF (1815-1899)			
ENGLISH SCHOOL			
20,582	F. Goodall	The Holy Well	182
LINTON, WILLIAM JAMES (1812-1898)			
ENGLISH SCHOOL			
11,042	H. Anelay	Defendants in 1884 State Trial	9
20,626	C. Branwhite	Moel Siabod Mountain, N.Wales	33
LIZARS, WILLIAM HOME (1788-1859)			
ENGLISH SCHOOL			
10,672	Reynolds of Dublin	Dr David MacBride	447
LODGE, JOHN (18TH CENTURY)			
?IRISH SCHOOL			
10,041(1)	R. Pool & J. Cash	Map of Dublin, 1780	410
10,041(2)	R. Pool & J. Cash	Speed's map of Dublin	411
10,041(3)	R. Pool & J. Cash	Frontispiece	411
10,041(4-5)	R. Pool & J. Cash	Dublin Castle	411
10,041(7)	R. Pool & J. Cash	House of Commons, Dublin	411
10,041(8-11)	R. Pool & J. Cash	Trinity College, Dublin	411-412
10,041(13)	R. Pool & J. Cash	The Royal Exchange, Dublin	412
10,041(14)	R. Pool & J. Cash	Queen's & Essex Bridges, Dublin	412
10,041(15	R. Pool & J. Cash	Newgate Gaol, Dublin	412
10,041(16)	R. Pool & J. Cash	Marine School, Dublin	413
10,041(17)	R. Pool & J. Cash	Lying-in Hospital, Dublin	413
10,041(19)	R. Pool & J. Cash	Dr Steevens's Hospital, Dublin	413
10,041(20)	R. Pool & J. Cash	Christchurch Cathedral, Dublin	413
10,041(22)	R. Pool & J. Cash	St Werburgh's Church, Dublin	413
10,041(23)	R. Pool & J. Cash	St Thomas's Church, Dublin	413
10,041(24)	R. Pool & J. Cash	St Catherine's Church, Dublin	414
10,041(28)	R. Pool & J. Cash	Baron Bowes monument	414
10,041(29)	R. Pool & J. Cash	Leinster House, Dublin	414
10,041(30)	R. Pool & J. Cash	Powerscourt House, Dublin	414
10,041(31)	R. Pool & J. Cash	Charlemont House, Dublin	414
10,041(32)	R. Pool & J. Cash	Tyrone House, Dublin	414
11,707	R. Pool & J. Cash	Marine School, Dublin	415
11,708	R. Pool & J. Cash	St Thomas's Church, Dublin	415
11,709	R. Pool & J. Cash	Trinity College, Dublin	415
11,710	R. Pool & J. Cash	Provost's House, TCD, Dublin	415
11,711	R. Pool & J. Cash	Trinity College, Dublin	415
11,725	R. Pool & J. Cash	Leinster House, Dublin	415
11,726	R. Pool & J. Cash	Lying-in Hospital, Dublin	416
11,734	R. Pool & J. Cash	Powerscourt House, Dublin	416
11,740	R. Pool & J. Cash	Dublin Bridges	416

Engraver	Artist	Short title	Page
LOMBART, PIERRE (1612-1682)			
FRENCH SCHOOL			
10,069	?P.Lely	John Ogilby	348
LUCAS, DAVID (1802-1881)			
ENGLISH SCHOOL			
10,033	W. Stevenson	Sir Philip Crampton	483
10,109	R. Rothwell	1st Baron Plunket	464
10,116	W. Stevenson	Sir Philip Crampton	484
10,411	W. Stevenson	Charles Kendal Bushe	484
10,725	T.C. Thompson	Charles Boyton	501
10,749	M. Cregan	Abraham Colles	92
20,327	C. Tomkins	Dieppe Beach, France	508
LUCAS, JOHN (1807-1874)			
ENGLISH SCHOOL			
20,055	J. Lucas	The Ninth Plague of Egypt	357
LUPTON, THOMAS GOFF (1791-1873)			
ENGLISH SCHOOL			
10,094	J. Ramsay	Sir John Newport	425
10,243	J.P. Knight	William Sharman Crawford	326
10,798	J. Comerford	1st Baron Downes	77
10,824	A. Wivell	George IV, King of England	545
20,009	J.M.W. Turner	Solway Moss, Cumberland	521
20,013	J.M.W. Turner	Dunblane Cathedral, Scotland	522
20,019	J.M.W. Turner	Watercress Gatherers	523
20,026	J.M.W. Turner	Ben Arthur, Scotland	524
20,112	T. Lawrence	Bishop John Jebb	336
20,326	N. Maes	The Listening Housewife	361
20,664(1)	G.C. Stuart	Richard Earlom	491
20,789	W. Velde the Elder & Younger	A gale	532
LUTTERELL, EDWARD (FL.C.1673-1724)			
IRISH SCHOOL			
10,022 (C.S.10 I/of II)	E. Lutterell	Francis Higgins	357
10,136 (C.S.7 II/of III)	P. Lely	1st Earl of Essex	348
10,774 (C.S.7 III/of III)	P. Lely	1st Earl of Essex	348
LYNCH, JAMES HENRY (FL.1815-1868)			
IRISH SCHOOL			
10,263	R. Fenton	Sir George De Lacy Evans	153
10,685	L. Gluckman	Sir William Wilde	177
10,893	M. Leighton	'The Ladies of Llangollen'	344
10,990	L. Gluckman	Patrick O'Donoghue	177
11,035	B.R. Green	Frederick Shaw	185
11,076	F.W. Burton	Edward Pennefather	46
11,226	?J. Comerford	Henry Joy McCracken	77
11,267	French School c.1796	Batholomew Teeling	166
11,329	J. Comerford	Archibald Hamilton Rowan	77
11,430	L. Gluckman	Dr Robert Graves	177
11,936	L. Gluckman	John Blake Dillon	178
11,939	L. Gluckman	Patrick O'Donoghue	178

Engraver	Artist	Short title	Page
LYONS, EDWARD (1726-1801)			
IRISH SCHOOL			
?10,232	Irish School 18C	John Murphy	265
?10,919	Irish School 18C	John Murphy	265
MAAS, THEODOR (1659-1717)			
ANGLO-DUTCH SCHOOL			
10,003	T. Maas	The Battle of the Boyne	358
20,800	T. Maas	The Battle of the Boyne	358
McARDELL, JAMES (1728/29-1765)			
IRISH SCHOOL			
?10,008	J. Tudor	Trinity College, Dublin	510
10,026 (C.S. [Brooks] 5 I/of II)	F. Bindon	Archbishop Hugh Boulter	29
10,060 (C.S. 123 I/of III)	J. Reynolds	Charles Lucas	440
10,087 (C.S.21 II/of II)	C. Chalmers	Baron William Blakeney	61
10,088 (C.S.113 II/of III; R.113 III/ of IV)	J. Reynolds	20th Earl of Kildare	440
10,104 (C.S.149 I/of II)	?F. Hayman	James Quin	215
10,114 (C.S.126 II/of II)	T. Hudson	Edward Maurice	255
10,123 (C.S.189 I/of II)	F. Hayman	Henry Woodward	215
10,149 (C.S.99 I/of III)	B. Wilson	1st Earl Harcourt	542
10,165 (C.S.20)	English School 18C	John Blachford	133
10,168 (C.S.61)	T. Hudson	2nd Earl of Egmont	255
10,175 (C.S.55 I/of II)	G. Kneller	1st Duke of Dorset	318
10,180 (C.S.54 II/of II; R.54 III/of III)	W. Hoare	Arthur Dobbs	227
10,189 (C.S.176; R.176 I/of IV)	T. Hudson	1st Marquess Townshend	255
10,216 (C.S.74 II/of II)	T. Gainsborough	Bishop John Garnett	169
?10,220 (C.S.108 II/of II)	R. Hunter	Rev. John Mears	257
10,319 (C.S.188)	A. Pond	Margaret Woffington	410
10,338 (C.S.67 II/of II; R.67 II/of III)	J. Reynolds	Lady Charlotte FitzWilliam	440
10,343 (C.S.97 I/of II; R.97 II/of III)	F. Cotes	Duchess of Hamilton and Brandon	89
10,344 (C.S.112 I/of II; R.112 I/of IV)	J. Reynolds	Countess of Kildare	440
10,366 (C.S.188)	A. Pond	Margaret Woffington	410
10,374 (C.S.47 I/of II; R.47 II/of III)	F. Cotes	Countess of Coventry	89
10,389 (C.S.52 1/of II; R.52 II/of III)	J. Reynolds	Lady Anne Dawson	440
10,396 (C.S.48 I/of III; R.48 I/of IV)	G. Hamilton	Countess of Coventry	194

Engraver	Artist	Short title	Page
10,401 (C.S.91 III/of III)	P. Lely	Countess of Gramont	348
10,440 (C.S.35)	R. Hunter	Sir Charles Burton	257
10,677 (C.S.99 II/of III)	B. Wilson	1st Earl Harcourt	542
10,755 (C.S.44 pre-1/of III)	N. Hone the Elder	Rev. Emmanuel Collins	241
10,804 (C.S.65 III/of III; R.65 IV/of IV)	N. Hone the Elder	Sir John Fielding	241
10,830 (C.S.48 II/of III; R.48 III/of IV)	G. Hamilton	Countess of Coventry	194
10,846 (C.S.66 II/of II)	A. Soldi	Hon. Susanna Fitzpatrick	480
10,852 (C.S.84; R.84 I/of II)	D. Lüders	George, Prince of Wales	357
10,855 (C.S.114)	T. Hudson	William King	256
11,056 (C.S.157 II/of II; R.157 III/of IV)	J. Reynolds	10th Earl of Rothes	441
11,906	J. Tudor	Parliament House, Dublin	510
MCCLATCHIE, A. (FL.1828-1834) ?SCOTTISH SCHOOL			
20,377	W. Tombleson	Maidstone, Kent	506
MACDONALD, DANIEL (1821-1853) IRISH SCHOOL			
10,916	D. MacDonald	Rev. Theobald Mathew	358
MCDOWALL (19TH CENTURY) IRISH SCHOOL			
11,291	Lady M. Bingham	Patrick Sarsfield	30
MACKENZIE, E. (19TH CENTURY) AMERICAN SCHOOL			
10,674	C.W. Peale	General Richard Montgomery	392
MACKENZIE, FREDERICK (1787-1854) SCOTTISH SCHOOL			
11,122	W.M. Craig	Maria Edgeworth	92
11,130	?G.C. Stuart	1st Earl of Clare	491
MACKENZIE, K. (19TH CENTURY) ENGLISH SCHOOL			
10,801	T. Phillips	Lord John Hutchinson	406
MACLISE, DANIEL (1806-1870) IRISH SCHOOL			
10,288	D. Maclise	William Maguire	359
10,601	D. Maclise	Daniel O'Connell	360
10,675	D. Maclise	Thomas Moore	360
MACLURE & MACDONALD (FL.1840S-1880S) SCOTTISH SCHOOL			
10,970	H. Newton	Daniel O'Connell	382

Engraver	Artist	Short title	Page
MCCRAE, J.C. (19TH CENTURY)			
?IRISH SCHOOL			
10,284	Irish School c.1870	Sir Charles Gavan Duffy	299
MAGUIRE, CHARLES E. (FL.C.1820)			
IRISH SCHOOL			
11,838	C.E. Maguire	Isaac Willis Advertisement	361
MAGUIRE, PATRICK (FL.1783-1820)			
IRISH SCHOOL			
10,277	G.C. Stuart	John Foster	472
10,293	Irish School c.1800	Charles Thorp	284
10,602	J. Cullen	Edward Lysaght	96
10,629	J. Petrie	Henry Howley	404
10,630	J. Petrie	Henry Howley	404
10,654	J. Reynolds	2nd Earl of Moira	441
10,783 *(COPYIST)*	H.D. Hamilton	Richard Dawson	196
10,863 *(COPYIST)*	H.D. Hamilton	1st Viscount Kilwarden	197
11,211	J. Petrie	2nd Earl of Carhampton	404
11,221	Irish School late 18C	Leonard MacNally	283
11,555	Irish School late 18C	1st Viscount O'Neill	283
MAGUIRE, THOMAS HERBERT (1821-1895)			
IRISH SCHOOL			
10,684	T.H. Maguire	Sir William Wilde	361
10,871	T.H. Maguire	Bishop Samuel Hinds	361
MAILE, GEORGE (1800-1842)			
ENGLISH SCHOOL			
10,423	G. Dawe	1st Baron Decies	103
10,477	G. Maile	General Sir William Ponsonby	362
MALONE, D. (FL.C.1748-1766)			
IRISH SCHOOL			
20,123	G. Kneller	William III, King of England	318
20,124	G. Kneller	Queen Mary	318
MALTON, JAMES (c.1760-1803)			
ENGLISH SCHOOL			
11,567	J. Speed	Survey of Dublin, 1610	480
11,568	J. Malton	Upper Yard, Dublin Castle	363
11,569	J. Malton	The Custom House, Dublin	363
11,570	J. Malton	The Royal Exchange, Dublin	363
11,573	J. Malton	St Patrick's Cathedral, Dublin	363
11,574	J. Malton	The Tholsel, Dublin	363
11,577	J. Malton	Royal Barracks, Dublin	364
11,579	J. Malton	St Patrick's Cathedral, Dublin	364
11,580	J. Malton	The Provost's House, TCD	364
11,581	J. Malton	Royal Hospital, Kilmainham	364
11,582	J. Malton	Royal Military Infirmary, Dublin	364
11,583	J. Malton	Powerscourt House, Dublin	364
11,585	J. Malton	The Rotunda, Dublin	365
11,586	J. Malton	Marine School, Dublin	365
11,587	J. Malton	St Stephen's Green, Dublin	365
11,588	J. Malton	Dublin from Phoenix Park	365
11,591	J. Malton	The Blue-Coat School, Dublin	365

Engraver	Artist	Short title	Page
11,592	J. Malton	The Four Courts, Dublin	365
11,634	J. Malton	The Custom House, Dublin	366
11,640	J. Malton	The Custom House, Dublin	366
11,690	J. Malton	Arms of the City of Dublin	366
11,816	J. Malton	Dublin Bay, 1795	366
MALTON, THOMAS (1726-1801) ENGLISH SCHOOL			
11,645	F. Wheatley	Dublin Bay, 1785	539
11,902	F. Wheatley	Sheds of Clontarf	539
MANSFELD, JOHANN GEORG (1764-1817) AUSTRIAN SCHOOL			
11,103	J.G. Mansfeld	Count de Browne	366
MARCHI, GIUSEPPE FILIPPO LIBERATI (FL.1752-1808) ANGLO-ITALIAN SCHOOL			
10,028 (C.S.7 III/of III)	J. Reynolds	Oliver Goldsmith	441
10,471 (C.S.11 Pre-I; R.11 I/of III)	J. Zoffany	John Moody	550
MARIESCHI, MICHELE (1696-1743) VENETIAN SCHOOL			
11,662	M. Marieschi	Piazza S. Marco, Venice	367
MARKS, J.L. (FL.1822-1839) ENGLISH SCHOOL			
11,704	Irish School 19C	The Four Courts, Dublin	289
MARSHALL, WILLIAM (FL.1591-1649) ENGLISH SCHOOL			
11,005	English School 17C	Archbishop James Ussher	127
MARTINET, ACHILLE LOUIS (1806-1877) FRENCH SCHOOL			
11,486	P. Delaroche	Virgin and Child	108
MARTYN, JOHN (FL.1794-1828) IRISH SCHOOL			
10,279	F. Bindon	Turlough O'Carolan	29
10,838	A. Pope	Henry Grattan	419
11,105	W. Brocas	Rev. Thomas Betagh	38
11,148	A. Pope	Henry Grattan	419
11,770	Irish School early 19C	St George's Church, Dublin	290
MASQUELIER LE JEUNE, NICOLAS FRANCOIS JOSEPH (1760-1809) FRENCH SCHOOL			
20,058	S. Vouet	The Flagellation	533
MASSARD (18TH CENTURY) FRENCH SCHOOL			
10,302	?Irish School c.1750	Bishop Richard Chenevix	267
MASSON, ALPHONSE CHARLES (1814-1898) FRENCH SCHOOL			
20,084	Titian	The Entombment	506

Engraver	Artist	Short title	Page
MATISSE, HENRI (1869-1954) FRENCH SCHOOL			
20,839	H. Matisse	Ballet Dancer	368
MAUGIN, MARGUERITE THERESE (1736-1787) FRENCH SCHOOL			
10,042	J. Pillement	A first view of Ireland	408
MAURAND, CHARLES (FL.1863-1786) FRENCH SCHOOL			
20,635 (COPYIST)	French School 19C	A fox and a rabbit	167
MAZELL, PETER (FL.C.1761-1788) ENGLISH SCHOOL			
11,600	R. Omer	House of Commons, Dublin	386
20,814	R. Omer	House of Lords, Dublin	386
MAYER, CARL (1798-1868) NUREMBERG SCHOOL			
10,045	Continental School early 19C	John Field	80
MEADOWS, ROBERT MITCHELL (1798-1812) ENGLISH SCHOOL			
10,147	Marchioness of Thomond	Murrough O'Brien	501
MECHEL, CHRISTIAN DE (1737-1817) SWISS SCHOOL			
20,675(2)	N. Guibal	The Genius of the Arts	192
MEDLAND, THOMAS (1755-1833) ENGLISH SCHOOL			
10,055	A.M. Bigari	Christchurch Cathedral, Dublin	28
11,603	J. Carr	The Four Courts, Dublin	55
11,927	T. Cocking	Baggotsrath Castle, Co. Dublin	69
20,324	A. Cuyp	Landing of Prince Frederick at Nijmegen	97
MELLAN, CLAUDE (1598-1688) FRENCH SCHOOL			
20,125	C. Mellan	Abbé Pierre Gasendi	370
MELVILLE, HENRY (FL.1826-1877) ENGLISH SCHOOL			
20,248(89)	G. Barret the Younger	Retirement	13
METZ, CONRAD MARTIN (1749-1827) ANGLO-GERMAN SCHOOL			
20,236	C.M. Metz	Putti playing with a bird	372
20,237	C.M. Metz	Putti fishing	372
20,238	C.M. Metz	Bacchic party	372
20,239	C.M. Metz	Putti playing with goats	372
MEYER, HENRY HOPPNER (1783-1847) ENGLISH SCHOOL			
10,126	T.C. Thompson	Francis Johnston	501
10,200	J. Comerford	George Ensor	78
10,270	J. Jackson	4th Duke of Richmond	302
10,409	A.W. Devis	Eliza O'Neill	109
10,638	A. Wivell the Elder	Michael Kelly	545

Engraver	Artist	Short title	Page
MOORE, J. (FL.1831-1837) ENGLISH SCHOOL			
20,546	W. Hogarth	Incorrect perspective	231
MOORE, J. (FL.1851-1861) ENGLISH SCHOOL			
11,027	J. Mayall	Barry Sullivan	369
MONTAGU, DOMENICO (D.C.1750) ITALIAN SCHOOL			
20,674(9)	J. Barbault	Temple of Concord, Rome	11
MORISON & CO. (FL.1865-1880) IRISH SCHOOL			
11,632	Irish School 1880	New Theatre Royal, Dublin	299
11,840	Irish School c.1865	Findlater's Church, Dublin	299
MORRIS, J. (18TH CENTURY) ENGLISH SCHOOL			
20,094	English School 18C	A Gothick garden gate	134
MORRIS, THOMAS (C.1750-C.1802) ENGLISH SCHOOL			
20,083	R. Wilson	River Dee, Cheshire	543
MORRIS & CO (19TH CENTURY) ENGLISH SCHOOL			
10,482	English School 19C	Arthur MacMorrough Kavanagh	143
MOSSE, G. (19TH CENTURY) ENGLISH SCHOOL			
11,663	D. Wilkie	The Village Holiday	541
?MOSSOP, WILLIAM STEPHEN (1788-1827) IRISH SCHOOL			
11,222	W.S. Mossop	Self-Portrait	377
MOTE, WILLIAM HENRY (FL.1830-1858) ENGLISH SCHOOL			
10,784	J. Hayter	Emily Mary Dawson	216
10,791	E. Lamont	Baroness Dufferin and Clandeboye	328
10,891	C.L. Eastlake	Blanche Augusta Bury	122
11,309	A.E. Chalon	Penelope, Princess of Capua	62
11,333	J. Ross	Viscountess Powerscourt	463
MOTTE, CHARLES ETIENNE PIERRE (1785-1836) FRENCH SCHOOL			
20,721(63)	R.A.Q. Monvoisin	Roman sleeping	374
MOTTRAM, CHARLES (1807-1876) ENGLISH SCHOOL			
20,486	G. Pickering	Grassmere Lake, Cumbria	407
MOYREAU, JEAN (18TH CENTURY) FRENCH SCHOOL			
20,690(80)	P. Wouverman	Departure for the hunt	

Engraver	Artist	Short title	Page
MULCAHY, JEREMIAH HODGES (FL.1831-1889) IRISH SCHOOL			
20,168	J.H. Mulcahy	Grindstone and Waterwheel	377
20,323	J.H. Mulcahy	Rothesay Pier, Isle of Bute	377
MULLER, JOHANN SEBASTIAN (1715-1785) ANGLO-GERMAN SCHOOL			
11,347	J.S. Muller	Book Illustration	377
MULRENIN, BERNARD (1803-1868) IRISH SCHOOL			
10,971	?B. Mulrenin	Daniel O'Connell	378
11,233	B. Mulrenin	1st Marquess of Anglesey	378
MURPHY, A. (19TH CENTURY) IRISH SCHOOL			
20,246	A. Murphy	The Broomseller	378
MURPHY, JOHN (FL.1778-1820) IRISH SCHOOL			
10,106 (C.S.11 II/of II)	M.W. Peters	Matthew Peters	396
10,166 (C.S.4)	C. Grignon the Younger	Captain George Farmer	191
11,475 (C.S.13 I/of II)	J. Reynolds	3rd Duke of Portland	441
10,541 (C.S.1 I/of II)	J. Murphy	Rev. James Arthur	379
20,731(89) (C.S.16 III/of IV)	School of Titian	So-called portraits	506
MYERS (18TH CENTURY) ENGLISH SCHOOL			
11,754	Irish School late 18C	Parliament House, Dublin	283
NASH, JOSEPH (1808-1878) ENGLISH SCHOOL			
11,497	J. Nash	Kenilworth Castle, England	380
NATTIER, JEAN MARC (1685-1766) FRENCH SCHOOL			
20,678(1) *(COPYIST)*	?A. Van Dyck	Peter Paul Rubens	527
20,678(6) *(COPYIST)*	P.P. Rubens	Marriage of Marie de Medici	467
NEEDHAM, JONATHAN (FL.1850-1874) ENGLISH SCHOOL			
20,338	D. Cox	'The Labourer's Return'	92
NEWMAN AND CO., JOHN (FL.1860s-1870s) ENGLISH SCHOOL			
11,761	Irish School 19C	St Patrick's Cathedral, Dublin	289
NEWMAN, J. (19TH CENTURY) ENGLISH SCHOOL			
20,624	?J. Newman	Trinity College, Dublin	382

Engraver	Artist	Short title	Page
NEWTON, JAMES (1748-1804) ENGLISH SCHOOL			
20,216	E. Edwards	The Entrance to Strawberry Hill	123
NICOLLET, BENEDICT ALPHONSE (1743-1806) FRENCH SCHOOL			
20,724(24)	? Giorgione	Milo of Croton	175
NIQUET, CLAUDE (C.1770-1831) FRENCH SCHOOL			
20,201	N. Poussin	St John Baptising	421
NOBLE, SAMUEL (1779-1853) ENGLISH SCHOOL			
20,430	E. Dayes	Middleham Castle, Yorkshire	103
NOLEL, T. (18TH CENTURY) IRISH SCHOOL			
11,543	T. Nolel	Counsellor Blackbourne	383
NUGENT, THOMAS (FL.1785-1798) IRISH SCHOOL			
10,743	H. Hone	1st Earl of Charlemont	236
11,123	H. Hone	1st Earl of Charlemont	236
NUNZER, ENGELHARD H. (D.1733) GERMAN SCHOOL			
11,260	English School 17C	George Walker	128
NUTIER, WILLIAM (1754-1802) ENGLISH SCHOOL			
11,094	S. Shelley	Colonel Henry Barry	474
NUTTING, JOSEPH (C.1660-1722) ENGLISH SCHOOL			
11,101	English School late 17C	James Bonnell	131
OGBORNE, JOHN (C.1755-1795) ENGLISH SCHOOL			
10,341	G. Romney	Mrs Jordan	461
OKEY, SAMUEL (FL.1765-1780) ANGLO-AMERICAN SCHOOL			
?10,327 (C.S.4a)	J. M....	The Gunning Sisters	358
10,339 (C.S.7 II/of II)	J. Reynolds	Nelly O'Brien	442
O'NEILL, HENRY (1798-1880) IRISH SCHOOL			
10,064	L. Gluckman	William Smith O'Brien	178
10,102	L. Gluckman	John Martin	178
10,121	L. Gluckman	Terence Bellew McManus	178
10,179	L. Gluckman	Charles Gavan Duffy	179
10,521	L. Gluckman	William Smith O'Brien	179
10,522	L. Gluckman	Richard O'Gorman Junior	179
10,523	L. Gluckman	Thomas Francis Meagher	179
10,525	L. Gluckman	Charles Gavan Duffy	180

Engraver	Artist	Short title	Page
10,526	L. Gluckman	John Martin	180
10,553	L. Gluckman	Terence Bellew McManus	180
10,710	L. Gluckman	George Baldwin	180
10,722	L. Gluckman	Lt.-General Sir Edward Blakeney	181
10,789	W.H. Collier	William Hamilton Drummond	69
10,980	H. O'Neill	Daniel O'Connell	387
11,934	L. Gluckman	John Martin	181
11,935	L. Gluckman	Charles Gavan Duffy	181
11,937	L. Gluckman	Richard O'Gorman Junior	181
11,938	L. Gluckman	Thomas Francis Meagher	181
11,940	L. Gluckman	Terence Bellew McManus	182
OPFFER, IVAN (1897-1980) DANISH SCHOOL			
20,837	I. Opffer	William Butler Yeats	387
O'REILLY, B. (19TH CENTURY) IRISH SCHOOL			
10,066	J. Gubbins	Daniel O'Connell	191
ORME, DANIEL (1766-1802) ENGLISH SCHOOL			
20,104	M. Brown	King George III and Officers	43
OUTRIM, JOHN (FL.1840-1874) ENGLISH SCHOOL			
20,260	W. Collins	'Rustic Civility'	70
P...., H. (18TH CENTURY) ENGLISH SCHOOL			
10,527	J. Reynolds	Lawrence Sterne	442
11,320	French School 18C	Guillaume Thomas Raynal	165
P...., T. (19TH CENTURY) IRISH SCHOOL			
11,861	T. Bridgford	'The Masquerader'	34
PAGE, ROBERT (19TH CENTURY) ENGLISH SCHOOL			
11,214	J. Jackson	Rev. Adam Clarke	302
PARK, THOMAS (C.1760-1834) ENGLISH SCHOOL			
10,323 (C.S.7 II/of III; R.7 III/of V)	J. Reynolds	Hon. Lincoln Stanhope	442
10,408 (C.S.5; R.5 III/of III)	J. Hoppner	Mrs Jordan	247
11,415 (C.S.2 I/of II; R.2 II/of III)	J. Hoppner	Lord Henry FitzGerald	247
PARKER, GEORGE (FL.1820-1834) ENGLISH SCHOOL			
10,986	J. Comerford	1st Marquess of Ormonde	78
PARKES, ROBERT BOWYER (1830-C.1891) ENGLISH SCHOOL			
10,711	J. Reynolds	Colonel Edward Bligh	442
10,720	J. Reynolds	1st Marquess of Drogheda	442

Engraver	Artist	Short title	Pag
PARR (18TH CENTURY) ENGLISH SCHOOL			
11,904	J. Tudor	Custom House, Dublin	51
11,905	J. Tudor	Dublin Castle	51
PARRY, T.H. (19TH CENTURY) ENGLISH SCHOOL			
11,193	T. Lawrence	John Wilson Croker	336
PAYNE, ALBERT HENRY (1812-1902) ENGLISH SCHOOL			
20,278	W. Tombleson	Bridge over the Rhine	507
20,412	G. Cattermole	Watermill, Cumbria	57
PAYNE, GEORGE T. (FL.1830-1860) ENGLISH SCHOOL			
10,705	R. Sayers	1st Viscount Beresford	470
PEARSON, JOHN (1777-1813) ENGLISH SCHOOL			
11,250	J.G. Eccard	Margaret Woffington	122
PELHAM, PETER (C.1680-1751) ANGLO-AMERICAN SCHOOL			
10,012 (C.S.27 I/of II)	T. Gibson	1st Viscount Molesworth	175
10,569 (C.S.30)	M. Dahl	2nd Duke of Ormonde	99
10,997 (C.S.[Beckett]30 IV/of IV; R.30a II/of II)	G. Kneller	1st Duke of Devonshire	319
11,022 (C.S.126 II/of III; R.126 III/of IV)	English School 17C	so-called Jonathan Swift	128
11,396 (C.S.13 II/of II)	R. Walker	so-called Oliver Cromwell	535
PELLETIER, JOSEPH LAURENT (1811-1892) FRENCH SCHOOL			
20,318	J.L. Pelletier	Rocks and bushes	392
20,319	J.L. Pelletier	Pathway to a cottage	392
PENNELL, JOSEPH (1860-1926) AMERICAN SCHOOL			
11,454	J. Pennell	Exeter	392
11,455	J. Pennell	Barnstaple, Devon	392
11,456	J. Pennell	Bideford, Devon	392
11,457	J. Pennell	New York	393
11,458	J. Pennell	Valley of Dart, Devon	393
11,459	J. Pennell	Kensington Gardens, London	393
11,460	J. Pennell	Times Building, New York	393
11,461	J. Pennell	Brooklyn, New York	393
11,462	J. Pennell	Statue of Liberty, New York	393
11,463	J. Pennell	New York	394
11,464	J. Pennell	Café	394
11,465	J. Pennell	Exeter Hall, London	394
11,466	J. Pennell	Brooklyn, New York	394
11,467	J. Pennell	Illfracombe, Devon	394

Engraver	Artist	Short title	Page
11,468	J. Pennell	Fig tree, London	394
11,469	J. Pennell	New York bridges	395
11,470	J. Pennell	Cortland Street, New York	395
20,693(1)	J. Pennell	Schiedam, Holland	395
PERRET, J.J. (18TH CENTURY) ENGLISH SCHOOL			
11,886	J.Rocque	Plan of Dublin, 1753	458
PETERKIN, JAMES (19TH CENTURY) IRISH SCHOOL			
10,452	C. Grey	Daniel O'Connell	191
PETERS, WILHELM OTTO (1851-AFTER 1923) NORWEGIAN SCHOOL			
20,068	W.O. Peters	Norwegian Fishermen	397
PETRIE, JAMES (1750-1819) IRISH SCHOOL			
10,156	J.Petrie	James Napper Tandy	405
PHILIPS, G.F. (FL.1815-1832) ENGLISH SCHOOL			
10,308	H. Hone	Mrs Sarah Siddons	236
PHILLIPS, CHARLES (1737-AFTER 1783) ENGLISH SCHOOL			
10,378 (C.S.1 II/of III)	N. Hone the Elder	Lydia Hone	241
10,699 (C.S.1 III/of III)	N. Hone the Elder	Lydia Hone	242
PHILLIPS, I. (19TH CENTURY) ENGLISH SCHOOL			
20,805	T.C. Croker	Man selling spectacles	95
PICART, CHARLES (C.1780-C.1837) ENGLISH SCHOOL			
10,185	T. Lawrence	Galbraith Lowry Cole	337
10,707	W. Evans	James Barry	152
10,800	C. Robertson	4th Duke of Dorset	453
PICOT, VICTOR MARIE (1744-1805) ANGLO-FRENCH SCHOOL			
11,257	N. Hone the Elder	Rev. George Whitefield	242
PINELLI, BARTOLOMEO (1781-1835) ITALIAN SCHOOL			
20,709(3)	B. Pinelli	The Grape Gatherers	408
PIRANESI, GIOVANNI BATTISTA (1720-1778) ITALIAN SCHOOL			
20,525	G.B. Piranesi	Temple of Polo, Istria	409
20,526	G.B. Piranesi	Arch of Augustus, Rimini	409
20,527	G.B. Piranesi	Campus Martius, Rome	409
20,528	G.B. Piranesi	Venetian Ambassador's Palace	409
20,530	G.B. Piranesi	Pontis Triumphalis, Rome	409

Engraver	Artist	Short title	Page
20,531	G.B. Piranesi	Temple of Vespasian, Rome	409
20,532	G.B. Piranesi	Tomb of the Scipios, Rome	409
20,533	G.B. Piranesi	Temple of Pola, Istria	409
20,534	G.B. Piranesi	Temple of Concord, Rome	410
20,832	G.B. Piranesi	Trevi Fountain, Rome	410
PLACE, FRANCIS (1647-1728) ENGLISH SCHOOL			
10,907 (C.S.6)	R. Walker	Major General John Lambert	535
POLLARD, ROBERT (1755-1838) ENGLISH SCHOOL			
10,777	N. Hone the Elder	General George Eliott	242
PONTIUS, PAUL (1603-1638) FLEMISH SCHOOL			
20,114	A. Van Dyck	Hendrik van Balen the Elder	529
20,116	A. Van Dyck	Jan Caspar Gevartius	529
PORTER, H. (19TH CENTURY) ENGLISH SCHOOL			
20,797	H. Porter	Sheep by Moonlight	420
POSSELWHITE, JAMES (1798-1884) ENGLISH SCHOOL			
10,885	W.J. Newton	George Alexander Hamilton	382
10,886	W.J. Newton	George Alexander Hamilton	383
11,308	J. Robertson	Marchioness of Sligo	454
POUNCEY, BENJAMIN THOMAS (FL.1772-1799) ENGLISH SCHOOL			
20,389	T.T. Hearne	Kenilworth, Warwickshire	217
POUND, D.J. (FL.1842-1877) ENGLISH SCHOOL			
10,567	J. Mayall	James Whiteside	369
10,860	J. Mayall	Sir Henry Singer Keating	369
10,927	J. Mayall	Daniel Maclise	369
11,023	J. Mayall	William Shee	370
POWLE, GEORGE (FL.1764-1771) ENGLISH SCHOOL			
10,290	English School 16C	Sir John Perrot	124
PRIOR, THOMAS ABIEL (1809-1886) ENGLISH SCHOOL			
11,341	T. Lawrence & English School c.1830	Group Portrait	337
11,346	G. Kneller & C. Jervas	Pope, Addison and Swift	326
11,372	English School 19C	British Prime Ministers	143
11,373	Lely & J. Closterman	Ray, Temple and Wren	349
11,374	G. Kneller & T. Worlidge	Kings George I and II	326
11,375	G. Kneller	Queen Anne	319
11,384	T. Lawrence & A. Wivell	Politicians	546

Engraver	Artist	Short title	Page
PROUT, SAMUEL (1783-1852) ENGLISH SCHOOL			
20,559	S. Prout	Gothic Archway	422
20,560	S. Prout	Farmyard, Devon	422
20,561	S. Prout	Cottage, Devon	422
20,562	S. Prout	Cottage, Devon	422
20,563	S. Prout	Cottage at Pennycross	422
20,564	S. Prout	Cottage at Ide,, Devon	423
20,565	S. Prout	Cottages at Glastonbury	423
20,567	S. Prout	Cottages	423
PRUDHON, PIERRE PAUL (1758-1823) *FRENCH SCHOOL*			
20,691(1) *(COPYIST)*	Raphael	Virgin and Child with St John	425
PURCELL, RICHARD (FL.1746-C.1766) IRISH SCHOOL			
10,011 (C.S.47)	C. Jervas	Archbishop William King	305
10,034 (C.S.31)	J. Reynolds	David Garrick	442
10,053 (C.S.8 I/of II)	G. Soest	Archbishop Michael Boyle	479
10,163 (C.S.4 ?I/ofII)	G. Chalmers	General William Blakeney	62
10,322 (C.S.61)	N. Hone the Elder	Mrs Laetitia Pilkington	242
10,683 (C.S.93 II/of II)	F. Van der Mijn	so-called Peg Woffington	526
?10,829 (C.S.Class III:46 IV/of V)	F. Cotes	Countess of Coventry	90
?10,831 (C.S.Class III:46 I/of V)	F. Cotes	Countess of Coventry	90
10,923 (C.S.54 I/of II)	R. Hunter	Rev. Samuel Madden	258
10,924 (C.S.54 II/of II)	R. Hunter	Rev. Samuel Madden	258
11,069 (C.S.61)	N. Hone the Elder	Mrs Laetitia Pilkington	242
11,249 (C.S.93 pre-I)	F. Van der Mijn	So-called Peg Woffington	526
PYE, JOHN (1782-1874) ENGLISH SCHOOL			
20,799	J.M.W. Turner	Ehrenbreitstein	511
QUILLEY, JOHN P. (FL. 1823-1842) ENGLISH SCHOOL			
10,975	J. Gubbins	Daniel O'Connell	191
RADCLYFFE, EDWARD (1809-1863) ENGLISH SCHOOL			
11,674	J.E. Jones	Monasterboice	306
11,675	J.E. Jones	Beaulieu House	306
11,676	J.E. Jones	Dominican Priory, Drogheda	307
11,677	J.E. Jones	Ardgillan Castle	307

Engraver	Artist	Short title	Page
11,678	J.E. Jones	Gormanstown Castle	307
11,685	J.E. Jones	Rush and the Skerries	307
11,686	J.E. Jones	Portrane and Lambay Island	307
11,687	J.E. Jones	Malahide	307
11,688	J.E. Jones	Malahide Castle	307
11,758	J.E. Jones	Lusk Church	308
RADCLYFFE THE ELDER, WILLIAM (1783-1855) ENGLISH SCHOOL			
11,609	P. Byrne	St Patrick's Cathedral	48
11,759	P. Byrne	St Patrick's Cathedral	48
11,798	J.M.W. Turner	Mantes-La-Jolie, France	512
20,206	T. Gainsborough	The Watering Place	169
20,424	J.D. Harding	Fiesole Cathedral, Italy	209
RADDON, WILLIAM (FL.1817-1862) ENGLISH SCHOOL			
20,615	A. Cooper	A Mule Pheasant	83
RAINALDI, FRANCESCO (1770-1805) ITALIAN SCHOOL			
20,676(1)	Raphael	Loggia of the Vatican	425
RANCATI, ANTONIO (1784-1816) ITALIAN SCHOOL			
20,467	Italian School late 18C	Chinese Porters	301
RANSON, THOMAS FRAZER (1784-1828) ENGLISH SCHOOL			
10,048	G. Petrie	Christchurch Cathedral, Dublin	400
20,076	F. Nicholson	Fanny with her puppies	383
RAPHAEL, JOSEPH (1872-1950) AMERICAN SCHOOL			
11,449	J. Raphael	Tree Trunk and Bust	427
11,450	J. Raphael	Strolling Players	427
11,451	J. Raphael	S. Giorgio Maggiore, Venice	427
11,452	J. Raphael	Women of Italy	427
11,453	J. Raphael	Sailing boats	427
RAUNHEIM, HERMAN (1817-1895) GERMAN SCHOOL			
20,176	U. Gréther	The Oath of the Grüli	185
RAVENET THE ELDER, SIMON FRANCOIS (1706-1746) ANGLO-FRENCH SCHOOL			
10,528	J. Reynolds	Lawrence Sterne	443
11,205	English School 17C	2nd Earl of St Albans	128
RAZÉ, L.L. (19TH CENTURY) FRENCH SCHOOL			
20,566	L.L. Razé	Rustic Buildings	428
20,569	L.L. Razé	A ruined castle	428
20,588	L.L. Razé	Porta Maggiore, Rome	428

Engraver	Artist	Short title	Page
READ, WILLIAM (FL.1824-1837)			
ENGLISH SCHOOL			
10,583	A. Wivell the Elder	Roger O'Connor	545
10,779	English School 19C	Robert Emmet	143
10,989	Irish School 1830s	Fergus O'Connor	296
READ AND CO. (19TH CENTURY)			
ENGLISH SCHOOL			
10,306	L. Gluckman	Thomas Francis Meagher	182
REDAWAY,JAMES C. (FL.1818-1857)			
ENGLISH SCHOOL			
20,265	T. Allom	Durham Cathedral	4
20,266	T. Allom	Grotto, Castle Eden Dean	4
REEVE, R.G. (FL.1811-1837)			
ENGLISH SCHOOL			
11,496	F.T.L. Francia	Calais, France	164
REGNIER, CHARLES (1811-1862)			
FRANCO-GERMAN SCHOOL			
20,061	German School 950/1050	Virgin and Child & St Nicholas	172
?20,064	German School 1520/1530	Decorative Panels	173
20,065	German School 1546/1555	Tankard	173
RETZCH, FRIEDRICH MORITZ AUGUST (1779-1857)			
GERMAN SCHOOL			
20,730(6)	F.M.A. Retzch	Love reposing	430
REYNOLDS THE ELDER, SAMUEL WILLIAM (1773-1835)			
ENGLISH SCHOOL			
10,422	C.F. Von Breda	Bishop Thomas Hussey	533
10,461	W. Owen	Archbishop William Stuart	389
10,466	M.W. Peters	1st Viscount O'Neill	396
10,469	J. Hoppner	1st Marquess of Thomond	247
10,491	T.C. Thompson	3rd Earl Talbot	502
10,701	W. Owen	Archbishop William Stuart	389
10,888	S.W. Reynolds the Younger	General Sir George Hewitt	447
20,024	J.M.W. Turner	East Gate, Winchelsea, Sussex	524
20,028	J.M.W. Turner	Christ and the Woman of Samaria	524
20,819	S.W. Reynolds the Elder	Passing of the Reform Bill	447
REYNOLDS THE YOUNGER, SAMUEL WILLIAM (1794-1872)			
ENGLISH SCHOOL			
20,132	A. Vandercabel	A Sailing boat	526
20,137	?Correggio	St Mary Magdalen	86
RICCIANI, ANTONIO (1775-1836)			
ROMAN SCHOOL			
20,714(16)	A. Canova	Napoleon I	54
RICHARDSON, GEORGE K. (FL.1836-1891)			
ENGLISH SCHOOL			
20,434	W.H. Bartlett	Powerscourt House, Co. Wicklow	21
20,436	W.H. Bartlett	Old Weir Bridge, Killarney	21
20,600	W.H. Bartlett	Salmon Leap, Leixlip	21

Engraver	Artist	Short title	Page
RICHARDSON, WILLIAM (FL. 1840-1877)			
ENGLISH SHCOOL			
20,282	D.O. Hill	Barskimming, Scotland	225
RIDLEY, WILLIAM (1764-1838)			
ENGLISH SCHOOL			
10,643	L.F. Abbott	Admiral Sir Robert Kingsmill	1
10,644	A. Kauffmann	Self-Portrait	311
10,656	English School c.1780	2nd Earl of Moira	137
10,657	English School c.1780	2nd Earl of Moira	137
10,669	N. Dance	Arthur Murphy	101
11,084	R. Home	Hugh Boyd	234
11,136	S. Drummond	William Thomas Fitzgerald	118
11,157	N. Hone the Elder	Francis Grose	243
11,174	T. Robinson	Rev. William Cooper	457
11,204	S. Drummond	Andrew Cherry	119
11,286	J. Steele	Dr Samuel Solomon	482
20,834	C. Allingham	Thomas Dermody	2
ROBERTS, P. (FL.1795-1828)			
ENGLISH SCHOOL			
11,145	P. Fitzpatrick	Henry Grattan	160
ROBINSON, HENRY (FL. 1827-1872)			
ENGLISH SCHOOL			
10,979	J. Stewart	Daniel O'Connell	485
20,155	E. Stone	Alice	486
20,157	L. Sharpe	The Maid of Athens	472
ROBINSON, JOHN CHARLES (1824-1912)			
ENGLISH SCHOOL			
20,082	J.C. Robinson	Nine Barrow Down, Dorset	454
ROBINSON, JOHN HENRY (1796-1871)			
ENGLISH SCHOOL			
10,370	F. Stone	Baroness Dufferin & Clandeboye	486
10,570	G. Kneller	2nd Duke of Ormonde	319
20,204	T. Lawrence	Lady Henrietta Grantham	337
20,331	T. Woodward	The Tempting Present	547
20,474	J.H. Robinson	Neath Abbey, Wales	455
ROBINSON, THOMAS (C.1770-1810)			
ENGLISH SCHOOL			
10,043	T. Robinson	1st Viscount Avonmore	457
ROFFE, F.R. (19TH CENTURY)			
ENGLISH SCHOOL			
20,209 *(COPYIST)*	J. Bell	The Children in the Wood	25
20,210 *(COPYIST)*	J.H. Foley	Ino and Bacchus	160
ROFFE, WILLIAM (FL.1848-1884)			
ENGLISH SCHOOL			
20,209	J. Bell	The Children in the Wood	25
20,210	J.H. Foley	Ino and Bacchus	160
ROGERS, JAMES EDWARD (1838-1896)			
IRISH SCHOOL			
11,737	T.N. Deane & B. Woodward	Dublin drinking Fountains	104

Engraver	Artist	Short title	Page
ROGERS, JOHN (C.1808-1888) ENGLISH SCHOOL			
20,514	W.H. Bartlett	Limerick Bridge	21
ROGERS, JOHN (FL. 1820'S-1850'S) ENLGISH SCHOOL			
10,704	J. Haslock	1st Viscount Beresford	211
ROLLS, CHARLES (C.1800-C.1857) ENGLISH SCHOOL			
10,754	J. Comerford	Bishop William Coppinger	78
20,136	T. Lawrence	The Morning Walk	337
ROMANET, ANTOINE LOUIS (1742/43-AFTER 1810) FRENCH SCHOOL			
20,723(14)	Raphael	Virgin and Child	427
20,725(56)	N. Poussin	The Eucharist	421
ROOKER, EDWARD (18TH CENTURY) IRISH SCHOOL			
11,669	T. Ivory	Marino Casino	301
ROSAPINA, FRANCESCO BOLOGNESE SCHOOL			
20,682(62)	G. Reni	Virgin and Child	430
ROWE, GEORGE (1797-1864) ENGLISH SCHOOL			
20,353	G. Rowe	Glendalough, Co. Wicklow	465
20,354	G. Rowe	Glen Malure, Co. Wicklow	465
ROWLANDSON, THOMAS (1756-1827) ENGLISH SCHOOL			
11,409	T. Rowlandson	Henry Munro	465
11,503	F. Wheatley	Irish Peasants	540
RYALL, HENRY THOMAS (1811-1867) ENGLISH SCHOOL			
10,361	A.E. Chalon	Countess of Blessington	62
RYLAND, WILLIAM WYNNE (1732-1783) ENGLISH SCHOOL			
11,258	T. Hudson	Admiral Sir Peter Warren	256
SABATIER, LEON JEAN BAPTISTE (FL.1827-1887) FRENCH SCHOOL			
20,316	E. Isabey	Fishing Community	300
20,317	E. Isabey	Boat under repair	300
SADELER, AEGIDIUS (C.1570-1629) FLEMISH SCHOOL			
20,229	F. Barocci	The Entombment of Christ	12
SADLER THE ELDER, WILLIAM (FL.1765-1788) IRISH SCHOOL			
10,417	R. Hunter	2nd Earl Temple	258

Engraver	Artist	Short title	Page
SAILLIAR, LEWIS (1748-C.1795)			
ENGLISH SCHOOL			
10,140	R. Cosway	George 1V, King of England	88
SANDERS, GEORGE (1810-C.1876)			
ENGLISH SCHOOL			
10,421	S. Catterson Smith the Elder	4th Earl of Clarendon	59
10,456	S. Catterson Smith the Elder	Francis Blackburne	59
10,468	S. Catterson Smith the Elder	3rd Duke of Leinster	59
10,483	S. Catterson Smith the Elder	Sir Henry Marsh	60
10,505	S. Catterson Smith the Elder	13th Earl of Eglington & Winton	60
10,506	S. Catterson Smith the Elder	Archbishop Richard Whateley	60
10,510	S. Catterson Smith the Elder	Archbishop De La Poer Beresford	60
10,544	S. Catterson Smith the Elder	Sir Philip Crampton	60
10,690	S. Catterson Smith the Elder	Charles William Wall	61
10,815	F.W. Burton	Arthur Guinness of Beaumont	47
11,856	S. Catterson Smith the Elder	Sir Edward Blakeney	61
20,768	S. Catterson Smith the Elder	Richard Ponsonby	61
SANDS, JAMES (FL.1832-1844)			
ENGLISH SCHOOL			
20,365	W.L. Leitch	Argyrd Castle, Albania	344
20,414	W.L. Leitch	Lake Garda, Italy	345
20,421	W.A. Nesfield	Wressel Castle, Yorkshire	381
20,442	W. Brockedom	Val Angrona, Italy	38
SANDS, ROBERT (1792-1855)			
ENGLISH SCHOOL			
11,086	F. Cotes & J. Ramberg	George Anne Bellamy	91
20,398	T. Allom	Buttermere, Cumberland	4
20,432	W. Tombleson	Henley-on-Thames, Berkshire	507
SANDYS, EDWIN (FL.1685-1708)			
IRISH SCHOOL			
10,285	D. Loggan	Sir William Petty	356
SANGSTER, SAMUEL (C.1804-1872)			
ENGLISH SCHOOL			
10,868	C. Jagger	General Sir Henry Johnston	303
SARGENT, HENRY (1795-1857)			
ENGLISH SCHOOL			
	W. Sadler the Younger	Poolbeg Light House	469
SAY, WILLIAM (1768-1834)			
ENGLISH SCHOOL			
10,083	G.C. Stuart	Archbishop Charles Agar	492
10,369	G.H. Harlow	Countess of Wicklow	210
10,372	J.J. Masquerier	Eliza O'Neill	368
10,455	J. Ramsay	Lt.-General Sir John Doyle	425
10,478	G.C. Stuart	1st Viscount Pery	492
11,979	J.M.W. Turner	Juvenile Tricks	516
11,981	J.M.W. Turner	Yorkshire Coast	517
11,984	J.M.W. Turner	Grand Junction Canal	517
11,986	J.M.W. Turner	Marine Dabblers	517
11,987	J.M.W. Turner	Near Blair Athol, Scotland	518

Engraver	Artist	Short title	Page
11,991	J.M.W. Turner	Martello Tower, Sussex	518
11,995	J.M.W. Turner	Hindu Ablutions	519
20,006	J.M.W. Turner	The Alps, France	521
20,010	J.M.W. Turner	Solitude	521
20,018	J.M.W. Turner	The Tenth Plague of Egypt	523
20,025	J.M.W. Turner	Isis	524
SCARLETT, DAVIS J. (1804-1845/46) ENGLISH SCHOOL			
10,775	W. Robinson	2nd Earl of Enniskillen	457
SCHENCK, PIETER (1660-1718/19) DUTCH SCHOOL			
10,560	?P.Lely	William of Orange	349
10,821	G. Kneller	George, Prince of Denmark	319
10,865	P. Schenck	James II, King of England	470
10,998	English School 17C	2nd Duke of Ormonde	128
SCHIAVONETTI, LEWIS (1765-1810) ANGLO-ITALIAN SCHOOL			
10,951	H. Edridge	1st Earl Macartney	123
20,722(15)	J. Barry	Pandora	18
SCOTIN, JEAN BAPTISTE GERARD (1698-AFTER 1733) ANGLO-FRENCH SCHOOL			
20,069	Genoese School 17C	Belisarius Recognised	171
SCOTT, JAMES (C.1809-1889) ENGLISH SCHOOL			
11,232	G. Lance	James Knowles	329
SCOTT, EDMUND (C.1746-C.1810) ENGLISH SCHOOL			
11,038	R. Stewart	Thomas Sheridan	485
SCRIVEN, EDWARD (1775-1841) ENGLISH SCHOOL			
10,437	A. Pope	Henry Grattan	419
10,529	F. Bindon	Dean Jonathan Swift	30
10,533	G. Kneller	1st Duke of Ormonde	319
10,679	J. Comerford	Thomas Williams	78
10,782	?M. Miereveld	1st Earl of Danby	373
10,925	N. Dance	Arthur Murphy	101
11,029	G.F. Joseph	Sir John Stevenson	309
11,030	G.F. Joseph	Sir John Stevenson	309
11,036	F. Cruickshank	Frederick Shaw	95
11,039	J. Moore	Sir Edward Burtenshaw Sugden	374
11,208	M.A. Shee	Countess of Cavan	473
11,218	W. Haines	John Croker	193
11,404	F.P. Stephanoff	Admiral Sir Edward Nagle	483
11,417	G. Romney	Mary Tighe	461
20,658	W.E. West	Felicia Dorothea Hemans	538
SEALE, RICHARD WILLIAM (FL.1732-1775) ENGLISH SCHOOL			
11,877	R.W. Seale	Plans of Irish Towns	471

Engraver	Artist	Short title	Page
SIMON, PETER (C.1750-C.1810)			
ENGLISH SCHOOL			
20,686(16)	M.W. Peters	Hero, Ursula and Beatrice	396
SINGLETON, JOHN (FL.1788-1799)			
ENGLISH SCHOOL			
10,283	B. Stoker	Robert Jephson	485
SKELTON, WILLIAM (1763-1848)			
ENGLISH SCHOOL			
10,984	W. Lane	2nd Earl of Upper Ossory	329
11,081	English School 18C	Rev. George Berkeley	134
SLACK (18TH CENTURY)			
?IRISH SCHOOL			
11,691	J. Tudor	Dublin from Phoenix Park	510
SLATER, JOSEPH			
ENGLISH SCHOOL			
10,271	J. Slater	John MacGregor Skinner	479
SLY, S. (FL.1833-1842)			
ENGLISH SCHOOL			
20,640	Irish School 19C	Old Bridge, Milltown	289
20,641	Irish School 19C	Newbridge	289
SMITH, BENJAMIN (1775-1833)			
ENGLISH SCHOOL			
10,744	H. Hone	1st Earl of Charlemont	236
10,745	H. Hone	1st Earl of Charlemont	236
SMITH, EDWARD (FL. 1823-1851)			
ENGLISH SCHOOL			
11,126	T. Hargreaves	Lt.-General John Devereux	210
11,265	T. Lawrence	1st Duke of Wellington	338
20,151	H. Melville	Wycoller Hall, Lancashire	371
20,152	G. Cattermole	Albert of Gierstein	57
20,219	David Wilkie	The Jew's Harp	541
SMITH, JOHN (1652-1742)			
ENGLISH SCHOOL			
10,002 (C.S.194)	G. Kneller	2nd Duke of Ormonde	320
10,009 (C.S.239 II/of III)	G. Kneller	Edward Southwell	320
10,010 (C.S.54 II/of III)	G. Kneller	William Congreve	321
10,030 (C.S.244 II/of III)	J. Richardson the Elder	Richard Steele	447
10,071 (C.S.200 II/of III)	G. Kneller	Sir John Percival	321
10,095 (C.S.143 II/of III)	G. Kneller	James 11, King of England	321
10,161 (C.S.240 II/of II)	G. Kneller	Sir Robert Southwell	321
10,213 (C.S.227 II/of III; R.227 III/of V)	G. Kneller	1st Duke of Schomberg	321

Engraver	Artist	Short title	Page
10,218 (C.S.267)	G. Kneller	1st Earl of Wharton	322
10,226 (C.S.15 II/of III)	G. Kneller	1st Earl of Athlone	322
10,227 (C.S.86 I/of II)	G. Kneller	2nd Duke of Grafton	322
10,229 (C.S.201 II/of III; R.201 II/of III)	J. Closterman	Sir William Petty	69
10,238 (C.S.156 II/of III)	G. Kneller	3rd Duke of Schomberg	322
10,317 (C.S.75)	G. Kneller	Baroness Elizabeth Cutts	322
10,333 (C.S.196 I/of II)	G. Kneller	Duchess of Ormonde	323
10,347 (C.S.195 II/of II)	G. Kneller	Duchess of Ormonde	323
10,534 (C.S.209 I/of II)	G. Kneller	Countess of Ranelagh	323
10,540 (C.S.268 II/of III)	G. Kneller	Queen Caroline	323
10,559 (C.S.275 II/of II)	W. Wissing	William III, King of England	544
10,691 (C.S.278 I/of II)	W. Wissing	Self-Portrait	544
10,719 (C.S.237 II/of III)	F.W. Weidemann	Sophia Dorothea of Zeil	536
10,728 (C.S.268 I/of III)	G. Kneller	Queen Caroline	324
10,785 (C.S.77 II/of III)	G. Kneller	Count D'Auverquerk	324
10,809 (C.S.58 I/of II; R.58 III/of 1V)	H. Howard	Arcangelo Corelli	248
10,904 (C.S. 58 III/of IV)	G. Kneller	Viscountess Lisburne	324
10,929 (C.S.169 I/of II)	G. Kneller	Mary of Modena	324
10,930 (C.S.180 II/of II)	J.B. Closterman	General Thomas Maxwell	69
10,996 (C.S.193 III/of III)	G. Kneller	2nd Duke of Ormonde	324
11,184 (C.S.78 II/of II; R.78 II/of III)	F.W. Weideman	Madame D'Auverquerck	537
11,185 (C.S.78 I/of II; R.78 I/of III)	F.W. Weideman	Madame D'Auverquerck	537

SMITH, JOHN ORRIN (1799-1843)
ENGLISH SCHOOL

Engraver	Artist	Short title	Page
20,628	T. Danby	A Moonlight feast	99

SMITH, JOHN RAPHAEL (1752-1812)
ENGLISH SCHOOL

Engraver	Artist	Short title	Page
10,058 (C.S.50 I/of II; R.50 I/of III)	T. Lawrence	John Philpot Curran	338
10,192 (C.S.165; R.165 II/of II)	W. Cuming	Baron Tyrawley	96
10,203 (C.S.29)	J.R. Smith	William Burgh	479

Engraver	Artist	Short title	Page
10,330 (C.S.86 III/of IV)	N. Hone the Elder	Lydia Hone	243
10,348 (C.S.123 II/of II; R.123 III/of III)	M.W. Peters	The Hon. Mrs John O'Neil	396
10,354 (C.S.62 II/of III; R.62 III/of IV)	J. Reynolds	Lady Anne Fitzpatrick	443
10,356 (C.S.158 II/of III; R.158 III/of IV)	J. Reynolds	The Hon. Mrs Eliza Stanhope	443
10,376 (C.S.44 I/of I11; R.44 II/of VI)	T. Gainsborough	Margaret Mary Coghlan	170
10,380 (C.S.51 IV/of IV)	J. Reynolds	The Hon. Mrs Damer	443
10,406 (C.S.160 II/of II; R.160 III/of III)	Wright of Derby	Sir Walter Synnot's Children	549
10,438 (C.S.18 I/of II; R.18 II/of III)	J. Reynolds	Archbishop Joseph Bourke	443
10,472 (C.S.101 I/of II)	J. Reynolds	Anthony Malone	444
10,697 (R.85a II/of III)	N. Hone the Elder	John Camillus Hone	243
10,805 (C.S.61 pre-II; R.61 III/of V)	N. Hone the Elder	Sir John Fielding	243
11,012 (C.S.148 II/of II)	N. Hone the Elder	Rev. William Sclater	244
11,414 (R.85a II/of III)	N. Hone the Elder	John Camillus Hone	244
11,665 (C.S.32; R.32 II/of III)	R. Cosway	Wisdom directing Beauty	88
SMITH, JOHN THOMAS (1766-1833) ENGLISH SCHOOL			
10,426	Reynolds of Dublin	Dr David MacBride	447
SMITH, JOSEPH CLARENDON (1778-1810) ENGLISH SCHOOL			
20,411	E. Dayes	Dovedale, Derbyshire	104
SMITH, RICHARD (19TH CENTURY) ENGLISH SCHOOL			
11,280	Irish School 19C	Archbishop Le Poer Trench	289
SMITH, W. (19TH CENTURY) IRISH SCHOOL			
11,608	P. Byrne	St Patrick's Cathedral, Dublin	48
SMITH, WILLIAM RAYMOND (FL.1818-1848) ENGLISH SCHOOL			
20,331	T. Woodward	The Tempting Present	547
20,386	G.F. Robson	Llyn Idwall, Wales	458
20,431	J.D. Harding	Dieppe, France	209
20,607	Claude Lorrain	The Flight into Egypt	67
SMITH & GRAVES (19TH CENTURY) ENGLISH SCHOOL			
11,548	English School 1836	Bill-Head for James Trevor	150
SMYTH (19TH CENTURY) IRISH SCHOOL			
11,878	Irish School 1846	Aerial view of Dublin	297

Engraver	Artist	Short title	Page
SORNIQUE, DOMINIQUE (1708-1756)			
FRENCH SCHOOL			
20,198	F.A. Kraus	The Money Lender	326
SPARROW (FL.1773-1795)			
ENGLISH SCHOOL			
11,748	English School 18C	Country House	134
SPECCHI, ALESSANDRO (1668-1729)			
ITALIAN SCHOOL			
20,677(2))	A. Specchi	St Peter's, Rome	480
SPILSBURY, JOHN (C.1730-1795)			
ENGLISH SCHOOL			
10,787 (C.S.15)	J. Russell	Rev. Richard De Courcy	468
10,851 (C.S.17 I/of II; R.17 II/of V)	J. Spilsbury	Frederick, Prince of Wales	481
SPOONER, CHARLES (C.1720-1767)			
IRISH SCHOOL			
10,013 (C.S.33)	J. Van Nost the Younger	Thomas Prior	531
10,101 (C.S.29)	J. Van Nost the Younger	Rev. Samuel Madden	531
10,221 (C.S.30)	Irish School c.1750	Anthony Malone	268
10,337 (C.S.31; R.31 I/of II)	J. Reynolds	Nelly O'Brien	444
10,358 (C.S.21 I/of II; R.21 I/of III)	F. Cotes	Catherine Gunning	90
10,375 (C.S.9)	F. Cotes	Countess of Coventry	90
STADLER, JOHANN (1804-1859)			
AUSTRIAN SCHOOL			
10,982	Doussin-Dubreuil	Daniel O'Connell	113
STADLER, JOSEPH CONSTANTINE (FL.1780-1812)			
GERMAN SCHOOL			
11,643	J.J. Barralet	The Rutland Fountain, Dublin	13
STAINES, ROBERT (1805-1849)			
ENGLISH SCHOOL			
20,271	H.S. Melville	Melrose Abbey, Scotland	370
STANIER, R. (FL.1770-1791)			
ENGLISH SCHOOL			
10,653	J. Reynolds	2nd Earl of Moira	444
STARLING, WILLIAM FRANCIS (FL.1833-1845)			
ENGLISH SCHOOL			
20,397	J. Martin	Titus before Jerusalem	368
20,453	W.H. Bartlett	Castle near Tripoli	21

Engraver	Artist	Short title	Page
STEPHENSON, JAMES (1808-1886) ENGLISH SCHOOL			
20,455	W.H. Bartlett	Seleuceia, Turkey	21
STEVENSON, WILLIAM (FL.1839-1844) IRISH SCHOOL			
11,115	W. Stephenson	Charles Kendal Bushe	484
STOCKS, LUMB (1812-1892) ENGLISH SCHOOL			
20,140	C.R. Leslie	Autolycus	350
STORER, HENRY SARGENT (1795-1857) ENGLISH SCHOOL			
11,769	W. Sadler the Younger	Poolbeg Lighthouse	469
11,788	G. Petrie	Dublin from Phoenix Park	401
STORER, JAMES (1781-1853) ENGLISH SCHOOL			
11,769	W. Sadler the Younger	Poolbeg Lighthouse	469
11,788	G. Petrie	View of Dublin	401
20,134	J. Storer	St Bartholomew's London	486
STRANGWAYS, LEONARD R. (20TH CENTURY) IRISH SCHOOL			
11,884	L.R. Strangways	Map of Dublin	487
STRIXNER, NEPOMUK JOHANN (1782-1855) GERMAN SCHOOL			
20,758(34)	R. Van Der Weyden	The Annunciation	538
STURT, JOHN (1658-1730) ENGLISH SCHOOL			
10,051	English School 17C	Bishop Ezekiel Hopkins	129
10,627	English School 17C	Bishop Ezekiel Hopkins	129
SULLIVAN, DENNIS (19TH CENTURY) IRISH SCHOOL			
10,039(1-25)	D. Sullivan	Tour through Ireland	493-97
SURUGUE, PIERRE LOUIS (1710-1772) FRENCH SCHOOL			
11,522	J.-B.-S. Chardin	'Les Tours de Cartes'	64
11,623	J.-B.-S. Chardin	'Les Tours de Cartes'	64
SWEBACH, JACQUES FRANCOIS JOSE (1769-1823) FRENCH SCHOOL			
20,707(66)	A. Ostade	The Schoolmaster	388
?SWISS SCHOOL (19TH CENTURY)			
20,648	?Swiss School 19C	Grimsel Hospice, Switzerland	497

Engraver	Artist	Short title	Page
SYER, JOHN (1815-1885)			
ENGLISH SCHOOL			
20,223	J. Syer	Stormy sea	497
20,348	J. Syer	Fishing boats	497
20,350	J. Syer	Bristol Docks	497
20,369	J. Syer	A Beach	497
TANGENA, JOHANNES (17TH CENTURY)			
DUTCH SCHOOL			
10,004	Dutch School 1691	Taking of Athlone	121
20,762 *(COPYIST)*	Dutch School 1691	Taking of Athlone	121
TANJE, PIETER (1706-1761)			
AMSTERDAM SCHOOL			
10,994	?G. Kneller	1st Duke of Marlborough	324
TARDIEU, AMBROSE (1788-1841)			
FRENCH SCHOOL			
11,074	English School c.1810	Charles Phillips	144
TARDIEU, NICOLAS HENRI (1674-1749)			
FRENCH SCHOOL			
20,672(7)	Titian	Noli me Tangere	506
TAYLOR, CHARLES (1756-1823)			
ENGLISH SCHOOL			
20,202	English School 18C	'Tasting'	134
20,203	English School 18C	'Feeling'	134
TAYLOR THE ELDER, ISAAC (1730-1807)			
ENGLISH SCHOOL			
10,041(6)	R. Pool & J. Cash	Parliament House, Dublin	416
10,041(12)	R. Pool & J. Cash	The Royal Exchange, Dublin	416
10,041(18)	R. Pool & J. Cash	Blue-Coat School, Dublin	416
10,041(21)	R. Pool & J. Cash	St Patrick's Cathedral	417
10,041(25)	R. Pool & J. Cash	Thomas Smyth monument	417
10,041(26)	R. Pool & J. Cash	Earl of Kildare monument	417
10,041(27)	R. Pool & J. Cash	Thomas Prior monument	417
11,753	R. Pool & J. Cash	Parliament House, Dublin	417
11,755	R. Pool & J. Cash	The Royal Exchange Dublin	418
TAYLOR, WELD (FL.1836-1852)			
ENGLISH SCHOOL			
10,162	W. Taylor	Philip Meadows Taylor	498
TAYLOR, WILLIAM (FL.1832-1852)			
ENGLISH SCHOOL			
20,267	T. Gainsborough	The Market Cart	170
20,380	W. Tombleson	Near Greenwich	507
TAYLOR, WILLIAM BENJAMIN (1781-1850)			
IRISH SCHOOL			
11,621	W.B. Taylor	Front Square, T.C.D.	498
11,622	W.B. Taylor	The Old Museum, T.C.D.	498
TELL, WILLIAM (19TH CENTURY)			
IRISH SCHOOL			
10,512	W. Tell	Hints and Hits No. 1	498
10,513	W. Tell	Hints and Hits No. 2	498

Engraver	Artist	Short title	Page
TEMPLETON, JOHN SAMUEL (FL.1819-1857)			
IRISH SCHOOL			
10,786	F.W. Burton	Thomas Osborne Davis	47
11,072	R. Rothwell	A Flower Seller	464
20,138	J.H. Robinson	River Towy, Wales	456
20,287	J.H. Robinson	Swansea, Wales	456
20,294	J.H. Robinson	Caldecut Castle, Wales	456
20,368	J.H. Robinson	Dynevor Castle, Wales	456
20,472	J.H. Robinson	Llanstephan Castle, Wales	456
TENIERS THE YOUNGER, DAVID			
(1610-1690)			
FLEMISH SCHOOL			
11,660	D. Teniers the Younger	Old Man with two dogs	500
20,716(10) *(COPYIST)*	Giorgione	Three Philosophers	176
THOMAS, N. (C.1750-C.1812)			
FRENCH SCHOOL			
20,688(108)	Roman Antique	The Young Faustina	459
THIBAULT, CHARLES EUGENE			
(1835-AFTER 1880)			
FRENCH SCHOOL			
20,796	J. Aubert	Dreaming	10
THOMAS, WILLIAM (FL.1780-1799)			
ENGLISH SCHOOL			
11,752	R. Pool & J. Cash	Parliament House, Dublin	418
THOMPSON, D. (FL.1832-1838)			
ENGLISH SCHOOL			
20,450	W.H. Bartlett	Besherrai, Syria	22
THOMSON, JAMES (1789-1850)			
ENGLISH SCHOOL			
10,336	A.E. Chalon	Marchioness of Londonderry	63
10,806	W.C. Ross	Lady Elizabeth Ferguson	463
11,203	J. Neagle	Matthew Carey	381
11,236	J. Jackson	Thomas Carey	302
11,278	S. Drummond	Peter Turnerelli	119
THURSTON, JOHN (1774-1822)			
ENGLISH SCHOOL			
10,763 *(COPYIST)*	T. Bewick	John Cunningham	28
11,285 *(COPYIST)*	C. Jervas	Dean Jonathan Swift	305
THURWANGER, MARGUERITE (FL. C.1877)			
FRENCH SCHOOL			
20,602	M. Thurwanger	Deer	503
20,603	M. Thurwanger	Shepherd with his family	503
TILLIARD, JEAN BAPTISTE (1742-1813)			30
FRENCH SCHOOL	Lady M. Bingham	Patrick Sarsfield	
10,093	C. Le Brun	Hercules	340
20,725(74)			
TILLIARD, MME. M. ANGELIQUE			
(?1743-1782)			
FRENCH SCHOOL			
10,093	Lady M. Bingham	Patrick Sarsfield	30

Engraver	Artist	Short title	Page
TINGLE, JAMES (FL.1830-1860) ENGLISH SCHOOL			
11,823(1-2)	T.H. Shepherd	Regent's Park, London	474-75
TISDALL, A.C. (19TH CENTURY) ?IRISH SCHOOL			
20,623	A.C. Tisdall	Marston House	504
20,624	A.C. Tisdall	Marston House	504
20,625	A.C. Tisdall	Marston House garden	504
TOFANELLI, AGOSTINO (1770-1834) ITALIAN SCHOOL			
11,659 *(COPYIST)*	Guercino	David with head of Goliath	192
TOGNOLI, GIOVANNI (1786-1862) ITALIAN SCHOOL			
20,714(16) *(COPYIST)*	A. Canova	Napoleon I	54
TOMBLESON, WILLIAM (FL.1814-1840) ENGLISH SCHOOL			
20,433	W. Tombleson	Clifton Hampden	507
20,485	T. Allom	Colwith force, Cumbria	4
TOMKINS, CHARLES ALGERNON (1821-1903) ENGLISH SCHOOL			
10,898	L. Lehmann	4th Duke of Leinster	344
10,905	L. Lehmann	Duchess of Leinster	344
TOMKINS, PELTRO WILLIAM (1760-1840) ENGLISH SCHOOL			
20,156 (COPYIST)	F. Barocci	'La Madonna del Gatto'	12
20,704	G. Moroni	'The School Master'	375
20,727(12)	A.R. Mengs	Robert Wood	371
TOMLINSON, JOHN (FL.1805-1824) ENGLISH SCHOOL			
11,692	J. Carr	The Four Courts, Dublin	55
TONE, CATHERINE SAMPSON (FL.1825-1858) IRISH SCHOOL			
10,433 (COPYIST)	Irish School c.1800	Wolfe Tone	284
TOPHAM, FRANCIS WILLIAM (1808-1877) ENGLISH SCHOOL			
11,763	W.H. Bartlett	St Patrick's Cathedral	22
20,590	W.H. Bartlett	St Patrick's Cathedral	22
TOURFAUT, LEON ALEXANDRE (FL.1876-1883) FRENCH SCHOOL			
11,723	?N. Clarget	The Four Courts, Dublin	66
TOUSSAINT, CHARLES HENRI (1849-1911) FRENCH SCHOOL			
20,079	C.H. Toussaint	King's College, Cambridge	509

Engraver	Artist	Short title	Page
TOWNLEY, CHARLES (1746-1800) ENGLISH SCHOOL			
10,439 (C.S.8; R.8 II/of II)	G. Romney	The Hon. John Forbes	461
10,953 (C.S.14 II/of II)	S. De Koster	1st Earl Macartney	107
TOWNSEND, T.S. (FL. C.1880) ENGLISH SCHOOL			
20,081	T.S. Townsend	Dog on a wooded lane	509
TRIERRE, PHILIPPE (1756-C.1815) FRENCH SCHOOL			
20,723(7)	A. Allori	Venus and Cupid	5
TROYEN, JAN VAN (C.1610-C.1666) FLEMISH SCHOOL			
20,716(10)	Giorgione	The Three Philosophers	176
TROUVAIN, ANTOINE (1656-1708) FRENCH SCHOOL			
20,678(6)	P.P. Rubens	Marriage of Marie de Medici	467
TURNER, CHARLES (1773-1857) ENGLISH SCHOOL			
10,061	H. O'Neill	Bartholomew Lloyd	387
10,075	J. Simpson	Tyrone Power	478
10,107	T. Lawrence	Bishop John Porter	338
10,164	J. Hoppner	Sir Henry Blackwood	247
10,170	J. Lonsdale	Michael Kelly	356
10,178	J.J. Masquerier	1st Baron de Blaquiere	368
10,207	H.D. Hamilton	Archbishop Charles Broderick	198
10,419	J. Ramsay	Henry Grattan	425
10,427	T.C. Thompson	Sir Thomas McKenny	502
10,453	J. Hoppner	1st Viscount Nelson	248
10,458	T. Lawrence	2nd Marquess of Londonderry	338
10,487	M.A. Shee	2nd Duke of Leinster	473
10,492	J. Reynolds	1st Marquess Townsend	444
10,507	J. Bauzil	1st Duke of Wellington	24
10,547	W. Cuming	2nd Earl Annesley	96
10,554	R. Rothwell	2nd Earl of Caledon	464
10,689	T. Lawrence	1st Earl Whitworth	338
10,724	T. Lawrence	Archbishop Beresford	339
10,812	J. Hoppner	1st Earl of Clare	248
10,842	T.C. Thompson	Charles Grabt	502
10,848	T.C. Thompson	8th Earl of Fingal	503
10,854	S. Ker	Richard Graves Ker	313
10,869	Continental School c.1620	Family of King James I	79
10,954	T. Lawrence	Sir John McMahon	339
10,966	T.C. Thompson	James McKenny	503
11,032	M. Cregan	James Stewart	93
11,959-11,978	J.M.W. Turner	'Liber Studiorum'	513-16
11,983	J.M.W. Turner	'Liber Studiorum'	517
20,014	J.M.W. Turner	'Liber Studiorum'	522
20,022	J.M.W. Turner	'Liber Studiorum'	523
20,113	?I. Oliver	Queen Elizabeth I	386
20,384	J.M.W. Turner	Totnes, Devon	512
20,445	R. Westall	The Cottage Door	538
20,663	T. Lawrence	George Canning	339

Engraver	Artist	Short title	Page
TURNER, JOSEPH MALLORD WILLIAM (1775-1851) ENGLISH SCHOOL			
11,958-11,999	J.M.W. Turner	'Liber Studiorum'	513-20
20,000-20,028	J.M.W. Turner	'Liber Studiorum'	520-23
TURNER, MRS MARY (1774-1850) ENGLISH SCHOOL			
10,926	T. Phillips	William Marsden	407
TYPO ETCHING COMPANY (19TH CENTURY) ENGLISH SCHOOL			
11,843	H. Furniss	Manchester 1887 Exhibition	168
TYRRELL, EDWIN (19TH CENTURY) ENGLISH SCHOOL			
20,212	T. Hills	The Cottage Door	225
VAILLANT, WALLERANT DUTCH SCHOOL			
20,732(57)	?W. Vaillant	A seated boy drawing	525
VALET, GUILLAUME (1632-1704) FRENCH SCHOOL			
10,144	C. Maratta	Father Luke Wadding	366
VAN BLEECK, PIETER (1700-1764) ANGLO-DUTCH SCHOOL			
10,112 (C.S.7 I/of II; R.7 II/of II)	P. Van Bleeck	Owen Macswinny	525
VAN DE PASSE, WILLEM (C.1598-1637) ANGLO-GERMAN SCHOOL and VAN DE PASSE, MAGDALENA (C.1600-C.1640) ANGLO-GERMAN SCHOOL			
11,037	?English School 16C	Sir Henry Sidney	124
VANDERBANCK, PETER (1649-1697) ANGLO-FRENCH SCHOOL			
10,414	G. Kneller	1st Duke of Schomberg	325
10,565	G. Kneller	George Walker	325
11,418	P. Lely	Thomas Butler	349
VANDERGUCHT, G. (1696-1776) ENGLISH SCHOOL			
10,282	J. Highmore	Thomas Emlyn	224
VANDERGUCHT, MICHAEL (1660-1725) ANGLO-FLEMISH SCHOOL			
10,625	English School 17C	Bishop Ezekiel Hopkins	129
10,626	English School 17C	Bishop Ezekiel Hopkins	129
10,636	S. Cooper	General Henry Ireton	84
10,729	H. Howard	Arcangelo Corelli	249
11,213	G. Kneller	William Congreve	325

Engraver	Artist	Short title	Page
VANDERVAART, JAN (1641-1721) ANGLO-DUTCH SCHOOL			
10,105 (C.S.7)	G. Morphey	Archbishop Oliver Plunkett	376
10,132 (C.S.9 pre-I; R.9 I/of IV)	J. Vandervaart	Bishop Edward Wetenhall	526
VAN HAECKEN, ALEXANDER (C.1701-1757) ANGLO-DUTCH SCHOOL			
10,142 (C.S.16 I/of III; R.16 I/of IV)	Markham	Dean Jonathan Swift	367
VAN SOMER THE YOUNGER, PAUL (1649-C.1694) ANGLO-DUTCH SCHOOL			
10,321 (C.S.8)	P. Mignard	Countess of Meath	373
VAN VOERST, ROBERT (1597-1635/36) ANGLO-FLEMISH SCHOOL			
10,191	M. Gheeraerts the Younger	1st Earl of Totnes	174
VARRALL, JOHN CHARLES (FL.1818-1848) ENGLISH SCHOOL			
20,552	R. Wilson	Children of Niobe	543
VELDE THE ELDER, JAN VAN DE (1598-C.1670) ANGLO-DUTCH SCHOOL			
10,245	R. Walker	Oliver Cromwell	535
VENDENBERG (18TH CENTURY) FRENCH SCHOOL			
20,723(14) (COPYIST)	Raphael	Virgin and Child	427
VERNON, THOMAS (1825-1872) ENGLISH SCHOOL			
20,141	C.R. Leslie	Olivia	350
VERTUE, GEORGE (1684-1750) ENGLISH SCHOOL			
10,124	English School 17C	Sir James Ware	129
10,214	C. Jervas	Dean Jonathan Swift	305
10,771	English School 17C	2nd Baron Coleraine	126
10,799	G. Kneller	1st Duke of Dorset	325
VINTER, JOHN ALFRED (C.1828-1905) ENGLISH SCHOOL			
10,190	S. Catterson Smith the Elder	Peter Purcell	61
VIZETELLY, HENRY (1820-1894) ENGLISH SCHOOL			
20,577	M.B. Foster	'March Primrose'	162
VON DALL'ARMI, ANDREAS (1788-1846) GERMAN SCHOOL			
20,759(9)	G. Fossati	Roman Temples	162
20,760(6)	G. Fossati	Roman Temples	162

Engraver	Artist	Short title	Page
VORSTERMANS THE YOUNGER, LUCAS (1624-1667)			
FLEMISH SCHOOL			
20,715	Titian	Ecce Homo	506
WAGSTAFF, CHARLES EDWARD (1808-1850)			
ENGLISH SCHOOL			
10,735	G. Patten	Prince Albert	391
11,197	T. Lawrence	John Philpot Curran	339
20,150	J. Inskipp	Portrait of a Lady	260
20,164	J. Inskipp	Girl with a sickle	260
20,166	J. Inskipp	Girl holding a dog	260
20,804	T. Lawrence	John Philpot Curran	339
?WAKER (FL. C.1800)			
IRISH SCHOOL			
20,659	?Waker	Printseller's label	534
WALKER, ANTHONY (1726-1765)			
ENGLISH SCHOOL			
11,506	Rembrandt	Tobit and the Angel	429
11,903	J. Tudor	Royal Barracks	510
20,541	English School 18C	Pyramus and Thisbe	134
WALKER, EMMERY (17TH CENTURY)			
ENGLISH SCHOOL			
10,717	G. Soest	Colonel Thomas Blood	480
WALKER, JAMES (1748-1808)			
ENGLISH SCHOOL			
10,864 (C.S.8 I/of II)	G. Romney	Eyles Irwin	461
?11,093	?D. Dodd	Ann Barry	111
11,225	D. Dodd	Charles Macklin	111
11,284	French School late 18C	Pierre Suffren	166
11,689	G. Holmes	Poolbeg Lighthouse	232
WALKER, WILLIAM (1791/93-1867)			
ENGLISH SCHOOL			
10,958	H.W. Phillips	Sir Samuel Martin	405
11,026	J.W. Gordon	Bishop Daniel Sandford	183
20,819	S.W. Reynolds the Elder	Passing of 1832 Reform Bill	447
WALLIS, HENRY (1804-1890)			
ENGLISH SCHOOL			
20,284	T. Allom	Burnshead Hall, Cumbria	4
20,285	T. Allom	Clare Moss, Cumbria	5
WALLIS, ROBERT (1794-1878)			
ENGLISH SCHOOL			
11,795	J.M.W. Turner	Tours, France	512
20,214	W.C. Stanfield	Boats near Murano	482
20,276	G. Barret the Younger	Bavarian Alps	14
20,413	W.C. Stanfield	Godesberg Castle, Germany	462
20,425	F. Abresch	Sulina, Romania	1
20,441	W.H. Bartlett	Istanbul, Turkey	22
20,504	T. Creswick	Lough Leane, Co. Kerry	94
20,513	T. Creswick	Glengarrif Castle, Co. Cork	94

Engraver	Artist	Short title	Page
WALLIS, WILLIAM (1796-AFTER 1846) ENGLISH SCHOOL			
20,403	H. Gastineau	Caerphilly Castle, Wales	171
20,404	H. Gastineau	Caerphilly Castle, Wales	171
WALSH, NICHOLAS (1839-1877) IRISH SCHOL			
20,655	J.H. Hogan	Thomas Osborne Davis	227
WALTON AND CO., C.W. (19TH CENTURY) ENGLISH SCHOOL			
11,075	C.W. Walton & Co.	7th Viscount Powerscourt	536
WARD, GEORGE RAPHAEL (1797-1879) ENGLISH SCHOOL			
10,449	M. Cregan	Bishop Richard Mant	93
WARD, JAMES (1769-1859) ENGLISH SCHOOL			
10,146 (C.S.7 III/of IV; R.7 III/of V)	J. Reynolds	Richard Burke	445
10,210 (C.S.4 III/of III)	J. Northcote	William Betty	383
10,435 (C.S.6 pre-III; R.6 II/of V)	J. Hickey	Edmund Burke	223
10,498 (C.S.13 II/of II; R.13 III/of III)	W. Beechey	1st Marquess Cornwallis	25
10,718 (C.S.3; R.3 II/of III)	H. J. Burch the Younger	William Betty	46
WARD THE ELDER, WILLIAM (1766-1826) ENGLISH SCHOOL			
10,050 (C.S.52 I/of II)	H.D. Hamilton	Rev. Walter Kirwan	199
10,067 (C.S.65)	J.D. Herbert	Arthur O'Connor	223
10,100 (C.S.50 II/of III)	M.A. Shee	John Johnstone	473
10,268 (C.S.72 I/of II)	G.C. Stuart	Robert Shaw	492
10,450 (C.S.23 I/of II)	T. Stewardson	George Canning	484
10,457 (C.S.29 pre-I)	W. Cuming	Edward Cooke	96
10,474 (C.S.63 II/of II)	N. Dance	Arthur Murphy	102
10,776 (C.S.36 I/of III; R.36 II/of V)	J. Jackson	1st Baron Dover	303
10,780 (C.S.32a)	W. Cuming	Lt.-Colonel John Doyle	96
10,797 (C.S.32a)	W. Cuming	Lt.-Colonel John Doyle	97
11,033 (C.S.72 II/of II)	G.C. Stuart	Robert Shaw	492
11,654 (C.S.55)	J.J. Barralet	Richard Maguire saved at sea	13

Engraver	Artist	Short title	Page
WARD THE YOUNGER, WILLIAM JAMES (1800-1840) ENGLISH SCHOOL			
10,000	J.P. Haverty	Daniel O'Connell	213
10,231	J. Constable	Prebendary John Wingfield	79
10,249	T. Foster	Bishop Thomas Elrington	162
20,126	T. Foster	Bishop Thomas Elrington	162
WARREN, ALFRED WILLIAM (FL.1830s-1840s) ENGLISH SCHOOL			
11,285	C. Jervas	Dean Jonathan Swift	305
WATKINS, W.G. (FL.1828-1848) ENGLISH SCHOOL			
20,429	J. Livesey	Gainsborough, Lincolnshire	354
WATSON, CAROLINE (1761-1814) IRISH SCHOOL			
10,307	G. Romney	Mary Tighe	462
11,045	T.A. Hayley	George Romney	215
11,046	G. Romney	Three Self-Portraits	462
WATSON, JAMES (C.1740-1790) IRISH SCHOOL			
10,068 (C.S.75 I/of II)	N. Hone the Elder	Horace Hone as David	244
10,078 (C.S.109 I/of III; R.109 I/of IV)	F. Cotes	William O'Brien	91
10,129 (C.S.63)	P. Batoni	3rd Duke of Grafton	23
10,139 (C.S.161)	N. Hone the Elder	The Brickdust Man	244
10,235 (C.S.150 III/of IV)	A. Van Dyck	Sir Roland Wandesford	530
10,236 (C.S.131)	F.R. West	Archbishop Arthur Smyth	537
10,237 (C.S.131)	F.R. West	Archbishop Arthur Smyth	538
10,254 (C.S.20 II/of IV)	J. Reynolds	Edmund Burke	445
10,257 (C.S.20 III/of IV)	J. Reynolds	Edmund Burke	445
10,332 (C.S.108 II/of III; R.108 III/of IV)	F. Cotes	Lady Susan O'Brien	91
10,334 (C.S.34 I/of II)	H.D. Hamilton	Countess of Cork and Orrery	199
10,345 (C.S.80 I/of II; R.80 I/of III)	J. Reynolds	Mrs Joshua Irwin	445
10,383 (C.S.95; R.95 II/of II)	J. Reynolds	Countess of Clanwilliam	445
10,392 (C.S.10)	A. Kauffmann	Lady Margaret Bingham	311
10,397 (C.S.135 II/of II; R.135 III/of III)	J. Reynolds	The Hon. Lady Anne Stanhope	446
10,424 (C.S.79 I/of II; R.79 II/of II)	J. Reynolds	John Hely-Hutchinson	446

Engraver	Artist	Short title	Page
10,459 (C.S.125 I/of II)	M.W. Peters	Sir William Robinson	397
10,563 (C.S.150	A. Van Dyck	Sir Roland Wandesford	530
10,700 (C.S.75 II/of II)	N. Hone the Elder	Horace Hone as David	244
11,018 (C.S.133)	J. Barrett	John Stacpoole	14
11,387 (C.S.161)	N. Hone the Elder	The Brickdust Man	245
20,731(92) (C.S.149 III/of III)	J.-B. Van Loo	Sir Horace Walpole	531
WATSON, THOMAS (1743-1781) ENGLISH SCHOOL			
10,351	J. Reynolds	Mrs Sheridan as St Cecilia	446
10,355	J. Reynolds	Mrs Sheridan as St Cecilia	446
10,853	J. Reynolds	George III, King of England	433
WATTS, S. (18TH-19TH CENTURY) ENGLISH SCHOOL			
11,128	B. Stoker	Henry Flood	486
11,288	W. Yellowless	Charles Phillips	549
WEBB, EDWARD (1805-1854) ENGLISH SCHOOL			
20,362	R. Hills & G.F. Robson	Deer in Scotland	225
WEBB, J. (18TH CENTURY) ENGLISH SCHOOL			
10,398	J. Reynolds	Mrs Sarah Siddons	446
WEGER, AUGUST (1823-1892) GERMAN SCHOOL			
10,858	English School c.1850	James Knowles	150
WEGER, T. (19TH CENTURY) LEIPZIG SCHOOL			
10,900	?Irish School 19C	Ron Levey	289
WEHRSCHMIDT, DANIEL ALBERT (1861-1932) AMERICAN SCHOOL			
11,855	F. Holl the Younger	1st Earl of Dufferin and Ava	232
WERFF, ADRIAEN VAN DER (1659-1722) DUTCH SCHOOL			
11,379 *(COPYIST)*	?R. Walker	Oliver Cromwell	534
WEST, CHARLES (BORN C.1750) ENGLISH SCHOOL			
20,731(136)	Rosalba	Diana	463
WESTALL, WILLIAM (1781-1850) ENGLISH SCHOOL			
20,324 *(COPYIST)*	A. Cuyp	Landing of Prince Frederick at Nijmegen	97

Engraver	Artist	Short title	Page
WHEATLEY, SAMUEL (FL.1744-1771)			
ENGLISH SCHOOL			
10,445	W. Hoare	4th Earl of Chesterfield	226
(C.S.[Houston]28)			
11,376	R. Barber	Dean Jonathan Swift	11
WHITE, CHARLES WILLIAM (FL.1750-1785)			
ENGLISH SCHOOL			
11,859	E. Crewe	The Good Mother	94
20,119	T. Worlidge	George II, King of England	548
WHITE, GEORGE (1671 OR 89-1732)			
ENGLISH SCHOOL			
10,266	School of P. Lely	Erasmus Smith	349
(C.S.43 II/of III)			
11,089	English School 17C	Colonel Thomas Blood	130
(C.S.5 II/of II)			
WHITE, ROBERT (1645-1703)			
ENGLISH SCHOOL			
10,611	R. White	General Sir George Rawdon	540
WHYMPER, EDWARD (1840-1911)			
ENGLISH SCHOOL			
20,269	E. Whymper	Scala Regia, Vatican, Rome	541
20,270	E. Whymper	St Peter's, Rome	541
WHYMPER, JOSIAH WOOD (1813-1903)			
ENGLISH SCHOOL			
20,630	J.C. Hook	Dream of ancient Venice	245
20,631	J.C. Hook	Market morning	245
WICAR, JEAN-BAPTISTE (1762-1834)			
FRENCH SCHOL			
20,687(46) *(COPYIST)*	Raphael	Virgin and Child	426
20,688(108) *(COPYIST)*	Roman Antique	Young Faustina	459
WILLIAMS, ROBERT or ROGER			
(FL.1680-1704)			
ENGLISH SCHOOL			
10,001	W. Wissing	1st Duke of Ormonde	545
(C.S.42 II/of III; R.42 II/of IV)			
10,016	W. Wissing	Baron Cutts	545
(C.S.17)			
10,199	T. Hill	1st Earl of Athlone	225
(C.S.18)			
WILLIAMSON, THOMAS (C.1800-1840)			
ENGLISH SCHOOL			
11,248	J.J. Jenkins	Queen Victoria	304
WILLMORE, JAMES TILBITTS (1800-1863)			
ENGLISH SCHOOL			
11,697	T. Creswick	12, Aungier Street, Dublin	94
11,796	J.M.W. Turner	River Seine, Normandy	512
11,797	J.M.W. Turner	Tancarville Château	512
20,139	W. Linton	The ruins of Carthage	354

Engraver	Artist	Short title	Page
20,418	W.H. Bartlett and T. Creswick	Pissevache Cascade	23
20,483	J.M.W. Turner	Le Havre, France	512
20,599	J.M.W. Turner	Barnard Castle	513
WILSON, BENJAMIN (1721-1788) ENGLISH SCHOOL			
10,128	B. Wilson	Dr Bryan Robinson	542
10,296	R. Barber	Dean Jonathan Swift	11
10,297	R. Barber	Dean Jonathan Swift	12
10,388	B. Wilson	Countess of Coventry	543
WINKLES, BENJAMIN (FL.1829-1842) ENGLISH SCHOOL			
11,776	G. Petrie	St Audeon's Church, Dublin	401
11,782	G. Petrie	Phoenix Pillar, Dublin	401
11,785	G. Petrie	Bank of Ireland, Dublin	401
11,786	G. Petrie	Bank of Ireland, Dublin	401
20,286	W. Tombleson	Waterfalls, Switzerland	507
WINKLES, HENRY (FL.1818-1842) ENGLISH SCHOOL			
20,376	W. Tombleson	Rochester Castle, Kent	507
20,379	W. Tombleson	Teddington Lock, London	508
WINKLES, RICHARD (FL.1829-1836) ENGLISH SCHOOL			
11,771	W.H. Bartlett	St George's Church, Dublin	22
20,611	W.H. Bartlett	St George's Church, Dublin	22
20,612	G. Petrie	Nelson Pillar, Dublin	401
WOOD, JOHN (1720-1780) ENGLISH SCHOOL			
11,427	Rembrandt	Rest on the Flight	429
WOODMAN THE YOUNGER, RICHARD (1784-1859) ENGLISH SCHOOL			
20,118	J. Jackson	John Flaxman	303
WOOLLETT, WILLIAM (1735-1785) ENGLISH SCHOOL			
11,664	B. West	Destruction of French Fleet	537
20,085	C. Dusart	The Jocund Peasants	120
WOOLNOTH, THOMAS (1785-C.1839) ENGLISH SCHOOL			
10,688	A. Stewart	Princess Victoria	485
WORRALL, JOHN (19TH CENTURY) IRISH SCHOOL			
20,524	J.H. Mulcahy	Baker's Place, Limerick	377
WORTHINGTON, WILLIAM HENRY (C.1795-C.1839) ENGLISH SCHOOL			
10,763	T. Bewick	John Cunningham	28

Engraver	Artist	Short title	Page
WRIGHT, JAMES HENRY (FL.1808-1818) ENGLISH SCHOOL 20,680(7)	L. Lotto	Virgin and Child	356
WRIGHT, JOHN (C.1745-1820) *ENGLISH SCHOOL* 10,751 *(COPYIST)*	W. Owen	John Wilson Croker	389
WRIGHT, THOMAS (1757-1834) *ENGLISH SCHOOL* 10,818 *(COPYIST)*	J. Comerford	George Forbes	74
YOUNG, E. (FL. C.1832) ENGLISH SCHOOL 20,262	T. Allom	Durham Cathedral	5
ZANCON, GAETANO (1771-1816) ITALIAN SCHOOL 20,468	Italian School late 18C	Chinese building	301
ZOBEL, GEORGE J. (1810-1881) ENGLISH SCHOOL 10,772	R. Buckner	Sir George De Lacy Evans	45
10,813	E. Eddis	4th Baron Fortescue	122
11,007	D.Y. Blakiston	Dr Robert Todd	31
11,043	F. Grant	6th Baron Rokeby	184
ZOCCHI, GIUSEPPE (1711-1767) ITALIAN SCHOOL 20,669(4)	G. Zocchi	Florence	549
ZUCCHI, LORENZO (1704-1779) ITALIAN SCHOOL 10,084	J. Tusch	Count Maguire	524

APPENDIX 3

PUBLISHERS

An alphabetical listing of publishers with the catalogue numbers of their prints. Addresses are given where they are found on prints or can be inferred.

Ackermann, Rudolph (1764-1834)
London print and book publisher
10,688; 10,733; 11,409; 11,593; 20,542; 20,559; 20,581 (101, Strand).

Ackermann & Co. (fl.1830-1856)
London publishers
11,057; 20,056; 20,111; 20,167; 20,222; 20,224; 20,225; 20,320; 20,321; 20,325; 20,347; 20,375; 20,695-20,700 (96, Strand).

Adlard, Alfred (fl.1825-1869)
London engraver and publisher
20,502-20,504; 20,510; 20,513.

Aertssens, Henri (17th century)
Antwerp publisher
20,716.

A.H.H. & Co. (20th century)
American publishers
11,412.

Aliamet, Jacques (1726-1788)
Paris engraver, printer and publisher
20,162 (Rue des Mathurins).

Allan, Bell & Co. (19th century)
London publishers
20,159.

Allard, Carel (1648-1709)
Amsterdam engraver and publisher
11,655.

Allegrini, Giuseppe (18th century)
Florence publisher
20,669.

Allen's (fl.1820s)
Dublin lithographers and publishers
10,915; 11,861 (Trinity Street).

Allen, M. (19th century)
Dublin printer
11,673.

Allen, M.H. & J.W. (19th century)
Dublin publishers
20,246 (32, Dame Street).

Allen, William (fl.1787-1829)
Dublin publisher
10,050; 10,780; 10,797; 11,033 (-). 11,601; 11,617; 11,627; 11,718 (32, Dame Street). 10,924 (88, Dame Street).

Allen & Sons (fl.1820s)
Dublin publishers
11,649-11,651 (Dame Street).

Allen's, Messrs. (fl.1820s-1830s)
Dublin and London publishers
10,491, 10,725 (Dame Street). 10,909 (13, Henrietta Street, Cavendish Square). 10,971 (Dame Street). 20,663 (Dublin).

The Amulet (1826-1836)
London magazine
20,136.

The Anaglyphic Company (fl.1840s)
London publishers
10,970; 20,240; 20,313; 20,314; 20,341; 20,342; 20,462; 20,488; 20,490 (25, Berners Street, Oxford Street).

Anselin, Jean Louis (1754-1823)
Paris engraver and publisher
10,906 (Rue de Seine F.B.S.G. no. 55).

Appleton & Co. (19th century)
New York publishers
11,333.

L'Art (1875-1907)
Paris magazine
11,487, 11,495; 11,502; 20,068.

Art Union of London (founded 1836)
Supporter of the Fine Arts and London publisher
20,495.

Asperne, James (fl.1803-1822)
London publisher
10,579; 10,644; 10,656; 10,657; 10,669; 11,136; 11,143; 11,204; 11,261;11,278; 11,330 (Bible, Crown and Constitution, 32, Cornhill).

Atkinson, George (1880-1941)
Dublin painter, sculptor, engraver and printer
10,502 (97, St Stephen's Green).

Austin, William (1721-1820)
London engraver, drawing master and publisher
10,252 (185, Piccadilly); 10,253, 10,390, 10,475 (41, St James's Street); 10,768 (185, Piccadilly).

Aze (19th century)
Paris printer
20,055.

Badger, George (mid 17th century)
London publisher
11,005 (St Dunstan's Churchyard in Fleet Street).

Baillie, (Captain) William (1723-1792)
Irish engraver and publisher
?10,532; ?10,942; ?10,944; ?10,945.

Baily, Ward & Co. (19th century)
New York publishers
10,970; 20,054.

Bakewell, Elizabeth (mid 18th century)
London publisher
10,139; 11,387 (Cornhill opposite Birchin Lane).

Baldrey, Joshua Kirby (1754-1828)
London engraver and publisher
?11,047 (20, Sherrard Street).

Baldwin & Cradock (19th century)
London publishers
20,615.

Baldwin, Cradock & Joy (fl.1820s)
London publishers
10,048; 11,700; 11,773; 11,775; 11,777-11,781; 11,783; 11,784; 11,789-11,791.

Bance et Aumont (19th century)
Paris publishers
20,100 (Rue J.J. Rousseau, no. 10).

Barclay, G. (19th century)
London printer
20,264 (Castle Street, Leicester Square).

Barnard, William S. (1774-1849)
London engraver and publisher
10,808 (1, Fitzroy Street, Fitzroy Square).

Barney, M.W. (fl.1800s)
London publisher
10,177 (16, College Street, Westminster).

Barralet, John James (1747-1815)
Irish artist and Dublin publisher
11,654.

Barron, H. (fl.1780s)
London publisher
11,011 (7, King Street, Covent Garden).

Barry, James (1741-1806)
Irish artist, engraver and London publisher
11,858. 20,722(1-15) (when 1st issued).

Bartolozzi, Francesco (1727-1815)
London engraver and publisher
10,310; 10,313-10,315; 10,819; 11,957.

Baumgärtners Buchhandlung (mid 19th century)
Leipzig bookseller's and publisher
10,858.

Beckett, G. (17th century)
London bookseller and publisher
11,025 (Ye Golden Head in ye Old Bayly).

Beckett, Isaac (1653-1719)
London engraver and publisher
10,080; 10,244; 10,328; 10,373; 10,561; 11,863.

Bell, John (1745-1831)
London publisher
10,316. (owned *La Belle Assemblée* and *Weekly Messenger*)

The Benchers of the Honorable Society of King's Inns
Dublin publishers
10,502.

Bengo, A. (fl.1820s)
London publisher
10,308 (38, Maiden Lane, Covent Garden).

Bensley & Son (early 19th century)
London printers
20,680; 20,704; 20,705; 20,726; 20,727. (Bolt Court, Fleet Street).

Bentley, Richard (fl.1830s-1860s)
London publisher
11,111; 11,377.

Bentley & Colburn (19th century)
London publishers
11,507.

Bertauts (19th century)
Paris printer
20,143.

Betty, William Henry West (1791-1874)
London child actor
10,718 (23, Cockspur Street).

Bickham the Younger, George (fl.1736-1758)
London engraver and publisher
10,531 (May's Buildings, Covent Garden).

Birchall, James (fl.1780s)
London publisher
11,606 (473, Strand).

Bird, Thomas (fl. c.1800)
Dublin printer
11,751.

Black and Armstrong (fl.1840s)
London publishers
20,280.

Blackie & Son (19th century)
London, Glasgow and Edinburgh publishers
11,088; 20,282; 20,460; 20,461.

Blaquiere, Jean de Blaquiere, 1st Baron de (1732-1812)
Dublin publisher
11,643.

Blooteling, Abraham (1640-1690)
Amsterdam engraver and publisher (in London 1672-78)
10,025; 10,495; ?10,706; 10,856; 11,263; 11,264.

Blyth, R. (fl.1780s)
London publisher
20,034 (27, Great Castle Street, Cavendish Square); 20,036, 20,066 (105 New Bond Street).

Bogue, David (fl.1840s-1850s)
London publisher
10,791 (Fleet Street). 10,784.

Bonyer, Jonah (18th century)
London publisher
10,047.

Boone, T. & W. (19th century)
London publishers
11,011 (29, New Bond Street). 20,030.

Bornabo & Lazzarini (mid 18th century)
Rome printers
20,833.

Bouchard et Gravier (18th century)
Paris publishers
20,674 (Rue du Cours, près Saint Marcel).

Bougeard (mid 19th century)
Antwerp printer
11,489.

Bouilliard, Jacques (1774-1806)
Paris engraver and publisher
20,723 (23, Rue St Thomas du Louvre).

Bovi, Marino (1760-c.1821)
London engraver and publisher
10,312, 20,103 (207, Piccadilly). 20,038 (12, Piccadilly).

Bow Bells (1862-1887)
London magazine
20,627. 20,632. 20,633.

Bowles, Carington (1724-1793)
London publisher
10,034; 10,272; 10,410; 10,542; 10,787; 11,557-11,562; 20,040-20,047; 20,050 (St Paul's Churchyard). ?10,686; ?10,828.

Bowles, Carington (1724-1793) & Carver (fl. c.1769)
London publishers
10,680; 11,256 (69, St Paul's Churchyard).

Bowles, John (1701-1779)
London publisher; brother of Thomas Bowles
10,542; 11,022; 11,096; (-). 10,027; 10,085; 10,359; 10,730; 10,731; 10,997; 11,021 (Black Horse, Cornhill). 10,007 (Cornhill). 10,577; 11.201; 11,393 (12, Cornhill). 10,015, 10,219; 11,396; 11,889 (Mercers Hall, Cornhill). 10,131; 11,396 (against Stocks Market).

Bowles, Thomas (1712-1767)
London publisher
10,027; 10,096; 10,219; 10,375; 10,826 (Next the Chapter House, St Paul's Churchyard).

Bowyer, R. & Parks, M. (fl.1820s)
London publishers
10,428 (Pall Mall).

Boydell, John (1719-1804)
London Engraver and London publisher
10,166; 10,171; 10,235; 10,382; 10,424; 10,443; 10,556; 10,765; 11,506; 11,826; 11,943; 20,035; 20,085; 20,090 (Cheapside).

Boydell, John (1719-1804) & Boydell, Josiah (1760-1817)
London publishers
10,341; 20,686; 20,712; 20,731 (Shakespeare Gallery, Pall Mall & 90, Cheapside).

Boydell & Co., Messrs
London publishers
10,409; 11,909; 20,653; 20,665; 20,666; 20,718; 20,719 (90, Cheapside).

Boys, Thomas (fl.1840s-1859)
London publisher
10,447 (11 Golden Square, Regent Street).

Bradshaw, T. (fl.1770s-1790s)
London publisher
10,697; 11,414 (James Street, Covent Garden).

Brain & Payne (19th century)
London publishers
10,978 (12, Paternoster Row).

Brandard, Robert (1805-1862)
London engraver and publisher
20,283; 20,492; 20,493 (1, Cloudesley Terrace, Islington). ?20,609.

Bretherton, James (fl.1770s-1780s)
London publisher
10,068; 10,700 (134, New Bond Street).

Brocas, William (1794-1868)
Dublin artist and engraver
?10,965 (5, Henry Street).

Brooks, John (fl.1730-1756)
Dublin mezzotinter and publisher
10,023; 10,026; 10,044; 10,115; 10,117; 10,159; 10,173; 10,187; 10,195; 10,197; 10,240; 10,242; 10,255; ?10,167; 10,267; 10,280; 10,418; 10,481; 10,760; 10,899 (Sir Isaac Newton's Head, Cork Hill).

Brooks (Vincent Robert Alfred), Day & Son (fl. from 1862)
London lithographers and publishers
11,078; 11,398; 11,400.

Brouilliard, J. (late 18th century)
Paris publisher
20,723.

Browne, Alexander (fl.1660-1680s)
London engraver and publisher
10,259; 10,756; 10,759 (Ye Blew Balcony in Little Queen Street).

Brownrigg, John (fl.1780s)
Dublin publisher
11,893 (64, Grafton Street).

Bry, Auguste (mid 19th century)
Paris printer
20,318; 20,319 (Rue du Bac 134).

Brydon, J. (fl.1790s)
London publisher
10,953 (Charing Cross).

Bull, Edward (fl.1830s)
London publisher
11,208; 11,308 (26, Holles Street).

Bull, Edward (fl.1830s) & Churton, Edward (1800-1874)
London publishers
11,119 (26, Holles Street, Cavendish Square).

Bulla Frères et Jouy (19th century)
Paris, Barcelona and New York publishers
11,486; 11,875.

Bulla, J. et Delarue, François (mid 19th century)
Paris publishers
(Rue J.J. Rousseau 10). 20,313; 20,314.

Bulmer & Co. W. (fl.1770s-1819)
London printers
20,665; 20,666; 20,686; 20,712; 20,719; 20,722 (Cleveland Row, St James's).

Bunney & Gold (fl.1800s)
London publishers
10,643 (Shoe Lane).

Cadell, Thomas (1742-1802)
London bookseller and publisher
10,294 (Strand).

Cadell, Thomas (1773-1836)
London publisher
10,751 (Strand).

Cadell, Thomas (1773-1836) & Davies, William (d.1819)
London publishers
10,062; 10,135; 10,151; 10,185; 10,260; 10,707; 10,739; 10,744; 10,745; 10,770; 10,801; 10,837; 10,883; 10,925; 10,951; 11,085; 11,741; 11,762; 11,764; 11,814; 11,831; 20,048; 20,156; 20,324; 20,680; 20,704; 20,705; 20,726; 20,727 (Strand).

Callaghan, Cornelius (fl.1780s)
Dublin publisher
10,464 (Great Britain Street).

Campen, J. van (17th century)
Venetian publisher
11,481; 11,498.

Cardon, Anthony (1772-1813)
London engraver and publisher
10,713; 11,220 (31, Clipstone Street, Fitzroy Square).

Carey, William (1759-1839)
London author, antiquarian and publisher
11,203.

Carey & Watson (18th century)
London publishers
10,804 (35, Mary le Bonne Street, Piccadilly).

Carfax & Co. (fl. early 20th century)
London publishers
11,446 (24, Bury Street).

Carpenter's Political Letter (1830-31)
Dublin journal of William Carpenter (1797-1874)
10,977.

Cassell, Petter & Galpin (19th century)
London, Paris and New York publishers
20,694.

Cattier (fl.1840s)
Paris lithographic printer
20,316; 20,317; 20,340-20,342; 20,462; 20,488-20,491; 20,494; 20,505-20,508; 20,652 (Rue de Lancry 12).

Caulfield, James (1764-1826)
London publisher
10,872; 10,873; 11,125; 11,133; 11,154; 11,277 (-). 11,392 (33, Titchfield Street).

Chapman & Hall (fl. from 1831)
London publishers
20,346; 20,358; 20,361; 20,370; 20,405-10,410; 20,428; 20,446; 20,447; 20,463-20,465.

Chater, N. (fl.1820s)
London printer
11,596.

Chesham, Francis (late 18th century)
London publisher
20,032 (8, Terrace, Walworth).

Churton, Edward (1800-1874)
London publisher
20,609 (Holles Street, Cavendish Square).

City Printing & Litho. Co. Ltd (late 19th century)
Dublin printers
20,644 (William Street).

Clarke, Mr (fl.1780s)
Dublin textile manufacturer
11,870 (Irish Furniture Cotton-warehouse, Werburgh Street).

Clarke, W. (fl.1817-1824)
London publisher
20,479 (New Bond Street).

Claudet, Antoine François Jean (1797-1867)
London daguerreotyper and publisher
11,057 (18, King William Street, Charing Cross & Collosseum, Regents Park). 10,582; 11,166.

Clay (early 19th century)
London bookseller and publisher
11,661.

Clément, A. (19th century)
Paris printer
11,495; 11,502; 20,068.

Clint, George (1758-1810)
London engraver and publisher
10,489 (21, Church Street, Soho). 10,948 (Hind Court, Fleet Street).

Clowes, B. (fl.1770s)
London publisher
10,332; 10,392 (18, Gutter Lane, Cheapside).

Cochin, Charles Nicolas (1715-1790)
Paris engraver and publisher
11,656 (Rue St Jacques à St Thomas d'Aquin).

Colburn, Henry (d.1855)
London publisher
10,658; 10,937; 10,959; 11,229; 11,234; 11,714 (Conduit Street). 10,615 (Great Marlborough Street). 10,959 (8, New Burlington Street). 10,638.

Colburn & Bentley (19th century)
London publishers
11,507.

Collyer, R.J. (fl.1790s)
London publisher
10,118 (Constitution Row, Gray's Inn Road).

Colnaghi (19th century)
London publishers
10,453; 10,772; 20,722.

Colnaghi & Co., Paul (1751-1833) and Dominic (1790-1879)
London publishers
10,094; 10,231; 10,449; 10,509; 10,790; 11,007; 11,489; 20,663. (13 & 14, Pall Mall East).

Colnaghi & Co. (fl.1790s-1830s)
London publishers
10,050; 10,210; 10,416; 10,478; 10,491; 10,701; 10,718; 10,725; 10,776; 11,048; 11,070; 11,647-11,651; ?11,661; 11,696; 20,039 (23, Cockspur Street). 10,164; 10,174; 10,775; 20,733 (Pall Mall East). 10,422; ?10,453; 10,469; 10,689; 10,842; 10,916; 10,949; 11,596; 11,698.

Colnaghi & Puckle (fl.1840s)
London publishers
10,949 (Cockspur Street, Charing Cross).

Colnaghi, Martin (fl.1820s-1830s)
London publisher
10,094; 10,882 (23, Cockspur Street).

Colnaghi, Sala & Co., late Torre (late 18th century)
London publishers
20,067 (132, Pall Mall).

Constable & Co., A. (fl. from 1814)
Edinburgh publishers
11,198.

Cooke, George (1781-1834)
London engraver and publisher
20,540.

Cooke, W.B. (1778-1855)
London engraver and publisher
20,333; 20,384 (9, Soho Square).

Cooper, E. (fl. c.1685-c.1725)
London publisher
10,001; 10,003; 10,012; 10,032; 10,331; 10,371; 10,385; 10,559; 10,569; 10,822; 10,921; 10,922; 10,993; 10,995; 20,800. (3 Pidgeons, Bedford Street).

Cooper the Younger, Richard (c.1740-?1814)
London engraver and publisher
10,546 (sold at Mr David Wilson's, bookseller near York Buildings in the Strand).

Cooper, Thomas Bird (fl.1800s)
Dublin printer
11,751 (56, Great George's Street South).

Copley, John Singleton (1737-1815)
American artist and London publisher
10,432 (George Street, Hanover Square).

Corcoran, B. (fl.1790s)
Dublin publisher
10,262.

Corr, Mathieu Erin (1805-1862)
Antwerp engraver and publisher
11,482; 11,489; 20,806.

Cosway, Richard (1742-1821)
English artist and publisher
10,140.

Couché, Jacques (1759-after 1808)
Paris engraver and publisher
20,723 (Rue St Hyacinthe no. 51). 20,724-20,725 (Rue de la Harpe).

Cowen, George (fl. 1790s)
London and Dublin publisher
10,092; 10,150; 10,217; 10,247; 10,251; 10,494; 10,501; 10,726 (at T. Macklin's Poets Gallery, Fleet Street and at his house Grafton Street). 11,568-11,570; 11,573-11,574; 11,579-11,582 (Grafton Street).

Cowen, Robert (fl. c. 1800)
London and Dublin publisher
10,702; 10,861-10.862 (39, Fleet Street & Grafton Street).

Cox, David (fl. 1810s)
London publisher
10,372 (9, Ball Alley, Lombard Street).

Cox, W. (fl. 1800s)
Dublin publisher
11,343.

Cranfield, Thomas (fl. 1850s-1880s)
Dublin publisher
10,421; 10,441; 10,456; 10,505; 10,506; 10,510; 10,815; 11,556 (115, Grafton Street). 10,710; 20,110 (23, Westmorland Street). 10,468; 10,544; 10,880.

Crepy (18th century)
Paris publisher
10,042 (Rue St Jacques à St Pierre).

Creuzbacher & Co. (19th century)
Carlsruhe publishers
20,376-20,380; 20,432; 20,433.

Cribb, R. (fl. 1780s-1820s)
London publisher
10,320 (288, Holborn).

Cribb, W. (fl. 1810s-1830s)
London publisher
10,098 (Tavistock Street).

Cuming, William (1769-1852)
Irish artist and Dublin publisher
10,547 (34, Anglena Street). 10,192.

Curry Junior and Co., William (fl. 1830s-1840s)
Dublin publishers
10,287; 10,592; 10,596; 10,613; 10,665; 11,082; 11,090; 11,100; 11,100; 11,104; 11,109; 11,156; 11,161; 11,192; 11,216; 11,217; 11,227; 11,254; 11,270; 11,273; 11,292; 11,293; 11,302; 11,311; 11,423.

Cyclopaedian Magazine (1807-1808)
Dublin magazine
11,221; 11,301.

D'Alton, John (1792-1867)
Irish historian and Dublin publisher
11,674-11,678; 11,685-11,688; 11,758.

Danckerts, Justus (1635-1701)
Amsterdam publisher
11,849.

Daniell, William (1769-1837)
London engraver and publisher
10,049; 10,196; 10,746; 11,860 (9, Cleveland Street, Fitzroy Square).

Daniell & Co., James (fl. 1800s)
London publisher
20,702 (480, Strand).

Darling and Thompson (fl. 1790s)
London publishers
10,118; 20,089 (Great Newport Street).

Darton, William (fl. 1810-1837) & T. (19th century)
London publishers
20,662 (58, Holborn Hill).

D'Aubert et Cie (19th century)
Paris printers
10,976.

Davies, Thomas (c. 1712-1785)
London actor, bookseller and publisher
10,014.

Davis, J. (fl. 1810s)
London publisher
11,117 (38, Essex Street, Strand).

Dawe, George (1781-1829)
London artist, engraver and publisher
10,423; 10,991 (22, Newman Street).

Day, William (1797-1845)
London lithographer and printer
20,344; 20,374 (17, Gate Street).

Day, William (1797-1845) & Haghe, William Louis (1806-1885)
London lithographers, printers and publishers
10,265; 10,615; 10,893; 11,040; 11,115; 11,267; 20,149; 20,222; 20,347; 20,580.

Day & Son (fl. c. 1830-1862)
London lithographers, printers and publishers
10,190; 10,263; 11,035; 11,040; 11,772; 20,264 (17, Gate Street, Lincoln's Inn Fields). 20,338; 20,369.

Dayes, Mrs (Susan, wife of Edward Dayes) (fl. 1797-after 1805)
London miniature painter, bookseller and publisher
20,411; 20,430 (42, Devonshire Street, Queen's Square).

Dean, John (c. 1750-1798)
London engraver and publisher
10,090; 10,911 (Church Street, Soho). ?10,549.

Dean & Co. (19th century)
London lithographers and publishers
10,594; 10,595; 20,798 (Threadneedle Street).

Dean & Munday (early 19th century)
London publishers
11,006 (Threadneedle Street).

De Antoni, Nicola (19th century)
Rome publisher
20,676 (Presso Nicola de Antoni in via del Corso no. 35).

De Antoni, Nicola & Pavon, Ignazio (19th century)
Rome printers and publishers
20,709 (Piazza di Spagna no. 84).

Debrett, J. (fl. 1780s-1790s)
London publisher
11,147 (Piccadilly).

De la Feuille, Daniel (18th century)
Amsterdam publisher
10,224.

De la Houe, Paul (early 17th century)
French publisher
10,311.

Delarue, François (mid 19th century)
Paris publisher
20,145; 20,147; 20,310-20,312; 20,315-20,319 (Rue J.J. Rousseau 10).

Del Vecchio, James (fl.1810s-1820s)
Dublin publisher
10,427; 11,647; 11,648; 11,696; 11,910; 20,659; (26, Westmorland Street). 10,848; 10,966.

De Mechel, Chretien (late 18th century)
Basle publisher
20,675.

Depeuille (fl.1790s)
Paris publisher
10,877 (Rue des Mathurins St Jacque aux deux pilastres d'or).

De Pogg, A.C. (fl.1790s)
London publisher
10,498 (91, New Bond Street).

De Rossi, Domenico (late 17th century)
Rome publisher
20,221.

De Rubeis, Johannes Jacobus (17th century)
Rome publisher
20,684 (S. Maria della Pace).

Dickenson & Co. (late 18th century)
London publishers
11,340.

Dickinson, J. (fl.1820s-1830s)
London publisher
10,703; 10,941 (144, New Bond Street).

Dickinson, William (1746-1823)
London engraver and publisher
10,479; 11,002 (Henrietta Street, Covent Garden). 11,028 (at Mrs Sledges, Covent Garden). 10,250; 10,352; 10,377; 10,475; 10,810 (158, New Bond Street). 10,490 (24, Old Bond Street).

Dickinson, William (1746-1823) & Watson, Thomas (1743-1781)
London engravers and publishers
10,381 (Dickinson at Henrietta Street; Watson at 142 Bond Street). 10,346; 10,351; 10,355; 10,462; 10,853 (158 New Bond Street).

Dickinson & Co. (19th century)
London lithographers and publishers
20,701 (144, New Bond Street).

Dicksee, John Robert (1817-1905)
London lithographer and publisher
20,111 (Holland Street, Fitzroy Square).

Didot L'Ainé, Jules (19th century)
Paris printer
20,679; 20,683; 20,685; 20,707 (Rue du Pont-du-Lodi).

Diemar, E.M. (fl.1790s)
London publisher
10,309; 10,753.

Dilly, Charles (late 18th century)
London bookseller and publisher
11,038.

Dixon, John (c.1740-1811)
Dublin and London engraver and publisher
10,158 (at Thomas Dixon's house on Cork Hill). 10,467.

Donbar, T. (late 17th century)
London printer
10,105.

Doo, George Thomas (1800-1886)
London engraver and publisher
10,402 (10 Adams Terrace, Camden Town).

Dorigny, Nicolas (1652-1746)
French engraver and London publisher
20,678(15).

Drouart (19th century)
Paris printer
11,486 (Rue du Fouarre).

The Dublin Builder (1859-1866)
11,737.

Dublin Magazine (1762)
(Ed. P. Wilson)
11,616

Dublin Magazine (1798-1800)
10,598; 10,599; 10,655; 11,305.

Dublin Monthly Museum (1814)
11,141; 11,142.

Duchange, Gaspard (1662-1757)
Paris engraver and publisher
20,678 (Rue St Jacques au dessus de la rue des Mathurins).

Ducôte, A. (fl.1829-1840s)
London lithographic printer
11,544(57-64); 11,852-11,854; 20,165; 20,172; 20,173; 20,175 (70, St Martin's Lane).

Ducôte & Stephen's (fl.1850s)
London lithographic printers
20,169; 20,170; 20,174; 20,243; 20,345; 20,402 (70, St Martin's Lane).

Dumont (19th century)
Paris Printer
11,496.

Duncan, James (fl.1830s)
London publisher
10,631.

Duncan, W. & D. (19th century)
Glasgow printers
20,282; 20,460; 20,461.

Dunton, J. (late 17th century)
London publisher
20,728.

Einslie, S. (fl.1785-1808)
London miniature painter, mezzotinter and publisher
10,387.

Engelmann & Co. (19th century)
London lithographic printers and publishers (Graf and Candet possibly omitted)
20,138; 20,288; 20,289; 20,294; 20,473 (14, Newman Street).

Engelmann, Graf, Coindet & Co. (fl.1820s-1830s)
London lithographic printers and publishers
10,288; 10,601; 10,675; 10,969; 11,020; 20,287; 20,289-20,293; 20,328; 20,334; 20,368; 20,471; 20,472; 20,474; 20,522 (14, Newman Street).

Esnauts (18th century)
Paris publisher
11,505.

Evans, B.B. (fl. c.1800)
London publisher
10,430; 20,032 (Poultry).

Evans, Edward (1789-1835)
London bookseller and publisher
10,788 (Great Queen Street, Lincoln's Inn Fields).

Ewart, J. (fl.1750s)
London publisher
10,357 (Beehive opposite Hartshorn Lane in the Strand).

Faber the Younger, John (c.1684-1756)
London engraver and publisher
10,867 (Fountain Court, Strand). 10,029; 10,031; 10,111; 10,125; 10,173; 10,176; 10,269; 10,843 (Golden Head, Bloomsbury Square). 10,193; 10,219 (Green Door, Craven Buildings, Drury Lane). 10.017; ?10,120; 10,160; ?10,393; ?10,420; ?10,548; 10,676; 10,709; 10,721; 10,845; 11,041; 20,244.

Faden, W. (fl.1790s)
London publisher
11,887 (Charing Cross).

Fairland, Thomas (1804-1852)
London artist, lithographer and printer
20,352.

Farrell & Son (19th century)
Dublin publishers
10,284.

Faulkner, George (?1699-1775)
Publisher and proprietor of *Faulkner's Journal* in Dublin
10,296; 10,297

Fennell, Robert (fl. c.1800)
London publisher
10,493.

Fenner, R. (fl.1820s)
London printer
11,700; 11,773; 11,775; 11,777-11,779; 11,780; 11,781; 11,783; 11,784; 11,789-11,791.

Ferrero, Giovanni Francesco (19th century)
Rome engraver and publisher
20,757.

Fielding, J. (fl.1780s)
London publisher
10,514; 10,516-10,518; 11,147; 11,284; 11,345 (Paternoster Row).

Fielding, J. & Walker, James (1748-1808)
London publishers
11,093; 11,095; 11,225; 11,282.

Filhol, Antoine Michel (1769-1812)
Paris engraver and publisher
20,201 (Rue de L'Odeon, no. 35).

Finden, William (1787-1852) & Finden, Edward Francis (1791-1857)
London engravers and publishers
10,370; 10,727; 10,769; 10,891; 10,943; 20,329; 20,383 (18 & 19, Southampton Place, Euston Square).

Finlay, John (fl.1820s-1850s)
Glasgow bookseller and publisher
10,970; 11,661.

Finlayson, John (c.1730-c.1776)
London engraver and publisher
11,386 (Berwick Street, Soho). 10,353; 10,391; 10,394; 10,933 (Orange Street, Leicester Fields).

Fisher, Edward (1722-1785)
Irish engraver and London publisher
10,194; 10,363; 10,401 (Golden head, Leicester Square). ?10,545.

Fisher, Henry (fl.1820s)
London publisher
11,693 (Caxton).

Fisher, Jonathan (fl.1763-1809)
Dublin artist, engraver and publisher
10,040 (Great Ship Street). 11,549; 11,628; 11,719.

Fisher, Son & Co. (fl.1820s-1840s)
London and Paris publishers
10,289; 10,972 (Newgate Street). 10,597; 10,632; 10,986; 11,193; 11,197; 11,283; 11,749; 11,771; 11,774; 11,776; 11,782; 11,785; 11,786; 11,787; 11,794; 20,151; 20,262; 20,263; 20,265; 20,266; 20,271; 20,279; 20,281; 20,284; 20,285; 20,356; 20,365; 20,367; 20,398; 20,399; 20,414; 20,419; 20,420; 20,424; 20,448-20,459; 20,477; 20,480; 20,485; 20,486; 20,611; 20,612.

Fittler, James (1758-1835)
London engraver and publisher
10,473 (Upper Charlotte Street, Rathbone Place).

Fleischer, E. (19th century)
Leipzig publisher
20,730.

Flemming, C. (fl.1830s)
Dublin publisher
10,973 (30, Upper Ormond Quay).

Ford, James (fl.1772-1812)
Dublin engraver and publisher
10,274 (15, Essex Quay, near Essex Bridge).

Ford, Michael (fl.1742-1765)
Dublin artist, mezzotinter and publisher
10,088; 10,206; 10,221; 10,221; 10,344; 10,504 (Ford's Print Shop on Cork Hill opposite Lucas's Coffee House). 10,024 (Vandykes Head on Cork Hill). 10,157; 10,500.

Formentin et Cie (19th century)
Paris printers
20,339 (Rue des Sts Pères 10).

Franzetti, Agapito (early 19th century)
Rome publisher
11,659 (Corso alle Convertite).

Fraser, James (d.1841)
London publisher
10,155; 10,288; 10,601; 10,675; 10,840; 10,894; 10,895; 10,913; 11,036; 11,039 (215, Regent Street).

Friedel, A. (fl.1820s)
London engraver and publisher
20,077 (15, Southampton Street, Strand).

Frye, Thomas (1710-1762)
Irish artist, mezzotinter and London publisher
10,465; 10,551; 10,552 (The Golden Head, Hatton Garden). 10,298; ?10,550; 10,551.

Fuller, Samuel & J. (19th century)
London publishers
20,169; 20,170; 20,174; 20,243; 20,261; 20,344; 20,345; 20,374; 20,402 (34, Rathbone Place).

Fumagalli, Paolo (19th century)
Florence publisher
20,154; 20,157.

Galignani, A. & W. (19th century)
Paris publishers
20,679; 20,683; 20,685; 20,707 (Rue Vivienne).

Gambart & Co., Ernest (fl. 1840s-1869)
London publishers
11,482; 11,486; 11,875; 20,311 (25 Berners Street: Oxford Street).

Gambart, Junin & Co. (fl. 1840s)
London publishers
20,147; 20,310; 20,312; 20,315-20,319; 20,343 (25 Berners Street: Oxford Street).

Garof, P. (fl. c.1810)
Edinburgh publisher
10,948 (Hanover Street).

Gattliffe, J. (fl. 1740s)
London publisher
10,403.

Gaven, George (fl. 1750-1775)
Dublin artist and publisher
10,108.

Gazette des Beaux-Arts (founded 1859)
Paris magazine
11,380.

Geller, William Overend (fl. 1834-1857)
London engraver and publisher
10,451 (4, Stanhope Place, Mornington Crescent).

General Advertiser (1837-1914)
Dublin publisher
20,644 (13, Fleet Street).

General Post Office Directory (19th century)
Dublin publishers
11,811.

Gentleman's Magazine (1731-1807)
London magazine
11,668; 11,706; 11,720; 11,721; 11,727; 11,728; 11,730; 11,731; 11,739; 11,742; 11,743; 11,744; 11,756; 11,767; 11,768; 11,832; 11,836; 11,837; 11,913-11,918; 11,920; 11,921; 11,923; 11,925.

Gillé Fils (early 19th century)
Paris printer
20,201.

Gilling, W. T. (early 19th century)
London publisher
20,732 (Suffolk Street)

Gilpin, C. (fl. c.1800)
London publisher
20,111 (Bishopgate Street Without).

Ginger, J. (late 18th century)
London publisher
10,796 (Old Bond Street).

Giraldon-Bovinez (19th century)
Paris publishers
20,088; 20,663 (Passage Vivienne no. 26).

Gluckman, (Professor) Leon (fl. 1843-1867)
Dublin daguerreotyper and publisher
10,064; 10,102; 10,119; 10,121; 10,179; 10,521-10,526; 10,553; 10,722; 10,990; ?11,430; 11,934-11,940 (24, Upper Sackville Street).

Goggins, J.J. (fl. 1890s)
Dublin publisher
10,433 (Gardiners Grove & Cabra).

Gole, Jacobus (1660-1737)
Amsterdam engraver and publisher
10,564; 11,024.

Goupil & Co. (fl. 1840s)
Paris, Berlin and New York publishers
10,263; 11,484.

Goupil & Vibert (fl. 1840s)
Paris publishers
10,970; 11,482; 11,489; 20,240; 20,340; 20,341; 20,343; 20,462; 20,488; 20,505; 20,506; 20,506-20,508 (15, Boulevard Montmartre & 7, Rue de Lancry).

Goyer (19th century)
Paris publisher
20,466 (Passage Dauphine 7).

Graf, J. (fl. 1840s)
London printer
10,757; 10,859; 11,065-11,067; 11,695; 20,336; 20,761.

Graf & Soret (fl. 1840s)
London printers
10,882.

Grant & Bolton (fl. 1830s-1840s)
Dublin publishers
10,449.

The Graphic (1869-1932)
London magazine
20,578.

E. Graves & Co. - late Colnaghi & Co. (fl. 1830s)
London publishers
10,249; 10,566; 10,806; 20,126 (23, Cockspur Street, Charing Cross).

Frs. Graves & Co., - late Colnaghi & Co. (fl. 1830s)
London publishers
11,044 (23, Cockspur Street, Charing Cross).

Henry Graves & Co. (fl. 1847-1894)
London publishers
10,188; 10,711; 10,720; 10,898; 10,903; 10,905; 11,663 (6, Pall Mall).

Green, Valentine (1739-1813)
London mezzotinter and publisher
10,130; 10,400; 10,405; ?11,034 (29, Newman Street, Oxford Street).

Griffin, E. (mid 18th century)
London publisher
10,123 (next the Globe Tavern, Fleet Street).

Gunst, Pieter van (1659-?1724)
Amsterdam engraver and publisher
10,349.

Habnit, Giuseppe A. (19th century)
Venice publisher
20,390 (Piazza S. Marco no. 102).

Hackert, Georg Abraham (1755-1805)
German engraver and Naples publisher
20,769.

Hailes, N. (fl. 1820s)
London publisher
20,212 (Piccadilly).

Hall, Arthur (19th century)
London publisher
11,035 (25, Paternoster Row).

Hall, John (1739-1797)
London engraver and publisher
10,152; 10,460 (83, Berwick Street).

Halpin, Patrick (fl.1755-1787)
Dublin engraver and publisher
10,091 (Blackamoor Yard, off Anglesea Street).

Halton, W. (19th century)
London printer
10,870.

Hanbury, Michael (fl.1748-1756)
Dublin publisher
10,141 (The Bear in George's Lane).

Hanhart, M. & N. (fl. c.1820-1865)
London lithographic printers and publishers
10,685; 10,722; 10,786; 10,789; 10,857; 10,871; 10,901; 11,057; 11,072; 11,076; 11,430; 11,857; 20,111; 20,181; 20,223; 20,348; 20,350; 20,766; 20,767.

Harding, Edward (1755-1840)
London bookseller and publisher
10,662; 10,663; 10,920 (Fleet Street).

Harding, George Perfect (c.1780-1853)
English watercolourist and London publisher
10,807; 11,052 (Hercules Buildings, Lambeth).

Harding, Sylvester (1745-1809)
London artist, bookseller and publisher
11,266 (727, Pall Mall).

Harding, Sylvester (1745-1809) & Edward (1755-1840)
London publishers
10,576; 10,614; 11,107; 11,543 (102, Pall Mall).

Harding & Lepard (fl.1820s-1830s)
London publishers
10,570; 10,782 (Pall Mall East).

Harding, Mavor & Lepard (fl.1820s)
London publishers
10,533.

Hardy, Thomas (fl.1790s)
London publisher
10,103 (4, Great Marlborough Street).

Harpur, Mr (fl.1768-1786)
Leixlip printer
11,870.

Harrison (fl.1780s-1790s)
London publisher
20,836.

Haskell & Allen (19th century)
Boston publishers
10,723 (61, Hanover Street).

Havell the Elder, Robert (1800-1840)
London engraver and publisher
11,705 (79, Newman Street: Oxford Street). 11,842 (77, Oxford Street).

Haverty, Joseph Patrick (1794-1864)
Irish artist, lithographer and occasional publisher
11,845 (London). 10,000.

Hawkins, G. (fl.1750s)
London publisher
10,087 (Milton's Head, Fleet Street).

Hawkins, S. (fl.1840s)
London printer
10,968.

Hayward & Co., James (mid 19th century)
London publishers
11,280.

Heath, Mr (fl.1810s)
London publisher
11,048 (15, Russell Place, Fitzroy Square).

Heffernan, Edward (19th century)
Dublin engineer and publisher
11,885 (12, Charleville Road, Rathmines).

Heissig, Franz Carl (fl. from 1770)
Augsburg engraver and publisher
10,752.

Henecy & Fitzpatrick (fl.1790s)
Dublin engravers and publishers
10,277.

Herbert, James Dowling (1762/63-1837)
Dublin and London actor, artist and publisher
10,067 (London). 10,291 (53, South Great George's Street).

Herbert, William (1718-1795)
London publisher
10,005; 10,223; 10,228; 10,241; 10,415; 10,434; 10,481; 10,537; 10,820; 10,825; 10,914; 11,062.

Herhan, L. E. (early 19th century)
Paris printer
20,691.

Hibernian Magazine (1771-1812)
Dublin magazine: *Walker's Hibernian Magazine* from 1786
10,292; 10,293; 10,527; 10,573; 10,585; 10,612; 10,651; 10,668; 11,083; 11,091; 11,102; 11,110; 11,129; 11,139; 11,175; 11,194; 11,211; 11,238; 11,242; 11,321; 11,323; 11,324; 11,328 11,331; 11,342; 11,344; 11,350; 11,381.

Hickey, John (1756-1795)
Irish sculptor and London publisher
10,435 (128, Oxford Street).

Hill, Alexander (fl.1847-1865)
Edinburgh publisher
20,168; 20,323 (67, Princes Street).

Hinton, John (fl.1747-1781)
London publisher
11,244; 11,614; 11,080; 11,712; 11,747 (King's Arms, St Paul's Churchyard).

Hinton, W. (late 18th century)
London publisher
11,645 (Sweetings Alley, Cornhill).

Hodges & McArthur (fl.1810s-1820s)
Dublin publishers
10,950.

Hodges & Smith (fl.1810s-1860s)
Dublin booksellers and publishers
10,690 (104, Grafton Street). 10,300; 10,591; 10,672; 10,749

Hodgson & Graves (fl.1830s-1840s)
London publishers
10,154; 10,735 (6, Pall Mall).

Hoeye, Rombout van den (b.1622)
Amsterdam engraver and publisher
10,245.

Höfelich, J. (19th century)
Vienna printer
10,938; 10,982.

Hogarth, William (1697-1764)
London artist, engraver and publisher
11,509-11,520.

Hogg, Alexander (fl.1780s-c.1810)
London publisher
11,680; 11,681; 11,713; 11,757 (16, Paternoster Row).

Holbrooke, William Henry (fl.1827-1848)
Dublin engraver and publisher
10,983. 11,240 (4, Crow Street).

Hollyer, S. (fl.1830s-1840s)
London publisher
10,968 (89, Chancery Lane). 20,327 (2, Everett Street).

Holmes, G. (fl.1790s)
London publisher
10,457.

Hone, Horace (1756-1825)
Irish miniaturist and Dublin publisher
10,745.

Hone the Elder, Nathaniel (1718-1784)
Irish artist and engraver; London publisher
10,072 (-). 20,822 (St James's Palace).

Hooper, A. (fl.1770s)
London publisher
11,665 (25, Ludgate Hill).

Hooper, Samuel (fl.1773-1793)
London publisher
10,055; 11,927 (212, High Holborn).

Houston, Richard (1721-1775)
Irish mezzotinter and London publisher
?10,342 (-). 11,068 (Ye Golden Head in Broad Court, Covent Garden).

How & Parsons (19th century)
London publishers
20,503 (132, Fleet Street). 20,502; 20,504; 20,510; 20,513.

Howlett & Brimmer (19th century)
London publishers
20,205; 20,241-20,242; 20,427 (-). 20,708 (Frith Street, Soho).

Huband, Willcocks (1776-1834)
Dublin amateur etcher and publisher
20,692.

Hulett, James (fl.1740-1771)
London engraver and publisher
10,181.

Hullmandel, Charles Joseph (1789-1850)
London lithographic printer and publisher
10,271; 10,703; 10,775; 10,794; 10,941; 11,233; 11,327; 11,610; 11,611; 20,127-20,131; 20,224; 20,225; 20,259; 20,273; 20,274; 20,296-20,307; 20,330.

Humphrey, H. (fl. c.1800)
London publisher
10,398 (18, New Bond Street). 10,939; 11,545 (27, St James's Street).

Humphrey, William (c.1740-1810)
London engraver and publisher
10,059; 10,380; 10,696; 11,058; 11,228 (Gerrard Street). 11,012 (St Martin's Lane).

Humphreys, G. (fl. c.1800)
London publisher
10,874 (St James's Street).

Hunter, R. (fl.1810s-1820s)
London publisher
11,167 (St Paul's Churchyard).

Hurst, Robinson & Co., successors to J. & J. Boydell (fl.1810s-1820s)
London publishers
11,649-11,651; 20,666 (Cheapside).

Illustrated London News (founded 1843)
11,595; 11,878; 20,570-20,576.

Illustrated News of the World (1858-1863)
London magazine
10,567; 10,927; 11,023.

L'Imprimerie de Komarek (18th century)
Paris printers
20,674.

L'Imprimerie de la Galerie de Florence (18th century)
Florence printers
20,687; 20,688.

Ireland's Mirror (1804-06)
Dublin magazine
11,087; 11,348; 11,349; 11,351.

Irish Catholic Magazine
Dublin magazine
10,587.

Irish Law Recorder (1828-1838)
Dublin magazine
10,875.

Irish Magazine (1807-1815)
Dublin magazine
10,067; 10,589; 10,650; 11,163; 11,338; 11,343.

Jackson, Zachariah (fl.1790s)
Dublin publisher
11,500 (5, Sackville Street). 11,709; 11,710 (5 New Buildings, Sackville Street & 18, Great Ship Street). 11,707; 11,708; 11,711; 11,725; 11,726; 11,734; 11,740; 11,753; 11,755.

Jackson, Michael (fl.1736-c.1753)
Irish mezzotinter and London publisher
?10,134.

Jacomme et Cie (19th century)
Paris printers
20,337; 20,470; 20,487; 20,497-20,500; 20,521 (Rue de Lancry no. 12). 20,145; 20,496 (Rue de Lancry no. 16).

Jazet, Jean Pierre Marie (1788-1871)
Paris engraver and publisher
20,100 (Rue de Lancry no. 4).

Jeannin, H. (mid 19th century)
Paris publisher
20,340-20,342; 20,462; 20,488; 20,490; 20,491; 20,505-20,508 (Place du Louvre, 20).

Jeanron, Victor et Charnoz, Edouard (mid 19th century)
Paris publishers
20,084 (46, Rue Richer).

Jefferys, Thomas (?1695-1771)
London publisher
10,005; 10,223; 10,228; 10,234; 10,241; 10,434; 10,537; 10,820; 10,825; 10,827; 10,914 (St Martin's Lane, Charing Cross). 10,851.

Jeffryes, John (fl.1790-c.1800)
London publisher
10,812 (Clapham Road).

Johnson, Wilson & Co. (19th century)
New York publishers
10,773.

Jones, G. (fl.1810s)
London publisher
10,910.

Jones, J. (18th century)
Dublin bookseller
11,547 (39, College Green).

Jones, John (c.1745-1797)
London engraver and publisher
11,388 (63, Great Portland Street). 10,089; 10,386; 10,442; 10,476; 10,499; 10,503; 10,508 (75, Great Portland Street).

Jones, R.G. (fl.1820s)
London publisher
20,088 (Brewer Street, Golden Square).

Jones, William (fl.1790s)
11,281 (86, Dame Street).

Jones & Co. (fl.1820s-1850s)
London publishers
11,823-11,825 (3, Acton Place, Kingsland Road). 20,245; 20,267; 20,403; 20,404; 20,476 (Temple of the Muses, Finsbury Square).

Jouret, Henry (18th century)
London picture frame maker and publisher
10,180 (at the Golden Frame in Maiden Lane).

Jouy (19th century)
Paris printer
20,100.

Jukes, Francis (1745-1812)
London engraver and publisher
11,732; 11,733 (Howland Street).

Keating, George (1762-1842)
London engraver, bookseller and publisher
10,250 (4, Air Street, Piccadilly).

Keating, George (1762-1842) & Brown (d.1837)
London publishers 1816-1840
10.572; 11,231 (38, Duke Street, Grosvenor Square).

Keating, George (1762-1842), Brown (d.1837) and Keating, Patrick (1734-1816)
London publishers 1800-1816
11,337 (37, Duke Street, Grosvenor Square).

Kelly, Thomas (fl.1810s-1830s)
London publisher
11,353-11,369 (Paternoster Row).

Kelly, W.J. (19th century)
Dublin publisher
10,974 (18, Nassau Street).

Kirkwood, John (fl.1826-1853)
Dublin engraver and publisher
11,701 (11, Crow Street). 20,110 (Westmorland Street). ?10,673 (Crow Street).

Kitchin, T. (fl. c.1750)
London engraver and publisher
11,652 (59, Holburn Hill).

Knapton, John (d.1770) & Paul (d.1755)
London printers and publishers
10,212; 10,839; 10,987.

Knight, Charles (1743-c.1826)
London engraver and publisher
10,082 (Hammersmith).

Knight, Charles (1791-1873)
London engraver and publisher
20,118 (Pall Mall East).

Kohl-Weigand, Franz Joseph (20th century)
St Ingbert publisher
20,660.

Königlich Lithographisches Institut (19th century)
Berlin lithographic publishers
10,758.

La Belle Assemblée (1803-1836)
London magazine
10,316; 11,118.

Lacey, E. (fl.1830s)
London publisher
20,211; 20,518 (16, St Paul's).

Lacombe, Etienne (fl.1779-1789)
Paris publisher
20,687; 20,688 (84, Rue de la Harpe).

Lady's Magazine (1770-1819)
London magazine
11,717.

Lahee, James (fl.1810-1852)
London printer
10,065; 10,824.

Lamb, Francis (fl.1820s)
Edinburgh publisher
11,661.

Landley, Thomas (fl.1810s)
Armagh publisher
10,461.

Landseer, H. (fl.1800s)
London engraver and publisher
10,949 (Northend, Fulham).

Lane, R. (fl.1780s)
London publisher
11,644; 11,826.

Laporte (early 19th century)
Paris engraver and publisher
20,724; 20,725 (Rue de Savoie, no. 5).

Laurent, Pierre François (1739-1809)
Paris publisher
20,691.

Laurie, Robert (c.1755-1836) & Whittle, James (18th-19th century)
London publishers
11,813; 11,839 (53, Fleet Street).

Lawrence, Sir Thomas (1769-1830)
English artist and London publisher
10,057.

Lee & Hurst (fl.1790s)
London publishers
10,275 (32, Paternoster Row).

Leith, S. (19th century)
Edinburgh printer
20,168; 20,323.

Lemaitre, Augustin François (1797-1870)
Paris engraver and publisher
11,699; 11,702.

Lemercier, Imprimerie (mid 19th century)
Paris printers
11,875; 20,558 (57, Rue de la Seine). 11,874; 20,147; 20,148; 20,176; 20,308-20,313; 20,315; 20,343; 20,556; 20,602; 20,603; 20,830.

Lenoir (18th century)
Paris publisher
20,158 (14, Rue St Jacques).

Le Petit, J. (fl. 1800-1820s)
Dublin publisher
10,952 (Anglesea Street). 10,823; 11,945; 11,946; 11,947; 11,948 (20, Capel Street). 11,703; 11,953-11,956 (24, Grafton Street). 11,944; 11,949; 11,950.

Le Prince, Jean-Baptiste (1734-1781)
French artist, engraver and publisher
20,711

Lesage, A. (fl. 1840s)
Dublin publisher
10,970 (40, Lower Sackville Street).

Lewis, N. (fl. 1820s)
London printer
10,039 (1-25), (25 Finch Lane, Cornhill).

Liénard, François (19th century)
Paris printer
11,380; 11,504; 20,080.

Linnell, John (1792-1882)
London artist, engraver and publisher
11,044 (38, Porchester Terrace, Bayswater).

Lipschitz, S. (19th century)
London publisher
11,407 (84, Brush Street, Bishopgate).

Livesay, R. (?Richard, 1753-1823)
London publisher
10,692; 10,693.

Lloyd Bros. and Co., Messrs. (fl. 1847-1866)
London publishers
10,421; 11,873 (22, Ludgate Hill).

Lloyd, J. (late 17th century)
London publisher
10,136; 11,207.

London Magazine (1732-1785)
20,122.

Longacre (19th century)
Philadelphia publisher
11,297.

Longman (fl. 1810s)
London publisher.
10,307; 10,637; 11,417.

Longman & Co. (fl. 1810s-1870s)
London publishers
10,056; 10,572; 10,950; 11,333; 11,697; 11,792; 11,860; 20,155; 20,207; 20,208; 20,213; 20,214; 20,413; 20,483; 20,484; 20,589; 20,791 (Paternoster Row).

Longman & Co. and Kennedy & Brown (fl. 1820s)
10,572.

Longman, Hurst, Rees & Orme (early 19th century), (Thomas Norton Longman, 1771-1842; Owen Rees, 1770-1837 and others)
London publishers
20,156 (Paternoster Row).

Longman, Hurst, Rees, Orme & Brown (19th century: see above)
London publishers
20,704; 20,705; 20,726; 20,727; 20,733 [& Green] (Paternoster Row). 20,048; 20,324; 20,680; 20,681.

Lucarme (19th century)
Paris lithographic printer
20,088.

Lowry, Wilson (1762-1824)
London engraver and publisher
20,389 (57, Titchfield Street).

Lupton, Thomas Goff (1791-1873)
London engraver and publisher
10,243 (4, Keppel Street, Russell Square). 20,112 (7, Leigh Street, Burton Crescent).

Lutterell, M. (late 17th century)
London publisher
10,022 (in Westminster Hall).

Lyons, Edward (1726-1801)
Dublin engraver and publisher
10,232; 10,919 (on Essex Bridge).

McArdell, James (1728/29-1765)
Irish mezzotinter; Dublin and London publisher
10,008; 10,104; 10,852 (The Golden Head, Covent Garden). 10,060; 10,114; ?10,149 10,165; 10,343; ?10,374 ?10,389; ?10,755; ?10,846; ?10,855; ?11,056.

McCleary, William (fl. c.1810-1830s)
Dublin publisher
11,867 (32, Nassau Street).

McCormick, J. (fl. 1830s)
London publisher
11,801; 20,352; 20,482; 20,514 (147, Strand).

McCormick, James (1840s)
Dublin publisher
10,512; 10,513 (16, Christchurch Place).

McCreery, J. (fl. 1820s)
London printer
20,720; 20,733 (Tooks Court).

McDonald, D. (19th century)
Cork publisher
10,916.

McGlashan, James (fl. 1840s-1850s)
Dublin publisher
10,617; 10,624; 10,641; 10,666; 11,099; 11,108; 11,127; 11,178; 11,202; 11,237; 11,268; 11,269; 11,271; 11,306; 11,307; 11,310; 11,312; 11,334; 11,378; 11,421; 11,422; 11,864.

MacGregor, Polson & Co. (19th century)
Dublin publishers
11,180; 11,199.

MacGregor, Polson, Sutherland & Co. (19th century)
Dublin publishers
10,639; 11,255.

MacKenzie, William (mid 19th century)
Glasgow, Edinburgh, London and New York publisher
10,645.

Mackintosh (fl. 1820s)
Edinburgh bookseller and publisher
11,661.

Macklin, Thomas (fl. 1779- after 1793)
London engraver and publisher
10,777 (29, Fleet Street). 10,092; 10,150; 10,217; 10,247; 10,251; 10,484; 10,494; 10,501; 10,726 (at T. Macklin's Poets Gallery, Fleet Street).

McLean, E. (fl. 1830s)
London publisher
10,035 (14, St Martin's Court, Leicester Square).

McLean, Thomas (fl. 1820s-1850s)
London publisher
10,039 (1-25); 10,265; 10,908; 10,973; 10,975; 11,401; 11,403; 11,544(56-67); 11,852-11,854; 11,891; 20,165 (26, Haymarket).

Maclure, Macdonald & Co. (late 19th century)
Glasgow printers
11,682.

McQueen (mid 19th century)
London printer
10,361; 10,477; 10,736; 10,847; 10,894; 10,895; 10,943; 11,803; 20,057; 20,207; 20,495.

Madden & Co. (Richard Robert Madden 1798-1886)
Irish writer and London publisher
10,582; 10,616; 10,628; 10,633; 10,646; 10,647; 10,649; 10,660; 10,661; 10,671; 11,137; 11,138; 11,164-11,166; 11,169-11,173; 11,182; 11,189; 11,226; 11,272; 11,294; 11,295; 11,298-11,300; 11,326 (-). 11,267; 11,329 (Leadenhall Street).

Madden, W. (fl.1770s)
Dublin publisher
10,479 (20, Moore Street).

Madeley, George E. (fl.1830s-1850s)
London lithographic printer
20,167; 20,325; 20,375 (3, Wellington Street, Strand).

Major (18th century)
London publisher
20,198.

Malouët, Baron (early 19th century)
Paris publisher
10,906 (Ministre de la Marine, Rue de Seine, F.B.S.G. no. 55).

Malton, James (c.1760-1803)
English artist, engraver and London publisher
11,567; 11,568-11,570; 11,573; 11,574; 11,577; 11,579; 11,580-11,583; 11,585-11,588; 11,591; 11,592; 11,634; 11,640; 11,690; 11,816.

Malton, Thomas (1726-1801)
English artist, engraver and London publisher
11,645; 11,902 (6, Conduit Street, Hanover Square).

March, T.G. (fl.1840s)
London publisher
10,847 (4, Hanover Square).

Marchand, D. (19th century)
Paris publisher
20,602; 20,603 (10, Boulevard des filles du Calvaire).

Mariette, Pierre (1634-1716)
Paris bookseller and publisher
20,231 (Rue St Jacques à L'Esperance).

Mariette Fils, Pierre Joseph (d.1729)
Paris engraver and publisher
20,232 (Rue St Jacques aux collomnes d'Hercule).

Marlow Brothers (fl.1850s)
Dublin publishers
11,630 (10, Merchants' Quay).

Marshall, R. (fl.1770s)
London publisher
10,330 (4, Aldermary Churchyard).

Marshall, W. (fl.1820s-1850s)
London publisher
11,683; 11,684; 20,295; 20,517; 20,519 (1, Holborn Bars).

Marshall & Simpkin (fl.1830s)
London publishers
20,152; 20,412; 20,415; 20,421-20,423; 20,426; 20,443; 20,444; 20,492; 20,493.

M'Arte Edizioni (20th century)
Milan publishers
11,424; 20,509; 20,536; 20,829.

Martin, Henry (fl.1830s)
London printer
10,962.

Martin, R. (fl.1830s)
London printer
10,980 (124, High Holburn).

Martyn, John (fl.1794-1828)
Dublin engraver and publisher
10,279 (24, Lower Ormond Quay).

Mason, W. (fl.1800s-1820s)
London printer
11,045; 11,046.

Mason, William Monck (1775-1859)
Irish historian and Dublin publisher
10,529; 11,608; 11,609; 11,759.

Mellan, Claude (1598-1688)
French engraver and publisher
20,125.

Merlen, I. van (17th century)
Antwerp publisher
20,215 (Rue St Jacques).

Metz, Conrad Martin (1749-1827)
London artist, engraver and publisher
20,236-20,239 (13, Thayr Street, Manchester Square).

Meyer, Henry Hoppner (1783-1847)
London engraver and publisher
10,270 (62, Great Russell Street, Bloomsbury).

Miller, Andrew (fl.1737-1763)
Dublin mezzotinter and publisher
10,074; 10,076; 10,099; 10,113; 10,122; 10,133; 10,186; 10,256; 10,335; 10,367; 10,436 (On Hog Hill near the Round Church). ?10,018; ?10,081; ?10,480; ?10,558; ?10,678; ?10,917.

Miller, William (fl.1800s-1810s)
London publisher
20,673 (Albemarle Street).

Milliken, Andrew (fl.1840s)
Dublin bookseller and publisher
10,033; 10,116; 10,411.

Milliken, Richard (fl.1810s-1820s)
Dublin publisher
11,649-11,651 (Grafton Street).

Milton, Thomas (1743-1827)
English engraver; Dublin and London publisher
11,615 (35, Great George's Street). 11,654 (40, Great Queen Street, Lincoln's Inn Fields).

Mitchell, Edward (fl. c.1805-c.1822)
Edinburgh engraver and publisher
10,258.

Mitchell, J. (fl.1830s-1860s)
London publisher
10,736; 11,410.

Mitchell, John (fl.1836-1854)
London publisher
10,757; 10,859; 11,065-11,067 (Royal Library, 33, Old Bond Street).

Moll, Herman (1688-1745)
London bookseller and publisher
11,666.

Molteno, J. (fl.1820s)
London publisher
10,065; 10,094; 20,733 (Pall Mall).

Molteno & Graves (fl.1820s)
London publishers
10,969; 11,020 (28, Pall Mall).

Monaco, Pietro (fl.1735-1775)
Venice engraver and publisher
11,488.

The Monthly Pantheon
Dublin magazine
11,071.

Moon, Sir Francis Graham (1796-1871)
London publisher
10,155; 10,411; 10,840; 10,913; 10,955; 11,036; 11,039; 20,139; 20,149 (20, Threadneedle Street).

Moon, Boys & Graves (fl.1825-1832)
London publishers
10,094; 20,057 (6, Pall Mall).

Morgan, S. (fl.1800s)
London publisher
20,033.

Morris & Co. (19th century)
London publisher
10,482 (292, Strand).

Motte, C. (fl.1820s-1830s)
London lithographic printer
11,403 (23, Leicester Square).

Motte, Charles Etienne Pierre (1785-1836)
Paris publisher
20,721 (Rue Saint-Honoré no. 290).

Moyes, J. (early 19th century)
London printer
20,664; 20,673 (Greville Street).

Moyreau, Jean (1690-1762)
Paris engraver and publisher
20,689; 20,690 (Rue Gallande vis à vis St Blaise).

Murphy, John (fl.1778-1820)
Irish engraver and London publisher
10,106 (4, Air Street, Piccadilly). 10,541 (26, Upper Berkeley Street, Edgware Road). 20,059 (19, Howland Street, Fitzroy Square). 20,060 (Northside, Paddington Green).

Murray, John (1745-1843)
Edinburgh and London publisher
11,116 (50 Albernatle Street).

Naval Chronicle (1799-1818)
London magazine
10,643.

Naylor, Sir George (?1764-1831)
London publisher
10,740 (College of Arms). 11,404.

Neumann, L.T. (19th century)
Vienna publisher
10,938; 10,982.

New London Magazine (1785-1797)
11,754.

Newman, J. (19th century)
London engraver and publisher
20,642 (Bridge Row).

J. Newman & Co. (fl.1860s-1870s)
London publishers
11,761 (Watling Street).

Newenham, Frederick (1807-1859)
Irish artist and London publisher
10,928 (3, Thayer Street, Manchester Square).

New Sporting Magazine (1831-1870)
London magazine
20,615.

J. Nichols & Co., (fl.1810s)
London publishers
10,946.

Nicol, G. (fl. c.1800)
London publisher
10,622 (Pall Mall). 10,952.

Nugent, Thomas (fl.1785-1798)
Irish engraver and London publisher
10,797 (Pall Mall). 10,743; 10,780; 11,123.

Okey, Samuel (fl.1765-1780)
London engraver and publisher
10,327 (under St Dunstans Church, Fleet Street).

O'Reilly, B. (fl.1820s)
Dublin engraver and publisher
10,066 (176, North King Street).

Orme, Edward (fl. late 18th century-c.1838)
London publisher
10,767 (Bond Street Corner off Brook Street); 20,104 (25, Conduit Street, Hanover Square).

Orpin, I. (fl.1740s)
Dublin publisher
10,052 (Crane Lane).

Ostervald Ainé (19th century)
Paris publisher
20,087 (Quai des Augustins, no. 32).

Ottley, William Young (1771-1836)
London author and publisher
20,720 (Kensington).

Overton, Henry (d.1751)
London publisher
10,021 (Newgate).

Palmer & Clayton (19th century)
London printers
11,042 (Crane Court, Fleet Street).

Palser, Thomas (fl.1800s-1810s)
London publisher
10,486 (Surreyside, Westminster Bridge).

Park, Thomas (1759-1834)
London engraver and publisher
10,408 (22, Jermyn Street). 10,323 (4, St Margaret Street). 11,415.

Parker, Henry (fl.1770s-1770s)
London publisher
10,376; 11,386 (82, Cornhill). 10,139; 10,337 (Opposite Birchin Lane, Cornhill). 11,387.

Parsons, J. (fl.1790s)
London publisher
20,119 (Paternoster Row).

Payne, Olive (18th century)
London bookseller and publisher
20,667 (Horace's Head in Round Court in the Strand).

Payne the Younger, Thomas (1752-1831)
London publisher
11,045; 11,046 (Pall Mall).

Pelham, Henry (1749-1806)
Irish miniature painter and publisher
10,788 (Bere Island, Co. Kerry).

Pelham, Peter (c.1680-1751)
London engraver and publisher
11,396.

Pen and Pencil (1869-1932)
London magazine
20,621.

Penny National Library Office (19th century)
London publishers
10,962 (369, Strand).

Perronneau, H. (fl. c.1800)
Paris printer
20,723-20,725.

Peterkin, James (fl.1840s)
Dublin engraver and publisher
10,452 (Parkgate Street).

Petrie, James (1750-1819)
Dublin artist, engraver and publisher
10,156 (82, Dame Street).

Phillips, Charles (1737-after 1783)
London engraver and publisher
?10,378.

Phillips & Co. (Sir Richard Phillips, 1767-1840)
London author, bookseller, patent medecin vendor and publisher
11,603 (6, New Bridge Street, Blackfriars). 10,583.

Pollard, Robert (1755-1838)
London engraver and publisher
10,777; 11,637 (15, Brains Row, Spaitalfields).

Pope, Alexander (1763-1835)
Irish actor, artist and London publisher
10,437 (7, Albany Court, Piccadilly).

Potrelle (late 18th century)
Paris publisher
10,878 (Rue St Honoré, no. 54).

Potts, J. (fl.1760s)
Dublin publisher
20,729 (Swift's Head, Dame Street).

Publicité Wall (20th century)
Paris publishers
11,565 (14, Rue Lafayette).

2nd Queen Victoria's Own Sappers and Miners (fl.1920s)
Bangalore lithographers and publishers
11,809; 11,841.

Ramboz (early 19th century)
Paris printer
(20,685)(13)

Ramsay, James (1786-1849)
London artist and publisher
10,419 (23, Great Pultney Street).

Ranew, Nathaniel (late 17th century)
?London publisher
10,627.

Ransome, G. (19th century)
Hon. Sec. of Ipswich Museum and publisher
10,871.

Rapilly (18th century)
Coutances publisher
11,505 (Rue St Jacques).

Read & Co. (19th century)
London engravers and publishers
10,306; 11,620 (10, Johnson's Court, Fleet Street).

Reynolds, Sir Joshua (1723-1792)
London artist and publisher
10,338.

Reynolds the Elder, Samuel William (1773-1835)
London engraver and publisher
10,491 (Bayswater).

Reynolds the Younger, Samuel William (1794-1872)
London engraver and publisher
20,132.

Reynolds, W. (fl.1810s)
London publisher
11,288 (137, Oxford Street).

Reynolds & Allen (fl.1830s)
London printers
20,164.

Richards, C. William (fl.1780s-c.1800)
London printer
10,152; 10,460.

Richardson, William (fl. c.1800)
London publisher
11,210 (Castle Street, Leicester Fields). 10,278; 10,593 (York House, 31 Strand). 10,750; 11,003.

Richardson Junior, William (early 19th century)
London publisher
10,610 (York House, Strand).

Richter & Co., A. (fl.1830s)
London publisher
20,730 (Soho Square).

Rittner (19th century)
Paris publisher
20,087 (Boulevard Montmartre).

Ritner et Goupil (19th century)
Paris publishers
20,054; 20,055 (12, Boulevard Montmartre).

Roberts, Thomas Sautell (1760-1826)
Irish artist and London publisher
20,838(1-12).

Robertson, James George (19th century)
Kilkenny antiquary and publisher
11,671; 11,672.

Robertson, William (19th century)
Kilkenny architect and publisher
11,673.

Robillard-Péronville (d.1809)
Paris publisher
20,691.

Robins, J. (fl.1820s)
London publisher
11,289.

Robins & Co. J. (fl.1820s-1830s)
London and Dublin publishers
11,214 (Ivy lane, Paternoster Row). 10,600; 10,981; 11,313; 11,314.

Robinson, G. (fl. c.1810)
London publisher
10,286; 10,687; 10,708; 10,714; 10,715; 10,742; 10,748; 10,761; 10,778; 10,783; 10,793; 10,795; 10,803; 10,811; 10,816; 10,818; 10,836; 10,863; 10,881; 10,936; 10,940; 10,947; 11,049; 20,790.

Robinson, G.G. & J. (fl.1790s)
London publishers
10,283.

Robinson, J.O. (19th century)
London publisher
20,679; 20,683; 20,685; 20,707 (Poultry).

Robinson, Thomas (c.1770-1810)
Irish artist, engraver and Dublin publisher
10,043.

Robinson & Co. (fl.1820s)
London publishers
20,331 (90, Cheapside & 8, Pall Mall).

Rocque, John (fl.1746-1762)
London and Dublin mapmaker and publisher
11,806; 11,886.

Rocque, Mary Ann (wife of John Rocque)
London publisher
11,880 (near Old Round Court in the Strand).

Rodwell & Martin (19th century)
London publishers
20,330 (40, Argyll Street & 46, New Bond Street).

Rogerson, Joseph (fl.1840s)
London publisher
11,079 (24, Norfolk Street, Strand).

Rosapina, Francesco (19th century)
Bologna publisher
20,682.

Rosi, Settimo (19th century)
Rome publisher
20,759; 20,760 (Via della Croce no. 78a).

Rossi, Giovanni (fl. c.1700)
Rome publisher
20,677.

Rowe, George (1797-1864)
English artist, lithographer and publisher
20,353; 20,354.

Rowney & Co. G. (19th century)
London publishers
20,181; 20,223; 20,348; 20,350; 20,369 (51, Rathbone Place).

Royal Irish Art Union (1839-1851)
Society for the encouragement of the Fine Arts and Dublin publishers
11,605.

Royal Society of Arts (founded 1754)
Society for encouragement of Arts and Industry
10,712.

Royston, Richard (1599-1686)
London publisher
10,281 (The Angell, Joy Lane).

Ryall, Henry Thomas (1811-1867)
London engraver and publisher
10,155; 11,036 (3, Euston Square). 10,913 (8, Regent Street).

Ryall, J. & Withy, R. (fl.1750s)
London publishers
10,163 (Hogarth's Head, Fleet Street).

Ryland, M. (fl.1790s)
London publisher
10,118.

Ryland, William Wynne (1732-1783)
London engraver and publisher
10,999; 11,000 (Near Somerset House, Strand). 10,379; 10,395.

Ryland, William Wynne (1732-1783) & Bryer, Henry (d.1799)
London publishers
10,339; 10,397; 10,401; 11,098 (At the King's Arms in Cornhill).

Ryley & Co., R. (fl.1830s)
London publishers
10,840; 10,955; 11,039 (8, Regent Street).

Sackse, L. (19th century)
Berlin publisher
10,970.

Salmon, A. (late 19th century)
Paris printer
11,487.

Sams, W. (fl.1820s)
London publisher
10,170; 10,824 (Royal Library, St James's Street).

Saunders, J. (fl.1820s-1830s)
London and Lincoln publisher
20,429.

Saunders & Otley (19th century)
London publishers
20,730 (Conduit Street).

Say, William (1768-1834)
London artist, engraver and publisher
10,369 (92, Norton Street, Marylebone).

Sayer, Robert (1724/25-1794)
London publisher
10,034; 10,357; 10,683; 10,830; 11,903-11,906 (Golden Buck, opposite Fetter Lane, Fleet Street). 10,028; 10,153; 10,234; 10,257; 10,329; 10,334; 10,496; 10,695; 11,063; 11,064; 11,106; 11,140; 11,151 (53, Fleet Street). 10,827; 11,557-11,562; 20,085 (Fleet Street). 10,337 (Near Serjeants Inn, Fleet Street). 10,350; 10,470; ?11,249.

Sayers, Reuben (mid 19th century)
London publisher
10,705 (1, St Peter's Square, Hammersmith).

Scalé, Bernard (fl.1760-1787)
Dublin publisher
11,629 (Lower Abbey Street). 11,600; 11,883; 20,814.

Schenck, Pieter (1660-1718/19)
Amsterdam engraver and publisher
10,560; 10,821; 10,865; 10,998.

Schuberth & Niemeyer (19th century)
Hamburg and Jtzehoe publishers
10,045.

Scott, Edmund (1746-1810)
London and Brighton engraver and publisher
11,051.

Scott, John (fl.1790s-1800s)
London publisher
11,050 (442, Strand).

Scott & Co. (fl.1860s)
London publishers
11,007 (Pall Mall).

Scudellari, Jean (18th century)
Rome publisher
20,703 (18-19, Rue Condotti).

Sentimental and Masonic Magazine (1792-1795)
Dublin magazine
10,578; 11,176.

Sewell, J. (fl.1780s-1800s)
London publisher
10,653; 10,670; 11,084; 11,147; 11,157; 11,190; 11,191; 11,224; 11,250; 11,262; 11,679; 11,752 (32, Cornhill).

Sharpe, John (1777-1860)
London publisher
20,204; 20,512.

Shepherd Bros. (fl.1886-1901)
London publishers
10,360 (27, King Street, St James's Square).

Sherwin, John Keyse (?1751-1790)
English artist; London engraver and publisher
10,448 (67, New Bond Street).

Sherwood & Co. (fl.1820s)
London publishers
11,236; 11,769.

Sherwood, Jones & Co. (fl.1820s)
London publishers
11,788.

Sherwood, Neely and Jones & Co. (fl.1810s-1820s)
London publishers
11,692 (Paternoster Row).

Shirley, G. (fl.1820s)
London publisher
20,076 (31, Wilderness Row).

Short, J. (fl.1760s)
London publisher
10,168.

Sidebotham, James (fl. c.1800-1820s)
Dublin publisher (also London from 1816)
10,264; 11,031; 11,851 (24, Lower Sackville Street).

Silcock, Thomas (fl.1750s)
Dublin publisher and fan seller
10,011; 10,013; 10,101; 10,413; 10,440; 10,511. (Silcock's Print Shop or at the Royal Fan, Nicholas Street).

Simon, John (1675-1751)
London engraver and publisher
10,021 (Against Cros Lane in Long Acre). 10,215 (The Golden Eagle in Villars Street, York Buildings). 10,184; 10,204; ?10,248; 10,535; 10,536; 10,682; 10,732.

Simpkin & Marshall (fl.1830s)
London publishers
20,152; 20,283; 20,412; 20,415; 20,421; 20,422; 20,423; 20,426; 20,443; 20,444; 20,492; 20,493; 20,610 (Stationers Court).

Simpson, E. (fl.1830s)
London publisher
10,075.

Simpson, T. (fl.1790-1815)
London publisher
10,118; 10,246; 20,089 (St Paul's Churchyard).

Skelton, William (1763-1848)
London engraver and publisher
11,830 (Stafford Place, Pimlico).

Smeeton, George (fl.1800-1828)
London publisher
11,133 (3, Old Baily). 20,115 (St Martin's Lane).

Smith, A. (fl.1830s)
London publisher
11,912 (Fleet Street).

Smith, A. (fl.1830s)
? Dublin publisher
11,222.

Smith, E. (fl.1810s)
Liverpool publisher
11,126.

Smith, G. (mid 18th century)
London publisher
10,208 (Near Temple Bar, Fleet Street).

Smith, George (19th century)
Liverpool publisher
20,276; 20,371.

Smith, H. (fl.1790s)
London publisher
11,145 (4, Red Lion Court, Fleet Street).

Smith, John (1652-1742)
London mezzotinter; map and print publisher
10,834 (Hogarth's Head in Cheapside). 10,002; 10,030; 10,095; 10,218; 10,333; 10,347; 10,534; 10,539; 10,540; 10,719; 10,728; 10,785; 10,904; 10,929; 10,996 (Lyon and Crown, Russell Street, Covent Garden). 10,010; 10,071; 10,226; 10,229; 10,238; ?10,691; 10,774; 10,930; ?11,184; ?11,185.

Smith, John (fl.1750s-1770s)
London publisher
10,396 (Hogarth's Head opposite Wood Street, Cheapside).

Smith, John Raphael (1752-1812)
London mezzotinter and publisher
10,805; 11,665 (4, Exeter Court, Strand). 10,348; 10,354; 10,472; 10,697; 11,414 (10, Bateman's Buildings, Soho). 10,192 (31, King Street, Covent Garden). 10,203 (33, Newman Street). 10,356; 10,406; 10,438 (83, Oxford Street, opposite the Pantheon).

Smith, Nathaniel (fl.1790s)
London publisher
10,426 (18, Great Mary's Buildings, St Martin's Lane).

Smith, P. (fl.1740s)
Dublin publisher
10,052; 10,133; 10,256; 10,335 (Crane Lane).

Smith, W. (fl.1810s)
London publisher
11,122 (23, Lisle Street, Leicester Square).

Soffe, W. (19th century)
London publisher
20,322 (180 Strand, corner of Southampton Street).

Sprigg, R.A. (mid 19th century)
London publisher
20,248 (106, Great Russell Street, Bedford Square),

Squire & Co., Henry (fl.1840s)
London publisher
10,555 (23, Cockspur Street).

Stevens, J.W. (fl.1830s)
London publisher
20,152; 20,412; 20,415; 20,421; 20,422; 20,426; 20,443; 20,444; 20,610 (10 Derby Street, King's Cross).

Stevenson, W. (fl.1840s)
Dublin publishers
11,115.

Stockdale, John Joseph (1770-1847)
London publisher
11,551 (Pall Mall).

Stratford, J. (fl. c.1800-c.1810)
London publisher
10,586.

Sunday at Home
London magazine
20,269; 20,270.

Sunday Magazine
London magazine
11,390; 20,619.

Surugue, Pierre Louis de (1710-1772)
Paris engraver and publisher
10,172; 11,522; 11,623 (Rue des Noyers, vis-à-vis St Yves).

D.G. Sutherland & Co. (19th century)
Belfast publishers
11,199.

Tallis & Co., John (19th century)
London and New York publishers
11,027.

Tangena, Johannes (17th century)
Leiden engraver and publisher
10,004; 11,846; 11,847; 11,882; 20,822.

Tardieu, Ambrose (1788-1841)
Paris engraver and publisher
11,074.

Tavernier, Melchior (1544-1641)
Paris engraver and publisher
20,235 (L'Isle du Pallais).

Taylor, Charles (1756-1823)
London engraver and publisher
20,202; 20,203 (10, near Castle Street, Holborn).

Taylor, J. (mid 19th century)
London publisher
11,673 (High Holborn).

Taylor, Weld (fl.1836-1852)
London artist and lithographer
10,162 (5, Southampton Street, Fitzroy Square).

Taylor, William Benjamin Sarsfield (1781-1850)
Dublin artist, engraver and publisher
11,621; 11,622.

Taylor & Hessey (fl.1820s)
London publishers
20,720 (13, Waterloo Place & 93, Fleet Street).

Tegg, T.T. & J. (early 19th century)
London publishers
10,764 (Cheapside).

Thomason, John (fl.1800s)
London publisher
10,318 (Great Newport Street).

Thompson (fl.1810s)
London publisher
10,455 (26, St James's Street).

Thompson, J. (fl.1830s)
London publisher
10,967 (334, Strand).

Thompson, John P. (fl.1800s-1810s)
London publisher
10,474 (Great Newport Street). 11,048 (St James's Street).

Thompson, Thomas Clement (c.1780-1857)
Irish artist and London publisher
10,491; 10,966.

Tilt, Charles (fl.1830s-1840s)
London publisher
10,361; 20,054; 20,150; 20,153; 20,164; 20,166; 20,172; 20,173; 20,175; 20,182-20,196; 20,226; 20,272; 20,360; 20,362; 20,366; 20,373; 20,381; 20,382; 20,385; 20,386; 20,478; 20,481; 20,520; 20,649 (86, Fleet Street).

Tombleson & Co. (William Tombleson, fl.1818-1840)
London artist and publisher
20,278; 20,286; 20,376; 20,377; 20,378-20,380; 20,432; 20,433 (11, Paternoster Row).

Tomkins, Peltro William (1759-1840)
London engraver and publisher
20,048; 20,156; 20,324; 20,680; 20,681; 20,704; 20,705; 20,726; 20,727 (54, New Bond Street).

Toms, William Henry (c.1700-1758)
London engraver and publisher
20,667 (Union Court, near Hatton Garden, Holborn).

Torbruck, J. (fl.1740s)
Dublin publisher
10,530 (Ye Bear in Skinner Row).

Townley, Charles (1746-1800)
London engraver and publisher
10,439 (5, Paradise Row, Chelsea College).

Treuttel et Wurtz (fl.1830s)
Paris and Strasburg publishers
20,730.

Triggs, H. (fl.1820s)
London printer
20,136.

Turner, Charles (1773-1857)
London Engraver and publisher
10,061; 10,107; 10,164; 10,178; 10,207; 10,419; 10,458; 10,492; 10,507; 10,554; 10,689; 10,724; 10,854; 10,954; 20,663 (50, Warren Street, Fitzroy Square).

Turner, Joseph Mallord William (1775-1851)
English artist, engraver and London publisher
11,959-11,963 (Harley Street). 11,964-11,978 (50, Warren Street, Fitzroy Square). 11,979-20,028 (Queen Ann Street West).

Tyrell, Gerard (fl.1830s)
Dublin publisher
11,888 (11, Lower Sackville Street).

The Union (1887-1890)
Dublin and London magazine
11,059.

Universal Magazine (1747-1803)
London magazine
10,654; 11,080; 11,134; 11,177; 11,200; 11,319; 11,322; 11,712; 11,747.

Vanderbanck, Peter (1649-1697)
Anglo-Dutch engraver and publisher in London (from 1674)
10,414; 10,565.

Van Haecken, Alexander (c.1701-1750)
Anglo-Dutch engraver and publisher in London 1735-40
?10,142.

Visscher, Nicolaus (late 17th century)
Belgian publisher
10,340.

Van Somer, Paul (c.1649-1694)
Anglo-Dutch artist, engraver and publisher in London
10,321 (Newport Street).

Vatout, J. et Quénot, J.P. (19th century)
Paris publishers
20,721 (Au bureau de la Galerie Lithographiée de S.A.R. Mgr. le Duc D'Orléans, Rue des Marais, Fbg. St Germain no. 13).

Vernor & Hood (1798-1806)
London publishers
20,834 (31, Poultry).

Vernor, Hood & Sharpe (fl. from 1806)
London publishers
11,209 (Poultry).

Villain (19th century)
Paris printer
20,087; 20,101.

Virtue, George (?1793-1868)
London publisher
20,161; 20,219; 20,234; 20,372; 20,417; 20,418; 20,434-20,442 (26, Ivy Lane). 10,704; 10,844; 10,885-10,887; 10,992; 11,009; 11,010; 11,060; 11,061.

Virtue & Co. (fl. from 1850s)
London publishers
20,140-20,142; 20,197; 20,796.

Virtue, James Sprent (1829-1892)
London publisher
11,335; 20,209; 20,210.

Volpi, Natale (early 19th century)
Florence publisher
20,388 (Lungo L'Arno no. 81).

Wakeman, William Frederick (fl.1830s)
Dublin bookseller and publisher
20,351 (9, D'Olier Street).

Walker, E. (fl.1790s)
London publisher
20,032 (7, Cornhill).

Walker, James (1748-1808)
London engraver and publisher
10,864; 11,689 (Paternoster Row).

Walker, T. (fl.1770s-1780s)
Dublin publisher
11,304 (Dame Street).

Walker, W. (fl.1820s-1850s)
London publisher
10,763 (8, Gray's Inn Square).

Walker, W. (fl.1830s)
Dublin publisher
10,725 (Suffolk Street).

Walker, William (1791/93-1867)
London and Edinburgh engraver and publisher
10,097; 10,958; 11,026; 20,819 (64, Margaret Street, Cavendish Square and 22, London Street).

Walter, J. (fl.1780s)
London publisher
10,865; 11,594; 11,604; 11,750; 20,277 (Charing Cross).

C.W. Walton & Co. (19th century)
London lithographers and publishers
11,075 (103, Shaftesbury Avenue W.).

Ward, James (1769-1859)
London engraver and publisher
10,146 (13, Southampton Row, Paddington).

Ward the Elder, William (1766-1826)
London engraver and publisher
10,450 (24, Buckingham Place, Fitzroy Square).

Ward & Co., Marcus (fl.1850s-1880s)
Belfast publishers
11,892.

Wards & Co., Messrs. (fl.1800s)
London publishers
10,100 (6, Newman Street).

Watson, James (c.1740-1790)
Irish engraver and publisher in London
10,345 (16, Craven Buildings, Drury Lane). 10,332; 10,392 (45, Little Queen Ann Street). 10,254 (Queen Ann Street). 10,078 (Upper end of Great Portland Street near Cavendish Square). 10,459; 11,018; ?10,383.

Weekly Messenger
London magazine
11,248.

Weger, August (1823-1892)
Leipzig engraver and publisher
10,858.

Welch & Gwynn (fl.1830s-1840s)
London publishers
10,222; 10,399 (24, St James's Street).

Wesson, I. (18th century)
London publisher
10,471.

Westley & Davis (19th century)
London publishers
20,212 (Stationers Court).

Whitaker, G. & W. (fl.1820s)
London publishers
11,303.

White, Charles William (fl.1750-1785)
London engraver and publisher
11,859 (Kemp Row, Chelsea).

White (& Co.), J. (fl.1810-1831)
London publishers
20,048; 20,156; 20,324; 20,680; 20,681.

Whittaker & Co. (fl.1820s-1830s)
London publishers
20,121; 20,260 (Ave Maria Lane). 20,276; 20,371.

Wild (19th century)
Paris publisher
20,176 (38, Passage du Saumon).

Wilkinson, H. (fl.1850s)
Dublin printer
11,127.

Wilkinson, Robert (fl.1750s-1810s)
London publisher (successor to John Bowles)
10,448; 11,276; 11,557-11,562; 11,657; 11,658 (58, Cornhill). 11,230 (Fenchurch Street).

Wilkinson, Thomas (fl.1750s)
Dublin publisher
10,221 (Toyshop at the corner of Christchurch Lane).

Wilkinson, William (mid 18th century)
Dublin publisher and picture cleaner
10,053; 10,923 (Chequers Lane).

Wilkinson & Dawe (fl.1830s)
London printers
10,155; 10,840; 10,913; 10,955; 11,036; 11,039.

Willanson, G. (fl.1800s)
London publisher
10,949 (Cornhill).

Williams, J. (fl. c.1780)
Dublin publisher
10,041 (21, Skinner's Row).

Williams, Matthew (fl.1750s)
Dublin publisher
10,221 (Dame Street).

Williams, R. (late 17th century)
London publisher
10,199 (Against ye Royal Bagnio in Long Acre). 10,016.

Williams, T. (fl. c.1800-c.1810)
London publisher
11,174 (Stationers Court).

Williamson, M. (fl.1790s)
Dublin publisher
11,850 (Grafton Street).

Willis, Isaac (early 19th century)
Dublin music seller and pianoforte maker
11,838 (Royal Harmonic saloon & circulating library, 7, Westmoreland Street).

Willis, J. (early 19th century)
Dublin publisher
11,029 (Westmoreland Street).

Wilson, Benjamin (1721-1788)
English engraver and publisher in Dublin and London
10,128; 10,388.

Wilson, William (fl.1790s)
Dublin cartographer and publisher
11,810 (6, Dame Street). 11,812.

Wolstenholme, John (early 19th century)
York publisher
10,203.

Woodburn, R. (fl.1800s)
Dublin publisher
10,416.

Woodburn, S. (fl.1810s)
London publisher
10,869 (112, St Martin's Lane). 11,112; 20,113.

Woodfall, George (fl.1760s)
London publisher
10,410 (Charing Cross).

Woollett, William (1735-1785)
London engraver and publisher
20,085 (Charlotte Street, Rathbone Place).

Wright & Bell (fl.1820s)
London publishers
11,946; 11,947 (Duke Street, Bloomsbury).

Yates, James (fl.1840s)
London printer
11,333.

APPENDIX 4

IDENTIFIED PORTRAITS

Abercorn, James Hamilton, 8th Earl of
T. Gainsborough/J. Dean (10,549)

Abercromby, General Sir Ralph
J. Hoppner/S. Close the Elder (10,584)

Aberdeen, George Hamilton Gordon, 4th Earl of
(British Prime Minister)
English School 19C/?T.A. Prior (11,372)*(group)*

Abernethy, John
J. Latham/J. Brooks (10,241)

Abington, Mrs
(née Frances Barton)
R. Cosway/W. Lane (11,340)

Addison, Joseph
G. Kneller/C. Jervas (11,346)
G. Kneller/J. Simon (10,539)

Agar, Charles
(P. Archbishop of Cashel; Archbishop of Dublin; 1st Viscount Somerton; 1st Earl of Normanton)
G.C. Stuart/W. Say (10,083)

Agar-Ellis, M.P., George James Welbore
(1st Baron Dover)
J. Jackson/W. Ward the Elder (10,776)

Agrippa, Marcus
J. Barry/J. Barry (20,722)(11)*(group)*

Albemarle, Henry FitzJames, 1st Duke of
R. De Hooghe/R. De Hooghe (11,655)*(group)*

Albert of Gierstein
G. Cattermole/E. Smith (20,152)

Albert of Saxe-Coburg-Gotha, Prince
(Consort of Queen Victoria)
E. Day/*E.H. Corbould*/F. Holl (10,736)
J. Doyle/J. Doyle (11,544)(66)*(group)*
G. Patten/C.E. Wagstaff (10,735)

Aldborough, Ann Elizabeth, Countess of
(née Henniker; wife of 2nd Earl of Aldborough)
J. Hoppner/S. Einslie (10,387)

Aldrich, William
(Lord Mayor of Dublin in 1742 & 1744)
A. Lee/J. Brooks (10,228)

Alexander the Great
J. Barry/J. Barry (20,722)(10)*(group)*

Alexander 1
(Emperor of Russia)
English School c.1815/English School 1815 (11,367)

Alexander, Du Pré
(2nd Earl of Caledon; Lord Lieutenant of Co. Tyrone)
R. Rothwell/C. Turner (10,554)

Alexander, James Du Pré, Viscount
(3rd Earl of Caledon)
T. Phillips/R.J. Lane (10,737)

Alexander, Lady Elizabeth
J.P. Haverty/R. Havell the Elder & Younger (11,650)*(group)*

Alexander, Mabella
(Lady Blayney, wife of 11th Baron)
J.P. Haverty/R. Havell the Elder & Younger (11,650)*(group)*

Alfred, King
J. Barry/J. Barry (20,722)(9)*(group)*

Allingham, William
A. Munro (8116)

Allnut, Anna
T. Lawrence/C. Rolls (20,136)

Allnut, Mrs Elizabeth
(née Douce)
T. Lawrence/C. Rolls (20,136)

Andrews, Christopher Stephen
('Todd' Andrews)
O. Kelly (8263)

Anglesey, Henry William Paget, 1st Marquess of
(2nd Earl of Uxbridge; Lord Lieutenant of Ireland)
English School c.1815/English School 1815 (11,359)
B. Mulrenin/B. Mulrenin (11,233)

Ann, Princess
(daughter of King Charles I of England)
A. Van Dyck/A. Browne (10,756)*(group)*
A. Van Dyck/R. Cooper (10,546)*(group)*

Anne, Princess
(daughter of King George II of England)
P. Mercier/J. Simon (10,535)
P. Mercier/J. Simon (10,536)

Anne
(Queen of England)
C. Boit/J. Simon (10,371)
G. Kneller/J. Houbraken (10,543)
G. Kneller/T.A. Prior (11,375)

Anne of Denmark
(Queen of King James I of England)
Continental School c.1620/C. Turner (10,869)*(group)*

Annesley, Lady Catherine
A.W. Devis/R. Cooper (11,118)

Annesley, Catherine Jane
(Mrs Prendergast)
J.H. Foley (8045)

Annesley, James
G. King/G. Bickham the Younger (10,531)
W. Lawrence/A. Miller (10,530)
J. Pope-Stevens the Elder/J. Brooks (10,208)

Annesley, Richard Annesley, 2nd Earl
W. Cuming/C. Turner (10,547)

Anster, John
W. Stevenson/J. Kirkwood (11,120)

Antrim, Ann Catherine McDonnel, Countess of
Mrs J. Mee/H.R. Cook (11,119)

Archer, Rev. James
J. Murphy/J. Murphy (10,541)

Archimedes
J. Barry/J. Barry (20,722)(7)*(group)*

Ardagh, John Richardson, P. Bishop of
English School 1653/English School 1804 (10,278)

Argyll, Elizabeth, Duchess of
(née Gunning; wife of 5th Duke of Argyll; also Duchess of Hamilton and Brandon, wife of 6th Duke and Baroness Hamilton)
F. Cotes/R. Brookshaw (11,150)
F. Cotes/R. Brookshaw (11,151)
F. Cotes/R. Houston (10,342)
F. Cotes/J. McArdell (10,343)
G. Hamilton/J. Faber the Younger (10,393)
G. Hamilton/J. Faber the Younger (10,834)
J. M..../S. Okey (10,327)
C. Read/J. Finlayson (10,394)

Armagh, John George Beresford, P. Archbishop of
S. Catterson Smith the Elder/G. Sanders (10,510)
T. Lawrence/C. Turner (10,724)

Armagh, Marcus Gervais Beresford, P. Archbishop of
S. Catterson Smith the Elder/J.R. Jackson (10,441)

Armagh, Hugh Boulter, P. Archbishop of
M. Ashton/T. Beard (10,202)
F. Bindon/J. McArdell (10,026)

Armagh, Michael Boyle, P. Archbishop of
(Lord Chancellor of Ireland)
G. Soest/R. Purcell (10,053)

Armagh, John Hoadly, P. Archbishop of
I. Woods/J. Faber the Younger (10,029)

Armagh, William Newcome, P. Archbishop of
H.D. Hamilton/C. Knight (10,082)

Armagh, Oliver Plunkett, R.C. Archbishop of
?G. Morphey/English School 1804 (11,337)
?G. Morphey/Irish School 1808 (11,338)
G. Morphey/R. Laurie (10,201)
?G. Morphey/?R. Laurie (11,073)
G. Morphey/J. Vandervaart (10,105)

Armagh, Richard Robinson, P. Archbishop of
J. Reynolds/R. Houston (10,410)
J.K. Sherwin/J.K. Sherwin (11,657-11,658)*(group)*
J.K. Sherwin/J.K. Sherwin (11,827-11,829)*(group)*

Armagh, The Hon. William Stuart, P. Archbishop of
W. Owen/S.W. Reynolds the Elder (10,461)
W. Owen/S.W. Reynolds the Elder (10,701)

Armagh, James Ussher, P. Archbishop of
English School 17C/W. Marshall (11,005)
English School 17C/A. Miller (10,133)
English School c.1645/G. Glover (10,281)
English School c.1650/J.G. Seiller (11,004)
English School c.1650/English School 17C (11,252)
W. Hollar/W. Hollar (20,763)*(group)*
R. Home/*C. Grey*/J. Kirkwood (11,254)
?P. Lely/English School 17C (11,251)
?P. Lely/W. Faithorne the Elder (11,253)
?P. Lely/S. Freeman (11,255)

Armit, John
F. Wheatley/J. Collyer (11,644)*(group)*
F. Wheatley/J. Collyer (11,826)*(group)*

Armstrong, Sir Walter
E.O. Ford (8143)

Arnaud, Antoine
J. Barry/J. Barry (20,722)(10)*(group)*

Arnold, Lydia
(Countess of Cavan; 2nd wife of 2nd Earl)
M.A. Shee/E. Scriven (11,208)

Arran, Arthur Saunders Gore, 4th Earl of
J.K. Sherwin/J.K. Sherwin (11,657-11,658)*(group)*
J.K. Sherwin/J.K. Sherwin (11,827-11,829)*(group)*

Asgill Bt., Captain Sir Charles
English School c.1786/English School c.1786 (10,514)

Ashbourne, William Gibson, 2nd Baron of
M. Bayser-Gratry (8025)

Athlone, Godert de Ginkel, 1st Earl of
Dutch School 1691/J. Tangena (10,004)*(group)*
T. Hill/R. Williams (10,199)
G. Kneller/T.S. Smith (10,226)

Atkinson, Richard
(Lord Mayor of Dublin)
G.B. Black/G.B. Black (10,734)

Auchmuty Bt., General Sir Samuel
(Commander-in-Chief in Ireland)
L.F. Abbot/A. Cardon (11,117)

Augusta, Princess
(Duchess of Brunswick; Sister of King George III)
J. Reynolds/R. Houston (10,542)

Austin, S.J., Rev. John
J. Petrie/H. Brocas the Elder (10,262)

Austria, Francis I, Emperor of
English School c.1815/English School 1815 (11,357)

Avonmore, Barry Yelverton, 1st Viscount
(Lord Chief Baron of the Exchequer)
T. Robinson/Irish School 1791 (11,242)
T. Robinson/T. Robinson (10,043)

Aylmer, Lord Henry
J.P. Haverty/R. Havell the Elder and Younger (11,650)*(group)*

Aylmer, Louisa Ann, Lady
(née Call; wife of 4th Baron Aylmer)
J.P. Haverty/R. Havell the Elder and Younger (11,620)*(group)*

Bacon, Francis
J. Barry/J. Barry (20,722)(7)*(group)*

Bacon, Roger
J. Barry/J. Barry (20,722)(7)*(group)*

Baillie, Captain William
?N. Hone the Elder/W. Baillie (10,225)

Baird, Lady
J.P. Haverty/R. Havell the Elder and Younger (11,650)*(group)*

Baird, Sir D.
J.P. Haverty/R. Havell the Elder and Younger (11,650)*(group)*

Baldwin, George
H. O'Neill/L. Gluckman (10,710)

Bale, John
(P. Bishop of Ossory)
?English School 16C/Continental School 17C (10,046)

Balen the Elder, Hendrik van
A. Van Dyck/P. Pontius (20,114)

Balfe, Michael William
T. Farrell (8044)
C. Grey/Irish School 1851 (11,099)

Ball, John
J. Comerford/J. Heath (10,714)

Baltimore, Cecil Calvert, 2nd Baron
Irish School c.1657/A. Blooteling (10,706)
J. Barry/J. Barry (20,772)(9)*(group)*

Banim, John
Irish School c.1820/English School 19C (11,088)

Banks, M.D., Sir John Thomas
O. Sheppard (8159)

Barré, M.P., Isaac
H.D. Hamilton/R. Houston (10,153)
G.C. Stuart/*W. Evans*/W.T. Fry (10,739)
G.C. Stuart/J. Hall (10,152)

Barrett, John
Irish School 19C/J. Kirkwood (11,109)

Barrett, Richard
J.P. Haverty/J.P. Haverty (11,857)*(group)*

Barrett, S.
Irish School c.1806/C. Doyle (11,087)

Barrington, Sir Jonah
H.D. Hamilton/*J. Comerford*/J. Heath (10,715)

Barry, Mrs Spranger
(née Ann Street)
D. Dodd/?J. Walker (11,093)
T. Kettle/J.S. De Wilde (10,325)

so-called Barry, Mrs. Spranger
T. Kettle/J.S. De Wilde (11,096)

Barry, Colonel Henry
S. Shelley/W. Nutter (11,094)

Barry, James
J. Barry/J. Barry (10,205)
J. Barry/J. Barry (20,722)(3)*(group)*
J. Barry/W.C. Edwards (11,116)
J. Barry/J. Heath (10,712)
G. Dance/W. Daniel (10,196)
W. Evans/C. Picart (10,707)

Barry, Spranger
D. Dodd/T. Cook (11,095)
J. Gwim/M. Jackson (10,134)

Barrymore, James Barry, 4th Earl of
T. Ottway/M. Ford (10,206)

Barton, Frances
(Mrs Abington)
R. Cosway/W. Lane (11,340)

Bastard, Mrs William
(née Ann Worsley)
J. Reynolds/W. Brookshaw (11,097)

Baulière, Charlotte Elizabeth de
(Duchess of Orleans)
H. Rigaud/F. Guibert (20,725)(76)

Baxter, Richard
English School c.1689/English School 1689 (20,728)

Beauclerk, Lady Mary
(wife of Charles Spencer)
J. Reynolds/W. Dickinson (11,028)

Bective, Thomas Taylor, 1st Earl of
J.K. Sherwin/J.K. Sherwin (11,657-11,658)*(group)*
J.K. Sherwin/J.K. Sherwin (11,827-11,829)*(group)*

Bedford, Francis Russell, 5th Duke of
J. Gillray/J. Gillray (11,545)*(group)*

Bedford, John Russell, 6th Duke of
J. Doyle/J. Doyle (11,854)*(group)*

Beecher, William
J. Comerford/Irish School 1825 (10,716)

Behan, Brendan Francis
D. MacNamara (8268)

Bellamy, George Anne
F. Cotes & J. Ramberg/R. Sands (11,086)

Belmore, Juliana, Countess of
(née Butler; wife of 2nd Earl)
J.P. Haverty/R. Havell the Elder and Younger (11,650)*(group)*

Bentinck, William
(1st Earl of Portland, 2nd creation)
R. De Hooghe/R. De Hooghe (11,655)*(group)*
T. Maas/T. Maas (10,003)*(group)*
T. Maas/T. Maas (20,800)*(group)*
J. Wyck/J. Brooks (11,652)*(group)*

Bentivoglio, Cardinal Guido
F. Duquesnoy (8030)

Beresford, M.P., John
(First Commissioner of Revenue in Ireland)
G.C. Stuart/C.H. Hodges (10,150)

Beresford, John Claudius
J.K. Sherwin/J.K. Sherwin (11,657-11,658)*(group)*
J.K. Sherwin/J.K. Sherwin (11,827-11,829)*(group)*

Beresford, John George
(son of 1st Marquess of Waterford; P. Archbishop of Armagh)
S. Catterson Smith the Elder/G. Sanders (10,510)
T. Lawrence/C. Turner (10,724)

Beresford, Marcus Gervais
(P. Archbishop of Armagh)
S. Catterson Smith the Elder/J.R. Jackson (10,144)
S. Catterson Smith the Elder/J.R. Jackson (11,556)

Beresford, Scrope
J.K. Sherwin/J.K. Sherwin (11,657-11,658)*(group)*
J.K. Sherwin/J.K. Sherwin (11,827-11,829)*(group)*

Beresford, William
(1st Baron Decies; P. Archbishop of Tuam)
G. Dawe/G. Maile (10,423)

Beresford, William Carr, 1st Viscount
J. Haslock/J. Rogers (10,704)
J.P. Haverty/R. Havell the Elder and Younger (11,650)*(group)*
R. Sayers/G.T. Payne (10,705)

Berkeley, George
(P. Bishop of Cloyne; Dean of Derry)
J. Latham/J. Brooks (10,023)
J. Latham/English School 1776 (11,080)

Berkeley, Rev. George
(Prebendary of Canterbury Cathedral)
English School 18C/W. Skelton (11,081)

Bermingham, Anne
(Countess of Charlemont, wife of 2nd Earl)
C. Moore (8265)

Bernard, Jeanne Françoise Julie Adelaide
(Madame Récamier)
R. Cosway/A. Cardon (10,318)

Bert, Paul
E. Guillaume (8192)

Berwick, James Fitzjames, 1st Duke of
R. De Hooghe/R. De Hooghe (11,655) *(group)*

Bery, John
English School 18C/English School 1820 (10,873)

Bessborough, William Ponsonby, 2nd Earl of
J.S. Copley/R. Dunkarton (10,432)

Bessborough, Frederick Ponsonby, 3rd Earl of
(Viscount Duncannon)
J. Reynolds/J. Grozier (10,253)

Bessborough, John William Ponsonby, 4th Earl of (Viscount Duncannon)
J. Doyle/J. Doyle (11,891)(group)

Bessborough, Henrietta Frances, Countess of
(née Spencer; wife of Viscount Duncannon, later 3rd Earl of Bessborough)
J. Downman/F. Bartolozzi (10,320)

Betagh, Rev. Thomas
W. Brocas/J. Martyn (11,105)

Betham, Sir William
D. Maclise/W. Drummond (10,265)

Betty, William Henry West
H. J. Burch the Younger/J. Ward (10,718)
J. Northcote/J. Ward (10,210)

Bewick, James FitzJames, 1st Duke of
R. De Hooghe/R. De Hooghe (11,655)*(group)*

Bianconi, Charles
J.P. Haverty/J. P. Haverty (11,857)*(group)*

Bingham, Charles
(1st Baron and 1st Earl of Lucan)
J.Reynolds/J. Jones (10,089)

Bisle, M.P., Thomas
J. Doyle/J. Doyle (11,403)*(group)*

Blachford, John
(Chancellor of St Patrick's Cathedral & Rector of St Werburgh's, Dublin)
English School 18C/J. McArdell (10,165)

Blachford, Mary
(Mrs Tighe)
R.E. Drummond/J. Hopwood the Younger (11,006)
G. Romney/E. Scriven (11,417)
G. Romney/*J. Comerford*/C. Watson (10,307)

Blackbourne, Counsellor
T. Nolel/T. Nolel (11,543)

Blackburne, Francis
(Lord Chancellor of Ireland)
S. Catterson Smith the Elder/G. Sanders (10,456)
C. Grey/J. Kirkwood (11,090)

Blacker, Colonel William
(Vice-Treasurer of Ireland)
C. Grey/J. Kirkwood (11,100)
H.W. Phillips/H. Cook (11,079)

Blacker, Rev. George
J.P. Haverty/R. Havell the Elder and Younger (11,650)*(group)*

Blackwood, Frederick Temple
(1st Earl and 1st Marquess of Dufferin and Ava)
F. Holl the Younger/D.A. Wehrschmidt (11,855)

Blackwood, Vice-Admiral Sir Henry
J. Hoppner/C. Turner (10,164)

Blakeney, Field-Marshal Sir Edward
S. Catterson Smith the Elder/G. Sanders (11,856)
L. Gluckman/H. O'Neill (10,722)
J.P. Haverty/R. Havell the Elder & Younger (11,649)*(group)*
J.P. Haverty/R. Havell the Elder and Younger (11,651)*(group)*

Blakeney, William Blakeney, 1st Baron
(Lt.-Governor of Minorca)
G. Chalmers/J. McArdell (10,087)
G. Chalmers/R. Purcell (10,163)
T. Hudson/J. Faber the Younger (10,709)

Bland, Dorothea
(Mrs Jordan)
J. Hoppner/J. Jones (10,386)
J. Hoppner/T. Park (10,408)
G. Romney/J. Ogbourne (10,341)

Blaney, Andrew Thomas, 11th Baron
J.P. Haverty/R. Havell the Elder and Younger (11,650)*(group)*

Blayney, Cadwallader Blayney, 9th Baron
(Lord Lieutenant of Co. Monaghan)
W. Thomson/Irish School 18C (10,738)

Blayney, Mabella, Lady
(née Alexander; wife of 11th Baron)
J.P. Haverty/R. Havell the Elder and Younger (11,650)*(group)*

Blessington, Marguerite, Countess of
(née Power; 2nd wife of the 2nd Earl)
A.C. Chalon/J.J. Hinchcliff (10,326)
A.E. Chalon/H.T. Ryall (10,361)
E. Landseer/English School c.1839 (11,065)

Bligh, Colonel Edward
J. Reynolds/R.B. Parkes (10,711)

Blood, Colonel Thomas
English School 17C/G. White (11,089)
G. Soest/E. Walker (10,717)

Bloomfield, Sir Benjamin
J.P. Haverty/R. Havell the Elder and Younger (11,650)*(group)*

Blount, Charles
(8th Baron Mountjoy; 1st Earl of Devonshire, Lord Deputy of Ireland)
P. Van Somer/V. Green (10,443)

Bohemia, King and Queen of
(with seven children)
Continental School c.1620/C. Turner (10,869)*(group)*

Bolton, Robert
J.P. Haverty/R. Havell the Elder and Younger (11,650)*(group)*

Bonnell, James
English School late 17C/J. Nutting (11,101)

Borromeo, St Charles
J. Barry/J. Barry (20,722)(10)*(group)*

Bossuet, James
J. Barry/J. Barry (20,722)(10)(*group*)

Boucicault, Dion
J. Rogers (8013)
L.M. Ward/J.R.A. Brooks (11,078)

Boulter, Hugh
(P. Archbishop of Armagh)
M. Ashton/T. Beard (10,202)
F. Bindon/J. McArdell (10,026)

Bourcher, Cardinal
English School 19C/English School 19C (20,039)

Bourke, John
(1st Baron Naas; 1st Earl of Mayo)
R. Hunter/W. Dickinson (10,454)

Bourke, Joseph Deane
(P. Archbishop of Tuam; 3rd Earl of Mayo)
J. Reynolds/J.R. Smith (10,438)

Bouverie, Jacob
(Viscount Folkestone; 2nd Earl of Radnor)
J. Reynolds/R. Brookshaw (11,098)

Bowes of Clonlyon, John Bowes, 1st Baron
(Lord Chief Baron of the Exchequer, Lord Chancellor of Ireland)
English or Irish School c.1741/J. Brooks (10,197)
R. Pool & J. Cash/I. Taylor the Elder (10,041)(28)

Boyd, Hugh
R. Home/W. Evans (11,085)
R. Home/W. Ridley (11,084)

Boydell, John
G. Stuart/Facius (20,665)(1)

Boyle, Charles
R. Cosway/?J. Jones (11,388)

Boyle, Courtenay
R. Cosway/?J. Jones (11,388)

Boyle, Lady Dorothy
(Countess of Euston, daughter of 3rd Earl of Blessington
Countess of Burlington/J. Faber the Younger (10,362)

Boyle, Edmund
(Viscount Dungarvan, 8th Earl of Cork and Orrery)
R. Cosway/?J. Jones (11,388)

Boyle, Henrietta
(The Hon. Mrs John O' Neill)
M.W. Peters/J. Smith (10,348)

Boyle, M.P., Henry
(1st Earl of Shannon)
English School c.1740/J. Brooks (10,255)
English School c.1740/J. Brooks (10,537-10,538)

Boyle, John Boyle, Baron
(5th Earl of Orrery; 6th Earl of Cork and Orrery)
J. Faber the Younger/J. Faber the Younger (10,017)

Boyle, Juliana
(Countess of Carrick, wife of 1st Earl)
R. Cosway/J.R. Smith (11,665)

Boyle, Michael
(P. Archbishop of Armagh; Lord Chancellor of Ireland)
G. Soest/R. Purcell (10,053)

Boyle, Richard
(1st Earl of Cork; Lord High Treasurer of Ireland)
Circle of M. Gheeraerts the Younger/English School 1803 (10,750)

Boyle, Richard
(2nd Earl of Shannon)
J.K. Sherwin/J.K. Sherwin (11,657-11,658)(*group*)
J.K. Sherwin/J.K. Sherwin (11,827-11,829)(*group*)

Boyle, Richard
(2nd Viscount Shannon)
G.Kneller/J. Faber the Younger (10,721)

Boyle, The Hon. Robert
J. Kerseboom/A. Miller (10,256)
M. Rysbrack/J. Faber the Younger (10,027)

Boyne, Gustavus Hamilton, 2nd Viscount
W. Hogarth/A. Miller (10,436)

Boyton, Rev. Charles
T.C. Thompson/D. Lucas (10,725)

Brady, Hugh
(President of St Anne's College, Louvain)
Q. Boel/Q. Boel (10,276)

Brady, Sir Nicholas
J.P. Haverty/R. Havell the Elder and Younger (11,650)(*group*)

Braganza, Catherine of
(Queen of King Charles II of England)
P. Lely/A. Blooteling (10,365)
P. Lely/A. Blooteling (11,207)

Brandenburg-Ansbach, Caroline of
(Queen of King George II of England)
G. Kneller/J. Smith (10,728)
J. Vanderbank/J. Faber the Younger (10,548)

Brecknock, William
Irish School c.1786/Irish School 1786 (11,102)

Breen, Dan
J. Behan (8054)

Brereton, Sir William
(1st Baron Brereton; Lord Justice of Ireland)
G. Gower/J. Basire the Elder (10,741)

Bridgford, Thomas
(Self-Portrait)
T. Bridgford/T. P.... (11,861)

Bristol, Frederick Augustus Hervey, 4th Earl of
(P. Bishop of Derry; the Earl-Bishop)
A. Kauffman/?T. Burke (10,209)

British Prime Ministers
George Hamilton Gordon, 4th Earl of Aberdeen
George Canning
Edward Geoffrey Smith Stanley, 14th Earl of Derby
Augustus Henry Fitzroy
William Ewart Gladstone
Charles Grey, 2nd Earl Grey
Frederick North, 2nd Earl of Guilford
William Petty, 2nd Earl of Shelburne; 1st Marquess of Lansdowne
Robert Banks Jenkinson, 2nd Earl of Liverpool
William Lamb, 2nd Viscount Melbourne
William Pitt the Younger
William Henry Cavendish-Bentick, 3rd Duke of Portland
John Russell, 1st Earl Russell
Arthur Wellesley, 1st Duke of Wellington

Brodrick, Charles
(P. Archbishop of Cashel)
H.D. Hamilton/C. Turner (10,207)

Broghill, John Boyle, Baron
(Baron Boyle; 5th Earl of Orrery; 6th Earl of Cork and Orrery)
J. Faber the Younger/J. Faber the Younger (10,017)

Brooke, John Charles
T. Maynard/E. Bell (10,740)

Brooke, Henry
H. Brooke/R. Clamp (11,107)
J. Lewis/Irish School 1852 (11.108)
J. Lewis/A. Miller (10,198)

Brougham and Vaux, Henry Peter Brougham, 1st Baron
(Lord Chancellor)
J. Doyle/J. Doyle (11,544)(55)*(group)*
J. Doyle/J. Doyle (11,544)(57)*(group)*
J. Doyle/J. Doyle (11,544)(61)*(group)*
J. Doyle/J. Doyle (11,544)(63)*(group)*
T. Lawrence & A. Wivell/?T.A. Prior (11,384)*(group)*

Browne, George, Comte de
J.G. Mansfield/J.G. Mansfield (11,103)

Browne, John Denis
(1st Marquess of Sligo)
J. Opie/W.W. Barney (10,177)

Browne, M.P., R.D.
J.P. Haverty/M. & N. Hanhart (11,857)*(group)*

Brownlow, M.P., William
Irish School c.1791/Irish School c.1791 (11,083)
G.C. Stuart/C.H. Hodges (10,251)
G.C. Stuart/C.H. Hodges (10,726)

Bruce, Mrs Samuel
(née Rose Rainey)
C. Andras (8080)

Bruce, Dr William
T.C. Thompson/T. Hodgetts (10,230)

Brugha, Cathal
O. Sheppard (8104)

Brunswick, Princess Augusta, Duchess of
(sister of King George III of England)
J. Reynolds/R. Houston (10,542)

'Duke of Brunswick'
(in fact Rowland Hill, 1st Viscount Hill)
English School c.1815/English School 1816 (11,354)

Brunswick, William Frederick, Duke of
English School c.1815/English School 1815 (11,364)

Brutus, Lucius Junius
J. Barry/J. Barry (20,722)(8)*(group)*

Brydges, Lucy
(Viscountess of Lisburne, wife of 1st Viscount)
G. Kneller/J. Smith (10,904)

Buchon, Madame
(née Helena Felicité Diziain)
G. Courbet (8050)

Buckingham, George Nugent-Grenville-Temple, 1st Marquess of
(2nd Earl Temple; Lord Lieutenant of Ireland; 1st Grand Master of the Knights of St Patrick)
T. Gainsborough/J.K. Sherwin (10,448)
R. Hunter/W. Sadler the Elder (10,417)
J.K. Sherwin/J.K. Sherwin (11,657-11,658)*(group)*
J.K. Sherwin/J.K. Sherwin (11,827-11,829)*(group)*

Buckinghamshire, John Hobart, 2nd Earl of
J.K. Sherwin/J.K. Sherwin (11,657-11,658)*(group)*
J.K. Sherwin/J.K. Sherwin (11,827-11,829)*(group)*

Bunting, Edward
W. Brocas/W. Brocas (10,264)
Irish School 19C/Irish School 1864 (11,864)

Bull, Mrs Elizabeth
R.E. Pine/R. Brookshaw (11,106)

Burgh, M.P., Walter Hussey
(Prime Serjeant and Chief Baron of the Exchequer of Ireland)
H.D. Hamilton/W.S. Barnard (10,233)
Irish School c.1779/Irish School 1779 (10,651)
Irish School c.1799/Irish School 1779 (11,110)

Burgh, M.P., William
J.R. Smith/J.R. Smith (10,203)

Burgherst, Lord
(A.D.C. to George IV)
J.P. Haverty/R. Havell the Elder and Younger (11,650)*(group)*

Burke, Augustus Nicholas
J. Woodhouse (8156)

Burke, M.P., Edmund
E.H. Baily (8224)
English School late 18C/H. Kingsbury (10,275)
J. Hickey/J. Ward (10,435)
T.R. Poole/English School 1791 (10,609)
J. Reynolds/J. Watson (10,254)
J. Reynolds/J. Watson (10,257)
G. Romney/J. Jones (10,442)

Burke, M.P., Richard
J. Reynolds/J. Ward (10,146)

Burke, Father Thomas
American School 19C/American School 19C (10,723)

Burney, Dr Charles
J. Barry/J. Barry (20,722)(4)*(group)*

Burton, Judge Charles
T. Kirk (8052)

Burton, M.P., Sir Charles
(Lord Mayor of Dublin)
R. Hunter/J. McArdell (10,440)

Burton, Sir Frederic William
J. Hughes (8097)

Burton-Conyngham, M.P., William
G.C. Stuart/J. Farn (11,190)
G.C. Stuart/J. Farn (11,191)

Bury, Blanche Augusta
(Mrs Lyons)
C.L. Eastlake/W.H. Mote (10,891)

Bushe, Charles Kendal
(Lord Chief Justice of Ireland)
C. Grey/J. Kirkwood (11,082)
W. Stevenson/D. Lucas (10,411)
P. Turnerelli (8188)

Bushe, Letitia
(Self-Portrait)
L. Bushe/J. Brown (11,111)

Bute, John Stuart, 1st Marquess of
(Baron Mountstuart)
N. Hone the Elder/W. Baillie (10,942)
N. Hone the Elder/W. Baillie (10,944)
N. Hone the Elder/W. Baillie (10,945)

Butler, Joseph
(Bishop of Bristol, also Durham)
J. Barry/J. Barry (20,722)(10)*(group)*

Butler, Elizabeth
(Countess of Chesterfield, 2nd wife of the 2nd Earl)
P. Lely/I. Beckett (10,373)

Butler, Humphrey Butler
(4th Viscount & 1st Earl of Lanesborough)
C. Brown/J. Brooks (10,481)

Butler, Humphrey
J. Comerford/J. Heath (10,748)
J. Comerford/Irish School 1825 (10,747)

Butler, James
(1st Duke of Ormonde)
G. Kneller/E. Scriven (10,533)
W. Wissing/R. Williams (10,001)

Butler, James
(2nd Duke of Ormonde)
?M. Dahl/English School early 18C (10,568)
M. Dahl/P. Pelham (10,569)
M. Dahl/J. Simon (10,995)
English School 17C/P. Schenck (10,998)
G. Kneller/J.H. Robinson (10,570)
G. Kneller/J. Smith (10,002)
G. Kneller/J. Smith (10,996)
J. Wyck/J. Brooks (11,652)*(group)*

Butler, James Wandesford
(19th Earl of Ormonde and Ossory; 1st Marquess of Ormonde)
J. Comerford/R. Graves (10,985)
J. Comerford/G. Parker (10,986)

Butler, Juliana
(Countess Belmore, wife of 2nd Earl)
J.P. Haverty/R. Havell the Elder and Younger (11,650)*(group)*

Butler, Lady Eleanor Charlotte
(daughter of 16th Earl of Ormonde)
M. Leighton/J.H. Lynch (10,893)

Butler, Simon
Irish School 18C/Irish School 18C (11,092)

Butler, Thomas
(Earl of Ossory)
G. Kneller/J. Smith (10,333)
P. Lely/P. Vanderbanck (11,418)

Butler, William Archer
C. Grey/J. Kirkwood (11,104)

Cabot, Sebastian
J. Barry/J. Barry (20,722)(4)*(group)*

Cadogen. William Cadogen, 1st Earl of
L. Laguerre the Elder/J. Simon (10,204)

Caldbeck, Counsellor
F. Wheatley/J. Collyer (11,644)*(group)*
F. Wheatley/J. Collyer (11,826)*(group)*

Caledon, Catherine, Countess of
(née Freeman; wife of 3rd Earl)
J.P. Haverty/R. Havell the Elder and Younger (11,650)*(group)*

Caledon, Dupré Alexander, 2nd Earl of
(Lord Lieutenant of Co. Tyrone)
R. Rothwell/C. Turner (10,554)

Caledon, James Dupré Alexander, 3rd Earl of
T. Phillips/R.J. Lane (10,737)

Call, Louisa Ann
(wife of 4th Baron Aylmer)
J.P. Haverty/R. Havell the Elder and Younger (11,650)*(group)*

Callaghan, M.P., Cornelius
English or Irish School 18C/J. Brooks (10,187)
English or Irish School 18C/J. Brooks (10,760)

Calvert, Cecil
(2nd Baron Baltimore)
J. Barry/J. Barry (20,772)(9)*(group)*
Irish School c.1657/A. Blooteling (10,706)

Campbell, Harriet Charlotte Beaujolais
(Countess of Charleville, wife of 3rd Earl)
J. Hayter/W. Finden (10,727)

Campbell, Rev. Thomas
(Rector of Galloon; Chancellor of Clogher)
Irish School c.1795/Irish School c.1795 (10,299)
Irish School c.1795/Irish School c.1795 (11,894)

Canning, M.P., George
(British Prime Minister)
T. Lawrence/C. Turner (20,663)
T. Stewardson/W. Ward the Elder (10,450)

Capel, Arthur
(1st Earl of Essex)
P. Lely/E. Lutterell (10,136)
P. Lely/E. Lutterell (10,774)

Capua, Penelope, Princess of
(née Smyth; wife of Prince Charles of Capua)
A.E. Chalon/W.H. Mote (11,309)

Carew, Sir George
(Baron of Clapton; 1st Earl of Totnes; Lord President of Munster)
M. Gheeraerts the Younger/English School c.1800 (11,210)
M. Gheeraerts the Younger/R. Van Voerst (10,191)

Carew, Henry
(1st Viscount Falkland)
P. Van Somer/*G.P. Harding*/J. Brown (10,807)

Carey, Matthew
J. Neagle/J. Thomson (11,203)

Carhampton, Henry Lawes Luttrell, 2nd Earl of
J. Petrie/P. Maguire (11,211)

Carhampton, Judith Maria, Viscountess
(née Lawes; wife of 1st Viscount, later 1st Earl of Carhampton)
J.K. Sherwin/J.K. Sherwin (11,657-11,658)*(group)*
J.K. Sherwin/J.K. Sherwin (11,827-11,829)*(group)*

Carhampton, Simon Luttrell, 1st Earl of
(Baron Irnham)
Irish School 1768/81/Irish School 1768/81 (11,212)

Carleton, John
F. Wheatley/J. Collyer (11,644)*(group)*
F. Wheatley/J. Collyer (11,826)*(group)*

Carleton, William
J. Hogan (8196)
C. Grey/J. Kirkwood (11,216)
C. Grey/J. Kirkwood (11,217)

Carlisle, Dean of
(Thomas Percy; Bishop of Dromore)
J. Reynolds/W. Dickinson (10,086)
J. Reynolds/English School 1811 (11,330)

Carlisle, George Willliam Frederick Howard, 7th Earl of
(Lord Lieutenant of Ireland)
English School 1864/English School 1864 (11,595)*(group)*
Irish School 1853/Irish School 1853 (11,722)*(group)*
C. Moore (8088)
G. Richmond/F. Holl (10,425)

Caroline of Brandenburg-Ansbach
(Queen of King George 111 of England)
G. Kneller/J. Smith (10,540)
G. Kneller/J. Smith (10,728)
J. Vanderbank/J. Faber the Younger (10,548)

Carr, William
(1st Viscount Beresford)
J. Haslock/J. Rogers (10,704)
J.P. Haverty/J.P. Haverty (11,650)*(group)*
R. Sayes/G.T. Payne (10,705)

Carracci, Annibale
J. Barry/J. Barry (20,722)(11)*(group)*

Carrick, Juliana, Countess of
(née Boyle; wife of 1st Earl of Carrick)
R. Cosway/J.R. Smith (11,665)

Carrick, Lady Harriet & Lady Margaret
R. Cosway/J.R. Smith (11,665)

Castlecoote, Charles Henry Coote, 1st Baron
J.K. Sherwin/J.K. Sherwin (11,657-11,658)*(group)*
J.K. Sherwin/J.K. Sherwin (11,827-11,829)*(group)*

Carter, M.P., Thomas
(Master of the Rolls in Ireland)
C. Jervas/J. Brooks (10,148)

Carteret, Baroness Frances
(née Worsley; 1st wife of Baron John Carteret)
C. D'Agar/J. Simon (10,730)

Carve, Thomas
Continental School 17C/English School 1795 (11,206)

Casement, Roger
A. Weckbecker (8032)
A. Weckbecker (8275)
A. Weckbecker (8282)

Cashel, P. Archbishop of
(Charles Agar; Archbishop of Dublin; 1st Viscount Somerton; 1st Earl of Normanton)
G.C. Stuart/W. Say (10,083)

Cashel, P. Archbishop of
(Charles Broderick)
H.D. Hamilton/C. Turner (10,207)

Cassiodorus
J. Barry/J. Barry (20,722)(11)*(group)*

Castlereagh, Frederick William Robert Stuart, Viscount
(4th Marquess of Londonderry)
F. Kruger/F. Kruger (10,758)

Castlereagh, Robert Stewart, Viscount
(2nd Marquess of Londonderry)
T. Lawrence/C. Turner (10,458)

Catherine of Braganza
(Queen of King Charles II of England)
P. Lely/A. Blooteling (10,356)
P. Lely/A. Blooteling (11,207)

Catherine of France
(Queen of King Henry V of England)
T. Stothard/A. Cardon (20,067)*(group)*

Cato the Younger, Marcus
J. Barry/J. Barry (20,772)(8)*(group)*

Caulfeild or Clements family, a Lady of
C. Moore (8266)

Caulfeild, James
(1st Earl of Charlemont)
G. Dance/W. Daniell (10,746)
W. Hogarth/English School 1784 (11,186)
W. Hogarth/English School 1784 (11,187)
W. Hogarth/J. Haynes (11,124)
H. Hone/J. Heath (10,742)
H. Hone/T. Nugent (10,743)
H. Hone/T. Nugent (11,123)
H. Hone/B. Smith (10,744)
Irish School 1783/Irish School 1783 (11,870)*(group)*
Irish School c.1780/Irish School c.1780 (11,188)
R. Livesay/J. Dean (10,464)
J. Mossop (8164)
J.K. Sherwin/J.K. Sherwin (11,657-11,658)*(group)*
J.K. Sherwin/J.K. Sherwin (11,827-11,829)*(group)*

Cavan, Lydia, Countess of
(née Arnold, 2nd wife of 2nd Earl)
M.A. Shee/E. Scriven (11,208)

Cavendish, Lord Frederick Charles
(Chief Secretary for Ireland)
W.B. Richmond/J.D. Miller (10,188)

Cavendish, Lord John
J. Reynolds/J. Grozer (10,768)

Cavendish, William
(1st Duke of Devonshire)
G. Kneller/P. Pelham (10,997)

Cavendish, William
(3rd Duke of Devonshire; Lord Lieutenant of Ireland)
J. Reynolds/J. Faber the Younger (10,176)

Cavendish-Bentinck, William Henry
(3rd Duke of Portland; Lord Lieutenant of Ireland, later Prime Minister of Britain)
J. Reynolds/J. Murphy (10,475)

Ceannt, Eamon
D. O Murchadha (8004)

Cecil, James
(1st Marquess of Salisbury; Lord Chamberlain of the Household)
M. Brown/D. Orme (20,104)*(group)*

Cecil, Margaret
(Countess of Ranelagh, 2nd wife of 1st Earl of Ranelagh)
G. Kneller/J. Smith (10,534)

Chamberlane, Frances
(Mrs Thomas Sheridan)
English School 18C/English School 1824 (11,303)

Chantery, Sir Francis Legatt
J. Heffernan (8264)

Charlemont, Anne, Countess of
(née Bermingham)
C. Moore (8265)

Charlemont, James Caulfeild, 1st Earl of
G. Dance/W. Daniell (10,746)
W. Hogarth/English School 1784 (11,186)
W. Hogarth/English School 1784 (11,187)
W. Hogarth/J. Haynes (11,124)
H. Hone/J. Heath (10,742)
H. Hone/T. Nugent (10,743)
H. Hone/T. Nugent (11,123)
H. Hone/B. Smith (10,744)
Irish School 1783/Irish School 1783 (11,870)*(group)*
Irish School c.1780/Irish School c.1780 (11,188)
R. Livesay/J. Dean (10,464)
J. Mossop (8164)
J.K. Sherwin/J.K. Sherwin (11,657-11,658)*(group)*
J.K. Sherwin/J.K. Sherwin (11,827-11,829) *(group)*

Charles I
(King of England)
Continental School c.1620/C. Turner (10,869)*(group)*
A. Van Dyck/J. Simon (10,248)

Charles II
(King of England)
P. Lely/A. Blooteling (10,495)
P. Lely/A. Blooteling (10,025)
P. Lely/A. Browne (10,759)

Charles II
(when Prince of Wales)
A. Van Dyck/A. Blooteling (11,215)
A. Van Dyck/A. Browne (10,756)*(group)*
A. Van Dyck/R. Cooper (10,546)*(group)*

Charles V, Duke of Burgundy
G. Cattermole/E. Smith (20,152)

Charles, Prince
(son of King of Bohemia)
Continental School c.1620/C. Turner (10,869)*(group)*

Charles, Brenda
J. Connor (8232)
J. Connor (8233)

Charleville, Harriet Charlotte Beaujolais, Countess of
(née Cambell; wife of 3rd Earl)
J. Hayter/W. Finden (10,727)

Charlotte Sophia of Mecklenburg-Stelitz
(Queen of King George III, of England)
J. Barry/J. Barry (20,722)(11)*(group)*
T. Frye/T. Frye (10,551)
A. Kauffmann/T. Burke (10,379)

Chatham, William Pitt the Elder, 1st Earl of
J. Barry/J. Barry (20,722)(3)*(group)*
W. Hoare/R. Houston (11,068)

Chenevix, Richard
(P. Bishop of Waterford and Lismore)
Irish School 18C/J. Hall (11,195)
?Irish School c.1750/Massard (10,302)

Cherry, Andrew
S. Drummond/W. Ridley & W. Holl the Elder (11,204)

Chesterfield, Elizabeth, Countess of
(née Butler; 2nd wife of the 2nd Earl of Chesterfield)
P. Lely/I. Beckett (10,373)

Chesterfield, Katherine, Countess of
(née Wotton; titled suo jure)
A. Van Dyck/*A. Houbraken*/P. Gunst (10,349)

Chesterfield, Philip Dormer Stanhope, 4th Earl of
(Lord Lieutenant of Ireland)
T. Gainsborough/E. Bell (10,183)
W. Hoare/J. Brooks (10,418)
W. Hoare/R. Houston & S. Wheatley (10,445)
W. Hoare/A. Miller (10,186)
W. Hoare/J. Simon (10,184)
J.P. Haverty/R. Havell the Elder and Younger (11,650)*group*

Chetwynd, Charles
(3rd Earl Talbot; Lord Lieutenant of Ireland)
T.C. Thompson/S.W. Reynolds the Elder (10,491)

Cheyne, Selina
(Mrs Charles Graves)
J.H. Foley (8269)

Chinnery, George Robert
J. Slater/F.C. Lewis the Elder (11,389)

Cholmondely, George Cholmondely, 4th Earl of
J. Gillray/J. Gillray (11,545)*(group)*

Churchill, John
(1st Duke of Marlborough)
G. Kneller/P. Tanjé (10,994)

Cimabue, Giovanni
?A. Bonaiuto/English School 18C (20,120)

Clanbrassil, James Hamilton, 4th Earl of
J.K. Sherwin/J.K. Sherwin (11,657-11,658)*(group)*
J.K. Sherwin/J.K. Sherwin (11,827-11,829)*(group)*

Clanricarde, Henry De Burgh, 12th Earl & 1st Marquess of (2nd creation)
R. Hunter/W. Sedgewick (10,497)
J.K. Sherwin/J.K. Sherwin (11,657-11,658)*(group)*
J.K. Sherwin/J.K. Sherwin (11,827-11,829)*(group)*

Clanricarde, Ulick De Burgh, 1st Marquess of
(2nd Earl of St Albans)
English School 17C/S.F. Ravenet the Elder (11,205)

Clanwilliam, Theodosia, Countess of
(née Magill; wife of 1st Earl)
J. Reynolds/J. Watson (10,383)

Clapton, Sir George Carew, 1st Earl of
(Lord President of Munster)
M. Gheeraerts the Younger/English School c.1800 (11,210)
M. Gheeraerts the Younger/R. Van Voerst (10,191)

Clare, Elizabeth de
English School 17C/English School 1815 (10,733)

Clare, John Fitzgibbon, 1st Earl of
(Lord Chancellor of Ireland)
J. Comerford/J. Heath (10,811)
R. Cosway/F. Bartolozzi (10,810)
J. Hoppner/C. Turner (10,812)
G.C. Stuart/C.H. Hodges (10,494)
G.C. Stuart/F. Mackenzie (11,130)
J.K. Sherwin/J.K. Sherwin (11,657-11,658)*(group)*
J.K. Sherwin/J.K. Sherwin (11,827-11,829)*(group)*
F. Wheatley/J. Collyer (11,644)*(group)*
F. Wheatley/J. Collyer (11,826)*(group)*

Clarendon, George William Frederick Villiers, 4th Earl of (Lord Lieutenant of Ireland)
S. Catterson Smith the Elder/G. Sanders (10,421)

Clarke, Rev. Adam
W. Derby/J. Mollison (10,764)
J.Jackson/R. Page (11,214)

Clarke, Thomas James
A. Power (8005)
A. Power (8290)

Claude Lorrain
Claude Lorrain/J. Boydell (20,718)(1)

Clements, M.P., Sir Henry John
T. Kirk (8267)

Clive, Kitty
J. Faber the Younger/W.J. Alais (11,121)

Clogher, Thomas Parnell, P. Archdeacon of
?Irish School 18C/?J. Dixon (10,014)

Clogher, John Garnett, P. Bishop of
T. Gainsborough/J. McArdell (10,216)

Clogher, John Porter, P. Bishop of
T. Lawrence/C. Turner (10,107)

Clogher, John Stearne, P. Bishop of
T. Carlton/T. Beard (10,143)

Clogher, Chancellor of (Rev. T. Campbell, Rector of Galloon)
Irish School c.1795/Irish School c.1795 (10,299)
Irish School c.1795/Irish School c.1795 (11,894)

Clonmel, John Scott, 1st Earl of (Lord Chief Justice of the King's Bench in Ireland)
R. Cosway/P. Condé (10,137)

Cloyne, George Berkeley, P. Bishop of
J. Latham/J. Brooks (10,023)
J. Latham/English School (11,080)

Cloyne and Ross, William Coppinger, P. Bishop of
J. Comerford/C. rolls (10,754)

Cobbe, Charles (P. Archbishop of Dublin)
F. Bindon/A. Miller (10,024)
?F. Bindon/A. Miller (10,444)

Cobden, Richard
English School 19C/?T.A. Prior (11,372)*(group)*

Coghlan, Margaret Mary (wife of Viscount Mount-Earl, later 1st Earl of Dunraven)
T. Gainsborough/J.R. Smith (10,376)

Colbert, Jean-Baptiste
J. Barry/J. Barry (20,722)(11)*(group)*

Cole, Henrietta Frances (Lady Grantham; Countess De Grey, wife of 1st Earl)
A.E. Chalon/R.A. Arlett (10,814)
T. Lawrence/J.H. Robinson (20,204)

Cole, John Willoughby (2nd Earl of Eniskillen)
W. Robinson/D.J. Scarlett (10,775)

Cole, Lieut.-General Sir Galbraith Lowry
T. Lawrence/C. Picart (10,185)

Coleraine, Henry Hare, 2nd Baron
English School 17C/W. Faithorne the Elder (10,771)

Colles, Dr Abraham
M. Cregan/D. Lucas (10,749)

Collins, Rev. Emmanuel
N. Hone the Elder/J. McArdell (10,755)

Collins, Michael
F.W. Doyle-Jones (8001)
A. Power (8070)
T. Spicer-Simpson (8139)
T. Spicer-Simpson (8216)

Colum, Padraic
T. Spicer-Simpson (8221)

Columbus, Christopher
J. Barry/J. Barry (20,722)(8)*(group)*

Congreve, William
G. Kneller/J. Smith (10,010)
G. Kneller/M. Vandergucht (11,213)

Connolly, James
S. Murphy (8006)

Conolly, M.P., Thomas
R. Bull/J. Collyer (10,753)
R. Bull/W. Sidgwick (11,194)

Conolly, William
T. Carter the Elder/Irish School 18C (11,642)
C. Jervas/P. Fourdinier (10,019)

Conolly, Mrs William (née Katherine Conyngham)
T. Carter the Elder/Irish School 18C (11,642)

Conroy, Lady Alicia (née Parsons; wife of Sir Edward Conroy, 2nd Bt.)
C.I. Baseley/W. Finden (10,769)

Conway, Field Marshal Henry Seymour
T. Gainsborough/G. Dupont (10,496)

Conway, Anne Seymour (the Hon. Mrs John Damer)
J. Reynolds/J.R. Smith (10,380)

Conyngham, Elizabeth, Marchioness of (née Denison, wife of 1st Marquess)
J.P. Haverty/R. Havell the Elder and Younger (11,650)*(group)*

Conyngham, Katherine (Mrs William Conolly)
T. Carter the Elder/Irish School 18C (11,642)

Conyngham, William (1st Baron Plunket)
C. Moore (8066)

Conyngham, William Burton (Teller of the Irish Exchequer; Treasurer of the Royal Irish Academy)
H.D. Hamilton/V. Green (10,182)
G.C. Stuart/C.H. Hodges (10,247)

Cook, Captain James
J. Barry/J. Barry (20,722)(4)*(group)*

Cook, William
A. Pope/English School 1807 (11,209)

Cooke, Edward (Under-Secretary of State for Ireland)
W. Cuming/W. Ward the Elder (10,457)

Cooke, Bt., Sir Samuel (Lord Mayor of Dublin, 1741)
J. Latham/J. Faber the Younger (10,240)

Cooper, Anthony
(3rd Earl of Shaftesbury)
J. Barry/J. Barry (20,722)(8)*(group)*

Cooper, Rev. William
T. Robinson/W. Ridley (11,174)

Coote, Charles Henry
(1st Baron Castlecoote)
J.K. Sherwin/J.K. Sherwin (11,657-11,658)*(group)*
J.K. Sherwin/J.K. Sherwin (11,827-11,829)*(group)*

Coote, Major-General Sir Eyre
W.P.J. Lodder/A. Cardon (10,713)

Copernicus, Nicolaus
J. Barry/J. Barry (20,722)(7)*(group)*

Copley, John Singleton
(Lord Chancellor; 1st Baron Lyndhurst)
J. Doyle/J. Doyle (11,544)(63)*(group)*
T. Lawrence and A. Wivell/?T.A. Prior (11,384)*(group)*

Coppingher, Stephen
J.P. Haverty/J.P. Haverty (11,020)*(group)*

Coppingher, William
(P. Bishop of Cloyne and Ross)
J. Comerford/C. Rolls (10,754)

Corbet, Miles
English School 17C/English School 1810 (10,610)

Corbett, William
(United Irishman)
Continental School 19C/T.W. Huffam (11,189)

Corelli, Arcangelo
H. Howard/J. Smith (10,809)
H. Howard/M. Vandergucht (10,729)

Cork, Francis Moynan, R.C. Bishop of
Irish School c.1800/English School 1816 (11,231)

Cork, Richard Boyle, 1st Earl of
(Lord High Treasurer of Ireland)
Circle of M. Gheeraerts the Younger/English School 1803 (10,750)

Cork and Orrery, Anne, Countess of
(née Courtney; 1st wife of 7th Earl)
H.D. Hamilton/F.C. Heissig (10,752)
H.D. Hamilton/J. Watson (10,334)

Cork and Orrery, Edmund Boyle, 8th Earl of
(Viscount Dungarvan)
R. Cosway/?J. Jones (11,388)

Cork and Orrery, John Boyle, 6th Earl of
(Baron Boyle of Marston)
J. Faber the Younger/J. Faber the Younger (10,017)

Cork and Ross, Edward Wetenhall, P. Bishop of
(Bishop of Kilmore and Ardagh)
J. Vandervaart/J. Vandervaart (10,132)

Cornwallis, Charles Cornwallis, 1st Marquess
(Lord Lieutenant of Ireland)
W. Beechey/W. Ward (10,498)
J. Comerford/J. Heath (10,761)
D. Gardner/J. Jones (10,499)

Corrigan, Sir Dominic
J.H. Foley (8191)

Cosgrave, William
G.F. Waters (8147)

Cosway, Mrs Richard
(née Maria Hadfield)
M. Cosway/V. Green (10,405)

Courtenay, Anne
(Countess of Cork and Orrery; 1st wife of 7th Earl)
H.D. Hamilton/F.C. Heissig (10,752)
H.D. Hamilton/J. Watson (10,334)

Courtown, James Stopford, 1st Earl of
J.K. Sherwin/J.K. Sherwin (11,657-11,658)*(group)*
J.K. Sherwin/J.K. Sherwin (11,827-11,829)*(group)*

Coventry, Maria, Countess of
(née Gunning; wife of 9th Earl)
F. Cotes/J. McArdell (10,374)
F. Cotes/?R. Purcell (10,829)
F. Cotes/?R. Purcell (10,831)
F. Cotes/C. Spooner (10,375)
G. Hamilton/J. McArdell (10,396)
G. Hamilton/J. McArdell (10,830)
J. M..../S. Okey (10,327)
C. Read/J. Finlayson (10,391)
B. Wilson/B. Wilson (10,388)

so-calledc Coventry, Maria, Countess of
J.E. Liotard/R. Houston (10,384)

Cowper, Frances Elizabeth
(daughter of 5th Earl Cowper; Countess Roden, wife of 1st Earl; Viscountess Jocelyn, 2nd wife of 1st Viscount)
J. Hayter/W.H. Egleton (10,860)

Cradock, Lieut.-General Sir John Francis
(1st Baron Howden)
T. Lawrence/J. Godby (10,767)

Cradock, William
(Dean of St Patrick's Cathedral, Dublin)
J.K. Sherwin/J.K. Sherwin (11,657-11,658)*(group)*
J.K. Sherwin/J.K. Sherwin (11,827-11,829)*(group)*

Crampton, Bt., Sir Philip
S. Catterson Smith the Elder/G. Sanders (10,544)
A.G.G. D'Orsay/A.G.G. D'Orsay (10,757)
W. Stevenson/D. Lucas (10,116)
W. Stevenson/D. Lucas (10,033)

Cranley, Thomas
(P. Archbishop of Dublin)
English School 15C/*J. Carter*/ J. Basire the Elder (10,766)

Crawford, M.P., John
J. Reynolds/J. Grozer (10,762)

Crawford, M.P., William Sharman
J.P. Knight/T. Lupton (10,243)

Crewe, Elizabeth
(Mrs John Hinchcliff)
J. Reynolds/R. Brookshaw (11,201)

Crewe, Sarah
(Mrs Obediah Langton)
J. Reynolds/R. Brookshaw (11,201)

Croker, John
(Surveyor-General of Customs and Excise in Ireland)
W. Haines/E. Scriven (11,218)

Croker, M.P., John Wilson
C. Grey/J. Kirkwood (11,192)
T. Lawrence/T.H. Parry (11,193)

Croker, Thomas Crofton
C. Grey/Irish School 1849 (11,202)

Cromwell, Oliver
(Lord Protector)
S. Cooper/R. Brookshaw (11,393)
S. Cooper/*J. Bulfinch*/R. Cooper (11,392)
English School 17C/English School 17C (11,395)
R. Walker/*M. Ford*/A. Miller (10,500)
?R. Walker/*A. van der Werff*/P. Drevet (11,379)
?R. Walker/English School 17C (11,394)
R. Walker/J. Velde the Elder (10,245)

so-called Cromwell, Oliver
?R. Walker/P. Pelham (11,396)

Crosbie, Diana, Viscountess
(née Sackville-Germain; wife of Viscount Crosbie, later 2nd Earl of Glandore)
J. Reynolds/W. Dickinson (10,407)

Crosbie, Mr
F. Wheatley/J. Collyer (11,644)*(group)*
F. Wheatley/J. Collyer (11,826)*(group)*

Crow, Crazy (George Hendrick)
Irish School c.1754/R. Graves (11,125)

Cuffe, Grace
(Countess of Farnham, wife of 1st Earl)
J.P. Haverty/R. Havell the Elder and Younger (11,650)*(group)*

Cuffe, James
(Baron Tyrawley)
W. Cuming/J.R. Smith (10,192)

Cumberland, Ernest Augustus, Duke of (son of King George III)
J. Doyle/J. Doyle (11,544)(57)*(group)*

Cumberland, Richard
G. Romney/V. Green (10,765)

Cunningham, John
T. Bewick/*J. Thurston*/W.H. Worthington (10,763)

Curran, M.P. John Philpot
(Master of the Rolls in Ireland)
J. Doyle/J. Doyle (11,403)*(group)*
H. Hopson/H. Houston (11,200)
Irish School 1806/14/*J.B. Lane*/S. Freeman (10,770)
Irish School 19C/Irish School 19C (11,867)
Irish School 1817 (8132)
J.B. Lane/S. Freeman (10,151)
T. Lawrence & S. Freeman/S. Freeman (11,199)
T. Lawrence/H. H. Meyer (11,198)
T. Lawrence/J.R. Smith (10,058)
T. Lawrence/C.E. Wagstaff (11,197)
T. Lawrence/C.E. Wagstaff (20,804)

Cutts, John Cutts, 1st Baron
G. Kneller/J. Simon (10,732)
W. Wissing/R. Williams (10,016)

Cutts, Elizabeth, Baroness
(née Pickering; 2nd wife of 1st Baron)
G. Kneller/J. Smith (10,317)

Damer, the Hon. Mrs John
(née Anne Seymour Conway)
J. Reynolds/J.R. Smith (10,380)

Danby, Francis
C. Moore (8059)

Danby, Henry Danvers, 1st Earl of
?M.J. Mierevelt/*W. Derby*/E. Scriven (10,782)

Dargan, William
T. Farrell (8277)
Irish School 1853/Irish School 1853 (11,630)
J.E. Jones (8024)
After J.E. Jones (8111)
G.F. Mulvany/W.V. Edwards (11,127)

Daschkov, Princess
F. Wheatley/J. Collyer (11,644)*(group)*
F. Wheatley/J. Collyer (11,826)*(group)*

D'Auverquerck, Madame
F.W. Weideman/J. Smith (11,184)
F.W. Weideman/J. Smith (11,185)

D'Avaux, Earl
Dutch School c.1690/Dutch School c.1690 (11,866)*(group)*

Davis, Thomas Osborne
W.F. Burton/J.S. Templeton (10,786)
J.P. Haverty/J.P. Haverty (11,857)*(group)*
J. Hogan/N. Walsh (20,655)

Dawson, Lady Anne
(née Lady Anne Fermor, daughter of the 1st Earl of Pomfert; wife of Thomas Dawson)
J. Reynolds/J. McArdell (10,389)

Dawson, Mrs Arthur
J.P. Haverty/R. Havell the Elder and Younger (11,650)*(group)*

Dawson, Emily Mary
(Mrs J.H. Wyndham King)
J. Hayter/W.H. Mote (10,784)

Dawson, M.P., Richard
H.D. Hamilton/*P. Maguire*/J. Heath (10,783)

Deane, Robert Tilson
(1st Baron Muskerry)
J.K. Sherwin/J.K. Sherwin (11,657-11,658)*(group)*
J.K. Sherwin/J.K. Sherwin (11,827-11,829)*(group)*

Deane, Sir Thomas Newenham
J. Hughes (8097)

Deane, William
H.D. Hamilton/R. Cooper (10,781)

De Blaquiere, John De Blaquiere, 1st Baron
(Chief Secretary to the Lord Lieutenant of Ireland)
J. Comerford/J. Heath (10,708)
J.J. Masquerier/C. Turner (10,178)

De Burgh, Henry
(12th Earl & 1st Marquess of Clanricarde, 2nd creation)
R. Hunter/W. Sedgewick (10,497)
J.K. Sherwin/J.K. Sherwin (11,657-11,658)*(group)*
J.K. Sherwin/J.K. Sherwin (11,827-11,829)*(group)*

De Burgh, Lady Hester Catherine
(daughter of the 13th Earl of Clanricarde; Marchioness of Sligo, wife of 2nd Marquess)
Mrs J. Robertson/J. Posselwhite (11,308)

De Burgh, Ulick
(2nd Earl of St Albans; 1st Marquess of Clanricarde)
English School 17C/S.F. Ravenet the Elder (11,205)

Decies, William Beresford, 1st Baron
(P. Archbishop of Tuam)
G. Dawe/G. Maile (10,423)

De Courcy, Rev. Richard
J. Russell/J. Spilsbury (10,787)

De Crillon, Louis De Berton, Duc
P. Le Grand/O. Birrell (10,516)

De Duras, Louis
(1st Earl of Feversham)
R. De Hooghe/R. De Hooghe (11,847)(9)*(group)*

De Ginkel, Godert
(1st Earl of Athlone)
Dutch School 1691/J. Tangena (10,004)*(group)*
T. Hill/R. Williams (10,199)
G. Kneller/J. Smith (10,226)

De Grasse, François Joseph Paul, Comte
W. Miller/A. Birrell (11,345)

De Grey, Countess Henrietta Frances
(née Cole; wife of 3rd Baron Grantham later 1st Earl de Grey)
A.E. Chalon/R.A. Arlett (10,814)

De Grey, Thomas Philip Weddell Robinson, 2nd Earl
(Baron Grantham; Lord Lieutenant of Ireland)
J. Doyle/J. Doyle (11,544)(56)*(group)*
J. Doyle/J. Doyle (11,544)(58)*(group)*
W. Robinson/*W. Brett*/S. Cousins (10,841)
J. Wood/J. Brown (10,840)

De Lacy, Maurice, Count
Irish School 19C (8165)

De Lacy Evans, M.P., General Sir George
R. Buckner/G.J. Zobel (10,772)
R. Fenton/J.H. Lynch (10,263)

De La Poer, George
(Earl of Tyrone; 1st Marquess of Waterford)
J.K. Sherwin/J.K. Sherwin (11,657-11,658)*(group)*
J.K. Sherwin/J.K. Sherwin (11,827-11,829)*(group)*

De Las Casas, Bartolomé
J. Barry/J. Barry (20,722)(14)*(group)*

Delaval, Anne Hussey
(Lady Stanhope; wife of Sir William Stanhope)
J. Reynolds/J. Watson (10,397)
B. Wilson/J. Basire (10,404)

De Levis, Marie
(Viscomtesse de Sarsfield)
French School 18C/V. Green (11,034)

Delvin, George Frederick Nugent, Baron (7th Earl of Westmeath)
J.K. Sherwin/J.K. Sherwin (11,657-11,658)*(group)*
J.K. Sherwin/J.K. Sherwin (11,827-11,829)*(group)*

De Marselaer, Frederick
A. Van Dyck/C. Galle the Elder (11,491)

De Melchthal, Arnold
G. Ulyssé/H. Raunheim (20,176)

De Moivre, Abraham
J. Highmore/J. Faber the Younger (10,173)

Denison, Elizabeth
(Marquess of Conyngham, wife of 1st Marquess)
J.P. Haverty/R. Havell the Elder and Younger (11,650)*(group)*

Denmark, George, Prince of
(Consort of Quenn Anne)
J. Wyck/J. Brooks (11,632)*(group)*

De Nassau, Amelia
(Countess of Ossory; wife of Count Thomas)
W. Wissing/I. Beckett (10,331)
W. Wissing/I. Beckett (10,993)

Derby, Edward George Stanley, 14th Earl of
(Prime Minister of Britain)
J. Doyle/J. Doyle (11,853)*(group)*
English School 19C/?T.A. Prior (11,372)*(group)*

Dermody, Thomas
C. Allingham/Ridley (20,834)

Derrick, Samuel
F.X. Vispré/English School 18C (11,183)

Derry, Frederick Augustus Hervey, P. Bishop of
(4th Earl of Bristol)
A. Kauffman/?T. Burke (10,209)

Derry, John Hickman, P. Bishop of
A. Russell/S. Gribelin (10,047)

Derry, Ezekiel Hopkins, P. Bishop of
English School 17C/J. Sturt (10,051)
English School 17C/J. Sturt (10,627)
English School 17C/M. Vandergucht (10,625-10,626)

Derry, The Hon. Richard Ponsonby, P. Bishop of
S. Catterson Smith the Elder/G. Sanders (20,768)

De Ruvigny, Henry Massue de Ruvigny, 2nd Marquess
(Earl of Galway)
P. De Graves/J. Simon (10,032)

De Salignac, François
(Archbishop De La Mothe-Fénlon)
French School 18C/French School 18C (20,359)

Descartes, René
J. Barry/J. Barry (20,722)(7)

D'Esterre, Mr
Irish School 19C/Irish School 19C (11,241)

D'Esterre Darby, Captain Henry
W. Beechey/R. Earlom (10,430)

De Suijlicum, Monsieur
T. Maas/T. Maas (10,003)*(group)*
T. Maas/T. Maas (20,800)*(group)*

De Valera, Eamon
J. Connor (8053)

De Vaudémont, Nicolas
(Duc de Mercoeur)
Attrib. to B. Prieur (8036)

Devereux, Lieutenant General John
T. Hargreaves/E. Smith (11,126)

Devitt, J.M.
J.P. Haverty/J.P. Haverty (11,857)*(group)*

Devonshire, Charles Blount, 1st Earl of
(8th Baron Mountjoy; Lord Duputy of Ireland)
P. Van Somer/V. Green (10,443)

Devonshire, Georgiana, Duchess of
(née Spencer; 1st wife of 5th Duke)
J. Barry/J. Barry (20,722)(5)*(group)*

Devonshire, William Cavendish, 1st Duke of
G. Kneller/P. Pelham (10,997)

Devonshire, William Cavendish, 3rd Duke of (Lord Lieutenant of Ireland)
J. Reynolds/J. Faber the Younger (10,176)

Dickson, William (P. Bishop of Down & Connor)
J. Comerford/J. Heath (10,795)

Dillon, John Blake
L. Gluckman/J.H. Lynch (11,936)

Dillon, Count Theobald
Irish School c.1792/Irish School 1792 (11,175)

Dillon, Admiral Sir William
C. Baugniet/C. Baugniet (10,802)

Diocres, Raymond
E. Le Sueur/P.L.H. Laurent (20,070)*(group)*

Dobbs, Arthur
W. Hoare/J. McArdell (10,180)

Dodley, J.
J.P. Haverty/R. Havell the Elder & Younger (11,650)*(group)*

Doherty, John
J. Hayter/F.C. Lewis (10,261)
Irish School c.1840/W. Griffiths (11,178)

Dolores (4th portrait)
J. Epstein (8074)

Dombrain, James
W. Howis the Elder/D. Lowes (20,127-20,131)

Domenichino
J. Barry/J. Barry (20,722)(10)*(group)*

Donoughmore, Lieut.-Colonel John Hely-Hutchinson, 2nd Earl of
Irish School c.1792/English School 1792 (11,177)
T. Phillips/*W. Evans*/K. Mackenzie (10,801)

Donoughmore, Richard Hely-Hutchinson, 1st Earl of (2nd Baron Hely-Hutchinson)
B. Stoker/H. Brocas the Elder (11,176)

Doria, Andrea
J. Barry/J. Barry (20,722)(10)*(group)*

Dorset, John Frederick Sackville, 3rd Duke of
J. Reynolds/T. Hardy (10,796)

Dorset, Lionel Cranfield Sackville, 1st Duke of (Lord Lieutenant of Ireland)
G. Kneller/J. McArdell (10,175)
G. Kneller/G. Virtue (10,799)

Douce, Elizabeth (Mrs Allnutt)
T. Lawrence/C. Rolls (20,136)

Douglas, Rev. Archibald
Irish School c.1805/Irish School 1805 (11,351)

Dover, George James Welborne Agar Ellis, 1st Baron
J. Jackson/W. Ward the Elder (10,776)

Down & Connor, William Dickson, P. Bishop of
?J. Comerford/J. Heath (10,795)

Down, Connor & Dromore, Richard Mant, P. Bishop of
M. Cregan/G.R. Ward (10,449)

Down, Connor & Dromore, Jeremy Taylor, P. Bishop of
English School 17C/W. Faithorne the Elder (11,275)

Downes, William Downes, 1st Baron (Lord Chief Justice of the King's Bench in Ireland)
J. Comerford/T. Lupton (10,798)
Irish School c.1811/Irish School 1811 (11,851)*(group)*

Downshire, Maria, Marchioness of (née Windsor; wife of 3rd Marquess)
J.P. Haverty/R. Havell the Elder and Younger (11,650)*(group)*

Downshire, William Hill, 1st Marquess of (1st Earl of Hillsborough)
?H.D. Hamilton/Irish School 18C (10,619)

Doyle, Major General Sir Charles William (Colonel of the 10th Royal Veteran Battalion)
M.S. Carpenter/T. Hodgetts (10,174)

Doyle, James Warren (R.C. Bishop of Kildare and Leighlin)
S. Catterson Smith the Elder/R. Cooper (11,179)
J.P. Haverty/J.P. Haverty (10,794)
Irish School 19C (8101)
Irish School c.1820/T. Kelly (11,180)

Doyle, John ('HB')
C. Moore (8298)

Doyle, General Sir John
W. Cuming/?Irish School 19C (11,325)

Doyle, Lieutenant-General Sir John (Lieutenant-Governor of Guernsey)
J. Ramsay/W. Say (10,455)

Drake, Sir Francis
J. Barry/J. Barry (20,722)(4)

Drogheda, Charles Moore, 6th Earl and 1st Marquess of
J. Reynolds/R.B. Parkes (10,720)
J.K. Sherwin/J.K. Sherwin (11,657-11,658)*(group)*
J.K. Sherwin/J.K. Sherwin (11,827-11,829)*(group)*

Dromore, Thomas Percy, P. Bishop of (Dean of Carlisle)
J. Reynolds/W. Dickinson (10,086)
J. Reynolds/English School 1811 (11,330)

Drummond, Thomas (Under-Secretary in Ireland)
H.W. Pickersgill/H. Cousins (10,790)

Drummond, William Hamilton
W.H. Collier/H. O'Neill (10,789)

Dublin, P. Archbishops of
Charles Agar
Charles Cobbe
Thomas Cranley
Robert Fowler
John Hoadly
William King
Arthur Smyth
Thomas Smyth
Richard Whateley

Dublin, Lord Mayors of
William Aldrich
Richard Atkinson
Sir Charles Burton, M.P.
Sir Samuel Cooke Bt.
Sir Humphrey French, M.P.
Thomas How

Sir Abraham King Bt.
Thomas McKenny
Daniel O'Connell, M.P.
Charles Thorp

Dufferin and Ava, Frederick Temple Blackwood, 1st Earl and 1st Marquess of
F. Holl the Younger/D.A. Wehrschmidt (11,855)

Dufferin and Clandeboye, Baroness Anna Dorothea
(née Foster; wife of 2nd Baron)
R. Rothwell/T. Hodgetts (10,792)

Dufferin and Clandeboye, Baroness Helena Selina
(née Sheridan; wife of the 4th Baron; Countess of Gifford)
F. Stone/J.H. Robinson (10,370)
E. Lamont/W.H. Mote (10,791)

Duffy, Sir Charles Gavan
M. De Carnowsky (8285)
L. Gluckman/H. O'Neill (10,179)
L. Gluckman/H. O'Neill (10,525)
L. Gluckman/H. O'Neill (11,935)
J.P. Haverty/J.P. Haverty (11,857)*(group)*
Irish School c.1870/J.C. McRae (10,284)

Duigenan, Dr Patrick
J. Comerford/J. Heath (10,793)

Duncannon, Frederick Ponsonby, Viscount (3rd Earl of Bessborough)
J. Reynolds/J. Grozier (10,253)

Duncannon, John William Ponsonby, Viscount (4th Earl of Bessborough)
J. Doyle/J. Doyle (11,891)*(group)*

Duncannon, Viscountess Henrietta Frances (née Spencer; wife of Viscount Duncannon, later 3rd Earl of Bessborough)
J. Downman/F. Bartolozzi (10,320)
Countess F. Spencer/F. Bartolozzi (10,352)
J. Reynolds/J. Grozer (10,390)

Dundas, Charlotte
M.W. Peters/H.H. Houston (11,601)

Dungarvan, Edmund Boyle, Viscount (8th Earl of Cork and Orrery)
R. Cosway/?J. Jones (11,388)

Dunluce, Harriet Charlotte Campbell, Viscountess
(Countess of Charleville)
J. Hayter/W. Finder (10,727)

Dunsany, Edward John Moreton Drax Plunkett, 18th Baron
T. Spicer-Simson (8223)

Durham, Charles William Lambton, 1st Earl of
T. Lawrence/S. Cousins (10,447)

Dwyer, Michael
(United Irishman)
Irish School c.1800/Irish School c.1800 (11,181)
J. Petrie/English School 1846 (11,182)

Earlom, Richard
G.C. Stuart/T.G. Lupton (20,664)

Edgeworth, Maria
A. Buck/English School 19C (11,508)*(group)*
A. Chappel/American School 1873 (10,773)
W.M. Craig/F. Mackenzie (11,122)

Edgeworth, Mrs Richard Lovell
(née Elizabeth Sneyd)
A. Buck/English School 19C (11,508)*(group)*

Edgeworth, Richard Lovell
A. Buck/English School 19C (11,508)*(group)*

Edinburgh, Daniel Sandford, P. Bishop of
J.G. Watson/W. Walter (11,026)

Edward V
(King of England)
English School 19C/English School 19C (20,039)

Edward VII
(King of England, when Prince of Wales)
English School c.1860/English School c.1860 (10,988)

Efferdi, Derriche
M. Brown/D. Orme (20,104)*(group)*

Egan, John
J. Comerford/J. Heath (10,778)

Eglington and Winton, Archibald William Montgomerie, 13th Earl of
(Lord Lieutenant of Ireland)
S. Catterson Smith the Elder/G. Sanders (10,505)

Egmont, John Percival, 2nd Earl of
(Viscount Perceval)
T. Hudson/J. McArdell (10,168)

Eliot, Edward Granville
(3rd Earl of Saint Germains; Lord Lieutenant of Ireland)
Irish School 1853/Irish School 1853 (11,722)

Eliott, General George Augustus
(1st Baron Heathfield)
N. Hone the Elder/R. Pollard (10,777)

Elizabeth I
(Queen of England)
I. Oliver/French School c.1600 (10,311)
I. Oliver/C. Turner (20,113)

so-called Elizabeth I
English School 17C/A. Miller (10,335)
M. Gheeraerts the Younger/J. Faber the Younger (10,403)

Elizabeth, Princess
(daughter of King Charles I of England)
A. Van Dyck/A. Browne (10,756)*(group)*
A. Van Dyck/R. Cooper (10,546)*(group)*

Elizabeth, Princess
(daughter of King of Bohemia)
Continental School c.1620/C. Turner (10,869)*(group)*

Elizabeth, Queen of Edward IV of England
English School 19C/English School 19C (20,039)

Elley, Sir John
J.P. Haverty/R. Havell the Elder & Younger (11,650)*(group)*

Ellis, Thomas
J.P. Haverty/R. Havell the Elder & Younger (11,650)*(group)*

Elrington, Thomas
(P. Bishop of Leighlin and Ferns; Provost of Trinty College Dublin)
T. Foster/W. Ward the Younger (10,249)
T. Foster/W. Ward the Younger (20,126)

Emlyn, Thomas
(1st Unitarian Minster in England)
J. Highmore/G. Vandergucht (10,282)
J. Highmore/J. Hopworth the Elder (11,168)

Emmet, Robert
(United Irishman)
English School 19C/English School 19C (11,407)
English School 19C/W. Read (10,779)
J. Petrie (8130)
J. Petrie (8293)
J. Petrie/English School 1846 (11,164)
J. Petrie/English School 1846 (11,165)
J. Petrie/*A.F.J. Claudet*/English School 1846 (11,166)
J. Petrie/Irish School 19C (11,219)
J. Petrie/Irish School c.1803 (11,352)*(group)*
J. Petrie/Irish School ?1808 (11,163)

Emmet, Thomas
(United Irishman)
L.F. Aubry/T.W. Huffam (11,171-11,173)
J.D. Herbert/T.W. Huffam (11,169)
J.D. Herbert/T.W. Huffam (11,170)

Enniskillen, John Willoughby Cole, 2nd Earl of
W. Robinson/D.J. Scarlett (10,775)

Ensor, George
J. Comerford/H. Meyer (10,200)

Epaminondas
J. Barry/J. Barry (20,722)(8)*(group)*

Essex, Arthur Capel, 1st Earl of
P. Lely/E. Lutterell (10,136)
P. Lely/E. Lutterell (10,774)

Esterhazy, Prince and Princess
J.P. Haverty/R. Havell the Elder and Younger (11,650)*(group)*

Eugénie, Empresss
(née Dona Eugénie Maria de Montijo de Guzman; wife of Napoleon III)
J.B. Carpeaux (8040)

Euston, Dorothy, Countess of
(née Lady Boyle; daughter of 3rd Earl of Burlington)
Countess of Burlington/J. Faber the Younger (10,362)

Euston, Charles Fitzroy, Lord
(2nd Duke of Grafton; Lord Lieutenant of Ireland)
G. Kneller/J. Smith (10,227)

Falconer, Eliza
(The Hon. Mrs Stanhope)
J. Reynolds/J.R. Smith (10,356)

Falkiner, Sir Frederick
W. Osborne/R.W. Hester (10,849)

Falkland, Henry Carey, 1st Viscount
P. Van Somer/*G.P. Harding*/J. Brown (10,807)

Fane, Lady Georgiana
(daughter of 10th Earl of Westmoreland)
T. Lawrence/C. Armstrong (20,211)

Fane, John
(10th Earl of Westmoreland; Lord Lieutenant of Ireland)
G. Romney/J. Jones (10,508)

Farmer, Captain George
C. Grignon the Younger/J. Murphy (10,166)

Farnham, Grace, Countess of
(née Cuffe; wife of 2nd Earl)
J.P. Haverty/R. Havell the Elder and Younger (11,650)*(group)*

Farrel. Owen
H.F. Gravelot/English School 1820 (11,133)
H.F. Gravelot/J. Hulett (10,181)

Faucit, Helen
(Lady Martin, wife of Sir Theodore Martin)
J.H. Foley (8042)

Faulkner, George
(Alderman of Dublin)
Irish School c.1750/W. Sharp (10,145)
Irish School c.1750/W. Sharp (11,416)

Feilding, The Hon. Mary
(née Swift, daughter of 1st Viscount Carlingford; wife of The Hon. Robert Feilding)
P. Lely/I. Beckett (10,328)

Ferguson, Lady Elizabeth
W.C. Ross/J. Thomson (10,806)

Fermor, Lady Anne
(daughter of 1st Earl of Pomfret; wife of Thomas Dawson)
J. Reynolds/J. McArdell (10,389)

Ferns, William Preston, P. Bishop of
G.C. Stuart/W. Dickinson (10,110)

Ferrard, Anna Dorothea
(Lady Dufferin and Claneboye, wife of 2nd Baron)
R. Rothwell/T. Hodgetts (10,792)

Feversham, Louis de Duras, 1st Earl of
R. De Hooghe/R. De Hooghe (11,847)(9)*(group)*

ffrench, Charles Austin ffrench, 3rd Baron
J.P. Haverty/J.P. Haverty (11,857)*(group)*

Field, John
Continental School early 19C/C. Mayer (10,045)

Fielding, Anna Maria
(Mrs Samuel Carter Hall)
English School 19C/English School 19C (10,884)

Fielding, Sir John
N. Hone the Elder/J. McArdell (10,804)
N. Hone the Elder/J.R. Smith (10,805)

Fingall, Arthur James Plunkett, 8th Earl of
Irish School c.1811/Irish School 1811 (11,350)
T.C. Thompson/C. Turner (10,848)

Fisher, Catherine Maria (Kitty)
J. Reynolds/E. Fisher (10,357)

FitzGerald, Augustus Frederick
(3rd Duke of Leinster)
S. Catterson Smith the Elder/G. Sanders (10,468)

FitzGerald, Charles William
(4th Duke of Leinster)
L. Lehmann/C.A. Tomkins (10,898)

FitzGerald, Elizabeth
(daughter of 9th Earl of Kildare; Countess of Lincoln, 2nd wife of 1st Earl)
English School 16C/O. Humphrey (11,135)

FitzGerald, Lady Margaretta
(daughter of 19th Earl of Kildare; Countess of Hillsborough, wife of 1st Earl)
R. Pool & J. Cash/I. Taylor the Elder (10,041)(26)*(group)*

FitzGerald, Lady Mary
(née O'Brien; wife of 19th Earl of Kildare)
R. Pool & J. Cash/I. Taylor the Elder (10,041)(26)*(group)*

FitzGerald, Lord Edward
(son of 1st Duke of Leinster)
H. Hone/T.W. Huffam (11,137)
H. Hone/T.W. Huffam (11,138)
T. Nugent/W.T. Annis (10,211)

FitzGerald, Lord Henry
(son of 1st Duke of Leinster)
J.J. Barralet/H. Ward the Elder (11,654)*(group)*
A. Buck/Irish School 1790 (11,134)
J. Hoppner/T. Park (11,415)

Fitzgerald, M.P., James
J. Comerford/J. Heath (10,803)

FitzGerald, James
(20th Earl of Kildare; 1st Duke of Leinster)
R. Pool & J. Cash/I. Taylor the Elder (10,041)(26)*(group)*
J. Reynolds/J. McArdell (10,088)

FitzGerald, Robert
(19th Earl of Kildare)
R. Pool & J. Cash/I. Taylor the Elder (10,041)(26)*(group)*

FitzGerald, William Robert
(2nd Duke of Leinster)
Irish School c.1785 (8256)
J. Reynolds/J. Dixon (10,467)
M.A. Shee/C. Turner (10,487)
J.K. Sherwin/J.K. Sherwin (11,657-11,658)*(group)*
J.K. Sherwin/J.K. Sherwin (11,827-11,829)*(group)*
G.C. Stuart/C.H. Hodges (10,092)
G.C. Stuart/Irish School c.1790 (10,635)
G.C. Stuart/Irish School c.1795 (10,079)
F. Wheatley/J. Collyer (11,644)*(group)*
F. Wheatley/J. Collyer (11,826)*(group)*

Fitzgerald, William Thomas
S. Drummond/W. Ridley (11,136)

Fitzgibbon, Anne, Viscountess
(née Whaley; wife of Viscount Fitzgibbon, later 1st Earl of Clare)
G. Chinnery/H. Brocas the Elder (11,344)

Fitzgibbon, Gerald
J.C. Harrison/G. Atkinson (10,502)

Fitzgibbon, John
(Viscount Fitzgibbon; 1st Earl of Clare; Lord Chancellor of Ireland)
J. Comerford/J. Heath (10,811)
R. Cosway/F. Bartolozzi (10,810)
J. Hoppner/C. Turner (10,812)
J.K. Sherwin/J.K. Sherwin (11,657-11,658)*(group)*
J.K. Sherwin/J.K. Sherwin (11,827-11,829)*(group)*
G.C. Stuart/C.H. Hodges (10,494)
?G.C. Stuart/F. Mackenzie (11,130)
F. Wheatley/J. Collyer (11,644)*(group)*
F. Wheatley/J. Collyer (11,826)*(group)*

FitzJames, Henry
(1st Duke of Albemarle)
R. De Hooghe/R. De Hooghe (11,655)*(group)*

FitzJames, James
(1st Duke of Berwick)
R. De Hooghe/R. De Hooghe (11,655)*(group)*

Fitzpatrick, Lady Anne
(daughter of 2nd Earl of Upper Ossory)
J. Reynolds/J.R. Smith (10,354)

Fitzpatrick, Lady Gertrude
(daughter of 2nd Earl of Upper Ossory)
J. Reynolds/J. Dean (10,377)

Fitzpatrick, Sir Jerome
S. Drummond/W. Barnard (10,493)

Fitzpatrick, John
(2nd Earl of Upper Ossory)
W. Lane/W. Skelton (10,984)

Fitzpatrick, Mr P.V.
J.P. Haverty/J.P. Haverty (11,857)*(group)*

Fitzpatrick, The Hon. Susanna
(née Usher)
A. Soldi/J. McArdell (10,846)

Fitzroy, Augustus Henry
(3rd Duke of Grafton; British Prime Minister)
P. Batoni/J. Watson (10,129)

Fitzroy, Charles
(Lord Euston; 2nd Duke of Grafton; Lord Lieutenant of Ireland)
G. Kneller/J. Faber the Younger (10,845)
G. Kneller/J. Smith (10,227)

Fitzroy, Henry
(1st Duke of Grafton)
W. Wissing/I. Beckett (10,244)
J. Wyck/J. Brooks (11,652)*(group)*

Fitzsimon, Mr C.
J.P. Haverty/J.P. Haverty (11,857)*(group)*

FitzWilliam, Lady Charlotte
(daughter of 1st Earl FitzWilliam)
J. Reynolds/English School c.1770 (11,140)
J. Reynolds/H. McArdell (10,338)

FitzWilliam, Richard FitzWilliam, 7th Viscount
H. Howard/R. Earlom (10,431)

FitzWilliam, William Wentworth FitzWilliam, 2nd Earl
(Lord Lieutenant of Ireland)
Irish School c.1795/Irish School c.1795 (11,139)
J. Reynolds/J. Grozer (10,252)
G.C. Stuart/Irish School c.1795 (10,079)

FitzWygram, Bt., M.P., Sir Robert
T. Phillips/J. Brown (10,844)

Flaxman, John
J. Jackson/R. Woodman the Younger (20,118)

Fleming, Jane
(Countess of Harrington, wife of 3rd Earl)
English School 18C/R. Cooper (10,316)
J. Reynolds/F. Bartolozzi (10,313-10,315)
J. Reynolds/V. Green (10,400)

Fletcher, William
Irish School c.1814/T. Blood (11,143)
Irish School c.1814/H. Brocas the Elder (11,141-11,142)

Flood, M.P., Henry
Irish School c.1770/Irish School 18C (10,138)
Irish School c.1785/Irish School 1785 (11,129)
B. Stoker/*J. Comerford*/S. Watts (11,128)
G.C. Stuart/Irish School c.1795 (10,079)

Foley, John Henry
C.B. Birch (8157)

Folkestone, Jacob Bouverie, Viscount
(2nd Earl of Radnor)
J. Reynolds/R. Brookshaw (11,098)

Folliott Ponsonby, The Hon. Mrs Jane
(née Taylor)
J. Worsdale/J. Brooks (11,062)

Forbes, George
(6th Earl of Granard)
?J. Comerford/J. Heath (10,818)

Forbes, The Hon. John
G. Romney/C. Townley (10,439)

Forrest, Theodosius
N. Hone the Elder/N. Hone the Elder (11,848)

Fortescue, Hugh Fortescue, 4th Baron and 2nd Earl
(Lord Lieutenant of Ireland)
J. Doyle/J. Doyle (11,544)(62)*(group)*
J. Doyle/J. Doyle (11,544)(63)*(group)*
E. Eddis/J.G. Zobell (10,813)

Fortescue, Lady Louisa
A. Robertson/E.F. Finden (10,847)

Foster, Anna Dorothea
(Baroness Dufferin and Clandeboye, wife of 2nd Baron)
R. Rothwell/T. Hodgetts (10,792)

Foster, John
(1st Baron Oriel)
Irish School c.1790/Irish School c.1790 (11,132)
J.K. Sherwin/J.K. Sherwin (11,657-11,658)*(group)*
J.K. Sherwin/J.K. Sherwin (11,827-11,829)*(group)*
G.C. Stuart/C.H. Hodges (10,501)
G.C. Stuart/Irish School 1799 (11,131)
G.C. Stuart/P. Maguire (10,277)

Foubert, Major
T. Hudson/J. Faber the Younger (10,843)
J. Wyck/J. Brooks (11,652)*(group)*

Fowler, Robert
(P. Archbishop of Dublin)
J.K. Sherwin/J.K. Sherwin (11,657-11,658)*group)*
J.K. Sherwin/J.K. Sherwin (11,827-11,829)*(group)*

Fox, M.P., Charles James
L.F. Abbott/W. Barnard (10,808)
J.Gillray/J. Gillray (11,545)*(group)*

Fox, Henry
(3rd Baron Holland)
J. Doyle/J. Doyle (11,544)(57)*(group)*

Fox-Strangeways, Lady Susan Sarah Louisa
(daughter of 1st Earl of Ilchester; wife of William O'Brien)
F. Cotes/J. Watson (10,332)

Francis I,
(Emperor of Austria)
English School c.1815/English School 1815 (11,357)

Francis I
(King of France)
J. Barry/J. Barry (20,722)(11)*(group)*

Frederick Augustus
(Duke of York and Albany)
R. Bowyer/J.C. Bromley (10,428)

Frederick, Prince
(son of King of Bohemia)
Continental School c.1620/C. Turner (10,869)*(group)*

Frederick, Prince of Wales
(son of King George II of England)
T. Frye/T. Frye (10,550)

Frederick William III
(King of Prussia)
English School c.1815/English School 1815 (11,363)

Freeman, Catherine
(Countess of Caledon, wife of 3rd Earl)
J.P. Haverty/R. Havell the Elder and Younger (11,650)

Freemantle, John
J.K. Sherwin/J.K. Sherwin (11,657-11,658)*(group)*
J.K. Sherwin/J.K. Sherwin (11,827-11,829)*(group)*

French, M.P., Sir Humphrey
(Lord Mayor of Dublin)
Irish School c.1732/Irish School c.1732 (10,020)

Frye, Thomas
(Self-portrait)
T. Frye/T. Frye (10,298)
T. Frye/T. Frye (10,465)
T. Frye/T. Frye (10,552)

Furlong, Thomas
J.P. Haverty/J.P. Haverty (11,020)*(group)*

Frederick, Prince of Hesse-Kassel
R. De Hooghe/R. De Hooghe (11,655)*(group)*

Fürst, Walter
G. Ulyssé/H. Raunheim (20,176)

Galilei, Galileo
J. Barry/J. Barry (20,722)(7)*(group)*

Galloon, Rector of
(Rev. T. Campbell; Chancellor of Clogher)
Irish School c.1795/Irish School c.1795 (10,299)
Irish School c.1795/Irish School c.1795 (11,894)

Galway, Henry Massue de Ruvigny, Earl of
(2nd Marquess de Ruvigny)
P. de Graves/J. Simon (10,032)

Gandon, James
J. Comerford/H. Meyer (11,152)
H.Hone/H. Meyer (10,833)
H.Hone/H. Meyer (11,153)

Gardiner, M.P., Luke
(Vice-Treasurer of Ireland)
C. Jervas/J. Brooks (10,242)
C. Jervas/J. Brooks (10,825)

Gardiner, M.P., Luke
(grandson of Luke Gardiner; 1st Viscount Mountjoy)
J.D. Herbert/H. Brocas the Elder (10,291)
Irish School c.1778/Irish School 1778 (11,381)
F. Wheatley/J. Collyer (11,644)*(group)*
F. Wheatley/J. Collyer (11,826)*(group)*

Garrick, David
Irish School 18C/W. Esdall (11,149)
J. Reynolds/R. Purcell (10,034)

Gasendi, Abbé Pierre
C. Mellan/C. Mellan (20,125)

Gast, Rev. John
(P. Archbishop of Glendalough)
Irish School 18C/H. Brocas the Elder (11,160)

Gavazzi, Fr. Alessandro
J.R. Dicksee/J.R. Dicksee (20,111)

George
(Prince of Denmark; Consort of Queen Anne)
G. Kneller/T.A.Prior (11,375)
G. Kneller/P. Schenck (10,821)
J. Wyck/J. Brooks (11,652)*(group)*

George I
(King of England)
G. Kneller & T. Worlidge/T.A. Prior (11,374)
D. Stevens/J. Faber the Younger (10,131)

George II
(King of England)
W.H. Bartlett/J. Heath (11,749)
G. Kneller/J. Faber the Younger (10,826)
G. Kneller & T. Worlidge/T.A. Prior (11,374)
R.E. Pine/W. Dickinson (10,828)
T. Worlidge/R. Houston (10,234)
T. Worlidge/R. Houston (10,827)
T. Worlidge/C.W. White (20,119)

George III
(King of England)
J. Barry/J. Barry (20,722)(13)*(group)*
M. Brown/D. Orme (20,104)*(group)*
English School c.1815/English School 1816 (11,361)
S. Drummond/J. Thomson (11,278)
D. Lüders/J. McArdell (10,852)
J. Reynolds/*W. Dickinson*/W. Watson (10,853)
E. Smyth (8038)
?J. Spilsbury/?J. Spilsbury (10,851)
B. West/E. Fischer (10,850)

George IV
(King of England)
J. Barry/J. Barry (20,722)(5)*(group)*
?H. Brocas the Elder/H. Brocas the Elder (11,155)
R. Cosway/L. Sailliar (10,140)
Sir T. Hammond/English School 1822 (11,596)
Sir T. Hammond/English School 1822 (11,698)
J.P. Haverty/R. Havell the Elder and Younger (11,649-11,651)*(group)*
Irish School c.1820/Irish School c.1820 (10,823)
A. Wivell/T. Lupton (10,824)

Geraldine, The Fair
(Elizabeth Fitzgerald, Countess of Lincoln; 2nd wife of 1st Earl)
English School 16C/O. Humphrey (11,135)

Gevartius, Jan Caspar
A. Van Dyck/P. Pontius (20,116)

Gibson, William
(2nd Baron Ashbourne)
M. Bayser-Gratry (8025)

Giffard, John
(High Sheriff of Dublin)
Irish School 18C/Irish School 18C (11,162)

Gifford, Bonaventure
(R.C. Bishop of Madura)
H. Hysing/T. Burford (10,817)

Gifford, Helina Selina, Countess of
(née Sheridan; Baroness Dufferin and Clandeboye; wife of 4th Baron)
E. Lamont/W.H. Mote (10,791)
F. Stone/J.H. Robinson (10,370)

Gladstone, William Ewart
(British Prime Minster)
S.F. Lynn (8235)

Glandore, Diana, Countess of
(née Sackville-Germain; wife of Viscount Crosbie, later 2nd Earl of Glandore)
J. Reynolds/W. Dickinson (10,407)

Glendalough, John Gast, P. Archbishop of
Irish School 18C/H. Brocas the Elder (11,160)

Glenelf, Charles Grant, 1st Baron
T.C. Thompson/C. Turner (10,842)

Gloucester, William Frederick, Duke of
J. Doyle/J. Doyle (11,544)(57)*(group)*

Gogarty, Oliver St John
T. Spicer-Simson (8222)

Gold, Thomas
J. Comerford/J. Heath (10,816)

Goldsmith, Oliver
J. Reynolds/G.F. Marchi (10,028)

Goodwin, Mrs A.
(née Jane Wenman)
A. Van Dyck/J. Boydell (10,556)

Goor, Count
T. Maas/T. Maas (10,008)*(group)*
T. Maas/T. Maas (20,800)*(group)*

Gordon, George Hamilton
(4th Earl of Aberdeen; British Prime Minster)
English School 19C/?T.A. Prior (11,372)*(group)*

Gore, Arthur Saunders
(4th Earl of Arran)
J.K. Sherwin/J.K. Sherwin (11,657-11,658)*(group)*
J.K. Sherwin/J.K. Sherwin (11,827-11,829)*(group)*

Gort, General-Colonel Charles Vereker, 2nd Viscount
J. Comerford/J. Heath (10,687)
C. Grey/J. Kirkwood (11,156)

Gough, Hugh Gough, 1st Viscount
F. Grant/S. Cousins (10,485)

Grady, Thomas
H. Brocas the Elder/H. Brocas the Elder (11,159)

Grafton, Henry Fitzroy, 1st Duke of
W. Wissing/I. Beckett (10,244)
J. Wyck/J. Brooks (11,652)*(group)*

Grafton, Charles Fitzroy, 2nd Duke of
(Lord Lieutenant of Ireland)
G. Kneller/J. Faber the Younger (10,845)
G. Kneller/J. Smith (10,227)

Grafton, Augustus Henry Fitzroy, 3rd Duke of
(British Prime Minster)
P. Batoni/ J. Watson (10,129)

Gramont, Elizabeth, Countess of
(née Hamilton)
P. Lely/J. McArdell (10,401)

Granard, George Forbes, 6th Earl of
?J. Comerford/J. Heath (10,818)

Grant, Charles
(1st Baron Glenelg)
T.C. Thompson/C. Turner (10,842)

Grant, Sir Colquin
J.P. Haverty/R. Havell the Elder and Younger (11,650)*(group)*

Grantham, Thomas Philip Weddell Robinson, Baron
(2nd Earl De Grey; Lord Lieutenant of Ireland)
J. Doyle/J. Doyle (11,544)(56)*(group)*
J. Doyle/J. Doyle (11,544)(58)*(group)*
W. Robinson/*W. Brett*/S. Cousins (10,841)
J. Wood/J. Brown (10,840)

Grantham, Lady Henrietta Frances
(née Cole; wife of 3rd Baron Grantham, later 1st Earl De Grey)
A.E. Chalon/R.A. Artlett (10,814)
T. Lawrence/J.H. Robinson (20,204)

Grattan, M.P., Henry
J. Comerford/J. Heath (10,835)
J. Comerford/J. Heath (10,836)
J. Doyle/J. Doyle (11,403)*(group)*
P. Fitzpatrick/P. Roberts (11,145)
J.P. Haverty/J.P. Haverty (11,857)*(group)*
Irish School c.1780/Irish School 1780 (11,146)
Irish School c.1782/Irish School 1782 (11,147)
N. Kenny/F.C. Lewis (11,144)
A. Pope/J. Godby (10,837)
A. Pope/J. Martyn (10,838)
A. Pope/J. Martyn (11,148)
A. Pope/E. Scriven (10,437)
J. Ramsay/C. Turner (10,419)
G.C. Stuart/C.H. Hodges (10,217)
G.C. Stuart/Irish School c.1795 (10,079)
P. Turnerelli (8107)
After P. Turnerelli (8228)

Graves, Charles
(P. Bishop of Limerick)
J.H. Foley (8252)

Graves, Mrs Charles
(née Selina Cheyne)
J.H. Foley (8269)

Graves, Dr Robert James
L. Gluckman/J.H. Lynch (11,430)
C. Grey/J. Kirkwood (11,161)

Gray, Edward Dwyer
M. Redmond-Dunne (8145)

Gray, Dr J.
J.P. Haverty/J.P. Haverty (11,857)*(group)*

Greatrakes, Valentine
?W. Faithorne the Elder/W. Faithorne the Elder (10,832)

Greene, Sir Jonas
J.P. Haverty/R. Havell the Elder and Younger (11,650)*(group)*

Gregory, Lady Augusta
(née Persse)
T. Spicer-Simson (8140)
T. Spicer-Simson (8218)

Grenville, William Grenville, 1st Baron
M. Brown/D. Orme (20,104)*(group)*
J.K. Sherwin(J.K. Sherwin (11,657-11,658)*(group)*
J.K. Sherwin/J.K. Sherwin (11,827-11,829)*(group)*

Grey, Charles Grey, 2nd Earl
(British Prime Minster)
J. Doyle/J. Doyle (11,544)(56)*(group)*
J. Doyle/J. Doyle (11,544)(58)*(group)*
T. Lawrence/S. Cousins (10,057)

Grey, Samuel
(Commissioner of Revenue in Ireland)
J. Worsdale/J. Brooks (10,167)
J. Worsdale/J. Brooks (10,820)

Griffith, Arthur
A. Power (8100)

Grose, Francis
N. Dance/F. Bartolozzi (10,819)
J. Doyle/J. Doyle (11,158)
N. Hone the Elder/*N. Dance*/W. Ridley (11,157)
N. Hone the Elder/N. Hone the Elder (11,848)

Grouthead, Bishop Robert
J. Barry/J. Barry (20,722)(7)*(group)*

Guilford, Frederick North, 2nd Earl of
(Lord North; British Prime Minister)
N. Dance/T. Burke (10,999)
N. Dance/T. Burke (11,000)

Guillamore, Standish O'Grady, 1st Viscount
(Lord Chief Baron of the Exchequer in Ireland)
Irish School c.1811/Irish School 1811 (11,851)*(group)*

Guinness, Arthur
(of Beaumont)
F.W. Burton/G. Sanders (10,815)

Gunning, Catherine
(wife of Robert Travis; sister of Maria and Elizabeth)
F. Cotes/R. Houston (10,359)
F. Cotes/C. Spooner (10,358)

Gunning, Elizabeth
(sister of Catherine and Maria; Duchess of Hamilton and Brandon, wife of 6th Duke; also Duchess of Argyll, wife of 5th Duke and Baroness Hamilton)
F. Cotes/R. Brookshaw (11,150)
F. Cotes/R. Brookshaw (11,151)
F. Cotes/R. Houston (10,342)
F. Cotes/J. McArdell (10,343)
G. Hamilton/J. Faber the Younger (10,393)
G. Hamilton/J. Faber the Younger (10,834)
J. M..../S. Okey (10,327)
C. Read/J. Finlayson (10,394)

Gunning, John
(father of Catherine, Elizabeth and Maria)
English or Irish School c.1760/R. Houston (10,127)

Gunning, Maria
(sister of Catherine and Elizabeth; Countess of Coventry, wife of 9th Earl)
F. Cotes/J. McArdell (10,374)
F. Cotes/C. Spooner (10,375)
F. Cotes/?R. Purcell (10,829)
F. Cotes/?R. Purcell (10,831)
G. Hamilton/J. McArdell (10,396)
G. Hamilton/J. McArdell (10,830)
J. M..../S. Okey (10,327)
C. Read/J. Finlayson (10,391)
B. Wilson/B. Wilson (10,388)

so called Gunning, Maria
J.E. Liotard/R. Houston (10,384)

Hadfield, Maria
(Mrs Richard Cosway)
M. Cosway/V. Green (10,405)

Haddington, Thomas Hamilton, 9th Earl of
(Lord Lieutenant of Ireland)
R. McInnes/J. Brown (10,887)

Hall, Mrs Samuel Carter
(née Anne Maria Fielding)
English School 19C/English School 19C (10,884)

Hamilton, Count Anthony
Continental School 17C/*S. Harding*/W.N. Gardiner (10,614)
French School 17C/French School 17C (20,117)

Hamilton, Cecil Frances
(Countess of Wicklow, wife of 4th Earl)
G.H. Harlow/W. Say (10,369)

Hamilton, Elizabeth
(Countess of Gramont)
P. Lely/J. McArdell (10,401)

Hamilton, Mrs Elizabeth
H. Raeburn/*J. Jackson*/H. Meyer (10,883)

Hamilton, Lady Frances
(Duchess of Tyrconnell, wife of 1st Duke)
R. De Hooghe/R. De Hooghe (11,655)*(group)*

Hamilton, George
(1st Earl of Orkney)
M. Maingaud/J. Houbraken (10,987)

Hamilton, M.P., George Alexander
W.J. Newton/J. Posselwhite (10,885)
W.J. Newton/J. Posselwhite (10,886)

Hamilton, Gustavus
(2nd Viscount Boyne)
W. Hogarth/A. Miller (10,436)

Hamilton, Hugh
(P. Bishop of Ossory)
G.C. Stuart/W. Evans (10,622)

Hamilton, Hugh Douglas
Irish School c.1811/H. Brocas the Elder (10,612)

Hamilton, James
(4th Earl of Clanbrassil)
J.K. Sherwin/J.K. Sherwin (11,657-11,658)*(group)*
J.K. Sherwin/J.K. Sherwin (11,827-11,829)*(group*

Hamilton, James
(8th Earl of Abercorn)
T. Gainsborough/J. Dean (10,549)

Hamilton, Thomas
(9th Earl of Haddington; Lord Lieutenant of Ireland)
R. McInnes/J. Brown (10,887)

Hamilton, Sir William Rowan
T. Kirk (8260)
C. Grey/J. Kirkwood (10,613)

Hamilton and Brandon, Elizabeth, Duchess of
(née Gunning; wife of 6th Duke; Duchess of Argyll, wife of 5th Duke)
F. Cotes/R. Brookshaw (11,151)
F. Cotes/R. Houston (10,342)
F. Cotes/J. McArdell (10,343)
G. Hamilton/J. Faber the Younger (10,393)
G. Hamilton/J. Faber the Younger (10,834)
J. M..../S. Okey (10,327)
C. Read/J. Finlayson (10,394)

Hammond, Sir F.T.
J.P. Haverty/R. Havell the Elder and Younger (11,650)*(group)*

Harborough, Philip Sherard, 2nd Earl of
N. Hone the Elder/J. Greenwood (11,408)

Harcourt, Simon Harcourt, 1st Earl of
R. Hunter/E. Fisher (10,194)
B. Wilson/J. McArdell (10,149)
B. Wilson/J. McArdell (10,677)

Hardy M.P., Francis
J.R. Maguire/J. Heath (10,881)

Hardwicke, Philip Yorke, 3rd Earl of
(Lord Lieutenant of Ireland)
T. Lawrence/W. Giller (10,154)

Hare, Henry
(2nd Baron Coleraine)
English School 17C/W. Faithorne the Elder (10,771)

Harley, Robert
(1st Earl of Oxford)
J. Wyck/J. Brooks (11,652)*(group)*

Harrington, Jane, Countess of
(née Fleming; wife of 3rd Earl)
English School 18C/R. Cooper (10,316)
J. Reynolds/F. Bartolozzi (10,313-10,315)
J. Reynolds/V. Green (10,400)

Harrington, William Stanhope, 1st Earl of
(Lord Lieutenant of Ireland)
B. Du Pan/M. Ford (10,157)
J. Fayram/J. Faber the Younger (10,193)

Harrington, Charles Stanhope, 4th Earl of
(Viscount Petersham)
J. Reynolds/F. Bartolozzi (10,313-10,315)

Hart, Sir Anthony
(Lord Chancellor of Ireland)
T. Cahill/Irish School c.1827 (10,875)
English School c.1800/English School c.1800 (10,874)

Harvey, William
J. Barry/J. Barry (20,722)(8)*(group)*

Hastings, Francis Rawdon-Hastings, 1st Marquess of
(2nd Earl of Moira)
English School c.1780/W. Ridley (10,656-10,657)
English School c.1813/Irish School 1813 (10,655)
J. Gillray/J. Gillray (11,545)*(group)*
H.D. Hamilton/J. Heath (10,947)
J. Hoppner/*F. Bartolozzi*/H. Landseer (10,949)
S. Percy (8160)
J. Reynolds/J.K. Baldrey (11,047)
J. Reynolds/J. Jones (10,503)
J. Reynolds/J. Jones (10,946)
J. Reynolds/P. Maguire (10,654)
J. Reynolds/R. Stanier (10,653)
M.A. Shee/G. Clint (10,948)
G.C. Stuart/J. Collyer (10,118)

Hastings, Lady Flora Elizabeth
(daughter of 1st Marquess of Hastings)
E. Hawkins/W. Finden (10,943)

Hatton, Lady Anne
J.K. Sherwin/J.K. Sherwin (11,657-11,658)*(group)*
J.K. Sherwin/J.K. Sherwin (11,827-11,829)*(group)*

Haugh, Jack
(alias Mill-Cushin)
Irish School c.1750/R. Graves (11,154)
Irish School c.1750/?M. Hanbury (10,141)

?Haverty, Joseph Patrick
J.P. Haverty/J.P. Haverty (11,020)*(group)*

Hawkins, James E.
P.F. Gethin/P.F. Gethin (11,429)

Hawkins, William
J.K. Sherwin/J.K. Sherwin (11,657-11,658)*(group)*
J.K. Sherwin/J.K. Sherwin (11,827-11,829)*(group)*

Hay, Edward
Irish School c.1800/Irish School c.1800 (10,620)

Hayes, Catherine
Irish School c.1850/Irish School 1850 (11,378)

Head, Richard
English School 17C/English School 1795 (10,872)

Headfort, Thomas Taylor, 1st Marquess of
J.P. Haverty/R. Havell the Elder & Younger (11,650)*(group)*

Healy, Rev. James
L.J. Chavalliaud (8189)

Healy, M.P., Timothy Michael
C. Dupechez/C. Dupechez (10,889)

Heathfield, General George Augustus Eliott, 1st Baron
N. Hone the Elder/R. Pollard (10,777)

Heffel of Rowton House
W. Sickert/W. Sickert (11,437)

Hely-Hutchinson, M.P., Christopher
(son of John Hely-Hutchinson)
Irish School 19C/P. Dillon (10,623)

Hely-Hutchinson, John
(Provost of Trinity College, Dublin; Secretary of State for Ireland)
J. Reynolds/J. Watson (10,424)

Hely-Hutchinson, M.P., Lt.-Colonel John
(2nd Earl of Donoughmore)
Irish School c.1792/English School 1792
T. Phillips/*W. Evans*/K. Mackenzie (10,801)

Hely-Hutchinson, Richard Hely-Hutchinson, 2nd Baron
(1st Earl of Donoughmore)
B. Stoker/H. Brocas the Elder (11,176)

Hemans, Felicia Dorothea
W.E. West/E. Scriven (20,658)

Hendrick, George (Crazy Crow)
Irish School c.1754/R. Graves (11,125)

Henniker, Ann Elizabeth
(Countess of Aldborough, wife of 2nd Earl)
J. Hoppner/S. Einslie (10,387)

Henry, Prince
(son of King James I of England)
Continental School c.1620/C. Turner (10,869)*(group)*

Henry IV
(King of France)
J. Barry/J. Barry (20,722)(10)*(group)*
P.P. Rubens/*J.M. Nattier*/A. Trouvain (20,678)(6)*(group)*

Henry V
(King of England)
T. Stothard/A. Cardon (20,067)*(group)*

so-called Hensey, Florence
English School 18C/English School 1820 (10,873)

Hertford, Francis Seymour-Conway, 4th Marquess of
(Lord Lieutenant of Ireland)
J. Astley/J. Dixon (10,412)

Hervey, Frederick Augustus
(P. Bishop of Derry; 4th Earl of Bristol; 'The Earl-Bishop')
A. Kauffmann/?T. Burke (10,209)

Hesse-Kassel, Frederick, Prince of
R. De Hooghe/R. De Hooghe (11,655)*(group)*

Hessen-Darmstadt, Prince of
Dutch School 1691/J. Tangena (10,004)*(group)*

Hewett, General Sir George
S.W. Reynolds the Younger/S.W. Reynolds the Elder & S. Cousins (10,888)

Hewitt, James
(1st Baron and 1st Viscount Lifford; Lord Chancellor of Ireland)
W. Madden/W. Dickinson (10,479)
J. Reynolds/R. Dunkarton (10,484)
J.K. Sherwin/J.K. Sherwin (11,657-11,658)*(group)*
J.K. Sherwin/J.K. Sherwin (11,827-11,829)*(group)*

Hewson, Colonel John
English School 17C/English School c.1816 (10,618)

Hickman, John
(P. Bishop of Derry)
A. Russell/S. Gribelin (10,047)

Higgins, Rev. Francis
E. Lutterell/E. Lutterell (10,022)

Hill, Anne
(Countess of Mornington, wife of 1st Earl)
Lady Burghersh/T. Hodgetts (10,399)

Hill, Lord Arthur
J.P. Haverty/R. Havell the Elder & Younger (11,650)*(group)*

Hill, Arthur Marcus Cecil
(3rd Baron Sandys)
J. Holmes/M. Gauci (10,621)

Hill, Rowland
English School 19C/?T.A. Prior (11,372)*(group)*

Hill, Rowland Hill, 1st Viscount
English School c.1815/English School 1816 (11,354)

Hillsborough, Margaretta, Countess of
(née FitzGerald; wife of 1st Earl)
R. Pool & J. Cash/I. Taylor the Elder (10,041)(26)*(group)*

Hillsborough, Wills Hill, 1st Earl of
(1st Marquess of Downshire)
?H.D. Hamilton/Irish School late 18C (10,619)

Hinchliffe, Mrs John
(née Elizabeth Crewe)
J. Reynolds/R. Brookshaw (11,201)

Hings, Samuel
(Bishop of Norwich)
T.H. Maguire/T.H. Maguire (10,871)

Hippocrates
J.Barry/J. Barry (20,722)(8)*(group)*

Hoadly, Benjamin
(Bishop of Winchester)
I. Gosset/*N. Hone the Elder*/J. Basire the Elder (10,879)

Hoadly, John
(P. Archbishop of Dublin; Archbishop of Armagh)
I. Woods/J. Faber the Younger (10,029)

Hobart, John
(2nd Earl of Buckinghamshire)
J.K. Sherwin/J.K. Sherwin (11,657-11,658)*(group)*
J.K. Sherwin/J.K. Sherwin (11,827-11,829)*(group)*

Hoche, General Lazare
French School c.1799/French School 1799 (10,877)
French School 18C/F. Lefebvre (10,878)

Hogan, John
C. Grey/Irish School 1850 (10,617)

Holland, Henry Fox, 3rd Baron
J. Doyle/J. Doyle (11,544)(57)*(group)*

Holmes, Robert
E. Hayes/S. Bellin (10,870)
Irish School c.1848/H. Griffiths (10,624)

Holmes, M.P., William
J. Moore/M. Gauci (10,882)

Holt, Joseph
Irish School 1798/R.J. Hamerton (10,615)

Honan, Martin
J.P. Haverty/M. & N. Hanhart (11,857)*(group)*

Hone, Amelia
(Mrs Ambrose Rigg)
N. Hone the Elder/J. Greenwood (10,329)
N. Hone the Elder/J. Greenwood (10,695)

Hone, Horace
(son of Nathaniel Hone the Elder)
N. Hone the Elder/J. Watson (10,068)
N. Hone the Elder/J. Watson (10,700)

Hone, John Camillus
(son of Nathaniel Hone the Elder)
N. Hone the Elder/W. Baillie (10,532)
N. Hone the Elder/W. Humphrey (10,696)
N. Hone the Elder/J.R. Smith (11,414)
N. Hone the Elder/J.R. Smith (10,697)

Hone, Lydia
(daughter of Nathaniel Hone the Elder)
N. Hone the Elder/C. Phillips (10,378)
N. Hone the Elder/C. Phillips (10,699)
N. Hone the Elder/J.R. Smith (10,330)

Hone the Elder, Nathaniel
(Self-Portrait)
N. Hone the Elder/E. Fisher (10,070)
N. Hone the Elder/E. Fisher (10,698)
N. Hone the Elder/N. Hone the Elder (10,072)

Hope, James
Irish School c.1843/T.W. Huffam (10,616)

Hopkins, M.P., Edward
G. Kneller/J. Faber the Younger (10,676)

Hopkins, Ezekiel
(P. Bishop of Derry)
English School 17C/J. Sturt (10,051)
English School 17C/J. Sturt (10,627)
English School 17C/M. Vandergucht (10,625)
English School 17C/M. Vandergucht (10,626)

Hort, Josiah
(P. Archbishop of Tuam)
J. Wills/A. Miller (10,018)

How, Thomas
(Lord Mayor of Dublin)
J. Latham/J. Brooks (10,195)

Howard, George
(Viscount Morpeth)
J. Doyle/J. Doyle (11,544)(62)*(group)*
J. Doyle/J. Doyle (11,544)(67)*(group)*
J. Doyle/J. Doyle (11,853)*(group)*

Howard, George William Frederick
(7th Earl of Carlisle; Lord Lieutenant of Ireland)
English School 1864/English School 1864 (11,595)
C. Moore (8088)
G. Richmond/F. Holl (10,425)

Howard, Hugh
M. Dahl/J. Faber the Younger (10,125)

Howard, Thomas
(4th Duke of Norfolk)
English School c.1560/J. Houbraken (11,942)

Howden, John Francis Cradock, 1st Baron
T. Lawrence/J. Godby (10,767)

Howden, Lord
J.P. Haverty/R. Havell the Elder & Younger (11,650)*(group)*

Howley, Henry
J. Petrie/P. Maguire (10,629)
J. Petrie/P. Maguire (10,630)

so-called Hudson, Edward
(United Irishman)
W. Cuming/T.S. Engleheart (10,628)

Hughes, Admiral Sir Edward
English School c.1786/English School 1786 (10,518)

Hume, Gustavus
J. Comerford/J. Carver (10,876)

Hume, Joseph
J. Doyle/J. Doyle (11,854)*(group)*

Hunter, Robert
T.A. Jones/Irish School late 19C (10,880)

Hunter, Dr William
J. Barry/J. Barry (20,722)(5)*(group)*

Hurley, Edward Timothy
E.T. Hurley/E.T. Hurley (11,016)
E.T. Hurley/E.T. Hurley (11,017)

Hussey, Giles
J. Barry/J. Barry (20,722)(11)*(group)*

Hussey, Thomas
(R.C. Bishop of Waterford and Lismore; 1st President of Maynooth College)
C.F. Von Breda/S.W. Reynolds the Elder (10,422)

Hutchinson, Lieut.-General John
(2nd Earl of Donoughmore)
T. Phillips/*W. Evans*/K. Mackenzie (10,801)

Hutton, Annie
C. Moore (8060)

Hyde, Douglas
(1st President of Ireland)
T. Spicer-Simson (8141)
T. Spicer-Simson (8217)

Hyde, Laurence
(1st Earl of Rochester; Lord Lieutenant of Ireland)
G. Kneller/J. Houbraken (10,212)

Inchiquin, Murrough O'Brien, 5th Earl of
(1st Marquess of Thomond)
J. Hoppner/S.W. Reynolds the Elder (10,469)
J.K. Sherwin/J.K. Sherwin (11,657-11,658)*(group)*
J.K. Sherwin/J.K. Sherwin (11,827-11,829)*(group)*
Marchioness of Thomond/R.W. Meadows (10,147)

Inchiquin, Mary, Countess of
(née Palmer; 2nd wife of 4th Earl)
T. Lawrence/W. Bond (10,368)

Ingram, Catherine
(Mrs Woodhull)
J. Zoffany/R. Houston (10,350)

Ireland, Attorney General for
William Saurin

Ireland, Chancellor of the Exchequer of
Anthony Malone
Thomas Spring Rice, 1st Baron Monteagle

Ireland, Chief Baron of the Exchequer of
Barry Yelverton, 1st Viscount Avonmore
John Bowes, 1st Baron Bowes
Walter Hussey Burgh, M.P.

Ireland, Chief Secretary for
Lord Frederick Charles Cavendish
George Macartney, 1st Earl Macartney

Ireland, Chief Secretary to the Lord Lieutenant of
John De Blaquiere, 1st Baron De Blaquiere

Ireland, Commander-in-Chief in
General Sir Samuel Auchmuty Bt.
Sir George Murray
John Leslie, 10th Earl of Rothes

Ireland, Commissioner of Revenue in
Samuel Grey
Hon. John Monck Mason, M.P.

Ireland, First Commissioner of Revenue in
John Beresford, M.P

Ireland, Lord Chancellor of
Francis Blackburne
John Bowes, 1st Baron Bowes
Michael Boyle, P. Archbishop of Armagh
Henry Brougham, M.P.; 1st Baron Brougham and Vaux
John Fitzgibbon, 1st Earl of Clare
Sir Anthony Hart
James Hewitt, 1st Viscount Lifford
Robert Jocleyn; Baron Newport; 1st Viscount Jocelyn
Thomas Manners-Sutton, 1st Baron Manners
John Methuen
Sir Joseph Napier Bt., M.P.
Sir John Newport Bt., M.P.
Sir Constantine Phipps
William Conyngham Plunket, 1st Baron Plunket
George Ponsonby, M.P.

Ireland, Lord Chief Justice of
Arthur Wolfe, 1st Viscount Kilwarden
George Augustus Chichester May
Charles Kendal Bushe
James Whiteside, M.P.

Ireland, Lord Chief Justice of the Common Pleas in
Standish O'Grady, 1st Viscount Guillamore
John Toler, 1st Earl of Norbury
Sir Henry Sydney

Ireland, Lord Chief Justice of the King's Bench in
William Downes, 1st Baron Downes
John Scott, 1st Earl of Clonmel

Ireland, Lord Deputy of
Charles Blount; 8th Baron Mountjoy; 1st Earl of Devonshire
Sir William Russel; 1st Baron Russel
Sir Henry Sydney
Henry Treton

Ireland, Lord High Treasurer of
Richard Boyle, 1st Earl of Cork

Ireland, Lord Justice of
Sir William Brereton; 1st Baron Brereton
Sir William Parsons

Ireland, Lord Lieutenant of
Henry William Paget, 1st Marquess of Anglesey
George Nugent-Grenville-Temple, 1st Marquess of Buckingham
George William Frederick Howard, 7th Earl of Carlisle
Philip Dormer Stanhope, 4th Earl of Chesterfield
George William Frederick Villiers, 4th Earl of Clarendon
Charles Cornwallis, 1st Marquess of Cornwallis
Thomas Philip Wedell Robinson, 2nd Earl De Grey
William Cavendish, 3rd Duke of Devonshire
Lionel Cranfield Sackville, 1st Duke of Dorset
Archibald William Montgomerie, 13th Earl of Eglington and Winton
William Wentworth, 2nd Earl FitzWilliam
Hugh Fortescue, 4th Baron Fortescue
Charles Fitzroy, 2nd Duke of Grafton
Thomas Hamilton, 9th Earl of Haddington
Simon Harcourt, 1st Earl Harcourt
Philip Yorke, 3rd Earl of Hardwicke
William Stanhope, 1st Earl of Harrington
Francis Seymour-Conway, 4th Marquess of Hertford
Major-General John Lambert
Constantine Phipps, 1st Marquess of Normandy
Hugh Percy, 1st Duke of Northumberland
James Butler, 1st Duke of Ormonde
James Butler, 2nd Duke of Ormonde
William Henry Cavendish-Bentinck, 3rd Duke of Portland
John Robartes, 1st Earl of Radnor
Charles Lennox, 4th Duke of Richmond
Laurence Hyde, 1st Earl of Rochester
Charles Manners, 4th Duke of Rutland
Edward Granville Eliot, 3rd Earl of Saint Germains
Thomas Wentworth, 1st Earl of Strafford
Charles Chetwynd-Talbot, 2nd Earl Talbot
George Townsend, 1st Marquess of Townsend
Richard Talbot, Earl and Titular Duke of Tyrconnel
Richard Wellesley, 1st Marquess Wellesley
John Fane, 10th Earl of Westmoreland
Thomas Wharton, 1st Marquess Wharton
Charles Whitworth, 1st Earl Whitworth

Ireland, Master of the Rolls in
Thomas Carter
John Philpot Curran, M.P.

Ireland, Secretary of State for
John Hely-Hutchinson
William Lingen
William Lamb, 2nd Viscount Melbourne
Sir Robert Southwell

Ireland, Solicitor General for
John Doherty

Ireland, Surveyor General of
Sir William Parsons

Ireland, Teller of the Exchequer in
William Burton Conyngham

Ireland, Under-Secretary of State for
Edward Cooke

Ireland, Vice-Treasurer of
Colonel William Blacker
Luke Gardiner, M.P.

Irnham, Simon Luttrell, Baron
(1st Earl of Carhampton)
Irish School 1768/81//Irish School 1768/81 (11,212)

Irwin, Anne
(Mrs Joshua Irwin)
J. Reynolds/J. Watson (10,345)

Irwin, Eyles
G. Romney/J. Walker (10,864)

Isaak, Monsieur
T. Maas/T. Maas (10,003)*(group)*
T. Maas/T. Maas (20,800)*(group)*

Isabella
(Queen of Spain)
J. Barry/J. Barry (20,722)(14)*(group)*

Ivanovitch, Matvei
(Count Platov)
English School c.1815/English School 1815 (11,358)

Jackson, Henry
(United Irishman)
J.D. Herbert/T.W. Huffam (10,633)

James I
(King of England)
Continental School c.1620/C. Turner (10,869)*(group)*
A. Van Dyck/J. Faber the Younger (10,096)

James II
(King of England)
R. De Hooghe/R. De Hooghe (11,655)*(group)*
R. De Hooghe/R. De Hooghe (11,847)(2-12)*(group)*
Dutch School c.1690/Dutch School c.1690 (11,865-11,866)*(group)*
G. Kneller/J. Gole (10,006)
G. Kneller/J. Smith (10,095)
After Larson (8095)
T. Maas/T. Maas (10,003)*(group)*
T. Maas/T. Maas (20,800)*(group)*
P. Schenck/P. Schenck (10,865)
A. Van Dyck/A. Browne (10,756)*(group)*
A. Van Dyck/R. Cooper (10,546)*(group)*

Jebb, John
(P. Bishop of Limerick, also Ardfert and Aghadoe)
T. Lawrence/T. Lupton (20,112)
G. Richmond/H. Adlard (10,631)

Jeffrey, Francis
(Lord Advocate)
C. Smith/S. Cousins (10,097)

Jenkinson, Robert Banks
(2nd Earl of Liverpool; British Prime Minister)
T. Lawrence & A. Wivell/?T.A. Prior (11,384)*(group)*

Jennings, Francis
(Lady Hamilton, wife of Sir George; Duchess of Tyrconnell, wife of 1st Duke)
R. De Hooghe/R. De Hooghe (11,655)*(group)*

Jennings, M.P., Sir John
G. Kneller/J. Faber the Younger (10,867)

Jephson, Robert
B. Stoker/J. Singleton (10,283)

Jersey, Julia Beatrice, Countess of
(née Peel; daughter of Sir Robert Peel; wife of 6th Earl of Jersey)
T. Lawrence/S. Cousins (10,446)

Jocelyn, Elizabeth Francis Charlotte
(Viscountess Powerscourt, wife of 6th Viscount; Marchioness of Londonderry, wife of 4th Marquess)
J. Ross/W.H. Mote (11,333)

Jocelyn, Elizabeth Frances, Viscountess
(daughter of 5th Earl Cowper; wife of 1st Earl Roden, also 2nd wife of 1st Viscount Jocelyn)
J. Hayter/W.H. Egleton (10,866)

Jocelyn ,Robert
(Baron Newport; Lord Chancellor of Ireland; 1st Viscount Jocelyn)
?J. Brooks/J. Brooks (10,434)
J. Pope-Stevens the Elder/A. Miller (10,099)

Jocelyn, Robert
(2nd Earl of Roden)
J. Oldham/J. Heath (11,048)

Jocelyn, Robert
(3rd Earl of Roden)
F.R. Say/J. Kirkwood (11,293)

Johnson, Bt., General Sir Henry
C. Jagger/S. Sangster (10,868)

Johnson, Major-General Henry
R. Woodburn/R. Dunkarton (10,416)

Johnson, Dr James
J. Wood/W. Holl the Younger (10,632)

Johnson, Samuel
J. Barry/J. Barry (20,722)(5)*(group)*

Johnston, Denis
V.H. Lines/V.H. Lines (11,554)

Johnston, Francis
T.C. Thompson/H. Meyer (10,126)

Johnston Bt., Sir John Allen
F. Wheatley/J. Collyer (11,644)*(group)*
F. Wheatley/J. Collyer (11,826)*(group)*

Johnstone, John Henry
M.A. Shee/W. Ward the Elder (10,100)

Joly, Jaspar
F. Wheatley/J. Collyer (11,644)*(group)*
F. Wheatley/J. Collyer (11,826)*(group)*

Jones, Elizabeth
(Countess of Kildare, 2nd wife of 18th Earl)
W. Wissing/I. Beckett (11,863)

Jones, John Gale
English School 18C/English School 19C (10,634)

Jordan, Mrs
(née Dorothy Bland)
J. Hoppner/J. Jones (10,386)
G. Romney/J. Ogborne (10,341)
J. Hoppner/T. Park (10,408)

Julius II, Pope
J. Barry/J. Barry (20,722)(10)*(group)*

Kane, Sir Robert
G.F. Mulvany/S. Freeman (10,645)

Kauffmann, Angelica
(Self-Portrait)
A. Kauffmann/W. Ridley (10,644)

Kavanagh, M.P., Arthur MacMorrough
English School 19C/Morris and Co. (10,482)

Keating, M.P., Sir Henry Singer
J. Mayall/D.J. Pound (10,860)

Kelly, Hugh
H.D. Hamilton/J. Boydell (10,294)

Kelly, Michael
J. Lonsdale/C. Turner (10,170)
A. Wivell the Elder/H. Meyer (10,638)

Kemble, Sarah
(Mrs Siddons)
H. Hone/F. Bartolozzi (10,310)
H. Hone/G.F. Philips (10,308)
J. Reynolds/J. Webb (10,398)

Kempenfelt, Admiral Richard
English School c.1780/English School 1786 (10,517)

Kennedy, Dr Evory
C. Grey/J. Kirkwoood (20,110)

Kent, Mr
(in his aquatic velocipede)
J.P. Haverty/R. Havell the Elder & Younger (11,649)*(group)*
J.P. Haverty/R. Havell the Elder & Younger (11,651)*(group)*

Ker, Richard Graves
S. Ker/C. Turner (10,854)

Kettle, Thomas
A. Power (8010)

Kickham, Charles Joseph
Irish School 1882 (8155)
Irish School 1882 (8206)

Kildare, Elizabeth, Countess of
(née Jones; 2nd wife of 18th Earl)
W. Wissing/I. Beckett (11,863)

Kildare, Emilia Mary, Countess of
(née Lennox; wife of 20th Earl of Kildare and 1st Duke of Leinster)
J. Reynolds/J. McArdell (10,344)

Kildare, Mary, Countess of
(née Mary O'Brien; wife of 19th Earl)
R. Pool & J. Cash/I. Taylor the Elder (10,041)(26)*(group)*

Kildare, James FitzGerald, 20th Earl of
(1st Duke of Leinster)
R. Pool & J. Cash/I. Taylor the Elder (10,041)(26)*(group)*
J. Reynolds/J. McArdell (10,088)

Kildare, Robert FitzGerald, 19th Earl of
R. Pool & J. Cash/I. Taylor the Elder (10,041)(26)*(group)*

Kildare and Leighlin, James Warren Doyle, R.C. Bishop of
S. Catterson Smith the Elder/R. Cooper (11,179)
J.P.Haverty/J.P. Haverty (10,794)
Irish School 19C (8101)
Irish School c.1820/T. Kelly (11,180)

Kildare, Richard Robinson, P. Bishop of
(Archbishop of Armagh; 1st Baron Rokeby)
J. Reynolds/R. Houston (10,410)
J.K. Sherwin/J.K. Sherwin (11,657-11,658)*(group)*
J.K. Sherwin/J.K. Sherwin (11,827-11,829)*(group)*

Killala, Walter Blake Kirwan, P. Dean of
M.A. Shee/T. Blood (10,637)
M.A. Shee/G. Clint (10,489)

Killaloe, Edward Parry, P. Bishop of
Irish School 17C/J. Dickson (10,305)

Killarey, Rector of
(Rev. Sir Harcourt Lees, Bt.)
T.C.Thompson/?Irish School c.1824 (10,604)

Killigrew, Anne
A. Killigrew/A. Blooteling (10,856)

Kilmore and Ardagh, William Sheridan, P. Bishop of
?Irish School c.1700/W. Sheridan (10,301)

Kilmore and Ardagh, Edward Weterhall, P. Bishop of
J. Vandervaart/J. Vandervaart (10,132)

Kilwarden, Arthur Wolfe, 1st Viscount
(Lord Chief Justice of Ireland)
H.D. Hamilton/F. Bartolozzi (10,702)
H.D. Hamilton/F. Bartolozzi (10,861-10,862)
H.D. Hamilton/P. Lightfoot (10,640)
H.D. Hamilton/*P. Maguire*/J. Heath (10,863)
G.F. Joseph/S. Freeman (10,639)

King, Sir A.B.
(Lord Mayor of Dublin)
J.P. Haverty/R. Havell the Elder & Younger (11,650)*(group)*

King Bt., Sir Abraham
(Lord Mayor of Dublin)
Irish School c.1779/Irish School c.1779 (10,642)

King, William
(Archbishop of Dublin)
M. Dahl/T. Beard (10,063)
T. Hudson/J. McArdell (10,885)
C. Jervas/R. Purcell (10,011)

Kingsmill Bt., Admiral Sir Robert
L.F. Abbot/W. Ridley (10,643)

Kirwan, Walter Blake
(P. Bishop of Killala)
H.D. Hamilton/W. Ward the Elder (10,050)
M.A. Shee/T. Blood (10,637)
M.A. Shee/G. Clint (10,489)
J.K. Sherwin/J.K. Sherwin (11,657-11,658)*(group)*
J.K. Sherwin/J.K. Sherwin (11,827-11,829)*(group)*

Knowles, James Sheridan
A.G.G. D'Orsay/A.G.G. D'Orsay (10,859)
English School c.1850/A. Weger (10,858)
C. Grey/Irish School 1852 (10,641)
G. Lance/J. Scott (11,232)

Knox, Rev. James
W. Foy/G. Foggo (10,857)

Ladrière, Brigadier
R. De Hooghe/R. De Hooghe (11,655)*(group)*

Lake, Major-General Francis Gerard (2nd Viscount Lake)
R. Dighton/R. Dighton (10,908)

Lally-Tolendal, Trophime Gérard, Comte de
French School late 18C & J. Duplessi-Bertaux/C.F.G. Lavachez & J. Duplessi-Bertaux (11,008)
J.M. Moreau/W.N.M. Courbe (10,605)
C.P. Verhulst/J.L. Anselin (10,906)

Lamb, William (2nd Viscount Melbourne; Secretary of State for Ireland; British Prime Minister)
J. Doyle/J. Doyle (11,544)(55)*(group)*
J. Doyle/J. Doyle (11,544)(58)*(group)*
J. Doyle/J. Doyle (11,544)(59)*(group)*
J. Doyle/J. Doyle (11,544)(61)*(group)*
J. Doyle/J. Doyle (11,544)(64)*(group)*
J. Doyle/J. Doyle (11,544)(65)*(group)*
J. Doyle/J. Doyle (11,544)(66)*(group)*
T. Lawrence & English School c.1830/?T.A. Prior (11,341)*(group)*

Lambert, Frances Thomasing (Countess of Talbot, wife of 3rd Earl)
C. Robertson/J.S. Agar (10,324)

Lambert, John
R. Walker/*M. Ford*/A. Miller (10,500)

Lambert, Major-General John (Lord Lieutenant of Ireland)
R. Walker/F. Place (10,907)

Lambton, Charles William (1st Earl of Durham)
T. Lawrence/S. Cousins (10,447)

La Meloniere, Brigadier
Dutch School 1691/J. Tangena (10,004)*(group)*

Lamothe-Fénelon, François De Salignac, Archbishop of
French School 18C/French School 18C (20,359)

Lane, Denny
J. Lawlor (8150)

Lanesborough, Elizabeth, Countess of (née La Touche; wife of 3rd Earl)
H. Hone/F. Bartolozzi (10,309)

Lanesborough, Humphrey Butler, 4th Viscount and 1st Earl of
C. Brown/J. Brooks (10,481)

Langton, Mrs Obediah (née Sarah Crewe)
J. Reynolds/R. Brookshaw (11,201)

Lansdowne, William Petty, 1st Marquess of (2nd Earl of Shelburne; British Prime Minister)
J. Gillray/J. Gillray (11,545)*(group)*
Irish School c.1780/Irish School 1780 (11,304)

Larderia, Prince
J.P. Haverty/R. Havell the Elder & Younger (11,650)*(group)*

Larrey, Dominique Jean
P.J. David D'Angers (8166)

Las Casas
J. Barry/J. Barry (20,722)(14)*(group)*

La Touche, M.P., David (Digues De)
H.D. Hamilton/J. Fittler (10,897)
H.D. Hamilton/J.K. Sherwin (10,896)
F. Wheatley/J. Collyer (11,644)*(group)*
F. Wheatley/J. Collyer (11,826)*(group)*

La Touche, Elizabeth (Countess of Lanesborough; wife of 3rd Earl)
H. Hone/F. Bartolozzi (10,309)

Lauzun, Antoine De Caumont, Duke of
R. De Hooghe/R. De Hooghe (11,655)*(group)*

Lawes, Judith Maria (Viscountess Carhampton; wife of 1st Viscount later 1st Earl Carhampton)
J.K. Sherwin/J.K. Sherwin (11,657-11,658)*(group)*
J.K. Sherwin/J.K. Sherwin (11,827-11,829)*(group)*

Lawes Lutterell, Henry (2nd Earl Carhampton)
J. Petrie/P. Maguire (11,211)

Lawless, Jack
J. Doyle/J. Doyle (10,035)*(group)*
English School 1828/English School 1828 (11,401)
J.P. Haverty/J.P. Haverty (11,020)*(group)*

Lawrence, Sir Thomas
L. Gahagan (8068)
T. Lawrence/F.C. Lewis (11,420)

Leberecht, Gebhard (Field-Marshal Blücher)
English School c.1815/English School 1815 (11,366)

Lees, Bt., Rev. Sir Harcourt (Rector of Killarey, Co. Down)
T.C. Thompson/?Irish School c.1824 (10,604)
T.C. Thompson/H. Meyer (10,909)

Leeson, Edward Nugent (6th Earl of Milltown)
H. Thornycroft (8098)
H. Thornycroft (8205)

Le Fanu, Brinsley Sheridan
Irish School 1873 (8275)

Leighlin and Ferns, P. Bishop of (Thomas Elrington; Provost of Trinity College Dublin)
T. Foster/W. Ward the Elder (10,249)
T. Foster/W.J. Ward the Elder (20,126)

Leinster, Augustus Frederick FitzGerald, 3rd Duke of
S. Catterson Smith the Elder/G. Sanders (10,468)

Leinster, Caroline, Duchess of (née Lady Lutherford-Leveson-Gower; wife of 4th Duke)
L. Lehmann/C.A. Tomkins (10,905)

Leinster, Charles William FitzGerald, 4th Duke of
L. Lehmann/C.A. Tomkins (10,898)

Leinster, Charlotte Augusta, Duchess of (née Stanhope; wife of 3rd Duke)
J.P. Haverty/R. Havell the Elder & Younger (11,650)*(group)*

Leinster, Emilia Mary, Duchess of (née Lennox; wife of 1st Duke)
J. Reynolds/R. Josey (10,903)
J. Reynolds/J. McArdall (10,344)

Leinster, Emilia Olivia, Duchess of (née Usher St George; wife of 2nd Duke)
J. Reynolds/W. Dickinson (10,346)

Leinster, James FitzGerald, 1st Duke of
(20th Earl of Kildare)
R. Pool & J. Cash/I. Taylor the Elder (10,041)(26)*(group)*
J. Reynolds/J. McArdell (10,088)

Leinster, Meinhardt Schomberg, Duke of
(Baron Tara; Earl of Bangor; 3rd Duke of Schomberg)
G. Kneller/J. Smith (10,238)

Leinster, William Robert FitzGerald, 2nd Duke of
Irish School c.1785 (8256)
J. Reynolds/J. Dixon (10,467)
M.A. Shee/C. Turner (10,487)
J.K. Sherwin/J.K. Sherwin (11,657-11,658)*(group)*
J.K. Sherwin/J.K. Sherwin (11,827-11,829)*(group)*
G.C. Stuart/C.H. Hodges (10,092)
G.C. Stuart/Irish School c.1790 (10,635)
G.C. Stuart/Irish School c.1795 (10,079)
F. Wheatley/J. Collyer (11,644)*(group)*
F. Wheatley/J. Collyer (11,826)*(group)*

Leland, John
A. Lee/G. Byrne (10,603)
A. Lee/J. Chapman (10,910)

Leland, Thomas
J. Reynolds/J. Dean (10,090)
J. Reynolds/J. Dean (10,911)

Le Maistre, Mrs Stephen
(née Mary Roche; Baroness Nolcken)
E.F. Calze/V. Green (10,382)

Lendrum, Rev. Thomas
Irish School 18C/R. Earlom (10,912)

Lennard, Elizabeth
(Countess of Meath)
P. Mignard/P. Van Somer the Younger (10,321)

Lennox, Charles
(4th Duke of Richmond; Lord Lieutenant of Ireland; Governor General of Canada)
J. Jackson/H. Meyer (10,270)
E. Scott/C. Knight (11,051)

Lennox, Charles
(9th Duke of Richmond; Lord Lieutenant of Ireland)
Irish School 1808/Irish School 1808 (11,735)*(group)*

Lennox, Emilia Mary
(Duchess of Leinster, wife of 1st Duke)
J. Reynolds/R. Josey (10,903)
J. Reynolds/J. McArdell (10,344)

Lerey, Brigadier
R. De Hooghe/R. De Hooghe (11,655)*(group)*

Leslie, John
(10th Earl of Rothes; Commander-in-Chief in Ireland)
J. Reynolds/J. McArdell (11,056)

Leslie, Rev. Charles
A.S. Belle/English School 18C (10,607)
A.S. Belle/?J. Simon (11,413)

L'Estrange, Rev. F.J.
J.P. Haverty/J.P. Haverty (11,020)*(group)*

Levy, Ron
?Irish School 19C/T. Weger (10,900)

Lewis, Prince
(son of King of Bohemia)
Continental School c.1620/C. Turner (10,869)*(group)*

Lifford, James Hewitt, 1st Baron and 1st Viscount
W. Madden/W. Dickinson (10,479)
J. Reynolds/R. Dunkarton (10,484)
J.K. Sherwin/J.K. Sherwin (11,657-11,658)*(group)*
J.K. Sherwin/J.K. Sherwin (11,827-11,829)*(group)*

Limerick, Thomas Barnard, P. Bishop of
G. Dance/W. Daniell (10,049)

Limerick, Charles Graves, P. Bishop of
J.H. Foley (8252)

Limerick, John Webb, P. Bishop of
T. Lawrence/T. Lupton (20,122)
G. Richmond/H. Adlard (10,631)

Limerick, George Webb, P. Bishop of
?English School 17C/T. Cross the Elder (10,304)

Limerick, Edmund Henry Pery, 1st Earl of
G. Dawe/T.A. Dean (10,894)

Lincoln, Elizabeth, Countess of
(née Fitzgerald; daughter of 9th Earl of Kildare, 2nd wife of 1st Earl of Lincoln)
English School 16C/D. Humphrey (11,135)

Lindsey, Colonel
J.P. Haverty/R. Havell the Elder & Younger (11,650)*(group)*

Lingen, William
(Irish Secretary of State)
A. Lee/J. Brooks (10,899)

Linley, Elizabeth Ann
(Mrs Richard Brinsley Sheridan)
J. Reynolds/W. Dickinson (10,381)
J. Reynolds/T. Watson (10,351)
J. Reynolds/T. Watson (10,355)

Lisburne, Lucy, Viscountess of
(née Brydges; wife of 1st Viscount)
G. Kneller/J. Smith (10,904)

Liverpool, Robert Banks Jenkinson, 2nd Earl of
(British Prime Minister)
T. Lawrence & A. Wivell/?T.A. Prior (11,384)

Lloyd, Bartholemew
T. Kirk (8043)
H. O'Neill/C. Turner (10,061)

Locke, John
J. Barry/J. Barry (20,722)(8)*(group)*

Locke-King, M.P., John
English School 19C/English School 19C (20,620)

Londonderry, Rev. George Walker, Governor of
R. De Hooghe/R. De Hooghe (11,655)*(group)*
English School 17C/E. Nurzer (11,260)
Irish School 18C/Irish School 18C (11,259)
G. Kneller/A. Haelwegh (10,224)
G. Kneller/P. Vanderbanck (10,565)
J. Wyck/J. Brooks (11,652)*(group)*

Londonderry, Robert Stewart, 1st Marquess of
(Viscount Castlereagh)
G. Dance the Younger/W. Daniell (10,902)
T. Lawrence/C. Turner (10,458)

Londonderry, Charles William Stewart, 3rd Marquess of
J. Bostok/J.J. Jenkins (10,913)

Londonderry, Frederick William Robert, 4th Marquess of (Viscount Castlereagh)
F. Kruger/F. Kruger (10,758)

Londonderry, Elizabeth Frances Charlotte, Marchioness of (née Jocelyn; wife of 4th Marquess; Viscountess Powerscourt, wife of 6th Viscount)
J. Ross/W.H. Mote (11,333)

Londonderry, Frances Anne, Marchioness of (née Vane-Tempest; 2nd wife of 3rd Marquess)
A.E. Chalon/J. Thomson (10,336)

Long, William
F. Wheatley/J. Collyer (11,644)*(group)*
F. Wheatley/J. Collyer (11,826)*(group)*

Lord, Percival Barton
C. Grey/J. Kirkwood (11,292)

Louis XIII (King of France)
French School 1634/French School 1634 (20,235-20,836)

Louis XIV (King of France)
J. Barry/J. Barry (20,722)(10)*(group)*
R. De Hooghe/R. De Hooghe (11,847)(12)*(group)*

Louisa, Princess (daughter of King of Bohemia)
Continental School c.1620/C. Turner (10,869)*(group)*

Louth, Lord
English School 18C/English School 18C (10,606)

Lover, Samuel
C. Baugniet/C. Baugniet (10,901)
English School c.1860/English School c.1860 (10,608)
Irish School 19C (8234)

Lowry-Corry, Juliana (née Butler; Countess Belmore, wife of 2nd Earl)
J.P. Haverty/R. Havell the Elder & Younger (11,650)*(group)*

Lowry-Corry, Lady Margaret (née Butler)
R. Cosway/J.R. Smith (11,665)

Lucan, Patrick Sarsfield, Earl of
Lady M. Bingham/McDowall (11,291)
Lady M. Bingham/J.B. Tilliard (10,093)

Lucan, Charles Bingham, 1st Baron and 1st Earl of
J. Reynolds/J. Jones (10,089)

Lucas, M.P., Charles
T. Hickey/P. Halpin (10,091)
W. Jones/A. Miller (10,074)
W. Jones/A. Miller (10,480)
J. Reynolds/J. McArdell (10,060)

Lutherford-Leveson-Gower, Lady Caroline (Duchess of Leinster, wife of 4th Duke)
L. Lehmann/C.A. Tomkins (10,905)

Luttrell, Henry Lawes (2nd Earl of Carhampton)
J. Petrie/P. Maguire (11,211)

Luttrell, Simon (1st Earl of Carhampton)
Irish School 18C/Irish School 18C (11,196)
Irish School 1768/81//Irish School 1768/81 (11,212)

Lycurgus
J. Barry/J. Barry (20,722)(9)*(group)*

Lyndhurst, John Singleton Copley, 1st Baron (Lord Chancellor)
J. Doyle/J. Doyle (11,544)(63)*(group)*
T. Lawrence & A. Wivell/?T.A. Prior (11,384)*(group)*

Lyons, Mrs (née Augusta Blanche Bury)
C.L. Eastlake/W.H. Mote (10,891)

Lyons, Thomas
J.P. Haverty/M. & N. Hanhart (11,857)*(group)*

Lysaght, Edward
J. Cullen/P. Maguire (10,602)

Lyster, John
J. Comerford/Irish School 1825 (10,892)

Maastrent, Heinrich (Count of Solms)
T. Maas/T. Maas (10,003)*(group)*
T. Maas/T. Maas (20,800)*(group)*
J. Wyck/J. Brooks (11,652)*(group)*

McArdell, James
J. McArdell/R. Earlom (10,470)

Macartney, George Macartney, 1st Earl (Chief Secretary for Ireland)
M. Brown/H. Hudson (10,246)
S. De Koster/C. Townley (10,953)
H. Edridge/L. Schiavonetti (10,951)
T. Hickey/J. Hall (10,952)

Macartney, James
J. Keenan/T.W. Fry (10,950)

Macbride, Dr David
Reynolds of Dublin/W.H. Lizars (10,672)
Reynolds of Dublin/J.T. Smith (10,426)

Macbride, Captain John
J. Northcote/J. Fittler (10,473)

McCracken, Henry Joy (United Irishman)
?J. Comerford/J.H. Lynch (11,226)

MacDiarmada, Seán
A. Power (8007)

MacDonagh, Thomas
O. Kelly (8008)

MacDonnell, Anne Katherine (Countess of Antrim)
J.P. Haverty/R. Havell the Elder & Younger (11,650)*(group)*
J. Mee/H.R. Cook (11,119)

MacDowell, Patrick
C. Grey/Irish School 1851 (10,666)

MacGuire, Richard
J.J. Barralet/J. Ward the Elder (11,654)*(group)*

McKenny Bt., Sir Thomas (Lord Mayor of Dublin)
W. Brocas/W. Brocas (10,965)
T.C. Thompson/C. Turner (10,427)
T.C. Thompson/C. Turner (10,966)

MacKercher, Daniel
J. Pope-Stevens the Elder/J. Brooks (10,115)

Macklin, Charles
D. Dodd/J. Walker (11,225)
J.C. Lochée/J. Corner (11,224)
J. Opie/H. Brocas the Elder (11,223)

McLaughlin, M.P., Mr C.
J.P. Haverty/J.P. Haverty (11,857)*(group)*

Maclise, Daniel
T. Bridgford/Irish School 1847 (11,237)
J. Mayall/D.J. Pound (10,927)
J. Thomas (8113)
J. Thomas (8184)

McLoghlin, Mrs Eliza
A. Gilbert (8077)

McMahon, Rev. Dr
English School 1828/English School 1828 (11,401)*(group)*

McMahon Bt., M.P., Sir John
T. Lawrence/C. Turner (10,954)

McManus, Terence Bellew
L. Gluckman/Irish School 19C (20,217)
L. Gluckman/H. O'Neill (10,121)
L. Gluckman/H. O'Neill (10,553)
L. Gluckman/H. O'Neill (11,940)

MacNally, Leonard
Irish School 18C/P. Maguire (11,221)

MacNeven, M.P., William James
J.D. Herbert/T.W. Huffam (10,671)

Macswinny, Owen
P. Van Bleeck/P. Van Bleeck (10,112)
J.P. Van Loo/J. Faber the Younger (10,120)

Madden, Richard Robert
?A.F.J. Claudet/T.W. Huffam (10,660)
?A.F.J. Claudet/T.W. Huffam (10,661)
J. Hardy/T.W. Huffam (10,934)

Madden, Rev. Samuel
?J. Brooks/J. Brooks (10,117)
R. Hunter/S. Harding (10,670)
R. Hunter/R. Purcell (10,923)
R. Hunter/R. Purcell (10,924)
J. Van Nost the Younger/C. Spooner (10,101)
After J. Van Nost the Younger (8201)

Madura, Bishop of
(Bonaventure Gifford)
H. Hysing/T. Burford (10,817)

Magellan, Ferñao de
J. Barry/J. Barry (20,722)(14)*(group)*

Magill, Theodosia
(Countess of Clanwilliam; wife of the 1st Earl)
J. Reynolds/J. Watson (10,383)

Maginn, William
D. Maclise/D. Maclise (10,288)
S. Skillin/J. Kirkwood (10,287)

Maguire, Count John Sigismund
J. Tusch/L. Zucchi (10,084)

Maguire, Sir Richard
J.J. Barralet/W. Ward the Elder (11,654)*(group)*

Maguire, Fr. Thomas
C. O'Donnell/H. Brocas the Elder (10,964)
J.P. Haverty/J.P. Haverty (10,963)

Mahon M.P., Colonel Charles James Patrick
('The O'Gorman Mahon')
J. Adams-Acton (8109)
English School 1828/English School 1828 (11,401)
J.P. Haverty/J.P. Haverty (10,969)*(group)*

Malone, M.P., Anthony
(Chancellor of the Exchequer in Ireland)
Irish School c.1750/C. Spooner (10,221)
J. Reynolds/J.R. Smith (10,472)

Malone, Edmond
J. Reynolds/C. Knight (10,662)
J. Reynolds/C. Knight (10,663)
J. Reynolds/C. Knight (10,664)

Manners, Charles
(4th Duke of Rutland; Lord Lieutenant of Ireland)
H. Hone/English School 1790 (11,322)
Irish School c.1784/Irish School 1784 (11,321)
J. Reynolds/W. Dickinson (10,490)

Manners, Thomas Manners-Sutton, 1st Baron
(Lord Chancellor of Irelnad)
J. Comerford/A. Cardon (11,220)
J. Comerford/A. Cardon (20,357)
Irish School c.1811/Irish School 1811 (11,851)*(group)*

Mannix, Dr
A. Power (8099)

Mant, Richard
(P. Bishop of Down, Connor & Dromore)
M. Cregan/G.R. Ward (10,449)

Marcus Aurelius
J. Barry/J. Barry (20,722)(9)*(group)*

Marie De Medici
(Queen of Henri IV of France)
P.P. Rubens/*J.M. Nattier*/A. Trouvain (20,678)(6)*(group)*

Marius, Caius
W. Linton/J.T. Willmore (20,139)

Marlay, Richard
(P. Bishop of Waterford)
H.D. Hamilton/J. Heath (10,286)

Marlborough, John Churchill, 1st Duke of
G. Kneller/P. Tanjé (10,994)

Marsden, William
T. Phillips/M. Turner (10,926)

Marsh, Sir Henry
(President of the Royal College of Physicians of Ireland)
S. Catterson Smith the Elder/G. Sanders (10,483)

Marsham, Robert
(2nd Baron Romney)
J. Barry/J. Barry (20,722)(5)*(group)*

Martin, Lady Helen
(née Faucit; wife of Sir Theodore Martin)
J.H. Foley (8042)

Martin, John
L. Gluckman/H. O'Neill (10,102)
L. Gluckman/H. O'Neill (10,526)
L. Gluckman/H. O'Neill (11,934)

Martin, Sir Samuel
H.W. Phillips/W. Walker (10,958)

Mary, Princess of Orange
(Queen of William III, King of England)
R. De Hooghe/R. De Hooghe (11,849)(5)*(group)*
R. De Hooghe/R. De Hooghe (11,882)*(group)*
G. Kneller/D. Malone (20,124)
P. Lely/A. Blooteling (11,264)

Mary, Princess
(daughter of Charles I, King of England)
A. Van Dyck/A. Browne (10,756)*(group)*
A. Van Dyck/R. Cooper (10,546)*(group)*

Mary, Princess
(daughter of James I, King of England)
Continental School c.1620/C. Turner (10,869)*(group)*

Mary II
(Queen of England)
English School 1692/J. Goldar (20,836)*(group)*
English School 17C/J. Gole (10,340)
English School 17C/B. Lens (10,921)
J. Vandervaart/W. Faithorne the Younger (10,385)
W. Wissing/B. Lens (10,922)

Mary, Queen of Scots
H.J. Fradelle/A. Duncan (20,057)
J. Barry/J. Barry (20,712)(9)*(group)*

Mary Beatrice of Modena
(Queen of James II, King of England)
R. De Hooghe/R. De Hooghe (11,847)(2-4)*(group)*
G. Kneller/J. Smith (10,929)

Mason, M.P., The Hon. John Monck
(Commissioner of Revenue for Ireland)
S. Harding/C. Knight (10,920)

Mathew, The Hon. Montague
English School 18C/English School 18C (10,659)
J. Petrie/J. Heath (10,936)

Mathew, Rev. Theobald
Allen/Allen (10,915)
A. Buck/J. Kirkwood (10,673)
D. MacDonald/D. MacDonald (10,916)
S. West/W.O. Geller (10,451)

Maturin, Rev. Charles Robert
W. Brocas/H. Meyer (10,658)
W. Brocas/H. Meyer (10,937)

Maule, Henry
(P. Bishop of Meath)
A. Lee/A. Miller (10,112)
A. Lee/A. Miller (10,113)

Maurice, Edward
(P. Bishop of Ossory)
T. Hudson/J. McArdell (10,114)

Maurice, Prince
(son of King of Bohemia)
Continental School c.1620/C. Turner (10,869)*(group)*

Mavrondi, Chevalier
M. Brown/R. Orme (20,104)*(group)*

Maxwell, General Thomas
J.B. Closterman/J. Smith (10,930)

Maxwell, Rev. William Hamilton
C. Grey/J. Kirkwood (10,665)

May, Frederick
S. Murphy (8245)

May, George Augustus Chichester
(Lord Chief Justice of Ireland)
English School c.1877/M. & N. Hanhart (10,429)

Mayne, Sir Richard
English School 19C/?T. Langer (10,918)

Mayo, John Bourke, 1st Earl of
(1st Baron Naas)
R. Hunter/W. Dickinson (10,454)

Mayo, Joseph Deane Bourke, 3rd Earl of
(P. Archbishop of Tuam)
J. Reynolds/J.R. Smith (10,438)

Meade, Lady Selina
(daughter of 2nd Earl Clanwilliam)
T. Lawrence/G.T. Doo (10,402)

Meagher, Thomas Francis
L. Gluckman/H. O' Neill (10,523)
L. Gluckman/H. O' Neill (11,938)
L. Gluckman/Read & Co. (10,306)

Mears, Rev. John
R. Hunter/J. McArdell (10,220)

Meath, Elizabeth, Countess of
(née Lennard, wife of 3rd Earl)
P. Mignard/P. Van Somer the Younger (10,321)

Meath, Henry Maule, P. Bishop of
A. Lee/A. Miller (10,113)
A. Lee/A. Miller (10,122)

Mecklenburgh-Strelitz, Charlotte Sophia of
(Queen of George III of England)
A. Kauffman/T. Burke (10,379)
T. Frye/T. Frye (10,551)

Medici, Cosimo
J. Barry/J. Barry (20,722)(10)*(group)*

Melbourne, William Lamb, 2nd Viscount
(Secretary of State for Ireland; British Prime Minister)
J. Doyle/J. Doyle (11,544)(55)*(group)*
J. Doyle/J. Doyle (11,544)(58)*(group)*
J. Doyle/J. Doyle (11,544)(59)*(group)*
J. Doyle/J. Doyle (11,544)(61)*(group)*
J. Doyle/J. Doyle (11,544)(64)*(group)*
J. Doyle/J. Doyle (11,544)(65)*(group)*
J. Doyle/J. Doyle (11,544)(66)*(group)*
J. Doyle/J. Doyle (11,891)*(group)*
T. Lawrence & English School c.1830/?T.A. Prior (11,341)*(group)*

Mercoeur, Nicolas De Vaudémont, Duc de
Attrib. to B. Prieur (8036)

Metcalfe, Eleanor or Mary
N. Hone the Elder/J. Finlayson (10,353)

Methuen, John
(Lord Chancellor of Ireland)
English School c.1774/W. Humphrey (11,228)

Miley, Rev. Dr
J.P. Haverty/J.P. Haverty (11,857)*(group)*

Mill-Cushin
(Jack Haugh; Irish Beggar from Mount Mellick)
Irish School c.1750/?M. Hanbury (10,141)

Miller, George
C. Grey/J. Kirkwood (11,227)

Miller, Joe
C. Stoppelaer/A. Miller (10,917)

Milltown, Edward Nugent Leeson, 6th Earl of
H. Thornycroft (8098)
H. Thornycroft (8205)

Mitchell, Mr A.
J.P. Haverty/R. Havell the Elder & Younger (11,650)*(group)*

Mitchel, John
T. Farrell (8133)
L. Gluckman/M. & N. Hanhart (10,119)
L. Gluckman/M. & N. Hanhart (10,524)

Modena, Mary of
(Queen of James II, King of England)
P. Lely/J. Griffier the Elder (10,364)

Moira, Francis Rawdon-Hastings, 2nd Earl of
(1st Marquess of Hastings)
English School c.1780/W. Ridley (10,656-10,657)
English School c.1813/Irish School 1813 (10,655)
J. Gillray/J. Gillray (11,545)*(group)*
H.D. Hamilton/J. Heath (10,947)
J. Hoppner/*F. Bartolozzi*/H. Landseer (10,949)
S. Percy (8160)
J. Reynolds/J.K. Baldrey (11,047)
J. Reynolds/J. Jones (10,503)
J. Reynolds/J. Jones (10,946)
J. Reynolds/P. Maguire (10,654)
J. Reynolds/R. Stanier (10,653)
M.A. Shee/G. Clint (10,948)
G.C. Stuart/J. Collyer (10,118)

Moira, Helena, Countess of
(née Lady Percival; wife of 1st Baron Rawdon, later 1st Earl of Moira)
J. Latham/J. Brooks (10,914)

Molesworth, Robert Molesworth, 1st Viscount
T. Gibson/P. Pelham (10,012)

Molyneux, William
R. Home/?Irish School 18C (10,931)

Moncrieff, Richard
F. Wheatley/J. Collyer (11,644)*(group)*
F. Wheatley/J. Collyer (11,644)*(group)*

Montagu, Henry
(6th Baron Rokeby)
F. Grant/G.J. Zobell (11,043)

Montague, Mrs Elizabeth
J. Barry/J. Barry (20,722)(5)*(group)*

Montalt, Lady
J.K. Sherwin/J.K. Sherwin (11,657-11,658)*(group)*
J.K. Sherwin/J.K. Sherwin (11,827-11,829)*(group)*

Monteagle, Thomas Spring Rice M.P., 1st Baron
(Chancellor of the Exchequer)
J. Comerford/R. Cooper (11,313)
J. Comerford/R. Cooper (11,314)
J. Doyle/J. Doyle (11,544)(64)*(group)*
J. Doyle/J. Doyle (11,544)(65)*(group)*
J. Doyle/J. Doyle (11,891)*(group)*
J. Linnell the Elder/J. Linnell the Elder (11,044)
L. MacDonald (8203)

Montgomerie, Archibald William
(13th Earl of Eglington & Winton; Lord Lieutenant of Ireland)
S. Catterson Smith the Elder/G. Sanders (10,505)

Montgomery, Rev. Richard
C.W. Peale/E. MacKenzie (10,674)

Montijo De Guzman, Dona Eugenia Maria de
(Empress Eugenie, wife of Napoleon III, Emperor of France)
J.B. Carpeaux (8040)

Moody, John
T. Hardy/T. Hardy (10,103)
J.J. Zoffany/G.F.L. Marchi (10,471)

Moore, Charles
(6th Earl and 1st Marquess of Drogheda)
J. Reynolds/R.B. Parkes (10,720)
J.K. Sherwin/J.K. Sherwin (11,657-11,658)*(group)*
J.K. Sherwin/J.K. Sherwin (11,827-11,829)*(group)*

Moore, George
Irish School 1933 (8129)

Moore, Lorenzo
J.K. Sherwin/J.K. Sherwin (11,657-11,658)*(group)*
J.K. Sherwin/J.K. Sherwin (11,827-11,829)*(group)*

Moore, Thomas
J. Comerford/Irish School 1825 (10,961)
English School c.1833/B. Holl (10,962)
J. Hogan (8061)
J. Hogan (8244)
J. Hogan (8284)
Irish School 1790s/Irish School early 19C (11,235)
Irish School c.1800/H.H. Meyer (10,960)
J. Jackson/J. Thomson (11,236)
D. Maclise/J. Kirkwood (11,423)
D. Maclise/D. Maclise (10,675)
C. Moore (8067)

Moray, James Stewart, Earl of
H. Melville/R. Staines (20,271)*(group)*

More, Sir Thomas
J. Barry/J. Barry (20,772)(8)*(group)*

Moreau, Jean Victor
English School c.1815/English School 1815 (11,365)

Morgan, Lady Sydney
(née Owenson; wife of Sir Thomas Morgan)
W. Behnes/H. Meyer (11,553)
T. Lawrence/J. Godby (11,551)
S. Lover/R. Cooper (10,959)
C.T. Wageman/H.H. Meyer (11,229)

Morgan, M.P., Sir Thomas
A. Van Dyck/*C.W. Bampfylde*/English School 1814 (20,115)

Mornington, Anne, Countess of
(née Hill; wife of 1st Earl)
Lady P. Burghersh/T. Hodgetts (10,399)

Mornington, Richard Wellesley, 2nd Earl of
(1st Marquess Wellesley; Lord Lieutenent of Ireland)
C. Moore (8202)
J.K. Sherwin/J.K. Sherwin (11,657-11,658)*(group)*
J.K. Sheriwn/J.K. Sheriwn (11,827-11,829)*(group)*

Morpeth, George Howard, Viscount
J. Doyle/J. Doyle (11,544)(62)*(group)*
J. Doyle/J. Doyle (11,544)(67)*(group)*
J. Doyle/J. Doyle (11,853)*(group)*

Moss, Mr
De Grifft/H. Brocas the Elder (10,667)

Mosse, Dr Bartholomew
Continental School 1730s/Irish School c.1847 (10,300)

Mossop, William Stephen
W.S. Mossop/?W.S. Mossop (11,222)

Mount-Earl, Margaret Mary, Viscountess (née Coghlan; wife of Viscount Mount-Earl, later 1st Earl of Dunraven)
T. Gainsborough/J.R. Smith (10,376)

Mountgarret, Harriet, Viscountess (née Butler; wife of 11th Viscount)
R. Cosway/J.R. Smith (11,665)

Mountjoy, Charles Blount, 8th Baron (Earl of Devonshire; Lord Deputy of Ireland)
P. Van Somer/V. Green (10,443)

Mountjoy, Luke Gardiner, Baron & 1st Viscount
J.D. Herbert/H. Brocas the Elder (10,291)
Irish School c.1778/Irish School 1778 (11,381)
F. Wheatley/J. Collyer (11,644)*(group)*
F. Wheatley/J. Collyer (11,826)*(group)*

Mountsandford, George Sandford, 3rd Baron
F. Newenham/F. C. Lewis (10,928)

Mountstuart, John Stuart, Baron (1st Marquess of Bute)
N. Hone the Elder/W. Baillie (10,942)
N. Hone the Elder/W. Baillie (10,944)
N. Hone the Elder/W. Baillie (10,945)

Moynan, Francis (R.C. Bishop of Cork)
Irish School c.1800/English School 1816 (11,231)

Mulready, William
C.W. Cope/C.W. Cope (10,957)

Mulvany, George Francis
J. Watkins (8032)

Munro, Henry
T. Rowlandson/T. Rowlandson (11,409)

Murphy, Arthur
N. Dance/*J. Jackson*/E. Scriven (10,925)
N. Dance/W. Ridley (10,669)
N. Dance/W. Ward the Elder (10,474)
S. Drummond/Irish School 1798 (10,668)

Murphy, Fr. John
Irish School 18C/?E. Lyons (10,232)
Irish School 18C/C. Lyons (10,919)

Murray, Dr Daniel
J. Hogan (8034)

Murray, M.P., Sir George (Commander-in-Chief in Ireland)
T. Lawrence/J. Cochran (10,995)

Muskerry, Robert Tilson Deane, 1st Baron
J.K. Sherwin/J.K. Sherwin (11,657-11,658)*(group)*
J.K. Sherwin/J.K. Sherwin (11,827-11,829)*(group)*

Naas, John Bourke, 1st Baron (1st Earl of Mayo)
R. Hunter/W. Dickinson (10,454)

Nagle, Admiral Sir Edmund
F.P. Stephanoff/E. Scriven (11,404)

Napier, General Sir Charles James
W.F.P. Francis/English School 19C (11,001)

Napier Bt., M.P., Sir Joseph (Lord Chancellor of Ireland)
C. Grey/Irish School 1853 (11,421)
C. Grey/Irish School 1853 (11,422)

Napoleon I (Emperor of France)
A. Canova/A. Ricciani (20,714)(16)
English School c.1815/English School 1815 (11,353)

Nares, Sir George
N. Hone the Elder/W. Dickinson (11,002)

Nary, Dr Cornelius
?J. Brooks/J. Brooks (20,802)
English School early 18C/A. Miller (10,081)

Nassau, Henry (Count D'Auverquerck)
G. Kneller/J. Smith (10,785)

Nelson, Admiral Horatio (1st Viscount Nelson)
J. Hoppner/C. Turner (10,453)

Netherlands, King William II of (Prince William of Orange)
English School c.1815/English School 1816 (11,356)

Newcome, William (P. Archbishop of Armagh)
H.D. Hamilton/C. Knight (10.082)

Newenham, M.P., Sir Edward
Irish School c.1778/Irish School 1778 (11,342)
F. Wheatley/J. Collyer (11,644)*(group)*
F. Wheatley/J. Collyer (11,826)*(group)*

Newport, Robert Jocelyn, Baron (1st Viscount Jocelyn; Lord Chancellor of Ireland)
?J. Brooks/J. Brooks (10,434)

Newport, Bt., Sir John (Lord Chancellor of Ireland)
J. Ramsay/T.G. Lupton (10,094)

Newton, Sir Isaac
J. Barry/J. Barry (20,722)(7)*(group)*

Nielson, Samuel (United Irishman)
C. Byrne/T.W. Huffam (10,646)
C. Byrne/T.W. Huffam (10,647)

Nolan, Michael
English School c.1819/English School 1819 (10,098)

?Nolan, William
English School 1840/English School 1840 (11,040)

Nolcken, Mary, Baroness (née Roche; wife of Mr Stephen Le Maistre)
E.F. Calze/V. Green (10,382)

Norbury, John Toler, 1st Earl of (Lord Chief Justice of the Common Pleas in Ireland)
English School 1790s/English School 1790s (10,652)
Irish School c.1811/Irish School 1811 (11,851)*(group)*

Norfolk, Thomas Howard, 4th Duke of
English School c.1560/J. Houbraken (11,942)

Normandy, Constantine Phipps, 1st Marquess of (Lord Lieutenant of Ireland)
J. Doyle/J. Doyle (11,544)(60)*(group)*
J. Doyle/J. Doyle (11,544)(62)*(group)*

Normanton, Charles Agar, 1st Earl of (1st Viscount Somerton; Archbishop of Cashel; Archbishop of Dublin)
G.C. Stuart/W. Say (10,083)

North, Lord Frederick (British Prime Minister; 2nd Earl of Guilford)
N. Dance/T. Burke (10,999)
N. Dance/T. Burke (11,000

Northampton, Simon Luttrell, 1st Earl of
?Irish School 18C/?Irish School 18C (11,196)

Northumberland, Elizabeth, Duchess of (née Seymour; wife of 1st Duke)
J. Barry/J. Barry (20,722)(5)*(group)*

Northumberland, Hugh Percy, 2nd Earl and 1st Duke of (Lord Lieutenant of Ireland)
W. Hoare/W. Hoare (11,230)

Norwich, Samuel Hings, Bishop of
T.H. Maguire/T.H. Maguire (10,871)

Nugent, Lady Anne Lucy (née Poulet; wife of 3rd Baron Nugent)
T. Lawrence/R.J. Lane (10,941)

Nugent, George Frederick (7th Earl of Westmeath)
Irish School c.1793/Irish School 1793 (11,245)
J.K. Sherwin/J.K. Sherwin (11,657-11,658)*(group)*
J.K. Sherwin/J.K. Sherwin (11,827-11,829)*(group)*

Nugent-Grenville-Temple, George (2nd Earl Temple; 1st Marquess of Buckingham; Lord Lieutenant of Ireland)
T. Gainsborough/J.K. Sherwin (10,448)
R. Hunter/W. Sadler (10,417)
J.K. Sherwin/J.K. Sherwin (11,657-11,658)*(group)*
J.K. Sherwin/J.K. Sherwin (11,827-11,829)*(group)*

Nugent, Count Lavell G.
J. Kriehuber/J. Krichuber (10,938)

Nugent, Thomas (6th Earl of Westmeath)
J.K. Sherwin/J.K. Sherwin (11,657-11,658)*(group)*
J.K. Sherwin/J.K. Sherwin (11,827-11,829)*(group)*

Numa Pompilius
J. Barry/J. Barry (20,722)(9)*(group)*

O'Brien, Lady Susan Sarah Louisa (née Fox-Strangeways, daughter of 1st Earl of Ilchester; wife of William O'Brien)
F. Cotes/J. Watson (10,332)

O'Brien, James (United Irishman)
A.F.J. Claudet/English School 1846 (10,582)
Irish School c.1800/Irish School c.1800 (10,581)

O'Brien, M.E.
Irish School c.1795/Irish School 1795 (10,578)

O'Brien, Mary (Lady Fitzgerald; wife of 19th Earl of Kildare)
R. Pool, J. Cash/I. Taylor the Elder (10,041)(26)*(group)*

O'Brien, Mary (Countess of Orkney, daughter of future 1st Marquess of Thomond)
J. Reynolds/J. Dixon (10,395)

O'Brien, Murrough (1st Marquess of Thomond)
J. Hoppner/P.W. Reynolds the Elder (10,469)
J.K. Sherwin/J.K. Sherwin (11,657-11,658)*(group)*
J.K. Sherwin/J.K. Sherwin (11,827-11,829)*(group)*
Marchioness of Thomond/R.M. Meadows (10,147)

O'Brien, Nelly
J. Reynolds/English School 1760s (10,577)
J. Reynolds/S. Okey (10,339)
J. Reynolds/C. Spooner (10,337)

O'Brien, Mr P.
J.P. Haverty/J.P. Haverty (11,857)*(group)*

O'Brien, William
F. Cotes/J. Watson (10,078)

O'Brien, William (2nd Marquess of Thomond)
Titani/S. Freeman (11,000)
Titani/S. Freeman (11,010)

O'Brien, M.P., William S.
J.P. Haverty/J.P. Haverty (11,857)*(group)*

O'Carolan, Turlough
F. Bindon/J. Martyn (10,279)
Irish School c.1809/Irish School 1809 (11,343)

O'Conaire, Padraig
A. Power (8114)

O'Connell, M.P., Daniel
T.H. Carrick/W. Holl the Younger (10,289)
T.H. Carrick/W. Holl the Younger (10,597)
T.H. Carrick/W. Holl the Younger (10,972)
S. Catterson Smith the Elder/R. Cooper (10,981)
?S. Catterson Smith the Elder/Irish School c.1830 (10,977)
J. Comerford/T. Heaphy (10,065)
A.G.G. D'Orsay (8142)
Doussin-Dubreuil/French School 19C (10,976)
Doussin-Dubreuil/J. Stadler (10,982)
J. Doyle/J. Doyle (10,035)*(group)*
J. Doyle/J. Doyle (11,403)*(group)*
J. Doyle/J. Doyle (11,544)(55)*(group)*
J. Doyle/J. Doyle (11,544)(56)*(group)*
J. Doyle/J. Doyle (11,544)(58)*(group)*
J. Doyle/J. Doyle (11,544)(59)*(group)*
J. Doyle/J. Doyle (11,544)(62-67)*(group)*
J. Doyle/J. Doyle (11,852-11,854)*(group)*
J. Doyle/J. Doyle (11,891)*(group)*
English School 1828/English School 1828 (11,401)
J.H. Foley (8200)
C. Grey/J. Peterkin (10,452)
J. Gubbins/B. O'Reilly (10,066)
J. Gubbins/J.P. Quigley (10,975)
J.P. Haverty/J.P. Haverty (11,857)*(group)*
J.P. Haverty/J.P. Haverty (10,969)*(group)*
J. Haverty/W. Ward the Younger (10,000)
R.M. Hodgetts/R.M. Hodgetts (10,968)
W.H. Holbrooke/W.H. Holbrooke (10,983)
W.H. Holbrooke/W.H. Holbrooke (11,240)*(group)*
Irish School c.1813/English School 1823 (10,600)
Irish School 19C/Irish School 19C (11,241)

Irish School c.1813/Irish School 1813 (10,598)
Irish School c.1813/Irish School 1813 (10,599)
Irish School c.1831/Irish School 1831 (10,973)
Irish School c.1840/Irish School c.1840 (11,862)
Irish School 1840s/Irish School 1840s (10,974)
Irish School c.1841/J. Kirkwood (10,596)
After J. Jones (8071)
J.S. Jordan (8237)
E.H. Latilla/H.B. Hall the Elder (10,967)
J. Lewis/J. Lewis (10,978)
J. Lewis/J. Lewis (10,979)
D. Maclise/D. Maclise (10,601)
?B. Mulrenin/B. Mulrenin (10,971)
H O'Neill/H. O'Neill (10,980)
H. Newton/Maclure & MacDonald (10,970)
W. Tell/W. Tell (10,512)
W. Tell/W. Tell (10,513)

O'Connell, Morgan
J.P. Haverty/J.P. Haverty (11,857)*(group)*

O'Connor, M.P., Arthur
(United Irishman)
B.F. Gerard/J. Godefroy (10,077)
J.D. Herbert/Irish School 1809 (10,589)
J.D. Herbert/W. Ward (10,067)
Irish School c.1797/Irish School 1797 (10,588)
Irish School c.1797/Irish School 1797 (10,590)

O'Connor M.P., Fergus
Irish School 1830s/W. Read (10,989)

O'Connor, Frank
S. Murphy (8082)

O'Connor, Phelim
Irish School c.1808/Irish School 1808 (10,587)

O'Connor, Roger
(United Irishman)
A. Buck/Irish School 1798 (10,585)
A. Wivell the Elder/W. Read (10,583)

O'Donoghue, Patrick
L. Gluckman/J.H. Lynch (10,939)
L. Gluckman/J.H. Lynch (10,990)

O'Flaherty, Liam
A. Stones (8305)

Ogilby, John
?P. Lely/P. Lombart (10,069)

Ogle, M.P., George
Irish School c.1777/Irish School 1777 (10,573)

O'Gorman Junior, Richard
L. Gluckman/H. O'Neill (10,522)
L. Gluckman/H. O'Neill (11,937)

The O'Gorman Mahon
(Charles James Patrick Mahon, M.P.)
J.A. Acton (8109)
English School 1828/English School 1828 (11,401)
J.P. Haverty/J.P. Haverty (10,969)

O'Grady, Standish
(1st Viscount Guillamore; Lord Chief Baron of the Exchequer in Ireland)
Irish School c.1811/Irish School 1811 (11,851)

O'Hagan, Thomas
J.P. Haverty/J.P. Haverty (11,857)*(group)*

O'Halloran, Sylvester
Irish School 18C/Irish School 1847 (10,591)

O'Hara, Kane
Irish School 1770s/E. Dorrell (10,593)

O'Kelly, Patrick
F.J. O'Kelly/Dean & Co. (10,594)
F.J. O'Kelly/Dean & Co. (10,595)

O'Higgins, Kevin
O. Sheppard (8046)

O'Leary, Rev. Arthur
Irish School 18C/Irish School 18C (10,571)
J. Murphy/W. Bond (10,572)
J. Murphy/G. Keating (10,250)

Oliver, Mr
J. Barralet/W. Ward the Elder (11,654)

O'Loghlen Bt., Sir Colman
J.P. Haverty/J.P. Haverty (11,857)*(group)*

O'Meara, Brigadier-General Thomas
Irish School c.1792/Irish School c.1793 (10,580)

O'Meara, Dr
T. Rowlandson/J. Hopwood the Younger (10,586)

O'Neill, Charles Henry St John O'Neill, 1st Earl
T. Phillips/J. Brown (10,992)

O'Neill, Eliza
(Lady Wrixon-Becher, wife of Sir William)
A.W. Devis/H. Meyer (10,409)
G. Dawe/F.C. Lewis the Elder (10,991)
S. Drummond/T. Blood (10,579)
J.J. Masquerier/W. Say (10,372)

O'Neill, John O'Neill, 1st Viscount
J.D. Herbert/S.W. Reynolds the Elder (10,446)
Irish School late 18C/P. Maguire (11,555)

O'Neill, The Hon. Mrs John
(née Henrietta Boyle)
M.W. Peters/J. Smith (10,348)

O'Neill, Sir Phelim
Irish School 17C/English School 17C (10,574)

O'Neill, John, 1st Viscount
J.D. Herbert/S.W. Reynolds (10,466)

O'Reilly, Mr
Irish School 18C/Irish School 18C (10,575)

Orford, Robert Walpole, 1st Earl of
J.B. Van Loo/J. Watson (20,731)(92)

Orford, Horatio Walpole, 4th Earl of
T. Lawrence/T. Evans (20,093)

Oriel, John Foster, 1st Baron
Irish School c.1790/Irish School c.1790 (11,132)
J.K. Sherwin/J.K. Sherwin (11,657-11,658)*(group)*
J.K. Sherwin/J.K. Sherwin (11,827-11,829)*(group)*
G.C. Stuart/C.H. Hodges (10,501)
G.C. Stuart/Irish School 1799 (11,131)
G.C. Stuart/P. Maguire (10,277)

Origen
J. Barry/J. Barry (20,722)(10)(*group*)

Orkney, George Hamilton, 1st Earl of
M. Maingaud/J. Houbraken (10,987)

Orkney, Mary, Countess of
(née O'Brien; daughter of future 1st Marquess of Thomond)
J. Reynolds/J. Dixon (10,395)

Orléans, Charlotte Elizabeth, Duchess of
(nee De Baulière)
H. Rigaud/F. Guibert (20,725)(76)

Orléans, Marie Amélie, Duchess of
(daughter of Ferdinand IV, King of Sicily)
F. Gérard/H. Grévedon (20,721)(1)

Ormonde, James Butler, 1st Duke of
G. Kneller/E. Scriven (10,533)
W. Wissing/R. Williams (10,001)

Ormonde, James Butler, 2nd Duke of
?M. Dahl/English School early 18C (10,568)
M. Dahl/P. Pelham (10,569)
M. Dahl/J. Simon (10,995)
English School 17C/P. Schenck (10,998)
G. Kneller/J.H. Robinson (10,570)
G. Kneller/J. Smith (10,002)
G. Kneller/J. Smith (10,996)
J. Wyck/J. Brooks (11,652)(*group*)

Ormonde, James Wandesford Butler, 1st Marquess of
(19th Earl of Ossory and Ormonde)
J. Comerford/R. Graves (10,985)
J. Comerford/G. Parker (10,986)

Ormonde, Mary, Duchess of
(née Somerset; 2nd wife of 2nd Duke)
G. Kneller/J. Smith (10,347)
G. Kneller/J. Smith (10,333)

Orrery, John Boyle, 5th Earl of
(Baron Boyle of Marston; 6th Earl of Cork & Orrery)
J. Faber the Younger/J. Faber the Younger (10,041)

O'Shauchnesey
J. Nixon/E. Harding (10,576)

Ossory, John Bale, P. Bishop of
English School 16C/A. B.... (10,046)

Ossory, Hugh Hamilton, P. Bishop of
G.C. Stuart/W. Evans (10,622)

Ossory, Edward Maurice, P. Bishop of
T. Hudson/J. McArdell (10,114)

Ossory, Amelia, Countess of
(née De Nassau; wife of Count Thomas)
W. Wissing/I. Beckett (10,331)
W. Wissing/I. Beckett (10,993)

Ossory, Thomas Butler, Earl of
G. Kneller/J. Smith (10,333)
P. Lely/P. Vanderbanck (11,418)

O'Sullivan, Denis
D. Wood (8119)

Ottway, Rev. Caesar
W. Stevenson/J. Kirkwood (10,592)

Overkirk, M.G.
T. Maas/T. Maas (10,003)(*group*)
T. Maas/T. Maas (20,800)(*group*)

Owenson, Miss Sydney
(Lady Morgan; wife of Sir Thomas)
W. Behnes/H. Meyer (11,553)
T. Lawrence/J. Godby (11,551)
S. Lover/R. Cooper (10,959)
C.T. Wageman/H.H. Meyer (11,229)

Oxford, Robert Harley, 1st Earl of
J. Wyck/J. Brooks (11,652)(*group*)

Paget, Henry William
(2nd Earl of Uxbridge; 1st Marquess of Anglesey; Lord Lieutenant of Ireland)
English School c.1815/English School 1815 (11,359)
B. Mulrenin/B. Mulrenin (11,233)

Palmer, Mary
(Countess of Inchiquin; 2nd wife of 4th Earl)
T. Lawrence/W. Bond (10,368)

Palmerston, Henry John Temple, 3rd Viscount
(British Prime Minister)
S.F. Lynn (8236)
T. Lawrence/?T.A. Prior (11,341)(*group*)

Parker, General Gervis
A. Lee/A. Miller (10,076)

Parnell, Charles Stewart
R. Barter (8086)

Parnell, M.P., Sir John
G.C. Stuart/Irish School c.1795 (10,079)

Parnell, Thomas
(Archdeacon of Clogher)
?Irish School 18C/?J. Dixon (10,014)

Parry, Edward
(P. Bishop of Killaloe)
Irish School 17C/J. Dickson (10,305)

Parsons, Alicia
(Lady Conroy; wife of Sir Edward Conroy, 2nd Bt.)
C.I. Baseley/W.F. Finden (10,769)

Parsons, Lawrence
(2nd Earl of Rosse)
J. Comerford/J. Heath (11,049)
J. Comerford/J. Heath (20,790)

Parsons, Sir William
(Surveyor General and Lord Justice of Ireland)
English School 17C/J. Paul (10,059)

Pascal, Blaise
J. Barry/J. Barry (20,722)(10)(*group*)

Paulet, Charles Ingoldsby
(13th Marquess of Winchester)
J.P. Haverty/R. Havell the Elder and Younger (11,650)(*group*)

Peel, Julia Beatrice
(daughter of Sir Robert Peel; Countess of Jersey, wife of 6th Earl)
T. Lawrence/S. Cousins (10,446)

Peel, Sir Robert
J. Doyle/J. Doyle (11,544)(55)(*group*)
W. Tell/W. Tell (10,512)
W. Tell/W. Tell (10,513)

Penn, William
J. Barry/J. Barry (20,722)(9)(*group*)

Perceval, John Perceval, Viscount
(2nd Earl of Egmont)
T. Hudson/J. McArdell (10,168)

Percival, M.P., Lieut.-Colonel Alexander
English School 1830s/Jenkinson (11,060-11,061)

Percival, Lady Helena
(Lady Rawdon; Countess of Moira, wife of 1st Earl)
J. Latham/J. Brooks (10,914)

Percival Bt., Sir John
G. Kneller/J. Smith (10,071)

Percy, Hugh
(2nd Earl and 1st Duke of Northumberland; Lord Lieutenant of Ireland)
W. Hoare/W. Hoare (11,230)

Percy, Thomas
(Dean of Carlisle; Bishop of Dromore)
J. Reynolds/W. Dickinson (10,086)
J. Reynolds/English School 1811 (11,330)

Perrin, Judge Louis
C. Moore (8108)

Perrot, Sir John
G. Powle/V. Green (10,290)

Pery, Edmond Henry
(1st Earl of Limerick)
G. Dawe/T.A. Dean (10,894)

Pery, Edmund Sexton, 1st Viscount
Irish School c.1777/Irish School 1777 (11,331)
G.C. Stuart/W. Say (10,478)

Peter the Great, Czar
J. Barry/J. Barry (20,722)(10)*(group)*
J.M. Rysbrack (8015)

Peters, Matthew
M.W. Peters/J. Murphy (10,106)

Petersham, Viscount Charles
(4th Earl of Harrington)
J. Reynolds/F. Bartolozzi (10,313)
J. Reynolds/F. Bartolozzi (10,314)
J. Reynolds/F. Bartolozzi (10,315)

Pethard, Counsellor
F. Wheatley/J. Collyer (11,644)*(group)*
F. Wheatley/J. Collyer (11,826)*(group)*

Petrie, George
Irish School 1866 (8154)

Petty, Sir William
J. Closterman/J. Smith (10,229)
D. Loggan/E. Sandys (10,285)

Petty, William
(2nd Earl of Shelburne; British Prime Minister; 1st Marquess of Lansdowne)
J. Gillray/J. Gillray (11,545)*(group)*
Irish School c.1780/Irish School 1780 (11,304)

Phillips, Charles
S. Drummond/H. Meyer (11,261)
English School c.1810/A. Tardieu (11,074)
W. Yellowless/S. Watts (11,288)

Phipps, Constantine
(1st Marquess of Normandy; Lord Lieutenant of Ireland)
J. Doyle/J. Doyle (11,544)(60)*(group)*
J. Doyle/J. Doyle (11,544)(62)*(group)*

Phipps, Sir Constantine
(Lord Chancellor of Ireland)
G. Kneller/J. Simon (10,021)

Pickering, Elizabeth
(Baroness Elizabeth Cutts; 2nd wife of Baron Cutts)
G. Kneller/J. Smith (10,317)

Picton, Sir Thomas
English School c.1815/English School 1815 (11,369)

Pilkington, Mrs Laetitia
(née Van Lewer; wife of John Carteret Pilkington)
N. Hone the Elder/R. Purcell (10,322)
N. Hone the Elder/R. Purcell (11,069)

Pitt, M.P., William
(1st Earl of Chatham)
J. Barry/J. Barry (20,772)(3)*(group)*
W. Hoare/R. Houston (11,068)

Pitt the Younger, M.P., William
(British Prime Minister)
M. Brown/D. Orme (20,104)*(group)*
J. Hoppner/G. Clint (11,070)
G. Romney/J. Jones (10,476)

Plaistow, Catherine
(Mrs Trapaud)
J. Reynolds/E. Fisher (10,363)

Plato
J. Barry/J. Barry (20,722)(8)*(group)*

Platov, M. Ivanovitch, Count
English School c.1815/English School 1815 (11,358)

Pluche, Abbé Noel Antoine
N. Blakey/L.J. Cathelin (20,770)

Plunket, William Conyngham Plunket, 1st Baron
(Lord Chancellor)
J. Doyle/J. Doyle (11,403)
Irish School c.1827/Irish School c.1827 (11,322)
R. Rothwell/D. Lucas (10,109)

Plunket, M.P., David Robert
(1st Baron Rathmore)
T. Fitzpatrick/T. Fitzpatrick (11,059)

Plunket, Edward John Moreton Drax
(18th Baron Dunsany)
T. Spicer-Simson (8223)

Plunket, William Conyngham Plunket, 1st Baron
(Lord Chancellor of Ireland)
C. Moore (8066)
C. Moore (8187)
J. Doyle/English School 1830 (11,403)*(group)*
Irish School c.1827/Irish School c.1827 (11,332)

Plunkett, Arthur James
(8th Earl of Fingall)
Irish School c.1811/Irish School 1811 (11,350)
T.C. Thompson/C. Turner (10,848)

Plunkett, Joseph Mary
P. Grant (8009)

Plunkett, (St) Oliver
(R.C. Archbishop of Armagh)
?G. Morphey/English School 1804 (11,337)
?G. Morphey/Irish School 1808 (11,338)
?G. Morphey/?R. Laurie (10,201)
?G. Morphey/?R. Laurie (11,073)
G. Morphey/J. Vandervaart (10,105)

Ponsonby, Frederick
(Viscount Duncannon; 3rd Earl of Bessborough)
J. Reynolds/J. Grozier (10,253)

Ponsonby, M.P., George
(Lord Chancellor of Ireland)
A. Hope/J. Godby (10,062)
Irish School c.1801/Irish School 1801 (11,238)

Ponsonby, John
G. Gaven/J. Gainer (10,108)

Ponsonby, John William
(Viscount Duncannon; 4th Earl of Bessborough)
J. Doyle/J. Doyle (11,891)(*group*)

Ponsonby, The Hon. Richard
(P. Bishop of Derry and Raphoe)
S. Catterson Smith the Elder/G. Sanders (20,768)

Ponsonby, M.P., Sir William
G. Maile/G. Maile (10,477)

Ponsonby, Sarah
Lady Leighton/J.H. Lynch (10,893)

Ponsonby, William
(2nd Earl of Bessborough)
J.S. Copley/R. Dunkarton (10,432)

Pope, Alexander
G. Kneller/C. Jervas (11,346)

Porter, John
(Bishop of Clogher)
T. Lawrence/C. Turner (10,107)

Porter, J. Scott
E. Crawford/R. Josey (11,077)

Porter, William
F. Wheatley/J. Collyer (11,826)(*group*)
F. Wheatley/J. Collyer (11,644)(*group*)

Portland, Hans Willem Bentinck, 5th Earl of
T. Maas/T. Maas (10,003)(*group*)
T. Maas/T. Maas (20,800)(*group*)
J. Wyck/J. Brooks (11,652)(*group*)

Portland, William Henry Cavendish-Bentinck, 3rd Duke of
(Lord Lieutenant of Ireland; British Prime Minister)
J. Reynolds/J. Murphy (10,475)

Pottinger Bt., Sir Henry
English School 1850/J. Brown (11,335)
S. Lawrence/H. Griffiths (11,334)

Poulet, Anne Lucy
(Baroness Nugent, wife of 3rd Baron)
T. Lawrence/R.J. Lane (10,941)

Powell, M.P., C.
J.P. Haverty/J.P. Haverty (11,857)(*group*)

Powell, Harriet
(Countess of Seaforth, 2nd wife of 1st Earl)
C. Read/R. Houston (11,064)
J. Reynolds/R. Houston (11,063)

Power Le Poer-Trench, William
(P. Archbishop of Tuam)
Irish School 19C/R. Smith (11,280)

Power, Marguerite
(Countess of Blessington, 2nd wife of 1st Earl)
A.E. Chalon/J.J. Hinchcliff (10,326)
A.E. Chalon/H.T. Ryall (10,361)
W. Drummond/W.H. Egleton (11,336)
E. Landseer/English School c.1839 (11,065)

Power, Richard
J. Comerford/Irish School 1825 (11,370)

Power, William Grattan Tyrone
A.G.G. D'Orsay/A.G.G. D'Orsay (11,066)
J. Simpson/C. Turner (10,075)

Powerscourt, Elizabeth Frances Charlotte, Viscountess
(née Jocelyn; wife of 6th Viscount; Marchioness of Londonderry, wife of 4th Marquess)
J. Ross/W.H. Mote (11,333)

Powerscourt, Richard Wingfield, 6th Viscount
A.G.G. D'Orsay/A.G.G. D'Orsay (11,067)

Powerscourt, Mervyn Wingfield, 7th Viscount
C.W. Walton & Co./C.W. Walton & Co. (11,075)

Praeger, Robert Lloyd
S.R. Praeger (8035)

Prendergast, Mrs Catherine Jane
(née Annesley)
J.H. Foley (8045)

Preston, William
(P. Bishop of Ferns)
G.C. Stuart/W. Dickinson (10,110)

Prior, Thomas
R. Pool & J. Cash/I. Taylor the Elder (10,041)
J. Van Nost the Younger/C. Spooner (10,013)

Purcell of Halverstown, Peter
S. Catterson Smith the Elder/J.A. Vintner (10,190)

Quadri, Giovanni Ludovico
Bolognese School 18C/Bolognese School 18C (10,515)

Quentin, Sir George
J.P. Haverty/R. Havell the Elder and Younger (11,650)(*group*)

Quin, James
English School 18C/English School 18C (10,272)
F. Hayman/J. McArdell (10,104)
T. Hudson/J. Faber the Younger (10,111)

Quin, Patrick
E. Trotter/H. Brocas the Elder (11,071)

Quinton, Richard
J.P. Haverty/R. Havell the Elder and Younger (11,650)(*group*)

Radnor, John Robartes, 1st Earl of
(Baron Robartes of Truro; Lord Lieutenant of Ireland)
S. Cooper/English School 1806 (11,050)

Radnor, Jacob Bouverte, 2nd Earl of
(Viscount Folkstone)
J. Reynolds/R. Brookshaw (11,098)

Raffalovitch, Madame
E. Guillaume (8193)

Rainey, Rose
(Mrs Samuel Bruce)
C. Andras (8080)

so-called Raleigh, Lady
(née Elizabeth Throgmorton)
English School 1603/R.C. Bell (11,055)

Raleigh, Sir Walter
J. Barry/J. Barry (20,722)(4)(*group*)
English School 1602/English School late 18C (11,239)

so-called Raleigh, Sir Walter
?W. Segar/C.R. Bell (11,053-11,054)

Ranelagh, Margaret, Countess of
(née Cecil; 2nd wife of 1st Earl)
G. Kneller/J. Smith (10,534)

Rathmore, David Robert Plunkett, 1st Baron of
T. Fitzpatrick/T. Fitzpatrick (11,059)

Rawdon, Bt., General Sir George
R. White/R. White (10,611)

Rawdon, Lady Helena
(née Lady Perceval; wife of Sir John Rawdon Bt., later 1st Earl of Moira)
J. Latham/J. Brooks (10,914)

Rawdon-Hastings, Francis
(Baron Rawdon; 2nd Earl of Moira; 1st Marquess of Hastings)
English School c.1780/W. Ridley (10,656)
English School c.1813/Irish School 1813 (10,657)
J. Gillray/J. Gillray (11,545)*(group)*
J. Gillray/J. Gillray (10,655)
H.D. Hamilton/J. Heath (10,947)
J. Hoppner/*F. Bartolozzi*/H. Landseer (10,949)
S. Percy (8160)
J. Reynolds/J.K. Baldrey (11,047)
J. Reynolds/J. Jones (10,503)
J. Reynolds/J. Jones (10,946)
J. Reynolds/P. Maguire (10,654)
J. Reynolds/R. Stanier (10,653)
M.A. Shee/G. Clint (10,948)
G.C. Stuart/J. Collyer (10,118)

Ray, John
P. Lely & ?J. Closterman/T.A. Prior (11,373)*(group)*

Raynal, Guillaume Thomas
French School 18C/H. P.... (11,320)

Recamier, Madame
(née Jeanne François Julie Adelaide Bernard)
R. Cosway/A. Cardon (10,318)

Redmond, John Edward
F.W. Doyle-Jones (8001)

Redmond, M.P., John Edward
J.G. Day/J.G. Day (11,419)
M. Lawlor (8239)

'Rembrandt's Mother'
Rembrandt/R. Earlom (10,171)

Reynolds, J.
J.P. Haverty/J.P. Haverty (11,857)*(grouup)*

Reynolds, Sir James
(Lord Chief Justice of the Common Pleas in Ireland; Chief Baron of the Exchequer in England)
J. Parmentier/J. Faber the Younger (10,269)

Reynolds, Sir Joshua
J. Barry/J. Barry (20,722)(11)*(group)*
J. Reynolds/W.C. Edwards (10,239)

Rice, Thomas Spring
(1st Baron Monteagle, Chancellor of the Exchequer)
J. Comerford/R. Cooper (11,313)
J. Comerford/R. Cooper (11,314)
J. Doyle/J. Doyle (11,544) (64)*(group)*
J. Doyle/J. Doyle (11,544) (65)*(group)*
J. Linnell the Elder/J. Linnell the Elder (11,044)
L. MacDonald (8203)

Richardson, John
(P. Bishop of Ardagh)
English School 1653/English School 1804 (10,278)

Richmond, Charles Lennox, 4th Duke of
(Lord Lieutenant of Ireland)
Irish School 1808/Irish School 1808 (11,753)*(group)*
Irish School 1808/Irish School 1808 (11,735)*(group)*
J. Jackson/H. Meyer (10,270)
E. Scott/C. Knight (11,051)

Riddal, Sir Jaspar
J.P. Haverty/R. Havell the Elder and Younger (11,650)*(group)*

Rigg, Mrs Ambrose
(née Amelia Hone)
N. Hone the Elder/J. Greenwood (10,329)
N. Hone the Elder/J. Greenwood (10,695)

Robartes, John
(Baron Robartes of Truro; 1st Earl of Radnor; Lord Lieutenant of Ireland)
S. Cooper/English School 1806 (11,050)

Robinson Bt., Sir William
M.W. Peters/J. Watson (10,459)

Robinson, Dr Bryan
(President of the Royal College of Physicians)
B. Wilson/B. Wilson (10,128)

Robinson, Richard
(P. Bishop of Kildare; Archbishop of Armagh; 1st Baron Rokeby)
J. Reynolds/R. Houston (10,410)
J.K. Sherwin/J.K. Sherwin (11,657-11,658)*(group)*
J.K. Sherwin/J.K. Sherwin (11,827-11,829)*(group)*

Robinson-Morris, Matthew
(2nd Baron Rokeby of Armagh)
T. Arrowsmith/T. Barrow (11,315)

Robinson, Thomas Philip Weddell
(Baron Grantham; 2nd Earl De Grey; Lord Lieutenant of Ireland)
W. Robinson/*W. Brett*/S. Cousins (10,841)
J. Wood/J. Browne (10,840)

Roche, Mary
(Mrs Stephen Le Maistre; Baroness Nolcken)
E.F. Calze/V. Green (10,382)

Roche, Sir Boyle
J.K. Sherwin/J.K. Sherwin (11,657-11,658)*(group)*
J.K. Sherwin/J.K. Sherwin (11,827-11,829)*(group)*

Rochester, Lawrence Hyde, 1st Earl of
(Lord Lieutenant of Ireland)
G. Kneller/J. Houbraken (10,212)

Roden, Frances Elizabeth, Countess of
(daughter of 5th Earl Cowper; wife of 1st Earl of Roden; also 2nd wife of 1st Viscount Jocelyn)
J. Hayter/W.H. Egleton (10,866)

Roden, Robert Jocelyn, 2nd Earl of
J. Oldham/J. Heath (11,048)

Roden, Robert Jocelyn, 3rd Earl of
F.R. Say/J. Kirkwood (11,293)

Rokeby, Dr Richard Robinson, 1st Baron
(P. Bishop of Kildare; Archbishop of Armagh)
J. Reynolds/R. Houston (10,410)
J.K. Sherwin/J.K. Sherwin (11,657-11,658)*(group)*
J.K. Sherwin/J.K. Sherwin (11,827-11,829)*(group)*

Rokeby, Matthew Robinson Morris, 2nd Baron
T. Arrowsmith/T. Barrow (11,315)

Rokeby, Henry Montagu, 6th Baron
F. Grant/G.J. Zobell (11,043)

Romney, George
T.A. Hayley/M. Denman (11,045)
G. Romney/C. Watson (11,046)

Romney, Robert Marsham, 2nd Baron
J. Barry/J. Barry (20,722)(5)*(group)*

Rosse, Lawrence Parsons, 2nd Earl of
J. Comerford/J. Heath (11,049)
J. Comerford/J. Heath (20,790)

Rothes, John Leslie, 10th Earl of
(Commander in Chief in Ireland)
J. Reynolds/J. McArdell (11,056)

Routh, George
J. Comerford/Irish School 1825 (11,371)

Rowan, Archibald Hamilton
(United Irishman)
J. Comerford/J. Comerford (11,327)
J. Comerford/J.H. Lynch (11,329)
Irish School c.1794/Irish School 1794 (11,328)

Rowley Bt., Rear Admiral Sir Josias
J.P. Haverty/R. Havell the Elder & Younger (10,650)

Rowley, Sir William
English School c.1740/J. Brooks (10,267)

Rubens, Peter Paul
?A. Van Dyck/*J.M. Nattier*/J. Audran (20,678)(1)
School of P.P. Rubens/B. Baron (20,040)

Rudd, Margaret Caroline
(née Youngson)
D. Dodd/G. Sibelius (11,058)

Rupert, Prince
(son of King of Bohemia)
Continental School c.1620/C. Turner (10,869)*(group)*

Russell, Francis
(5th Duke of Bedford)
J. Gillray/J. Gillray (11,545)*(group)*

Russell ('AE'), George
O. Sheppard (8092)
T. Spicer-Simson (8138)
T. Spicer-Simson (8219)

Russell, John
(6th Duke of Bedford)
J. Doyle/J. Doyle (11,854)*(group)*

Russell, John Russell, 1st Earl
(British Prime Minister)
J. Doyle/J. Doyle (11,544)(59)*(group)*
J. Doyle/J. Doyle (11,544)(64-65)*(group)*
J. Doyle/J. Doyle (11,544)(67) *(group)*
J. Doyle/J. Doyle (11,852-11,854)*(group)*
J. Doyle/J. Doyle (11,891)*(group)*

Russell, Thomas
(United Irishman)
Irish School c.1803/T.W. Huffam (11,326)
Irish School c.1803/Irish School 1803 (11,323)
Irish School c.1803/Irish School 1803 (11,324)

Russell, Sir William
(1st Baron Russell of Thornhaugh, Lord Deputy of Ireland)
English School c.1580/*G.P. Harding*/W. Greatbach (11,052)

Rutland, Charles Manners, 4th Duke of
(Lord Lieutenant of Ireland)
H. Hone/English School 1790 (11,322)
Irish School c.1784/Irish School 1784 (11,321)
J. Reynolds/W. Dickinson (10,490)

Rutland, Mary Isabella, Duchess of
(née Somerset, daughter of 4th Duke of Beaufort; wife of 4th Duke of Rutland)
M.W. Peters/H.H. Houston (11,601)
J. Barry/J. Barry (20,722)(5)*(group)*
Mrs O'Neill/English School c.1790 (11,319)

Ryan, Captain Luke
Irish School 18C/Irish School 18C (11,318)

Ryder, Thomas
Irish School 18C/Irish School 18C (11,317)
M.A. Shee/J. Ford (10,274)

Ryland, Williams Wynne
Irish School 18C/Irish School 18C (11,316)

Sackville-Germain, Diana
(Viscountess Crosbie; wife of Viscount Crosbie, later 2nd Earl of Glandore)
J. Reynolds/W. Dickinson (10,407)

Sackville, John Frederick
(3rd Duke of Dorset)
J. Reynolds/T. Hardy (10,796)

Sackville, Lionel Cranfield
(1st Duke of Dorset; Lord Lieutenant of Ireland)
G. Kneller/J. McArdell (10,175)
G. Kneller/G. Vertue (10,799)

St Albans, Ulick de Burgh, 2nd Earl of
(1st Marquess of Clanricarde)
English School 17C/S.F. Raveneth the Elder (11,205)

Saint Germans, Edward Granville Eliot, 3rd Earl of
(Lord Lieutenant of Ireland)
Irish School 1853/Irish School 1853 (11,722)

St George, Brigadier General Richard
F. Bindon/J. Brooks (10,044)

St Leonards, Edward Burtenshaw Sugden, 1st Baron
J. Moore/E. Scriven (11,039)

St Patrick's Cathedral, Dublin, Chancellor of
(John Blackford)
English School 18C/J. McArdell (10,165)

St Patrick's Cathedral, Dublin, Dean of
(William Cradock)
J.K.Sherwin/J.K.Sherwin (11,657-11,658) *(group)*
J.K.Sherwin/J.K.Sherwin (11,827-11,659) *(group)*

St Patrick's Cathedral, Dublin, Dean of
(Jonathan Swift)
R. Barber/S. Wheatley (11,376)
R. Barber/B. Wilson (10,296)
R. Barber/B. Wilson (11,377)
F. Bindon/A. Miller (10,052)
F. Bindon/A. Miller (20,801)

Sophia, Princess
(daughter of James I of England)
Contintental School c.1620/C. Turner (10,869)*(group)*

Southerne, Thomas
J. Worsdale/J. Simon (10,215)

Southill, M.P., Edward
(Secretary of State for Ireland)
G. Kneller/J. Smith (10,161)

Spencer, Lady Mary
(née Beauclerk; wife of Charles Spencer)
J. Reynolds/W. Dickinson (11,028)

Spencer, Henrietta Frances
(Viscountess Duncannon, wife of Viscount Duncannon, later 3rd Earl of Bessborough)
J. Downman/F. Bartolozzi (10,320)
J. Reynolds/J. Grozer (10,390)
Countess Spencer/F. Bartolozzi (10,352)

Spratt, Rev. John
Irish School c.1850/Irish School c.1850 (11,383)

Spring Rice, M.P., Thomas
(1st Baron Monteagle; Chancellor of the Exchequer)
J. Comerford/R. Cooper (11,313)
J. Comerford/R. Cooper (11,314)
J. Doyle/J. Doyle (11,544)(64-65) *(group)*
J. Doyle/J. Doyle (11,891)*(group)*

Stack, Austin
A. Power (8120)

Stacpoole, John
J. Barrett/J. Watson (11,018)

Stanhope, Algernon Russell Gayleard
R. Westmacott (8209)

Stanhope, Lady Anne Hussey
(née Delaval; wife of Sir William Stanhope)
J. Reynolds/J. Watson (10,397)
B. Wilson/J. Basire (10,404)

Stanhope, Charlotte Augusta
(Duchess of Leinster, wife of 4th Duke)
J.P. Haverty/R. Havell the Elder & Younger (11,650)

Stanhope, the Hon. Mrs Eliza
(née Falconer)
J. Reynolds/J.R. Smith (10,356)

Stanhope, Elizabeth William
English School 19C (8225)

Stanhope, The Hon. Lincoln Edwin Robert
J. Reynolds/F. Bartolozzi (10,313)
J. Reynolds/F. Bartolozzi (10,314)
J. Reynolds/T. Park (10,323)

Stanhope, Philip Dormer
(4th Earl of Chesterfield; Lord Lieutenant of Ireland)
T. Gainsborough/E. Bell (10,183)
W. Hoare/J. Brooks (10,418)
W. Hoare/R. Houston & S. Wheatley (10,445)
W. Hoare/A. Miller (10,186)
W. Hoare/J. Simon (10,184)

Stanhope, William
(1st Earl of Harrington; Lord Lieutenant of Ireland)
B. Du Pan/M. Ford (10,157)
J. Fayram/J. Faber the Younger (10,193)

Stanley, Edward George
(14th Earl of Derby)
J. Doyle/J. Doyle (11,853)*(group)*
English School 19C/?T.A. Prior (11,372)*(group)*

Stanley, Sir Edward
C. Panormo (8300)
I. Parkes (8158)

Stanley, Mr J.
J.P. Haverty/R. Havell the Elder & Younger (11,650)

Stannard, M.P., Eaton
J. Latham/A. Miller (10,413)

Stauffacher, Werner
G. Ulyssé/H, Raunheim (20,176)

Staunton, Michael
J.P. Haverty/J.P. Haverty (11,020)*(group)*

Stearne, John
(P. Bishop of Clogher)
T. Carlton/T. Beard (10,143)

Steele, M.P., Sir Richard
G. Kneller/J. Faber the Younger (11,041)
J. Richardson the Elder/J. Smith (10,030)

Steele, Thomas
J.P. Haverty/J.P. Haverty (10,969)*(group)*
J.P. Haverty/J.P. Haverty (11,857)*(group)*

Stephens, James
E.T. Hurley/E.T. Hurley (11,013-11,015)
E. Quinn (8002)
T. Spicer-Simson (8220)

Sterne, Laurence
L. Carrogis/?French School 19C (10,273)
J. Reynolds/E. Fisher (10,545)
J. Reynolds/H. P.... (10,527)
J. Reynolds/S.F. Ravenet the Elder (10,528)

Stevenson, Sir John Andrew
W. Brocas/W. Brocas (11,031)
E. Jones/H. Brocas the Elder (11,301)
G.F. Joseph/E. Scriven (11,029)

Stewart, Charles William
(3rd Marquess of Londonderry)
J. Bostok/J.J. Jenkins (10,913)

Stewart, Frederick William Robert
(Viscount Castlereagh; 4th Marquess of Londonderry)
F. Kruger/F. Kruger (10,758)

Stewart, M.P., James
M. Cregan/C. Turner (11,032)

Stewart, James
(Earl of Moray)
H. Melville/R. Staines (20,271)

Stewart, Robert
(1st Marquess of Londonderry)
G. Dance the Younger/W. Daniell (10,902)

Stewart, Robert
(Viscount Castlereagh; 2nd Marquess of Londonderry)
T. Lawrence/C. Turner (10,458)

Stokes, Dr Whitley
C. Grey/H. Griffiths (11,311)

Stokes, Dr William
English School 1840/English School 1840 (11,040)

Stopford, Admiral Robert
H. MacManus/J. Kirkwood (11,302)

Stopford, James
(1st Earl of Courtown)
J.K. Sherwin/J.K. Sherwin (11,657-11,658)*(group)*
J.K. Sherwin/J.K. Sherwin (11,827-11,829)*(group)*

Strafford, Thomas Wentworth, 1st Earl of
(Lord Lieutenant of Ireland)
W. Hollar/W. Hollar (20,763)*(group)*
A. Van Dyck/A. Browne (10,259)

Street, Ann
(Mrs Spranger Barry)
?D. Dodd/J. Walker (11,093)
T. Kettle/J.S. Paul (10,325)
T. Kettle/J.S. Paul (11,096)

Stronge, Lady
J.P. Haverty/R. Havell the Elder & Younger (11,650)

Stuart, Gilbert Charles
S. Goodridge/A.B. Durand (11,297)

Stuart, The Hon. William
(P. Archbishop of Armagh)
W. Owen/S.W. Reynolds (10,461)
W. Owen/S.W. Reynolds (10,701)

Suffren, Pierre André
French School 18C/J. Walker (11,284)

Sullivan, Barry
J. Mayall/J. Moore (11,027)

Sugden, Sir Edward Burtenshaw
(Lord Chancellor; 1st Baron St Leonards)
J. Moore/E. Scriven (11,039)

Sullivan, Alexander Martin
T. Farrell (8183)

Swan, John
H. Barron/V. Green (11,011)

Swift, Jonathan
(Dean of St Patrick's Cathedral, Dublin)
R. Barber/S. Wheatley (11,376)
R. Barber/B. Wilson (10,296)
R. Barber/B. Wilson (10,297)
F. Bindon/E. Miller (10,052)
F. Bindon/A. Miller (20,801)
F. Bindon/E. Scriven (10,529)
P. Cunningham (8026)
P. Cunningham/Irish School c.1770 (11,287)
C. Jervas/P. Fourdrinier (10,169)
C. Jervas/G. Vertue (10,214)
C. Jervas/*J. Thurston*/A.W. Warren (11,285)
C. Kneller & C. Jervas/T.A. Prior (11,346)
Markham/T. Burford (10,085)
Markham/T. Burford (11,021)
Markham/A. Van Haecken (10,142)

so-called Swift, Jonathan
English School 17C/P. Pelham (11,022)

Swift, Mary
(The Hon. Mary Feilding, daughter of Viscount Carlingford)
P. Lely/I. Beckett (10,328)

Sydney, Sir Henry
(Lord Deputy of Ireland)
?English School 16C/W. & M. De Passe (11,037)

Synnot, Marcus
J. Wright of Derby/J.R. Smith (10,406)

Synnot, Maria Eliza
J. Wright of Derby/J.R. Smith (10,406)

Synnot, Walter
J. Wright of Derby/J.R. Smith (10,406)

Taafe, Nicholas Taafe, 6th Viscount
R. Hunter/J. Dixon (10,158)
R. Hunter/S. Harding (11,266)

Talbot, Charles Chetwynd-Talbot, 2nd Earl
(Lord Lieutenant of Ireland)
J.P. Haverty/R. Havell the Elder & Younger (11,650) *(group)*
T.C. Thompson/S.W. Reynolds the Elder (10,491)

Talbot, Frances Thomasina, Countess of
(née Lambert; wife of 3rd Earl)
C. Robertson/J.S. Agar (10,324)

Talbot, Colonel Richard
J.K. Sherwin/J.K. Sherwin (11,657-11,658)*(group)*
J.K. Sherwin/J.K. Sherwin (11,827-11,829)*(group)*

Talbot, Richard
(Earl and Titular Duke of Tyrconnel; Lord Lieutenant of Ireland)
Dutch School 17C/Dutch School 17C (11,274)

Talmask, Major
Dutch School 1691/J. Tangera (10,004)*(group)*

Tandy, James Napper
(United Irishman)
J. Gillray/J. Gillray (10,939)
J. Petrie/English School 1843 (10,649)
Irish School c.1798/Irish School c.1798 (10,648)
J. Petrie/Irish School 1843 (10,649)
J. Petrie/Irish School 1808 (10,650)
J. Petrie/J. Heath (10,940)
J. Petrie/J. Petrie (10,156)
F. Wheatley/J. Collyer (11,644) *(group)*
F. Wheatley/J. Collyer (11,826) *(group)*

Tara, Meinhardt Schomberg, Baron
(Earl of Bangor; Duke of Leinster; 3rd Duke of Schomberg)
G. Kneller/J. Smith (10,238)

Taylor, Jane
(The Hon. Jame Ffolliott Ponsonby)
J. Worsdale/J. Brooks (11,062)

Taylor, Jeremy
(P. Bishop of Down, Connor and Dromore)
English School 17C/W. Faithorne the Elder (11,275)

Taylor, Philip Meadows
C. Grey/J. Kirkwood (11,273)
W. Taylor/W. Taylor (10,162)

Taylour, Thomas
(1st Earl of Bective)
J.K. Sherwin/J.K. Sherwin (11,657-11,658)*(group)*
J.K. Sherwin/J.K. Sherwin (11,827-11,829)*(group)*

Taylour, Thomas
(1st Marquess of Headfort)
J.P. Haverty/R. Havell the Elder & Younger (11,650)*(group)*

Teeling, Bartholomew
(United Irishman)
French School c.1796/J.H. Lynch (11,267)

Temple, George Nugent-Grenville-Temple, 2nd Earl
(1st Marquess of Buckingham and Lord Lieutenant of Ireland)
T. Gainsborough/J.K. Sherwin (10,448)
R. Hunter/W. Sadler the Elder (10,417)

J.K. Sherwin/J.K. Sherwin (11,657-11,658)*(group)*
J.K. Sherwin/J.K. Sherwin (11,827-11,829)*(group)*

Temple, Henry John
(3rd Viscount Palmerston)
T. Lawrence & English School c.1830/?T.A. Prior (11,341)
S.F. Lynn (8236)

Temple, Mary Elizabeth, Countess
(wife of 2nd Earl Temple and 1st Marquess of Buckingham; Baroness Nugent)
J.K. Sherwin/J.K. Sherwin (11,657-11,658) *(group)*
J.K. Sherwin/J.K. Sherwin (11,827-11,829) *(group)*

Temple, Sir William
P. Lely & ?J. Closterman/T.A. Prior (11,373)*(group)*

Teniers the Younger, David
D. Teniers the Younger/J.P. Lebas (11,868)*(group)*

Tennent, M.P., Sir James Emerson
C. Grey/Irish School 1852 (11,271)
G. Richmond/R.A. Artlett (10,155)

Tetteau, Major
Dutch School 1691/J. Tangera (10,004)*(group)*

Thales
J. Barry/J. Barry (20,722)(7)*(group)*

Thomas, Barnard
(Bishop of Limerick)
G. Dance/W. Daniell (10,049)

Thome, Francis
J.P. Haverty/R. Havell the Elder & Younger (11,650)*(group)*

Thomas, Percy
(Dean of Carlisle; Bishop of Dromore)
J. Reynolds/W. Dickinson (10,086)

Thomond, Murrough O'Brien, 1st Marquess of
(5th Earl of Inchiquin)
J. Hoppner/S.W. Reynolds the Elder (10,147)
J. Hoppner/S.W. Reynolds the Elder (10,469)
J.K. Sherwin/J.K. Sherwin (11,657-11,658)*(group)*
J.K. Sherwin/J.K. Sherwin (11,827-11,829)*(group)*
Marchioness of Thomond/R.W. Meadows (10,147)

Thomond, William O'Brien, 2nd Marquess of
Titani/S. Freeman (11,009-11,010)

Thornhaugh, Sir William Russell of
(Lord Deputy of Ireland)
English School c.1580/*G.P. Harding*/W. Greatbach (11,052)

Thornton, Mr
J.J. Barralet/W. Ward the Elder (11,654)*(group)*

Thorp, Charles
(Lord Mayor of Dublin)
Irish School c.1800/P. Maguire (10,293)

Throgmorton, so-called Elizabeth
(Lady Raleigh)
English School 1603/R.C. Bell (11,055)

Tierney, Rev. Dr
J.P. Haverty/J.P. Haverty (11,857)*(group)*

Tiffin, Captain William
N. Hone the Elder/J. Greenwood (11,408)

Tighe, Mary
(née Blanchford)
R.E. Drummond/J. Hopwood the Younger (11,006)
G. Romney/*J. Comerford*/C. Watson (10,307)
G. Romney/E. Scriven (11,417)

Tisdal, Mr
F. Wheatley/J. Collyer (11,644)*(group)*
F. Wheatley/J. Collyer (11,826)*(group)*

Titus, Emperor
J. Barry/J. Barry (20,722)(10)*(group)*

Todd, Robert Bentley
D.Y. Blakiston/G. Zobel (11,007)

Toler, John
(Chief Justice of the Common Pleas in Ireland; 1st Earl of Norbury)
English School 1790s/English School 1790s (10,652)
Irish School c.1811/Irish School 1811 (11,851)

Tollemache, Lieut.-General Thomas
G. Kneller/J. Houbraken (20,133)

Tone, Theobald Wolfe
(United Irishman)
Irish School 1798 (8128)
Irish School 1798 (8294)
Irish School c.1800/*C.S. Tone*/J.J. Goggins (10,433)
Irish School c.1790/T.W. Huffam (11,272)
Irish School 1798/Irish School 1798 (10,292)

Torrens, Major-General Sir Henry
T. Lawrence/T.A. Dean (11,283)

Totnes, Sir George Carew, 1st Earl of
(Baron of Clapton, Lord President of Munster)
M. Gheeraerts the Younger/English School c.1800 (11,210)
M. Gheeraerts the Younger/R. Van Voerst (10,191)

Tottenham, M.P., Charles
J. Pope-Stevens the Elder/A. Miller (10,511)

Townley, Charles Gostling
H. Room/J. Cochran (11,279)

Townshend, George Townshend, 4th Viscount & 1st Marquess
(Lord Lieutenant of Ireland)
T. Hudson/J. McArdell (10,189)
J. Reynolds/C. Turner (10,492)

Trapaud, Mrs Cyrus
(née Catherine Plaistow)
J. Reynolds/E. Fisher (10,363)

Trajan, Emperor
J. Barry/J. Barry (20,722)(10)*(group)*

Travis, Mrs Robert
(née Catherine Gunning)
F. Cotes/R. Houston (10,359)
F. Cotes/C. Spooner (10,358)

Tresham, Henry
A. Pope/A. Cardon (10,135)

Treton, Henry
(Lord Deputy of Ireland)
S. Cooper/M. Vandergucht (10,636)

Troy, John Thomas
(R.C. Archbishop of Dublin)
P. Turnerelli (8199)

Truro, John Robartes, Baron of
(Lord Lieutenant of Ireland, 1st Earl of Radnor)
S. Cooper/English School 1806 (11,050)

Tuam, William Beresford, P. Archbishop of
G. Dawe/G. Maile (10,423)

Tuam, Joseph Deane Bourke, P. Archbishop of
(3rd Earl of Mayo)
J. Reynolds/J.R. Smith (10,438)

Tuam, William Power Le Poer-Trench, P. Archbishop of
Irish School 19C/R. Smith (11,280)

Tuam, Josiah Hort, Archbishop of
J. Wills/A. Miller (10,018)

Turner, James
N. Hone the Elder/R. Graves (11,277)
N. Hone the Elder/N. Hone the Elder (11,278)

Turnerelli, Peter
S. Drummond/J. Thomson (11,278)

Tyrawley, James Cuffe, Baron
W. Cuming/J.R. Smith (10,192)

Tyrconnel, Frances, Duchess of
(née Hamilton, wife of 1st Duke of Tyrconnel)
R. De Hooghe/R. De Hooghe (11,655)*(group)*

Tyrconnel, Richard Talbot, Earl and Titular Duke of
(Lord Lieutenant of Ireland)
Dutch School 17C/Dutch School 17C (11,274)

Tyrone, George de la Poer, 1st Earl of
(Marquess of Waterford)
J.K. Sherwin/J.K. Sherwin (11,657-11,658)*(group)*
J.K. Sherwin/J.K. Sherwin (11,827-11,829)*(group)*

United Irishmen
Samuel Butler
William Corbett
Michael Dwyer
William Dwyer
Robert Emmet
Thomas Addis Emmet
Lord Edward Fitzgerald
James Hope
Edward Hudson
Henry Jackson
Richard Robert Madden
William James MacNevan, M.P.
Henry Joy MacCracken
Samuel Nielson
James O'Brien
James O'Brien
Arthur O'Connor, M.P.
Roger O'Connor
Archibald Hamilton Rowan
Thomas Russell
William Samson
Henry Sheares
John Sheares
James Napper Tandy
Bartholomew Teeling
Theobald Wolfe Tone

United States of America, Woodrow Wilson, President of
J. S. Sargent/T. Cole (11,412)

Upper Ossory, John Fitzpatrick, 2nd Earl of
W. Lane/W. Skelton (10,984)

Urwick, Rev. William
Maull & Polybank/J. Cochran (11,243)

Usher, Susanna
(The Hon. Susanna Fitzpatrick)
A. Soldi/J. McArdell (10,846)

Usher St George, Emilia Olivia
(wife of the 2nd Duke of Leinster)
J. Reynolds/W. Dickinson (10,346)

Ussher, James
(P. Archbishop of Armagh)
English School 17C/W. Marshall (11,005)
English School 17C/A. Miller (10,133)
English School c.1645/G. Glover (10,281)
English School c.1650/J.G. Seiller (11,004)
English School c.1650/English School 17C (11,252)
W. Hollar/W. Hollar (20,763)*(group)*
R. Home/*C. Grey*/J. Kirkwood (11,254)
?P. Lely/English School 17C (11,251)
?P. Lely/W. Faithorne the Elder (11,253)
?P. Lely/S. Freeman (11,255)

Uxbridge, Henry William Paget, 2nd Earl of
(1st Marquess of Anglesey; Lord Lieutenant of Ireland)
English School c.1815/English School 1815 (11,359)

Vallancey, Lieut.-General Charles
G. Chinnery/Irish School 1804 (11,246-11,247)

Van Lewen, Laetitia
(wife of John Carteret Pilkington)
N. Hone the Elder/R. Purcell (10,322)
N. Hone the Elder/R. Purcell (11,069)

Vane-Tempest, Frances Anne
(Marchioness of Londonderry, 2nd Wife of the 3rd Marquess)
A.E. Chalon/J. Thomson (10,336)

Vereker, Charles
(2nd Viscount Gort)
J. Comerford/J. Heath (10,687)
C. Grey/J. Kirkwood (11,156)

Victoria, Princess
(later Victoria, Queen of England)
S.P. Denning/J.W. Chapman (10,360)
J.J. Jenkins/T. Williamson (11,248)
A. Steward/T. Woolworth (10,688)

Victoria
(Queen of England)
J. Doyle/J. Doyle (11,544)(55)*(group)*
J. Doyle/J. Doyle (11,544)(60)*(group)*
J. Doyle/J. Doyle (11,544)(64)*(group)*
J. Doyle/J. Doyle (11,544)(65)*(group)*
J. Doyle/J. Doyle (11,544)(66)*(group)*
English School c.1850/English School c.1850(11,382)
J.H. Foley 8251
O.J. Jones/Dickinson and Co. (20,701)*(group)*
A.C. & W. Wyon (8278)

Vigée-Le Brun, Elizabeth Louise
(Self-Portrait)
E.L. Vigée-Le Brun/G.J. Hart (11,876)

Vigée-Le Brun, Jeanne Lucie Louise
E.L. Vigée-le Brun/G.J. Hart (11,876)

Villiers, George William Frederick (4th Earl of Clarendon; Lord Lieutenant of Ireland)
S. Catterson Smith the Elder/G. Sanders (10,421)

Von Blücher, Prince Gebhard Leberecht
English School c.1815/English School 1815
P. Turnerelli (8274)

Von Bülow, Frederick William
English School c.1815/English School 1816 (11,355)

Wadding, Father Luke (Founder of the Irish College, Rome)
C. Maratta/G. Valet (10,144)

Wainwright, John
J. Latham/J. Brooks (10,159)

Wales, Charles, Prince of — see Charles II

Wales, Frederick, Prince of (son of George II of England)
T. Frye/T. Frye (10,550)

Wales, George Frederick, Prince of (George III of England)
D. Lüders/J. McArdell (10,852)

Wales, George, Prince of (Prince Regent; George IV of England)
J. Barry/J. Barry (20,772)(5)*(group)*
R. Cosway/L. Sailliar (10,728)

Wales, Charlotte Augusta, Princess of (daughter of the Prince Regent)
S. Percy (8057)

Walker, Rev. George (Governor of Londonderry)
R. De Hooghe/R. De Hooghe (11,655)*(group)*
English School 17C/E. Nunzer (11,260)
Irish School 18C/Irish School 18C (11,259)
G. Kneller/A. Haelwegh (10,224)
G. Kneller/P. Vanderbanck (10,565)
J. Wyck/J. Brooks (11,652)*(group)*

Wall, Charles William
S. Catterson Smith the Elder/G. Sanders (10,690)

Wallace Bt., Sir Richard
P.J.A. Baudry/J.F. Jacquemart (11,380)

Walpole, Horatio (4th Earl of Orford)
T. Lawrence/T. Evans (20,093)

Walpole, Sir Robert (1st Earl of Orford)
J.B. Van Loo/J. Watson (20,731) (92)

Walsh, Rev. Robert
J. Comerford/J. Kirkwood (11,270)

Wandesford, Sir James
(Lord Chief Baron Wandesford)
A. Van Dyck/*G. Farrington*/J. Watson (10,235)
A. Van Dyck/*G. Farrington*/J. Watson (10,563)

Warburton, Henry
J. Doyle/J. Doyle (11,854)*(group)*

Ware, Sir James
English School 17C/G. Vertue (10,124)

Warren, Admiral Sir Peter
T. Hudson/W.W. Ryland (11,258)

Waterford, George de la Poer, Marquess of (Earl of Tyrone)
J.K. Sherwin/J.K. Sherwin (11,657-11,658) *(group)*
J.K. Sherwin/J.K. Sherwin (11,827-11,829)*(group)*

Waterford, Richard Marlay, P. Bishop of
H.D. Hamilton/J. Heath (10,286)

Waterford and Lismore, Richard Chenevix, P. Bishop of
Irish School 18C/J. Hall (11,195)
Irish School c.1750/Massard (10,302)

Waterford and Lismore, Thomas Hussey, R.C. Bishop of (1st President of Maynooth College)
C.F. Von Breda/S.W. Reynolds the Elder (10,422)

Webb, George (P. Bishop of Limerick)
?English School 17C/T. Cross the Elder (10,304)

Weir, Julian Alden
O.L. Warner (8161)

Wellesley, Arthur (1st Duke of Wellington; Field-Marshal; British Prime Minister)
J. Bauzil/C. Turner (10,507)
J. Doyle/J. Doyle (11,544)(55)*(group)*
J. Doyle/J. Doyle (11,544)(57)*(group)*
J. Doyle/J. Doyle (11,544)(61)*(group)*
English School c.1815/English School 1815 (11,362)
J. Hoppner/G. Clint (10,486)
J.P. Lassouquère/J.P. Lassouquère (10,555)
T. Lawrence/S. Cousins (10,509)
T. Lawrence/E. Smith (11,265)
R.R. Scanlan/H.R. Cook (10,562)
W. Tell/W. Tell (10,512-10,513)
P. Turnerelli (8273)

Wellesley, Richard Wellesley, 1st Marquess (2nd Earl of Mornington; Lord Lieutenant of Ireland; brother of Arthur Wellesley)
T. Lawrence/S. Cousins (10,222)
C. Moore (8202)
J.K. Sherwin/J.K. Sherwin (11,657-11,658)*(group)*
J.K. Sherwin/J.K. Sherwin (11,827-11,829)*(group)*

Wenman, Jane (Mrs Arthur Goodwin)
A. Van Dyck/J. Boydell (10,556)

Wentworth, Thomas (1st Earl of Strafford; Lord Lieutenant of Ireland)
W. Hollar/W. Hollar (20,763)(63) *(group)*
A. Van Dyck/A. Browne (10,259)

Wentworth-FitzWilliam, William (2nd Earl FitzWilliam)
J. Reynolds/J. Grozer (10,252)
G.C. Stuart/Irish School c.1795 (10,079)

West, Benjamin
G.H. Harlow/H. Meyer (20,122)

Westmeath, Thomas Nugent, 6th Earl of
J.K. Sherwin/J.K. Sherwin (11,657-11,658)*(group)*
J.K. Sherwin/J.K. Sherwin (11,827-11,829)*(group)*

Westmeath, George Frederick Nugent, 7th Earl of
Irish School c1793/Irish School 1793 (11,245)
J.K. Sherwin/J.K. Sherwin (11,657-11,658)*(group)*
J.K. Sherwin/J.K. Sherwin (11,827-11,829)*(group)*

Westmoreland, John Fane, 10th Earl of
(Lord Lieutenant of Ireland)
G. Romney/J. Jones (10,508)

Wetenhall, Edward
(P. Bishop of Cork and Ross; Bishop of Kilmore and Ardagh)
J. Vandervaart/J. Vandervaart (10,132)

Whaley, Anne
(Viscountess Fitzgibbon, wife of Viscount Fitzgibbon, later 1st Earl of Clare)
G. Chinnery/H. Brocas the Elder (11,344)

Wharton, Philip Wharton, 1st Duke of
C. Jervas/J. Simon (10,682)

Wharton, Thomas Wharton, 1st Earl & 1st Marquess of
(Lord Lieutenant of Ireland)
G. Kneller/English School 18C (11,244)
G. Kneller/J. Smith (10,218)

Whateley, Richard
(P. Archbishop of Dublin)
W. Bennes/F.C. Lewis (10,566)
S. Catterson Smith the Elder/G. Sanders (10,506)
S. L..../G. & E. Dalziel (11,390)

Whitford, Sir George
J.P. Haverty/R. Havell the Elder & Younger (11,650)*(group)*

Whitman, Walt
J. Connor (8012)

Whitefield, Rev. George
N. Hone the Elder/English School 18C (11,256)
N. Hone the Elder/J. Greenwood (10,680)
N. Hone the Elder/V.M. Picot (11,257)

Whiteside, James
C. Grey/Irish School 1849 (11,268) (11,269)

Whiteside, M.P., James
(Lord Chief Justice of Ireland)
J. Mayall/D.J. Pound (10,567)

Whitworth, Charles Whitworth, 1st Viscount & 1st Earl
(Lord Lieutenant of Ireland)
T. Lawrence/C. Turner (10,689)

Whyte, Samuel
H.D. Hamilton/H. Brocas the Elder (10,295)

Wicklow, Cecilia Frances, Countess of
(née Hamilton; wife of 4th Earl)
G.H. Harlow/W. Say (10,369)

Wilde, Sir William Robert Wills
L. Gluckman/J.H. Lynch (10,685)
T.H. Maguire/T.H. Maguire (10,684)

Wilks, Robert
J. Ellys/J. Faber the Younger (10,219)

William II
(King of The Netherlands)
English School c.1815/English School 1816 (11,356)

William III (King of England)
R. De Hooghe/R. De Hooghe (11,847)(1)
R. De Hooghe/R. De Hooghe (11,655)*(group)*
R. De Hooghe/R. De Hooghe (11,849)(3)
English School 1692/J. Goldar (20,836)
G. Kneller/J. Brooks (10,223)
G. Kneller/T. Chambars (10,519)
G. Kneller/M. Ford (10,504)
G. Kneller/D. Malone (20,123)
G. Kneller/A. Miller (10,558)
T. Maas/T. Maas (10,003)*(group)*
T. Maas/T. Maas (20,800)*(group)*
R. Pool & J. Cash/J. Lodge (10,041)(3)
W. Wissing/J. Smith (10,559)
J. Wyck/J. Brooks (11,652)*(group)*
J. Wyck/J. Faber the Younger (10,420)

William III as Prince of Orange
R. De Hooghe/R. De Hooghe (11,846)*(group)*
R. De Hooghe/R. De Hooghe (11,849)*(group)*
R. De Hooghe/R. De Hooghe (11,849)(1-2)*(group)*
R. De Hooghe/R. De Hooghe (11,849)(4)*(group)*
P. Lely/I. Beckett (10,561) (10,080)
P. Lely/A. Blooteling (11,263)
?P. Lely/P. Schenck(10,560)

William IV
(King of England)
English School c.1830/English School 1830 (10,703)

Williams, Rev. Thomas
J. Comerford/E. Scriven (10,679)
English School 18C/A. Miller (10,678)

Williams-Wynn Bt., Sir Watkin
C. Hewetson (8063)

Wilson Croker, M.P., John
W. Owen/*J. Wright*/H. Meyer (10,751)

Wilson, Gavin
Irish School late 18C/English School late 18C (11,739)

Wilson, Thomas
(Bishop of Sodor and Man)
R. Philips/J. Simon (10,694)

Wilson, Woodrow
(President of United States of America)
J.S. Sargent/T. Cole (11,142)

Winchester, Benjamin Hoadly, Bishop of
I. Gosset/*N. Hone the Elder*/J. Basire the Elder (10,879)

Winchester, Charles Ingoldsby Paulet, 13th Marquess of
J.P. Haverty/R. Havell the Elder & Younger (11,650) *(group)*

Windsor, Maria
(Marchioness of Downshire, wife of 3rd Marquess)
J.P. Haverty/R. Havell the Elder & Younger (11,650)*(group)*

Wingfield, Dr John
J. Constable/W.J. Ward the Younger (10,231)

Wingfield, Mervyn
(7th Viscount Powerscourt)
C.W. Walton & Co./C.W. Walton & Co. (11,075)

Wingfield, Richard
(6th Viscount Powerscourt)
A.G.G. D'Orsay/A.G.G. D'Orsay (11,967)

Winstanley, John
Irish School 18C/J. Brooks (10,280)

Wirtenberg, Duke of
Dutch School 1691/J. Tangera (10,004)*(group)*

Wissing, William
(Self-Portrait)
W. Wissing/J. Smith (10,691)

Wodhull, Mrs
(née Catherine Ingram)
J. Zoffany/R. Houston (10,350)

Woffington, Margaret (Peg)
J.G. Eccard/A. Miller (10,367)
J. G. Eccard/J. Pearson (11,250)
H. Pickering/J. Faber the Younger (10,031)
A. Pond/J. McArdell (10,319)
A. Pond/J. McArdell (10,366)

so-called Woffington, Margaret (Peg)
F. Van der Mijn/R. Purcell (10,683)
F. Van der Mijn/R. Purcell (11,249)

Wolfe, Arthur
(1st Viscount Kilwarden; Lord Chief Justice of Ireland)
H.D. Hamilton/F. Bartolozzi (10,072)
H.D. Hamilton/F. Bartolozzi (10,861-10,862)
H.D. Hamilton/*P. Maguire*/J. Heath (10,863)
H.D. Hamilton/P. Lightfoot (10,640)
G.F. Joseph/S. Freeman (10,639)

Wolfe, Theobald
R. Home/F. Bartolozzi (10,692)
R. Home/F. Bartolozzi (10,693)

Wood, Richard
A.R. Mengs/P.W. Thomas (20,727) (12)

Woods, Lady
A. Power (8198)

Woodward, Henry
F. Hayman/J. McArdell (10,123)
R.E. Pine/W. Dickinson (10,686)

Worsdale, James
R.E. Pine/W. Dickinson (10,686)

Worsley, Anne
(Mrs William Bastard)
J. Reynolds/R. Brookshaw (11,097)

Worsley, Frances
(Baroness Carteret, 1st wife of Baron John Carteret)
C. D'Agar/J. Simon (10,730-10,731)

Wotton, Katherine
(Suo jure Countess of Chesterfield)
A. Van Dyck/*A. Houbraken*/P. Gunst (10,349)

Wren, Sir Christopher
P. Lely & ?J. Closterman/T.A. Prior (11,373)*(group)*

Wrixon-Becher, Lady Eliza
(née O'Neill)
A.W. Devis/H. Meyer (10,409)
G. Dawes/F.C. Lewis the Elder (10,991)
S. Drummond/T. Blood (10,579);
J.J. Masquerier/W.Say (10,372)

Wyndham King, Mrs. J.H.
(née Emily Mary Dawson)
J. Hayter/W.H. Mote (10,784)

Wyse, M.P., Sir Thomas
Cossos and Brontos (8185)
J.P. Haverty/J.P. Haverty (11,020)*(group)*

Yeats, John Butler
E. Quinn (8145)

Yeats, William Butler
A. John/A. John (20,764)
A. Power (8048)
A. Power (8292)
T. Spicer-Simson (8215)

Yelverton, Barry
(1st Viscount Avonmore; Lord Chief Baron of the Exchequer)
T. Robinson/Irish School 1791 (11,242)
T. Robinson/T. Robinson (10,043)

Yonge, John
Irish School 17C/English School 1794 (11,003)

York, James, Duke of — see James II

York and Albany, Frederick Augustus, Duke of
R. Bowyer/J.C. Bromley (10,428)

Yorke, Philip
(3rd Earl of Harwicke; Lord Lieutenant of Ireland)
T. Lawrence/W. Giller (10,154)

Young, Arthur
J. Rising/W. Hinton (11,262)

Youngson, Margaret Caroline
D. Dodd/G. Sibelius (11,058)

Zamparini, Madame Anna
N. Hone the Elder/G. Cook (11,377)

Zeno
J. Barry/J. Barry (20,722)(8)*(group)*

APPENDIX 5

IDENTIFIED VIEWS

Abbeville, N. France (St Wulfran's)
D. Roberts/A.R. Freebairn (20,371)

Aghaboe Abbey, Co. Laois
D. Sullivan/D. Sullivan (10,039)(9)

Alphington, near Exeter, Devon
J.D. Harding/J.D. Harding (20,185)

The Alps (from Grenoble to Chambéry)
J.M.W. Turner/J.M.W. Turner & W. Say (20,006)

Amboise Château, France
J.M.W. Turner/J.B. Allen (20,482)

Amsterdam (Buiten singel)
Baronne C. Rothschild/T.N. Chauvel (20,080)

Andernach Castle, Germany
J.D. Harding/J.D. Harding (20,193)

Ardgillan Castle, Balbriggan, Co. Dublin
J.E. Jones/E. Radclyffe (11,667)

Ard Loch, Scotland
G.F. Robson/E.F. Finden (20,478)

Argyro-Castro Castle, Albania
W.L. Leitch/J. Sands (20,365)

Armoy Round Tower, Co. Antrim
Irish School 19C/Irish School 19C (11,746)

Arran Isle, Scotland
D.Y. Cameron/D.Y. Cameron (11,682)

Arthur's Seat, Edinburgh, Scotland
P. Nasmyth/S. Lacey (20,519)

Athlone, Co. Westmeath (view and plan)
Dutch School 1691/*J. Tangena*/Dutch School c.1691
R.W. Seale/R.W. Seale (11,877)

Aveiron River, Chamonix, France
J.M.W. Turner/J.M.W. Turner (20,017)

Avoca, Co. Wicklow
D. Sullivan/D. Sullivan (10,039)(3)

Avonbeg River, Co. Wicklow
T. Fairland/T. Fairland (20,352)
G. Rowe/G. Rowe (20,354)

Aydon Castle, Northumberland
T. Allom/T. Allom (20,419)

Ayr, Scotland (Auld Brig of Doon bridge)
D.O. Hill/W. Forrest (20,461)

Ayr River, Scotland
D.O. Hill/W. Richardson (20,282)

Baggotsrath Castle, Co. Dublin
T. Cocking/T. Mèdland (11,927)

Balregan Castle, Co. Louth
D. Sullivan/D. Sullivan (10,039)(11)

Bantry Bay, Co. Cork
T. Creswick/R. Wallis (20,513)

Barnard Castle, Co. Durham
J.M.W. Turner/J.T. Willemore (20,599)

Barnstable, Devon
J. Pennell/J. Pennell (11,455)

Barskimming, Scotland
D.O. Hill/W. Richardson (20,282)

Basle, Switzerland
J.M.W. Turner/J.M.W. Turner & C. Turner (11,962)

Bavarian Alps, Germany
G. Barret the Younger/R. Wallis (20,276)

Beaulieu House, Drogheda, Co. Louth
J.E. Jones/E. Radclyffe (11,675)

Beau-Parc, Co. Meath
T. Roberts/T. Milton (20,277)

Belfast, Co. Antrim (plan and view)
R.W. Seale/R.W. Seale (11,877)
D. Sullivan/D. Sullivan (10,039)(14)

Belfast Lough, Co. Antrim
D. Sullivan/D. Sullivan (10,039)(13)

Belgrade, Yugoslavia
F. Abresch/*W.H. Bartlett*/Brandard (20.475)

Belstein, Germany
J.D. Harding/J.D. Harding (20,306)

Ben Arthur, Scotland
J.M.W. Turner/J.M.W. Turner & T.G. Lupton (20,026)

Ben Lomond, Scotland
T. Allom/E.F. Finden (20,478)

Bexhill, Sussex (Martello towers)
J.M.W. Turner/J.M.W. Turner & W. Say (11,991)

Bideford, Devon
J. Pennell/J. Pennell (11,456)

Birkland, Ullswater, Cumbria
J.D. Harding/J.D. Harding (20,303)

Bishopscourt, Co. Dublin
Irish School 19C/Irish School 19C (11,241)

Blackrock Castle, Co. Cork
T. Creswick/R. Brandard (20,510)
T.S. Roberts/J.W. Edy (20,838)(7)

Blackwater River, Co. Waterford
T.S. Roberts/S. Alken (20,838)(12)

Blair Athol, Scotland
J.M.W. Turner/J.M.W. Turner & W. Say (11,987)

Blarney Castle, Co. Cork
T.S. Roberts/S. Alken (20,838)(8)

Bonneville, E. France (Château de St Michel)
J.M.W. Turner/J.M.W. Turner & H. Dawe (20,021)

Boppard, Germany
J.D. Harding/J.D. Harding (20,194)

Boreragh, Co. Derry (Ancient tomb)
Irish School 19C/Irish School 19C (20,815)

Boulac, France
A.G. Decamps/A.G. Decamps (20,332)

Bow Fell, Cumbria
T. Allom/W.H. Kersall (20,457)

Boyne river
R. De Hooghe/R. De Hooghe (11,655)
Irish School c.1798/English School 1798 (11,679)
J.E. Jones/E. Radclyffe (11,675)
T. Maas/T. Maas (10,003)
T. Maas/T. Maas (20,800)
T. Roberts/T. Milton (20,277)
J. Wyck/J. Brooks (11,652)

Delphi Lodge, Lough Doo, Co. Mayo
W.H. Bartlett/J. Cousen (20,438-20,439)

Derrynane Abbey, Co. Kerry
J. Fogarty/R. Havell the Elder & Younger (11,842)

Devinish, Co. Fermanagh
D. Sullivan/D. Sullivan (10,039)(5)

Dieppe, N. France (views and Old Royal Hotel)
J.D. Harding/W.R. Smith (20,431)
W. Sickert/W. Sickert (11,443)
C. Tomkins/D. Lucas (20,327)

Dijle River, Mechlin, Belgium
?J. Shury the Elder/J. Shury the Elder & Younger (20,280)

Doo Lough, Co. Mayo
W.H. Bartlett/J. Cousen (20,438)
W.H. Bartlett/J. Cousen (20,439)

Dorney Common, Buckinghamshire
J.D. Harding/J.D. Harding (20,186)

Dovedale, Derbyshire
E. Dayes/Smith (20,411)

Downpatrick, Co. Down
D. Sullivan/D. Sullivan (10,039)(17)

Downpatrick Cathedral, Co. Down
M. Cregan/G.R. Ward (10,449)

Drogheda, Co. Louth (view and plan
Irish School c.1798/English School 1798 (11,679)
J.E. Jones/E. Radclyffe (11,676)
R.W. Seale/R.W. Seale (11,877)

Dromona, Co. Waterford
T.S. Roberts/S. Alken (20,838)(12)

Dryslwyn Castle, S. Wales
J.H. Robinson/J.S. Templeton (20,138)

Co. Dublin, Map of
J. Rocque/English School 1799 (10,813)

DUBLIN

Maps and Plans
C. Brooking/J. Bowles (10,015)
J. Cooke/J. Cooke (11,888)
W. Faden/W. Faden (11,887)
E. Heffernan/Irish School 1868 (11,685)
Irish School c.1717/Irish School 1717 (11,881)
Irish School c.1728/E. Bowen (11,889)
Irish School c.1753/Irish School 1753 (11,667)
J. Kirkwood/J. Kirkwood (11,811)
H. Moll/H. Moll (11,666)
R. Pool & J. Cash/J. Lodge (10,041)(1)
R. Pool & J. Cash/J. Lodge (10,041)(2)
J. Rocque/A. Dury & P. Halpin (11,806)
J. Rocque/English School 1762 (11,880)
J. Rocque/J.J. Perret (11,886)
R.W. Seale/R.W. Seale (11,877)
T. Sherrard/Irish School 1803 (11,807)
J. Speed/J. Malton (11,567)
L.R. Strangways/L.R. Strangways (11,884)
W. Wilson/B. Baker (11,812)

General Views
E. Heffernan/Irish School 1868 (11,885)
E. Heffernan/Irish School 1868 (11,885)(8)
Irish School 18C/Irish School 18C (11,713)
Irish School c.1785/Irish School c.1785 (11,901)
Irish School late 18C/Irish School late 18C (11,715)
Irish School c.1800/Irish School c.1800 (11,718)
Irish School 1846/Smyth (11,878)
G. Petrie/E. Goodall (11,787)
G. Petrie/English School 1821 (11,789)
T.S. Roberts/R. Havell the Elder & Younger (11,909)

Dublin from the Phoenix Park
J. Fisher/J. Fisher (11,639)
J. Fisher/J. Fisher (11,719)
E. Heffernan/Irish School 1868 (11,885)(4)
Irish School 1784/English School 1784 (11,901)
J. Malton/J. Malton (11,588)
G. Petrie/J. Storer & H. Sargent (11,788)
J. Tudor/F. Cary (11,716)
J. Tudor/English School 1774 (11,717)
J. Tudor/Slack (11,691)

Áras an Uachtarain, Phoenix Park (was the Lord Lieutenant's Residence; Vice-regal lodge)
J.J. Barralet/T. Milton (11,604)
E. Heffernan/Irish School 1868 (11,885)(22)
Irish School late 18C/Irish School late 18C (11,618)

Assembly Rooms (now the Gate Theatre)
E. Heffernan/Irish School 1868 (11,885)(15)
J. Malton/J. Malton (11,585)

No. 12, Aungier street (birthplace of Thomas Moore)
T. Creswick/J.T. Willmore (11,697)

Bank of Ireland, College Green (former Parliament House) - exterior
S.F. Brocas/H. Brocas the Younger (11,952)
W. Brocas/R. Havell the Elder & Younger (11,638)
W. Brocas/R. Havell the Elder & Younger (11,646)
J. Cooke/J. Cooke (11,888)(1)
E. Heffernan/Irish School 1868 (11,885)(1)
Irish School c.1779/Irish School c.1800 (11,627)
Irish School 1784/English School 1784 (11,626)
Irish School 1784/English School 1784 (11,898)
Irish School 1784/English School 1784 (11,900)
Irish School c.1787/English School 1787 (11,730-11,731)
Irish School 1792/English School 1792 (11,728)
Irish School 1792/English School 1792 (11,914)
Irish School late 18C/Myers (11,754)
Irish School 19C/M. Jackson (11,729)
T. Kelly/T. Kelly (11,850)
R. Omer/P. Halpin (11,629)
G. Petrie/T. Barber (11,777)
G. Petrie/B. Winkles (11,785-11,786)
R. Pool & J. Cash/I. Taylor the Elder (10,041)(6)
R. Pool & J. Cash/I. Taylor the Elder (11,753)

R. Pool & J. Cash/W. Thomas (11,752)
A. Pope/C. Scriven (10,437)*(detail)*
T.S. Roberts/J. Bluck (11,593)
J. Tudor/?J. McArdell (11,906)
F. Wheatley/J. Collyer (11,644)
F. Wheatley/J. Collyer (11,826)

- interior
R. Omer/Irish School 1767 (11,883)
R. Omer/P. Mazell (11,600)
R. Omer/P. Mazell (20,814)
R. Pool & J. Cash/J. Lodge (10,041)(7)
F. Wheatley/English School 1801 (11,830)

Barrack bridge (now rebuilt)
G. Petrie/T. Barber (11,792)

Beresford Place fountain (now destroyed)
T.N. Deane & B. Woodward/J.C. Rogers (11,737)

The Blew-Coat Hospital, Queen Street (now demolished)
C. Brooking/J. Bowles (10,015)(9)
Irish School c.1762/Irish School 1762 (11,616)

The Blue-Coat School, Blackhall Place, (now the Incorporated Law Society)
J. Cooke/J. Cooke (11,888)(2)
J. Malton/J. Malton (11,591)
R. Pool & J. Cash/I. Taylor the Elder (10,041)(18)

Carlisle (now O'Connell) Bridge
R. Pool & J. Cash/J. Lodge (11,740)
Irish School c.1880/Irish School c.1880 (11,724)

The Castle - exterior
S.F. Brocas/H. Brocas the Younger (11,944)
S.F. Brocas/H. Brocas the Younger (11,950)
C. Brooking/J. Bowles (10,015)(13)
J. Cooke/J. Cooke (11,888)(5)
J. Cooke/J. Cooke (11,888)(6)
Sir T. Hammond/English School 1822 (11,596)
Sir T. Hammond/English School 1822 (11,698)
E. Heffernan/Irish School 1868 (11,885)(6)
E. Heffernan/Irish School 1868 (11,885)(7)
Irish School 1784/English School 1784 (11,895)
J. Malton/A.F. Lemaitre (11,699)
J. Malton/J. Malton (11,568)
G. Petrie/English School 1821 (11,773)
G. Petrie/E. Goodall (11,774)
G. Petrie/T. Higham (11,700)
R. Pool & J. Cash/J. Lodge (10,041)(4)
R. Pool & J. Cash/J. Lodge (10,041)(5)
J. Tudor/Parr (11,905)

- Chapel Royal (now Chapel of the Holy Trinity)
S.F. Brocas/H. Brocas the Younger (11,955)

- St Patrick's Hall
J.K. Sherwin/J.K. Sherwin (11,657-11,658)
J.K. Sherwin/J.K. Sherwin (11,827-11,829)

Castle Street
Irish School c.1788/English School 1788 (11,917)

Castle Street wooden house (now demolished)
Irish School 19C/Irish School 19C (11,922)

Charlemont House, Rutland (now Parnell) Square
R. Pool & J. Cash/J. Lodge (10,041)(31)

Chief Secretary's Lodge, Phoenix Park (now American Ambassador's Residence)
E. Heffernan/Irish School 1868 (11,885)(2)

Christchurch Cathedral - exterior
A.M. Bigari/T. Medland (10,055)
H. Grattan/J. Greig (10,054)
G. Petrie/T. Barber (10,056)
G. Petrie/T.F. Ranson (10,048)
R. Pool & J. Cash/J. Lodge (10,041)(20)

- interior
R. Pool & J. Cash/J. Lodge (10,041)(28)
R. Pool & J. Cash/I. Taylor the Elder (10,041)(26)
R. Pool & J. Cash/I. Taylor the Elder (10,041)(27)

City Basin
C. Brooking/J. Bowles (10,015)(20)

City Hall, Cork Hill (was the Royal Exchange)
S.F. Brocas/H. Brocas the Younger (11,951)
J. Cooke/J. Cooke (11,888)(19)
Irish School 1784/English School 1784 (11,896)
J. Malton/J. Malton (11,570)
G. Petrie/English School 1821 (11,781)
R. Pool & J. Cash/J. Lodge (10,041)(13)
R. Pool & J. Cash/I. Taylor the Elder (10,041)(12)
R. Pool & J. Cash/I. Taylor the Elder (11,755)

Clarendon Market (now demolished; plan of proposed alterations)
S. Sproule/Irish School 1783 (11,818)

Clontarf
Irish School 18C/Irish School 18C (11,713)

Clontarf Castle (now altered)
Irish School c.1787/English School 1787 (11,837)

Clontarf sheds
F. Wheatley/T. Malton (11,902)

College Green
C. Brooking/J. Bowles (10,015)(5-6)
Irish School c.1779/Irish School c.1800 (11,627)
Irish School 1784/English School 1784 (11,626)
Irish School 1784/English School 1784 (11,900)
T. Kelly/T. Kelly (11,850)
R. Pool & J. Cash/J. Lodge (10,041)(3)
T.S. Roberts/J. Bluck (11,593)
J. Tudor/?J. McArdell (11,906)
F. Wheatley/J. Collyer (11,644)
F. Wheatley/J. Collyer (11,826)

College Street
G. Petrie/E. Winkles (11,788)

Collins (was the Royal) Barracks
C. Brooking/J. Bowles (10,015)(15)
J. Malton/J. Malton (11,577)

The Corn Exchange, Burgh Quay (now rebuilt)
S.F. Brocas/H. Brocas the Younger (11,946)
J. Cooke/J. Cooke (11,888)(3)

Corn Market, Thomas Street (now demolished)
C. Brooking/J. Bowles (10,015)(18)

(Old) Courts of Justice, St Michael's Hill (now demolished)
Irish School c.1788/English School 1788 (11,743)
Irish School c.1788/English School 1788 (11,921)

(Old) Custom House, Burgh Quay (now demolished)
C. Brooking/J. Bowles (10,015)(14)
Irish School c.1785/Irish School c.1785 (11,899)
J. Tudor/Parr (11,904)

The Custom House
S.F. Brocas/H. Brocas the Younger (11,703)
S.F. Brocas/H. Brocas the Younger (11,954)
J. Cooke/J. Cooke (11,888)(4)
E. Heffernan/Irish School 1868 (11,885)(3)
H. Hone/H. Meyer (10,833)
H. Hone/H. Meyer (11,153)
Irish School 1792/English School 1792 (11,720)
Irish School 1792/English School 1792 (11,721)
J. Kirkwood/J. Kirkwood (11,701)
J. Malton/A.F. Lemaitre (11,702)
J. Malton/J. Malton (11,569)
J. Malton/J. Malton (11,634)
J. Malton/J. Malton (11,640)
T.S. Roberts/J. Bluck (11,909)

The Dáil and Seanad, Kildare Street (was Duke of Leinster's house)
R. Pool & J. Cash/J. Lodge (10,041)(29)
R. Pool & J. Cash/J. Lodge (11,725)

Daly's Club House, College Green (now partially demolished)
S.F. Brocas/H. Brocas the Younger (11,951)
S.F. Brocas/H. Brocas the Younger (11,953)
Irish School 1790/English School 1790 (11,923)
T. Kelly/T. Kelly (11,850)

D'Olier Street
S.F. Brocas/H. Brocas the Younger (11,947)

Essex (now rebuilt Grattan) Bridge
C. Brooking/J. Bowles (10,015)(12)
Irish School c.1755/B. Cole (11,768)
Irish School 1784/English School 1784 (11,899)
R. Pool & J. Cash/J. Lodge (10,041)(14)
R. Pool & J. Cash/J. Lodge (11,740)
J. Tudor/Parr (11,904)

Father Mathew Bridge - see Whitworth Bridge

Findlater's Church, Rutland (now Parnell) Square
Irish School c.1845/Morison & Co. (11,840)

Fortfield House, Terenure
T. Robinson/T. Robinson (10,043)

The Foundling Hospital and Workhouse, James's Street (later St Kevin's Hospital; now demolished)
C. Brooking/J. Bowles (10,015)(11)
Irish School c.1817/English School 1817 (11,831)

The Four Courts, Inns Quay
S.F. Brocas/H. Brocas the Younger (11,945)
J. Carr/T. Medland (11,603)
?N. Clarget/L.A. Tourfaut (11,723)
J. Cooke/J. Cooke (11,888)(7)
Irish School 19C/J.L. Marks (11,704)
E. Heffernan/Irish School 1868 (11,885)(9)
Irish School c.1811/Irish School 1811 (11,591)
J. Malton/J. Malton (11,592)
G. Petrie/English School 1821 (11,783)
T.S. Roberts/J. Bluck (11,911)
T.S. Roberts/R. Havell the Elder and Younger (11,912)

The Gate Theatre, Cavendish Row (former Assembly Rooms)
E. Heffernan/Irish School 1868 (11,885)(15)
J. Malton/J. Malton (11,585)

The General Post Office, Sackville (now O'Connell) Street
S.F. Brocas/H. Brocas the Younger (11,948)
J. Cooke/J. Cooke (11,888)(8)
?C. Corley/C. Corley (11,835)
E. Heffernan/Irish School 1868 (11,885)(10)
F. Johnston/R. Havell the Elder & Younger (11,705)
T.S. Roberts/R. Havell the Elder & Younger (11,910)

George I statue (was on Essex Bridge)
C. Brooking/J. Bowles (10,015)(12)

Grand Canal Hotel, Portobello (now Portobello House)
J. Ford/J. Ford (11,624)

Harcourt Bridge, Grand Canal
J.J. Barralet/J.J. Barralet (11,641)

Harcourt Street Station (disused; formerly Dublin and Wicklow Railway terminus)
E. Heffernan/Irish School 1868 (11,885)(5)

Heuston (was King's Bridge) Station
E. Heffernan/Irish School 1868 (11,885)(11)

The Hibernian Military School, Phoenix Park (now St Mary's Hospital)
E. Heffernan/Irish School 1868 (11,885)(12)

Homes Hotel, Ussher's Quay (now demolished)
J. Cooke/J. Cooke (11,888)(9)

Irishtown
Irish School 18C/Irish School 18C (11,713)

Islandbridge
J. Fisher/J. Fisher (11,639)
J. Fisher/J. Fisher (11,719)
E. Heffernan/Irish School 1868 (11,885)(4)
Irish School 18C/Irish School 18C (11,715)
Irish School 1784/English School 1784 (11,901)
Irish School late 18C/English School late 18C (11,739)
J. Malton/J. Malton (11,588)
G. Petrie/E. Goodall (11,794)

G. Petrie/J. Storer & H. Sargent (11,788)
J. Tudor/F. Cary (11,716)
J. Tudor/English School 1774 (11,717)
J. Tudor/Slack (11,691)

James's Street Obelisk fountain
Irish School c.1790/English School 1790 (11,832)

King's (now Heuston) Bridge)
G. Petrie/T. Higham (11,793)

King's Bridge (now Heuston) Station
E. Heffernan/Irish school 1868 (11,885)(11)

King's Inns, Henrietta Street
J. Cooke/J. Cooke (11,888)(10)
E. Heffernan/Irish School 1868 (11,885)(14)
G. Petrie/English School 1821 (11,784)

La Touche Bank, Castle Street (now demolished)
Irish School c.1788/English School 1788 (11,917)

Leinster House Lawn
J.J. Barralet/T. Milton (11,615)
J.J. Barralet/T. Milton (11,750)
Irish School 1853/Irish School 1853 (11,722)

Leinster House, Kildare Street (now Dáil and Seanad)
R. Pool & J. Cash/J. Lodge (10,041)(29)
R. Pool & J. Cash/J. Lodge (11,725)

The Linen Hall, Halston Street (now demolished)
C. Brooking/J. Bowles (10,015)(2)
J. Cooke/J. Cooke (11,888)(11)
W. Hincks/W. Hincks (11,637)

The Lying-in (now Rotunda) Hospital, Great Britain (now Parnell) Street
S.F. Brocas/H. Brocas the Younger (11,949)
J. Cooke/J. Cooke (11,888)(12)
J.P. Haverty/R. Havell the Elder & Younger (11,650)
E. Heffernan/Irish School 1868 (11,885)(15)
Irish School c.1785/Irish School c.1785 (11,897)

J. Malton/J. Malton (11,585)
G. Petrie/English School 1821 (11,780)
R. Pool & J. Cash/J. Lodge (10,041)(17)
R. Pool & J. Cash/J. Lodge (11,726)

The Mansion House (now refaced)
C. Brooking/J. Bowles (10,015)(8)

Marrowbone Lane house (demolished)
B. Clayton the Elder/B. Clayton the Elder (11,924)

Marino Casino
T. Ivory/E. Rooker (11,669)
F. Wheatley/T. Milton (11,594)

The Marine School, Sir John Rogerson's Quay (now demolished)
J. Malton/J. Malton (11,586)
R. Pool & J. Cash/J. Lodge (10,041)(16)
R. Pool & J. Cash/J. Lodge (11,707)

The Meath Infirmary, the Coombe (now demolished)
Irish School c.1786/Irish School 1786 (11,668)

The Metropolitan Chapel, Marlborough Street (now Pro-Cathedral)
J. Cooke/J. Cooke (11,888)(13)
J. Cooke/J. Cooke (11,888)(14)

The Mint House of King James II, Capel Street (now demolished)
T. Archdeakon/T. Archdeakon (11,919)

Nelson Pillar, Sackville Street (now demolished)
S.F. Brocas/H. Brocas the Younger (11,948)
Irish School 1808/Irish School 1808 (11,735)
J. Cooke/J. Cooke (11,888)(15)
G. Petrie/R. Winkles (20,612)

Newcomen Bank, Castle Street (now Civic offices)
S.F. Brocas/H. Brocas the Younger (11,944
S.F. Brocas/H. Brocas the Younger (11,950)
Irish School 1784/English School 1784 (11,895)
Irish School c.1788/English School 1788 (11,917)

New Stamp Office (Powerscourt House, William Street South)
J. Ford/J. Ford (11,625)
Irish School c.1790/English School 1790 (11,832)
J. Malton/J. Malton (11,583)
R. Pool & J. Cash/J. Lodge (10,041)(30)

New Theatre Royal, Hawkins Street (now demolished)
J. Cooke/J. Cooke (11,888)(16)
Irish School 1880/Morison and Co. (11,632)
G. Petrie/T. Barber (11,779)

Newgate Jail (now demolished)
R. Pool & J. Cash/J. Lodge (10,041)(15)

O'Connell (was Carlisle) Bridge
Irish School c.1880/Irish School c.1880 (11,724)
R. Pool & J. Cash/J. Lodge (11,740)

O'Connell (was Sackville) Street
S.F. Brocas/H. Brocas the Younger (11,948)
J. Cooke/J. Cooke (11,888)(15)
?C. Corley/C. Corley (11,835)
E. Heffernan/Irish School 1868 (11,885)(20)
Irish School c.1750/J. Jones (11,633)
Irish School c.1880/Irish School c.1880 (11,734)
G. Petrie/T. Barber (11,790-11,791)
G. Petrie/R. Winkles (20,612)

O'Donovan Rossa Bridge - see Richmond Bridge

Parkgate Street fountain (partially destroyed)
T.N. Deane & B. Woodward/J.E. Rogers (11,737)

Parliament House, College Green (Bank of Ireland from 1800)
- exterior
S.F. Brocas/H. Brocas the Younger (11,952)
W. Brocas/R. Havell the Elder & Younger (11,638)
W. Brocas/R. Havell the Elder & Younger (11,646)
J. Cooke/J. Cooke (11,888)(1)
E. Heffernan/Irish School 1868 (11,885)(1)
Irish School 1784/English School 1784 (11,626)

Irish School 1784/English School 1784 (11,900)
Irish School c.1787/English School 1787 (11,730-11,731)
Irish School 1792/English School 1792 (11,728)
Irish School 1792/English School 1792 (11,914)
Irish School c.1779/Irish School c.1800 (11,627)
Irish School late 18C/Myers (11,754)
Irish School 19C/M. Jackson (11,729)
T. Kelly/T. Kelly (11,850)
R. Omer/P. Halpin (11,629)
G. Petrie/T. Barber (11,777)
G. Petrie/B. Winkles (11,785-11,786)
R. Pool & J. Cash/I. Taylor the Elder (10,041)(6)
R. Pool & J. Cash/I. Taylor the Elder (11,753)
R. Pool & J. Cash/W. Thomas (11,752)
A. Pope/E. Scriver (10,437)*(detail)*
T.S. Roberts/J. Bluck (11,593)
J. Tudor/?J. McArdell (11,906)
F. Wheatley/J. Collyer (11,644)
F. Wheatley/J. Collyer (11,826)

- interior
R. Omer/Irish School 1767 (11,883)
R. Omer/P. Mazell (11,600)
R. Omer/P. Mazell (20,814)
R. Pool & J. Cash/J. Lodge (10,041)(7)
F. Wheatley/English School 1801 (11,830)

Phoenix Park
see Áras an Uachtaráin
see Chief Secretary's Residence
see Dublin from the Phoenix Park
see Hibernian Military School
see Wellington Testimonial
Irish School 1783/Irish School 1783 (11,870)

Phoenix Pillar, Phoenix Park
G. Petrie/B. Winkles (11,782)

Poor House, James's Street (now demolished)
C. Brooking/J. Bowles (10,015)(11)

Portobello House, Grand Canal (was Grand Canal Hotel)
J. Ford/J. Ford (11,624)

Powder Magazine, Phoenix Park
?F. Jukes/F. Jukes (11,732-11,733)

Powerscourt House, William Street South
J. Ford/J. Ford (11,625)
Irish School c.1790/Irish School 1790 (11,832)
J. Malton/J. Malton (11,583)
R. Pool & J. Cash/J. Lodge (10,041)(30)
R. Pool & J. Cash/J. Lodge (11,734)

Pro-Cathedral, Marlborough Street (was the Metropolitan Chapel
J. Cooke/J. Cooke (11,888)(13)
J. Cooke/J. Cooke (11,888)(14)

Queen's (now Queen Maev) Bridge
G. Petrie/T. Barber (11,792)
R. Pool & J. Cash/J. Lodge (10,041)(14)
R. Pool & J. Cash/J. Lodge (11,740)

Richmond (now O'Donovan Rossa) Bridge
S.F. Brocas/H. Brocas the Younger (11,945)
J. Carr/T. Medland (11,603)
Irish School 19C/J.L. Marks (11,704)
G. Petrie/English School 1821 (11,783)
T.S. Roberts/R. Havell the Elder & Younger (11,912)

Richmond Tower (now at Kilmainham)
G. Petrie/T. Barber (11,792)

Ringsend
Irish School 18C/Irish School 18C (11,713)
Irish School c.1796/Irish School c.1796 (11,602)
W. Jones/G. King (10,007)

Ringsend dock with floating chapel
Irish School late 18C/Irish School late 18C (11,738)

The Rotunda (was part of Lying-in Hospital; now a cinema)
see Rotunda Hospital
J. Malton/J. Malton (11,585)

Rotunda Hospital (was Lying-in Hospital)
S.F. Brocas/H. Brocas the Younger (11,949)
J. Cooke/J. Cooke (11,888)(12)
J.P. Haverty/R. Havell the Elder & Younger (11,650)
E. Heffernan/Irish School 1868 (11,885)(15)
Irish School 1784/English School 1784 (11,897)
J. Malton/J. Malton (11,585)

G. Petrie/English School 1821 (11,780)
R. Pool & J. Cash/J. Lodge (10,041)(17)
R. Pool & J. Cash/J. Lodge (11,726)

Round Church (St. Andrew's, Suffolk Street; now rebuilt)
English School 1836/Smith & Graves (11,548)

The Royal (now Allied Irish) Bank, Foster Place
E. Heffernan/Irish School 1868 (11,885)(16)

Royal (now Collins) Barracks
C. Brooking/J. Bowles (10,015)(15)
J. Malton/J. Malton (11,577)
J. Tudor/A. Walker

Royal Canal
W.M. Craig/T. Dixon (11,693)

Royal Canal harbour
G. Petrie/English School 1821 (11,784)

Royal Charter School, Clontarf (now demolished)
Irish School c.1787/English School 1787 (11,918)

Royal College of Surgeons, St Stephen's Green
J. Cooke/J. Cooke (11,888)(17)
German School 19C/German School 19C (11,834)
E. Heffernan/Irish School 1868 (11,885)(17)
Irish School c.1820/Irish School c.1820 (11,736)

Royal Dublin Society Headquarters, Ballsbridge
J. Cooke/J. Cooke (11,888)(18)

The Royal Exchange, Cork Hill (now City Hall)
S.F. Brocas/H. Brocas the Younger (11,951)
J. Cooke/J. Cooke (11,888)(19)
Irish School 1784/English School 1784 (11,896)
G. Petrie/English School 1821 (11,781)
R. Pool & J. Cash/J. Lodge (10,041)(13)
R. Pool & J. Cash/I. Taylor the Elder (10,041)(12)
R. Pool & J. Cash/I. Taylor the Elder (11,755)

Royal Hospital, Kilmainham
C. Brooking/J. Bowles (10,015)(16)
Irish School c.1750/English School 1750 (10,005)
E. Heffernan/Irish School 1868 (11,885)(18)
J. Malton/J. Malton (11,581)

Royal Military Infirmary, Phoenix Park (now Army GHQ)
?J. Ford/J. Ford (11,694)
Irish School c.1790/English School 1790 (11,727)
J. Malton/J. Malton (11,582)

The Rutland Fountain, Merrion Square
J.J. Barralet/J.C. Stadler (11,643)

Sackville (now O'Connell) Street
S.F. Brocas/H. Brocas the Younger (11,948)
J. Cooke/J. Cooke (11,888)(15)
?C. Corley/C. Corley (11,835)
E. Heffernan/Irish School 1868 (11,885)(20)
Irish School c.1750/J. Jones (11,633)
Irish School c.1880/Irish School c.1880 (11,724)
G. Petrie/T. Barber (11,790-11,791)
G. Petrie/B. Winkles (20,612)

26, St Andrew's Street (now demolished)
English School 1836/Smith & Graves (11,548)

St Andrew's Church, Suffolk Street (now rebuilt)
?English School 1836/Smith & Graves (11,548)
Irish School c.1790/English School 1790 (11,832)

St Ann's Church, Dawson Street (now refaced)
C. Brooking/J. Bowles (10,015)(17)
Irish School c.1786/English School 1786 (11,668)
Irish School c.1786/English School 1786 (11,920)

St Audeon's Church (C of I), High Street
G. Petrie/B. Winkles (11,776)

St Audeon's Church (RC), High Street
Irish School c.1850/Irish School c.1850 (11,766)

St Catherine's Church, Thomas Street
R. Pool & J. Cash/J. Lodge (10,041)(24)

St George's Church, Hardwicke Place
W.H. Bartlett/R. Winkles (11,771)
W.H. Bartlett/R. Winkles (20,611)
J. Cooke/J. Cooke (11,888)(20)
Irish School 19C/J. Martyn (11,770)
Irish School c.1817/English School 1817 (11,741)
G. Petrie/T. Barber (11,778)

St John the Evangelist Church, Fishamble Street (now demolished)
Irish School c.1785/English School 1785 (11,915)

St Kevin's Hospital, James's Street (was the Foundling Hospital; now demolished)
Irish School c.1817/English School 1817 (11,831)

St Mary's Hospital, Phoenix Park (was the Hibernian Military School)
E. Heffernan/Irish School 1868 (11,885)(12)

St Michan's Church, Church Street
Irish School c.1790/English School 1790 (11,832)

St Nicholas-within Church, Christchurch Place (now demolished)
Irish School c.1786/English School 1786 (11,742)
Irish School c.1786/English School 1786 (11,916)

St Patrick's Cathedral - exterior
W.H. Bartlett/F.W. Topham (11,763)
W.H. Bartlett/F.W. Topham (20,590)
P. Byrne/W. Smith (11,608)
E. Heffernan/Irish School 1868 (11,885)(19)
Irish School early 18C/Irish School early 18C (11,833)
Irish School 19C/J. Newman and Co. (11,761)
Irish School c.1817/English School 1817 (11,762)
J. Malton/English School 1817 (11,764)
J. Malton/A.F. Lemaitre (11,765)
J. Malton/J. Malton (11,573)
J. Malton/J. Malton (11,579)
R. O'C. Newenham/J.D. Harding (11,610)
G. Petrie/T. Higham (11,775)
R. Pool & J. Cash/I. Taylor the Elder (10,041)(21)

- interior
P. Byrne/W. Radclyffe (11,609)
P. Byrne/W. Radclyffe (11,759)
R. Carpenter/T.T. Bury (11,722)
J. Cooke/J. Cooke (11,888)(21)
Irish School 19C/Irish School 19C (11,760)
R. O'C. Newenham/J.D. Harding (11,611
R. Pool & J. Cash/I. Taylor the Elder (10,041)(25)

St Stephen's Green (now re-landscaped)
J. Brooking/J. Bowles (10,015)(4)
J. Malton/J. Malton (11,587)
J. Tudor/English School 1749 (11,614); (11,712)

St Thomas's Church, Marlborough Street (now demolished)
R. Pool & J. Cash/J. Lodge (10,041)(23)
R. Pool & J. Cash/J. Lodge (11,708)

St Werburgh's Church, Werburgh Street
C. Brooking/J. Bowles (10,015)(1)
R. Pool & J. Cash/J. Lodge (10,041)(22)

Sarah Bridge (now Island Bridge)
Irish School late 18C/Irish School late 18C (11,739)
G. Petrie/E. Goodall (11,794)
G. Petrie/J. Storer & H. Sargent (11,788)

Simpson's Hospital, Great Britain Street (now demolished)
Irish School c.1785/English School 1785 (11,706
Irish School c.1785/English School 1785 (11,836)

Skinners Row
C. Brooking/J. Bowles (10,015)(10)

Smock Alley Theatre (now demolished)
Irish School c.1789/Irish School 1789 (11,925)

The Stamp Office, William Street South (Powerscourt House)
J. Cooke/J. Cooke (11,888)(22)
J. Malton/J. Malton (11,583)

Dr Steevens's Hospital, Steevens Lane
C. Brooking/J. Bowles (10,015)(3)
R. Pool & J. Cash/J. Lodge (10,041)(19)

Stevens Street Hospital (now demolished)
C. Brooking/J. Bowles (10,015)(19)

Stove Tenter House, Weavers Square (now demolished)
Irish School c.1818/B. Brunton (11,767)

The Tholsel, Skinners Row (now demolished)
C. Brooking/J. Bowles (10,015)(10)

Trinity College - exterior
S.F. Brocas/H. Brocas the Younger (11,953)
S.F. Brocas/H. Brocas the Younger (11,956)
W. Brocas/R. Havell the Elder & Younger (11,646)
C. Brooking/C. Brooking (10,015)(6-7)
J. Cooke/J. Cooke (11,888)(23)
E. Heffernan/Irish School 1868 (11,885)(21)
Irish School c.1779/Irish School c.1800 (11,627)
Irish School 1784/English School 1784 (11,626)
Irish School 1784/English School 1784 (11,898)
Irish School 1784/English School 1784 (11,900)
Irish School 19C/M. Jackson (11,729)
Irish School 19C/J. Kirkwood (11,109)
T. Kelly/T. Kelly (11,850)
J. Newman/J. Newman (20,642)
G. Petrie/T. Barber (11,777)
R. Pool & J. Cash/J. Lodge (10,041)(8)
R. Pool & J. Cash/J. Lodge (11,711)
T.S. Roberts/J. Bluck (11,593)
F. Wheatley/J. Collyer (11,644)
F. Wheatley/J. Collyer (11,826)

- front/principal square
R. Pool & J. Cash/J. Lodge (10,041)(9-10)
R. Pool & J. Cash/J. Lodge (11,709)
W.B. Taylor/W.B. Taylor & J. Black (11,621)

- library
C. Brooking/J. Bowles (10,015)(7)
S. Catterson Smith the Elder/G. Sanders (10,510)
J. Tudor/J. McArdell (10,008)

- old museum
W.B. Taylor/R. Havell the Elder & Younger (11,622)

- Provost's House
J. Malton/J. Malton (11,580)
R. Pool & J. Cash/J. Lodge (10,041)(11)
R. Pool & J. Cash/J. Lodge (11,710)

Tyrone House, Marlborough Street (now Department of Education
R. Pool & J. Cash/J. Lodge (10,041)(32)

Viceregal Lodge - see Aras an Uachtarain

Wellington Testimonial, Phoenix Park
J. Cooke/J. Cooke (11,888)(24)
G. Petrie/E. Goodall (11,794)
G. Petrie/J. Storer & H. Sargent (11,788)

Westmoreland Street
S.F. Brocas/H. Brocas the Younger (11,947)

Whitworth (now Father Mathew) Bridge
S.F. Brocas/H. Brocas the Younger (11,945)
?N. Clarget/L.A. Tourfaut (11,723)
Irish School 19C/J.L. Marks (11,704)
T.S. Roberts/R. Havell the Elder & Younger (11,912)

William III statue (destroyed; was on College Green)
C. Brooking/J. Bowles (10,015)(3)
R. Pool & J. Cash/J. Lodge (10,041)(3)

Dublin Bay
G. Collins/English School 17C (11,879)
J. Fisher/J. Fisher (11,628)
Irish School 18C/Irish School 18C (11,713)
Irish School 18C/Irish School 18C (11,817)
Irish School c.1816/English School 1816 (11,714)
Irish School c.1817/Irish School 1817 (11,814)
W. Jones/G. King (10,007)
J. Malton/J. Malton (11,816)
T.L. Rowbotham the Elder/D. Havell (11,648)
F. Wheatley/T. Malton (11,645)

Dunamase Castle, Co. Laois
D. Sullivan/D. Sullivan (10,039)(22)

Dunblane Cathedral, Scotland
J.M.W. Turner/J.M.W. Turner (20,013)

Dunbrody Abbey, Co. Wexford
T.S. Roberts/S. Alken (20,838)(4)

Duncannon, Co. Wexford (plan)
R.W. Seale/R.W. Seale (11,877)

Dun Laoghaire (was Kingstown)
J.P. Haverty/R. Havell the Elder & Younger (11,649)
J.P. Haverty/R. Havell the Elder & Younger (11,651)

Dunloe Gap, Killarney. Co. Kerry
T. Creswick/S. Bradshaw (20,502)
T. Creswick/S. Bradshaw (20,606)

Douro River, Portugal
J.B. Forrester/G. Childs (20,592-20,593)
J.B. Forrester/G. Childs (20,595)

Dunmow Castle, Co. Meath
G. Petrie/T. Higham (20,791)

Dunsink Observatory, Co. Dublin
Irish School c.1788/English School 1788 (11,743-11,744)

Dunstanborough Castle, Northumberland
J.M.W. Turner/J.M.W. Turner & C. Turner (11,971)

Durham, Co. Durham (Castle and Cathedral)
T. Allom/J. Redaway (20,265)
G.F. Robson/E.F. Finden (20,481)

Dynevor Castle, S. Wales
J.H. Robinson/J.S. Templeton (20,368)

Eden Vale, Co. Wexford
T.S. Roberts/S. Alken (20,838)(11)

Edinburgh, Scotland (Tolbooth)
A. Nasmyth/E.F. Finden (20,360)

Elai River, S. Wales
J.H. Robinson/G. Childs (20,291)

Ellisland, Scotland
D.O. Hill/T. Jeavons (20,460)

Enniskillen, Co. Fermananagh
Dutch School c.1690/Dutch School c.1690 (11,866)

Epping Forest, Essex
J.D. Harding/J.D. Harding (20,273)

Esthwaite Lake, Cumbria
G. Pickering/A. Le Petit (20,458)

Etna, Sicily
P.E. Grandsire/C. Barbant (20,619)

Etretat, Normandy, N. France
J.D. Harding/J.D. Harding (20,187)

Ewenny River, S. Wales
J.H. Robinson/G. Childs (20,293)

Exeter Cathedral, Devon
J. Pennell/J. Pennell (11,454)

Fécamp, Normandy, N. France
C. Stanfield/J. Cousen (20,208)

Feldrich Tyrol, Austria
J.D. Harding/J.D. Harding (20,428)

Fiesole, N. Italy (Duomo)
J.D. Harding/J.D. Harding (20,424)

Flint Castle, N. Wales
J.M.W. Turner/J.M.W. Turner & C. Turner (11,961)

Florence, Italy (Duomo and view from Arno River)
G. Carocci/G. Carocci (20,387)
G. Zocchi/G. Zocchi & B.C. Sgrilli (20,669)(4)

Fonthill Abbey, Wiltshire
J.M.W. Turner/T. Crostick (20,512)

Forest Hall Mountains, Cumbria
P. De Wint/J.H. Kernot (20,382)

Foyle River, Co. Derry
Dutch School 1689/Dutch School c.1689 (11,819)

Gainsborough, Lincolnshire
J. Livesey/W.G. Watkins (20,429)

Galway (plan)
R.W. Seale/R.W. Seale (11,877)

Ganges River, India
T. Allom/J.H. Kernot (20,454)

Gartmore, Scotland
J.D. Harding/J.D. Harding (20,581)

Geneva Lake, Switzerland
S. Prout/J.B. Allen (20,459)

Giant's Causeway, Co. Antrim
D. Sullivan/D. Sullivan (10,039)(10)

Glasgow, Scotland (St Mungo's Well)
English School 19C/English School 19C (20,576)

Glashaboy River, Co. Cork
T.S. Roberts/S. Alken (20,838)(9)

Glastonbury, Somerset
S. Prout/S. Prout (20,565)

Glencoe Pass, Scotland
R. Hills/B.P. Gibbon (20,362)

Glendalough, Co. Wicklow
G. Rowe/G. Rowe (20,353)

Glengariff Castle, Co. Cork
T. Creswick/R. Wallis (20,513)

Glenmalure, Co. Wicklow
G. Rowe/G. Rowe (20,354)

Godesberg Castle, Germany
W.C. Stanfield/R. Wallis (20,413)

Goodrich Castle, Herefordshire
P. De Wint/W. Floyd (20,493
A.V.D. Copley-Fielding/E.F. Finden (20,591)

Gormanstown Castle, Co. Meath
J.E. Jones/E. Radclyffe (11,678)

Grand Canal (plan from Dublin to Monasterevin)
J. Brownrigg/J. Ford (11,893)

Near the Grande Chartreuse, E. France
J.M.W. Turner/H. Dawe (20,011)

Grasmere Lake and Village, Cumbria
G. Pickering/C. Mottram (20,486)

Great Munden Park, Hertfordshire
J.D. Harding/J.D. Harding (20,302)

Greta Bridge and River, Yorkshire
J.D. Harding/J.D. Harding (20,259)
J.D. Harding/J.D. Harding (20,274)
J.D. Harding/J.D. Harding (20,296)

Grimsel-See Hospice, Switzerland
?Swiss School 19C/Swiss School 19C (20,648)

Gungotri, India
T. Allom/J.H. Kernot (20,454)

Harfleur, N. France
J.M.W. Turner/J. Cousen (11,799)

Harristown, Co. Kilkenny (Cromlech)
Irish School 19C/Irish School 19C (11,672)

Hastings, Sussex
English School 19C/English School 19C (20,355)
English School 19C/English School 19C (20,391)

Henley-on-Thames, Berkshire
W. Tombleson/R. Sands (20,432)

Hind Head, Surrey
J.M.W. Turner/J.M.W. Turner & R. Dunkarton (11,982)

Holyhead Lighthouse, Anglesey, N. Wales
W. Daniell/W. Daniell (11,860)

Howth, Co. Dublin
A. Concanen/E. Chavane (11,620)
J.P. Haverty/R. Havell the Elder & Younger (11,649)
J.P. Haverty/R. Havell the Elder & Younger (11,651)
Irish School 1788/English School 1789 (11,756)
Irish School c.1816/English School 1816 (11,714)
W. Jones/G. King (10,007)
T.L. Rowbotham the Elder/D. Havell (11,647)
T.L. Rowbotham the Elder/D. Havell (11,696)

Howth Castle, Co. Dublin
F. Wheatley/T. Milton (11,683)

Ideford, Devon
S. Prout/S. Prout (20,564)

Idrone, Co. Carlow (map of Barony)
P. Keere/P. Keere (20,765)

Ilfracombe, Devon
J. Pennell/J. Pennell (11,467)

Inverary Castle, Scotland
J.M.W. Turner/J.M.W. Turner & C. Turner (20,022)

Inverary Pier, Scotland
J.M.W. Turner/J.M.W. Turner (11,992)

Ireland, a first view of
J. Pillement/M.T. Maugin (10,042)

Ireland's Eye, off Howth, Co. Dublin
Irish School 18C/Irish School 18C (11,713)
Irish School 1788/English School 1789 (11,756)

Ischia, Bay of Naples
C. Stanfield/E. Goodall (20,495)

Isle of Man (map)
R. Philips/J. Simon (10,694)

Isle O'Valla, Strangford Lough
Countess of Harrington/M. & N. Hanhart (20,766)

Istanbul, Turkey
W.H. Bartlett/R. Wallis (20,441)

Istria, Italy (Temple of Pola)
G.B. Piranesi/G.B. Piranesi (20,525)
G.B. Piranesi/G.B. Piranesi (20,533)

Jericho, Israel
R. Roberts/W. Day & W.L. Haghe (20,149)

Kadesha (now Orontes) River, Syria
W.H. Bartlett/W.F. Starling (20,453)

Kelso Abbey, Scotland
D. Roberts/W.A. Le Petit (20,443)

Kelty River, Scotland
J.D. Harding/J.D. Harding (20,581)

Kendal, Cumbria
T. Allom/T. Allom (20,448)(2)

Kenilworth Castle, Warwickshire
English School 1829/English School 1829 (20,596-20,598)
T. Hearne/B.J. Pouncy (20,389)
J. Nash/J. Nash (11,497)

Kentmere Head and slate quarries, Cumbria
T. Allom/S. Bradshaw (20,448)(1)

Kidwelly, S. Wales
J.H. Robinson/G. Childs (20,334)

Kilkenny (market cross and plan)
Irish School 18C/J.H. Burgess (11,892)
R.W. Seale/R.W. Seale (11,877)

Killarney, Co. Kerry (views of area)
W.H. Bartlett/G.K. Richardson (20,436)
T. Creswick/S. Bradshaw (20,502)
T. Creswick/S. Bradshaw (20,606)
T. Creswick/R. Hill (20,503)
T. Creswick/R. Wallis (20,504)
D. Sullivan/D. Sullivan (10,039)(7)

Killiney, Co. Dublin
J.P. Haverty/J.P. Haverty (11,695)
J.P. Haverty/J.P. Haverty (20,336)
Irish School 18C/Irish School 18C (11,757)

Kingstown, Co. Dublin (now Dun Laoghaire)
J.P. Haverty/R. Havell the Elder & Younger (11,649)
J.P. Haverty/R. Havell the Elder & Younger (11,651)

Kinsale Harbour (plan)
R.W. Seale/R.W. Seale (11,877)

Kirkstall Abbey, Yorkshire
J.M.W. Turner/J.M.W. Turner (11,996)

Lake Garda, N. Italy
W.L. Leitch/J. Sands (20,414)

Lake Maggiore, N. Italy
J. Raphael/J. Raphael (11,450)

Lambay Island
Irish School 1788/English School 1789 (11,756)

Lancaster, Lancashire
J. Henderson/W. Finden (20,367)

Laufenburg, Switzerland
J.M.W. Turner/J.M.W. Turner & T. Hodgetts (11,988)

Lausanne, Switzerland
W.H. Bartlett/H. Jordan (20,372)

Leane Lough, Killarney, Co. Kerry
T. Creswick/R. Wallis (20,504)
D. Sullivan/D. Sullivan (10,039)(7)

Lee River, Co. Cork
T. Creswick/R. Brandard (20,510)
T.S. Roberts/J.W. Edy (20,838)(7)

Le Havre, N. France
J.M.W. Turner/J.B. Allen (11,800)
J.M.W. Turner/J.T. Willmore (20,483)

Leixlip Castle, Co. Kildare
Irish School c.1750/English School 1751 (11,747)

Leixlip (Salmon Leap), Co. Kildare
W.H. Bartlett/G.K. Richardson (20,600)
Irish School c.1750/English School 1751 (11,747)
D. Sullivan/D. Sullivan (10,039)(21)

Liffey River (outside Dublin)
J. Fisher/J. Fisher (11,549)
W. Howis the Younger/W. Howis the Younger (20,250)
Irish School 19C/?S. Sly (20,644)

Limerick (- plan)
R.W. Seale/R.W. Seale (11,877)

- Baker's Place houses
J.H. Mulcahy/J. Worrall (20,524)

- Exchange (now demolished)
Irish School 18C/Irish School 18C (11,670)

- King John's Castle
W.H. Bartlett/J. Cousen (20,605)
W.H. Bartlett/J. Rogers (20,574)
P. Sandby/T. Cook (20,029)
D. Sullivan/D. Sullivan (10,039)(25)

Lindisfarne Priory, off Northumberland
J.M.W. Turner/J.M.W. Turner & C. Turner (11,968)

Lismore Castle, Co. Waterford
W.H. Bartlett/E. Benjamin (20,437)
T.S. Roberts/S. Alken (20,838)(5)

Littlehampton, Sussex
J.D. Harding/J.D. Harding (20,188)

Llanstephan Castle, S. Wales
J.H. Robinson/J.S. Templeton (20,472)

Llyn Idwall, N. Wales
G.F. Robson/W.R. Smith (20,386)

Loire River, France
J.M.W. Turner/R. Brandard (11,803)

LONDON

- Bridewell Prison (now demolished)
W. Hogarth/W. Hogarth (11,520)

- Cambridge Terrace, Regent's Park
T.H. Shepherd/R. Acon (11,824)(2)

- *Chelsea Hospital*
  W. Tombleson/S. Lacey (20,378)

- *The City (before the Fire of London)*
  English School 17C/English School 17C (11,820)

- *Clifford Street (James Trevor, Military & Merchant Tailor)*
  English School 1836/Smith & Graves (11,548)

- *Cumberland Terrace, Regent's Park*
  T.H. Shepherd/J. Tingle (11,823)(2)

- *Exeter Hall*
  J. Pennell/J. Pennell (11,465)

- *Fig Tree House, Lincoln's Inn*
  J. Pennell/J. Pennell (11,468)

- *Greenwich*
  W. Tombleson/W. Taylor (20,380)
  J.M.W. Turner/J.M.W. Turner & C. Turner (11,983)

- *Hertford Villa (now St Dunstan's) Regent's Park*
  T.H. Shepherd/J. Tingle (11,823)(1)

- *Isleworth shooting lodge*
  J.M.W. Turner/J.M.W. Turner & H. Dawe (20,020)

- *Kensington Gardens*
  J. Pennell/J. Pennell (11,459)

- *Maple Street*
  W. Sickert/W. Sickert (11,439)
  W. Sickert/W. Sickert (11,445)

- *Middlesex Music Hall (now demolished)*
  W. Sickert/W. Sickert (11,438)

- *Mill Hill*
  G. Childs/G. Childs (20,375)

- *Newgate Prison (now demolished)*
  English School 18C/English School 18C (10,606)

- *Pimlico*
  A. McEvoy/W. Sickert (11,448)

- *Pinner*
  J.D. Harding/J.D. Harding (20,301)

- *Regent's Park*
  T.H. Shepherd/R. Acon (11,824)(2)
  T.H. Shepherd/T. Barber (11,825)(1-2)
  T.H. Shepherd/J. Tingle (11,823)(1)

- *Regent Street*
  T.H. Shepherd/R. Acon (11,824)(1)

- *St Bartholomew the Great Priory, Smithfield*
  J. Storer/J. Storer (20,134)

- *St James's Palace Gate*
  W. Hogarth/W. Hogarth (11,516)

- *St Paul's Church, Covent Garden*
  H.F. Gravelot/J. Hulett (10,181)

- *Strawberry Hill*
  E. Edwards/J. Newton (20,216)
  W. Marlow/Godfrey (20,029)
  W. Pars/Godfrey (20,096-20,098)

- *Tower of London*
  W. Hollar/W. Hollar (20,763)

- *Twickenham*
  J.D. Harding/J.D. Harding (20,307)

- *York Terrace, Regent's Park*
  T.H. Shepherd/T. Barber (11,825)(2)

Londonderry, Co. Derry
- *plans*
  Dutch School 1689/Dutch School c.1689 (20,835
  R.W. Seale/R.W. Seale (11,877)

- *Cathedral*
  A. Kauffman/?T. Burke (10,209)

- *walls*
  Irish School 19C/Irish School 19C (11,635)
  Irish School 19C/Irish School 19C (20,816)

Loughlinstown, Co. Dublin
  Irish School 18C/Irish School 18C (11,821)

Lower Glanmire, Co. Cork
  T.S. Roberts/S. Alken (20,838)(9)

Lucan House demesne, Co. Dublin
  T. Roberts/T. Milton (20,295)

Luggala Lodge, Co. Wicklow
  W.H. Bartlett/H. Adlard (20,440)

Lugnaquilla, Co. Wicklow
  D. Sullivan/D. Sullivan (10,039)(4)

Lune River, Lancashire
  J. Henderson/W. Finden (20,367)

Lusk Church, Co. Dublin
  J.E. Jones/E. Radclyffe (11,758)

Lynn River, Devon
  J.B. Pyne/R. Brandard (20,422)

Maas River, Holland
  C. Stanfield/W. Miller (20,207)

Macosquin, Co. Derry (high cross)
  Irish School 19C/Irish School 19C (20,818)

Maghera Church doorway, Co. Derry
  Irish School 19C/Irish School 19C (11,636)
  Irish School 19C/Irish School 19C (20,817)

Mah Chung Keow, Canton, China
  R.J. Elliot/*S. Austin*/W.A. Le Petit (20,356)

Maidstone, Kent
  W. Tombleson/A. McClatchie (20,377)

Malahide, Co. Dublin
  J.E. Jones/E. Radclyffe (11,687-11,688)

Malahide Castle, Co. Dublin
  W.H. Bartlett/E. Challis (20,234)
  F. Wheatley/T. Milton (11,684)

Manaber Castle, S. Wales
  J.H. Robinson/G. Childs (20,292)

Mantes-la-Jolie, France
  J.M.W. Turner/W. Radclyffe (11,798)

Marston Hall, Co. Cork
  A.C. Tisdall/A.C. Tisdall (20,623-20,625)

Marston Hall, Somerset
  J. Faber the Younger/J. Faber the Younger (10,017)

Mechlin, Belgium (Brussels Gate)
  ?J. Shurer the Elder/J. Shurer the Elder & Younger (20,280)

Medway River, Kent
W. Tombleson/A. McClatchie (20,377
W. Tombleson/A. Winkles (20,376)

Meeting of the Waters, Avoca, Co. Wicklow
T. Fairland/T. Fairland (20,357)

Melrose Abbey and Cross, Scotland
H. Melville/R. Staines (20,271)

Middleham Castle, Yorkshire
E. Dayes/S. Noble (20,430)

Milan (S. Giorgio Maggiore)
G. Castellini/G. Castellini (20,393)

Milltown, Co. Dublin (Old Bridge, now rebuilt)
Irish School 19C/S. Sly (20,640)

Moel Siabod Mountains, N. Wales
C. Branwhite/W. Linton (20,625)

Monasterboice, Co. Louth
J.E. Jones/E. Radclyffe (11,674)

Monkstown, Co. Dublin (St John's Church and Montpelier Parade)
Irish School c.1787/Irish School 1787 (11,730)
S. Close the Elder/S. Close the Elder (11,751)

Mont St Gothard, Switzerland
J.M.W. Turner/J.M.W. Turner & C. Turner (11,966)

Mount Etna, Sicily
P.E. Grandsire/C. Barbant (20,619)

Mount Lebanon, Syria
W.H. Bartlett/D. Thompson (20,450)

Mount Snowdon, N. Wales
J.C. Bentley/J.C. Bentley (20,415)
J.C. Bentley/J.C. Bentley (20,610)
J.D. Harding/J.D. Harding (20,183)
J.D. Harding/J.D. Harding (20,649)

Morpeth, Northumberland
J.M.W. Turner/J.M.W. Turner & C. Turner (11,978)

Mona Inch Abbey, Co. Tipperary
D. Sullivan/D. Sullivan (10,039)(6)

Mountains of Mourne, Co. Down
D. Sullivan/D. Sullivan (10,039)(16)

Muckross Lake, Killarney, Co. Kerry
W.H. Bartlett/G.K. Richardson (20,436)
T. Creswick/R. Hill (20,503)

Naples, S. Italy
W. Linton/E. Goodall (20,511)

Neagh Lough, Co. Down
D. Sullivan/D. Sullivan (10,039)(18)

Nealagh River, Co. Cork
D. Sullivan/D. Sullivan (10,039)(20)

Neath Abbey, S. Wales
J.H. Robinson/J.H. Robinson (20,474)

Nérac, S. France
E. Sabatier/French School 19C (20,466)

New York (Brooklyn and Manhattan)
J. Pennell/J. Pennell (11,457)
J. Pennell/J. Pennell (11,460-11,463)
J. Pennell/J. Pennell (11,466)
J. Pennell/J. Pennell (11,469-11,470)

Nijmegen, Holland
A. Cuyp/*W. Westall*/T. Medland & J. Bailey (20,324)

Nine barrow Down, Dorset
J.C. Robinson/J.C. Robinson (20,082)

The Nore, off Sheerness, Kent
J.M.W. Turner/J.M.W. Turner & C. Turner (11,977)

Norham Castle, Scotland
J.M.W. Turner/J.M.W. Turner & C. Turner (20,014)

The North Foreland, Kent
G. Chambers/R. Brandard (20,283)

Oberwesel, Germany
J.D. Harding/J.D. Harding (20,226)

Old Court, Co. Down
Countess of Harrington/M. & N. Hanhart (20,767)

Old Kilcullen, Co. Kildare (high crosses)
D. Sullivan/D. Sullivan (10,039)(2)

Oporto, Portugal (religious buildings)
J.B. Forrester/G. Childs (20,592-20,595)

Orontes (was Kadesha) River, Syria
W.H. Bartlett/T. Higham (20,399)
W.H. Bartlett/W.F. Starling (20,453)
W.H. Bartlett/S. Stephenson (20,455)

Oxwich Bay, S. Wales
J.H. Robinson/G. Childs (20,522)

Oystermouth Castle, S. Wales
J.H. Robinson/J.S. Templeton (20,287)

Paignton, Devon
W.I. Hocker/T. Higham (20,479)

Palmerston, Co. Dublin (Secretary of State's house)
J. Fisher/J. Fisher (11,549)

Paris
- Gaité Rochechouart
W. Sickert/W. Sickert (11,442)
W. Sickert/W. Sickert (11,447)

Institut de France and Port S. Nicolas
C. Lapostolet/L.C. Beauparlant (11,502)

Pays de Caux, N. France
R.P. Bonington/W. Millar (20,484)

Pays de Vaud, Switzerland
W.H. Bartlett/J. Jordan (20,372)

Pembury Mill, Kent
J.M.W. Turner/J.M.W. Turner & C. Turner (11,969)

Penshurst, Kent (cottage)
J.D. Harding/J.D. Harding (20,184)

Pentargon Bay waterfall and stone quarry, Cornwall
T. Allom/W.A. Le Petit (20,452)

Pen-y-Gwryd, N. Wales
J.C. Bentley/J.C. Bentley (20,415)
J.C. Bentley/J.C. Bentley (20,610)

Peveril Castle, Derbyshire
T. Allom/T. Clark (20,279)

Pisa, N. Italy (Baptistery and Duomo)
G. Carocci/G. Carocci (20,392)
G. Corsi/G. Corsi (20,388)

Pissevache Cascade, Valais, Switzerland
W.H. Bartlett/J.T. Wilmore (20,418)

Poolbeg Lighthouse, South Wall, Dublin Bay
G. Holmes/J. Walker (11,789)
Irish School 18C/Irish School 18C (11,713)
W. Sadler the Younger/J. Storer & H. Sargent (11,769)

Portrane, Co. Dublin
J.E. Jones/E. Radclyffe (11,686)

Porth yr Ogof, S. Wales
H. Gastineau/S. Lacey (20,476)

Powerscourt House, Co. Wicklow
W.H. Bartlett/G.K. Richardson (20,434)

Prestwold Park, Leicestershire
J.D. Harding/J.D. Harding (20,275)

Quoile Valley, Co. Down
D. Sullivan/D. Sullivan (10,039)(17)

Raglan Castle, S. Wales
J.M.W. Turner/J.M.W. Turner (20,015)

Rainham Marshes, Kent
J.D. Harding/J.D. Harding (20,182)

Rathmichael Monastery, Co. Dublin
Irish School 19C/Irish School 19C (11,745)

Rhine River, Germany
J.D. Harding/J.D. Harding (20,193)
J.D. Harding/J.D. Harding (20,226)
W.L. Leitch/W. Floyd (20,281)
C.W. Stanfield/R. Wallis (20,413)
W. Tombleson/A.H. Payne (20,278)

Richmond Park, Surrey (tree)
W.H. B..../English School 19C (20,616)

Rietz, near Saumur, N. France
J.M.W. Turner/R. Brandard (11,803)

Rievaulx Abbey, Yorkshire
J.M.W. Turner/J.M.W. Turner & H. Dawe (20,008)

Rimini, Italy (Arch of Augustus)
G.B. Piranesi/G.B. Piranesi (20,526)

Ringwood, Hampshire
English School 19C/English School 19C (20,325)

Roche Castle, Co. Louth
D. Sullivan/D. Sullivan (10,039)(12)

Rochester Castle, Kent
W. Tombleson/H. Winkles (20,376)

Roffla Gorge, Switzerland
W. Tombleson/H. Winkles (20,286)

Rokeby, Yorkshire
J.D. Harding/J.D. Harding (20,296)
J.D. Harding/J.D. Harding (20,305)

Near Rome (tomb of Nero
D. Amici/D. Amici (20,749)

ROME
- *Arch of Constantine*
D. Amici/D. Amici (20,748)

- *Arch of Drusus*
D. Amici/D. Amici (20,741)

- *Arch of Gallienus*
D. Amici/D. Amici (20, 742)

- *Arch of Janus*
D. Amici/D. Amici (20,734)

- *Arch of Septimus Severus*
D. Amici/D. Amici (20,735)

- *Arch of Settimo Severo*
D. Amici/D. Amici (20,743)

- *Arch of Titus*
D. Amici/D. Amici (20,736)

- *Basilica of Maxentius*
D. Amici/D. Amici (20,751)

- *Campus Martius*
G.B. Piranesi/G.B. Piranesi (20,527)
G.B. Piranesi/G.B. Piranesi (20,530)

- *Castel Sant'Angelo*
English School 18C/English School 18C (20,537)

- *Colosseum*
D. Amici/D. Amici (20,754)
Italian School c.1741/Italian School 1741 (20,833)(3)
A. Locatelli/W. Austin (20,247)(16)

- *Column of Marcus Aurelius*
D. Amici/D. Amici (20,744)

- *Column of Phocas*
D. Amici/D. Amici (20,739)

- *Column of Trajan*
D. Amici/D. Amici (20,740)

- *Forum of Augustus*
D. Amici/D. Amici (20,745)

- *Mausoleum of Augustus (reconstruction)*
English School 18C/J. Basire the Elder (20,535)

- *Piazza Navona*
G.P. Panini/*J. Dumont the Elder*/C.N. Cochin (11,656)

- *Pantheon*
D. Amici/D. Amici (20,755)

- *Piazza di S. Marco*
G.B. Piranesi/G.B. Piranesi (20,528)

- *Porticus of Octavia*
D. Amici/D. Amici (20,753)

- *Pyramid of Caius Cestius*
D. Amici/D. Amici (20,737)
G.P. Panini/?French School 18C (20,544)

- *Sts. Cosmas and Damian Church*
A. Locatelli/W. Austin (20,247)(16)

- *S. Maria Maggiore Church*
D. Amici/D. Amici (20,755)

- *St Peter's basilica*
English School 18C/English School 18C (20,537)
A. Specchi/A. Specchi (20,677)(2)
E. Whymper/E. Whymper (20,270)

- *Scala Regia, The Vatican*
E. Whymper/E. Whymper (20,269)

- *Temple of Antoninus and Faustina*
D. Amici/D. Amici (20,750)

- *Temple of Concorde*
J. Barbault/D. Montagu (20,674)(9)
G. Fossati/A. Von Dall'Armi (20,759)(9)
G.B. Piranesi/G.B. Piranesi (20,534)

- *Temple of Mars Ultor*
D. Amici/D. Amici (20,745)

- *Temple of Minerva*
D. Amici/D. Amici (20,747)

- *Temple of Rome*
G. Fossati/A. Von Dall'Armi (20,760)(6)

- Temple of the Sibyls
J.P. Hackert/G.A. Hackert (20,769)

- Temple of Venus
D. Amici/D. Amici (20,746)
G. Fossati/A. Von Dall'Armi (20,760)(6)

- Temple of Vespasian
G. Fossati/A. Von Dall'Armi (20,759)(9)
G.B. Piranesi/G.B. Piranesi (20,530)

- Temple of Vesta
D. Amici/D. Amici (20,752)

- Theatre of Marcellus (reconstruction)
English School 18C/J. Basire the Elder (20,535)

- Tiber River
English School 18C/English School 18C (20,537)
G.B. Piranesi/G.B. Piranesi (20,530)

- Tomb of Cecilia Metella
D. Amici/D. Amici (20,738)

- Trevi Fountain
G.B. Piranesi/G.B. Piranesi (20,832)

- Vatican Loggia
Raphael/*L. Comparini*/G. Balzar & F. Rainaldi (20.676)(1)

Rothesay pier, Isle of Bute, Scotland
English School 19C/English School 19C (20,323)

Rouen, N. France
J.M.W. Turner/R. Brandard (11,802)

Roughty Bridge, Co. Kerry
T. Walmsley/W. Cartwright (20,702)

Rush and Skerries, Co. Dublin
J.E. Jones/E, Radclyffe (11,685)

St Catherine's Hill and Chapel, Surrey
J.M.W. Turner/J.M.W. Turner & J.C. Easling (11,990)

St Fagan's Castle, S. Wales
J.H. Robinson/G. Childs (20,291)

Saint-Gervais-les-Bains, Switzerland
W.H. Bartlett/W. Cooke (20,417)

St Gothard Pass, Switzerland
J.M.W. Turner/J.M.W. Turner & C. Turner (11,976)

St Kelly's Castle, Co. Waterford
D. Sullivan/D. Sullivan (10,039)(24)

St Michael's Mount, Cornwall
W.C. Stanfield/W.A. Le Petit (20,423)

Salmon Leap, Leixlip, Co. Kildare
W.H. Bartlett/G.K. Richardson (20,600)
Irish School c.1750/English School 1751 (11,747)
D. Sullivan/D. Sullivan (10,039)(21)

Near Saverne, Alsace, E. France
J.C. Brand/J. Aliamet (20,162)

Schiedam, Holland
J.Pennell/J. Pennell (20,693)

Schönburg Castle, Oberwesel, Germany
J.D. Harding/J.D. Harding (20,226)

Seine River, France
C. Lapostolet/L.C. Beauparlant (11,502)
J.M.W. Turner/J.B. Allen (11,801)
J.M.W. Turner/R. Brandard (11,802)
J.M.W. Turner/R. Brandard (11,804)
J.M.W. Turner/J.T. Willmore (11,796)

Seleucia Port, Turkey
W.H. Bartlett/J. Stephenson (20,455)

Severn River, S. Wales
J.M.W. Turner/J.M.W. Turner (11,985)

Shannon River
W.H. Bartlett/J. Rogers (20,514)
D. Sullivan/D. Sullivan (10,039)(15)

Skiddaw, Cumbria
P. De Wint/E.F. Finden (20,520)

Solway Moss, Cumbria
J.M.W. Turner/J.M.W. Turner (20,009)

Somme River, France
D. Roberts/A.R. Freebairn (20,371)

Southall Mill, Grand Junction Canal
J.M.W. Turner/J.M.W. Turner & W. Say (11,984)

Southampton, Hampshire
A.V. Copley-Fielding/G. Cooke (20,373)
English School 19C/English School 19C (20,516)

Suir River, Co. Tipperary
Irish School 19C/?A.R. Branston (20,639)
T.S. Roberts/J.W. Edy (20,838)(5)

Sulina, Romania
F. Abresch/*W.H. Bartlett*/R. Wallis (20,425)

Swansea, S. Wales
J.B. Pyne/R. Brandard (20,492)
J.H. Robinson/J.S. Templeton (20,287)

Tancarville Château, Normandy, N. France
J.M.W. Turner/R. Brandard (11,804)
J.M.W. Turner/J.T. Willmore (11,797)

Tay Lough, Co. Wicklow
W.H. Bartlett/H. Adlard (20,440)

Teddington, Surrey
W. Pars/Godfrey (20,099)
W. Tombleson/H. Winkles (20,379)

Tees River, Yorkshire
J.D. Harding/J.D. Harding (20,274
J.D. Harding/J.D. Harding (20,298)

Teifi River, S. Wales
J.H. Robinson/G. Childs (20,473)

Thames River
English School pre-1666/English School 17C (11,820)
J.D. Harding/J.D. Harding (20,186)
J.D. Harding/J.D. Harding (20,191-20,192)
J.D. Harding/J.D. Harding (20,300)
W. Pars/Godfrey (20,099)
W. Tombleson/S. Lacey (20,378)
W. Tombleson/W. Taylor (20,380)
W. Tombleson/H. Winkles (20,379)
J.M.W. Turner/J.M.W. Turner & C. Turner (11,970)
J.M.W. Turner/J.M.W. Turner & W. Say (20,025)

Thun and Thun Lake, Switzerland
J.M.W. Turner/J.M.W. Turner & T. Hodgetts (20,016)
J.M.W. Turner/J.M.W. Turner & C. Turner (11,972)

Thurnberg Castle, Germany ('The Mouse')
W.L. Leitch/W. Floyd (20,281)

Tintagel Castle and Head, Cornwall
T. Allom/W.A. Le Petit (20,451)

Tivoli (Temple of Sibyl or Vesta)
J.P. Hackert/G.A. Hackert (20,769)

Torc Mountain, Killarney, Co. Kerry
T. Creswick/R. Hill (20,503)

Totnes, Devon
J.M.W. Turner/J.M.W. Turner & C. Turner (20,384)

Touraine landscape, France
K. Girardet/English School 19C (20,575)

Tours, France
J.M.W. Turner/R. Wallis (11,595)

Towy River, S. Wales
J.H. Robinson/J.S. Templeton (20,138)
J.H. Robinson/J.S. Templeton (20,368)

Trier, Germany
J.D. Harding/J.D. Harding (20,358)

Trim Castle, Co. Meath
D. Sullivan/D. Sullivan (10,039)(9)

Tubrid, Co. Kilkenny (cromlech)
Irish School 19C/Irish School 19C (11,671)

The Twelve Pins, Connemara, Co. Galway
G. Petrie/N. Fielding (20,351)

Val Angrogna, N. Italy
W. Brockedon/J. Sands (20,442)

Venice, N. Italy - Doge's Palace
Canaletto/C. Dietro (20,390)
S. Prout/E. Goodall)

- Murano Island
W.C. Stanfield/R. Wallis (20,214)

- Piazza S. Marco
English School 18C/English School 18C (20,538)
M. Marieschi/M. Marieschi (11,662)

- Rialto Bridge
Canaletto/J.C. Bromley (20,333)

- Riva degli Schiavone
R.C. Goff/R.C. Goff (11,871)

- S. Giorgio Maggiore
J. Raphael/J. Raphael (11,451)

- S. Silvestro gondolas
W. Sickert/W. Sickert (11,444)

Vienna (St Charles Borromeo Church)
J.B. Fisher von Erlach/German School c.1721 (20,670)(61)

Villerville, Normandy, N. France
U.L.A. Butin/U.L.A. Butin (11,487)

Waterford (views and plan)
T.S. Roberts/S. Alken (20,838)(1)
T.S. Roberts/J.W. Edy (20,838)(3)
W. Seale/W. Seale (11,877)

- Commins Hotel
M.A. Hayes/J. Harris the Younger (20,700)

- Harbour
T.S. Roberts/J.W. Edy (20,838)(6)

- Reginald's Tower
R. O'C. Newenham/J.D. Harding (20,030)

Wedbley Castle, S. Wales
J.H. Robinson/G. Childs (20,471)

Welmich, Germany
W.L. Leitch/W. Floyd (20,281)

Wessel Castle, Yorkshire
W.A. Nesfield/J. Sands (20,421)

Co. Wicklow cottages
D. Sullivan/D. Sullivan (10,039)(1)

Co. Wicklow goldmines
T.S. Roberts/J. Bluck (11,653)
D. Sullivan/D. Sullivan (10,039)(3)

Winchelsea, Sussex
J.M.W. Turner/J.M.W. Turner & J.C. Easling (11,999)
J.M.W. Turner/J.M.W. Turner & S.W. Reynolds the Elder (20,024)

Windermere Lake, Cumbria
G. Pickering/A. Le Petit (20,458)

Windsor Castle, Berkshire
English School 19C/English School 19C (20,608)
English School c.1815/English School 1816 (11,361)

Windsor Forest, Berkshire
J.D. Harding/J.D. Harding (20,299)

Wye River
A.V.D. Copley-Fielding/E.F. Finden (20,591)
J.H. Robinson/G. Childs (20,288)
J.M.W. Turner/J.M.W. Turner (11,985)

Yorkshire coast
J.M.W. Turner/J.M.W. Turner & W. Say (11,981)

Zachringen suspension bridge, Fribourg, Switzerland
A. Bader/A. Bader (20,400)

APPENDIX 6

RELIGIOUS, MYTHOLOGICAL, HISTORICAL AND LITERARY SUBJECTS

Abel
H. Singleton/J. Godby (20,060)

Abraham
J. Bassand/P. Monaco (11,488)

Abundance and Cupid
?English School early 19C/?English School early 19C (11,426)

Achilles
P.P. Rubens/B. Baron (20,041-20,047)

Actaeon
Titian/J. Couché (20,724)(11)

Adam
Michelangelo/F.C. Lewis (20,720)(28)

Adam bearing the murdered body of Abel
H. Singleton/J. Godby (20,060)

Adonis
J. Le Pautre/J. Le Pautre (20,231)
F.M. Poncet (8135)

Advertisement for Isaac Willis, music seller and pianoforte maker
C.E.. Maguire/C.E. Maguire (11,838)

Aesacus Discarding Hesperia (from Ovid's 'Metamorphoses')
J.M.W. Turner/J.M.W. Turner (20,023)

Agamemnon
P.P. Rubens/B. Baron (20,044)

Alexander
C. Le Brun/R. Shepherd (20,049-20,053)

Alexander receives the defeated King Porus
C. Le Brun/R. Shepherd (20,549)

Alexander shows compassion and respect for the defeated Porus
C. Le Brun/R. Shepherd (20,051)

Alexander with the family of the Persian King Darius before him
C. Le Brun/R. Shepherd (20,049)

Allegory of the Flourishing of the Arts
P. Quila/P. Aquila (20,684)(4)

Allegory of Time Revealing Truth
G. Kneller/P. Tanjé (10,994)

Amphitrite
J. Thiery/French School 17C (10,230)

Angel carrying the spirit of a child to heaven
M.W. Peters/H.H. Houston (11,601)

Angel holding the crowned Arms of Castille and Leon
Spanish School 15C (8325)

The Angel departing from Tobit and his family
Rembrandt/A. Walker (11,500)

Annette (from Marmontel's book, 'Contes Moraux')
H. Fragonard/English School 1827 (20,205)

The Annunciation
R. Van Der Weyden/N.J. Strixner (20,758)(34)

'Another heavy blow. . .'
(Political Cartoon)
J. Doyle/J. Doyle (11,544)(66)

Apollo
Roman Antique (8033)
M. Stapleton (8021)

Apollo Belvedere
Roman School early 19C (8144)
F. Saunders (8152)

Apostles
see App. 1: E. Hone (12,069)

'An Aquatic Fête at Dort'
A. Cuyp/*W. Westall*/T. Medland & J. Bailey (20,324)

Argus
Claude Lorrain/R. Earlom (20,665)(150)
Claude Lorrain/R. Earlom (20,719)(149)

Arms of the City of Dublin
J. Malton/J. Malton (11,690)

Arrival of the Lord Lieutenant, at the Dublin Great Exhibition, Leinster Lawn, 1853
Irish School 1853/Irish School 1853 (11,722)

Ascanius Shooting the Stag of Silvia
Claude Lorrain/R. Earlom (20,664)(93)

Assumption of the Virgin
Bolognese School 17C/Bolognese School 17C (20,228)
J. Le Pautre/J. Le Pautre (20,232)

Atalanta
After P.P. Rubens/F. Lamb (11,661)

Aurora
?Roman Antique/English School early 19C (20,654)

Autolycus (from Shakespeare's play 'A Winter's Tale)
C.R. Leslie/L. Stocks (20,140)

Bacchus
J.H. Foley/*F. Roffe*/W. Roffe (20,210)

'Ball-room Scene'
(Political Cartoon)
J. Doyle/J. Doyle (11,544)(60)

The Battle of Ballyshannon, Co. Donegal, 17th October 1593
J. Thomas/Army Litho School 20C (11,841)

The Battle of the Boyne, Co. Louth, 1st July 1690
R. De Hooghe/R. De Hooghe (11,655)
G. Kneller/J. Brooks (10,223)
T. Maas/T. Maas (10,003)
T. Maas/T. Maas (20,800)
R.W. Seale/R.W. Seale (11,877)*(detail)*
J. Wyck/J. Brooks (11,652)

The Battle of Trafalgar, 21st October 1805
J. Hoppner/C. Turner (10,453)

The Battle of Waterloo, 18th June 1815
English School c.1815/English School 1816 (11,360)

Beatrice (from Shakespeare's play 'Much Ado about Nothing')
M.W. Peters/P. Simon (20,686)(16)

Beauty
R. Cosway/J.R. Smith (11,665)

Belisarius
Genoese School 17C/J. Goupy (20,069)

Belvidera (from C. Otway's 'Venice Preserved')
A.W. Devis/H.H. Meyer (10,409)

The Birth or Triumph of Cupid
F. Chauveau/F. Chauveau (20,215)

The Blind Girl of Castle Cuille (from Longfellow's poem)
J. Lawlor (8083)

The Blinding of Elymas
Raphael/C. Du Bosc (11,494)

Borghese Gladiator
Roman School early 19C (8117)

Lord Brackenbury
(Play by A.B. Edwards, 1880)
L. Fildes/English School 1830 (20,578)

Brutus, Marcus Lucius
J. Barry/J. Barry (20,772)(8)

Cain
H. Singleton/J. Godby (20,059)

The Caledonian Boar Hunt
After P.P. Rubens/F. Lamb (11,661)

The Captive (from Sterne's novel 'A Sentimental Journey')
J.H. Mortimer/R. Blyth (20,034)

Car Travelling in the South of Ireland in the year 1856
M.A. Hayes/J. Harris the Younger (20,695-20,700)

Caractacus or The Norseman
J.H. Foley (8258)

Castille and Leon, Arms of
Spanish School 15C (8325)

Catherine of Aragon (from Shakespeare's play 'King Henry VIII)
C.R. Leslie/C.W. Sharpe (20,142)

Catherine of France meets her future husband King Henry V of England at the Treaty of Troyes, 1420
T. Stothard/A. Cardon (20,067)

'The Catholic Triumvirate'
(Political Cartoon)
H. Doyle/H. Doyle (10,035)

Cephalus and Procris reunited by Diana
Claude Lorrain/English School 1827 (20,242)
Claude Lorrain/J.B. Allen (20,245)

Cephalus discovers he has killed his wife Procris
J.M.W. Turner/J.M.W. Turner & G. Clint (11,998)

The Charge to St Peter
Raphael/N. Dorigny (20,678)(15)

Charity (detail)
Irish School 18C/Irish School 18C (10,919)

Earl of Charlemont at the Provincial Review in Phoenix Park Dublin, 3rd June 1782
Irish School 1783/Irish School 1783 (11,870)

Charlotte Sophia, Queen of George III of England, raising the Genius of the Fine Arts
A. Hauffmann/T. Burke (10,379)

Chastelard playing the lute to Mary, Queen of Scots
H.J. Fradelle/A. Duncan (20,057)

The Children of Lir
O. Kelly (8262)
O. Sheppard (8136)

Chiron the Centaur
P.P. Rubens/B. Baron (20,042)

Christ
F. Barocci/A. Sadeler (20,229)
Claude Lorrain/W.R. Smith (20,607)
P. Delaroche/L.P. Henriquel-Dupont (11,484)
Italian School 16C/M.E. Corr (11,482)
Italian School 16C/M.E. Corr (20,806)
B. Luini/M. Bovi (20,038)
J. Drouais-Germain/Duval (20,106)
P. Perugino/C. Duflos (20,671)(3)
N. Poussin/G.F. Ferrero (20,757)(138)
Raphael/N. Dorigny (20,678)(15)
Rembrandt/English School 1827 (20,708)(19)
E.S. Schwartz/A. Friedl (20,077)
Titian/F. Chauveau (20,107)
Titian/A.C. Masson (20,084)
Titian/L. Vorstermans the Younger (20,715)
J.M.W. Turner/J.M.W. Turner & S.W. Reynolds the Elder (20,028)
?W. Vaillant/W. Vaillant (20,732)(57)
A. Van Dyck/M.E. Corr (11,489)
S. Vouet/N.F.J. Masquelier le Jeune (20,058)

Christ among the Doctors
B. Luiri/N. Bori (20,038)

Christ and the woman of Cana
J. Drouais-Germain/L. Duval (20,106)

Christ and the woman of Samaria
J.M.W. Turner/J.M.W. Turner & S.W. Reynolds the Elder (20,028)

Chronos eating one of his Children
F. Dietz (8081)

Chryseis
P.P. Rubens/B. Baron (20,044)

Cicero
Roman Antique (8287)

'A Classical Subject'
(Political Cartoon)
J. Doyle/J. Doyle (11,853)

Cock and Pot (The Betrayal)
see App. 1: E. Hone (12,066)

Comedy
J. Reynolds/R. Purcell (10,034)

'The Committee'
(Play by R. Howard)
C. Stoppelaer/A. Miller (10,917)

'The Company of Undertakers'
W. Hogarth/W. Hogarth (11,521)

'Comus'
(Masque by Milton)
T. Lawrence/R.J. Lane (10,941)

'Contes Moraux'
(Book by Marmontel)
H. Fragonard/English School c.1827 (20,205)

'A Contrast'
(Political Cartoon)
J. Doyle/J. Doyle (11,544)(61)

Cordelia (from Shakespeare's play 'King Lear')
J. Barry/F. Legat (20,712)(40)

Cornelia (mother of the Gracchi)
F. Bartolozzi/M. Bovi (20,103)

Coriolanus (from Shakespeare's play)
English School 18C/English School 18C (10,272)

'A Council of War'
(Political Cartoon)
J. Doyle/J. Doyle (11,544)(62)

'The Country Boy'
(poem by Walcot)
W. Collins/E.F. Finden (20,383)

The Creation of Adam
Michelangelo/F.C. Lewis (20,720)(28)

The Creation of Eve
M. Heemskerk/M. Heemskerk (20,710)(1)

The Crossing of the River Granique-Alexander defeats Darius
C. Le Brun/R. Shepherd (20,052)

The Crowning with thorns
C.S. Schwartz/A. Friedl (20,077)

Crucifix
Roman School c.1620 (8014)
Spanish School 17C (12,049)

The Crucifixion
German School 17C (12,048)
A. O'Connor (8238)
A. Van Dyck/M.E. Corr (11,489)

Cruelty, Stages of
W. Hogarth/W. Hogarth (11,511-11,514)

Cupid
A. Allori/*A. Borel*/P. Trierre (20,723)(7)
F. Chauveau/F. Chaveau (20,215)
J. McArdell/R. Earlom (10,470)
P.P. Rubens/B. Brandard (20,047)

Cupid Bound
M. Stapleton (8016)

Cupid Drawing Venus with Swans
M. Stapleton (8018)

Cupid on a Pedestal
M. Stapleton (8017)

Cyrus
B. Castiglione/*R. Earlom*/J. Boydell (11,943)

A Dancing Faun
S. Angelis (8289)

Dante
E. Delacroix/L.D. Carred (11,495)

'The Darranane Conjuror or More Wigs on the Green'
(Political Cartoon)
J. Doyle/English School 1830 (11,403)

David, the Shepherd Boy
N. Hone the Elder/J. Watson (10,068)
N. Hone the Elder/J. Watson (10,700)

David with the Head of Goliath
Guercino/*A. Tofanelli*/G.B. Leonetti (11,659)

'Death of Abel', Book V
(by S. Gessner)
H. Singleton/J. Godby (20,059)

Death of Actaeon
Titian/J. Couché (20,724)(2)

The Death of Pyramus and Thisbe (from Ovid's 'Metamorphoses')
English School 18C/A. Walker (20,541)

The Death of Samson
L.C.P.G. Doré/C. Laplante (20,694)(72)

The Defeat of the Indian King Porus by Alexander
C. Le Brun/R. Shepherd (20,050)

Defendents in the State Trial of 1844
H. Anelay/W.J. Linton (11,042)

The Delivery of St Peter out of Prison
Claude Lorrain/R. Earlom (20,666)(51)

The Departure of Abraham for Canaan
J. Bassano/P. Monaco (11,488)

The Departure of Cain and His Family
H. Singleton/J. Godby (20,059)

The Departure of William, Prince of Orange from Holland, 2nd November 1688
R. De Hooghe/R. De Hooghe (11,846)

The Departure of William, Prince of Orange from Holland, 2nd November 1688 and his arrival in England on 15th November
R. De Hooghe/R. De Hooghe (11,849)

The Deposition
P. Delaroche/L.P. Henriquel-Dupont (11,484)

'The Deserted Village'
(poem by Goldsmith)
English School early 19C/English School early 19C (20,662)

The Destruction of the Children of Niobe
R. Wilson/J.C. Varrall (20,552)

The Destruction of the French Fleet at La Hogue, 1692
B. West/W. Woollett (11,664)

The Devil and the Jack-Ass, dissolving the Polling Board
Irish School 1804/06/Irish School 1804/06 (11,348)

Diagora of Athens
J. Barry/J. Barry (20,722)(3)

Diagorides Victors
J. Barry/J. Barry (20,722)(12)

Diana
Claude Lorrain/J.B. Allen (20,245)
Claude Lorrain/English School 1827 (20,242)
J. Reynolds/J. McArdell (10,389)
Rosalba/C. West (20,731)(43)
Titian/J. Couché (20,724)(2)

Diana and Adonis
J. Le Pautre/J. Le Pautre (20,231)

Diana and her Nymphs Bathing
N.N. Coypel/J.P. Lebas (20,678)(14)

Diana on her Chariot
M. Stapleton (8023)

Diana preparing for the Chase
English School 19C/English School 19C (20,826)

Diomedes's Horses
C. Le Brun/A. Lafitte & J.-B. Tilliard (20,725)(74)

The Distribution of Premiums at the Society of Arts
J. Barry/J. Barry (20,772)(5)

Divine Justice
J. Barry/J. Barry (20,772)(10)

The Dublin Volunteers on College Green, 4th November 1779, commemorating the birthday of King William III
F. Wheatley/J. Collyer (11,644)
F. Wheatley/J. Collyer (11,826)

The Dublin Volunteers on College Green, commemorating the birthday of King William III
Irish School c.1779/Irish School 1800 (11,627)
Irish School 1784/English School 1784 (11,900)

The Earl of Essex
(play by H. Jones)
D. Dodd/T. Cook (11,095)

Ecce Homo
Titian/L. Vorstermans the Younger (20,715)

The Ecstasy of St Cecilia
Raphael/*A. Dutertre*/F.J.E. Beisson (20,679)(18)

Elias
J.A. Villabrille y Ron (8031)

Elisha witnessing the Assumption of Elija
?English School 19C/?English School 19C (11,499)

Elizabeth, Queen of Edward IV, giving up her son, Edward V, to Cardinal Bourchier
English School 19C/English School 19C (20,039)

Elymas
Raphael/C. Du Bosc (11,494)

Elymas Struck Blind
Raphael/W. Huband (11,538)

Elysium
J. Barry/J. Barry (20,722)(10)

Elysium and Tartarus
J. Barry/J. Barry (20,722)(6)

The Embarkation of King George IV at Kingstown, 3rd September 1821
J.P. Haverty/R. Havell the Elder & Younger (11,649)

The Entombment of Christ
F. Barocci/A. Sadeler (20,229)
N. Poussin/G.F. Ferrero (20,757)(138)
Titian/A.C. Masson (20,084)
Titian/F. Chauveau (20,107)

Entrance of King George IV into the Upper Yard, Dublin Castle, 17th August 1821
Sir T. Hammond/English School 1822 (11,596)
Sir T. Hammond/English School 1822 (11,698)

Erato (muse of lyric poetry)
N.R. Roskell (8207)

Erymanthian Boar
F. Tacca (8123)

Esther
W. Poorter/L. Beyer (11,933)

The Eucharist
N. Poussin/H.G. Bertaux & A.L. Romanet (20,725)(56)

Euphrosyne
J. Hoopner/T. Park (10,408)

Europa and the Bull (inset)
J.M.W. Turner/J.M.W. Turner & J.C. Easling (11,958)

Eurydice
L. MacDonald (8303)

Eve
M. Heemskerk/M. Heemskerk (20,710)(1)

The Execution of Thomas, Earl of Strafford, on Tower Hill, London, 16th May 1641
W. Hollar/W. Hollar (20,763)

'The Exposition of Cyrus'
B. Castliglione/*R. Earlom*/J. Boydell (11,943)

The Faierie Queen
(poem by E. Spenser)
J.M.W. Turner/J.M.W. Turner & T. Hodgetts (11,993)

The Fall of Icarus
A. Power (8089)

Falstaff (from Shakespeare's play 'Henry IV')
F. Hayman/J. McArdell (10,104)

The Family of the Persian King Darius before Alexander
C. Le Brun/R. Shepherd (20,049)

Fate
Willis (8197)

The Fate of the children of Lir
O. Kelly (8262)
O. Shepherd (8136)

Father Foigard (from Farquhar's play 'The Beaux Stratagem')
J. Zoffany/G.F.L. Marchi (10,471)

Father Luke (from 'Poor Soldier')
Irish School c.1793/Irish School 1793 (11,245)

Faun with Grapes
B. Cavaceppi (8242)

Faun with a Kid
B. Cavaceppi (8243)

Faust (from Goethe's play 'Faust')
G. Cattermole/J.C. Bentley (20,444)

Faustine the Young
Roman Antique/*J.B. Wicar*/N. Thomas (20,688)(108)

Felix, Don (from T. Park's play 'The Wonder')
J. Hoppner/T. Park (11,415)

The Flagellation
S. Vouet/N.F.J. Masquelier le Jeune (20,058)

The Flight into Egypt
Claude Lorrain/W.R. Smith (20,607)
Rembrandt/English School 1827 (20,708)(19)

The Flight of King James II from Ireland on the 12th July 1690
R. De Hooghe/R. De Hooghe (11,655)

'Flora or Hob-in-the-Wall'
(farce by J. Hippisley)
Irish School 18C/Irish School 18C (11,317)

'Friar Tuck and Little John'
(political cartoon)
J. Doyle/J. Doyle (11,852)

David Garrick, between the Muses of Tragedy and Comedy
J. Reynolds/R. Purcell (10,034)

George III and the Officers of State receiving the Turkish Ambassadors and Suit
M. Brown/D. Orme (20,014)

The Genius of the Arts
N. Guibal/C. Mechel (20,675)(2)

'The Gipsy Child'
(poem by Routledge)
English School 19C/English School 19C (20,617)

The Glorious Sextumvirate, showing Epaminondas, Socrates, Brutus, Cato the Younger, Thomas Moore and Marcus Junius Brutus
J. Barry/J. Barry (20,722)(8)

Goliath
Guercino/*A. Tofanelli*/G.B. Leonetti (11,659)

The Great Industrial Exhibition, Dublin 1853
Irish School 1853/Irish School 1853 (11,630)

'Greece'
(poem by Wordsworth)
W. Purser/J.C. Bentley (20,200)

Hagar and Ishmael in the Desert
F.J. Navez/M.E. Corr (11,483)

Hamlet (from Shakespeare's play)
J. Mayall/J. Moore (11,027)

'A Harlot's Progress'
(Hogarth's Series, Plate 4)
W. Hogarth/W. Hogarth (11,520)

Haydée
C.L. Bazin/J.B.A. Lafosse (11,875)

'HB Discovered'
(political cartoon)
J. Doyle/J. Doyle (11,544)(63)

The Heart of Midlothian
(novel by Sir Walter Scott)
A. Nasmyth/E.F. Finden (20,360)
G.F. Robson/E.F. Finden (20,481)

Hector
P.P. Rubens/B. Baron (20,046)

Hercules and the Erymanthian Boar
F. Tacca (8123)

Hercules defeating the Horses of Diomedes
C. Le Brun/A. Lafitte (20,725)(74)

Hercules slaying the Lernaean Hydra
F. Tacca (8121)

Hercules slaying the Nemean Lion
F. Tacca (1824)

Hercules with the Pillars
F. Tacca (8125)

The Hermit of Cabinteely, Co. Dublin (S. Barrett)
Irish School c.1806/C. Doyle (11,087)

Hero, Ursula and Beatrice listening (from Shakespeare's play 'Much Ado About Nothing')
M.W. Peters/P. Simon (20,686)(16)

Hesperia (from Ovid's 'Metamorphoses')
J.M.W. Turner/J.M.W. Turner (20,023)

The History of Achilles
(by Homer)
P.P. Rubens/B. Baron (20,041-20,047)

'Hob' (from T. Hippisley's farce 'Flora or Hob-in-the-Wall)
Irish School 18C/Irish School 18C (11,317)

The Holy Family with St Anne and St John the Baptist
N. Berrettoni/B. Clayton the Elder (11,500)

The Holy Family with St John the Baptist
F. Barocci/*P.W. Tomkins & W.W. Hodgson*/A. Cardon (20,156)

Homage to Rubens (from Rubens's 'The History of Achilles')
School of P.P. Rubens/B. Baron (20,040)

The Horatii and the Curiatii
(political cartoon)
J. Doyle/J. Doyle (11,544) (57)

The Hunting of the Caledonian Boar
After P.P. Rubens/F. Lamb (11,661)

Hypolita (from Cibber's play 'She would and she would not')
J. Hoppner/J. Jones (10,386)

Icarus
A. Power (8089)

'The Iliad'
(poem by Homer)
P.P. Rubens/B. Baron (20,041-20,047)

Ino and Bacchus
J.H. Foley/*F. Roffe*/W. Roffe (20,210)

The Installation Banquet of the Knights of St Patrick in the Great Hall, Dublin Castle, 17th March 1783
J.K. Sherwin/J.K. Sherwin (11,657-11,658)
J.K. Sherwin/J.K. Sherwin (11,827-11,829)

Io
Claude Lorrain/R. Earlom (20,719)

'An Irish Subject'
(political cartoon)
J. Doyle/J. Doyle (11,544)(64)

'The Irish Tutor'
(political cartoon)
J. Doyle/J. Doyle (11,891)

Ishmael
F.J. Navez/M.E. Corr (11,483)

James II, former King of England and the Earl of D'Avaux are defeated by the Protestants at Enniskillen
Dutch School c.1690/Dutch School c.1690 (11,866)

James II, former King of England lands at Kinsale, 12th March 1689
Dutch School c.1690/Dutch School c.1690 (11,865)

Jason and the Serpent
J.M.W. Turner/J.M.W. Turner & C. Turner (11,963)

'Jerusalem Delivered'
(poem by Tasso)
G.B. Cipriani/F. Bartolozzi (11,957)

The Jew's Harp
D. Wilkie/E. Smith (20,219)

'John Gilpin'
(political cartoon)
J. Doyle/J. Doyle (11,544)(56)

The Judgement of Paris
Italian School 18C (8212)

Judith with the Head of Holofernes
Flemish School 17C (8331)

Juliet (from Shakespeare's play 'Romeo and Juliet')
G. Dawe/F.C. Lewis the Elder (10,991)
L. Sharpe/J.C. Edwards (20,154)

Juno
J. Barry/J. Barry (11,858)
P.P. Rubens/B. Baron (20,045)

Juno committing Io to the care of Argus
Claude Lorrain/R. Earlom (20,719)

Jupiter
P.P. Rubens/B. Baron (20,045)

Jupiter and Juno on Mount Ida
J. Barry/J. Barry (11,858)

Justice
R. De Hooghe/R. De Hooghe (11,849)(3)

King Lear weeping over the Body of Cordelia (from Shakespeare's play, 'King Lear')
J. Barry/F. Legat (20,712)(40)

King Henry VIII (from Shakespeare's play, 'King Henry VIII')
C.R. Leslie/C.W. Sharpe (20,142)

Lamentation over the dead Christ
P. Perugino/C. Duflos (20,671)(3)

The Landing of Prince Frederick Henry at Nijmegen, Holland
A. Cuyp/*W. Westall*/T. Medland & J. Bailey (20,324)

The Laocoon
Hellenistic School 1C/*P. Bouillon*/Bervic (20,683)(59)
Hellenistic School 1C/English School 1809 (20,653)
Roman School early 19C (8127)

Lazarus
Sebastiano del Piombo/R. Delaunay (20,723)(22)

Leonora (from I. Bickerstaffe's play, 'The Padlock')
J. Reynolds/R. Houston (11,063)

Lernaean Hydra
F. Tacca (8121)

'Lethe'
(play by D. Garrick)
F. Hayman/J. McArdell (10,123)

Louis XIV, King of France, receives James II at St Germain-en-Laye
R. De Hooghe/R. De Hooghe (11,847)(12)

Louis XIII, King of France creating Chevaliers de St Michel the day before the ceremony of the Order of St Esprit
French School 1634/French School 1634 (20,235)

'Love à La Mode'
(play by C. Macklin)
M.A. Shee/W. Ward the Elder (10,100)

Lycomedes, the daughters of
P.P. Rubens/B. Baron (20,043)

Macbeth (from Shakespeare's play)
J. Gwim/M. Jackson (10,134)

Macbeth, Lady (from Shakespeare's play)
English School c.1820 (8231)

'The Maid of Athens' (from Lord Byron's play)
L. Sharpe/H. Robinson (20,157)

Margaret meets Faust in the Summer House (from Goethe's play 'Faust')
G. Cattermole/J.C. Bentley (20,444)

Mars Gradius
Italian School late 18C (8115)

'Marriage à la Mode'
(plates from Hogarth's Series)
W. Hogarth/English School c.1750 (11,557-11,662)

The Marriage of Marie de Medici and Henry IV
P.P. Rubens/*J.M. Nattier*/A. Trouvain (20,678)(6)

The Martyrdom of St Peter Martyr
Titian/V. Lefebvre (11,481)

Maynooth College, 1st President of
(Thomas Hussey, R.C. Bishop of Waterford and Lismore)
C.F. Von Breda/S.W. Reynolds the Elder (10,422)

The Meeting of Solomon and the Queen of Sheba
Raphael/S. Bianchi (20,703)(47)

Meleager and Atalanta or the Hunting of the Caledonian Boar
After P.P. Rubens/F. Lamb (11,661)

Melozzo da Forli medallion struck for the fifth centenary of his birth
P. Morbiducci (8170)

Mercury charming Argus to sleep
Claude Lorrain/R. Earlom (20,665)(150)

Metamorphoses
(by Ovid)
L. Bramer/P.C. Canot (20,035)
F. Chauveau/F. Chauveau (20,215)
English School 18C/A. Walker (20,541)
J.M.W. Turner/J.M.W. Turner (20,023)

Midas (from the play by O'Hara)
De Grifft/H. Brocas the Elder (10,667)

'A Midnight Modern Conversation'
W. Hogarth/W. Hogarth (11,509)

Milo of Croton
?Giorgione/B.A. Nicollet (20,724)(24)

Minerva
R. De Hooghe/R. De Hooghe (11,849)(3)

Miraculous draught of fishes
J.B. Jouvenet/J.B. Jouvenet (20,529)

The Monster Meeting of the 20th September at Clifden in the Irish Highlands
J.P. Haverty/J.P. Haverty (11,857)

Moses striking the Rock
F. Chesham/F. Chesham (20,032)

Mount Ida
J. Barry/J. Barry (11,858)

Mount Olympia
J. Barry/J. Barry (20,772)(3)

Mounts Olympus and Ossa from the plains of Thessalay (from Wordsworth's poem 'Greece')
W. Purser/J.C. Bentley (20,200)

'Much Ado about Nothing'
(play by Shakespeare)
M.W. Peters/P. Simon (20,686)(16)

Naval Engagement between the Turks and Russians
English School 18C/English School 18C (20,803)

Nemean Lion
F. Tacca (8124)

Nestor
P.P. Rubens/B. Brandard (20,044)

Niobe mourning the Death of her children
Roman Antique/R. Audengerd (20,221)

Noli me Tangere
Titian/N.H. Tardieu (20,672)(7)

The Norseman (Caratacus)
J.H. Foley (8258)

Nymph Sleeping
After A. Canova (8103)

The Oath of the Grütli, Arnold de Melchthac, Walter Furst and Werner Stauffacher, 1307
G. Ulyssé/H. Raunheim (20,176)

O'Brallaghan, Sir Callaghan (from Macklin's play, 'Love à la Mode')
M.A. Shee/W. Ward the Elder (10,100)

Oedipe Roi de Thebes'
(play by Saint Georges de Bouhelier)
K. Van Dongen/French School 20C (11,565)

Olivia (from Shakespeare's play 'Twelfth Night')
C.R. Leslie/T. Vernon (20,141)

'Omnibus Race'
(political cartoon)
J. Doyle/J. Doyle (11,544)(67)

Orlando being prevented from stabbing himself (from Ariosto's poem 'Orlando Furioso' Canto XL)
G.B. Cipriani/F. Bartolozzi (20,031)

Orpheus instructing a Savage people in Theology and the Arts of Social Life
J. Barry/J. Barry (20,722)(1)

'The Padlock'
(play by I. Bickerstaff)
J. Reynolds/R. Houston (11,063)

Pallas
P.P. Rubens/B. Brandard (20,044)

Pandora
J. Barry/J. Barry (20,722)(15)

Paris
P.P. Rubens/B. Baron (20,047)

Paris deserted by his army
C. Le Brun/R. Shepherd (20,050)

Passing of the Reform Bill in the House of Lords, 1832
S.W. Reynolds/S.W. Reynolds (20,819)

Patroclus
P.P. Rubens/B. Baron (20,046)

Peace and War
P.P. Rubens/*W.M. Craig*/C. Heath (20,705)(7)

Pegasus and Aurora
?Roman Antique/English School early 19C (20,654)

Peggy (from 'The Country Dealer')
G. Romney/J. Ogborne (10,341)

Pericles
J. Barry/J. Barry (20,722)(3)

Phillida (from Cibber's play 'Damon and Phillida')
J. Faber the Younger/W.J. Alais (11,121)

The Piping Boy
(John Camillus Hone)
N. Hone the Elder/W. Baillie (10,532)

'A Pitiful Looking Group'
(political cartoon)
J. Doyle/J. Doyle (11,854)

The Fifth Plague of Egypt
(Diseased Cattle)
J.M.W. Turner/J.M.W. Turner & C. Turner (11,973)

The Ninth Plague of Egypt
(Plague of Darkness)
J. Lucas/J. Lucas (20,055)

The Tenth Plague of Egypt
(Death of the First Born)
J.M.W. Turner/J.M.W. Turner & W. Say (20,018)

Politeness
G.M. Woodward/English School 1808 (11,544)(8)

'Poor Soldier' (play)
Irish School c.1793/Irish School 1793 (11,245)

Porcia
Roman School 18C (8295)

Porus
C. Le Brun/R. Shepherd (20,050-20,051)
C. Le Brun/R. Shepherd (20,549)

Preparation for the Fête and Firework Display in Rome, 30th November 1729, on the Birth of a Dauphin to King Louis XIV of France
G.P. Panini/*J. Dumont the Elder*/C.N. Cochin (11,656)

The Preservation of Richard MacGuire, 12th May 1781, after his balloon crashed in the sea off the Irish coast
J.J. Barralet/W. Ward the Elder (11,654)

Procris
Claude Lorrain/J.B. Allen (20,245)
Claude Lorrain/English School 1827 (20,242)
J.M.W. Turner/J.M.W. Turner & G. Clint (11,998)

Truth
G. Kneller/P. Tanjé (10,994)

Truth and Falsehood
A.G. Stevens (8075)

'Twelfth Night'
(play by Shakespeare)
C.R. Leslie/T. Vernon (20,141)

Unitarian Minister in England, the First
(Thomas Emlyn)
J. Highmore/G. Vandergucht (10,282)

'The Upsetting of the Reform Coach'
(Political Cartoon)
J. Doyle/J. Doyle (11,544) (58)

Ursula (from Shakespeare's play, 'Much Ado About Nothing')
M.W. Peters/P. Simon (20,686)(16)

Valour and Cowardice
A.G. Stevens (8075)

Vanderfeld, Lord S.Q. (from Hogarth's 'Marriage à la Mode', Plate 1)
W. Hogarth/English School c.1750 (11,557)

'Venice Preserved' (play by C. Otway)
A.W. Devis/H.H. Meyer (10,409)

Venus
M. Stapleton (8018) (8020)
Roman School early 19C (8110)
Roman School early 19C (8226)
G. Vanelli (8186)

Venus and Adonis
Italian School 18C (8213)

Venus and Cupid
A. Allori/*A. Borel*/P. Trierre (20,723)(7)

Victors being Crowned at Mount Olympia
J. Barry/J. Barry (20,722)(3)

Virgil
E. Delacroix/L.D. Carred (11,495)

The Virgin
L. Richier (8246)

The Virgin (in narrative scenes)
Bolognese School 17C/Bolognese School 17C (20,228)
Claude Lorrain/W.R. Smith (20,607)
P. Delaroche/L.P. Henriquel Dupont (11,484)
J. Le Pautre/J. Le Pautre (20,232)
Perugino/C. Duflos (20,671)(3)
G.B. Piazzetta/P.A. Kilian (20,218)
Rembrandt/English School 1827 (20,708)(19)

The Virgin and Christchild
German School (950/1050)/C. Regnier (20,001)
Circle of L. Ghiberti (8049)
L. Lotto/*W.M. Craig*/J.H. Wright (20,680)(7)
Raphael/*P.P. Prudhon*/P. Audouin (20,691)(1)
Raphael/*J.B. Wicar*/C.E. Duponchel (20,687)(46)
Raphael/*Vendenberg*/A.L. Romanet (20,723)(14)
M. Schongauer/English School 1826 (20,733)(39)
Titian/V. Lefebvre (11,492)

Virtue
R. Cosway/J.R. Smith (11,665)

Vulcan
P.P. Rubens/B. Brandard (20,045)

Vulcan's Forge
?H.R. Devilliers/H.R. Devilliers (20,102)

William III at the Siege of Namur, 1695
J. Wyck/J. Faber the Younger (10,420)

'A Winter's Tale'
(play by Shakespeare)
C.R. Leslie/L. Stocks (20,140)

Wisdom Directing Beauty and Virtue to Sacrifice at the Altar of Diana
R. Cosway/J.R. Smith (11,665)

'The Wonder'
(play by T. Park)
J. Hoppner/T. Park (11,415)

Wrangle, Sir Gilbert (from C. Cibber's play 'The Refusal')
D. Dodd/J. Walker (11,225)

The Wreck of the Dunraven off S. Wales
J.H. Robinson/G. Childs (20,328)

The Wreck of the Queen Victoria on Howth Rocks, 15th February 1853
A. Concanen/E. Chavane (11,620)

The Young Sophocles leading the Chorus of Victory after the Battle of Salamis
J. Donoghue (8037)

APPENDIX 7

ILLUSTRATIONS FOR BOOKS AND MAGAZINES NOT IN THE COLLECTION

'The Amulet', 1829
(pl. of Mrs Elizabeth Allnutt)
T. Lawrence/C. Rolls (20,136)
(pl. of Lady Georgiana Fane)
T. Lawrence/C. Armstrong (20,211)

'An authentic account of the Embassy from the King of Great Britain to the Emperor of China', 1797
(by Sir g. Staunton; pl. of 1st Earl Macartney)
T. Hickey/J. Hall (10,952)

'Ancient Historical Pictures', 1844
(by Harding; pl. of 1st Viscount Falkland)
P. Van Somer/*G.P. Harding*/J. Brown (10,807)
(pl. of Sir William Russell)
English School c.1580/*G.P. Harding*/W. Greatbach (11,052)

'The Anniversary', 1829
(pl. of Fonthill abbey, Wiltshire)
J.M.W. Turner/T. Crostick (20,512)

'Annotations', 1655
(by John Richardson; pl. of author)
English School 1653/English School 1804 (10,278)

'The Antiquarian Itinerary', 1817
(pl. of a cross at Paignton, Devon)
W.I. Hocker/T. Higham (20,479)

'The Antiquities of Ireland', 1791-95
(by F. Grose; pl. of Baggotsrath castle)
T. Cocking/T. Medland (11,927)
(pl. of Christchurch Cathedral)
A.M. Bigari/T. Medland (10,055)

'Antiquities and Scenery of County Kilkenny', 1851
(by J.G. Robertson; pl. of Callan church)
Irish School 19C/Irish School 19C (11,673)

'Art Journal', 1849
(pl. of Ino and Bacchus)
J.H. Foley/*F.R. Roffe*/W. Roffe (20,210)

'Art Journal', 1853
(pl. of the children in the wood)
J. Bell/*F.R. Roffe*/W. Roffe (20,209)

'Art Journal', 1863
(pl. of Olivia from Shakespeare's play 'Twelfth Night')
C.R. Leslie/T. Vernon (20,141)

'Art Journal', 1867
(pl. of Autolycus from Shakespeare's play 'A Winter's Tale')
C.R. Leslie/L. Stocks (20,140)

'Art Journal', 1868
(pl. of a sunny day)
A. Cuyp/J.C. Bentley (20,161)

'Art Journal', 1873
(pl. of Catherine of Aragon from Shakespeare's play 'King Henry VIII')
C.R. Leslie/C.W. Sharpe (20,142)

'Art Union Monthly', 1839
(pl. of pilgrims at Jericho)
D. Roberts/W. Day & W.L. Haghe (20,149)

'Athenaeum Portraits', 1836
(by T. Maclean; pl. of William Betham)
D. Maclise/W. Drummond (10,265)

'The Beauties of the Bosphorus', 1839-40
(by J. Pardoe; pl. of Istanbul, Turkey)
W.H. Bartlett/R. Wallis (20,441)

'The Biographical Mirror', 1793
(by E. & S. Harding; pl. of Henry Brooke)
H. Brooke/R. Clamp (11,107)

'Body of Divinity', 1647
(by J. Ussher, frontispiece of James Ussher)
English School 17C/W. Marshall (11,005)

'Book of Beauty', 1839
(by Heath; pl. of Viscountess Powerscourt)
J. Ross/W.H. Mote (11,333)

'Book of Beauty', 1842
(by Heath; pl. of Miss Marguerite A. Power)
W. Drummond/W.H. Egleton (11,336)
(pl. of Viscountess Powerscourt)
J. Ross/W.H. Mote (11,333)
(pl. of Penelope, Princess of Capua)
A.E. Chalon/W.H. Mote (11,309)

'Bow Bell's', May 1867
(pl. of The Young Mother)
F. Geefs/English School 1867 (20,633)

'Bow Bell's Almanack', 1867
(pl. of The Nurse)
K. Piloty/English School 1867 (20,632)
(pl. of The Sick Boy)
English School c.1867/English School 1867 (20,627)

'The British Gallery of Pictures', 1818
(pl. of the Holy Family with St John the Baptist)
F. Barocci/*P.W. Tomkins & W.W. Hodgson*/A. Cardon (20,156)

'Caverns of the Kickapoo'
W.H. Brooke/W.H. Brooke (20,811)

'Chronicles of Eri', 1822
(by R. O'Connor; frontispiece of Roger O'Connor)
A. Buck/Irish School 1798 (10,585)

'Church Magazine', 1841
(pl. of William Power Le Poer Trench)
Irish School 19C/R. Smith (11,280)

'Les Cinquante Deux Tableaux', 1788
(pl. of the meeting of Solomon and the Queen of Sheba)
Raphael/S. Bianchi (20,703)(47)

'Collectanea de Rebus Hibernicis', 1804
(by Vallancey; pl. of Charles Vallancey)
G. Chinnery/Irish School 1804 (11,246-11,247)

'Collection des Portraits de Députés de l'Assemblée Nationale', 1789
(pl. of Comte de Lally-Tolendal)
J.M. Moreau/W.N.M. Courbe (10,605)

'A Collection of Portraits sketched from life since the year 1793 by George Dance', 1809-14
(pl. of James Barry)
G. Dance/W. Daniell (10,196)

'A Complete History of England', 1757
(by T.G. Smollett; pl. of Queen Anne)
G. Kneller/J. Houbraken (10,543)
(pl. of Ulick De Burgh)
English School 17C/S.F. Ravenet the Elder (11,205)
(pl. of Admiral Sir Peter Warren)
T. Hudson/W.W. Ryland (11,258)

'Contemporary Portraits', 1822
(by T. Cadell & W. Davies; pl. of Isaac Barré, M.P.)
G.C. Stuart/*W. Evans*/W.T. Fry (10,739)
(pl. of Earl of Charlemont)
H. Hone/B. Smith (10,744-10,745)
(pl. of John Wilson Croker, M.P.)
W. Owen/*J. Wright*/H. Meyer (10,751)
(pl. of John Philpot Curran, M.P.)
Irish School 1806/1814/*J.B. Lane*/S. Freeman (10,151)
Irish School 1806/1814/*J.B. Lane*/S. Freeman (10,770)
(pl. of Henry Grattan, M.P.)
A. Pope/J. Godby (10,837)
(pl. of Elizabeth Hamilton)
H. Raeburn/*J. Jackson*/H. Meyer (10,883)
(pl. of Lord John Huchinson)
T. Philips/*W. Evans*/K. Mackenzie (10,801)
(pl. of Arthur Murphy)
N. Dance/*J. Jackson*/E. Scriven (10,925)
(pl. of George Ponsonby)
A. Hope/J. Godby (10,062)
(pl. of Martin Archer Shee)
J. Jackson/W.T. Fry (10,260)
(pl. of Henry Tresham)
A. Pope/A. Cardon (10,135)

'Continental Tourist', c.1849
(pl. of Brussels gate, Mechlin)
?J. Shury the Elder/J. Shury the Elder and J. Shury the Younger (20,280)

'Continuation of Rapin', 1787
(by N. Tindal; pl. of Medals of William III and Queen Mary)
English School 1692/J. Goldar (20,836)

'Continuation of Rapin's History of England', 1757-59 edition
(by N. Tindal; pls. of William and Mary)
G. Kneller/O. Malone (20,123-20,124)

'Counties of Cheshire', 1836
(by T. Noble & T. Rose; pl. of the castle of the Peverils, in the Peak, Derbyshire)
T. Allom/T. Clark (20,279)

'Court Album', 1852
(by D. Bogue; pl. of Miss Emily Mary Dawson)
J. Hayter/W.H. Mote (10,784)
(pl. of Baroness Helen Dufferin and Clandeboye)
E. Lamont/W.H. Mote (10,791)

'Court Magazine', 1832
(by Bell; pl. of Hester Catherine, Marchioness of Sligo)
Mrs. J. Robertson/J. Posselwhite (11,308)

'Court Magazine', April 1834
(by Bell; pl. of Anne Catherine McDonnell)
Mrs J. Mee/H.R. Cook (11,119)

'Critical and Familiar Notices on the Art of Etching upon Copper', 1810
(by W. Huband; pl. of Elymas Struck Blind)
Raphael/WS. Huband (11,538)
(pl. of a Man with arm in Coat)
W. Huband/W. Huband (11,533)
(pl. of a Profile of a Young Man)
W. Huband/W. Huband (11,537)

'Cumberland', 1832
(by T. Rose; pl. of Buttermere)
T. Allom/R. Sands (20,398)
(pl. of Castle Crag)

T. Allom/J.C. Bentley (20,477)
(pl. of Colwith Force, Cumbria)
T. Allom/W. Tombleson (20,485)
(pl. of Mardale Head)
T. Allom/E. Challis (20,480)
(pl. of Windermere, Esthwaite and Coniston Lakes)
G. Pickering/W. Le Petit (20,458)

'Cyclopaedian Magazine', April 1807
(pl. of Sir John Andrew Stevenson)
E. Jones/H. Brocas the Elder (11,301)

'Cyclopaedian Magazine', October 1808
(pl. of Leonard Macnally)
J. Petrie/P. Maguire (11,221)

'The Danube', 1844
(by W. Beattie; pl. of Belgrade, Yugoslavia)
F. Abresch/*W.H. Bartlett*/E. Brandard (20,475)
(pl. of Sulina, Romania)
F. Abresch/*W.H. Bartlett*/R. Wallis (20,425)

'David Restored, or an antidote against the prosperity of the wicked', 1660
(by E. Parry; frontispiece of Edward Parry)
Irish School 17C/J. Dickson (10,305)

'Death of Abel', 1800
(by S. Gessner; pl. of Cain and family)
H. Singleton/J. Godby (20,059)

'Death Disarmed', 1712
(by Ezekiel Hopkins; frontispiece of author)
English School 17C/M. Vandergucht (10,625-10,626)

'Devonshire and Cornwall illustrated', 1832
(by J. Britton and E.W. Brayley; pl. of Tintagel castle, Cornwall)
T. Allom/W.A. Le Petit (20,451)

'Dramatic Works', 1778
(by H. Kelly; frontispiece of Hugh Kelly)
H.D. Hamilton/J. Boydell (10,294)

'Drawing Book of Animals and Rustic Groups', 1853
(by T.S. Cooper; pl. of shire horses)
T.S. Cooper/T.S. Cooper (20,169)
(pl. of halt at the Bell Inn)
T.S. Cooper/T.S. Cooper (20,170)
(pl. of donkeys)
T.S. Cooper/T.S. Cooper (20,174)
(pl. of deer)
T.S. Cooper/T.S. Cooper (20,243)
(pl. of sheep and carthorses)
T.S. Cooper/T.S. Cooper (20,345)
(pl. of donkey and donkey with rider)
T.S. Cooper/T.S. Cooper (20,402)

'Drawing Book of Landscapes', 1843
(by H. Bright; pl. of castle entrance)
H. Bright/W. Day & W.L. Haghe (20,222)
(pl. of a cabin)
H. Bright/W. Day & W.L. Haghe (20,347)

'Drawing Room Portrait Gallery of Eminent Personages', 1859
(pl. of Daniel Maclise)
J. Mayall/D.J. Pound (10,927)
(pl. of William Shee)
J. Mayall/D.J. Pound (11,023)
(pl. of James Whiteside, M.P.)
J. Mayall/D.J. Pound (10,567)

'Drawing Room Table Book', 1851
(by J. Tallis; pl. of Barry Sullivan)
J. Mayall/J. Moore (11,027)

'The Dublin Builder', 1st February 1861
(pl. of Dublin drinking fountains)
T.N. Deane & B. Woodward/J.C. Rogers (11,737)

'Dublin and London Magazine', 1825
(pl. of Richard Lalor Sheil, M.P.)
S. Catterson Smith the Elder/R. Cooper (11,289)

'Dublin Magazine', August 1762
(pl. of the front of the Blew-Coat school)
Irish School c.1762/Irish School 1762 (11,616)

'Dublin Magazine', April 1799
(pl. of William Saurin)
Irish School c.1799/Irish School 1799 (11,305)

'Dublin Magazine', March 1813
(pl. of Daniel O'Connell)
Irish School c.1813/Irish School 1813 (10,598-10,599)

'Dublin Magazine', May 1813
(pl. of 2nd Earl of Moira)
English School c.1813/Irish School 1813 (10,655)

'Dublin Monthly Museum', September 1814
(pl. of William Fletcher)
Irish School c.1814/H. Brocas the Elder (11,141-11,142)

'Dublin University Magazine', October 1839
(pl. of Rev. Caesar Otway)
W. Stevenson/J. Kirkwood (10,592)

'Dublin University Magazine', November 1839
(pl. of John Anster)
W. Stevenson/J. Kirkwood (11,120)

'Dublin University Magazine', January 1840
(pl. of 3rd Earl of Roden)
F.R. Say/J. Kirkwood (11,293)

'Dublin University Magazine', February 1840
(pl. of Rev. Robert Walsh)
J. Comerford/J. Kirkwood (11,270)

'Dublin University Magazine', January 1841
(pl. of William Carleton)
C. Grey/J. Kirkwood (11,216-11,217)

'Dublin University Magazine', February 1841
(pl. of James Ussher)
R. Home/*C. Grey*/J. Kirkwood (11,254)

'Dublin University Magazine', March 1841
(pl. of Daniel O'Connell)
Irish School c.1841/J. Kirkwood (10,596)

'Dublin University Magazine', April 1841
(pl. of Philip Taylor)
C. Grey/J. Kirkwood (11,273)

'Dublin University Magazine', May 1841
(pl. of Colonel William Blacker)
?C. Grey/J. Kirkwood (11,100)

'Dublin University Magazine', June 1841
(pl. of Rev. George Miller)
C. Grey/J. Kirkwood (11,227)

'Dublin University Magazine', July 1841
(pl. of Charles Kendel Bushe)
C. Grey/J. Kirkwood (11,082)

'Dublin University Magazine', August 1841
(pl. of Rev. William Hamilton Maxwell)
C. Grey/J. Kirkwood (10,665)

'Dublin University Magazine', September 1841
(pl. of Rev. John Barrett)
Irish School c.1841/J. Kirkwood (11,109)

'Dublin University Magazine', January 1842
(pl. of Sir William Rowan Hamilton)
C. Grey/J. Kirkwood (10,613)

'Dublin University Magazine', February 1842
(pl. of Dr Robert James Graves)
C. Grey/J. Kirkwood (11,161)

'Dublin University Magazine', March 1842
(pl. of Charles, 2nd Viscount Gort)
C. Grey/J. Kirkwood (11,156)

'Dublin University Magazine', April 1842
(pl. of Rev. William Butler)
C. Grey/J. Kirkwood (11,104)
(pl. of Thomas Moore)
D. Maclise/J. Kirkwood (11,423)

'Dublin University Magazine', June 1842
(pl. of John Wilson Croker, M.P.)
C. Grey/J. Kirkwood (11,192)

'Dublin University Magazine', July 1842
(pl. of Sir Robert Stopford)
H. MacManus/J. Kirkwood (11,302)

'Dublin University Magazine', September 1843
(pl. of Percival Barton Lord)
C. Grey/J. Kirkwood (11,292)

'Dublin University Magazine', January 1844
(pl. of William Maginn)
S. Skillin/J. Kirkwood (10,287)

'Dublin University Magazine', October 1844
(pl. of Francis Blackburne)
C. Grey/J. Kirkwood (11,090)

'Dublin University Magazine', August 1845
(pl. of Dr Whitley Stokes)
C. Grey/H. Griffiths (11,311)

'Dublin University Magazine', May 1846
(pl. of Sir Martin Archer Shee)
T. Bridgford/H. Griffiths (11,310)
T. Bridgford/H. Griffiths (11,312)

'Dublin University Magazine', August 1846
(pl. of Sir Robert Henry Sale)
English School 19C/H. Griffiths
(11,306-11,307)

'Dublin University Magazine', October 1846
(pl. of Sir Henry Pottinger)
S. Laurence/H. Griffiths (11,334)

'Dublin University Magazine', January 1847
(pl. of Edward Bunting)
Irish School 19C/Irish School 1847 (11,864)

'Dublin University Magazine', May 1847
(pl. of Daniel Maclise)
T. Bridgford/Irish School 1847 (11,237)

'Dublin University Magazine', June 1847
(pl. of John Doherty)
Irish School c.1847/H. Griffiths (11,178)

'Dublin University Magazine', January 1848
(pl. of Robert Holmes)
Irish School c.1848/H. Griffiths (10,624)

'Dublin University Magazine', March 1849
(pl. of James Whiteside)
C. Grey/Irish School 1849 (11,268-11,269)

'Dublin University Magazine', August 1849
(pl. of Thomas Crofton Croker)
?C. Grey/Irish School 1849 (11,202)

'Dublin University Magazine', January 1850
(pl. of John Hogan)
C. Grey/Irish School 1850 (10,617)

'Dublin University Magazine', November 1850
(pl. of Catherine Hayes)
Irish School c.1850/Irish School 1850 (11,378)

'Dublin University Magazine', July 1851
(pl. of Michael William Balfe)
C. Grey/Irish School 1851 (11,099)

'Dublin University Magazine', November 1851
(pl. of Patrick MacDowell)
C. Grey/Irish School 1851 (10,666)

'Dublin University Magazine', January 1852
(pl. of Sir James Emerson Tennent, M.P.)
C. Grey/Irish School 1852 (11,271)

'Dublin University Magazine', February 1852
(pl. of Henry Brooke)
J. Lewis/Irish School 1852 (11,108)

'Dublin University Magazine', October 1852
(pl. of James Sheridan Knowles)
C. Grey/Irish School 1852 (10,641)

'Dublin University Magazine', March 1853
(pl. of Joseph Napier, M.P.)
C. Grey/Irish School 1853 (11,421-11,422)

'Durham and Northumberland' 1832
(by T. Rose; pl. of Aydon castle, Northumberland)
T. Allom/D. Buckle (20,419-20,420)
(pl. of Bynell Hall)
T. Allom/D. Buckle (20,420)

'Effigies Poetical', 1821
(pl. of John Cunningham)
T. Bewick/*J. Thurston*/W.H. Worthington (10,763)

'Elementary Drawing Book of Landscapes and Buildings', 1821
(by S. Prout; various rustic plates)
S. Prout/S. Prout (20,559-20,565)
S. Prout/S. Prout (20,567)

'European Magazine', August 1782
(pl. of Henry Grattan)
Irish School c.1782/English School 1782 (11,147)

'European Magazine', February 1784
(pl. of Earl of Charlemont)
W. Hogarth/English School 1784 (11,186-11,187)

'European Magazine', December 1787
(pl. of Charles Macklin)
J.C. Lochée/J. Corner (11,224)

'European Magazine', January 1791
(pl. of Francis Rawdon)
J. Reynolds/R. Stanier (10,653)

'European Magazine', April 1792
(pl. of Parliament house, Dublin)
R. Pool & J. Cash/W. Thomas (11,752)

'European Magazine', March 1794
(pl. of William Burton-Conyngham, M.P.)
G.C. Stuart/J. Farn (11,190-1)

'European Magazine', February 1795
(pl. of Peg Woffington)
J.G. Eccard/J. Pearson (11,250)

'European Magazine', August 1795
(pl. of Arthur Young)
J. Rising/W. Hinton (11,262)

'European Magazine', June 1797
(pl. of Francis Grose)
N. Hone the Elder/*N. Dance*/W. Ridley (11,157)

'European Magazine', April 1798
(pl. of Drogheda, Co. Louth)
Irish School c.1798/English School 1798 (11,679)

'European Magazine', May 1800
(pl. of Hugh Boyd)
R. Home/W. Ridley (11,084)

'European Magazine', April 1802
(pl. of Rev. Samuel Madden)
R. Hunter/S. Harding (10,670)

'European Magazine', April 1804
(pl. of William Thomas Fitzgerald)
S. Drummond/W. Ridley (11,136)

'European Magazine', August 1805
(pl. of Arthur Murphy)
N. Dance/W. Ridley (10,669)

'European Magazine', April 1806
(pl. of Andrew Cherry)
S. Drummond/W. Ridley & W. Holl the Elder (11,204)

'European Magazine', May 1809
(pl. of Angelica Kauffmann)
A. Kauffmann/W. Ridley (10,644)

'European Magazine', August 1811
(pl. of Francis Rawdon)
English School c.1780/W. Ridley (10,656-10,657)

'European Magazine', December 1814
(pl. of Eliza O'Neill)
S. Drummond/T. Blood (10,579)

'European Magazine', January 1815
(pl. of William Fletcher)
Irish School c.1814/T. Blood (11,143)

'European Magazine', December 1816
(pl. of Charles Philips)
S. Drummond/H. Meyer (11,261)

'European Magazine', June 1821
(pl. of Peter Turnerelli)
S. Drummond/J. Thomson (11,278)

'European Magazine', April 1824
(pl. of Thomas Moore)
J. Jackson/J. Thomson (11,236)

'Excursions through Ireland', 1820
(by T.K. Cromwell; pl. of Christchurch Cathedral)
G. Petrie/T. Barber (10,056)
(pl. of Queen's Bridge and Richmond Tower)
G. Petrie/T. Barber (11,792)

'An Excursion through the Principle parts of Yorkshire and Derbyshire', 1805
(pl. of Middleham castle, Yorkshire)
E. Dayes/S. Noble (20,430)

'Female Aristocracy of the Court of Queen Victoria', 1849
(by W. Finden; pl. of Miss Blanche Bury)
C.L. Castlake/W.H. Mote (10,891)
(pl. of Countess of Charleville)
J. Hayter/W. Finden (10,727)
(pl. of Lady Alice Conroy)
C.I. Baseley/W. Finden (10,769)
(pl. of Lady Selina Dufferin and Clandeboye)
F. Stone/J.H. Robinson (10,370)
(pl. of Lady Flora Hastings)
E. Hawkins/W. Finden (10,943)

'Flora or Hob-in-the-Wall'
(by J.H. Hippisley; frontispiece of T. Ryder)
Irish School 18C/Irish School 18C (11,317)

'Galerie du Musée de France', 1814
(pl. of St John baptising in the Jordan)
N. Poussin/*Dufraine*/J. Duplessi-Bertaux & C. Niquet (20,201)

'A Gallery of Illustrious Literary Characters', 1830-38
(by Fraser; pl. of William Maginn)
D. Maclise/D. Maclise (10,288)
(pl. of Thomas Moore)
D. Maclise/D. Maclise (10,675)
(pl. of O'Connell and Sheil)
D. Maclise/D. Maclise (10,601)

'Gallery of Modern British Artists', 1834
(pl. of Goodrich castle)
P. De Wint/W. Floyd (20,493)

'Gallery of Portraits', 1833-37
(by C. Knight; pl. of John Flaxman)
J. Jackson/R. Woodman the Younger (20,118)

'Gallery of Rare Portraits', 1816
(by S. Woodburn; pl. of Colonel John Hewson)
English School 17C/English School c.1816 (10,618)

'Gallery of the Society of Painters in Watercolours', 1833
(pl. of Southampton harbour)
A.V.D. Copley-Fielding/G. Cooke (20,373)
(pl. of the Forest Hall mountains)
P. De Wint/J.H. Kernot (20,382)

'Garanga'
W.H. Brooke/W.H. Brooke (11,507)
W.H. Brooke/W.H. Brooke (20,809-20,810)
W.H. Brooke/W.H. Brooke (20,812)

'Gems of Ancient Art', 1827
(pl. of Annette)
H. Fragonard/English School 1827
(pl. of Cephalus and Procris)
Claude/English School 1827
(pl. of Leicestershire)
G. Morland/English School 1827
(pl. of Pastoral Landscape)
Claude/English School 1827

'Gems of Art', 1824
(pl. of The Listening Housewife)
N. Maes/T. Lupton (20,326)
(pl. of the Rialto bridge, Venice)
Canaletto/J.C. Bromley (20,333)

'Gems of European Art', 1846
(by S.C. Hall; pl. of Cottage Door)
R. Westall/C. Turner (20,445)
(pl. of the Jew's Harp)
D. Wilkie/E. Smith (20,219)
(pl. of Olden Hospitality)

J.R. Herbert/H.C. Shenton the Elder (20,583)
(pl. of St Mary Magdalen reading)
?Correggio/S.W. Reynolds the Younger (20,137)
(pl. of a Sunny Day)
A. Cuyp/J.C. Bentley (20,161)

'The General Advertiser', 21st April 1883
(pl. of an advertisement for Pim Brothers furniture warehouses)
Irish School 1883/Irish School 1883 (20,644)

'Gentleman's Magazine', May 1785
(pl. of St Roch and an angel, etc)
Irish School c.1785/English School 1785 (11,836)
(pl. of Simpson's hospital)
Irish School c.1785/English School 1785 (11,706)

'Gentleman's Magazine', August 1785
(pl. of St John's church, Fishamble Street)
Irish School c.1785/English School 1785 (11,915)

'Gentleman's Magazine', May 1786
(pl. of the Meath Infirmary; St Ann's church, Dawson street)
Irish School c.1786/English School 1786 (11,668)
(pl. of St Ann's Church, Dawson street)
Irish School c.1786/English School 1786 (11,920)
(pl. of St Nicholas-Within Church, Christchurch place)
Irish School c.1786/English School 1786 (11,742)
Irish School c.1786/English School 1786 (11,916)

'Gentleman's Magazine', October 1787
(pl. of College Green post office)
Irish School c.1787/English School 1787 (11,913)
(pl. of the Parliament House; St John's, Monkstown)
Irish School c.1787/English School 1787 (11,730-11,731)

'Gentleman's Magazine', December 1787
(pl. of Clontarf castle)
Irish School c.1787/English School 1787 (11,837)
(pl. of the Royal Charter school)
Irish School c.1787/English School 1787 (11,918)

'Gentleman's Magazine', April 1788
(pl. of Dunsink observatory)
Irish School c.1788/English School 1788 (11,743-11,744)
(pl. of Four Courts, St. Michael's Hill)
Irish School c.1788/English School 1788 (11,921)

'Gentleman's Magazine', December 1788
(pl. of Castle street)
Irish School c.1788/English School 1788 (11,917)

'Gentleman's Magazine', June 1789
(pl. of Smock Alley theatre)
Irish School c.1789/English School 1789 (11,925)

'Gentleman's Magazine', October 1789
(pl. of Howth, Ireland's Eye, and Lambay Island)
Irish School c.1789/English School 1789 (11,756)

'Gentleman's Magazine', May 1790
(pl. of Daly's Club House)
Irish School c.1790/English School 1790 (11,923)
(pl. of Royal Military Infirmary)
Irish School c.1790/English School 1790 (11,727)

'Gentleman's Magazine', November 1790
(pl. of the New Stamp Office, etc)
Irish School c.1790/English School 1790 (11,832)

'Gentleman's Magazine', April 1792
(pl. of the Custom House)
Irish School 1792/English School 1792 (11,720-11,721)
(pl. of the Parliament House)
Irish School 1792/English School 1792 (11,728)
Irish School 1792/English School 1792 (11,914)

'Gentleman's Magazine', February 1818
(pl. of Stove Tenter House)
Irish School c.1818/B. Brunton (11,767)

'Gentleman's Magazine'
(pl. of Essex bridge)
Irish School c.1755/B. Cole (11,768)

'Gentleman's Magazine'
(pl. of Sarah bridge)
Irish School late 18C/English School late 18C (11,739)

'Genuine Edition of Hume's England'
(by J. Parson; pl. of George II, King of England)
T. Worlidge/C.W. White (20,119)

'The Graphic', May 1880
(pl. of illustration to serial)
L. Fildes/English School 1880 (20,578)

'Great Britain's Coasting Pilot', 1693
(pl. of Dublin Bay)
G. Collins/English School 17C (11,879)

'Greece', 1839
(by W. Wordsworth; pl. of Mounts Olympus and Ossa)
W. Purser/J.C. Bentley (20,200)

'Guy Mannering', 1832
(by Lord Byron; pl. of Skiddaw, Cumbria)
P. De Wint/E. Finden (20,520)

'The Heads of Illustrious Persons of Great Britain', 1747-52
(by T. Birch; pl. of Charles Fleetwood)
R. Walker/J. Houbraken (10,839)
(pl. of 1st Earl of Orkney)
M. Maingaud/J. Houbraken (10,987)
(pl. of Lieut. General Thomas Tollemache)
G. Kneller/J. Houbraken (20,133)
R. Walker/J. Houbraken (10,839)

'Herwologia', 1620
(by H. Holland; pl. of Sir Henry Sidney)
?English School 16C/W. Van De passe & M. Van De Passe (11,037)

'Hiberniae Delineatio', 1685
(by Sir William Petty; frontispiece of author)
D. Loggan/E. Sandys (10,285)

'Hibernian Magazine', March 1774
(pl. of Lawrence Sterne)
J. Reynolds/H. P.... (10,527)

'Hibernian Magazine', September 1777
(pl. of Edmund Sexton Pery)
Irish School c.1777/Irish School 1777 (11,331

'Hibernian Magazine', December 1777
(pl. of George Ogle)
Irish School c.1777/Irish School 1777 (10,573)

'Hibernian Magazine', March 1778
(pl. of Sir Edward Newenham)
Irish School c.1778/Irish School 1778 (11,342)

'Hibernian Magazine', June 1778
(pl. of Luke Gardiner, M.P.)
Irish School c.1778/Irish School 1778 (11,381)

'Hibernian Magazine', December 1779
(pl. of Walter Hussey Burgh)
Irish School c.1779/Irish School 1779 (10,651)
Irish School c.1779/Irish School 1779 (11,110)

'Hibernian Magazine', April 1784
(pl. of Charles Manners)
Irish School c.1784/Irish School 1784 (11,321)

'Hibernian Magazine', April 1785
(pl. of Henry Flood, M.P.)
Irish School c.1785/Irish School 1785 (11,129)

'Hibernian Magazine', June 1786
(pl. of Timothy Brecknock)
Irish School c.1786/Irish School 1786 (11,102)

'Hibernian Magazine', February 1791
(pl. of Barry Yelverton)
T. Robinson/Irish School 1791 (11,242)

'Hibernian Magazine', September 1791
(pl. of William Brownlow, M.P.)
Irish School c.1791/Irish School 1791 (11,083)

'Hibernian Magazine', July 1792
(pl. of Count Theobald Dillon)
Irish School c.1792/Irish School 1792 (11,175)

'Hibernian Magazine', November 1792
(pl. of Edward Byrne)
Irish School c.1792/Irish School 1792 (11,091)

'Hibernian Magazine', April 1793
(pl. of 7th Earl of Westmeath)
Irish School c.1793/Irish School 1793 (11,245)

'Hibernian Magazine', February 1794
(pl. of Archibald Hamilton Rowan)
Irish School c.1794/Irish School 1794 (11,328)

'Hibernian Magazine', March 1794
(pl. of Anne, Viscountess Fitzgibbon)
G. Chinnery/H. Brocas the Elder (11,344)

'Hibernian Magazine', March 1795
(pl. of William, Earl FitzWilliam)
Irish School c.1795/Irish School 1795 (11,139)

'Hibernian Magazine', May 1796
(pl. of Thomas Conolly)
R. Bull/W. Sidgwick (11,194)

'Hibernian Magazine', December 1797
(pl. of 2nd Earl Carhampton)
J. Petrie/P. Maguire (11,211)

'Hibernian Magazine', March 1798
(pl. of Roger O'Connor)
A. Buck/Irish School 1798 (10,585)

'Hibernian Magazine', November 1798
(pl. of Theobald Wolfe Tone)
Irish School c.1798/Irish School 1798 (10,292)

'Hibernian Magazine', December 1798
(pl. of Arthur Murphy)
S. Drummond/Irish School 1798 (10,668)

'Hibernian Magazine', October 1800
(pl. of Sir Charles Thorpe)
Irish School c.1800/P. Maguire (10,293)

'Hibernian Magazine', February 1801
(pl. of George Ponsonby)
Irish School c.1801/Irish School 1801 (11,238)

'Hibernian Magazine', October 1803
(pl. of Thomas Russell)
Irish School c.1803/Irish School 1803
(11,323-11,324)

'Hibernian Magazine', April 1811
(pl. of Hugh Douglas Hamilton)
Irish School c.1811/H. Brocas the Elder
(10,612)

'Hibernian Magazine', November 1811
(pl. of Arthur James Plunkett)
Irish School c.1811/Irish School 1811 (11,350)

'Histoire de L'Angleterre', 1697-1713
(by J. de Larrey; pl. of Oliver Cromwell)
?R. Walker/*A. van der Werff*/P. Devet (11,379)

'Historic Anecdotes and Secret Memoirs', 1809-15
(by Sir J. Barrington; pl. of John Ball)
J. Comerford/J. Heath (10,714)
(pl. of Sir Jonah Barrington)
H.D. Hamilton/*J. Comerford*/J. Heath (10,715)
(pl. of John Blacquiere)
J. Comerford/J. Heath (10,708)
(pl. of Humphrey Butler)
J. Comerford/J. Heath (10,748)
(pl. of Earl of Charlemont)
H. Hone/J. Heath (10,742)
pl. of Charles Cornwallis)
J. Comerford/J. Heath (10,761)
(pl. of Richard Dawson, M.P.)
H.D. Hamilton/*P. Maguire*/J. Heath (10,783)
(pl. of William Dickson)
?J. Comerford/J. Heath (10,795)
(pl. of Dr Patrick Duigenan)
J. Comerford/J. Heath (10,793)
(pl. of John Egan)
J. Comerford/J. Heath (10,778)
(pl. of James Fitzgerald)
J. Comerford/J. Heath (10,803)
(pl. of John Fitzgibbon)
J. Comerford/J. Heath (10,811)
(pl. of George Forbes)
?J. Comerford/J. Heath (10,818)
(pl. of Thomas Gold)
J. Comerford/J. Heath (10,816)
(pl. of Henry Grattan)
J. Comerford/J. Heath (10,836)
(pl. of Francis Hardy, M.P.)
J.R. Maguire/J. Heath (10,881)
(pl. of Viscount Kilwarden)
H.D. Hamilton/*P. Maguire*/J. Heath (10,863)
(pl. of Richard Marlay)
H.D. Hamilton/J. Heath (10,286)
(pl. of Hon. Montague Mathew)
J. Petrie/J. Heath (10,936)
(pl. of Earl of Moira)
H.D. Hamilton/J. Heath (10,947)
(pl. of 2nd Earl of Rosse)
J. Comerford/J. Heath (11,049)
J. Comerford/J. Heath (20,790)
(pl. of Col. Charles Vereker, M.P.)
J. Comerford/J. Heath (10,687)

'An Historical Guide to Ancient and Modern Dublin', 1821
(by G.N. Wright; Christchurch Cathedral and Dublin from the South East)
G. Petrie/T.F. Ranson (10,048)
(pl. of Dublin from the north)
G. Petrie/English School 1821 (11,789)
(pl. of Dublin castle)
G. Petrie/English School 1821 (11,773)
G. Petrie/T. Higham (11,700)
(pl. of the Four Courts and Richmond bridge)
G. Petrie/English School 1821 (11,783)
(pl. of the King's Inns and Royal Canal harbour)
G. Petrie/English School 1821 (11,784)
(pl. of the New Theatre Royal)
G. Petrie/T. Barber (11,779)
(pl. of Rotunda hospital)
G. Petrie/English School 1821 (11,780)
(pl. of the Royal Exchange)
G. Petrie/English School 1821 (11,781)
(pl. of Sackville street)
G. Petrie/T. Barber (11,790-11,791)
(pl. of Christchurch Cathedral)
G. Petrie/T.F. Ranson (10,048)
(pl. of St George's church, Hardwick place)
G. Petrie/T. Barber (11,778)
(pl. of St Patrick's Cathedral)
G. Petrie/T. Higham (11,775)
(pl. of Trinity College Dublin)
G. Petrie/T. Barber (11,777)

'The History and Antiquities of the Collegiate and Cathedral Church of St Patrick near Dublin', 1819
(by W. Mason; pl. of St Patrick's Cathedral)
P. Byrne/W. Radclyffe the Elder (11,609)
(pl. of St Patrick's Cathedral)
P. Byrne/W. Radclyffe the Elder (11,759)
(pl. of St Patrick's Cathedral, exterior)
P. Byrne/W. Smith (11,608)
(pl. of Jonathan Swift)
F. Bindon/E. Scriven (10,529)

'History of the Colleges of Cambridge', 1815
(by R. Ackermann; pl. of Elizabeth de Clare)
English School 17C/English School 1815 (10,733)

'History of the City of Dublin', 1818
(by J. Warburton, J. White and R. Walsh; pl. of the Foundling Hospital)
Irish School c.1817/English School 1817 (11,831)
(pl. of St George's church)
Irish School c.1817/English School 1817 (11,741)
(pl. of St Patrick's Cathedral)
Irish School c.1817/English School 1817 (11,762)
J. Malton/English School 1817 (11,764)

'History of the Coronation of George IV', 1839
(by Sir George Nayler; pl. of Admiral Sir Edmund Nagle)
F.P. Stephanoff/E. Scriven (11,404)

'History of Drogheda with its Environs', 1844
(by J. d'Alton; pl. of Ardgillan Castle)
J.C. Jones/E. Radclyffe (11,677)
(pl. of Beaulieu House)
J.C. Jones/E. Radclyffe (11,675)
(pl. of Dominican Priory, Drogheda)
J.C. Jones/E. Radclyffe (11,676)
(pl. of Gormanstown Castle)
J.C. Jones/E. Radclyffe (11,678)
(pl. of Lusk Church and Round Tower)
J.C. Jones/E. Radclyffe (11,758)
(pl. of Malahide)
J.C. Jones/E. Radclyffe (11,687)
(pl. of Malahide Castle)
J.C. Jones/E. Radclyffe (11,688)
(pl. of Monasterboice)
J.C. Jones/E. Radclyffe (11,674)
(pl. of Portrane and Lambay Island)
J.C. Jones/E. Radclyffe (11,686)
(pl. of Rush and Skerries)
J.C. Jones/E. Radclyffe (11,685)

'History of the French Revolution, and of the Wars resulting from that Event', 1816-27
(by J.J. McGregor; pl. of 1st Duke of Wellington)
T. Lawrence/E. Smith (11,265)

'History of the French Revolution', 1817
(by C. Kelly; series of equestrian portraits)
England School c.1815/English School 1815 or 1816 (11,353-11,369)

'History of the Grand Rebellion', 1713
(by E. Ward; pl. of Henry Treton)
S. Cooper/M. Vandergucht (10,636)

'History of Lancaster', 1836
(by E. Baine; pl. of Lancaster)
J. Henderson/W. Finden (20,367)
(pl. of Christmas at Wycoller Hall, Lancashire in 1650)
H. Melville/E. Smith (20,151)

'History of Wales', 1853
(pl. of Porth yr Ogof)
H. Gastineau/S. Lacey (20,476)
(pl. of Caerphilly Castle)
H. Gastineau/W. Wallis (20,403-20,404)

'History of the War with America, France, Spain and Holland', 1785-86
(by J. Andrews; pl. of Capt. Sir Charles Asgill, Bt.)
English School c.1786/English School 1786 (10,514)
(pl. of de Crillon)
?P. Le Grand/O. Birrell (10,516)
(pl. of Comte François Joseph Paul de Grasse)
W. Miller/A. Birrell (11,345)
(pl. of Admiral Sir Edward Hughes)
English School c.1786/English School 1786 (10,518)
(pl. of Admiral Kempelfelt)
English School c.1786/English School 1786 (10,517)
(pl. of Pierre Andre Suffren)
French School late 18C/J. Walker (11,284)

'Holy Living', 1653
(by J. Taylor; frontispiece of author)
English School 17C/W. Faithorne (11,275)

'The Houghton Gallery', 1778
(pl. of Sir Rowland Wandesford)
A. Van Dyck/*G. Farrington*/J. Watson (10,235)
A. Van Dyck/*G. Farrington*/J. Watson (10,563)
(pl. of Jane Wenman)
A. Van Dyck/J. Boydell (10,556)

'Illustrated London News', 1846
(pl. of Aerial view of Dublin)
Irish School 1846/Smyth (11,878)

'Illustrated London News, 1861
(pl. of 'Rouge et Noir')
P. Levin/English School 1861 (20,570)

'Illustrated London News', 1862
(pl. of Prince of Wales' visit to Egypt)
English School 1862/English School 1862 (20,571)
(pl. of Checkmate, next move)
J.C. Horsely/H. Harral (20,572)

'Illustrated London News', 1864
(pl. of Opening of NGI)
English School 1864/English School 1864 (11,595)

'Illustrated London News', 1865
(pl. of The Civil War in America)
M. Jackson/English School 1865 (20,573)

'Illustrated London News', 1869
(pl. of St Mungo's Well)
English School c.1869/English School 1869 (20,576)

'Illustrations of Shakespeare', 1833
(pl. of Titus)
J. Martin/W.F. Starling (20,397)

'Imitations of Modern Drawings', 1786
(by T. Rowlandson; pl. of a Group of Gypsies)
F. Wheatley/T. Rowlandson (11,503)

'Indian Empire', 1857
(by R. Martin; pl. of Gungotri)
G.F. White/T. Allom & J.H. Kernot (20,454)

'Ipswich Museum Portraits', 1851
(pl. of Samuel Hinds)
T.H. Maguire/T.H. Maguire (10,871)

'Ireland Illustrated', 1831
(by G.N. Wright; pl. of Bank of Ireland)
G. Petrie/E. Goodall (11,785-11,786)
(pl. of Dublin from Blaquire Bridge)
G. Petrie/E. Goodall (11,787)
(pl. of Dublin Castle)
G. Petrie/E. Goodall (11,774)
(pl. of King George II statue)
W. H. Bartlett/J. Heath (11,749)
(pl. of Nelson Pillar, Sackville Street)
G. Petrie/E. Goodall (20,612)
(pl. of St Audeon's Church)
G. Petrie/B. Winkles (11,776)
(pl. of St George's Church)
W.H. Bartlett/R. Winkles (11,771)
W.H. Bartlett/R. Winkles (20,611)
(pl. of Sarah Bridge, Wellington Testimonial)
G. Petrie/E. Goodall (11,794)

'Ireland, its Scenery, Character etc.', 1841-43
(by S.C. and A.M. Hall; pl. of the Gap of Dunloe, Killarney, Co. Kerry)
T. Creswick/S. Bradshaw (20,502)
(pl. of the Gap of Dunloe, Co. Kerry)
T. Creswick/S. Bradshaw (20,606)
(pl. of King John's castle, Limerick)
W.H. Bartlett/J. Cousen (20,605)
(pl. of Lough Leane, Killarney)
T. Creswick/R. Wallis (20,504)
(pl. of Old Weir Bridge, Killarney)
W.H. Bartlett/G.K. Richardson (20,436)
(pl. of the River Dargle, Co Wicklow)
W.H. Bartlett/J.C. Bentley (20,601)
(pl. of St Patrick's Cathedral, Dublin)
W.H. Bartlett/F.W. Topham (11,763)
W.H. Bartlett/F.W. Topham (20,590)
(pl. of Torc Mountain and Muckross Lake)
T. Creswick/R. Hill (20,503)

'Ireland's Mirror', March 1805
(pl. of Rev. Archibald Douglas)
Irish School c.1805/Irish School 1805 (11,351)

'Ireland's Mirror', April 1806
(pl. of S. Barrett)
Irish School c.1806/C. Doyle (11,087)

'Irish Catholic Magazine', January 1808
(pl. of Phelim O'Connor)
Irish School c.1808/Irish School 1808 (10,587)

'The Irish Industrial Exhibition of 1853', 1854
(by Sproule; frontispiece of William Dargan)
G.F. Mulvany/W.J. Edwards (11,127)

'Irish Magazine', March 1808
(pl. of Oliver Plunkett)
?G. Morphey/English School 19C (11,338)

'Irish Magazine', September 1808
(pl. of James Napper Tandy)
J. Petrie/Irish School 1808 (10,650)

'Irish Magazine', November 1808
(pl. of Robert Emmet)
J. Petrie/Irish School 1808 (11,163)

'Irish Magazine', April 1809
(pl. of Arthur O'Connor, M.P.)
J.D. Herbert/Irish School 1809 (10,589)

'Irish Magazine', April 1809
(pl. of Arthur O'Connor, M.P.)
J.D. Herbert/W. Ward the Elder (10,067)

'Irish Magazine', October 1809
(pl. of Turlough O'Carolan)
Irish School c.1809/Irish School 1809 (11,343)

'The Keepsake', 1831
(pl. of Juliet)
L. Sharpe/J.C. Edwards (20,154)
(pl. of Sunset)
R.P. Bonington/W. Miller (20,484)
R.P. Bonington/W. Miller (20,589)

'La Belle Assemblée', October 1808
(pl. of Jane, Countess ofHarrington)
English School 18C/R. Cooper (10,316)

'La Belle Assemblée', December 1811
(pl. of Lady Annesley)
A.W. Devis/R. Cooper (11,118)

'La Belle Assemblée', November 1822
(pl. of Maria Edgeworth)
W.M. Craig/F. Mackenzie (11,122)

'La Belle Assemblée', February 1824
(pl. of Mrs Francis Sheridan)
English School 18C/English School 1824

'La Belle Assemblée', August 1824
(pl. of Lady Morgan)
W. Behnes/H. Meyer (10,553)

'La Henriade', 1768
(by Voltaire; pl. for Voltaire's novel)
H.F. Gravelot/J.C. Le Vasseur (20,037)

'Lady's Magazine', October 1774
(pl. of Dublin and Islandbridge)
J. Tudor/English School 1774 (11,717)

'Lady's Monthly Museum', February 1805
(pl. of George Anne Bellamy)
F. Cotes & J. Ramberg/R. Sands (11,086)

'Lady's Monthly Museum', 1818
(pl. of Mary Tighe)
R.E. Drummond/J. Hopwood the Younger (11,006)

'Lancashire', 1842
(by G.N. Wright; pl. of Christmas at Wycoller Hall)
H. Melville/E. Smith (20,151)

'Land of Burns', 1840
(by J. Wilson and R. Chambers; pl. of Barskimming on the River Ayr, Scotland)
D. O. Hill/W. Richardson (20,282)
(pl. of Ellisland, Scotland)
D. O. Hill/T. Jeavons (20,460)

'Landscape Illustrations of the Waverly Novels', 1832
(pl. of Durham)
G.F. Robson/E.F. Finden (20,481)
(pl. of Lochard)
G.F. Robson/E.F. Finden (20,478)

'Letters of Mrs Delany', 1861
(by Lady Llanover; pl. of Letitia Bushe)
L. Bushe/J. Brown (11,111)

'Letters on Love', 1718
(by W. Congreve; frontispiece of William Congreve)
G. Kneller/M. Vandergucht (11,213)

'Life of Bishop Jebb', 1836
(by C. Foster; frontispiece of John Jebb)
G. Richmond/H. Adlard (10,631)

'Life of Romney', 1809
(by W. Hayley; pl of the artist)
T.A. Hayley/*M. Denman*/C. Watson (11,045)
(pl. of three Self Portraits)
G. Romney/C. Watson (11,046)

'The Life of James Gandon', 1846
(by T. Mulvany; pl. of James Gandon)
H. Hone/H. Meyer (10,833)
H. Hone/H. Meyer (11,153)

'Lithographic Drawing Book for the Year 1835'
(by Hullmandel; pl. of Fishing Boats by the Shore)
J.D. Harding/J.D. Harding (20,224)
(pl. of a Shepherd driving Sheep toward a Village)
J.D. Harding/J.D. Harding (20,225)

'Lives of Illustrious and Distinguished Irishmen', 1839-47
(by J. Wills; pl. of Arthur Wolfe)
G.F. Joseph/S. Freeman (10,639)
(pl. of James Ussher
?P. Lely/S. Freeman (11,255)

'The Lives of the most eminent British painters, sculptors and architects'
(by A. Cunningham; pl. of James Barry)
J. Barry/W.C. Edwards (11,116)

'London and its Environs in the 19th Century', 1829
(by T.A. Shepherd; pls. of Regent Park)
T.H. Shepherd/J. Tingle (11,823)(1-2)
T.H. Shepherd/R. Acon (11,824)(1-2)
T.H. Shepherd/T. Barber (11,825)(1-2)

'London Magazine', April 1820
(by Golf & Northouse; pl. of Benjamin West)
G.H. Harlow/H. Meyer (20,122)

'Magnificentiores selectioresque Urbis Venetiarum Prospectus', 1741
(pl. of Piazza S. Marco, Venice)
M. Marieschi/M. Marieschi (11,662)

'The Mansions of England in the Olden Time', c.1849
(by Nash; pl. of Interior of Kenilworth Castle)
J. Nash/J. Nash (11,497)

'Maps and Plans of Tindal's Continuation of Rapin's History of England', 1785-c.90
(pl. of Irish plans)
R.W. Seale/R.W. Seale (11,877)

'Masonic Magazine', May 1795
(pl. of M.E. O'Brien)
Irish School c.1795/Irish School 1795 (10,578)

'Medical Portrait Gallery', 1838
(by Pettigrew; pl. of Dr James Johnson)
J. Wood/W. Holl the Younger (10,632)

'Memoirs of Lord Chesterfield', 1777
(by Maty; pl. of Richard Chenevix)
Irish School 18C/J. Hall (11,195)

'Memoirs of Count de Grammont', 1794
(by Count Hamilton; pl. of author)
Continental School 17C/*S. Harding*/W.N. Gardiner (10,614)

'Memoir of the Life and Times of Henry Grattan', 1839-46
(by Henry Grattan Jnr.; pl. of Henry Grattan, M.P.)
N. Kenny/F.C. Lewis (11,144)

'Memoirs of Joseph Holt', 1838
(by Joseph Holt; frontispiece of author)
Irish School 1798/R. J. Hamerton (10,615)

'Memoirs of George Selwyn and his Contemporaries', 1843
(by J. Jesse; pl. of Madame Anna Zamparini)
N. Hone the Elder/G. Cook (11,377)

'Metamorphoses', 1636
(by Ovid; frontispiece)
F. Chauveau/F. Chauveau (20,215)

'Monthly Mirror', September 1802
(pl. of Thomas Dermody)
C. Allingham/W. Ridley (20,834)

'Monthly Mirror', December 1807
(pl. of William Cook)
A. Pope/English School 1807 (11,209)

'The Monthly Pantheon', October 1809
(pl. of Patrick Quinn)
E. Trotter/H. Brocas the Elder (11,071)

'Narrative of a Residence in Ireland during 1814 and 1815', 1817
(by A. Plumptre; pl. of Dublin Bay and Howth)
Irish School c.1816/English School 1816 (11,714)

'National Portrait Gallery', 1844
(by W. Cooke Taylor; pl. of Daniel O'Connell)
T.H. Carrick/W. Holl the Younger (10,289)
T.H. Carrick/W. Holl the Younger (10,597)
T.H. Carrick/W. Holl the Younger (10,972)

'National Portrait Gallery of Distinguished Americans', 1837
(by Longacre and Herring; pl. of Gilbert Charles Stuart)
S. Goodridge/A.B. Durand (11,297)

'National Portrait Gallery of Illustrious and Eminent Personages of the 19th Century', 1830-34
(by W. Jerdan; pl. of John Philpot Curran)
T. Lawrence/W.E. Wagstaff (11,197)
T. Lawrence/W.E. Wagstaff (20,804)
(pl. of Sir Henry Torrens)
T. Lawrence/T.A. Dean (11,283)

'Naval Chronicle', 1801
(pl. of Admiral Sir Robert Kingsmill)
L.F. Abbot/W. Ridley (10,643)

'New Complete and Universal System of Geography'
(by Millar; pl. of Dublin from Phoenix Park)
J. Tudor/F. Cary (11,716)

'New London Magazine', March 1790
(pl. of the Parliament House)
Irish School late 18C/Myers (11,754)

'New Monthly Magazine and Universal Register', August 1818
(pl. of Thomas Moore)
Irish School c.1800/H.H. Meyer (10,960)
Irish School c.1800/H.H. Meyer (11,234)

'New Monthly Magazine and Universal Register', September 1818
(pl. of Lady Sydney Morgan)
C.T. Wageman/H.H. Meyer (11,229)

'New Monthly Magazine and Universal Register', March 1819
(pl. of Rev. Charles Robert Maturin)
W. Brocas/H.H. Meyer (10,658)
W. Brocas/H.H. Meyer (10,937)

'New Sporting Magazine', June 1832
(pl. of a Mule Pheasant)
A. Cooper/W. Raddon (20,615)

'New System of Universal Geography', 1793
(by J. Payne; views of Dublin)
R. Pool & J. Cash/J. Lodge (11,707-11,711)
R. Pool & J. Cash/J. Lodge (11,725-11,726)
R. Pool & J. Cash/J. Lodge (11,734)
R. Pool & J. Cash/J. Lodge (11,740)
R. Pool & J. Cash/I. Taylor the Elder (11,753)
R. Pool & J. Cash/I. Taylor the Elder (11,755)

'Les Noms, Surnoms, Qualitez, Armes et Blasons des Chevaliers de l'Ordre du Sainct-Esprit creèz par Louis le Juste XIII du Nom, Roy de France et Navarre', 1634
(by Hozier; frontispiece of King of France, creating Chevaliers de St Michel)
French School 1634/French School 1634 (20,235)

'No. III, or the Nosegay: third letter of the Country Post-bag', 1816
(by Thomas Grady; pl. of Thomas Grady)
H. Brocas the Elder/H. Brocas the Elder (11,159)

'The Oriental Annual', 1836
(pl. of Oriental Birds)
W. Daniell/R. Brandard (20,609)

'Orlando Furioso', 1773
(by Ariosto, Canto XL)
G.B. Cipriani/F. Bartolozzi (20,031)

'Pacanta Hibernia', 1633
(by Sir Thomas Stafford; frontispiece of Sir George Carew)
M. Gheeraerts the Younger/R. Van Voerst (10,191)

'The Park and the Forest', 1841
(by J.D. Harding; various plates)
J.D. Harding/J.D. Harding (20,259)
J.D. Harding/J.D. Harding (20,273-20,274)
J.D. Harding/J.D. Harding (20,296-20,307)

'Pen and Pencil', 11th May 1889
(pl. of Mother and Child)
English School c.1889/English School 1889 (20,621)

'Picturesque Annuals', 1832
(by C. Heath; pl. of Boats near the Island of Murano, Venice)
W.C. Stanfield/R. Wallis (20,214)

'Picturesque Annuals', 1833
(by C. Heath; pl. of leaving the River Maas, Holland)
C. Stanfield/W. Miller (20,207)

'Picturesque Annuals', 1834
(by C. Heath; pl. of Fécamp, France)
W.C. Stanfield/J. Cousen (20,208)

'The Picturesque Beauties of Great Britain', 1832
(by G. Virtue; pl. of Malahide Castle, Co. Dublin)
W.H. Bartlett/C. Challis (20,234)

'Picturesque Beauties of the Rhine', 1832
(by W.G. Fearnside; pl. of the first stone bridge over the River Rhine)
W. Tombleson/A.H. Payne (20,278)

'A picturesque and descriptive view of the City of Dublin described in a series of the most interesting scenes taken in the year 1791', 1799
J. Malton/J. Malton (11,568-11,570)
J. Malton/J. Malton (11,573-11,574)
J. Malton/J. Malton (11,577)
J. Malton/J. Malton (11,579-11,583)
J. Malton/J. Malton (11,585-11,588)
J. Malton/J. Malton (11,591-11,592)
J. Speed/J. Malton (11,567)

'Picturesque Sketches of some of the Finest Landscape and Coast Scenery of Ireland', 1835
(pl. of The Twelve Pins, Co. Galway)
G. Petrie/N. Fielding (20,351)

'Picturesque Views of the Antiquities of Ireland', 1830
(by R. O'C. Newenham; pl. of Reginald's Tower)
R. O'C. Newenham/J.D. Harding (20,030)

'Piedmont and Italy', c.1855
(by D. Costello; pl. of Val Angrogna)
W. Brockedon/J. Sands (20,442)

'Poems', 1795
(by S. Whyte; frontispiece of author)
H.D. Hamilton/H. Brocas the Elder (10,295)

'Poems', 1811
(by E. Lysaght; frontispiece of author)
J. Cullen/P. Maguire (10,602)

'Poems written occasionally', 1742
(by J. Winstanley; frontispiece of author)
Irish School 18C/J. Brooks (10,280)

'Poetical Fragments', 1689
(by R. Baxter; pl. of author)
English School c.1689/English School 1689 (20,728)

'The Portrait Gallery of Distinguished Females', 1833
(by J. Burke; pl. of Lydia, Countess of Cavan)
M.A. Shee/E. Scriven (11,208)

'Portrait Gallery of Eminent Men & Women of Europe and America', 1873
(by E. Duyckink; pl. of Maria Edgeworth)
A. Chappel/American School 1873 (10,773)

'Portraits of Eminent Conservative Statesmen', 1836
(by H.T. Ryall; pl. of Sir Frederick Shaw)
F. Cruickshank/E. Scriven (11,036)
(pl. of James Tennent)
G. Richmond/R. Artlett (10,155)

'Portraits of Eminent Conservative Statesmen', 2nd Series', 1846
(by H.T. Ryall; pl. of 1st Viscount Beresford)
J. Haslock/J. Rogers (10,704)
(pl. of Sir Robert FitzWygram)
T. Phillips/J. Brown (10,844)
(pl. of 9th Earl of Haddington)
R. McInnes/J. Brown (10,887)
(pl. of George Hamilton, M.P.)
W.J. Newton/J. Posselwhite (10,885-10,886)
(pl. of 3rd Marquess of Londonderry)
J. Bostok/J.J. Jenkins (10,913)
(pl. of Sir George Murray, M.P.)
T. Lawrence/J. Cochran (10,955)
(pl. of 1st Earl O'Neill)
T. Phillips/J. Brown (10,992)
(pl. of Lt.-Colonel Perceval)
English School 1830s/Jenkinson (11,060-11,061)
(pl. of Sir Edward Burtenshaw Sugden)
J. Moore/E. Scriven (11,039)
(pl. of Sir James Tennent M.P.)
G. Richmond/R.A. Artlett (10,155)
(pl. of 2nd Marquess of Thomond)
Titani/S. Freeman (11,009-11,010)

'Portraits of Illustrious Personages of Great Britain', 1821-28
(by E. Lodge; pl. of Henry Danvers)
?M. Miereveld/*W. Derby*/E. Scriven (10,782)
(pl. of 1st Duke of Ormonde)
G. Kneller/E. Scriven (10,533)

'Portraits, Memoirs and Characters of Remarkable Persons', 1820
(by J. Caulfield; pl. of Crazy Crow)
Irish School c.1754/R. Graves (11,125)
(pl. of Owen Farrell)
H.F. Gravelot/English School 1820 (11,133)
(pl. of Jack Haugh)
Irish School 17C/R. Graves (11,154)
(pl. of Richard Head)
English School 17C/English School 1795 (10,872)
(pl. of Florence Hensey)
English School 18C/English School 1820 (10,873)
(pl. of James Turner)
N. Hone the Elder/R. Graves (11,277)

'The Practice of Quietness', 1705
(by G. Webb; frontispiece of George Webb)
?English School 17C/T. Cross the Elder (10,304)

'Principali Vedute di Milano e de Contorini'
(by G. Castellani; pl. of S. Lorenzo)
G. Castellani/G. Castellani (20,393)

'Principles and Practice of Art', 1845
(by J.D. Harding; various plates)
J.D. Harding/J.D. Harding (20,361)
J.D. Harding/J.D. Harding (20,370)
J.D. Harding/J.D. Harding (20,405-20,410)
J.D. Harding/J.D. Harding (20,428)
J.D. Harding/J.D. Harding (20,446-20,447)
J.D. Harding/J.D. Harding (20,463-20,465)

'The Private Theatre of Kilkenny', 1825
(pl. of William Beecher)
J. Comerford/Irish School 1825 (10,716)
(pl. of Humphrey Butler)
J. Comerford/Irish School 1825 (10,747)
(pl. of Henry Grattan, M.P.)
J. Comerford/J. Heath (10,835)
(pl. of John Lyster)
J. Comerford/Irish School 1825 (10,892)
(pl. of Thomas Moore)
J. Comerford/Irish School 1825 (10,961)
(frontispiece of Richard Power)
J. Comerford/Irish School 1825 (11,370)
(pl. of George Routh)
J. Comerford/Irish School 1825 (11,371)
(pl. of Miss Smyth)
J. Comerford/Irish School 1825 (10,557)

'Psyche, or the Legend of Love', 1811
(by Mary Tighe; frontispiece of Mary Tighe)
G. Romney/*J. Comerford*/C. Watson (10,307)
G. Romney/*J. Comerford*/C. Watson (11,417)

'Psyche or the Legend of Love', 1816 edition
G. Romney/*J. Comerford*/E. Scriven (11,417)

'Public Life of Earl Macartney', 1807
(by Barrow; pl. of 1st Earl Macartney)
H. Edridge/L. Schiavonetti (10,951)

'The Real Story of John Carteret Pilkington', 1760
(by Mrs L. Pilkington; frontispiece of author)
N. Hone the Elder/R. Purcell (10,322)
N. Hone the Elder/R. Purcell (11,069)

'Remarks on Life and Writing of Swift', 1752
(by Lord Orrery; frontispiece of Jonathan Swift)
R. Barber/B. Wilson (10,297)

'Reminiscences', 1825
(by Michael Kelly; frontispiece of author)
A. Wivell the Elder/H. Meyer (10,638)

'Revolution Française', 1801
(by Girardon; pl. of Comte de Lally-Tolendal)
French School late 18C & J. Duplessi-Bertaux/G.F.G. Lavachez & J. Duplessi-Bertaux (11,008)

'Rivers of England', 1827
(by W.B. Cooke; pl. of Totnes)
J.M.W. Turner/C. Turner (20,384)

'Roman Portraits', 1794
(by Robert Jephson; frontispiece of author)
B. Stoker/J. Singleton (10,283)

'Royal Gallery of British Art', 1838-49
(by E. & W. Finden; pl. of Carthage)
W. Linton/J.T. Willmore (20,139)
(pl. of 'Happy as a King')
E.F. Finden/W. Collins (20,383)
(pl. of Highlander's cottage)
E. Landseer/W. Finden (20,329)

'Royal Military Chronicle', 1811
(pl. of General Sir Samuel Auchmuty)
L.F. Abbot/A. Cardon (11,117)

'Rustic Figures', ?1850
(by G.E. Hicks; pl. of Figure Studies)
G.E. Hicks/G.E. Hicks (20,181)

'The Scenery and Antiquities of Ireland', 1842
(by N. Willis and S. Coyne; pls. of Delphi Lodge, Co. Mayo)
W.H. Bartlett/J. Cousen (20,438-20,439)
(pl. of Luggala Lodge, Co. Wicklow)
W.H. Bartlett/H. Adlard (20,440)
(pl. of Lismore Castle, Co. Waterford)
W.H. Bartlett/E. Benjamin (20,437)
(pl. of Old Weir Bridge, Killarney)
W.H. Bartlett/G.K. Richardson (20,436)
(pl. of Pontoon Bridge)
W.H. Bartlett/H. Adlard (20,435)
(pl. of Powerscourt House)
W.H. Bartlett/G.K. Richardson (20,434)
(pl. of river Dargle)
W.H. Bartlett/J.C. Bentley (20,601)
(pl. of Salmon Leap at Leixlip)
W.H. Bartlett/G.K. Richardson (20,600)

'Scenery of Ireland', 1796
(by J. Fisher; pl. of Dublin and Islandbridge)
J. Fisher/J. Fisher (11,639)
J. Fisher/J. Fisher (11,719)
(pl. of View of Dublin Harbour)
J. Fisher/J. Fisher (11,628)
(pl. of Secretary of State's House)
J. Fisher/J. Fisher (11,549)

'The Seats and Desmesnes of the Nobility and Gentry in Ireland', 1783-93
(by T. Milton; pl. of Beau-Parc)
T. Roberts/T. Milton (20,277)
(pl. of Howth Castle)
F. Wheatley/T. Milton (11,683)
(pl. of Leinster Lawn)
J.J. Barralet/T. Milton (11,615)
J.J. Barralet/T. Milton (11,750)
(pl. of Malahide Castle)
F. Wheatley/T. Milton (11,684)
(pl. of Lord Charlemont's Casino at Marino)
F. Wheatley/T. Milton (11,594)
(pl. of Vice-Regal Lodge)
J.J. Barralet/T. Milton (11,604)

'Sentimental and Masonic Magazine', August 1792
(pl. of Richard Hely-Hutchinson)
B. Stoker/H. Brocas the Elder (11,176)

'A Sentimental Journey'
(by Sterne; pl. of The Captive)
J.H. Mortimer/R. Blyth (20,034)

'Sermons', 1691
(by E. Hopkins; frontispiece of author)
English School 17C/J. Sturt (10,627)

'Sermons, 1705
(by William Sheridan; frontispiece of author)
Irish School c.1700/W. Sherwin (10,301)

'Sermons', 1724
(by C. Hickman, pl. of the author)
A. Russell/S. Gribelin (10,047)

'Sermons', 1742
(by Thomas Emlyn; frontispiece of author)
J. Highmore/G. Vandergucht (10,282)

'Sermons', 1760
(by L. Sterne; frontispiece of author)
J. Reynolds/S.F. Ravenet the Elder (10,528)

'Shakespeare Illustrated', 1789-93
(by S. Harding; pl. of Edmund Malone)
J. Reynolds/C. Knight (10,662-10,663)
(pl. of John Monck Mason, M.P.)
S. Harding/C. Knight (10,920)

'Sketches from Nature', 1795
(by J. Nixon; pl. of O'Shaughnesey)
J. Nixon/E. Harding (10,576)

'Specimens of English Ecclesiastical Costume', 1817
(by J. Carter; pl. of Thomas Cranley, Archbishop of Dublin)
English School 15C/*J. Carter*/J. Basire the Elder (10,766)

'Studies of Heads from Nature', 1838
(by J. Inskipp)
J. Inskipp/C.E. Wagstaff (20,150)
J. Inskipp/C.E. Wagstaff (20,164)
J. Inskipp/C.E. Wagstaff (20,166)

'Studies from the Portfolios of Various Artists, Drawn on Stone', 1851
(pl. of Stormy Sea)
J. Syer/J. Syer (20,223)
(pl. of Fishing Boats in a Cave)
J. Syer/J. Syer (20,348)
(pl. of Bristol Docks, Avon)
J. Syer/J. Syer (20,350)

'Sunday at Home', March 1870
(pl. of the Scala Regia, Vatican)
E. Whymper/E. Whymper (20,269)

'Sunday at Home', June 1870
(pl. of interior of St Peter's, Rome)
E. Whymper/E. Whymper (20,270)

'Sunday Magazine', December 1886
(pl. of Richard Whately)
S. L. . . ./G. Dalziel & E. Dalziel (11,390)

'Sunday Magazine', November 1887
(pl. of Mount Etna, Sicily)
P.E. Grandsire/C. Barbant (20,619)

'Supplement to the Irish Fireside', September 1885
(pl. of Terence Bellew McManus)
L. Gluckman/Irish School 1885 (20,217)

'Switzerland', 1836
(by Beattie; pl. of Baths at St-Gervais-les-Bains, Switzerland)
W.H. Bartlett/W.B. Cooke (20,417)
(pl. of Pays de Vaud)
W.H. Bartlett/H. Jordan (20,372)

'Syria', 1836-38
(by J. Carne; pl. of Besherrai Village, Mount Lebanon)
W.H. Bartlett/D. Thompson (20,450)
(pl. of a Castle near Tripoli)
W.H. Bartlett/W.F. Starling (20,453)
(pl. of Port of Seleucia)
W.H. Bartlett/J. Stephenson (20,455)
(pl. of scene on River Orantes)
W.H. Bartlett/T. Higham (20,399)

'The Talisman', 1831
(pl. of Barnard Castle, Durham)
J.M.W. Turner/J.T. Willemore (20,599)

'Theatrum Europaeum', 1698
(pl. of Siege of Londonderry)
Dutch School 1689/Dutch School c.1689 (11,819)
Dutch School 1689/Dutch School c.1689 (20,835)
(pl. of the Taking of Athlone)
Dutch School 1691/J. Tangena & Dutch School c.1691 (20,762)

'Tisdal's continuation of Rapin's History of England', c.1785
(pl. of plans)
R.W. Seale/R.W. Seale (11,877)

'Tisdal's continuation of Rapin', 1787
(Harrison's Edition; pl. of Medals of King William III and Queen Mary)
English School 1692/J. Goldar (20,836)

'Tombleson's Thames', 1834
(by W.C. Fearnside; pl. of Chelsea Hospital)
W. Tombleson/S. Lacey (20,378)
(pl. of Clifden Hampden, Oxfordshire)
W. Tombleson/E. Tombleson (20,433)
(pl. of view near Greenwich)
W. Tombleson/W. Tombleson (20,380)
(pl. of view near Henley-on-Thames)
W. Tombleson/R. Sands (20,432)
(pl. of Maidstone, Kent)
W. Tombleson/A. McClatchie (20,377)
(pl. of Rochester Castle, Kent)
W. Tombleson/H. Winkles (20,376)
(pl. of Teddington Locks, Surrey)
W. Tombleson/W. Tombleson (20,379)

'Tombleson's Upper Rhine', 1832
(by W.C. Fearnside; pl. of Waterfalls in the Roffla Gorge, Switzerland)
W. Tombleson/H. Winkles (20,286)

'Tourist in Switzerland', 1830
(by T. Rose; pl. of Chillon Castle, Lake Geneva)
S. Prout/J.B. Allen (20,459)

'Trackten Christlichen Mittelaltens', 1840-54
(by J.H. Van Hoffner-Altenecks; pl. of a Court Cupboard)
German School 1490/1530/J. Klipphahn (20,062)
(pl. of drinking cup and cover)
German School 1519/J. Klipphahn (20,063)
(pl. of an Ivory with the Virgin and Child)
German School 950/1050/C. Regnier (20,061)
(pl. of a Tankard)
German School 1546/55/C. Regnier (20,065)

'Transactions of the Society of Arts', 1804
(frontispiece of James Barry)
J. Barry/J. Heath (10,712)

'Traverstie, or School of Modern Manners', 1808
(by Earl of Chesterfield: pl. of 'Politeness')
G.M. Woodward/English School 1808 (11,644)(8)

'Trial of the Duke of York', 1809
(pl. of Dr O'Meara)
T. Rowlandson/J. Hopwood the Younger (10,586)

'Turner's Annual Tour — the Loire', 1833
(pl. of Rietz)
J.M.W. Turner/R. Brandard (11,803)

'Turner's Annual Tour — the Seine', 1834
(pl. of Harfleur)
J.M.W. Turner/J. Cousen (11,799)
(pl. of Le Harvre)
J.M.W. Turner/J.B. Allen (11,800)
(pl. of Mantes-La-Jolie)
J.M.W. Turner/W. Radclyffe (11,798)
(pl. of the River Seine)
J.M.W. Turner/J.T. Willmore (11,796)
(pl. of the River Seine)
J.M.W. Turner/J.B. Allen (11,801)
(pl. of Rouen)
J.M.W. Turner/R. Brandard (11,802)
(pl. of Tancarville Château, Normandy)
J.M.W. Turner/J.T. Willmore (11,797)
J.M.W. Turner/R. Brandard (11,804)

'The Union', February 1887
(pl. of D.R. Plunket, M.P.)
T. Fitzpatrick/T. Fitzpatrick (11,059)

'Union Magazine', May 1801
(pl. of Poolbeg Lighthouse)
G. Holmes/J. Walker (11,689)

'Universal Magazine, May 1790
(pl. of Lord Henry Fitzgerald)
A. Buck/Irish School 1790 (11,134)

'United Irishmen', 2nd Series 1843
(by R.R. Madden; pl. of Thomas Addis Emmet)
L.F. Aubry/T.W. Huffam (11,171-11,173)
(pl. of Thomas Addis Emmet)
J.D. Herbert/T.W. Huffam (11,169-11,170)
(pl. of Lord Edward FitzGerald)
H. Hone/T.W. Huffam (11,137-11,138)
(pl. of James Hope)
Irish School c.1843/T.W. Huffam (10,616)
(pl. of Henry Jackson)
J.D. Herbert/T.W. Huffam (10,633)
(pl. of Henry Joy McCracken)
J. Comerford/J.H. Lynch (11,226)
(pl. of William James McNeven)
J.D. Herbert/T.W. Huffam (10,671)
(pl. of Samuel Neilson)
C. Byrne/T.W. Huffam (10,646-10,647)
(pl. of Archibald Hamilton Rowan)
J. Comerford/J.H. Lynch (11,329)
(pl. of Henry Sheares)
?A. Buck/T.W. Huffam (11,295)
(pl. of of John Sheares)
A. Buck/T.W. Huffam (11,294)
(pl. of James Napper Tandy)
J. Petrie/English School 1843 (10,649)
(pl. of Wolfe Tone)
Irish School c.1790/T.W. Huffam (11,272)

'United Irishmen', 3rd Series 1846
(by R.R. Madden; pl. of William Corbett)
Continental School 19C/T.W. Huffam (11,189)
(by R. Madden; pl. of Michael Dwyer)
J. Petrie/English School 1846 (11,182)
(pl. of Robert Emmet)
J. Petrie/Irish School 1846 (11,164-11,165)
(pl. of death mask of Robert Emmet)
J. Petrie/*A.F.J. Claudet*/English School 1846 (11,166)
(pl. of Richard Robert Madden)
A.F.J. Claudet/T.W. Huffam (10,660-10,661)
(pl. of James O'Brien)
A.F.J. Claudet/English School 1846 (10,582)
(pl. of Thomas Russell)
Irish School c.1803/T.W. Huffam (11,326)
(pl. of William Samson)
C.S. Tone/English School 1846 (11,298-11,300)
(pl. of Bartholomew Teeling)
French School c.1796/J.H. Lynch (11,267)

'Universal Magazine', April 1749
(pl. of Illuminations and Fireworks)
J. Tudor/English School 1749 (11,614);(11,712)

'Universal Magazine', October 1751
(pl. of Leixlip Castle)
Irish School c.1750/English School 1751 (11,747)

'Universal Magazine', December 1776
(pl. of George Berkeley)
J. Latham/English School 1776 (11,080)

'Universal Magazine', February 1790
(pl. of Charles Manners)
H. Hone/English School 1790 (11,322)

'Universal Magazine', May 1790
(pl. of Lord Henry FitzGerald)
A. Buck/Irish School 1790 (11,134)

'Universal Magazine', February 1791
(pl. of John Philpot Curran)
H. Hopson/H. Houston (11,200)

'Universal Magazine', July 1791
(pl. of Francis Rawdon)
J. Reynolds/P. Maguire (10,654)

'Universal Magazine', April 1792
(pl. of Lieut.-Colonel J. Hely Hutchinson)
Irish School c.1792/English School 1792 (11,177)

'Universal Magazine', February 1797
(pl. of John Philpot Curran)
H. Hopson/H. Houston (11,200)

'Vanity Fair', December 1882
(pl. of Dion Boucicault)
L.M. Ward/V.R.A. Brooks (11,078)

'Views in the East', 1830-33
(by E. Roberts; pl. of Mah Chung Keow, Canton)
R.J. Elliot/*S. Austin*/W. Le Petit (20,356)

'Views of Italy, France and Switzerland', 1836
(by J.D. Harding; pl. of the Campanile at Fiesole)
J.D. Harding/W. Radclyffe (20,424)

'The Virtuosi's Museum', Vol. II, 1781
(pl. of King John's Castle)
P. Sandby/T. Cook (20,029)

'The Wahconda's Son'
W.H. Brooke/W.H. Brooke (20,808)

'Weekly Messenger', January 1832
(by Bell; pl. of Princess Victoria)
J.J. Jenkins/T. Williamson (11,248)

'Westmorland', 1832
(by T. Rose; pl. of Bowfield, Cumbria)
T. Allom/T. Allom (20,457)
(pl. of Burnshead Hall, Westmorland)
T. Allom/H. Wallis (20,284)
(pl. of Clare Moss from Langdale Head)
T. Allom/H. Wallis (20,285)
(pl. of Grassmere Lake and Village, Cumbria)
G. Pickering/C. Mottram (20,486)
(pl. of Kendal)
T. Allom/S. Bradshaw (20,440)(2)
(pl. of Kentmere Head)
T. Allom/S. Bradshaw (20,448)(1)
(pl. of view from Langdale Pikes)
T. Allom/W.H. Kelsall (20,456)

'The Whole Works of Sir James Ware', 1739-64
(by Sir James Ware; frontispiece of author)
English School 17C/G. Vertue (10,124)

'Worcestershire', 1776
(by J.N. Nash; pl. of Sir John Perrot)
English School 16C/G. Powle & V. Green (10,290)

'Works', 1773
(by B. Hoadly; frontispiece of author)
I. Gosset/*N. Hone the Elder*/J. Basire the Elder (10,879)

'Works', 1807
(by H. Hamilton; frontispiece of author)
G.C. Stuart/W. Evans (10,622)

'Works', 1839
(by F.D. Hemans; frontispiece of author)
W.E. West/E. Scriven (20,658)

'Works of James Barry', 1809
(frontispiece of the artist)
W. Evans/C. Picart (10,707)

'Works of the late Edward Dayes containing 'An excursion through the principle parts of Derbyshire and Yorkshire', 1805
(pl. of Dovedale, Derbyshire)
E. Dayes/J. Smith (20,411)
(pl. of Middleham Castle)
E. Dayes/S. Noble (20,430)

'Works of Lord Chesterfield', 1777
(pl. of George Faulkner)
Irish School c.1750/W. Sharp (10,145)
Irish School c.1750/W. Sharp (11,416)

'The Works of Horatio Walpole, Earl of Orford', 1798
(by H. Walpole; pl. of a Gothick Garden Gate)
English School 18C/J. Morris (20,094)
(pls. of Strawberry Hill, Middlesex)
E. Edwards/J. Newton (20,216)
W. Marlow/Godfrey (20,095)
W. Pars/Godfrey (20,096-20,098)
(pl. of the River Thames)
W. Pars/Godfrey (20,099)
(pl. of Horatio Walpole)
T. Lawrence/T. Evans (20,093)

APPENDIX 8

ENGRAVED BOOKS AND ALBUMS IN THE COLLECTION

10,039 *A Picturesque tour through Ireland by Dennis Sullivan*
25 illustrations
Published: T. McLean, London, 1824, price £2 12s. 6d.
Printed: N. Lewis
20.5 × 27
All included in catalogue:
D. Sullivan/D. Sullivan (10,039)(1-25)
Purchased, Lewes, Bow Windows Bookshop, 1968.

10,041 *Views of the most remarkable public buildings, monuments and other edifices in the city of Dublin*
Maps of 1610 and 1780, also 32 illustrations
Published: J. Williams, Dublin, 1780
24.3 × 19.1
All illustrations in catalogue:
R. Pool & J. Cash/J. Lodge & I. Taylor the Elder (10,041)(1-32)
Purchased, London, Sabin & Co., 1969

11,424 *Still by Samuel Beckett*
Illustrated by Stanley William Hayter
9th copy of 133
Published: M'Artc Edizioni, Milan, 1974
38.5 × 29.5
All illustrations in catalogue:
S.W. Hayter/S.W. Hayer (11,424)(1-3)
Purchased, Dublin, The Neptune Gallery, 1974

11,544 *An Album with 54 mounted caricatures (by Rowlandson, Woodward, Cruikshank and Williams) and 12 cartoons by John Doyle 'HB'*
44.6 x 31
Examples in catalogue:
G.M. Woodward/English School 1808 (11,544)(8)
J. Doyle/J. Doyle (11,544)(55-67)
Milltown Gift, 1902

11,932 *An Album of Kernoff prints- 72 woodcuts, calendar illustrations, portraits, views and genre scenes*
All signed and some dated by the artist
Example in catalogue: H. Kernoff/H. Kernoff (11,932)(7)
Presented, Mr T. Ryan P.R.H.A., 1981

20,247 *Bound copy of 28 Views of Rome and Environs by Andrea Locatelli*
23.7 x 30.5
Example in catalogue: A. Locatelli/W. Austin (20,247)(16)
Purchased, Lusk, Mr de Courcy Donovan, 1971

20,248 *The London Art and Union Prize Annual of 1846*
250 Illustrations
Published: R.A. Sprigg, London
34.6 x 24.6
Example in catalogue: G. Barret the Younger/H.Melville (20,248)(89)
Purchased, Lusk, Mr de Courcy Donovan, 1971

20,264 *Lessons on trees by J. D. Harding*
30 Illustrations
Published: Day & Son, London, 1852
Printed: G. Barclay, London
38.5 x 28
Example in catalogue: J.D. Harding/J.D. Harding (20,264)(26)
Purchased, Lusk, Mr de Courcy Donovan, 1971

20,660 *Zwanzig farblithographien zu gestalten und symbolen aus dem Werk von Ernst Jünger*
Published: F.-J. Kohl-Weigrand, St Ingbert, 29th March 1970
58 x 45.7
Example in catalogue: A. Huberti/A. Huberti (20,660)(13)
Provenance Unknown

20,664 *Liber Veritatis or a collection of two hundred prints after the original designs of Claude Le Lorrain, in the collection of his Grace the Duke of Devonshire, executed by Richard Earlom.... Vol. 3*
1 Frontispiece and 100 Illustrations
Dedicated: *To his Grace the Duke of Devonshire....John Boydell*
Published: Messrs. Boydell & Co.,
Printed: J. Moyes
London, 2nd May 1817
29 × 42.6
Examples in catalogue:
G.C. Stuart/T.G. Lupton (20,664)(1)
Claude Lorrain/R. Earlom (20,664)(93)
Bequeathed, Judge J. Murnaghan, 1976

20,665 *Liber Veritatis or a Collection of two hundred prints after the original designs of Claude Le Lorrain, in the collection of his Grace the Duke of Devonshire, executed by Richard Earlom.... Vol. 2*
1 Frontispiece and 100 Illustrations
Published: Messrs. Boydell & Co., London, 1777
Printed: W. Bulmer & Co., London
42.6 x 29
Examples in catalogue:
G.C. Stuart/Facius (20,665)(1)
Claude Lorrain/R. Earlom (20,665)(150)
Bequeathed, Judge J. Murnaghan, 1976

20,666 *Liber Veritatis or a Collection of prints after the original designs of Claude Le Lorrain, in the collection of his Grace the Duke of Devonshire, executed by Richard Earlom... Vol. 1*
1 Frontispiece and 100 Illustrations
Dedicated: *To His Grace the Duke of Devonshire...Josiah Boydell*
Published: Messrs. Boydell & Co., London, 1777
Printed: W. Bulmer & Co.
42.6 x 29
Example in catalogue: Claude Lorrain/R. Earlom (20,666)(51)
Bequeathed, Judge J. Murnaghan, 1976

20,667 *The Portraits of the most Eminent Painters and Other Famous Artists By F. Bouttats, P. De Jode Senior & Junior, W. Hollar, P. Pontius, J. Vorsterman, C. Wallmans &c from Original Paintings of Sir Anthony van Dyck, Gonzalo Coques, Peter Dunkerse de Ry, Cornelis Janssens, James Jordaens, John Meyssens, Erasmus Quellinius, Guido Rheni, Nicholas De Helt Stocade, David Teniers, Thomas Willeborts Bossaert, and other celebrated Masters with an account of their Lives, Characters and their most considerable Works, in French and English*
102 Portraits
Published: O. Payne; also W.H. Toms, London, 1739
31.1 x 25.2
Example in catalogue: D. Heil/C. Caukercken (20,667)(37)
Provenance Unknown

20,669 *Scelta di XXIV Vedute delle principali Contrade, Piazze, Chiese e Palazzi della Atta di Firenze*
1 Frontispiece and 24 Illustrations
Dedicated: *Alla Sacra Reale Apostolica Maestra di Maria Teresa ....*
Published: G. Allegrini, Florence, 1744
57.9 x 39.9
Example in catalogue: G. Zocchi/G. Zocchi & B.S. Sgrilli (20,669)(4)
(Also bound with it)
Vedute delle Ville, e d'altri Luoghi della Toscana
Frontispiece, Title Page and 24 Illustrations
Provenance Unknown

20,670 *Entwürf einer Historischen Architectur Vol. 1, by Fischer Von Erlach*
2 Frontispieces and 83 Illustrations
Published: Vienna, 1721 & Leipzig, 1725
38.1 x 52.5
Example in catalogue: J.B. Fischer Von Erlach/German School c.1721 (20,670)(61)
Provenance Unknown

20,671 *Receuil d'Estampes d'après les plus beaux tableaux et d'après les plus beaux dessins qui sont en France dans le Cabinet du Roy.... Vol.1*
2 Vignettes and 88 Illustrations; 33 Illustrations missing
Published: L'Imprimerie Royale, Paris, 1729
62.5 x 47.9
Example in catalogue:
P. Perugino/C. Duflos (20,671)(3)
Provenance Unknown

20,672 *Recueil d'Estampes d'après les plus beaux tableaux et d'après les plus beaux dessins qui sont en France dans le Cabinet du Roy.... Vol.2*
2 Vignettes and 88 Illustrations: 28 Illustrations missing
Published: 1742
62.5 x 48
Example in catalogue: Titian/N.H. Tardieu (20,672)(7)
Provenance Unknown

20,673 *The British Gallery of Engravings from Pictures of the Italian, Flemish, Dutch and English Schools now in the possession of the King and several Noblemen and Gentlemen of the United Kingdoms: with some account of each Picture by Edward Forster*
52 Illustrations

Dedicated: To Sir Richard Colt Hoare Bt. This Work is respectfully dedicated by his most obediant and much obliged servant, William Miller
Published: W. Miller, London, 1807
Printed: J. Moyes, London
48.2 x 33.9
Example in catalogue: G. Metsu/J. Burnet (20,673)(37)
Bequeathed, Judge J. Murnaghan, 1976

20,674 *Les plus beaux Monuments de Rome Ancienne ou Recueil des plus beaux Morceaux de L'Antique Romaine qui existaient encore*
1 Frontispiece, 1 Vignette and 43 Illustrations
Dedicated: A Son Excellance Monseigneur Jean Francois Joseph De Rochechouart Evêque Duc De Laon, Pair de France, Grand Aumonier de la Reine.
Published: Bouchard & Gravier, Paris
Printed: L'Imprimerie de Komarek
53.5 × 38
Example in catalogue: J. Barbault/D. Montagu (20,674)(9)
Bequeathed, Judge J. Murnaghan, 1976

20,675 *La Galerie Electorale de Dusseldorf*
No plates, only 1 coat of arms and 6 Vignettes
Published: 1778
30.4 x 39.2
Example in catalogue: N. Guibal/C. von Mechel (20,675)(2)
Bequeathed, Judge J. Murnaghan, 1976

20,676 *Logge del Vaticano*
1 Frontispiece and 13 Figures with 26 details of the Painted Wall Pilasters by Raphael in the Vatican Loggia taken under the direction of Francesco Rainaldi (1770-1805)
Published: N. de Antoni, Rome, 1802
65.4 x 46.4
Example in catalogue: Raphael/*L. Comparini*/G. Balzar & F. Rainaldi (20,676)(1)
Provenance Unknown

20,677 *Views of Rome*
23 Illustrations
Published: G. Rossi, Rome
52.6 x 41.3
Example in catalogue: A. Speechi/A. Speechi (20,677)(2)
Provenance Unknown

20,678 *La Gallerie du Palais Luxembourg peinte par Rubens, dessiné par les S. Nattier, et gravée par les plus Illustres Graveurs du Temps*
13 Illustrations
Dedicated: Dediée Au Roy
Published: G. Duchange, Paris, 1710
59.6 x 45.6
(Also bound with it, 1 painting after N. Coypel & 4 of the Raphael Cartoons)
Examples in catalogue:
?A. Van Dyck/*J. M. Nattier*/J. Audran (20,678)(1)
P.P. Rubens/*J.M. Nattier*/A. Trouvain (20,678)(6)
N.N. Coypel/J.P. Lebas (20,678)(14)
Raphael/N. Dorigny (20,678)(15)
Provenance unknown

20,679 *Musée Francais. Recueil des plus beaux Tableaux, Statues, et Bas-reliefs qui existaient au Louvre avant 1815. Avec l'explication des sujets, et des discours historiques sur la peinture, la sculpture, et la gravure, par Duchesne áine- Ecole Italienne*
3 Vignettes and 70 Illustrations
Published: A. & W. Galignani, Paris; also J.O. Robinson, London
Printed: J. Didot L'Ainé, Paris
63 x 48.2
Example in catalogue: Raphael/*A. Dutertre*/F.J.E. Beisson (20,679)(18)
Provenance Unknown

20,680 *Engravings of the most noble the Marquis of Stafford's Collection of Pictures in London arranged according to Schools and in chronological order, with remarks on each Picture, by William Ottley, Vol.2*
31 Plates (67 Illustrations)
Published: Longman, Hurst, Rees, Orme & Brown; also J. White; also Cadell & Davies; also P.W. Tomkins, London, 1st June 1816
Printed: Bensley & Son, London
60.7 x 44.5
Example in catalogue: L. Lotto/*W.M. Craig*/J.H. Wright (20,680)(7)
Provenance Unknown

20,681 *Engravings of the most noble the Marquis of Stafford's Collection of Pictures in London arranged according to Schools, in chronological order, with remarks on each picture, by William Ottley, Vol.4*
34 Plates (78 Illustrations)
Published: Longman, Hurst, Rees, Orme & Brown; also J. White; also Cadell & Davies; also P. Tomkins, London, 1st May 1816

Printed: Bensley & Son, London
60.7 x 44.5
Example in catalogue: J. Os/*W.M. Craig*/E. Byrne (20,681)(155)
Bequeathed, Judge J. Murnaghan, 1976

20,682 *La Pinacoteca della Pontificia Accademia delle Belle Arti in Bologna*
63 Illustrations
Published: F. Rosapina, Bologna, 1830
46.1 x 34
Example in catalogue: G. Reni/F. Rosapina (20,682)(62)
Provenance Unknown

20,683 *Musée Francais. Recueil des plus beaux Tableaux, Statues et Bas-reliefs qui existaient au Louvre avant 1815, avec l'explication des sujets et des discours historiques sur la peinture, la sculpture et la gravure, par Duchesse Ainé. Statues*
1 Frontispiece, 4 Vignettes and 80 Illustrations
Published: A. & W. Galignani, Paris; also J.O. Robinson, London
Printed: J. Didot L'Ainé, L'Imprimeur du Roi, Paris
62.8 x 48.2
Example in catalogue: Hellenistic School 1C/*P. Bouillon*/Bervic (20,683)(59)
Provenance Unknown

20,684 *Galeriae Farnesianae Icones Romae in Aedibus Sereniss.*
Details of the Carracci Frescoes in the Galleria of the Palazzo Farnese, Rome
1 Frontispiece, 2 Vignettes and 21 Illustrations
Published: J.J. de Rubeis, Rome
72 x 49.6
Example in catalogue: P. Aquila/P. Aquila (20,684)(4)
Provenance Unknown

20,685 *Musée Français. Recueil des plus beaux Tableaux, Statues, et Bas-reliefs qui existaient au Louvre avant 1815, avec l'explication des sujets, et des discours historiques sur la peinture, la Sculpture, la Gravure par Duchesne Ainé - Ecole Française*
1 Frontispiece, 4 Vignettes and 51 Illustrations
Published: A. & W. Galignani, Paris; also J.O. Robinson, London
Printed: J. Didot L'Ainé, Paris
62.9 x 47.6
Example in catalogue: N. Poussin/*A.E. Fragonard*/A. Girardet (20,685)(13)
Provenance Unknown

20,686 *Collection of Prints and Pictures painted for the purpose of Illustrating the Dramatic Works of Shakespeare by the Artists of Great Britain - Vol.1*
1 Frontispiece, 1 Vignette and 45 Illustrations
Published: John & Josiah Boydell, London, 25th March 1805
Printed: W. Bulmer and Co., London
69.2 x 53.8
Example in catalogue: M.W. Peters/P. Simon (20,686)(16)
Bequeathed, Judge J. Murnaghan, 1976

20,687 *Galerie de Florence et du Palais Pitti Vol.1 - Tableaux, Statues, Bas-reliefs et Camées de la Galerie de Florence et du Palais Pitti*
1 Frontispiece and 159 Illustrations of Pictures and Sculptures alternating with Antique Gems
Dedicated: A La Glorie de Pierre Leopold-Joseph, Souverain Chéri, sage Législator de la Toscane, Protecteur Eclareé des Science et des Arts.... dédié par son trés humble serviteur, Lacombe
Published: E. Lacombe, Paris 1789
Printed: Galerie de Florence Press
53.7 x 35.5
Example in catalogue: Raphael/*J.B. Wicar*/C.E. Duponchel (20,687)(46)
Provenance Unknown

20,688 *Galerie de Florence et du Palais Pitti Vol.2*
177 Illustrations (as no. 20,687)
Printed & Published with 20,687
53.8 x 35.2
Example in catalogue: Roman Antique/*J.B. Wicar*/N. Thomas (20,688)(108)
Provenance Unknown

20,689 *Oeuvres de P. Wouverman, Hollandois, Gravées d'aprés ses meilleures tableaux qui sont dans les plus beaux Cabinets de Paris et ailleurs Vol.1*
1 Vignette and 52 Illustrations
Dedicated: Dediées á son Altesse Serenissime Monseigneurie Comte de Clermont, Prince du Sang Par son tres humble et tres obeissant Serviteur I. Moyreau, Graveur du Roy 1737
Published: J. Moyreau, Paris, 1737 (prints dated 1733-46)
66 x 44.5
Example in catalogue: P. Wouwerman/P. Filloueul (20,689)(25)
Bequeathed, Judge J. Murnaghan, 1976

20,690 *Oeuvres de P. Wouverman... Vol.2*
Dedicated: *Dediées á Monsieur Le Marquis de Marigny, Conseiller du Roy en ses Conseils Directeur et Ordannateur Général des Batiments et Jardins de sa Majesté, Arts Academies et Manufactures de France*
51 Illustrations, 2 missing
Published: J. Moyreau, Paris, 1756
66 x 44.5
Example in catalogue: P. Wouwerman/J. Moyreau (20,690)(80)
Bequeathed, Judge J. Murnaghan, 1976

20,691 *Musée Français. Recueil Complet des Tableaux, Statues et Bas-reliefs, qui composent la collection nationale; avec l'explication des sujets et des discours historiques sur la peinture, et la sculpture et la Gravure par S.C. Croze-Magnan*
3 Vignettes and 86 Illustrations
Dedicated: *À Bonaparte. Citoyen premier consul. Dans le cours de vos victoires vous avez conquis les principaux chef-d'oeuvres des beaux-arts, et vous en avez enrichi la France. La Collection des gravures qui peut les faire connaitre á l'Europe entiére est un hommage qui vous est dû. Nous vous l'offrons avec reconnaissance et respect. Les Editeurs du Musée Français*
Published: Robillard-Peronville et Laurent, Paris, 1803
Printed: L.E. Herhan
63.7 x 48.5
Example in catalogue: Raphael/ *P.P. Prudhon*/P. Audouin (20,691)(1)
Bequeathed, Judge J. Murnaghan, 1976

20,692 *Critical and Familiar Notices on the Art of etching upon copper. Through which are interpersed, some prints, etched by an Amateur.*
6 Illustrations
Published: W. Huband, Dublin, 1810
21.9 x 17.7
(These individual prints of illustrations in the book are included in the catalogue)
W. Huband/W. Huband (11,533)
A. Ostade/W. Huband (11,532)
A. Ostade/W. Huband (11,536)
Raphael/W. Huband (11,538)
Provenance Unknown

20,693 *A Limited Edition of 58 copies containing three lithographs by Joseph Pennell, of which this is no. 53*
31.3 x 23.5
Example in catalogue: J. Pennell/J. Pennell (20,693)(1)
Presented, Mrs B. Ganly, 1978

20,694 *Plates from the Doré Gallery: Containing two hundred and fifty beautiful engravings, selected from the Doré Bible, Milton, Dante's Inferno, Dante's Purgatorio and Paradiso, Atala, Fontaine, Fairy Realm, Don Quixote, Baron Munchausen, Croquemitaine, &c. &c.*
90 Illustrations
Published: Cassell, Petter & Galpin, London, Paris, & New York
37.8 x 30
Example in catalogue: L.C.P.G. Doré/C. Laplante (20,694)(72)
Provenance Unknown

20,703 *Les cinquante deux tableaux representant les faits les plus célébres du vieux et du nouveau Testament peints á fresque par Raphael D'Urbin aux Voutes des Galeries du Vatican*
1 Frontispiece, 1 Vignette and 52 Illustrations
Dedicated: *Dédiés á S.S. Pie VI. Souverain Pont.*
Published: J. Scudellari, Rome
27.9 x 41
Example in catalogue; Raphael/S. Bianchi (20,703)(47)
Purchased, Miss White, 1936

20,704 *Engravings of the Most Noble the Marquis of Stafford's Collection of Pictures in London arranged according to Schools and in Chronological order with remarks on each Picture. Vols. 1 & 2 (bound together)*
13 plans of the Stafford Gallery and 24 Plates (48 illustrations) in Vol.1, 31 Plates (67 illustrations) in Vol.2
Dedicated: *To the King's Most Excellant Majesty, Patron: his royal Highness the Prince of Wales, Vice-Patron; The Earl of Dartmouth, President; and the Rest of the Noblemen and Gentlemen, Governors of the British Institution for promoting the Fine Arts in the United Kingdom*
Published: Longman, Hurst, Rees, Orme, & Brown; also Cadell & Davies; also P. W. Tomkins, London, 1818
Printed: Bensley & Son, London
42.4 x 34
Example in Catalogue: G. Moroni/*W.N. Craig*/P.W. Tomkins (20,704)(8)
Bequeathed, Judge J. Murnaghan, 1976

20,705 *Engravings of the Most Noble the Marquis of Stafford's Collection of Pictures in London, arranged according to Schools and in chronological order, with remarks on each Picture. Vols. 3 & 4 (bound together)*
36 Plates (103 illustrations) in Vol. 3,
34 Plates (78 illustrations) in Vol.4
Published: Longman, Hurst, Rees, Orme & Brown; also Cadell & Davies; also P.W. Tomkins, London, 1st March 1815
Printed: Bensley & Son, London
42.4 x 34
Example in catalogue: P.P. Rubens/ *W.M. Craig*/C. Heath (20,705)(7)
Bequeathed, Judge J. Murnaghan, 1976

20,706 *Gli Antichi Sepolcri, overo Mausolei Romani, ed Etruschi Trovati in Roma, ed in altri Luoghi celebri....*
1 Frontispiece and 110 Illustrations
Published: Rome, 1768
29.6 x 20.4
Example in catalogue: Roman Antique /P.S. Bartoli (20,706)(47)
Provenance Unknown

20,707 *Musée Francais. Recueil des Plus Beaux Tableaux, Statues et Bas-reliefs qui existaient au Louvre avant 1815, avec explication des sujets, et des discours historiques sur le peinture, la Sculpture, et la Gravure, par Duchesne Ainé. Ecole Allemande (sic)*
1 Frontispiece, 4 Vignettes and 116 Illustrations
Published: A.& W. Galignani, Paris; also J.O. Robinson, London
Printed: J. Didot L'Ainé, Paris
63 x 47.8
Example in catalogue: A. Ostade/*Swebach*/Bovinet (20,707)(66)
Provenance Unknown

20,708 *Gems of Ancient Art, or select Specimens from the Old Masters, consisting of Forty Engravings, by Eminent Artists*
39 Illustrations
Published: Howlett & Brimmer, London, 1827
33.2 x 26.4
Example in catalogue: Rembrandt/English School 1827 (20,708)(19)
Bequeathed, Judge J. Murnaghan, 1976

20,709 *Nuova Raccolta Di Cinquanta Pittoreschi incisi all'acqua forte da Bartolomeo Pinelli Romano*
10 Illustrations
Dedicated: *Dedicati a Sua Eccellenza il Sigr. Cavaliere Hitroft, General Maggiore delle Armate di S. M. J. L'Imperatore di tutte le Russie...., e protettore Zelante delle belle Arti*
Published: N. de Antoni & I. Pavon, Rome, 1816
28 x 40.9
Example in catalogue: B. Pinelli/B. Pinelli (20,709)(3)
Purchased, Miss White, 1936

20,710 *Book of Maarten Heemskerk Engravings*
9 Illustrations
Originally issued 1548-1549
40 x 27.7
Example in catalogue: M. Heemskerk/M. Heemskerk (20,710)(1)
Provenance Unknown

20,711 *Divers Ajustements et Usage de Russie*
1 Frontispiece, I Title-Page and 66 Illustrations
Dedicated: *Dédiés á Monsieur Boucher Peintre du Roy, Recteur en son Academie Royale de Peinture et Sculpture et sur Inspecteur de la Fabrique des Gobelins par son trés humble et trés obeissant serviteur et son élève Le Prince*
Published: J.B. La Prince, Paris, 1763-65
29.8 x 21.8
Example in catalogue: J.B. Le Prince/J.B. Le Prince (20,711)(36)
Bequeathed, Judge J. Murnaghan, 1976

20,712 *A Collection of prints from Pictures painted for the purpose of illustrating the Dramatic Works of Shakespeare Vol.2 1803*
1 Frontispiece, 1 Vignette and 50 Illustrations
Published: J. & J. Boydell, London, 1st August 1792
Printed: W. Bulmer & Co.
69.3 x 54.3
Example in catalogue:J. Barry/F. Legat (20,712)(40)
Provenance Unknown

20,713 Another copy of 20,670
Provenance Unknown

20,714 *Oeuvre de Canova. Recueil de Statues, Groupes, Bustes, Mausolées, Colosses et Monuments de tout genre, executés par Canova. Dessinés et Gravés sous les yeux de l'auteur á Rome*
1 Frontispiece and 74 Illustrations
Published: Rome, 1819
86.9 x 67
Example in catalogue: A. Canova/*G. Tognoli*/A. Ricciani (20,714)(16)
Provenance Unknown

20,716 *Le Theatre des Peintures de David Teniers, natif d'Anvers, Peintre et Ayde de Chambre des Serenissimes Princes Leopolde GVIL Archiduc, et Don Jean d'Austriche: auquel sont representez les dessins tracés de sa main, et gravés en cuivre par ses soins, sur les Originaux Italiens, que le Serme Archiduc a assemblé en son Cabinet de le Cour de Brusselles*
1 Title-Page, 4 Vignettes and 144 Illustrations
Dedicated: *Dediée au dit Prince Serme Leopolde Gvil. Archiduc etc.*
Published: H. Aertssens, Antwerp, 1660
41.5 x 27.7
Example in catalogue: Giorgione/J. Van Troyen (20,716)(10)
Provenance Unknown

20,717 *Petrus Lapidus Meteris Regiorum Negotiorum summus Procurator apud Mediomatrices, Tullios e Viridumenses*
171 Roman Tombs, Inscriptions and Sepuchral Statues. No Artist, Engraver or Publisher given
Example in catalogue: Roman Antique/Italian School 17C (20,717)(89)
Provenance Unknown

20,718 Another copy of 20,666
Example in catalogue: Claude Lorrain/J. Boydell (20,718)(1)
Bequeathed, Judge J. Murnaghan, 1976

20,719 Another copy of 20,665
Example in catalogue: Claude Lorrain/R. Earlom (20,719)(149)
Bequeathed, Judge J. Murnaghan, 1976

20,720 *The Italian School of Design: being a Series of Fac-Similes of Original Drawings by the most Eminent Painters and Sculptors of Italy: with biographical notices of the artists, and observations on their works*
1 Frontispiece and 84 Illustrations (13 missing)
Published: Taylor & Hessey, London, 1823
Printed: J. McCreery
50.7 x 35.7
Example in catalogue: Michelangelo/F.C. Lewis (20,720)(28)
Provenance Unknown

20,721 *Galerie Lithographiée de son Altesse Royale, Monseigneur Duc D'Orléans, Vol.1*
1 Title-Page, 1 Frontispiece and 76 Illustrations
Dedicated: *Á son altesse Royale la Princess Marie Amélie, Duchesse D'Orléans*
Published: J. Vatout et J.P. Quenot
Printed: C. Motte, Lithographer to the Duc D'Orléans, Paris
54.5 x 36.4
Examples in catalogue:
F.P.S. Gérard/H. Grévedon (20,721)(1)
R.A.Q. Monvoisin/C.E.P. Motte (20,721)(63)
Bequeathed, Judge J. Murnaghan, 1976

20,722 *A Series of Etchings by James Barry, Esq. from his original and justly celebrated paintings, in the Great Room of the Society of Arts, Manufacturers and Commerce, Adelphi.*
15 Illustrations
Published: Colnaghi, London, 1808
Printed: W. Bulmer & Co.
69 x 52
Examples in catalogue: J. Barry/J. Barry (20,722)(1-14)
J. Barry/L. Schiavonetti (20,722)(15)
Provenance Unknown

20,723 *Galerie du Palais Royal Gravée d'aprés les tableaux des differentes Ecoles qui la composent: Avec un abrégé de la vie des peintres et une description historique de chaque tableau par Mr. L'Abbé de Fontenay, Vol.1*
1 Title Page, 6 Vignettes and 130 Illustrations
Dedicated: *Dediée á S.A.S. Monseigneur le Duc D'Orleans premier Prince du Sang par J. Couché Graveur de son Cabinet*

Published: J. Couché; also J. Bouilliard, Paris, 1786
Printed: H. Perronneau
51.8 x 34.4
Examples in catalogue:
Bronzino/*A. Borel*/P. Trierre (20,723)(7)
Raphael/*Vendenberg*/A.L. Romanet (20,723)(14)
Sebastiano del Piombo/R. Delaunay (20,723)(22)
Bequeathed, Judge J. Murnaghan, 1976

20,724 *Galerie du Palais Royal. Gravée d'aprés les Tableaux des Différentes Ecoles qui la composent, avec un abrégé de la vie des peintres, et une Description Historique de chaque tableau, Vol. 2*
140 Illustrations
Published: J. Couché; also Laporte, Paris, 1808
Printed: H. Perronneau
51.8 x 34.4
Examples in catalogue:
Titian/J. Couché (20,724)(2)
?Giorgione/B.A. Nicollet (20,724)(24)
Bequeathed, Judge J. Murnaghan, 1976

20,725 *Galerie du Palais Royal. Gravée d'aprés les Tableaux des differentes écoles qui la composent, avec un abrégé de la vie des peintres, et un description historique de chaque tableau, Vol. 3*
77 Illustrations
Published: J. Couché; also Laporte, Paris, 1808
Printed: H. Perronneau
50.7 x 35.7
Examples in catalogue:
C. Le Brun/A. Lafitte & J.-B. Tilliard (20,725)(74)
N. Poussin/H.G. Bertaux & A. L. Ronanet (20,725)(56)
H. Rigaud/F. Guibert (20,725)(76)
Bequeathed, Judge J. Murnaghan, 1976

20,726 Another copy of 20,704
Example in catalogue: N. Poussin/C. Heath (20,726)(14)
Presented, Mr G. F. Mulvany, 1868

20,727 Another copy of no. 20,705
Example in catalogue: A.R. Mengs/P.W. Tomkins & W.M. Craig (20,727)(12)
Presented, Mr G. F. Mulvany, 1868

20,728 *Poetical Fragments: Heart-Imployment with God and Itself. The Concordant Discord of a Broken-healed Heart.... by Richard Baxter*
Second Edition
1 Frontispiece
Published: J. Dunton, London, 1689
14.8 x 8.7
Example in catalogue: English School c.1689/English School 1689 (20,728)(1)
Provenance Unknown

20,729 *The Art of Drawing and Painting in Water-colours*
2 Illustrations
Printed: J. Potts, Dublin, 1768
16.6 x 9.9
Example in catalogue: Irish School c.1768/Irish School 1768 (20,729)(1)
Provenance Unknown

20,730 *Fancies. A Series of Subjects in outline, now first published from the original plates. Designed and etched by Moritz Retzsch with prefatory remarks and descriptions by Mrs Jameson*
6 Illustrations
Published: Saunders & Otley; also A. Richter & Co., London; also Treuttel & Wurtz, Paris & Strasbourg; also E. Fleischer, Leipzig, 1834
20.1 x 23
Example in catalogue: F.M.A. Retzsch/F.M.A. Retzsch (20,730)(6)
Provenance Unknown

20,731 *A Set of Prints Engraved after the Most Capital Paintings in the collection of Her Imperial Majesty the Empress of Russia, lately in the possession of the Earl of Orford, at Houghton Hall in Norfolk with Plans, elevations, Sections, Chimney Pieces and Ceilings, Vols. 1 & 2, ('The Houghton Gallery')*
1 Frontispiece, 2 Vignettes, 28 Plates and Elevations and 158 Illustrations in Vol. 1. 1 Frontispiece, 1 Vignette and 69 Illustrations in Vol. 2
Dedicated: To Her Most Sacred Majesty, Catherine II, Empress of all the Russias, whose transcendant wisdom, admirable policy & parental affection, extended to every part of her vast dominions, have completed the immense task begun by the Immortal Peter. As a just tribute to this August Princess, the avowed Patroness of Genius, & universal Protectoress of Art, Science and Literature. These volumes are with the profoundest repect and gratitude dedicated by her Imperial Majesty's most obediant and most devoted servant - John Boydell

Published: John & Josiah Boydell, London, 1st January 1788
68.2 x 52.3
Examples in catalogue:
School of Titian/J. Murphy (20,731)(89)
J.B. Van Loo/J. Watson (20,731)(92)
Rosalba/C. West (20,731)(136)
Bequeathed, Judge J. Murnaghan, 1976

20,732 *A Collection of Engravings from Paintings and Drawings by the Most Celebrated Masters containing a Series of fine specimens after Van Dyck, Annibale Carracci, Murillo, Carlo Dolci, Salvator Rosa, Teniers, Rembrandt, Van de Velde, Brauwer, Netcher*
1 Frontispiece and 89 Illustrations
Published: W.T. Gilling, London, ?1807
42.6 x 29.6
Example in catalogue: ?W. Vaillant/W. Vaillant (20,732)(57)
Bequeathed, Judge J. Murnaghan, 1976

20,733 *A Collection of Fac-Similes of Scarce and Curious Prints by the Early Masters of the Italian, German, and Flemish Schools, illustrative of the History of Engraving, from the invention of the Art by Maso Finiguerra, in the Middle of the 15C, to the end of the following century; with introductory remarks, and a catalogue of the Plates, by William Young Ottley Esq. F.S.A., member of the Society of Arts and Sciences at Utrecht. Vol.1*
1 Frontispiece and 99 Plates (132 Illustrations)
Dedicated: To Francis Douce, esq. F.S.A. this Work is respectfully dedicated by the Editor
Printed: J. McCreery
Published: Longman, Hurst, Rees, Orme, Brown and Green; also Molteno; also Colnaghi & Co., London, 1826
38.6 x 28.6
Example in catalogue: M. Schongauer/English School 1826 (20,733)(39)
Presented, Mr G. F. Mulvany, 1867

20,757 *A Collection of the Best Works of Raphael, Domenichino and other celebrated Painters, designed and Engraved by G.F. Ferrero, Ex-Pensionnaire of the King of Sardinia*
1 Frontispiece and 150 Illustrations
Published: G.F. Ferrero, Rome
24.7 x 33.3
Example in catalogue: N. Poussin/G.F. Ferrero (20,757)(138)
Provenance Unknown

20,758 *Die Sammlung Alt-Nieder und Ober-Deutscher Gemälde der Brüder Sulpiz (b.1783) und Melchior (b.1786), Boisseree und Johann Bertram. Lithographiert von Johann Nepomuk Strissener. Mit Nachrichten uber die Altdeutschen Maler von den Besitzern Stuttgart bei den Herausgebern, 1821*
36 Illustrations
dedicated: Seiner Majestat dem Konig Wilhelm von Wurtemberg...
Published: Stuttgart, 1821
82.2 x 63.2
Example in catalogue: R. Weyden/N.J. Strixner (20,758)(34)
Provenance Unknown

20,759 *Views of Rome by G. Fossati*
10 Illustrations
Published: S. Rosi, Rome, c.1830
28.6 x 43.1
Example in catalogue: G. Fossati/A. Von Dall'Armi (20,759)(9)
Provenance Unknown

20,760 *Views of Rome by G. Fossati*
10 Illustrations
Published: S. Rosi, Rome, c.1830
29.5 x 44.7
Example in catalogue: G. Fossati/A. Von Armi Dall'Armi (20,760)(6)
Provenance Unknown

20,833 *Roma Antica. Distincta par Regioni (Di Sesto Rufo, Vittore e Nardini) Tuomo Primo*
1 Frontispiece and 19 Illustrations
Printed: Bornabo & Lazzarini
Published: Rome, 1741
16.9 x 11.2
Example in catalogue: Italian School c.1741/Italian School 1741 (20,833)(3)
Provenance Unknown

APPENDIX 9

PROVENANCES

Key:
B = bequest
C = commissioned
G = gift
P = purchase
T = transfer

Adam's (P1984)
A. John/A. John (20,764)

Mrs J. Adams-Acton (P1912)
J. Adams-Acton (8109)

Mr D. Alexander (G1986)
N. Blakey/L.J. Cathelin (20,770)

Mr R.B. Armstrong (G1907)
S. Percy (8160)

Mr R.B. Armstrong (G1909)
English School early 19C (8231)

Mr R.B. Armstrong (G1911)
J. Reynolds/J. Baldrey (11,047)

Sir Walter Armstrong (G1892)
N. Hone the Elder/R. Purcell (11,069)

Sir Walter Armstrong (G1893)
W. Poorter/L. Beyer (11,933)

Miss Ashford (P1918)
English School 19C/Morris & Co. (10,482)

M.W. Balfe Memorial Committee (G1879)
T. Farrell (8044)

Mr F.E. Ball (G1905)
J.P. Haverty/J.P. Haverty (11,695)

Mrs N. Ball (P1890)
C. Moore (8088)

Messrs. Barry (P1957)
J. Hogan (8047)

Mrs E.H. Bartlett (B1974)
Irish School 19C (8234)

Mr R. Bateman (P1913)
A. Buck/Irish School 1790 (11,134)

Battersby & Co. (P1943)
T. Kirk (8000)

Mr J. Behan (G1968)
J. Behan (8054)

Bennett's (P1885)
J. Tusch/L. Zucchi (10,084)
J. Barry/J. Barry (10,205)

Bennett's (P1900)
Irish School 1866 (8154)

Messrs. Benson (P1908)
A.G.G. D'Orsay (8142)

Sir H. Beresford Pierce (P1903)
School of F. Chantrey (8241)

Mrs E. Bishop (G1942)
W. Hogarth/W. Hogarth (11,509-11,515)
W. Hogarth/W. Hogarth (11,520-11,521)

Mrs A. Bodkin (G1974)
J.S. Jorden (8237)

Dr T. Bodkin (G1925)
J.B.S. Chardin/B.F. Lepicié (11,490)
J.B.S. Chardin/P.L. Surugue (11,623)
P.P. Rubens/B. Baron (20,040-20,047)

Dr T. Bodkin (G1934)
T. Farrell (8183)

Mr W. Booth Pearsall (G1901)
J. Woodhouse (8156)

Mr R.V. Bourke (P1924)
E.H. Baily (8224)

Bow Windows bookshop (P1968)
D. Sullivan/D. Sullivan (10,039)

Mr H.A.J. Breun (P1909)
C. Brown/J. Brooks (10,481)
W. Cuming/W. Ward (10,780)
W. Fox/G. Foggo (10,857)
J. Hoppner/S.W. Reynolds (10,469)
J. Northcote/J. Fittler (10,473)
F.R. West/J. Watson (10,236)

Mr H.A.J. Breun (P1910)
C. Baugniet/C. Baugniet (10,802)
Countess of Burlington/J. Faber the Younger (10,362)
W. Hogarth/A. Miller (10,436)
T. Lawrence/J. Godby (10,767)
T.H. Maguire/T.H. Maguire (10,684-10,685)
H.W. Philips/H. Cook (11,079)

Mr H.A.J. Breun (P1911)
?J. Comerford/J.L. Lynch (11,226)
J. M..../?S. Okey (10,327)

British Museum (G1981)
C. Smith (8254)

Rev. Stopford A. Brooke (G1903)
J.M.W. Turner/J.M.W. Turner and others (11,958-11,999; 20,000-20,028)

Browne & Philips (P1907)
R. Bull/J. Collyer (10,753)

The Misses Bruce (G1911)
T.C. Thompson/T. Hodgetts (10,230)

Sir Bernard Burke (G1873)
J.K. Sherwin/J.K. Sherwin (11,657)

Rev. C. Burke (G1864)
J. Hogan (8034)

Mr D. Burke (P1949)
J. Constable/W. Ward the Younger (10,231)

Mr F.V. Burnidge, through Sarah Purser (G1926)
P.F. Gethin/P.F. Gethin (11,428-11,429)
P.F. Gethin/P.F. Gethin (11,480)
P.F. Gethin/P.F. Gethin (11,619)
P.F. Gethin/P.F. Gethin (11,869)

Mrs Carmichael (G1863)
G. Vanelli (8085)
G. Vanelli (8186)

Mr E.N. Carrothers (G1963)
S.R. Praeger (8035)

Mr S. Catterson Smith the Younger (G1884)
W. Stevenson/D. Lucas (10,033)

Lady Cavendish (G1899)
W. Richmond/J. Miller (10,188)

Mrs Chadwick (P1896)
T.C. Thompson/C. Turner (10,848)

Central Catholic Library (G1974)
A. O'Connor (8238)

1st Chaloner Smith sale (Christie's), (P21-29 March, 1887)
L.F. Abbott/W. Barnard (10,808)
H. Barron/V. Green (11,011)
F. Bindon/J. Brooks (10,044)
F. Bindon/J. McArdell (10,026)

F. Bindon/A. Miller (10,024)
F. Bindon/A. Miller (10,052)
F. Bindon/A. Miller (20,801)
?J. Brooks/J. Brooks (10,117)
?J. Brooks/J. Brooks (10,415)
?J. Brooks/J. Brooks (10,434)
M. Brown/H. Hudson (10,246)
E.F. Calze/V. Green (10,382)
T. Carlton/T. Beard (10,143)
S. Cooper/R. Brookshaw (11,393)
M. Cosway/V. Green (10,405)
F. Cotes/R. Brookshaw (11,150)
F. Cotes/R. Brookshaw (11,151)
F. Cotes/R. Houston (10,342)
F. Cotes/R. Houston (10,359)
F. Cotes/J. McArdell (10,343)
F. Cotes/J. McArdell (10,374)
M. Dahl/T. Beard (10,063)
M. Dahl/P. Pelham (10,569)
N. Dance/T. Burke (10,999)
N. Dance/T. Burke (11,000)
N. Dance/W. Dickinson (10,462)
S. Drummond/W. Barnard (10,493)
J.G. Eccard/A. Miller (10,367)
English School 17C/S. De Wilde (10,059)
English School 17C/J. Gole (10,340)
English School 17C/J. Gole (10,564)
English School 17C/B. Lens (10,921)
English School 17C/A. Miller (10,133)
English School c.1740/J. Brooks (10,255)
English School c.1740/J. Brooks (10,267)
English School c.1740/J. Brooks (10,537)
English School c.1740/J. Brooks (10,538)
English or Irish School 18C/J. Brooks (10,760)
English or Irish School c.1741/J. Brooks (10,197)
English or Irish School c.1760/R. Houston (10,127)
J. Faber the Younger/J. Faber the Younger (10,017)
French School 18C/V. Green (11,034)
T. Frye/T. Frye (10,298)
T. Frye/T. Frye (10,465)
T. Frye/T. Frye (10,550)
T. Frye/T. Frye (10,551)
T. Gainsborough/T. Bell (10,183)
T. Gainsborough/J. Dean (10,549)
T. Gainsborough/G. Dupont (10,496)
D. Gardner/J. Jones (10,499)
G. Gaven/J. Gainer (10,108)
M. Gheeraerts the Younger/J. Faber the Younger (10,403)
T. Gibson/T. Pelham (10,012)
C. Grignon the Younger/J. Murphy (10,166)
J. Gwim/M. Jackson (10,134)
G. Hamilton/J. Faber the Younger (10,393)
G. Hamilton/J. Faber the Younger (10,394)
G. Hamilton/J. McArdell (10,396)
H.D. Hamilton/W. Barnard (10,233)
H.D. Hamilton/J. Boydell (10,294)
H.D. Hamilton/V. Green (10,182)
H.D. Hamilton/R. Houston (10,153)
?F. Hayman/J. McArdell (10,104)
F. Hayman/J. McArdell (10,123)
W. Hoare/R. Houston (11,068)
W. Hoare/R. Houston & S. Wheatley (10,445)
W. Hoare/J. McArdell (10,180)
N. Hone the Elder/J. Greenwood (10,695)
N. Hone the Elder/N. Hone the Elder (10,072)
N. Hone the Elder/W. Humphrey (10,696)
N. Hone the Elder/C. Phillips (10,378)
N. Hone the Elder/C. Phillips (10,699)
J. Hoppner/G. Clint (10,486)
J. Hoppner/S. Einslie (10,387)
J. Hoppner/J. Jones (10,386)
J. Hoppner/T. Park (10,408)
J. Hoppner/T. Park (11,415)
H. Howard/R. Earlom (10,431)
T. Hudson/J. McArdell (10,189)
T. Hudson/J. McArdell (10,855)
R. Hunter/J. Dixon (10,158)
R. Hunter/E. Fisher (10,194)
R. Hunter/J. McArdell (10,440)
H. Hysing/T. Burford (10,817)
C. Jervas/J. Brooks (10,148)
C. Jervas/J. Brooks (10,242)
C. Jervas/J. Brooks (10,825)
W. Jones/A. Miller (10,074)
W. Jones/A. Miller (10,480)
A. Kauffmann/T. Burke (10,379)
T. Kettle/S. De Wilde (10,235)
T. Kettle/S. De Wilde (11,096)
A. Killigrew/A. Blooteling (10,586)
G. Kneller/J. Brooks (10,223)
G. Kneller/J. Faber the Younger (10,826)
G. Kneller/J. Faber the Younger (10,827)
G. Kneller/M. Ford (10,504)
G. Kneller/J. Gole (10,006)
G. Kneller/J. Gole (11,024)
G. Kneller/J. McArdell (10,175)
G. Kneller/P. Schenck (10,821)
J. Latham/J. Brooks (10,023)
J. Latham/J. Brooks (10,195)
J. Latham/A. Miller (10,413)
W. Lawrence/A. Miller (10,530)
P. Lely/I. Beckett (10,080)
P. Lely/I. Beckett (10,328)
P. Lely/I. Beckett (10,373)
P. Lely/I. Beckett (10,561)
P. Lely/A. Blooteling (10,025)
P. Lely/A. Blooteling (10,365)
P. Lely/A. Blooteling (10,495)
P. Lely/A. Blooteling (11,207)
P. Lely/A. Blooteling (11,263)
P. Lely/A. Blooteling (11,264)
P. Lely/A. Blooteling (10,759)
P. Lely/J. Griffier (10,364)
P. Lely/E. Lutterell (10,136)
P. Lely/E. Lutterell (10,774)
?P. Lely/P. Schenck (10,560)
J. Lewis/A. Miller (10,198)
J.E. Liotard/R. Houston (10,384)
R. Livesay/J. Dean (10,464)
D. Lüders/J. McArdell (10,852)
E. Lutterell/E. Lutterell (10,022)
W. Madden/W. Dickinson (10,479)
J. McArdell/R. Earlom (10,470)
P. Mignard/W. Faithorne the Elder (11,025)
J. Murphy/J. Murphy (10,541)
M.W. Peters/J. Murphy (10,106)
H. Pickering/J. Faber the Younger (10,031)
R.E. Pine/W. Dickinson (10,828)
J. Pope-Stevens/J. Brooks (10,208)
J. Pope-Stevens/A. Miller (10,511)
C. Read/J. Finalyson (10,391)
C. Read/R. Houston (11,064)
J. Reynolds/J. Dean (10,377)
J. Reynolds/W. Dickinson (10,086)
J. Reynolds/W. Dickinson (10,346)
J. Reynolds/W. Dickinson (10,407)
J. Reynolds/W. Dickinson (10,490)
J. Reynolds/W. Dickinson (11,028)
J. Reynolds/W. Dickinson & T. Watson (10,853)
J. Reynolds/J. Dixon (10,395)
J. Reynolds/R. Dunkarton (10,484)
J. Reynolds/English School c.1770 (11,140)
J. Reynolds/J. Faber the Younger (10,176)
J. Reynolds/E. Fisher (10,363)
J. Reynolds/J. Grozer (10,390)
J. Reynolds/J. Grozer (10,762)
J. Reynolds/J. Grozer (10,768)
J. Reynolds/T. Hardy (10,796)
J. Reynolds/R. Houston (11,063)
J. Reynolds/J. McArdell (10,060)
J. Reynolds/J. McArdell (10,088)
J. Reynolds/J. McArdell (10,334)
J. Reynolds/J. McArdell (10,338)
J. Reynolds/J. McArdell (10,389)
J. Reynolds/S. Okey (10,339)

G. Romney/V. Green (10,765)
G. Romney/J. Jones (10,442)
G. Romney/J. Jones (10,476)
G. Romney/J. Jones (10,508)
J.M. Rysbrack/J. Faber the Younger (10,027)
P. Schenck/P. Schenck (10,865)
A. Soldi/J. McArdell (10,846)
D. Stevens/J. Faber the Younger (10,131)
C. Stoppelaer/A. Miller (10,917)
G.C. Stuart/W. Dickinson (10,110)
G.C. Stuart/C.H. Hodges (10,092)
G.C. Stuart/C.H. Hodges (10,150)
G.C. Stuart/C.H. Hodges (10,494)
G.C. Stuart/C.H. Hodges (10,726)
J. Vanderbank/J. Faber the Younger (10,548)
J. Vandervaart/W. Faithorne the Younger (10,385)
A. Van Dyck/J. Boydell (10,556)
A. Van Dyck/A. Browne (10,259)
A. Van Dyck/A. Browne (10,756)
A. Van Dyck/J. Faber the Younger (10,096)
P. Van Somer/V. Green (10,443)
R. Walker/*M. Ford*/A. Miller (10,500)
R. Walker/P. Pelham (11,396)
R. Walker/F. Place (10,907)
R. Walker/J. Velde the Elder (10,245)
B. West/E. Fisher (10,850)
J. Wills/A. Miller (10,018)
B. Wilson/J. McArdell (10,149)
B. Wilson/J. McArdell (10,677)
W. Wissing/I. Beckett (10,244)
W. Wissing/I. Beckett (10,331)
W. Wissing/I. Beckett (10,993)
W. Wissing/I. Beckett (11,863)
W. Wissing/B. Lens (10,922)
W. Wissing/J. Smith (10,691)
T. Worlidge/R. Houston (10,234)
T. Worlidge/R. Houston (10,827)
J. Worsdale/J. Brooks (10,167)
J. Worsdale/J. Brooks (10,820)
J. Wyck/J. Faber the Younger (10,420)
J. Zoffany/G.F.L. Marchi (10,471)

2nd Chaloner Smith sale (Christie's), (P25 April-4 May, 1888)
J.J. Barralet/W. Ward the Elder (11,654)
H.J. Burch the Younger/J. Ward (10,718)
T. Carter the Elder/Irish School 18C (11,642)
R. Cosway/J.R. Smith (11,665)
F. Cotes/C. Spooner (10,358)
F. Cotes/C. Spooner (10,375)
F. Cotes/J. Watson (10,332)
C. D'Agar/J. Simon (10,730)
C. D'Agar/J. Simon (10,731)
M. Dahl/J. Simon (10,822)
M. Dahl/J. Simon (10,995)
P. De Graves/J. Simon (10,032)
S. De Koster/C. Townley (10,953)
English School 17C/English School 17C (11,395)
English School 17C/P. Pelham (11,022)
T. Gainsborough/J.R. Smith (10,376)
H.D. Hamilton/J. Watson (10,334)
T. Hill/R. Williams (10,199)
W. Hoare/J. Simon (10,184)
N. Hone the Elder/J.R. Smith (10,330)
N. Hone the Elder/J. Watson (10,068)
R. Hunter/R. Purcell (10,923)
R. Hunter/R. Purcell (10,924)
Irish School c.1750/C. Spooner (10,221)
J. Jackson/W. Ward the Elder (10,776)
C. Jervas/R. Purcell (10,011)
C. Jervas/J. Simon (10,682)
A. Kauffmann/J. Watson (10,392)
J. Kerseboom/A. Miller (10,256)
?G. Kneller/J. Simon (10,021)
G. Kneller/J. Simon (10,732)
G. Kneller/J. Smith (10,009)
G. Kneller/J. Smith (10,161)
G. Kneller/J. Smith (10,238)
G. Kneller/J. Smith (10,317)
G. Kneller/J. Smith (10,333)
G. Kneller/J. Smith (10,347)
G. Kneller/J. Smith (10,534)
G. Kneller/J. Smith (10,540)
G. Kneller/J. Smith (10,728)
G. Kneller/J. Smith (10,785)
T. Lawrence/J.R. Smith (10,058)
E. Lilly/*C. Boit*/J. Simon (10,371)
Markham/T. Burford (10,085)
Markham/T. Burford (11,021)
Markham/A. Van Haecken (10,142)
P. Mercier/J. Simon (10,535)
P. Mercier/J. Simon (10,536)
P. Mignard/P. Van Somer the Younger (10,321)
G. Morphey/J. Vandervaart (10,105)
J. Northcote/J. Ward (10,210)
M.W. Peters/J.R. Smith (10,348)
J. Ramsay/W. Say (10,455)
J. Ramsay/C. Turner (10,419)
J. Reynolds/J.R. Smith (10,380)
J. Reynolds/J.R. Smith (10,438)
J. Reynolds/J.R. Smith (10,472)
J. Reynolds/C. Spooner (10,337)
J. Reynolds/J. Ward (10,146)
J. Reynolds/J. Watson (10,345)
J. Reynolds/J. Watson (10,383)
G. Romney/C. Townley (10,539)
G. Romney/J. Walker (10,864)
J. Russell/J. Spilsbury (10,787)
J. Spilsbury/J. Spilsbury (10,851)
G. Soest/R. Purcell (10,053)
T. Stewardson/W. Ward the Elder (10,450)
J. Vandervaart/J. Vandervaart (10,132)
A. Van Dyck/J. Simon (10,248)
J. Van Nost the Younger/C. Spoone (10,013)
J. Van Nost the Younger/C. Spoone (10,101)
?R. Walker/English School 17C (11,394)
F.W. Weideman/J. Smith (11,184)
F.W. Weideman/J. Smith (11,185)
B. Wilson/B. Wilson (10,388)
W. Wissing/R. Williams (10,001)
W. Wissing/R. Williams (10,016)
J. Wright of Derby/J.R. Smith (10,406)

3rd Chaloner Smith Sale (Christie's), (P3-6 Feb, 1896)
H. Brocas the Elder/H. Brocas the Elder (11,159)
W. Brocas/W. Brocas (10,965)
W. Brocas/H. Meyer (10,658)
W. Brocas/H. Meyer (10,937)
G. Chalmers/J. McArdell (10,087)
R. Cosway/F. Bartolozzi (10,810)
?R. Cosway/J. Jones (11,388)
J. Downman/F. Bartolozzi (10,320)
English School 18C/J. McArdell (10,165)
English School late 18C/English School late 18C (11,114)
E. Jones/H. Brocas the Elder (11,301)
School of P. Lely/G. White (10,266)
T. Nugent/W. Annis (10,211)
C. O'Donnell/H. Brocas the Elder (10,964)
J. Opie/H. Brocas the Elder (11,223)
G.C. Stuart/W. Say (10,083)
G.C. Stuart/W. Say (10,478)
G.C. Stuart/W. Ward the Elder (11,033)
G.C. Stuart/W. Ward the Elder (10,268)

J.M. Caulfeild, 3rd Earl of Charlemont (G1873)
C. Moore (8067)

Mr R. Charles (G1973)
J. Connor (8232)

Sir Alfred Chester Beatty (G1953)
Attributed to E.A. Bourdelle (8093)
J. Epstein (8074)
M. Lambert (8064)
Roman Antique (8033)
T. Rosandic (8168)
S. Stoyanovitch (8167)

Mr A.G.F. Chittenden (G1898)
R. White/R. White (10,611)

Christie's (P1982)
J.H. Foley (8257)
J.H. Foley (8258)
G. Geefs (8259)
J. Heffernan (8264)

Christie's (Mr & Mrs R. Slazenger sale), (P1984)
L. MacDonald (8303)

City of Dublin Steam Packet Company (G1924)
W. Daniell/W. Daniell (11,860)

Mrs S. Clarke (G1980)
V.H. Lines/V.H. Lines (11,554)

Mr M. Clements (P1983)
T. Kirk (8267)
C. Moore (8265)
C. Moore (8266)

V. Lawless, 4th Baron Cloncurry (B1929)
Rembrandt/R. Earlom (10,171)

The Hon. F. Lawless, later 5th Baron Cloncurry (G1919)
M.W. Peters/J. Watson (10,459)

The Hon. F. Lawless. later 5th Baron Cloncurry (G1926)
J. Donoghue (8037)

F. Lawless, 5th Baron Cloncurry (P1929)
J.P. Hackert/G.A. Hackert (20,769)

The Misses Colles (G1890/98)
M. Cregan/D. Lucas (10,749)

Colnaghi's (P1938)
P. Troubetzkoy (8105)

Commissioners of Public Works (G1909)
Irish School c.1728/E. Bowen (11,889)
J. Kirkwood/J. Kirkwood (11,811)

Miss I.C. Conan (G1918)
W.H. Brooke/W.H. Brooke (20,808-20,812)

Mrs N. Connell (B1958)
See App. 1: E. Hone (12,069-70)

Major B.R. Cooper (G1927)
J.H. Foley (8045)

Mr M. Corr van der Maeren (G1864)
Italian School 16C/M.E. Corr (11,482)
F.J. Navez/M.E. Corr (11,483)

Mr W.T. Cosgrave (G1927)
G.F. Waters (8147)

Miss A.L. Cousins (P1901)
P. Cunningham (8026)

Mr Cox (P1874)
J. Thomas (8113)

Cranfield's (P1876)
J. Barrett/J. Watson (11,018)
H.D. Hamilton/Fittler (10,897)

Mr J. Culwick (G1901)
J. Fisher/J. Fisher (11,628)
J. Fisher/J. Fisher (11,639)

Alfred Daber (P1966)
A. Renoir (8011)

Alfred Daber (P1968)
G. Courbet (8050)

Mrs Daley (P1896)
T. Robinson/T. Robinson (10,043)

Mr W.V. Daniell (P1901)
?J. Comerford/J. Heath (10,818)
G. Dawe/T.A. Dean (10,894)
J. Hayter/W.H. Egleton (10,866)
R. Home/?Irish School 18C (10,931)
G. Kneller/A. Haelwegh (10,224)
T. Phillips/J. Brown (10,992)
F.P. Stephanoff/E. Scriven (11,404)
W. Taylor/W. Taylor (10,162)
(Mr W.V. Daniell (P1913)
J. Brownrigg/J. Ford (11,893)
Dutch School 1689/Dutch School c.1689 (11,819)
R.W. Seale/R.W. Seale (11,877)
T. Sherrard/Irish School 1803 (11,807)
S. Sproule/Irish School 1783 (11,818)

Mr J.F. D'Arcy (G1903)
S. Angelis (8289)

W. Dargan Committee for the NGI (G1863)
T. Farrell (8277)

Lady Deane (G1903)
J. Hughes (8097)

Hon. G. De Brún (G1978)
S. Murphy (8245)

Mr de Courcy Donovan (P1971)
T. Allom/J.C. Bentley (20,477)
T. Allom/S. Bradshaw (20,448)(1-2)
T. Allom/D. Buckle (20,419-20,420)
T. Allom/E. Challis (20,480)
T. Allom/T. Clark (20,279)
T. Allom/W.H. Kelsall (20,456-20,457)
T. Allom/S. Lacey (20,263)
T. Allom/W.A. Le petit (20,451-20,452)
T. Allom/J. Redaway (20,265-20,266)
T. Allom/R. Sands (20,398)
T. Allom/W. Tombleson (20,485)
T. Allom/H. Wallis (20,284-20,285)
T. Allom/E. Young (20,262)
F. Barocci/A. Sadeler (20,229)
F. Barocci/*P.W. Tomkins*/A. Cardon (20,156)
G. Barret the Younger/R. Wallis (20,276)
W.H. Bartlett/H. Adlard (20,435)
W.H. Bartlett/H. Adlard (20,440)
W.H. Bartlett/E. Benjamin (20,437)
W.H. Bartlett/E.P. Brandard (20,475)
W.H. Bartlett/E. Challis (20,434)
W.H. Bartlett/W.B. Cooke (20,417)
W.H. Bartlett/J. Cousen (20,438-20,439)
W.H. Bartlett/T. Higham (20,399)
W.H. Bartlett/G.K. Richardson (20,434)
W.H. Bartlett/G.K. Richardson (20,436)
W.H. Bartlett/J. Rogers (20,514)
W.H. Bartlett/W.F. Starling (20,453
W.H. Bartlett/J. Stephenson (20,455
W.H. Bartlett/D. Thompson (20,450
W.H. Bartlett/R. Wallis (20,425)
W.H. Bartlett/R. Wallis (20,441)
W.H. Bartlett & T. Creswick/J.T. Willmore (20,418)
J. Bell/*R. Roffe*/W. Roffe (20,209)
S. della Bella/S. della Bella (20,792-20,795)
J.C. Bentley/J.C. Bentley (20,415)
N. Berchem/English School 18C (20,135)
N. Berchem/English School 19C (20,146)
A. Biasoli/A. Biasoli (20,171)
Bolognese School 17C/Bolognese School 17C (20,228)

A. da Bonaiuto/English School 18C
20,120)
R.P. Bonington/W. Miller (20,484)
.C. Brand/J. Aliament (20,162)
I. Bright/W. Day & W.L. Haghe
20,222)
V. Brockedon/J. Sands (20,442)
. Calame/A. Calame (20,145)
. Calame/A. Calame (20,337)
. Calame/A. Calame (20,340)
. Calame/A. Calame
20,342-20,343)
. Calame/A. Calame
20,469-20,470)
. Calame/A. Calame (20,487)
. Calame/A. Calame
20,489-20,491)
. Calame/A. Calame (20,494)
. Calame/A. Calame
20,496-20,500)
. Calame/A. Calame
20,505-20,508)
. Calame/A. Calame (20,521)
. Calame & F.F.A. Ferogio/A.
alame & F.F.A. Ferogio (20,341)
. Calame & F.F.A. Ferogio/A.
alame & F.F.A. Ferogio (20,462)
A. Calame & F.F.A. Ferogio/A.
alame & F.F.A. Ferogio (20,488)
analetto/J.C. Bromley (20,333)
analetto/P. Chevalier (20,390)
. Carocci/G. Carocci (20,387)
. Carocci/G. Carocci (20,392)
A. Carracci/English School 19C
20,268)
G. Castellini/G. Castellini (20,393)
G. Cattermole/A.H. Payne (20,412)
G. Cattermole/J.C. Bentley (20,444)
G. Cattermole/E. Smith (20,152)
G. Chambers/R. Brandard (20,283)
F. Chauveau/F. Chauveau (20,215)
G. Childs/G. Childs (20,167)
G. Childs/G. Childs (20,375)
Claude Lorrain/T.B. Allen (20,245)
Claude Lorrain/English School 1827
(20,242)
Claude Lorrain/English School 1827
(20,427)
W. Collins/W. Collins (20,330)
W. Collins/J. Outrim (20,260)
W. Collins/E.F. Finden (20,383)
J. Comerford/A. Cardon (20,307)
T.S. Cooper/T.S. Cooper (20,165)
T.S. Cooper/T.S. Cooper
(20,169-20,170)
T.S. Cooper/T.S. Cooper (20,174)
T.S. Cooper/T.S. Cooper (20,243)
T.S. Cooper/T.S. Cooper (20,345)
T.S. Cooper/T.S. Cooper (20,402)
A.V.D. Copley-Fielding/G. Cooke
(20,373)

A.V.D. Copley-Fielding/W.J. Cooke
(20,517)
?Correggio/S.W. Reynolds the
Younger (20,137)
G. Corsi/G. Corsi (20,388)
D. Cox/R. Brandard (20,426)
D. Cox/W.J. Cooke (20,385)
D. Cox/J. Needham (20,338)
T. Creswick/S. Bradshaw (20,502)
T. Creswick/R. Hill (20,503)
T. Creswick/S. Lacey (20,518)
T. Creswick/R. Wallis (20,504)
T. Creswick/R. Wallis (20,513)
A. Cuyp/J.C. Bentley (20,161)
A. Cuyp/*W. Westall*/T. Medland &
J. Bailey (20,324)
E. Dayes/S. Noble (20,430)
E. Dayes/J.C. Smith (20,411)
A.G. Decamps/A.G. Decamps
(20,332)
S. della Bella/S. della Bella (20,233)
P. De Wint/E.F. Finden (20,520)
P. De Wint/W. Floyd (20,493)
P. De Wint/J.H. Kernot (20,382)
J.R. Dicksee/J.R. Dicksee (20,111)
C.W.E. Dietrich/J.-B. Fosseyeux
(20,158)
G. Dou/English School 19C (20,159)
A. Drulin/A. Drulin (20,401)
E. Edwards/J. Newton (20,216)
R.J. Elliot/*S. Austin*/W. Le Petit
(20,356)
English School 18C/C. Taylor
(20,202-20,203)
English School 19C/English School
19C (20,144)
English School 19C/English School
19C (20,163)
English School 19C/English School
19C (20,197)
English School 19C/English School
19C (20,220)
English School 19C/English School
19C (20,320-20,321)
English School 19C/English School
19C (20,349)
English School 19C/English School
19C (20,363-20,364)
English School 19C/English School
19C (20,416)
English School 19C/English School
19c (20,515-20,516)
English School c.1835/English School
c.1835 (20,325)
Engraved book (20,247)
Engraved book (20,248)
Engraved book (20,264)
W. Evans/C. Fox (20,153)
T. Fairland/T. Fairland (20,352)
F.F.A. Ferogio/F.F.A. Ferogio
(20,147-20,148)

F.F.A. Ferogio/F.F.A. Ferogio
(20,308-20,314)
J.H. Foley/*F.R. Roffe*/W. Roffe
(20,210)
T. Foster/W.J. Ward the Elder
(20,126)
H. Fragonard/English School 1827
(20,205)
French School 17C/French School
17C (20,117)
French School 1634/French School
1634 (20,235)
French School 18C/French School
18C (20,359)
T. Gainsborough/W. Radclyffe
(20,206)
T. Gainsborough/W. Taylor (20,267)
H. Gastineau/S. Lacey (20,476)
H. Gastineau/W. Wallis
(20,403-20,404)
L. Gluckman/Irish School 1885
(20,217)
U. Gréthier/H. Raunheim (20,176)
J.D. Harding/E. Goodall (20,381)
J.D. Harding/J.D. Harding
(20,182-20,196)
J.D. Harding/J.D. Harding
(20,224-20,226)
J.D. Harding/J.D. Harding (20,249)
J.D. Harding/J.D. Harding (20,259)
J.D. Harding/J.D. Harding
(20,273-20,275)
J.D. Harding/J.D. Harding
(20,296-20,307)
J.D. Harding/J.D. Harding (20,355)
J.D. Harding/J.D. Harding (20,358)
J.D. Harding/J.D. Harding (20,361)
J.D. Harding/J.D. Harding (20,370)
J.D. Harding/J.D. Harding (20,391)
J.D. Harding/J.D. Harding
(20,405-20,406)
J.D. Harding/J.D. Harding
(20,407)(1-2)
J.D. Harding/J.D. Harding
(20,409-20,410)
J.D. Harding/J.D. Harding
(20,428)
J.D. Harding/J.D. harding
(20,446)(1-2)
J.D. Harding/J.D. Harding
(20,463)(1-3)
G.H. Harlow/H. Meyer (20,122)
T. Hearne/B.T. Pouncy (20,389)
J. Henderson/W. Finden (20,367)
G.E. Hicks/G.E. Hicks (20,181)
D.O. Hill/W. Forrest (20,461)
D.O. Hill/T. Jeavons (20,460)
D.O. Hill/W. Richardson (20,282)
R. Hills/B.P. Gibbon (20,362)
T. Hills/E. Tyrrell (20,212)
W.I. Hocker/T. Higham (20,479)

G.A. Williams/G. Augustus (20,501)
T. Woodward/W.R. Smith & J.H. Robinson (20,331)
T. Worlidge/C.W. White (20,119)

Mr A. Denson (P1966)
J. Connor (8012)

Dillon & Co., (P1901)
S. Catterson Smith the Elder/Irish School c.1830 (10,977)
J. Comerford/T. Heaphy (10,065)
N. Dance/F. Bartolozzi (10,819)
Irish School c.1813/English School c.1823 (10,600)
E.H. Latilla/H.B. Hall the Elder (10,967)
J. Lewis/J. Lewis (10,978)
?B. Mulrenin/B. Mulrenin (10,971)
J. Stewart/H. Robinson (10,979)
J. Wood/J. Brown (10,840)

Mr H. Doyle (G date unknown)
L.C. & W. Wyon (8278)

Mr H. Doyle (G1873)
J. Doyle/J. Doyle (10,035)

Mr H. Doyle (G1889)
Irish School 1840s/Irish School 1840s (10,974)
G. Kneller/P. Vanderbanck (10,565)
?V. Kriehuber/V. Kriehuber (10,938)
J.G. Mansfield/J.G. Mansfield (11,103)

Mr F.W. Doyle-Jones (P1924)
F.W. Doyle-Jones (8001)

Dublin Library (P1882)
P. Turnerelli (8107)

Harriet, Marchioness of Dufferin (G1902)
F. Holl/D. Wehrschmidt (11,855)

Miss Duffy (G1904)
M. De Carnowsky (8285)

Sir Charles Gavan Duffy (G1903)
F.W. Burton/J. Templeton (10,786)
L. Gluckman/H. O'Neill (10,179)

Mr C. Dupechez (G1931)
C. Dupechez/C. Dupechez (10,889)

Durlacher Bros. (P1902)
After W. Larson (8095)

Mr F. Elrington Ball (G1909)
J.P. Haverty/J.P. Haverty (11,695)

Mr J. Elrington Ball (G1903)
T. Foster/W.J. Ward the Younger (10,249)

English Property Corporation Ltd. (G1974)
S.F. Lynn (8235)
S.F. Lynn (8236)

Mr T. Farrell (P1907)
T. Farrell (8133)

Mr Fausset (G1908)
A. Munro (8116)

Fine Art Society Ltd. (P1980)
E. Foley (8249)

Lord Frederick FitzGerald (G1899)
J. Reynolds/R. Josey (10,903)

Forli Municipality (G1939)
P. Morbiducci (8170)

Mrs Fox Pym (P1949)
A. Power (8090)

Signor U. Franchini (G1978)
U. Franchini/U. Franchini (11,929)
U. Franchini/U. Franchini (20,823-20,825)

Friends of the National Collections of Ireland (G1940)
H. Matisse/H. Matisse (20,839)

Mr J.F. Fuller (G1914)
Irish School c.1752/Irish School 1752 (20,831)
Irish School c.1753/Irish School 1753 (11,667)

Mrs B. Ganly (G1978)
Engraved book (20,693)

Mrs Gibbons (G1913)
C. Moore (8059)

Sir John T. Gilbert (G1891)
Lady M. Bingham/J.B. Tilliard (10,093)

Gombridge's (P1914)
A. Lee/A. Miller (10,076)

Mr A.B. Goor (G1968)
J. Watkins (8153)

Miss S. Gorry (B1917)
R. Barter (8086)

The Government (G1963)
P. Grant (8009)
O. Kelly (8008)
S. Murphy (8006)
D. O Murchadha (8004)
A. Power (8005)
A. Power (8007)
A. Power (8120)
A. Power (8290)
O. Sheppard (8104)

Governors and Guardians of the NGI (C1955)
A. Weckbecker (8282)

Governors and Guardians of the NGI (C1958)
O. Sheppard (8136-8137)

Governors and Guardians of the NGI (C1968)
A. Power (8048)

Governors and Guardians of the NGI (C1973)
J. Connor (8233)

Governors and Guardians of the NGI (C1977)
J. Hogan (8244)

Governors and Guardians of the NGI (C1983)
O. Kelly (8262)
D. MacNamara (8268)

Governors and Guardians of the NGI (C1984)
A. Stones (8305)

Dr W.H. Grattan Flood (P1920)
Continental School early 19C/C. Mayer (10,045)

H. Graves & Co. (P1886)
F. Grant/S. Cousins (10,485)

Mr C. Gregory (P1905)
T.S. Roberts/R. Havell the Elder & Younger (11,912)
(Mr E. Guntrip (P1930)
T. Frye/T. Frye (10,552)

Arthur H. Hanlo & Co. (P1919)
J.S. Sargent/T. Cole (11,412)

Miss S.C. Harrison (G1904)
A. Legros/A. Legros (11,473-11,479)

Hartley Fine Arts (P1982)
T. Kirk (8260)

Mr J. Healy (G1931)
C. Moore (8066)

Heim (P1966)
Roman School c.1620 (8014)
J.M. Rysbrack (8015)

Heim (P1967)
Attributed to A. Brustolon (8028-8029)
F. Dietz (8081)
F. Duquesnoy (8030)
Attributed to B. Prieur (8036)
Attributed to J.A. Villabrille-y-Ron (8031)

Heim (P1968)
L. Gahagan (8058)
Workshop of L. Ghiberti (8049)
Venetian School 16C (8055)

Heim (P1969)
C. Hewetson (8063)

Heim (P1971)
J. Lawlor (8083)

Mrs Hepburn (G1918)
L. Gluckman/J.H. Lynch (11,430)
J. Keenan/W.F. Fay (10,950)
J. Steel/W. Ridley & W. Holl the Elder & T. Blood (11,286)

Hibernian Antiques (P1971)
T. Kirk (8096)

Mrs C. Hone (G1925)
N. Hone the Elder/J. Finlayson (10,933)
N. Hone the Elder/J.R. Smith (11,414)
N. Hone the Elder/J. Watson (11,387)
(Miss E. Hone (B1912)
S. Cooper/English School 1806 (11,050)
J. Doyle/J. Doyle (11,158)
I. Gosset/N. Hone the Younger (10,879)
H. Hone/F. Bartolozzi (10,309-10,310)
H. Hone/H. Meyer (10,833)
H. Hone/M. Meyer (11,133)
H. Hone/T. Nugent (11,127)
H. Hone/R. Purcell (11,322)
H. Hone/B. Smith (10,745)
H. Hone & A. B..../G.F. Philips & T. Levens (10,308)
N. Hone the Elder/W. Baillie (10,532)
N. Hone the Elder/W. Baillie (10,942)
N. Hone the Elder/W. Baillie (10,944-10,945)
N. Hone the Elder/G. Cook (11,377)
N. Hone the Elder/W. Dickinson (11,002)
N. Hone the Elder/English School 18C (11,256)
N. Hone the Elder/J. Finlayson (10,353)
N. Hone the Elder/J. Finlayson (11,386)
N. Hone the Elder/E. Fisher (10,698)
N. Hone the Elder/R. Graves (11,277)
N. Hone the Elder/J. Greenwood (10,329)
N. Hone the Elder/J. Greenwood (10,680)
N. Hone the Elder/J. Greenwood (11,408)
N. Hone the Elder/N. Hone the Elder (11,276)
N. Hone the Elder/N. Hone the Elder (11,848)
N. Hone the Elder/J. McArdell (10,755)
N. Hone the Elder/J. McArdell (10,804)
N. Hone the Elder/C. Phillips (10,378)
N. Hone the Elder/V.M. Picot (11,257)
N. Hone the Elder/R. Pollard (11,777)
N. Hone the Elder/J.R. Smith (10,697)
N. Hone the Elder/J.R. Smith (10,805)
N. Hone the Elder/J.R. Smith (11,012)
N. Hone the Elder/J. Watson (10,139)
N. Hone the Elder/J. Watson (10,700)
I. Oliver/French School c.1600 (10,311)
Rembrandt/A. Walker (11,506)

Cyril Humphris (P1969)
Florentine School late 16C (8062)

Cyril Humphris (P1970)
P. Turnerelli (8078)

Cyril Humphris (G1970)
L. Gahagan (8068)

Mr J. Hunt (B1977)
Flemish School 17C (8331)
French School 16C (8330)
French School 17C (8332)
French or German School c.1600 (8329)
German School 17C (8327)
Attributed to J. Sansovino (8326)
Spanish School 1600/1650 (8328)
Spanish or Italian School c.1300 (8324)

Mr E.T. Hurley (G1935)
E.T. Hurley/E.T. Hurley (11,013-11,017)

Miss M.B. Hutton (P1954)
C. Moore (8060)

Mrs M.B. Hutton (G date unknown)
C. Andras (8080)

Mr H. Johnston (G1879/90)
W. Evans/C. Picart (10,707)
T.C. Thompson/H. Meyer (10,126)

Jones Saleroom (presumed P1879)
F. Bindon/J. Martyn (10,279)
J. Closterman/J. Smith (10,229)
T. Hardy/T. Hardy (10,103)
Irish School 1806/14/*J.B. Lane*/S. Freeman (10,151)
G. Kneller/J. Smith (10,010)
J.P. Knight/T.G. Lupton (10,243)
T. Lawrence/S. Cousins (10,722)
T. Lawrence/C. Turner (10,458)
J. Reynolds/J. Hall (10,460)
J. Reynolds/J.F.L. Marchi (10,028)
J. Reynolds/J. Watson (10,254)
J. Reynolds/J. Watson (10,424)
J. Richardson the Elder/J. Smith (10,030)
M.A. Shee/C. Turner (10,487)
W. Stevenson/D. Lucas (10,411)
F. Wheatley/V. Green (10,130)
I. Woods/J. Faber the Younger (10,029)

Captain Kelly (G1910)
J. Carré (8106)

Gerald Kelly (P1966)
M. Stapleton (8016-8023)

O. Kelly family (G1982)
O. Kelly (8263)

Mr J.H. Kilgour (P1910)
T. Rowbotham/D. Havell (11,647-11,648)

Miss R.S.R. Kirkpatrick (B1979)
A. Gleizes/A. Gleizes (11,566)
A. Gleizes/A. Gleizes (20,813)
K. Van Dongen/French School 20C (11,565)
see App. 1: E. Hone (12,065-67)

Mrs G. Lane (G1919)
P. Gethin/P. Gethin (11,869)

Sir Hugh Lane (B1918)
A.L. Barye (8162-8163)
J.-B.S. Chardin/B.F. Lepicié the Elder (10,172)
A.J. Dalou (8056)
A.J. Dalou (8069)
A. Maillol (8094)
A. Maillol (8270)
A. Maillol (8271)
A. Rodin (8039)
A. Rodin (8072)
A. Rodin (8073)
A.G. Stevens (8075)
A.G. Stevens (8076)

Mr R. Langton Douglas (P1906)
S. Catterson Smith the Elder/G. Sanders (10,690)
H.D. Hamilton/W. Ward the Elder (10,050)
R. Philips/J. Simon (10,694)
J. Reynolds/J. Grozer (10,253)
T.C. Thompson/D. Lucas (10,725)

Miss Latterman (G1909)
O. Sheppard (8159)

Mr G. Lausen (P1895)
S. Catterson Smith the Elder/J. Jackson (10,441)
S. Catterson Smith the Elder/G. Sanders (10,456)
S. Catterson Smith the Elder/G. Sanders (10,506)
M. Cregan/C. Turner (11,032)
W. Cuming/J.R. Smith (10,192)
D. Dodd/G. Sibelius (11,058)
?G. Dou/N. Grogan (10,788)
English or Irish 18C/J. Brooks (10,187)
M. Gheeraerts the Younger/R. Van Voerst (10,191)
R. Hodgetts/R. Hodgetts (10,968)
J. Hoppner/C. Turner (10,164)
?Irish 18C/?J. Dixon (10,014)
P. Lely/P. Vanderbanck (11,418)
M. Maingaud/J. Houbraken (10,987)
M.W. Peters/*J.D. Herbert*/S. Reynolds (10,466)
M. Shee/G. Clint (10,489)
G.C. Stuart/C.H. Hodges (10,247)

The Hon. F. Lawless - see 5th Baron Cloncurry

Mr B. Le Fanu (G1914)
Irish School 1873 (8275)

C.W. FitzGerald, 4th Duke of Leinster (G1878)
F.M. Poncet (8135)

M. FitzGerald, 7th Duke of Leinster (G1913)
J. Rocque/English School 1762 (11,880)
J. Rocque/J. Perret (11,886)

Sir James Linton (P1908)
J. Malton/J. Malton (11,634)

Miss E. Lloyd (B1891)
T. Kirk (8043)

Mr E.M. Lloyd (B1952)
A. Claudet/English School 1846 (10,582)

Mr T.H. Longfield (G1898)
M. Marieschi/M. Marieschi (11,622)

Mr T.H. Longfield (G1903)
?P. Lely/P. Lombart (10,069)

Mr J.V. McAlpine (P1896)
L. Abbott/A. Cardon (11,117)
J. Comerford/R. Cooper (11,313)
J. Comerford/R. Cooper (11,314)
A. De St Aubyn/A. Cardon (11,167)
H.D. Hamilton/C. Knight (10,082)
J. Haslock/J. Rogers (10,704)
J. Hoppner/C. Turner (10,812)
J. Mee/H. Cook (11,119)
J. Reynolds/C. Knight (10,662)
J. Reynolds/C. Knight (10,663)

Mr J.V. McAlpine (P1897)
T. Hudson/J. McArdell (10,168)

Mr J.V. McAlpine (P1898)
F.W. Burton/G. Sanders (10,815)
English School 19C/W. Read (10,583)
H.D. Hamilton/F. Bartolozzi (10,861)
H.D. Hamilton/F. Bartolozzi (10,862)
Irish School 1830s/W. Read (10,989)
C. Jervas/P. Foudrinier (10,019)
A. Wivell the Elder/W. Read (10,583)

Mr J.V. McAlpine (P1899)
F.W. Burton/J.H. Lynch (11,076)
S. Catterson Smith the Elder/G. Sanders (10,510)
J.B. Closterman/J. Smith (10,930)
Continental School 17C/*S. Harding*/W.N. Gardiner (10,614)
M. Dahl/J. Faber the Younger (10,125)
English School 15C/*J. Carter*/J. Basire the Elder (10,766)
Circle of M. Gheeraerts the Younger/English School 1803 (10,750)
L. Gluckman/J.H. Lynch (10,990)
J. Hickey/J. Ward (10,435)
A. Hope/J. Godby (10,062)
J. Jackson/W.T. Fry (10,260)
G. Kneller/J. Houbraken (10,212)
G. Kneller/J. Smith (10,002)
G. Kneller/J. Smith (10,904)
T. Lawrence/W. Giller (10,154)
T. Lawrence/C. Picart (10,185)
H. Raeburn/*J. Jackson*/H. Meyer (10,883)
E. Scott/C. Knight (11,051)
M.A. Shee/W. Ward the Elder (10,100)
R. Stewart/E. Scott (11,038)
R. Walker/J. Houbraken (10,839)

Mr J.V. McAlpine (G1901)
E. Hayes/S. Bellin (10,870)
Irish School c.1779/Irish School c.1800 (11,627)
J.J. Jenkins/T. Williamson (11,248)
B. Mulrenin/B. Mulrenin (11,233)
R. Omer/P. Mazell (11,600)
J. Tudor/English 1749 (11,614)
J. Tudor/?J. McArdell (11,906)

Mr J.V. McAlpine (P1901)
S.F. Brocas/H. Brocas the Younger (11,944)
Lady Burghersh/T. Hodgetts (10,399)
G. Chalmers/R. Purcell (10,163)
L. Gluckman/H. O'Neill (10,064)
J.P. Haverty/J.P. Haverty (10,794)
W. Hoare/A. Miller (10,186)
T. Hudson/J. Faber the Younger (10,709)
G. Kneller/J. Faber the Younger (10,160)
J. Parmentier/J. Faber the Younger (10,269)
J. Reynolds/J. Jones (10,946)
T. Lawrence/H. Bond (10,368)
T.C. Thompson/S.W. Reynolds the Elder (10,491)
J. Worsdale/J. Simon (10,215)

Mr J. V. McAlpine (P1903)
G.B. Black/G.B. Black (10,734)
English School 1840/English School 1840 (11,040)
L. Gluckman/H. O'Neill (10,722)
H. O'Neill/C. Turner (10,061)

Mr J. V. McAlpine (P1904)
W. Brocas/R. Havell the Elder & Younger (11,638)
L. Bushe/J. Brown (11,111)
T. Cahill/Irish School c.1827 (10,875)
M. Cregan/G.R. Ward (10,449)
G. Dawe/T.A. Dean (10,895)
English School c.1580/*G.P. Harding*/W. Greatbach (11,052)
English School 17C/G. White (11,089)
English School c.1645/G. Glover (10,281)
?G. Gower/J. Basire (10,741)
F. Grant/G.J. Zobel (11,043)
T. Lawrence/C. Turner (10,107)
A. Lee/J. Brooks (10,228)
H. Newton/Maclure & MacDonald (10,970)
J. Petrie/J. Petrie (10,156)
T.S. Roberts/R. Havell the Elder & Younger (11,909)
R. Rothwell/C. Turner (10,554)
P. Van Somer/*G.P. Harding*/J. Brown (10,807)
B. Wilson/B. Wilson (10,128)

Mr J. V. McAlpine (P1905)
Irish School 19C/Irish School 19C (11,867)
F. Newenham/F.C. Lewis (10,928)
T. Lawrence/C. Turner (10,724)
W. Owen/S.W. Reynolds (10,461)
G.C. Stuart/J.Collyer (10,118)

Mr J. V. McAlpine (P1906)
R. Cosway/P. Condé (10,137)
F. Cotes/?R. Purcell (10,829)
W. Cuming/C. Turner (10,547)
English School 17C/G. Vertue (10,124)
English School 1653/English School 1804 (10,278)
English School c.1819/English School 1819 (10,098)
T. Gainsborough/J. McArdell (10,216)
C. Grey/Irish School 1852 (10,461)
Irish School 18C/J. Hall (11,195)
Irish School late 18C/P. Maguire (11,221)
G. Kneller/J. Faber the Younger (10,721)
G. Kneller/J. Smith (10,218)
J.C. Lochee/J. Corner (11,224)
D. Loggan/E. Sandys (10,285)
?H.J. Mierevelt/*W. Derby*/E. Scriven (10,782)
W. Owen/*J. Wright*/H. Meyer (10,751)
J. Pope-Stevens/J. Brooks (10,115)
J. Reynolds/J. Dean (10,090)
Countess Spencer/F. Bartolozzi (10,352)

Mr J. V. McAlpine (P1909)
J.J. Barralet/J.C. Stadler (11,643)
A.S. Belle/English School 18C (10,607)
T. Bewick/*J. Thurston*/W.H. Worthington (10,763)
Q. Boel/Q. Boel (10,276)
G. Dance/W. Daniell (10,049)
W. Derby/J. Mollison (10,764)
?English School 16C/A. B.... (10,046)
English School 17C/W. Faithorne the Elder (11,275)
English School late 17C/J. Nutting (11,101)
English School 1819/English School 1819 (10,098)
H.F. Gravelot/J. Hulett (10,181)
J. Highmore/J. Emlyn (11,168)
R. Home/W. Evans (11,085)
R. Home/W. Ridley (11,084)
Irish School c.1700/W. Sherwin (10,301)
Irish School c.1750/R. Graves (11,154)
Irish School c.1800/Irish School 1816 (11,231)
C. Jagger/S. Sangster (10,868)
C. Jervas/*J. Thurston*/A. Warren (11,285)
A. Lee/J. Chapman (10,910)
S. Lover/R. Cooper (10,959)
J. Nixon/E. Harding (10,576)
C. Peale/E. Mackenzie (10,674)
A. Pope/English School 1807 (11,209)
T. Rowlandson/J. hopwood the Younger (10,586)
A. Russell/S. Gribelin (10,047)

Mr J. V. McAlpine (P1910)
A. Kauffmann/?T. Burke (10,209)

Mr J. V. McAlpine (P1911)
W. Collier/H. O'Neill (10,789)
J. Herbert/H. Brocas the Elder (10,291)
Irish School 1853/Irish School 1853 (11,630)
G. Kneller/G. Vertue (10,799)
J. Linnell/J. Linnell (11,044)
H.W. Pickersgill/H. Cousins (10,79
J. Reynolds/R. Parkes (10,720)
C. Robertson/C. Picart (10,800)

Mr J. V. McAlpine (P1913)
W. Bewnes/F.C. Lewis (10,566)
T. Brigford/H. Griffiths (11,310)
T. Brigford/H. Griffiths (11,312)
R. Buckner/G.J. Zobel (10,722)
G. Chinnery/Irish School 1804 (11,246)
English School 19C/H. Griffiths (11,306-11,307)
C. Grey/H. Griffiths (11,311)
C. Grey/Irish School 1851 (10,666)
C. Grey/Irish School 1851 (11,099)
C. Grey/Irish School 1852 (11,271)
C. Grey/J. Kirkwood (11,082)
C. Grey/J. Kirkwood (11,090
C. Grey/J. Kirkwood (11,104)
C. Grey/J. Kirkwood (11,292)
S. Harding/C. Knight (10,920)
Irish School 18C/H. Brocas the Elde (11,160)
Irish School c.1850/Irish School 185 (11,378)
J. Latham/J. Faber the Younger (10,240)
S. Lawrence/H. Griffiths (11,334)
J. Lewis/Irish School 1852 (11,108)
R. McInnes/J. Brown (10,887)
H. McManus/J. Kirkwood (11,302)
W. Newton/J. Posselwhite (10,886)
J. Petrie & Irish School c.1803/Irish School c.1803 (11,352)
J. Rocque/A. Drury & P. Halpin (11,806)
R. Sayers/G. Payne (10,705)
Titani/S. Freeman (11,010)

Mr J. V. McAlpine (P1914)
J. Tudor/A. Walker (11,903)

Mr J. V. McAlpine (P1919)
G. Kneller/J. Faber the Younger (10,845)

Colonel McClintock (G1927)
J. Thomas/Army Litho School 20C (11,809)
J. Thomas/Army Litho School 20C (11,841)

Mr McDonnell (G1888)
T.H. Carrick/W. Holl the Younger (10,289)
T.H. Carrick/W. Holl the Younger (10,597)

Dr E. MacDowel Cosgrave (G1905)
J. Tudor/J. McArdell (10,008)

Dr E. MacDowel Cosgrave G1907)
W.H. Bartlett/R. Winkles (11,771)
F. Byrne/W. Radclyffe the Elder (11,609)
F. Byrne/W. Smith (11,608)
T. Cocking/T. Medland (11,927)
Irish School early 18C/Irish School early 18C (11,833)
Irish School c.1755/B. Cole (11,768)
Irish School 1783/Irish School 1783 (11,870)
Irish School late 18C/Myers (11,754)
Irish School c.1820/Irish School c.1820 (11,736)
Irish School 1853/Irish School 1853 (11,722)
J. Kirkwood/J. Kirkwood (11,701)
H. Moll/H. Moll (11,666)
R. O'C. Newenham/J.D. Harding (11,610)
R. O'C. Newenham/J.D. Harding (11,611)
R. Omer/Irish School 1767 (11,883)
G. Petrie/T. Barber (11,777-11,779)
G. Petrie/T. Barber (11,790-11,792)
G. Petrie/English School 1821 (11,773)
G. Petrie/English School 1821 (11,780-11,781)
G. Petrie/English School 1821 (11,783-11,784)
G. Petrie/English School 1821 (11,789)
G. Petrie/E. Goodall (11,774)
G. Petrie/E. Goodall (11,787)
G. Petrie/E. Goodall (11,794)
G. Petrie/T. Higham (11,700)
G. Petrie/T. Higham (11,775)
G. Petrie/T. Higham (11,793)
G. Petrie/J. Storer & H. Sargent (11,788)
G. Petrie/B. Winkles (11,776)
G. Petrie/B. Winkles (11,782)
G. Petrie/B. Winkles (11,785-11,786)
J. Tudor/F. Cary (11,716)
F. Wheatley/T. Milton (11,594)
F. Wheatley/T. Milton (11,683-11,684)

Mr H.P. McIlhenny (G1981)
Irish School c.1785 (8256)
J. Van Nost the Younger (8255)

Mr E.J. McKean (G1918)
R. Carpenter/T. Bury (11,772)
?Irish School 18C/Barclay (11,680)

Dr J. Mackey (G1969)
J. Hogan (8061)

Mrs E. McLoghlin (G1921)
A. Gilbert (8077)

Mr H. McManus (G1877)
G.C. Stuart/C.H. Hodges (10,217)

McMullan & Co. (P1930)
C. Moore (8108)

Mr J. McGlade (P1964)
J. Fisher/J. Fisher (11,549)

Miss M.A. McNeill (B1985)
English School 1692/J. Goldar (20,836)
J. Miers/J. Miers (20,668)
Attributed to S. Percy (8322)
J. Tassie (8320-8321)

Maggs Bros. (P1904)
H.D. Hamilton/J.K. Sherwin (10,896)
J. Reynolds/J. McArdell (11,056)

Maggs Bros. (P1905)
English School 18C/English School 18C (10,272)
J. Lonsdale/C. Turner (10,170)
S.W. Reynolds/S.W. Reynolds & S. Cousins (10,888)
T.C. Thompson/C. Turner (10,842)

Dr W.J. Maloney (G1938)
J. Pennell/J. Pennell (11,458)

Mr T. Mansfield (P1956)
A. Watteau/C. Dupois (11,845)

Mr L. Marks (P1898)
S.F. Brocas/H. Brocas the Younger (11,945-11,949)
S.F. Brocas/H. Brocas the Younger (11,952-11,956)
Irish School late 18C/English School 1799 (11,839)
T.S. Roberts/R. Havell the Elder & Younger (11,910)

Mr L. Marks (P1904)
S.F. Brocas/H. Brocas the Younger (11,953)

Mr L. Marks (P1911)
W. Taylor/R. Bluck (11,621)
W. Taylor/R. Havell the Elder & Younger (11,622)

Lady Martin (B1907)
J.H. Foley (8191)

Mrs J. Martin (G1907)
L. Gluckman/M. & N. Hanhart (10,119)

Mrs W.M. Martin (G1906)
L. Gluckman/H. O'Neill (10,526)

Mr E. Martyn (B1924)
A.G.G. D'Orsay/A.G.G. D'Orsay (11,410)

Mr Justice Mathew (G1903)
S. West/W. Geller (10,451)

Mrs E.C. May (G1905)
English School c.1877/M. & N. Hanhart (10,429)

Rev. C.P. Meehan (G1884)
C. Maratta/C. Valet (10,144)

Mr L. Meier (P1950)
English School 19C/English School 19C (11,407)

Mrs M.R. Middleton (G1892)
J. Thomas (8184)

Mr Miller (P1893)
J. Doyle/J. Doyle (11,403)
J. Doyle/J. Doyle (11,852-11,854)
J. Doyle/J. Doyle (11,891)

Mr R. Miller (P1896)
Irish School 19C (8101)
C. Moore (8298)
T.C. Thompson/C. Turner (10,848)

Milltown Gift (G1902)
After A. Canova (8103)
B. Cavaceppi (8242-8243)
English School 19C (8225)
French School 19C (8102)
Italian School 18C (8212-8213)
Italian School late 18C (8115)
J. Moyse (8281)
G.B. Piamontini (8210-8211)
Roman Antique (8276)
Roman Antique (8279)
Roman Antique (8287)
Roman School 18C (8288)
Roman School 18C (8295)
Roman School 18C (8299)

Mrs D. Molloy (G1981)

G.B. Piranesi/G.B. Piranesi (20,526-20,528)
G.B. Piranesi/G.B. Piranesi (20,530-20,534)
N. Poussin/F. Ertinger (20,545)
S. Prout/S. Prout (20,559-20,565)
S. Prout/S. Prout (20,567)
L.L. Razé/L.L. Razé (20,566)
L.L. Razé/L.L. Razé (20,569)
L.L. Razé/L.L. Razé (20,588)
Roman Antique/English School 19C (20,557)
Roman Antique/English School early 19C (20,654)
S. Rosa/English School 18C (20,551)
P.P. Rubens/English School 19C (20,634)
D. Stoop/G. Cooke (20,540)
?Swiss School 19C??Swiss School 19C (20,648)
M. Thurwanger/M. Thurwanger (20,602-20,603)
A.C. Tisdall/Irish School 19C (20,625)
A.C. Tisdall/A.C. Tisdall (20,623-20,624)
J.M.W. Turner/J.T. Willmore (20,599)
C. White/J. Linton (20,626)
R. Wilson/J.C. Varrall (20,552)

Mr K. Monaghan (P1967)
J.H. Foley (8042)

F.S. Rice, 4th Baron Monteagle (G1935)
L. MacDonald (8203)
P. Turnerelli (8228)

Mr A. Montgomery (G1889)
F. Chantrey (8151)

Mrs T.G. Moorehead (G1960)
Irish School c.1795/Irish School c.1795 (10,229)
?G. Morphey/?R. Laurie (10,201)

Dr T. Moore Madden (G1901)
C. Byrne/T.W. Huffam (10,647)
A.F.J. Claudet/T.W. Huffam (10,660)
J. Petrie/English School 1846 (11,164)
C.S. Tone/English School 1846 (11,298)

Mr W. Morrissey (P1955)
J. Lawlor (8150)

Mr J. Mulhall (G1907)
J.K. Sherwin/J.K. Sherwin (11,827-11,828)

Mr G.F. Mulvany (G1867)
Engraved book (20,733)

Mr G.F. Mulvany (G1868)
Engraved books (20,726; 20,727)

Judge J. Murnaghan (B1976)
Engraved books (20,665-20,667; 20,673-20,675; 20,681; 20,686; 20,690-20,691; 20,704-20,705; 20,708; 20,711; 20,718-20,719; 20,721; 20,723-20,725; 20,731-20,732)

Mr S. Murphy (P1970)
S. Murphy (8082)

Mrs M. Murphy (G1976)
J. Higgins (8240)

Mr J.C. Nairn (P1900)
Continental School 17C/C. Turner (10,869)
W. Robinson/W. Brett & S. Cousins (10,841)

National Library of Ireland (T1968)
Irish School 1933 (8129)

National Museum of Ireland (T1967)
M. Bayser-Gratry (8025)
Roman School 19C (8296)

National Museum of Ireland (T1968)
S. Percy (8057)

Mr G. Natorp (G1896)
G. Natorp (8084)

Mr H. Naylor (P1905)
S. Catterson Smith the Elder/G. Sanders (10,468)

Mr H. Naylor (P1909)
Irish School 18C/?E. Lyons (10,232)
Irish School c.1780/Irish School c.1780 (11,612)
Irish School 1787/Irish School 1787 (11,613)

Mr H. Naylor (P1933)
Irish School 1784/English School 1784 (11,895-11,901)

The Neptune Gallery (P1975)
S.W. Hayter/S.W. Hayter (11,424)(1-3)
S.W. Hayter/S.W. Hayter (20,509)
S.W. Hayter/S.W. Hayter (20,536)
S.W. Hayter/S.W. Hayter (20,829)

Mr F. Newland Price (G1925)
O.L. Warner (8161)

Mr J.H. North (P1894)
M. Murphy/G. Keating (10,250)

Mrs Noseda (P1875)
C. Allingham/W. Ridley (20,834)

Mrs Noseda (G1882)
J.D. Herbert/W. Ward (10,067)
G. Kneller/J. Smith (10,213)
G. Kneller/J. Smith (20,226)
J. Opie/W.W. Barney (10,177)
J. reynolds/T. Watson (10,351)
G. Romney/J. Ogborne (10,341)

Mrs Noseda (P1886)
J. Reynolds/J. Grozer (10,252)

Mrs Noseda (P1887)
F. Cotes/J. Watson (10,078)
J.J. Masquerier/W. Say (10,372)
J. Simpson/C. Turner (10,075)

Dr B. O'Brien (G1982)
L. Gluckman/J.H. Lynch (11,936)
L. Gluckman/J.H. Lynch (11,939)
L. Gluckman/H. O'Neill (11,934)
L. Gluckman/H. O'Neill (11,935)
L. Gluckman/H. O'Neill (11,937-11,938)
L. Gluckman/H. O'Neill (11,940)

Mrs W. O'Brien (G1932)
E. Guillaume (8192-8193)

Mr L. O'Callaghan (G1926)
F. Johnston/R. Havell the Elder & Younger (11,705)

Mr A.J. Onderdonk (P1969)
J. Pillement/M.T. De Maugin (10,042)

Mrs I. Opffer (P1986)
I. Opffer/I. Opffer (20,837)

Mr J.P. O'Reilly (G1903)
L. Gluckman/H. O'Neill (10,121)

Mr M. O'Shaughnessy (G1881)
R. Rothwell/D. Lucas (10,109)
W. Stevenson/W. Stevenson (11,115)
A. Van Dyck/*G. Farrington*/J. Watson (10,235)

Mr N. O'Siochain (G1985)
Dutch School 1689/Dutch School c.1689 (20,835)
Dutch School 1691/*J. Tangena*/Dutch School c.1691 (20,762)
W. Hollar/W. Hollar (20,763)
P. Keere/P. Keere (20,765)

Signora E. Papascogli (G1953)
M. Redmond Dunne (8145)

Mrs Page (G1905)
L. Gluckman/H. O'Neill (10,102)

The Parker Gallery (P1983)
M.A. Hayes/MJ. Harris (20,695-20,700)
O.J. Jones/Dickinson & Co. (20,701)
R. O'C. Newenham/J.D. Harding (20,030)
P. Sandby/T. Cook (20,029)
T. Walmsley/W. Cartwright (20,702)

The Parker Gallery (P1984)
W. Joy/J. Brandard (20,761)

Mr W.B. Pearsall (G1902)
J. Barry/J. Barry (11,858)
Rev. W. Fitzgerald/Rev. W. Fitzgerald (20,771-20,788)

Mr G.A. Phillips (G1905)
J.E. Jones (8204)

Mrs H. Piatt (G1925)
J. Hogan (8131)
Irish School 1882 (8155)

Portobello Market Antiques (P1983)
G.B. Castiglione/*R. Earlom*/J. Boydell (11,943)

Mr O. Power (P1968)
T. Kirk (8052)

Mr E. Quinn (G1926)
E. Quinn (8194)

Miss P. Quinlan (G1984)
Countess of Harrington/M. & N. Hanhart (20,766-20,767)

Mrs Ramsay (G1928)
E. Quinn (8002)

Miss Ray (P1905)
J.P. Haverty/J.P. Haverty (11,857)

Mr J. Ribton Garstin (G1895)
Irish School 1784/English School 1784 (11,626)

Mr J. Ribton Garstin (G1904)
J. Tudor/Irish School 1749 (11,712)

Mr E.S. Robertson (G1906)
C. Panormo (8300)

Mr F.G. Robertson (P1895)
J.-B. Van Loo/J. Faber the Younger (10,120)

Mr J.G. Robertson (P1883)
J. Comerford/C. Rolls (10,754)

Mr J.C. Robinson (G1883)
Rembrandt/J. Wood (10,754)

Rodman's (P1915)
E. Crawford/R. Josey (11,077)

Mrs Rogers (P1950)
R. Rothwell/J. Templeton (11,072)

Mr A. Roth (P1895)
T. Arrowsmith/T. Barrow (11,315)
S. Carpenter/T. Hodgetts (10,174)
A.F.J. Claudet/Bosley (11,057)
W. Cuming/W. Ward the Elder (10,457)
G. Dance the Younger/W. Daniell (10,902)
English School 17C/P. Schenck (10,998)
Irish School 17C/English School 17C (10,574)
T. Phillips/*W. Evans*/K. Mackenzie (10,801)
D. Maclise/W. Drummond (10,265)
A. Pope/A. Cardon (10,135)

Mr A. Roth (P1896)
American School 19C/American School 19C (10,723)
A.E. Chalon/R.A. Artlett (10,814)
A.E. Chalon/H.T. Ryall (10,361)
A.E. Chalon/J. Thomson (10,336)
J. Comerford/H. Meyer (10,200)
J. Copley/R. Dunkarton (10,432)
A.W. Devis/R. Cooper (11,118)
Dutch School c.1690/Dutch School c.1690 (11,274)
C.L. Eastlake/W.L. Mote (10,891)
English School 1828/English School 1828 (11,401)
R. Fenton/J.H. Lynch (10,263)
G.H. Harlow/W. Say (10,369)
E. Hawkins/W. Finden (10,943)
?N. Hone the Elder/W. Baillie (10,225)
Irish School c.1632/Irish School c.1632 (10,020)
G. Kneller/P. Pelham (10,997)
?G. Kneller/P. Tanjé (10,994)
J.P. Lassouquère/J.P. Lassouquère (10,555)
J. Latham/J. Brooks (10,241)
T. Lawrence/G.T. Doo (10,402)
T. Lawrence/R. Lane (10,941)
J.J. Masquerier/C. Turner (10,178)
H. Phillips/W. Walker (10,958)
J. Reynolds/J. Dean (10,911)
W. Robinson/D.J. Scarlett (10,775)
F. Stone/J. Robinson (10,370)
G.C. Stuart/J. Hall (10,152)
A. Wivell the Elder/H. Meyer (10,638)

Mr A. Roth (P1897)
D. Blakiston/G. Zobel (11,007)
J. Comerford/E. Scriven (10,679)
English School 17C/J. Sturt (10,051)
Irish School 17C/R. Dunkarton (11,112)
G.C. Stuart/*W. Evans*/W.T. Fry (10,739)

Mr A. Roth (P1898)
Continental School 17C/English School 1795 (11,206)
English School 17C/English School 1815 (10,733)
English School 1830s/Jenkinson (11,060)
B.R. Green/J.H. Lynch (11,035)
R. Hunter/J. McArdell (10,220)
Irish School 18C/Irish School 18C (10,919)
W. Lodder/A. Caron (10,713)
J.P. Haverty/J.P. Haverty (10,969)
J.P. Haverty/J.P. Haverty (11,020)
T. Lawrence/J. Cochran (10,955)
J. Moore/E. Scriven (11,039)
T.C. Thompson/C. Turner (10,427)

Mr A. Roth (P1901)
English School 17C/W. Faithorne the Elder & G. Vertue (10,771)
G.F. Joseph/E. Scriven (11,029-11,030)
J. Moore/M. Gauci (10,882)

Royal Hibernian Academy (G1912)
Irish School 1817 (8132)

Sabin & Co. (P1969)
Engraved book (10,041)

Frank T. Sabin (P1911)
A. Lee/A. Miller (10,113)

Mr T. Sadlier (G1915)
T.H. Maguire/T.H. Maguire (10,871)

Mr V. Scully (G1885)
After J.E. Jones (8071)

Mr S. Shannon Millin (G1915)
J. Highmore/G. Vandergucht (10,282)

Mr S. Shannon Millin (P1919)
J. Hogan (8196)

Shepherd Bros. (P1902)
S. Denning/J. Chapman (10,360)

Miss C. Sheppard (P1942)
O. Sheppard (8091)

Miss C. Sheppard (G1985)
O. Sheppard (8311-8319)

Mr O. Sheppard (P1936)
O. Sheppard (8092)

The Sickert Trust (G1947)
T. Lessore/T. Lessore (11,431-11,436)
A. McEvoy/W. Sickert (11,448)
W. Sickert/W. Sickert (11,437-11,438)
W. Sickert/W. Sickert (11,439)

Mr J. Simington (P1898)
P. Van Bleeck/P. Van Bleeck (10,112)

Sotheby's (P1980)
J.H. Foley (8252)
J.H. Foley (8269)

Sotheby's (P1982)
J. Lawlor (8261)

Sotheby's (P1984)
P. Turnerelli (8273-8274)

Mr T. Spicer-Simson (G1924)
T. Spicer-Simson (8138-8141)

Mr T. Spicer-Simson (P1940)
T. Spicer-Simson (8215-8223)

Mr G. Stacpoole (P1980)
P. MacDowell (8250)

Mr F. Stewart (G1912)
Continental School 18C (8165)

Mr W.G. Strickland (G1906)
T. Archdeakon/T. Archdeakon (11,919)
J.J. Barralet/T. Milton (11,604)
J.J. Barralet/T. Milton (11,615)
A.M. Bigari/T. Medland (10,055)
?B. Clayton the Elder/B. Clayton the Elder (11,924)
J. Comerford/J. Carver (10,876)
J. Cooke/J. Cooke (11,888)
J. Ford/J. Ford (11,624-11,625)
H. Grattan/J. Greg (10,054)
Irish School c.1750/English School 1750 (10,005)
Irish School c.1785/English School 1785 (11,915)
Irish School c.1786/English School 1786 (11,916)
Irish School c.1786/English School 1786 (11,920)
Irish School c.1787/English School 1787 (11,913)
Irish School c.1787/English School 1787 (11,918)
Irish School c.1788/English School 1788 (11,921)
Irish School c.1788/English School 1788 (11,917)
Irish School c.1789/English School 1789 (11,925)
Irish School c.1790/English School 1790 (11,923)
Irish School 1792/English School 1792 (11,914)
Irish School c.1796/Irish School c.1796 (11,602)
Irish School late 18C/Irish School late 18C (11,618)
Irish School 19C/Irish School 19C (11,922)
Irish School c.1817/English School 1817 (11,741)
Irish School c.1817/English School 1817 (11,762)
Irish School c.1817/English School 1817 (11,831)
J. Malton/English School 1817 (11,764)
G. Petrie/T. Barber (10,056)
R.E. Pine/W. Dickinson (10,686)
M.A. Shee/J. Ford (10,274)
G.C. Stuart/P. Maguire (10,277)

Subscribers (G1907)
D. Wood (8119)

Serjeant A.M. Sullivan (G1921)
T. Farrell (8195)

Mr G.F. Sweeny (P1897)
G. Kneller/J. Smith (10,071)

H. Labouchere, 1st Baron Taunton (G1856)
C. Moore (8065)

Mr R. Thomas (P1925)
G.C. Stuart/C.H. Hodges (10,501)

Mr A. Thompson (P1986)'
T.S. Roberts/S. Alken & J.W. Edy (20,838)(1-12)

Mr H.Y. Thompson (G1895)
L.J. Chavalliaud (8189)

Mr C. Tindall (G1914)
T. Brigford/T. P.... (11,861)

Dr Torney (G1887)
J. Ramsay/T.G. Lupton (10,094)

Mr P. Traynor (P1898)
L.F. Aubry/T.W. Huffam (11,171-11,173)
R. Barber/S. Wheatley (11,376)
R. Barber/B. Wilson (10,297)
Lady Bingham/McDowall (11,291)
T. Brigford/Irish School 1847 (11,237)
W. Brocas/W. Brocas (10,264)
W. Brocas/J. Martyn (11,105)
A. Buck/T.W. Huffam (11,294)
?A. Buck/T.W. Huffam (11,295)
A. Buck/Irish School 1798 (10,585)
A. Buck/T. Kirkwood (10,673)
R. Bull/W. Sedgwick (11,194)
C. Byrne/T.W. Huffam (10,646)
G. Chinnery/H. Brocas the Elder (11,344)
A.F.J. Claudet/T.W. Huffam (10,661)
S. Catterson Smith the Elder/R. Cooper (11,179)
J. Comerford/J. Comerford (11,327)
J. Comerford/Irish School c.1825 (10,961)
J. Comerford/J. Kirkwood (11,270)
J. Comerford/J.H. Lynch (11,329)
Continental School 1730s/Irish School c.1847 (10,300)
Continental School 19C/T.W. Huffam (11,189)
J. Cullen/P. Maguire (10,602)
P. Cunningham/Irish School c.1770 (11,287)
N. Dance/W. Ridley (10,669)
De Grifft/H. Brocas the Elder (10,667)
R.E. Drummond/J. Hopwood the Younger (11,006)
S. Drummond/T. Blood (10,579)
S. Drummond/Irish School 1798 (10,668)

J. Petrie/*A.F.J. Claudet*/English School 1843 (11,166)
J. Petrie/English School 1843 (10,649)
J. Petrie/English School 1846 (11,165)
J. Petrie/English School 1846 (11,182)
J. Petrie/Irish School 1808 (10,650)
J. Petrie/Irish School 1808 (11,163)
J. Petrie/P. Maguire (10,629-10,630)
J. Petrie/P. Maguire (11,211)
J. Reynolds/R. Stanier (10,653)
Reynolds of Dublin/W.H. Lizars (10,672)
T. Rising/W. Hinton (11,262)
G. Romney/*J. Comerford*/E. Scriven (11,417)
G. Romney/*J. Comerford*/C. Watson (10,307)
F.R. Say/J. Kirkwood (10,287)
S. Skillen/J. Kirkwood (10,287)
W. Stevenson/J. Kirkwood (10,592)
W. Stevenson/J. Kirkwood (11,120)
B. Stoker/H. Brocas the Elder (11,176)
B. Stoker/*J. Comerford*/S. Watts (11,128)
G.C. Stuart/J. Farn (11,190-11,191)
T.C. Thompson/?Irish School c.1824 (10,604)
T.C. Thompson/H. Meyer (10,909)
C.S. Tone/English School 1846 (11,299-11,300)

Mr P. Traynor (P1899)
W. Jones/G. King (10,007)
J. Malton/J. Malton (11,640)

Mr J. Vickers (P1902)
T. Hudson/J. McArdell (10,114)

Mr J. Vickers (P1903)
T. Hudson/J. Faber the Younger (10,843)
C. Moore (8187)
P. Turnerelli (8188)

Mr G. Von Pirch (P1909)
C.B. Birch (8157)

Mr P. Wallraf (P1968)
J.J. Caffieri (8051)

Mrs Watkins (P1891)
J. Watkins (8190)

Mr E. Watson (G1924)
J. Slater/J. Slater (10,271)

Mr A. Webb (G1903)
W. Beechey/R. Earlom (10,430)

Mr W.E. Wheeler (P1966)
J. Rogers (8013)

Miss White (P1936)
Engraved books (20,703; 20,709-20,710)

Mrs C. White (G1937)
J. Pennell/J. Pennell (11,454-11,457)
J. Pennell/J. Pennell (11,459-11,470)

C.R. Howard, 6th Earl of Wicklow (G1884)
R. De Hooghe/R. De Hooghe (11,846-11,847)
R. De Hooghe/R. De Hooghe (11,849)
G. Kneller/P. Vanderbanck (10,414)
C.F. Von Breda/S.W. Reynolds the Elder (10,422)

Mrs J.D.H. Widdess (P1981)
J. Hogan (8253)

Friends and pupils of R.H.A. Willis (G1907)
R.H.A. Willis (8197)

Wolfe Cherrick Antiques (P1967)
J. Hogan (8024)

Miss Wyse (G1907)
Cossos & Brontos (8185)

APPENDIX 10

CURRENT ATTRIBUTION

Permanent Catalogue Number and Sculptor (8000s)
Permanent Catalogue Number and Artist/*Copyist*/Engraver (10,000 plus)

SCULPTURES

8000 T. Kirk
8001 F.W. Doyle-Jones
8002 E. Quinn
8003 F.W. Doyle-Jones
8004 D. O Murchadha
8005 A. Power
8006 S. Murphy
8007 A. Power
8008 O. Kelly
8009 P. Grant
8010 A. Power
8011 A. Renoir
8012 J. Connor
8013 J. Rogers
8014 Roman School c.1620
8015 J.M. Rysbrack
8016 M. Stapleton
8017 M. Stapleton
8018 M. Stapleton
8019 M. Stapleton
8020 M. Stapleton
8021 M. Stapleton
8022 M. Stapleton
8023 M. Stapleton
8024 J. Hogan
8025 M. Bayser-Gratry
8026 P. Cunningham
8027 No Entry
8028 Attr. to A. Brustolon
8029 Attr. to A. Brustolon
8030 F. Duquesnoy
8031 J.A. Villabrille y Ron
8032 A. Weckbecker
8033 Roman Antique
8034 J. Hogan
8035 R. Praeger
8036 Attr. to B. Prieur
8037 J. Donoghue
8038 E. Smyth
8039 A. Rodin
8040 J.B. Carpeaux
8041 No Entry
8042 J.H. Foley
8043 T. Kirk
8044 T. Farrell
8045 J.H. Foley
8046 O. Sheppard
8047 J. Hogan
8048 A. Power
8049 Workshop of L. Ghiberti
8050 G. Courbet
8051 School of J.J. Caffieri
8052 T. Kirk
8053 J. Connor
8054 J. Behan
8055 Venetian School 16C
8056 A.J. Dalou
8057 S. Percy
8058 L. Gahagan
8059 C. Moore
8060 C. Moore
8061 J. Hogan
8062 Florentine School late 16C
8063 C. Hewetson
8064 M. Lambert
8065 C. Moore
8066 C. Moore
8067 C. Moore
8068 L. Gahagan
8069 A.J. Dalou
8070 A. Power
8071 After J.E. Jones
8072 A. Rodin
8073 A. Rodin
8074 J. Epstein
8075 A. Stevens
8076 A. Stevens
8077 A. Gilbert
8078 P. Turnerelli
8079 F. Cuairan
8080 C. Andras
8081 F. Dietz
8082 S. Murphy
8083 J. Lawlor
8084 G. Natorp
8085 G. Vanelli
8086 R. Barter
8087 No Entry
8088 C. Moore
8089 A. Power
8090 A. Power
8091 O. Sheppard
8092 O. Sheppard
8093 E.A. Bourdelle
8094 A. Maillol
8095 After W. Larson
8096 T. Kirk
8097 J. Hughes
8098 H. Thornycroft
8099 A. Power
8100 A. Power
8101 Irish School 19C
8102 French School 19C
8103 After A. Canova
8104 O. Sheppard
8105 P. Troubetzkoy
8106 J.S.M. Carre
8107 P. Turnerelli
8108 C. Moore
8109 J.A. Acton
8110 After B. Thorwaldsen
8111 After J.E. Jones
8112 Roman School early 19C
8113 J. Thomas
8114 A. Power
8115 Italian School late 18C
8116 A. Munro
8117 Roman School early 19C
8118 No Entry
8119 D. Wood
8120 A. Power
8121 F. Tacca
8122 M. Soldani
8123 F. Tacca
8124 F. Tacca
8125 F. Tacca
8126 Roman School early 19C
8127 Roman School early 19C
8128 Irish School 1798
8129 Irish School 1933
8130 J. Petrie
8131 J. Hogan
8132 Irish School 1817
8133 T. Farrell
8134 J. Hughes
8135 F.M. Poncet
8136 O. Sheppard
8137 O. Sheppard
8138 T. Spicer-Simson
8139 T. Spicer-Simson
8140 T. Spicer-Simson
8141 T. Spicer-Simson
8142 A.G.G. D'Orsay
8143 E.O. Ford
8144 Roman School early 19C
8145 M. Redmond-Dunne
8146 J. Coplans
8147 G.F. Waters
8148 E. Boehm
8149 H. Thornycroft
8150 J. Lawlor
8151 F. Chantrey
8152 F. Sanders
8153 J. Watkins
8154 Irish School 1866
8155 Irish School 1882
8156 J. Woodhouse
8157 C.B. Birch
8158 I. Parkes
8159 O. Sheppard
8160 S. Percy
8161 O.L. Warner
8162 A.L. Barye
8163 A.L. Barye
8164 W. Mossop
8165 Continental School 18C
8166 P.J. David D'Angers
8167 S. Stoyanovitch
8168 T. Rosandic
8169 A. Bonnetain
8170 P. Morbiducci
8171 No Entry
8172 No Entry
8173 No Entry
8174 No Entry
8175 No Entry

8176 No Entry
8177 No Entry
8178 No Entry
8179 No Entry
8180 No Entry
8181 No Entry
8182 No Entry
8183 T. Farrell
8184 J. Thomas
8185 Cossos and Brontos
8186 G. Vanelli
8187 C. Moore
8188 P. Turnerelli
8189 L.J. Chavalliaud
8190 J. Watkins
8191 J.H. Foley
8192 E. Guillaume
8193 E. Guillaume
8194 E. Quinn
8195 T. Farrell
8196 J. Hogan
8197 R.H.A. Willis
8198 A. Power
8199 P. Turnerelli
8200 J.H. Foley
8201 After J. Van Nost the Younger
8202 C. Moore
8203 L. MacdDonald
8204 J.E. Jones
8205 H. Thornycroft
8206 Irish School 1882
8207 N.R. Roskell
8208 J.E. Jones
8209 R. Westmacott the Younger
8210 G.B. Piamontini
8211 G.B. Piamontini
8212 Italian School 18C
8213 Italian School 18C
8214 W. Mossop
8215 T. Spicer-Simson
8216 T. Spicer-Simson
8217 T. Spicer-Simson
8218 T. Spicer-Simson
8219 T. Spicer-Simson
8220 T. Spicer-Simson
8221 T. Spicer-Simson
8222 T. Spicer-Simson
8223 T. Spicer-Simson
8224 E.H. Baily
8225 English School 19C
8226 Roman School early 19C
8227 After B. Thorvaldsen
8228 After P. Turnerelli
8229 No Entry
8230 No Entry
8231 English School ?c.1820
8232 J. Connor
8233 J. Connor
8234 Irish School 19C
8235 S.F. Lynn
8236 S.F. Lynn
8237 J.S. Jordan
8238 A. O'Connor
8239 No Entry
8240 J. Higgins
8241 School of F. Chantrey
8242 B. Cavaceppi
8243 B. Cavaceppi
8244 J. Hogan
8245 S. Murphy
8246 L. Richier
8247 L. Richier
8248 Irish School c.1919
8249 E. Foley
8250 P. MacDowell
8251 J.H. Foley
8252 J.H. Foley
8253 J. Hogan
8254 C. Smith
8255 J. Van Nost the Younger
8256 Irish School c.1785
8257 J.H. Foley
8258 J.H. Foley
8259 G. Geefs
8260 T. Kirk
8261 J. Lawlor
8262 O. Kelly
8263 O. Kelly
8264 J. Heffernan
8265 C. Moore
8266 C. Moore
8267 T. Kirk
8268 D. Mac Namara
8269 J.H. Foley
8270 A. Maillol
8271 A. Maillol
8272 A. Weckbecker
8273 P. Turnerelli
8274 P. Turnerelli
8275 Irish School 1873
8276 Roman Antique
8277 T. Farrell
8278 L.C. and W. Wyon
8279 Roman Antique
8280 C. Moore
8281 J. Moyse
8282 A. Weckbecker
8283 Irish School 19C
8284 J. Hogan
8285 M. De Carnowsky
8286 Roman School 19C
8287 Roman School 19C
8288 Roman School ?18C
8289 S. Angelis
8290 A. Power
8291 J. Hogan
8292 A. Power
8293 J. Petrie
8294 Irish School 1798
8295 Roman School 18C
8296 Roman School 19C
8297 P. Turnerelli
8298 C. Moore
8299 Roman School ?18C
8300 C. Panormo
8301 Irish School 19C
8302 Continental School 19C
8303 L. MacDonald
8304 S. Murphy
8305 A. Stones
8306 G. Herbert
8307 No Entry
8308 No Entry
8309 No Entry
8310 French School 19C
8311 O. Sheppard
8312 O. Sheppard
8313 O. Sheppard
8314 O. Sheppard
8315 O. Sheppard
8316 O. Sheppard
8317 O. Sheppard
8318 O. Sheppard
8319 O. Sheppard
8320 J. Tassie
8321 J. Tassie
8322 Attr. to S. Percy
8323 Sèvres 19C
8324 Spanish School c.1300
8325 Spanish School 15C
8326 Attr. to J. Sansovino
8327 German School 17C
8328 Spanish School 1600/1650
8329 French or German School c.1600
8330 French School 16C
8331 Flemish School 17C
8332 French School 17C
8333 French School late 17C
8334 French School late 17C

PRINTS

10,000 J.P. Haverty/W.J. Ward the Younger
10,001 W. Wissing/R. Williams
10,002 G. Kneller/J. Smith
10,003 T. Maas/T. Maas
10,004 Dutch School 1691/J. Tangena
10,005 Irish School c.1750/English School 1750
10,006 G. Kneller/J. Gole
10,007 W. Jones/G. King
10,008 J. Tudor/J. McArdell
10,009 G. Kneller/J. Smith
10,010 G. Kneller/J. Smith
10,011 C. Jervas/R. Purcell
10,012 T. Gibson/P. Pelham
10,013 J. Van Nost the Younger/C. Spooner
10,014 ?Irish School 18C/?J. Dixon
10,015 C. Brooking/C. Brooking
10,015 (1-20) details of C. Brooking/C. Brooking
10,016 W. Wissing/R. Williams

10,017 J. Faber the Younger/J. Faber the Younger
10,018 J. Wills/A. Miller
10,019 C. Jervas/P. Fourdrinier
10,020 Irish School c.1732/Irish School c.1732
10,021 ?G. Kneller/J. Simon
10,022 E. Lutterell/E. Lutterell
10,023 J. Latham/J. Brooks
10,024 F. Bindon/A. Miller
10,025 P. Lely/A. Blooteling
10,026 F. Bindon/J. McArdell
10,027 J. M. Rysbrack/J. Faber the Younger
10,028 J. Reynolds/G.F.L. Marchi
10,029 I. Woods/J. Faber the Younger
10,030 J. Richardson the Elder/J. Smith
10,031 H. Pickering/J. Faber the Younger
10,032 P. De Graves/J. Simon
10,033 W. Stevenson/D. Lucas
10,034 J. Reynolds/R. Purcell
10,035 J. Doyle/J. Doyle
10,036 No Entry
10,037 No Entry
10,038 No Entry
10,039 (1-25) D. Sullivan/D. Sullivan
10,040 No Entry
10,041 (1-32) R. Pool & J. Cash/ J. Lodge & I. Taylor the Elder
10,042 J. Pillement/M.T. Maugin
10,043 T. Robinson/T. Robinson
10,044 F. Bindon/J. Brooks
10,045 Continental School early 19C/C. Mayer
10,046 ?English School 16C/A. B....
10,047 A. Russell/S. Gribelin
10,048 G. Petrie/T.F. Ranson
10,049 G. Dance/W. Daniell
10,050 H.D. Hamilton/W. Ward the Elder
10,051 English School 17C/J. Sturt
10,052 F. Bindon/A. Miller
10,053 G. Soest/R. Purcell
10,054 H. Grattan/J. Greig
10,055 A.M. Bigari/T. Medland
10,056 G. Petrie/T. Barber
10,057 T. Lawrence/S. Cousins
10,058 T. Lawrence/J.R. Smith
10,059 English School 17C/S. De Wilde
10,060 J. Reynolds/J. McArdell
10,061 H. O'Neill/C. Turner
10,062 A. Hope/J. Godby
10,063 M. Dahl/T. Beard
10,064 L. Gluckman/H. O'Neill
10,065 J. Comerford/T. Heaphy
10,066 J. Gubbins/B. O'Reilly
10,067 J.D. Herbert/W. Ward the Elder
10,068 N. Hone the Elder/J. Watson
10,069 ?P. Lely/P. Lombart
10,070 N. Hone the Elder/E. Fisher
10,071 G. Kneller/J.Smith
10,072 N. Hone the Elder/N. Hone the Elder
10,073 No Entry
10,074 W. Jones/A. Miller
10,075 J.Simpson/C. Turner
10,076 A. Lee/A. Miller
10,077 F.P.S. Gérard/J. Godefroy
10,078 F. Cotes/J. Watson
10,079 G.C. Stuart/ Irish School c.1795
10,080 P. Lely/ I. Beckett
10,081 English School early 18C/A. Miller
10,082 H.D. Hamilton/C. Knight
10,083 G.C. Stuart/W. Say
10,084 J. Tusch/L. Zucchi
10,085 Markham/T. Burford
10,086 J. Reynolds/W. Dickinson
10,087 G. Chalmers/J. McArdell
10,088 J. Reynolds/J. McArdell
10,089 J. Reynolds/J. Jones
10,090 J. Reynolds/J. Dean
10,091 T. Hickey/P. Halpin
10,092 G.C. Stuart/C.H. Hodges
10,093 Lady M. Bingham/J.B. & M.A. Tilliard
10,094 J. Ramsay/T.G. Lupton
10,095 G. Kneller/J. Smith
10,096 A. Van Dyck/J. Faber the Younger
10,097 C. Smith/S. Cousins
10,098 English School c.1819/English School 1819
10,099 J. Pope-Stevens the Elder/A. Miller
10,100 M.A. Shee/W. Ward the Elder
10,101 J. Van Nost the Younger/C. Spooner
10,102 L. Gluckman/H. O'Neill
10,103 T. Hardy/T. Hardy
10,104 ?F. Hayman/J. McArdell
10,105 G. Morphey/ J. Vandervaart
10,106 M.W. Peters/J. Murphy
10,107 T. Lawrence/C. Turner
10,108 G. Gaven/J. Gainer
10,109 R. Rothwell/D. Lucas
10,110 G.C. Stuart/W. Dickinson
10,111 T. Hudson/J. Faber the Younger
10,112 P. Van Bleeck/P. Van Bleeck
10,113 A. Lee/A. Miller
10,114 T. Hudson/J. McArdell
10,115 J. Pope-Stevens the Elder/J. Brooks
10,116 W. Stevenson/D. Lucas
10,117 ?J. Brooks/J. Brooks
10,118 G.C. Stuart/J. Collyer
10,119 L. Gluckman/M. & N. Hanhart
10,120 J. B. Van Loo/J. Faber the Younger
10,121 L. Gluckman/H. O'Neill
10,122 A. Lee/A. Miller
10,123 F. Hayman/J. McArdell
10,124 English School 17C/G. Vertue
10,125 M. Dahl/J. Faber the Younger
10,126 T.C. Thompson/H. Meyer
10,127 English or Irish School c.1760 /R. Houston
10,128 B. Wilson/B. Wilson
10,129 P. Batoni/J. Watson
10,130 F. Wheatley/V. Green
10,131 D. Stevens/J. Faber the Younger
10,132 J. Vandervaart/J. Vandervaart
10,133 English School 17C/A. Miller
10,134 J.Gwim/M. Jackson
10,135 A. Pope/A. Cardon
10,136 P. Lely/E. Lutterell
10,137 R. Cosway/P. Condé
10,138 Irish School c.1770/Irish School 18C
10,139 N. Hone the Elder/J. Watson
10,140 R. Cosway/L. Sailliar
10,141 Irish School c.1750/?M. Hanbury
10,142 Markham/A. Van Haecken
10,143 T. Carlton/T. Beard
10,144 C. Maratta/G. Valet
10,145 Irish School c.1750/W. Sharp
10,146 J. Reynolds/J. Ward
10,147 Marchioness of Thomond/R.M. Meadows
10,148 C. Jervas/J. Brooks
10,149 B. Watson/J. McArdell
10,150 G.C. Stuart/C.H. Hodges
10,151 Irish School 1806/14//*J.B. Lane*/S. Freeman
10,152 G.C. Stuart/J. Hall
10,153 H.D. Hamilton/R. Houston
10,154 T. Lawrence/W. Giller
10,155 G. Richmond/R.A. Artlett
10,156 J. Petrie/J. Petrie
10,157 B. Du Pan/M. Ford
10,158 R. Hunter/J. Dixon
10,159 J. Latham/J. Brooks
10,160 G.Kneller/J. Faber the Younger
10,161 G. Kneller/J. Smith
10,162 W. Taylor/W. Taylor
10,163 G. Chalmers/R. Purcell
10,164 J. Hoppner/C. Turner
10,165 English School 18C/J. McArdell
10,166 C. Grignon the Younger/J. Murphy
10,167 J. Worsdale/J. Brooks
10,168 T. Hudson/J. McArdell

10,169 C. Jervas/P. Fourdrinier
10,170 J. Lonsdale/C. Turner
10,171 Rembrandt/R. Earlom
10,172 J.-B.-S. Chardin/B. F. Lépicié the Elder
10,173 J. Highmore/J. Faber the Younger
10,174 M.S. Carpenter/T. Hodgetts
10,175 G. Kneller/J. McArdell
10,176 J. Reynolds/J. Faber the Younger
10,177 J. Opie/W.W. Barney
10,178 J.J. Masquerier/C. Turner
10,179 L. Gluckman/H. O'Neill
10,180 W. Hoare/J. McArdell
10,181 H.F. Gravelot/J. Hulett
10,182 H.D. Hamilton/V. Green
10,183 T. Gainsborough/E. Bell
10,184 W. Hoare/J.L. Simon
10,185 T. Lawrence/C. Picart
10,186 W. Hoare/A. Miller
10,187 English or Irish School 18C/J. Brooks
10,188 W.B. Richmond/J.D. Miller
10,189 T. Hudson/J. McArdell
10,190 S. Catterson Smith the Elder/J.A. Vinter
10,191 M. Gheeraerts the Younger/R. Van Voerst
10,192 W. Cuming/J.R. Smith
10,193 J. Fayram/J. Faber the Younger
10,194 R. Hunter/E. Fisher
10,195 J. Latham/J. Brooks
10,196 G. Dance/W. Daniell
10,197 English or Irish School c.1741/J. Brooks
10,198 J. Lewis/A. Miller
10,199 T. Hill/R. Williams
10,200 J. Comerford/H. Meyer
10,201 ?G. Morphey/R. Laurie
10,202 M. Ashton/T. Beard
10,203 J.R. Smith/J.R. Smith
10,204 L. Laguerre the Elder/J. Simon
10,205 J. Barry/J. Barry
10,206 T. Ottway/M. Ford
10,207 H.D. Hamilton/C. Turner
10,208 J. Pope-Stevens the Elder/J. Brooks
10,209 A. Kauffmann/?T. Burke
10,210 J. Northcote/J. Ward
10,211 T. Nugent/W.T. Annis
10,212 G. Kneller/J. Houbraken
10,213 G. Kneller/J. Smith
10,214 C. Jervas/G. Vertue
10,215 J. Worsdale/J. Simon
10,216 T. Gainsborough/J. McArdell
10,217 G.C. Stuart/C.H. Hodges
10,218 G. Kneller/J. Smith
10,219 J. Ellys/J. Faber the Younger
10,220 R. Hunter/?J. McArdell
10,221 Irish School c.1750/C. Spooner
10,222 T. Lawrence/S. Cousins
10,223 G. Kneller/J. Brooks
10,224 G. Kneller/A. Haelwegh
10,225 ?N. Hone the Elder/W. Baillie
10,226 G. Kneller/J. Smith
10,227 G. Kneller/J. Smith
10,228 A. Lee/J. Brooks
10,229 J. Closterman/J. Smith
10,230 T.C. Thompson/T. Hodgetts
10,231 J. Constable/W.J. Ward the Younger
10,232 Irish School 18C/?E. Lyons
10,233 H.D. Hamilton/W.S. Barnard
10,234 T. Worlidge/R. Houston
10,235 A. Van Dyck/*G. Farrington*/J. Watson
10,236 F.R. West/J. Watson
10,237 F.R. West/J. Watson
10,238 G. Kneller/J. Smith
10,239 J. Reynolds/W.C. Edwards
10,240 J. Latham/J. Faber the Youngerr
10,241 J. Latham/J. Brooks
10,242 C. Jervas/J. Brooks
10,243 J.P. Knight/T.G. Lupton
10,244 W. Wissing/I. Beckett
10,245 R. Walker/J. Van de Velde the Elder
10,246 M. Brown/H. Hudson
10,247 G.C. Stuart/C.H. Hodges
10,248 A. Van Dyck/J. Simon
10,249 T. Foster/W.J. Ward the Younger
10,250 M. Murphy/G. Keating
10,251 G.C. Stuart/C.H. Hodges
10,252 J. Reynolds/J. Grozer
10,253 J. Reynolds/J. Grozer
10,254 J. Reynolds/J. Watson
10,255 English School c.1740/J. Brooks
10,256 J. Kerseboom/A. Miller
10,257 J. Reynolds/J. Watson
10,258 H. Raeburn/E. Mitchell
10,259 A. Van Dyck/A. Browne
10,260 J. Jackson/W.T. Fry
10,261 J. Hayter/F.C. Lewis
10,262 J. Petrie/H. Brocas the Elder
10,263 R. Fenton/J.H. Lynch
10,264 W. Brocas/W. Brocas
10,265 D. Maclise/W. Drummond
10,266 School of P. Lely/G. White
10,267 English School c.1740/J. Brooks
10268 G.C. Stuart/W. Ward the Elder
10,269 J. Parmentier/J. Faber the Younger
10,270 J. Jackson/H. Meyer
10,271 J. Slater/J. Slater
10,272 English School 18C/English School 18C
10,273 L. Carrogis/?French School 19C
10,274 M.A. Shee/J. Ford
10,275 English School late 18C/H. Kingsbury
10,276 Q. Boel/Q. Boel
10,277 G.C. Stuart/P. Maguire
10,278 English School 1653/English School 1804
10,279 F. Bindon/J. Martyn
10,280 Irish School 18C/J. Brooks
10,281 English School c.1645/G. Glover
10,282 J. Highmore/G. Vandergucht
10,283 B. Stoker/J. Singleton
10,284 Irish School c.1870/J.C. McRae
10,284 B. Stoker/J. Singleton
10,285 D. Loggan/E. Sandys
10,286 H.D. Hamilton/J. Heath
10,287 S. Skillin/J. Kirkwood
10,288 D. Maclise/D. Maclise
10,289 T.H. Carrick/W. Holl the Younger
10,290 English School 16C/V. Green
10,291 J.D. Herbert/H. Brocas the Elder
10,292 Irish School 1798/Irish School 1798
10,293 Irish School c.1800/P. Maguire
10,294 H.D. Hamilton/J. Boydell
10,295 H.D. Hamilton/H. Brocas the Elder
10,296 R. Barber/B. Wilson
10,297 R. Barber/B. Wilson
10,298 T. Frye/T. Frye
10,299 Irish School c.1795/Irish School c.1795
10,300 Continental School 1730s/Irish School c.1847
10,301 ?Irish School c.1700/W. Sherwin
10,302 ?Irish School c.1750/Massard
10,303 No Entry
10,304 ?English School 17C/T. Cross the Elder
10,305 Irish School 17C/J. Dickson
10,306 L. Gluckman/Read & Co.
10,307 G. Romney/*J. Comerford*/C. Watson
10,308 H. Hone & A. B.../G.F. Philips & T. Levens
10,309 H. Hone/F. Bartolozzi
10,310 H. Hone/F. Bartolozzi
10,311 I. Oliver/French School c.1600
10,312 G.B. Cipriani/M. Bovi
10,313 J. Reynolds/F. Bartolozzi
10,314 J. Reynolds/F. Bartolozzi
10,315 J. Reynolds/F. Bartolozzi

10,316 English School 18C/R. Cooper
10,317 G. Kneller/J. Smith
10,318 R. Cosway/A. Cardon
10,319 A. Pond/J. McArdell
10,320 J. Downman/F. Bartolozzi
10,321 P. Mignard/P. Van Somer the Younger
10,322 N. Hone the Elder/R. Purcell
10,323 J. Reynolds/T. Park
10,324 C. Robertson/J.S. Agar
10,325 T. Kettle/J.S. De Wilde
10,326 A.E. Chalon/J.J. Hinchcliff
10,327 J. M..../?S. Okey
10,328 P. Lely/I. Beckett
10,329 N. Hone the Elder/J. Greenwood
10,330 N. Hone the Elder/J.R. Smith
10,331 W. Wissing/I. Beckett
10,332 F. Cotes/J. Watson
10,333 G. Kneller/J. Smith
10,334 H.D. Hamilton/J. Watson
10,335 English School 17C/A. Miller
10,336 A.E. Chalon/J. Thomson
10,337 J. Reynolds/C. Spooner
10,338 J. Reynolds/J. McArdell
10,339 J. Reynolds/S. Okey
10,340 English School 17C/J. Gole
10,341 G. Romney/J. Ogborne
10,342 F. Cotes/R. Houston
10,343 F. Cotes/J. McArdell
10,344 J. Reynolds/J. McArdell
10,345 J. Reynolds/J. Watson
10,346 J. Reynolds/W. Dickinson
10,347 G. Kneller/J. Smith
10,348 M.W. Peters/J.R. Smith
10,349 A. Van Dyck/*A. Houbraken*/P. Gunst
10,350 J. Zoffany/R. Houston
10,351 J. Reynolds/T. Watson
10,352 Countess Spencer/F. Bartolozzi
10,353 N. Hone the Elder/J. Finlayson
10,354 J. Reynolds/J.R. Smith
10,355 J. Reynolds/T. Watson
10,356 J. Reynolds/J.R. Smith
10,357 J. Reynolds/E. Fisher
10,358 F. Cotes/C. Spooner
10,359 F. Cotes/R. Houston
10,360 S.P. Denning/J.W. Chapman
10,361 A.E. Chalon/H.T. Ryall
10,362 Countess of Burlington/J. Faber the Younger
10,363 J. Reynolds/E. Fisher
10,364 P. Lely/J. Griffier the Elder
10,365 P. Lely/A. Blooteling
10,366 A. Pond/J. McArdell
10,367 J.G. Eccard/A. Miller
10,368 T. Lawrence/W. Bond
10,369 G.H. Harlow/W. Say
10,370 F. Stone/J.H. Robinson
10,371 E. Lilly/*C. Boit*/J. Simon
10,372 J.J. Masquerier/W. Say
10,373 P. Lely/I. Beckett
10,374 F. Cotes/J. McArdell
10,375 F. Cotes/C. Spooner
10,376 T. Gainsborough/J.R. Smith
10,377 J. Reynolds/J. Dean
10,378 N. Hone the Elder/C. Phillips
10,379 A. Kauffmann/T. Burke
10,380 J. Reynolds/J.R. Smith
10,381 J. Reynolds/W. Dickinson
10,382 E.F. Calze/V. Green
10,383 J. Reynolds/J. Watson
10,384 J.E. Liotard/R. Houston
10,385 J. Vandervaart/W. Faithorne the Younger
10,386 J. Hoppner/J. Jones
10,387 J. Hoppner/S. Einslie
10,388 B. Wilson/B. Wilson
10,389 J. Reynolds/J. McArdell
10,390 J. Reynolds/J. Grozer
10,391 C. Read/J. Finlayson
10,392 A. Kauffmann/J. Watson
10,393 G. Hamilton/J. Faber the Younger
10,394 C. Read/J. Finlayson
10,395 J. Reynolds/J. Dixon
10,396 G. Hamilton/J. McArdell
10,397 J. Reynolds/J. Watson
10,398 J. Reynolds/J. Webb
10,399 Lady Burghersh/T. Hodgetts
10,400 J. Reynolds/V. Green
10,401 P. Lely/J. McArdell
10,402 T. Lawrence/G.T. Doo
10,403 M. Gheeraerts the Younger/J. Faber the Younger
10,404 B. Wilson/J. Basire
10,405 M. Cosway/V. Green
10,406 J. Wright of Derby/J.R. Smith
10,407 J. Reynolds/W. Dickinson
10,408 J. Hoppner/T. Park
10,409 A.W. Devis/H. Meyer
10,410 J. Reynolds/R. Houston
10,411 W. Stevenson/D. Lucas
10,412 J. Astley/J. Dixon
10,413 J. Latham/A. Miller
10,414 G. Kneller/P. Vanderbanck
10,415 ?J. Brooks/J. Brooks
10,416 R. Woodburn/R. Dunkarton
10,417 R. Hunter/W. Sadler the Elder
10,418 W. Hoare/J. Brooks
10,419 J. Ramsay/C. Turner
10,420 J. Wyck/J. Faber the Younger
10,421 S. Catterson Smith the Elder/G. Sanders
10,422 C.F. Von Breda/S.W. Reynolds the Elder
10,423 G. Dawe/G. Maile
10,424 J. Reynolds/J. Watson
10,425 G. Richmond/F. Holl
10,426 Reynolds of Dublin/J.T. Smith
10,427 T.C. Thompson/C. Turner
10,428 R. Bowyer/J.C. Bromley
10,429 English School c.1877/M. & N. Hanhart
10,430 W. Beechey/R. Earlom
10,431 H. Howard/R. Earlom
10,432 J.S. Copley/R. Dunkarton
10,433 Irish Schoool c.1800/*C.S. Tone*/J.J. Goggins
10,434 ?J. Brooks/J. Brooks
10,435 J. Hickey/J. Ward
10,436 W. Hogarth/A. Miller
10,437 A. Pope/E. Scriven
10,438 J. Reynolds/J.R. Smith
10,439 G. Romney/C. Townley
10,440 R. Hunter/J. McArdell
10,441 S. Catterson Smith the Elder/J.R. Jackson
10,442 G. Romney/J. Jones
10,443 P. Van Somer/V. Green
10,444 ?F. Bindon/A. Miller
10,445 W. Hoare/R. Houston & S. Wheatley
10,446 T. Lawrence/S. Cousins
10,447 T. Lawrence/S. Cousins
10,448 T. Gainsborough/J.K. Sherwin
10,449 M. Cregan/G.R. Ward
10,450 T. Stewardson/W. Ward the Elder
10,451 S. West/W.O. Geller
10,452 C. Grey/J. Peterkin
10,453 J. Hoppner/C. Turner
10,454 R. Hunter/W. Dickinson
10,455 J. Ramsay/W. Say
10,456 S. Catterson Smith the Elder/G. Sanders
10,457 W. Cuming/W. Ward the Elder
10,458 T. Lawrence/C. Turner
10,459 M.W. Peters/J. Watson
10,460 J. Reynolds/J. Hall
10,461 W. Owen/S.W. Reynolds the Elder
10,462 N. Dance/W. Dickinson
10,463 No Entry
10,464 R. Livesay/J. Dean
10,465 T. Frye/T. Frye
10,466 M.W. Peters/*J.D. Herbert*/S.W. Reynolds the Elder
10,467 J. Reynolds/J. Dixon
10,468 S. Catterson Smith the Elder/G. Sanders
10,469 J. Hoppner/S.W. Reynolds the Elder
10,470 J. McArdell/R. Earlom
10,471 J. Zoffany/G.F.L. Marchi
10,472 J. Reynolds/J.R. Smith
10,473 J. Northcote/J. Fittler
10,474 N. Dance/W. Ward the Elder
10,475 J. Reynolds/J. Murphy
10,476 G. Romney/J. Jones
10,477 G. Maile/G. Maile

0,478 G.C. Stuart/W. Say
0,479 W. Madden/W. Dickinson
0,480 W. Jones/A. Miller
0,481 C. Brown/J. Brooks
0,482 English School 19C/Morris & Co.
0,483 S. Catterson Smith the Elder/G. Sanders
0,484 J. Reynolds/R. Dunkarton
0,485 F. Grant/S. Cousins
0,486 J. Hoppner/G. Clint
0,487 M.A. Shee/C. Turner
0,489 M.A. Shee/G. Clint
0,490 J. Reynolds/W. Dickinson
0,491 T.C. Thompson/S.W. Reynolds the Elder
10,492 J. Reynolds/C. Turner
0,493 S. Drummond/W.S. Barnard
10,494 G.C. Stuart/C.H. Hodges
10,495 P. Lely/A. Blooteling
10,496 T. Gainsborough/G. Dupont
10,497 R. Hunter/W. Sedgwick
10,498 W. Beechey/J. Ward
10,499 D. Gardner/J. Jones
10,500 R. Walker/*M. Ford*/A. Miller
10,501 G.C. Stuart/C.H. Hodges
10,502 J.C. Harrison/G. Atkinson
10,503 J. Reynolds/J. Jones
10,504 G. Kneller/M. Ford
10,505 S. Catterson Smith the Elder/G. Sanders
10,506 S. Catterson Smith the Elder/G. Sanders
10,507 J. Bauzil/C. Turner
10,508 G. Romney/J. Jones
10,509 T. Lawrence/S. Cousins
10,510 S. Catterson Smith the Elder/G. Sanders
10,511 J. Pope-Stevens the Elder/A. Miller
10,512 W. Tell/W. Tell
10,513 W. Tell/W. Tell
10,514 English School c.1786/English School 1786
10,515 Bolognese School 18C/Bolognese School 18C
10,516 ?P. Le Grand/O. Birrell
10,517 English School c.1786/English School 1786
10,518 English School c.1786/English School 1786
10,519 G. Kneller/T. Chambars
10,520 No Entry
10,521 L. Gluckman/H. O'Neill
10.522 L. Gluckman/H. O'Neill
10,523 L. Gluckman/H. O'Neill
10,524 L. Gluckman/M. & N. Hanhart
10,525 L. Gluckman/H. O'Neill
10,526 L. Gluckman/H. O'Neill
10,527 J. Reynolds/H. P...
10,528 J. Reynolds/S.F. Ravenet the Elder
10,529 F. Bindon/E. Scriven
10,530 W. Lawrence/A. Miller
10,531 G. King/G. Bickham the Younger
10,532 N. Hone the Elder/W. Baillie
10,533 G. Kneller/E. Scriven
10,534 G. Kneller/J. Smith
10,535 P. Mercier/J. Simon
10,536 P. Mercier/J. Simon
10,537 English School c.1740/J. Brooks
10,538 English School c.1740/J. Brooks
10,539 G. Kneller/J. Simon
10,540 G. Kneller/J. Smith
10,541 J. Murphy/J. Murphy
10,542 J. Reynolds/R. Houston
10,543 G. Kneller/J. Houbraken
10,544 S. Catterson Smith the Elder/G. Sanders
10,545 J. Reynolds/E. Fisher
10,546 A. Van Dyck/R. Cooper
10,547 W. Cuming/C. Turner
10,548 J. Vanderbank/J. Faber the Younger
10,549 T. Gainsborough/J. Dean
10,550 T. Frye/T. Frye
10,551 T. Frye/T. Frye
10,552 T. Frye/T. Frye
10,553 L. Gluckman/H. O'Neill
10,554 R. Rothwell/C. Turner
10,555 J.P. Lassouquère/J.P. Lassouquère
10,556 A. Van Dyck/J. Boydell
10,557 J. Comerford/Irish School 1825
10,558 G. Kneller/A. Miller
10,559 W. Wissing/J. Smith
10,560 ?P. Lely/P. Schenck
10,561 P. Lely/I. Beckett
10,562 R.R. Scanlan/H.R. Cook
10,563 A. Van Dyck/*G. Farrington*/J. Watson
10,564 English School 17C/J. Gole
10,565 G. Kneller/P. Vanderbank
10,566 W. Bewnes/F.C. Lewis
10,567 Mayall/D.J. Pound
10,568 ?M. Dahl/English School early 18C
10,569 M. Dahl/P. Pelham
10,570 G. Kneller/J.H. Robinson
10,571 Irish School 18C/Irish School 18C
10,572 J. Murphy/W. Bond
10,573 Irish School c.1777/Irish School 1777
10,574 Irish School 17C/English School 17C
10,575 Irish School 18C/Irish School 18C
10,576 J. Nixon/E. Harding
10,577 J. Reynolds/English School 1760s
10,578 Irish School c.1795/Irish School 1795
10,579 S. Drummond/T. Blood
10,580 Irish School c.1792/Irish School c.1793
10,581 Irish School c.1800/Irish School c.1800
10,582 A.F.J. Claudet/English School 1846
10,583 A. Wivell the Elder/W. Read
10,584 J. Hoppner/S. Close the Elder
10,585 A. Buck/Irish School 1798
10,586 T. Rowlandson/J. Hopwood the Younger
10,587 Irish School c.1808/Irish School 1808
10,588 Irish School c.1797/Irish School 1797
10,589 J.D. Herbert/Irish School 1809
10,590 Irish School c.1797/Irish School 1797
10,591 Irish School 18C/Irish School 1847
10,592 W. Stevenson/J. Kirkwood
10,593 Irish School 1770s/E. Dorrell
10,594 F.J. O'Kelly/Dean & Co.
10,595 F.J. O'Kelly/Dean & Co.
10,596 Irish School c.1841/J. Kirkwood
10,597 T.H. Carrick/W. Holl the Younger
10,598 Irish School c.1813/Irish School 1813
10,599 Irish School c.1813/Irish School 1813
10,600 Irish School c.1813/English School 1823
10,601 D. Maclise/D. Maclise
10,602 J. Cullen/P. Maguire
10,603 A. Lee/G. Byrne
10,604 T.C. Thompson/?Irish School c.1824
10,605 J.M. Moreau/W.N.M. Courbe
10,606 English School 18C/English School 18C
10,607 A.S. Belle/English School 18C
10,608 English School c.1860/English School c.1860
10,609 T.R. Poole/English School 1791/94
10,610 English School 17C/English School 1810
10,611 R. White/R. White
10,612 Irish School c.1811/H. Brocas the Elder
10,613 C. Grey/J. Kirkwood
10,614 Continental School 17C/*S. Harding*/W.N. Gardiner

10,615 Irish School 1798/R.J. Hamerton

10,616 Irish School c.1843/T.W. Huffam

10,617 C.Grey/Irish School 1850

10,618 English School 17C/English School c.1816

10,619 ?H.D. Hamilton/Irish School 18C

10,620 Irish School c.1808/Irish School c.1808

10,621 J. Holmes/M. Gauci

10,622 G.C. Stuart/W. Evans

10,623 Irish School early 19C/P. Dillon

10,624 Irish School c.1848/H. Griffiths

10,625 English School 17C/M. Vandergucht

10,626 English School 17C/M. Vandergucht

10,627 English School 17C/J. Sturt

10,628 W. Cuming/T.S. Engleheart

10,629 J. Petrie/P. Maguire

10,630 J. Petrie/P. Maguire

10,631 G. Richmond/H. Adlard

10,632 J. Wood/W. Holl the Younger

10,633 J.D. Herbert/T.W. Huffam

10,634 English School 19C/English School 19C

10,635 G.C. Stuart/Irish School c.1790

10,636 S. Cooper/M. Vandergucht

10,637 M.A. Shee/T. Blood

10,638 A. Wivell the Elder/H. Meyer

10,639 G.F. Joseph/S. Freeman

10,640 H.D. Hamilton/P. Lightfoot

10,641 C. Grey/Irish School 1852

10,642 Irish School c.1779/Irish School c. 1779

10,643 L.F. Abbot/?W. Ridley

10,644 A. Kauffmann/W. Ridley

10,645 G. Mulvany/S. Freeman

10,646 C. Byrne/T.W. Huffam

10,647 C. Byrne/T.W. Huffam

10,648 Irish School c.1798/Irish School c.1798

10,649 J. Petrie/English School 1843

10,650 J. Petrie/Irish School 1808

10,651 Irish School c.1779/Irish School 1779

10,652 English School 1790s/English School 1790s

10,653 J. Reynolds/R. Stanier

10,654 J. Reynolds/P. Maguire

10,655 English School c.1813/Irish School 1813

10,656 English School c.1780/W. Ridley

10,657 English School c.1780/W. Ridley

10,658 W. Brocas/H. Meyer

10,659 English School 18C/English School 18C

10,660 A.F.J. Claudet/T.W. Huffam

10,661 A.F.J. Claudet/T.W. Huffam

10,662 J. Reynolds/C. Knight

10,663 J. Reynolds/C. Knight

10,664 J. Reynolds/English School late 18C

10,665 C. Grey/J. Kirkwood

10,666 C. Grey/Irish School 1851

10,667 De Grifft/H. Brocas the Elder

10,668 S. Drummond/Irish School 1798

10,669 N. Dance/W. Ridley

10,670 R. Hunter/S. Harding

10,671 J.D. Herbert/T.W. Huffam

10,672 Reynolds of Dublin/W.H. Lizars

10,673 A. Buck/J. Kirkwood

10,674 C.W. Peale/E. Mackenzie

10,675 D. Maclise/D. Maclise

10,676 G. Kneller/J. Faber the Younger

10,677 B. Wilson/J. McArdell

10,678 English School 18C/A. Miller

10,679 J. Comerford/E. Scriven

10,680 N. Hone the Elder/J. Greenwood

10,681 No Entry

10,682 C. Jervas/J. Simon

10,683 F. Van Der Mijn/R. Purcell

10,684 T.H. Maguire/T.H. Maguire

10,685 L. Gluckman/J.H. Lynch

10,686 R.E. Pine/W. Dickinson

10,687 J. Comerford/J. Heath

10,688 A. Stewart/T. Woolnoth

10,689 T. Lawrence/C. Turner

10,690 S. Catterson Smith the Elder/G. Sanders

10,691 W. Wissing/J. Smith

10,692 R. Home/F. Bartolozzi

10,693 R. Home/F. Bartolozzi

10,694 R. Philips/J. Simon

10,695 N. Hone the Elder/J. Greenwood

10,696 N. Hone the Elder/W. Humphrey

10,697 N. Hone the Elder/J.R. Smith

10,698 N. Hone the Elder/E. Fisher

10,699 N. Hone the Elder/C. Phillips

10,700 N. Hone the Elder/J. Watson

10,701 W. Owen/S.W. Reynolds the Elder

10,702 H.D. Hamilton/F. Bartolozzi

10,703 English School c.1830/English School 1830

10,704 J. Haslock/J. Rogers

10,705 R. Sayers/G.T. Payne

10,706 Irish School c.1657/A. Blooteling

10,707 W. Evans/C. Picart

10,708 J. Comerford/J. Heath

10,709 T. Hudson/J. Faber the Younger

10,710 L. Gluckman/H. O'Neill

10,711 J. Reynolds/R.B. Parkes

10,712 J. Barry/J. Heath

10,713 W.P.J. Lodder/A. Cardon

10,714 J. Comerford/J. Heath

10,715 H.D. Hamilton/*J. Comerford*/J Heath

10,716 J. Comerford/Irish School 182

10,717 G. Soest/E. Walker

10,718 H.J. Burch the Younger/J. Ward

10,719 F.W. Weidemann/J. Smith

10,720 J. Reynolds/R.B. Parkes

10,721 G. Kneller/J. Faber the Younger

10,722 L. Gluckman/H. O'Neill

10,723 American School 19C/American School 19C

10,724 T. Lawrence/C. Turner

10,725 T.C. Thompson/D. Lucas

10,726 G.C. Stuart/C.H. Hodges

10,727 J. Hayter/W. Finden

10,728 G. Kneller/J. Smith

10,729 H. Howard/M. Vandergucht

10,730 C. D'Agar/J. Simon

10,731 C. D'Agar/J. Simon

10,732 G. Kneller/J. Simon

10,733 English School 17C/English School 1815

10,734 G.B. Black/G.B. Black

10,735 G. Patten/C.E. Wagstaff

10,736 E. Day/*E.H. Corbould*/?F. Holl

10,737 T. Phillips/R.J. Lane

10,738 W. Thomson/Irish School 18C

10,739 C.G. Stuart/*W. Evans*/W.T. Fry

10,740 T. Maynard/E. Bell

10,741 ?G. Gower/J. Basire the Elder

10,742 H. Hone/J. Heath

10,743 H. Hone/T. Nugent

10,744 H. Hone/B. Smith

10,745 H. Hone/B. Smith

10,746 G. Dance/W. Daniell

10,747 J. Comerford/Irish School 1825

10,748 J. Comerford/J. Heath

10,749 M. Cregan/D. Lucas

10,750 Circle of M. Gheeraerts the Younger/English School 1803

10,751 W. Owen/*J. Wright*/H. Meyer

10,752 H.D. Hamilton/F.C. Heissig

10,753 R. Bull/J. Collyer

10,754 J. Comerford/C. Rolls

10,755 N. Hone the Elder/J. McArdell

10,756 A. Van Dyck/A. Browne

10,757 A.G.G. D'Orsay/A.G.G. D'Orsay

10,758 F. Kruger/F. Kruger

10,759 P. Lely/A. Browne
10,760 English or Irish School 18C/J. Brooks
10,761 J. Comerford/J. Heath
10,762 J. Reynolds/J. Grozer
10,763 T. Bewick/*J. Thurston*/W.H. Worthington
10,764 W. Derby/J. Mollison
10,765 G. Romney/V. Green
10,766 English School 15C/*J. Carter*/J. Basire the Elder
10,767 T. Lawrence/J.Godby
10,768 J. Reynolds/J. Grozer
10,769 C.I. Baseley/W. Finden
10,770 Irish School 1806/14/*J.B. Lane*/S. Freeman
10,771 English School 17C/W. Faithorne the Elder & G. Vertue
10,772 R. Buckner/G.J. Zobel
10,773 A. Chappel/American School 1873
10,774 P. Lely/E. Lutterell
10,775 W. Robinson/D.J. Scarlett
10,776 J. Jackson/W. Ward the Elder
10,777 N. Hone the Elder/R. Pollard
10,778 J. Comerford/J. Heath
10,779 English School 19C/W. Read
10,780 W. Cuming/W. Ward the Elder
10,781 H.D. Hamilton/R. Cooper
10,782 ?M. Miereveld/*W. Derby*/E. Scriven
10,783 H.D. Hamilton/*P. Maguire*/J. Heath
10,784 J. Hayter/W.H. Mote
10,785 G. Kneller/J. Smith
10,786 F.W. Burton/J.S. Templeton
10,787 J. Russell/J. Spilsbury
10,788 After Rembrandt/N. Grogan
10,789 W.H. Collier/H. O'Neill
10,790 H.W. Pickersgill/H. Cousins
10,791 E. La Monte/W.H. Mote
10,792 R. Rothwell/T. Hodgetts
10,793 J. Comerford/J. Heath
10,794 J.P. Haverty/J.P. Haverty
10,795 ?J. Comerford/J. Heath
10,796 J. Reynolds/T. Hardy
10,797 W. Cuming/W. Ward the Elder
10,798 J. Comerford/T.G. Lupton
10,799 G. Kneller/G. Vertue
10,800 C. Robertson/C. Picart
10,801 T. Phillips/*W. Evans*/K. MacKenzie
10,802 C. Baugniet/C. Baugniet
10,803 J. Comerford/J. Heath
10,804 N. Hone the Elder/J. McArdell
10,805 N. Hone the Elder/J.R. Smith
10,806 W.C. Ross/J. Thomson
10,807 P. Van Somer/*G.P. Harding*/J. Brown
10,808 L.F. Abbott/W.S. Barnard
10,809 H. Howard/J. Smith
10,810 R. Cosway/F. Bartolozzi
10,811 J. Comerford/J. Heath
10,812 J. Hoppner/C. Turner
10,813 E.U. Eddis/G.J. Zobel
10,814 A.E. Chalon/R.A. Artlett
10,815 F.W. Burton/G. Sanders
10,816 J. Comerford/J. Heath
10,817 H. Hysing/T. Burford
10,818 ?J. Comerford/*T. Wright*/J. Heath
10,819 N. Dance/F. Bartolozzi
10,820 J. Worsdale/J. Brooks
10,821 G. Kneller/P. Schenck
10,822 M. Dahl/J. Simon
10,823 Irish School c.1820/Irish School c.1820
10,824 A. Wivell/T.G. Lupton
10,825 C. Jervas/J. Brooks
10,826 G. Kneller/J. Faber the Younger
10,827 T. Worlidge/R. Houston
10,828 R.E. Pine/W. Dickinson
10,829 F. Cotes/?R. Purcell
10,830 G. Hamilton/J. McArdell
10,831 F. Cotes/?R. Purcell
10,832 ?W. Faithorne the Younger/W. Faithorne the Younger
10,833 H. Hone/H.H. Meyer
10,834 G. Hamilton/J. Faber the Younger
10,835 J. Comerford/J. Heath
10,836 J. Comerford/J. Heath
10,837 A. Pope/J. Godby
10,838 A. Pope/J. Martyn
10,839 R. Walker/J. Houbraken
10,840 J. Wood/J. Brown
10,841 W. Robinson/W. Brett & S. Cousins
10,842 T.C. Thompson/C. Turner
10,843 T. Hudson/J. Faber the Younger
10,844 T. Phillips/J. Brown
10,845 G. Kneller/J. Faber the Younger
10,846 A. Soldi/J. McArdell
10,847 A. Robertson/E.F. Finden
10,848 T.C. Thompson/C. Turner
10,849 No Entry
10,850 B. West/E. Fisher
10,851 J. Spilsbury/J. Spilsbury
10,852 D. Lüders/J. McArdell
10,853 J. Reynolds/W. Dickinson & T. Watson
10,854 S. Ker/C. Turner
10,855 T. Hudson/J. McArdell
10,856 A. Killigrew/A. Blooteling
10,857 W. Foy/G. Foggo
10,858 English School c.1850/A. Weger
10,859 A.G.G. D'Orsay/A.G.G. D'Orsay
10,860 J. Mayall/D.J. Pound
10,861 H.D. Hamilton/F. Bartolozzi
10,862 H.D. Hamilton/F. Bartolozzi
10,863 H.D. Hamilton/*P. Maguire*/J. Heath
10,864 G. Romney/J. Walker
10,865 P. Schenck/P. Schenck
10,866 J. Hayter/W.H. Egleton
10,867 G. Kneller/J. Faber the Younger
10,868 C. Jagger/S. Sangster
10,869 Continental School c.1620/C. Turner
10,870 E. Hayes/S. Bellin
10,871 T.H. Maguire/T.H. Maguire
10,872 English School 17C/English School 1795
10,873 English School 18C/English School 1820
10,874 English School c.1800/English School c.1800
10,875 T. Cahill/Irish School c.1827
10,876 J. Comerford/J. Carver
10,877 French School c.1799/French School 1799
10,878 French School 18C/F. Lefebvre
10,879 I. Gosset/*N. Hone the Elder*/J. Basire the Elder
10,880 T.A. Jones/Irish School late 19C
10,881 J.R. Maguire/J. Heath
10,882 J. Moore/M. Gauci
10,883 H. Raeburn/*J. Jackson*/H.H. Meyer
10,884 English School 19C/English School 19C
10,885 W.J. Newton/J. Posselwhite
10,886 W.J. Newton/J. Posselwhite
10,887 R. McInnes/J. Brown
10,888 S.W. Reynolds the Younger/S.W. Reynolds the Elder & S. Cousins
10,889 C. Dupéchez/C. Dupéchez
10,890 No Entry
10,891 C.L. Eastlake/W.H. Mote
10,892 J. Comerford/Irish School 1825
10,893 M. Leighton/J.H. Lynch
10,894 G. Dawe/T.A. Dean
10,895 G. Dawe/T.A. Dean
10,896 H.D. Hamilton/J.K. Sherwin
10,897 H.D. Hamilton/J. Fittler
10,898 L. Lehmann/C.A. Tomkins
10,899 A. Lee/J. Brooks
10,900 ?Irish School 19C/T. Weger
10,901 C. Baugniet/C. Baugniet
10,902 G. Dance the Younger/W. Daniell

10,903 J. Reynolds/R. Josey
10,904 G. Kneller/J. Smith
10,905 L. Lehmann/C.A. Tomkins
10,906 C.P. Verhulst/J.-L. Anselin
10,907 R. Walker/F. Place
10,908 R. Dighton/R. Dighton
10,909 T.C. Thompson/H.H. Meyer
10,910 A. Lee/J. Chapman
10,911 J. Reynolds/J. Dean
10,912 Irish School 18C/R. Earlom
10,913 J. Bostock/J.J. Jenkins
10,914 J. Latham/J. Brooks
10,915 Allen/Allen
10,916 D. MacDonald/D. MacDonald
10,917 C. Stoppelaer/A. Miller
10,918 English 19C/?T. Langer
10,919 Irish School 18C/?E. Lyons
10,920 S. Harding/C. Knight
10,921 English School 17C/B. Lens
10,922 W. Wissing/B. Lens
10,923 R. Hunter/R. Purcell
10,924 R. Hunter/R. Purcell
10,925 N. Dance/*J. Jackson*/E. Scriven
10,926 T. Phillips/Mrs M. Turner
10,927 J. Mayall/D.J. Pound
10,928 F. Newenham/F.C. Lewis
10,929 G. Kneller/J. Smith
10,930 J.B. Closterman/J. Smith
10,931 R. Home/?Irish School 18C
10,932 No Entry
10,933 N. Hone the Elder/J. Finlayson
10,934 J. Hardy/T.W. Huffam
10,935 J. Hardy/T.W. Huffam
10,936 J. Petrie/J. Heath
10,937 W. Brocas/H.H. Meyer
10,938 ?J. Kriehuber/J. Kriehuber
10,939 J. Gillray/J. Gillray
10,940 J. Petrie/J. Heath
10,941 T. Lawrence/R.J. Lane
10,942 N. Hone the Elder/W. Baillie
10,943 E. Hawkins/W. Finden
10,944 N. Hone the Elder/W. Baillie
10,945 N. Hone the Elder/W. Baillie
10,946 J. Reynolds/J. Jones
10,947 H.D. Hamilton/J. Heath
10,948 M.A. Shee/G. Clint
10,949 J. Hoppner/*F. Bartolozzi*/H. Landseer
10,950 J. Keenan/W.T. Fry
10,951 H. Edridge/L. Schiavonetti
10,952 T. Hickey/J. Hall
10,953 S. De Koster/C. Townley
10,954 T. Lawrence/C. Turner
10,955 T. Lawrence/J. Cochran
10,956 No Entry
10,957 C.W. Cope/C.W. Cope
10,958 H.W. Phillips/W. Walker
10,959 S. Lover/R. Cooper
10,960 Irish School c.1800/H.H. Meyer
10,961 J. Comerford/Irish School 1825
10,962 English School c.1833/B. Holl
10,963 J.P. Haverty/J.P. Haverty
10,964 C. O'Donnell/H. Brocas the Elder
10,965 W. Brocas/W. Brocas
10,966 T.C. Thompson/C. Turner
10,967 E.H. Latilla/H.B. Hall the Elder
10,968 R.M. Hodgetts/R.M. Hodgetts
10,969 J.P. Haverty/J.P. Haverty
10,970 H. Newton/Maclure & MacDonald
10,971 B. Mulrenin/B. Mulrenin
10,972 T.H. Carrick/W. Holl the Younger
10,973 Irish School c.1831/Irish School 1831
10,974 Irish School 1840s/Irish School 1840s
10,975 J. Gubbins/J.P. Quilley
10,976 Doussin-Dubreuil/French School 19C
10,977 ?S. Catterson Smith the Elder/Irish School c.1830
10,978 J. Lewis/J. Lewis
10,979 J. Stewart/H. Robinson
10,980 H. O'Neill/H. O'Neill
10,981 S. Catterson Smith the Elder/R. Cooper
10,982 Doussin-Dubreuil/J. Stadler
10,983 W.H. Holbrooke/W.H. Holbrooke
10,984 W. Lane/W. Skelton
10,985 J. Comerford/R. Graves
10,986 J. Comerford/G. Parker
10,987 M. Maingaud/J. Houbraken
10,988 English School c.1860/English School c.1860
10,989 Irish School 1830s/W. Read
10,990 L. Gluckman/J.H. Lynch
10,991 G. Dawe/F.C. Lewis the Elder
10,992 T. Phillips/J. Brown
10,993 W. Wissing/I. Beckett
10,994 ?G. Kneller/P. Tanjé
10,995 M. Dahl/J. Simon
10,996 G. Kneller/J. Smith
10,997 G. Kneller/P. Pelham
10,998 English School 17C/P. Schenck
10,999 N. Dance/T. Burke
11,000 N. Dance/T. Burke
11,001 W.F.P. Napier/English School 19C
11,002 N. Hone the Elder/W. Dickinson
11,003 Irish School 17C/English School 1794
11,004 English School c.1650/J.G. Seiller
11,005 English School 17C/W. Marshall
11,006 R.E. Drummond/J. Hopwood the Younger
11,007 D.Y. Blakiston/G.J. Zobel
11,008 French School late 18C & J. Duplessi-Bertaux/ C.F.G. Lavachez & J. Duplessi-Bertaux
11,009 Titani/S. Freeman
11,010 Titani/S. Freeman
11,011 H. Barron/V. Green
11,012 N. Hone the Elder/J.R. Smith
11,013 E.T. Hurley/E.T. Hurley
11,014 E.T. Hurley/E.T. Hurley
11,015 E.T. Hurley/E.T. Hurley
11,016 E.T. Hurley/E.T. Hurley
11,017 E.T. Hurley/E.T. Hurley
11,018 J. Barrett/J. Watson
11,019 Irish School c.1843/J. Kirkwood
11,020 J.P. Haverty/J.P. Haverty
11,021 Markham/T. Burford
11,022 English School 17C/P. Pelham
11,023 J. Mayall/D.J. Pound
11,024 G. Kneller/J. Gole
11,025 P. Mignard/W. Faithorne the Younger
11,026 J.W. Gordon/W. Walker & S. Cousins
11,027 J. Mayall/J. Moore
11,028 J. Reynolds/W. Dickinson
11,029 G.F. Joseph/E. Scriven
11,030 G.F. Joseph/E. Scriven
11,031 W. Brocas/W. Brocas
11,032 M. Cregan/C. Turner
11,033 G.C. Stuart/W. Ward the Elder
11,034 French School 18C/V. Green
11,035 B.R. Green/J.H. Lynch
11,036 F. Cruikshank/E. Scriven
11,037 ?English School 16C/W. & M. Van De Passe
11,038 R. Stewart/E. Scott
11,039 J. Moore/E. Scriven
11,040 English School 1840/English School 1840
11,041 G. Kneller/J. Faber the Younger
11,042 H. Anelay/W.J. Linton
11,043 F. Grant/G.J. Zobel
11,044 J. Linnell the Elder/J. Linnell the Elder
11,045 T.A. Hayley/*M. Denman*/C. Watson
11,046 G. Romney/C. Watson
11,047 J. Reynolds/J.K. Baldrey
11,048 J. Oldham/J. Heath
11,049 J. Comerford/J. Heath
11,050 S. Cooper/English School 1806
11,051 E. Scott/C. Knight
11,052 English School c.1580/*G.P. Harding*/W. Greatbach

11,053 ?W. Segar/R.C. Bell
11,054 ?W. Segar/R.C. Bell
11,055 English School 1603/R.C. Bell
11,056 J. Reynolds/J. McArdell
11,057 A.F.J. Claudet/Bosley
11,058 D. Dodd/Sibelius
11,059 T. Fitzpatrick/T. Fitzpatrick
11,060 English School 1830s/Jenkinson
11,061 English School 1830s/Jenkinson
11,062 J. Worsdale/J. Brooks
11,063 J. Reynolds/R. Houston
11,064 C. Read/R. Houston
11,065 E. Landseer/English School c.1839
11,066 A.G.G. D'Orsay/A.G.G. D'Orsay
11,067 A.G.G. D'Orsay/A.G.G. D'Orsay
11,068 W. Hoare/R. Houston
11,069 N. Hone the Elder/R. Purcell
11,070 J. Hoppner/G. Clint
11,071 E.H. Trotter/H. Brocas the Elder
11,072 R. Rothwell/J.S. Templeton
11,073 ?G. Morphey/?R. Laurie
11,074 English School c.1810/A. Tardieu
11,075 C.W. Walton & Co./C.W. Walton & Co.
11,076 F.W. Burton/J.H. Lynch
11,077 E. Crawford/R. Josey
11,078 L.M. Ward/V.R.A. Brooks
11,079 H.W. Phillips/H.R. Cook
11,080 J. Latham/English School 1776
11,081 English School 18C/W. Skelton
11,082 C. Grey/J. Kirkwood
11,083 Irish School c.1791/Irish School 1791
11,084 R. Home/W. Ridley
11,085 R. Home/W. Evans
11,086 F. Cotes & J. Ramberg/R. Sands
11,087 Irish School c.1806/C. Doyle
11,088 Irish School c.1820/English School 19C
11,089 English School 17C/G. White
11,090 C. Grey/J. Kirkwood
11,091 Irish School c.1792/Irish School 1792
11,092 Irish School 18C/Irish School 18C
11,093 ?D. Dodd/?J. Walker
11,094 S. Shelley/W. Nutter
11,095 D. Dodd/T. Cook
11,096 T. Kettle/S. De Wilde
11,097 J. Reynolds/R. Brookshaw
11,098 J. Reynolds/R. Brookshaw
11,099 C. Grey/Irish School 1851
11,100 ?C. Grey/J. Kirkwood
11,101 English School late 17C/J. Nutting
11,102 Irish School c.1786/Irish School 1786
11,103 J.G. Mansfield/J.G. Mansfield
11,104 C. Grey/J. Kirkwood
11,105 W. Brocas/J. Martyn
11,106 R.E. Pine/R. Brookshaw
11,107 H. Brooke/R. Clamp
11,108 J. Lewis/Irish School 1852
11,109 Irish School c.1841/J. Kirkwood
11,110 Irish School c.1779/Irish School 1779
11,111 L. Bushe/J. Brown
11,112 Irish School 17C/R. Dunkarton
11,113 No Entry
11,114 English School late 18C/English School late 18C
11,115 W. Stevenson/W. Stevenson
11,116 J. Barry/W.C. Edwards
11,117 L.F. Abbott/A. Cardon
11,118 A.W. Devis/R. Cooper
11,119 J. Mee/H.R. Cook
11,120 W. Stevenson/J. Kirkwood
11,121 P. Van Bleeck/*J. Faber the Younger*/W.J. Alais
11,122 W.M. Craig/F. Mackenzie
11,123 H. Hone/T. Nugent
11,124 W. Hogarth/J. Haynes
11,125 Irish School c.1754/R. Graves
11,126 T. Hargreaves/E. Smith
11,127 G. F. Mulvany/W.J. Edwards
11,128 B. Stoker/*J. Comerford*/S. Watts
11,129 Irish School c.1785/Irish School 1785
11,130 ?G.C. Stuart/F. Mackenzie
11,131 G.C. Stuart/?Irish School 1799
11,132 Irish School c.1790/Irish School c.1790
11,133 H.F. Gravelot/English School 1820
11,134 A. Buck/Irish School c.1790
11,135 English School 16C/O. Humphrey/
11,136 S. Drummond/W. Ridley
11,137 H. Hone/T.W. Huffam
11,138 H. Hone/T.W. Huffam
11,139 Irish School c.1795/Irish School 1795
11,140 J. Reynolds/English School c.1770
11,141 Irish School c.1814/H. Brocas the Elder
11,142 Irish School c.1814/H. Brocas the Elder
11,143 Irish School c.1814/T. Blood
11,144 N. Kenny/F.C. Lewis
11,145 P. Fitzpatrick/P. Roberts
11,146 Irish School c.1780/Irish School c.1780
11,147 Irish School c.1782/English School 1782
11,148 A. Pope/J. Martyn
11,149 Irish School 18C/W. Esdall
11,150 F. Cotes/R. Brookshaw
11,151 F. Cotes/R. Brookshaw
11,152 J. Comerford/H. Meyer
11,153 H. Hone/H. Meyer
11,154 Irish School c.1750/R. Graves
11,155 ?H. Brocas the Elder/H. Brocas the Elder
11,156 C. Grey/J. Kirkwood
11,157 N. Hone the Elder/*N. Dance*/W. Ridley
11,158 J. Doyle/J. Doyle
11,159 H. Brocas the Elder/H. Brocas the Elder
11,160 Irish School 18C/H. Brocas the Elder
11,161 C. Grey/J. Kirkwood
11,162 Irish School late 18C/Irish School late 18C
11,163 J. Petrie/Irish School 1808
11,164 J. Petrie/English School 1846
11,165 J. Petrie/English School 1846
11,166 J. Petrie/*A.F.J. Claudet*/English School 1846
11,167 A. De Saint Aubyn/A. Cardon
11,168 J. Highmore/J. Hopwood the Elder
11,169 J.D. Herbert/T.W. Huffam
11,170 J.D. Herbert/T.W. Huffam
11,171 L.F. Aubry/T.W. Huffam
11,172 L.F. Aubry/T.W. Huffam
11,173 L.F. Aubry/T.W. Huffam
11,174 T. Robinson/W. Ridley
11,175 Irish School c.1792/Irish School 1792
11,176 B. Stoker/H. Brocas the Elder
11,177 Irish School c.1792/English School 1792
11,178 Irish School c.1847/H. Griffiths
11,179 S. Catterson Smith the Elder/R. Cooper
11,180 Irish School c.1820/T. Kelly
11,181 Irish School c.1800/Irish School c.1800
11,182 J. Petrie/English School 1846
11,183 F.X. Vispre/English School 18C
11,184 F.W. Weideman/J. Smith
11,185 F.W. Weideman/J. Smith
11,186 W. Hogarth/English School 1784
11,187 W. Hogarth/English School 1784
11,188 Irish School c.1780/Irish School c.1780
11,189 Continental School 19C/T.W. Huffam
11,190 G.C. Stuart/J. Farn
11,191 G.C. Stuart/J. Farn
11,192 C. Grey/J. Kirkwood

11,193 T. Lawrence/T.H. Parry
11,194 R. Bull/W. Sidgwick
11,195 Irish School 18C/J. Hall
11,196 ?Irish School 18C/?Irish School 18C
11,197 T. Lawrence/C.E. Wagstaff
11,198 T. Lawrence/H.H. Meyer
11,199 T. Lawrence/S. Freeman
11,200 H. Hopson/H.H. Houston
11,201 J. Reynolds/R. Brookshaw
11,202 ?C. Grey/Irish School 1849
11,203 J. Neagle/J. Thomson
11,204 S. Drummond/W. Ridley & W. Holl the Elder
11,205 English School 17C/S.F. Ravenet the Elder
11,206 Continental School 17C/English School 1795
11,207 P. Lely/A. Blooteling
11,208 M.A. Shee/E. Scriven
11,209 A. Pope/English School 1807
11,210 M. Gheeraerts the Younger/English School c.1800
11,211 J. Petrie/P. Maguire
11,212 Irish School 1768/1781//Irish School 1768/1781
11,213 G. Kneller/M. Vandergucht
11,214 J. Jackson/R. Page
11,215 A. Van Dyck/A. Blooteling
11,216 C. Grey/J. Kirkwood
11,217 C. Grey/J. Kirkwood
11,218 W. Haines/E. Scriven
11,219 J. Petrie/Irish School 19C
11,220 J. Comerford/A. Cardon
11,221 Irish School late 18C/P. Maguire
11,222 W.S. Mossop/?W.S. Mossop
11,223 J. Opie/H. Brocas the Elder
11,224 J.C. Lochée/J. Corner
11,225 D. Dodd/J. Walker
11,226 ?J. Comerford/J.H. Lynch
11,227 C. Grey/J. Kirkwood
11,228 English School c.1774/W. Humphrey
11,229 C.T. Wageman/H.H. Meyer
11,230 W. Hoare/W. Hoare
11,231 Irish School c.1800/English School 1816
11,232 G. Lance/J. Scott
11,233 B. Mulrenin/B. Mulrenin
11,234 Irish School c.1800/H.H. Meyer
11,235 Irish School 1790s/Irish School early 19C
11,236 J. Jackson/J. Thomson
11,237 T. Bridgford/Irish School 1847
11,238 Irish School c.1801/Irish School 1801
11,239 English School 1602/English School late 18C
11,240 W.H. Holbrooke/W.H. Holbrooke
11,241 Irish School 19C/Irish School 19C
11,242 T. Robinson/Irish School 1791
11,243 Maull & Polyblank/J. Cochran
11,244 G. Kneller/English School 18C
11,245 Irish School c.1793/Irish School 1793
11,246 G. Chinnery/Irish School 1804
11,247 G. Chinnery/Irish School 1804
11,248 J.J. Jenkins/T. Williamson
11,249 F. Van Der Mijn/R. Purcell
11,250 J.G. Eccard/J. Pearson
11,251 ?P. Lely/English School 17C
11,252 English School c.1650/English School 17C
11,253 ?P. Lely/W. Faithorne the Elder
11,254 R. Home/*C. Grey*/J. Kirkwood
11,255 ?P. Lely/S. Freeman
11,256 N. Hone the Elder/English School 18C
11,257 N. Hone the Elder/V.M. Picot
11,258 T. Hudson/W.W. Ryland
11,259 Irish School 18C/Irish School 18C
11,260 English School 17C/E. Nunzer
11,261 S. Drummond/H. Meyer
11,262 J. Rising/W. Hinton
11,263 P. Lely/A. Blooteling
11,264 P. Lely/A. Blooteling
11,265 T. Lawrence/E. Smith
11,266 R. Hunter/S. Harding
11,267 French School c.1796/J.H. Lynch
11,268 C. Grey/Irish School 1849
11,269 C. Grey/Irish School 1849
11,270 J. Comerford/J. Kirkwood
11,271 C. Grey/Irish School 1852
11,272 Irish School c.1790/T.W. Huffam
11,273 C. Grey/J. Kirkwood
11,274 Dutch School c.1690/Dutch School c.1690
11,275 English School 17C/W. Faithorne the Elder
11,276 N. Hone the Elder/N. Hone the Elder
11,277 N. Hone the Elder/R. Graves
11,278 S. Drummond/J. Thomson
11,279 H. Room/J. Cochran
11,280 Irish School 19C/R. Smith
11,281 J.C. Lochée/J. Heath
11,282 D. Dodd/T. Cook
11,283 T. Lawrence/T.A. Dean
11,284 French School late 18C/J. Walker
11,285 C. Jervas/*J. Thurston*/A.W. Warren
11,286 J. Steel/W. Ridley & W. Holl the Elder & T. Blood
11,287 P. Cunnignham/Irish School c.1770
11,288 W. Yellowless/S. Watts
11,289 S. Catterson Smith the Elder/R. Cooper
11,290 Irish School 19C/Irish School 19C
11,291 Lady M. Bingham/McDowall
11,292 C. Grey/J. Kirkwood
11,293 F.R. Say/J. Kirkwood
11,294 A. Buck/T.W. Huffam
11,295 ?A. Buck/T.W. Huffam
11,296 Irish School 18C/Irish School late 18C
11,297 S. Goodridge/A.B. Durand
11,298 C.S. Tone/English School 1846
11,299 C.S. Tone/English School 1846
11,300 C.S. Tone/English School 1846
11,301 E. Jones/H. Brocas the Elder
11,302 H. MacManus/J. Kirkwood
11,303 English School 18C/English School 1824
11,304 Irish School c.1780/Irish School 1780
11,305 Irish School c.1799/Irish School 1799
11,306 English School 19C/H. Griffiths
11,307 English School 19C/H. Griffiths
11,308 J. Robertson/J. Posselwhite
11,309 A.E. Chalon/W.H. Mote
11,310 T. Bridgford/H. Griffiths
11,311 C. Grey/H. Griffiths
11,312 T. Bridgford/H. Griffiths
11,313 J. Comerford/R. Cooper
11,314 J. Comerford/R. Cooper
11,315 T. Arrowsmith/T. Barrow
11,316 Irish School late 18C/Irish School late 18C
11,317 Irish School 18C/Irish School 18C
11,318 Irish School late 18C/Irish School late 18C
11,319 Mrs O'Neill/English School c.1790
11,320 French School 18C/H. P....
11,321 Irish School c.1784/Irish School 1784
11,322 H. Hone/English School 1790's
11,323 Irish School c.1803/Irish School 1803
11,324 Irish School c.1803/Irish School 1803
11,325 W. Cuming/?Irish School 19C
11,326 Irish School c.1803/T.W. Huffam
11,327 J. Comerford/J. Comerford

11,328 Irish School c.1794/Irish School 1794
11,329 J. Comerford/J.H. Lynch
11,330 J. Reynolds/English School 1811
11,331 Irish School c.1777/Irish School 1777
11,332 Irish School c.1827/Irish School c.1827
11,333 J. Ross/W.H. Mote
11,334 S. Lawrence/H. Griffiths
11,335 English School c.1850/J. Brown
11,336 W. Drummond/W.H. Egleton
11,337 ?G. Morphey/English School 1804
11,338 ?G. Morphey/Irish School 1808
11,339 M. Carpenter/W. Carpenter
11,340 R. Cosway/W. Lane
11,341 T. Lawrence & English School c.1830/?T.A. Prior
11,342 Irish School c.1778/Irish School 1778
11,343 Irish School c.1809/Irish School 1809
11,344 G. Chinnery/H. Brocas the Elder
11,345 W. Miller/O. Birrell
11,346 G. Kneller & C. Jervas/T.A. Prior
11,347 J.S. Muller/J.S. Muller
11,348 Irish School 1804/06/Irish School 1804/06
11,349 Irish School 1804/06/Irish School 1804/06
11,350 Irish School c.1811/Irish School 1811
11,351 Irish School c.1805/Irish School 1805
11,352 J. Petrie & Irish School c.1803/Irish School c.1803
11,353 English School c.1815/English School 1815
11,354 English School c.1815/English School 1816
11,355 English School c.1815/English School 1816
11,356 English School c.1815/English School 1816
11,357 English School c.1815/English School 1815
11,358 English School c.1815/English School 1815
11,359 English School c.1815/English School 1815
11,360 English School c.1815/English School 1816
11,361 English School c.1815/English School 1816
11,362 English School c.1815/English School 1815
11,363 English School c.1815/English School 1815
11,364 English School c.1815/English School 1815
11,365 English School c.1815/English School 1815
11,366 English School c.1815/English School 1815
11,367 English School c.1815/English School 1815
11,368 English School c.1815/English School 1815
11,369 English School c.1815/English School 1815
11,370 J. Comerford/Irish School 1825
11,371 J. Comerford/Irish School 1825
11,372 English School 19C/?T.A. Prior
11,373 P. Lely & ?J. Closterman/ T.A. Prior
11,374 G. Kneller & T. Worlidge/T.A. Prior
11,375 G. Kneller/T.A. Prior
11,376 R. Barber/S. Wheatley
11,377 N. Hone the Elder/G. Cook
11,378 Irish School c.1850/Irish School 1850
11,379 ?R. Walker/*A. van der Werff*/P. Drevet
11,380 P.J.A. Baudry/J.F. Jacquemart
11,381 Irish School c.1778/Irish School 1778
11,382 English School c.1850/English School c.1850
11,383 Irish School c.1850/Irish School c.1850
11,384 A. Wivell & T. Lawrence/?T.A. Prior
11,385 No Entry
11,386 N. Hone the Elder/J. Finlayson
11,387 N. Hone the Elder/J. Watson
11,388 R. Cosway/?J. Jones
11,389 J. Slater/F.C. Lewis the Elder
11,390 S. L..../G. Dalziel & E. Dalziel
11,391 No Entry
11,392 S. Cooper/*J. Bulfinch*/R. Cooper
11,393 S. Cooper/R. Brookshaw
11,394 ?R. Walker/English School 17C
11,395 English School 17C/English School 17C
11,396 ?R. Walker/P. Pelham
11,397 No Entry
11,398 No Entry
11,399 No Entry
11,400 No Entry
11,401 English School 1828/English School 1828
11,402 No Entry
11,403 J. Doyle/J. Doyle
11,404 F.P. Stephanoff/E. Scriven
11,405 No Entry
11,406 No Entry
11,407 English School 19c/English School 19C
11,408 N. Hone the Elder/J. Greenwood
11,409 T. Rowlandson/T. Rowlandson
11,410 A.G.G. D'Orsay/A.G.G. D'Orsay
11,411 Irish School 19C/Irish School 19C
11,412 J.S. Sargent/T. Cole
11,413 A.S. Belle/?J. Simon
11,414 N. Hone the Elder/J.R. Smith
11,415 J. Hoppner/T. Park
11,416 Irish School c.1750/W. Sharp
11,417 G. Romney/*J. Comerford*/E. Scriven
11,418 P. Lely/P. Vanderbanck
11,419 J.G. Day/J.G. Day
11,420 T. Lawrence/F.C. Lewis the Elder
11,421 C. Grey/Irish School 1853
11,422 C. Grey/Irish School 1853
11,423 D. Maclise/J. Kirkwood
11,424 Book: See Appendix 8
11,424 (1) S.W. Hayter/S.W. Hayter
11,424 (2) S.W. Hayter/S.W. Hayter
11,424 (3) S.W. Hayter/S.W. Hayter
11,425 ?English School early 19C/?English School early 19C
11,426 ?English School early 19C/?English School early 19c
11,427 Rembrandt/J. Wood
11,428 P.F. Gethin/P.F. Gethin
11,429 P.F. Gethin/P.F. Gethin
11,430 L. Gluckman/J.H. Lynch
11,431 T. Lessore/T. Lessore
11,432 T. Lessore/T. Lessore
11,433 T. Lessore/T. Lessore
11,434 T. Lessore/T. Lessore
11,435 T. Lessore/T. Lessore
11,436 T. Lessore/T. Lessore
11,437 W. Sickert/W. Sickert
11,438 W. Sickert/W. Sickert
11,439 W. Sickert/W. Sickert
11,440 W. Sickert/W. Sickert
11,441 W. Sickert/W. Sickert
11,442 W. Sickert/W. Sickert
11,443 W. Sickert/W. Sickert
11,444 W. Sickert/W. Sickert
11,445 W. Sickert/W. Sickert
11,446 W. Sickert/W. Sickert
11,447 W. Sickert/W. Sickert
11,448 A. McEvoy/W. Sickert
11,449 J. Raphael/J. Raphael
11,450 J. Raphael/J. Raphael
11,451 J. Raphael/J. Raphael

11,452 J. Raphael/J. Raphael
11,453 J. Raphael/J. Raphael
11,454 J. Pennell/J. Pennell
11,455 J. Pennell/J. Pennell
11,456 J. Pennell/J. Pennell
11,457 J. Pennell/J. Pennell
11,458 J. Pennell/J. Pennell
11,459 J. Pennell/J. Pennell
11,460 J. Pennell/J. Pennell
11,461 J. Pennell/J. Pennell
11,462 J. Pennell/J. Pennell
11,463 J. Pennell/J. Pennell
11,464 J. Pennell/J. Pennell
11,465 J. Pennell/J. Pennell
11,466 J. Pennell/J. Pennell
11,467 J. Pennell/J. Pennell
11,468 J. Pennell/J. Pennell
11,469 J. Pennell/J. Pennell
11,470 J. Pennell/J. Pennell
11,471 English School 20C/English School 20C
11,472 English School 20C/English School 20C
11,473 A. Legros/A. Legros
11,474 A. Legros/A. Legros
11,475 A. Legros/A. Legros
11,476 A. Legros/A. Legros
11,477 A. Legros/A. Legros
11,478 A. Legros/A. Legros
11,479 A. Legros/A. Legros
11,480 P.F. Gethin/P.F. Gethin
11,481 Titan/V. Lefebvre
11,482 Italian School 16C/M.E. Corr
11,483 F.J. Navez/M.E. Corr
11,484 P. Delaroche/L.P. Henriquel-Dupont
11,485 Continental School 19C/Continental School 19C
11,486 P. Delaroche/A.L. Martinet
11,487 U.L.A. Butin/U.L.A. Butin
11,488 J. Bassano/P. Monaco
11,489 A. Van Dyck/M.E. Corr
11,490 J.B.S. Chardin/B.F. Lépicié
11,491 A. Van Dyck/C. Galle the Elder
11,492 Titian/V. Lefebvre
11,493 Titian/F. Chauveau
11,494 Raphael/C. Du Bosc
11,495 E. Delacroix/L. D. Carred
11,496 F.T.L. Francia/R.G. Reeve
11,497 J. Nash/J. Nash
11,498 Titian/V. Lefebvre
11,499 ?English School 19C/?English School 19C
11,500 N. Berrettoni/B. Clayton the Elder
11,501 G.B. Tiepolo/Italian School 18C
11,502 C. Lapostolet/L.C. Beauparlant
11,503 F. Wheatley/T. Rowlandson
11,504 J.C. Vermeyen/E.G. Bocourt
11,505 P.P. Rubens/French School 18C
11,506 Rembrandt/A. Walker
11,507 W.H. Brooke/W.H. Brooke
11,508 A. Buck/English School 19C
11,509 W. Hogarth/W. Hogarth
11,510 W. Hogarth/W. Hogarth
11,511 W. Hogarth/W. Hogarth
11,512 W. Hogarth/W. Hogarth
11,513 W. Hogarth/W. Hogarth
11,514 W. Hogarth/W. Hogarth
11,515 W. Hogarth/W. Hogarth
11,516 W. Hogarth/W. Hogarth
11,517 W. Hogarth/W. Hogarth
11,518 W. Hogarth/W. Hogarth
11,519 W. Hogarth/W. Hogarth
11,520 W. Hogarth/W. Hogarth
11,521 W. Hogarth/W. Hogarth
11,522 J.-B.-S. Chardin/P.L. Surugue
11,523 G.J. Huband/G.J. Huband
11,524 G.J. Huband/G.J. Huband
11,525 G.J. Huband/G.J. Huband
11,526 G.J. Huband/G.J. Huband
11,527 G.J. Huband/G.J. Huband
11,528 G.J. Huband/G.J. Huband
11,529 G.J. Huband/G.J. Huband
11,530 G.J. Huband/G.J. Huband
11,531 No Entry
11,532 A. Ostade/W. Huband
11,533 W. Huband/W. Huband
11,534 W. Huband/W. Huband
11,535 W. Huband/W. Huband
11,536 A. Ostade/W. Huband
11,537 W. Huband/W. Huband
11,538 Raphael/W. Huband
11,539 W. Huband/W. Huband
11,540 W. Huband/W. Huband
11,541 G.J. Huband/G.J. Huband
11,542 P. Loutherbourg/W. Huband
11,543 T. Nolel/T. Nolel
11,544 Book: see Appendix 8
11,544 (8) G.M. Woodward/English School 1808
11,544 (55) J. Doyle/J. Doyle
11,544 (56) J. Doyle/J. Doyle
11,544 (57) J. Doyle/J. Doyle
11,544 (58) J. Doyle/J. Doyle
11,544 (59) J. Doyle/J. Doyle
11,544 (60) J. Doyle/J. Doyle
11,544 (61) J. Doyle/J. Doyle
11,544 (62) J. Doyle/J. Doyle
11,544 (63) J. Doyle/J. Doyle
11,544 (64) J. Doyle/J. Doyle
11,544 (65) J. Doyle/J. Doyle
11,544 (66) J. Doyle/J. Doyle
11,544 (67) J. Doyle/J. Doyle
11,545 J. Gillray/J. Gillray
11,546 Irish School 1789/Irish School 1789
11,547 Irish School 18C/Irish Schoc 18C
11,548 English School 1836/Smith & Graves
11,549 J. Fisher/J. Fisher
11,550 ?Italian School 1856/?Italian School 1856
11,551 T. Lawrence/J. Godby
11,552 No Entry
11,553 W. Behnes/H. Meyer
11,554 V.H. Lines/V.H. Lines
11,555 Irish School late 18C/P. Maguire
11,556 S. Catterson Smith the Elder/J.R. Jackson
11,557 W. Hogarth/English School c.1750
11,558 W. Hogarth/English School c.1750
11,559 W. Hogarth/English School c.1750
11,560 W. Hogarth/English School c.1750
11,561 W. Hogarth/English School c.1750
11,562 W. Hogarth/English School c.1750
11,563 No Entry
11,564 No Entry
11,565 K. Van Dongen/French Scho 20C
11,566 A. Gleizes/A. Gleizes
11,567 J. Speed/J. Malton
11,568 J. Malton/J. Malton
11,569 J. Malton/J. Malton
11,570 J. Malton/J. Malton
11,571 No Entry
11,572 No Entry
11,573 J. Malton/J. Malton
11,574 J. Malton/J. Malton
11,575 No Entry
11,576 No Entry
11,577 J. Malton/J. Malton
11,578 No Entry
11,579 J. Malton/J. Malton
11,580 J. Malton/J. Malton
11,581 J. Malton/J. Malton
11,582 J. Malton/J. Malton
11,583 J. Malton/J. Malton
11,584 No Entry
11,585 J. Malton/J. Malton
11,586 J. Malton/J. Malton
11,587 J. Malton/J. Malton
11,588 J. Malton/J. Malton
11,589 No Entry
11,590 No Entry
11,591 J. Malton/J. Malton
11,592 J. Malton/J. Malton
11,593 T.S. Roberts/J. Bluck
11,594 F. Wheatley/T. Milton

11,595 English School 1864/English School 1864
11,596 Sir T. Hammond/English School 1822
11,597 No Entry
11,598 No Entry
11,599 No Entry
11,600 R. Omer/P. Mazell
11,601 M.W. Peters/H.H. Houston
11,602 Irish School c.1796/Irish School c.1796
11,603 J. Carr/T. Medland
11,604 J.J. Barralet/T. Milton
11,605 N.J. Crowley/C.W. Sharpe
11,606 J.H. Ramberg/F. Bartolozzi
11,607 No Entry
11,608 P. Byrne/W. Smith
11,609 P. Byrne/W. Radclyffe the Elder
11,610 R.O'C. Newenham/J.D. Harding
11,611 R.O'C. Newenham/J.D. Harding
11,612 Irish School c.1780/Irish School c.1780
11,613 Irish School 1787/Irish School 1787
11,614 J. Tudor/T. Chambars
11,615 J.J. Barralet/T. Milton
11,616 Irish School c.1762/Irish School 1762
11,617 M.W. Peters/H.H. Houston
11,618 Irish School late 18C/Irish School late 18C
11,619 P.F. Gethin/P.F. Gethin
11,620 A. Concanen/E. Chavane
11,621 W.B. Taylor/W.B. Taylor & J. Bluck
11,622 W.B. Taylor/W.B. Taylor & R. Havell the Elder &Younger
11,623 J.-B.-S. Chardin/P.L. Surugue
11,624 J. Ford/J. Ford
11,625 J. Ford/J. Ford
11,626 Irish School 1784/English School 1784
11,627 Irish School c.1779/Irish School c.1800
11,628 J. Fisher/J. Fisher
11,629 R. Omer/P. Halpin
11,630 Irish School 1853/Irish School 1853
11,631 No Entry
11,632 Irish School 1880/Morison & Co.
11,633 Irish School c.1750/J. Jones
11,634 J. Malton/J. Malton
11,635 Irish School 19C/Irish School 19C
11,636 Irish School 19c/Irish School 19C
11,637 W. Hincks/W. Hincks
11,638 W. Brocas/R. Havell the Elder & Younger
11,639 J. Fisher/J. Fisher
11,640 J. Malton/J. Malton
11,641 J.J. Barralet/J.J. Barralet
11,642 T. Carter the Elder/Irish School 18C
11,643 J.J. Barralet/J.C. Stadler
11,644 F. Wheatley/J. Collyer
11,645 F. Wheatley/T. Malton
11,646 W. Brocas/R. Havell the Elder & Younger
11,647 T.L. Rowbotham the Elder/D. Havell
11,648 T.L. Rowbotham the Elder/D. Havell
11,649 J.P. Haverty/R. Havell the Elder & Younger
11,650 J.P. Haverty/R. Havell the Elder & Younger
11,651 J.P. Haverty/R. Havell the Elder & Younger
11,652 J. Wyck/J. Brooks
11,653 T.S. Roberts/J. Bluck
11,654 J.J. Barralet/W. Ward the Elder
11,655 R. De Hooghe/R. De Hooghe
11,656 G.P. Panini/*J. Dumont the Elder*/C.N. Cochin
11,657 J.K. Sherwin/J.K. Sherwin
11,658 J.K. Sherwin/J.K. Sherwin
11,659 Guercino/*A. Tofanelli*/G.B. Leonetti
11,660 D. Teniers the Younger/D. Teniers the Younger
11,661 After P.P. Rubens/F. Lamb
11,662 M. Marieschi/M. Marieschi
11,663 D. Wilkie/G. Mosse
11,664 B. West/W. Woollett
11,665 R. Cosway/J.R. Smith
11,666 H. Moll/H. Moll
11,667 Irish School c.1753/Irish School 1753
11,668 Irish School c.1786/Irish School 1786
11,669 T. Ivory/E. Rooker
11,670 Irish School 18C/Irish School 18C
11,671 Irish School 19C/Irish School 19C
11,672 Irish School 19C/Irish School 19C
11,673 Irish School 19C/Irish School 19C
11,674 J.E. Jones/E. Radclyffe
11,675 J.E. Jones/E. Radclyffe
11,676 J.E. Jones/E. Radclyffe
11,677 J.E. Jones/E. Radclyffe
11,678 J.E. Jones/E. Radclyffe
11,679 Irish School c.1798/English School 1798
11,680 ?Irish School 18C/Barclay
11,681 ?Irish School 18C/Barclay
11,682 D.Y. Cameron/D.Y. Cameron
11,683 F. Wheatley/T. Milton
11,684 F. Wheatley/T. Milton
11,685 J.E. Jones/E. Radclyffe
11,686 J.E. Jones/E. Radclyffe
11,687 J.E. Jones/E. Radclyffe
11,688 J.E. Jones/E. Radclyffe
11,689 G. Holmes/J. Walker
11,690 J. Malton/J. Malton
11,691 J. Tudor/Slack
11,692 J. Carr/J. Tomlinson
11,693 W.M. Craig/T. Dixon
11,694 ?J. Ford/J. Ford
11,695 J.P. Haverty/J.P. Haverty
11,696 T.L. Rowbothom the Elder/D. Havell
11,697 T. Creswick/J. T. Willmore
11,698 Sir T. Hammond/English School 1822
11,699 J. Malton/A.F. Lemaitre
11,700 G. Petrie/T. Higham
11,701 J. Kirkwood/J. Kirkwood
11,702 J. Malton/A.F. Lemaitre
11,703 S.F. Brocas/H. Brocas the Younger
11,704 Irish School 19C/J.L. Marks
11,705 F. Johnston/R. Havell the Elder & Younger
11,706 Irish School c.1785/English School 1785
11,707 R. Pool & J. Cash/J. Lodge
11,708 R. Pool & J. Cash/J. Lodge
11,709 R. Pool & J. Cash/J. Lodge
11,710 R. Pool & J. Cash/J. Lodge
11,711 R. Pool & J. Cash/J. Lodge
11,712 J. Tudor/English School 1749
11,713 Irish School 18C/Irish School 18C
11,714 Irish School c.1816/English School 1816
11,715 Irish School late 18C/Irish School late 18C
11,716 J. Tudor/F. Cary
11,717 J. Tudor/English School 1774
11,718 Irish School c.1800/Irish School c.1800
11,719 J. Fisher/J. Fisher
11,720 Irish School 1792/English School 1792
11,721 Irish School 1792/English School 1792
11,722 Irish School 1853/Irish School 1853
11,723 ?N. Clarget/L.A. Tourfaut
11,724 Irish School c.1880/Irish School c.1880
11,725 R. Pool & J. Cash/J. Lodge

11,726 R. Pool & J. Cash/J. Lodge
11,727 Irish School c.1790/English School 1790
11,728 Irish School 1792/English School 1792
11,729 Irish School 19C/M. Jackson
11,730 Irish School c.1787/English School 1787
11,731 Irish School c.1787/English School 1787
11,732 ?F. Jukes/F. Jukes
11,733 ?F. Jukes/F. Jukes
11,734 R. Pool & J. Cash/J. Lodge
11,735 Irish School 1808/Irish School 1808
11,736 Irish School c.1820/Irish School c.1820
11,737 T.N. Deane & B. Woodward/J.E. Rogers
11,738 Irish School late 18C/Irish School late 18C
11,739 Irish School late 18C/English School late 18C
11,740 R. Pool & J. Cash/J. Lodge
11,741 Irish School c.1817/English School 1817
11,742 Irish School c.1786/English School 1786
11,743 Irish School c.1788/English School 1788
11,744 Irish School c.1788/English School 1788
11,745 Irish School 19C/Irish School 19C
11,746 Irish School 19C/Irish School 19C
11,747 Irish School c.1750/English School 1751
11,748 English School 18C/Sparrow
11,749 W.H. Bartlett/J. Heath
11,750 J.J. Barralet/T. Milton
11,751 S. Close the Elder/S. Close the Elder
11,752 R. Pool & J. Cash/W. Thomas
11,753 R. Pool & J. Cash/I. Taylor the Elder
11,754 Irish School late 18C/Myers
11,755 R. Pool & J. Cash/I. Taylor the Elder
11,756 Irish School 1788/English School 1789
11,757 Irish School 18C/Irish School 18C
11,758 J.E. Jones/E. Radclyffe
11,759 P. Byrne/W. Radclyffe
11,760 Irish School 19C/Irish School 19C
11,761 Irish School 19C/J. Newman & Co.
11,762 Irish School c.1817/English School 1817
11,763 W.H. Bartlett/F.W. Topham
11,764 J. Malton/English School 1817
11,765 J. Malton/A.F. Lemaitre
11,766 Irish School c.1850/Irish School c.1850
11,767 Irish School c.1818/B. Brunton
11,768 Irish School c.1755/B. Cole
11,769 W. Sadler the Younger/J. Storer & H. Sargent
11,770 Irish School early 19C/J. Martyn
11,771 W.H. Bartlett/R. Winkles
11,772 R. Carpenter/T.T. Bury
11,773 G. Petrie/English School 1821
11,774 G. Petrie/E. Goodall
11,775 G. Petrie/T. Higham
11,776 G. Petrie/B. Winkles
11,777 G. Petrie/T. Barber
11,778 G. Petrie/T. Barber
11,779 G. Petrie/T. Barber
11,780 G. Petrie/English School 1821
11,781 G. Petrie/English School 1821
11,782 G. Petrie/B. Winkles
11,783 G. Petrie/English School 1821
11,784 G. Petrie/English School 1821
11,785 G. Petrie/B. Winkles
11,786 G. Petrie/B. Winkles
11,787 G. Petrie/E. Goodall
11,788 G. Petrie/J. Storer & H. Sargent
11,789 G. Petrie/English School 1821
11,790 G. Petrie/T. Barber
11,791 G. Petrie/T. Barber
11,792 G. Petrie/T. Barber
11,793 G. Petrie/T. Higham
11,794 G. Petrie/E. Goodall
11,795 J.M.W. Turner/R. Wallis
11,796 J.M.W. Turner/J.T. Willmore
11,797 J.M.W. Turner/J.T. Willmore
11,798 J.M.W. Turner/W. Radclyffe
11,799 J.M.W. Turner/J. Cousen
11,800 J.M.W. Turner/J.B. Allen
11,801 J.M.W. Turner/J.B. Allen
11,802 J.M.W. Turner/R. Brandard
11,803 J.M.W. Turner/R. Brandard
11,804 J.M.W. Turner/R. Brandard
11,805 No Entry
11,806 J. Rocque/A. Dury & P. Halpin
11,807 T. Sherrard/Irish School 1803
11,808 No Entry
11,809 J. Thomas/Army Litho School 20C
11,810 No Entry
11,811 J. Kirkwood/J. Kirkwood
11,812 W. Wilson/B. Baker
11,813 J. Rocque/English School 1799
11,814 Irish School c.1817/English School 1817
11,815 No Entry
11,816 J. Malton/J. Malton
11,817 Irish School 18C/Irish School 18C
11,818 S. Sproule/Irish School 1783
11,819 Dutch School 1689/Dutch school c.1689
11,820 English School pre-1666/English School 17C
11,821 Irish School 18C/Irish School 18C
11,822 No Entry
11,823 (1-2) T.H. Shepherd/J. Tingle
11,824 (1-2) T.H. Shepherd/R. Acon
11,825 (1-2) T.H. Shepherd/T. Barber
11,826 F. Wheatley/J. Collyer
11,827 J.K. Sherwin/J.K. Sherwin
11,828 J.K. Sherwin/J.K. Sherwin
11,829 J.K. Sherwin/J.K. Sherwin
11,830 F. Wheatley/English School 1801
11,831 Irish School c.1817/English School 1817
11,832 Irish School c.1790/English School 1790
11,833 Irish School early 18C/Irish School early 18C
11,834 German School 19C/German School 19C
11,835 ?C. Corley/C. Corley
11,836 English School c.1785/English School 1785
11,837 Irish School c.1787/English School 1787
11,838 C.E. Maguire/C.E. Maguire
11,839 Irish School late 18C/English School 1799
11,840 Irish School c.1865/Morison & Co.
11,841 J. Thomas/Army Litho School 20C
11,842 J. Fogarty/R. Havell the Elder and Younger
11,843 H. Furniss/Typo Etching Company
11,844 No Entry
11,845 A. Watteau/C. Dupuis
11,846 R. De Hooghe/R. De Hooghe
11,847 R. De Hooghe/R. De Hooghe
11,847 (1-12) details of R. De Hooghe/R. De Hooghe
11,848 N. Hone the Elder/N. Hone the Elder
11,849 R. De Hooghe/R. De Hooghe
11,849 (1-5) details of R. De Hooghe/R. De Hooghe
11,850 T. Kelly/T. Kelly
11,851 Irish School c.1811/Irish School 1811
11,852 J. Doyle/J. Doyle
11,853 J. Doyle/J. Doyle
11,854 J. Doyle/J. Doyle

11,855 F. Holl the Younger/D.A. Wehrschmidt
11,856 S. Catterson Smith the Elder/G. Sanders
11,857 J.P. Haverty/J.P. Haverty
11,858 J. Barry/J. Barry
11,859 E. Crewe/C.W. White
11,860 W. Daniell/W. Daniell
11,861 T. Bridgford/T. P....
11,862 Irish School c.1840/Irish School c.1840
11,863 W. Wissing/I. Beckett
11,864 Irish School 19C/Irish School 1847
11,865 Dutch School c.1690/Dutch School c.1690
11,866 Dutch School c.1690/Dutch School c.1690
11,867 Irish School 19C/Irish School 19C
11,868 D. Teniers the Younger/J.P. Lebas
11,869 P.F. Gethin/P.F. Gethin
11,870 Irish School 1783/Irish School 1783
11,871 R.C. Goff/R.C. Goff
11,872 No Entry
11,873 J. Bateman/T.J. Engleheart
11,874 B.R. Julien/B.R. Julien
11,875 C.L. Bazin/J.B.A. Lafosse
11,876 E.L. Vigée-Le Brun/G.J. Hart
11,877 R.W. Seale/R.W. Seale
11,878 Irish School 1846/Smyth
11,879 G. Collins/English School 17C
11,880 J. Rocque/English School 1762
11,881 Irish School c.1717/Irish School 1717
11,882 R. De Hooghe/R. De Hooghe
11,883 R. Omer/Irish School 1767
11,884 L.R. Strangways/L.R. Strangways
11,885 E. Heffernan/Irish School 1868
11,885 (1-22) details of E. Heffernan/Irish School 1868
11,886 J. Rocque/J.J. Perret
11,887 W. Faden/W. Faden
11,888 J. Cooke/J. Cooke
11,888 (1-24) details of J. Cooke/J. Cooke
11,889 Irish School c.1728/E. Bowen
11,890 No Entry
11,891 J. Doyle/J. Doyle
11,892 Irish School 18C/J.H. Burgess
11,893 J. Brownrigg/J. Ford
11,894 Irish School c.1795/Irish School c.1795
11,895 Irish School 1784/English School 1784
11,896 Irish School 1784/English School 1784
11,897 Irish School 1784/English School 1784
11,898 Irish School 1784/English School 1784
11,899 Irish School 1784/English School 1784
11,900 Irish School 1784/English School 1784
11,901 Irish School 1784/English School 1784
11,902 F. Wheatley/T. Malton
11,903 J. Tudor/A. Walker
11,904 J. Tudor/Parr
11,905 J. Tudor/Parr
11,906 J. Tudor/?J. McArdell
11,907 No Entry
11,908 No Entry
11,909 T.S. Roberts/R. Havell the Elder & Younger
11,910 T.S.Roberts/R.Havell the Elder & Younger
11,911 T.S. Roberts/J. Bluck
11,912 T.S. Roberts/R. Havell the Elder & Younger
11,913 Irish School c.1787/English School 1787
11,914 Irish School 1792/English School 1792
11,915 Irish School c.1785/English School 1785
11,916 Irish School c.1786/English School 1786
11,917 Irish School c.1788/English School 1788
11,918 Irish School c.1787/English School 1787
11,919 T. Archdeakon/T. Archdeakon
11,920 Irish School c.1786/English School 1786
11,921 Irish School c.1788/English School 1788
11,922 Irish School 19C/Irish School 19C
11,923 Irish School c.1790/Irish School 1790
11,924 B. Clayton the Elder/B. Clayton the Elder
11,925 Irish School c.1789/Irish School 1789
11,926 No Entry
11,927 T. Cocking/T. Medland
11,928 No Entry
11,929 U. Franchini/U. Franchini
11,930 M.M. Kennedy/M.M. Kennedy
11,931 J.D. Burns/J.D. Burns
11,932 Album: See Appendix 8
11,932 (7) H. Kernoff/H. Kernoff
11,933 W. Poorter/L. Beyer
11,934 L. Gluckman/H. O'Neill
11,935 L. Gluckman/H. O'Neill
11,936 L. Gluckman/J.H. Lynch
11,937 L. Gluckman/H. O'Neill
11,938 L. Gluckman/H. O'Neill
11,939 L. Gluckman/J.H. Lynch
11,940 L. Gluckman/H. O'Neill
11,941 No Entry
11,942 English School c.1560/J. Houbraken
11,943 G.B. Castiglione/*R. Earlom*/J. Boydell
11,944 S.F. Brocas/H. Brocas the Younger
11,945 S.F. Brocas/H. Brocas the Younger
11,946 S.F. Brocas/H. Brocas the Younger
11,947 S.F. Brocas/H. Brocas the Younger
11,948 S.F. Brocas/H. Brocas the Younger
11,949 S.F. Brocas/H. Brocas the Younger
11,950 S.F. Brocas/H. Brocas the Younger
11,951 S.F. Brocas/H. Brocas the Younger
11,952 S.F. Brocas/H. Brocas the Younger
11,953 S.F. Brocas/H. Brocas the Younger
11,954 S.F. Brocas/H. Brocas the Younger
11,955 S.F. Brocas/H. Brocas the Younger
11,956 S.F. Brocas/H. Brocas the Younger
11,957 G.B. Cipriani/F. Bartolozzi
11,958 J.M.W. Turner/J.M.W. Turner & J.C. Easling
11,959 J.M.W.Turner/J.M.W.Turner & C. Turner
11,960 J.M.W. Turner/J.M.W. Turner & C. Turner
11,961 J.M.W. Turner/J.M.W. Turner & C. Turner
11,962 J.M.W. Turner/J.M.W. Turner & C. Turner
11,963 J.M.W. Turner/J.M.W. Turner & C. Turner
11,964 J.M.W. Turner/J.M.W. Turner & C. Turner
11,965 J.M.W. Turner/J.M.W. Turner & C. Turner
11,966 J.M.W. Turner/J.M.W. Turner & C. Turner
11,967 J.M.W. Turner/J.M.W. Turner & C. Turner
11,968 J.M.W. Turner/J.M.W. Turner & C. Turner
11,969 J.M.W. Turner/J.M.W. Turner & C. Turner

11,970 J.M.W. Turner/J.M.W. Turner & C. Turner
11,971 J.M.W. Turner/J.M.W. Turner & C. Turner
11,972 J.M.W. Turner/J.M.W. Turner & C. Turner
11,973 J.M.W. Turner/J.M.W. Turner & C. Turner
11,974 J.M.W. Turner/J.M.W. Turner & C. Turner
11,975 J.M.W. Turner/J.M.W. Turner & C. Turner
11,976 J.M.W. Turner/J.M.W. Turner & C. Turner
11,977 J.M.W. Turner/J.M.W. Turner & C. Turner
11,978 J.M.W. Turner/J.M.W. Turner & C. Turner
11,979 J.M.W. Turner/J.M.W. Turner & W. Say
11,980 J.M.W. Turner/J.M.W. Turner & R. Dunkarton
11,981 J.M.W. Turner/J.M.W. Turner & W. Say
11,982 J.M.W. Turner/J.M.W. Turner & R. Dunkarton
11,983 J.M.W. Turner/J.M.W. Turner & C. Turner
11,984 J.M.W. Turner/J.M.W. Turner & W. Say
11,985 J.M.W. Turner/J.M.W. Turner
11,986 J.M.W. Turner/J.M.W. Turner & W. Say
11,987 J.M.W. Turner/J.M.W. Turner & W. Say
11,988 J.M.W. Turner/J.M.W. Turner & T. Hodgetts
11,989 J.M.W. Turner/J.M.W. Turner & R. Dunkarton
11,990 J.M.W. Turner/J.M.W. Turner & J.C. Easling
11,991 J.M.W. Turner/J.M.W. Turner & W. Say
11,992 J.M.W. Turner/J.M.W. Turner
11,993 J.M.W. Turner/J.M.W. Turner & T. Hodgetts
11,994 J.M.W. Turner/J.M.W. Turner & R. Dunkarton
11,995 J.M.W. Turner/J.M.W. Turner & W. Say
11,996 J.M.W. Turner/J.M.W. Turner
11,997 J.M.W. Turner/J.M.W. Turner & W.T. Annis & J.C. Easling
11,998 J.M.W. Turner/J.M.W. Turner & G. Clint
11,999 J.M.W. Turner/J.M.W. Turner & J.C. Easling
20,000 J.M.W. Turner/J.M.W. Turner & F.C. Lewis the Elder
20,001 J.M.W. Turner/J.M.W. Turner
20,002 J.M.W. Turner/J.M.W. Turner & G. Clint
20.003 J.M.W. Turner/J.M.W. Turner & R. Dunkarton
20,004 J.M.W. Turner/J.M.W. Turner & J.C. Easling
20,005 J.M.W. Turner/J.M.W. Turner & W.T. Annis
20,006 J.M.W. Turner/J.M.W. Turner & W. Say
20,007 J.M.W. Turner/J.M.W. Turner
20,008 J.M.W. Turner/J.M.W. Turner & H. Dawe
20,009 J.M.W. Turner/J.M.W. Turner & T.G. Lupton
20,010 J.M.W. Turner/J.M.W. Turner & W. Say
20,011 J.M.W. Turner/H. Dawe
20,012 J.M.W. Turner/J.M.W. Turner
20,013 J.M.W. Turner/J.M.W. Turner & T.G. Lupton
20,014 J.M.W. Turner/J.M.W. Turner & C. Turner
20,015 J.M.W. Turner/J.M.W. Turner
20,016 J.M.W. Turner/J.M.W. Turner & T. Hodgetts
20,017 J.M.W. Turner/J.M.W. Turner
20,018 J.M.W. Turner/J.M.W. Turner & W. Say
20,019 J.M.W. Turner/J.M.W. Turner & T.G. Lupton
20,020 J.M.W. Turner/J.M.W. Turner & H. Dawe
20,021 J.M.W. Turner/H. Dawe
20,022 J.M.W. Turner/J.M.W. Turner & C. Turner
20,023 J.M.W. Turner/J.M.W. Turner
20,024 J.M.W. Turner/J.M.W. Turner & S.W. Reynolds the Elder
20,025 J.M.W. Turner/J.M.W. Turner & W. Say
20,026 J.M.W. Turner/J.M.W. Turner & T.G. Lupton
20,027 J.M.W. Turner/J.M.W. Turner
20,028 J.M.W. Turner/J.M.W. Turner & S.W. Reynolds the Elder
20,029 P. Sandby/T. Cook
20,030 R. O'C. Newenham/J.D. Harding
20,031 G.B. Cipriani/F. Bartolozzi
20,032 F. Chesham/F. Chesham
20,033 E. Dayes/T. Gaugain & J. Mitan
20,034 J.H. Mortimer/R. Blyth
20,035 L. Bramer/P.C. Canot
20,036 J.H. Mortimer/R. Blyth
20,037 H. Gravelot/J.C. Le Vasseur
20,038 B. Luini/M. Bovi
20,039 English School 19C/English School 19C
20,040 School of P.P. Rubens/B. Baron
20,041 P.P. Rubens/B. Baron
20,042 P.P. Rubens/B. Baron
20,043 P.P. Rubens/B. Baron
20,044 P.P. Rubens/B. Baron
20,045 P.P. Rubens/B. Baron
20,046 P.P. Rubens/B. Baron
20,047 P.P. Rubens/B. Baron
20,048 Venetian School 16C/*W. Hodgson*/A. Cardon
20,049 C. Le Brun/R. Shepherd
20,050 C. Le Brun/R. Shepherd
20,051 C. Le Brun/R. Shepherd
20,052 C. Le Brun/R. Shepherd
20,053 C. Le Brun/R. Shepherd
20,054 H.L. Garnier/A.L. Lemercier
20,055 J. Lucas/J. Lucas
20,056 H.P. Parker/W.O. Geller
20,057 H.J. Fradelle/A. Duncan
20,058 S. Vouet/N.F.J. Masquelier Le Jeune
20,059 H. Singleton/J. Godby
20,060 H. Singleton/J. Godby
20,061 German School 950/1050//C. Regnier
20,062 German School 1490/1530//J. Klipphahn
20,063 German School 1519/J. Klipphahn
20,064 German School 1520/1530//?C. Regnier
20,065 German School 1546/1555//C. Regnier
20,066 J.H. Mortimer/R. Blyth
20,067 T. Stothard/A. Cardon
20,068 W.O. Peters/W.O. Peters
20,069 Genoese School 17C/J. Goupy & J.B.G. Scotin
20,070 E. Le Sueur/P.L.H. Laurent
20,071 E. Le Sueur/P.L.H. Laurent
20,072 G. Metsu/A. Chaitaigner
20,073 P. Rossi/A. Chaitaigner
20,074 J. Steen/G.R. Le Vilain
20,075 D. Teniers the Younger/R. Delaunay
20,076 F. Nicholson/T.F. Ranson
20,077 C. Schwartz/A. Friedel
20,078 D. Teniers the Younger/R. Cooper

20,079 C.H. Toussaint/C.H. Toussaint
20,080 C. Rothschild/T.N. Chauvel
20,081 T.S. Townsend/T.S. Townsend
20,082 J.C. Robinson/J.C. Robinson
20,083 R. Wilson/T. Morris
20,084 Titian/A.C. Masson
20,085 C. Dusart/J. Browne & W. Woollett
20,086 D. Teniers the Younger/J.N. Lerouge
20,087 Heigeleg/French School 1868
20,088 C.M. Dubufe/C.M. Dubufe
20,089 J. Ward/English School 1795
20,090 I. Ostade/P.C. Canot
20,091 No Entry
20,092 No Entry
20,093 T. Lawrence/T. Evans
20,094 English School 18C/J. Morris
20,095 W. Marlow/Godfrey
20,096 W. Pars/Godfrey
20,097 W. Pars/Godfrey
20,098 W. Pars/Godfrey
20,099 W. Pars/Godfrey
20,100 French School 19C/J.P.M. Jazet
20,101 A.E. Fragonard/Barthier
20,102 ?H.R. Devilliers/H.R. Devilliers
20,103 ?Titian/*F. Bartolozzi*/M. Bovi
20,104 M. Brown/D. Orme
20,105 Dutch School 17C/J.M.F. Geissler
20,106 J. Drouais-Germain/L. Duval
20,107 Titian/F. Chauveau
20,108 D. Teniers the Younger/R. Delaunay
20,109 D. Teniers the Younger/G. Hulbeste
20,110 C. Grey/J. Kirkwood
20,111 J.R. Dicksee/J. R. Dicksee
20,112 T. Lawrence/T.G. Lupton
20,113 ?I. Oliver/C. Turner
20,114 A. Van Dyck/P. Pontius
20,115 A. Van Dyck/*C. W. Bampfylde*/English School 1814
20,116 A. Van Dyck/P. Pontius
20,117 French School 17C/French School 17C
20,118 J. Jackson/R. Woodman the Younger
20,119 T. Worlidge/C.W. White
20,120 ?A. da Bonaiuto/English School 18C
20,121 G.S. Newton/Gibbs
20,122 G.H. Harlow/H. Meyer
20,123 G. Kneller/D. Malone
20,124 G. Kneller/D. Malone
20,125 C. Mellan/C. Mellan
20,126 T. Foster/W.J. Ward the Younger
20,127 W. Howis the Elder/L. Dickinson
20,128 W. Howis the Elder/L. Dickinson
20,129 W. Howis the Elder/L. Dickinson
20,130 W. Howis the Elder/L. Dickinson
20,131 W. Howis the Elder/L. Dickinson
20,132 A. Vandercabel/S.W. Reynolds the Younger
20,133 G. Kneller/J. Houbraken
20,134 J. Storer/J. Storer
20,135 N. Berchem/English School 18C
20,136 T. Lawrence/C. Rolls
20,137 ?Correggio/S.W. Reynolds the Younger
20,138 J.H. Robinson/J.S. Templeton
20,139 W. Linton/J.T. Willmore
20,140 C.R. Leslie/L. Stocks
20,141 C.R. Leslie/T. Vernon
20,142 C.R. Leslie/C.W. Sharpe
20,143 E. Leroux/E. Leroux
20,144 English School 19C/English School 19C
20,145 A. Calame/A. Calame
20,146 N. Berchem/English School 19C
20,147 F.F.A. Ferogio/F.F.A. Ferogio
20,148 F.F.A. Ferogio/F.F.A. Ferogio
20,149 D. Roberts/W. Day & W.L. Haghe
20,150 J. Inskipp/C.E. Wagstaff
20,151 H. Melville/E. Smith
20,152 G. Cattermole/E. Smith
20,153 W. Evans/C. Fox
20,154 L. Sharpe/J.C. Edwards
20,155 E. Stone/H. Robinson
20,156 F. Barocci/*P. W. Tomkins & W. W. Hodgson*/A. Cardon
20,157 L. Sharpe/H. Robinson
20,158 C.W.E. Dietrich/J.-B. Fosseyeux
20,159 G. Dou/English School 19C
20,160 D. Teniers the Younger/English School 19C
20,161 A. Cuyp/J.C. Bentley
20,162 J.C. Brand/J. Aliamet
20,163 English School 19C/English School 19C
20,164 J. Inskipp/C.E. Wagstaff
20,165 T.S. Cooper/T.S. Cooper
20,166 J. Inskipp/C.E. Wagstaff
20,167 G. Childs/G. Childs
20,168 J.H. Mulcahy/J.H. Mulcahy
20,169 T.S. Cooper/T.S. Cooper
20,170 T.S. Cooper/T.S. Cooper
20,171 A. Biasioli/A. Biasioli
20,172 W. Howis the Elder/W. Howis the Elder
20,173 W. Howis the Elder/W. Howis the Elder
20,174 T.S. Cooper/T.S. Cooper
20,175 W. Howis the Elder/W. Howis the Elder
20,176 U. Gréther/H. Raunheim
20,177 Roman Antique/Continental School 19C
20,178 Roman Antique/Continental School 19C
20,179 L. Rossi/French School 19C
20,180 L. Rossi/French School 19C
20,181 G.E. Hicks/G.E. Hicks
20,182 J.D. Harding/J.D. Harding
20,183 J.D. Harding/J.D. Harding
20,184 J.D. Harding/J.D. Harding
20,185 J.D. Harding/J.D. Harding
20,186 J.D. Harding/J.D. Harding
20,187 J.D. Harding/J.D. Harding
20,188 J.D. Harding/J.D. Harding
20,189 J.D. Harding/J.D. Harding
20,190 J.D. Harding/J.D. Harding
20,191 J.D. Harding/J.D. Harding
20,192 J.D. Harding/J.D. Harding
20,193 J.D. Harding/J.D. Harding
20,194 J.D. Harding/J.D. Harding
20,195 J.D. Harding/J.D. Harding
20,196 J.D. Harding/J.D. Harding
20,197 English School 19C/English School 19C
20,198 F.A. Kraus/D. Sornique
20,199 E. Landseer/F.C. Lewis the Elder
20,200 W. Purser/J.C. Bentley
20,201 N. Poussin/*Dufraine*/J. Duplessi-Bertaux & C. Niquet
20,202 English School 18C/?C. Taylor
20,203 English School 18C/?C. Taylor
20,204 T. Lawrence/J.H. Robinson
20,205 H. Fragonard/English School 1827
20,206 T. Gainsborough/W. Radclyffe
20,207 W.C. Stanfield/W. Miller
20,208 W.C. Stanfield/J. Cousen
20,209 J. Bell/*F.R. Roffe*/W. Roffe
20,210 J.H. Foley/*F.R. Roffe*/W. Roffe
20,211 T. Lawrence/C. Armstrong
20,212 T. Hills/E. Tyrrell
20,213 W.C. Stanfield/J. Cousen
20,214 W.C. Stanfield/R. Wallis
20,215 F. Chauveau/F. Chauveau
20,216 E. Edwards/J. Newton
20,217 L. Gluckman/Irish School 1885
20,218 G.B. Piazzetta/P.A. Kilian
20,219 D. Wilkie/E. Smith
20,220 English School 19C/English School 19C

20,221 Roman Antique/R. Audengerd
20,222 H. Bright/W. Day & W.L. Haghe
20,223 J. Syer/J. Syer
20,224 J.D. Harding/J.D. Harding
20,225 J.D. Harding/J.D. Harding
20,226 J.D. Harding/J.D. Harding
20,227 J. Wijnants/English School 19C
20,228 Bolognese School 17C/Bolognese School 17C
20,229 F. Barocci/A. Sadeler
20,230 J. Thierry/French School 17C
20,231 J. Le Pautre/J. Le Pautre
20,232 J. Le Pautre/J. Le Pautre
20,233 S. della Bella/S. della Bella
20,234 W.H. Bartlett/E. Challis
20,235 French School 1634/French School 1634
20,236 C.M. Metz/C.M. Metz
20,237 C.M. Metz/C.M. Metz
20,238 C.M. Metz/C.M. Metz
20,239 C.M. Metz/C.M. Metz
20,240 E. Ciceri/E. Ciceri
20,241 G. Morland/English School 1827
20,242 Claude Lorrain/English School 1827
20,243 T.S. Cooper/T.S. Cooper
20,244 ?A. Van Dyck/J. Faber the Younger
20,245 Claude Lorrain/J.B. Allen
20,246 A. Murphy/A. Murphy
20,247 Book: See Appendix 8
20,247 (16) A. Locatelli/W. Austin
20,248 Book: See Appendix 8
20,248 (89) G. Barret the Younger/H. Melville
20,249 J.D. Harding/J.D. Harding
20,250 W. Howis the Younger/ W. Howis the Younger
20,251 W. Howis the Younger/W. Howis the Younger
20,252 W. Howis the Younger/W. Howis the Younger
20,253 W. Howis the Elder/W. Howis the Elder
20,254 W. Howis the Younger/W. Howis the Younger
20,255 W. Howis the Younger/W. Howis the Younger
20,256 W. Howis the Elder/W. Howis the Elder
20,257 W. Howis the Elder/W. Howis the Elder
20,258 W. Howis the Elder/W. Howis the Elder
20,259 J.D. Harding/J.D. Harding
20,260 W. Collins/J. Outrim
20,261 S.R. Lines/S.R. Lines
20,262 T. Allom/E. Young
20,263 T. Allom/S. Lacey
20,264 Book: See Appendix 8
20,264 (26) J.D. Harding/J.D. Harding
20,265 T. Allom/J. Redaway
20,266 T. Allom/J.C. Redaway
20,267 T. Gainsborough/W. Taylor
20,268 A. Carracci/English School 19C
20,269 E. Whymper/E. Whymper
20,270 E. Whymper/E. Whymper
20,271 H.S. Melville/R. Staines
20,272 D. Roberts/E.F. Finden
20,273 J.D. Harding/J.D. Harding
20,274 J.D. Harding/J.D. Harding
20,275 J.D. Harding/J.D. Harding
20,276 G. Barret the Younger/R. Wallis
20,277 T. Roberts/T. Milton
20,278 W. Tombleson/A.H. Payne
20,279 T. Allom/T. Clark
20,280 ?J. Shury the Elder/J. Shury the Elder & Younger
20,281 W. L. Leitch/W. Floyd
20,282 D.O. Hill/W. Richardson
20,283 G. Chambers/R. Brandard
20,284 T. Allom/H. Wallis
20,285 T. Allom/H. Wallis
20,286 W. Tombleson/H. Winkles
20,287 J.H. Robinson/J.S. Templeton
20,288 J.H. Robinson/G. Childs
20,289 J.H. Robinson/G. Childs
20,290 J.H. Robinson/G. Childs
20,291 J.H. Robinson/G. Childs
20,292 J.H. Robinson/G. Childs
20,293 J.H. Robinson/G. Childs
20,294 J.H. Robinson/J.S. Templeton
20,295 T. Roberts/ T. Milton
20,296 J.D. Harding/J.D. Harding
20,297 J.D. Harding/J.D. Harding
20,298 J.D. Harding/J.D. Harding
20,299 J.D. Harding/J.D. Harding
20,300 J.D. Harding/J.D. Harding
20,301 J.D. Harding/J.D. Harding
20,302 J.D. Harding/J.D. Harding
20,303 J.D. Harding/J.D. Harding
20,304 J.D. Harding/J.D. Harding
20,305 J.D. Harding/J.D. Harding
20,306 J.D. Harding/J.D. Harding
20,307 J.D. Harding/J.D. Harding
20,308 F.F.A. Ferogio/F.F.A. Ferogio
20,309 F.F.A. Ferogio/F.F.A. Ferogio
20,310 F.F.A. Ferogio/F.F.A. Ferogio
20,311 F.F.A. Ferogio/F.F.A. Ferogio
20,312 F.F.A. Ferogio/F.F.A. Ferogio
20,313 F.F.A. Ferogio/F.F.A. Ferogio
20,314 F.F.A. Ferogio/F.F.A. Ferogio
20,315 L.J. Jacottet & A.J.B.Bayot/L.J. Jacottet & A.J.B. Bayot
20,316 E. Isabey/L.J.-B. Sabatier
20,317 E. Isabey/L.J.-B. Sabatier
20,318 J.L. Pelletier/J.L. Pelletier
20,319 J.L. Pelletier/J.L. Pelletier
20,320 English School 19C/English School 19C
20,321 English School 19C/English School 19C
20,322 N. Pocock/D. Havell & R. Havell the Elder
20,323 J.H. Mulcahy/J.H. Mulcahy
20,324 A. Cuyp/*W. Westall*/T. Medland & J. Bailey
20,325 English School c.1835/English School 1835
20,326 N. Maes/T. Lupton
20,327 C. Tomkins/D. Lucas
20,328 J.H. Robinson/G. Childs
20,329 E. Landseer/W. Finden
20,330 W. Collins/W. Collins
20,331 T. Woodward/W.R. Smith & J.H. Robinson
20,332 A.G. Decamps/A.G. Decamps
20,333 Canaletto/J.C. Bromley
20,334 J.H. Robinson/G. Childs
20,335 ?S. Rosa/A. G....
20,336 J.P. Haverty/J.P. Haverty
20,337 A. Calame/A. Calame
20,338 D. Cox/ J. Needham
20,339 J.B.L. Hubert/J.B.L. Hubert
20,340 A. Calame/A. Calame
20,341 A. Calame & F.F.A. Ferogio/A. Calame & F.F.A. Ferogio
20,342 A. Calame/A. Calame
20,343 ?A. Calame/?A. Calame
20,344 S.R. Lines/S.R. Lines
20,345 T.S. Cooper/T.S. Cooper
20,346 English School 19C/English School 19C
20,347 H. Bright/W. Day & W.L. Haghe
20,348 J. Syer/J. Syer
20,349 English School 19C/English School 19C
20,350 J. Syer/J. Syer
20,351 G. Petrie/N. Fielding
20,352 T. Fairland/T. Fairland
20,353 G. Rowe/G. Rowe
20,354 G. Rowe/G. Rowe
20,355 J.D. Harding/J.D. Harding
20,356 R.J. Elliot/*S. Austin*/W. Le Petit
20,357 J. Comerford/A. Cardon
20,358 J.D. Harding/J.D. Harding
20,359 French School 18C/French School 18C
20,360 A. Nasmyth/E.F. Finden
20,361 J.D. Harding/J.D. Harding
20,362 R. Hills & R.G. Fennell/B.P. Gibbon & E. Webb

20,363 English School 19C/English School 19C
20,364 English School 19C/English School 19C
20,365 W.L. Leitch/J. Sands
20,366 S. Prout/E. Goodall
20,367 J. Henderson/W. Finden
20,368 J.H. Robinson/J.S. Templeton
20,369 J. Syer/J. Syer
20,370 J.D. Harding/J.D. Harding
20,371 D. Roberts/A.R. Freebairn
20,372 W.H. Bartlett/H. Jordan
20,373 A.V.D. Copley Fielding/G. Cooke
20,374 S.R. Lines/S.R. Lines
20,375 G. Childs/G. Childs
20,376 W. Tombleson/H. Winkles
20,377 W. Tombleson/A. McClatchie
20,378 W. Tombleson/S. Lacey
20,379 W. Tombleson/H. Winkles
20,380 W. Tombleson/W. Taylor
20,381 J.D. Harding/E. Goodall
20,382 P. De Wint/J.H. Kernot
20,383 W. Collins/E.F. Finden
20,384 J.M.W. Turner/C. Turner
20,385 D. Cox/W.J. Cooke
20,386 G.F. Robson/W.R. Smith
20,387 G. Carocci/G. Carocci
20,388 G. Corsi/G. Corsi
20,389 T. Hearne/B.T. Pouncey
20,390 Canaletto/P. Chevalier
20,391 J.D. Harding/J.D. Harding
20,392 G. Carocci/G. Carocci
20,393 G. Castellini/G. Castellini
20,394 Irish School 19C/Irish School 19C
20,395 Irish School 19C/Irish School 19C
20,396 Irish School 19C/Irish School 19C
20,397 J. Martin/W.F. Starling
20,398 T. Allom/R. Sands
20,399 W.H. Bartlett/T. Higham
20,400 A. Bader/A. Bader
20,401 A. Drulin/A. Drulin
20,402 T.S. Cooper/T.S. Cooper
20,403 H. Gastineau/W. Wallis
20,404 H. Gastineau/W. Wallis
20,405 J.D. Harding/J.D. Harding
20,406 J.D. Harding/J.D. Harding
20,407 (1) J.D. Harding/J.D. Harding
20,407 (2) J.D. Harding/J.D. Harding
20,408 No Entry
20,409 J.D. Harding/J.D. Harding
20,410 J.D. Harding/J.D. Harding
20,411 E. Dayes/J.C. Smith
20,412 G. Cattermole/A.H. Payne
20,413 W.C. Stanfield/R. Wallis
20,414 W.L. Leitch/J. Sands
20,415 J.C. Bentley/J.C. Bentley
20,416 English School 19C/English School 19C
20,417 W.H. Bartlett/W.B. Cooke
20,418 W.H. Bartlett & T. Creswick/J.T. Willmore
20,419 T. Allom/D. Buckle
20,420 T. Allom/D. Buckle
20,421 W.A. Nesfield/J. Sands
20,422 J.B. Pyne/R. Brandard
20,423 W.C. Stanfield/W.A. Le Petit
20,424 J.D. Harding/W. Radclyffe
20,425 F. Abresch/ *W.H. Bartlett*/R. Wallis
20,426 D. Cox/R. Brandard
20,427 Claude Lorrain/English School 1827
20,428 J.D. Harding/J.D. Harding
20,429 J. Livesay/W.G. Watkins
20,430 E. Dayes/S. Noble
20,431 J.D. Harding/W.R. Smith
20,432 W. Tombleson/R. Sands
20,433 W. Tombleson/W. Tombleson
20,434 W.H. Bartlett/G.K. Richardson
20,435 W.H. Bartlett/H. Adlard
20,436 W.H. Bartlett/G.K. Richardson
20,437 W.H. Bartlett/E. Benjamin
20,438 W.H. Bartlett/J. Cousen
20,439 W.H. Bartlett/J. Cousen
20,440 W.H. Bartlett/H. Adlard
20,441 W.H. Bartlett/R. Wallis
20,442 W. Brockedon/J. Sands
20,443 D. Roberts/W. Le Petit
20,444 G. Cattermole/J.C. Bentley
20,445 R. Westall/C. Turner
20,446 (1) J.D. Harding/J.D. Harding
20,446 (2) J.D. Harding/J.D. Harding
20,447 No Entry
20,448 (1) T. Allom/S. Bradshaw
20,448 (2) T. Allom/S. Bradshaw
20,449 No Entry
20,450 W.H. Bartlett/D. Thompson
20,451 T. Allom/W.A. Le Petit
20,452 T. Allom/W.A. Le Petit
20,453 W.H. Bartlett/W.F. Starling
20,454 G.F. White/*T. Allom*/J.H. Kernot
20,455 W.H. Bartlett/J. Stephenson
20,456 T. Allom/W.H. Kelsall
20,457 T. Allom/W.H. Kelsall
20,458 G. Pickering/W.A. Le Petit
20,459 S. Prout/J.B. Allen
20,460 D.O. Hill/T. Jeavons
20,461 D.O. Hill/W. Forrest
20,462 A. Calame & F.F.A. Ferogio/A. Calame & F.F.A. Ferogio
20,463 (1) J.D. Harding/J.D. Harding
20,463 (2) J.D. Harding/J.D. Harding
20,463 (3) J.D. Harding/J.D. Harding
20,464 No Entry
20,465 No Entry
20,466 E. Sabatier/French School 19C
20,467 Italian School late 18C/A. Rancati
20,468 Italian School late 18C/G. Zancon
20,469 A. Calame/A. Calame
20,470 A. Calame/A. Calame
20,471 J.H. Robinson/G. Childs
20,472 J.H. Robinson/J.S. Templeton
20,473 J.H. Robinson/G. Childs
20,474 J.H. Robinson/J.H. Robinson
20,475 F. Abresch/ *W.H. Bartlett*/E.P. Brandard
20,476 H. Gastineau/S. Lacey
20,477 T. Allom/J.C. Bentley
20,478 G.F. Robson/E.F. Finden
20,479 W.I. Hocker/T. Higham
20,480 T. Allom/E. Challis
20,481 G.F. Robson/E.F. Finden
20,482 J.M.W. Turner/J.B. Allen
20,483 J.M.W. Turner/J.T. Willmore
20,484 R.P. Bonington/W. Miller
20,485 T. Allom/W. Tombleson
20,486 G. Pickering/C. Mottram
20,487 A. Calame/A. Calame
20,488 A. Calame & F.F.A. Ferogio/A. Calame & F.F.A. Ferogio
20,489 A. Calame/A. Calame
20,490 A. Calame/A. Calame
20,491 A. Calame/A. Calame
20,492 J.B. Pyne/R. Brandard
20,493 P. De Wint/W. Floyd
20,494 A. Calame/A. Calame
20,495 C. Stanfield/E. Goodall
20,496 A. Calame/A. Calame
20,497 A. Calame/A. Calame
20,498 A. Calame/A. Calame
20,499 A. Calame/A. Calame
20,500 A. Calame/A. Calame
20,501 G.A. Williams/English School 19C
20,502 T. Creswick/S. Bradshaw
20,503 T. Creswick/R. Hill
20,504 T. Creswick/R. Wallis
20,505 A. Calame/A. Calame
20,506 A. Calame/A. Calame
20,507 A. Calame/A. Calame
20,508 A. Calame/A. Calame
20,509 W.S. Hayter/W.S. Hayter
20,510 T. Creswick/R. Brandard
20,511 W. Linton/E. Goodall
20,512 J.M.W. Turner/T. Crostick
20,513 T. Creswick/R. Wallis
20,514 W.H. Bartlett/J. Rogers
20,515 English School 19C/English School 19C
20,516 English School 19C/English School 19C

20,517 A.V.D. Copley-Fielding/W.J. Cooke
20,518 T. Creswick/S. Lacey
20,519 P. Nasmyth/S. Lacey
20,520 P. De Wint/E.F. Finden
20,521 A. Calame/A. Calame
20,522 J.H. Robinson/G. Childs
20,523 B. Langley/English School 18C
20,524 J.H. Mulcahy/J. Worrall
20,525 G.B. Piranesi/G.B. Piranesi
20,526 G.B. Piranesi/G.B. Piranesi
20,527 G.B. Piranesi/G.B. Piranesi
20,528 G.B. Piranesi/G.B. Piranesi
20,529 J.B. Jouvenet/W.H. Egleton
20,530 G.B. Piranesi/G.B. Piranesi
20,531 G.B. Piranesi/G.B. Piranesi
20,532 G.B. Piranesi/G.B. Piranesi
20,533 G.B. Piranesi/G.B. Piranesi
20,534 G.B. Piranesi/G.B. Piranesi
20,535 English School 18C/J. Basire
20,536 W.S. Hayter/W.S. Hayter
20,537 English School 18C/English School 18C
20,538 English School 18C/English School 18C
20,539 ?Parmigianino/English School early 19C
20,540 D. Stoop/G. Cooke
20,541 English School 18C/A. Walker
20,542 G. Barret the Younger/A.R. Freebairn
20,543 English School c.1840/English School c.1840
20,544 G.P. Panini/French School 18C
20,545 N. Poussin/F. Ertinger
20,546 W. Hogarth/J. Moore
20,547 N. Berchem/?English School 18C
20,548 N. Berchem/?English School 18C
20,549 C. Le Brun/R. Shepherd
20,550 A. Fraser/J. Burnett
20,551 S. Rosa/English School 18C
20,552 R. Wilson/J.C. Varrell
20,553 Style of Claude Lorrain/English School 19C
20,554 Irish School 1861/Irish School 1861
20,555 Irish School 19C/Irish School 19C
20,556 French School 19C/French School 19C
20,557 Roman Antique/English School 19C
20,558 French School 19C/French School 19C
20,559 S. Prout/S. Prout
20,560 S. Prout/S. Prout
20,561 S. Prout/S. Prout
20,562 S. Prout/S. Prout
20,563 S. Prout/S. Prout
20,564 S. Prout/S. Prout
20,565 S. Prout/S. Prout
20,566 L.L. Razé/L.L. Razé
20,567 S. Prout/S. Prout
20,568 English School 19C/English School 19C
20,569 L.L. Razé/L.L. Razé
20,570 P. Levin/English School 1861
20,571 English School 1862/English School 1862
20,572 J.C. Horsley/H. Harral
20,573 M. Jackson/English School 1865
20,574 English School 19C/English School 19C
20,575 K. Girardet/English School 19C
20,576 English School c.1869/English School 1869
20,577 M.B. Foster/H. Vizetelley
20,578 L. Fildes/English School 1880
20,579 J.D. Harding/J.D. Harding
20,580 ?J.D. Harding/?J.D. Harding
20,581 J.D. Harding/J.D. Harding
20,582 F. Goodall/H.D. Linton
20,583 J.R. Herbert/H.C. Shenton the Elder
20,584 English School 19C/English School 19C
20,585 English School 19C/English School 19C
20,586 English School 19C/English School 19C
20,587 English School 19C/English School 19C
20,588 L.L. Razé/L.L. Razé
20,589 R.P. Bonington/W. Miller
20,590 W.H. Bartlett/F.W. Topham
20,591 A.V.D. Copley-Fielding/E.F. Finden
20,592 J.J. Forrester/G. Childs
20,593 J.J. Forrester/G. Childs
20,594 J.J. Forrester/G. Childs
20,595 J.J. Forrester/G. Childs
20,596 English School 1829/English School 1829
20,597 English School 1829/English School 1829
20,598 English School 1829/English School 1829
20,599 J.M.W. Turner/J.T. Willmore
20,600 W.H. Bartlett/G.K. Richardson
20,601 W.H. Bartlett/J.C. Bentley
20,602 M. Thurwanger/M. Thurwanger
20,603 M. Thurwanger/M. Thurwanger
20,604 English School c.1830/English School c.1830
20,605 W.H. Bartlett/J. Cousen
20,606 T. Creswick/S. Bradshaw
20,607 Claude Lorrain/W.R. Smith
20,608 English School 19C/English School 19C
20,609 W. Daniell/R. Brandard
20,610 J.C. Bentley/J.C. Bentley
20,611 W.H. Bartlett/R. Winkles
20,612 G. Petrie/R. Winkles
20,613 No Entry
20,614 English School 19C/English School 19C
20,615 A. Cooper/W. Raddon
20,616 W.H. B..../English School 19C
20,617 English School 19C/English School 19C
20,618 N. Berchem/L. Dujardin
20,619 P.E. Grandsire/C. Barbant
20,620 R. L..../English School 19C
20,621 English School c.1889/English School 1889
20,622 Irish School 19C/Irish School 19C
20,623 A.C. Tisdall/A.C. Tisdall
20,624 A.C. Tisdall/A.C. Tisdall
20,625 A.C. Tisdall/A.C. Tisdall
20,626 C. Branwhite/W.J. Linton
20,627 English School c.1687/English School 1867
20,628 T. Danby/J.O. Smith
20,629 J.H. Mulcahy/English School 1859
20,630 J.C. Hook/J.W. Whymper
20,631 J.C. Hook/J.W. Whymper
20,632 K. Piloty/English School 1867
20,633 F. Geefs/English School 1867
20,634 P.P. Rubens/English School 19C
20,635 French School 19C/C. Maurand
20,636 W. Kalf/English School 19C
20,637 No Entry
20,638 No Entry
20,639 Irish School 19C/?A.R. Branston
20,640 Irish School 19C/S. Sly
20,641 Irish School 19C/?S. Sly
20,642 ?J. Newman/J. Newman
20,643 ?Dutch School 18C/English School 19C
20,644 Irish School 1883/Irish School 1883
20,645 English School late 19C/English School late 19C
20,646 English School 19C/English School 19C
20,647 F.R. Lee/J. Fussell & M. Jackson
20,648 ?Swiss School 19C/?Swiss School 19C
20,649 J.D. Harding/J.D. Harding

20,650 English School c.1840/English School c.1840
20,651 English School 19C/English School 19C
20,652 A. Calame/A. Calame
20,653 Hellenistic School 1C A.D./English School 1809
20,654 ?Roman Antique/English School early 19C
20,655 J. Hogan/N. Walsh
20,656 No Entry
20,657 No Entry
20,658 W.E. West/E. Scriven
20,659 ?Waker/?Waker
20,660 Book: See Appendix 8
20,660 (13) A. Huberti/A. Huberti
20,661 English School 18C/W. Green & W. Darling
20,662 English School early 19C/W. Darton the Younger
20,663 T. Lawrence/C. Turner
20,664 Book: See Appendix 8
20,664 (1) G.C. Stuart/T.G. Lupton
20,664 (93) Claude Lorrain/R. Earlom
20,665 Book: See Appendix 8
20,665 (1) G.C. Stuart/Facius
20,665 (150) Claude Lorrain/R. Earlom
20,666 Book: See Appendix 8
20,666 (51) Claude Lorrain/R. Earlom
20,667 Book: See Appendix 8
20,667 (37) D. Heil/C. Coukercken
20,668 J. Miers/J. Miers
20,669 Book: See Appendix 8
20,669 (4) G. Zocchi/G. Zocchi & B.S. Sgrilli
20,670 Book: See Appendix 8
20,670 (61) J.B. Fischer Von Erlach/German School c.1725
20,671 Book: See Appendix 8
20,671 (3) P. Perugino/C. Duflos
20,672 Book: See Appendix 8
20,672 (7) Titian/N.H. Tardieu
20,673 Book: See Appendix 8
20,673 (37) G. Metsu/J. Burnet
20,674 Book: See Appendix 8
20,674 (9) J. Barbault/D. Montagu
20,675 Book: See Appendix 8
20,675 (2) N. Guibal/C. Mechel
20,676 Book: See Appendix 8
20,676 (1) Raphael/*L. Comparani*/G. Balzar & F. Rainaldi
20,677 Book: See Appendix 8
20,677 (2) A. Specchi/A. Specchi
20,678 Book: See Appendix 8
20,678 (1) ?A. Van Dyck/*J.M. Nattier*/J. Audran
20,678 (6) P.P. Rubens/*J.M. Nattier*/A. Trouvain
20,678 (14) N.N. Coypel/J.P. Lebas
20,678 (15) Raphael/N. Dorigny
20,679 Book: See Appendix 8
20,679 (18) Raphael/*A. Dutertre*/F.J.E. Beisson
20,680 Book: See Appendix 8
20,680 (7) L. Lotto/*W.M. Craig*/J.H. Wright
20,681 Book: See Appendix 8
20,681 (155) J. Os/*W.M. Craig*/E. Byrne
20,682 Book: See Appendix 8
20,682 (62) G. Reni/F. Rosapina
20,683 Book: See Appendix 8
20,683 (59) Hellenistic School 1C/*P. Bouillon*/Bervic
20,684 Book: See Appendix 8
20,684 (4) P. Aquila/P. Aquila
20,685 Book: See Appendix 8
20,685 (13) N. Poussin/*A.E. Fragonard*/A. Girardet
20,686 Book: See Appendix 8
20,686 (16) M.W. Peters/P. Simon
20,687 Book: See Appendix 8
20,687 (46) Raphael/*J.B. Wicar*/C.E. Duponchel
20,688 Book: See Appendix 8
20,688 (108) Roman Antique/*J.B. Wicar*/N. Thomas
20,689 Book: See Appendix 8
20,689 (25) P. Wouwerman/P. Filloeul
20,690 Book: See Appendix 8
20,690 (80) P. Wouwerman/J. Moyreau
20,691 Book: See Appendix 8
20,691 (1) Raphael/*P.P. Prudhon*/P. Audouin
20,692 Book: See Appendix 8
20,693 Book: See Appendix 8
20,693 (1) J. Pennell/J. Pennell
20,694 Book: See Appendix 8
20,694 (72) L.C.P.G. Doré/C. Laplante
20,695 M.A. Hayes/J. Harris the Younger
20,696 M.A. Hayes/J. Harris the Younger
20,697 M.A. Hayes/J. Harris the Younger
20,698 M.A. Hayes/J. Harris the Younger
20,699 M.A. Hayes/J. Harris the Younger
20,700 M.A. Hayes/J. Harris the Younger
20,701 ?O.J. Jones/Dickinson & Co.
20,702 T. Walmsley/W. Cartwright
20,703 Book: See Appendix 8
20,703 (47) Raphael/S. Bianchi
20,704 Book: See Appendix 8
20,704 (8) G. Moroni/*W.M. Craig*/P.W. Tomkins
20,705 Book: See Appendix 8
20,705 (7) P.P. Rubens/*W.M. Craig*/C. Heath
20,706 Book: See Appendix 8
20,706 (47) Roman Antique/P.S. Bartoli
20,707 Book: See Appendix 8
20,707 (66) A. Ostade/*?B.E. Swebach*/Bovinet
20,708 Book: See Appendix 8
20,708 (19) Rembrandt/English School 1827
20,709 Book: See Appendix 8
20,709 (3) B. Pinelli/B. Pinelli
20,710 Book: See Appendix 8
20,710 (1) M. Heemskerk/M. Heemskerk
20,711 Book: See Appendix 8
20,711 (36) J.B. Le Prince/J.B. Le Prince
20,712 Book: See Appendix 8
20,712 (40) J. Barry/F. Legat
20,713 Book. See Appendix 8
20,714 Book: See Appendix 8
20,714 (16) A. Canova/*G. Tognoli*/A. Ricciani
20,715 Titian/L. Vorstermans the Younger
20,716 Book: See Appendix 8
20,716 (10) Giorgione/*D. Teniers the Younger*/J. Van Troyen
20,717 Book: See Appendix 8
20,717 (89) Roman Antique/Italian School 17C
20,718 Book: See Appendix 8
20,718 (1) Claude Lorrain/J. Boydell
20,719 Book: See Appendix 8
20,719 (149) Claude Lorrain/R. Earlom
20,720 Book: See Appendix 8
20,720 (28) Michelangelo/F.C. Lewis
20,721 Book: See Appendix 8
20,721 (1) F.P.S. Gérard/H. Grévedon
20,721 (63) R.A.Q. Monvoisin/*H.L.V.J.B. Aubry-Lecomte*/ C.E.P. Motte
20,722 Book: See Appendix 8
20,722 (1-15) J. Barry/J. Barry
20,723 Book: See Appendix 8
20,723 (7) A. Allori/*A. Borel*/P. Trierre
20,723 (14) Raphael/*Vendenberg*/A.L. Romanet
20,723 (22) Sebastiano del Piombo/R. Delaunay
20,724 Book: See Appendix 8
20,724 (11) Titian/J. Couché
20,724 (24) ?Giorgione/B.A. Nicollet
20,725 Book: See Appendix 8
20,725 (56) N. Poussin/H.G. Bertaux & A.L. Romanet

20,725 (74) C. Le Brun/A. Lafitte & J.-B. Tilliard

20,725 (76) H. Rigaud/F. Guibert

20,726 Book: See Appendix 8

20,726 (14) N. Poussin/C. Heath

20,727 Book: See Appendix 8

20,727 (12) A.R. Mengs/*W.M. Craig*/P.W. Tomkins

20,728 Book: See Appendix 8

20,728 (1) English School c.1689/English School 1689

20,729 Book: See Appendix 8

20,729 (1) Irish School c.1768/Irish School c.1768

20,730 Book: See Appendix 8

20,730 (6) F.M.A. Retzch/F.M.A. Retzch

20,731 Book: See Appendix 8

20,731 (89) School of Titian/J. Murphy

20,731 (92) J.-B. Van Loo/J. Watson

20,731 (136) Rosalba/C. West

20,732 Book: See Appendix 8

20,732 (57) ?W. Vaillant/W. Vaillant

20,733 Book: See Appendix 8

20,733 (39) M. Schongauer/English School 1826

20,734 D. Amici/D. Amici

20,735 D. Amici/D. Amici

20,736 D. Amici/D. Amici

20,737 D. Amici/D. Amici

20,738 D. Amici/D. Amici

20,739 D. Amici/D. Amici

20,740 D. Amici/D. Amici

20,741 D. Amici/D. Amici

20,742 D. Amici/D. Amici

20,743 D. Amici/D. Amici

20,744 D. Amici/D. Amici

20,745 D. Amici/D. Amici

20,746 D. Amici/D. Amici

20,747 D. Amici/D. Amici

20,748 D. Amici/D. Amici

20,749 D. Amici/D. Amici

20,750 D. Amici/D. Amici

20,751 D. Amici/D. Amici

20,752 D. Amici/D. Amici

20,753 D. Amici/D. Amici

20,754 D. Amici/D. Amici

20,755 D. Amici/D. Amici

20,756 D. Amici/D. Amici

20,757 Book: See Appendix 8

20,757 (138) N. Poussin/G.F. Ferrero

20,758 Book: See Appendix 8

20,758 (34) R. Weyden/N.J. Strixner

20,759 Book: See Appendix 8

20,759 (9) G. Fossati/A. Von dall'Armi

20,760 Book: See Appendix 8

20,760 (6) G. Fossati/A.V.D. Armi

20,761 W. Joy/J. Brandard

20,762 Dutch School 1691/*J. Tangena*/Dutch School c.1691

20,763 W. Hollar/W. Hollar

20,764 A. John/A. John

20,765 P. Keere/P. Keere

20,766 Countess of Harrington/M. & N. Hanhart

20,767 Countess of Harrington/M. & N. Hanhart

20,768 S. Catterson Smith the Elder/G. Sanders

20,769 J.P. Hackert/G.A. Hackert

20,770 N. Blakey/L.J. Cathelin

20,771 Rev. W. Fitzgerald/Rev. W. Fitzgerald

20,772 Rev. W. Fitzgerald/Rev. W. Fitzgerald

20,773 Rev. W. Fitzgerald/Rev. W. Fitzgerald

20,774 Rev. W. Fitzgerald/Rev. W. Fitzgerald

20,775 Rev. W. Fitzgerald/Rev. W. Fitzgerald

20,776 Rev. W. Fitzgerald/Rev. W. Fitzgerald

20,777 Rev. W. Fitzgerald/Rev. W. Fitzgerald

20,778 Rev. W. Fitzgerald/Rev. W. Fitzgerald

20,779 Rev. W. Fitzgerald/Rev. W. Fitzgerald

20,780 Rev. W. Fitzgerald/Rev. W. Fitzgerald

20,781 Rev. W. Fitzgerald/Rev. W. Fitzgerald

20,782 Rev. W. Fitzgerald/Rev. W. Fitzgerald

20,783 Rev. W. Fitzgerald/Rev. W. Fitzgerald

20,784 Rev. W. Fitzgerald/Rev. W. Fitzgerald

20,785 Rev. W. Fitzgerald/Rev. W. Fitzgerald

20,786 Rev. W. Fitzgerald/Rev. W. Fitzgerald

20,787 Rev. W. Fitzgerald/Rev. W. Fitzgerald

20,788 Rev. W. Fitzgerald/Rev. W. Fitzgerald

20,789 W. Velde the Elder & Younger/T.G. Lupton

20,790 J. Comerford/J. Heath

20,791 G. Petrie/T. Higham

20,792 S. della Bella/S. della Bella

20,793 S. della Bella/S. della Bella

20,794 S. della Bella/S. della Bella

20,795 S. della Bella/S. della Bella

20,796 ?J. Aubert/?Thibault

20,797 H. Porter/H. Porter

20,798 I.F. Marshall/T. Fairland

20,799 J.M.W. Turner/J. Pye

20,800 T. Maas/T. Maas

20,801 F. Bindon/A. Miller

20,802 ?J. Brooks/J. Brooks

20,803 English School 18C/English School 18C

20,804 T. Lawrence/C.E. Wagstaff

20,805 T.C. Croker/I. Phillips

20,806 Italian School 16C/M.E. Corr

20,807 F. Bartolozzi/F. Bartolozzi

20,808 W.H. Brooke/W.H. Brooke

20,809 W.H. Brooke/W.H. Brooke

20,810 W.H. Brooke/W.H. Brooke

20,811 W.H. Brooke/W.H. Brooke

20,812 W.H. Brooke/W.H. Brooke

20,813 A. Gleizes/A. Gleizes

20,814 R. Omer/P. Mazell

20,815 Irish School 19c/Irish School 19C

20,816 Irish School 19C/Irish School 19C

20,817 Irish School 19C/Irish School 19C

20,818 Irish School 19C/Irish School 19C

20,819 S.W. Reynolds the Elder/S.W. Reynolds the Elder & W. Walker

20,820 J.P. Haverty/R. Havell the Elder & Younger

20,821 J.P. Haverty/R. Havell the Elder & Younger

20,822 No Entry

20,823 U. Franchini/U. Franchini

20,824 U. Franchini/U. Franchini

20,825 U. Franchini/U. Franchini

20,826 ?English School early 19C/English School early 19C

20,827 No Entry

20,828 No Entry

20,829 W.S. Hayter/W.S. Hayter

20,830 K. Lang/K. Lang

20,831 Irish School c.1752/Irish School 1752

20,832 G.B. Piranesi/?G.B. Piranesi

20,833 Book: See Appendix 8

20,833 (3) Italian School c.1741/Italian School 1741

20,834 C. Allingham/W. Ridley

20,835 Dutch School 1689/Dutch School c.1689

20,836 English School 1692/J. Goldar

20,837 I. Opffer/I. Opffer

20,838 (1-12) T.S. Roberts/S. Alken & W. Edy

20,839 H. Matisse/H. Matisse